CAMBRIDGE International Examinations

Advanced Level Mathematics
Pure Mathematics 1
Hugh Neill and Douglas Quadling

 CAMBRIDGE UNIVERSITY PRESS

PUBLISHED BY THE PRESS SYNDICATE OF THE UNIVERSITY OF CAMBRIDGE
The Pitt Building, Trumpington Street, Cambridge, United Kingdom

CAMBRIDGE UNIVERSITY PRESS
The Edinburgh Building, Cambridge CB2 2RU, UK
40 West 20th Street, New York, NY 10011–4211, USA
477 Williamstown Road, Port Melbourne, VIC 3207, Australia
Ruiz de Alarcón 13, 28014 Madrid, Spain
Dock House, The Waterfront, Cape Town 8001, South Africa

http://www.cambridge.org

First published 2002
Third printing 2004

Printed in the United Kingdom at the University Press, Cambridge

Typefaces Times, Helvetica   *Systems* Microsoft® Word, MathType™

A catalogue record for this book is available from the British Library

ISBN 0 521 53011 3   paperback

Cover image: © James L. Amos/CORBIS

Contents

Introduction

Cambridge International Examinations (CIE) Advanced Level Mathematics has been created especially for the new CIE mathematics syllabus. There is one book corresponding to each syllabus unit, except that units P2 and P3 are contained in a single book. This book covers the first Pure Mathematics unit, P1.

The syllabus content is arranged by chapters which are ordered so as to provide a viable teaching course. The early chapters develop the foundations of the syllabus; students may already be familiar with some of these topics. Later chapters, however, are largely independent of each other, and teachers may wish to vary the order in which they are used.

Some chapters, particularly Chapters 2, 3 and the first four sections of Chapter 8, contain material which is not in the examination syllabus for P1, and which therefore cannot be the direct focus of examination questions. Some of this is necessary background material, such as indices and surds; some is useful knowledge, such as graphs of powers of x, the use and meaning of modulus, and work on sequences.

A few sections include important results which are difficult to prove or outside the syllabus. These sections are marked with an asterisk (*) in the section heading, and there is usually a sentence early on explaining precisely what it is that the student needs to know.

Occasionally within the text paragraphs appear in *this type style*. These paragraphs are usually outside the main stream of the mathematical argument, but may help to give insight, or suggest extra work or different approaches.

Graphic calculators are not permitted in the examination, but they are useful aids in learning mathematics. In the book the authors have noted where access to a graphic calculator would be especially helpful but have not assumed that they are available to all students.

Numerical work is presented in a form intended to discourage premature approximation. In ongoing calculations inexact numbers appear in decimal form like 3.456..., signifying that the number is held in a calculator to more places than are given. Numbers are not rounded at this stage; the full display could be, for example, 3.456 123 or 3.456 789. Final answers are then stated with some indication that they are approximate, for example '1.23 correct to 3 significant figures'.

There are plenty of exercises, and each chapter ends with a Miscellaneous exercise which includes some questions of examination standard. Three Revision exercises consolate work in preceeding chpaters. The book concludes with two Practice examination papers.

In some exercises a few of the later questions may go beyond the likely requirements of the P1 examination, either in difficulty or in length or both. Some questions are marked with an asterisk, which indicates that they require knowledge of results outside the syllabus.

Cambridge University Press would like to thank OCR (Oxford, Cambridge and RSA Examinations), part of the University of Cambridge Local Examinations Syndicate (UCLES) group, for permission to use past examination questions set in the United Kingdom.

The authors thank UCLES and Cambridge University Press, in particular Diana Gillooly, for their help in producing this book. However, the responsibility for the text, and for any errors, remains with the authors.

1 Coordinates, points and lines

This chapter uses coordinates to describe points and lines in two dimensions. When you have completed it, you should be able to

- find the distance between two points
- find the mid-point of a line segment, given the coordinates of its end points
- find the gradient of a line segment, given the coordinates of its end points
- find the equation of a line though a given point with a given gradient
- find the equation of the line joining two points
- recognise lines from different forms of their equations
- find the point of intersection of two lines
- tell from their gradients whether two lines are parallel or perpendicular.

1.1 The distance between two points

When you choose an origin, draw an x-axis to the right on the page and a y-axis up the page and choose scales along the axes, you are setting up a coordinate system. The coordinates of this system are called **cartesian coordinates** after the French mathematician René Descartes, who lived in the 17th century.

In Fig. 1.1, two points A and B have cartesian coordinates $(4,3)$ and $(10,7)$. The part of the line AB which lies between A and B is called a **line segment**. The length of the line segment is the distance between the points.

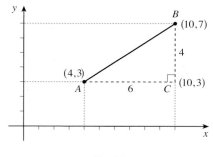

Fig. 1.1

A third point C has been added to Fig. 1.1 to form a right-angled triangle. You can see that C has the same x-coordinate as B and the same y-coordinate as A; that is, C has coordinates $(10,3)$.

It is easy to see that AC has length $10 - 4 = 6$, and CB has length $7 - 3 = 4$. Using Pythagoras' theorem in triangle ABC shows that the length of the line segment AB is

$$\sqrt{(10-4)^2 + (7-3)^2} = \sqrt{6^2 + 4^2} = \sqrt{36 + 16} = \sqrt{52}.$$

You can use your calculator to give this as $7.21\ldots$, if you need to, but often it is better to leave the answer as $\sqrt{52}$.

The idea of coordinate geometry is to use algebra so that you can do calculations like this when A and B are any points, and not just the particular points in Fig. 1.1. It often helps to use a notation which shows at a glance which point a coordinate refers to. One way of doing this is with suffixes, calling the coordinates of the first point (x_1, y_1), and the coordinates of the second point (x_2, y_2). Thus, for example, x_1 stands for 'the x-coordinate of the first point'.

Fig. 1.2 shows this general triangle. You can see that C now has coordinates (x_2, y_1), and that $AC = x_2 - x_1$ and $CB = y_2 - y_1$. Pythagoras' theorem now gives

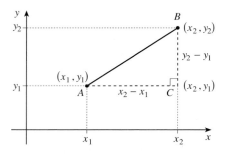

$$AB = \sqrt{(x_2 - x_1)^2 + (y_2 - y_1)^2}.$$

Fig. 1.2

An advantage of using algebra is that this formula works whatever the shape and position of the triangle. In Fig. 1.3, the coordinates of A are negative, and in Fig. 1.4 the line slopes downhill rather than uphill as you move from left to right. Use Figs. 1.3 and 1.4 to work out for yourself the length of AB in each case. You can then use the formula to check your answers.

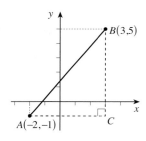

Fig. 1.3

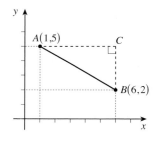

Fig. 1.4

In Fig. 1.3,

$$x_2 - x_1 = 3 - (-2) = 3 + 2 = 5 \quad \text{and} \quad y_2 - y_1 = 5 - (-1) = 5 + 1 = 6,$$

so $$AB = \sqrt{(3 - (-2))^2 + (5 - (-1))^2} = \sqrt{5^2 + 6^2} = \sqrt{25 + 36} = \sqrt{61}.$$

And in Fig. 1.4,

$$x_2 - x_1 = 6 - 1 = 5 \quad \text{and} \quad y_2 - y_1 = 2 - 5 = -3,$$

so $$AB = \sqrt{(6 - 1)^2 + (2 - 5)^2} = \sqrt{5^2 + (-3)^2} = \sqrt{25 + 9} = \sqrt{34}.$$

Also, it doesn't matter which way round you label the points A and B. If you think of B as 'the first point' (x_1, y_1) and A as 'the second point' (x_2, y_2), the formula doesn't change. For Fig. 1.1, it would give

$$BA = \sqrt{(4 - 10)^2 + (3 - 7)^2} = \sqrt{(-6)^2 + (-4)^2} = \sqrt{36 + 16} = \sqrt{52}, \text{ as before.}$$

The distance between the points (x_1, y_1) and (x_2, y_2) (or the length of the line segment joining them) is

$$\sqrt{(x_2 - x_1)^2 + (y_2 - y_1)^2}.$$

1.2 The mid-point of a line segment

You can also use coordinates to find the mid-point of a line segment.

Fig. 1.5 shows the same line segment as in Fig. 1.1, but with the mid-point M added. The line through M parallel to the y-axis meets AC at D. Then the lengths of the sides of the triangle ADM are half of those of triangle ACB, so that

$$AD = \tfrac{1}{2}AC = \tfrac{1}{2}(10 - 4) = \tfrac{1}{2}(6) = 3,$$
$$DM = \tfrac{1}{2}CB = \tfrac{1}{2}(7 - 3) = \tfrac{1}{2}(4) = 2.$$

The x-coordinate of M is the same as the x-coordinate of D, which is

$$4 + AD = 4 + \tfrac{1}{2}(10 - 4) = 4 + 3 = 7.$$

The y-coordinate of M is

$$3 + DM = 3 + \tfrac{1}{2}(7 - 3) = 3 + 2 = 5.$$

So the mid-point M has coordinates $(7, 5)$.

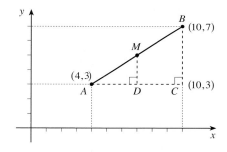

Fig. 1.5

In Fig. 1.6 points M and D have been added in the same way to Fig. 1.2. Exactly as before,

$$AD = \tfrac{1}{2}AC = \tfrac{1}{2}(x_2 - x_1), \qquad DM = \tfrac{1}{2}CB = \tfrac{1}{2}(y_2 - y_1).$$

So the x-coordinate of M is

$$x_1 + AD = x_1 + \tfrac{1}{2}(x_2 - x_1) = x_1 + \tfrac{1}{2}x_2 - \tfrac{1}{2}x_1$$
$$= \tfrac{1}{2}x_1 + \tfrac{1}{2}x_2 = \tfrac{1}{2}(x_1 + x_2).$$

The y-coordinate of M is

$$y_1 + DM = y_1 + \tfrac{1}{2}(y_2 - y_1) = y_1 + \tfrac{1}{2}y_2 - \tfrac{1}{2}y_1$$
$$= \tfrac{1}{2}y_1 + \tfrac{1}{2}y_2 = \tfrac{1}{2}(y_1 + y_2).$$

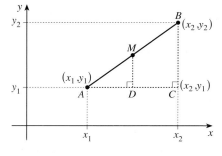

Fig. 1.6

The mid-point of the line segment joining (x_1, y_1) and (x_2, y_2) has coordinates

$$\left(\tfrac{1}{2}(x_1 + x_2), \tfrac{1}{2}(y_1 + y_2)\right).$$

Now that you have an algebraic form for the coordinates of the mid-point M you can use it for any two points. For example, for Fig. 1.3 the mid-point of AB is

$$\left(\tfrac{1}{2}((-2)+3),\tfrac{1}{2}((-1)+5)\right)=\left(\tfrac{1}{2}(1),\tfrac{1}{2}(4)\right)=\left(\tfrac{1}{2},2\right).$$

And for Fig. 1.4 it is $\left(\tfrac{1}{2}(1+6),\tfrac{1}{2}(5+2)\right)=\left(\tfrac{1}{2}(7),\tfrac{1}{2}(7)\right)=\left(3\tfrac{1}{2},3\tfrac{1}{2}\right).$

Again, it doesn't matter which you call the first point and which the second. In Fig. 1.5, if you take (x_1,y_1) as $(10,7)$ and (x_2,y_2) as $(4,3)$, you find that the mid-point is $\left(\tfrac{1}{2}(10+4),\tfrac{1}{2}(7+3)\right)=(7,5)$, as before.

1.3   The gradient of a line segment

The gradient of a line is a measure of its steepness. The steeper the line, the larger the gradient.

Unlike the distance and the mid-point, the gradient is a property of the whole line, not just of a particular line segment. If you take any two points on the line and find the increases in the x- and y-coordinates as you go from one to the other, as in Fig. 1.7, then the value of the fraction

$$\frac{y\text{-step}}{x\text{-step}}$$

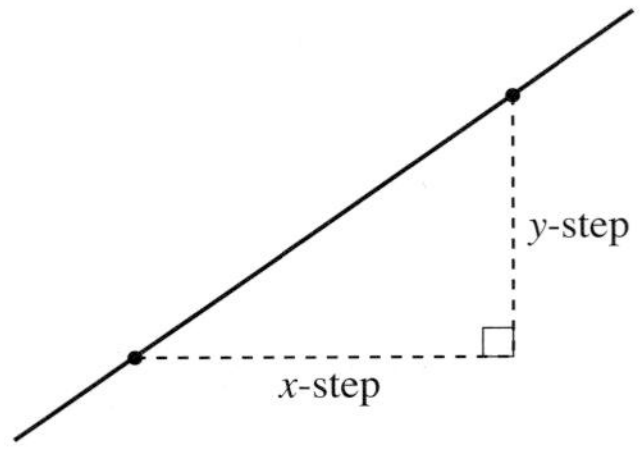

Fig. 1.7

is the same whichever points you choose. This is the **gradient** of the line.

In Fig. 1.2 on page 2 the x-step and y-step are x_2-x_1 and y_2-y_1, so that:

> The gradient of the line joining (x_1,y_1) to (x_2,y_2) is $\dfrac{y_2-y_1}{x_2-x_1}$.

This formula applies whether the coordinates are positive or negative. In Fig. 1.3, for example, the gradient of AB is $\dfrac{5-(-1)}{3-(-2)}=\dfrac{5+1}{3+2}=\dfrac{6}{5}$.

But notice that in Fig. 1.4 the gradient is $\dfrac{2-5}{6-1}=\dfrac{-3}{5}=-\tfrac{3}{5}$; the negative gradient tells you that the line slopes downhill as you move from left to right.

As with the other formulae, it doesn't matter which point has the suffix 1 and which has the suffix 2. In Fig. 1.1, you can calculate the gradient as either $\dfrac{7-3}{10-4}=\dfrac{4}{6}=\dfrac{2}{3}$, or $\dfrac{3-7}{4-10}=\dfrac{-4}{-6}=\dfrac{2}{3}$.

Two lines are **parallel** if they have the same gradient.

Example 1.3.1

The ends of a line segment are $(p-q, p+q)$ and $(p+q, p-q)$. Find the length of the line segment, its gradient and the coordinates of its mid-point.

For the length and gradient you have to calculate

$$x_2 - x_1 = (p+q) - (p-q) = p+q-p+q = 2q$$

and $y_2 - y_1 = (p-q) - (p+q) = p-q-p-q = -2q.$

The length is $\sqrt{(x_2 - x_1)^2 + (y_2 - y_1)^2} = \sqrt{(2q)^2 + (-2q)^2} = \sqrt{4q^2 + 4q^2} = \sqrt{8q^2}$.

The gradient is $\dfrac{y_2 - y_1}{x_2 - x_1} = \dfrac{-2q}{2q} = -1.$

For the mid-point you have to calculate

$$x_1 + x_2 = (p-q) + (p+q) = p-q+p+q = 2p$$

and $y_1 + y_2 = (p+q) + (p-q) = p+q+p-q = 2p.$

The mid-point is $\left(\frac{1}{2}(x_1 + x_2), \frac{1}{2}(y_1 + y_2)\right) = \left(\frac{1}{2}(2p), \frac{1}{2}(2p)\right) = (p, p).$

Try drawing your own figure to illustrate the results in this example.

Example 1.3.2

Prove that the points $A(1,1)$, $B(5,3)$, $C(3,0)$ and $D(-1,-2)$ form a parallelogram.

You can approach this problem in a number of ways, but whichever method you use, it is worth drawing a sketch. This is shown in Fig. 1.8.

Method 1 (using distances)   In this method, find the lengths of the opposite sides. If both pairs of opposite sides are equal, then $ABCD$ is a parallelogram.

$$AB = \sqrt{(5-1)^2 + (3-1)^2} = \sqrt{20}.$$
$$DC = \sqrt{(3-(-1))^2 + (0-(-2))^2} = \sqrt{20}.$$
$$CB = \sqrt{(5-3)^2 + (3-0)^2} = \sqrt{13}.$$
$$DA = \sqrt{(1-(-1))^2 + (1-(-2))^2} = \sqrt{13}.$$

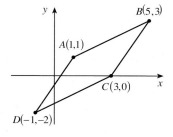

Fig. 1.8

Therefore $AB = DC$ and $CB = DA$, so $ABCD$ is a parallelogram.

Method 2 (using mid-points)   In this method, begin by finding the mid-points of the diagonals AC and BD. If these points are the same, then the diagonals bisect each other, so the quadrilateral is a parallelogram.

The mid-point of AC is $\left(\frac{1}{2}(1+3), \frac{1}{2}(1+0)\right)$, which is $\left(2, \frac{1}{2}\right)$. The mid-point of BD is $\left(\frac{1}{2}(5+(-1)), \frac{1}{2}(3+(-2))\right)$, which is also $\left(2, \frac{1}{2}\right)$. So $ABCD$ is a parallelogram.

Method 3 (using gradients)   In this method, find the gradients of the opposite sides. If both pairs of opposite sides are parallel, then $ABCD$ is a parallelogram.

The gradients of AB and DC are $\dfrac{3-1}{5-1} = \dfrac{2}{4} = \dfrac{1}{2}$ and $\dfrac{0-(-2)}{3-(-1)} = \dfrac{2}{4} = \dfrac{1}{2}$ respectively, so AB is parallel to DC. The gradients of DA and CB are both $\dfrac{3}{2}$, so DA is parallel to CB. As the opposite sides are parallel, $ABCD$ is a parallelogram.

Exercise 1A

Do not use a calculator. Where appropriate, leave square roots in your answers.

1   Find the lengths of the line segments joining these pairs of points. In parts (e) and (h) assume that $a > 0$; in parts (i) and (j) assume that $p > q > 0$.

   (a) $(2,5)$ and $(7,17)$ (b) $(-3,2)$ and $(1,-1)$

   (c) $(4,-5)$ and $(-1,0)$ (d) $(-3,-3)$ and $(-7,3)$

   (e) $(2a,a)$ and $(10a,-14a)$ (f) $(a+1,2a+3)$ and $(a-1,2a-1)$

   (g) $(2,9)$ and $(2,-14)$ (h) $(12a,5b)$ and $(3a,5b)$

   (i) (p,q) and (q,p) (j) $(p+4q,p-q)$ and $(p-3q,p)$

2   Show that the points $(1,-2)$, $(6,-1)$, $(9,3)$ and $(4,2)$ are vertices of a parallelogram.

3   Show that the triangle formed by the points $(-3,-2)$, $(2,-7)$ and $(-2,5)$ is isosceles.

4   Show that the points $(7,12)$, $(-3,-12)$ and $(14,-5)$ lie on a circle with centre $(2,0)$.

5   Find the coordinates of the mid-points of the line segments joining these pairs of points.

   (a) $(2,11),(6,15)$ (b) $(5,7),(-3,9)$

   (c) $(-2,-3),(1,-6)$ (d) $(-3,4),(-8,5)$

   (e) $(p+2,3p-1),(3p+4,p-5)$ (f) $(p+3,q-7),(p+5,3-q)$

   (g) $(p+2q,2p+13q),(5p-2q,-2p-7q)$ (h) $(a+3,b-5),(a+3,b+7)$

6   $A(-2,1)$ and $B(6,5)$ are the opposite ends of the diameter of a circle. Find the coordinates of its centre.

7   $M(5,7)$ is the mid-point of the line segment joining $A(3,4)$ to B. Find the coordinates of B.

8   $A(1,-2)$, $B(6,-1)$, $C(9,3)$ and $D(4,2)$ are the vertices of a parallelogram. Verify that the mid-points of the diagonals AC and BD coincide.

9   Which one of the points $A(5,2)$, $B(6,-3)$ and $C(4,7)$ is the mid-point of the other two? Check your answer by calculating two distances.

10   Find the gradients of the lines joining the following pairs of points.

   (a) $(3,8),(5,12)$ (b) $(1,-3),(-2,6)$

   (c) $(-4,-3),(0,-1)$ (d) $(-5,-3),(3,-9)$

   (e) $(p+3,p-3),(2p+4,-p-5)$ (f) $(p+3,q-5),(q-5,p+3)$

   (g) $(p+q-1,q+p-3),(p-q+1,q-p+3)$ (h) $(7,p),(11,p)$

11 Find the gradients of the lines AB and BC where A is $(3,4)$, B is $(7,6)$ and C is $(-3,1)$. What can you deduce about the points A, B and C?

12 The point $P(x,y)$ lies on the straight line joining $A(3,0)$ and $B(5,6)$. Find expressions for the gradients of AP and PB. Hence show that $y = 3x - 9$.

13 A line joining a vertex of a triangle to the mid-point of the opposite side is called a median. Find the length of the median AM in the triangle $A(-1,1)$, $B(0,3)$, $C(4,7)$.

14 A triangle has vertices $A(-2,1)$, $B(3,-4)$ and $C(5,7)$.

(a) Find the coordinates of M, the mid-point of AB, and N, the mid-point of AC.

(b) Show that MN is parallel to BC.

15 The points $A(2,1)$, $B(2,7)$ and $C(-4,-1)$ form a triangle. M is the mid-point of AB and N is the mid-point of AC.

(a) Find the lengths of MN and BC.   (b) Show that $BC = 2MN$.

16 The vertices of a quadrilateral $ABCD$ are $A(1,1)$, $B(7,3)$, $C(9,-7)$ and $D(-3,-3)$. The points P, Q, R and S are the mid-points of AB, BC, CD and DA respectively.

(a) Find the gradient of each side of $PQRS$.   (b) What type of quadrilateral is $PQRS$?

17 The origin O and the points $P(4,1)$, $Q(5,5)$ and $R(1,4)$ form a quadrilateral.

(a) Show that OR is parallel to PQ.   (b) Show that OP is parallel to RQ.

(c) Show that $OP = OR$.   (d) What shape is $OPQR$?

18 The origin O and the points $L(-2,3)$, $M(4,7)$ and $N(6,4)$ form a quadrilateral.

(a) Show that $ON = LM$.   (b) Show that ON is parallel to LM.

(c) Show that $OM = LN$.   (d) What shape is $OLMN$?

19 The vertices of a quadrilateral $PQRS$ are $P(1,2)$, $Q(7,0)$, $R(6,-4)$ and $S(-3,-1)$.

(a) Find the gradient of each side of the quadrilateral.

(b) What type of quadrilateral is $PQRS$?

20 The vertices of a quadrilateral are $T(3,2)$, $U(2,5)$, $V(8,7)$ and $W(6,1)$. The mid-points of UV and VW are M and N respectively. Show that the triangle TMN is isosceles.

21 The vertices of a quadrilateral $DEFG$ are $D(3,-2)$, $E(0,-3)$, $F(-2,3)$ and $G(4,1)$.

(a) Find the length of each side of the quadrilateral.

(b) What type of quadrilateral is $DEFG$?

22 The points $A(2,1)$, $B(6,10)$ and $C(10,1)$ form an isosceles triangle with AB and BC of equal length. The point G is $(6,4)$.

(a) Write down the coordinates of M, the mid-point of AC.

(b) Show that $BG = 2GM$ and that BGM is a straight line.

(c) Write down the coordinates of N, the mid-point of BC.

(d) Show that AGN is a straight line and that $AG = 2GN$.

1.4   What is meant by the equation of a straight line or of a curve?

How can you tell whether or not the points $(3,7)$ and $(1,5)$ lie on the curve $y = 3x^2 + 2$? The answer is to substitute the coordinates of the points into the equation and see whether they fit; that is, whether the equation is **satisfied** by the coordinates of the point.

For $(3,7)$: the right side is $3 \times 3^2 + 2 = 29$ and the left side is 7, so the equation is not satisfied. The point $(3,7)$ does not lie on the curve $y = 3x^2 + 2$.

For $(1,5)$: the right side is $3 \times 1^2 + 2 = 5$ and the left side is 5, so the equation is satisfied. The point $(1,5)$ lies on the curve $y = 3x^2 + 2$.

> The equation of a line or curve is a rule for determining whether or not the point with coordinates (x, y) lies on the line or curve.

This is an important way of thinking about the equation of a line or curve.

1.5   The equation of a line

Example 1.5.1
Find the equation of the line with gradient 2 which passes through the point $(2,1)$.

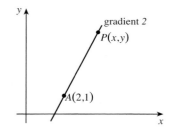

Fig. 1.9 shows the line of gradient 2 through $A(2,1)$, with another point $P(x,y)$ lying on it. P lies on the line if (and only if) the gradient of AP is 2.

Fig. 1.9

The gradient of AP is $\dfrac{y-1}{x-2}$. Equating this to 2 gives $\dfrac{y-1}{x-2} = 2$, which is $y - 1 = 2x - 4$, or $y = 2x - 3$.

In the general case, you need to find the equation of the line with gradient m through the point A with coordinates (x_1, y_1). Fig. 1.10 shows this line and another point P with coordinates (x,y) on it. The gradient of AP is $\dfrac{y - y_1}{x - x_1}$.

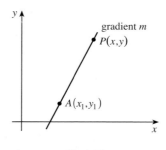

Fig. 1.10

Equating to m gives $\dfrac{y - y_1}{x - x_1} = m$, or $y - y_1 = m(x - x_1)$.

> The equation of the line through (x_1, y_1) with gradient m is $y - y_1 = m(x - x_1)$.

Notice that the coordinates of $A(x_1, y_1)$ satisfy this equation.

Example 1.5.2

Find the equation of the line through the point $(-2,3)$ with gradient -1.

Using the equation $y - y_1 = m(x - x_1)$ gives the equation $y - 3 = -1(x - (-2))$, which is $y - 3 = -x - 2$ or $y = -x + 1$. As a check, substitute the coordinates $(-2,3)$ into both sides of the equation, to make sure that the given point does actually lie on the line.

Example 1.5.3

Find the equation of the line joining the points $(3,4)$ and $(-1,2)$.

To find this equation, first find the gradient of the line joining $(3,4)$ to $(-1,2)$. Then you can use the equation $y - y_1 = m(x - x_1)$.

The gradient of the line joining $(3,4)$ to $(-1,2)$ is $\dfrac{2-4}{(-1)-3} = \dfrac{-2}{-4} = \dfrac{1}{2}$.

The equation of the line through $(3,4)$ with gradient $\frac{1}{2}$ is $y - 4 = \frac{1}{2}(x - 3)$. After multiplying out and simplifying you get $2y - 8 = x - 3$, or $2y = x + 5$.

Check this equation mentally by substituting the coordinates of the other point.

1.6 Recognising the equation of a line

The answers to Examples 1.5.1–1.5.3 can all be written in the form $y = mx + c$, where m and c are numbers.

It is easy to show that any equation of this form is the equation of a straight line. If $y = mx + c$, then $y - c = m(x - 0)$, or

$$\frac{y - c}{x - 0} = m \qquad \text{(except when } x = 0\text{)}.$$

This equation tells you that, for all points (x,y) whose coordinates satisfy the equation, the line joining $(0,c)$ to (x,y) has gradient m. That is, (x,y) lies on the line through $(0,c)$ with gradient m.

The point $(0,c)$ lies on the y-axis. The number c is called the **y-intercept** of the line.

To find the x-intercept, put $y = 0$ in the equation, which gives $x = -\dfrac{c}{m}$. But notice that you can't do this division if $m = 0$. In that case the line is parallel to the x-axis, so there is no x-intercept.

When $m = 0$, all the points on the line have coordinates of the form $(\text{something}, c)$. Thus the points $(1,2)$, $(-1,2)$, $(5,2)$, ... all lie on the straight line $y = 2$, shown in Fig. 1.11. As a special case, the x-axis has equation $y = 0$.

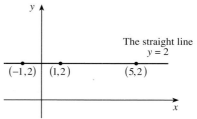

Fig. 1.11

Similarly, a straight line parallel to the y-axis has an equation of the form $x = k$. All points on it have coordinates $(k, \text{something})$. Thus the points $(3,0)$, $(3,2)$, $(3,4)$, ... all lie on the line $x = 3$, shown in Fig. 1.12. The y-axis itself has equation $x = 0$.

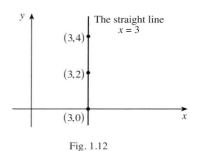

Fig. 1.12

The line $x = k$ does not have a gradient; its gradient is undefined. Its equation cannot be written in the form $y = mx + c$.

1.7   The equation $ax + by + c = 0$

Suppose you have the equation $y = \frac{2}{3}x + \frac{4}{3}$. It is natural to multiply by 3 to get $3y = 2x + 4$, which can be rearranged to get $2x - 3y + 4 = 0$. This equation is in the form $ax + by + c = 0$ where a, b and c are constants.

Notice that the straight lines $y = mx + c$ and $ax + by + c = 0$ both contain the letter c, but it doesn't have the same meaning. For $y = mx + c$, c is the y-intercept, but there is no similar meaning for the c in $ax + by + c = 0$.

A simple way to find the gradient of $ax + by + c = 0$ is to rearrange it into the form $y = \dots$. Here are some examples.

Example 1.7.1
Find the gradient of the line $2x + 3y - 4 = 0$.

Write this equation in the form $y = \dots$, and then use the fact that the straight line $y = mx + c$ has gradient m.

From $2x + 3y - 4 = 0$ you find that $3y = -2x + 4$ and $y = -\frac{2}{3}x + \frac{4}{3}$. Therefore, comparing this equation with $y = mx + c$, the gradient is $-\frac{2}{3}$.

Example 1.7.2
One side of a parallelogram lies along the straight line with equation $3x - 4y - 7 = 0$. The point $(2,3)$ is a vertex of the parallelogram. Find the equation of one other side.

The line $3x - 4y - 7 = 0$ is the same as $y = \frac{3}{4}x - \frac{7}{4}$, so its gradient is $\frac{3}{4}$. The line through $(2,3)$ with gradient $\frac{3}{4}$ is $y - 3 = \frac{3}{4}(x - 2)$, or $3x - 4y + 6 = 0$.

1.8   The point of intersection of two lines

Suppose that you have two lines with equations $2x - y = 4$ and $3x + 2y = -1$. How do you find the coordinates of the point of intersection of these lines?

You want the point (x, y) which lies on both lines, so the coordinates (x, y) satisfy both equations. Therefore you need to solve the equations simultaneously.

From these two equations, you find $x = 1$, $y = -2$, so the point of intersection is $(1, -2)$.

This argument applies to straight lines with any equations provided they are not parallel. To find points of intersection, solve the equations simultaneously. The method can also be used to find the points of intersection of two curves.

Exercise 1B

1 Test whether the given point lies on the straight line (or curve) with the given equation.

   (a) $(1, 2)$ on $y = 5x - 3$ (b) $(3, -2)$ on $y = 3x - 7$

   (c) $(3, -4)$ on $x^2 + y^2 = 25$ (d) $(2, 2)$ on $3x^2 + y^2 = 40$

   (e) $\left(1, 1\tfrac{1}{2}\right)$ on $y = \dfrac{x + 2}{3x - 1}$ (f) $\left(5p, \dfrac{5}{p}\right)$ on $y = \dfrac{5}{x}$

   (g) $\left(p, (p-1)^2 + 1\right)$ on $y = x^2 - 2x + 2$ (h) $\left(t^2, 2t\right)$ on $y^2 = 4x$

2 Find the equations of the straight lines through the given points with the gradients shown. Your final answers should not contain any fractions.

   (a) $(2, 3)$, gradient 5   (b) $(1, -2)$, gradient -3

   (c) $(0, 4)$, gradient $\tfrac{1}{2}$ (d) $(-2, 1)$, gradient $-\tfrac{3}{8}$

   (e) $(0, 0)$, gradient -3 (f) $(3, 8)$, gradient 0

   (g) $(-5, -1)$, gradient $-\tfrac{3}{4}$ (h) $(-3, 0)$, gradient $\tfrac{1}{2}$

   (i) $(-3, -1)$, gradient $\tfrac{3}{8}$ (j) $(3, 4)$, gradient $-\tfrac{1}{2}$

   (k) $(2, -1)$, gradient -2 (l) $(-2, -5)$, gradient 3

   (m) $(0, -4)$, gradient 7   (n) $(0, 2)$, gradient -1

   (o) $(3, -2)$, gradient $-\tfrac{5}{8}$ (p) $(3, 0)$, gradient $-\tfrac{3}{5}$

   (q) $(d, 0)$, gradient 7   (r) $(0, 4)$, gradient m

   (s) $(0, c)$, gradient 3   (t) $(c, 0)$, gradient m

3 Find the equations of the lines joining the following pairs of points. Leave your final answer without fractions and in one of the forms $y = mx + c$ or $ax + by + c = 0$.

   (a) $(1, 4)$ and $(3, 10)$ (b) $(4, 5)$ and $(-2, -7)$

   (c) $(3, 2)$ and $(0, 4)$ (d) $(3, 7)$ and $(3, 12)$

   (e) $(10, -3)$ and $(-5, -12)$ (f) $(3, -1)$ and $(-4, 20)$

   (g) $(2, -3)$ and $(11, -3)$ (h) $(2, 0)$ and $(5, -1)$

   (i) $(-4, 2)$ and $(-1, -3)$ (j) $(-2, -1)$ and $(5, -3)$

   (k) $(-3, 4)$ and $(-3, 9)$ (l) $(-1, 0)$ and $(0, -1)$

   (m) $(2, 7)$ and $(3, 10)$ (n) $(-5, 4)$ and $(-2, -1)$

   (o) $(0, 0)$ and $(5, -3)$ (p) $(0, 0)$ and (p, q)

   (q) (p, q) and $(p + 3, q - 1)$ (r) $(p, -q)$ and (p, q)

   (s) (p, q) and $(p + 2, q + 2)$ (t) $(p, 0)$ and $(0, q)$

4 Find the gradients of the following lines.

(a) $2x + y = 7$

(b) $3x - 4y = 8$

(c) $5x + 2y = -3$

(d) $y = 5$

(e) $3x - 2y = -4$

(f) $5x = 7$

(g) $x + y = -3$

(h) $y = 3(x + 4)$

(i) $7 - x = 2y$

(j) $3(y - 4) = 7x$

(k) $y = m(x - d)$

(l) $px + qy = pq$

5 Find the equation of the line through $(-2, 1)$ parallel to $y = \frac{1}{2}x - 3$.

6 Find the equation of the line through $(4, -3)$ parallel to $y + 2x = 7$.

7 Find the equation of the line through $(1, 2)$ parallel to the line joining $(3, -1)$ and $(-5, 2)$.

8 Find the equation of the line through $(3, 9)$ parallel to the line joining $(-3, 2)$ and $(2, -3)$.

9 Find the equation of the line through $(1, 7)$ parallel to the x-axis.

10 Find the equation of the line through $(d, 0)$ parallel to $y = mx + c$.

11 Find the points of intersection of the following pairs of straight lines.

(a) $3x + 4y = 33, \ 2y = x - 1$

(b) $y = 3x + 1, \ y = 4x - 1$

(c) $2y = 7x, \ 3x - 2y = 1$

(d) $y = 3x + 8, \ y = -2x - 7$

(e) $x + 5y = 22, \ 3x + 2y = 14$

(f) $2x + 7y = 47, \ 5x + 4y = 50$

(g) $2x + 3y = 7, \ 6x + 9y = 11$

(h) $3x + y = 5, \ x + 3y = -1$

(i) $y = 2x + 3, \ 4x - 2y = -6$

(j) $ax + by = c, \ y = 2ax$

(k) $y = mx + c, \ y = -mx + d$

(l) $ax - by = 1, \ y = x$

12 Let P, with coordinates (p, q), be a fixed point on the 'curve' with equation $y = mx + c$ and let Q, with coordinates (r, s), be any other point on $y = mx + c$. Use the fact that the coordinates of P and Q satisfy the equation $y = mx + c$ to show that the gradient of PQ is m for all positions of Q.

13 There are some values of a, b and c for which the equation $ax + by + c = 0$ does not represent a straight line. Give an example of such values.

1.9 The gradients of perpendicular lines

In Section 1.3 it is stated that two lines are parallel if they have the same gradient. But what can you say about the gradients of two lines which are perpendicular?

Firstly, if a line has a positive gradient, then the perpendicular line has a negative gradient, and vice versa. But you can be more exact than this.

In Fig. 1.13, if the gradient of PB is m, you can draw a 'gradient triangle' PAB in which PA is one unit and AB is m units.

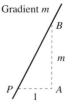

Fig. 1.13

In Fig 1.14, the gradient triangle PAB has been rotated through a right-angle to $PA'B'$, so that PB' is perpendicular to PB. The y-step for $PA'B'$ is 1 and the x-step is $-m$, so

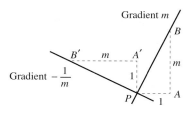

Fig. 1.14

$$\text{gradient of } PB' = \frac{y\text{-step}}{x\text{-step}} = \frac{1}{-m} = -\frac{1}{m}.$$

Therefore the gradient of the line perpendicular to PB is $-\dfrac{1}{m}$.

Thus if the gradients of the two perpendicular lines are m_1 and m_2, then $m_1 m_2 = -1$. It is also true that if two lines have gradients m_1 and m_2, and if $m_1 m_2 = -1$, then the lines are perpendicular. To prove this, see Miscellaneous exercise 1 Question 22.

> Two lines with gradients m_1 and m_2 are perpendicular if
>
> $$m_1 m_2 = -1, \quad \text{or} \quad m_1 = -\frac{1}{m_2}, \quad \text{or} \quad m_2 = -\frac{1}{m_1}.$$

Notice that the condition does not work if the lines are parallel to the axes. However, you can see that a line $x = \text{constant}$ is perpendicular to one of the form $y = \text{constant}$.

Example 1.9.1
Show that the points $(0,-5)$, $(-1,2)$, $(4,7)$ and $(5,0)$ form a rhombus.

You could tackle this question in several ways. This solution shows that the points form a parallelogram, and then that its diagonals are perpendicular.

The mid-points of the diagonals are $\left(\frac{1}{2}(0+4),\frac{1}{2}(-5+7)\right)$, or $(2,1)$, and $\left(\frac{1}{2}((-1)+5),\frac{1}{2}(2+0)\right)$, or $(2,1)$. As these are the same point, the quadrilateral is a parallelogram.

The gradients of the diagonals are $\dfrac{7-(-5)}{4-0} = \dfrac{12}{4} = 3$ and $\dfrac{0-2}{5-(-1)} = \dfrac{-2}{6} = -\dfrac{1}{3}$. As the product of the gradients is -1, the diagonals are perpendicular. Therefore the parallelogram is a rhombus.

Example 1.9.2
Find the coordinates of the foot of the perpendicular from $A(-2,-4)$ to the line joining $B(0,2)$ and $C(-1,4)$.

Always draw a diagram, like Fig. 1.15; it need not be to scale. The foot of the perpendicular is the point of intersection, P, of BC and the line through A perpendicular to BC. First find the gradient of BC and its equation.

The gradient of BC is $\dfrac{4-2}{-1-0} = \dfrac{2}{-1} = -2$.

The equation of BC is $y - 2 = -2(x-0)$,
which simplifies to $2x + y = 2$.

The gradient of the line through A
perpendicular to BC is $-\dfrac{1}{-2} = \tfrac{1}{2}$.

The equation of this line is

$$y - (-4) = \tfrac{1}{2}(x - (-2)),$$

or $x - 2y = 6$.

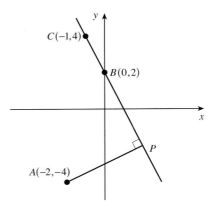

Fig. 1.15

These lines meet at the point P, whose
coordinates satisfy the simultaneous
equations $2x + y = 2$ and $x - 2y = 6$.
This is the point $(2,-2)$.

Exercise 1C

1   In each part write down the gradient of a line which is perpendicular to one with the given gradient.

(a) 2   (b) -3 (c) $\frac{3}{4}$ (d) $-\frac{5}{6}$

(e) -1 (f) $1\frac{3}{4}$ (g) $-\dfrac{1}{m}$ (h) m

(i) $\dfrac{p}{q}$ (j) 0   (k) $-m$ (l) $\dfrac{a}{b-c}$

2   In each part find the equation of the line through the given point which is perpendicular to the given line. Write your final answer so that it doesn't contain fractions.

(a) $(2,3)$, $y = 4x + 3$ (b) $(-3,1)$, $y = -\frac{1}{2}x + 3$

(c) $(2,-5)$, $y = -5x - 2$ (d) $(7,-4)$, $y = 2\frac{1}{2}$

(e) $(-1,4)$, $2x + 3y = 8$ (f) $(4,3)$, $3x - 5y = 8$

(g) $(5,-3)$, $2x = 3$ (h) $(0,3)$, $y = 2x - 1$

(i) $(0,0)$, $y = mx + c$ (j) (a,b), $y = mx + c$

(k) (c,d), $ny - x = p$ (l) $(-1,-2)$, $ax + by = c$

3   Find the equation of the line through the point $(-2,5)$ which is perpendicular to the line $y = 3x + 1$. Find also the point of intersection of the two lines.

4   Find the equation of the line through the point $(1,1)$ which is perpendicular to the line $2x - 3y = 12$. Find also the point of intersection of the two lines.

5   A line through a vertex of a triangle which is perpendicular to the opposite side is called an altitude. Find the equation of the altitude through the vertex A of the triangle ABC where A is the point $(2,3)$, B is $(1,-7)$ and C is $(4,-1)$.

6 $P(2,5)$, $Q(12,5)$ and $R(8,-7)$ form a triangle.

    (a) Find the equations of the altitudes (see Question 5) through (i) R and (ii) Q.

    (b) Find the point of intersection of these altitudes.

    (c) Show that the altitude through P also passes through this point.

Miscellaneous exercise 1

1 Show that the triangle formed by the points $(-2,5)$, $(1,3)$ and $(5,9)$ is right-angled.

2 Find the coordinates of the point where the lines $2x + y = 3$ and $3x + 5y - 1 = 0$ meet.

3 A triangle is formed by the points $A(-1,3)$, $B(5,7)$ and $C(0,8)$.

    (a) Show that the angle ACB is a right angle.

    (b) Find the coordinates of the point where the line through B parallel to AC cuts the x-axis.

4 $A(7,2)$ and $C(1,4)$ are two vertices of a square $ABCD$.

    (a) Find the equation of the diagonal BD.

    (b) Find the coordinates of B and of D.

5 A quadrilateral $ABCD$ is formed by the points $A(-3,2)$, $B(4,3)$, $C(9,-2)$ and $D(2,-3)$.

    (a) Show that all four sides are equal in length.

    (b) Show that $ABCD$ is not a square.

6 P is the point $(7,5)$ and l_1 is the line with equation $3x + 4y = 16$.

    (a) Find the equation of the line l_2 which passes through P and is perpendicular to l_1.

    (b) Find the point of intersection of the lines l_1 and l_2.

    (c) Find the perpendicular distance of P from the line l_1.

7 Prove that the triangle with vertices $(-2,8)$, $(3,20)$ and $(11,8)$ is isosceles. Find its area.

8 The three straight lines $y = x$, $7y = 2x$ and $4x + y = 60$ form a triangle. Find the coordinates of its vertices.

9 Find the equation of the line through $(1,3)$ which is parallel to $2x + 7y = 5$. Give your answer in the form $ax + by = c$.

10 Find the equation of the perpendicular bisector of the line joining $(2,-5)$ and $(-4,3)$.

11 The points $A(1,2)$, $B(3,5)$, $C(6,6)$ and D form a parallelogram. Find the coordinates of the mid-point of AC. Use your answer to find the coordinates of D.

12 The point P is the foot of the perpendicular from the point $A(0,3)$ to the line $y = 3x$.

    (a) Find the equation of the line AP.

    (b) Find the coordinates of the point P.

    (c) Find the perpendicular distance of A from the line $y = 3x$.

13 Points which lie on the same straight line are called collinear. Show that the points $(-1,3)$, $(4,7)$ and $(-11,-5)$ are collinear.

14 Find the equation of the straight line that passes through the points $(3,-1)$ and $(-2,2)$, giving your answer in the form $ax + by + c = 0$. Hence find the coordinates of the point of intersection of the line and the x-axis.   (OCR)

15 The coordinates of the points A and B are $(3,2)$ and $(4,-5)$ respectively. Find the coordinates of the mid-point of AB, and the gradient of AB.

    Hence find the equation of the perpendicular bisector of AB, giving your answer in the form $ax + by + c = 0$, where a, b and c are integers.   (OCR)

16 The curve $y = 1 + \dfrac{1}{2+x}$ crosses the x-axis at the point A and the y-axis at the point B.

    (a) Calculate the coordinates of A and of B.

    (b) Find the equation of the line AB.

    (c) Calculate the coordinates of the point of intersection of the line AB and the line with equation $3y = 4x$.   (OCR)

17 The straight line p passes through the point $(10,1)$ and is perpendicular to the line r with equation $2x + y = 1$. Find the equation of p.

    Find also the coordinates of the point of intersection of p and r, and deduce the perpendicular distance from the point $(10,1)$ to the line r.   (OCR)

18 Show by calculation that the points $P(0,7)$, $Q(6,5)$, $R(5,2)$ and $S(-1,4)$ are the vertices of a rectangle.

19 The line $3x - 4y = 8$ meets the y-axis at A. The point C has coordinates $(-2,9)$. The line through C perpendicular to $3x - 4y = 8$ meets it at B. Calculate the area of the triangle ABC.

20 The points $A(-3,-4)$ and $C(5,4)$ are the ends of the diagonal of a rhombus $ABCD$.

    (a) Find the equation of the diagonal BD.

    (b) Given that the side BC has gradient $\frac{5}{3}$, find the coordinates of B and hence of D.

21 Find the equations of the medians (see Exercise 1A Question 13) of the triangle with vertices $(0,2)$, $(6,0)$ and $(4,4)$. Show that the medians are concurrent (all pass through the same point).

22 Two lines have equations $y = m_1 x + c_1$ and $y = m_2 x + c_2$, and $m_1 m_2 = -1$. Prove that the lines are perpendicular.

2 Surds and indices

The first part of this chapter is about expressions involving square and cube roots. The second part is about index notation. When you have completed it, you should

- be able to simplify expressions involving square, cube and other roots
- know the rules of indices
- know the meaning of negative, zero and fractional indices
- be able to simplify expressions involving indices.

2.1 Different kinds of number

At first numbers were used only for counting, and $1, 2, 3, \ldots$ were all that was needed. These are **natural numbers**, or **positive integers**.

Then it was found that numbers could also be useful for measurement and in commerce. For these purposes fractions were also needed. Integers and fractions together make up the **rational numbers**. These are numbers which can be expressed in the form $\frac{p}{q}$ where p and q are integers, and q is not 0.

One of the most remarkable discoveries of the ancient Greek mathematicians was that there are numbers which cannot be expressed in this way. These are called **irrational numbers**. The first such number to be found was $\sqrt{2}$, which is the length of the diagonal of a square with side 1 unit, by Pythagoras' theorem. The argument that the Greeks used to prove that $\sqrt{2}$ cannot be expressed as a fraction can be adapted to show that the square root, cube root, ... of any positive integer is either an integer or an irrational number. Many other numbers are now known to be irrational, of which the most well known is π.

Rational and irrational numbers together make up the **real numbers**. Integers, rational and irrational numbers, and real numbers can be either positive, negative or zero.

When rational numbers are written as decimals, they either come to a stop after a number of places, or the sequence of decimal digits eventually starts repeating in a regular pattern. For example,

$$\frac{7}{10} = 0.7, \quad \frac{7}{11} = 0.6363\ldots, \quad \frac{7}{12} = 0.5833\ldots, \quad \frac{7}{13} = 0.538\,461\,538\,461\,53\ldots,$$
$$\frac{7}{14} = 0.5, \quad \frac{7}{15} = 0.466\ldots, \quad \frac{7}{16} = 0.4375, \quad \frac{7}{17} = 0.411\,764\,705\,882\,352\,941\,176\ldots$$

The reverse is also true: if a decimal number stops or repeats indefinitely then it is a rational number. So if an irrational number is written as a decimal, the pattern of the decimal digits never repeats however long you continue the calculation.

2.2 Surds and their properties

When you met expressions such as $\sqrt{2}$, $\sqrt{8}$ and $\sqrt{12}$ before, it is likely that you used a calculator to express them in decimal form. You might have written

$$\sqrt{2} = 1.414\ldots \quad \text{or} \quad \sqrt{2} = 1.414 \text{ correct to 3 decimal places} \quad \text{or} \quad \sqrt{2} \approx 1.414.$$

Why is the statement '$\sqrt{2} = 1.414$' incorrect?

Expressions like $\sqrt{2}$ or $\sqrt[3]{9}$ are called **surds**. This section is about calculating with surds. You need to remember that $\sqrt{x}$ always means the *positive* square root of x (or zero when $x = 0$).

The main properties of surds that you will use are:

$$\sqrt{xy} = \sqrt{x} \times \sqrt{y} \quad \text{and} \quad \sqrt{\frac{x}{y}} = \frac{\sqrt{x}}{\sqrt{y}}.$$

You can see that as $\left(\sqrt{x} \times \sqrt{y}\right) \times \left(\sqrt{x} \times \sqrt{y}\right) = \left(\sqrt{x} \times \sqrt{x}\right) \times \left(\sqrt{y} \times \sqrt{y}\right) = x \times y = xy$, and as $\sqrt{x} \times \sqrt{y}$ is positive, it is the square root of xy. Therefore $\sqrt{xy} = \sqrt{x} \times \sqrt{y}$. Similar reasoning will convince you that $\sqrt{\frac{x}{y}} = \frac{\sqrt{x}}{\sqrt{y}}$.

The following examples illustrate these properties:

$$\sqrt{8} = \sqrt{4 \times 2} = \sqrt{4} \times \sqrt{2} = 2\sqrt{2}; \quad \sqrt{12} = \sqrt{4 \times 3} = \sqrt{4} \times \sqrt{3} = 2\sqrt{3};$$

$$\sqrt{18} \times \sqrt{2} = \sqrt{18 \times 2} = \sqrt{36} = 6; \quad \frac{\sqrt{27}}{\sqrt{3}} = \sqrt{\frac{27}{3}} = \sqrt{9} = 3.$$

It is well worth checking some or all of the calculations above on your calculator.

Example 2.2.1
Simplify   (a) $\sqrt{28} + \sqrt{63}$,   (b) $\sqrt{5} \times \sqrt{10}$.

Alternative methods of solution may be possible, as in part (b).

(a) $\sqrt{28} + \sqrt{63} = \left(\sqrt{4} \times \sqrt{7}\right) + \left(\sqrt{9} \times \sqrt{7}\right) = 2\sqrt{7} + 3\sqrt{7} = 5\sqrt{7}$.

(b) **Method 1** $\sqrt{5} \times \sqrt{10} = \sqrt{5 \times 10} = \sqrt{50} = \sqrt{25 \times 2} = 5\sqrt{2}$.

     Method 2 $\sqrt{5} \times \sqrt{10} = \sqrt{5} \times \left(\sqrt{5} \times \sqrt{2}\right) = \left(\sqrt{5} \times \sqrt{5}\right) \times \sqrt{2} = 5\sqrt{2}$.

It is sometimes useful to be able to remove a surd from the denominator of a fraction such as $\dfrac{1}{\sqrt{2}}$. You can do this by multiplying top and bottom by $\sqrt{2}$: $\dfrac{1 \times \sqrt{2}}{\sqrt{2} \times \sqrt{2}} = \dfrac{\sqrt{2}}{2}$.

Results which it is often helpful to use are:

$$\frac{x}{\sqrt{x}} = \sqrt{x} \text{ , and its reciprocal } \frac{1}{\sqrt{x}} = \frac{\sqrt{x}}{x} \text{ .}$$

Removing the surd from the denominator is called **rationalising the denominator**.

Example 2.2.2
Rationalise the denominator in the expressions   (a) $\dfrac{6}{\sqrt{2}}$,   (b) $\dfrac{3\sqrt{2}}{\sqrt{10}}$.

(a) $\dfrac{6}{\sqrt{2}} = \dfrac{3 \times 2}{\sqrt{2}} = 3 \times \dfrac{2}{\sqrt{2}} = 3\sqrt{2}.$

(b) $\dfrac{3\sqrt{2}}{\sqrt{10}} = \dfrac{3 \times \sqrt{2}}{\sqrt{5} \times \sqrt{2}} = \dfrac{3}{\sqrt{5}} = \dfrac{3\sqrt{5}}{5}.$

Similar rules to those for square roots also apply to cube roots and higher roots.

Example 2.2.3
Simplify   (a) $\sqrt[3]{16}$,   (b) $\sqrt[3]{12} \times \sqrt[3]{18}$.

(a) $\sqrt[3]{16} = \sqrt[3]{8 \times 2} = \sqrt[3]{8} \times \sqrt[3]{2} = 2 \times \sqrt[3]{2}.$

(b) $\sqrt[3]{12} \times \sqrt[3]{18} = \sqrt[3]{12 \times 18} = \sqrt[3]{216} = 6.$

Example 2.2.4
Fig. 2.1 shows the vertical cross-section of a roof of a building as a right-angled triangle ABC, with $AB = 15$ m. The height of the roof, BD, is 10 m. Calculate x and y.

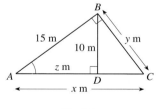

Fig. 2.1

Starting with triangle ADB, by Pythagoras' theorem $z^2 + 10^2 = 15^2$, so $z^2 = 225 - 100 = 125$ and

$$z = \sqrt{125} = \sqrt{25 \times 5} = 5\sqrt{5}.$$

Now notice that the triangles ADB and ABC are similar. You can see the similarity more clearly by flipping triangle ADB over to make the side AB horizontal, as in Fig. 2.2. The sides of triangles ADB and ABC must therefore be in the same proportion, so

$$\frac{x}{15} = \frac{y}{10} = \frac{15}{z}. \text{ Since } \frac{15}{z} = \frac{15}{5\sqrt{5}} = \frac{3}{\sqrt{5}} = \frac{3\sqrt{5}}{5},$$

$$x = 15 \times \frac{3\sqrt{5}}{5} = 9\sqrt{5} \quad \text{and} \quad y = 10 \times \frac{3\sqrt{5}}{5} = 6\sqrt{5}.$$

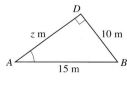

Fig. 2.2

Use Pythagoras' theorem in triangle ABC to check that $x^2 = 15^2 + y^2$.

Exercise 2A

1 Simplify the following without using a calculator.

(a) $\sqrt{3} \times \sqrt{3}$ (b) $\sqrt{10} \times \sqrt{10}$ (c) $\sqrt{16} \times \sqrt{16}$ (d) $\sqrt{8} \times \sqrt{2}$

(e) $\sqrt{32} \times \sqrt{2}$ (f) $\sqrt{3} \times \sqrt{12}$ (g) $5\sqrt{3} \times \sqrt{3}$ (h) $2\sqrt{5} \times 3\sqrt{5}$

(i) $3\sqrt{6} \times 4\sqrt{6}$ (j) $2\sqrt{20} \times 3\sqrt{5}$ (k) $\left(2\sqrt{7}\right)^2$ (l) $\left(3\sqrt{3}\right)^2$

(m) $\sqrt[3]{5} \times \sqrt[3]{5} \times \sqrt[3]{5}$ (n) $\left(2\sqrt[4]{3}\right)^4$ (o) $\left(2\sqrt[3]{2}\right)^6$ (p) $\sqrt[4]{125} \times \sqrt[4]{5}$

2 Simplify the following without using a calculator.

(a) $\sqrt{18}$ (b) $\sqrt{20}$ (c) $\sqrt{24}$ (d) $\sqrt{32}$

(e) $\sqrt{40}$ (f) $\sqrt{45}$ (g) $\sqrt{48}$ (h) $\sqrt{50}$

(i) $\sqrt{54}$ (j) $\sqrt{72}$ (k) $\sqrt{135}$ (l) $\sqrt{675}$

3 Simplify the following without using a calculator.

(a) $\sqrt{8} + \sqrt{18}$ (b) $\sqrt{3} + \sqrt{12}$ (c) $\sqrt{20} - \sqrt{5}$

(d) $\sqrt{32} - \sqrt{8}$ (e) $\sqrt{50} - \sqrt{18} - \sqrt{8}$ (f) $\sqrt{27} + \sqrt{27}$

(g) $\sqrt{99} + \sqrt{44} + \sqrt{11}$ (h) $8\sqrt{2} + 2\sqrt{8}$ (i) $2\sqrt{20} + 3\sqrt{45}$

(j) $\sqrt{52} - \sqrt{13}$ (k) $20\sqrt{5} + 5\sqrt{20}$ (l) $\sqrt{48} + \sqrt{24} - \sqrt{75} + \sqrt{96}$

4 Simplify the following without using a calculator.

(a) $\dfrac{\sqrt{8}}{\sqrt{2}}$ (b) $\dfrac{\sqrt{27}}{\sqrt{3}}$ (c) $\dfrac{\sqrt{40}}{\sqrt{10}}$ (d) $\dfrac{\sqrt{50}}{\sqrt{2}}$

(e) $\dfrac{\sqrt{125}}{\sqrt{5}}$ (f) $\dfrac{\sqrt{54}}{\sqrt{6}}$ (g) $\dfrac{\sqrt{3}}{\sqrt{48}}$ (h) $\dfrac{\sqrt{50}}{\sqrt{200}}$

5 Rationalise the denominator in each of the following expressions, and simplify them.

(a) $\dfrac{1}{\sqrt{3}}$ (b) $\dfrac{1}{\sqrt{5}}$ (c) $\dfrac{4}{\sqrt{2}}$ (d) $\dfrac{6}{\sqrt{6}}$

(e) $\dfrac{11}{\sqrt{11}}$ (f) $\dfrac{2}{\sqrt{8}}$ (g) $\dfrac{12}{\sqrt{3}}$ (h) $\dfrac{14}{\sqrt{7}}$

(i) $\dfrac{\sqrt{6}}{\sqrt{2}}$ (j) $\dfrac{\sqrt{2}}{\sqrt{6}}$ (k) $\dfrac{3\sqrt{5}}{\sqrt{3}}$ (l) $\dfrac{4\sqrt{6}}{\sqrt{5}}$

(m) $\dfrac{7\sqrt{2}}{2\sqrt{3}}$ (n) $\dfrac{4\sqrt{2}}{\sqrt{12}}$ (o) $\dfrac{9\sqrt{12}}{2\sqrt{18}}$ (p) $\dfrac{2\sqrt{18}}{9\sqrt{12}}$

6 Simplify the following, giving each answer in the form $k\sqrt{3}$.

(a) $\sqrt{75} + \sqrt{12}$ (b) $6 + \sqrt{3}\left(4 - 2\sqrt{3}\right)$ (c) $\dfrac{12}{\sqrt{3}} - \sqrt{27}$

(d) $\dfrac{2}{\sqrt{3}} + \dfrac{\sqrt{2}}{\sqrt{6}}$ (e) $\sqrt{2} \times \sqrt{8} \times \sqrt{27}$ (f) $\left(3 - \sqrt{3}\right)\left(2 - \sqrt{3}\right) - \sqrt{3} \times \sqrt{27}$

7 *ABCD* is a rectangle in which $AB = 4\sqrt{5}$ cm and $BC = \sqrt{10}$ cm. Giving each answer in simplified surd form, find

(a) the area of the rectangle,   (b) the length of the diagonal *AC*.

8 Solve the following equations, giving each answer in the form $k\sqrt{2}$.

(a) $x\sqrt{2} = 10$

(b) $2y\sqrt{2} - 3 = \dfrac{5y}{\sqrt{2}} + 1$

(c) $z\sqrt{32} - 16 = z\sqrt{8} - 4$

9 Express in the form $k\sqrt[3]{3}$

(a) $\sqrt[3]{24}$,

(b) $\sqrt[3]{81} + \sqrt[3]{3}$,

(c) $\left(\sqrt[3]{3}\right)^4$,

(d) $\sqrt[3]{3000} - \sqrt[3]{375}$.

10 Find the length of the third side in each of the following right-angled triangles, giving each answer in simplified surd form.

(a)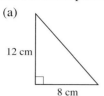

(b)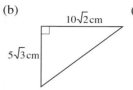

(c)

(d)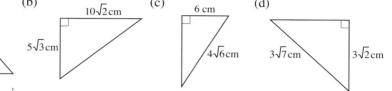

11 You are given that, correct to 12 decimal places, $\sqrt{26} = 5.099\,019\,513\,593$.

(a) Find the value of $\sqrt{104}$ correct to 10 decimal places.

(b) Find the value of $\sqrt{650}$ correct to 10 decimal places.

(c) Find the value of $\dfrac{13}{\sqrt{26}}$ correct to 10 decimal places.

12 Solve the simultaneous equations $7x - \left(3\sqrt{5}\right)y = 9\sqrt{5}$ and $\left(2\sqrt{5}\right)x + y = 34$.

13 Simplify the following.

(a) $\left(\sqrt{2} - 1\right)\left(\sqrt{2} + 1\right)$

(b) $\left(2 - \sqrt{3}\right)\left(2 + \sqrt{3}\right)$

(c) $\left(\sqrt{7} + \sqrt{3}\right)\left(\sqrt{7} - \sqrt{3}\right)$

(d) $\left(2\sqrt{2} + 1\right)\left(2\sqrt{2} - 1\right)$

(e) $\left(4\sqrt{3} - \sqrt{2}\right)\left(4\sqrt{3} + \sqrt{2}\right)$

(f) $\left(\sqrt{10} + \sqrt{5}\right)\left(\sqrt{10} - \sqrt{5}\right)$

(g) $\left(4\sqrt{7} - \sqrt{5}\right)\left(4\sqrt{7} + \sqrt{5}\right)$

(h) $\left(2\sqrt{6} - 3\sqrt{3}\right)\left(2\sqrt{6} + 3\sqrt{3}\right)$

14 In Question 13, every answer is an integer. Copy and complete each of the following.

(a) $\left(\sqrt{3} - 1\right)\left(\qquad\right) = 2$

(b) $\left(\sqrt{5} + 1\right)\left(\qquad\right) = 4$

(c) $\left(\sqrt{6} - \sqrt{2}\right)\left(\qquad\right) = 4$

(d) $\left(2\sqrt{7} + \sqrt{3}\right)\left(\qquad\right) = 25$

(e) $\left(\sqrt{11} + \sqrt{10}\right)\left(\qquad\right) = 1$

(f) $\left(3\sqrt{5} - 2\sqrt{6}\right)\left(\qquad\right) = 21$

The examples in Questions 15 and 16 indicate a method for rationalising the denominator in cases which are more complicated than those in Question 5.

15 (a) Explain why $\dfrac{1}{\sqrt{3} - 1} = \dfrac{1}{\sqrt{3} - 1} \times \dfrac{\sqrt{3} + 1}{\sqrt{3} + 1}$ and hence show that $\dfrac{1}{\sqrt{3} - 1} = \dfrac{\sqrt{3} + 1}{2}$.

(b) Show that $\dfrac{1}{2\sqrt{2} + \sqrt{3}} = \dfrac{2\sqrt{2} - \sqrt{3}}{5}$.

16 Rationalise the denominators and simplify these fractions.

(a) $\dfrac{1}{2 - \sqrt{3}}$

(b) $\dfrac{1}{3\sqrt{5} - 5}$

(c) $\dfrac{4\sqrt{3}}{2\sqrt{6} + 3\sqrt{2}}$

2.3 Working with indices

In the 16th century, when mathematics books began to be printed, mathematicians were finding how to solve cubic and quartic equations. They found it was more economical to write and to print the products xxx and $xxxx$ as x^3 and x^4.

This is how index notation started. But it turned out to be much more than a convenient shorthand. The new notation led to important mathematical discoveries, and mathematics as it is today would be inconceivable without index notation.

You will already have used simple examples of this notation. In general, the symbol a^m stands for the result of multiplying m as together:

$$a^m = \overbrace{a \times a \times a \times \ ... \ \times a}^{m \text{ of these}}.$$

The number a is called the **base**, and the number m is the **index** (plural 'indices'). Notice that, although a can be any kind of number, m must be a positive integer. Another way of describing this is 'a raised to the mth power', or more shortly 'a to the power m'. Expressions in index notation can often be simplified by using a few simple rules.

One of these is the **multiplication rule**,

$$a^m \times a^n = \overbrace{a \times a \times \ ... \ \times a}^{m \text{ of these}} \times \overbrace{a \times a \times \ ... \ \times a}^{n \text{ of these}} = \overbrace{a \times a \times \ ... \ \times a}^{m+n \text{ of these}} = a^{m+n}.$$

This is used, for example, in finding the volume of a cube of side a:

$$\text{volume} = \text{base area} \times \text{height} = a^2 \times a = a^2 \times a^1 = a^{2+1} = a^3.$$

Closely linked with this is the **division rule**,

$$a^m \div a^n = \overbrace{(a \times a \times \ ... \ \times a)}^{m \text{ of these}} \div \overbrace{(a \times a \times \ ... \ \times a)}^{n \text{ of these}}$$

$$= \overbrace{a \times a \times \ ... \ \times a}^{m-n \text{ of these}} \quad \text{(since } n \text{ of the } a\text{s cancel out)}$$

$$= a^{m-n}, \quad \text{provided that } m > n.$$

Another rule is the **power-on-power rule**,

$$(a^m)^n = \overbrace{\overbrace{a \times a \times \ ... \ \times a}^{m \text{ of these}} \times \overbrace{a \times a \times \ ... \ \times a}^{m \text{ of these}} \times ... \times \overbrace{a \times a \times \ ... \ \times a}^{m \text{ of these}}}^{n \text{ of these brackets}}$$

$$= \overbrace{a \times a \times \ ... \ \times a}^{m \times n \text{ of these}} = a^{m \times n}.$$

One further rule, the **factor rule**, has two bases but just one index:

$$(a \times b)^m = \overbrace{(a \times b) \times (a \times b) \times ... \times (a \times b)}^{m \text{ of these brackets}} = \overbrace{a \times a \times \ ... \ \times a}^{m \text{ of these}} \times \overbrace{b \times b \times \ ... \ \times b}^{m \text{ of these}} = a^m \times b^m.$$

In explaining these rules multiplication signs have been used. But, as in other parts of algebra, they are usually omitted if there is no ambiguity. For completeness, here are the rules again.

Multiplication rule: $a^m \times a^n = a^{m+n}$

Division rule: $a^m \div a^n = a^{m-n}$,   provided that $m > n$

Power-on-power rule: $(a^m)^n = a^{m \times n}$

Factor rule: $(a \times b)^m = a^m \times b^m$

Example 2.3.1
Simplify $(2a^2b)^3 \div (4a^4b)$.

$$(2a^2b)^3 \div (4a^4b) = \left(2^3(a^2)^3b^3\right) \div (4a^4b) \qquad \text{factor rule}$$
$$= (8a^{2\times3}b^3) \div (4a^4b) \qquad \text{power-on-power rule}$$
$$= (8 \div 4) \times (a^6 \div a^4) \times (b^3 \div b^1) \qquad \text{rearranging}$$
$$= 2a^{6-4}b^{3-1} \qquad \text{division rule}$$
$$= 2a^2b^2.$$

2.4   Zero and negative indices

The definition of a^m in Section 2.3, as the result of multiplying m as together, makes no sense if m is zero or a negative integer. You can't multiply -3 as or 0 as together. But extending the meaning of a^m when the index is zero or negative is possible, and useful, since it turns out that the rules still work with such index values.

Look at this sequence: $2^5 = 32$, $2^4 = 16$, $2^3 = 8$, $2^2 = 4$, ...

On the left sides, the base is always 2, and the indices go down by 1 at each step. On the right, the numbers are halved at each step. So you might continue the process

$$\ldots , \; 2^2 = 4, \; 2^1 = 2, \; 2^0 = 1, \; 2^{-1} = \tfrac{1}{2}, \; 2^{-2} = \tfrac{1}{4}, \; 2^{-3} = \tfrac{1}{8}, \; \ldots$$

and you can go on like this indefinitely. Now compare

$$2^1 = 2 \text{ with } 2^{-1} = \tfrac{1}{2}, \qquad 2^2 = 4 \text{ with } 2^{-2} = \tfrac{1}{4}, \qquad 2^3 = 8 \text{ with } 2^{-3} = \tfrac{1}{8}.$$

It looks as if 2^{-m} should be defined as $\dfrac{1}{2^m}$, with the special value in the middle $2^0 = 1$.

This observation, extended to any base a (except 0), and any positive integer m, gives the **negative power rule**.

Negative power rule: $a^{-m} = \dfrac{1}{a^m}$ and $a^0 = 1$.

Here are some examples to show that, with these definitions, the rules established in Section 2.3 for positive indices still work with negative indices. Try making up other examples for yourself.

Multiplication rule: $\quad a^3 \times a^{-7} = a^3 \times \dfrac{1}{a^7} = \dfrac{1}{a^7 \div a^3}$

$$= \dfrac{1}{a^{7-3}} \qquad \qquad \text{using the division rule}$$
$$\text{for positive indices}$$

$$= \dfrac{1}{a^4} = a^{-4} = a^{3+(-7)}.$$

Power-on-power rule: $\quad (a^{-2})^{-3} = \left(\dfrac{1}{a^2}\right)^{-3} = \dfrac{1}{(1/a^2)^3} = \dfrac{1}{1/(a^2)^3}$

$$= \dfrac{1}{1/a^6} \qquad \qquad \text{using the power-on-power}$$
$$\text{rule for positive indices}$$

$$= a^6 = a^{(-2)\times(-3)}.$$

Factor rule: $\qquad (ab)^{-3} = \dfrac{1}{(ab)^3} = \dfrac{1}{a^3 b^3} \qquad \qquad \text{using the factor rule}$
$$\text{for positive indices}$$

$$= \dfrac{1}{a^3} \times \dfrac{1}{b^3} = a^{-3}b^{-3}.$$

Example 2.4.1

If $a = 5$, find the value of $4a^{-2}$.

The important thing to notice is that the index -2 goes only with the a and not with the 4. So $4a^{-2}$ means $4 \times \dfrac{1}{a^2}$. When $a = 5$, $4a^{-2} = 4 \times \dfrac{1}{25} = 0.16$.

Example 2.4.2

Simplify $\quad$ (a) $4a^2 b \times (3ab^{-1})^{-2}$, $\quad$ (b) $\left(\dfrac{MLT^{-2}}{L^2}\right) \div \left(\dfrac{LT^{-1}}{L}\right)$.

(a) **Method 1** $\quad$ Turn everything into positive indices.

$$4a^2 b \times (3ab^{-1})^{-2} = 4a^2 b \times \dfrac{1}{(3a \times 1/b)^2} = 4a^2 b \times \dfrac{1}{9a^2 \times 1/b^2} = 4a^2 b \times \dfrac{b^2}{9a^2}$$

$$= \tfrac{4}{9}b^{1+2} = \tfrac{4}{9}b^3.$$

Method 2 $\quad$ Use the rules directly with positive and negative indices.

$$4a^2 b \times (3ab^{-1})^{-2} = 4a^2 b \times \left(3^{-2}a^{-2}(b^{-1})^{-2}\right) \qquad \qquad \text{factor rule}$$

$$= 4a^2 b \times (3^{-2}a^{-2}b^2) \qquad \qquad \text{power-on-power rule}$$

$$= \left(4 \times \dfrac{1}{3^2}\right) \times (a^2 a^{-2}) \times (bb^2) = \tfrac{4}{9}a^0 b^3 = \tfrac{4}{9}b^3.$$

(b) This is an application in mechanics: M, L, T stand for dimensions of mass, length and time in the measurement of viscosity. Taking the brackets separately,

$$\left(\dfrac{MLT^{-2}}{L^2}\right) = ML^{1-2}T^{-2} = ML^{-1}T^{-2} \quad \text{and} \quad \left(\dfrac{LT^{-1}}{L}\right) = L^{1-1}T^{-1} = L^0 T^{-1} = T^{-1},$$

so $\left(\dfrac{MLT^{-2}}{L^2}\right) \div \left(\dfrac{LT^{-1}}{L}\right) = \left(ML^{-1}T^{-2}\right) \div T^{-1} = ML^{-1}T^{-2-(-1)} = ML^{-1}T^{-1}.$

One application of negative indices is in writing down very small numbers. You probably know how to write very large numbers in standard form, or scientific notation. For example, it is easier to write the speed of light as $3.00 \times 10^8 \text{ m s}^{-1}$ than as $300\,000\,000 \text{ m s}^{-1}$. Similarly, the wavelength of red light, about $0.000\,000\,75$ metres, is more easily appreciated written as 7.5×10^{-7} metres.

Computers and calculators often give users the option to work in scientific notation, and if numbers become too large (or too small) to be displayed in ordinary numerical form they will switch into standard form, for example 3.00E8 or 7.5E±7. The symbol E stands for 'exponent', which is yet another word for 'index'. You can write this in scientific notation by simply replacing the symbol Em by $\times 10^m$, for any integer m.

Example 2.4.3

Calculate the universal constant of gravitation, G, from $G = \dfrac{gR^2}{M}$ where, in SI units, $g \approx 9.81$, $R \approx 6.37 \times 10^6$ and $M \approx 5.97 \times 10^{24}$. ($R$ and M are the earth's radius and mass, and g is the acceleration due to gravity at the earth's surface.)

$$G \approx \frac{9.81 \times (6.37 \times 10^6)^2}{5.97 \times 10^{24}} = \frac{9.81 \times (6.37)^2}{5.97} \times \frac{(10^6)^2}{10^{24}}$$

$$\approx 66.7 \times \frac{10^{12}}{10^{24}} = 6.67 \times 10^1 \times 10^{-12} = 6.67 \times 10^{1-12} = 6.67 \times 10^{-11}.$$

Exercise 2B

1 Simplify the following expressions.

(a) $a^2 \times a^3 \times a^7$ (b) $(b^4)^2$ (c) $c^7 \div c^3$

(d) $d^5 \times d^4$ (e) $(e^5)^4$ (f) $(x^3y^2)^2$

(g) $5g^5 \times 3g^3$ (h) $12h^{12} \div 4h^4$ (i) $(2a^2)^3 \times (3a)^2$

(j) $(p^2q^3)^2 \times (pq^3)^3$ (k) $(4x^2y)^2 \times (2xy^3)^3$ (l) $(6ac^3)^2 \div (9a^2c^5)$

(m) $(3m^4n^2)^3 \times (2mn^2)^2$ (n) $(49r^3s^2)^2 \div (7rs)^3$ (o) $(2xy^2z^3)^2 \div (2xy^2z^3)$

2 Simplify the following, giving each answer in the form 2^n.

(a) $2^{11} \times (2^5)^3$ (b) $(2^3)^2 \times (2^2)^3$ (c) 4^3 (d) 8^2

(e) $\dfrac{2^7 \times 2^8}{2^{13}}$ (f) $\dfrac{2^2 \times 2^3}{(2^2)^2}$ (g) $4^2 \div 2^4$ (h) $2 \times 4^4 \div 8^3$

3 Express each of the following as an integer or a fraction.

(a) 2^{-3} (b) 4^{-2} (c) 5^{-1} (d) 3^{-2}

(e) 10^{-4} (f) 1^{-7} (g) $\left(\frac{1}{2}\right)^{-1}$ (h) $\left(\frac{1}{3}\right)^{-3}$

(i) $\left(2\frac{1}{2}\right)^{-1}$ (j) 2^{-7} (k) 6^{-3} (l) $\left(1\frac{1}{3}\right)^{-3}$

4 If $x = 2$, find the value of each of the following.

(a) $4x^{-3}$ (b) $(4x)^{-3}$ (c) $\frac{1}{4}x^{-3}$

(d) $\left(\frac{1}{4}x\right)^{-3}$ (e) $(4 \div x)^{-3}$ (f) $(x \div 4)^{-3}$

5 If $y = 5$, find the value of each of the following.

(a) $(2y)^{-1}$ (b) $2y^{-1}$ (c) $\left(\frac{1}{2}y\right)^{-1}$

(d) $\frac{1}{2}y^{-1}$ (e) $\frac{1}{(2y)^{-1}}$ (f) $\frac{2}{\left(y^{-1}\right)^{-1}}$

6 Express each of the following in as simple a form as possible.

(a) $a^4 \times a^{-3}$ (b) $\frac{1}{b^{-1}}$ (c) $(c^{-2})^3$

(d) $d^{-1} \times 2d$ (e) $e^{-4} \times e^{-5}$ (f) $\frac{f^{-2}}{f^3}$

(g) $12g^3 \times (2g^2)^{-2}$ (h) $(3h^2)^{-2}$ (i) $(3i^{-2})^{-2}$

(j) $\left(\frac{1}{2}j^{-2}\right)^{-3}$ (k) $(2x^3y^{-1})^3$ (l) $(p^2q^4r^3)^{-4}$

(m) $(4m^2)^{-1} \times 8m^3$ (n) $(3n^{-2})^4 \times (9n)^{-1}$ (o) $(2xy^2)^{-1} \times (4xy)^2$

(p) $(5a^3c^{-1})^2 \div (2a^{-1}c^2)$ (q) $(2q^{-2})^{-2} \div \left(\frac{4}{q}\right)^2$ (r) $(3x^{-2}y)^2 \div (4xy)^{-2}$

7 Solve the following equations.

(a) $3^x = \frac{1}{9}$ (b) $5^y = 1$ (c) $2^z \times 2^{z-3} = 32$

(d) $7^{3x} \div 7^{x-2} = \frac{1}{49}$ (e) $4^y \times 2^y = 8^{120}$ (f) $3^t \times 9^{t+3} = 27^2$

8 The length of each edge of a cube is 3×10^{-2} metres.

(a) Find the volume of the cube.   (b) Find the total surface area of the cube.

9 An athlete runs 2×10^{-1} km in 7.5×10^{-3} hours. Find her average speed in km h^{-1}.

10 The volume, $V \text{ m}^3$, of l metres of wire is given by $V = \pi r^2 l$, where r metres is the radius of the circular cross-section.

(a) Find the volume of 80 m of wire with radius of cross-section 2×10^{-3} m.

(b) Another type of wire has radius of cross-section 5×10^{-3} m. What length of this wire has a volume of $8 \times 10^{-3} \text{ m}^3$?

(c) Another type of wire is such that a length of 61 m has a volume of $6 \times 10^{-3} \text{ m}^3$. Find the radius of the cross-section.

11 An equation which occurs in the study of waves is $y = \dfrac{\lambda d}{a}$.

(a) Calculate y when $\lambda = 7 \times 10^{-7}$, $d = 5 \times 10^{-1}$ and $a = 8 \times 10^{-4}$.

(b) Calculate λ when $y = 10^{-3}$, $d = 0.6$ and $a = 2.7 \times 10^{-4}$.

12 Solve the equation $\dfrac{3^{5x+2}}{9^{1-x}} = \dfrac{27^{4+3x}}{729}$.

2.5   Fractional indices

In Section 2.4, you saw that the four index rules still work when m and n are integers, but not necessarily positive. What happens if m and n are not necessarily integers?

If you put $m = \frac{1}{2}$ and $n = 2$ in the power-on-power rule, you find that

$$\left(x^{\frac{1}{2}}\right)^2 = x^{\frac{1}{2} \times 2} = x^1 = x.$$

Putting $x^{\frac{1}{2}} = y$, this equation becomes $y^2 = x$, so $y = \sqrt{x}$ or $y = -\sqrt{x}$, which is $x^{\frac{1}{2}} = \sqrt{x}$ or $-\sqrt{x}$. *Defining* $x^{\frac{1}{2}}$ to be the positive square root of x, you get $x^{\frac{1}{2}} = \sqrt{x}$.

Similarly, if you put $m = \frac{1}{3}$ and $n = 3$, you can show that $x^{\frac{1}{3}} = \sqrt[3]{x}$. More generally, by putting $m = \dfrac{1}{n}$, you find that $\left(x^{\frac{1}{n}}\right)^n = x^{\frac{1}{n} \times n} = x$, which leads to the result

$$x^{\frac{1}{n}} = \sqrt[n]{x}.$$

Notice that for the case $x^{\frac{1}{2}} = \sqrt{x}$, you must have $x \geqslant 0$, but for the case $x^{\frac{1}{3}} = \sqrt[3]{x}$ you do not need $x \geqslant 0$, because you can take the cube root of a negative number.

A slight extension of the $x^{\frac{1}{n}} = \sqrt[n]{x}$ rule can show you how to deal with expressions of the form $x^{\frac{2}{3}}$. There are two alternatives:

$$x^{\frac{2}{3}} = x^{\frac{1}{3} \times 2} = \left(x^{\frac{1}{3}}\right)^2 = \left(\sqrt[3]{x}\right)^2 \quad \text{and} \quad x^{\frac{2}{3}} = x^{2 \times \frac{1}{3}} = \left(x^2\right)^{\frac{1}{3}} = \sqrt[3]{x^2}.$$

(If x has an exact cube root it is usually best to use the first form; otherwise the second form is better.) In general, similar reasoning leads to the **fractional power rule**.

Fractional power rule: $x^{\frac{m}{n}} = \left(\sqrt[n]{x}\right)^m = \sqrt[n]{x^m}$.

Fractional powers can also be written as $x^{1/2}$, $x^{m/n}$ *and so on.*

Example 2.5.1
Simplify   (a) $9^{\frac{1}{2}}$,   (b) $3^{\frac{1}{2}} \times 3^{\frac{3}{2}}$,   (c) $16^{-\frac{3}{4}}$.

(a) $9^{\frac{1}{2}} = \sqrt{9} = 3$.   (b) $3^{\frac{1}{2}} \times 3^{\frac{3}{2}} = 3^{\frac{1}{2} + \frac{3}{2}} = 3^2 = 9$.

(c) **Method 1** $16^{-\frac{3}{4}} = \left(2^4\right)^{-\frac{3}{4}} = 2^{-3} = \frac{1}{8}$.

Method 2 $16^{-\frac{3}{4}} = \dfrac{1}{16^{\frac{3}{4}}} = \dfrac{1}{\left(\sqrt[4]{16}\right)^3} = \dfrac{1}{2^3} = \dfrac{1}{8}$.

There are often good alternative ways for solving problems involving indices, and you should try experimenting with them. Many people prefer to think with positive indices rather than negative ones; if you are one of them, writing $16^{-\frac{3}{4}} = \dfrac{1}{16^{\frac{3}{4}}}$, as in method 2 of Example 2.5.1(c), makes good sense as a first step.

Example 2.5.2

Simplify   (a) $\left(2\frac{1}{4}\right)^{-\frac{1}{2}}$,   (b) $2x^{\frac{1}{2}} \times 3x^{-\frac{5}{2}}$,   (c) $\dfrac{\left(2x^2y^2\right)^{-\frac{1}{2}}}{\left(2xy^{-2}\right)^{\frac{3}{2}}}$.

(a) $\left(2\frac{1}{4}\right)^{-\frac{1}{2}} = \left(\frac{9}{4}\right)^{-\frac{1}{2}} = \left(\frac{4}{9}\right)^{\frac{1}{2}} = \sqrt{\frac{4}{9}} = \frac{2}{3}$.

(b) $2x^{\frac{1}{2}} \times 3x^{-\frac{5}{2}} = 6x^{\frac{1}{2}-\frac{5}{2}} = 6x^{-2} = \dfrac{6}{x^2}$.

(c) **Method 1**   The numerator is $\left(2x^2y^2\right)^{-\frac{1}{2}} = \dfrac{1}{\left(2x^2y^2\right)^{\frac{1}{2}}} = \dfrac{1}{2^{\frac{1}{2}}xy}$, so

$$\dfrac{\left(2x^2y^2\right)^{-\frac{1}{2}}}{\left(2xy^{-2}\right)^{\frac{3}{2}}} = \dfrac{1}{2^{\frac{1}{2}}xy} \times \dfrac{1}{2^{\frac{3}{2}}x^{\frac{3}{2}}y^{-3}} = \dfrac{1}{2^2 x^{\frac{5}{2}}y^{-2}} = \dfrac{y^2}{4x^{\frac{5}{2}}}.$$

Method 2   Dividing by $\left(2xy^{-2}\right)^{\frac{3}{2}}$ is equivalent to multiplying by $\left(2xy^{-2}\right)^{-\frac{3}{2}}$, so

$$\dfrac{\left(2x^2y^2\right)^{-\frac{1}{2}}}{\left(2xy^{-2}\right)^{\frac{3}{2}}} = \left(2x^2y^2\right)^{-\frac{1}{2}}\left(2xy^{-2}\right)^{-\frac{3}{2}} = \left(2^{-\frac{1}{2}}x^{-1}y^{-1}\right)\left(2^{-\frac{3}{2}}x^{-\frac{3}{2}}y^3\right) = 2^{-2}x^{-\frac{5}{2}}y^2.$$

Notice that in part (c) the final answer has been given in different forms for the two methods. Which is 'simpler' is a matter of taste.

Exercise 2C

1 Evaluate the following without using a calculator.

(a) $25^{\frac{1}{2}}$ (b) $8^{\frac{1}{3}}$ (c) $36^{\frac{1}{2}}$ (d) $32^{\frac{1}{5}}$

(e) $81^{\frac{1}{4}}$ (f) $9^{-\frac{1}{2}}$ (g) $16^{-\frac{1}{4}}$ (h) $49^{-\frac{1}{2}}$

(i) $1000^{-\frac{1}{3}}$ (j) $(-27)^{\frac{1}{3}}$ (k) $64^{\frac{2}{3}}$ (l) $(-125)^{-\frac{4}{3}}$

2 Evaluate the following without using a calculator.

(a) $4^{\frac{1}{2}}$ (b) $\left(\frac{1}{4}\right)^2$ (c) $\left(\frac{1}{4}\right)^{-2}$ (d) $4^{-\frac{1}{2}}$

(e) $\left(\frac{1}{4}\right)^{-\frac{1}{2}}$ (f) $\left(\frac{1}{4}\right)^{\frac{1}{2}}$ (g) 4^2 (h) $\left(\left(\frac{1}{4}\right)^{\frac{1}{4}}\right)^2$

3 Evaluate the following without using a calculator.

(a) $8^{\frac{2}{3}}$ (b) $4^{\frac{3}{2}}$ (c) $9^{-\frac{3}{2}}$ (d) $27^{\frac{4}{3}}$

(e) $32^{\frac{2}{5}}$ (f) $32^{\frac{3}{5}}$ (g) $64^{-\frac{5}{6}}$ (h) $4^{2\frac{1}{2}}$

(i) $10\,000^{-\frac{3}{4}}$ (j) $\left(\frac{1}{125}\right)^{-\frac{4}{3}}$ (k) $\left(3\frac{3}{8}\right)^{\frac{2}{3}}$ (l) $\left(2\frac{1}{4}\right)^{-\frac{1}{2}}$

4 Simplify the following expressions.

(a) $a^{\frac{1}{3}} \times a^{\frac{5}{3}}$

(b) $3b^{\frac{1}{2}} \times 4b^{-\frac{3}{2}}$

(c) $\left(6c^{\frac{1}{4}}\right) \times \left(4c\right)^{\frac{1}{2}}$

(d) $(d^2)^{\frac{1}{3}} \div \left(d^{\frac{1}{3}}\right)^2$

(e) $\left(2x^{\frac{1}{2}} y^{\frac{1}{3}}\right)^6 \times \left(\frac{1}{2} x^{\frac{1}{4}} y^{\frac{3}{4}}\right)^4$

(f) $(24e)^{\frac{1}{3}} \div (3e)^{\frac{1}{3}}$

(g) $\dfrac{(5p^2 q^4)^{\frac{1}{3}}}{(25pq^2)^{-\frac{1}{3}}}$

(h) $(4m^3 n)^{\frac{1}{4}} \times (8mn^3)^{\frac{1}{2}}$

(i) $\dfrac{(2x^2 y^{-1})^{-\frac{1}{4}}}{(8x^{-1} y^2)^{-\frac{1}{2}}}$

5 Solve the following equations.

(a) $x^{\frac{1}{2}} = 8$

(b) $x^{\frac{1}{3}} = 3$

(c) $x^{\frac{2}{3}} = 4$

(d) $x^{\frac{3}{2}} = 27$

(e) $x^{-\frac{3}{2}} = 8$

(f) $x^{-\frac{2}{3}} = 9$

(g) $x^{\frac{3}{2}} = x\sqrt{2}$

(h) $x^{\frac{3}{2}} = 2\sqrt{x}$

6 The time, T seconds, taken by a pendulum of length l metres to complete one swing is given by $T = 2\pi l^{\frac{1}{2}} g^{-\frac{1}{2}}$ where $g \approx 9.81 \text{ m s}^{-2}$.

(a) Find the value of T for a pendulum of length 0.9 metres.

(b) Find the length of a pendulum which takes 3 seconds for a complete swing.

7 The radius, r cm, of a sphere of volume V cm^3 is given by $r = \left(\dfrac{3V}{4\pi}\right)^{\frac{1}{3}}$. Find the radius of a sphere of volume 1150 cm^3.

8 Solve the following equations.

(a) $4^x = 32$

(b) $9^y = \frac{1}{27}$

(c) $16^z = 2$

(d) $100^x = 1000$

(e) $8^y = 16$

(f) $8^z = \frac{1}{128}$

(g) $(2^t)^3 \times 4^{t-1} = 16$

(h) $\dfrac{9^y}{27^{2y+1}} = 81$

Miscellaneous exercise 2

1 Simplify

(a) $5(\sqrt{2} + 1) - \sqrt{2}(4 - 3\sqrt{2})$,

(b) $\left(\sqrt{2}\right)^4 + \left(\sqrt{3}\right)^4 + \left(\sqrt{4}\right)^4$,

(c) $\left(\sqrt{5} - 2\right)^2 + \left(\sqrt{5} - 2\right)\left(\sqrt{5} + 2\right)$,

(d) $\left(2\sqrt{2}\right)^5$.

2 Simplify

(a) $\sqrt{27} + \sqrt{12} - \sqrt{3}$,

(b) $\sqrt{63} - \sqrt{28}$,

(c) $\sqrt{100\,000} + \sqrt{1000} + \sqrt{10}$,

(d) $\sqrt[3]{2} + \sqrt[3]{16}$.

3 Rationalise the denominators of the following.

(a) $\dfrac{9}{2\sqrt{3}}$

(b) $\dfrac{1}{5\sqrt{5}}$

(c) $\dfrac{2\sqrt{5}}{3\sqrt{10}}$

(d) $\dfrac{\sqrt{8}}{\sqrt{15}}$

4 Simplify

(a) $\dfrac{4}{\sqrt{2}} - \dfrac{4}{\sqrt{8}}$,

(b) $\dfrac{10}{\sqrt{5}} + \sqrt{20}$,

(c) $\dfrac{1}{\sqrt{2}}\left(2\sqrt{2} - 1\right) + \sqrt{2}\left(1 - \sqrt{8}\right)$,

(d) $\dfrac{\sqrt{6}}{\sqrt{2}} + \dfrac{3}{\sqrt{3}} + \dfrac{\sqrt{15}}{\sqrt{5}} + \dfrac{\sqrt{18}}{\sqrt{6}}$.

5 Express $\dfrac{5}{\sqrt{7}}$ in the form $k\sqrt{7}$ where k is a rational number.

(OCR)

6   Justify the result $\sqrt{12} \times \sqrt{75} = 30$

    (a) using surds,   (b) using fractional indices.

7   In the diagram, angles ABC and ACD are right angles. Given that $AB = CD = 2\sqrt{6}$ cm and $BC = 7$ cm, show that the length of AD is between $4\sqrt{6}$ cm and $7\sqrt{2}$ cm.

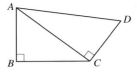

8   In the triangle PQR, Q is a right angle, $PQ = \left(6 - 2\sqrt{2}\right)$ cm and $QR = \left(6 + 2\sqrt{2}\right)$ cm.

    (a) Find the area of the triangle.   (b) Show that the length of PR is $2\sqrt{22}$ cm.

9   Simplify $\sqrt[3]{36} \times \sqrt[6]{\dfrac{4}{3}} \times \sqrt{27}$ by writing each factor in index notation.

10   In the triangle ABC, $AB = 4\sqrt{3}$ cm, $BC = 5\sqrt{3}$ cm and angle B is $60°$. Use the cosine rule to find, in simplified surd form, the length of AC.

11   Solve the simultaneous equations $5x - 3y = 41$ and $\left(7\sqrt{2}\right)x + \left(4\sqrt{2}\right)y = 82$.

12   Use the 'raise to power' key on your calculator to find, correct to 5 significant figures,

    (a) $\dfrac{1}{3.7^5}$,   (b) $\sqrt[5]{3.7}$.

13   The coordinates of the points A and B are $(2,3)$ and $(4,-3)$ respectively. Find the length of AB and the coordinates of the midpoint of AB.   (OCR)

14   (a) Find the equation of the line l through the point $A(2,3)$ with gradient $-\frac{1}{2}$.

    (b) Show that the point P with coordinates $(2 + 2t, 3 - t)$ will always lie on l whatever the value of t.

    (c) Find the values of t such that the length AP is 5 units.

    (d) Find the value of t such that OP is perpendicular to l (where O is the origin). Hence find the length of the perpendicular from O to l.

15   P and Q are the points of intersection of the line

$$\frac{x}{a} + \frac{y}{b} = 1 \qquad (a > 0, \ b > 0)$$

with the x- and y-axes respectively. The distance PQ is 20 and the gradient of PQ is -3. Find the values of a and b.

16   The sides of a parallelogram lie along the lines $y = 2x - 4$, $y = 2x - 13$, $x + y = 5$ and $x + y = -4$. Find the length of one side, and the perpendicular distance between this and the parallel side. Hence find the area of the parallelogram.

17   Evaluate the following without using a calculator.

    (a) $\left(\frac{1}{2}\right)^{-1} + \left(\frac{1}{2}\right)^{-2}$ (b) $32^{-\frac{4}{5}}$ (c) $\left(4^{\frac{3}{2}}\right)^{-\frac{1}{3}}$ (d) $\left(1\frac{7}{9}\right)^{1\frac{1}{2}}$

18   Express $\left(9a^4\right)^{-\frac{1}{2}}$ as an algebraic fraction in simplified form.   (OCR)

19   By letting $y = x^{\frac{1}{3}}$, or otherwise, find the values of x for which $x^{\frac{1}{3}} - 2x^{-\frac{1}{3}} = 1$.   (OCR)

20   Solve the equation $4^{2x} \times 8^{x-1} = 32$.

21 Express $\dfrac{1}{\left(\sqrt{a}\right)^{\frac{4}{3}}}$ in the form a^n, stating the value of n. (OCR)

22 Simplify

(a) $\left(4p^{\frac{1}{4}}q^{-3}\right)^{\frac{1}{2}}$,

(b) $\dfrac{(5b)^{-1}}{\left(8b^6\right)^{\frac{1}{3}}}$,

(c) $\left(2x^6y^8\right)^{\frac{1}{4}}\times\left(8x^{-2}\right)^{\frac{1}{4}}$,

(d) $\left(m^{\frac{1}{3}}n^{\frac{1}{2}}\right)^2\times\left(m^{\frac{1}{6}}n^{\frac{1}{3}}\right)^4\times(mn)^{-2}$.

23 Given that, in standard form, $3^{236}\approx4\times10^{112}$, and $3^{-376}\approx4\times10^{-180}$, find approximations, also in standard form, for

(a) 3^{376},　　(b) 3^{612},　　(c) $\left(\sqrt{3}\right)^{236}$,　　(d) $\left(3^{-376}\right)^{\frac{5}{2}}$.

24 The table below shows, for three of the planets in the solar system, details of their mean distance from the sun and the time taken for one orbit round the sun.

Planet	Mean radius of orbit r metres	Period of revolution T seconds
Mercury	5.8×10^{10}	7.6×10^6
Jupiter	7.8×10^{11}	3.7×10^8
Pluto	5.9×10^{12}	7.8×10^9

(a) Show that r^3T^{-2} has approximately the same value for each planet in the table.

(b) The earth takes one year for one orbit of the sun. Find the mean radius of the earth's orbit around the sun.

25 Simplify

(a) $2^{-\frac{3}{2}}+2^{-\frac{1}{2}}+2^{\frac{1}{2}}+2^{\frac{3}{2}}$, giving your answer in the form $k\sqrt{2}$,

(b) $\left(\sqrt{3}\right)^{-3}+\left(\sqrt{3}\right)^{-2}+\left(\sqrt{3}\right)^{-1}+\left(\sqrt{3}\right)^0+\left(\sqrt{3}\right)^1+\left(\sqrt{3}\right)^2+\left(\sqrt{3}\right)^3$, giving your answer in the form $a+b\sqrt{3}$.

26 Express each of the following in the form 2^n.

(a) $2^{70}+2^{70}$　　(b) $2^{-400}+2^{-400}$　　(c) $2^{\frac{1}{3}}+2^{\frac{1}{3}}+2^{\frac{1}{3}}+2^{\frac{1}{3}}$

(d) $2^{100}-2^{99}$　　(e) $8^{0.1}+8^{0.1}+8^{0.1}+8^{0.1}+8^{0.1}+8^{0.1}+8^{0.1}+8^{0.1}$

27 Solve the equation $\dfrac{125^{3x}}{5^{x+4}}=\dfrac{25^{x-2}}{3125}$.

28 The formulae for the volume and the surface area of a sphere are $V=\frac{4}{3}\pi r^3$ and $S=4\pi r^2$ respectively, where r is the sphere's radius. Find expressions for

(a) S in terms of V,　　(b) V in terms of S,

giving your answer in the form $(S\text{ or }V)=2^m3^n\pi^p(V\text{ or }S)^q$.

29 The kinetic energy, K joules, possessed by an object of mass m kg moving with speed v m s^{-1} is given by the formula $K=\frac{1}{2}mv^2$. Find the kinetic energy possessed by a bullet of mass 2.5×10^{-2} kg moving with speed 8×10^2 m s^{-1}.

3 Functions and graphs

This chapter introduces the idea of a function and investigates the graphs representing functions of various kinds. When you have completed it, you should

- understand function notation, and the terms 'domain' and 'range'
- know the shapes of graphs of powers of x
- know the shapes of graphs of functions of the form $f(x) = ax^2 + bx + c$
- be able to suggest possible equations of such functions from their graphs
- know how to use factors to sketch graphs
- be able to find the point(s) of intersection of two graphs.

If you have access to a graphic calculator or a computer with graph-plotting software, you can use it to check for yourself the graphs which accompany the text, and to carry out further research along similar lines.

3.1 The idea of a function

You are already familiar with formulae which summarise calculations that need to be performed frequently, such as:

the area of a circle with radius x metres is πx^2 square metres;

the volume of a cube of side x metres is x^3 cubic metres;

the time to travel k kilometres at x kilometres per hour is $\dfrac{k}{x}$ hours.

You will often have used different letters from x in these formulae, such as r for radius or s for speed, but in this chapter x will always be used for the letter in the formula, and y for the quantity you want to calculate. Notice that some formulae also involve other letters, called **constants**; these might be either a number like π, which is irrational and cannot be written out in full, or a quantity like the distance k, which you choose for yourself depending on the distance you intend to travel.

Expressions such as πx^2, x^3 and $\dfrac{k}{x}$ are examples of **functions** of x. Having chosen a value for x, you can get a unique value of y from it.

It is often useful to have a way of writing functions in general, rather than always having to refer to particular functions. The notation which is used for this is $f(x)$ (read 'f of x', or sometimes just 'f x'). The letter f stands for the function itself, and x for the number for which you choose to evaluate it.

If you want to refer to the value of the function when x has a particular value, say $x = 2$, then you write the value as $f(2)$. For example, if $f(x)$ stands for the function x^3, then $f(2) = 2^3 = 8$.

If a problem involves more than one function, you can use a different letter for each function. Two functions can, for example, be written as $f(x)$ and $g(x)$.

Functions are not always defined by algebraic formulae. Sometimes it is easier to describe them in words, or to define them using a flow chart or a computer program. All that matters is that each value of x chosen leads to a unique value of $y = f(x)$.

3.2   Graphs, domain and range

You know how to draw graphs. You set up a coordinate system for cartesian coordinates using x- and y-axes, and choose a scale on each axis.

The axes divide the plane of the paper or screen into four quadrants, numbered as shown in Fig. 3.1. The first quadrant is in the top right corner, where x and y are both positive. The other quadrants then follow in order going anticlockwise round the origin.

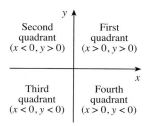

Fig. 3.1

Example 3.2.1
In which quadrants is $xy > 0$?

> If the product of two numbers is positive, either both are positive or both are negative. So either $x > 0$ and $y > 0$, or $x < 0$ and $y < 0$. The point (x, y) therefore lies in either the first or the third quadrant.

It is often convenient to describe the direction of the y-axis as 'vertical', and the x-axis as 'horizontal'. But of course if you are drawing the graph on a horizontal surface like a table, these descriptions are not strictly accurate.

The graph of a function $f(x)$ is made up of all the points whose coordinates (x, y) satisfy the equation $y = f(x)$. When you draw such a graph by hand, you choose a few values of x and work out $y = f(x)$ for these. You then plot the points with coordinates (x, y), and join up these points by eye, usually with a smooth curve. If you have done this accurately, the coordinates of other points on the curve will also satisfy the equation $y = f(x)$. Calculators and computers make graphs in much the same way, but they can plot many more points much more quickly.

When you produce a graph of $y = mx + c$ or $y = x^2$ you cannot show the whole graph. However small the scale, and however large the screen or the paper, the graph will eventually spill over the edge. This is because x can be any real number, as large as you like in both positive and negative directions. When you have to draw a graph like this, the skill is to choose the values of x between which to draw the graph so that you include all the important features.

You have met some functions which can't be defined for all real numbers. Examples are $\frac{1}{x}$, which has no meaning when x is 0; and $\sqrt{x}$, which has no meaning when x is negative.

Here is another example for which there is a restriction on the values of x you can choose.

Example 3.2.2

Draw the complete graph of $f(x) = \sqrt{4 - x^2}$.

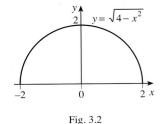

Fig. 3.2

You can only calculate the values of the function $f(x) = \sqrt{4 - x^2}$ if x is between -2 and 2 inclusive.

If $x > 2$ or $x < -2$, the value of $4 - x^2$ is negative, and a negative number does not have a square root.

Also $y = f(x)$ cannot be negative (recall that square roots are positive or zero by definition) and it can't be greater than $\sqrt{4} = 2$. So the graph of $f(x) = \sqrt{4 - x^2}$, shown in Fig. 3.2, lies between -2 and 2 inclusive in the x-direction, and between 0 and 2 inclusive in the y-direction.

Even when you use a function which has a meaning for all real numbers x, you may be interested in it only when x is restricted in some way. For example, the formula for the volume of a cube is $V = x^3$. Although you can calculate x^3 for any real number x, you would only use this formula for $x > 0$.

Here is an example in which x is restricted to a finite interval.

Example 3.2.3

A wire of length 4 metres is cut into two pieces, and each piece is bent into a square. How should this be done so that the two squares together have
(a) the smallest area,   (b) the largest area?

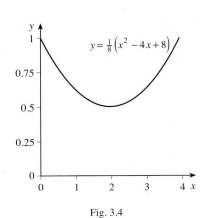

Fig. 3.3

Let the two pieces have lengths x metres and $(4 - x)$ metres. The areas of the squares in Fig. 3.3 are then $\left(\frac{1}{4}x\right)^2$ and $\left(\frac{1}{4}(4 - x)\right)^2$ square metres. So the total area, y square metres, is given by

$$y = \tfrac{1}{16}\left(x^2 + \left(16 - 8x + x^2\right)\right) = \tfrac{1}{8}\left(x^2 - 4x + 8\right).$$

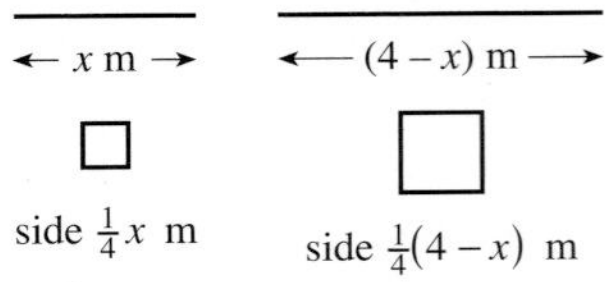

Notice that, since $(x - 2)^2 = x^2 - 4x + 4$, this can be written as

$$y = \tfrac{1}{8}\left((x - 2)^2 + 4\right).$$

You can evaluate this expression for any real number x, but the problem only has meaning if $0 < x < 4$. Fig. 3.4 shows the graph of the area function for this interval. As $(x - 2)^2 \geqslant 0$, the area is least when $x = 2$, when it is 0.5 m^2 .

From the graph it looks as if the largest area is 1 m^2 , when $x = 0$ and $x = 4$; but these values of x are excluded, since they do not produce two pieces of wire. You can get areas as near to 1 m^2 as you like, but you cannot achieve this target. There is therefore no largest area.

Fig. 3.4

So two possible reasons why a function $f(x)$ might not be defined for all real numbers x are
- the algebraic expression for $f(x)$ may have meaning only for some x
- only some x are relevant in the context in which the function is being used.

The set of numbers x for which a function $f(x)$ is defined is called the **domain** of the function. For example, the domains of the functions in Examples 3.2.2 and 3.2.3 are the intervals $-2 \le x \le 2$ and $0 < x < 4$. The largest possible domain of the function $\dfrac{1}{x}$ is all the real numbers except 0, but if the function is used in a practical problem you may choose a smaller domain, such as all positive real numbers.

Once you have decided the domain of a function $f(x)$, you can ask what values $f(x)$ can take. This set of values is called the **range** of the function.

In Example 3.2.2 the range is $0 \le y \le 2$. In Example 3.2.3 the graph shows that the range is $\frac{1}{2} \le y < 1$. Note that the value $y = \frac{1}{2}$ is attained when $x = 2$, but the value $y = 1$ is not attained if $0 < x < 4$.

The function $f(x) = \dfrac{1}{x}$, with domain all real numbers except 0, takes all values except 0.

Exercise 3A

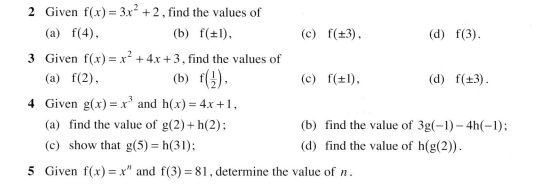

1 Given $f(x) = 2x + 5$, find the values of
   (a) $f(3)$,   (b) $f(0)$,   (c) $f(-4)$,   (d) $f\left(-2\frac{1}{2}\right)$.

2 Given $f(x) = 3x^2 + 2$, find the values of
   (a) $f(4)$,   (b) $f(\pm 1)$,   (c) $f(\pm 3)$,   (d) $f(3)$.

3 Given $f(x) = x^2 + 4x + 3$, find the values of
   (a) $f(2)$,   (b) $f\left(\frac{1}{2}\right)$,   (c) $f(\pm 1)$,   (d) $f(\pm 3)$.

4 Given $g(x) = x^3$ and $h(x) = 4x + 1$,
   (a) find the value of $g(2) + h(2)$;   (b) find the value of $3g(-1) - 4h(-1)$;
   (c) show that $g(5) = h(31)$;   (d) find the value of $h(g(2))$.

5 Given $f(x) = x^n$ and $f(3) = 81$, determine the value of n.

6 Given that $f(x) = ax + b$ and that $f(2) = 7$ and $f(3) = 12$, find a and b.

7 Find the largest possible domain of each of the following functions.
   (a) $\sqrt{x}$ (b) $\sqrt{-x}$ (c) $\sqrt{x - 4}$ (d) $\sqrt{4 - x}$
   (e) $\sqrt{x(x - 4)}$ (f) $\sqrt{2x(x - 4)}$ (g) $\sqrt{x^2 - 7x + 12}$ (h) $\sqrt{x^3 - 8}$
   (i) $\dfrac{1}{x - 2}$ (j) $\dfrac{1}{\sqrt{x - 2}}$ (k) $\dfrac{1}{1 + \sqrt{x}}$ (l) $\dfrac{1}{(x - 1)(x - 2)}$

8 The domains of these functions are the set of all positive real numbers. Find their ranges.
   (a) $f(x) = 2x + 7$ (b) $f(x) = -5x$ (c) $f(x) = 3x - 1$
   (d) $f(x) = x^2 - 1$ (e) $f(x) = (x + 2)^2 - 1$ (f) $f(x) = (x - 1)^2 + 2$

9 Find the range of each of the following functions. All the functions are defined for all real values of x.

(a) $f(x) = x^2 + 4$ 　　　　　(b) $f(x) = 2(x^2 + 5)$ 　　　　　(c) $f(x) = (x-1)^2 + 6$

(d) $f(x) = -(1-x)^2 + 7$ 　　　(e) $f(x) = 3(x+5)^2 + 2$ 　　　(f) $f(x) = 2(x+2)^4 - 1$

10 These functions are each defined for the given domain. Find their ranges.

(a) $f(x) = 2x$ for $0 \leqslant x \leqslant 8$ 　　　　　　(b) $f(x) = 3 - 2x$ for $-2 \leqslant x \leqslant 2$

(c) $f(x) = x^2$ for $-1 \leqslant x \leqslant 4$ 　　　　　　(d) $f(x) = x^2$ for $-5 \leqslant x \leqslant -2$

11 Find the range of each of the following functions. All the functions are defined for the largest possible domain of values of x.

(a) $f(x) = x^8$ 　　　(b) $f(x) = x^{11}$ 　　　(c) $f(x) = \dfrac{1}{x^3}$ 　　　(d) $f(x) = \dfrac{1}{x^4}$

(e) $f(x) = x^4 + 5$ 　　(f) $f(x) = \tfrac{1}{4}x + \tfrac{1}{8}$ 　　(g) $f(x) = \sqrt{4 - x^2}$ 　　(h) $f(x) = \sqrt{4 - x}$

12 A piece of wire 24 cm long has the shape of a rectangle. Given that the width is w cm, show that the area, A cm^2, of the rectangle is given by the function $A = 36 - (6 - w)^2$. Find the greatest possible domain and the corresponding range of this function in this context.

13 Sketch the graph of $y = x(8 - 2x)(22 - 2x)$.
Given that y cm^3 is the volume of a cuboid with height x cm, length $(22 - 2x)$ cm and width $(8 - 2x)$ cm, state an appropriate domain for the function given above.

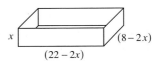

3.3 Graphs of powers of x

(i) Positive integer powers

Consider first the graphs of functions of the form $f(x) = x^n$, where n is a positive integer. Notice that $(0,0)$ and $(1,1)$ satisfy the equation $y = x^n$ for all these values of n, so that all the graphs include the points $(0,0)$ and $(1,1)$.

First look at the graphs when x is positive. Then x^n is also positive, so that the graphs lie entirely in the first quadrant. Fig. 3.5 shows the graphs for $n = 1, 2, 3$ and 4 for values of x from 0 to somewhere beyond 1.

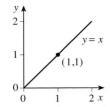 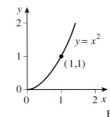 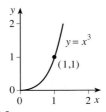 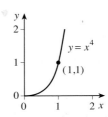

Fig. 3.5

Points to notice are:

- $n = 1$ is a special case: it gives the straight line $y = x$ through the origin, which makes an angle of $45°$ with each axis.

- For $n > 1$ the x-axis is a tangent to the graphs at the origin. This is because, when x is small, x^n is very small. For example, $0.1^2 = 0.01$, $0.1^3 = 0.001$, $0.1^4 = 0.0001$.
- For each increase in the index n, the graph stays closer to the x-axis between $x = 0$ and $x = 1$, but then climbs more steeply beyond $x = 1$. This is because $x^{n+1} = x \times x^n$, so that $x^{n+1} < x^n$ when $0 < x < 1$ and $x^{n+1} > x^n$ when $x > 1$.

What happens when x is negative depends on whether n is odd or even. To see this, suppose $x = -a$, where a is a positive number.

If n is even, $f(-a) = (-a)^n = a^n = f(a)$. So the value of y on the graph is the same for $x = -a$ and $x = a$. This means that the graph is symmetrical about the y-axis. This is illustrated in Fig. 3.6 for the graphs of $y = x^2$ and $y = x^4$. Functions with the property that $f(-a) = f(a)$ for all values of a are called **even functions**.

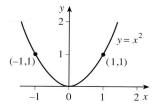
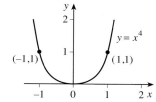

Fig. 3.6

If n is odd, $f(-a) = (-a)^n = -a^n = -f(a)$. The value of y for $x = -a$ is minus the value for $x = a$. Note that the points with coordinates (a, a^n) and $(-a, -a^n)$ are symmetrically placed on either side of the origin. This means that the whole graph is symmetrical about the origin. This is illustrated in Fig. 3.7 for the graphs of $y = x$ and $y = x^3$. Functions with the property that $f(-a) = -f(a)$ for all values of a are called **odd functions**.

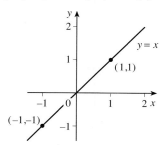
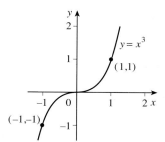

Fig. 3.7

(ii) Negative integer powers

You can write a negative integer n as $-m$, where m is a positive integer. Then x^n becomes x^{-m}, or $\dfrac{1}{x^m}$.

It is again simplest to begin with the part of the graph for which x is positive. Then $\dfrac{1}{x^m}$ is also positive, so the graph lies in the first quadrant. Just as when n is positive, the point $(1,1)$ lies on the graph. But there is an important difference when $x = 0$, since then $x^m = 0$ and $\dfrac{1}{x^m}$ is not defined. So there is no point on the graph for which $x = 0$.

To look at this more closely, take a value of x close to 0, say 0.01. Then for $n = -1$ the corresponding value of y is $0.01^{-1} = \frac{1}{0.01^1} = \frac{1}{0.01} = 100$; and for $n = -2$ it is $0.01^{-2} = \frac{1}{0.01^2} = \frac{1}{0.0001} = 10\ 000$. Even if you use a very small scale, the graph of x^n will disappear off the top of the page or screen as x is reduced towards zero.

What happens if x is large? For example, take $x = 100$. Then for $n = -1$ the corresponding value of y is $100^{-1} = \frac{1}{100^1} = \frac{1}{100} = 0.01$; and for $n = -2$ it is $100^{-2} = \frac{1}{100^2} = \frac{1}{10\ 000} = 0.0001$. So x^n becomes very small, and the graph comes very close to the x-axis.

Now consider the part of the graph for which x is negative. You found in (i) above that, for positive n, this depends on whether n is odd or even. The same is true when n is negative, and for the same reason. If n is even, x^n is an even function and its graph is symmetrical about the y-axis. If n is odd, x^n is an odd function and its graph is symmetrical about the origin.

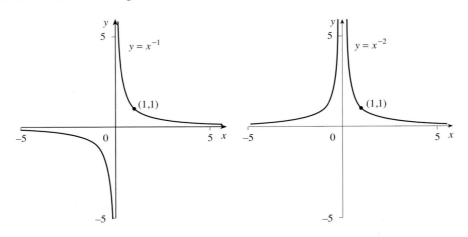

Fig. 3.8

All these properties are shown by the graphs of $y = x^n$ for $n = -1$ and $n = -2$ in Fig. 3.8.

(iii) Fractional powers

When n is a fraction, the function x^n may or may not be defined for negative values of x. For example, $x^{\frac{1}{3}}$ (the cube root of x) and $x^{-\frac{4}{5}}$ have values when $x < 0$, but $x^{\frac{1}{2}}$ (the square root of x) and $x^{-\frac{3}{4}}$ do not. Even when x^n is defined for negative x, some calculators and computers are not programmed to do the calculation. So it is simplest to restrict the discussion to values of $x \geqslant 0$.

It is easy to sketch the graphs of many of these functions by comparing them with graphs of integer powers of x. Here are two examples.

The graph of $y = x^{\frac{5}{2}}$ must lie between the graphs of $y = x^2$ and $y = x^3$.

The graph of $y = x^{-\frac{1}{2}}$ is not defined when $x = 0$; its graph resembles the graph of $y = x^{-1}$ (see Fig. 3.8), but lies below it when $x < 1$ and above it when $x > 1$.

If you are able to experiment for yourself with other fractional powers using a calculator or a computer, you will find that:

- It is still true that the graph of $y = x^n$ contains the point $(1,1)$.
- If n is positive the graph also contains the point $(0,0)$.
- If $n > 1$ the x-axis is a tangent to the graph; if $0 < n < 1$ the y-axis is a tangent. (To show this convincingly you may need to zoom in on a section of the graph close to the origin.)

Much the most important of these graphs is that of $y = x^{\frac{1}{2}}$, or $y = \sqrt{x}$. The clue to finding the shape of this graph is to note that if $y = x^{\frac{1}{2}}$, then $x = y^2$. The graph can therefore be obtained from that of $y = x^2$ by swapping the x- and y-axes. This has the effect of tipping the graph on its side, so that instead of facing upwards it faces to the right.

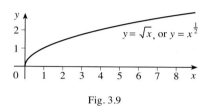

Fig. 3.9

But this is not quite the whole story. If $x = y^2$, then either $y = +\sqrt{x}$ or $y = -\sqrt{x}$. Since you want only the first of these possibilities, you must remove the part of the graph of $x = y^2$ below the x-axis, leaving only the part shown in Fig. 3.9 as the graph of $y = x^{\frac{1}{2}}$, or $y = \sqrt{x}$.

3.4   The modulus of a number

Suppose that you want to find the difference between the heights of two people. With numerical information, the answer is straightforward: if their heights are 90 cm and 100 cm, you would answer 10 cm; and if their heights were 100 cm and 90 cm, you would still answer 10 cm. But how would you answer the question if their heights were H cm and h cm? The answer is, it depends which is bigger: if $H > h$, you would answer $(H - h)$ cm; if $h > H$ you would answer $(h - H)$ cm; and if $h = H$ you would answer 0 cm, which is either $(H - h)$ cm or $(h - H)$ cm.

Questions like this, in which you want an answer that is always positive or zero, lead to the idea of the modulus.

> The **modulus** of x, written $|x|$ and pronounced 'mod x', is defined by
>
> $$|x| = x \qquad \text{if } x \geqslant 0,$$
> $$|x| = -x \qquad \text{if } x < 0.$$

Using the modulus notation, you can now write the difference in heights as $|H - h|$ whether $H > h$, $h > H$ or $h = H$.

Another situation in which the modulus is useful is when you want to talk about numbers which are large numerically, but which are negative, such as -1000 or $-1000\,000$. You can describe these as 'negative numbers with large modulus'.

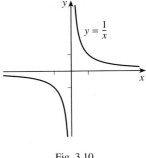

Fig. 3.10

For example, for large positive values of x, the value of $\dfrac{1}{x}$ approaches 0. The same is true for negative values of x with large modulus. So you can say that, when $|x|$ is large, $\left|\dfrac{1}{x}\right|$ is close to zero; or in a numerical example, when $|x| > 1000$, $\left|\dfrac{1}{x}\right| < 0.001$. (See Fig. 3.10.)

Some calculators have a key which converts any number in the display to its modulus. This key is often labelled [ABS], which stands for 'absolute value'.

Exercise 3B

If you have access to a graphic calculator, use it to check your answers to Questions 4, 5 and 6.

1   Sketch the graphs of
    (a) $y = x^5$,
    (b) $y = x^6$,
    (c) $y = x^{10}$,
    (d) $y = x^{15}$.

2   Three graphs have equations   (p) $y = x^{-2}$,   (q) $y = x^{-3}$,   (r) $y = x^{-4}$.
    A line $x = k$ meets the three graphs at points P, Q and R, respectively. Give the order of the points P, Q and R on the line (from the bottom up) when k takes the following values.
    (a) 2
    (b) $\frac{1}{2}$
    (c) $-\frac{1}{2}$
    (d) -2

3   For what values of x are these inequalities satisfied? Sketch graphs illustrating your answers.
    (a) $0 < x^{-3} < 0.001$
    (b) $x^{-2} < 0.0004$
    (c) $x^{-4} \geqslant 100$
    (d) $8x^{-4} < 0.000\,05$

4   Sketch the graphs of these equations for $x > 0$.
    (a) $y = x^{\frac{3}{2}}$
    (b) $y = x^{\frac{1}{3}}$
    (c) $y = -2x^{\frac{1}{2}}$
    (d) $y = 4x^{-\frac{1}{4}}$
    (e) $y = x^{-\frac{4}{3}}$
    (f) $y = x^{\frac{2}{3}} - x^{-\frac{2}{3}}$

5   Sketch these graphs, including negative values of x where appropriate.
    (a) $y = x^{\frac{2}{3}}$
    (b) $y = x^{\frac{3}{4}}$
    (c) $y = x^{\frac{4}{5}}$
    (d) $y = x^{-\frac{1}{3}}$
    (e) $y = x^{\frac{4}{3}}$
    (f) $y = x^{-\frac{3}{2}}$

6   Draw sketch graphs with these equations.
    (a) $y = x^2 + x^{-1}$
    (b) $y = x + x^{-2}$
    (c) $y = x^2 - x^{-1}$
    (d) $y = x^{-2} - x^{-1}$
    (e) $y = x^{-2} - x^{-3}$
    (f) $y = x^{-2} - x^{-4}$

7   Of the following functions, one is even and two are odd. Determine which is which.
    (a) $y = x^7$
    (b) $y = x^4 + 3x^2$
    (c) $y = x(x^2 - 1)$

8 State the values of the following.

    (a) $|-7|$ (b) $\left|-\frac{1}{200}\right|$ (c) $|9-4|$

    (d) $|4-9|$ (e) $|\pi-3|$ (f) $|\pi-4|$

9 Find the values of $\left|x-x^2\right|$ when x takes the values

    (a) 2,   (b) $\frac{1}{2}$,   (c) 1,

    (d) -1,   (e) 0.

10 You are given that $y=\dfrac{1}{x^2}$. What can you say about y if

    (a) $|x|>100$,   (b) $|x|<0.01$?

11 You are given that $y=\dfrac{1}{x^3}$.

    (a) What can you say about y if $|x|<1000$?

    (b) What can you say about x if $|y|>1000$?

12 The number, N, of people at a football match was reported as '37 000 to the nearest thousand'. Write this statement as an inequality using the modulus sign.

13 The mathematics marks, m and n, of two twins never differ by more than 5. Write this statement as an inequality using the modulus sign.

14 A line has length x cm. You are given that $|x-5.23|<0.005$. How would you explain this in words?

3.5 Graphs of the form $y=ax^2+bx+c$

In Chapter 1, you found out how to sketch graphs of straight lines, and what the constants m and c mean in the equation $y=mx+c$.

Exercise 3C gives you experience of plotting the graphs of functions with equations of the form $y=ax^2+bx+c$.

If you have access to a graphic calculator, use it and do all the questions; if not, work in a group and share out the tasks.

A summary of the main points appears after the exercise.

Exercise 3C

1 Draw, on the same set of axes, the graphs of

    (a) $y=x^2-2x+5$,   (b) $y=x^2-2x+1$,   (c) $y=x^2-2x$.

2 Draw, on the same set of axes, the graphs of

    (a) $y=x^2+x-4$,   (b) $y=x^2+x-1$,   (c) $y=x^2+x+2$.

3 The diagram shows the graph of $y = ax^2 - bx$. On a copy of the diagram, sketch the graphs of

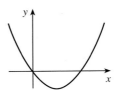

(a) $y = ax^2 - bx + 4$,

(b) $y = ax^2 - bx - 6$.

4 What is the effect on the graph of $y = ax^2 + bx + c$ of changing the value of c?

5 Draw the graphs of

(a) $y = x^2 - 4x + 1$, (b) $y = x^2 - 2x + 1$,

(c) $y = x^2 + 1$, (d) $y = x^2 + 2x + 1$.

6 Draw the graph of $y = 2x^2 + bx + 4$ for different values of b. How does changing b affect the curve $y = ax^2 + bx + c$?

7 Draw the graphs of

(a) $y = x^2 + 1$, (b) $y = 3x^2 + 1$,

(c) $y = -3x^2 + 1$, (d) $y = -x^2 + 1$.

8 Draw the graphs of

(a) $y = -4x^2 + 3x + 1$, (b) $y = -x^2 + 3x + 1$,

(c) $y = x^2 + 3x + 1$, (d) $y = 4x^2 + 3x + 1$.

10 How does changing a affect the shape of the graph of $y = ax^2 + bx + c$?

11 Which of the following could be the equation of the curve shown in the diagram?

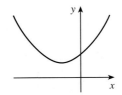

(a) $y = x^2 - 2x + 5$

(b) $y = -x^2 - 2x + 5$

(c) $y = x^2 + 2x + 5$

(d) $y = -x^2 + 2x + 5$

12 Which of the following could be the equation of the curve shown in the diagram?

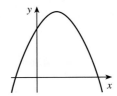

(a) $y = -x^2 + 3x + 4$

(b) $y = x^2 - 3x + 4$

(c) $y = x^2 + 3x + 4$

(d) $y = -x^2 - 3x + 4$

3.6 The shapes of graphs of the form $y = ax^2 + bx + c$

In Exercise 3C, you should have discovered a number of results, which are summarised in the box below.

All the graphs have the same general shape, which is called a **parabola**. These parabolas have a vertical **axis of symmetry**. The point where a parabola meets its axis of symmetry is called the **vertex**.

Changing c moves the graph up and down in the y-direction.

Changing b moves the axis of symmetry of the graph in the x-direction. If a and b have the same sign the axis of symmetry is to the left of the y-axis; if a and b have opposite signs the axis of symmetry is to the right of the y-axis.

If a is positive the vertex is at the lowest point of the graph; if a is negative the vertex is at the highest point. The larger the size of $|a|$ the more the graph is elongated, that is, lengthened in the y-direction.

3.7 The point of intersection of two graphs

The principle for finding the point of intersection of two curves is the same as that for finding the point of intersection of two graphs which are straight lines.

Suppose that you have two graphs, with equations $y = f(x)$ and $y = g(x)$. You want the point (x, y) which lies on both graphs, so the coordinates (x, y) satisfy both equations. Therefore x must satisfy the equation $f(x) = g(x)$.

Example 3.7.1

Find the points of intersection of the line $y = 2$ with the graph $y = x^2 - 3x + 4$ (see Fig. 3.11).

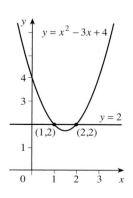

Solving these equations simultaneously gives $x^2 - 3x + 4 = 2$, which reduces to $x^2 - 3x + 2 = 0$.

Factorising gives $(x - 1)(x - 2) = 0$, so

$$x = 1 \text{ or } x = 2.$$

Substituting these values in either equation ($y = 2$ is obviously easier!) to find y, the points of intersection are $(1, 2)$ and $(2, 2)$.

Fig. 3.11

Example 3.7.2

Find the point of intersection of the line $y = 2x - 1$ with the graph $y = x^2$ (see Fig. 3.12).

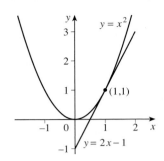

Solving these equations gives $2x - 1 = x^2$, which is $x^2 - 2x + 1 = 0$. This factorises as $(x-1)^2 = 0$, giving $x = 1$.

Substituting these values in either equation to find y gives the point of intersection as $(1,1)$.

The reason that there is only one point of intersection is that this line is a tangent to the graph. If you have access to a graphic calculator, draw the graph to check this statement.

Fig. 3.12

Example 3.7.3

Find the points of intersection of the graphs $y = x^2 - 2x - 6$ and $y = 12 + x - 2x^2$.

Solving these equations simultaneously gives $x^2 - 2x - 6 = 12 + x - 2x^2$, which is $3x^2 - 3x - 18 = 0$. Dividing by 3 gives $x^2 - x - 6 = 0$, which factorises as $(x+2)(x-3) = 0$, giving $x = -2$ or $x = 3$.

Substituting these values in either equation to find y gives the points of intersection as $(-2,2)$ and $(3,-3)$.

Exercise 3D

1 Find the point or points of intersection for the following lines and curves.

(a) $x = 3$ and $y = x^2 + 4x - 7$ (b) $y = 3$ and $y = x^2 - 5x + 7$

(c) $y = 8$ and $y = x^2 + 2x$ (d) $y + 3 = 0$ and $y = 2x^2 + 5x - 6$

2 Find the points of intersection for the following lines and curves.

(a) $y = x + 1$ and $y = x^2 - 3x + 4$ (b) $y = 2x + 3$ and $y = x^2 + 3x - 9$

(c) $y = 3x + 11$ and $y = 2x^2 + 2x + 5$ (d) $y = 4x + 1$ and $y = 9 + 4x - 2x^2$

(e) $3x + y - 1 = 0$ and $y = 6 + 10x - 6x^2$

3 In both the following, show that the line and curve meet only once and find the point of intersection.

(a) $y = 2x + 2$ and $y = x^2 - 2x + 6$ (b) $y = -2x - 7$ and $y = x^2 + 4x + 2$

4 Find the points of intersection between the curve $y = x^2 - x$ and the line

(a) $y = x$,   (b) $y = x - 1$.

If you have access to a graphic calculator, use it to see how the curve and lines are related.

5 Find the points of intersection between the curve $y = x^2 + 5x + 18$ and the lines

(a) $y = -3x + 2$,   (b) $y = -3x + 6$.

If you have access to a graphic calculator, use it to see how the curve and lines are related.

6 Find the points of intersection between the line $y = x + 5$ and the curves

(a) $y = 2x^2 - 3x - 1$,　　　　(b) $y = 2x^2 - 3x + 7$.

If you have access to a graphic calculator, use it to see how the line and curves are related.

7 Find the points of intersection of the following curves.

(a) $y = x^2 + 5x + 1$ and $y = x^2 + 3x + 11$

(b) $y = x^2 - 3x - 7$ and $y = x^2 + x + 1$

(c) $y = 7x^2 + 4x + 1$ and $y = 7x^2 - 4x + 1$

8 Find the points of intersection of the following curves.

(a) $y = \frac{1}{2}x^2$ and $y = 1 - \frac{1}{2}x^2$　　　　(b) $y = 2x^2 + 3x + 4$ and $y = x^2 + 6x + 2$

(c) $y = x^2 + 7x + 13$ and $y = 1 - 3x - x^2$　　(d) $y = 6x^2 + 2x - 9$ and $y = x^2 + 7x + 1$

(e) $y = (x - 2)(6x + 5)$ and $y = (x - 5)^2 + 1$　(f) $y = 2x(x - 3)$ and $y = x(x + 2)$

9 Find the point or points of intersection of these pairs of graphs. Illustrate your answers with sketch graphs.

(a) $y = 8x^2, y = 8x^{-1}$　　(b) $y = x^{-1}, y = 3x^{-2}$　　(c) $y = x, y = 4x^{-3}$

(d) $y = 8x^{-2}, y = 2x^{-4}$　(e) $y = 9x^{-3}, y = x^{-5}$　(f) $y = \frac{1}{4}x^4, y = 16x^{-2}$

3.8 Using factors to sketch graphs

The graphs of some functions of the form $f(x) = ax^2 + bx + c$ which factorise can also be drawn in another way. For example, take the functions

$$f(x) = x^2 - 6x + 5 = (x - 1)(x - 5),$$

$$g(x) = 12x - 4x^2 = -4x(x - 3).$$

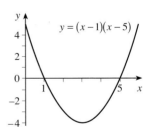

Fig. 3.13

In the first case, $f(1) = 0$ and $f(5) = 0$, so that the points $(1,0)$ and $(5,0)$ lie on the graph of $f(x)$. This is shown in Fig. 3.13.

Similarly $g(0) = g(3) = 0$, so that $(0,0)$ and $(3,0)$ lie on the graph of $g(x)$. This is shown in Fig. 3.14.

You can draw the graph of any function of this type which can be factorised as

$$a(x - r)(x - s),$$

by first noting that it cuts the x-axis at the points $(r,0)$ and $(s,0)$. The sign of the constant a tells you whether it 'bends upwards' (like $y = x^2$) or 'bends downwards'.

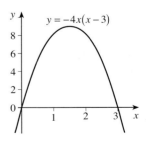

Fig. 3.14

In Figs. 3.13 and 3.14 different scales have been used on the two axes. If equal scales had been used the elongation in both figures would have been more obvious.

Example 3.8.1

Sketch the graph of $f(x) = 3x^2 - 2x - 1$.

You can factorise the expression as $f(x) = (3x+1)(x-1)$, but to apply the factor method you need to write it as

$$f(x) = 3\left(x + \tfrac{1}{3}\right)(x - 1).$$

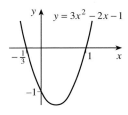

So the graph passes through $\left(-\tfrac{1}{3}, 0\right)$ and $(1, 0)$. The constant 3 tells you that the graph faces upwards and is elongated.

This is enough information to give a good idea of the shape of the graph, from which you can draw a sketch like Fig. 3.15. It is also worth noting that $f(0) = -1$, so that the graph cuts the y-axis at the point $(0, -1)$.

Fig. 3.15

Note that the sketch does not have marks against the axes, except to say where the graph cuts them.

You can extend the factor method to drawing graphs of functions with more than two factors. For example,

$$f(x) = a(x - r)(x - s)(x - t)$$

defines a function whose equation, when multiplied out, starts with $f(x) = ax^3 - \dots$.

The graph passes through the points $(r, 0)$, $(s, 0)$ and $(t, 0)$. The constant a tells you whether, for large values of x, the graph lies in the first or the fourth quadrant.

This is shown in Figs. 3.16 and 3.17, which show the graphs of $y = 2x(x-1)(x-4)$ and $y = -(x+2)(x-1)^2$.

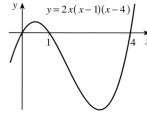

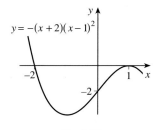

Notice that, in Fig. 3.17, the factor $(x-1)$ is squared, so that there are only two points of the graph on the x-axis. At $(1, 0)$ the x-axis is a tangent to the graph.

Fig. 3.16   Fig. 3.17

3.9 Predicting functions from their graphs

You can also use the factor form to predict the equation of a function of the type $f(x) = ax^2 + bx + c$, if you know the points where its graph crosses the x-axis and the coordinates of one other point on the graph.

Example 3.9.1

Find the equation of the graph of the type $y = ax^2 + bx + c$ which crosses the x-axis at the points $(1,0)$ and $(4,0)$ and also passes through the point $(3,-4)$.

Since the curve cuts the axes at $(1,0)$ and $(4,0)$, as in Fig. 3.18, the equation has the form

$$y = a(x-1)(x-4).$$

Since the point $(3,-4)$ lies on this curve,
$-4 = a(3-1)(3-4)$, giving $-4 = -2a$, so $a = 2$.
The equation of the curve is therefore

$$y = 2(x-1)(x-4), \quad \text{or} \quad y = 2x^2 - 10x + 8.$$

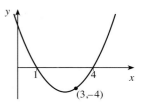

Fig. 3.18

Exercise 3E

1 Sketch the following graphs.

(a) $y = (x-2)(x-4)$ (b) $y = (x+3)(x-1)$ (c) $y = x(x-2)$

(d) $y = (x+5)(x+1)$ (e) $y = x(x+3)$ (f) $y = 2(x+1)(x-1)$

2 Sketch the following graphs.

(a) $y = 3(x+1)(x-5)$ (b) $y = -2(x-1)(x-3)$ (c) $y = -(x+3)(x+5)$

(d) $y = 2\left(x + \frac{1}{2}\right)(x-3)$ (e) $y = -3(x-4)^2$ (f) $y = -5(x-1)\left(x + \frac{4}{5}\right)$

3 By first factorising the function, sketch the following graphs.

(a) $y = x^2 - 2x - 8$ (b) $y = x^2 - 2x$ (c) $y = x^2 + 6x + 9$

(d) $y = 2x^2 - 7x + 3$ (e) $y = 4x^2 - 1$ (f) $y = -(x^2 - x - 12)$

(g) $y = -x^2 - 4x - 4$ (h) $y = -(x^2 - 7x + 12)$ (i) $y = 11x - 4x^2 - 6$

4 Find the equation, in the form $y = x^2 + bx + c$, of the parabola which

(a) crosses the x-axis at the points $(2,0)$ and $(5,0)$,

(b) crosses the x-axis at the points $(-7,0)$ and $(-10,0)$,

(c) passes through the points $(-5,0)$ and $(3,0)$,

(d) passes through the points $(-3,0)$ and $(1,-16)$.

5 Sketch the following graphs.

(a) $y = (x+3)(x-2)(x-3)$ (b) $y = x(x-4)(x-6)$

(c) $y = x^2(x-4)$ (d) $y = x(x-4)^2$

(e) $y = -(x+6)(x+4)(x+2)$ (f) $y = -3(x+1)(x-3)^2$

6 Find the equation, in the form $y = ax^2 + bx + c$, of the parabola which

(a) crosses the x-axis at $(1,0)$ and $(5,0)$ and crosses the y-axis at $(0,15)$,

(b) crosses the x-axis at $(-2,0)$ and $(7,0)$ and crosses the y-axis at $(0,-56)$,

(c) passes through the points $(-6,0)$, $(-2,0)$ and $(0,-6)$,

(d) crosses the x-axis at $(-3,0)$ and $(2,0)$ and also passes through $(1,16)$,

(e) passes through the points $(-10,0)$, $(7,0)$ and $(8,90)$.

7 Sketch the following graphs.

(a) $y = x^2 - 4x - 5$ (b) $y = 4x^2 - 4x + 1$ (c) $y = -x^2 - 3x + 18$

(d) $y = 2x^2 - 9x + 10$ (e) $y = -(x^2 - 4x + 9)$ (f) $y = 3x^2 + 9x$

8 Here are the equations of nine parabolas.

A $y = (x - 3)(x - 8)$ B $y = 14 + 5x - x^2$ C $y = 6x^2 - x - 70$

D $y = x(3 - x)$ E $y = (x + 2)(x - 7)$ F $y = -3(x + 3)(x + 7)$

G $y = x^2 + 2x + 1$ H $y = x^2 + 8x + 12$ I $y = x^2 - 25$

Answer the following questions without drawing the graphs of these parabolas.

(a) Which of the parabolas cross the y-axis at a positive value of y?

(b) For which of the parabolas is the vertex at the highest point of the graph?

(c) For which of the parabolas is the vertex to the left of the y-axis?

(d) Which of the parabolas pass through the origin?

(e) Which of the parabolas do not cross the x-axis at two separate points?

(f) Which of the parabolas have the y-axis as their axis of symmetry?

(g) Which two of the parabolas have the same axis of symmetry?

(h) Which of the parabolas have the vertex in the fourth quadrant?

9 Suggest a possible equation for each of the graphs shown below.

(a) 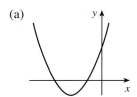 (b) 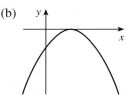 (c)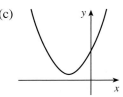

(d) 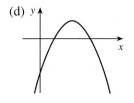 (e) 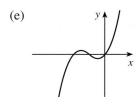 (f)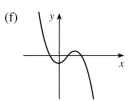

Miscellaneous exercise 3

1 The function f is defined by $f(x) = 7x - 4$.

(a) Find the values of $f(7)$, $f\left(\frac{1}{2}\right)$ and $f(-5)$.

(b) Find the value of x such that $f(x) = 10$.

(c) Find the value of x such that $f(x) = x$.

(d) Find the value of x such that $f(x) = f(37)$.

2 The function f is defined by $f(x) = x^2 - 3x + 5$. Find the two values of x for which $f(x) = f(4)$.

3 The diagram shows the graph of $y = x^n$, where n is an integer. Given that the curve passes between the points $(2, 200)$ and $(2, 2000)$, determine the value of n.

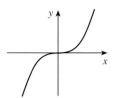

4 Find the points of intersection of the curves $y = x^2 - 7x + 5$ and $y = 1 + 2x - x^2$.

5 Find the points of intersection of the line $y = 2x + 3$ and the curve $y = 2x^2 + 3x - 7$.

6 Find the coordinates of the point at which the line $3x + y - 2 = 0$ meets the curve $y = (4x - 3)(x - 2)$.

7 Find the coordinates of any points of intersection of the curves $y = (x - 2)(x - 4)$ and $y = x(2 - x)$. Sketch the two curves to show the relationship between them.

8 Given that k is a positive constant, sketch the graphs of

   (a) $y = (x + k)(x - 2k)$,

   (b) $y = (x + 4k)(x + 2k)$,

   (c) $y = x(x - k)(x - 5k)$,

   (d) $y = (x + k)(x - 2k)^2$.

9 The function f is defined by $f(x) = ax^2 + bx + c$. Given that $f(0) = 6$, $f(-1) = 15$ and $f(1) = 1$, find the values of a, b and c.

10 Find the point where the line $y = 3 - 4x$ meets the curve $y = 4(4x^2 + 5x + 3)$.

11 Sketch the graphs of

   (a) $y = (x + 4)(x + 2) + (x + 4)(x - 5)$,

   (b) $y = (x + 4)(x + 2) + (x + 4)(5 - x)$.

12 A function f is defined by $f(x) = ax + b$. Given that $f(-2) = 27$ and $f(1) = 15$, find the value of x such that $f(x) = -5$.

13 A curve with equation $y = ax^2 + bx + c$ crosses the x-axis at $(-4, 0)$ and $(9, 0)$ and also passes through the point $(1, 120)$. Where does the curve cross the y-axis?

14 The curve $y = ax^2 + bx + c$ passes through the points $(-1, 22)$, $(1, 8)$, $(3, 10)$, $(-2, p)$ and $(q, 17)$. Find the value of p and the possible values of q.

15 Show that the curves $y = 2x^2 + 5x$, $y = x^2 + 4x + 12$ and $y = 3x^2 + 4x - 6$ have one point in common and find its coordinates.

16 Given that the curves $y = x^2 - 3x + c$ and $y = k - x - x^2$ meet at the point $(-2, 12)$, find the values of c and k. Hence find the other point where the two curves meet.

17 Find the value of the constant p if the three curves $y = x^2 + 3x + 14$, $y = x^2 + 2x + 11$ and $y = px^2 + px + p$ have one point in common.

18 The straight line $y = x - 1$ meets the curve $y = x^2 - 5x - 8$ at the points A and B. The curve $y = p + qx - 2x^2$ also passes through the points A and B. Find the values of p and q.

19 The line $y = 10x - 9$ meets the curve $y = x^2$. Find the coordinates of the points of intersection.

20 Suggest a possible equation for each of the graphs shown below.

(a)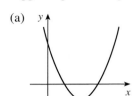

(b)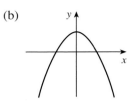

(c)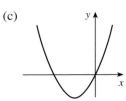

(d)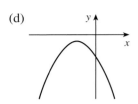

(e)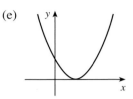

(f)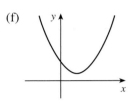

(g)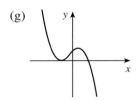

(h)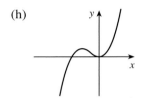

(i)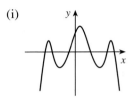

21 Find, in surd form, the points of intersection of the curves $y = x^2 - 5x - 3$ and $y = 3 - 5x - x^2$.

22 The line $y = 6x + 1$ meets the curve $y = x^2 + 2x + 3$ at two points. Show that the coordinates of one of the points are $\left(2 - \sqrt{2}, 13 - 6\sqrt{2}\right)$, and find the coordinates of the other point.

23 Show that the curves $y = 2x^2 - 7x + 14$ and $y = 2 + 5x - x^2$ meet at only one point. Without further calculation or sketching, deduce the number of points of intersection of

(a) $y = 2x^2 - 7x + 12$ and $y = 2 + 5x - x^2$,   (b) $y = 2x^2 - 7x + 14$ and $y = 1 + 5x - x^2$,

(c) $y = 2x^2 - 7x + 34$ and $y = 22 + 5x - x^2$.

24 What can you say about $\dfrac{|x|}{x}$ if   (a) $x > 0$,   (b) $x < 0$?

4 Quadratics

This chapter is about quadratic expressions of the form $ax^2 + bx + c$ and their graphs. When you have completed it, you should

- know how to complete the square in a quadratic expression
- know how to locate the vertex and the axis of symmetry of the quadratic graph $y = ax^2 + bx + c$
- be able to solve quadratic equations
- know that the discriminant of the quadratic expression $ax^2 + bx + c$ is the value of $b^2 - 4ac$, and know how to use it
- be able to solve a pair of simultaneous equations involving a quadratic equation and a linear equation
- be able to recognise and solve equations which can be reduced to quadratic equations by a substitution.

4.1 Quadratic expressions

You know that the equation $y = bx + c$ has a graph which is a straight line. The expression $y = bx + c$ is called a linear equation. You know from Chapter 3 that if you add on a term ax^2, giving $y = ax^2 + bx + c$, the graph is a parabola. The expression $ax^2 + bx + c$, where a, b and c are constants, is called a **quadratic**. Thus x^2, $x^2 - 6x + 8$, $2x^2 - 3x + 4$ and $-3x^2 - 5$ are all examples of quadratics.

You can write any quadratic as $ax^2 + bx + c$, where a, b and c are constants. The values of b and c can be any numbers you please, including 0, but a cannot be 0 (the expression would not then be a quadratic). The numbers a, b and c are called **coefficients**: a is the coefficient of x^2, b is the coefficient of x and c is often called the constant term.

The coefficients of x^2 and x in $2x^2 - x + 4$ are 2 and -1, and the constant term is 4.

4.2 Completed square form

You can write a quadratic expression such as $x^2 - 6x + 8$ in a number of ways. These include the factor form $(x - 4)(x - 2)$, useful for finding where the parabola $y = x^2 - 6x + 8$, shown in Fig. 4.1, cuts the x-axis; and the form $(x - 3)^2 - 1$, useful for locating the vertex of the parabola and also for finding the range of the function $f(x) = x^2 - 6x + 8$, as shown in Example 3.2.3.

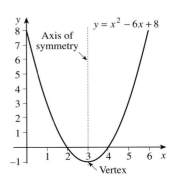

Fig. 4.1

Note that you cannot always write a quadratic expression in factor form. For instance, try $x^2 + 1$ or $x^2 + 2x + 3$.

If you write the equation of the graph $y = x^2 - 6x + 8$ in the form $y = (x-3)^2 - 1$, you can locate the axis of symmetry and the vertex quite easily. Since $(x-3)^2$ is a perfect square its value is always greater than or equal to 0, and is 0 only when $x = 3$. That is, $(x-3)^2 \geq 0$, and since $y = (x-3)^2 - 1$, it follows that $y \geq -1$. Since $(x-3)^2 = 0$ when $x = 3$, the vertex is at the point $(3, -1)$. The axis of symmetry is the line $x = 3$.

The form $(x-3)^2 - 1$ is called the **completed square form**. Here are some more examples of its use.

Example 4.2.1

Locate the vertex and the axis of symmetry of the quadratic graph $y = 3 - 2(x+2)^2$.

Since $2(x+2)^2 \geq 0$, and $2(x+2)^2 = 3 - y$, it follows that $3 - y \geq 0$, so $y \leq 3$. As $(x+2)^2 = 0$ when $x = -2$, the vertex of the graph is the point with coordinates $(-2, 3)$, the greatest value of y is 3 and the axis of symmetry is $x = -2$.

Example 4.2.2

Solve the equation $3(x-2)^2 - 2 = 0$.

As $3(x-2)^2 - 2 = 0$, $3(x-2)^2 = 2$ and $(x-2)^2 = \frac{2}{3}$.

Therefore $(x-2) = \pm\sqrt{\frac{2}{3}}$, so $x = 2 \pm \sqrt{\frac{2}{3}}$.

4.3 Completing the square

When you try to write the quadratic expression $x^2 + bx + c$ in completed square form, the key point is to note that when you square $x + \frac{1}{2}b$ you get

$$\left(x + \tfrac{1}{2}b\right)^2 = x^2 + bx + \tfrac{1}{4}b^2, \text{ so } x^2 + bx = \left(x + \tfrac{1}{2}b\right)^2 - \tfrac{1}{4}b^2.$$

Now add c to both sides:

$$x^2 + bx + c = \left(x^2 + bx\right) + c = \left\{\left(x + \tfrac{1}{2}b\right)^2 - \tfrac{1}{4}b^2\right\} + c.$$

Example 4.3.1

Write $x^2 + 10x + 32$ in completed square form.

$$x^2 + 10x + 32 = \left(x^2 + 10x\right) + 32 = \left\{(x+5)^2 - 25\right\} + 32 = (x+5)^2 + 7.$$

Don't try to memorise the form $x^2 + bx + c = \left(x + \tfrac{1}{2}b\right)^2 - \tfrac{1}{4}b^2 + c$. *Learn that you halve the coefficient of* x, *and write* $x^2 + bx = \left(x + \tfrac{1}{2}b\right)^2 - \tfrac{1}{4}b^2$. *Then add* c *to both sides.*

If you need to write $ax^2 + bx + c$ in completed square form, but the coefficient a of x^2 is not 1, you can rewrite $ax^2 + bx + c$ by taking out the factor a from the first two terms:

$$ax^2 + bx + c = a\left(x^2 + \frac{b}{a}x\right) + c.$$

Then complete the square of the quadratic expression $x^2 + \dfrac{b}{a}x$ inside the bracket.

Example 4.3.2

Express $2x^2 + 10x + 7$ in completed square form.

Start by taking out the factor 2 from the terms which involve x:

$$2x^2 + 10x + 7 = 2(x^2 + 5x) + 7.$$

Dealing with the term inside the bracket,

$$x^2 + 5x = \left(x + \tfrac{5}{2}\right)^2 - \tfrac{25}{4},$$

so $\quad 2x^2 + 10x + 7 = 2(x^2 + 5x) + 7 = 2\left\{\left(x + \tfrac{5}{2}\right)^2 - \tfrac{25}{4}\right\} + 7$

$$= 2\left(x + \tfrac{5}{2}\right)^2 - \tfrac{25}{2} + 7 = 2\left(x + \tfrac{5}{2}\right)^2 - \tfrac{11}{2}.$$

It's worth checking your result mentally at this stage.

If the coefficient of x^2 is negative, the technique is similar, as shown in Example 4.3.3.

Example 4.3.3

Express $3 - 4x - 2x^2$ in completed square form.

Start by taking out the factor -2 from the terms which involve x:

$$3 - 4x - 2x^2 = 3 - 2(x^2 + 2x).$$

Dealing with the term inside the bracket, $x^2 + 2x = (x+1)^2 - 1$,

so $\quad 3 - 4x - 2x^2 = 3 - 2(x^2 + 2x) = 3 - 2\{(x+1)^2 - 1\}$

$$= 3 - 2(x+1)^2 + 2 = 5 - 2(x+1)^2.$$

Example 4.3.4

Express $12x^2 - 7x - 12$ in completed square form, and use your result to find the factors of $12x^2 - 7x - 12$.

$$12x^2 - 7x - 12 = 12\left(x^2 - \tfrac{7}{12}x\right) - 12 = 12\left\{\left(x - \tfrac{7}{24}\right)^2 - \tfrac{49}{576}\right\} - 12$$

$$= 12\left\{\left(x - \tfrac{7}{24}\right)^2 - \tfrac{625}{576}\right\} = 12\left\{\left(x - \tfrac{7}{24}\right)^2 - \left(\tfrac{25}{24}\right)^2\right\}.$$

You can now use the formula $a^2 - b^2 = (a - b)(a + b)$ with a as $x - \tfrac{7}{24}$ and b as $\tfrac{25}{24}$ to factorise the expression inside the brackets as the difference of two squares:

$$12\left\{\left(x - \tfrac{7}{24}\right)^2 - \left(\tfrac{25}{24}\right)^2\right\} = 12\left(x - \tfrac{7}{24} - \tfrac{25}{24}\right)\left(x - \tfrac{7}{24} + \tfrac{25}{24}\right)$$

$$= 12\left(x - \tfrac{4}{3}\right)\left(x + \tfrac{3}{4}\right) = 3\left(x - \tfrac{4}{3}\right) \times 4\left(x + \tfrac{3}{4}\right)$$

$$= (3x - 4)(4x - 3).$$

Example 4.3.5

Express $x^2 - 8x + 12$ in completed square form. Use your result to find the range of the function $f(x) = x^2 - 8x + 12$, which is defined for all real values of x.

$$x^2 - 8x + 12 = (x - 4)^2 - 4.$$

As $(x - 4)^2 \geq 0$ for all values of x,

$$x^2 - 8x + 12 = (x - 4)^2 - 4 \geq -4, \text{ so } f(x) \geq -4.$$

Writing $f(x)$ as y, the range is $y \geq -4$.

Exercise 4A

1 Find (i) the vertex and (ii) the equation of the line of symmetry of each of the following quadratic graphs.

(a) $y = (x - 2)^2 + 3$
(b) $y = (x - 5)^2 - 4$
(c) $y = (x + 3)^2 - 7$

(d) $y = (2x - 3)^2 + 1$
(e) $y = (5x + 3)^2 + 2$
(f) $y = (3x + 7)^2 - 4$

(g) $y = (x - 3)^2 + c$
(h) $y = (x - p)^2 + q$
(i) $y = (ax + b)^2 + c$

2 Find (i) the least (or, if appropriate, the greatest) value of each of the following quadratic expressions and (ii) the value of x for which this occurs.

(a) $(x + 2)^2 - 1$
(b) $(x - 1)^2 + 2$
(c) $5 - (x + 3)^2$

(d) $(2x + 1)^2 - 7$
(e) $3 - 2(x - 4)^2$
(f) $(x + p)^2 + q$

(g) $(x - p)^2 - q$
(h) $r - (x - t)^2$
(i) $c - (ax + b)^2$

3 Solve the following quadratic equations. Leave surds in your answer.

(a) $(x - 3)^2 - 3 = 0$
(b) $(x + 2)^2 - 4 = 0$
(c) $2(x + 3)^2 = 5$

(d) $(3x - 7)^2 = 8$
(e) $(x + p)^2 - q = 0$
(f) $a(x + b)^2 - c = 0$

4 Express the following in completed square form.

(a) $x^2 + 2x + 2$
(b) $x^2 - 8x - 3$
(c) $x^2 + 3x - 7$

(d) $5 - 6x + x^2$
(e) $x^2 + 14x + 49$
(f) $2x^2 + 12x - 5$

(g) $3x^2 - 12x + 3$
(h) $7 - 8x - 4x^2$
(i) $2x^2 + 5x - 3$

5 Use the completed square form to factorise the following expressions.

(a) $x^2 - 2x - 35$
(b) $x^2 - 14x - 176$
(c) $x^2 + 6x - 432$

(d) $6x^2 - 5x - 6$
(e) $14 + 45x - 14x^2$
(f) $12x^2 + x - 6$.

6 Use the completed square form to find as appropriate the least or greatest value of each of the following expressions, and the value of x for which this occurs.

(a) $x^2 - 4x + 7$
(b) $x^2 - 3x + 5$
(c) $4 + 6x - x^2$

(d) $2x^2 - 5x + 2$
(e) $3x^2 + 2x - 4$
(f) $3 - 7x - 3x^2$

7 Each of the following functions is defined for all real values of x. By completing the square write $f(x)$ as $(x - p)^2 + q$, and hence find their ranges.

(a) $f(x) = x^2 - 6x + 10$ (b) $f(x) = x^2 + 7x + 1$ (c) $f(x) = x^2 - 3x + 4$

8 By completing the square find (i) the vertex, and (ii) the equation of the line of symmetry, of each of the following parabolas.

(a) $y = x^2 - 4x + 6$ (b) $y = x^2 + 6x - 2$ (c) $y = 7 - 10x - x^2$

(d) $y = x^2 + 3x + 1$ (e) $y = 2x^2 - 7x + 2$ (f) $y = 3x^2 - 12x + 5$

9 The domain of each of the following functions is the set of all positive real numbers. Find the range of each function.

(a) $f(x) = (x + 2)(x + 1)$ (b) $f(x) = (x - 1)(x - 2)$ (c) $f(x) = (2x - 1)(x - 2)$

4.4 Solving quadratic equations

You will be familiar with solving quadratic equations of the form $x^2 - 6x + 8 = 0$ by factorising $x^2 - 6x + 8$ into the form $(x - 2)(x - 4)$, and then using the argument:

> if $(x - 2)(x - 4) = 0$
> then either $x - 2 = 0$ or $x - 4 = 0$
> so $x = 2$ or $x = 4$.

The **solution** of the equation $x^2 - 6x + 8 = 0$ is $x = 2$ or $x = 4$. The numbers 2 and 4 are the **roots** of the equation.

If the quadratic expression has factors which you can find easily, then this is certainly the quickest way to solve the equation. However, the expression may not have factors, or they may be hard to find: try finding the factors of $30x^2 - 11x - 30$.

If you cannot factorise a quadratic expression easily to solve an equation, then use the quadratic formula:

> The solution of $ax^2 + bx + c = 0$, where $a \neq 0$, is
>
> $$x = \frac{-b \pm \sqrt{b^2 - 4ac}}{2a}.$$

It is useful to know how this formula is derived by expressing $ax^2 + bx + c$ in completed square form. Start by dividing both sides of the equation by a (which cannot be zero, otherwise the equation would not be a quadratic equation):

$$x^2 + \frac{b}{a}x + \frac{c}{a} = 0.$$

Completing the square of the expression on the left side, you find that

$$x^2 + \frac{b}{a}x + \frac{c}{a} = \left(x + \frac{b}{2a}\right)^2 - \frac{b^2}{4a^2} + \frac{c}{a} = \left(x + \frac{b}{2a}\right)^2 - \frac{b^2 - 4ac}{4a^2}.$$

So you can continue with the equation

$$\left(x + \frac{b}{2a}\right)^2 - \frac{b^2 - 4ac}{4a^2} = 0, \quad \text{which is} \quad \left(x + \frac{b}{2a}\right)^2 = \frac{b^2 - 4ac}{4a^2}.$$

There are two possibilities,

$$x + \frac{b}{2a} = +\sqrt{\frac{b^2 - 4ac}{4a^2}} \quad \text{or} \quad -\sqrt{\frac{b^2 - 4ac}{4a^2}},$$

giving

$$x = -\frac{b}{2a} \pm \frac{\sqrt{b^2 - 4ac}}{2a} = \frac{-b \pm \sqrt{b^2 - 4ac}}{2a}.$$

This shows that if $ax^2 + bx + c = 0$ and $a \neq 0$, then $x = \dfrac{-b \pm \sqrt{b^2 - 4ac}}{2a}$.

Example 4.4.1

Use the quadratic formula to solve the equations
(a) $2x^2 - 3x - 4 = 0$,   (b) $2x^2 - 3x + 4 = 0$,   (c) $30x^2 - 11x - 30 = 0$.

(a) Comparing this with $ax^2 + bx + c = 0$, put $a = 2$, $b = -3$ and $c = -4$. Then

$$x = \frac{-(-3) \pm \sqrt{(-3)^2 - 4 \times 2 \times (-4)}}{2 \times 2} = \frac{3 \pm \sqrt{9 + 32}}{4} = \frac{3 \pm \sqrt{41}}{4}.$$

Sometimes you will be expected to leave the roots in surd form. At other times you may be required to give the roots in the form $\dfrac{3 + \sqrt{41}}{4} \approx 2.35$ and $\dfrac{3 - \sqrt{41}}{4} \approx -0.85$. Try substituting these numbers in the equation and see what happens.

(b) Putting $a = 2$, $b = -3$ and $c = 4$,

$$x = \frac{-(-3) \pm \sqrt{(-3)^2 - 4 \times 2 \times 4}}{2 \times 2} = \frac{3 \pm \sqrt{9 - 32}}{4} = \frac{3 \pm \sqrt{-23}}{4}.$$

But -23 does not have a square root. This means that the equation $2x^2 - 3x + 4 = 0$ has no roots.

Try putting $2x^2 - 3x + 4$ in completed square form; what can you deduce about the graph of $y = 2x^2 - 3x + 4$?

(c) Putting $a = 30$, $b = -11$ and $c = -30$,

$$x = \frac{-(-11) \pm \sqrt{(-11)^2 - 4 \times 30 \times (-30)}}{2 \times 30} = \frac{11 \pm \sqrt{121 + 3600}}{60}$$

$$= \frac{11 \pm \sqrt{3721}}{60} = \frac{11 \pm 61}{60}.$$

So $x = \frac{72}{60} = \frac{6}{5}$ or $x = -\frac{50}{60} = -\frac{5}{6}$.

This third example factorises, but the factors are difficult to find. But once you know the roots of the equation you can deduce that $30x^2 - 11x - 30 = (6x + 5)(5x - 6)$.

4.5 The discriminant $b^2 - 4ac$

If you look back at Example 4.4.1 you will see that in part (a) the roots of the equation involved surds, in part (b) there were no roots, and in part (c) the roots were fractions.

You can predict which case will arise by calculating the value of the expression under the square root sign, $b^2 - 4ac$, and thinking about the effect that this value has in the quadratic formula $x = \dfrac{-b \pm \sqrt{b^2 - 4ac}}{2a}$.

- If $b^2 - 4ac$ is a perfect square, the roots will be integers or fractions.
- If $b^2 - 4ac > 0$, the equation $ax^2 + bx + c = 0$ will have two roots.
- If $b^2 - 4ac < 0$, there will be no roots.
- If $b^2 - 4ac = 0$, the roots are given by $x = \dfrac{-b \pm 0}{2a} = -\dfrac{b}{2a}$, and there is one root only. Sometimes it is said that there are two coincident roots, or a **repeated root**, because the root values $\dfrac{-b + 0}{2a}$ and $\dfrac{-b - 0}{2a}$ are equal.

The expression $b^2 - 4ac$ is called the **discriminant** of the quadratic expression $ax^2 + bx + c$ because, by its value, it discriminates between the types of solution of the equation $ax^2 + bx + c = 0$.

Example 4.5.1
What can you deduce from the values of the discriminants of the quadratics in the following equations?
(a) $2x^2 - 3x - 4 = 0$ (b) $2x^2 - 3x - 5 = 0$
(c) $2x^2 - 4x + 5 = 0$ (d) $2x^2 - 4x + 2 = 0$

(a) As $a = 2$, $b = -3$ and $c = -4$, $b^2 - 4ac = (-3)^2 - 4 \times 2 \times (-4) = 9 + 32 = 41$. The discriminant is positive, so the equation $2x^2 - 3x - 4 = 0$ has two roots. Also, as 41 is not a perfect square, the roots are irrational.

(b) As $a = 2$, $b = -3$ and $c = -5$, $b^2 - 4ac = (-3)^2 - 4 \times 2 \times (-5) = 9 + 40 = 49$. The discriminant is positive, so the equation $2x^2 - 3x - 5 = 0$ has two roots. Also, as 49 is a perfect square, the roots are rational.

(c) $b^2 - 4ac = (-4)^2 - 4 \times 2 \times 5 = 16 - 40 = -24$. As the discriminant is negative, the equation $2x^2 - 4x + 5 = 0$ has no roots.

(d) $b^2 - 4ac = (-4)^2 - 4 \times 2 \times 2 = 16 - 16 = 0$. As the discriminant is zero, the equation $2x^2 - 4x + 2 = 0$ has only one (repeated) root.

Example 4.5.2
The equation $kx^2 - 2x - 7 = 0$ has two real roots. What can you deduce about the value of the constant k ?

The discriminant is $(-2)^2 - 4 \times k \times (-7) = 4 + 28k$. As the equation has two real roots, the value of the discriminant is positive, so $4 + 28k > 0$, and $k > -\frac{1}{7}$.

Example 4.5.3
The equation $3x^2 + 2x + k = 0$ has a repeated root. Find the value of k .

The equation has repeated roots if $b^2 - 4ac = 0$; that is, if $2^2 - 4 \times 3 \times k = 0$. This gives $k = \frac{1}{3}$.

Notice how, in the above examples, there is no need to solve the quadratic equation. You can find all you need to know from the discriminant.

<hr>

Exercise 4B

1   Use the quadratic formula to solve the following equations. Leave irrational answers in surd form. If there is no solution, say so. Keep your answers for use in Question 8.

(a) $x^2 + 3x - 5 = 0$
(b) $x^2 - 4x - 7 = 0$
(c) $x^2 + 6x + 9 = 0$
(d) $x^2 + 5x + 2 = 0$
(e) $x^2 + x + 1 = 0$
(f) $3x^2 - 5x - 6 = 0$
(g) $2x^2 + 7x + 3 = 0$
(h) $8 - 3x - x^2 = 0$
(i) $5 + 4x - 6x^2 = 0$

2   Use the value of the discriminant $b^2 - 4ac$ to determine whether the following equations have two roots, one root or no roots.

(a) $x^2 - 3x - 5 = 0$
(b) $x^2 + 2x + 1 = 0$
(c) $x^2 - 3x + 4 = 0$
(d) $3x^2 - 6x + 5 = 0$
(e) $2x^2 - 7x + 3 = 0$
(f) $5x^2 + 9x + 4 = 0$
(g) $3x^2 + 42x + 147 = 0$
(h) $3 - 7x - 4x^2 = 0$

In parts (i) and (j), the values of p and q are positive.

(i) $x^2 + px - q = 0$
(j) $x^2 - px - q = 0$

3   The following equations have a repeated root. Find the value of k in each case. Leave your answers as integers, exact fractions or surds.

(a) $x^2 + 3x - k = 0$
(b) $kx^2 + 5x - 8 = 0$
(c) $x^2 - 18x + k = 0$
(d) $-3 + kx - 2x^2 = 0$
(e) $4x^2 - kx + 6 = 0$
(f) $kx^2 - px + q = 0$

4   The following equations have the number of roots shown in brackets. Deduce as much as you can about the value of k .

(a) $x^2 + 3x + k = 0$ (2)
(b) $x^2 - 7x + k = 0$ (1)
(c) $kx^2 - 3x + 5 = 0$ (0)
(d) $3x^2 + 5x - k = 0$ (2)
(e) $x^2 - 4x + 3k = 0$ (1)
(f) $kx^2 - 5x + 7 = 0$ (0)
(g) $x^2 - kx + 4 = 0$ (2)
(h) $x^2 + kx + 9 = 0$ (0)

5 Use the value of the discriminant to determine the number of points of intersection of the following graphs with the x-axis.

(a) $y = x^2 - 5x - 5$ (b) $y = x^2 + x + 1$ (c) $y = x^2 - 6x + 9$

(d) $y = x^2 + 4$ (e) $y = x^2 - 10$ (f) $y = 3 - 4x - 2x^2$

(g) $y = 3x^2 - 5x + 7$ (h) $y = x^2 + bx + b^2$ (i) $y = x^2 - 2qx + q^2$

6 If a and c are both positive, what can be said about the graph of $y = ax^2 + bx - c$?

7 If a is negative and c is positive, what can be said about the graph of $y = ax^2 + bx + c$?

8 You will need your answers to Question 1, in rational or surd form, not decimals.

(A) For Question 1(a), (b) and (d), find (i) the sum and (ii) the product of the roots. What do you notice? What happens if there is only one (repeated) root?

(B) If α and β are the roots of the quadratic equation $x^2 + bx + c = 0$ then these arise from factors $(x - \alpha)$ and $(x - \beta)$ of $x^2 + bx + c$. Show that the equation $x^2 + bx + c = 0$ has roots which have sum $-b$ and product c.

(C) Extend (B) to find expressions in terms of a, b and c for (i) the sum and (ii) the product of the roots of the equation $ax^2 + bx + c = 0$.

4.6 Simultaneous equations

This section shows how to solve a pair of simultaneous equations such as $y = x^2$ and $5x + 4y = 21$. This takes forward the ideas in Section 3.7.

Example 4.6.1
Solve the simultaneous equations $y = x^2$, $x + y = 6$.

These equations are usually best solved by finding an expression for x or y from one equation and substituting it into the other. In this case, it is easier to substitute for y from the first equation into the second, giving $x + x^2 = 6$. This rearranges to $x^2 + x - 6 = 0$, so $(x + 3)(x - 2) = 0$, giving $x = 2$ or $x = -3$.

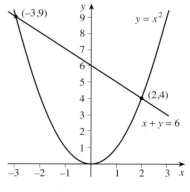

Fig. 4.2

You can find the corresponding y-values from the equation $y = x^2$. They are $y = 4$ and $y = 9$ respectively.

The solution is therefore $x = 2, y = 4$ or $x = -3, y = 9$.

Check that, for each pair of values, $x + y = 6$.

Note that the answers go together in pairs. It would be wrong to give the answer in the form $x = 2$ or $x = -3$ and $y = 4$ or $y = 9$, because the pairs of values $x = 2$, $y = 9$ and $x = -3$, $y = 4$ do not satisfy the original equations. You can see this if you interpret the question as finding the points of intersection of the graphs $y = x^2$ and $x + y = 6$, as in Fig. 4.2.

Example 4.6.2

Solve the simultaneous equations $x^2 - 2xy + 3y^2 = 6$ and $2x - 3y = 3$.

It is not easy to find expressions for either x or y from the first equation, so begin with the second equation. You are less likely to make mistakes if you avoid fractions. From the second equation, $2x = 3 + 3y$, so, squaring this equation,

$$4x^2 = (3 + 3y)^2 = 9 + 18y + 9y^2.$$

You now have expressions for $4x^2$ and $2x$, so you would like to substitute for them in the first equation. It is helpful to multiply the first equation by 4. Then

$$4x^2 - 8xy + 12y^2 = 24, \quad \text{or} \quad 4x^2 - 4y \times 2x + 12y^2 = 24;$$

so $(9 + 18y + 9y^2) - 4y(3 + 3y) + 12y^2 = 24$.

This reduces to $9y^2 + 6y - 15 = 0$, and, dividing by 3, to $3y^2 + 2y - 5 = 0$. Solving this equation gives $(y - 1)(3y + 5) = 0$, so $y = 1$ or $y = -\frac{5}{3}$.

Substituting in the second equation to find x, you obtain $x = 3$ and $x = -1$ respectively. Therefore the solution is $x = 3, y = 1$ and $x = -1, y = -\frac{5}{3}$.

Example 4.6.3

At how many points does the line $x + 2y = 3$ meet the curve $2x^2 + y^2 = 4$?

From $x + 2y = 3$, $x = 3 - 2y$. Substituting for x in $2x^2 + y^2 = 4$, $2(3 - 2y)^2 + y^2 = 4$, so $2(9 - 12y + 4y^2) + y^2 = 4$, which reduces to $9y^2 - 24y + 14 = 0$.

The discriminant of this equation is $24^2 - 4 \times 9 \times 14 = 576 - 504 = 72$. As this is positive, the equation has two solutions, so the line meets the curve at two points.

4.7   Equations which reduce to quadratic equations

Sometimes you will come across equations which are not quadratic, but which can be changed into quadratic equations, usually by making the right substitution.

Example 4.7.1

Solve the equation $t^4 - 13t^2 + 36 = 0$.

This is called a quartic equation because it has a t^4 term, but if you let x stand for t^2, the equation becomes $x^2 - 13x + 36 = 0$, which is a quadratic equation in x.

Then $(x - 4)(x - 9) = 0$, so $x = 4$ or $x = 9$.

Now recall that $x = t^2$, so $t^2 = 4$ or $t^2 = 9$, giving $t = \pm 2$ or $t = \pm 3$.

Example 4.7.2

Solve the equation $\sqrt{x} = 6 - x$
(a) by letting y stand for $\sqrt{x}$ (b) by squaring both sides of the equation.

(a) Letting $\sqrt{x} = y$, the equation becomes $y = 6 - y^2$ or $y^2 + y - 6 = 0$. Therefore $(y + 3)(y - 2) = 0$, so $y = 2$ or $y = -3$. But, as $y = \sqrt{x}$, and $\sqrt{x}$ is never negative, the only solution is $y = 2$, giving $x = 4$.

(b) Squaring both sides gives $x = (6 - x)^2 = 36 - 12x + x^2$ or $x^2 - 13x + 36 = 0$. Therefore $(x - 4)(x - 9) = 0$, so $x = 4$ or $x = 9$. Checking the answers shows that when $x = 4$, the equation $\sqrt{x} = 6 - x$ is satisfied, but when $x = 9$, $\sqrt{x} = 3$ and $6 - x = -3$, so $x = 9$ is not a root. Therefore $x = 4$ is the only root.

This is important. If you square you will find the root or roots of the equation $\sqrt{x} = -(6 - x)$ as well as the roots that you are actually looking for. Notice that $x = 9$ does satisfy this last equation, but $x = 4$ doesn't! The moral is that, when you square an equation in the process of solving it, it is essential to check your answers.

Exercise 4C

1 Solve the following pairs of simultaneous equations.

(a) $y = x + 1$, $x^2 + y^2 = 25$

(b) $x + y = 7$, $x^2 + y^2 = 25$

(c) $y = x - 3$, $y = x^2 - 3x - 8$

(d) $y = 2 - x$, $x^2 - y^2 = 8$

(e) $2x + y = 5$, $x^2 + y^2 = 25$

(f) $y = 1 - x$, $y^2 - xy = 0$

(g) $7y - x = 49$, $x^2 + y^2 - 2x - 49 = 0$

(h) $y = 3x - 11$, $x^2 + 2xy + 3 = 0$

2 Find the coordinates of the points of intersection of the given straight lines with the given curves.

(a) $y = 2x + 1$, $y = x^2 - x + 3$

(b) $y = 3x + 2$, $x^2 + y^2 = 26$

(c) $y = 2x - 2$, $y = x^2 - 5$

(d) $x + 2y = 3$, $x^2 + xy = 2$

(e) $3y + 4x = 25$, $x^2 + y^2 = 25$

(f) $y + 2x = 3$, $2x^2 - 3xy = 14$

(g) $y = 2x - 12$, $x^2 + 4xy - 3y^2 = -27$

(h) $2x - 5y = 6$, $2xy - 4x^2 - 3y = 1$

3 In each case find the number of points of intersection of the straight line with the curve.

(a) $y = 1 - 2x$, $x^2 + y^2 = 1$

(b) $y = \frac{1}{2}x - 1$, $y = 4x^2$

(c) $y = 3x - 1$, $xy = 12$

(d) $4y - x = 16$, $y^2 = 4x$

(e) $3y - x = 15$, $4x^2 + 9y^2 = 36$

(f) $4y = 12 - x$, $xy = 9$

4 Solve the following equations; give irrational answers in terms of surds.

(a) $x^4 - 5x^2 + 4 = 0$

(b) $x^4 - 10x^2 + 9 = 0$

(c) $x^4 - 3x^2 - 4 = 0$

(d) $x^4 - 5x^2 - 6 = 0$

(e) $x^6 - 7x^3 - 8 = 0$

(f) $x^6 + x^3 - 12 = 0$

5 Solve the following equations. (In most cases, multiplication by an appropriate expression will turn the equation into a form you should recognise.)

(a) $x = 3 + \dfrac{10}{x}$

(b) $x + 5 = \dfrac{6}{x}$

(c) $2t + 5 = \dfrac{3}{t}$

(d) $x = \dfrac{12}{x + 1}$

(e) $\sqrt{t} = 4 + \dfrac{12}{\sqrt{t}}$

(f) $\sqrt{t}\left(\sqrt{t} - 6\right) = -9$

(g) $x - \dfrac{2}{x + 2} = \frac{1}{3}$

(h) $\dfrac{20}{x + 2} - 1 = \dfrac{20}{x + 3}$

(i) $\dfrac{12}{x + 1} - \dfrac{10}{x - 3} = -3$

(j) $\dfrac{15}{2x + 1} + \dfrac{10}{x} = \frac{55}{2}$

(k) $y^4 - 3y^2 = 4$

(l) $\dfrac{1}{y^2} - \dfrac{1}{y^2 + 1} = \frac{1}{2}$

6 Solve the following equations.

  (a) $x - 8 = 2\sqrt{x}$ (b) $x + 15 = 8\sqrt{x}$ (c) $t - 5\sqrt{t} - 14 = 0$

  (d) $t = 3\sqrt{t} + 10$ (e) $\sqrt[3]{x^2} - \sqrt[3]{x} - 6 = 0$ (f) $\sqrt[3]{t^2} - 3\sqrt[3]{t} = 4$

Miscellaneous exercise 4

1 Solve the simultaneous equations $x + y = 2$ and $x^2 + 2y^2 = 11$.   (OCR)

2 The quadratic polynomial $x^2 - 10x + 17$ is denoted by $f(x)$. Express $f(x)$ in the form $(x - a)^2 + b$ stating the values of a and b.

Hence find the least possible value that $f(x)$ can take and the corresponding value of x.   (OCR)

3 Solve the simultaneous equations $2x + y = 3$ and $2x^2 - xy = 10$.   (OCR)

4 For what values of k does the equation $2x^2 - kx + 8 = 0$ have a repeated root?

5 By expressing the function $f(x) = (2x + 3)(x - 4)$ in completed square form, find the range of the function $f(x)$.

6 (a) Solve the equation $x^2 - (6\sqrt{3})x + 24 = 0$, giving your answer in terms of surds, simplified as far as possible.

  (b) Find all four solutions of the equation $x^4 - (6\sqrt{3})x^2 + 24 = 0$ giving your answers correct to 2 decimal places.   (OCR)

7 Show that the line $y = 3x - 3$ and the curve $y = (3x + 1)(x + 2)$ do not meet.

8 Express $9x^2 - 36x + 52$ in the form $(Ax - B)^2 + C$, where A, B and C are integers. Hence, or otherwise, find the set of values taken by $9x^2 - 36x + 52$ for real x.   (OCR)

9 Find the points of intersection of the curves $y = 6x^2 + 4x - 3$ and $y = x^2 - 3x - 1$, giving the coordinates correct to 2 decimal places.

10 (a) Express $9x^2 + 12x + 7$ in the form $(ax + b)^2 + c$ where a, b, c are constants whose values are to be found.

  (b) Find the set of values taken by $\dfrac{1}{9x^2 + 12x + 7}$ for real values of x.   (OCR)

11 Find, correct to 3 significant figures, all the roots of the equation $8x^4 - 8x^2 + 1 = \frac{1}{2}\sqrt{3}$.   (OCR)

12 Find constants a, b and c such that, for all values of x,
$$3x^2 - 5x + 1 = a(x + b)^2 + c.$$

Hence find the coordinates of the minimum point on the graph of $y = 3x^2 - 5x + 1$. (Note: the minimum point or maximum point is the vertex.)   (OCR, adapted)

13 Find the points of intersection of the curve $xy = 6$ and the line $y = 9 - 3x$.   (OCR)

14 The equation of a curve is $y = ax^2 - 2bx + c$, where a, b and c are constants with $a > 0$.

    (a) Find, in terms of a, b and c, the coordinates of the vertex of the curve.

    (b) Given that the vertex of the curve lies on the line $y = x$, find an expression for c in

        terms of a and b. Show that in this case, whatever the value of b, $c \geqslant -\dfrac{1}{4a}$.

                                                                             (OCR, adapted)

15 (a) The diagram shows the graphs of $y = x - 1$ and $y = kx^2$, where k is a positive constant. The graphs intersect at two distinct points A and B. Write down the quadratic equation satisfied by the x-coordinates of A and B, and hence show that $k < \frac{1}{4}$.

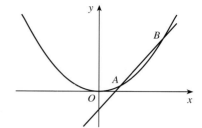

    (b) Describe briefly the relationship between the graphs of $y = x - 1$ and $y = kx^2$ in each of the cases   (i) $k = \frac{1}{4}$,   (ii) $k > \frac{1}{4}$.

    (c) Show, by using a graphical argument or otherwise, that when k is a negative constant, the equation $x - 1 = kx^2$ has two real roots, one of which lies between 0 and 1.

16 Use the following procedure to find the least (perpendicular) distance of the point $(1, 2)$ from the line $y = 3x + 5$, *without* having to find the equation of a line perpendicular to $y = 3x + 5$ (as you did in Chapter 1).

    (a) Let (x, y) be a general point on the line. Show that its distance, d, from $(1, 2)$ is given by $d^2 = (x - 1)^2 + (y - 2)^2$.

    (b) Use the equation of the line to show that $d^2 = (x - 1)^2 + (3x + 3)^2$.

    (c) Show that $d^2 = 10x^2 + 16x + 10$.

    (d) By completing the square, show that the minimum distance required is $\frac{3}{5}\sqrt{10}$.

17 Using the technique of Question 16,

    (a) find the perpendicular distance of $(2, 3)$ from $y = 2x + 1$,

    (b) find the perpendicular distance of $(-1, 3)$ from $y = -2x + 5$,

    (c) find the perpendicular distance of $(2, -1)$ from $3x + 4y - 7 = 0$.

18 Point O is the intersection of two roads which cross at right angles; one road runs from north to south, the other from east to west. Car A is 100 metres due west of O and travelling east at a speed of 20 m s^{-1}, and Car B is 80 metres due north of O and travelling south at 20 m s^{-1}.

    (a) Show that after t seconds their distance apart, d metres, is given by
$$d^2 = (100 - 20t)^2 + (80 - 20t)^2.$$

    (b) Show that this simplifies to $d^2 = 400\big((5 - t)^2 + (4 - t)^2\big)$.

    (c) Show that the minimum distance apart of the two cars is $10\sqrt{2}$ metres.

19 Point O is the intersection of two roads which cross at right angles; one road runs from north to south, the other from east to west. Find the least distance apart of two motorbikes A and B which are initially approaching O on different roads in the following cases.

(a) Both motorbikes are 10 metres from O. A is travelling at 20 m s^{-1}, B at 10 m s^{-1}.

(b) A is 120 metres from O travelling at 20 m s^{-1}, B is 80 metres from O travelling at 10 m s^{-1}.

(c) A is 120 metres from O travelling at 20 m s^{-1}, B is 60 metres from O travelling at 10 m s^{-1}.

20 (a) Express $2 - 4x - x^2$ and $24 + 8x + x^2$ in their completed square forms.

(b) Show that the graphs with equations $y = 2 - 4x - x^2$ and $y = 24 + 8x + x^2$ do not intersect.

(c) By giving an example, show that it is possible to find graphs with equations of the forms $y = A - (x - a)^2$ and $y = B + (x - b)^2$ with $A > B$ which do not intersect.

21 A recycling firm collects aluminium cans from a number of sites. It crushes them and then sells the aluminium back to a manufacturer.

The profit from processing t tonnes of cans each week is $\$p$, where

$$p = 100t - \tfrac{1}{2}t^2 - 200 \,.$$

By completing the square, find the greatest profit the firm can make each week, and how many tonnes of cans it has to collect and crush each week to achieve this profit.

5 Inequalities

This chapter is about inequality relationships, and how to solve inequalities. When you have completed it, you should

- know the rules for working with inequality symbols
- be able to solve linear inequalities
- be able to solve quadratic inequalities.

5.1 Notation for inequalities

You often want to compare one number with another and say which is the bigger. This comparison is expressed by using the inequality symbols $>$, $<$, $\leqslant$ and $\geqslant$. You have already met inequalities in Chapters 3 and 4.

The symbol $a > b$ means that a is greater than b. You can visualise this geometrically as in Fig. 5.1, which shows three number lines, with a to the right of b.

Notice that it does not matter whether a and b are positive or negative. The position of a and b in relation to zero on the number line is irrelevant. In all three lines, $a > b$. As an example, in the bottom line, $-4 > -7$.

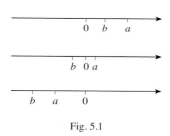

Fig. 5.1

Similarly, the symbol $a < b$ means that a is less than b. You can visualise this geometrically on a number line, with a to the left of b.

> These four expressions are equivalent.
>
> $a > b$ a is greater than b
> $b < a$ b is less than a

The symbol $a \geqslant b$ means 'either $a > b$ or $a = b$'; that is, a is greater than or equal to, but not less than, b. Similarly, the symbol $a \leqslant b$ means 'either $a < b$ or $a = b$'; that is, a is less than or equal to, but not greater than, b.

> These expressions are equivalent.
>
> $a \geqslant b$ a is greater than or equal to b
> $b \leqslant a$ b is not greater than a

The symbols $<$ and $>$ are called **strict** inequalities, and the symbols $\leqslant$ and $\geqslant$ are called **weak** inequalities.

5.2 Solving linear inequalities

When you solve an inequality such as $3x + 10 > 10x - 11$, you have to write a simpler statement with precisely the same meaning. In this case the simpler statement turns out to be $x < 3$. But how do you get from the complicated statement to the simple one?

Adding or subtracting the same number on both sides
You can add or subtract the same number on both sides of an inequality. For instance you can add the number 11 to both sides. In the example you would get

$$(3x + 10) + 11 > (10x - 11) + 11,$$
$$3x + 21 > 10x.$$

Justifying such a step involves showing that, for any number c, 'if $a > b$ then $a + c > b + c$'.

This is saying that if a is to the right of b on the number line, then $a + c$ is to the right of $b + c$. Fig. 5.2 shows that this is true whether c is positive or negative.

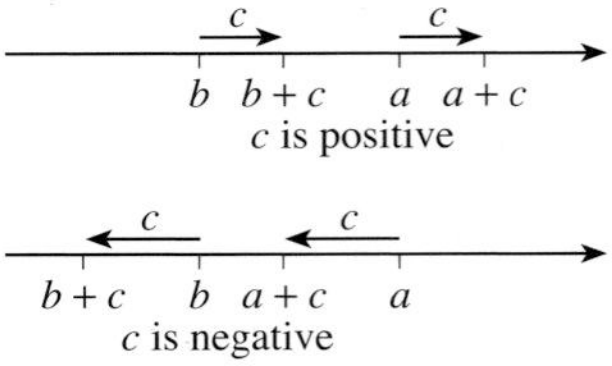

Since subtracting c is the same as adding $-c$, you can also subtract the same number from both sides.

Fig. 5.2

In the example, if you subtract $3x$ from both sides you get

$$(3x + 21) - 3x > 10x - 3x,$$
$$21 > 7x.$$

Multiplying both sides by a positive number
You can multiply (or divide) both sides of an inequality by a positive number. In the example above, you can divide both sides by the positive number 7 (or multiply both sides by $\frac{1}{7}$), and get:

$$21 \times \frac{1}{7} > 7x \times \frac{1}{7},$$
$$3 > x.$$

Here is a justification of the step, 'if $c > 0$ and $a > b$, then $ca > cb$'.

As $a > b$, a is to the right of b on the number line.

As $c > 0$, ca and cb are enlargements of the positions of a and b relative to the number 0.

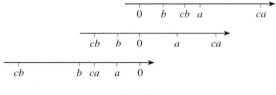

Fig. 5.3

Fig. 5.3 shows that, whether a and b are positive or negative, ca is to the right of cb, so $ca > cb$.

Multiplying both sides by a negative number

If $a > b$, and you subtract $a + b$ from both sides, then you get $-b > -a$, which is the same as $-a < -b$. This shows that if you multiply both sides of an inequality by -1, then you change the direction of the inequality. Suppose that you wish to multiply the inequality $a > b$ by -2. This is the same as multiplying $-a < -b$ by 2, so $-2a < -2b$.

You can also think of multiplying by -2 as reflecting the points corresponding to a and b in the origin, and then multiplying by 2 as an enlargement.

You can summarise this by saying that if you multiply (or divide) both sides of an inequality by a negative number, you must change the direction of the inequality. Thus if $c < 0$ and $a > b$, then $ca < cb$ (see Fig. 5.4).

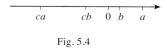

Fig. 5.4

Summary of operations on inequalities

> - You can add or subtract a number on both sides of an inequality.
> - You can multiply or divide an inequality by a positive number.
> - You can multiply or divide an inequality by a negative number, but you must change the direction of the inequality.

Solving inequalities is simply a matter of exploiting these three rules.

Example 5.2.1

Solve the inequality $-3x < 21$.

In this example you need to divide both sides by -3. Remembering to change the direction of the inequality, $-3x < 21$ becomes $x > -7$.

Example 5.2.2

Solve the inequality $\frac{1}{3}(4x + 3) - 3(2x - 4) \geqslant 20$.

Use the rule about multiplying by a positive number to multiply both sides by 3, in order to clear the fractions. In the solution, a reason is given only when an operation is carried out which affects the inequality.

$$\frac{1}{3}(4x + 3) - 3(2x - 4) \geqslant 20,$$
$$(4x + 3) - 9(2x - 4) \geqslant 60, \qquad \text{multiply both sides by 3}$$
$$4x + 3 - 18x + 36 \geqslant 60,$$
$$-14x + 39 \geqslant 60,$$
$$-14x \geqslant 21, \qquad \text{subtract 39 from both sides}$$
$$x \leqslant -\frac{3}{2}. \qquad \text{divide both sides by } -14, \text{ change } \geqslant \text{ to } \leqslant$$

Solving inequalities of this type is similar to solving equations. However, when you multiply or divide by a number, remember to reverse the inequality if that number is negative.

Exercise 5A

Solve the following inequalities.

1 (a) $x - 3 > 11$ (b) $x + 7 < 11$ (c) $2x + 3 \leqslant 8$ (d) $3x - 5 \geqslant 16$

    (e) $3x + 7 > -5$ (f) $5x + 6 \leqslant -10$ (g) $2x + 3 < -4$ (h) $3x - 1 \leqslant -13$

2 (a) $\dfrac{x + 3}{2} > 5$ (b) $\dfrac{x - 4}{6} \leqslant 3$ (c) $\dfrac{2x + 3}{4} < -5$ (d) $\dfrac{3x + 2}{5} \leqslant 4$

    (e) $\dfrac{4x - 3}{2} \geqslant -7$ (f) $\dfrac{5x + 1}{3} > -3$ (g) $\dfrac{3x - 2}{8} < 1$ (h) $\dfrac{4x - 2}{3} \geqslant -6$

3 (a) $-5x \leqslant 20$ (b) $-3x \geqslant -12$ (c) $5 - x < -4$ (d) $4 - 3x \leqslant 10$

    (e) $2 - 6x \leqslant 0$ (f) $6 - 5x > 1$ (g) $6 - 5x > -1$ (h) $3 - 7x < -11$

4 (a) $\dfrac{3 - x}{5} < 2$ (b) $\dfrac{5 - x}{3} \geqslant 1$ (c) $\dfrac{3 - 2x}{5} > 3$ (d) $\dfrac{7 - 3x}{2} < -1$

    (e) $\dfrac{5 - 4x}{2} \leqslant -3$ (f) $\dfrac{3 - 2x}{5} > -7$ (g) $\dfrac{3 + 2x}{4} < 5$ (h) $\dfrac{7 - 3x}{4} \leqslant -5$

5 (a) $x - 4 \leqslant 5 + 2x$ (b) $x - 3 \geqslant 5 - x$ (c) $2x + 5 < 4x - 7$

    (d) $3x - 4 > 5 - x$ (e) $4x \leqslant 3(2 - x)$ (f) $3x \geqslant 5 - 2(3 - x)$

    (g) $6x < 8 - 2(7 + x)$ (h) $5x - 3 > x - 3(2 - x)$ (i) $6 - 2(x + 1) \leqslant 3(1 - 2x)$

6 (a) $\frac{1}{3}(8x + 1) - 2(x - 3) > 10$ (b) $\frac{5}{2}(x + 1) - 2(x - 3) < 7$

    (c) $\dfrac{2x + 1}{3} - \dfrac{4x + 5}{2} \leqslant 0$ (d) $\dfrac{3x - 2}{2} - \dfrac{x - 4}{3} < x$

    (e) $\dfrac{x + 1}{4} + \dfrac{1}{6} \geqslant \dfrac{2x - 5}{3}$ (f) $\dfrac{x}{2} - \dfrac{3 - 2x}{5} \leqslant 1$

    (g) $\dfrac{x - 1}{3} - \dfrac{x + 1}{4} > \dfrac{x}{2}$ (h) $\dfrac{x}{3} \geqslant 5 - \dfrac{3x}{4}$

5.3 Quadratic inequalities

In Chapter 4, you saw that a quadratic function might take one of three forms:

$$f(x) = ax^2 + bx + c \qquad \text{the usual form}$$
$$f(x) = a(x - p)(x - q) \qquad \text{the factor form}$$
$$f(x) = a(x - r)^2 + s \qquad \text{the completed square form.}$$

If you need to solve a quadratic inequality of the form $f(x) < 0$, $f(x) > 0$, $f(x) \leqslant 0$ or $f(x) \geqslant 0$, by far the easiest form to use is the factor form.

Here are some examples which show ways of solving quadratic inequalities.

Example 5.3.1

Solve the inequality $(x-2)(x-4) < 0$.

Method 1 Sketch the graph of $y = (x-2)(x-4)$. The graph cuts the x-axis at $x = 2$ and $x = 4$. As the coefficient of x^2 is positive, the parabola bends upwards, as shown in Fig. 5.5.

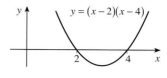

Fig. 5.5

You need to find the values of x such that $y < 0$.

From the graph you can see that this happens when x lies between 2 and 4, that is $x > 2$ and $x < 4$.

Remembering that $x > 2$ is the same as $2 < x$, you can write this as $2 < x < 4$, meaning that x is greater than 2 and less than 4.

When you write an inequality of the kind $r < x$ and $x < s$ in the form $r < x < s$, it is essential that $r < s$. It makes no sense to write $7 < x < 3$; how can x be both greater than 7 and less than 3?

An inequality of the type $r < x < s$ (or $r < x \leqslant s$ or $r \leqslant x < s$ or $r \leqslant x \leqslant s$) is called an **interval.**

Method 2 Find the values of x for which $(x-2)(x-4) = 0$. These values, $x = 2$ and $x = 4$, are called the **critical values** for the inequality.

Make a table showing the signs of the factors in the product $(x-2)(x-4)$.

	$x < 2$	$x = 2$	$2 < x < 4$	$x = 4$	$x > 4$
$x - 2$	$-$	0	$+$	$+$	$+$
$x - 4$	$-$	$-$	$-$	0	$+$
$(x-2)(x-4)$	$+$	0	$-$	0	$+$

Table 5.6

From Table 5.6 you can see that $(x-2)(x-4) < 0$ when $2 < x < 4$.

Example 5.3.2

Solve the inequality $(x+1)(5-x) \leqslant 0$.

Fig. 5.7 shows the graph of $y = (x+1)(5-x)$. As the coefficient of x^2 is negative, the parabola has its vertex at the top. So $y \leqslant 0$ when either $x \leqslant -1$ or $x \geqslant 5$.

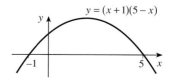

Fig. 5.7

Note that in this case the inequality is also satisfied by the critical values -1 and 5.

Example 5.3.3

Solve the inequality $x^2 \leqslant a^2$, where $a > 0$.

This is the same as $x^2 - a^2 \leqslant 0$ or $(x+a)(x-a) \leqslant 0$. The critical values are $x = -a$ and $x = a$.

	$x < -a$	$x = -a$	$-a < x < a$	$x = a$	$x > a$
$x + a$	−	0	+	+	+
$x - a$	−	−	−	0	+
$(x+a)(x-a)$	+	0	−	0	+

Table 5.8

Table 5.8 shows that, if $x^2 \leqslant a^2$, then $-a \leqslant x \leqslant a$. It also shows that, if $-a \leqslant x \leqslant a$, then $x^2 \leqslant a^2$.

The result of Example 5.3.3 is important. You can write it more shortly as:

> If $a > 0$, then these statements are equivalent.
>
> $$x^2 \leqslant a^2 \qquad -a \leqslant x \leqslant a$$

It is usually easiest to solve inequalities by using graphical or tabular methods. If you have access to a graphic calculator, you can use it to obtain the sketch, which makes the whole process even easier.

Example 5.3.4 shows how inequality arguments can be expressed in a more algebraic form.

Example 5.3.4

Solve the inequalities   (a) $(2x+1)(x-3) < 0$,   (b) $(2x+1)(x-3) > 0$.

(a) If the product of two factors is negative, one of them must be negative, and the other positive. So there are two possibilities to consider.

If $2x+1$ is negative and $x-3$ is positive, then $x < -\frac{1}{2}$ and $x > 3$. This is obviously impossible.

But if $2x+1$ is positive and $x-3$ is negative, then $x > -\frac{1}{2}$ and $x < 3$, which happens if $-\frac{1}{2} < x < 3$.

(b) If the product of two factors is positive, either both are positive or both are negative.

If both $2x+1$ and $x-3$ are positive, then $x > -\frac{1}{2}$ and $x > 3$, which happens if $x > 3$.

If both $2x+1$ and $x-3$ are negative, then $x < -\frac{1}{2}$ and $x < 3$, which happens if $x < -\frac{1}{2}$.

So $(2x+1)(x-3) > 0$ if $x > 3$ or $x < -\frac{1}{2}$.

You could solve both parts at once by constructing a table as in Example 5.3.3, and reading off the sign from the last line.

There may be times when you don't have access to a graphic calculator, or when factorising the given expression is difficult or impossible. In those cases, you should complete the square, as described in Section 4.3.

Example 5.3.5

Solve algebraically the inequalities   (a) $2x^2 - 8x + 11 \leqslant 0$,   (b) $2x^2 - 8x + 5 \leqslant 0$.

(a) By completing the square, $2x^2 - 8x + 11 = 2(x-2)^2 + 3$.
The smallest value of $2(x-2)^2 + 3$ is 3, and it occurs when $x = 2$. So there are no values of x for which $2x^2 - 8x + 11 \leqslant 0$.

(b) $2x^2 - 8x + 5 = 2(x-2)^2 - 3$,

so $2(x-2)^2 - 3 \leqslant 0$,

$\qquad (x-2)^2 - \frac{3}{2} \leqslant 0$,

$\qquad\quad (x-2)^2 \leqslant \frac{3}{2}$.

Using the result in the box on page 70,

$$-\sqrt{\tfrac{3}{2}} \leqslant x - 2 \leqslant \sqrt{\tfrac{3}{2}}, \quad \text{or} \quad 2 - \sqrt{\tfrac{3}{2}} \leqslant x \leqslant 2 + \sqrt{\tfrac{3}{2}}.$$

Exercise 5B

1 Use sketch graphs to solve the following inequalities.

(a) $(x-2)(x-3) < 0$ (b) $(x-4)(x-7) > 0$ (c) $(x-1)(x-3) < 0$

(d) $(x-4)(x+1) \geqslant 0$ (e) $(2x-1)(x+3) > 0$ (f) $(3x-2)(2x+5) \leqslant 0$

(g) $(x+2)(4x+5) \geqslant 0$ (h) $(1-x)(3+x) < 0$ (i) $(3-2x)(5-x) > 0$

(j) $(x-5)(x+5) < 0$ (k) $(3-4x)(3x+4) > 0$ (l) $(2+3x)(2-3x) \leqslant 0$

2 Use a table based on critical values to solve the following inequalities.

(a) $(x-3)(x-6) < 0$ (b) $(x-2)(x-8) > 0$ (c) $(x-2)(x+5) \leqslant 0$

(d) $(x-3)(x+1) \geqslant 0$ (e) $(2x+3)(x-2) > 0$ (f) $(3x-2)(x+5) \leqslant 0$

(g) $(x+3)(5x+4) \geqslant 0$ (h) $(2-x)(5+x) < 0$ (i) $(5-2x)(3-x) > 0$

(j) $(3x+1)(3x-1) \geqslant 0$ (k) $(2-7x)(3x+4) < 0$ (l) $(5+3x)(1-3x) \leqslant 0$

3 Use an algebraic method to solve the following inequalities. Leave irrational numbers in terms of surds. Some inequalities may be true for all values of x, others for no values of x.

(a) $x^2 + 3x - 5 > 0$ (b) $x^2 + 6x + 9 < 0$ (c) $x^2 - 5x + 2 < 0$

(d) $x^2 - x + 1 \geqslant 0$ (e) $x^2 - 9 < 0$ (f) $x^2 + 2x + 1 \leqslant 0$

(g) $2x^2 - 3x - 1 < 0$ (h) $8 - 3x - x^2 > 0$ (i) $2x^2 + 7x + 1 \geqslant 0$

4 Use any method you like to solve the following inequalities.

(a) $x^2 + 5x + 6 > 0$ (b) $x^2 - 7x + 12 < 0$ (c) $x^2 - 2x - 15 \leqslant 0$

(d) $2x^2 - 18 \geqslant 0$ (e) $2x^2 - 5x + 3 \geqslant 0$ (f) $6x^2 - 5x - 6 < 0$

(g) $x^2 + 5x + 2 > 0$ (h) $7 - 3x^2 < 0$ (i) $x^2 + x + 1 < 0$

(j) $2x^2 - 5x + 5 > 0$ (k) $12x^2 + 5x - 3 > 0$ (l) $3x^2 - 7x + 1 \leqslant 0$

Miscellaneous exercise 5

1 Solve the inequality $x^2 - x - 42 \leqslant 0$.

2 Solve the inequality $(x + 1)^2 < 9$.

3 Solve the inequality $x(x + 1) < 12$.   (OCR)

4 Solve the inequality $x - x^3 < 0$.

5 Solve the inequality $x^3 \geqslant 6x - x^2$.

Use the discriminant '$b^2 - 4ac$' in answering Questions 6 to 8. You may need to check the value $k = 0$ separately.

6 Find the values of k for which the following equations have two separate roots.

(a) $kx^2 + kx + 2 = 0$ (b) $kx^2 + 3x + k = 0$ (c) $x^2 - 2kx + 4 = 0$

7 Find the values of k for which the following equations have no roots.

(a) $kx^2 - 2kx + 5 = 0$ (b) $k^2x^2 + 2kx + 1 = 0$ (c) $x^2 - 5kx - 2k = 0$

8 Find the range of values of k for which the equation $x^2 + 3kx + k = 0$ has any roots.

9 Find the set of values of x for which $9x^2 + 12x + 7 > 19$.   (OCR)

10 Sketch, on the same diagram, the graphs of $y = \dfrac{1}{x}$ and $y = x - \dfrac{3}{2}$. Find the solution set of the inequality $x - \dfrac{3}{2} > \dfrac{1}{x}$.   (OCR)

11 Solve each of the following inequalities.

(a) $\dfrac{x}{x - 2} < 5$

(b) $x(x - 2) < 5$ (OCR, adapted)

Revision exercise 1

1 The line l_1 passes through the points $A(4,8)$ and $B(10,26)$. Show that an equation for l_1 is $y = 3x - 4$.

   The line l_1 intersects the line l_2, which has equation $y = 5x + 4$, at C. Find the coordinates of C.

2 Show that any root of the equation $5 + x - \sqrt{3 + 4x} = 0$ is also a root of the equation $x^2 + 6x + 22 = 0$. Hence show that the equation $5 + x - \sqrt{3 + 4x} = 0$ has no solutions.

3 Write $x^2 + 10x + 38$ in the form $(x + b)^2 + c$ where the values of b and c are to be found.
   (a) State the minimum value of $x^2 + 10x + 38$ and the value of x for which this occurs.
   (b) Determine the values of x for which $x^2 + 10x + 38 \geqslant 22$.

4 Simplify $\left(4x^{\frac{1}{2}}y\right)^2 \div \left(2x^{-1}y^2\right)$.

5 Solve the inequalities   (a) $2x^2 - 5x + 2 \leqslant 0$,   (b) $(2x - 3)^2 < 16$,   (c) $\frac{1}{3}x - \frac{1}{4}(2x - 5) < \frac{1}{5}$.

6 Show that the equation $2^{x+1} + 2^{x-1} = 160$ can be written in the form $2.5 \times 2^x = 160$. Hence find the value of x which satisfies the equation.

7 Find the values of k such that the straight line $y = 2x + k$ meets the curve with equation $x^2 + 2xy + 2y^2 = 5$ exactly once.

8 Display on the same axes the curves with equations $y = x^3$ and $y = \sqrt[3]{x}$, and give the coordinates of their points of intersection.

9 A mail-order photographic developing company offers a picture-framing service to its customers. It will enlarge and mount any photograph, under glass and in a rectangular frame. Its charge is based on the size of the enlargement. It charges $6 per metre of perimeter for the frame and $15 per square metre for the glass. Write down an expression for the cost of enlarging and mounting a photograph in a frame which is x metres wide and y metres high.

   A photograph was enlarged and mounted in a square frame of side z metres at a cost of $12. Formulate and solve a quadratic equation for z.

10 Find the equation of the straight line through $A(1,4)$ which is perpendicular to the line passing through the points $B(2,-2)$ and $C(4,0)$. Hence find the area of the triangle ABC, giving your answer in the simplest possible form.

11 Solve the inequalities
   (a) $2(3 - x) < 4 - (2 - x)$,   (b) $(x - 3)^2 < x^2$,   (c) $(x - 2)(x - 3) \geqslant 6$.

12 The quadratic equation $(p - 1)x^2 + 4x + (p - 4) = 0$ has a repeated root. Find the possible values of p.

13 Solve the simultaneous equations
$$2x + 3y = 5,$$
$$x^2 + 3xy = 4.$$

14 Prove that the triangle with vertices at the points $(1,2)$, $(9,8)$ and $(12,4)$ is right-angled, and calculate its area.

15 Find where the line $y = 5 - 2x$ meets the curve $y = (3 - x)^2$. What can you deduce from your answer?

16 A rhombus has opposite vertices at $(-1,3)$ and $(5,-1)$. Find the equations of its diagonals. One of the other vertices is $(0,-2)$. Find the fourth vertex.

17 Points A and B have coordinates $(-1,2)$ and $(7,-4)$ respectively.
   (a) Write down the coordinates of M, the mid-point of AB.
   (b) Calculate the distance MB.
   (c) The point P lies on the circle with AB as diameter and has coordinates $(2,y)$ where y is positive. Calculate the value of y, giving your answer in surd form.

18 Solve the inequalities (a) $x^2 - x - 2 > 0$,   (b) $(x+1)(x-2)(x-3) > 0$.

19 Two of the sides of a triangle have lengths 4 cm and 6 cm, and the angle between them is $120°$. Calculate the length of the third side, giving your answer in the form $m\sqrt{p}$, where m and p are integers, and p is prime.

20 A triangle has vertices $O(0,0)$, $A(2,6)$ and $B(12,6)$. Write down the equation of the perpendicular bisector of AB, and find the perpendicular bisector of OA. Find the coordinates of the point C where these lines meet, and calculate the distances of C from O, A and B.

   Write down the area of triangle OAB. Hence find the length of the perpendicular from A to OB, and deduce that angle AOB is $45°$.   (MEI, adapted)

21 A quadrilateral has vertices $A(-1,1)$, $B(1,2)$, $C(4,1)$ and $D(3,4)$. Find the lengths and the equations of the two diagonals AC and BD.   (OCR)

22 The quadratic function $f(x) = px^2 + qx + r$ has $f(0) = 35$, $f(1) = 20$ and $f(2) = 11$. Find the values of the constants p, q and r.

   Express $f(x)$ in the form $a(x+b)^2 + c$. Use your answer to find the smallest value of $f(x)$.   (OCR, adapted)

23 Use the substitution $y = 3^x$ to find the values of x which satisfy the equation $3^{2x+2} - 10 \times 3^x + 1 = 0$.

24 Show that $\sqrt{N+1} - \sqrt{N} = \dfrac{1}{\sqrt{N+1} + \sqrt{N}}$. Use this to explain why $\sqrt{101}$ is close to, but slightly less than, 10.05.

   Without using a calculator, find the roots of $x^2 + 7x - 13 = 0$, giving your answers correct to 2 decimal places.

25 If $ab^{0.4} = c$, express b in terms of a and c
   (a) in index notation,   (b) in surd notation.

6 Differentiation

This chapter is about finding the gradient of the tangent at a point on a graph. When you have completed it, you should be able to

- calculate an approximation to the gradient at a point on a curve, given its equation
- calculate the exact gradient at a point on a quadratic curve and certain other curves
- find the equations of the tangent and normal to a curve at a point.

This chapter is divided into two parts. In the first part, Sections 6.1 to 6.5, you will develop results experimentally and use them to solve problems about tangents to graphs. In the second part, Sections 6.6 and 6.7, the experimental results are proved. You may, if you wish, omit the second part of the chapter on a first reading, but you should still tackle Miscellaneous exercise 6 at the end of the chapter.

6.1 Calculating gradients of chords

Think of a simple curve such as the graph of $y = x^2$. As your eye moves along the x-axis, can you describe, in mathematical terms, how the direction of the curve changes?

Just as a straight line has a numerical gradient, so any curve, provided it is reasonably smooth, has a steepness or **gradient** which can be measured at any given point. The difference is that for the curve the gradient will change as you move along it; mathematicians use this gradient to describe the curve's direction.

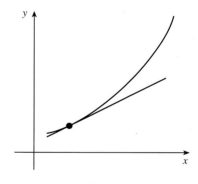

Fig. 6.1

In Chapter 1 you saw how to find the gradient of a straight line through two points when you know their coordinates. You cannot use this method directly on a curve because it is not a straight line. Instead you find the gradient of the **tangent** to the curve at the point you have chosen, since (as you can see from Fig. 6.1) the tangent has the same steepness as the curve at that point. However, this creates another difficulty; you can only find the gradient of a line if you know the coordinates of two points on it.

Fig. 6.2 shows three chords (straight lines through two points of the curve) which get closer and closer to the tangent line; it turns out that a good way to begin is by finding the gradient of these chords, because for these you *can* use the techniques of Chapter 1.

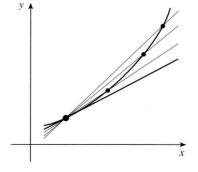

Fig. 6.2

Example 6.1.1
Find the gradient and the equation of the chord joining
the points on the curve $y = x^2$ with coordinates
$(0.4, 0.16)$ and $(0.7, 0.49)$.

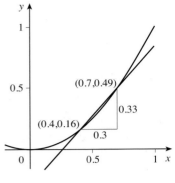

Fig. 6.3

From the formula in Section 1.3, the gradient of
the chord is

$$\frac{0.49 - 0.16}{0.7 - 0.4} = \frac{0.33}{0.3} = 1.1.$$

The formula in Section 1.5 then gives the
equation of the chord as

$$y - 0.16 = 1.1(x - 0.4), \quad \text{which is}$$
$$y = 1.1x - 0.28.$$

*Fig. 6.3 shows that this is the equation of the whole line through the two points, not just
the line segment between the two points which people often think of as the 'chord'.*

At this point it is useful to introduce some new notation. The Greek letter δ (delta) is
used as an abbreviation for 'the increase in'. Thus 'the increase in x' is written as δx,
and 'the increase in y' as δy. These are the quantities called the 'x-step' and 'y-step'
in Section 1.3. Thus in Example 6.1.1 from one end of the chord to the other the x-step
is $0.7 - 0.4 = 0.3$ and the y-step is $0.49 - 0.16 = 0.33$, so you can write

$$\delta x = 0.3, \quad \delta y = 0.33.$$

With this notation, you can write the gradient of the chord as $\dfrac{\delta y}{\delta x}$.

Some people use the capital letter Δ rather than δ. Either is acceptable.

Notice that, in the fraction $\dfrac{\delta y}{\delta x}$, you cannot 'cancel out' the deltas; they do not stand for a
number. While you are getting used to the notation it is a good idea to read δ as 'the
increase in', so that you are not tempted to treat it as an ordinary algebraic symbol.
Remember also that δx or δy could be negative, making the x-step or y-step a decrease.

Using this notation for the gradient of the chord, the first line of Example 6.1.1 would read

$$\frac{\delta y}{\delta x} = \frac{0.49 - 0.16}{0.7 - 0.4} = \frac{0.33}{0.3} = 1.1.$$

Example 6.1.2
Find the gradient of the chord joining the points on the curve $y = x^2$ with x-coordinates
0.4 and 0.41.

First you need to calculate the y-coordinates of the two points. They are
$0.4^2 = 0.16$ and $0.41^2 = 0.1681$.

Working in a similar way to Example 6.1.1,

$$\delta x = 0.41 - 0.4 = 0.01 \quad \text{and} \quad \delta y = 0.1681 - 0.16 = 0.0081,$$

so that the gradient of the chord is

$$\frac{\delta y}{\delta x} = \frac{0.0081}{0.01} = 0.81.$$

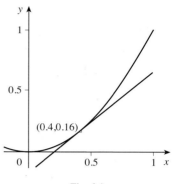

Fig. 6.4

Fig. 6.4 is not very useful as an illustration, because the two points are so close together. There is a small triangle there, like the triangle in Fig. 6.3, but you could be excused for missing it.

In Fig. 6.4 it has become difficult to distinguish between the chord joining two points close together and the tangent at the point with x-coordinate 0.4. This shows the way to find the gradient of the tangent at the point on the curve with $x = 0.4$.

In Example 6.1.3, the two points have become even closer together.

Example 6.1.3
Find the gradient of the chord joining the points on the curve $y = x^2$ with x-coordinates 0.4 and 0.400 01.

The coordinates of the two points are $\left(0.4, 0.4^2\right)$ and $\left(0.400\ 01, 0.400\ 01^2\right)$;

$$\delta x = 0.400\ 01 - 0.4 = 0.000\ 01 \quad \text{and} \quad \delta y = 0.400\ 01^2 - 0.4^2 = 0.000\ 008\ 000\ 1,$$

so that the gradient of the chord is

$$\frac{\delta y}{\delta x} = \frac{0.000\ 008\ 000\ 1}{0.000\ 01} = 0.800\ 01.$$

This result, being so close to 0.8, seems to indicate that the gradient of the tangent to the curve $y = x^2$ at $x = 0.4$ is 0.8. But it does not prove it, because you are still finding the equation of the chord joining two points, no matter how close those points are.

Exercise 6A

In Questions 2 and 3 the parts of questions could be divided, so that groups of students working together have answers to all the parts of each question, and can pool their results.

1 Find the equation of the line joining the points with x-values 1 and 2 on the graph $y = x^2$.

2 In each part of this question, find the gradient of the chord joining the two points with the given x-coordinates on the graph of $y = x^2$.

(a) 1 and 1.001   (b) 1 and 0.9999   (c) 2 and 2.002

(d) 2 and 1.999   (e) 3 and 3.000 001   (f) 3 and 2.999 99

3 In each part of this question find the gradient of the chord from the given point on the graph $y = x^2$ to a nearby point. Vary the distance between the point given and the nearby point; make sure that some of the points that you choose are to the left of the given point.

(a) $(-1,1)$ (b) $(-2,4)$ (c) $(10,100)$

4 Use the results of Questions 2 and 3 to make a guess about the gradient of the tangent at any point on the graph of $y = x^2$.

5 (a) Use a similar method to that of Questions 2 to 4 to make a guess about the gradients of the tangents at points on the graphs of $y = x^2 + 1$ and $y = x^2 - 2$.

(b) Use the results from part (a) to make a generalisation about the gradient at any point on the graph of $y = x^2 + c$, where c is any real number.

6.2 The gradient of a tangent to the curve $y = x^2 + c$

If you collect the results from Exercise 6A, you should suspect that the gradient of the tangent to the curve $y = x^2$ at any point is twice the value of the x-coordinate of the point. Another way of saying this is that the gradient formula for the curve $y = x^2$ is $2x$.

For example, at the point $(-3,9)$ on the curve $y = x^2$, the gradient is $2 \times (-3) = -6$. This means that the tangent to the curve at this point is the straight line which has gradient -6 and passes through the point $(-3,9)$.

To find the equation of this tangent, you can use the method in Section 1.5. The equation of the line is

$$y - 9 = -6(x - (-3)), \quad \text{which is}$$
$$y - 9 = -6x - 18, \text{ or } y = -6x - 9.$$

You should also see that the gradient formula holds for the curve $y = x^2 + c$ where c is any constant: the gradient at x is also $2x$. After all, the curve $y = x^2 + c$ has the same shape as the curve $y = x^2$, but it is shifted in the y-direction.

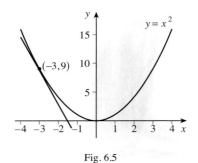

Fig. 6.5

Assume for the moment that these results can be proved. You will find proofs, when you need them, in Section 6.6.

6.3 The normal to a curve at a point

The line passing through the point of contact of the tangent with the curve which is perpendicular to the tangent is called the **normal** to the curve at that point.

Fig. 6.6 shows a curve with equation $y = f(x)$. The tangent and the normal at the point A have been drawn.

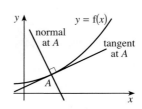

Fig. 6.6

If you know the gradient of the tangent at A, you can calculate the gradient of the normal by using the result of Section 1.9. If the gradient of the tangent is m, then the gradient of the normal is $-\dfrac{1}{m}$, provided that $m \neq 0$.

Example 6.3.1
Find the equation of the normal to the curve $y = x^2$ at the point for which
(a) $x = -3$,   (b) $x = 0$.

(a) You found in Section 6.2 that the gradient of the tangent at $(-3,9)$ is -6.

The normal has a gradient of $-\dfrac{1}{-6} = \tfrac{1}{6}$ and also passes through $(-3,9)$.

Therefore the equation of the normal is $y - 9 = \tfrac{1}{6}\big(x - (-3)\big)$, which simplifies to $6y = x + 57$.

(b) At $(0,0)$, the gradient of the tangent is 0, so the tangent is parallel to the x-axis. The normal is therefore parallel to the y-axis, so its equation is of the form $x = \text{something}$. As the normal passes through $(0,0)$, its equation is $x = 0$.

If you have access to a graphic calculator, try displaying the curve $y = x^2$, the tangent $y = -6x - 9$ and the normal $6y = x + 57$ on it. You may be surprised by the results.

You should realise that if you draw a curve together with its tangent and normal at a point, the normal will only appear perpendicular in your diagram if the scales are the same on both the x- and y-axes. However, no matter what the scales are, the tangent will always appear as a tangent.

At this stage you should recognise that you need to generalise this result to curves with other equations. In Section 6.2 you saw that the gradient of the tangent at x to the curve $y = x^2 + c$ is $2x$.

Exercise 6B

For Questions 9 to 12 the parts of questions could be divided, so that groups of students working together have answers to all the parts of each question, and can pool their results.

1 Find the gradient of the tangent to the graph of $y = x^2$, at each of the points with the given x-coordinate.

(a) 1	(b) 4	(c) 0	(d) −2
(e) −0.2	(f) −3.5	(g) p	(h) $2p$

2 Find the gradient of the tangent to the graph of $y = x^2 - 2$, at each of the points with the given x-coordinate.

(a) 1	(b) 4	(c) 0	(d) −2
(e) −0.2	(f) −3.5	(g) p	(h) $2p$

3 The y-coordinate of a point P on the graph of $y = x^2 + 5$ is 9. Find the two possible values of the gradient of the tangent to $y = x^2 + 5$ at P.

4 Find the equation of the tangent(s) to each of the following graphs at the point(s) whose
 x- or y-coordinate is given.

 (a) $y = x^2$ where $x = 2$ (b) $y = x^2 + 2$ where $x = -1$

 (c) $y = x^2 - 2$ where $y = -1$ (d) $y = x^2 - 2$ where $y = -2$

5 Find the equation of the normal to each of the following graphs at the point whose
 x-coordinate is given.

 (a) $y = x^2$ where $x = 1$ (b) $y = x^2 + 1$ where $x = -2$

 (c) $y = x^2 + 1$ where $x = 0$ (d) $y = x^2 + c$ where $x = \sqrt{c}$

6 The tangent at P to the curve $y = x^2$ has gradient 3. Find the equation of the normal at P.

7 A normal to the curve $y = x^2 + 1$ has gradient -1. Find the equation of the tangent there.

8 Find the point where the normal at $(2,4)$ to $y = x^2$ cuts the curve again.

9 In each part of this question, find the gradient of the chord joining the two points with the
 given x-coordinates on the graphs of $y = 2x^2$, $y = 3x^2$ and $y = -x^2$.

 (a) 1 and 1.001   (b) 1 and 0.9999   (c) 2 and 2.002

 (d) 2 and 1.999   (e) 3 and 3.000 001   (f) 3 and 2.999 99

10 In each part of this question find the gradient of the chord from the point with the given
 x-coordinate to a nearby point for each of the curves $y = \frac{1}{2}x^2$ and $y = \frac{1}{2}x^2 + 2$. Vary the
 distance between the point given and the nearby point which you choose; make sure that
 some of the points that you choose are to the left of the given point.

 (a) -1 (b) -2 (c) 10

11 Use the results of Questions 9 and 10 to make a guess about the gradient of the tangent at
 any point on the graphs of $y = ax^2$ and $y = ax^2 + c$, where a is any real number.

12 (a) Use a similar method to that of Questions 9 to 11 to make a guess about the gradients
   of the tangents at points on the graphs of $y = x^2 + 3x$ and $y = x^2 - 2x$.

 (b) Use the results from part (a) to make a generalisation about the gradient at any point on
   the graph of $y = x^2 + bx$, where b is any real number.

6.4 The gradient formula for quadratic graphs

Chapter 3 introduced the idea of the general quadratic graph, whose equation can be
written $y = ax^2 + bx + c$, where a, b and c are constants. What can you say about the
gradient of the tangent to this curve?

From the results of the questions in Exercise 6B you should have found that the gradient
formula for $y = ax^2$ is $2ax$. This means, for example, that the graph of $y = 3x^2$ is three
times as steep at any given value of x as the graph of $y = x^2$. You should also have found
that the gradient formula for $y = x^2 + bx$ is $2x + b$. This means that the gradient formula
for $y = x^2 + 4x$ is $2x + 4$, which is the sum of the gradient formulae for x^2 and $4x$.

You already know that $y = x^2$ and $y = x^2 + c$ have the same gradient formula whatever the value of c.

So it seems reasonable to expect that:

> The gradient formula for the curve with equation
> $y = ax^2 + bx + c$ is $2ax + b$.

The importance of this result is that you can find the gradient of a function which is the sum of several parts by finding the gradient of each part in turn, and adding the results. You can also find the gradient of a constant multiple of a function by taking the same multiple of the gradient.

Section 6.6 will show how these results can be proved. Meanwhile here are some examples of their use. But first it will help to have some new notation.

Let the equation of a curve be $y = f(x)$. Then the gradient formula is denoted by $f'(x)$. This is pronounced 'f dashed x'.

The process of finding the gradient of the tangent to a curve is called **differentiation**. When you find the gradient formula, you are **differentiating**.

Just as $f(2)$ stands for the value of the function where $x = 2$, so $f'(2)$ stands for the gradient of $y = f(x)$ at $x = 2$. Thus the dash in $f'(x)$ tells you to differentiate: you then substitute the value of x at which you wish to find the gradient.

The quantity $f'(2)$ is called the **derivative** of $f(x)$ at $x = 2$.

Thus to find the gradient at $x = 2$ on the curve with equation $y = f(x)$, find $f'(x)$, and then substitute $x = 2$ to get $f'(2)$.

Example 6.4.1
(a) Differentiate $y = 3x^2 - 2x + 5$.
(b) Find the equations of the tangent and the normal to the graph of $y = 3x^2 - 2x + 5$ at the point for which $x = 1$.

(a) Let $f(x) = 3x^2 - 2x + 5$. For this function $a = 3$, $b = -2$ and $c = 5$. So, differentiating, $f'(x) = 2 \times 3 \times x - 2 = 6x - 2$.

(b) The y-coordinate of the point on the curve for which $x = 1$ is $3 - 2 + 5 = 6$.

When $x = 1$ the gradient of the tangent is $f'(1) = 6 \times 1 - 2 = 4$.

The equation of the tangent is therefore $y - 6 = 4(x - 1)$, or $y = 4x + 2$.

The normal is perpendicular to the tangent, so its gradient is $-\frac{1}{4}$. The equation of the normal is therefore $y - 6 = -\frac{1}{4}(x - 1)$, which simplifies to $x + 4y = 25$.

Example 6.4.2

Differentiate   (a) $f(x) = 2(x^2 - 3x - 2)$,   (b) $g(x) = (x+2)(2x-3)$.

(a) **Method 1**   Multiplying out the bracket,

$$f(x) = 2(x^2 - 3x - 2) = 2x^2 - 6x - 4, \quad \text{so} \quad f'(x) = 4x - 6.$$

Method 2   If a given function is multiplied by a constant, the gradient of that function is multiplied by the same constant. In this case, the multiple is 2, so $f'(x) = 2(2x-3)$.

(b) For $g(x) = (x+2)(2x-3)$, you cannot use method 2 of part (a) because the multiple is not constant. But you can multiply out the brackets to get a quadratic which you can then differentiate.

$$g(x) = (x+2)(2x-3) = 2x^2 + x - 6, \quad \text{so} \quad g'(x) = 4x + 1.$$

If you cannot immediately differentiate a given function using the rules you know, see if you can write the function in a different form which enables you to apply one of the rules.

Example 6.4.3

Find the equation of the tangent to the graph of $y = x^2 - 4x + 2$ which is parallel to the x-axis.

From Section 1.6, a line parallel to the x-axis has gradient 0.

Let $f(x) = x^2 - 4x + 2$. Then $f'(x) = 2x - 4$.

To find when the gradient is 0 you need to solve $2x - 4 = 0$, giving $x = 2$.

When $x = 2$, $y = 2^2 - 4 \times 2 + 2 = -2$.

From Section 1.6, the equation of a line parallel to the x-axis has the form $y = c$. So the equation of the tangent is $y = -2$.

Exercise 6C

For Questions 13 to 16 the parts of questions could be divided, so that groups of students working together have answers to all the parts of each question, and can pool their results.

1 Find the gradient formula for each of the following functions.

(a) x^2　　　　(b) $x^2 - x$　　　　(c) $4x^2$　　　　(d) $3x^2 - 2x$

(e) $2 - 3x$　　　　(f) $x - 2 - 2x^2$　　　　(g) $2 + 4x - 3x^2$　　　　(h) $\sqrt{2}x - \sqrt{3}x^2$

2 For each of the following functions $f(x)$, find $f'(x)$. You may need to rearrange some of the functions before differentiating them.

(a) $3x - 1$　　　　(b) $2 - 3x^2$　　　　(c) 4　　　　(d) $1 + 2x + 3x^2$

(e) $x^2 - 2x^2$　　　　(f) $3(1 + 2x - x^2)$　　　　(g) $2x(1 - x)$　　　　(h) $x(2x+1) - 1$

3 Find the derivative of each of the following functions $f(x)$ at $x = -3$.

(a) $-x^2$ (b) $3x$ (c) $x^2 + 3x$ (d) $2x - x^2$

(e) $2x^2 + 4x - 1$ (f) $-\left(3 - x^2\right)$ (g) $-x(2 + x)$ (h) $(x - 2)(2x - 1)$

4 For each of the following functions $f(x)$, find x such that $f'(x)$ has the given value.

(a) $2x^2$ 3   (b) $x - 2x^2$ -1 (c) $2 + 3x + x^2$ 0

(d) $x^2 + 4x - 1$ 2   (e) $(x - 2)(x - 1)$ 0   (f) $2x(3x + 2)$ 10

5 Find the equation of the tangent to the curve at the point with the given x-coordinate.

(a) $y = x^2$ where $x = -1$ (b) $y = 2x^2 - x$ where $x = 0$

(c) $y = x^2 - 2x + 3$ where $x = 2$ (d) $y = 1 - x^2$ where $x = -3$

(e) $y = x(2 - x)$ where $x = 1$ (f) $y = (x - 1)^2$ where $x = 1$

6 Find the equation of the normal to the curve at the point with the given x-coordinate.

(a) $y = -x^2$ where $x = 1$ (b) $y = 3x^2 - 2x - 1$ where $x = 1$

(c) $y = 1 - 2x^2$ where $x = -2$ (d) $y = 1 - x^2$ where $x = 0$

(e) $y = 2\left(2 + x + x^2\right)$ where $x = -1$ (f) $y = (2x - 1)^2$ where $x = \frac{1}{2}$

7 Find the equation of the tangent to the curve $y = x^2$ which is parallel to the line $y = x$.

8 Find the equation of the tangent to the curve $y = x^2$ which is parallel to the x-axis.

9 Find the equation of the tangent to the curve $y = x^2 - 2x$ which is perpendicular to the line $2y = x - 1$.

10 Find the equation of the normal to the curve $y = 3x^2 - 2x - 1$ which is parallel to the line $y = x - 3$.

11 Find the equation of the normal to the curve $y = (x - 1)^2$ which is parallel to the y-axis.

12 Find the equation of the normal to the curve $y = 2x^2 + 3x + 4$ which is perpendicular to the line $y = 7x - 5$.

13 Use an exploration method similar to that of Exercise 6B Questions 9 and 10 to make a guess about the gradient formulae for the graphs of $y = x^3$ and $y = x^4$.

14 In each part of this question, find the gradient of the chord joining the two points with the given x-coordinates on the graph of $y = \sqrt{x}$.

(a)   1 and 1.001   (b)   1 and 0.9999   (c)   4 and 4.002

(d)   4 and 3.999   (e)   0.25 and 0.250 001   (f)   0.25 and 0.249 999

15 In each part of this question find the gradient of the chord from the given point to a nearby point for the curve $y = \dfrac{1}{x}$. Vary the distance between the given point and the nearby point which you choose; make sure that some of the points that you choose are to the left of the given point.

(a) $(-1, -1)$ (b) $(-2, -0.5)$ (c) $(10, 0.1)$

16   Use the results of Questions 14 and 15 to make a guess about the gradient of the tangent at any point on the graphs of $y = \sqrt{x}$ and $y = \dfrac{1}{x}$.

6.5   Some rules for differentiation

You already know the following rules:

> If $f(x) = ax^2 + bx + c$, then $f'(x) = 2ax + b$.
>
> If you add two functions, then the derivative of the sum is the sum of the derivatives: if $f(x) = g(x) + h(x)$, then $f'(x) = g'(x) + h'(x)$.
>
> If you multiply a function by a constant, you multiply its derivative by the same constant: if $f(x) = ag(x)$, then $f'(x) = ag'(x)$.

You will have found from Exercise 6C Question 13 that the derivative of $f(x) = x^3$ is $f'(x) = 3x^2$, and the derivative of $f(x) = x^4$ is $f'(x) = 4x^3$. You already know that if $f(x) = x^2$, then $f'(x) = 2x$, or $2x^1$. This suggests the rule:

> If $f(x) = x^n$, where n is a positive integer, then $f'(x) = nx^{n-1}$.

Example 6.5.1
Find the coordinates of the points on the graph of $y = x^3 - 3x^2 - 4x + 2$ at which the gradient is 5.

Let $f(x) = x^3 - 3x^2 - 4x + 2$. Then $f'(x) = 3x^2 - 6x - 4$. The gradient is 5 when $f'(x) = 5$, that is when $3x^2 - 6x - 4 = 5$. This gives the quadratic equation $3x^2 - 6x - 9 = 0$, which simplifies to $x^2 - 2x - 3 = 0$.

In factor form this is $(x + 1)(x - 3) = 0$, so $x = -1$ or $x = 3$.

Substituting these values into $y = x^3 - 3x^2 - 4x + 2$ to find the y-coordinates of the points, you find $y = (-1)^3 - 3 \times (-1)^2 - 4 \times (-1) + 2 = -1 - 3 + 4 + 2 = 2$ and $y = 3^3 - 3 \times 3^2 - 4 \times 3 + 2 = 27 - 27 - 12 + 2 = -10$. The coordinates of the required points are therefore $(-1, 2)$ and $(3, -10)$.

The results of Exercise 6C Questions 14 to 16 suggest two more rules:

> If $f(x) = \sqrt{x}$, then $f'(x) = \dfrac{1}{2\sqrt{x}}$.
>
> If $f(x) = \dfrac{1}{x}$, then $f'(x) = -\dfrac{1}{x^2}$.

In index notation, these results take the forms:

> If $f(x) = x^{\frac{1}{2}}$, then $f'(x) = \frac{1}{2}x^{-\frac{1}{2}}$.
>
> If $f(x) = x^{-1}$, then $f'(x) = -x^{-2} = (-1)x^{-2}$.

This suggests the following rule:

> If $f(x) = x^n$, where n is a rational number, then $f'(x) = nx^{n-1}$.

Example 6.5.2

Find the equation of the tangent to the graph of $y = 2\sqrt{x}$ at the point where $x = 9$.

Let $f(x) = 2\sqrt{x} = 2x^{\frac{1}{2}}$.

Then, using results in the boxes,

$$f'(x) = 2 \times \frac{1}{2}x^{-\frac{1}{2}} = x^{-\frac{1}{2}}.$$

When $x = 9$, $f'(9) = 9^{-\frac{1}{2}} = \frac{1}{\sqrt{9}} = \frac{1}{3}$.

The tangent passes through the point $(9, 2\sqrt{9}) = (9, 6)$, so its equation is

$$y - 6 = \tfrac{1}{3}(x - 9), \quad \text{or} \quad 3y - x = 9.$$

Example 6.5.3

Differentiate each of the functions (a) $x(1 + x^2)$, (b) $(1 + \sqrt{x})^2$, (c) $\dfrac{x^2 + x + 1}{x}$.

(a) Let $f(x) = x(1 + x^2)$.

Then $f(x) = x + x^3$, so $f'(x) = 1 + 3x^2$.

(b) Let $f(x) = (1 + \sqrt{x})^2$.

Then $f(x) = 1 + 2\sqrt{x} + x = 1 + 2x^{\frac{1}{2}} + x$, so $f'(x) = 2 \times \frac{1}{2}x^{-\frac{1}{2}} + 1 = x^{-\frac{1}{2}} + 1 = \frac{1}{\sqrt{x}} + 1$.

(c) Let $f(x) = \dfrac{x^2 + x + 1}{x}$.

Then, by division, $f(x) = x + 1 + \dfrac{1}{x} = x + 1 + x^{-1}$, so $f'(x) = 1 + (-1)x^{-2} = 1 - \dfrac{1}{x^2}$.

Example 6.5.4
Find the equation of the tangent to $y = \sqrt[3]{x}$ at the point $(8,2)$.

In index notation $\sqrt[3]{x} = x^{\frac{1}{3}}$. So the rule gives the derivative as $\frac{1}{3} x^{\left(\frac{1}{3}-1\right)}$ or $\frac{1}{3} x^{-\frac{2}{3}}$,

which in surd notation is $\dfrac{1}{3\left(\sqrt[3]{x}\right)^2}$. At $(8,2)$, this is $\dfrac{1}{3\left(\sqrt[3]{8}\right)^2} = \dfrac{1}{12}$.

Thus the equation of the tangent is $y - 2 = \frac{1}{12}(x - 8)$, or $x - 12y + 16 = 0$.

The results stated in this section can be assumed for the remainder of this book. Some of them are proved in Sections 6.6 and 6.7, but if you wish you may omit these final sections and, after working through Exercise 6D, go straight to Miscellaneous exercise 6.

Exercise 6D

1 Differentiate the following functions.

(a) $x^3 + 2x^2$
(b) $1 - 2x^3 + 3x^2$
(c) $x^3 - 6x^2 + 11x - 6$
(d) $2x^3 - 3x^2 + x$
(e) $2x^2\left(1 - 3x^2\right)$
(f) $(1 - x)\left(1 + x + x^2\right)$

2 Find $f'(-2)$ for each of the following functions $f(x)$.

(a) $2x - x^3$
(b) $2x - x^2$
(c) $1 - 2x - 3x^2 + 4x^3$
(d) $2 - x$
(e) $x^2(1 + x)$
(f) $(1 + x)\left(1 - x + x^2\right)$

3 For each of the following functions $f(x)$ find the value(s) of x such that $f'(x)$ is equal to the given number.

(a) x^3 12
(b) $x^3 - x^2$ 8
(c) $3x - 3x^2 + x^3$ 108
(d) $x^3 - 3x^2 + 2x$ -1
(e) $x(1 + x)^2$ 0
(f) $x(1 - x)(1 + x)$ 2

4 Differentiate the following functions.

(a) $2\sqrt{x}$
(b) $\left(1 + \sqrt{x}\right)^2$
(c) $y = x - \frac{1}{2}\sqrt{x}$
(d) $x\left(1 - \dfrac{1}{\sqrt{x}}\right)^2$

(e) $x - \dfrac{1}{x}$
(f) $\dfrac{x^3 + x^2 + 1}{x}$
(g) $\dfrac{(x + 1)(x + 2)}{x}$
(h) $\left(\dfrac{\sqrt{x} + x}{\sqrt{x}}\right)^2$

5 Find the equation of the tangent to the curve $y = x^3 + x$ at the point for which $x = -1$.

6 One of the tangents to the curve with equation $y = 4x - x^3$ is the line with equation $y = x - 2$. Find the equation of the other tangent parallel to $y = x - 2$.

7 Find the equation of the tangent at the point $(4,2)$ to the curve with equation $y = \sqrt{x}$.

8 Find the equation of the tangent at the point $\left(2, \frac{1}{2}\right)$ to the curve with equation $y = \dfrac{1}{x}$.

9 Find the equation of the normal at the point $(1,2)$ to the graph $y = x + \dfrac{1}{x}$.

10 The graphs of $y = x^2 - 2x$ and $y = x^3 - 3x^2 - 2x$ both pass through the origin. Show that they share the same tangent at the origin.

11 Find the equation of the tangent to the curve with equation $y = x^3 - 3x^2 - 2x - 6$ at the point where it crosses the y-axis.

12 A curve has equation $y = x(x - a)(x + a)$, where a is a constant. Find the equations of the tangents to the graph at the points where it crosses the x-axis.

13 Find the coordinates of the point of intersection of the tangents to the graph of $y = x^2$ at the points at which it meets the line with equation $y = x + 2$.

14 Differentiate each of these functions $f(x)$. Give your answers $f'(x)$ in a similar form, without negative or fractional indices.

(a) $\dfrac{1}{4x}$ (b) $\dfrac{3}{x^2}$ (c) x^0 (d) $\sqrt[4]{x^3}$

(e) $6\sqrt[3]{x}$ (f) $\dfrac{4}{\sqrt{x}}$ (g) $\dfrac{3}{x} + \dfrac{1}{3x^3}$ (h) $\sqrt{16x^5}$

(i) $x\sqrt{x}$ (j) $\dfrac{1}{\sqrt[3]{8x}}$ (k) $\dfrac{x-2}{x^2}$ (l) $\dfrac{1+x}{\sqrt[4]{x}}$

15 Find the equations of the tangent and the normal to $y = \sqrt[3]{x^2}$ at the point $(8, 4)$.

16 The tangent to the curve with equation $y = \dfrac{1}{x^2}$ at the point $\left(\tfrac{1}{2}, 4\right)$ meets the axes at P and Q. Find the coordinates of P and Q.

6.6* The gradient formula for any quadratic graph

If you wish, you can omit these final sections and go straight to Miscellaneous exercise 6.

The purpose of this section is to show you how to calculate the gradient of a quadratic graph without making any approximations.

Example 6.6.1
Find the gradient of the chord of $y = x^2$ joining the points with x-coordinates p and $p + h$.

The y-coordinates of the points are p^2 and $(p + h)^2$, so for this chord

$$\delta x = h, \quad \delta y = (p + h)^2 - p^2 = p^2 + 2ph + h^2 - p^2 = 2ph + h^2 = h(2p + h),$$

and the gradient is

$$\frac{\delta y}{\delta x} = \frac{h(2p + h)}{h} = 2p + h.$$

Notice that the gradients found in Examples 6.1.1 to 6.1.3 are special cases of this result, as shown in Table 6.7.

	p	$p+h$	h	$\dfrac{\delta y}{\delta x} = 2p + h$
Example 6.1.1	0.4	0.7	0.3	1.1
Example 6.1.2	0.4	0.41	0.01	0.81
Example 6.1.3	0.4	0.400 01	0.000 01	0.800 01

Table 6.7

The advantage of using algebra is that you don't have to work out the gradients each time from scratch. Table 6.8 shows some more results for $p = 0.4$ with different values of h, some positive and some negative.

Value of h	0.1	0.001	0.000 001	−0.1	−0.001	−0.000 001
Value of $\dfrac{\delta y}{\delta x}$	0.9	0.801	0.800 001	0.7	0.799	0.799 999

Table 6.8

If you have a graphic calculator, or some computer software for drawing graphs, it is interesting to produce a display showing the graph of $y = x^2$ and the chord through $(0.4, 0.16)$ with each of these gradients in turn. You will find that, when h is very close to 0, so that the two ends of the chord are very close together, it is almost impossible to distinguish the chord from the tangent to the curve. And you can see from Tables 6.7 and 6.8 that, for these chords, the gradient is very close to 0.8.

In fact, by taking h close enough to 0, you can make the gradient of the chord as close to 0.8 as you choose. From Example 6.6.1, the gradient of the chord is $0.8 + h$. So if you want to find a chord through $(0.4, 0.16)$ with a gradient between, say, 0.799 999 and 0.800 001, you can do it by taking h somewhere between −0.000 001 and +0.000 001.

The only value that you cannot take for h is 0 itself. But you can say that

'in the limit, as h tends to 0, the gradient of the chord tends to 0.8'.

The conventional way of writing this is

$$\lim_{h \to 0}(\text{gradient of chord}) = \lim_{h \to 0}(0.8 + h) = 0.8.$$

There is nothing special about taking p to be 0.4. You can use the same argument for any other value of p. Example 6.6.1 shows that the gradient of the chord joining (p, p^2) to $(p+h, (p+h)^2)$ is $2p + h$. If you keep p fixed, and let h take different values, then, by the same argument as before,

$$\lim_{h \to 0}(\text{gradient of chord}) = \lim_{h \to 0}(2p + h) = 2p.$$

Therefore the gradient at the point (p, p^2) on the curve $y = x^2$ is $2p$.

This shows that:

> The gradient formula for the curve $y = x^2$ is $2x$.

A similar approach can be used for any curve if
you know its equation.

Fig. 6.9 shows a curve which has an equation
of the form $y = f(x)$. Suppose that you want
the gradient of the tangent at the point P, with
coordinates $(p, f(p))$. The chord joining this
point to any other point Q on the curve with
coordinates $(p+h, f(p+h))$ has

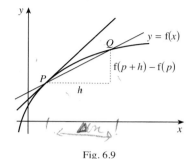

$$\delta x = h, \quad \delta y = f(p+h) - f(p)$$

so that its gradient is

$$\frac{\delta y}{\delta x} = \frac{f(p+h) - f(p)}{h}.$$

Fig. 6.9

Now let the value of h change so that the point Q takes different positions on the curve.
Then, if Q is close to P, so that h is close to 0, the gradient of the chord is close to the
gradient of the tangent at P, where $x = p$. In the limit, as h tends to 0, this expression
tends to $f'(p)$.

> If the curve $y = f(x)$ has a tangent at $(p, f(p))$, then its gradient is
>
> $$\lim_{h \to 0} \frac{f(p+h) - f(p)}{h}.$$
>
> This quantity is called the derivative of $f(x)$ at $x = p$; it is denoted by $f'(p)$.

Since p can stand for any value of x, you can write:

> The derivative of $f(x)$ for any value of x is $f'(x) = \lim_{h \to 0} \dfrac{f(x+h) - f(x)}{h}$.

Example 6.6.2

Find the derivative of the function $f(x) = 4x - 5$.

From the definition, $f'(x) = \lim\limits_{h \to 0} \dfrac{f(x+h) - f(x)}{h}$ with $f(x) = 4x - 5$.

The top line is

$$f(x+h) - f(x) = (4(x+h) - 5) - (4x - 5) = 4x + 4h - 5 - 4x + 5 = 4h.$$

Therefore

$$\frac{f(x+h) - f(x)}{h} = \frac{4h}{h} = 4.$$

Then in the limit, as h tends to 0,

$$f'(x) = \lim_{h \to 0} \frac{f(x+h) - f(x)}{h} = \lim_{h \to 0} 4 = 4.$$

Of course you could have predicted this result. From the work of Chapter 1, the graph of $f(x) = 4x - 5$ is a straight line with gradient 4. So it should not be a surprise that the derivative of $f(x) = 4x - 5$ is 4.

Similarly, you would expect the gradient of the function $f(x) = mx + c$, whose graph is the straight line $y = mx + c$, to be given by $f'(x) = m$.

Example 6.6.3

Find the derivative of the function $f(x) = 3x^2$.

For this function, $f(x+h) = 3(x+h)^2 = 3x^2 + 6xh + 3h^2$, so

$$f(x+h) - f(x) = \left(3x^2 + 6xh + 3h^2\right) - 3x^2 = 6xh + 3h^2 = h(6x + 3h)$$

and $\quad \dfrac{f(x+h) - f(x)}{h} = \dfrac{h(6x + 3h)}{h} = 6x + 3h.$

Then in the limit, as h tends to 0,

$$f'(x) = \lim_{h \to 0} \frac{f(x+h) - f(x)}{h} = \lim_{h \to 0}(6x + 3h) = 6x.$$

Notice that the derivative of $f(x) = x^2$ is $2x$ and the derivative of $f(x) = 3x^2$ is $6x$, which is $3 \times 2x$. This is an example of a general rule first seen in Section 6.5:

> If you multiply a function by a constant, then you multiply its derivative by the same constant.

Example 6.6.4

Find the derivative of the function $f(x) = 3x^2 + 4x - 5$.

For the function $f(x) = 3x^2 + 4x - 5$,

$$f(x+h) = 3(x+h)^2 + 4(x+h) - 5 = 3x^2 + 6xh + 3h^2 + 4x + 4h - 5,$$

so $f(x+h) - f(x) = \left(3x^2 + 6xh + 3h^2 + 4x + 4h - 5\right) - \left(3x^2 + 4x - 5\right)$

$$= 3x^2 + 6xh + 3h^2 + 4x + 4h - 5 - 3x^2 - 4x + 5$$

$$= 6xh + 3h^2 + 4h = h(6x + 3h + 4),$$

and $\dfrac{f(x+h) - f(x)}{h} = \dfrac{h(6x + 3h + 4)}{h} = 6x + 3h + 4.$

Then in the limit, as h tends to 0,

$$f'(x) = \lim_{h \to 0} \frac{f(x+h) - f(x)}{h} = \lim_{h \to 0} (6x + 3h + 4) = 6x + 4.$$

Examples 6.6.2 to 6.6.4 illustrate another general rule. The function in Example 6.6.4 is the sum of the functions in Examples 6.6.2 and 6.6.3, and the gradient in Example 6.6.4 is the sum of the gradients in Examples 6.6.2 and 6.6.3.

The general rule is:

> If you add two functions, then you find the derivative of the resulting function by adding the derivatives of the individual functions.

6.7* The gradient formula for some other functions

For some functions the method used in Section 6.6 lands you in some tricky algebra, and it is easier to use a different notation. Instead of finding the gradient of the chord joining the points with x-coordinates p and $p + h$ (or x and $x + h$), you can take the points to have coordinates $(p, f(p))$ and $(q, f(q))$, so that

$$\delta x = q - p \quad \text{and} \quad \delta y = f(q) - f(p).$$

Then the gradient is $\dfrac{\delta y}{\delta x} = \dfrac{f(q) - f(p)}{q - p}.$

To see how this works, here is Example 6.6.3 worked in this notation.

Example 6.7.1

Find the derivative at $x = p$ of the function $f(x) = 3x^2$.

For this function, $f(q) - f(p) = 3q^2 - 3p^2 = 3\left(q^2 - p^2\right) = 3(q - p)(q + p).$

So $\dfrac{\delta y}{\delta x} = \dfrac{\mathrm{f}(q) - \mathrm{f}(p)}{q - p} = \dfrac{3(q - p)(q + p)}{q - p} = 3(q + p).$

Now, in this method, q has taken the place of $p + h$, so that instead of taking the limit 'as h tends to 0' you take it 'as q tends to p'. It is easy to see that, as q tends to p, $3(q + p)$ tends to $3(p + p) = 3(2p) = 6p$.

Therefore, if $\mathrm{f}(x) = 3x^2$, $\mathrm{f}'(p) = 6p$. Since this holds for any value of p, you can write $\mathrm{f}'(x) = 6x$.

In this notation, the definition of the derivative takes the form:

> The derivative of $\mathrm{f}(x)$ at $x = p$ is $\mathrm{f}'(p) = \displaystyle\lim_{q \to p} \dfrac{\mathrm{f}(q) - \mathrm{f}(p)}{q - p}$.

Example 6.7.2
Find the derivative of the function $\mathrm{f}(x) = x^4$ at $x = p$.

At $x = p$, $\mathrm{f}(p) = p^4$, and at $x = q$, $\mathrm{f}(q) = q^4$. The chord joining $\left(p, p^4\right)$ and $\left(q, q^4\right)$ has $\delta x = q - p$, $\delta y = q^4 - p^4$.

Notice that you can write δy as $\left(q^2\right)^2 - \left(p^2\right)^2$, so you can use the difference of two squares twice to obtain

$$\delta y = \left(q^2 - p^2\right)\left(q^2 + p^2\right) = (q - p)(q + p)\left(q^2 + p^2\right).$$

Therefore

$$\frac{\delta y}{\delta x} = \frac{(q - p)(q + p)\left(q^2 + p^2\right)}{q - p} = (q + p)\left(q^2 + p^2\right).$$

Then in the limit, as q tends to p,

$$\mathrm{f}'(p) = \lim_{q \to p} \frac{\mathrm{f}(q) - \mathrm{f}(p)}{q - p} = \lim_{q \to p}\left((q + p)\left(q^2 + p^2\right)\right) = 2p\left(2p^2\right) = 4p^3.$$

Example 6.7.3
Find the derivative of the function $\mathrm{f}(x) = \sqrt{x}$ at $x = p$.

At $x = p$, $\mathrm{f}(p) = \sqrt{p}$, and at $x = q$, $\mathrm{f}(q) = \sqrt{q}$. The chord joining $\left(p, \sqrt{p}\right)$ and $\left(q, \sqrt{q}\right)$ has $\delta x = q - p$, $\delta y = \sqrt{q} - \sqrt{p}$.

Notice that you can write δx as the difference of two squares in the form

$$\delta x = q - p = \left(\sqrt{q}\right)^2 - \left(\sqrt{p}\right)^2 = \left(\sqrt{q} - \sqrt{p}\right)\left(\sqrt{q} + \sqrt{p}\right).$$

So $\dfrac{\delta y}{\delta x} = \dfrac{\sqrt{q} - \sqrt{p}}{\left(\sqrt{q} - \sqrt{p}\right)\left(\sqrt{q} + \sqrt{p}\right)} = \dfrac{1}{\sqrt{q} + \sqrt{p}}$.

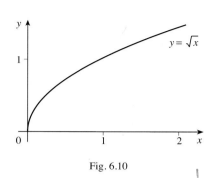

Fig. 6.10

Then in the limit, as q tends to p,

$$f'(p) = \lim_{q \to p} \frac{f(q) - f(p)}{q - p}$$

$$= \lim_{q \to p} \frac{1}{\sqrt{q} + \sqrt{p}}$$

$$= \frac{1}{\sqrt{p} + \sqrt{p}} = \frac{1}{2\sqrt{p}} = \tfrac{1}{2} p^{-\frac{1}{2}}.$$

Notice that this does not work when $p = 0$. In this case $\dfrac{\delta y}{\delta x} = \dfrac{1}{\sqrt{q}}$, which does

not have any limit as $q \to 0$. You can see from the graph of $y = \sqrt{x}$ in Fig. 6.10 that the tangent at $x = 0$ is the y-axis, which does not have a gradient.

Example 6.7.4

Find the derivative of the function $f(x) = \dfrac{1}{x}$ at $x = p$.

At $x = p$, $f(p) = \dfrac{1}{p}$, and at $x = q$, $f(q) = \dfrac{1}{q}$.

The chord joining $\left(p, \dfrac{1}{p}\right)$ and $\left(q, \dfrac{1}{q}\right)$ has $\delta x = q - p$, $\delta y = \dfrac{1}{q} - \dfrac{1}{p} = \dfrac{p - q}{qp} = -\dfrac{q - p}{qp}$,

and $\dfrac{\delta y}{\delta x} = \dfrac{-\left(\dfrac{q - p}{qp}\right)}{q - p} = -\dfrac{1}{qp}$.

Then, in the limit as q tends to p,

$$f'(p) = \lim_{q \to p} \frac{f(q) - f(p)}{q - p} = \lim_{q \to p}\left(-\frac{1}{qp}\right) = -\frac{1}{p^2} = -p^{-2}.$$

If you have access to a graphic calculator, display this curve and see why the gradient is always negative.

Exercise 6E*

Use the method of Section 6.7 in this exercise.

1 Find the derivative of the function $f(x) = x^3$ at $x = p$.

(You will need to use either the expansion $(p + h)^3 = p^3 + 3p^2 h + 3ph^2 + h^3$ or the product of factors $(q - p)(q^2 + qp + p^2) = q^3 - p^3$.)

2 Find the derivative of the function $f(x) = x^8$ at $x = p$. (Let $p + h = q$ and use the difference of two squares formula on $q^8 - p^8$ as often as you can.)

3　Find the derivative of the function $f(x) = \dfrac{1}{x^2}$ at $x = p$.

Miscellaneous exercise 6

1　Find the equation of the tangent to $y = 5x^2 - 7x + 4$ at the point $(2,10)$.

2　Given the function $f(x) = x^3 + 5x^2 - x - 4$, find
(a) $f'(-2)$,　　　　　(b) the values of a such that $f'(a) = 56$.

3　Find the equation of the normal to $y = x^4 - 4x^3$ at the point for which $x = \tfrac{1}{2}$.

4　Show that the equation of the tangent to $y = \dfrac{1}{x}$ at the point for which $x = p$ is

$p^2 y + x = 2p$. At what point on the curve is the equation of the tangent $9y + x + 6 = 0$?

5　The tangent to the curve $y = 6\sqrt{x}$ at the point $(4,12)$ meets the axes at A and B. Show that the distance AB may be written in the form $k\sqrt{13}$, and state the value of k.

6　Find the coordinates of the two points on the curve $y = 2x^3 - 5x^2 + 9x - 1$ at which the gradient of the tangent is 13.

7　Find the equation of the normal to $y = (2x - 1)(3x + 5)$ at the point $(1,8)$. Give your answer in the form $ax + by + c = 0$, where a, b and c are integers.

8　The curve $y = x^2 - 3x - 4$ crosses the x-axis at P and Q. The tangents to the curve at P and Q meet at R. The normals to the curve at P and Q meet at S. Find the distance RS.

9　The equation of a curve is $y = 2x^2 - 5x + 14$. The normal to the curve at the point $(1,11)$ meets the curve again at the point P. Find the coordinates of P.

10　At a particular point of the curve $y = x^2 + k$, the equation of the tangent is $y = 6x - 7$. Find the value of the constant k.

11　Show that the curves $y = x^3$ and $y = (x + 1)(x^2 + 4)$ have exactly one point in common, and use differentiation to find the gradient of each curve at this point.　　　　　　　(OCR)

12　At a particular point of the curve $y = 5x^2 - 12x + 1$ the equation of the normal is $x + 18y + c = 0$. Find the value of the constant c.

13　The graphs of $y = x^m$ and $y = x^n$ intersect at the point $P(1,1)$. Find the connection between m and n if the tangent at P to each curve is the normal to the other curve.

14　The tangents at $x = \tfrac{1}{4}$ to $y = \sqrt{x}$ and $y = \dfrac{1}{\sqrt{x}}$ meet at P. Find the coordinates of P.

15　The normals at $x = 2$ to $y = \dfrac{1}{x^2}$ and $y = \dfrac{1}{x^3}$ meet at Q. Find the coordinates of Q.

7 Applications of differentiation

In the last chapter you learnt what differentiation means and how to differentiate a lot of functions. This chapter shows how you can use differentiation to sketch graphs and apply it to real-world problems. When you have completed it, you should

- understand that the derivative of a function is itself a function
- appreciate the significance of positive, negative and zero derivatives
- be able to locate maximum and minimum points on graphs
- know that you can interpret a derivative as a rate of change of one variable with respect to another
- be familiar with the notation $\dfrac{dy}{dx}$ for a derivative
- be able to apply these techniques to solve real-world problems.

7.1 Derivatives as functions

In Chapter 6 you were introduced to differentiation by carrying out a number of 'explorations'. For example, in Exercise 6A Question 5(a) you were asked to make guesses about the gradient of the tangent at various points on the graph of $y = f(x)$, where $f(x) = x^2 - 2$. Table 7.1 shows the results you were expected to get.

p	-2	-1	1	2	3	10
$f(p)$	2	-1	-1	2	7	98
$f'(p)$	-4	-2	2	4	6	20

Table 7.1

What this suggests is that the gradient is also a function of x, given by the formula $2x$. In Chapter 6 this formula was called the derivative. But when you are thinking of it as a function rather than using its value for a particular x, it is sometimes called the **derived function**. It is denoted by $f'(x)$, and in this example $f'(x) = 2x$.

Also, just as you can draw the graph of the function $f(x)$, so it is possible to draw the graph of the derived function $f'(x)$. It is interesting to show these two graphs aligned one above the other on the page, as in Fig. 7.2.

On the left half of the graph, where $x < 0$, the graph of $f'(x)$ is below the x-axis, indicating that the gradient of $f(x)$ is negative. On the right, where the gradient of $f(x)$ is positive, the graph of $f'(x)$ is above the x-axis.

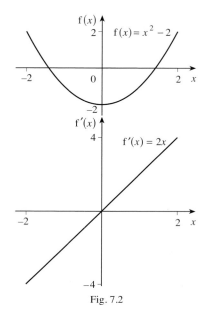

Fig. 7.2

You can now write down what you know about differentiation in terms of the derived function:

> If $f(x) = x^n$, where n is a rational number, then $f'(x) = nx^{n-1}$.
>
> The derived function of $f(x) + g(x)$ is $f'(x) + g'(x)$.
>
> The derived function of $cf(x)$, where c is a constant, is $cf'(x)$.

Example 7.1.1
Find the derived function of $f(x) = x^2 - \frac{1}{3}x^3$.

Using the results from the box, the derived function is $f'(x) = 2x - x^2$.

The graphs of $f(x)$ and $f'(x)$ in Example 7.1.1 are drawn in Fig. 7.3. Here are some points to notice.

When $x < 0$ the gradient of the graph of $f(x) = x^2 - \frac{1}{3}x^3$ is negative, and the values of the derived function are also negative.

When $x = 0$, the gradient of $f(x)$ is 0, and the value of $f'(0)$ is 0.

Between $x = 0$ and $x = 2$ the gradient of $f(x)$ is positive, and $f'(x)$ is positive.

When $x = 2$, the gradient of $f(x)$ is 0, and $f'(2) = 0$.

When $x > 2$, the gradient of $f(x)$ is negative, and the values of the derived function are also negative.

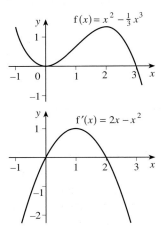

Fig. 7.3

Exercise 7A

1 Draw and compare the graphs of $y = f(x)$ and $y = f'(x)$ in each of the following cases.

   (a) $f(x) = 4x$ (b) $f(x) = 3 - 2x$ (c) $f(x) = x^2$

   (d) $f(x) = 5 - x^2$ (e) $f(x) = x^2 + 4x$ (f) $f(x) = 3x^2 - 6x$

2 Draw and compare the graphs of $y = f(x)$ and $y = f'(x)$ in each of the following cases.

   (a) $f(x) = (2 + x)(4 - x)$ (b) $f(x) = (x + 3)^2$ (c) $f(x) = x^4$

   (d) $f(x) = x^2(x - 2)$ (e) $f(x) = \sqrt{x}$ for $x \geqslant 0$ (f) $f(x) = \dfrac{1}{x}$ for $x \neq 0$

3 In each part of the question, the diagram shows the graph of $y = f(x)$. Draw a graph of the derived function $y = f'(x)$.

(a)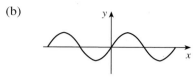

(b)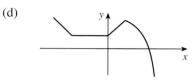

(c)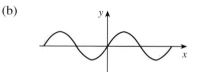

(d)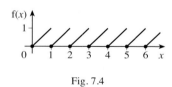

4 In each part of the question, the diagram shows the graph of the derived function $y = f'(x)$. Draw a possible graph of $y = f(x)$.

(a)

(b)

7.2 Increasing and decreasing functions

For simplicity, the word 'function' in this chapter will mean functions which are **continuous** within their domains. This includes all the functions you have met so far, but cuts out functions such as 'the fractional part of x', which is defined for all positive real numbers but whose graph (shown in Fig. 7.4) has jumps in it.

Fig. 7.4

You can use the idea that the derivative of a function is itself a function to investigate the shape of a graph from its equation.

Example 7.2.1
Find the interval in which $f(x) = x^2 - 6x + 4$ is increasing, and the interval in which it is decreasing.

The derivative is $f'(x) = 2x - 6 = 2(x - 3)$. This means that the graph has a positive gradient for $x > 3$. That is, $f(x)$ is increasing for $x > 3$.

For $x < 3$ the gradient is negative, and the values of y are getting smaller as x gets larger. That is, $f(x)$ is decreasing for $x < 3$.

The results are illustrated in Fig. 7.5 on the next page.

What about $x = 3$ itself? At first sight you might think that this has to be left out of both the increasing and the decreasing intervals, but this would be wrong! If you imagine moving along the curve from left to right, then as soon as you have passed through $x = 3$ the gradient becomes positive and the curve starts to climb. However close you are to $x = 3$, the value of y is greater than $f(3) = -5$. So you can say that $f(x)$ is increasing for $x \geqslant 3$; similarly, it is decreasing for $x \leqslant 3$.

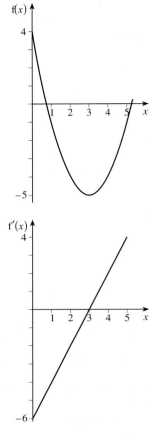

Fig. 7.5

You can use the reasoning in Example 7.2.1 for any function. Fig. 7.6 shows the graph of a function $y = f(x)$ whose derivative $f'(x)$ is positive in an interval $p < x < q$. You can see that larger values of y are associated with larger values of x. More precisely, if x_1 and x_2 are two values of x in the interval $p \leqslant x \leqslant q$, and if $x_2 > x_1$, then $f(x_2) > f(x_1)$. A function with this property is said to be **increasing** over the interval $p \leqslant x \leqslant q$.

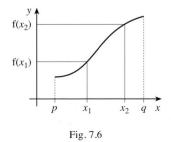

Fig. 7.6

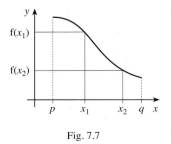

Fig. 7.7

If $f'(x)$ is negative in the interval $p < x < q$, as in Fig. 7.7, the function has the opposite property; if $x_2 > x_1$, then $f(x_2) < f(x_1)$. A function with this property is **decreasing** over the interval $p \leqslant x \leqslant q$.

> If $f'(x) > 0$ in an interval $p < x < q$, then $f(x)$ is increasing over the interval $p \leqslant x \leqslant q$.
>
> If $f'(x) < 0$ in $p < x < q$, then $f(x)$ is decreasing over $p \leqslant x \leqslant q$.

Notice that, for $f(x)$ to be increasing for $p \leqslant x \leqslant q$, the gradient $f'(x)$ does not have to be positive at the ends of the interval, where $x = p$ or $x = q$. At these points it may be 0, or even undefined. This may seem a minor distinction, but it has important consequences. It is a pay-off from the decision to work only with continuous functions.

The word 'interval' is used not only for values of x between finite end points, but also for values of x satisfying inequalities $x > p$ or $x < q$, which extend indefinitely in either the positive or negative direction.

Example 7.2.2

For the function $f(x) = x^4 - 4x^3$, find the intervals in which $f(x)$ is increasing and those in which it is decreasing.

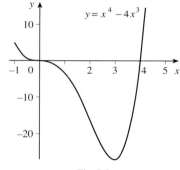

Fig. 7.8

Begin by expressing $f'(x)$ in factors as

$$f'(x) = 4x^3 - 12x^2 = 4x^2(x - 3).$$

As x^2 is always positive (except at $x = 0$), to find where $f'(x) > 0$ you need only solve the inequality $x - 3 > 0$, giving $x > 3$. So $f(x)$ is increasing over the interval $x \geqslant 3$, now including the end point.

The solution of $x - 3 < 0$ is $x < 3$; but to find where $f'(x) < 0$ you have to exclude $x = 0$, so that $f'(x) < 0$ if $x < 0$ or $0 < x < 3$. Therefore $f(x)$ is decreasing over the intervals $x \leqslant 0$ and $0 \leqslant x \leqslant 3$.

However, these last two intervals have the value $x = 0$ in common, so you can combine them as a single interval $x \leqslant 3$. It follows that $f(x)$ is decreasing over the interval $x \leqslant 3$.

Note also that $f'(x) = 0$ when $x = 0$ and $x = 3$. You can check all these properties from the graph of $y = f(x)$ shown in Fig. 7.8.

Example 7.2.2 shows that the rule given above, connecting the sign of $f'(x)$ with the property that $f(x)$ is increasing or decreasing, can be slightly relaxed.

> If $f'(x) > 0$ in an interval $p < x < q$ except at isolated points where $f'(x) = 0$, then $f(x)$ is increasing in the interval $p \leqslant x \leqslant q$.
>
> If $f'(x) < 0$ in an interval $p < x < q$ except at isolated points where $f'(x) = 0$, then $f(x)$ is decreasing over $p \leqslant x \leqslant q$.

The next example is about a function which involves fractional powers of x for $x < 0$. Fractional powers sometimes present problems, because some of them are not defined when x is negative. But the indices in this example involve only cube roots. There is no difficulty in taking the cube root of a negative number.

Example 7.2.3

Find the intervals in which the function $f(x) = x^{\frac{2}{3}}(1-x)$ is increasing and those in which it is decreasing.

To differentiate, write the function as $f(x) = x^{\frac{2}{3}} - x^{\frac{5}{3}}$, so that

$$f'(x) = \tfrac{2}{3}x^{-\frac{1}{3}} - \tfrac{5}{3}x^{\frac{2}{3}},$$

which you can write as

$$f'(x) = \tfrac{1}{3}x^{-\frac{1}{3}}(2 - 5x).$$

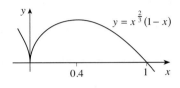

In this last expression, $x^{-\frac{1}{3}}$ is positive when $x > 0$ and negative when $x < 0$. The factor $2 - 5x$ is positive when $x < 0.4$ and negative when $x > 0.4$. Fig. 7.9 shows that

Fig. 7.9

$f(x)$ is increasing in the interval $0 \leqslant x \leqslant 0.4$,

$f(x)$ is decreasing in the intervals $x \leqslant 0$ and $x \geqslant 0.4$.

7.3 Maximum and minimum points

Example 7.2.1 showed that, for $f(x) = x^2 - 6x + 4$, $f(x)$ is decreasing for $x \leqslant 3$ and increasing for $x \geqslant 3$. It follows from the definition of decreasing and increasing functions that, if $x_1 < 3$, then $f(x_1) > f(3)$; and that, if $x_2 > 3$, then $f(x_2) > f(3)$. That is, for every value of x other than 3, $f(x)$ is greater than $f(3) = -5$. You can say that $f(3)$ is the minimum value of $f(x)$, and that $(3, -5)$ is the minimum point on the graph of $y = f(x)$.

A minimum point does not have to be the lowest point on the whole graph, but is the lowest point in its immediate neighbourhood. In Fig. 7.9, $(0,0)$ is a minimum point; this is shown by the fact that $f(x) > 0$ for every number $x < 1$ except $x = 0$ although $f(x) < 0$ when $x > 1$.

This leads to a definition, which is illustrated by Fig. 7.10.

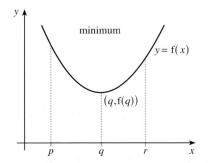
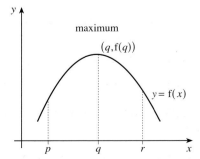

Fig. 7.10

A function $f(x)$ has a **minimum** at $x = q$ if there is an interval $p < x < r$ containing q in which $f(x) > f(q)$ for every value of x except q.

It has a **maximum** if $f(x) < f(q)$ for every value of x in the interval except q.

The point $(q, f(q))$ is called a **minimum point**, or a **maximum point**.

Thus, in Example 7.2.3, $f(x)$ has a minimum at $x = 0$, and a maximum at $x = 0.4$.

Minimum and maximum points are sometimes also called **turning points**.

You will see that at the minimum point in Fig. 7.8 and the maximum point in Fig. 7.9 the graph has gradient 0. But at the minimum point $(0,0)$ in Fig. 7.9 the tangent to the graph is the y-axis, so that the gradient is undefined. These examples illustrate a general rule:

If $(q, f(q))$ is a minimum or maximum point of the graph of $y = f(x)$, then either $f'(q) = 0$ or $f'(q)$ is undefined.

Notice, though, that Fig. 7.8 has another point at which the gradient is 0, which is neither a minimum nor a maximum, namely the point $(0,0)$. A point of a graph where the gradient is 0 is called a **stationary point**. So Figs. 7.8 and 7.9 illustrate the fact that a stationary point may be a minimum or maximum point, but may be neither.

A way to decide between a minimum and a maximum point is to find the sign of the gradient $f'(x)$ on either side of $x = q$. To follow the details you may again find it helpful to refer to the graphs in Fig. 7.10.

If $f'(x) < 0$ in an interval $p < x < q$, and $f'(x) > 0$ in an interval $q < x < r$, then $(q, f(q))$ is a minimum point.

If $f'(x) > 0$ in $p < x < q$, and $f'(x) < 0$ in $q < x < r$, then $(q, f(q))$ is a maximum point.

You may be happy to accept this on the evidence of the graphs, but it can also be argued from statements which you have already met. Consider the minimum case.

Suppose that x_1 is a number in $p < x < q$. Then, since $f'(x) < 0$ in that interval, it follows from Section 7.2 that $f(x_1) > f(q)$.

Now suppose that x_2 is a number in $q < x < r$. Since $f'(x) > 0$ in that interval, $f(q) < f(x_2)$.

This shows that, if x is any number in the interval $p < x < r$ other than q, then $f(x) > f(q)$. From the definition, this means that $f(x)$ has a minimum at $x = q$.

All these results can be summed up as a procedure.

To find the minimum and maximum points on the graph of $y = f(x)$:

Step 1 Decide the domain in which you are interested.

Step 2 Find an expression for $f'(x)$.

Step 3 List the values of x in the domain for which $f'(x)$ is either 0 or undefined.

Step 4 Taking each of these values of x in turn, find the sign of $f'(x)$ in intervals immediately to the left and to the right of that value.

Step 5 If these signs are $-$ and $+$ respectively, the graph has a minimum point. If they are $+$ and $-$ it has a maximum point. If the signs are the same, it has neither.

Step 6 For each value of x which gives a minimum or maximum, calculate $f(x)$.

Example 7.3.1

Find the minimum point on the graph with equation $y = \sqrt{x} + \dfrac{4}{x}$.

Let $f(x) = \sqrt{x} + \dfrac{4}{x}$.

Step 1 As $\sqrt{x}$ is defined for $x \geq 0$ but $\dfrac{1}{x}$ is not defined for $x = 0$, the largest possible domain for $f(x)$ is the positive real numbers.

Step 2 The derivative $f'(x) = \frac{1}{2} x^{-\frac{1}{2}} - 4x^{-2}$ can be written as $f'(x) = \dfrac{x^{\frac{3}{2}} - 8}{2x^2}$.

Step 3 The derivative is defined for all positive real numbers, and is 0 when $x^{\frac{3}{2}} = 8$. Raising both sides to the power $\frac{2}{3}$ and using the power-on-power rule,

$$x = \left(x^{\frac{3}{2}}\right)^{\frac{2}{3}} = 8^{\frac{2}{3}} = 4.$$

Step 4 If $0 < x < 4$, the bottom line, $2x^2$, is positive, and

$$x^{\frac{3}{2}} - 8 < 4^{\frac{3}{2}} - 8 = 8 - 8 = 0, \text{ so that } f'(x) < 0.$$

If $x > 4$, $2x^2$ is still positive, but $x^{\frac{3}{2}} - 8 > 4^{\frac{3}{2}} - 8 = 0$, so that $f'(x) > 0$.

Step 5 The sign of $f'(x)$ is $-$ on the left of 4 and $+$ on the right, so the function has a minimum at $x = 4$.

Step 6 Calculate $f(4) = \sqrt{4} + \dfrac{4}{4} = 2 + 1 = 3$. The minimum point is $(4, 3)$.

If you have a graphic calculator, it is interesting to use it to display $y = f(x)$ together with $y = \sqrt{x}$ and $y = \dfrac{4}{x}$, from which it is made up. You will find that $y = f(x)$ is very flat around the minimum; it would be difficult to tell by eye exactly where the minimum occurs.

Notice that this theory gives you another way to find the range of some functions. For the function in Example 7.3.1 with domain $x > 0$, the range is $y \geqslant 3$.

Exercise 7B

1 For each of the following functions $f(x)$, find $f'(x)$ and the interval in which $f(x)$ is increasing.

    (a) $x^2 - 5x + 6$ (b) $x^2 + 6x - 4$ (c) $7 - 3x - x^2$

    (d) $3x^2 - 5x + 7$ (e) $5x^2 + 3x - 2$ (f) $7 - 4x - 3x^2$

2 For each of the following functions $f(x)$, find $f'(x)$ and the interval in which $f(x)$ is decreasing.

    (a) $x^2 + 4x - 9$ (b) $x^2 - 3x - 5$ (c) $5 - 3x + x^2$

    (d) $2x^2 - 8x + 7$ (e) $4 + 7x - 2x^2$ (f) $3 - 5x - 7x^2$

3 For each of the following functions $f(x)$, find $f'(x)$ and any intervals in which $f(x)$ is increasing.

    (a) $x^3 - 12x$ (b) $2x^3 - 18x + 5$ (c) $2x^3 - 9x^2 - 24x + 7$

    (d) $x^3 - 3x^2 + 3x + 4$ (e) $x^4 - 2x^2$ (f) $x^4 + 4x^3$

    (g) $3x - x^3$ (h) $2x^5 - 5x^4 + 10$ (i) $3x + x^3$

4 For each of the following functions $f(x)$, find $f'(x)$ and any intervals in which $f(x)$ is decreasing. In part (i), n is an integer.

    (a) $x^3 - 27x$ for $x \geqslant 0$ (b) $x^4 + 4x^2 - 5$ for $x \geqslant 0$ (c) $x^3 - 3x^2 + 3x - 1$

    (d) $12x - 2x^3$ (e) $2x^3 + 3x^2 - 36x - 7$ (f) $3x^4 - 20x^3 + 12$

    (g) $36x^2 - 2x^4$ (h) $x^5 - 5x$ (i) $x^n - nx$ $(n > 1)$

5 For each of the following functions $f(x)$, find $f'(x)$, the intervals in which $f(x)$ is decreasing, and the intervals in which $f(x)$ is increasing.

    (a) $x^{\frac{3}{2}}(x - 1)$, for $x > 0$ (b) $x^{\frac{3}{4}} - 2x^{\frac{7}{4}}$, for $x > 0$ (c) $x^{\frac{2}{3}}(x + 2)$

    (d) $x^{\frac{3}{5}}\left(x^2 - 13\right)$ (e) $x + \dfrac{3}{x}$, for $x \neq 0$ (f) $\sqrt{x} + \dfrac{1}{\sqrt{x}}$, for $x > 0$

6 For the graphs of each of the following functions:

    (i)   find the coordinates of the stationary point;

    (ii)   say, with reasoning, whether this is a maximum or a minimum point;

    (iii) check your answer by using the method of 'completing the square' to find the vertex;

    (iv) state the range of values which the function can take.

    (a) $x^2 - 8x + 4$ (b) $3x^2 + 12x + 5$ (c) $5x^2 + 6x + 2$

    (d) $4 - 6x - x^2$ (e) $x^2 + 6x + 9$ (f) $1 - 4x - 4x^2$

7   Find the coordinates of the stationary points on the graphs of the following functions, and find whether these points are maxima or minima.

(a) $2x^3 + 3x^2 - 72x + 5$ (b) $x^3 - 3x^2 - 45x + 7$ (c) $3x^4 - 8x^3 + 6x^2$

(d) $3x^5 - 20x^3 + 1$ (e) $2x + x^2 - 4x^3$ (f) $x^3 + 3x^2 + 3x + 1$

(g) $x + \dfrac{1}{x}$ (h) $x^2 + \dfrac{54}{x}$ (i) $x - \dfrac{1}{x}$

(j) $x - \sqrt{x}$, for $x > 0$ (k) $\dfrac{1}{x} - \dfrac{3}{x^2}$ (l) $x^2 - \dfrac{16}{x} + 5$

(m) $x^{\frac{1}{3}}(4 - x)$ (n) $x^{\frac{1}{5}}(x + 6)$ (o) $x^4(1 - x)$

8   Find the ranges of each of these functions $f(x)$, defined over the largest possible domains.

(a) $x^2 + x + 1$ (b) $x^4 - 8x^2$ (c) $x + \dfrac{1}{x}$

7.4   Derivatives as rates of change

The quantities x and y in a relationship $y = f(x)$ are often called **variables**, because x can stand for any number in the domain and y for any number in the range. When you draw the graph you have a free choice of values of x, and then work out the values of y. So x is called the **independent variable** and y the **dependent variable**.

These variables often stand for physical or economic quantities, and then it is convenient to use other letters which suggest what these quantities are: for example, t for time, V for volume, C for cost, P for population, and so on.

To illustrate this consider a situation familiar to deep sea divers, that pressure increases with depth below sea level. The independent variable is the depth, z metres, below the surface.

It will soon be clear why the letter d was not used for the depth. The letter z is often used for distances in the vertical direction.

The dependent variable is the pressure, p, measured in bars. At the surface the diver experiences only atmospheric pressure, about 1 bar, but the pressure increases as the diver descends.

At off-shore (coastal) depths the variables are connected approximately by the equation

$p = 1 + 0.1z$.

The (z, p) graph is a straight line, shown in Fig. 7.11.

The constant 0.1 in the equation is the amount that the pressure goes up for each extra metre of depth. This is the 'rate of change of pressure with respect to depth'.

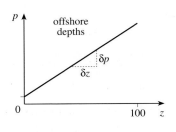

Fig. 7.11

If the diver descends a further distance of δz metres, the pressure goes up by δp bars; this rate of change is $\dfrac{\delta p}{\delta z}$.
It is represented by the gradient of the graph.

But at ocean depths the (z, p) graph is no longer a straight line: it has the form of Fig. 7.12. The quantity $\dfrac{\delta p}{\delta z}$ now represents the average rate of change over the extra depth δz. It is represented by the gradient of the chord in Fig. 7.12.

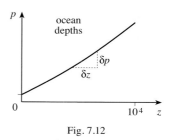

Fig. 7.12

The rate of change of pressure with respect to depth is the limit of $\dfrac{\delta p}{\delta z}$ as δz tends to 0. The $f'(\ )$ notation, which has so far been used for this limit, is not ideal because it does not mention p; it is useful to have a notation which includes both of the letters used for the variables. An alternative symbol $\dfrac{dp}{dz}$ was devised, obtained by replacing the letter δ in the average rate by d in the limit. Formally,

$$\frac{dp}{dz} = \lim_{\delta z \to 0} \frac{\delta p}{\delta z}.$$

There is no new idea here. It is just a different way of writing the definition of the derivative given in Chapter 6. The advantage is that it can be adapted, using different letters, to express the rate of change whenever there is a function relationship between two variables.

> If x and y are the independent and dependent variables respectively in a functional relationship, then the derivative,
>
> $$\frac{dy}{dx} = \lim_{\delta x \to 0} \frac{\delta y}{\delta x},$$
>
> measures the **rate of change of y with respect to x**.
>
> If $y = f(x)$, then $\dfrac{dy}{dx} = f'(x)$.

Although $\dfrac{dy}{dx}$ looks like a fraction, for the time being you should treat it as one inseparable symbol made up of four letters and a horizontal line. By themselves, the symbols dx and dy have no meaning. (Later on, though, you will find that in some ways the symbol $\dfrac{dy}{dx}$ *behaves* like a fraction. This is another of its advantages over the $f'(\ )$ notation.)

The notation can be used in a wide variety of contexts. For example, if the area of burnt grass, t minutes after a fire has started, is A square metres, then $\dfrac{dA}{dt}$ measures the rate at which the fire is spreading in square metres per minute. If, at a certain point on the Earth's surface, distances of x metres on the ground are represented by distances of y metres on a map, then $\dfrac{dy}{dx}$ represents the scale of the map at that point.

Example 7.4.1

A sprinter in a women's 100-metre race reaches her top speed of 12 metres per second after she has run 36 metres. Up to that distance her speed is proportional to the square root of the distance she has run. Show that until she reaches full speed the rate of change of her speed with respect to distance is inversely proportional to her speed.

Suppose that after she has run x metres her speed is S metres per second. You are told that, up to $x = 36$, $S = k\sqrt{x}$, and also that $S = 12$ when $x = 36$. So

$$12 = k\sqrt{36}, \quad \text{giving} \quad k = \tfrac{12}{6} = 2.$$

The (x, S) relationship is therefore

$$S = 2\sqrt{x} \text{ for } 0 < x < 36.$$

The rate of change of speed with respect to distance is the derivative $\dfrac{dS}{dx}$, and the derivative of $\sqrt{x}$ (from Section 6.5) is $\dfrac{1}{2\sqrt{x}}$. Therefore

$$\frac{dS}{dx} = 2 \times \frac{1}{2\sqrt{x}} = \frac{1}{\sqrt{x}}.$$

Since $\sqrt{x} = \dfrac{S}{2}$, $\dfrac{dS}{dx}$ can be written as $\dfrac{2}{S}$.

The rate of change is therefore inversely proportional to her speed.

If she maintains her top speed for the rest of the race, the rate of change of speed with respect to distance drops to 0 for $x > 36$. Fig. 7.13 shows that the gradient, which represents the rate of change, gets smaller as her speed increases, and then becomes zero once she reaches her top speed.

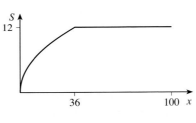

Fig. 7.13

Example 7.4.2

A line of cars, each 5 metres long, is travelling along an open road at a steady speed of S km per hour. There is a recommended separation between each pair of cars given by the formula $(0.18S + 0.006S^2)$ metres. At what speed should the cars travel to maximise the number of cars that the road can accommodate?

It is a good idea to write the separation formula as $(aS + bS^2)$, where $a = 0.18$ and $b = 0.006$. This gives a neater formula, and will also enable you to investigate the effect of changing the coefficients in the formula. But remember when you differentiate that a and b are simply constants, and you can treat them just like numbers.

A 'block', consisting of a car's length and the separation distance in front of it, occupies $5 + aS + bS^2$ metres of road, or $\dfrac{5 + aS + bS^2}{1000}$ km. For the largest number of blocks passing a checkpoint in an hour, the time T (in hours) for a single block to pass the checkpoint should be as small as possible. Since the block is moving at speed S km per hour,

$$TS = \frac{5 + aS + bS^2}{1000},$$

or $\quad T = \dfrac{5 + aS + bS^2}{1000S} = 0.001\left(5S^{-1} + a + bS\right).$

Now follow the procedure for finding the minimum value of T.

Step 1 Since the speed must be positive, the domain is $S > 0$.

Step 2 The derivative is $\dfrac{dT}{dS} = 0.001\left(-5S^{-2} + b\right)$.

Step 3 This derivative is defined everywhere in the domain, and is 0 when $-\dfrac{5}{S^2} + b = 0$, which is at $S = \sqrt{\dfrac{5}{b}}$.

Step 4 As S increases, $\dfrac{5}{S^2}$ decreases, so $-\dfrac{5}{S^2} + b$ increases. Since $\dfrac{dT}{dS}$ is 0 when $S = \sqrt{\dfrac{5}{b}}$, the sign of $\dfrac{dT}{dS}$ is $-$ when $S < \sqrt{\dfrac{5}{b}}$, and $+$ when $S > \sqrt{\dfrac{5}{b}}$.

Step 5 Since $\dfrac{dT}{dS}$ changes from $-$ to $+$, T is a minimum when $S = \sqrt{\dfrac{5}{b}}$.

Step 6 Substituting $a = 0.18$ and $b = 0.006$ gives $S = \sqrt{\dfrac{5}{0.006}} \approx 28.87$ and $T \approx 0.000\,526\,4$ at the minimum point.

This shows that the cars flow best at a speed of just under 29 km h^{-1}. (Each block then takes approximately $0.000\,526$ hours, or 1.89 seconds, to pass the checkpoint, so that the number of cars which pass in an hour is approximately $\frac{1}{0.000\,526} \approx 1900$.)

Example 7.4.3

A hollow cone with base radius a cm and height b cm is placed on a table. What is the volume of the largest cylinder that can be hidden underneath it?

The volume of a cylinder of radius r cm and height h cm is V cm^3, where

$$V = \pi r^2 h.$$

You can obviously make this as large as you like by choosing r and h large enough. But in this problem the variables are restricted by the requirement that the cylinder has to fit under the cone. Before you can follow the procedure for finding a maximum, you need to find how this restriction affects the values of r and h.

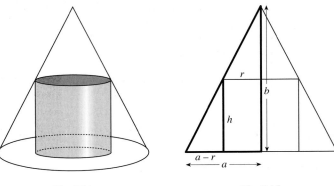

Fig. 7.14   Fig. 7.15

Fig. 7.14 shows the three-dimensional set-up, and Fig. 7.15 is a vertical section through the top of the cone. The similar triangles picked out with heavy lines in Fig. 7.15 show that r and h are connected by the equation

$$\frac{h}{a-r} = \frac{b}{a}, \text{ so that } h = \frac{b(a-r)}{a}.$$

Substituting this expression for h in the formula for V then gives

$$V = \frac{\pi r^2 b(a-r)}{a} = \left(\frac{\pi b}{a}\right)\left(ar^2 - r^3\right).$$

Notice that the original expression for V contains two independent variables r and h. The effect of the substitution is to reduce the number of independent variables to one; h has disappeared, and only r remains. This makes it possible to apply the procedure for finding a maximum.

The physical problem only has meaning if $0 < r < a$, so take this interval as the domain of the function. Differentiating by the usual rule (remembering that π, a and b are constants) gives

$$\frac{dV}{dr} = \left(\frac{\pi b}{a}\right)\left(2ar - 3r^2\right) = \left(\frac{\pi b}{a}\right)r(2a - 3r).$$

The only value of r in the domain for which $\dfrac{dV}{dr} = 0$ is $\frac{2}{3}a$. It is easy to check that the sign of $\dfrac{dV}{dr}$ is + for $0 < r < \frac{2}{3}a$ and − for $\frac{2}{3}a < r < a$.

So the cylinder of maximum volume has radius $\frac{2}{3}a$, height $\frac{1}{3}b$ and volume $\frac{4}{27}\pi a^2 b$. (Since the volume of the cone is $\frac{1}{3}\pi a^2 b$, the cylinder of maximum volume occupies $\frac{4}{9}$ of the space under the cone.)

Exercise 7C

1 In each part of this question express each derivative as 'the rate of change of ... with respect to ...', and state its physical significance.

(a) $\dfrac{dh}{dx}$, where h is the height above sea level, and x is the horizontal distance travelled, along a straight road

(b) $\dfrac{dN}{dt}$, where N is the number of people in a stadium at time t after the gates open

(c) $\dfrac{dM}{dr}$, where M is the magnetic force at a distance r from a magnet

(d) $\dfrac{dv}{dt}$, where v is the velocity of a particle moving in a straight line at time t

(e) $\dfrac{dq}{dS}$, where q is the rate at which petrol is used in a car in litres per km, and S is the speed of the car in km per hour

2 Defining suitable notation and units, express each of the following as a derivative.

(a) the rate of change of atmospheric pressure with respect to height above sea level

(b) the rate of change of temperature with respect to the time of day

(c) the rate at which the tide is rising

(d) the rate at which a baby's weight increases in the first weeks of life

3 (a) Find $\dfrac{dz}{dt}$ where $z = 3t^2 + 7t - 5$.   (b) Find $\dfrac{d\theta}{dx}$ where $\theta = x - \sqrt{x}$.

(c) Find $\dfrac{dx}{dy}$ where $x = y + \dfrac{3}{y^2}$.   (d) Find $\dfrac{dr}{dt}$ where $r = t^2 + \dfrac{1}{\sqrt{t}}$.

(e) Find $\dfrac{dm}{dt}$ where $m = (t+3)^2$.   (f) Find $\dfrac{df}{ds}$ where $f = 2s^6 - 3s^2$.

(g) Find $\dfrac{dw}{dt}$ where $w = 5t$.   (h) Find $\dfrac{dR}{dr}$ where $R = \dfrac{1-r^3}{r^2}$.

4 A particle moves along the x-axis. Its displacement at time t is $x = 6t - t^2$.

(a) What does $\dfrac{dx}{dt}$ represent?

(b) Is x increasing or decreasing when   (i) $t = 1$,   (ii) $t = 4$?

(c) Find the greatest (positive) displacement of the particle. How is this connected to your answer to part (a)?

5 Devise suitable notation to express each of the following in mathematical form.

(a) The distance travelled along the motorway is increasing at a constant rate.

(b) The rate at which a savings bank deposit grows is proportional to the amount of money deposited.

(c) The rate at which the diameter of a tree increases is a function of the air temperature.

6 At a speed of S km per hour a car will travel y kilometres on each litre of petrol, where

$$y = 5 + \tfrac{1}{5}S - \tfrac{1}{800}S^2.$$

Calculate the speed at which the car should be driven for maximum economy.

7 A ball is thrown vertically upwards. At time t seconds its height h metres is given by $h = 20t - 5t^2$. Calculate the ball's maximum height above the ground.

8 The sum of two real numbers x and y is 12. Find the maximum value of their product xy.

9 The product of two positive real numbers x and y is 20. Find the minimum possible value of their sum.

10 The volume of a cylinder is given by the formula $V = \pi r^2 h$. Find the greatest and least values of V if $r + h = 6$.

11 A loop of string of length 1 metre is formed into a rectangle with one pair of opposite sides each x cm. Calculate the value of x which will maximise the area enclosed by the string.

12 One side of a rectangular sheep pen is formed by a hedge. The other three sides are made using fencing. The length of the rectangle is x metres; 120 metres of fencing is available.

(a) Show that the area of the rectangle is $\tfrac{1}{2}x(120 - x)\,\mathrm{m}^2$.

(b) Calculate the maximum possible area of the sheep pen.

13 A rectangular sheet of metal measures 50 cm by 40 cm. Equal squares of side x cm are cut from each corner and discarded. The sheet is then folded up to make a tray of depth x cm. What is the domain of possible values of x? Find the value of x which maximises the capacity of the tray.

14 An open rectangular box is to be made with a square base, and its capacity is to be $4000\,\mathrm{cm}^3$. Find the length of the side of the base when the amount of material used to make the box is as small as possible. (Ignore 'flaps'.)

15 An open cylindrical wastepaper bin, of radius r cm and capacity $V\,\mathrm{cm}^3$, is to have a surface area of $5000\,\mathrm{cm}^2$.

(a) Show that $V = \tfrac{1}{2}r\left(5000 - \pi r^2\right)$.

(b) Calculate the maximum possible capacity of the bin.

16 A circular cylinder is to fit inside a sphere of radius 10 cm. Calculate the maximum possible volume of the cylinder. (It is probably best to take as your independent variable the height, or half the height, of the cylinder.)

Miscellaneous exercise 7

1 Use differentiation to find the coordinates of the stationary points on the curve

$$y = x + \frac{4}{x}$$

and determine whether each stationary point is a maximum point or a minimum point.

Find the set of values of x for which y increases as x increases. (OCR)

2 The rate at which a radioactive mass decays is known to be proportional to the mass remaining at that time. If, at time t, the mass remaining is m, this means that m and t satisfy the equation

$$\frac{dm}{dt} = -km$$

where k is a positive constant. (The negative sign ensures that $\frac{dm}{dt}$ is negative, which indicates that m is decreasing.)

Write down similar equations which represent the following statements.

(a) The rate of growth of a population of bacteria is proportional to the number, n, of bacteria present.

(b) When a bowl of hot soup is put in the freezer, the rate at which its temperature, $\theta\,°C$, decreases as it cools is proportional to its current temperature.

(c) The rate at which the temperature, $\theta\,°C$, of a cup of coffee decreases as it cools is proportional to the excess of its temperature over the room temperature, $\beta\,°C$.

3 A car accelerates to overtake a truck. Its initial speed is u, and in a time t after it starts to accelerate it covers a distance x, where $x = ut + kt^2$.

Use differentiation to show that its speed is then $u + 2kt$, and show that its acceleration is constant.

4 A car is travelling at $20\ \text{m s}^{-1}$ when the driver applies the brakes. At a time t seconds later the car has travelled a further distance x metres, where $x = 20t - 2t^2$. Use differentiation to find expressions for the speed and the acceleration of the car at this time. For how long do these formulae apply?

5 A boy stands on the edge of a cliff of height $60\ \text{m}$. He throws a stone vertically upwards so that its distance, $h\ \text{m}$, above the cliff top is given by $h = 20t - 5t^2$.

(a) Calculate the maximum height of the stone above the cliff top.

(b) Calculate the time which elapses before the stone hits the beach. (It just misses the boy and the cliff on the way down.)

(c) Calculate the speed with which the stone hits the beach.

6 Find the least possible value of $x^2 + y^2$ given that $x + y = 10$.

7 The sum of the two shorter sides of a right-angled triangle is $18\ \text{cm}$. Calculate

(a) the least possible length of the hypotenuse,

(b) the greatest possible area of the triangle.

8 (a) Find the stationary points on the graph of $y = 12x + 3x^2 - 2x^3$ and sketch the graph.

(b) How does your sketch show that the equation $12x + 3x^2 - 2x^3 = 0$ has exactly three real roots?

(c) Use your graph to show that the equation $12x + 3x^2 - 2x^3 = -5$ also has exactly three real roots.

(d) For what range of values of k does the equation $12x + 3x^2 - 2x^3 = k$ have
(i) exactly three real roots, (ii) only one real root?

9 Find the coordinates of the stationary points on the graph of $y = x^3 - 12x - 12$ and sketch the graph.

Find the set of values of k for which the equation $x^3 - 12x - 12 = k$ has more than one real solution. (OCR)

10 Find the coordinates of the stationary points on the graph of $y = x^3 + x^2$. Sketch the graph and hence write down the set of values of the constant k for which the equation $x^3 + x^2 = k$ has three distinct real roots.

11 Find the coordinates of the stationary points on the graph of $y = 3x^4 - 4x^3 - 12x^2 + 10$, and sketch the graph. For what values of k does the equation $3x^4 - 4x^3 - 12x^2 + 10 = k$ have

(a) exactly four roots,   (b) exactly two roots?

12 Find the coordinates of the stationary points on the curve with equation $y = x(x-1)^2$. Sketch the curve.

Find the set of real values of k such that the equation $x(x-1)^2 = k^2$ has exactly one real root. (OCR, adapted)

13 The cross-section of an object has the shape of a quarter-circle of radius r adjoining a rectangle of width x and height r, as shown in the diagram.

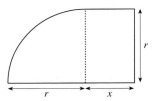

(a) The perimeter and area of the cross-section are P and A respectively. Express each of P and A in terms of r and x, and hence show that $A = \frac{1}{2}Pr - r^2$.

(b) Taking the perimeter P of the cross-section as fixed, find x in terms of r for the case when the area A of the cross-section is a maximum, and show that, for this value of x, A is a maximum and not a minimum. (OCR)

14 A curve has equation $y = \dfrac{1}{x} - \dfrac{1}{x^2}$. Use differentiation to find the coordinates of the stationary point and determine whether the stationary point is a maximum point or a minimum point. Deduce, or obtain otherwise, the coordinates of the stationary point of each of the following curves.

(a) $y = \dfrac{1}{x} - \dfrac{1}{x^2} + 5$ (b) $y = \dfrac{2}{x-1} - \dfrac{2}{(x-1)^2}$

15 The manager of a supermarket usually adds a mark-up of 20% to the wholesale prices of all the goods he sells. He reckons that he has a loyal core of F customers and that, if he lowers his mark-up to $x\%$ he will attract an extra $k(20-x)$ customers from his rivals. Each week the average shopper buys goods whose wholesale value is £A. Show that with a mark-up of $x\%$ the supermarket will have an anticipated weekly profit of

$$£\frac{1}{100}Ax((F + 20k) - kx).$$

Show that the manager can increase his profit by reducing his mark-up below 20% provided that $20k > F$. (OCR)

16 The costs of a firm which makes climbing boots are of two kinds:

> Fixed costs (plant, rates, office expenses): £2000 per week;
> Production costs (materials, labour): £20 for each pair of boots made.

Market research suggests that, if they price the boots at £30 a pair they will sell 500 pairs a week, but that at £55 a pair they will sell none at all; and between these values the graph of sales against price is a straight line.

If they price boots at £x a pair $(30 \leqslant x \leqslant 55)$ find expressions for

(a) the weekly sales,   (b) the weekly receipts,   (c) the weekly costs

(assuming that just enough boots are made).

Hence show that the weekly profit, £P, is given by

$$P = -20x^2 + 1500x - 24\,000\,.$$

Find the price at which the boots should be sold to maximise the profit.   (OCR)

17 Sketch the graph of an even function $f(x)$ which has a derivative at every point.

Let P be the point on the graph for which $x = p$ (where $p > 0$). Draw the tangent at P on your sketch. Also draw the tangent at the point P' for which $x = -p$.

(a) What is the relationship between the gradient at P' and the gradient at P? What can you deduce about the relationship between $f'(p)$ and $f'(-p)$? What does this tell you about the derivative of an even function?

(b) Show that the derivative of an odd function is even.

8 Sequences

This chapter is about sequences of numbers. When you have completed it, you should

- know that a sequence can be constructed from a formula or an inductive definition
- be familiar with triangle, factorial, Pascal and arithmetic sequences
- know how to find the sum of an arithmetic series.

8.1 Constructing sequences

Here are six rows of numbers, each forming a pattern of some kind. What are the next three numbers in each row?

(a) 1   4   9   16   25 ...

(b) $\frac{1}{2}$ $\frac{2}{3}$ $\frac{3}{4}$ $\frac{4}{5}$ $\frac{5}{6}$ ...

(c) 99   97   95   93   91 ...

(d) 1   1.1   1.21   1.331   1.4641 ...

(e) 2   4   8   14   22 ...

(f) 3   1   4   1   5 ...

Rows of this kind are called **sequences**, and the separate numbers are called **terms**.

The usual notation for the first, second, third, ... terms of a sequence is u_1, u_2, u_3, and so on. There is nothing special about the choice of the letter u, and other letters such as v, x, t and I are often used instead, especially if the sequence appears in some application. If r is a natural number, then the rth term will be u_r, v_r, x_r, t_r or I_r.

Sometimes it is convenient to number the terms $u_0, u_1, u_2, \ldots$, starting with $r = 0$, but you then have to be careful in referring to 'the first term': do you mean u_0 or u_1?

In (a) and (b) you would have no difficulty in writing a formula for the rth term of the sequence. The numbers in (a) could be rewritten as 1^2, 2^2, 3^2, 4^2, 5^2, and the pattern could be summed up by writing

$$u_r = r^2.$$

The terms of (b) are $\dfrac{1}{1+1}, \dfrac{2}{2+1}, \dfrac{3}{3+1}, \dfrac{4}{4+1}, \dfrac{5}{5+1}$, so $u_r = \dfrac{r}{r+1}$.

In (c), (d) and (e) you probably expect that there is a formula, but it is not so easy to find it. What is more obvious is how to get each term from the one before. For example, in (c) the terms go down by 2 at each step, so that $u_2 = u_1 - 2$, $u_3 = u_2 - 2$, $u_4 = u_3 - 2$, and so on. These steps can be summarised by the single equation

$$u_{r+1} = u_r - 2.$$

The terms in (d) are multiplied by 1.1 at each step, so the rule is

$$u_{r+1} = 1.1u_r.$$

Unfortunately, there are many other sequences which satisfy the equation $u_{r+1} = u_r - 2$. Other examples are $10, 8, 6, 4, 2, \ldots$ and $-2, -4, -6, -8, -10, \ldots$.

The definition is not complete until you know the first term. So to complete the definitions of the sequences (c) and (d) you have to write

(c) $u_1 = 99$ and $u_{r+1} = u_r - 2$,

(d) $u_1 = 1$ and $u_{r+1} = 1.1u_r$.

Definitions like these are called **inductive definitions**.

Sequence (e) originates from geometry. It gives the greatest number of regions into which a plane can be split by different numbers of circles. (Try drawing your own diagrams with $1, 2, 3, 4, \ldots$ circles.) This sequence is developed as $u_2 = u_1 + 2$, $u_3 = u_2 + 4$, $u_4 = u_3 + 6$, and so on. Since the increments 2, 4, 6, $\ldots$ are themselves given by the formula $2r$, this can be summarised by the inductive definition

$u_1 = 2$ and $u_{r+1} = u_r + 2r$.

For (f) you may have given the next three terms as 1, 6, 1 (expecting the even-placed terms all to be 1, and the odd-placed terms to go up by 1 at each step). In fact this sequence had a quite different origin, as the first five digits of π in decimal form! With this meaning, the next three terms would be 9, 2, 6.

This illustrates an important point, that a sequence can never be uniquely defined by giving just the first few terms. Try, for example, working out the first eight terms of the sequence defined by

$u_r = r^2 + (r-1)(r-2)(r-3)(r-4)(r-5)$.

You will find that the first five terms are the same as those given in (a), but the next three are probably very different from your original guess.

A sequence can only be described unambiguously by giving a formula, an inductive definition in terms of a general natural number r, or some other general rule.

Exercise 8A

1 Write down the first five terms of the sequences with the following definitions.

(a) $u_1 = 7$, $u_{r+1} = u_r + 7$

(b) $u_1 = 13$, $u_{r+1} = u_r - 5$

(c) $u_1 = 4$, $u_{r+1} = 3u_r$

(d) $u_1 = 6$, $u_{r+1} = \frac{1}{2}u_r$

(e) $u_1 = 2$, $u_{r+1} = 3u_r + 1$

(f) $u_1 = 1$, $u_{r+1} = u_r^2 + 3$

2 Suggest inductive definitions which would produce the following sequences.

(a) 2 4 6 8 10 $\ldots$

(b) 11 9 7 5 3 $\ldots$

(c) 2 6 10 14 18 $\ldots$

(d) 2 6 18 54 162 $\ldots$

(e) $\frac{1}{3}$ $\frac{1}{9}$ $\frac{1}{27}$ $\frac{1}{81}$ $\ldots$

(f) $\frac{1}{2}a$ $\frac{1}{4}a$ $\frac{1}{8}a$ $\frac{1}{16}a$ $\ldots$

(g) $b-2c$ $b-c$ b $b+c$ $\ldots$

(h) 1 -1 1 -1 1 $\ldots$

(i) $\dfrac{p}{q^3}$ $\dfrac{p}{q^2}$ $\dfrac{p}{q}$ $\ldots$

(j) $\dfrac{a^3}{b^2}$ $\dfrac{a^2}{b}$ a b $\ldots$

(k) x^3 $5x^2$ $25x$ $\ldots$

(l) 1 $1+x$ $(1+x)^2$ $(1+x)^3$ $\ldots$

3   Write down the first five terms of each sequence and give an inductive definition for it.

(a) $u_r = 2r + 3$ (b) $u_r = r^2$ (c) $u_r = \frac{1}{2}r(r+1)$

(d) $u_r = \frac{1}{6}r(r+1)(2r+1)$ (e) $u_r = 2 \times 3^r$ (f) $u_r = 3 \times 5^{r-1}$

4   For each of the following sequences give a possible formula for the rth term.

(a)   9   8   7   6   ...   (b)   6   18   54   162   ...

(c)   4   7   12   19   ...   (d)   4   12   24   40   60   ...

(e) $\frac{1}{4}$ $\frac{3}{5}$ $\frac{5}{6}$ $\frac{7}{7}$ ...   (f) $\frac{2}{2}$ $\frac{5}{4}$ $\frac{10}{8}$ $\frac{17}{16}$ ...

8.2   The triangle number sequence

The numbers of crosses in the triangular patterns in Fig. 8.1 are called triangle numbers. If t_r denotes the rth triangle number, you can see by counting the numbers of crosses in successive rows that

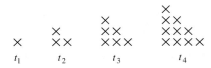

$$t_1 = 1, \quad t_2 = 1 + 2 = 3, \quad t_3 = 1 + 2 + 3 = 6,$$

Fig. 8.1

and in general $t_r = 1 + 2 + 3 + \dots + r$, where the dots indicate that all the natural numbers between 3 and r have to be included in the addition.

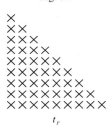

Fig. 8.2 shows a typical pattern of crosses forming a triangle number t_r. (It is in fact drawn for $r = 9$, but any other value of r could have been chosen.) An easy way of finding a formula for t_r is to make a similar pattern of 'noughts', and then to turn it upside down and place it alongside the pattern of crosses, as in Fig. 8.3. The noughts and crosses together then make a rectangular pattern, $r + 1$ objects wide and r objects high. So the total number of objects is $r(r+1)$, half of them crosses and half noughts. The number of crosses alone is therefore

Fig. 8.2

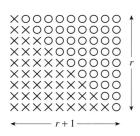

$$t_r = \tfrac{1}{2}r(r+1).$$

This shows that:

Fig. 8.3

> The sum of all the natural numbers from 1 to r
> is $\frac{1}{2}r(r+1)$.

You can put this argument into algebraic form. If you count the crosses from the top downwards you get

$$t_r = 1 + 2 + 3 + \ldots + (r-2) + (r-1) + r,$$

but if you count the noughts from the top downwards you get

$$t_r = r + (r-1) + (r-2) + \ldots + 3 + 2 + 1.$$

Counting all the objects in the rectangle is equivalent to adding these two equations:

$$2t_r = (r+1) + (r+1) + (r+1) + \ldots + (r+1) + (r+1) + (r+1).$$

with one $(r+1)$ bracket for each of the r rows. It follows that $2t_r = r(r+1)$, so that

$$t_r = \tfrac{1}{2}r(r+1).$$

It is also possible to give an inductive definition for the sequence t_r. Fig. 8.1 shows that to get from any triangle number to the next you simply add an extra row of crosses underneath. Thus $t_2 = t_1 + 2, t_3 = t_2 + 3, t_4 = t_3 + 4$, and in general

$$t_{r+1} = t_r + (r+1).$$

You can complete this definition by specifying either $t_1 = 1$ or $t_0 = 0$. If you choose $t_0 = 0$, then you can find t_1 by putting $r = 0$ in the general equation, as $t_1 = t_0 + 1 = 0 + 1 = 1$. So you may as well define the triangle number sequence by

$$t_0 = 0 \quad \text{and} \quad t_{r+1} = t_r + (r+1), \quad \text{where } r = 0, 1, 2, 3, \ldots .$$

8.3 The factorial sequence

If, in the definition of t_r, you go from one term to the next by multiplication rather than addition, you get the factorial sequence

$$f_{r+1} = f_r \times (r+1), \quad \text{where } r = 0, 1, 2, 3, \ldots .$$

There would be little point in defining f_0 to be 0 (think about why this is); instead take f_0 to be 1. (This may seem strange, but you will see the reason in the next chapter.) You then get

$$f_1 = f_0 \times 1 = 1 \times 1 = 1, \quad f_2 = f_1 \times 2 = 1 \times 2 = 2, \quad f_3 = f_2 \times 3 = 2 \times 3 = 6,$$

and if you go on in this way you find that, for any $r \geqslant 1$,

$$f_r = 1 \times 2 \times 3 \times \ldots \times r.$$

This sequence is so important that it has its own special notation, $r!$, read as 'factorial r' or 'r factorial' (or often, colloquially, as 'r shriek').

Factorial r is defined by $0! = 1$ and $(r+1)! = r! \times (r+1)$, where $r = 0, 1, 2, 3, \ldots .$

For $r \geqslant 1$, $r!$ is the product of all the natural numbers from 1 to r.

Many calculators have a special key labelled $[n!]$. For small values of n the display gives the exact value, but the numbers in the sequence increase so rapidly that from about $n = 14$ onwards only an approximate value in standard form can be displayed.

8.4 Pascal sequences

Another important type of sequence based on a multiplication rule is a Pascal sequence. You will find in the next chapter that these sequences feature in the expansion of expressions like $(x+y)^n$. A typical example has an inductive definition

$$p_0 = 1 \quad \text{and} \quad p_{r+1} = \frac{4-r}{r+1} p_r, \quad \text{where } r = 0, 1, 2, 3, \ldots .$$

Using the inductive definition for $r = 0, 1, 2, \ldots$ in turn produces the terms

$$p_1 = \tfrac{4}{1} p_0 = 4, \quad p_2 = \tfrac{3}{2} p_1 = 6, \quad p_3 = \tfrac{2}{3} p_2 = 4,$$

$$p_4 = \tfrac{1}{4} p_3 = 1, \quad p_5 = \tfrac{0}{5} p_4 = 0, \quad p_6 = \tfrac{(-1)}{6} p_5 = 0, \quad \text{and so on.}$$

You will see that at a certain stage the sequence has a zero term, and because it is formed by multiplication all the terms after that will be zero. So the complete sequence is

$$1, 4, 6, 4, 1, 0, 0, 0, 0, 0, \ldots .$$

This is only one of a family of Pascal sequences, and its terms also have a special notation, $\binom{4}{r}$. For example, $\binom{4}{0} = 1$, $\binom{4}{1} = 4$, $\binom{4}{2} = 6$, and so on. Other Pascal sequences have numbers different from 4 in the multiplying factor.

The general definition of a Pascal sequence, whose terms are denoted by $\binom{n}{r}$, is

$$\binom{n}{0} = 1 \quad \text{and} \quad \binom{n}{r+1} = \frac{n-r}{r+1} \binom{n}{r}, \quad \text{where } r = 0, 1, 2, 3, \ldots .$$

Check for yourself that the Pascal sequences for $n = 0, 1, 2, 3$ are

$$
\begin{array}{llccccc}
n = 0: & 1, & 0, & 0, & 0, & 0, & \ldots \\
n = 1: & 1, & 1, & 0, & 0, & 0, & \ldots \\
n = 2: & 1, & 2, & 1, & 0, & 0, & \ldots \\
n = 3: & 1, & 3, & 3, & 1, & 0, & \ldots
\end{array}
$$

The complete pattern of Pascal sequences, without the trailing zeros, is called **Pascal's triangle**. Its earliest recorded use was in China, but Blaise Pascal (a French mathematician of the 17th century, one of the originators of probability theory) was one of the first people in Europe to publish it. It is usually presented in isosceles form (Fig. 8.4), drawing attention to the symmetry of the sequence. But for its algebraic applications the format of Fig. 8.5 is often more convenient, since each column then corresponds to a particular value of r.

Fig. 8.4   Fig. 8.5

You may be surprised to notice that every number in the pattern in Fig. 8.4 except for the 1s is the sum of the two numbers most closely above it.

You have seen these numbers before: look back at sequence (d) in Section 8.1.

Exercise 8B

1   Using Fig. 8.3 as an example,

(a)   draw a pattern of crosses to represent the rth triangle number t_r;

(b)   draw another pattern of noughts to represent t_{r-1};

(c)   combine these two patterns to show that $t_r + t_{r-1} = r^2$.

(d)   Use the fact that $t_r = \frac{1}{2}r(r+1)$ to show the result in part (c) algebraically.

2   (a)   Find an expression in terms of r for $t_r - t_{r-1}$ for all $r \geqslant 1$.

(b)   Use this result and that in Question 1(c) to show that $t_r^2 - t_{r-1}^2 = r^3$.

(c)   Use part (b) to write expressions in terms of triangle numbers for 1^3, 2^3, 3^3, ... , n^3. Hence show that $1^3 + 2^3 + 3^3 + ... + n^3 = \frac{1}{4}n^2(n+1)^2$.

3   Without using a calculator, evaluate the following.

(a) $7!$ (b) $\dfrac{8!}{3!}$ (c) $\dfrac{7!}{4! \times 3!}$

4   Write the following in terms of factorials.

(a) $8 \times 7 \times 6 \times 5$ (b) $9 \times 10 \times 11 \times 12$ (c) $n(n-1)(n-2)$

(d) $n(n^2 - 1)$ (e) $n(n+1)(n+2)(n+3)$ (f) $(n+6)(n+5)(n+4)$

(g) $8 \times 7!$ (h) $n \times (n-1)!$

5   Simplify the following.

(a) $\dfrac{12!}{11!}$ (b) $23! - 22!$ (c) $\dfrac{(n+1)!}{n!}$ (d) $(n+1)! - n!$

6   Show that $\dfrac{(2n)!}{n!} = 2^n(1 \times 3 \times 5 \times ... \times (2n-1))$.

7   Use the inductive definition in Section 8.4 to find the Pascal sequences for

(a) $n = 5$,   (b) $n = 6$,   (c) $n = 8$.

8 Use the inductive definition for $\binom{n}{r}$ to show that $\binom{9}{6} = \dfrac{9 \times 8 \times 7}{1 \times 2 \times 3}$, and show that this can be written as $\dfrac{9!}{6! \times 3!}$.

Use a similar method to write the following in terms of factorials.

(a) $\binom{11}{4}$ (b) $\binom{11}{7}$ (c) $\binom{10}{5}$ (d) $\binom{12}{3}$ (e) $\binom{12}{9}$

9 The answers to Question 8 suggest a general result, that $\binom{n}{r} = \dfrac{n!}{r! \times (n-r)!}$. Assuming this to be true, show that $\binom{n}{r} = \binom{n}{n-r}$.

10 Show by direct calculation that

(a) $\binom{6}{3} + \binom{6}{4} = \binom{7}{4}$,   (b) $\binom{8}{5} + \binom{8}{6} = \binom{9}{6}$.

Write a general statement, involving n and r, suggested by these results.

11 The Pascal sequence for $n = 2$ is   1   2   1.

The sum of the terms in this sequence is $1 + 2 + 1 = 4$.

Investigate the sum of the terms in Pascal sequences for other values of n.

8.5 Arithmetic sequences

An **arithmetic sequence**, or **arithmetic progression**, is a sequence whose terms go up or down by constant steps. Sequence (c) in Section 8.1 is an example. The inductive definition for an arithmetic sequence has the form

$$u_1 = a, \quad u_{r+1} = u_r + d.$$

The number d is called the **common difference**.

Sequence (c) has first term $a = 99$ and common difference $d = -2$.

Example 8.5.1

Senne would like to give a sum of money to a charity each year for 10 years. She decides to give $100 in the first year, and to increase her contribution by $20 each year. How much does she give in the last year, and how much does the charity receive from her altogether?

> Although she makes 10 contributions, there are only 9 increases. So in the last year she gives $\$(100 + 9 \times 20) = \$280$.
>
> If the total amount the charity receives is $\$ S$, then
>
> $$S = 100 + 120 + 140 + \ldots + 240 + 260 + 280.$$
>
> With only 10 numbers it is easy enough to add these up, but you can also find the sum by a method similar to that used to find a formula for t_n. If you add up the numbers in reverse order, you get

$$S = 280 + 260 + 240 + \ldots + 140 + 120 + 100.$$

Adding the two equations then gives

$$2S = 380 + 380 + 380 + \ldots + 380 + 380 + 380,$$

where the number 380 occurs 10 times. So

$$2S = 380 \times 10 = 3800, \text{ giving } S = 1900.$$

Over the 10 years the charity receives \$1900.

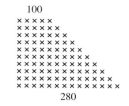

Fig. 8.6

This calculation can be illustrated with diagrams similar to Figs. 8.2 and 8.3. Senne's contributions are shown by Fig. 8.6, with the first year in the top row. (Each cross is worth \$20.) In Fig. 8.7 a second copy, with noughts instead of crosses, is put alongside it, but turned upside down. There are then 10 rows, each with 19 crosses or noughts and worth \$380.

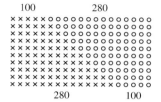

Fig. 8.7

Two features of Example 8.5.1 are typical of arithmetic progressions.

- They usually only continue for a finite number of terms.
- It is often interesting to know the sum of all the terms. In this case, it is usual to describe the sequence as a **series**.

In Example 8.5.1, the annual contributions

$$100, 120, 140, \ldots, 240, 260, 280$$

form an arithmetic sequence, but if they are added as

$$100 + 120 + 140 + \ldots + 240 + 260 + 280$$

they become an **arithmetic series**.

If the general arithmetic sequence

$$a, a+d, a+2d, a+3d, \ldots$$

has n terms in all, then from the first term to the last there are $n-1$ steps of the common difference d. Denote the last term, u_n, by l. Then

$$l = a + (n-1)d.$$

From this equation you can calculate any one of the four quantities a, l, n, d if you know the other three.

Let S be the sum of the arithmetic series formed by adding these terms. Then it is possible to find a formula for S in terms of a, n and either d or l.

Method 1   This generalises the argument used in Example 8.5.1.
The series can be written as

$$S = \quad a \quad +(a+d)+(a+2d)+\ldots+(l-2d)+(l-d)+l.$$

Turning this back to front,

$$S = \quad l \quad +(l-d)+(l-2d)+\ldots+(a+2d)+(a+d)+a.$$

Adding these,

$$2S = (a+l)+(a+l)+(a+l)+\ldots+(a+l)+(a+l)+(a+l),$$

where the bracket $(a+l)$ occurs n times. So

$$2S = n(a+l), \text{ which gives } S = \tfrac{1}{2}n(a+l).$$

Method 2   This uses the formula for triangle numbers found in Section 8.2.
In the series

$$S = a+(a+d)+(a+2d)+\ldots+(a+(n-1)d)$$

you can collect separately the terms involving a and those involving d:

$$S = (a+a+\ldots+a)+(1+2+3+\ldots+(n-1))d.$$

In the first bracket a occurs n times. The second bracket is the sum of the natural
numbers from 1 to $n-1$, or t_{n-1}; using the formula $t_r = \tfrac{1}{2}r(r+1)$ with $r = n-1$ gives
this sum as

$$t_{n-1} = \tfrac{1}{2}(n-1)((n-1)+1) = \tfrac{1}{2}(n-1)n.$$

Therefore

$$S = na + \tfrac{1}{2}(n-1)nd = \tfrac{1}{2}n(2a+(n-1)d).$$

Since $l = a+(n-1)d$, this is the same answer as that given by method 1.

Here is a summary of the results about arithmetic series.

An arithmetic series of n terms with first term a
and common difference d has last term

$$l = a+(n-1)d$$

and sum

$$S = \tfrac{1}{2}n(a+l) = \tfrac{1}{2}n(2a+(n-1)d).$$

Example 8.5.2

Find the sum of the first n odd natural numbers.

Method 1 The odd numbers $1, 3, 5, \ldots$ form an arithmetic series with first term $a = 1$ and common difference $d = 2$. So

$$S = \tfrac{1}{2} n(2a + (n-1)d) = \tfrac{1}{2} n(2 + (n-1)2) = \tfrac{1}{2} n(2n) = n^2 \,.$$

Method 2 Take the natural numbers from 1 to $2n$, and remove the n even numbers $2, 4, 6, \ldots, 2n$. You are left with the first n odd numbers.

The sum of the numbers from 1 to $2n$ is t_r where $r = 2n$, that is

$$t_{2n} = \tfrac{1}{2}(2n)(2n+1) = n(2n+1).$$

The sum of the n even numbers is

$$2 + 4 + 6 + \ldots + 2n = 2(1 + 2 + 3 + \ldots + n) = 2t_n = n(n+1).$$

So the sum of the first n odd numbers is

$$n(2n+1) - n(n+1) = n((2n+1) - (n+1)) = n(n) = n^2 \,.$$

Method 3 Fig. 8.8 shows a square of n rows with n crosses in each row (drawn for $n = 7$). You can count the crosses in the square by adding the numbers in the 'channels' between the dotted L-shaped lines, which gives

$$n^2 = 1 + 3 + 5 + \ldots \text{ (to } n \text{ terms)}.$$

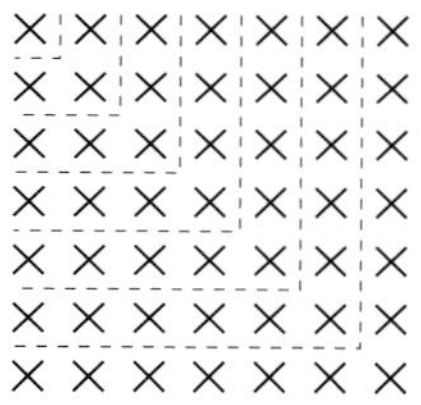

Fig. 8.8

Example 8.5.3

A student reading a 426-page book finds that he reads faster as he gets into the subject. He reads 19 pages on the first day, and his rate of reading then goes up by 3 pages each day. How long does he take to finish the book?

You are given that $a = 19$, $d = 3$ and $S = 426$. Since $S = \tfrac{1}{2} n(2a + (n-1)d)$,

$$426 = \tfrac{1}{2} n(38 + (n-1)3),$$
$$852 = n(3n + 35),$$
$$3n^2 + 35n - 852 = 0.$$

Using the quadratic formula,

$$n = \frac{-35 \pm \sqrt{35^2 - 4 \times 3 \times (-852)}}{2 \times 3} = \frac{-35 \pm 107}{6} \,.$$

Since n must be positive, $n = \dfrac{-35 + 107}{6} = \dfrac{72}{6} = 12$. He will finish the book in 12 days.

Exercise 8C

1 Which of the following sequences are the first four terms of an arithmetic sequence? For those that are, write down the value of the common difference.

  (a) 7   10   13   16   ...   (b) 3   5   9   15   ...   (c) 1   0.1   0.01   0.001   ...

  (d) 4   2   0 -2 ...   (e) 2 -3 4 -5 ...   (f) $p-2q$ $p-q$ p $p+q$ ...

  (g) $\frac{1}{2}a$ $\frac{1}{3}a$ $\frac{1}{4}a$ $\frac{1}{5}a$ ...   (h) x $2x$ $3x$ $4x$ ...

2 Write down the sixth term, and an expression for the rth term, of the arithmetic sequences which begin as follows.

  (a) 2   4   6   ...   (b) 17   20   23   ...   (c) 5   2 -1 ...

  (d) 1.3   1.7   2.1   ...   (e) 1 $1\frac{1}{2}$ 2   ...   (f) 73   67   61   ...

  (g) x $x+2$ $x+4$ ...   (h) $1-x$ 1 $1+x$ ...

3 In the following arithmetic progressions, the first three terms and the last term are given. Find the number of terms.

  (a) 4   5   6   ...   17   (b) 3   9   15   ...   525

  (c) 8   2 -4 ... -202 (d) $2\frac{1}{8}$ $3\frac{1}{4}$ $4\frac{3}{8}$ ... $13\frac{3}{8}$

  (e) $3x$ $7x$ $11x$ ... $43x$ (f) -3 $-1\frac{1}{2}$ 0   ...   12

  (g) $\frac{1}{6}$ $\frac{1}{3}$ $\frac{1}{2}$ ... $2\frac{2}{3}$ (h) $1-2x$ $1-x$ 1   ... $1+25x$

4 Find the sum of the given number of terms of the following arithmetic series.

  (a) $2+5+8+...$ (20 terms)   (b) $4+11+18+...$ (15 terms)

  (c) $8+5+2+...$ (12 terms)   (d) $\frac{1}{2}+1+1\frac{1}{2}+...$ (58 terms)

  (e) $7+3+(-1)+...$ (25 terms)   (f) $1+3+5+...$ (999 terms)

  (g) $a+5a+9a+...$ (40 terms)   (h) $-3p-6p-9p-...$ (100 terms)

5 Find the number of terms and the sum of each of the following arithmetic series.

  (a) $5+7+9+...+111$ (b) $8+12+16+...+84$

  (c) $7+13+19+...+277$ (d) $8+5+2+...+(-73)$

  (e) $-14-10-6-...+94$ (f) $157+160+163+...+529$

  (g) $10+20+30+...+10\,000$ (h) $1.8+1.2+0.6+...+(-34.2)$

6 In each of the following arithmetic sequences you are given two terms. Find the first term and the common difference.

  (a) 4th term $=15$,   9th term $=35$ (b) 3rd term $=12$,   10th term $=47$

  (c) 8th term $=3.5$,   13th term $=5.0$ (d) 5th term $=2$,   11th term $=-13$

  (e) 12th term $=-8$,   20th term $=-32$ (f) 3rd term $=-3$,   7th term $=5$

  (g) 2nd term $=2x$,   11th term $=-7x$ (h) 3rd term $=2p+7$,   7th term $=4p+19$

7 Find how many terms of the given arithmetic series must be taken to reach the given sum.

  (a) $3+7+11+...$,   sum $=820$ (b) $8+9+10+...$,   sum $=162$

  (c) $20+23+26+...$,   sum $=680$ (d) $27+23+19+...$,   sum $=-2040$

  (e) $1.1+1.3+1.5+...$,   sum $=1017.6$ (f) $-11-4+3+...$,   sum $=2338$

8 A squirrel is collecting nuts. It collects 5 nuts on the first day of the month, 8 nuts on the second, 11 on the third and so on in arithmetic progression.

(a) How many nuts will it collect on the 20th day?

(b) After how many days will it have collected more than 1000 nuts?

9 Kulsum is given an interest-free loan to buy a car. She repays the loan in unequal monthly instalments; these start at $30 in the first month and increase by $2 each month after that. She makes 24 payments.

(a) Find the amount of her final payment.   (b) Find the amount of her loan.

10 (a) Find the sum of the natural numbers from 1 to 100 inclusive.

(b) Find the sum of the natural numbers from 101 to 200 inclusive.

(c) Find and simplify an expression for the sum of the natural numbers from $n+1$ to $2n$ inclusive.

11 An employee starts work on 1 January 2000 on an annual salary of $30,000. His pay scale will give him an increase of $800 per annum on the first of January until 1 January 2015 inclusive. He remains on this salary until he retires on 31 December 2040. How much will he earn during his working life?

<hr>

Miscellaneous exercise 8

1 A sequence is defined inductively by $u_{r+1} = 3u_r - 1$ and $u_0 = c$.

(a) Find the first five terms of the sequence if (i) $c = 1$, (ii) $c = 2$, (iii) $c = 0$, (iv) $c = \frac{1}{2}$.

(b) Show that, for each of the values of c in part (a), the terms of the sequence are given by the formula $u_r = \frac{1}{2} + b \times 3^r$ for some value of b.

(c) Show that, if $u_r = \frac{1}{2} + b \times 3^r$ for some value of r, then $u_{r+1} = \frac{1}{2} + b \times 3^{r+1}$.

2 The sequence $u_1, u_2, u_3, \ldots$ is defined by
$$u_1 = 0, \quad u_{r+1} = (2 + u_r)^2.$$
Find the value of u_4.

3 The sequence $u_1, u_2, u_3, \ldots$, where u_1 is a given real number, is defined by
$$u_{n+1} = \sqrt{(4 - u_n)^2}.$$

(a) Given that $u_1 = 1$, evaluate u_2, u_3 and u_4, and describe the behaviour of the sequence.

(b) Given alternatively that $u_1 = 6$, describe the behaviour of the sequence.

(c) For what value of u_1 will all the terms of the sequence be equal to each other?

(OCR, adapted)

4 The sequence $u_1, u_2, u_3, \ldots$, where u_1 is a given real number, is defined by
$$u_{n+1} = u_n^2 - 1.$$

(a) Describe the behaviour of the sequence for each of the cases $u_1 = 0, u_1 = 1$ and $u_1 = 2$.

(b) Given that $u_2 = u_1$, find exactly the two possible values of u_1.

(c) Given that $u_3 = u_1$, show that $u_1^4 - 2u_1^2 - u_1 = 0$.

(OCR)

5   The rth term of an arithmetic progression is $1 + 4r$. Find, in terms of n, the sum of the first n terms of the progression.   (OCR)

6   The sum of the first two terms of an arithmetic progression is 18 and the sum of the first four terms is 52. Find the sum of the first eight terms.   (OCR)

7   The sum of the first twenty terms of an arithmetic progression is 50, and the sum of the next twenty terms is -50. Find the sum of the first hundred terms of the progression.

(OCR)

8   An arithmetic progression has first term a and common difference -1. The sum of the first n terms is equal to the sum of the first $3n$ terms. Express a in terms of n.   (OCR)

9   Find the sum of the arithmetic progression $1, 4, 7, 10, 13, 16, \dots, 1000$.

Every third term of the above progression is removed, i.e. $7, 16$, etc. Find the sum of the remaining terms.   (OCR)

10   The sum of the first hundred terms of an arithmetic progression with first term a and common difference d is T. The sum of the first 50 odd-numbered terms, i.e. the first, third, fifth, $\dots$, ninety-ninth, is $\frac{1}{2}T - 1000$. Find the value of d.   (OCR)

11   In the sequence $1.0, 1.1, 1.2, \dots, 99.9, 100.0$, each number after the first is 0.1 greater than the preceding number. Find

   (a)   how many numbers there are in the sequence,

   (b)   the sum of all the numbers in the sequence.   (OCR)

12   The sequence $u_1, u_2, u_3, \dots$ is defined by $u_n = 2n^2$.

   (a)   Write down the value of u_3.

   (b)   Express $u_{n+1} - u_n$ in terms of n, simplifying your answer.

   (c)   The differences between successive terms of the sequence form an arithmetic progression. For this arithmetic progression, state its first term and its common difference, and find the sum of its first 1000 terms.   (OCR)

13   A small company producing children's toys plans an increase in output. The number of toys produced is to be increased by 8 each week until the weekly number produced reaches 1000. In week 1, the number to be produced is 280; in week 2, the number is 288; etc. Show that the weekly number produced will be 1000 in week 91.

From week 91 onwards, the number produced each week is to remain at 1000. Find the total number of toys to be produced over the first 104 weeks of the plan.   (OCR)

14   In 1971 a newly-built flat was sold with a 999-year lease. The terms of the sale included a requirement to pay 'ground rent' yearly. The ground rent was set at £28 per year for the first 21 years of the lease, increasing by £14 to £42 per year for the next 21 years, and then increasing again by £14 at the end of each subsequent period of 21 years.

   (a)   Find how many complete 21-year periods there would be if the lease ran for the full 999 years, and how many years there would be left over.

   (b)   Find the total amount of ground rent that would be paid in all of the complete 21-year periods of the lease.   (OCR)

15 An arithmetic progression has first term a and common difference 10. The sum of the first n terms of the progression is $10\,000$. Express a in terms of n, and show that the nth term of the progression is

$$\frac{10\,000}{n} + 5(n-1).$$

Given that the nth term is less than 500, show that $n^2 - 101n + 2000 < 0$ and hence find the largest possible value of n. (OCR)

16 Three sequences are defined inductively by

(a) $u_0 = 0$ and $u_{r+1} = u_r + (2r+1)$,

(b) $u_0 = 0$, $u_1 = 1$ and $u_{r+1} = 2u_r - u_{r-1}$ for $r \geqslant 1$,

(c) $u_0 = 1$, $u_1 = 2$ and $u_{r+1} = 3u_r - 2u_{r-1}$ for $r \geqslant 1$.

For each sequence calculate the first few terms, and suggest a formula for u_r. Check that the formula you have suggested does in fact satisfy all parts of the definition.

17 A sequence F_n is constructed from terms of Pascal sequences as follows:

$$F_0 = \binom{0}{0}, \quad F_1 = \binom{1}{0} + \binom{0}{1}, \quad F_2 = \binom{2}{0} + \binom{1}{1} + \binom{0}{2}, \text{ and in general}$$

$$F_n = \binom{n}{0} + \binom{n-1}{1} + \ldots + \binom{1}{n-1} + \binom{0}{n}$$

Show that terms of the sequence F_n can be calculated by adding up numbers in Fig. 8.5 along diagonal lines. Verify by calculation that, for small values of n, $F_{n+1} = F_n + F_{n-1}$. (This is called the *Fibonacci sequence*, after the man who introduced algebra from the Arabic world to Italy in about the year 1200.)

Use the Pascal sequence property $\binom{n}{r} + \binom{n}{r+1} = \binom{n+1}{r+1}$ (see Exercise 8B Question 10) to explain why $F_3 + F_4 = F_5$ and $F_4 + F_5 = F_6$.

9 The binomial theorem

This chapter is about the expansion of $(x+y)^n$, where n is a positive integer (or zero). When you have completed it, you should

- be able to use Pascal's triangle to find the expansion of $(x+y)^n$ when n is small
- know how to calculate the coefficients in the expansion of $(x+y)^n$ when n is large
- be able to use the notation $\binom{n}{r}$ in the context of the binomial theorem.

9.1 Expanding $(x+y)^n$

The binomial theorem is about calculating $(x+y)^n$ quickly and easily. It is useful to start by looking at $(x+y)^n$ for $n = 2, 3$ and 4.

The expansions are:

$$(x+y)^2 = x(x+y) + y(x+y) = x^2 + 2xy + y^2,$$

$$
\begin{aligned}
(x+y)^3 &= (x+y)(x+y)^2 = (x+y)\left(x^2 + 2xy + y^2\right) \\
&= x\left(x^2 + 2xy + y^2\right) + y\left(x^2 + 2xy + y^2\right) \\
&= \begin{array}{cccccccc}
x^3 & + & 2x^2y & + & xy^2 & & \\
& & + & x^2y & + & 2xy^2 & + & y^3 \\
\hline
x^3 & + & 3x^2y & + & 3xy^2 & + & y^3,
\end{array}
\end{aligned}
$$

$$
\begin{aligned}
(x+y)^4 &= (x+y)(x+y)^3 = (x+y)\left(x^3 + 3x^2y + 3xy^2 + y^3\right) \\
&= x\left(x^3 + 3x^2y + 3xy^2 + y^3\right) + y\left(x^3 + 3x^2y + 3xy^2 + y^3\right) \\
&= \begin{array}{cccccccccc}
x^4 & + & 3x^3y & + & 3x^2y^2 & + & xy^3 & & \\
& & + & x^3y & + & 3x^2y^2 & + & 3xy^3 & + & y^4 \\
\hline
x^4 & + & 4x^3y & + & 6x^2y^2 & + & 4xy^3 & + & y^4.
\end{array}
\end{aligned}
$$

You can summarise these results, including $(x+y)^1$, as follows. The coefficients are in bold type.

$$
\begin{aligned}
(x+y)^1 &= \mathbf{1}x + \mathbf{1}y \\
(x+y)^2 &= \mathbf{1}x^2 + \mathbf{2}xy + \mathbf{1}y^2 \\
(x+y)^3 &= \mathbf{1}x^3 + \mathbf{3}x^2y + \mathbf{3}xy^2 + \mathbf{1}y^3 \\
(x+y)^4 &= \mathbf{1}x^4 + \mathbf{4}x^3y + \mathbf{6}x^2y^2 + \mathbf{4}xy^3 + \mathbf{1}y^4
\end{aligned}
$$

Study these expansions carefully. Notice how the powers start from the left with x^n. The powers of x then successively reduce by 1, and the powers of y increase by 1 until reaching the term y^n.

Notice also that the coefficients form the pattern of Pascal's triangle, which you saw in Section 8.4 and which is shown again in Fig. 9.1.

A simple way of building up Pascal's triangleis as follows: start with 1; then add pairs of elements in the row above to get the entry positioned below and between them (as the arrows in Fig. 9.1 show); complete the row with a 1. This is identical to the way in which the two rows are added to give the final result in the expansions of $(x+y)^3$ and $(x+y)^4$ on the previous page.

Row 1				**1**		**1**			
Row 2			**1**		**2**		**1**		
Row 3		**1**		**3** ↘		↙ **3**		**1**	
Row 4	**1**		**4**		**6**		**4**		**1**

Fig. 9.1

You should now be able to predict that the coefficients in the fifth row are

1 5 10 10 5 1

and that

$$(x+y)^5 = x^5 + 5x^4y + 10x^3y^2 + 10x^2y^3 + 5xy^4 + y^5.$$

Example 9.1.1
Write down the expansion of $(1+y)^6$.

Use the next row of Pascal's triangle, continuing the pattern of powers and replacing x by 1:

$$\begin{aligned}(1+y)^6 &= (1)^6 + 6(1)^5y + 15(1)^4y^2 + 20(1)^3y^3 + 15(1)^2y^4 + 6(1)y^5 + y^6 \\ &= 1 + 6y + 15y^2 + 20y^3 + 15y^4 + 6y^5 + y^6.\end{aligned}$$

Example 9.1.2
Multiply out the brackets in the expression $(2x+3)^4$.

Use the expansion of $(x+y)^4$, replacing x by $(2x)$ and replacing y by 3:

$$\begin{aligned}(2x+3)^4 &= (2x)^4 + 4\times(2x)^3\times3 + 6\times(2x)^2\times3^2 + 4\times(2x)\times3^3 + 3^4 \\ &= 16x^4 + 96x^3 + 216x^2 + 216x + 81.\end{aligned}$$

Example 9.1.3
Expand $\left(x^2+2\right)^3$.

$$\left(x^2+2\right)^3 = \left(x^2\right)^3 + 3\times\left(x^2\right)^2\times2 + 3\times x^2\times2^2 + 2^3 = x^6 + 6x^4 + 12x^2 + 8.$$

Example 9.1.4
Find the coefficient of x^3 in the expansion of $(3x-4)^5$.

The term in x^3 comes third in the row with coefficients $1, 5, 10, \ldots$. So the term is

$$10\times(3x)^3\times(-4)^2 = 10\times27\times16x^3 = 4320x^3.$$

The required coefficient is therefore 4320.

Example 9.1.5

Expand $\left(1 + 2x + 3x^2\right)^3$.

To use the binomial expansion, you need to write $1 + 2x + 3x^2$ in a form with two terms rather than three. One way to do this is to consider $\left(1 + \left(2x + 3x^2\right)\right)^3$. Then

$$\left(1 + \left(2x + 3x^2\right)\right)^3 = 1^3 + 3 \times 1^2 \times \left(2x + 3x^2\right) + 3 \times 1 \times \left(2x + 3x^2\right)^2 + \left(2x + 3x^2\right)^3.$$

Now you can use the binomial theorem to expand the bracketed terms:

$$\left(1 + 2x + 3x^2\right)^3 = 1 + 3\left(2x + 3x^2\right) + 3\left(\left(2x\right)^2 + 2 \times \left(2x\right) \times \left(3x^2\right) + \left(3x^2\right)^2\right)$$
$$+ \left(\left(2x\right)^3 + 3 \times \left(2x\right)^2 \times \left(3x^2\right) + 3 \times \left(2x\right) \times \left(3x^2\right)^2 + \left(3x^2\right)^3\right)$$
$$= 1 + \left(6x + 9x^2\right) + \left(12x^2 + 36x^3 + 27x^4\right)$$
$$+ \left(8x^3 + 36x^4 + 54x^5 + 27x^6\right)$$
$$= 1 + 6x + 21x^2 + 44x^3 + 63x^4 + 54x^5 + 27x^6.$$

In this kind of detailed work, it is useful to check your answers. You could do this by expanding $\left(1 + 2x + 3x^2\right)^3$ in the form $\left(\left(1 + 2x\right) + 3x^2\right)^3$ to see if you get the same answer. Rather quicker is to give x a particular value, $x = 1$ for example. Then the left side is $(1 + 2 + 3)^3 = 6^3 = 216$; the right is $1 + 6 + 21 + 44 + 63 + 54 + 27 = 216$. It is important to note that the results are the same, it does not guarantee that the expansion is correct; but if they are different, it is certain that there is a mistake.

Exercise 9A

1   Write down the expansion of each of the following.

     (a) $(2x + y)^2$ (b) $(5x + 3y)^2$ (c) $(4 + 7p)^2$ (d) $(1 - 8t)^2$

     (e) $\left(1 - 5x^2\right)^2$ (f) $\left(2 + x^3\right)^2$ (g) $\left(x^2 + y^3\right)^3$ (h) $\left(3x^2 + 2y^3\right)^3$

2   Write down the expansion of each of the following.

     (a) $(x + 2)^3$ (b) $(2p + 3q)^3$ (c) $(1 - 4x)^3$ (d) $\left(1 - x^3\right)^3$

3   Find the coefficient of x in the expansion of

     (a) $(3x + 7)^2$,   (b) $(2x + 5)^3$.

4   Find the coefficient of x^2 in the expansion of

     (a) $(4x + 5)^3$,   (b) $(1 - 3x)^4$.

5   Expand each of the following expressions.

     (a) $(1 + 2x)^5$ (b) $(p + 2q)^6$ (c) $(2m - 3n)^4$ (d) $\left(1 + \frac{1}{2}x\right)^4$

6   Find the coefficient of x^3 in the expansion of

     (a) $(1 + 3x)^5$,   (b) $(2 - 5x)^4$.

7   Expand $\left(1 + x + 2x^2\right)^2$. Check your answer with a numerical substitution.

8   Write down the expansion of $(x + 4)^3$ and hence expand $(x + 1)(x + 4)^3$.

9 Expand $(3x+2)^2(2x+3)^3$.

10 In the expansion of $(1+ax)^4$, the coefficient of x^3 is 1372. Find the constant a.

11 Expand $(x+y)^{11}$.

12 Find the coefficient of x^6y^6 in the expansion of $(2x+y)^{12}$.

9.2   The binomial theorem

The treatment given in Section 9.1 is fine for finding the coefficients in the expansion of $(x+y)^n$ where n is small, but it is hopelessly inefficient for finding the coefficient of $x^{11}y^4$ in the expansion of $(x+y)^{15}$. Just think of all the rows of Pascal's triangle which you would have to write out! What you need is a formula in terms of n and r for the coefficient of $x^{n-r}y^r$ in the expansion of $(x+y)^n$.

Fortunately, the nth row of Pascal's triangle is the nth Pascal sequence given in Section 8.4. It was shown there that

$$\binom{n}{0}=1 \quad \text{and} \quad \binom{n}{r+1}=\frac{n-r}{r+1}\binom{n}{r}, \quad \text{where } r=0,1,2,\dots .$$

In fact, you can write Pascal's triangle as

Row 1 $\quad\quad\quad\quad\quad \binom{1}{0} \quad\quad \binom{1}{1}$

Row 2 $\quad\quad\quad \binom{2}{0} \quad\quad \binom{2}{1} \quad\quad \binom{2}{2}$

Row 3 $\quad\quad \binom{3}{0} \quad\quad \binom{3}{1} \quad\quad \binom{3}{2} \quad\quad \binom{3}{3}$

Row 4 $\quad \binom{4}{0} \quad\quad \binom{4}{1} \quad\quad \binom{4}{2} \quad\quad \binom{4}{3} \quad\quad \binom{4}{4}$

and so on.

This enables you to write down a neater form of the expansion of $(x+y)^n$.

> The **binomial theorem** states that, if n is a natural number,
>
> $$(x+y)^n = \binom{n}{0}x^n + \binom{n}{1}x^{n-1}y + \binom{n}{2}x^{n-2}y^2 + \dots + \binom{n}{n}y^n.$$

To calculate the coefficients, you can use the inductive formula given at the beginning of this section to generate a formula for $\binom{n}{r}$. For example, to calculate $\binom{4}{2}$, start by putting $n=4$. Then

$$\binom{4}{0}=1, \text{ so } \binom{4}{1}=\frac{4-0}{0+1}\binom{4}{0}=\frac{4}{1}\times 1=\frac{4}{1}, \text{ and } \binom{4}{2}=\frac{4-1}{1+1}\binom{4}{1}=\frac{3}{2}\times\frac{4}{1}=\frac{4\times 3}{1\times 2}.$$

In the general case,

$$\binom{n}{0}=1,\quad \binom{n}{1}=\frac{n-0}{0+1}\times 1=\frac{n}{1},\quad \binom{n}{2}=\frac{n-1}{1+1}\binom{n}{1}=\frac{n-1}{2}\times\frac{n}{1}=\frac{n(n-1)}{1\times 2},\quad\ldots.$$

Continuing in this way, you find that $\binom{n}{r}=\dfrac{n(n-1)\ldots(n-(r-1))}{1\times 2\times\ldots\times r}.$

You can also write $\binom{n}{r}$ in the form

$$\binom{n}{r}=\frac{n(n-1)\ldots(n-(r-1))}{1\times 2\times\ldots\times r}\times\frac{(n-r)\times(n-r-1)\times\ldots\times 2\times 1}{(n-r)\times(n-r-1)\times\ldots\times 2\times 1}=\frac{n!}{r!(n-r)!}.$$

Notice that this formula works for $r=0$ and $r=n$ as well as the values in between, since (from Section 8.3) $0!=1$.

The **binomial coefficients** are given by

$$\binom{n}{r}=\frac{n(n-1)\ldots(n-(r-1))}{1\times 2\times\ldots\times r},\quad\text{or}\quad\binom{n}{r}=\frac{n!}{r!(n-r)!}.$$

When you use the first formula to calculate any particular value of $\binom{n}{r}$, such as $\binom{10}{4}$ or $\binom{12}{7}$, it is helpful to remember that there are as many factors in the top line as there are in the bottom. So you can start by putting in the denominators, and then count down from 10 and 12 respectively, making sure that you have the same number of factors in the numerator as in the denominator.

$$\binom{10}{4}=\frac{10\times 9\times 8\times 7}{1\times 2\times 3\times 4}=210,\quad \binom{12}{7}=\frac{12\times 11\times 10\times 9\times 8\times 7\times 6}{1\times 2\times 3\times 4\times 5\times 6\times 7}=792.$$

Many calculators give you values of $\binom{n}{r}$, usually with a key labelled $[{}_nC_r]$. To find $\binom{10}{4}$, you would normally key in the sequence $[10,\ {}_nC_r,\ 4]$, but you may need to check your calculator manual for details.

Example 9.2.1
Calculate the coefficient of $x^{11}y^4$ in the expansion of $(x+y)^{15}$.

The coefficient is $\binom{15}{4}=\dfrac{15\times 14\times 13\times 12}{1\times 2\times 3\times 4}=1365.$

One other step is required before you can be sure that the values of $\binom{n}{r}$ are the values that you need for the binomial theorem. In Fig. 9.1 you saw that each term of Pascal's triangle, except for the 1s at the end of each row, is obtained by adding the two terms immediately above it. So it should be true that

$$\binom{n+1}{r+1} = \binom{n}{r} + \binom{n}{r+1}.$$

For example:

$$\binom{6}{3} + \binom{6}{4} = \frac{6 \times 5 \times 4}{1 \times 2 \times 3} + \frac{6 \times 5 \times 4 \times 3}{1 \times 2 \times 3 \times 4} = \frac{6 \times 5 \times 4 \times 4 + 6 \times 5 \times 4 \times 3}{1 \times 2 \times 3 \times 4}$$

$$= \frac{6 \times 5 \times 4}{1 \times 2 \times 3 \times 4} \times (4 + 3)$$

$$= \frac{7 \times 6 \times 5 \times 4}{1 \times 2 \times 3 \times 4}$$

$$= \binom{7}{4}.$$

The proof that $\binom{n+1}{r+1} = \binom{n}{r} + \binom{n}{r+1}$ is not easy. You may wish to accept the result and omit the proof, and jump to Example 9.2.2.

To prove this result, start from the right side.

$$\binom{n}{r} + \binom{n}{r+1} = \frac{n(n-1)\dots(n-(r-1))}{1 \times 2 \times \dots \times r} + \frac{n(n-1)\dots(n-r)}{1 \times 2 \times \dots \times r \times (r+1)}$$

$$= \frac{n(n-1)\dots(n-(r-1)) \times (r+1) + n(n-1)\dots(n-r)}{1 \times 2 \times \dots \times r \times (r+1)}$$

$$= \frac{n(n-1)\dots(n-(r-1))}{1 \times 2 \times \dots \times r \times (r+1)} \times \left((r+1) + (n-r)\right)$$

$$= \frac{n(n-1)\dots(n-(r-1))}{1 \times 2 \times \dots \times r \times (r+1)} \times (n+1)$$

$$= \frac{(n+1)n(n-1)\dots((n+1)-r)}{1 \times 2 \times \dots \times r \times (r+1)}$$

$$= \binom{n+1}{r+1}.$$

This completes the chain of reasoning which connects Pascal's triangle with the binomial coefficients.

The following example is one in which the value of x is assumed to be small. When this is the case, say for $x = 0.1$, the successive powers of x decrease by a factor of 10 each time and become very small indeed, so higher powers can be neglected in approximations.

In Example 9.2.2 you are asked to put the terms of a binomial expansion in order of **ascending powers** of x. This means that you start with the term with the smallest power of x, then move to the next smallest, and so on.

Example 9.2.2

Find the first four terms in the expansion of $(2-3x)^{10}$ in ascending powers of x. By putting $x = \frac{1}{100}$, find an approximation to 1.97^{10} correct to the nearest whole number.

$$(2-3x)^{10} = 2^{10} + \binom{10}{1} \times 2^9 \times (-3x) + \binom{10}{2} \times 2^8 \times (-3x)^2 + \binom{10}{3} \times 2^7 \times (-3x)^3 + \dots$$

$$= 1024 - 10 \times 512 \times 3x + \frac{10 \times 9}{1 \times 2} \times 256 \times 9x^2 - \frac{10 \times 9 \times 8}{1 \times 2 \times 3} \times 128 \times 27x^3 + \dots$$

$$= 1024 - 15\,360x + 103\,680x^2 - 414\,720x^3 + \dots .$$

The first four terms are therefore $1024 - 15\,360x + 103\,680x^2 - 414\,720x^3$.

Putting $x = \frac{1}{100}$ gives

$$1.97^{10} \approx 1024 - 15\,360 \times \tfrac{1}{100} + 103\,680 \times \left(\tfrac{1}{100}\right)^2 - 414\,720 \times \left(\tfrac{1}{100}\right)^3$$

$$= 880.353\,28.$$

Therefore $1.97^{10} \approx 880$.

The next term is actually $\binom{10}{4} \times 2^6 \times (3x)^4 = 1\,088\,640x^4 = 0.010\,886\,4$ and the rest are very small indeed.

Exercise 9B

1 Find the value of each of the following.

    (a) $\binom{7}{3}$ (b) $\binom{8}{6}$ (c) $\binom{9}{5}$ (d) $\binom{13}{4}$

    (e) $\binom{6}{4}$ (f) $\binom{10}{2}$ (g) $\binom{11}{10}$ (h) $\binom{50}{2}$

2 Find the coefficient of x^3 in the expansion of each of the following.

    (a) $(1+x)^5$ (b) $(1-x)^8$ (c) $(1+x)^{11}$ (d) $(1-x)^{16}$

3 Find the coefficient of x^5 in the expansion of each of the following.

    (a) $(2+x)^7$ (b) $(3-x)^8$ (c) $(1+2x)^9$ (d) $\left(1-\tfrac{1}{2}x\right)^{12}$

4 Find the coefficient of $x^6 y^8$ in the expansion of each of the following.

    (a) $(x+y)^{14}$ (b) $(2x+y)^{14}$ (c) $(3x-2y)^{14}$ (d) $\left(4x+\tfrac{1}{2}y\right)^{14}$

5 Find the first four terms in the expansion in ascending powers of x of the following.

    (a) $(1+x)^{13}$ (b) $(1-x)^{15}$ (c) $(1+3x)^{10}$ (d) $(2-5x)^7$

6 Find the first three terms in the expansion in ascending powers of x of the following.

    (a) $(1+x)^{22}$ (b) $(1-x)^{30}$ (c) $(1-4x)^{18}$ (d) $(1+6x)^{19}$

7 Find the first three terms in the expansion, in ascending powers of x, of $(1+2x)^8$. By substituting $x = 0.01$, find an approximation to 1.02^8.

8 Find the first three terms in the expansion, in ascending powers of x, of $(2+5x)^{12}$. By substituting a suitable value for x, find an approximation to 2.005^{12} to 2 decimal places.

9 Expand $(1+2x)^{16}$ up to and including the term in x^3. Deduce the coefficient of x^3 in the expansion of $(1+3x)(1+2x)^{16}$.

10 Expand $(1-3x)^{10}$ up to and including the term in x^2. Deduce the coefficient of x^2 in the expansion of $(1+3x)^2(1-3x)^{10}$.

11 Given that the coefficient of x in the expansion of $(1+ax)(1+5x)^{40}$ is 207, determine the value of a.

12 Simplify $(1-x)^8 + (1+x)^8$. Substitute a suitable value of x to find the exact value of $0.99^8 + 1.01^8$.

13 Given that the expansion of $(1+ax)^n$ begins $1+36x+576x^2$, find the values of a and n.

Miscellaneous exercise 9

1 Expand $(3+4x)^3$.

2 Find the first three terms in the expansions, in ascending powers of x, of

    (a) $(1+4x)^{10}$,   (b) $(1-2x)^{16}$.

3 Find the coefficient of a^3b^5 in the expansions of

    (a) $(3a-2b)^8$,   (b) $\left(5a + \tfrac{1}{2}b\right)^8$.

4 Expand $(3+5x)^7$ in ascending powers of x up to and including the term in x^2. By putting $x = 0.01$, find an approximation, correct to the nearest whole number, to 3.05^7.

5 Obtain the first four terms in the expansion of $\left(2 + \tfrac{1}{4}x\right)^8$ in ascending powers of x. By substituting an appropriate value of x into this expansion, find the value of 2.0025^8 correct to three decimal places.   (OCR)

6 Find, in ascending powers of x, the first three terms in the expansion of $(2-3x)^8$. Use the expansion to find the value of 1.997^8 to the nearest whole number.   (OCR)

7 Expand $\left(x^2 + \dfrac{1}{x}\right)^3$, simplifying each of the terms.

8 Expand $\left(2x - \dfrac{3}{x^2}\right)^4$.

9   Expand and simplify $\left(x + \dfrac{1}{2x}\right)^6 + \left(x - \dfrac{1}{2x}\right)^6$.   (OCR)

10   Find the coefficient of x^2 in the expansion of $\left(x^4 + \dfrac{4}{x}\right)^3$.

11   Find the term independent of x in the expansion of $\left(2x + \dfrac{5}{x}\right)^6$.

12   Find the coefficient of y^4 in the expansion of $(1 + y)^{12}$. Deduce the coefficient of
     (a) y^4 in the expansion of $(1 + 3y)^{12}$,
     (b) y^8 in the expansion of $\left(1 - 2y^2\right)^{12}$,
     (c) $x^8 y^4$ in the expansion of $\left(x + \tfrac{1}{2} y\right)^{12}$.

13   Determine the coefficient of $p^4 q^7$ in the expansion of $(2p - q)(p + q)^{10}$.

14   Find the first three terms in the expansion of $(1 + 2x)^{20}$. By substitution of a suitable value of x in each case, find approximations to
     (a) 1.002^{20},   (b) 0.996^{20}.

15   Write down the first three terms in the binomial expansion of $\left(2 - \dfrac{1}{2x^2}\right)^{10}$ in ascending powers of x. Hence find the value of 1.995^{10} correct to three significant figures.   (OCR)

16   Two of the following expansions are correct and two are incorrect. Find the two expansions which are incorrect.
     A: $(3 + 4x)^5 = 243 + 1620x + 4320x^2 + 5760x^3 + 3840x^4 + 1024x^5$
     B: $\left(1 - 2x + 3x^2\right)^3 = 1 + 6x - 3x^2 + 28x^3 - 9x^4 + 54x^5 - 27x^6$
     C: $(1 - x)(1 + 4x)^4 = 1 + 15x + 80x^2 + 160x^3 - 256x^5$
     D: $(2x + y)^2 (3x + y)^3 = 108x^5 + 216x^4 y + 171x^3 y^2 + 67x^2 y^3 + 13xy^4 + y^6$

17   Find and simplify the term independent of x in the expansion of $\left(\dfrac{1}{2x} + x^3\right)^8$.   (OCR)

18   Find the term independent of x in the expansion of $\left(2x + \dfrac{1}{x^2}\right)^9$.

19   Evaluate the term which is independent of x in the expansion of $\left(x^2 - \dfrac{1}{2x^2}\right)^{16}$.   (OCR)

20   Find the coefficient of x^{-12} in the expansion of $\left(x^3 - \dfrac{1}{x}\right)^{24}$.   (OCR)

21   Expand $\left(1 + 3x + 4x^2\right)^4$ in ascending powers of x as far as the term in x^2. By substituting a suitable of x, find an approximation to 1.0304^4.

22   Expand and simplify $(3x + 5)^3 - (3x - 5)^3$.
     Hence solve the equation $(3x + 5)^3 - (3x - 5)^3 = 730$.

23   Solve the equation $(7 - 6x)^3 + (7 + 6x)^3 = 1736$.

24 Find, in ascending powers of t, the first three terms in the expansions of

    (a) $(1+\alpha t)^5$,   (b) $(1-\beta t)^8$.

Hence find, in terms of α and β, the coefficient of t^2 in the expansion of $(1+\alpha t)^5(1-\beta t)^8$.

(OCR)

25 (a) Show that

    (i) $\dbinom{6}{4}=\dbinom{6}{2}$,   (ii) $\dbinom{10}{3}=\dbinom{10}{7}$,   (iii) $\dbinom{15}{12}=\dbinom{15}{3}$,   (iv) $\dbinom{13}{6}=\dbinom{13}{7}$.

    (b) State the possible values of x in each of the following.

    (i) $\dbinom{11}{4}=\dbinom{11}{x}$ (ii) $\dbinom{16}{3}=\dbinom{16}{x}$ (iii) $\dbinom{20}{7}=\dbinom{20}{x}$ (iv) $\dbinom{45}{17}=\dbinom{45}{x}$

    (c) Use the definition $\dbinom{n}{r}=\dfrac{n!}{r!(n-r)!}$ to prove that $\dbinom{n}{r}=\dbinom{n}{n-r}$.

26 The inductive property $\dbinom{n}{r+1}=\dfrac{n-r}{r+1}\dbinom{n}{r}$ was given in Section 8.4. Use this to prove the Pascal triangle property that $\dbinom{n}{r}+\dbinom{n}{r+1}=\dbinom{n+1}{r+1}$.

27 (a) Show that

    (i) $4\times\dbinom{6}{2}=3\times\dbinom{6}{3}=6\times\dbinom{5}{2}$,   (ii) $3\times\dbinom{7}{4}=5\times\dbinom{7}{5}=7\times\dbinom{6}{4}$.

    (b) State numbers a, b and c such that

    (i) $a\times\dbinom{8}{5}=b\times\dbinom{8}{6}=c\times\dbinom{7}{5}$,   (ii) $a\times\dbinom{9}{3}=b\times\dbinom{9}{4}=c\times\dbinom{8}{3}$.

    (c) Prove that $(n-r)\times\dbinom{n}{r}=(r+1)\times\dbinom{n}{r+1}=n\times\dbinom{n-1}{r}$.

28 Prove that $\dbinom{n}{r-1}+2\dbinom{n}{r}+\dbinom{n}{r+1}=\dbinom{n+2}{r+1}$.

29 Find the value of 1.0003^{18} correct to 15 decimal places.

30 (a) Expand $\left(2\sqrt{2}+\sqrt{3}\right)^4$ in the form $a+b\sqrt{6}$, where a and b are integers.

    (b) Find the exact value of $\left(2\sqrt{2}+\sqrt{3}\right)^5$.

31 (a) Expand and simplify $\left(\sqrt{7}+\sqrt{5}\right)^4+\left(\sqrt{7}-\sqrt{5}\right)^4$. By using the fact that $0<\sqrt{7}-\sqrt{5}<1$, state the consecutive integers between which $\left(\sqrt{7}+\sqrt{5}\right)^4$ lies.

    (b) Without using a calculator, find the consecutive integers between which the value of $\left(\sqrt{3}+\sqrt{2}\right)^6$ lies.

32 Find an expression, in terms of n, for the coefficient of x in the expansion

$$(1+4x)+(1+4x)^2+(1+4x)^3+\ldots+(1+4x)^n.$$

33 Given that

$$a+b(1+x)^3+c(1+2x)^3+d(1+3x)^3=x^3$$

for all values of x, find the values of the constants a, b, c and d.

10 Trigonometry

This chapter develops work on sines, cosines and tangents. When you have completed it, you should

- know the shapes of the graphs of sine, cosine and tangent for all angles
- know, or be able to find, exact values of the sine, cosine and tangent of certain special angles
- be able to solve simple trigonometric equations
- know and be able to use identities involving $\sin\theta°$, $\cos\theta°$ and $\tan\theta°$.

10.1 The graph of $\cos\theta°$

Letters of the Greek alphabet are often used to denote angles. In this chapter, θ (theta) and ϕ (phi) will usually be used.

You probably first used $\cos\theta°$ in calculations with right-angled triangles, so that $0 < \theta < 90$. Then you may have used it in any triangle, with $0 < \theta < 180$. However, if you have a graphic calculator, you will find that it produces a graph of $\cos\theta°$ like that in Fig. 10.3. This section extends the definition of $\cos\theta°$ to angles of any size, positive or negative.

Fig. 10.1 shows a circle of radius 1 unit with centre O; the circle meets the x-axis at A. Draw a line OP at an angle θ to the x-axis, to meet the circle at P. Draw a perpendicular from P to meet OA at N. Let $ON = x$ units and $NP = y$ units, so that the coordinates of P are (x,y).

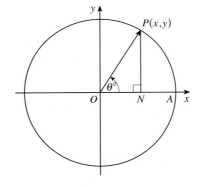

Look at triangle ONP. Using the definition $\cos\theta° = \dfrac{ON}{OP}$, you find that $\cos\theta° = \dfrac{x}{1} = x$.

This result, $\cos\theta° = x$, is used as the definition of $\cos\theta°$ for all values of θ.

You can see the consequences of this definition whenever θ is a multiple of 90.

Fig. 10.1

Example 10.1.1
Find the value of $\cos\theta°$ when   (a) $\theta = 180$,   (b) $\theta = 270$.

(a) When $\theta = 180$, P is the point $(-1,0)$. As the x-coordinate of P is -1, $\cos 180° = -1$.

(b) When $\theta = 270$, P is the point $(0,-1)$, so $\cos 270° = 0$.

As θ increases, the point P moves round the circle. When $\theta = 360$, P is once again at A, and as θ becomes greater than 360, the point P moves round the circle again. It follows immediately that $\cos(\theta - 360)° = \cos\theta°$, and that the values of $\cos\theta°$ repeat themselves every time θ increases by 360.

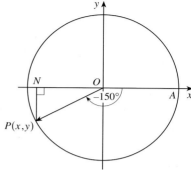

If $\theta < 0$, the angle θ is drawn in the opposite direction, starting once again from A. Fig. 10.2 shows the angle $-150°$ drawn. Thus, if $\theta = -150$, P is in the third quadrant, and, since the x-coordinate of P is negative, $\cos(-150)°$ is negative.

A calculator will give you values of $\cos\theta°$ for all values of θ. If you have access to a graphic calculator you should use it to display the graph of $\cos\theta°$, shown in Fig. 10.3.

Fig. 10.2

You will have to input the equation of the graph of $\cos\theta°$ *as* $y = \cos x$ *into the calculator, and make sure that the calculator is in degree mode.*

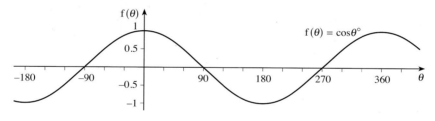

Fig. 10.3

Note that the range of the cosine function is $-1 \leqslant \cos\theta° \leqslant 1$. The maximum value of 1 is taken at $\theta = 0, \pm 360, \pm 720, \dots$, and the minimum of -1 at $\theta = \pm 180, \pm 540, \dots$.

The graph of the cosine function keeps repeating itself. Functions with this property are called **periodic**; the **period** of such a function is the smallest interval for which the function repeats itself. The period of the cosine function is therefore 360. The property that $\cos(\theta \pm 360)° = \cos\theta°$ is called the **periodic property**. Many natural phenomena have periodic properties, and the cosine is often used in applications involving them.

Example 10.1.2

The height in metres of the water in a harbour is given approximately by the formula $d = 6 + 3\cos 30t°$ where t is the time in hours from noon. Find (a) the height of the water at 9.45 p.m., and (b) the highest and lowest water levels, and when they occur.

(a) At 9.45 p.m., $t = 9.75$, so $d = 6 + 3\cos(30 \times 9.75)° = 6 + 3\cos 292.5° = 7.148\dots$. Therefore the height of the water is 7.15 metres, correct to 3 significant figures.

(b) The maximum value of d occurs when the value of the cosine function is 1, and is therefore $6 + 3 \times 1 = 9$. Similarly, the minimum value is $6 + 3 \times (-1) = 3$. The highest and lowest water levels are 9 metres and 3 metres. The first times that they occur after noon are when $30t = 360$ and $30t = 180$; that is, at midnight and 6.00 p.m.

10.2 The graphs of $\sin\theta°$ and $\tan\theta°$

Using the same construction as for the cosine (see Fig. 10.1), the sine function is defined by

$$\sin\theta° = \frac{NP}{OP} = \frac{y}{1} = y.$$

Like the cosine graph, the sine graph (shown in Fig. 10.4) is periodic, with period 360.
It also lies between -1 and 1 inclusive.

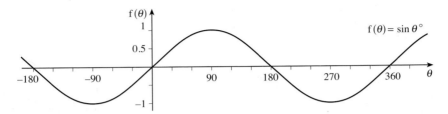

Fig. 10.4

If you return to Fig. 10.1, you will see that $\tan\theta° = \dfrac{NP}{ON} = \dfrac{y}{x}$; this is taken as the
definition of $\tan\theta°$. The domain of $\tan\theta°$ does not include those angles for which x is
zero, namely $\theta = \pm90, \pm270, \ldots$. Fig. 10.5 shows the graph of $\tan\theta°$.

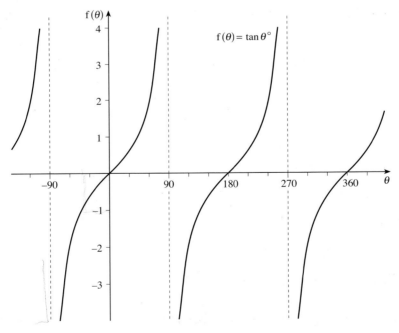

Fig. 10.5

Like the graphs of $\cos\theta°$ and $\sin\theta°$, the graph of $\tan\theta°$ is periodic, but its period is
180. Thus $\tan(\theta\pm180)° = \tan\theta°$.

As $\cos\theta° = x$, $\sin\theta° = y$ and $\tan\theta° = \dfrac{y}{x}$, it follows that $\tan\theta° = \dfrac{\sin\theta°}{\cos\theta°}$. You could use this as an alternative definition of $\tan\theta°$.

10.3 Exact values of some trigonometric functions

There are a few angles which are a whole number of degrees and whose sines, cosines and tangents you can find exactly. The most important of these are $45°$, $60°$ and $30°$.

To find the cosine, sine and tangent of $45°$, draw a right-angled isosceles triangle of side 1 unit, as in Fig. 10.6. The length of the hypotenuse is then $\sqrt{2}$ units. Then

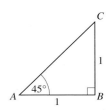

$$\cos 45° = \frac{1}{\sqrt{2}}, \quad \sin 45° = \frac{1}{\sqrt{2}}, \quad \tan 45° = 1.$$

If you rationalise the denominators you get

$$\cos 45° = \frac{\sqrt{2}}{2}, \quad \sin 45° = \frac{\sqrt{2}}{2}, \quad \tan 45° = 1.$$

Fig. 10.6

To find the cosine, sine and tangent of $60°$ and $30°$, draw an equilateral triangle of side 2 units, as in Fig. 10.7. Draw a perpendicular from one vertex, bisecting the opposite side. This perpendicular has length $\sqrt{3}$ units, and it makes an angle of $30°$ with AC. Then

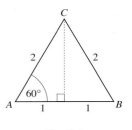

$$\cos 60° = \frac{1}{2}, \qquad \sin 60° = \frac{\sqrt{3}}{2}, \qquad \tan 60° = \sqrt{3};$$

$$\cos 30° = \frac{\sqrt{3}}{2}, \qquad \sin 30° = \frac{1}{2}, \qquad \tan 30° = \frac{1}{\sqrt{3}} = \frac{\sqrt{3}}{3}.$$

Fig. 10.7

You should learn these results, or be able to reproduce them quickly.

Example 10.3.1
Write down the exact values of   (a) $\cos 135°$,   (b) $\sin 120°$,   (c) $\tan 495°$.

(a) From Fig. 10.3, $\cos 135° = -\cos 45° = -\frac{1}{2}\sqrt{2}$.

(b) From Fig. 10.4, $\sin 120° = \sin 60° = \frac{1}{2}\sqrt{3}$.

(c) From Fig. 10.5, $\tan 495° = \tan(495 - 360)° = \tan 135° = -\tan 45° = -1$.

Exercise 10A

1   For each of the following values of θ find, correct to 4 decimal places, the values of
    (i) $\cos\theta°$,   (ii) $\sin\theta°$,   (iii) $\tan\theta°$.

   (a)   25   (b)   125   (c)   225   (d)   325

   (e)   −250   (f)   67.4   (g)   124.9   (h)   554

2 Find the maximum value and the minimum value of each of the following functions. In each case, give the least positive values of x at which they occur.

(a) $2 + \sin x°$

(b) $7 - 4\cos x°$

(c) $5 + 8\cos 2x°$

(d) $\dfrac{8}{3 - \sin x°}$

(e) $9 + \sin(4x - 20)°$

(f) $\dfrac{30}{11 - 5\cos\left(\frac{1}{2}x - 45\right)°}$

3 (Do not use a calculator for this question.) In each part of the question a trigonometric function of a number is given. Find all the other numbers x, $0 \leqslant x \leqslant 360$, such that the same function of x is equal to the given trigonometric ratio. For example, if you are given $\sin 80°$, then $x = 100$, since $\sin 100° = \sin 80°$.

(a) $\sin 20°$

(b) $\cos 40°$

(c) $\tan 60°$

(d) $\sin 130°$

(e) $\cos 140°$

(f) $\tan 160°$

(g) $\sin 400°$

(h) $\cos(-30)°$

(i) $\tan 430°$

(j) $\sin(-260)°$

(k) $\cos(-200)°$

(l) $\tan 1000°$

4 (Do not use a calculator for this question.) In each part of the question a trigonometric function of a number is given. Find all the other numbers x, $-180 \leqslant x \leqslant 180$, such that the same function of x is equal to the given trigonometric ratio. For example, if you are given $\sin 80°$, then $x = 100$, since $\sin 100° = \sin 80°$.

(a) $\sin 20°$

(b) $\cos 40°$

(c) $\tan 60°$

(d) $\sin 130°$

(e) $\cos 140°$

(f) $\tan 160°$

(g) $\sin 400°$

(h) $\cos(-30)°$

(i) $\tan 430°$

(j) $\sin(-260)°$

(k) $\cos(-200)°$

(l) $\tan 1000°$

5 Without using a calculator, write down the exact values of the following.

(a) $\sin 135°$

(b) $\cos 120°$

(c) $\sin(-30)°$

(d) $\tan 240°$

(e) $\cos 225°$

(f) $\tan(-330)°$

(g) $\cos 900°$

(h) $\tan 510°$

(i) $\sin 225°$

(j) $\cos 630°$

(k) $\tan 405°$

(l) $\sin(-315)°$

(m) $\sin 210°$

(n) $\tan 675°$

(o) $\cos(-120)°$

(p) $\sin 1260°$

6 Without using a calculator, write down the smallest positive angle which satisfies the following equations.

(a) $\cos \theta° = \frac{1}{2}$

(b) $\sin \phi° = -\frac{1}{2}\sqrt{3}$

(c) $\tan \theta° = -\sqrt{3}$

(d) $\cos \theta° = \frac{1}{2}\sqrt{3}$

(e) $\tan \theta° = \frac{1}{3}\sqrt{3}$

(f) $\tan \phi° = -1$

(g) $\sin \theta° = -\frac{1}{2}$

(h) $\cos \theta° = 0$

7 Without using a calculator, write down the angle with the smallest modulus which satisfies the following equations. (If there are two such angles, choose the positive one.)

(a) $\cos \theta° = -\frac{1}{2}$

(b) $\tan \phi° = \sqrt{3}$

(c) $\sin \theta° = -1$

(d) $\cos \theta° = -1$

(e) $\sin \phi° = \frac{1}{2}\sqrt{3}$

(f) $\tan \theta° = -\frac{1}{3}\sqrt{3}$

(g) $\sin \phi° = -\frac{1}{2}\sqrt{2}$

(h) $\tan \phi° = 0$

8 The water levels in a dock follow (approximately) a twelve-hour cycle, and are modelled by the equation $D = A + B\sin 30t°$, where D metres is the depth of water in the dock, A and B are positive constants, and t is the time in hours after 8 a.m.

Given that the greatest and least depths of water in the dock are 7.80 m and 2.20 m respectively, find the value of A and the value of B.

Find the depth of water in the dock at noon, giving your answer correct to the nearest cm.

10.4 Symmetry properties of the graphs of $\cos\theta°$, $\sin\theta°$ and $\tan\theta°$

If you examine the graphs of $\cos\theta°$, $\sin\theta°$ and $\tan\theta°$, you can see that they have many symmetry properties. The graph of $\cos\theta°$ is shown in Fig. 10.8.

The graph of $\cos\theta°$ is symmetrical about the vertical axis. This means that if you replace θ by $-\theta$ the graph is unchanged. Therefore

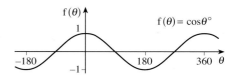

$$\cos(-\theta)° = \cos\theta° .$$

This shows that $\cos\theta°$ is an even function of θ (as defined in Section 3.3).

Fig. 10.8

There are other symmetry properties. For example, from Fig. 10.8 you can see that if you decrease (or increase) θ by 180 you change the sign of $f(\theta)$. Therefore

$$\cos(\theta - 180)° = -\cos\theta° .$$

This is called the translation property.

There is one more useful symmetry property. Using the even and translation properties,

$$\cos(180 - \theta)° = \cos(\theta - 180)° = -\cos\theta° .$$

You may have met this property in using the cosine formula for a triangle.

There are similar properties for the graph of $\sin\theta°$, which is shown in Fig. 10.9. You are asked to prove them as part of Exercise 10B. Their proofs are similar to those for the cosine.

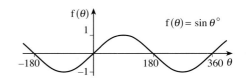

Fig. 10.9

The functions $\cos\theta°$ and $\sin\theta°$ have the following properties.

Periodic property: $\cos(\theta \pm 360)° = \cos\theta°$ $\sin(\theta \pm 360)° = \sin\theta°$

Odd property: $\cos(-\theta)° = \cos\theta°$ $\sin(-\theta)° = -\sin\theta°$

Translation property: $\cos(\theta - 180)° = -\cos\theta°$ $\sin(\theta - 180)° = -\sin\theta°$

  $\cos(180 - \theta)° = -\cos\theta°$ $\sin(180 - \theta)° = \sin\theta°$

If you refer back to the graph of $\tan\theta°$ in Fig. 10.5, and think in the same way as with the cosine and sine graphs, you can obtain similar results:

The function $\tan\theta°$ has the following properties.

Periodic property: $\qquad \tan(\theta \pm 180)° = \tan\theta°$

Odd property: $\qquad\qquad \tan(-\theta)° = -\tan\theta°$

$\qquad\qquad\qquad\qquad\quad \tan(180-\theta)° = -\tan\theta°$

Note that the period of the graph of $\tan\theta°$ is 180, and that the translation property of $\tan\theta°$ is the same as the periodic property.

There are also relations between $\cos\theta°$ and $\sin\theta°$. One is shown in Example 10.4.1.

Example 10.4.1
Establish the property that $\cos(90-\theta)° = \sin\theta°$.

This is easy if $0 < \theta < 90$: consider a right-angled triangle. But it can be shown for any value of θ.

If you translate the graph of $\cos\theta°$ by 90 in the direction of the positive θ-axis, you obtain the graph of $\sin\theta°$, so $\cos(\theta-90)° = \sin\theta°$. And since the cosine is an even function, $\cos(90-\theta)° = \cos(\theta-90)°$. Therefore $\cos(90-\theta)° = \sin\theta°$.

Another property, which you are asked to prove in Exercise 10B, is $\sin(90-\theta)° = \cos\theta°$.

Exercise 10B

1 Use the symmetric and periodic properties of the sine, cosine and tangent functions to establish the following results.

   (a) $\sin(90-\theta)° = \cos\theta°$ (b) $\sin(270+\theta)° = -\cos\theta°$

   (c) $\sin(90+\theta)° = \cos\theta°$ (d) $\cos(90+\theta)° = -\sin\theta°$

   (e) $\tan(\theta-180)° = \tan\theta°$ (f) $\cos(180-\theta)° = \cos(180+\theta)°$

   (g) $\tan(360-\theta)° = -\tan(180+\theta)°$ (h) $\sin(-\theta-90)° = -\cos\theta°$

2 Sketch the graphs of $y = \tan\theta°$ and $y = \dfrac{1}{\tan\theta°}$ on the same set of axes.
   Show that $\tan(90-\theta)° = \dfrac{1}{\tan\theta°}$.

3 In each of the following cases find the least positive value of α for which

   (a) $\cos(\alpha-\theta)° = \sin\theta°$,   (b) $\sin(\alpha-\theta)° = \cos(\alpha+\theta)°$,

   (c) $\tan\theta° = \tan(\theta+\alpha)°$,   (d) $\sin(\theta+2\alpha)° = \cos(\alpha-\theta)°$,

   (e) $\cos(2\alpha-\theta)° = \cos(\theta-\alpha)°$,   (f) $\sin(5\alpha+\theta)° = \cos(\theta-3\alpha)°$.

10.5 Solving equations involving the trigonometric functions

Solving the equation $\cos\theta° = k$

To solve the equation $\cos\theta° = k$, you need to assume that $-1 \leq k \leq 1$. If this is not true, there is no solution. In Fig. 10.10, a negative value of k is shown. Note that, in general, there are two roots to the equation $\cos\theta° = k$ in every interval of $360°$, the exceptions being when $k = \pm1$.

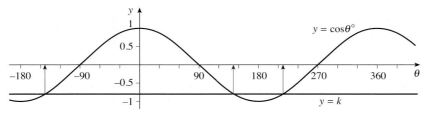

Fig. 10.10

To find an angle θ which satisfies the equation you can use the $[\cos^{-1}]$ key on your calculator (or, on some calculators, the [ARCCOS] key), but unfortunately it will only give you one answer. Usually you want to find all the roots of $\cos\theta° = k$ in a given interval (probably one of width 360). The problem then is how to find all the other roots in your required interval.

There are three steps in solving the equation of $\cos\theta° = k$.

Step 1 Find $\cos^{-1}k$.

Step 2 Use the symmetry property $\cos(-\theta)° = \cos\theta°$ to find another root.

Step 3 Use the periodic property $\cos(\theta \pm 360)° = \cos\theta°$ to find the roots in the required interval.

Example 10.5.1

Solve the equation $\cos\theta° = \frac{1}{3}$, giving all roots in the interval $0 \leq \theta \leq 360$ correct to 1 decimal place.

Step 1 Use your calculator to find $\cos^{-1}\frac{1}{3} = 70.52\ldots$. This is one root in the interval $0 \leq \theta \leq 360$.

Step 2 Use the symmetry property $\cos(-\theta)° = \cos\theta°$ to show that $-70.52\ldots$ is another root. Note that $-70.52\ldots$ is not in the required interval.

Step 3 Use the periodic property, $\cos(\theta \pm 360)° = \cos\theta°$, to obtain $-70.52\ldots + 360 = 289.47\ldots$, which is a root in the required interval.

Therefore the roots in the interval $0 \leq \theta \leq 360$ are 70.5 and 289.5, correct to 1 decimal place.

Example 10.5.2

Solve the equation $\cos 3\theta° = -\frac{1}{2}$, giving all the roots in the interval $-180 \leqslant \theta \leqslant 180$.

This example is similar to the previous example, except for an important extra step at the beginning, and another at the end.

Let $3\theta = \phi$. Then you have to solve the equation $\cos\phi° = -\frac{1}{2}$. But, as $3\theta = \phi$, if $-180 \leqslant \theta \leqslant 180$, then $3 \times (-180) \leqslant 3\theta \leqslant 3 \times 180$ so $-540 \leqslant \phi \leqslant 540$. So the original problem has become: solve the equation $\cos\phi° = -\frac{1}{2}$ giving all the roots in the interval $-540 \leqslant \phi \leqslant 540$. (You should expect six roots of the equation in this interval.)

Step 1 $\cos^{-1}\left(-\frac{1}{2}\right) = 120$.

Step 2   Another root is -120.

Step 3   Adding and subtracting multiples of 360 shows that $-120 - 360 = -480$, $-120 + 360 = 240$, $120 - 360 = -240$ and $120 + 360 = 480$ are also roots.

Therefore the roots of $\cos\phi° = -\frac{1}{2}$ in $-540 \leqslant \phi \leqslant 540$ are -480, -240, -120, 120, 240 and 480.

Returning to the original equation, and using the fact that $\theta = \frac{1}{3}\phi$, the roots are $-160, -80, -40, 40, 80$ and 160.

Solving the equation $\sin\theta° = k$

The equation $\sin\theta° = k$, where $-1 \leqslant k \leqslant 1$ is solved in a similar way. The only difference is that the symmetry property for $\sin\theta°$ is $\sin(180 - \theta)° = \sin\theta°$.

Step 1   Find $\sin^{-1}k$.

Step 2   Use the symmetry property
$\sin(180 - \theta)° = \sin\theta°$ to find another root.

Step 3   Use the periodic property $\sin(\theta \pm 360)° = \sin\theta°$ to find the roots in the required interval.

Example 10.5.3

Solve the equation $\sin\theta° = -0.7$, giving all the roots in the interval $-180 \leqslant \theta \leqslant 180$ correct to 1 decimal place.

Step 1   Use your calculator to find $\sin^{-1}(-0.7) = -44.42\ldots$. This is one root in the interval $-180 \leqslant \theta \leqslant 180$.

Step 2 Use the symmetry property $\sin(180 - \theta)° = \sin\theta°$ to show that $180 - (-44.42\ldots) = 224.42\ldots$ is another root. Unfortunately it is not in the required interval.

Step 3 Use the periodic property, $\sin(\theta \pm 360)° = \sin\theta°$, to obtain $224.42\ldots - 360 = -135.57\ldots$, which is a root in the required interval.

Therefore the roots in the interval $-180 \leqslant \theta \leqslant 180$ are -44.4 and -135.6, correct to 1 decimal place.

Example 10.5.4

Solve the equation $\sin\frac{1}{3}(\theta - 30)° = \frac{1}{2}\sqrt{3}$, giving all the roots in the interval $0 \leqslant \theta \leqslant 360$.

Let $\frac{1}{3}(\theta - 30) = \phi$, so that the equation becomes $\sin\phi° = \frac{1}{2}\sqrt{3}$, with roots required in the interval $-10 \leqslant \phi \leqslant 110$.

Step 1 $\sin^{-1}\left(\frac{1}{2}\sqrt{3}\right) = 60$. This is one root in the interval $-10 \leqslant \phi \leqslant 110$.

Step 2 Another root is $180 - 60 = 120$, but this is not in the required interval.

Step 3 Adding and subtracting multiples of 360 will not give any more roots in the interval $-10 \leqslant \phi \leqslant 110$.

Therefore the only root of $\sin\phi° = \frac{1}{2}\sqrt{3}$ in $-10 \leqslant \phi \leqslant 110$ is 60.

Returning to the original equation, since $\theta = 3\phi + 30$, the root is $\theta = 210$.

Solving the equation $\tan\theta° = k$

The equation $\tan\theta° = k$ is also solved in a similar way. Note that there is generally one root for every interval of 180. Other roots can be found from the periodic property, $\tan(180 + \theta)° = \tan\theta°$.

Step 1 Find $\tan^{-1}k$.

Step 2 Use the periodic property $\tan(180 \pm \theta)° = \tan\theta°$ to find the roots in the required interval.

Example 10.5.5

Solve the equation $\tan\theta° = -2$, giving all the roots correct to 1 decimal place in the interval $0 \leqslant \theta \leqslant 360$.

Step 1 Find $\tan^{-1}(-2) = -63.43\ldots$. Unfortunately, this root in not in the required interval.

Step 2 Add multiples of 180 to get roots in the required interval. This gives $116.56\ldots$ and $296.56\ldots$.

Therefore the roots of $\tan\theta° = -2$ in $0 \leqslant \theta \leqslant 360$ are 116.6 and 296.6, correct to 1 decimal place.

Revisiting Example 10.1.2, here is an application of solving equations of this type.

Example 10.5.6
The height in metres of the water in a harbour is given approximately by the formula $d = 6 + 3\cos 30t^\circ$ where t is the time measured in hours from noon. Find the time after noon when the height of the water is 7.5 metres for the second time.

To find when the height is 7.5 metres, solve $6 + 3\cos 30t^\circ = 7.5$. This gives $3\cos 30t^\circ = 7.5 - 6 = 1.5$, or $\cos 30t^\circ = 0.5$. After substituting $\phi = 30t$, the equation reduces to $\cos\phi^\circ = 0.5$.

Now $\cos^{-1} 0.5 = 60$, but this gives only the first root, $t = 2$. So, using the symmetry property of the cos function, another root is -60. Adding 360 gives $\phi = 300$ as the second root of $\cos\phi^\circ = 0.5$. Thus $30t = 300$, and $t = 10$.

The water is at height 7.5 metres for the second time at 10.00 p.m.

Exercise 10C

1 Find, correct to 1 decimal place, the two smallest positive values of θ which satisfy each of the following equations.

   (a) $\sin\theta^\circ = 0.1$ (b) $\sin\theta^\circ = -0.84$ (c) $\sin\theta^\circ = 0.951$

   (d) $\cos\theta^\circ = 0.8$ (e) $\cos\theta^\circ = -0.84$ (f) $\cos\theta^\circ = \sqrt{\dfrac{2}{3}}$

   (g) $\tan\theta^\circ = 4$ (h) $\tan\theta^\circ = -0.32$ (i) $\tan\theta^\circ = 0.11$

   (j) $\sin(180 + \theta)^\circ = 0.4$ (k) $\cos(90 - \theta)^\circ = -0.571$ (l) $\tan(90 - \theta)^\circ = -3$

   (m) $\sin(2\theta + 60)^\circ = 0.3584$ (n) $\sin(30 - \theta)^\circ = 0.5$ (o) $\cos(3\theta - 120)^\circ = 0$

2 Find all values of θ in the interval $-180 \leqslant \theta \leqslant 180$ which satisfy each of the following equations, giving your answers correct to 1 decimal place where appropriate.

   (a) $\sin\theta^\circ = 0.8$ (b) $\cos\theta^\circ = 0.25$ (c) $\tan\theta^\circ = 2$

   (d) $\sin\theta^\circ = -0.67$ (e) $\cos\theta^\circ = -0.12$ (f) $4\tan\theta^\circ + 3 = 0$

   (g) $4\sin\theta^\circ = 5\cos\theta^\circ$ (h) $2\sin\theta^\circ = \dfrac{1}{\sin\theta^\circ}$ (i) $2\sin\theta^\circ = \tan\theta^\circ$

3 Find all the solutions in the interval $0 < \theta \leqslant 360$ of each of the following equations.

   (a) $\cos 2\theta^\circ = \dfrac{1}{3}$ (b) $\tan 3\theta^\circ = 2$ (c) $\sin 2\theta^\circ = -0.6$

   (d) $\cos 4\theta^\circ = -\dfrac{1}{4}$ (e) $\tan 2\theta^\circ = 0.4$ (f) $\sin 3\theta^\circ = -0.42$

4 Find the roots in the interval $-180 \leqslant x \leqslant 180$ of each of the following equations.

   (a) $\cos 3x^\circ = \dfrac{2}{3}$ (b) $\tan 2x^\circ = -3$ (c) $\sin 3x^\circ = -0.2$

   (d) $\cos 2x^\circ = 0.246$ (e) $\tan 5x^\circ = 0.8$ (f) $\sin 2x^\circ = -0.39$

5 Find the roots (if there are any) in the interval $-180 \leqslant \theta \leqslant 180$ of the following equations.

(a) $\cos\frac{1}{2}\theta° = \frac{2}{3}$

(b) $\tan\frac{2}{3}\theta° = -3$

(c) $\sin\frac{1}{4}\theta° = -\frac{1}{4}$

(d) $\cos\frac{1}{3}\theta° = \frac{1}{3}$

(e) $\tan\frac{3}{4}\theta = 0.5$

(f) $\sin\frac{2}{5}\theta° = -0.3$

6 Without using a calculator, find the exact roots of the following equations, if there are any, giving your answers in the interval $0 < t \leqslant 360$.

(a) $\sin(2t - 30)° = \frac{1}{2}$

(b) $\tan(2t - 45)° = 0$

(c) $\cos(3t + 135)° = \frac{1}{2}\sqrt{3}$

(d) $\tan\left(\frac{3}{2}t - 45\right)° = -\sqrt{3}$

(e) $\cos(2t - 50)° = -\frac{1}{2}$

(f) $\sin\left(\frac{1}{2}t + 50\right)° = 1$

(g) $\cos\left(\frac{1}{5}t - 50\right)° = 0$

(h) $\tan(3t - 180)° = -1$

(i) $\sin\left(\frac{1}{4}t - 20\right)° = 0$

7 Find, to 1 decimal place, all values of z in the interval $-180 \leqslant z \leqslant 180$ satisfying

(a) $\sin z° = -0.16$,

(b) $\cos z°(1 + \sin z°) = 0$,

(c) $(1 - \tan z°)\sin z° = 0$,

(d) $\sin 2z° = 0.23$,

(e) $\cos(45 - z)° = 0.832$,

(f) $\tan(3z - 17)° = 3$.

8 Find all values of θ in the interval $0 \leqslant \theta \leqslant 360$ for which

(a) $\sin 2\theta° = \cos 36°$,

(b) $\cos 5\theta° = \sin 70°$,

(c) $\tan 3\theta° = \tan 60°$.

9 Find all values of θ in the interval $0 \leqslant \theta \leqslant 180$ for which $2\sin\theta°\cos\theta° = \frac{1}{2}\tan\theta°$.

10 For each of the following values, give an example of a trigonometric function involving (i) sine, (ii) cosine and (iii) tangent, with that value as period.

(a) 90

(b) 20

(c) 48

(d) 120

(e) 720

(f) 600

11 Sketch the graphs of each of the following in the interval $0 \leqslant \phi \leqslant 360$. In each case, state the period of the function.

(a) $y = \sin 3\phi°$

(b) $y = \cos 2\phi°$

(c) $y = \sin 4\phi°$

(d) $y = \tan\frac{1}{3}\phi°$

(e) $y = \cos\frac{1}{2}\phi°$

(f) $y = \sin\left(\frac{1}{2}\phi + 30\right)°$

(g) $y = \sin(3\phi - 20)°$

(h) $y = \tan 2\phi°$

(i) $y = \tan\left(\frac{1}{2}\phi + 90\right)°$

12 At a certain latitude in the northern hemisphere, the number d of hours of daylight in each day of the year is taken to be $d = A + B\sin kt°$, where A, B, k are positive constants and t is the time in days after the spring equinox.

(a) Assuming that the number of hours of daylight follows an annual cycle of 365 days, find the value of k, giving your answer correct to 3 decimal places.

(b) Given also that the shortest and longest days have 6 and 18 hours of daylight respectively, state the values of A and B. Find, in hours and minutes, the amount of daylight on New Year's Day, which is 80 days before the spring equinox.

(c) A town at this latitude holds a fair twice a year on those days having exactly 10 hours of daylight. Find, in relation to the spring equinox, which two days these are.

10.6 Relations between the trigonometric functions

In algebra you are used to solving equations, which involves finding a value of the unknown, often called x, in an equation such as $2x + 3 - x - 6 = 7$. You are also used to simplifying algebraic expressions like $2x + 3 - x - 6$, which becomes $x - 3$. You may not have realised, however, that these are quite different processes.

When you solve the equation $2x + 3 - x - 6 = 7$, you find that there is one solution, $x = 10$. But the expression $x - 3$ is identical to $2x + 3 - x - 6$ for *all* values of x. Sometimes it is important to distinguish between these two situations.

If two expressions take the same values for every value of x, they are said to be **identically equal**. This is written with the symbol $\equiv$, read as 'is identically equal to'. The statement

$$2x + 3 - x - 6 \equiv x - 3$$

is called an **identity**. Thus an identity in x is an equation which is true for all values of x.

Similar ideas occur in trigonometry. At the end of Section 10.2, it was observed that $\tan\theta° = \dfrac{\sin\theta°}{\cos\theta°}$, provided that $\cos\theta° \neq 0$. Thus

$$\tan\theta° \equiv \frac{\sin\theta°}{\cos\theta°}.$$

The identity symbol is used even when there are some exceptional values for which neither side is defined. In the example given, neither side is defined when θ is an odd multiple of 90, but the identity sign is still used.

There is another relationship which comes immediately from the definitions of $\cos\theta° = x$ and $\sin\theta° = y$ in Sections 10.1 and 10.2. As P lies on the circumference of a circle with radius 1 unit, Pythagoras' theorem gives $x^2 + y^2 = 1$, or $(\cos\theta°)^2 + (\sin\theta°)^2 \equiv 1$.

Conventionally, $(\cos\theta°)^2$ is written as $\cos^2\theta°$ and $(\sin\theta°)^2$ as $\sin^2\theta°$, so for all values of θ, $\cos^2\theta° + \sin^2\theta° \equiv 1$. This is sometimes called Pythagoras' theorem in trigonometry.

> For all values of θ:
>
> $$\tan\theta° \equiv \frac{\sin\theta°}{\cos\theta°}, \qquad \text{provided that } \cos\theta° \neq 0;$$
>
> $$\cos^2\theta° + \sin^2\theta° \equiv 1.$$

The convention of using $\cos^n\theta°$ to stand for $(\cos\theta°)^n$ is best restricted to positive powers. In any case, it should never be used with $n = -1$, because of the danger of confusion with $\cos^{-1}x$, which is used to stand for the angle whose cosine is x. If in doubt, you should write $(\cos\theta°)^n$ or $(\cos\theta°)^{-n}$, which could only mean one thing.

You can use the relation $\cos^2 \theta° + \sin^2 \theta° \equiv 1$ in the process of proving the cosine formula for a triangle.

Let ABC be a triangle, with sides $BC = a$, $CA = b$ and $AB = c$. Place the point A at the origin, and let AC lie along the x-axis in the positive x-direction, shown in Fig. 10.11.

The coordinates of C are $(b,0)$, and those of B are $(c \cos A°, c \sin A°)$, where A stands for the angle BAC. Then, using the distance formula (Section 1.1),

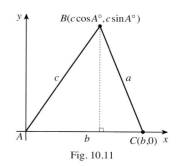

Fig. 10.11

$$a^2 = (b - c \cos A°)^2 + (c \sin A°)^2$$
$$= b^2 - 2bc \cos A° + c^2 \cos^2 A° + c^2 \sin^2 A°$$
$$= b^2 - 2bc \cos A° + c^2 \left(\cos^2 A° + \sin^2 A°\right)$$
$$= b^2 + c^2 - 2bc \cos A°,$$

using $\cos^2 A° + \sin^2 A° = 1$ at the end.

Example 10.6.1

Given that $\sin \theta° = \frac{3}{5}$, and that the angle $\theta°$ is obtuse, find, without using a calculator, the values of $\cos \theta°$ and $\tan \theta°$.

Since $\cos^2 \theta° + \sin^2 \theta° = 1$, $\cos^2 \theta° = 1 - \left(\frac{3}{5}\right)^2 = \frac{16}{25}$ giving $\cos \theta° = \pm \frac{4}{5}$. As the angle $\theta°$ is obtuse, $90 < \theta < 180$, so $\cos \theta°$ is negative. Therefore $\cos \theta° = -\frac{4}{5}$.

As $\sin \theta° = \frac{3}{5}$ and $\cos \theta° = -\frac{4}{5}$, $\tan \theta° = \dfrac{\sin \theta°}{\cos \theta°} = \dfrac{\frac{3}{5}}{-\frac{4}{5}} = -\frac{3}{4}$.

Example 10.6.2

Solve the equation $3 \cos^2 \theta° + 4 \sin \theta° = 4$, giving all the roots in the interval $-180 < \theta \leq 180$ correct to 1 decimal place.

As it stands you cannot solve this equation, but if you replace $\cos^2 \theta°$ by $1 - \sin^2 \theta°$ you will obtain the equation $3\left(1 - \sin^2 \theta°\right) + 4 \sin \theta° = 4$, which reduces to

$$3 \sin^2 \theta° - 4 \sin \theta° + 1 = 0.$$

This is a quadratic equation in $\sin \theta°$, which you can solve using factors:

$$(3 \sin \theta° - 1)(\sin \theta° - 1) = 0, \text{ giving } \sin \theta° = \frac{1}{3} \text{ or } \sin \theta° = 1.$$

One root is $\sin^{-1} \frac{1}{3} = 19.47\ldots$, and the other root, obtained from the symmetry of $\sin \theta°$, is $(180 - 19.47\ldots) = 160.52\ldots$.

The only root for $\sin \theta° = 1$ is $\theta = 90$, so the roots are 19.5, 90 and 160.5, correct to 1 decimal place.

Exercise 10D

1 For each triangle sketched below,

(i) use Pythagoras' theorem to find the length of the third side in an exact form;

(ii) write down the exact values of $\sin\theta°$, $\cos\theta°$ and $\tan\theta°$.

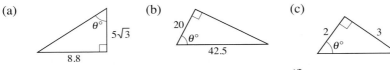

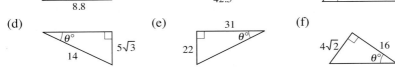

2 (a) Given that angle A is obtuse and that $\sin A° = \frac{5}{14}\sqrt{3}$, find the exact value of $\cos A°$.

(b) Given that $180 < B < 360$ and that $\tan B° = -\frac{21}{20}$, find the exact value of $\cos B°$.

(c) Find all possible values of $\sin C°$ for which $\cos C° = \frac{1}{2}$.

(d) Find the values of D for which $-180 < D < 180$ and $\tan D° = 5\sin D°$.

3 Use $\tan\theta° \equiv \dfrac{\sin\theta°}{\cos\theta°}$, $\cos\theta° \neq 0$, and $\cos^2\theta° + \sin^2\theta° \equiv 1$ to establish the following.

(a) $\dfrac{1}{\sin\theta°} - \dfrac{1}{\tan\theta°} \equiv \dfrac{1-\cos\theta°}{\sin\theta°}$

(b) $\dfrac{\sin^2\theta°}{1-\cos\theta°} \equiv 1+\cos\theta°$

(c) $\dfrac{1}{\cos\theta°} + \tan\theta° \equiv \dfrac{\cos\theta°}{1-\sin\theta°}$

(d) $\dfrac{\tan\theta°\sin\theta°}{1-\cos\theta°} \equiv 1 + \dfrac{1}{\cos\theta°}$

4 Solve the following equations for θ, giving all the roots in the interval $0 \leqslant \theta \leqslant 360$ correct to the nearest 0.1.

(a) $4\sin^2\theta° - 1 = 0$

(b) $\sin^2\theta° + 2\cos^2\theta° = 2$

(c) $10\sin^2\theta° - 5\cos^2\theta° + 2 = 4\sin\theta°$

(d) $4\sin^2\theta°\cos\theta° = \tan^2\theta°$

5 Find all values of θ, $-180 < \theta < 180$, for which $2\tan\theta° - 3 = \dfrac{2}{\tan\theta°}$.

Miscellaneous exercise 10

1 Write down the period of each of the following.

(a) $\sin x°$ (b) $\tan 2x°$ (OCR)

2 By considering the graph of $y = \cos x°$, or otherwise, express the following in terms of $\cos x°$.

(a) $\cos(360-x)°$ (b) $\cos(x+180)°$ (OCR)

3 Draw the graph of $y = \cos\frac{1}{2}\theta°$ for θ in the interval $-360 \leqslant \theta \leqslant 360$. Mark clearly the coordinates of the points where the graph crosses the θ- and y-axes.

4 Solve the following equations for θ, giving your answers in the interval $0 \leqslant \theta \leqslant 360$.

(a) $\tan\theta° = 0.4$ (b) $\sin 2\theta° = 0.4$ (OCR)

5 Solve the equation $3\cos 2x° = 2$, giving all the solutions in the interval $0 \le x \le 180$ correct to the nearest 0.1. (OCR)

6 (a) Give an example of a trigonometric function which has a period of 180.

(b) Solve for x the equation $\sin 3x° = 0.5$, giving all solutions in the interval $0 < x < 180$. (OCR)

7 Find all values of $θ°$, $0 \le θ \le 360$, for which $2\cos(θ + 30)° = 1$. (OCR)

8 (a) Express $\sin 2x° + \cos(90 - 2x)°$ in terms of a single trigonometric function.

(b) Hence, or otherwise, find all values of x in the interval $0 \le x \le 360$ for which $\sin 2x° + \cos(90 - 2x)° = -1$. (OCR)

9 Find the least positive value of the angle A for which

(a) $\sin A° = 0.2$ and $\cos A°$ is negative;   (b) $\tan A° = -0.5$ and $\sin A°$ is negative;

(c) $\cos A° = \sin A°$ and both are negative;   (d) $\sin A° = -0.2275$ and $A > 360$.

10 Prove the following identities.

(a) $\dfrac{1}{\sin θ°} - \sin θ° \equiv \dfrac{\cos θ°}{\tan θ°}$ (b) $\dfrac{1 - \sin θ°}{\cos θ°} \equiv \dfrac{\cos θ°}{1 + \sin θ°}$

(c) $\dfrac{1}{\tan θ°} + \tan θ° \equiv \dfrac{1}{\sin θ° \cos θ°}$ (d) $\dfrac{1 - 2\sin^2 θ°}{\cos θ° + \sin θ°} \equiv \cos θ° - \sin θ°$

11 For each of the following functions, determine the maximum and minimum values of y and the least positive values of x at which these occur.

(a) $y = 1 + \cos 2x°$ (b) $y = 5 - 4\sin(x + 30)°$

(c) $y = 29 - 20\sin(3x - 45)°$ (d) $y = 8 - 3\cos^2 x°$

(e) $y = \dfrac{12}{3 + \cos x°}$ (f) $y = \dfrac{60}{1 + \sin^2(2x - 15)°}$

12 Solve the following equations for $θ$, giving solutions in the interval $0 \le θ \le 360$.

(a) $\sin θ° = \tan θ°$ (b) $2 - 2\cos^2 θ° = \sin θ°$

(c) $\tan^2 θ° - 2\tan θ° = 1$ (d) $\sin 2θ° - \sqrt{3}\cos 2θ° = 0$

13 The function t is defined by $t(x) = \tan 3x°$.

(a) State the period of $t(x)$.

(b) Solve the equation $t(x) = \frac{1}{2}$ for $0 \le x \le 180$.

(c) Deduce the smallest positive solution of each of the following equations.

(i) $t(x) = -\frac{1}{2}$

(ii) $t(x) = 2$ (OCR)

14 In each of the following, construct a formula involving a trigonometric function which could be used to model the situations described.

(a) Water depths in a canal vary between a minimum of 3.6 metres and a maximum of 6 metres over 24-hour periods.

(b) Petroleum refining at a chemical plant is run on a 10-day cycle, with a minimum production of 15 000 barrels per day and a maximum of 28 000 barrels per day.

(c) At a certain town just south of the Arctic circle, the number of hours of daylight varies between 2 and 22 hours during a 360-day year.

15 A tuning fork is vibrating. The displacement, y centimetres, of the tip of one of the prongs from its rest position after t seconds is given by

$$y = 0.1\sin(100\ 000t)°.$$

Find

(a) the greatest displacement and the first time at which it occurs,

(b) the time taken for one complete oscillation of the prong,

(c) the number of complete oscillations per second of the tip of the prong,

(d) the total time during the first complete oscillation for which the tip of the prong is more than 0.06 centimetres from its rest position.

16 One end of a piece of elastic is attached to a point at the top of a door frame and the other end hangs freely. A small ball is attached to the free end of the elastic. When the ball is hanging freely it is pulled down a small distance and then released, so that the ball oscillates up and down on the elastic. The depth d centimetres of the ball from the top of the door frame after t seconds is given by

$$d = 100 + 10\cos 500t°.$$

Find

(a) the greatest and least depths of the ball,

(b) the time at which the ball first reaches its highest position,

(c) the time taken for a complete oscillation,

(d) the proportion of the time during a complete oscillation for which the depth of the ball is less than 99 centimetres.

17 An oscillating particle has displacement y metres, where y is given by $y = a\sin(kt + \alpha)°$, where a is measured in metres, t is measured in seconds and k and α are constants. The time for a complete oscillation is T seconds.

Find

(a) k in terms of T,

(b) the number, in terms of k, of complete oscillations per second.

18 The population, P, of a certain type of bird on a remote island varies during the course of a year according to feeding, breeding, migratory seasons and predator interactions. An ornithologist doing research into bird numbers for this species attempts to model the population on the island with the annually periodic equation

$$P = N - C\cos\omega t°,$$

where N, C and ω are constants, and t is the time in weeks, with $t = 0$ representing midnight on the first of January.

(a) Taking the period of this function to be 50 weeks, find the value of ω.

(b) Use the equation to describe, in terms of N and C,

   (i) the number of birds of this species on the island at the start of each year;

   (ii) the maximum number of these birds, and the time of year when this occurs.

19 The road to an island close to the shore is sometimes covered by the tide. When the water rises to the level of the road, the road is closed. On a particular day, the water at high tide is a height 4.6 metres above mean sea level. The height, h metres, of the tide is modelled by using the equation $h = 4.6\cos kt°$, where t is the time in hours from high tide; it is also assumed that high tides occur every 12 hours.

(a) Determine the value of k.

(b) On the same day, a notice says that the road will be closed for 3 hours. Assuming that this notice is correct, find the height of the road above sea level, giving your answer correct to two decimal places.

(c) In fact, a road repair has raised its level, and it is impassable for only 2 hours 40 minutes. By how many centimetres has the road level been raised? (OCR)

20 A simple model of the tides in a harbour on the south coast of Cornwall assumes that they are caused by the attractions of the sun and the moon. The magnitude of the attraction of the moon is assumed to be nine times the magnitude of the attraction of the sun. The period of the sun's effect is taken to be 360 days and that of the moon is 30 days. A model for the height, h metres, of the tide (relative to a mark fixed on the harbour wall), at t days, is

$$h = A\cos\alpha t° + B\cos\beta t°,$$

where the term $A\cos\alpha t°$ is the effect due to the sun, and the term $B\cos\beta t°$ is the effect due to the moon. Given that $h = 5$ when $t = 0$, determine the values of A, B, α and β.

(OCR, adapted)

11 Combining and inverting functions

This chapter develops the idea of a function, which you first met in Chapter 3. It introduces a kind of algebra of functions, by showing how to find a composite function. When you have completed it, you should

- be able to use correct language and notation associated with functions
- know when functions can be combined by the operation of composition, and be able to form the composite function
- appreciate that a sequence can be regarded as a function whose domain is the natural numbers, or a consecutive subset of the natural numbers
- know the 'one–one' condition for a function to have an inverse, and be able to form the inverse function
- know the relationship between the graph of a one–one function and the graph of its inverse function.

The references to calculators in the chapter may not exactly fit your own machine. For example, on some calculators the [=] key is labelled [EXE] (which stands for 'execute').

11.1 Function notation

In using a calculator to find values of a function, you carry out three separate steps:

Step 1   Key in a number (the 'input').

Step 2   Key in the function instructions.

Step 3   Read the number in the display (the 'output').

Step 2 sometimes involves just a single key, such as 'square root', 'change sign' or 'sine'. For example:

$$\begin{array}{ccc}
\text{Input} & & \text{Output} \\
4 & \rightarrow \ [\ \sqrt{\ }\ ] \ \rightarrow & 2 \\
3 & \rightarrow \ [+/\pm] \ \rightarrow & -3 \\
30 & \rightarrow \ [\sin] \ \rightarrow & 0.5
\end{array}$$

In this chapter sin, cos *and* tan *stand for these functions as operated by your calculator in degree mode. You enter a number* x*, and the output is* $\sin x°$*,* $\cos x°$ *or* $\tan x°$*.*

Other functions need several keys, such as 'subtract 3':

$$7 \ \rightarrow \ [-,\ 3,\ =] \ \rightarrow \ 4.$$

But the principle is the same. The important point is that it is the key sequence inside the square brackets that represents the function. This sequence is the same whatever number you key in as the input in Step 1.

You can think of a function as a kind of machine. Just as you can have a machine which takes fabric and turns it into clothes, so a function takes numbers in the domain and turns them into numbers in the range.

For a general input number x, you can write

$$x \rightarrow [\ +/\pm\ ] \rightarrow -x,$$
$$x \rightarrow [\ -,\ 3,\ =\ ] \rightarrow x-3,$$

and so on. And for a general function,

$$x \rightarrow [\ f\ ] \rightarrow f(x),$$

where f stands for the key sequence of the function.

This book has often used phrases like 'the function x^2', 'the function $\cos x°$', or 'the function $f(x)$', and you have understood what is meant. Working mathematicians do this all the time. But it is strictly wrong; x^2, $\cos x°$ and $f(x)$ are symbols for the *output* when the input is x, not for the function itself. When you need to use precise language, you should refer to 'the function square', 'the function cos' or 'the function f'.

Unfortunately only a few functions have convenient names like 'square' or 'cos'. There is no simple name for a function whose output is given by an expression such as $x^2 - 6x + 4$. The way round this is to decide for the time being to call this function f (or any other letter you like). You can then write

$$f : x \mapsto x^2 - 6x + 4.$$

You read this as ' f is the function which turns any input number x in the domain into the output number $x^2 - 6x + 4$'. Notice the bar at the blunt end of the arrow; it avoids confusion with the arrow which has been used to stand for 'tends to' in finding gradients of tangents.

Try to write a key sequence to represent this function. (You may need the memory keys.)

Example 11.1.1
If $f : x \mapsto x(5-x)$, what is $f(3)$?

The symbol $f(3)$ stands for the output when the input is 3. The function f turns the input 3 into the output $3(5-3) = 6$. So $f(3) = 6$.

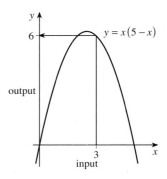

This idea of using an arrow to show the connection between the input and the output can be linked to the graph of the function. Fig. 11.1 shows the graph of $y = x(5-x)$, with the input number 3 on the x-axis. An arrow which goes up the page from this point and bends through a right angle when it hits the graph takes you to the output number 6 on the y-axis.

Fig. 11.1

11.2 Forming composite functions

If you want to work out values of $\sqrt{x-3}$, you would probably use the key sequence $\left[-,3,=,\sqrt{}\,\right]$ with hardly a thought. But if you look carefully, you will see that three numbers appear in the display during the process. For example, if you use the input 7, the display will show in turn your input number 7, then (after keying $[=]$) 4, and finally the output 2. In fact, you are really working out two functions, 'subtract 3' then 'square root', in succession. You could represent the whole calculation:

$$7 \;\rightarrow\; [-,3,=] \;\rightarrow\; 4 \;\rightarrow\; [\sqrt{}\,] \;\rightarrow\; 2.$$

The output of the first function becomes the input of the second.

Example 11.2.1
Find the outputs when the functions 'square' and 'sin' act in succession on the inputs of
(a) 30,   (b) x.

(a) $30 \;\rightarrow\; [\,\text{square}\,] \;\rightarrow\; 900 \;\rightarrow\; [\,\text{sin}\,] \;\rightarrow\; 0.$

(b) $x \;\rightarrow\; [\,\text{square}\,] \;\rightarrow\; x^2 \;\rightarrow\; [\,\text{sin}\,] \;\rightarrow\; \sin\!\left(x^2\right)^{\circ}.$

Since in (b) the input to the function $\sin$ is x^2, not x, the output is $\sin\!\left(x^2\right)^{\circ}$, not $\sin x^{\circ}$.

For a general input, and two general functions f and g, the process would be written:

$$x \;\rightarrow\; [\,\text{f}\,] \;\rightarrow\; \text{f}(x) \;\rightarrow\; [\,\text{g}\,] \;\rightarrow\; \text{g}(\text{f}(x)).$$

When you work out two functions in succession in this way, you are said to be 'composing' them. The result is a third function called the 'composite function'.

Since the output of the composite function is $\text{g}(\text{f}(x))$, the composite function itself is denoted by gf. Notice that gf must be read as 'first f, then g'. You must get used to reading the symbol gf from right to left. Writing fg means 'first g, then f', which is almost always a different function from gf. For instance, if you change the order of the functions in Example 11.2.1(a), instead of the output 0 you get

$$30 \;\rightarrow\; [\,\text{sin}\,] \;\rightarrow\; 0.5 \;\rightarrow\; [\,\text{square}\,] \;\rightarrow\; 0.25.$$

Example 11.2.2
Let $\text{f}:x \mapsto x+3$ and $\text{g}:x \mapsto x^2$. Find gf and fg. Show that there is just one number x such that $\text{gf}(x) = \text{fg}(x)$.

The composite function gf is represented by

$$x \;\rightarrow\; [\,\text{f}\,] \;\rightarrow\; x+3 \;\rightarrow\; [\,\text{g}\,] \;\rightarrow\; (x+3)^2$$

and fg is represented by

$$x \;\rightarrow\; [\,\text{g}\,] \;\rightarrow\; x^2 \;\rightarrow\; [\,\text{f}\,] \;\rightarrow\; x^2+3.$$

So $\text{gf}:x \mapsto (x+3)^2$ and $\text{fg}:x \mapsto x^2+3$.

If $\text{gf}(x) = \text{fg}(x)$, $(x+3)^2 = x^2+3$, so $x^2+6x+9 = x^2+3$, giving $x = -1$.

You can check this with your calculator. If you input -1 and then 'add 3' $[+, 3, =]$ followed by 'square', the display will show in turn $-1, 2, 4$. If you do 'square' followed by 'add 3', it will show $-1, 1, 4$. When the input is -1, the outputs are the same although the intermediate displays are different.

Example 11.2.3

If $f : x \mapsto \cos x°$ and $g : x \mapsto \dfrac{1}{x}$, calculate   (a) $gf(60)$,   (b) $gf(90)$.

(a)   With input 60, the calculator will show in turn $60, 0.5, 2$, so $gf(60) = 2$.

(b)   With input 90, the calculator will display 90, 0 and then give an error message! This is because $\cos 90° = 0$ and $\frac{1}{0}$ is not defined.

What has happened in Example 11.2.3(b) is that the number 0 is in the range of the function f, but it is not in the domain of g. You must always be aware that this may happen when you find the composite of two functions. It is time to look again at domains and ranges, so that you can avoid this problem.

11.3 Domain and range

When you see the letters x and y in mathematics, for example in an equation such as $y = 2x - 10$, it is generally understood that they stand for real numbers. But sometimes it is important to be absolutely precise about this. The symbol $\mathbb{R}$ is used to stand for 'the set of real numbers', and the symbol $\in$ for 'belongs to'. With these symbols, you can shorten the statement 'x is a real number', or 'x belongs to the set of real numbers', to $x \in \mathbb{R}$. So you can write

$$f : x \mapsto 2x - 10, \quad x \in \mathbb{R}$$

to indicate that f is the function whose domain is the set of real numbers which turns any input x into the output $2x - 10$.

Strictly, a function is not completely defined unless you state the domain as well as the rule for obtaining the output from the input. For the function above the range is also $\mathbb{R}$, although you do not need to state this in describing the function.

You know from Chapter 3 that for some functions the domain is only a part of $\mathbb{R}$, because the expression $f(x)$ only has meaning for some $x \in \mathbb{R}$. (Here $\in$ has to be read as 'belonging to' rather than 'belongs to'.) The set of real numbers for which $f(x)$ has a meaning will be called the 'natural domain' of f. With a calculator, if you input a number that is not in the natural domain, the output will be an 'error' display.

For the square root function, for example, the natural domain is the set of positive real numbers and zero, so you write

$$\text{square root} : x \mapsto \sqrt{x}, \quad \text{where } x \in \mathbb{R} \text{ and } x \geqslant 0.$$

If you are given a function described by a formula but no domain is stated, you should assume that the domain is the natural domain.

Example 11.3.1

Find the range of each of the functions

(a) $\sin$, with natural domain $\mathbb{R}$,   (b) $\sin$, with domain $x \in \mathbb{R}$ and $0 < x < 90$.

From the graph of $y = \sin x°$, shown in Fig. 11.2, you can read off the ranges:

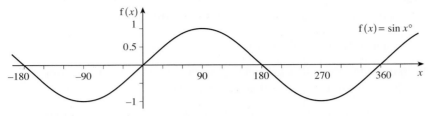

Fig. 11.2

(a)   For $x \in \mathbb{R}$, the range is $y \in \mathbb{R}, -1 \leqslant y \leqslant 1$.

(b)   For $x \in \mathbb{R}, 0 < x < 90$, the range is $y \in \mathbb{R}, 0 < y < 1$.

Example 11.3.1 has used the letter x in describing the domain, and y for the range, but other letters would work just as well. The expressions $y \in \mathbb{R}, 0 < y < 1$ and $x \in \mathbb{R}, 0 < x < 1$ and $t \in \mathbb{R}, 0 < t < 1$ all describe the same set of numbers.

It is especially important to understand this when you find composite functions. For example, in Example 11.2.3(a), the number 0.5 appears first as the output for the input 60 to the function $f : x \mapsto \cos x°$, so you might think of it as $y = \cos 60° = 0.5$.

But when it becomes the input to the function $g : x \mapsto \dfrac{1}{x}$, it is natural to write $x = 0.5$.

The number 0.5 belongs first to the range of f, then to the domain of g.

This is where Example 11.2.3(b) breaks down. The number 0, which is the output when the input to f is 90, is not in the natural domain of g. So although 90 is in the natural domain of f, it is not in the natural domain of gf.

The general rule is:

> To form the **composite function** gf, the domain D of f must be chosen so that the whole of the range of f is included in the domain of g. The function gf is then defined as $gf : x \mapsto g(f(x)), x \in D$.

For the functions in Example 11.2.3, the domain of g is the set $\mathbb{R}$ excluding 0, so the domain of f must be chosen to exclude the numbers x for which $\cos x° = 0$. These are $\ldots$, -450, -270, -90, $+90$, $+270$, $+450$, $\ldots$, all of which can be summed up by the formula $90 + 180n$, where n is an integer.

There is a neat way of writing this, using the standard symbol $\mathbb{Z}$ for the set of integers $\{\ldots, -3, -2, -1, 0, 1, 2, 3, \ldots\}$. The domain of f can then be expressed as $x \in \mathbb{R}, x \neq 90 + 180n, n \in \mathbb{Z}$.

Example 11.3.2
Find the natural domain and the corresponding range of the function $x \mapsto \sqrt{x(x-3)}$.

You can express the function as gf, where $f: x \mapsto x(x-3)$ and $g: x \mapsto \sqrt{x}$.

The natural domain of g is $x \in \mathbb{R}, x \geqslant 0$, so you want the range of f to be included in $y \in \mathbb{R}, y \geqslant 0$. (Switching from x to y is not essential, but you may find it easier.) The solution of the inequality $y = x(x-3) \geqslant 0$ is $x \geqslant 3$ or $x \leqslant 0$.

The natural domain of gf is therefore $x \in \mathbb{R}, x \geqslant 3$ or $x \leqslant 0$.

With this domain the range of f is $y \in \mathbb{R}, y \geqslant 0$, so the numbers input to g are given by $x \in \mathbb{R}, x \geqslant 0$. With this domain, the range of g is $y \in \mathbb{R}, y \geqslant 0$. This is therefore the range of the combined function gf.

If you have access to a graphic calculator, try to plot the graph $y = \sqrt{x(x-3)}$, using a window of $-1 \leqslant x \leqslant 4$ and $0 \leqslant y \leqslant 2$. You should find that no points are plotted for the 'illegal' values of x in the interval $0 < x < 3$. If you input a number in this interval, such as 1, you will get as far as $1(1-3) = -2$, but the final $[\sqrt{}]$ key will give you an error message or some display which does not represent a real number.

11.4 Sequences as functions

Not all functions have for their domain the set of real numbers or a restricted interval of the real numbers. For example, a function might have the set of natural numbers $\{1, 2, 3, \ldots\}$ for its domain. This set is denoted by the symbol $\mathbb{N}$.

Some games (such as chess and Scrabble) are played on a board ruled out in squares. If the board has r squares each way, then the total number of squares is r^2. So this defines a function

$$f: r \mapsto r^2, \quad \text{where } r \in \mathbb{N}.$$

This is a different function from

$$f: x \mapsto x^2, \quad \text{where } x \in \mathbb{R},$$

because the number of squares each way must be a whole number.

You can make a list of the successive values of $f(r)$:

$$f(1) = 1, \ f(2) = 4, \ f(3) = 9, \ f(4) = 16, \ f(5) = 25, \ldots .$$

Notice that these numbers are precisely those in sequence (a) in Section 8.1. This suggests that a sequence can be considered as a function whose domain is $\mathbb{N}$.

Some sequences have only a finite number of terms. Suppose, for example, that you have 6 identical coins, and $f(r)$ denotes the number of ways of splitting the coins into r piles. Thus $f(2) = 3$, because you can have piles of 1 coin and 5 coins, 2 coins and 4 coins, or 3 coins and 3 coins. Check for yourself that

$$f(1) = 1, \ f(2) = 3, \ f(3) = 3, \ f(4) = 2, \ f(5) = 1 \text{ and } f(6) = 1;$$

but $f(r)$ has no meaning for $r > 6$. The domain of the function is therefore the set $\{1, 2, 3, 4, 5, 6\}$, which is a subset of consecutive numbers in $\mathbb{N}$.

A sequence can therefore be defined as a function whose domain is $\mathbb{N}$ or a consecutive subset of $\mathbb{N}$. For sequences the notation u_r is normally used rather than $f(r)$, but that is simply for convenience.

You saw in Chapter 8 that it is simpler with some sequences to begin with $r = 0$ rather than $r = 1$. For those sequences the domain is $\{0, 1, 2, 3, \ldots\}$. The notation for describing this set is $\mathbb{N} \cup \{0\}$.

An important difference between $\mathbb{N}$ and $\mathbb{R}$ is that, for every natural number r, there is a 'next number'. This is what makes it possible to use an inductive definition to describe a sequence. There is no comparable way of defining a function $f(x)$, where $x \in \mathbb{R}$, because there is no such thing as the 'next real number'.

Exercise 11A

1 Given $f : x \mapsto (3x + 5)^2$, where $x \in \mathbb{R}$, find the values of
   (a) $f(2)$,   (b) $f(-1)$,   (c) $f(7)$.

2 Given $g : x \mapsto 3x^2 + 5$, where $x \in \mathbb{R}$, find the values of
   (a) $g(2)$,   (b) $g(-1)$,   (c) $g(7)$.

3 Given $f : x \mapsto \dfrac{4}{x + 5}$, where $x \in \mathbb{R}$ and $x \neq -5$, find the values of
   (a) $f(-1)$,   (b) $f(-4)$,   (c) $f(3)$.

4 Given $g : x \mapsto \dfrac{4}{x} + 5$, where $x \in \mathbb{R}$ and $x \neq 0$, find the values of
   (a) $g(-1)$,   (b) $g(-4)$,   (c) $g(3)$.

5 Find the output if the functions 'square' and 'subtract 4' act in succession on an input of
   (a) 2,   (b) -5,   (c) $\frac{1}{2}$,   (d) x.

6 Find the output if the functions 'cos', 'add 2', and 'cube' act in succession on an input of
   (a) 0,   (b) 90,   (c) 120,   (d) x.

7 Find the output if the functions 'square root', 'multiply by 2', 'subtract 10' and 'square' act in succession on an input of
   (a) 9,   (b) 16,   (c) $\frac{1}{4}$,   (d) x.

8 Determine the key sequence needed to represent each of the following functions.
   (a) $f : x \mapsto 4x + 9$ (b) $f : x \mapsto 4(x + 9)$ (c) $f : x \mapsto 2x^2 - 5$
   (d) $f : x \mapsto 2(x - 5)^2$ (e) $f : x \mapsto \left(\sqrt{x} - 3\right)^3$, $x \geqslant 0$ (f) $f : x \mapsto \sqrt{(x - 2)^2 + 10}$

9 Find the natural domain and corresponding range of each of the following functions.
   (a) $f : x \mapsto x^2$ (b) $f : x \mapsto \cos x°$ (c) $f : x \mapsto \sqrt{x - 3}$
   (d) $f : x \mapsto x^2 + 5$ (e) $f : x \mapsto \dfrac{1}{\sqrt{x}}$ (f) $f : x \mapsto x(4 - x)$
   (g) $f : x \mapsto \sqrt{x(4 - x)}$ (h) $f : x \mapsto x^2 + 4x + 10$ (i) $f : x \mapsto \left(1 - \sqrt{x - 3}\right)^2$

10 Given that $f : x \mapsto 2x + 1$ and $g : x \mapsto 3x - 5$, where $x \in \mathbb{R}$, find the value of the following.

(a) $gf(1)$ (b) $gf(-2)$ (c) $fg(0)$ (d) $fg(7)$

(e) $ff(5)$ (f) $ff(-5)$ (g) $gg(4)$ (h) $gg\left(2\frac{2}{9}\right)$

11 Given that $f : x \mapsto x^2$ and $g : x \mapsto 4x - 1$, where $x \in \mathbb{R}$, find the value of the following.

(a) $fg(2)$ (b) $gg(4)$ (c) $gf(-3)$

(d) $ff\left(\frac{1}{2}\right)$ (e) $fgf(-1)$ (f) $gfgf(2)$

12 Given that $f : x \mapsto 5 - x$ and $g : x \mapsto \dfrac{4}{x}$, where $x \in \mathbb{R}$ and $x \neq 0$ or 5, find the values of the following.

(a) $ff(7)$ (b) $ff(-19)$ (c) $gg(1)$ (d) $gg\left(\frac{1}{2}\right)$

(e) $gggg\left(\frac{1}{2}\right)$ (f) $fffff(6)$ (g) $fgfg(2)$ (h) $fggf(2)$

13 Given that $f : x \mapsto 2x + 5$, $g : x \mapsto x^2$ and $h : x \mapsto \dfrac{1}{x}$, where $x \in \mathbb{R}$ and $x \neq 0$ or $-\frac{5}{2}$, find the following composite functions.

(a) fg (b) gf (c) fh (d) hf

(e) ff (f) hh (g) gfh (h) hgf

14 Given that $f : x \mapsto \sin x°$, $g : x \mapsto x^3$ and $h : x \mapsto x - 3$, where $x \in \mathbb{R}$, find the following functions.

(a) hf (b) fh (c) fhg

(d) fg (e) hhh (f) gf

15 Given that $f : x \mapsto x + 4$, $g : x \mapsto 3x$ and $h : x \mapsto x^2$, where $x \in \mathbb{R}$, express each of the following in terms of f, g, h as appropriate.

(a) $x \mapsto x^2 + 4$ (b) $x \mapsto 3x + 4$ (c) $x \mapsto x^4$

(d) $x \mapsto 9x^2$ (e) $x \mapsto 3x + 12$ (f) $x \mapsto 3\left(x^2 + 8\right)$

(g) $x \mapsto 9x + 16$ (h) $x \mapsto x^2 + 8x + 16$ (i) $x \mapsto 9x^2 + 48x + 64$

16 In each of the following, find the natural domain and the range of the function gf.

(a) $f : x \mapsto \sqrt{x}$, $g : x \mapsto x - 5$ (b) $f : x \mapsto x + 3$, $g : x \mapsto \sqrt{x}$

(c) $f : x \mapsto x - 2$, $g : x \mapsto \dfrac{1}{x}$ (d) $f : x \mapsto \sin x°$, $g : x \mapsto \sqrt{x^2}$

(e) $f : x \mapsto \sqrt{(x-3)^2}$, $g : x \mapsto \sqrt{x}$ (f) $f : x \mapsto 16 - x^2$, $g : x \mapsto \sqrt[4]{x}$

(g) $f : x \mapsto x^2 - x - 6$, $g : x \mapsto \sqrt{x}$ (h) $f : x \mapsto x + 2$, $g : x \mapsto \dfrac{1}{\sqrt{-x}}$

17 Given that $f : x \mapsto x^2$ and $g : x \mapsto 3x - 2$, where $x \in \mathbb{R}$, find a, b and c such that

(a) $fg(a) = 100$,   (b) $gg(b) = 55$,   (c) $fg(c) = gf(c)$.

18 Given that $f : x \mapsto ax + b$ and that $ff : x \mapsto 9x - 28$, find the possible values of a and b.

19 For $f : x \mapsto ax + b$, $f(2) = 19$ and $ff(0) = 55$. Find the possible values of a and b.

20 The functions $f : x \mapsto 4x + 1$ and $g : x \mapsto ax + b$ are such that $fg = gf$ for all real values of x. Show that $a = 3b + 1$.

21 Use function notation to describe

(a) the triangle number sequence,

(b) the general arithmetic sequence with first term a and common difference d .

22 In prime number theory the following notation is used:

p_r is the r th prime number,

$\pi(r)$ is the number of prime numbers less than or equal to r .

For each of these functions, state

(a) the domain,   (b) the values for $1 \leqslant r \leqslant 10$,   (c) the range.

(*Note*: 1 is not a prime number.)

11.5 Reversing functions

If your sister is 2 years older than you, then you are 2 years younger than her. To get her age from yours you use the 'add 2' function; to get your age from hers you 'subtract 2'. The functions 'add 2' and 'subtract 2' are said to be **inverse functions** of each other. That is, 'subtract 2' is the inverse function of 'add 2' (and vice versa).

You know many pairs of inverse functions: 'double' and 'halve', and 'cube' and 'cube root' are simple examples.

Some functions are their own inverses, such as 'change sign'; to undo the effect of a change of sign, you just change sign again. Another example is 'reciprocal' $\left(x \mapsto \dfrac{1}{x} \right)$.

These functions are said to be **self-inverse**.

The inverse of a function f is denoted by the symbol f^{-1} . If f turns an input number x into an output number y , then f^{-1} turns y into x . You can illustrate this graphically by reversing the arrow which symbolises the function, as in Fig. 11.3. The range of f becomes the domain of f^{-1} , and the domain of f becomes the range of f^{-1} .

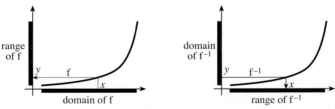

Fig. 11.3

You have already used inverse functions in calculations about triangles. Often you know an angle, and calculate the length of a side by using one of the trigonometric functions such as tan . But if you know the sides and want to calculate the angle you use the inverse function, which is denoted by $\tan^{-1}$.

On many calculators you find values of $\tan^{-1}$ *by using a sequence of two keys: first an 'inverse' key (which on some calculators is labelled 'shift' or '2nd function') and then 'tan'. In the following pages this is referred to as 'the* $\tan^{-1}$ *key', and similarly for the* $\sin^{-1}$ *and* $\cos^{-1}$ *functions.*

Example 11.5.1

Find the values of $\cos^{-1} y$ when   (a) $y = 0.5$,   (b) $y = -1$,   (c) $y = 1.5$.

Using the $[\cos^{-1}]$ key with inputs 0.5, -1, 1.5 in turn gives outputs of 60, 180, and an error message!

So, in degree mode, (a) $\cos^{-1} 0.5 = 60$,
(b) $\cos^{-1}(-1) = 180$, but (c) $\cos^{-1} 1.5$ has no meaning.

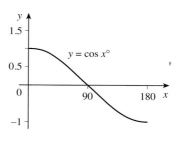

Fig. 11.4 shows the graph of $y = \cos x°$ with domain $x \in \mathbb{R}, 0 \leqslant x \leqslant 180$. This shows that the range of the function $\cos$ is $-1 \leqslant x \leqslant 1$. Since this is the domain of the inverse function, the result in part (c) is explained by the fact that 1.5 lies outside this interval.

Fig. 11.4

If you try to check by finding the cosines of the answers to this example, you get

(a) $0.5 \rightarrow [\cos^{-1}] \rightarrow 60 \rightarrow [\cos] \rightarrow 0.5,$

(b) $-1 \rightarrow [\cos^{-1}] \rightarrow 180 \rightarrow [\cos] \rightarrow -1.$

This is of course what you would expect; the function and its inverse cancel each other out. In general, if $-1 \leqslant y \leqslant 1$, then

$$y \rightarrow [\cos^{-1}] \rightarrow [\cos] \rightarrow y.$$

You may therefore be surprised by the result of the next example.

Example 11.5.2

If $f : x \mapsto \sin x°$ and $g : x \mapsto \sin^{-1} x$, evaluate   (a) $gf(50)$,   (b) $gf(130)$.

Work this example for yourself using the calculator sequence

$$x \rightarrow [\sin] \rightarrow [\sin^{-1}] \rightarrow gf(x).$$

You should get the answers (a) 50 (as you would expect) and (b) 50.

The answer to part (b) calls for a more careful look at the theory of inverse functions.

11.6 One–one functions

The answers to Example 11.5.2 can be explained by Fig. 11.5, which shows the graph of $y = \sin x°$ over the interval $0 \leqslant x \leqslant 180$. The graph rises from $y = 0$ to $y = 1$ over values for x for which the angle is acute, and then falls symmetrically back to $y = 0$ over values for which the angle is obtuse. This is because the sine of the obtuse angle $x°$ is equal to the sine of the supplementary angle $(180 - x)°$. So $\sin 130° = \sin 50°$, and the calculator gives the value $0.7660\ldots$ for both.

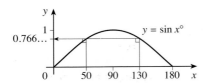
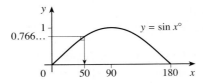

Fig. 11.5

When you use the $[\,\sin^{-1}\,]$ key to find $\sin^{-1}(0.7660\ldots)$, the calculator has to give the same answer in either case. It is programmed to give the answer with the smallest modulus, which in this case is 50.

Exactly the same problem arises whenever you try to reverse a function which has the same output for more than one input. And in mathematics, such ambiguity is not acceptable. The solution adopted is a drastic one, to refuse to define an inverse for any function which has the same output for more than one input. That is, the only functions which have an inverse function are those for which each output in the range comes from only one input. These functions are said to be 'one–one'.

> A function f defined for some domain D is **one–one** if, for each
> number y in the range R of f there is only one number $x \in D$
> such that $y = f(x)$. The function with domain R defined by
> $f^{-1} : y \mapsto x$, where $y = f(x)$, is the **inverse function** of f.

This definition was illustrated in Fig. 11.3, which was drawn to ensure that the function f was one–one.

In practice, this can be achieved by restricting its domain. For example, the function $x \mapsto \sin x^\circ$, $x \in \mathbb{R}$, whose graph is shown in Fig. 11.2 on page 160, is not one–one, so it does not have an inverse. But the function $x \mapsto \sin x^\circ$, where $x \in \mathbb{R}$ and $-90 \leqslant x \leqslant 90$, shown in Fig. 11.6, is one–one; it is the inverse of this function which is denoted by $\sin^{-1}$, and activated by the familiar key sequence on the calculator.

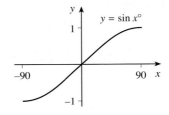

Fig. 11.6

Fig. 11.3 suggests that, if you compose a function with its inverse, you get back to the number you started with. That is,

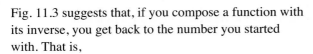
$$f^{-1}f(x) = x, \quad \text{and} \quad ff^{-1}(y) = y.$$

The functions $f^{-1}f$ and ff^{-1} are called **identity functions** because their inputs and outputs are identical. But there is a subtle difference between these two composite functions, since their domains may not be the same; the first has domain D and the second has domain R.

11.7 Finding inverse functions

For very simple functions it is easy to write down an expression for the inverse function. The inverse of 'add 2' is 'subtract 2', so

$$f : x \mapsto x + 2, x \in \mathbb{R} \quad \text{has inverse} \quad f^{-1} : x \mapsto x - 2, x \in \mathbb{R}.$$

Notice that the inverse could equally well be written as $f^{-1} : y \mapsto y - 2, y \in \mathbb{R}$.

You can sometimes break down more complicated functions into a chain of simple steps. You can then find the inverse by going backwards through each step in reverse order. (This is sometimes called the 'shoes and socks' process: you put your socks on before your shoes, but you take off your shoes before your socks. In mathematical notation, $(gf)^{-1} = f^{-1}g^{-1}$, where f denotes putting on your socks and g your shoes.)

However, this method does not always work, particularly if x appears more than once in the expression for the function. Another method is to write $y = f(x)$, and turn the formula round into the form $x = g(y)$. Then g is the inverse of f.

Example 11.7.1

Find the inverse of $f : x \mapsto 2x + 5, x \in \mathbb{R}$.

Note first that f is one–one, and that the range is $\mathbb{R}$.

Method 1 You can break the function down as

$$x \rightarrow [\text{double}] \rightarrow [\text{add 5}] \rightarrow 2x + 5.$$

To find f^{-1}, go backwards through the chain (read from right to left):

$$\tfrac{1}{2}(x - 5) \leftarrow [\text{halve}] \leftarrow [\text{subtract 5}] \leftarrow x.$$

So $f^{-1} : x \mapsto \tfrac{1}{2}(x - 5), x \in \mathbb{R}$.

Method 2 If $y = 2x + 5$,

$$y - 5 = 2x \quad \text{which gives} \quad x = \tfrac{1}{2}(y - 5).$$

So the inverse function is $f^{-1} : y \mapsto \tfrac{1}{2}(y - 5), y \in \mathbb{R}$.

The two answers are the same, even though different letters are used.

Example 11.7.2

Restrict the domain of the function $f : x \mapsto x^2 - 2x$, so that an inverse function exists. Find an expression for f^{-1}.

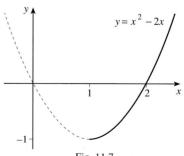

Fig. 11.7

Fig. 11.7 shows the graph of $y = x^2 - 2x, x \in \mathbb{R}$, which is quadratic with its vertex at $(1, -1)$. For $y > -1$ there are two values of x for each y, so the graph does not represent a one–one function. One way of making it one–one is to chop off the part of the graph to the left of its axis of symmetry. This restricts the domain to $x \in \mathbb{R}, x \geqslant 1$, but the range is still $y \in \mathbb{R}, y \geqslant -1$.

Method 1   Completing the square gives $f(x) = (x-1)^2 - 1$, so you can break the function down as

$$x \rightarrow [\text{subtract } 1] \rightarrow [\text{square}] \rightarrow [\text{subtract } 1] \rightarrow y.$$

In reverse,

$$1 + \sqrt{y+1} \leftarrow [\text{add } 1] \leftarrow [\sqrt{}\,] \leftarrow [\text{add } 1] \leftarrow y.$$

So the inverse function is $f^{-1} : y \mapsto 1 + \sqrt{y+1}, y \in \mathbb{R}, y \geq -1$.

Notice that the positive square root was chosen to make $x > 1$.

Method 2   If $y = x^2 - 2x$, then $x^2 - 2x - y = 0$.

This is a quadratic equation with roots

$$x = \frac{2 \pm \sqrt{4 + 4y}}{2} = 1 \pm \sqrt{1 + y}.$$

Since $x \geq 1$, you must choose the positive sign, giving $x = 1 + \sqrt{1+y}$. So the inverse function is $f^{-1} : y \mapsto 1 + \sqrt{y+1}, y \in \mathbb{R}, y \geq -1$.

Example 11.7.3

Find the inverse of the function $f(x) = \dfrac{x+2}{x-2}$, where $x \in \mathbb{R}$ and $x \neq 2$.

It is not obvious that this function is one–one, or what its range is. However, using the second method and writing $y = \dfrac{x+2}{x-2}$,

$$y(x-2) = x+2,$$
$$yx - 2y = x + 2,$$
$$yx - x = 2y + 2,$$
$$x(y-1) = 2(y+1),$$
$$x = \frac{2(y+1)}{y-1}.$$

This shows that, unless $y = 1$, there is just one value of x for each value of y. So f must be one–one, the inverse function therefore exists, and

$$f^{-1} : y \mapsto \frac{2(y+1)}{y-1}, \text{ where } y \in \mathbb{R} \text{ and } y \neq -1.$$

11.8 Graphing inverse functions

Fig. 11.8 shows the graph of $y = f(x)$, where f is a one–one function with domain D and range R. Since f^{-1} exists, with domain R and range D, you can also write the equation as $x = f^{-1}(y)$. You can regard Fig. 11.8 as the graph of both f and f^{-1}.

But you sometimes want to draw the graph of f^{-1} in the more conventional form, as $y = f^{-1}(x)$ with the domain along the x-axis. To do this you have to swap the x- and y-axes, which you do by reflecting the graph in Fig. 11.8 in the line $y = x$. (Make sure that you have the same scale on both axes!) Then the x-axis is reflected into the y-axis and vice versa, and the graph of $x = f^{-1}(y)$ is reflected into the graph of $y = f^{-1}(x)$. This is shown in Fig. 11.9.

> If f is a one–one function, the graphs of $y = f(x)$ and $y = f^{-1}(x)$
> are reflections of each other in the line $y = x$.

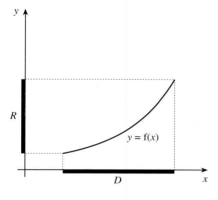

Fig. 11.8

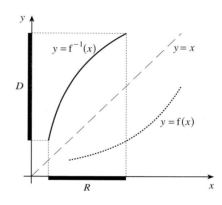

Fig. 11.9

Example 11.8.1
For the function in Example 11.7.2, draw the graphs of $y = f(x)$ and $y = f^{-1}(x)$.

Example 11.7.2 showed that
$f^{-1}(x) = 1 + \sqrt{x+1}$, $x \in \mathbb{R}$, $x \geqslant -1$.

Fig. 11.10 shows the graphs of
$y = f(x) = x^2 - 2x$ for $x \geqslant 1$ and
$y = f^{-1}(x) = 1 + \sqrt{x+1}$ for $x \geqslant -1$. You
can see that these graphs are reflections of
each other in the line $y = x$.

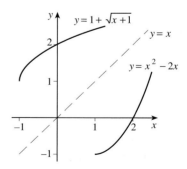

Fig. 11.10

Exercise 11B

1 Each of the following functions has domain $\mathbb{R}$. In each case use a graph to show that the function is one–one, and write down its inverse.

(a) $f : x \mapsto x + 4$ (b) $f : x \mapsto x - 5$ (c) $f : x \mapsto 2x$

(d) $f : x \mapsto \frac{1}{4}x$ (e) $f : x \mapsto x^3$ (f) $f : x \mapsto \sqrt[5]{x}$

2 Given the function $f : x \mapsto x - 6, x \in \mathbb{R}$, find the values of

  (a) $f^{-1}(4)$,   (b) $f^{-1}(1)$,   (c) $f^{-1}(-3)$,   (d) $ff^{-1}(5)$,   (e) $f^{-1}f(-4)$.

3 Given the function $f : x \mapsto 5x, x \in \mathbb{R}$, find the values of

  (a) $f^{-1}(20)$,   (b) $f^{-1}(100)$,   (c) $f^{-1}(7)$,   (d) $ff^{-1}(15)$,   (e) $f^{-1}f(-6)$.

4 Given the function $f : x \mapsto \sqrt[3]{x}, x \in \mathbb{R}$, find the values of

  (a) $f^{-1}(2)$,   (b) $f^{-1}\left(\frac{1}{2}\right)$,   (c) $f^{-1}(8)$,   (d) $f^{-1}f(-27)$,   (e) $ff^{-1}(5)$.

5 Each of the following functions has domain $\mathbb{R}$. Determine which are one–one functions.

  (a) $f : x \mapsto 3x + 4$ (b) $f : x \mapsto x^2 + 1$ (c) $f : x \mapsto x^2 - 3x$

  (d) $f : x \mapsto 5 - x$ (e) $f : x \mapsto \cos x°$ (f) $f : x \mapsto x^3 - 2$

  (g) $f : x \mapsto \frac{1}{2}x - 7$ (h) $f : x \mapsto \sqrt{x^2}$ (i) $f : x \mapsto x(x - 4)$

  (j) $f : x \mapsto x^3 - 3x$ (k) $f : x \mapsto x^9$ (l) $f : x \mapsto \sqrt{x^2 + 1}$

6 Determine which of the following functions, with the specified domains, are one–one.

  (a) $f : x \mapsto x^2, x > 0$ (b) $f : x \mapsto \cos x°, -90 \leqslant x \leqslant 90$

  (c) $f : x \mapsto 1 - 2x, x < 0$ (d) $f : x \mapsto x(x - 2), 0 < x < 2$

  (e) $f : x \mapsto x(x - 2), x > 2$ (f) $f : x \mapsto x(x - 2), x < 1$

  (g) $f : x \mapsto \sqrt{x}, x > 0$ (h) $f : x \mapsto x^2 + 6x - 5, x > 0$

  (i) $f : x \mapsto x^2 + 6x - 5, x < 0$ (j) $f : x \mapsto x^2 + 6x - 5, x > -3$

7 Each of the following functions has domain $x \geqslant k$. In each case, find the smallest possible value of k such that the function is one–one.

  (a) $f : x \mapsto x^2 - 4$ (b) $f : x \mapsto (x + 1)^2$ (c) $f : x \mapsto (3x - 2)^2$

  (d) $f : x \mapsto x^2 - 8x + 15$ (e) $f : x \mapsto x^2 + 10x + 1$ (f) $f : x \mapsto (x + 4)(x - 2)$

  (g) $f : x \mapsto x^2 - 3x$ (h) $f : x \mapsto 6 + 2x - x^2$ (i) $f : x \mapsto (x - 4)^4$

8 Use method 1 of Example 11.7.1 to find the inverse of each of the following functions.

  (a) $f : x \mapsto 3x - 1, x \in \mathbb{R}$ (b) $f : x \mapsto \frac{1}{2}x + 4, x \in \mathbb{R}$

  (c) $f : x \mapsto x^3 + 5, x \in \mathbb{R}$ (d) $f : x \mapsto \sqrt{x} - 3, x > 0$

  (e) $f : x \mapsto \dfrac{5x - 3}{2}, x \in \mathbb{R}$ (f) $f : x \mapsto (x - 1)^2 + 6, x \geqslant 1$

9 Use method 2 of Example 11.7.1 to find the inverse of each of the following functions.

  (a) $f : x \mapsto 6x + 5, x \in \mathbb{R}$ (b) $f : x \mapsto \dfrac{x + 4}{5}, x \in \mathbb{R}$

  (c) $f : x \mapsto 4 - 2x, x \in \mathbb{R}$ (d) $f : x \mapsto \dfrac{2x + 7}{3}, x \in \mathbb{R}$

  (e) $f : x \mapsto 2x^3 + 5, x \in \mathbb{R}$ (f) $f : x \mapsto \dfrac{1}{x} + 4, x \in \mathbb{R}$ and $x \neq 0$

  (g) $f : x \mapsto \dfrac{5}{x - 1}, x \in \mathbb{R}$ and $x \neq 1$ (h) $f : x \mapsto (x + 2)^2 + 7, x \in \mathbb{R}$ and $x \geqslant -2$

  (i) $f : x \mapsto (2x - 3)^2 - 5, x \in \mathbb{R}$ and $x \geqslant \frac{3}{2}$ (j) $f : x \mapsto x^2 - 6x, x \in \mathbb{R}$ and $x \geqslant 3$

10 For each of the following, find the inverse function and sketch the graphs of $y = f(x)$ and $y = f^{-1}(x)$.

(a) $f : x \mapsto 4x, x \in \mathbb{R}$

(b) $f : x \mapsto x + 3, x \in \mathbb{R}$

(c) $f : x \mapsto \sqrt{x}, x \in \mathbb{R}$ and $x \geq 0$

(d) $f : x \mapsto 2x + 1, x \in \mathbb{R}$

(e) $f : x \mapsto (x - 2)^2, x \in \mathbb{R}$ and $x \geq 2$

(f) $f : x \mapsto 1 - 3x, x \in \mathbb{R}$

(g) $f : x \mapsto \dfrac{3}{x}, x \in \mathbb{R}$ and $x \neq 0$

(h) $f : x \mapsto 7 - x, x \in \mathbb{R}$

11 Show that the following functions are self-inverse.

(a) $f : x \mapsto 5 - x, x \in \mathbb{R}$

(b) $f : x \mapsto -x, x \in \mathbb{R}$

(c) $f : x \mapsto \dfrac{4}{x}, x \in \mathbb{R}$ and $x \neq 0$

(d) $f : x \mapsto \dfrac{6}{5x}, x \in \mathbb{R}$ and $x \neq 0$

(e) $f : x \mapsto \dfrac{x + 5}{x - 1}, x \in \mathbb{R}$ and $x \neq 1$

(f) $f : x \mapsto \dfrac{3x - 1}{2x - 3}, x \in \mathbb{R}$ and $x \neq \frac{3}{2}$

12 Find the inverse of each of the following functions.

(a) $f : x \mapsto \dfrac{x}{x - 2}, x \in \mathbb{R}$ and $x \neq 2$

(b) $f : x \mapsto \dfrac{2x + 1}{x - 4}, x \in \mathbb{R}$ and $x \neq 4$

(c) $f : x \mapsto \dfrac{x + 2}{x - 5}, x \in \mathbb{R}$ and $x \neq 5$

(d) $f : x \mapsto \dfrac{3x - 11}{4x - 3}, x \in \mathbb{R}$ and $x \neq \frac{3}{4}$

13 The function $f : x \mapsto x^2 - 4x + 3$ has domain $x \in \mathbb{R}$ and $x > 2$.

(a) Determine the range of f.

(b) Find the inverse function f^{-1} and state its domain and range.

(c) Sketch the graphs of $y = f(x)$ and $y = f^{-1}(x)$.

14 The function $f : x \mapsto \sqrt{x - 2} + 3$ has domain $x \in \mathbb{R}$ and $x > 2$.

(a) Determine the range of f.

(b) Find the inverse function f^{-1} and state its domain and range.

(c) Sketch the graphs of $y = f(x)$ and $y = f^{-1}(x)$.

15 The function $f : x \mapsto x^2 + 2x + 6$ has domain $x \in \mathbb{R}$ and $x \leq k$. Given that f is one–one, determine the greatest possible value of k. When k has this value,

(a) determine the range of f,

(b) find the inverse function f^{-1} and state its domain and range,

(c) sketch the graphs of $y = f(x)$ and $y = f^{-1}(x)$.

16 The inverse of the function $f : x \mapsto ax + b, x \in \mathbb{R}$, is $f^{-1} : x \mapsto 8x - 3$. Find a and b.

17 The function $f : x \mapsto px + q, x \in \mathbb{R}$, is such that $f^{-1}(6) = 3$ and $f^{-1}(-29) = -2$. Find $f^{-1}(27)$.

18 The function $f : x \mapsto x^2 + x + 6$ has domain $x \in \mathbb{R}$ and $x > 0$. Find the inverse function and state its domain and range.

19 The function $f : x \mapsto -2x^2 + 4x - 7$ has domain $x \in \mathbb{R}$ and $x < 1$. Find the inverse function and state its domain and range.

20 For each of the following functions, sketch the graph of $y = f^{-1}(x)$.

(a) $f : x \mapsto \sin x°, x \in \mathbb{R}$ and $-90 \approx x \approx 90$

(b) $f : x \mapsto \cos x°, x \in \mathbb{R}$ and $0 \approx x \approx 180$

(c) $f : x \mapsto \tan x°, x \in \mathbb{R}$ and $-90 < x < 90$

Miscellaneous exercise 11

1 The functions f and g are defined by

$$f : x \mapsto 4x + 9, x \in \mathbb{R}, \qquad g : x \mapsto x^2 + 1, x \in \mathbb{R}.$$

Find the value of each of the following.

(a) $fg(2)$

(b) $fg(2\sqrt{3})$

(c) $gf(-2)$

(d) $ff(-3)$

(e) $gg(-4)$

(f) $fgf\left(\frac{1}{2}\right)$

2 Find the natural domain and corresponding range of each of the following functions.

(a) $f : x \mapsto 4 - x^2$

(b) $f : x \mapsto (x + 3)^2 - 7\square$

(c) $f : x \mapsto \sqrt{x + 2}$

(d) $f : x \mapsto 5x + 6$

(e) $f : x \mapsto (2x + 3)^2$

(f) $f : x \mapsto 2 - \sqrt{x}$

3 The functions f and g are defined by

$$f : x \mapsto x^3, x \in \mathbb{R}, \qquad g : x \mapsto 1 - 2x, x \in \mathbb{R}.$$

Find the functions

(a) fg,

(b) gf,

(c) gff,

(d) gg,

(e) g^{-1}.

4 The function f is defined by $f : x \mapsto 2x^3 - 6, x \in \mathbb{R}$. Find the values of the following.

(a) $f(3)$

(b) $f^{-1}(48)$

(c) $f^{-1}(-8)$

(d) $f^{-1}f(4)$

(e) $ff^{-1}(4)$

5 The function f is defined for all real values of x by $f(x) = x^{\frac{1}{3}} + 10$. Evaluate

(a) $ff(-8)$,

(b) $f^{-1}(13)$.   (OCR)

6 Show that the function $f : x \mapsto (x + 3)^2 + 1$, with domain $x \in \mathbb{R}$ and $x > 0$, is one–one and find its inverse.

7 The function f is defined by $f : x \mapsto 4x^3 + 3, x \in \mathbb{R}$. Give the corresponding definition of f^{-1}. State a relationship between the graphs of f and f^{-1}.   (OCR)

8 Given that $f(x) = 3x^2 - 4, x > 0$, and $g(x) = x + 4, x \in \mathbb{R}$, find

(a) $f^{-1}(x), x > -4$,

(b) $fg(x), x > -4$.   (OCR)

9 The functions f, g and h are defined by

$$f : x \mapsto 2x + 1, x \in \mathbb{R}, \qquad g : x \mapsto x^5, x \in \mathbb{R}, \qquad h : x \mapsto \frac{1}{x}, x \in \mathbb{R} \text{ and } x \neq 0.$$

Express each of the following in terms of f, g, h as appropriate.

(a) $x \mapsto (2x + 1)^5$

(b) $x \mapsto 4x + 3$

(c) $x \mapsto x^{\frac{1}{5}}$

(d) $x \mapsto 2x^{-5} + 1$

(e) $x \mapsto \dfrac{1}{2x^5 + 1}$

(f) $x \mapsto \dfrac{x - 1}{2}$

(g) $x \mapsto \sqrt[5]{\dfrac{2}{x^5} + 1}$

(h) $x \mapsto \dfrac{2}{x - 1}$

10 The function f is defined by $f : x \mapsto x^2 + 1, x \geqslant 0$. Sketch the graph of the function f and, using your sketch or otherwise, show that f is a one–one function. Obtain an expression in terms of x for $f^{-1}(x)$ and state the domain of f^{-1}.

The function g is defined by $g : x \mapsto x - 3, x \geqslant 0$. Give an expression in terms of x for $gf(x)$ and state the range of gf.   (OCR)

11 The functions f and g are defined by

$$f : x \mapsto x^2 + 6x, x \in \mathbb{R}, \qquad g : x \mapsto 2x - 1, x \in \mathbb{R}.$$

Find the two values of x such that $fg(x) = gf(x)$, giving each answer in the form $p + q\sqrt{3}$.

12 The function f is defined by $f : x \mapsto x^2 - 2x + 7$ with domain $x \leqslant k$. Given that f is a one–one function, find the greatest possible value of k and find the inverse function f^{-1}.

13 Functions f and g are defined by

$$f : x \mapsto x^2 + 2x + 3, x \in \mathbb{R}, \qquad g : x \mapsto ax + b, x \in \mathbb{R}.$$

Given that $fg(x) = 4x^2 - 48x + 146$ for all x, find the possible values of a and b.

14 The function f is defined by $f : x \mapsto 1 - x^2, x \leqslant 0$.

(a) Sketch the graph of f.

(b) Find an expression, in terms of x, for $f^{-1}(x)$ and state the domain of f^{-1}.

(c) The function g is defined by $g : x \mapsto 2x, x \leqslant 0$. Find the value of x for which $fg(x) = 0$.   (OCR)

15 Functions f and g are defined by $f : x \mapsto 4x + 5, x \in \mathbb{R}$, and $g : x \mapsto 3 - 2x, x \in \mathbb{R}$. Find

(a) f^{-1},   (b) g^{-1},   (c) $f^{-1}g^{-1}$,   (d) gf,   (e) $(gf)^{-1}$.

16 Functions f and g are defined by $f : x \mapsto 2x + 7, x \in \mathbb{R}$, and $g : x \mapsto x^3 - 1, x \in \mathbb{R}$. Find

(a) f^{-1},   (b) g^{-1},   (c) $g^{-1}f^{-1}$,   (d) $f^{-1}g^{-1}$,

(e) fg,   (f) gf,   (g) $(fg)^{-1}$,   (h) $(gf)^{-1}$.

17 Given the function $f : x \mapsto 10 - x, x \in \mathbb{R}$, evaluate

(a) $f(7)$,   (b) $f^2(7)$,   (c) $f^{15}(7)$,   (d) $f^{100}(7)$.

(The notation f^2 represents the composite function ff, f^3 represents fff, and so on.)

18 Given the function $f : x \mapsto \dfrac{x + 5}{2x - 1}, x \in \mathbb{R}$ and $x \neq \frac{1}{2}$, find

(a) $f^2(x)$,   (b) $f^3(x)$,   (c) $f^4(x)$,   (d) $f^{10}(x)$,   (e) $f^{351}(x)$.

19 Given the function $f(x) = \dfrac{2x - 4}{x}, x \in \mathbb{R}$ and $x \neq 0$, find

(a) $f^2(x)$,   (b) $f^{-1}(x)$,   (c) $f^3(x)$,

(d) $f^4(x)$,   (e) $f^{12}(x)$,   (f) $f^{82}(x)$.

20 Show that a function of the form $x \mapsto \dfrac{x + a}{x - 1}, x \in \mathbb{R}$ and $x \neq 1$, is self-inverse for all values of the constant a.

12 Extending differentiation

This chapter is about differentiating composite functions. When you have completed it, you should

- be able to differentiate composite functions of the form $f(F(x))$
- be able to apply differentiation to rates of change, and to related rates of change.

You may want to leave out Section 12.4 on a first reading; the exercises do not depend on it.

12.1 Differentiating $(ax+b)^n$

To differentiate a function like $(2x+1)^3$, the only method available to you at present is to use the binomial theorem to multiply out the brackets, and then to differentiate term by term.

Example 12.1.1

Find $\dfrac{dy}{dx}$ for (a) $y = (2x+1)^3$, (b) $y = (1-3x)^4$.

(a) Expanding by the binomial theorem,

$$y = (2x)^3 + 3 \times (2x)^2 \times 1 + 3 \times (2x) \times 1^2 + 1^3 = 8x^3 + 12x^2 + 6x + 1.$$

So $\dfrac{dy}{dx} = 24x^2 + 24x + 6$.

It is useful to express the result in factors, as $\dfrac{dy}{dx} = 6\left(4x^2 + 4x + 1\right) = 6(2x+1)^2$.

(b) Expanding by the binomial theorem,

$$y = 1^4 + 4 \times 1^3 \times (-3x) + 6 \times 1^2 \times (-3x)^2 + 4 \times 1 \times (-3x)^3 + (-3x)^4$$
$$= 1 - 12x + 54x^2 - 108x^3 + 81x^4.$$

So $\dfrac{dy}{dx} = -12 + 108x - 324x^2 + 324x^3 = -12\left(1 - 9x + 27x^2 - 27x^3\right) = -12(1-3x)^3.$

Exercise 12A

In Question 1, see if you can predict what the result of the differentiation will be. If you can predict the result, then check by carrying out the differentiation, and factorising your result. If you can't, differentiate and simplify and look for a pattern in your answers.

1 Find $\dfrac{dy}{dx}$ for each of the following functions. In parts (d) and (e), a and b are constants.

(a) $(x+3)^2$ (b) $(2x-3)^2$ (c) $(1-3x)^3$ (d) $(ax+b)^3$

(e) $(b-ax)^3$ (f) $(1-x)^5$ (g) $(2x-3)^4$ (h) $(3-2x)^4$

2 Suppose that $y = (ax + b)^n$, where a and b are constants and n is a positive integer. Guess a formula for $\dfrac{dy}{dx}$.

3 Use the formula you guessed in Question 2, after checking that it is correct, to differentiate each of the following functions, where a and b are constants.

(a) $(x+3)^{10}$ (b) $(2x-1)^5$ (c) $(1-4x)^7$ (d) $(3x-2)^5$

(e) $(4-2x)^6$ (f) $4(2+3x)^6$ (g) $(2x+5)^5$ (h) $(2x-3)^9$

In Exercise 12A, you were asked to predict how to differentiate a function of the form $(ax+b)^n$, where a and b are constants and n is a positive integer. The result was:

$$\text{If } y = (ax+b)^n, \text{ then } \frac{dy}{dx} = n(ax+b)^{n-1} \times a.$$

Now assume that the same formula works for all n, including fractional and negative values. There is a proof in Section 12.4, but you can skip it on a first reading. The result, however, is important, and you must be able to use it confidently.

> If a, b and n are constants, and $y = (ax+b)^n$, then $\dfrac{dy}{dx} = n(ax+b)^{n-1} \times a$.

Example 12.1.2

Find $\dfrac{dy}{dx}$ when   (a) $y = \sqrt{3x+2}$,   (b) $y = \dfrac{1}{1-2x}$.

(a) Writing $\sqrt{3x+2}$ in index form as $(3x+2)^{\frac{1}{2}}$ and using the result in the box,

$$\frac{dy}{dx} = \tfrac{1}{2}(3x+2)^{-\frac{1}{2}} \times 3 = \tfrac{3}{2}\frac{1}{(3x+2)^{\frac{1}{2}}} = \frac{3}{2\sqrt{3x+2}}.$$

(b) In index form $y = (1-2x)^{-1}$, so $\dfrac{dy}{dx} = -1(1-2x)^{-2} \times (-2) = \dfrac{2}{(1-2x)^2}$.

Example 12.1.3

Find any stationary points on the graph $y = \sqrt{2x+1} + \dfrac{1}{\sqrt{2x+1}}$, and determine whether they are maxima, minima or neither.

$\sqrt{2x+1}$ is defined for $x \geqslant -\tfrac{1}{2}$, and $\dfrac{1}{\sqrt{2x+1}}$ for $x > -\tfrac{1}{2}$. So the largest possible domain is $x > -\tfrac{1}{2}$.

$y = (2x+1)^{\frac{1}{2}} + (2x+1)^{-\frac{1}{2}}$, so

$$\frac{dy}{dx} = \tfrac{1}{2}(2x+1)^{-\frac{1}{2}} \times 2 + \left(-\tfrac{1}{2}\right)(2x+1)^{-\frac{3}{2}} \times 2 = (2x+1)^{-\frac{1}{2}} - (2x+1)^{-\frac{3}{2}}$$

$$= \frac{1}{(2x+1)^{\frac{1}{2}}} - \frac{1}{(2x+1)^{\frac{3}{2}}} = \frac{2x+1-1}{(2x+1)^{\frac{3}{2}}} = \frac{2x}{(2x+1)^{\frac{3}{2}}}.$$

Stationary points are those for which $\dfrac{dy}{dx} = 0$, which happens when $x = 0$.

To find the nature of the stationary point, notice that the denominator in the expression for $\dfrac{dy}{dx}$ is positive for all values of x in the domain, and that the numerator is positive for $x > 0$ and negative for $x < 0$. So y has a minimum at $x = 0$.

The result given in the box on page 175 is a special case of a more general result which you can use to differentiate any function of the form $\mathrm{f}(ax + b)$.

> If a and b are constants, and if $\dfrac{d}{dx}\mathrm{f}(x) = \mathrm{g}(x)$,
>
> then $\dfrac{d}{dx}\mathrm{f}(ax + b) = a\mathrm{g}(ax + b)$.

For the special case in this section, $\mathrm{f}(x) = x^n$ and $\mathrm{g}(x) = nx^{n-1}$. Then

$$\frac{d}{dx}(ax + b)^n = \frac{d}{dx}\mathrm{f}(ax + b) = a\mathrm{g}(ax + b) = an(ax + b)^{n-1}.$$

Exercise 12B

1 Find $\dfrac{dy}{dx}$ for each of the following.

(a) $y = (4x + 5)^5$ (b) $y = (2x - 7)^8$ (c) $y = (2 - x)^6$ (d) $y = \left(\tfrac{1}{2}x + 4\right)^4$

2 Find $\dfrac{dy}{dx}$ for each of the following.

(a) $y = \dfrac{1}{3x + 5}$ (b) $y = \dfrac{1}{(4 - x)^2}$ (c) $y = \dfrac{1}{(2x + 1)^3}$ (d) $y = \dfrac{4}{(4x - 1)^4}$

3 Find $\dfrac{dy}{dx}$ for each of the following.

(a) $y = \sqrt{2x + 3}$ (b) $y = \sqrt[3]{6x - 1}$ (c) $y = \dfrac{1}{\sqrt{4x + 7}}$ (d) $y = 5(3x - 2)^{-\frac{2}{3}}$

4 Given that $y = (2x + 1)^3 + (2x - 1)^3$, find the value of $\dfrac{dy}{dx}$ when $x = 1$.

5 Find the coordinates of the point on the curve $y = (1 - 4x)^{\frac{3}{2}}$ at which the gradient is -30.

6 Find the equation of the tangent to the curve $y = \dfrac{1}{3x + 1}$ at $\left(-1, -\tfrac{1}{2}\right)$.

7 Find the equation of the normal to the curve $y = \sqrt{6x + 3}$ at the point for which $x = 13$.

12.2 The chain rule: an informal treatment

When you differentiate $(ax + b)^n$ by using the methods of Section 12.1, you are actually differentiating the composite function

$$x \;\; \rightarrow \;\; [\times, a, +, b, =] \;\; \rightarrow \;\; ax + b \;\; \rightarrow \;\; [\text{ raise to power } n\,] \;\; \rightarrow \;\; (ax + b)^n\,.$$

That is, you are differentiating $f(F(x))$, where $F : x \mapsto ax + b$ and $f : u \mapsto u^n$.

You will soon see the reason for using different letters, x and u, in describing the two functions. Remember that the function is the same, whatever letter is used. (See Section 11.3.)

The rule at the end of Section 12.1 is a special case in which $F(x) = ax + b$. This section shows how the rule can be generalised to differentiate $f(F(x))$ where F is any function which can be differentiated. As a lead-in, here is a very simple example which suggests the general rule.

Example 12.2.1
Find the derivative of the composite function
$$x \;\; \rightarrow \;\; [\times, a, +, b, =] \;\; \rightarrow \;\; ax + b \;\; \rightarrow \;\; [\times, c, +, d, =] \;\; \rightarrow \;\; c(ax + b) + d\,.$$

If you let $y = c(ax + b) + d$, then
$$\frac{dy}{dx} = \frac{d}{dx}\big(c(ax + b) + d\big) = \frac{d}{dx}(cax + cb + d) = ca\,.$$

However, if you let u stand for the intermediate output $ax + b$, then $y = cu + d$.
So $\dfrac{dy}{du} = c$ and $\dfrac{du}{dx} = a$, and $\dfrac{dy}{dx} = ca$. That is, $\dfrac{dy}{dx} = \dfrac{dy}{du} \times \dfrac{du}{dx}$.

You can also think about this in terms of rates of change.

Recall that:

- $\dfrac{dy}{dx}$ is the rate at which y changes with respect to x,

- $\dfrac{dy}{du}$ is the rate at which y changes with respect to u,

- $\dfrac{du}{dx}$ is the rate at which u changes with respect to x.

The equation $\dfrac{dy}{du} = c$ means that y is changing c times as fast as u; similarly u is changing a times as fast as x. It is natural to think that if y is changing c times as fast as u, and u is changing a times as fast as x, then y is changing $c \times a$ times as fast as x. Thus, again,

$$\frac{dy}{dx} = \frac{dy}{du} \times \frac{du}{dx}\,.$$

Example 12.2.2

Find $\dfrac{dy}{dx}$ when $y = \left(1 + x^2\right)^3$.

So far there has been no alternative to expanding by the binomial theorem. You have had to write

$$y = \left(1 + x^2\right)^3 = 1 + 3x^2 + 3x^4 + x^6,$$

$$\frac{dy}{dx} = 6x + 12x^3 + 6x^5 = 6x\left(1 + 2x^2 + x^4\right)$$

$$= 6x\left(1 + x^2\right)^2.$$

But now the relation $\dfrac{dy}{dx} = \dfrac{dy}{du} \times \dfrac{du}{dx}$ suggests another approach. If you substitute $u = 1 + x^2$, so that $y = u^3$, then

$$\frac{dy}{du} = 3u^2 = 3\left(1 + x^2\right)^2 \text{ and } \frac{du}{dx} = 2x.$$

So $\quad \dfrac{dy}{du} \times \dfrac{du}{dx} = 3\left(1 + x^2\right)^2 \times 2x = 6x\left(1 + x^2\right)^2.$

So once again $\dfrac{dy}{dx} = \dfrac{dy}{du} \times \dfrac{du}{dx}$.

Assume now that this result, known as the chain rule, holds in all cases. It is also sometimes called the 'composite function' rule, or the 'function of a function' rule.

The chain rule is easy to remember because the term du appears to cancel, but bear in mind that this is simply a helpful feature of the notation. Cancellation has no meaning in this context.

Chain rule

If $y = f(F(x))$, and $u = F(x)$ so that $y = f(u)$, then $\dfrac{dy}{dx} = \dfrac{dy}{du} \times \dfrac{du}{dx}$.

A proof is given in Section 12.4, but you can omit it on a first reading.

Example 12.2.3

Differentiate $y = (2x + 1)^{\frac{1}{2}}$ with respect to x.

Substitute $u = 2x + 1$, so that $y = u^{\frac{1}{2}}$. Then $\dfrac{dy}{du} = \dfrac{1}{2}u^{-\frac{1}{2}} = \dfrac{1}{2}(2x + 1)^{-\frac{1}{2}}$ and $\dfrac{du}{dx} = 2$.

As $\dfrac{dy}{dx} = \dfrac{dy}{du} \times \dfrac{du}{dx}$, $\dfrac{dy}{dx} = \dfrac{1}{2}(2x + 1)^{-\frac{1}{2}} \times 2 = (2x + 1)^{-\frac{1}{2}} = \dfrac{1}{\sqrt{2x + 1}}$.

Example 12.2.4

Find $\dfrac{dy}{dx}$ when (a) $y = \dfrac{1}{1+x^2}$, (b) $y = \sqrt{1-x^2}$, (c) $y = \sqrt{1+\sqrt{x}}$.

(a) Substitute $u = 1 + x^2$, so $y = \dfrac{1}{u}$. Then $\dfrac{dy}{du} = -\dfrac{1}{u^2} = -\dfrac{1}{\left(1+x^2\right)^2}$ and $\dfrac{du}{dx} = 2x$.

So $\dfrac{dy}{dx} = \dfrac{dy}{du} \times \dfrac{du}{dx} = -\dfrac{1}{\left(1+x^2\right)^2} \times 2x = \dfrac{-2x}{\left(1+x^2\right)^2}$.

(b) Substitute $u = 1 - x^2$, so $y = \sqrt{u} = u^{\frac{1}{2}}$.

Then $\dfrac{dy}{du} = \tfrac{1}{2} u^{-\frac{1}{2}} = \dfrac{1}{2\sqrt{u}} = \dfrac{1}{2\sqrt{1-x^2}}$ and $\dfrac{du}{dx} = -2x$.

So $\dfrac{dy}{dx} = \dfrac{dy}{du} \times \dfrac{du}{dx} = \dfrac{1}{2\sqrt{1-x^2}} \times (-2x) = \dfrac{-x}{\sqrt{1-x^2}}$.

(c) Substitute $u = 1 + \sqrt{x}$, so $y = \sqrt{u}$.

Then $\dfrac{dy}{du} = \tfrac{1}{2} u^{-\frac{1}{2}} = \dfrac{1}{2\sqrt{u}} = \dfrac{1}{2\sqrt{1+\sqrt{x}}}$ and $\dfrac{du}{dx} = \dfrac{1}{2\sqrt{x}}$.

So $\dfrac{dy}{dx} = \dfrac{dy}{du} \times \dfrac{du}{dx} = \dfrac{1}{2\sqrt{1+\sqrt{x}}} \times \dfrac{1}{2\sqrt{x}} = \dfrac{1}{4\sqrt{x\left(1+\sqrt{x}\right)}}$.

Exercise 12C

1 Use the substitution $u = 5x + 3$ to differentiate the following with respect to x.

   (a) $y = (5x+3)^6$ 　　　　　　(b) $y = (5x+3)^{\frac{1}{2}}$ 　　　　　　(c) $y = \dfrac{1}{5x+3}$

2 Use the substitution $u = 1 - 4x$ to differentiate the following with respect to x.

   (a) $y = (1-4x)^5$ 　　　　　　(b) $y = (1-4x)^{-3}$ 　　　　　　(c) $y = \sqrt{1-4x}$

3 Use the substitution $u = 1 + x^3$ to differentiate the following with respect to x.

   (a) $y = \left(1+x^3\right)^5$ 　　　　　(b) $y = \left(1+x^3\right)^{-4}$ 　　　　　(c) $y = \sqrt[3]{1+x^3}$

4 Use the substitution $u = 2x^2 + 3$ to differentiate the following with respect to x.

   (a) $y = \left(2x^2+3\right)^6$ 　　　　　(b) $y = \dfrac{1}{2x^2+3}$ 　　　　　(c) $y = \dfrac{1}{\sqrt{2x^2+3}}$

5 Differentiate $y = \left(3x^4+2\right)^2$ with respect to x by using the chain rule. Confirm your answer by expanding $\left(3x^4+2\right)^2$ and then differentiating.

6 Differentiate $y = (2x^3 + 1)^3$ with respect to x

    (a) by using the binomial theorem to expand $y = (2x^3 + 1)^3$ and then differentiating term by term,

    (b) by using the chain rule.

    Check that your answers are the same.

7 Use appropriate substitutions to differentiate the following with respect to x.

    (a) $y = (x^5 + 1)^4$ (b) $y = (2x^3 - 1)^8$ (c) $y = (\sqrt{x} - 1)^5$

8 Differentiate the following with respect to x; try to do this without writing down the substitutions.

    (a) $y = (x^2 + 6)^4$ (b) $y = (5x^3 + 4)^3$ (c) $y = (x^4 - 8)^7$ (d) $y = (2 - x^9)^5$

9 Differentiate the following with respect to x.

    (a) $y = \sqrt{4x + 3}$ (b) $y = (x^2 + 4)^6$ (c) $y = (6x^3 - 5)^{-2}$ (d) $y = (5 - x^3)^{-1}$

10 Given that $f(x) = \dfrac{1}{1 + x^2}$, find   (a) $f'(2)$,   (b) the value of x such that $f'(x) = 0$.

11 Given that $y = \sqrt[4]{x^3 + 8}$, find the value of $\dfrac{dy}{dx}$ when $x = 2$.

12 Differentiate the following with respect to x.

    (a) $y = (x^2 + 3x + 1)^6$ (b) $y = \dfrac{1}{(x^2 + 5x)^3}$

13 Find the equation of the tangent to the curve $y = (x^2 - 5)^3$ at the point $(2, -1)$.

14 Find the equation of the tangent to the curve $y = \dfrac{1}{\sqrt{x} - 1}$ at the point $(4, 1)$.

15 Find the equation of the normal to the curve $y = \dfrac{8}{1 - x^3}$ at the point $(-1, 4)$.

16 Use the substitutions $u = x^2 - 1$ and $v = \sqrt{u} + 1$ with the chain rule in the form $\dfrac{dy}{dx} = \dfrac{dy}{dv} \times \dfrac{dv}{du} \times \dfrac{du}{dx}$ to differentiate $y = (\sqrt{x^2 - 1} + 1)^6$.

17 Use two substitutions to find $\dfrac{d}{dx}\left(\sqrt{1 + \sqrt{4x + 3}}\right)$.

18 A curve has equation $y = (x^2 + 1)^4 + 2(x^2 + 1)^3$. Show that $\dfrac{dy}{dx} = 4x(x^2 + 1)^2(2x^2 + 5)$ and hence show that the curve has just one stationary point. State the coordinates of the stationary point and, by considering the gradient of the curve on either side of the stationary point, determine its nature.

12.3 Related rates of change

You often need to calculate the rate at which one quantity varies with another when one of them is time. In Section 7.4 it was shown that if r is some quantity, then the rate of change of r with respect to time t is $\dfrac{dr}{dt}$.

But suppose that r is the radius of a spherical balloon, and you know how fast the volume V of the balloon is increasing. How can you find out how fast the radius is increasing?

Questions like this can be answered by using the chain rule. The situation is best described by a problem.

Example 12.3.1
Suppose that a spherical balloon is being inflated at a constant rate of $5 \text{ m}^3 \text{ s}^{-1}$. At a particular moment, the radius of the balloon is 4 metres. Find how fast the radius of the balloon is increasing at that instant.

First translate the information into a mathematical form.

Let $V \text{ m}^3$ be the volume of the balloon, and let r metres be its radius. Let t seconds be the time for which the balloon has been inflating. Then you are given that $\dfrac{dV}{dt} = 5$ and $r = 4$, and you are asked to find $\dfrac{dr}{dt}$ at that moment.

Your other piece of information is that the balloon is spherical, so that $V = \frac{4}{3}\pi r^3$.

The key to solving the problem is to use the chain rule in the form

$$\frac{dV}{dt} = \frac{dV}{dr} \times \frac{dr}{dt}.$$

You can now use $\dfrac{dV}{dr} = 4\pi r^2$. Substituting the various values into the chain rule formula gives

$$5 = \left(4\pi \times 4^2\right) \times \frac{dr}{dt}.$$

Therefore, rearranging this equation, you find that $\dfrac{dr}{dt} = \dfrac{5}{64\pi}$, so the radius is increasing at $\dfrac{5}{64\pi} \text{ m s}^{-1}$.

In practice you do not need to write down so much detail. Here is another example.

Example 12.3.2
The surface area of a cube is increasing at a constant rate of $24 \text{ cm}^2 \text{ s}^{-1}$. Find the rate at which its volume is increasing at the moment when the volume is 216 cm^3.

Let the side of the cube be x cm at time t seconds, let the surface area be $S \text{ cm}^2$ and let the volume be $V \text{ cm}^3$.

Then $S = 6x^2$, $V = x^3$ and $\dfrac{\mathrm{d}S}{\mathrm{d}t} = 24$, and you need to find $\dfrac{\mathrm{d}V}{\mathrm{d}t}$ when $V = 216$,

which is when $x^3 = 216$, or $x = 6$.

If you know S and want to find V you need to find x first. Similarly, when you know
$\dfrac{\mathrm{d}S}{\mathrm{d}t}$ *and want to find* $\dfrac{\mathrm{d}V}{\mathrm{d}t}$ *you should expect to find* $\dfrac{\mathrm{d}x}{\mathrm{d}t}$ *first.*

From the chain rule, $\dfrac{\mathrm{d}V}{\mathrm{d}t} = \dfrac{\mathrm{d}V}{\mathrm{d}x} \times \dfrac{\mathrm{d}x}{\mathrm{d}t} = 3x^2 \dfrac{\mathrm{d}x}{\mathrm{d}t}$, so, when $x = 6$, $\dfrac{\mathrm{d}V}{\mathrm{d}t} = 108 \dfrac{\mathrm{d}x}{\mathrm{d}t}$.

But $\dfrac{\mathrm{d}S}{\mathrm{d}t} = \dfrac{\mathrm{d}S}{\mathrm{d}x} \times \dfrac{\mathrm{d}x}{\mathrm{d}t} = 12x \dfrac{\mathrm{d}x}{\mathrm{d}t}$, so $24 = (12 \times 6) \times \dfrac{\mathrm{d}x}{\mathrm{d}t}$, giving $\dfrac{\mathrm{d}x}{\mathrm{d}t} = \tfrac{1}{3}$. Substituting

this in the equation $\dfrac{\mathrm{d}V}{\mathrm{d}t} = 108 \dfrac{\mathrm{d}x}{\mathrm{d}t}$ gives $\dfrac{\mathrm{d}V}{\mathrm{d}t} = 108 \times \tfrac{1}{3} = 36$.

Therefore the volume is increasing at a rate of $36 \text{ cm}^3 \text{ s}^{-1}$.

Exercise 12D

1   The number of bacteria present in a culture at time t hours after the beginning of an
    experiment is denoted by N. The relation between N and t is modelled by
    $N = 10\left(1 + \tfrac{3}{2}t\right)^3$. At what rate per hour will the number of bacteria be increasing when
    $t = 6$?   (OCR, adapted)

2   A metal bar is heated to a certain temperature and then the heat source is removed. At time
    t minutes after the heat source is removed, the temperature, θ degrees Celsius, of the
    metal bar is given by $\theta = \dfrac{280}{1 + 0.02t}$. At what rate is the temperature decreasing
    100 minutes after the removal of the heat source?   (OCR, adapted)

3   The length of the side of a square is increasing at a constant rate of 1.2 cm s^{-1}. At the
    moment when the length of the side is 10 cm, find

    (a) the rate of increase of the perimeter,

    (b) the rate of increase of the area.

4   The length of the edge of a cube is increasing at a constant rate of 0.5 mm s^{-1}. At the
    moment when the length of the edge is 40 mm, find

    (a) the rate of increase of the surface area,

    (b) the rate of increase of the volume.

5   A circular stain is spreading so that its radius is increasing at a constant rate of 3 mm s^{-1}.
    Find the rate at which the area is increasing when the radius is 50 mm.

6   A water tank has a rectangular base 1.5 m by 1.2 m. The sides are vertical and water is
    being added to the tank at a constant rate of 0.45 m^3 per minute. At what rate is the depth
    of water in the tank increasing?

7   Air is being lost from a spherical balloon at a constant rate of $0.6 \text{ m}^3 \text{ s}^{-1}$. Find the rate at
    which the radius is decreasing at the instant when the radius is 2.5 m.

8 The volume of a spherical balloon is increasing at a constant rate of $0.25 \text{ m}^3 \text{ s}^{-1}$. Find the rate at which the radius is increasing at the instant when the volume is 10 m^3.

9 A funnel has a circular top of diameter 20 cm and a height of 30 cm. When the depth of liquid in the funnel is 12 cm, the liquid is dripping from the funnel at a rate of $0.2 \text{ cm}^3 \text{ s}^{-1}$. At what rate is the depth of the liquid in the funnel decreasing at this instant?

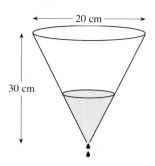

12.4* Deriving the chain rule

In Section 12.2 the chain rule was shown to work in a number of simple cases, and justified by an informal argument involving rates of change. This section shows how it can be proved, although the argument depends on some assumptions which need to be examined more carefully before the proof is complete. You may omit this section if you wish; there is no exercise depending on it.

In Section 7.4, $\dfrac{dy}{dx}$ is defined as

$$\frac{dy}{dx} = \lim_{\delta x \to 0} \frac{\delta y}{\delta x}.$$

By changing the letters in the definition,

$$\frac{dy}{du} = \lim_{\delta u \to 0} \frac{\delta y}{\delta u} \quad \text{and} \quad \frac{du}{dx} = \lim_{\delta x \to 0} \frac{\delta u}{\delta x}.$$

Now, in these expressions, when y is a function of u, where u is a function of x, then as x changes u changes and so y changes.

Take a particular value of x, and increase x by δx with a corresponding increase of δu in the value of u, which, in turn, increases the value of y by δy. Then

$$\frac{\delta y}{\delta x} = \frac{\delta y}{\delta u} \times \frac{\delta u}{\delta x}$$

because δy, δu and δx are numbers which you can cancel, assuming that $\delta u \neq 0$.

To find $\dfrac{dy}{dx}$, you must take the limit as $\delta x \to 0$, so

$$\frac{dy}{dx} = \lim_{\delta x \to 0} \frac{\delta y}{\delta x} = \lim_{\delta x \to 0}\left(\frac{\delta y}{\delta u} \times \frac{\delta u}{\delta x} \right).$$

Assuming that as $\delta x \to 0$, $\delta u \to 0$ and that $\lim\limits_{\delta x \to 0} \left(\dfrac{\delta y}{\delta u} \times \dfrac{\delta u}{\delta x} \right) = \lim\limits_{\delta x \to 0} \left(\dfrac{\delta y}{\delta u} \right) \times \lim\limits_{\delta x \to 0} \left(\dfrac{\delta u}{\delta x} \right)$,
it follows that

$$\begin{aligned}
\frac{dy}{dx} &= \lim_{\delta x \to 0} \frac{\delta y}{\delta x} = \lim_{\delta x \to 0} \left(\frac{\delta y}{\delta u} \times \frac{\delta u}{\delta x} \right) \\
&= \lim_{\delta x \to 0} \left(\frac{\delta y}{\delta u} \right) \times \lim_{\delta x \to 0} \left(\frac{\delta u}{\delta x} \right) = \lim_{\delta u \to 0} \left(\frac{\delta y}{\delta u} \right) \times \lim_{\delta x \to 0} \left(\frac{\delta u}{\delta x} \right) \\
&= \frac{dy}{du} \times \frac{du}{dx}.
\end{aligned}$$

This result, $\dfrac{dy}{dx} = \dfrac{dy}{du} \times \dfrac{du}{dx}$, is the chain rule for differentiating composite functions.

Note that the results in Section 12.1 are particular cases of the chain rule since, if
$u = ax + b$, $\dfrac{du}{dx} = a$.

Miscellaneous exercise 12

1 Differentiate $(4x - 1)^{20}$ with respect to x.   (OCR)

2 Differentiate $\dfrac{1}{(3 - 4x)^2}$ with respect to x.   (OCR)

3 Differentiate $2(x^4 + 3)^5$ with respect to x.

4 Find the equation of the tangent to the curve $y = (x^2 - 5)^6$ at the point $(2,1)$.

5 Given that $y = \sqrt{x^3 + 1}$, show that $\dfrac{dy}{dx} > 0$ for all $x > -1$.

6 Given that $y = \dfrac{1}{2x - 1} + \dfrac{1}{(2x - 1)^2}$, find the exact value of $\dfrac{dy}{dx}$ when $x = 2$.

7 Find the equation of the tangent to the curve $y = (4x + 3)^5$ at the point $\left(-\tfrac{1}{2}, 1 \right)$, giving your
answer in the form $y = mx + c$.   (OCR)

8 Find the coordinates of the stationary point of the curve with equation $y = \dfrac{1}{x^2 + 4}$.

9 Find the equation of the normal to the curve $y = \sqrt{2x^2 + 1}$ at the point $(2,3)$.

10 The radius of a circular disc is increasing at a constant rate of 0.003 cm s^{-1}. Find the rate at
which the area is increasing when the radius is 20 cm.   (OCR)

11 A viscous liquid is poured on to a flat surface. It forms a circular patch whose area grows at
a steady rate of $5 \text{ cm}^2 \text{ s}^{-1}$. Find, in terms of π,

   (a) the radius of the patch 20 seconds after pouring has commenced,

   (b) the rate of increase of the radius at this instant.   (OCR)

12 Find the equation of the tangent to the curve $y = \dfrac{50}{(2x-1)^2}$ at the point $(3,2)$, giving your answer in the form $ax + by + c = 0$, where a, b and c are integers. (OCR)

13 Sketch the graph of $y = (x-2)^2 - 4$ showing clearly on your graph the coordinates of any stationary points and of the intersections with the axes.

Find the coordinates of the stationary points on the graph of $y = (x-2)^3 - 12(x-2)$ and sketch the graph, giving the exact coordinates (in surd form, where appropriate) of the intersections with the axes. (OCR)

14 Differentiate $\sqrt{x + \dfrac{1}{x}}$ with respect to x. (OCR)

15 The formulae for the volume of a sphere of radius r and for its surface area are $V = \frac{4}{3}\pi r^3$ and $A = 4\pi r^2$ respectively. Given that, when $r = 5$ m, V is increasing at a rate of 10 m^3 s^{-1}, find the rate of increase of A at this instant. (OCR)

16 Using differentiation, find the equation of the tangent at the point $(2,1)$ on the curve with equation $y = \sqrt{x^2 - 3}$. (OCR)

17 Differentiate $\dfrac{1}{\left(3t^2 + 5\right)^2}$ with respect to t. (OCR)

18 (a) Curve C_1 has equation $y = \sqrt{4x - x^2}$. Find $\dfrac{dy}{dx}$ and hence find the coordinates of the stationary point.

(b) Show that the curve C_2 with equation $y = \sqrt{x^2 - 4x}$ has no stationary point.

19 A curve has equation $y = \frac{1}{12}(3x+1)^4 - 8x$.

(a) Show that there is a stationary point where $x = \frac{1}{3}$ and determine whether this stationary point is a maximum or a minimum.

(b) At a particular point of the curve, the equation of the tangent is $48x + 3y + c = 0$. Find the value of the constant c. (OCR)

20 If a hemispherical bowl of radius 6 cm contains water to a depth of x cm, the volume of the water is $\frac{1}{3}\pi x^2(18 - x)$. Water is poured into the bowl at a rate of 3 cm^3 s^{-1}. Find the rate at which the water level is rising when the depth is 2 cm.

21 An underground oil storage tank $ABCDEFGH$ is part of an inverted square pyramid, as shown in the diagram. The complete pyramid has a square base of side 12 m and height 18 m. The depth of the tank is 12 m.

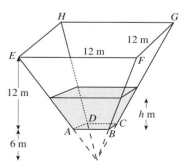

When the depth of oil in the tank is h metres, show that the volume V m^3 is given by
$V = \frac{4}{27}(h + 6)^3 - 32$.

Oil is being added to the tank at the constant rate of 4.5 m^3 s^{-1}. At the moment when the depth of oil is 8 m, find the rate at which the depth is increasing.

22 A curve has equation $y = (x^2 - 1)^3 - 3(x^2 - 1)^2$. Find the coordinates of the stationary points and determine whether each is a minimum or a maximum. Sketch the curve.

23 Find the coordinates of the stationary point of the curve $y = \dfrac{1}{2x+1} - \dfrac{1}{(2x+1)^2}$ and determine whether the stationary point is a maximum or a minimum.

24 Find the coordinates of the stationary point of the curve $y = \sqrt{4x-1} + \dfrac{9}{\sqrt{4x-1}}$ and determine whether the stationary point is a maximum or a minimum.

25 (a) Expand $(ax + b)^3$ using the binomial theorem. Differentiate the result with respect to x and show that the derivative is $3a(ax + b)^2$.

    (b) Expand $(ax + b)^4$ using the binomial theorem. Differentiate the result with respect to x and show that the derivative is $4a(ax + b)^3$.

    (c) Write down the expansion of $(ax + b)^n$ where n is a positive integer. Differentiate the result with respect to x. Show that the derivative is $na(ax + b)^{n-1}$.

Revision exercise 2

1 Find the equation of the tangent at $x = 3$ to the curve with equation $y = 2x^2 - 3x + 2$.

2 Find the coordinates of the vertex of the parabola with equation $y = 3x^2 + 6x + 10$

    (a) by using the completed square form,

    (b) by using differentiation.

3 Find the coordinates of the point on the curve $y = 2x^2 - 3x + 1$ where the tangent has gradient 1.

4 The normal to the curve with equation $y = x^2$ at the point for which $x = 2$ meets the curve again at P. Find the coordinates of P.

5 A normal to the curve $y = x^2$ has gradient 2. Find where it meets the curve.

6 Find the equation of the normal to the curve with equation $y = \sqrt{x}$ at the point $(1,1)$. Calculate the coordinates of the point at which this normal meets the graph of $y = -\sqrt{x}$.

7 The height, h centimetres, of a bicycle pedal above the ground at time t seconds is given by the equation

$$h = 30 + 15 \cos 90t°.$$

    (a) Calculate the height of the pedal when $t = 1\frac{1}{3}$.

    (b) Calculate the maximum and minimum heights of the pedal.

    (c) Find the first two positive values of t for which the height of the pedal is 43 cm. Give your answers correct to 2 decimal places.

    (d) How many revolutions does the pedal make in one minute?

8 (a) Calculate the gradient of the graph of $y = 12\sqrt[3]{x}$ at the point where $x = 8$ and hence find the equation of the tangent to the graph of $y = 12\sqrt[3]{x}$ at the point where $x = 8$.

    (b) Find the equation of the line passing through the points with coordinates $(15,30)$ and $(-31,-14)$.

    (c) Hence find the coordinates of the point where the tangent in part (a) meets the line in part (b).

9 Differentiate $x + \dfrac{1}{x}$, $2\sqrt{x}$, $\dfrac{3}{\sqrt{x}}$ and $\dfrac{\left(\sqrt{x} + 1\right)^2}{x}$ with respect to x.

10 Find the maximum and minimum values of $y = x^3 - 6x^2 + 9x - 8$.

11 A curve has equation $y = 2x^3 - 9x^2 + 12x - 5$. Show that one of the stationary points lies on the x-axis, and determine whether this point is a maximum or a minimum.

12 Solve the following equations, giving values of θ in the interval $-180 \leqslant \theta \leqslant 180$ correct to 1 decimal place.

(a) $3\sin^2\theta° - 2\cos^2\theta° = 1$ (b) $\cos\theta° \tan\theta° = -\frac{1}{2}$

(b) $3 + 4\tan 2\theta° = 5$ (d) $4\cos^2 2\theta° = 3$

13 (a) Solve the equation $\tan^2 2x° = \frac{1}{3}$ giving all solutions in the interval $0 \leqslant x \leqslant 360$.

(b) Prove that $\tan^2\theta° \equiv \dfrac{1}{\cos^2\theta°} - 1$.

(c) Write down the period of the graph of $y = \dfrac{3}{2 + \cos^2 2x°}$, and also the coordinates of a maximum value of y.

14 Differentiate $\sqrt{x} + \dfrac{1}{\sqrt{x}}$ and $\left(\sqrt{x} + \dfrac{1}{\sqrt{x}}\right)^2$ with respect to x.

15 By drawing suitable sketch graphs, determine the number of roots of the equation

$$\cos x° = \frac{10}{x}$$

which lie in the interval $-180 < x < 180$.   (OCR, adapted)

16 The function $x \mapsto \dfrac{1-x}{1+2x}, x \in \mathbb{R}, x \neq -\frac{1}{2}$, has an inverse. Find the inverse function, giving your answer in similar notation to the original.

17 The nth term of a series is $\frac{1}{2}(2n-1)$. Write down the $(n+1)$th term.

(a) Prove that the series is an arithmetic progression.

(b) Find, algebraically, the value of n for which the sum to n terms is 200.   (OCR)

18 (a) Determine the first three terms in the binomial expansion of $\left(x - \dfrac{1}{x}\right)^8$.

(b) Write down the constant term in the binomial expansion of $\left(2x + \dfrac{3}{x}\right)^4$.   (OCR)

19 Differentiate $y = \dfrac{1}{\sqrt{2x+3}}$ with respect to x. Draw a sketch of the curve.

20 (a) The function f is defined by $f(x) = x^2 - 2x - 1$ for the domain $-2 \leqslant x \leqslant 5$. Write $f(x)$ in completed square form. Hence find the range of f. Explain why f does not have an inverse.

(b) A function g is defined by $g(x) = 2x^2 - 4x - 3$. Write down a domain for g such that g^{-1} exists.   (OCR, adapted)

21 The tenth term of an arithmetic progression is 125 and the sum of the first ten terms is 260.

(a) Show that the first term in the progression is -73.

(b) Find the common difference.   (OCR)

22 The binomial expansion of $(1 + ax)^n$, where n is a positive integer, has six terms.

   (a) Write down the value of n.

   The coefficient of the x^3 term is $\frac{5}{4}$.

   (b) Find a. (OCR)

23 The function f is defined for the domain $x \geqslant 0$ by $f : x \mapsto 4 - x^2$.

   (a) Sketch the graph of f and state the range of f.

   (b) Describe a simple transformation whereby the graph of $y = f(x)$ may be obtained from the graph of $y = x^2$ for $x \geqslant 0$.

   (c) The inverse of f is denoted by f^{-1}. Find an expression for $f^{-1}(x)$ and state the domain of f^{-1}.

   (d) Show, by reference to a sketch, or otherwise, that the solution to the equation $f(x) = f^{-1}(x)$ can be obtained from the quadratic equation $x^2 + x - 4 = 0$. Determine the solution of $f(x) = f^{-1}(x)$, giving your value to 2 decimal places.

24 Find the coefficient of $\dfrac{1}{x^4}$ in the binomial expansion of $\left(1 + \dfrac{3}{x}\right)^6$.

25 An arithmetic progression has first term 3 and common difference 0.8. The sum of the first n terms of this arithmetic progression is 231. Find the value of n.

26 Differentiate each of the following functions with respect to x.

   (a) $\left(x^3 + 2x - 1\right)^3$ (b) $\sqrt{\dfrac{1}{x^2 + 1}}$

27 A spherical star is collapsing in size, while remaining spherical. When its radius is one million kilometres, the radius is decreasing at the rate of 500 km s^{-1}. Find

   (a) the rate of decrease of its volume,   (b) the rate of decrease of its surface area.

28 Write down the periods of the following trigonometric functions.

   (a) $\cos x°$ (b) $\cos \frac{1}{2} x°$ (c) $\cos \frac{3}{2} x°$

29 A woman started a business with a workforce of 50 people. Every two weeks the number of people in the workforce increased by 3 people.

   How many people were there in the workforce after 26 weeks?

   Each member of the workforce earned $600 per week. What was the total wage bill for this 26 weeks?

30 Sketch the graph of $y = \frac{1}{2} x^2 - 3x + 12$.

   The points P and Q on the graph have x-coordinates 0 and 8 respectively. The tangents at P and Q meet at R. Show that the point $(11, 9)$ is equidistant from P, Q and R. (OCR, adapted)

31 The origin O and a point $B(p, q)$ are opposite vertices of the square $OABC$. Find the coordinates of the points A and C.

   A line l has gradient $\dfrac{q}{p}$. Find possible values for the gradient of a line at $45°$ to l.

13 Vectors

This chapter introduces the idea of vectors as a way of doing geometry in two or three dimensions. When you have completed it, you should

- understand the idea of a translation, and how it can be expressed either in column form or in terms of basic unit vectors
- know and be able to use the rules of vector algebra
- understand the idea of displacement and position vectors, and use these to prove geometrical results
- appreciate similarities and differences between geometry in two and three dimensions
- know the definition of the scalar product, and its expression in terms of components
- be able to use the rules of vector algebra which involve scalar products
- be able to use scalar products to solve geometrical problems in two and three dimensions, using general vector algebra or components.

13.1 Translations of a plane

In Section 3.6 you saw that if you translate the graph $y = ax^2 + bx$ through a distance c in the y-direction its new equation is $y = ax^2 + bx + c$. In general, if you translate the graph $y = f(x)$ a distance c units in the y-direction its equation becomes $y = f(x) + c$. A practical way of doing this is to draw the graph on a transparent sheet placed over a coordinate grid, and then to move this sheet up the grid by c units.

The essential feature of a translation is that the sheet moves over the grid without turning. A general translation would move the sheet k units across and l units up the grid. This is shown in Fig. 13.1, where several points move in the same direction through the same distance. Such a translation is called a **vector** and is written $\begin{pmatrix} k \\ l \end{pmatrix}$.

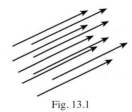

Fig. 13.1

For example, the translation of $y = f(x)$ described above would be performed by the vector $\begin{pmatrix} 0 \\ c \end{pmatrix}$; similarly the vector $\begin{pmatrix} k \\ 0 \end{pmatrix}$ performs a translation of k units across in the x-direction.

In practice, drawing several arrows, as in Fig. 13.1, is not a convenient way of representing a vector. It is usual to draw just a single arrow, as in Fig. 13.2. But you must understand that the position of the arrow in the (x,y)-plane is of no significance. This arrow is just one of infinitely many that could be drawn to represent the vector.

Fig. 13.2

You may meet uses of vectors in other contexts. For example, mechanics uses velocity vectors, acceleration vectors, force vectors, and so on. When you need to make the distinction, the vectors described here are called **translation vectors**. These are the only vectors used in this book.

13.2 Vector algebra

It is often convenient to use a single letter to stand for a vector. In print, bold type is used to distinguish vectors from numbers. For example, in $\mathbf{p} = \begin{pmatrix} k \\ l \end{pmatrix}$, $\mathbf{p}$ is a vector but k and l are numbers, called the **components** of the vector $\mathbf{p}$ in the x- and y-directions.

In handwriting vectors are indicated by a wavy line underneath the letter: $\underset{\sim}{p} = \begin{pmatrix} k \\ l \end{pmatrix}$. It is important to get into the habit of writing vectors in this way, so that it is quite clear in your work which letters stand for vectors and which stand for numbers.

If s is any number and $\mathbf{p}$ is any vector, then $s\mathbf{p}$ is another vector. If $s > 0$, the vector $s\mathbf{p}$ is a translation in the same direction as $\mathbf{p}$ but s times as large; if $s < 0$ it is in the opposite direction and $|s|$ times as large. A number such as s is often called a **scalar**, because it usually changes the scale of the vector.

The similar triangles in Fig. 13.3 show that $s\mathbf{p} = \begin{pmatrix} sk \\ sl \end{pmatrix}$. In particular, $(-1)\mathbf{p} = \begin{pmatrix} -k \\ -l \end{pmatrix}$, which is a translation of the same magnitude as $\mathbf{p}$ but in the opposite direction. It is denoted by $-\mathbf{p}$.

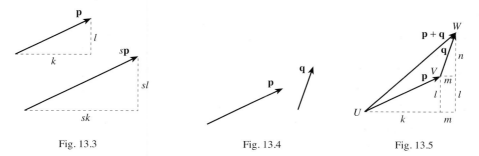

Fig. 13.3   Fig. 13.4   Fig. 13.5

Vectors are added by performing one translation after another. In Fig. 13.4, $\mathbf{p}$ and $\mathbf{q}$ are two vectors. To form their sum, you want to represent them as a pair of arrows by which you can trace the path of a particular point of the moving sheet. In Fig. 13.5, $\mathbf{p}$ is shown by an arrow from U to V, and $\mathbf{q}$ by an arrow from V to W. Then when the translations are combined, the point of the sheet which was originally at U would move first to V and then to W. So the sum $\mathbf{p} + \mathbf{q}$ is represented by an arrow from U to W.

Fig. 13.5 also shows that:

If $\mathbf{p} = \begin{pmatrix} k \\ l \end{pmatrix}$ and $\mathbf{q} = \begin{pmatrix} m \\ n \end{pmatrix}$, then $\mathbf{p} + \mathbf{q} = \begin{pmatrix} k + m \\ l + n \end{pmatrix}$.

To form the sum $\mathbf{q} + \mathbf{p}$ the translations are performed in the reverse order. In Fig. 13.6, $\mathbf{q}$ is now represented by the arrow from U to Z; and since $UVWZ$ is a parallelogram $\mathbf{p}$ is represented by the arrow from Z to W. This shows that

$$\mathbf{p} + \mathbf{q} = \mathbf{q} + \mathbf{p}.$$

This is called the **commutative rule for addition of vectors.**

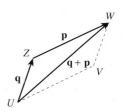

Fig. 13.6

Example 13.2.1

If $\mathbf{p} = \begin{pmatrix} 2 \\ -3 \end{pmatrix}$, $\mathbf{q} = \begin{pmatrix} 1 \\ 2 \end{pmatrix}$ and $\mathbf{r} = \begin{pmatrix} 5 \\ 3 \end{pmatrix}$, show that there is a number s such that $\mathbf{p} + s\mathbf{q} = \mathbf{r}$.

You can write $\mathbf{p} + s\mathbf{q}$ in column vector form as

$$\begin{pmatrix} 2 \\ -3 \end{pmatrix} + s \begin{pmatrix} 1 \\ 2 \end{pmatrix} = \begin{pmatrix} 2 \\ -3 \end{pmatrix} + \begin{pmatrix} s \\ 2s \end{pmatrix} = \begin{pmatrix} 2+s \\ -3+2s \end{pmatrix}.$$

If this is equal to $\mathbf{r}$, then both the x- and y-components of the two vectors must be equal. This gives the two equations

$$2 + s = 5 \quad \text{and} \quad -3 + 2s = 3.$$

Both these equations are satisfied by $s = 3$, so it follows that $\mathbf{p} + 3\mathbf{q} = \mathbf{r}$. You can check this for yourself using squared paper or a screen display, showing arrows representing $\mathbf{p}$, $\mathbf{q}$, $\mathbf{p} + 3\mathbf{q}$ and $\mathbf{r}$.

The idea of addition can be extended to three or more vectors. But when you write $\mathbf{p} + \mathbf{q} + \mathbf{r}$ it is not clear whether you first add $\mathbf{p}$ and $\mathbf{q}$ and then add $\mathbf{r}$ to the result, or whether you add $\mathbf{p}$ to the result of adding $\mathbf{q}$ and $\mathbf{r}$. Fig. 13.7 shows that it doesn't matter, since the outcome is the same either way. That is,

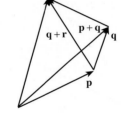

$$(\mathbf{p} + \mathbf{q}) + \mathbf{r} = \mathbf{p} + (\mathbf{q} + \mathbf{r}).$$

This is called the **associative rule for addition of vectors**.   Fig. 13.7

To complete the algebra of vector addition, the symbol $\mathbf{0}$ is needed for the **zero vector**, the 'stay-still' translation, which has the properties that, for any vector $\mathbf{p}$,

$$0\mathbf{p} = \mathbf{0}, \quad \mathbf{p} + \mathbf{0} = \mathbf{p}, \quad \text{and} \quad \mathbf{p} + (-\mathbf{p}) = \mathbf{0}.$$

Vector addition and multiplication by a scalar can be combined according to the two **distributive rules for vectors**:

$$s(\mathbf{p} + \mathbf{q}) = s\mathbf{p} + s\mathbf{q} \quad \text{(from the similar triangles in Fig. 13.8)}$$

and $\quad (s + t)\mathbf{p} = s\mathbf{p} + t\mathbf{p} \quad$ (see Fig. 13.9)

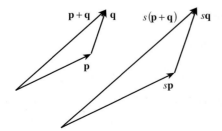

Fig. 13.8

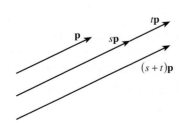

Fig. 13.9

Subtraction of vectors is defined by

$$\mathbf{p} + \mathbf{x} = \mathbf{q} \quad \Leftrightarrow \quad \mathbf{x} = \mathbf{q} - \mathbf{p}.$$

This is illustrated in Fig. 13.10. Notice that to show $\mathbf{q} - \mathbf{p}$ you represent $\mathbf{p}$ and $\mathbf{q}$ by arrows which both start at the same point; this is different from addition, where the arrow representing $\mathbf{q}$ starts where the $\mathbf{p}$ arrow ends.

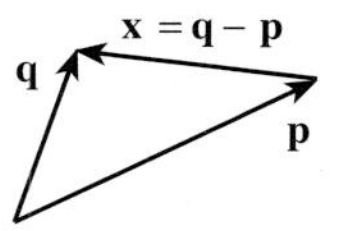

Fig. 13.10

Comparing Fig. 13.10 with Fig. 13.11 shows that

$$\mathbf{q} - \mathbf{p} = \mathbf{q} + (-\mathbf{p}).$$

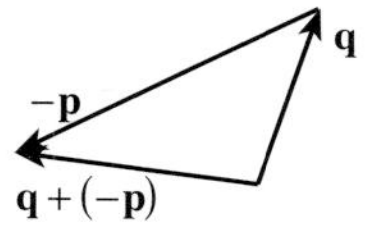

Fig. 13.11

In summary, the rules of vector addition, subtraction and multiplication by scalars look very similar to the rules of number addition, subtraction and multiplication. But the diagrams show that the rules for vectors are interpreted differently from the rules for numbers.

13.3 Basic unit vectors

If you apply the rules of vector algebra to a vector in column form, you can see that

$$\mathbf{p} = \binom{k}{l} = \binom{k+0}{0+l} = \binom{k}{0} + \binom{0}{l} = k\binom{1}{0} + l\binom{0}{1}.$$

The vectors $\binom{1}{0}$ and $\binom{0}{1}$ which appear in this last expression are called **basic unit vectors** in the x- and y-directions. They are denoted by the letters $\mathbf{i}$ and $\mathbf{j}$, so

$$\mathbf{p} = k\mathbf{i} + l\mathbf{j}.$$

This is illustrated by Fig. 13.12. The equation shows that any vector in the plane can be constructed as the sum of multiples of the two basic vectors $\mathbf{i}$ and $\mathbf{j}$.

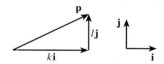

The vectors $k\mathbf{i}$ and $l\mathbf{j}$ are called the **component vectors** of $\mathbf{p}$ in the x- and y-directions.

Fig. 13.12

You now have two alternative notations for doing algebra with vectors. For example, if you want to find $3\mathbf{p} - 2\mathbf{q}$, where $\mathbf{p}$ is $\binom{2}{5}$ and $\mathbf{q}$ is $\binom{1}{-3}$, you can write either

$$3\binom{2}{5} - 2\binom{1}{-3} = \binom{6}{15} - \binom{2}{-6} = \binom{6-2}{15-(-6)} = \binom{4}{21}$$

or $3(2\mathbf{i} + 5\mathbf{j}) - 2(\mathbf{i} - 3\mathbf{j}) = (6\mathbf{i} + 15\mathbf{j}) - (2\mathbf{i} - 6\mathbf{j}) = 6\mathbf{i} + 15\mathbf{j} - 2\mathbf{i} + 6\mathbf{j} = 4\mathbf{i} + 21\mathbf{j}.$

You will find that sometimes one of these forms is more convenient than the other, but usually it makes no difference which you use.

Exercise 13A

When you are asked to illustrate a vector equation geometrically, you should show vectors as arrows on a grid of squares, either on paper or on screen.

1 Illustrate the following equations geometrically.

(a) $\begin{pmatrix} 4 \\ 1 \end{pmatrix} + \begin{pmatrix} -3 \\ 2 \end{pmatrix} = \begin{pmatrix} 1 \\ 3 \end{pmatrix}$

(b) $3\begin{pmatrix} 1 \\ -2 \end{pmatrix} = \begin{pmatrix} 3 \\ -6 \end{pmatrix}$

(c) $\begin{pmatrix} 0 \\ 4 \end{pmatrix} + 2\begin{pmatrix} 1 \\ -2 \end{pmatrix} = \begin{pmatrix} 2 \\ 0 \end{pmatrix}$

(d) $\begin{pmatrix} 3 \\ 1 \end{pmatrix} - \begin{pmatrix} 5 \\ 1 \end{pmatrix} = \begin{pmatrix} -2 \\ 0 \end{pmatrix}$

(e) $3\begin{pmatrix} -1 \\ 2 \end{pmatrix} - \begin{pmatrix} -4 \\ 3 \end{pmatrix} = \begin{pmatrix} 1 \\ 3 \end{pmatrix}$

(f) $4\begin{pmatrix} 2 \\ 3 \end{pmatrix} - 3\begin{pmatrix} 3 \\ 2 \end{pmatrix} = \begin{pmatrix} -1 \\ 6 \end{pmatrix}$

(g) $\begin{pmatrix} 2 \\ -3 \end{pmatrix} + \begin{pmatrix} 4 \\ 5 \end{pmatrix} + \begin{pmatrix} -6 \\ -2 \end{pmatrix} = \begin{pmatrix} 0 \\ 0 \end{pmatrix}$

(h) $2\begin{pmatrix} 3 \\ -1 \end{pmatrix} + 3\begin{pmatrix} -2 \\ 3 \end{pmatrix} + \begin{pmatrix} 0 \\ -7 \end{pmatrix} = \begin{pmatrix} 0 \\ 0 \end{pmatrix}$

2 Rewrite each of the equations in Question 1 using unit vector notation.

3 Express each of the following vectors as column vectors, and illustrate your answers geometrically.

(a) $\mathbf{i} + 2\mathbf{j}$ (b) $3\mathbf{i}$ (c) $\mathbf{j} - \mathbf{i}$ (d) $4\mathbf{i} - 3\mathbf{j}$

4 Show that there is a number s such that $s\begin{pmatrix} 1 \\ 2 \end{pmatrix} + \begin{pmatrix} -3 \\ 1 \end{pmatrix} = \begin{pmatrix} -1 \\ 5 \end{pmatrix}$. Illustrate your answer geometrically.

5 If $\mathbf{p} = 5\mathbf{i} - 3\mathbf{j}$, $\mathbf{q} = 2\mathbf{j} - \mathbf{i}$ and $\mathbf{r} = \mathbf{i} + 5\mathbf{j}$, show that there is a number s such that $\mathbf{p} + s\mathbf{q} = \mathbf{r}$. Illustrate your answer geometrically.

Rearrange this equation so as to express $\mathbf{q}$ in terms of $\mathbf{p}$ and $\mathbf{r}$. Illustrate the rearranged equation geometrically.

6 Find numbers s and t such that $s\begin{pmatrix} 5 \\ 4 \end{pmatrix} + t\begin{pmatrix} -3 \\ -2 \end{pmatrix} = \begin{pmatrix} 1 \\ 2 \end{pmatrix}$. Illustrate your answer geometrically.

7 If $\mathbf{p} = 4\mathbf{i} + \mathbf{j}$, $\mathbf{q} = 6\mathbf{i} - 5\mathbf{j}$ and $\mathbf{r} = 3\mathbf{i} + 4\mathbf{j}$, find numbers s and t such that $s\mathbf{p} + t\mathbf{q} = \mathbf{r}$. Illustrate your answer geometrically.

8 Show that it isn't possible to find numbers s and t such that $\begin{pmatrix} 4 \\ -2 \end{pmatrix} + s\begin{pmatrix} 3 \\ 1 \end{pmatrix} = \begin{pmatrix} -6 \\ 3 \end{pmatrix}$ and $\begin{pmatrix} 3 \\ 4 \end{pmatrix} + t\begin{pmatrix} -1 \\ 2 \end{pmatrix} = \begin{pmatrix} 1 \\ 1 \end{pmatrix}$. Give geometrical reasons.

9 If $\mathbf{p} = 2\mathbf{i} + 3\mathbf{j}$, $\mathbf{q} = 4\mathbf{i} - 5\mathbf{j}$ and $\mathbf{r} = \mathbf{i} - 4\mathbf{j}$, find a set of numbers f, g and h such that $f\mathbf{p} + g\mathbf{q} + h\mathbf{r} = \mathbf{0}$. Illustrate your answer geometrically. Give a reason why there is more than one possible answer to this question.

10 If $\mathbf{p} = 3\mathbf{i} - \mathbf{j}$, $\mathbf{q} = 4\mathbf{i} + 5\mathbf{j}$ and $\mathbf{r} = 2\mathbf{j} - 6\mathbf{i}$,

(a) can you find numbers s and t such that $\mathbf{q} = s\mathbf{p} + t\mathbf{r}$,

(b) can you find numbers u and v such that $\mathbf{r} = u\mathbf{p} + v\mathbf{q}$?

Give a geometrical reason for your answers.

13.4 Position vectors

If E and F are two points on a grid, there is a unique translation which takes you from E to F. This translation can be represented by the arrow which starts at E and ends at F, and it is denoted by the symbol $\overrightarrow{EF}$.

Some books use **EF** *in bold type rather than $\overrightarrow{EF}$ to emphasise that it is a vector.*

However, although this translation is unique, its name is not. If G and H are two other points on the grid such that the lines EF and GH are parallel and equal in length (so that $EFHG$ is a parallelogram, see Fig. 13.13), then the translation $\overrightarrow{EF}$ also takes you from G to H, so that it could also be denoted by $\overrightarrow{GH}$. In a vector equation $\overrightarrow{EF}$ could be replaced by $\overrightarrow{GH}$ without affecting the truth of the statement.

Vectors written like this are sometimes called **displacement vectors**. But they are not a different kind of vector, just translation vectors written in a different way.

There is, however, one especially important displacement vector. This is the translation that starts at the origin O and ends at a point A ($\overrightarrow{OA}$ in Fig. 13.13), so that $\overrightarrow{OA} = \overrightarrow{EF} = \overrightarrow{GH}$. The translation from O to A is called the **position vector** of A.

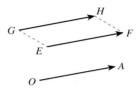

Fig. 13.13

There is a close link between the coordinates of A and the components of its position vector. If A has coordinates (u,v), then to get from O to A you must move u units in the x-direction and v units in the y-direction, so that the vector $\overrightarrow{OA}$ has components u and v.

> The position vector of the point A with coordinates (u,v) is
> $$\overrightarrow{OA} = \begin{pmatrix} u \\ v \end{pmatrix} = u\mathbf{i} + v\mathbf{j}.$$

A useful convention is to use the same letter for a point and its position vector. For example, the position vector of the point A can be denoted by $\mathbf{a}$. This 'alphabet convention' will be used wherever possible in this book. It has the advantages that it economises on letters of the alphabet and avoids the need for repetitive definitions.

13.5 Algebra with position vectors

Multiplication by a scalar has a simple interpretation in terms of position vectors. If the vector $s\mathbf{a}$ is the position vector of a point D, then:

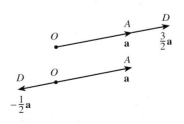

- If $s > 0$, D lies on the directed line OA (produced if necessary) such that $OD = sOA$.
- If $s < 0$, D lies on the directed line AO produced such that $OD = |s|OA$.

Fig. 13.14

This is shown in Fig. 13.14 for $s = \frac{3}{2}$ and $s = -\frac{1}{2}$.

To identify the point with position vector $\mathbf{a} + \mathbf{b}$ is not quite so easy, because the arrows from O to A and from O to B are not related in the way needed for addition (see Fig. 13.5). It is therefore necessary to complete the parallelogram $OACB$, as in Fig. 13.15.

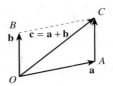

Then

Fig. 13.15

$$\mathbf{a} + \mathbf{b} = \overrightarrow{OA} + \overrightarrow{OB} = \overrightarrow{OA} + \overrightarrow{AC} = \overrightarrow{OC}.$$

This is called the **parallelogram rule of addition** for position vectors.

Subtraction can be shown in either of two ways. If you compare Fig. 13.16 with Fig. 13.10, you will see that $\mathbf{b} - \mathbf{a}$ is the displacement vector $\overrightarrow{AB}$. To interpret this as a position vector, draw a line OE equal and parallel to AB, so that $\overrightarrow{OE} = \overrightarrow{AB}$. Then E is the point with position vector $\mathbf{b} - \mathbf{a}$.

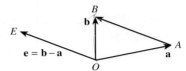

Fig. 13.16

Alternatively, you can write $\mathbf{b} - \mathbf{a}$ as $\mathbf{b} + (-\mathbf{a})$, and then apply the parallelogram rule of addition to the points with position vectors $\mathbf{b}$ and $-\mathbf{a}$. By comparing Figs. 13.16 and 13.17 you can see that this leads to the same point E.

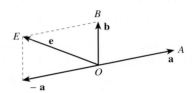

Fig. 13.17

Example 13.5.1

Points A and B have position vectors $\mathbf{a}$ and $\mathbf{b}$. Find the position vectors of
(a) the mid-point M of AB,
(b) the point of trisection T such that $AT = \frac{2}{3} AB$.

(a) **Method 1**   The displacement vector $\overrightarrow{AB} = \mathbf{b} - \mathbf{a}$, so $\overrightarrow{AM} = \frac{1}{2}(\mathbf{b} - \mathbf{a})$. Therefore

$$\mathbf{m} = \overrightarrow{OM} = \overrightarrow{OA} + \overrightarrow{AM} = \mathbf{a} + \tfrac{1}{2}(\mathbf{b} - \mathbf{a}) = \tfrac{1}{2}\mathbf{a} + \tfrac{1}{2}\mathbf{b}.$$

Method 2   If the parallelogram $OACB$ is completed (see Fig. 13.15) then $\mathbf{c} = \mathbf{a} + \mathbf{b}$. Since the diagonals of $OACB$ bisect each other, the mid-point M of AB is also the midpoint of OC. Therefore

$$\mathbf{m} = \tfrac{1}{2}\mathbf{c} = \tfrac{1}{2}(\mathbf{a} + \mathbf{b}) = \tfrac{1}{2}\mathbf{a} + \tfrac{1}{2}\mathbf{b}.$$

(b) The first method of (a) can be modified. The displacement vector $\overrightarrow{AT} = \frac{2}{3}\overrightarrow{AB} = \frac{2}{3}(\mathbf{b} - \mathbf{a})$, so

$$\mathbf{t} = \overrightarrow{OA} + \overrightarrow{AT} = \mathbf{a} + \tfrac{2}{3}(\mathbf{b} - \mathbf{a}) = \tfrac{1}{3}\mathbf{a} + \tfrac{2}{3}\mathbf{b}.$$

The results of this example can be used to prove an important theorem about triangles.

Example 13.5.2

In triangle ABC the mid-points of BC, CA and AB are D, E and F. Prove that the lines AD, BE and CF (called the **medians**) meet at a point G, which is a point of trisection of each of the medians (see Fig. 13.18).

From Example 13.5.1, $\mathbf{d} = \frac{1}{2}\mathbf{b} + \frac{1}{2}\mathbf{c}$, and the point of trisection on the median AD closer to D has position vector

$$\frac{1}{3}\mathbf{a} + \frac{2}{3}\mathbf{d} = \frac{1}{3}\mathbf{a} + \frac{2}{3}\left(\frac{1}{2}\mathbf{b} + \frac{1}{2}\mathbf{c}\right)$$
$$= \frac{1}{3}\mathbf{a} + \frac{1}{3}\mathbf{b} + \frac{1}{3}\mathbf{c}.$$

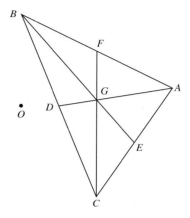

This last expression is symmetrical in $\mathbf{a}$, $\mathbf{b}$ and $\mathbf{c}$. It therefore also represents the point of trisection on the median BE closer to E, and the point of trisection on CF closer to F.

Therefore the three medians meet each other at a point G, with position vector $\mathbf{g} = \frac{1}{3}(\mathbf{a} + \mathbf{b} + \mathbf{c})$. This point is called the **centroid** of the triangle.

Fig. 13.18

Exercise 13B

In this exercise the alphabet convention is used, that $\mathbf{a}$ stands for the position vector of the point A, and so on.

1 The points A and B have coordinates $(3,1)$ and $(1,2)$. Plot on squared paper the points C, $D, \ldots , H$ defined by the following vector equations, and state their coordinates.

(a) $\mathbf{c} = 3\mathbf{a}$ (b) $\mathbf{d} = -\mathbf{b}$ (c) $\mathbf{e} = \mathbf{a} - \mathbf{b}$

(d) $\mathbf{f} = \mathbf{b} - 3\mathbf{a}$ (e) $\mathbf{g} = \mathbf{b} + 3\mathbf{a}$ (f) $\mathbf{h} = \frac{1}{2}(\mathbf{b} + 3\mathbf{a})$

2 Points A and B have coordinates $(2,7)$ and $(-3,-3)$ respectively. Use a vector method to find the coordinates of C and D, where

(a) C is the point such that $\overrightarrow{AC} = 3\overrightarrow{AB}$,   (b) D is the point such that $\overrightarrow{AD} = \frac{3}{5}\overrightarrow{AB}$.

3 C is the point on AB produced such that $\overrightarrow{AB} = \overrightarrow{BC}$. Express C in terms of $\mathbf{a}$ and $\mathbf{b}$. Check your answer by using the result of Example 13.5.1(a) to find the position vector of the mid-point of AC.

4 C is the point on AB such that $AC:CB = 4:3$. Express $\mathbf{c}$ in terms of $\mathbf{a}$ and $\mathbf{b}$.

5 If C is the point on AB such that $\overrightarrow{AC} = t\overrightarrow{AB}$, prove that $\mathbf{c} = t\mathbf{b} + (1-t)\mathbf{a}$.

6 Write a vector equation connecting $\mathbf{a}$, $\mathbf{b}$, $\mathbf{c}$ and $\mathbf{d}$ to express the fact that $\overrightarrow{AB} = \overrightarrow{DC}$. Deduce from your equation that

(a) $\overrightarrow{DA} = \overrightarrow{CB}$,

(b) if E is the point such that $OAEC$ is a parallelogram, then $OBED$ is a parallelogram.

7   ABC is a triangle. D is the mid-point of BC, E is the mid-point of AC, F is the mid-point of AB and G is the mid-point of EF. Express the displacement vectors $\overrightarrow{AD}$ and $\overrightarrow{AG}$ in terms of $\mathbf{a}$, $\mathbf{b}$ and $\mathbf{c}$. What can you deduce about the points A, D and G?

8   $OABC$ is a parallelogram, M is the mid-point of BC, and P is the point of trisection of AC closer to C. Express $\mathbf{b}$, $\mathbf{m}$ and $\mathbf{p}$ in terms of $\mathbf{a}$ and $\mathbf{c}$. Deduce that $\mathbf{p} = \frac{2}{3}\mathbf{m}$, and interpret this equation geometrically.

9   ABC is a triangle. D is the mid-point of BC, E is the mid-point of AD and F is the point of trisection of AC closer to A. G is the point on FB such that $\overrightarrow{FG} = \frac{1}{4}\overrightarrow{FB}$. Express $\mathbf{d}$, $\mathbf{e}$, $\mathbf{f}$ and $\mathbf{g}$ in terms of $\mathbf{a}$, $\mathbf{b}$ and $\mathbf{c}$, and deduce that G is the same point as E. Draw a figure to illustrate this result.

10 OAB is a triangle, Q is the point of trisection of AB closer to B and P is the point on OQ such that $\overrightarrow{OP} = \frac{2}{5}\overrightarrow{OQ}$. AP produced meets OB at R. Express $\overrightarrow{AP}$ in terms of $\mathbf{a}$ and $\mathbf{b}$, and hence find the number k such that $\overrightarrow{OA} + k\overrightarrow{AP}$ does not depend on $\mathbf{a}$. Use your answer to express $\mathbf{r}$ in terms of $\mathbf{b}$, and interpret this geometrically.

Use a similar method to identify the point S where BP produced meets OA.

13.6 Vectors in three dimensions

The power of vector methods is best appreciated when they are used to do geometry in three dimensions. This requires setting up axes in three directions, as in Fig. 13.19. The usual convention is to take x- and y-axes in a horizontal plane (shown shaded), and to add a z-axis pointing vertically upwards.

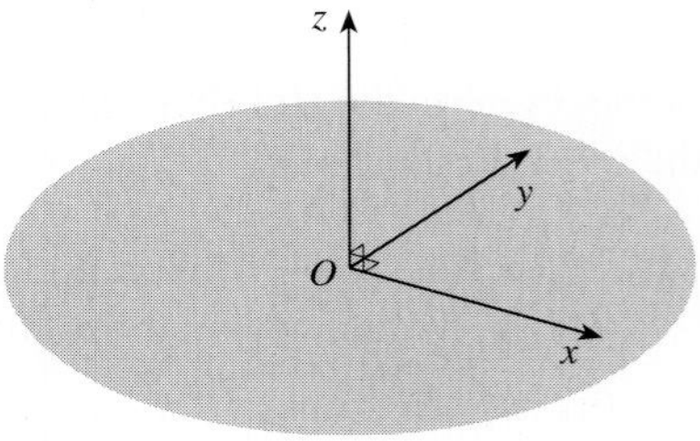

Fig. 13.19

These axes are said to be 'right-handed': if the outstretched index finger of your right hand points in the x-direction, and you bend your middle finger to point in the y-direction, then your thumb can naturally point up in the z-direction.

The position of a point is given by its three coordinates (x, y, z).

A vector $\mathbf{p}$ in three dimensions is a translation of the whole of space relative to a fixed coordinate framework. (You could imagine Fig. 13.1 as a rainstorm, with the arrows showing the translations of the individual droplets.)

It is written as $\begin{pmatrix} l \\ m \\ n \end{pmatrix}$, which is a translation of l, m and n units in the x-, y- and z-directions. It can also be written in the form $l\mathbf{i} + m\mathbf{j} + n\mathbf{k}$, where $\mathbf{i} = \begin{pmatrix} 1 \\ 0 \\ 0 \end{pmatrix}$, $\mathbf{j} = \begin{pmatrix} 0 \\ 1 \\ 0 \end{pmatrix}$, $\mathbf{k} = \begin{pmatrix} 0 \\ 0 \\ 1 \end{pmatrix}$ are basic unit vectors in the x-, y- and z-directions.

Almost everything that you know about coordinates in two dimensions carries over into three dimensions in an obvious way, but you need to notice a few differences:

- The axes can be taken in pairs to define coordinate planes. For example, the x- and y-axes define the horizontal plane, called the xy-plane. All points in this plane have z-coordinate zero, so the equation of the plane is $z = 0$. Similarly the xz-plane and the yz-plane have equations $y = 0$ and $x = 0$; these are both vertical planes.
- The idea of the gradient of a line does not carry over into three dimensions. However, you can still use a vector to describe the direction of a line. This is one of the main reasons why vectors are especially useful in three dimensions.
- In three dimensions lines which are not parallel may or may not meet. Non-parallel lines which do not meet are said to be **skew**.

Example 13.6.1

Points A and B have coordinates $(-5,3,4)$ and $(-2,9,1)$. Investigate whether or not the point C with coordinates $(-4,5,2)$ lies on the line passing through A and B.

The displacement vector $\overrightarrow{AB}$ is

$$\mathbf{b} - \mathbf{a} = \begin{pmatrix} -2 \\ 9 \\ 1 \end{pmatrix} - \begin{pmatrix} -5 \\ 3 \\ 4 \end{pmatrix} = \begin{pmatrix} 3 \\ 6 \\ -3 \end{pmatrix} = 3 \begin{pmatrix} 1 \\ 2 \\ -1 \end{pmatrix}.$$

The displacement vector $\overrightarrow{AC}$ is

$$\mathbf{c} - \mathbf{a} = \begin{pmatrix} -4 \\ 5 \\ 2 \end{pmatrix} - \begin{pmatrix} -5 \\ 3 \\ 4 \end{pmatrix} = \begin{pmatrix} 1 \\ 2 \\ -2 \end{pmatrix}.$$

As $\mathbf{c} - \mathbf{a}$ is not a multiple of $\mathbf{b} - \mathbf{a}$, it is not parallel to $\mathbf{b} - \mathbf{a}$. The points B and C are not in the same direction (or in opposite directions) from A, so C does not lie on the line passing through A and B.

Note that if you change the z-coordinate of C to 3, then C would lie on the line AB.

Example 13.6.2

Points P, Q and R have coordinates $(1,3,2)$, $(3,1,4)$ and $(4,1,-5)$ respectively.
(a) Find the displacement vectors $\overrightarrow{PQ}$ and $\overrightarrow{QR}$ in terms of the basic vectors $\mathbf{i}, \mathbf{j}$ and $\mathbf{k}$.
(b) Find $2\overrightarrow{PQ} - \frac{1}{2}\overrightarrow{PR} + \frac{1}{2}\overrightarrow{QR}$ in terms of the basic vectors $\mathbf{i}, \mathbf{j}$ and $\mathbf{k}$, and the coordinates of the point reached if you start at R and carry out the translation $2\overrightarrow{PQ} - \frac{1}{2}\overrightarrow{PR} + \frac{1}{2}\overrightarrow{QR}$.

(a) $\overrightarrow{PQ} = \mathbf{q} - \mathbf{p} = (3\mathbf{i} + \mathbf{j} + 4\mathbf{k}) - (\mathbf{i} + 3\mathbf{j} + 2\mathbf{k}) = 2\mathbf{i} - 2\mathbf{j} + 2\mathbf{k}$.

$\overrightarrow{QR} = \mathbf{r} - \mathbf{q} = (4\mathbf{i} + \mathbf{j} - 5\mathbf{k}) - (3\mathbf{i} + \mathbf{j} + 4\mathbf{k}) = \mathbf{i} - 9\mathbf{k}$.

(b) Note first that $\overrightarrow{PR} = \mathbf{r} - \mathbf{p} = (4\mathbf{i} + \mathbf{j} - 5\mathbf{k}) - (\mathbf{i} + 3\mathbf{j} + 2\mathbf{k}) = 3\mathbf{i} - 2\mathbf{j} - 7\mathbf{k}$.

Then $2\overrightarrow{PQ} - \frac{1}{2}\overrightarrow{PR} + \frac{1}{2}\overrightarrow{QR} = 2(2\mathbf{i} - 2\mathbf{j} + 2\mathbf{k}) - \frac{1}{2}(3\mathbf{i} - 2\mathbf{j} - 7\mathbf{k}) + \frac{1}{2}(\mathbf{i} - 9\mathbf{k})$

$= 4\mathbf{i} - 4\mathbf{j} + 4\mathbf{k} - \frac{3}{2}\mathbf{i} + \mathbf{j} + \frac{7}{2}\mathbf{k} + \frac{1}{2}\mathbf{i} - \frac{9}{2}\mathbf{k}$

$= 3\mathbf{i} - 3\mathbf{j} + 3\mathbf{k}.$

If you start from R, then the point reached has position vector

$$\mathbf{r} + (3\mathbf{i} - 3\mathbf{j} + \mathbf{k}) = (4\mathbf{i} + \mathbf{j} - 5\mathbf{k}) + (3\mathbf{i} - 3\mathbf{j} + 3\mathbf{k}) = 7\mathbf{i} - 2\mathbf{j} - 2\mathbf{k}.$$

The point is therefore $(7, -2, -2)$.

Exercise 13C

1 If $\mathbf{p} = 2\mathbf{i} - \mathbf{j} + 3\mathbf{k}$, $\mathbf{q} = 5\mathbf{i} + 2\mathbf{j}$ and $\mathbf{r} = 4\mathbf{i} + \mathbf{j} + \mathbf{k}$, calculate the vector $2\mathbf{p} + 3\mathbf{q} - 4\mathbf{r}$ giving your answer as a column vector.

2 A and B are points with coordinates $(2,1,4)$ and $(5,-5,-2)$. Find the vector $\overrightarrow{AB}$

   (a) as a column vector,

   (b) using $\mathbf{i}, \mathbf{j}$ and $\mathbf{k}$.

3 For each of the following sets of points A, B and C, determine whether the point C lies on the line AB.

   (a) $A(3,2,4)$, $B(-3,-7,-8)$, $C(0,1,3)$　　　　(b) $A(3,1,0)$, $B(-3,1,3)$, $C(5,1,-1)$

   If the answer is yes, draw a diagram showing the relative positions of A, B and C on the line.

4 (a) Using the points $A(2,-1,3)$, $B(3,1,-4)$ and $C(-1,1,-1)$, write $\overrightarrow{AB}$, $2\overrightarrow{AC}$ and $\frac{1}{2}\overrightarrow{BC}$ as column vectors.

   (b) If you start from B and the translation $\overrightarrow{AB} + 2\overrightarrow{AC} + \frac{1}{2}\overrightarrow{BC}$ takes you to D, find the coordinates of D.

5 Four points A, B, C and D have position vectors $3\mathbf{i} - \mathbf{j} + 7\mathbf{k}$, $4\mathbf{i} + \mathbf{k}$, $\mathbf{i} - \mathbf{j} + \mathbf{k}$ and $-2\mathbf{j} + 7\mathbf{k}$ respectively. Find the displacement vectors $\overrightarrow{AB}$ and $\overrightarrow{DC}$. What can you deduce about the quadrilateral $ABCD$?

6 Two points A and B have position vectors $\begin{pmatrix} 4 \\ -1 \\ 2 \end{pmatrix}$ and $\begin{pmatrix} 1 \\ 5 \\ 3 \end{pmatrix}$. C is the point on the line segment AB such that $\dfrac{AC}{CB} = 2$. Find

   (a) the displacement vector $\overrightarrow{AB}$,　　　　(b) the displacement vector $\overrightarrow{AC}$,

   (c) the position vector of C.

7 Four points A, B, C and D have coordinates $(0,1,-2)$, $(1,3,2)$, $(4,3,4)$ and $(5,-1,-2)$ respectively. Find the position vectors of

   (a) the mid-point E of AC,

   (b) the point F on BC such that $\dfrac{BF}{FD} = \frac{1}{3}$.

   Use your answers to draw a sketch showing the relative positions of A, B, C and D.

13.7 The magnitude of a vector

Any translation can be described by giving its magnitude and direction. The notation used for the magnitude of a vector $\mathbf{p}$, ignoring its direction, is $|\mathbf{p}|$.

If you have two vectors $\mathbf{p}$ and $\mathbf{q}$ which are not equal, but which have equal magnitudes, then you can write $|\mathbf{p}| = |\mathbf{q}|$.

If s is a scalar multiple of $\mathbf{p}$, then it follows from the definition of $s\mathbf{p}$ (see Section 13.2) that $|s\mathbf{p}| = |s||\mathbf{p}|$. This is true whether s is positive or negative (or zero).

The symbol for the magnitude of a vector is the same as the one for the modulus of a real number, because the concepts are similar. In fact, a real number x behaves just like the vector $x\mathbf{i}$ in one dimension, where $\mathbf{i}$ is a basic unit vector. The vector $x\mathbf{i}$ represents a displacement on the number line, and the modulus $|x|$ then measures the magnitude of the displacement, whether it is in the positive or the negative direction.

A vector of magnitude 1 is called a **unit vector**. The basic unit vectors $\mathbf{i}$, $\mathbf{j}$, $\mathbf{k}$ are examples of unit vectors, but there are others: there is a unit vector in every direction.

Unit vectors are sometimes distinguished by a circumflex accent ^ over the letter. For example, a unit vector in the direction of $\mathbf{r}$ may be denoted by $\hat{\mathbf{r}}$. This notation is especially common in mechanics, but it will not generally be used in this chapter.

13.8 Scalar products

So far vectors have been added, subtracted and multiplied by scalars, but they have not been multiplied together. The next step is to define the product of two vectors:

> The **scalar product**, or **dot product**, of vectors $\mathbf{p}$ and $\mathbf{q}$ is the number (or scalar) $|\mathbf{p}||\mathbf{q}|\cos\theta$, where θ is the angle between the directions of $\mathbf{p}$ and $\mathbf{q}$. It is written $\mathbf{p}.\mathbf{q}$ and pronounced 'p dot q'.

The angle θ may be acute or obtuse, but it is important that it is the angle between $\mathbf{p}$ and $\mathbf{q}$, and not (for example) the angle between $\mathbf{p}$ and $-\mathbf{q}$. It is best to show θ in a diagram in which the vectors are represented by arrows with their tails at the same point, as in Fig. 13.20.

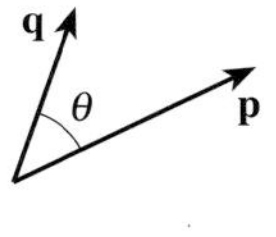

Fig. 13.20

The reason for calling this the 'scalar product', rather than simply the product, is that mathematicians also use another product, called the 'vector product'. But it is important to distinguish the scalar product from 'multiplication by a scalar'. To avoid confusion, many people prefer to use the alternative name 'dot product'.

For the same reason, you must always insert the 'dot' between $\mathbf{p}$ and $\mathbf{q}$ for the scalar product, but you must *not* insert a dot between s and $\mathbf{p}$ when multiplying by a scalar.

For example, you can never have a scalar product of three vectors, $\mathbf{p}\,.\,\mathbf{q}\,.\,\mathbf{r}$. You saw in Section 13.2 that the sum of these three vectors can be regarded as $(\mathbf{p}+\mathbf{q})+\mathbf{r}$ or as $\mathbf{p}+(\mathbf{q}+\mathbf{r})$, and that these expressions are equal. But $(\mathbf{p}\,.\,\mathbf{q})\,.\,\mathbf{r}$ has no meaning: $\mathbf{p}\,.\,\mathbf{q}$ is a scalar, and you cannot form a dot product of a scalar with the vector $\mathbf{r}$. Similarly, $\mathbf{p}\,.\,(\mathbf{q}\,.\,\mathbf{r})$ has no meaning.

However, $s(\mathbf{p}\,.\,\mathbf{q})$, where s is scalar, does have a meaning; as you would expect,

$$s(\mathbf{p}\,.\,\mathbf{q}) = (s\mathbf{p})\,.\,\mathbf{q}\,.$$

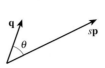

Fig. 13.21   Fig. 13.22

The proof depends on whether s is positive (see Fig. 13.21) or negative (see Fig. 13.22).

If $s > 0$, then the angle between $s\mathbf{p}$ and $\mathbf{q}$ is θ, so

$$(s\mathbf{p})\,.\,\mathbf{q} = \left|\,s\mathbf{p}\,\right|\left|\,\mathbf{q}\,\right|\cos\theta = \left|\,s\,\right|\left|\,\mathbf{p}\,\right|\left|\,\mathbf{q}\,\right|\cos\theta = \left|\,s\,\right|\left(\left|\,\mathbf{p}\,\right|\left|\,\mathbf{q}\,\right|\cos\theta\right) = s(\mathbf{p}\,.\,\mathbf{q})\,.$$

If $s < 0$, then the angle between $s\mathbf{p}$ and $\mathbf{q}$ is $\pi - \theta$, and $s = -\left|\,s\,\right|$, so

$$(s\mathbf{p})\,.\,\mathbf{q} = \left|\,s\mathbf{p}\,\right|\left|\,\mathbf{q}\,\right|\cos(\pi-\theta) = \left|\,s\,\right|\left|\,\mathbf{p}\,\right|\left|\,\mathbf{q}\,\right|(-\cos\theta) = -\left|\,s\,\right|\left(\left|\,\mathbf{p}\,\right|\left|\,\mathbf{q}\,\right|\cos\theta\right) = s(\mathbf{p}\,.\,\mathbf{q})\,.$$

Another property of the scalar product is that $\mathbf{p}\,.\,\mathbf{q} = \mathbf{q}\,.\,\mathbf{p}$, which follows immediately from the definition. This is called the **commutative rule for scalar products**.

There are two very important special cases, which you get by taking $\theta = 0$ and putting $\mathbf{p} = \mathbf{q}$, and taking $\theta = \frac{1}{2}\pi$, in the definition of scalar product.

> $\mathbf{p}\,.\,\mathbf{p} = \left|\,\mathbf{p}\,\right|^2$ ($\mathbf{p}\,.\,\mathbf{p}$ is sometimes written as $\mathbf{p}^2$).
>
> If neither $\mathbf{p}$ nor $\mathbf{q}$ is the zero vector,
>
> $\mathbf{p}\,.\,\mathbf{q} = 0$ if and only if $\mathbf{p}$ and $\mathbf{q}$ are in perpendicular directions.

These properties allow you to use vectors to find lengths and to identify right angles.

13.9 Scalar products in component form

The rules in the last section suggest that algebra with scalar products is much like ordinary algebra, except that some expressions (such as the scalar product of three vectors) have no meaning. You need one more rule to be able to use vectors to get geometrical results. This is the **distributive rule** for multiplying out brackets:

$$(\mathbf{p}+\mathbf{q})\,.\,\mathbf{r} = \mathbf{p}\,.\,\mathbf{r} + \mathbf{q}\,.\,\mathbf{r}\,.$$

For the present this will be assumed to be true. There is a proof in Section 13.10, but you may if you wish omit it on a first reading.

In the special cases at the end of Section 13.8, take $\mathbf{p}$ and $\mathbf{q}$ to be basic unit vectors. You then get:

For the basic unit vectors $\mathbf{i}$, $\mathbf{j}$, $\mathbf{k}$,

$$\mathbf{i}.\mathbf{i} = \mathbf{j}.\mathbf{j} = \mathbf{k}.\mathbf{k} = 1 \quad \text{and} \quad \mathbf{j}.\mathbf{k} = \mathbf{k}.\mathbf{i} = \mathbf{i}.\mathbf{j} = 0.$$

It follows that, if vectors $\mathbf{p}$ and $\mathbf{q}$ are written in component form as $\mathbf{p} = l\,\mathbf{i} + m\,\mathbf{j} + n\,\mathbf{k}$ and $\mathbf{q} = u\,\mathbf{i} + v\,\mathbf{j} + w\,\mathbf{k}$, then

$$
\begin{aligned}
\mathbf{p}.\mathbf{q} &= \left(l\,\mathbf{i} + m\,\mathbf{j} + n\,\mathbf{k} \right).\left(u\,\mathbf{i} + v\,\mathbf{j} + w\,\mathbf{k} \right) \\
&= lu\,\mathbf{i}.\mathbf{i} + lv\,\mathbf{i}.\mathbf{j} + lw\,\mathbf{i}.\mathbf{k} + mu\,\mathbf{j}.\mathbf{i} + mv\,\mathbf{j}.\mathbf{j} + mw\,\mathbf{j}.\mathbf{k} \\
&\qquad + nu\,\mathbf{k}.\mathbf{i} + nv\,\mathbf{k}.\mathbf{j} + nw\,\mathbf{k}.\mathbf{k} \qquad \text{(using the distributive rule)} \\
&= lu \times 1 + lv \times 0 + lw \times 0 + mu \times 0 + mv \times 1 + mw \times 0 \\
&\qquad + nu \times 0 + nv \times 0 + nw \times 1 \\
&= lu + mv + nw.
\end{aligned}
$$

In component form, the scalar product is

$$\begin{pmatrix} l \\ m \\ n \end{pmatrix}.\begin{pmatrix} u \\ v \\ w \end{pmatrix} = \left(l\,\mathbf{i} + m\,\mathbf{j} + n\,\mathbf{k} \right).\left(u\,\mathbf{i} + v\,\mathbf{j} + w\,\mathbf{k} \right) = lu + mv + nw.$$

This result has many applications. In particular, $\mathbf{p}.\mathbf{p} = l^2 + m^2 + n^2$, giving the length of $\mathbf{p}$:

$$\left| \mathbf{p} \right| = \sqrt{l^2 + m^2 + n^2}\,.$$

In two dimensions, if $\mathbf{p} = l\,\mathbf{i} + m\,\mathbf{j}$ and $\mathbf{q} = u\,\mathbf{i} + v\,\mathbf{j}$, then

$$\mathbf{p}.\mathbf{q} = lu + mv$$

so, in component form

$$\begin{pmatrix} l \\ m \end{pmatrix}.\begin{pmatrix} u \\ v \end{pmatrix} = lu + mv\,.$$

Example 13.9.1

Show that the vectors $\begin{pmatrix} 3 \\ 2 \end{pmatrix}$ and $\begin{pmatrix} -2 \\ 3 \end{pmatrix}$ are perpendicular.

Writing $\mathbf{p} = \begin{pmatrix} 3 \\ 2 \end{pmatrix}$ and $\mathbf{q} = \begin{pmatrix} -2 \\ 3 \end{pmatrix}$, and using $\mathbf{p}.\mathbf{q} = lu + mv$,

$$\mathbf{p}.\mathbf{q} = \begin{pmatrix} 3 \\ 2 \end{pmatrix}.\begin{pmatrix} -2 \\ 3 \end{pmatrix} = 3 \times (-2) + 2 \times 3 = -6 + 6 = 0,$$

Using the result in the box on page 202, since neither $\mathbf{p}$ nor $\mathbf{q}$ is the zero vector and $\mathbf{p}.\mathbf{q} = 0$, the vectors are perpendicular.

Example 13.9.2

Find the angle between the vectors $\mathbf{p} = 2\mathbf{i} - 2\mathbf{j} + \mathbf{k}$ and $\mathbf{q} = 12\mathbf{i} + 4\mathbf{j} - 3\mathbf{k}$, giving your answer correct to the nearest tenth of a degree.

The magnitudes of $\mathbf{p}$ and $\mathbf{q}$ are given by

$$|\mathbf{p}| = \sqrt{2^2 + (-2)^2 + 1^2} = \sqrt{4+4+1} = \sqrt{9} = 3$$

and

$$|\mathbf{q}| = \sqrt{12^2 + 4^2 + (-3)^2} = \sqrt{144 + 16 + 9} = \sqrt{169} = 13.$$

Using $\mathbf{p}.\mathbf{q} = |\mathbf{p}||\mathbf{q}|\cos\theta = lu + mv + nw$, where $\theta°$ is the angle between $\mathbf{p}$ and $\mathbf{q}$,

$$3 \times 13 \times \cos\theta° = 2 \times 12 + (-2) \times 4 + 1 \times (-3) = 24 - 8 - 3 = 13,$$

giving

$$\cos\theta° = \tfrac{13}{39} = \tfrac{1}{3}, \text{ and thus } \theta = 70.5\ldots.$$

The required angle is $70.5°$.

Vectors can give a good method for finding the angle between two straight lines, where it may not be easy or possible to draw a triangle containing the two lines.

Example 13.9.3

A barn (Fig. 13.23) has a rectangular floor $ABCD$ of dimensions 6 m by 12 m. The edges AP, BQ, CR and DS are each vertical and of height 5 m. The ridge UV is symmetrically placed above $PQRS$, and is height 7 m above $ABCD$. Calculate to the nearest tenth of a degree the angle between the lines AS and UR.

Take the unit vectors $\mathbf{i}, \mathbf{j}$ and $\mathbf{k}$ in the directions BC, BA and BQ.

Let $\overrightarrow{AS} = \mathbf{e}$ and $\overrightarrow{UR} = \mathbf{f}$.

Then

$$\mathbf{e} = 12\mathbf{i} + 5\mathbf{k} \text{ and } \mathbf{f} = 12\mathbf{i} - 3\mathbf{j} - 2\mathbf{k},$$

so $\quad |\mathbf{e}| = \sqrt{12^2 + 0^2 + 5^2} = \sqrt{169} = 13$

and $\quad |\mathbf{f}| = \sqrt{12^2 + (-3)^2 + (-2)^2} = \sqrt{157}.$

Denote the angle between the lines by $\theta°$.

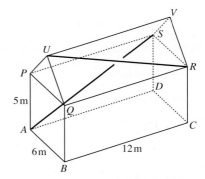

Fig. 13.23

Then $13 \times \sqrt{157} \cos\theta° = 12 \times 12 + 0 \times (-3) + 5 \times (-2) = 134$,

giving $\theta = 34.6$, correct to 1 decimal place.

So the angle between AS and UR is $34.6°$.

In this example AS and UR are skew lines. Since AS is parallel to BR, the angle between AS and UR is equal to the angle between AS and BR.

13.10* The distributive rule $(\mathbf{p}+\mathbf{q}).\mathbf{r} = \mathbf{p}.\mathbf{r} + \mathbf{q}.\mathbf{r}$

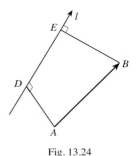

The proof of this needs a preliminary result. Fig. 13.24 shows a directed line l and two points A and B (in three dimensions). If lines AD and BE are drawn perpendicular to l, the directed length DE is called the **projection** of the displacement vector $\overrightarrow{AB}$ on l.

Here the word 'directed' means that a positive direction is selected on l, and that (in this diagram) DE is positive and ED is negative.

Fig. 13.24

Theorem   If $\mathbf{p}$ is the displacement vector $\overrightarrow{AB}$, and $\mathbf{u}$ is a unit vector in the direction of l, then the projection of $\overrightarrow{AB}$ on l is $\mathbf{p}.\mathbf{u}$.

Proof   You will probably find the proof is easiest to follow if l is drawn as a vertical line, as in Fig. 13.25. Recall that AD and BE are perpendicular to l, and so are horizontal. The shaded triangles ADM and NEB lie in the horizontal planes through D and E. The point N is such that AN is parallel to l and perpendicular to NB.

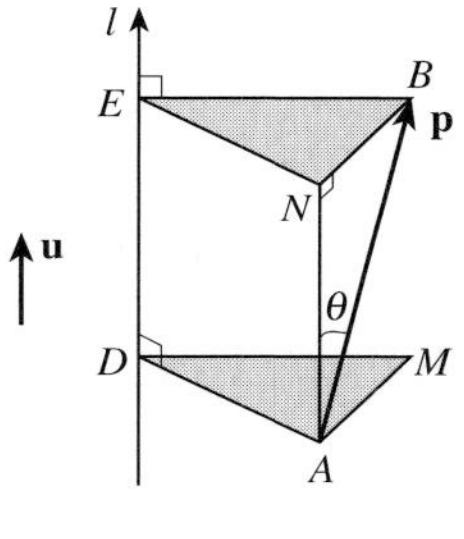

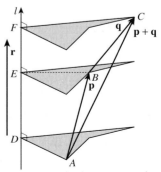

Then $DE = AN$, and $\mathbf{u}$ is a unit vector in the direction of AN. If the angle BAN is denoted by θ, then

Fig. 13.25

$$\mathbf{p}.\mathbf{u} = |\mathbf{p}| \times 1 \times \cos\theta = AB\cos\theta = AN = DE,$$

which is the projection of $\overrightarrow{AB}$ on l.

Notice that, if B were below A, then the angle between $\mathbf{p}$ and $\mathbf{u}$ would be obtuse, so $\mathbf{p}.\mathbf{u}$ would be negative. On l, E would be below D, so the directed length DE would also be negative.

When you have understood this proof with l vertical, you can try re-drawing Fig. 13.25 with l in some other direction, as in Fig. 13.24. If you then replace 'horizontal planes' by 'planes perpendicular to l', the proof will still hold.

Theorem   For any vectors $\mathbf{p}$, $\mathbf{q}$ and $\mathbf{r}$, $(\mathbf{p}+\mathbf{q}).\mathbf{r} = \mathbf{p}.\mathbf{r} + \mathbf{q}.\mathbf{r}$.

Proof   In Fig. 13.26 the displacement vectors $\overrightarrow{AB}$, $\overrightarrow{BC}$ and $\overrightarrow{AC}$ represent $\mathbf{p}$, $\mathbf{q}$ and $\mathbf{p}+\mathbf{q}$. The line l is in the direction of $\mathbf{r}$; this is again shown as a vertical line. The horizontal planes through A, B and C cut l at D, E and F respectively, so that AD, BE and CF are perpendicular to l. Let $\mathbf{u}$ be a unit vector in the direction of $\mathbf{r}$, and denote $|\mathbf{r}|$ by s, so that $\mathbf{r} = s\mathbf{u}$.

Fig. 13.26

Then

$$\mathbf{p} \cdot \mathbf{r} = \mathbf{p} \cdot (s\mathbf{u}) = s(\mathbf{p} \cdot \mathbf{u}) = s \times DE,$$

and similarly $\mathbf{q} \cdot \mathbf{r} = s \times EF$ and $(\mathbf{p} + \mathbf{q}) \cdot \mathbf{r} = s \times DF$.

Since DE, EF and DF are directed lengths, it is always true that $DE + EF = DF$, whatever the order of the points D, E and F on l.

Therefore

$$(\mathbf{p} + \mathbf{q}) \cdot \mathbf{r} = s \times DF = s \times (DE + EF) = s \times DE + s \times EF = \mathbf{p} \cdot \mathbf{r} + \mathbf{q} \cdot \mathbf{r}.$$

As before, when you have understood this proof with l vertical, you can adapt it for any other direction of l.

Exercise 13D

1   Let $\mathbf{a} = \begin{pmatrix} 3 \\ 2 \end{pmatrix}$, $\mathbf{b} = \begin{pmatrix} -4 \\ 2 \end{pmatrix}$ and $\mathbf{c} = \begin{pmatrix} 1 \\ 4 \end{pmatrix}$. Calculate $\mathbf{a} \cdot \mathbf{b}$, $\mathbf{a} \cdot \mathbf{c}$ and $\mathbf{a} \cdot (\mathbf{b} + \mathbf{c})$, and verify that $\mathbf{a} \cdot (\mathbf{b} + \mathbf{c}) = \mathbf{a} \cdot \mathbf{b} + \mathbf{a} \cdot \mathbf{c}$.

2   Let $\mathbf{a} = 2\mathbf{i} - \mathbf{j}$, $\mathbf{b} = 4\mathbf{i} - 3\mathbf{j}$ and $\mathbf{c} = -2\mathbf{i} - \mathbf{j}$. Calculate $\mathbf{a} \cdot \mathbf{b}$, $\mathbf{a} \cdot \mathbf{c}$ and $\mathbf{a} \cdot (\mathbf{b} + \mathbf{c})$, and verify that $\mathbf{a} \cdot (\mathbf{b} + \mathbf{c}) = \mathbf{a} \cdot \mathbf{b} + \mathbf{a} \cdot \mathbf{c}$.

3   Let $\mathbf{p} = \begin{pmatrix} 3 \\ -1 \\ 4 \end{pmatrix}$, $\mathbf{q} = \begin{pmatrix} -1 \\ -9 \\ 3 \end{pmatrix}$ and $\mathbf{r} = \begin{pmatrix} 33 \\ -13 \\ -28 \end{pmatrix}$. Calculate $\mathbf{p} \cdot \mathbf{q}$, $\mathbf{p} \cdot \mathbf{r}$ and $\mathbf{q} \cdot \mathbf{r}$. What can you deduce about the vectors $\mathbf{p}$, $\mathbf{q}$ and $\mathbf{r}$?

4   Which of the following vectors are perpendicular to each other?
   (a) $2\mathbf{i} - 3\mathbf{j} + 6\mathbf{k}$ (b) $2\mathbf{i} - 3\mathbf{j} - 6\mathbf{k}$ (c) $-3\mathbf{i} - 6\mathbf{j} + 2\mathbf{k}$ (d) $6\mathbf{i} - 2\mathbf{j} - 3\mathbf{k}$

5   Let $\mathbf{p} = \mathbf{i} - 2\mathbf{k}$, $\mathbf{q} = 3\mathbf{j} + 2\mathbf{k}$ and $\mathbf{r} = 2\mathbf{i} - \mathbf{j} + 5\mathbf{k}$. Calculate $\mathbf{p} \cdot \mathbf{q}$, $\mathbf{p} \cdot \mathbf{r}$ and $\mathbf{p} \cdot (\mathbf{q} + \mathbf{r})$ and verify that $\mathbf{p} \cdot (\mathbf{q} + \mathbf{r}) = \mathbf{p} \cdot \mathbf{q} + \mathbf{p} \cdot \mathbf{r}$.

6   Find the magnitude of each of the following vectors.
   (a) $\begin{pmatrix} -3 \\ 4 \end{pmatrix}$ (b) $\begin{pmatrix} -2 \\ 1 \end{pmatrix}$ (c) $\begin{pmatrix} -1 \\ -2 \end{pmatrix}$ (d) $\begin{pmatrix} 0 \\ -1 \end{pmatrix}$

   (e) $\begin{pmatrix} 1 \\ -2 \\ 2 \end{pmatrix}$ (f) $\begin{pmatrix} 4 \\ -3 \\ 12 \end{pmatrix}$ (g) $\begin{pmatrix} 0 \\ -3 \\ 4 \end{pmatrix}$ (h) $\begin{pmatrix} 2 \\ -1 \\ 1 \end{pmatrix}$

   (i) $\mathbf{i} - 2\mathbf{k}$ (j) $3\mathbf{j} + 2\mathbf{k}$ (k) $2\mathbf{i} - \mathbf{j} + 5\mathbf{k}$ (l) $2\mathbf{k}$

7   Let $\mathbf{a} = \begin{pmatrix} 4 \\ -3 \end{pmatrix}$. Find the magnitude of $\mathbf{a}$, and find a unit vector in the same direction as $\mathbf{a}$.

8   Find unit vectors in the same directions as $\begin{pmatrix} 1 \\ -2 \\ 2 \end{pmatrix}$ and $2\mathbf{i} - \mathbf{j} + 2\mathbf{k}$.

9 Use a vector method to calculate the angles between the following pairs of vectors, giving your answers in degrees to one place of decimals, where appropriate.

(a) $\begin{pmatrix} 2 \\ 1 \end{pmatrix}$ and $\begin{pmatrix} 1 \\ 3 \end{pmatrix}$ (b) $\begin{pmatrix} 4 \\ -5 \end{pmatrix}$ and $\begin{pmatrix} -5 \\ 4 \end{pmatrix}$ (c) $\begin{pmatrix} 4 \\ -6 \end{pmatrix}$ and $\begin{pmatrix} -6 \\ 9 \end{pmatrix}$

(d) $\begin{pmatrix} -1 \\ 4 \\ 5 \end{pmatrix}$ and $\begin{pmatrix} 2 \\ 0 \\ -3 \end{pmatrix}$ (e) $\begin{pmatrix} 1 \\ 2 \\ -3 \end{pmatrix}$ and $\begin{pmatrix} 2 \\ 3 \\ -4 \end{pmatrix}$ (f) $\begin{pmatrix} 2 \\ -1 \\ 3 \end{pmatrix}$ and $\begin{pmatrix} 5 \\ -2 \\ -4 \end{pmatrix}$

10 Let $\mathbf{r}_1 = \begin{pmatrix} x_1 \\ y_1 \end{pmatrix}$ and $\mathbf{r}_2 = \begin{pmatrix} x_2 \\ y_2 \end{pmatrix}$. Calculate $|\mathbf{r}_2 - \mathbf{r}_1|$ and interpret your result geometrically.

11 Find the angle between the line joining $(1,2)$ and $(3,-5)$ and the line joining $(2,-3)$ to $(1,4)$.

12 Find the angle between the line joining $(1,3,-2)$ and $(2,5,-1)$ and the line joining $(-1,4,3)$ to $(3,2,1)$.

13 Find the angle between the diagonals of a cube.

14 *ABCD* is the base of a square pyramid of side 2 units, and *V* is the vertex. The pyramid is symmetrical, and of height 4 units. Calculate the acute angle between *AV* and *BC*, giving your answer in degrees correct to 1 decimal place.

15 Two aeroplanes are flying in directions given by the vectors $300\mathbf{i} + 400\mathbf{j} + 2\mathbf{k}$ and $-100\mathbf{i} + 500\mathbf{j} - \mathbf{k}$. A person from the flight control centre is plotting their paths on a map. Find the acute angle between their paths on the map.

16 The roof of a house has a rectangular base of side 4 metres by 8 metres. The ridge line of the roof is 6 metres long, and centred 1 metre above the base of the roof. Calculate the acute angle between two opposite slanting edges of the roof.

Miscellaneous exercise 13

1 Find which pairs of the following vectors are perpendicular to each other.
   $\mathbf{a} = 2\mathbf{i} + \mathbf{j} - 2\mathbf{k}$ $\mathbf{b} = 2\mathbf{i} - 2\mathbf{j} + \mathbf{k}$ $\mathbf{c} = \mathbf{i} + 2\mathbf{j} + 2\mathbf{k}$ $\mathbf{d} = 3\mathbf{i} + 2\mathbf{j} - 2\mathbf{k}$

2 The vectors $\overrightarrow{AB}$ and $\overrightarrow{AC}$ are $\begin{pmatrix} -1 \\ 0 \\ 3 \end{pmatrix}$ and $\begin{pmatrix} 2 \\ 4 \\ 3 \end{pmatrix}$ respectively. The vector $\overrightarrow{AD}$ is the sum of $\overrightarrow{AB}$ and $\overrightarrow{AC}$. Determine the acute angle, in degrees correct to one decimal place, between the diagonals of the parallelogram defined by the points A, B, C and D. (OCR)

3 The vectors **AB** and **AC** are $\begin{pmatrix} -2 \\ 6 \\ -3 \end{pmatrix}$ and $\begin{pmatrix} -2 \\ -3 \\ 6 \end{pmatrix}$ respectively.

(a) Determine the lengths of the vectors.

(b) Find the scalar product **AB**.**AC**.

(c) Use your result from part (b) to calculate the acute angle between the vectors. Give the angle in degrees correct to one decimal place. (OCR)

4 The points A, B and C have position vectors $\mathbf{a} = \begin{pmatrix} 2 \\ 1 \\ 2 \end{pmatrix}$, $\mathbf{b} = \begin{pmatrix} -3 \\ 2 \\ 5 \end{pmatrix}$ and $\mathbf{c} = \begin{pmatrix} 4 \\ 5 \\ -2 \end{pmatrix}$

respectively, with respect to a fixed origin. The point D is such that $ABCD$, in that order, is a parallelogram.

(a) Find the position vector of D.

(b) Find the position vector of the point at which the diagonals of the parallelogram intersect.

(c) Calculate the angle BAC, giving your answer to the nearest tenth of a degree.

(OCR)

5 A vertical aerial is supported by three straight cables, each attached to the aerial at a point P, 30 metres up the aerial. The cables are attached to the horizontal ground at points A, B and C, each x metres from the foot O of the aerial, and situated symmetrically around it (see the diagrams).

Suppose that $\mathbf{i}$ is the unit vector in the direction $\overrightarrow{OA}$, $\mathbf{j}$ is the unit vector perpendicular to $\mathbf{i}$ in the plane of the ground, as shown in the Plan view, and $\mathbf{k}$ is the unit vector in the direction $\overrightarrow{OP}$.

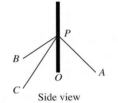

Side view

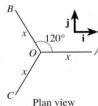

Plan view

(a) Write down expressions for the vectors $\overrightarrow{OA}$, $\overrightarrow{OB}$ and $\overrightarrow{OC}$ in terms of x, $\mathbf{i}$, $\mathbf{j}$ and $\mathbf{k}$.

(b) (i) Write down an expression for the vector $\overrightarrow{AP}$ in terms of vectors $\overrightarrow{OA}$ and $\overrightarrow{OP}$.

    (ii) Hence find expressions for the vectors $\overrightarrow{AP}$ and $\overrightarrow{BP}$ in terms of x, $\mathbf{i}$, $\mathbf{j}$ and $\mathbf{k}$.

(c) Given that $\overrightarrow{AP}$ and $\overrightarrow{BP}$ are perpendicular to each other, find the value of x. (OCR)

6 The position vectors of three points A, B and C with respect to a fixed origin O are $2\mathbf{i} - 2\mathbf{j} + \mathbf{k}$, $4\mathbf{i} + 2\mathbf{j} + \mathbf{k}$ and $\mathbf{i} + \mathbf{j} + 3\mathbf{k}$ respectively. Find unit vectors in the directions of $\overrightarrow{CA}$ and $\overrightarrow{CB}$. Calculate angle ACB in degrees, correct to 1 decimal place. (OCR)

7 (a) Find the angle between the vectors $2\mathbf{i} + 3\mathbf{j} + 6\mathbf{k}$ and $3\mathbf{i} + 4\mathbf{j} + 12\mathbf{k}$.

(b) The vectors $\mathbf{a}$ and $\mathbf{b}$ are non-zero.

    (i) Given that $\mathbf{a} + \mathbf{b}$ is perpendicular to $\mathbf{a} - \mathbf{b}$, prove that $|\mathbf{a}| = |\mathbf{b}|$.

    (ii) Given instead that $|\mathbf{a} + \mathbf{b}| = |\mathbf{a} - \mathbf{b}|$, prove that $\mathbf{a}$ and $\mathbf{b}$ are perpendicular.

(OCR)

8 $OABCDEFG$, shown in the figure, is a cuboid. The position vectors of A, C and D are $4\mathbf{i}$, $2\mathbf{j}$ and $3\mathbf{k}$ respectively. Calculate

(a) $|AG|$,

(b) the angle between AG and OB.

(OCR)

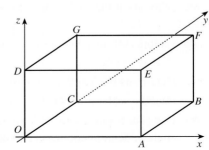

9   The three-dimensional vector $\mathbf{r}$, which has positive components, has magnitude 1 and makes angles of $60°$ with each of the unit vectors $\mathbf{i}$ and $\mathbf{j}$.

   (a) Write $\mathbf{r}$ as a column vector.

   (b) State the angle between $\mathbf{r}$ and the unit vector $\mathbf{k}$.

10 The points A, B and C have position vectors given respectively by $\mathbf{a} = 7\mathbf{i} + 4\mathbf{j} - 2\mathbf{k}$, $\mathbf{b} = 5\mathbf{i} + 3\mathbf{j} - 3\mathbf{k}$, $\mathbf{c} = 6\mathbf{i} + 5\mathbf{j} - 4\mathbf{k}$.

   (a) Find the angle BAC.   (b) Find the area of the triangle ABC.   (OCR)

11 The points A, B and C have position vectors $\mathbf{a}$, $\mathbf{b}$ and $\mathbf{c}$ respectively relative to the origin O. P is the point on BC such that $\overrightarrow{PC} = \frac{1}{10}\overrightarrow{BC}$.

   (a) Show that the position vector of P is $\frac{1}{10}(9\mathbf{c} + \mathbf{b})$.

   (b) Given that the line AP is perpendicular to the line BC, show that
$$(9\mathbf{c} + \mathbf{b}) \cdot (\mathbf{c} - \mathbf{b}) = 10\mathbf{a} \cdot (\mathbf{c} - \mathbf{b}).$$

   (c) Given also that OA, OB and OC are mutually perpendicular, prove that $OC = \frac{1}{3}OB$.
      (OCR)

12 A mathematical market trader packages fruit in three sizes. An Individual bag holds 1 apple and 2 bananas; a Jumbo bag holds 4 apples and 3 bananas; and a King-size bag holds 8 apples and 7 bananas. She draws two vector arrows $\mathbf{a}$ and $\mathbf{b}$ to represent an apple and a banana respectively, and then represents the three sizes of bag by vectors $\mathbf{I} = \mathbf{a} + 2\mathbf{b}$, $\mathbf{J} = 4\mathbf{a} + 3\mathbf{b}$ and $\mathbf{K} = 8\mathbf{a} + 7\mathbf{b}$. Find numbers s and t such that $\mathbf{K} = s\mathbf{I} + t\mathbf{J}$.

By midday she has sold all her King-size bags, but she has plenty of Individual and Jumbo bags left. She decides to make up some more King-size bags by using the contents of the other bags. How can she do this so that she has no loose fruit left over?

13 $ABCD$ is a parallelogram. The coordinates of A, B, D are $(4,2,3)$, $(18,4,8)$ and $(-1,12,13)$ respectively. The origin of coordinates is O.

   (a) Find the vectors $\overrightarrow{AB}$ and $\overrightarrow{AD}$. Find the coordinates of C.

   (b) Show that $\overrightarrow{OA}$ can be expressed in the form $\lambda\overrightarrow{AB} + \mu\overrightarrow{AD}$, stating the values of λ and μ. What does this tell you about the plane $ABCD$?   (MEI)

14 A balloon flying over flat land reports its position at 7.40 a.m. as $(7.8, 5.4, 1.2)$, the coordinates being given in kilometres relative to a checkpoint on the ground. By 7.50 a.m. its position has changed to $(9.3, 4.4, 0.7)$. Assuming that it continues to descend at the same speed along the same line, find the coordinates of the point where it would be expected to land, and the time when this would occur.

15 Prove that, if $(\mathbf{c} - \mathbf{b}) \cdot \mathbf{a} = 0$ and $(\mathbf{c} - \mathbf{a}) \cdot \mathbf{b} = 0$, then $(\mathbf{b} - \mathbf{a}) \cdot \mathbf{c} = 0$. Show that this can be used to prove the following geometrical results.

   (a) The lines through the vertices of a triangle ABC perpendicular to the opposite sides meet in a point.

   (b) If the tetrahedron $OABC$ has two pairs of perpendicular opposite edges, the third pair of edges is perpendicular.

Prove also that, in both cases, $OA^2 + BC^2 = OB^2 + CA^2 = OC^2 + AB^2$.

14 Geometric sequences

This chapter introduces another type of sequence. When you have completed it, you should

- recognise geometric sequences and be able to do calculations on them
- know and be able to obtain the formula for the sum of a geometric series
- know the condition for a geometric series to converge, and how to find its limiting sum.

14.1 Geometric sequences

In Chapter 8 you met arithmetic sequences, in which you get from one term to the next by adding a constant. A sequence in which you get from one term to the next by multiplying by a constant is called a geometric sequence.

A **geometric sequence**, or **geometric progression**, is a sequence defined by $u_1 = a$ and $u_{i+1} = ru_i$, where $i \in \mathbb{N}$ and $r \neq 0$ or 1.

The constant r is called the **common ratio** of the sequence.

You should notice two points about this definition. First, since the letter r is conventionally used for the common ratio, a different letter, i, is used for the suffixes.

Secondly, the ratios 0 and 1 are excluded. If you put $r = 0$ in the definition you get the sequence $a, 0, 0, 0, \dots$; if you put $r = 1$ you get $a, a, a, a, \dots$. Neither is very interesting, and some of the properties of geometric sequences break down if $r = 0$ or 1. However, r can be negative; in that case the terms are alternately positive and negative.

It is easy to give a formula for the ith term. To get from u_1 to u_i you multiply by the common ratio $i - 1$ times, so $u_i = r^{i-1} \times u_1$, which gives $u_i = ar^{i-1}$.

Example 14.1.1
A geometric sequence has first term $u_1 = 1$ and common ratio 1.1. Which is the first term greater than (a) 2, (b) 5, (c) 10, (d) 1000?

On many calculators you can keep multiplying by 1.1 by repeatedly pressing a single key. This makes it easy to display successive terms of a geometric sequence.

(a) This can easily be done experimentally, counting how many times you press the key until the display exceeds 2. You should find that after 8 presses you get 2.143 588 81, which is 1.1^8. The ith term of the sequence is $u_i = 1 \times 1.1^{i-1}$, so this is first greater than 2 when $i - 1 = 8$, or $i = 9$.

(b) Go on pressing the key. After another 8 presses you reach $(2.143\ 588\ 81)^2$, which is certainly greater than 4, so you will reach 5 quite soon. In fact it turns out that 1.1^{15} is already greater than 4, and two more presses take you to $1.1^{17} = 5.054\ldots$. So $u_{18} = 1 \times 1.1^{17}$ is the first term greater than 5.

(c) Since $1.1^8 > 2$ and $1.1^{17} > 5$, it is certainly true that $1.1^{25} = 1.1^8 \times 1.1^{17}$ is greater than 10. Rather than continuing to multiply, you can just use the power key to find $1.1^{25} = 10.834\ldots$. But you must check that 1.1^{24} is not already greater than 10. In fact it isn't, since $1.1^{24} = 9.849\ldots$. So the first term greater than 10 is $u_{26} = 1 \times 1.1^{25}$.

(d) Since $1.1^{24} < 10$ and $1.1^{25} > 10$, you can cube both sides to find that $1.1^{72} = \left(1.1^{24}\right)^3 < 1000$ and $1.1^{75} = \left(1.1^{25}\right)^3 > 1000$. So you only need to check 1.1^{73} and 1.1^{74}. Using the power key, $1.1^{73} = 1051.1\ldots$. So the first term greater than 1000 is $u_{74} = 1.1^{73}$.

The first terms greater than 2, 5, 10 and 1000 are u_9, u_{18}, u_{26} and u_{74}.

You can see from this example that, even with a common ratio only slightly greater than 1, the terms of a geometric sequence get big quite quickly.

14.2 Summing geometric series

Geometric sequences have many applications in finance, biology, mechanics and probability, and you often need to find the sum of all the terms. In this context it is usual to call the sequence a **geometric series**.

The method used in Chapter 8 to find the sum of an arithmetic series does not work for geometric series. You can see this by taking a simple geometric series like $1 + 2 + 4 + 8 + 16$ and placing an upside-down copy next to it, as in Fig. 14.1. When you did this with arithmetic series the two sets of crosses and noughts made a perfect join (see Fig. 8.7), so they could easily be counted; but for the geometric series there is a gap in the middle.

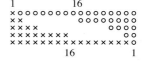

Fig. 14.1

For geometric series a different method is used. If you multiply the equation $S = 1 + 2 + 4 + 8 + 16$ by 2, then you get $2S = 2 + 4 + 8 + 16 + 32$. Notice that the right sides in these two equations have the terms $2 + 4 + 8 + 16$ in common; the sum of these terms is equal to $S - 1$, from the first equation, and $2S - 32$, from the second. So

$$S - 1 = 2S - 32, \text{ giving } S = 31.$$

You can use this method to find the sum of any geometric series. Let S be the sum of the first n terms of the series. Then

$$S = a + ar + ar^2 + \ldots + ar^{n-2} + ar^{n-1}.$$

If you multiply this equation by r, you get

$$Sr = ar + ar^2 + ar^3 + \ldots + ar^{n-1} + ar^n.$$

The right sides in these two equations have the terms $ar + ar^2 + \ldots + ar^{n-2} + ar^{n-1}$ in common; so

$$S - a = ar + ar^2 + \ldots + ar^{n-2} + ar^{n-1} = Sr - ar^n,$$

which gives

$$S(1 - r) = a(1 - r^n), \quad \text{or} \quad S = \frac{a(1 - r^n)}{1 - r}.$$

> The sum of the geometric series $a + ar + ar^2 + \ldots + ar^{n-1}$, with n terms, is
>
> $$\frac{a(1 - r^n)}{1 - r}.$$

You should notice that it has nowhere been assumed that r is positive. The formula is valid whether r is positive or negative. When $r > 1$, some people prefer to avoid fractions with negative numerators and denominators by using the result in the alternative form

$$S = \frac{a(r^n - 1)}{r - 1}.$$

Example 14.2.1

A child lives 200 metres from school. He walks 60 metres in the first minute, and in each subsequent minute he walks 75% of the distance he walked in the previous minute. Show that he takes between 6 and 7 minutes to get to school.

The distances walked in the first, second, third, ... , nth minutes are 60 m, 60×0.75 m, 60×0.75^2 m, ... , $60 \times 0.75^{n-1}$ m. In the first n minutes the child walks S_n metres, where

$$S_n = 60 + 60 \times 0.75^1 + 60 \times 0.75^2 + \ldots + 60 \times 0.75^{n-1}$$

$$= \frac{60(1 - 0.75^n)}{1 - 0.75} = \frac{60(1 - 0.75^n)}{0.25} = 240(1 - 0.75^n).$$

From this formula you can calculate that

$$S_6 = 240(1 - 0.75^6) = 240(1 - 0.177\ldots) = 197.2\ldots, \text{ and}$$

$$S_7 = 240(1 - 0.75^7) = 240(1 - 0.133\ldots) = 207.9\ldots \, .$$

So he has not reached school after 6 minutes, but (if he had gone on walking) he would have gone more than 200 m in 7 minutes. That is, he takes between 6 and 7 minutes to walk to school.

Example 14.2.2

Find a simple expression for the sum $p^6 - p^5 q + p^4 q^2 - p^3 q^3 + p^2 q^4 - pq^5 + q^6$.

This is a geometric series of 7 terms, with first term p^6 and common ratio $-\dfrac{q}{p}$. Its sum is therefore

$$\frac{p^6\left(1-(-q/p)^7\right)}{1-(-q/p)} = \frac{p^6\left(1-\left(-q^7/p^7\right)\right)}{1+q/p} = \frac{p^7\left(1+q^7/p^7\right)}{p(1+q/p)} = \frac{p^7+q^7}{p+q}.$$

Another way of writing the result of this example is

$$p^7 + q^7 = (p+q)\left(p^6 - p^5q + p^4q^2 - p^3q^3 + p^2q^4 - pq^5 + q^6\right).$$

You can use a similar method for any odd number n to express $p^n + q^n$ as the product of $p + q$ and another factor.

Exercise 14A

1 For each of the following geometric sequences find the common ratio and the next two terms.

   (a) $3, 6, 12, \ldots$ (b) $2, 8, 32, \ldots$ (c) $32, 16, 8, \ldots$

   (d) $2, -6, 18, -54, \ldots$ (e) $1.1, 1.21, 1.331, \ldots$ (f) $x^2, x, 1, \ldots$

2 Find an expression for the ith term of each of the following geometric sequences.

   (a) $2, 6, 18, \ldots$ (b) $10, 5, 2.5, \ldots$ (c) $1, -2, 4, \ldots$

   (d) $81, 27, 9, \ldots$ (e) $x, x^2, x^3, \ldots$ (f) $pq^2, q^3, p^{-1}q^4, \ldots$

3 Find the number of terms in each of these geometric progressions.

   (a) $2, 4, 8, \ldots, 2048$ (b) $1, -3, 9, \ldots, 531\,441$

   (c) $2, 6, 18, \ldots, 1458$ (d) $5, -10, 20, \ldots, -40\,960$

   (e) $16, 12, 9, \ldots, 3.796\,875$ (f) $x^{-6}, x^{-2}, x^2, \ldots, x^{42}$

4 Find the common ratio and the first term in the geometric progressions where

   (a) the 2nd term is 4 and the 5th term is 108,

   (b) the 3rd term is 6 and the 7th term is 96,

   (c) the 4th term is 19 683 and the 9th term is 81,

   (d) the 3rd term is 8 and the 9th term is 64,

   (e) the nth term is 16 807 and the $(n+4)$th term is 40 353 607.

5 Find the sum, for the given number of terms, of each of the following geometric series. Give decimal answers correct to 4 places.

   (a) $2 + 6 + 18 + \ldots$ 10 terms   (b) $2 - 6 + 18 - \ldots$ 10 terms

   (c) $1 + \frac{1}{2} + \frac{1}{4} + \ldots$ 8 terms   (d) $1 - \frac{1}{2} + \frac{1}{4} - \ldots$ 8 terms

   (e) $3 + 6 + 12 + \ldots$ 12 terms   (f) $12 - 4 + \frac{4}{3} - \ldots$ 10 terms

   (g) $x + x^2 + x^3 + \ldots$ n terms   (h) $x - x^2 + x^3 - \ldots$ n terms

   (i) $x + \dfrac{1}{x} + \dfrac{1}{x^3} + \ldots$ n terms   (j) $1 - \dfrac{1}{x^2} + \dfrac{1}{x^4} + \ldots$ n terms

6 Use the method in Section 14.2 to find the sum of each of the following geometric series. Give numerical answers as rational numbers.

(a) $1 + 2 + 4 + \ldots + 1024$

(b) $1 - 2 + 4 - \ldots + 1024$

(c) $3 + 12 + 48 + \ldots + 196\,608$

(d) $1 + \frac{1}{2} + \frac{1}{4} + \ldots + \frac{1}{512}$

(e) $1 - \frac{1}{3} + \frac{1}{9} - \ldots - \frac{1}{19\,683}$

(f) $10 + 5 + 2.5 + \ldots + 0.156\,25$

(g) $\frac{1}{4} + \frac{1}{16} + \frac{1}{64} + \ldots + \frac{1}{1024}$

(h) $1 + \frac{1}{2} + \frac{1}{4} + \ldots + \frac{1}{2^n}$

(i) $16 + 4 + 1 + \ldots + \dfrac{1}{2^{2n}}$

(j) $81 - 27 + 9 - \ldots + \dfrac{1}{(-3)^n}$

7 A well-known story concerns the inventor of the game of chess. As a reward for inventing the game it is rumoured that he was asked to choose his own prize. He asked for 1 grain of rice to be placed on the first square of the board, 2 grains on the second square, 4 grains on the third square and so on in geometric progression until all 64 squares had been covered. Calculate the total number of grains of rice he would have received. Give your answer in standard form!

8 A problem similar to that of Question 7 is posed by the child who negotiates a pocket money deal of 1 cent on 1 February, 2 cents on 2 February, 4 cents on 3 February and so on for 28 days. How much should the child receive in total during February?

9 If x, y and z are the first three terms of a geometric sequence, show that x^2, y^2 and z^2 form another geometric sequence.

10 Different numbers x, y and z are the first three terms of a geometric progression with common ratio r, and also the first, second and fourth terms of an arithmetic progression.

(a) Find the value of r.

(b) Find which term of the arithmetic progression will next be equal to a term of the geometric progression.

11 Different numbers x, y and z are the first three terms of a geometric progression with common ratio r and also the first, second and fifth terms of an arithmetic progression.

(a) Find the value of r.

(b) Find which term of the arithmetic progression will next be equal to a term of the geometric progression.

12 Consider the geometric progression

$$q^{n-1} + q^{n-2}p + q^{n-3}p^2 + \ldots + qp^{n-2} + p^{n-1}.$$

(a) Find the common ratio and the number of terms.

(b) Show that the sum of the series is equal to $\dfrac{q^n - p^n}{q - p}$.

(c) By considering the limit as $q \to p$ deduce expressions for $f'(p)$ in the cases

(i) $f(x) = x^n$,   (ii) $f(x) = x^{-n}$,   for all positive integers n.

14.3 Convergent sequences

Take any sequence, such as the sequence of triangle numbers $t_1 = 1$, $t_2 = 3$, $t_3 = 6$, ... (see Section 8.2). Form a new sequence whose terms are the sums of successive triangle numbers:

$$S_1 = t_1 = 1, \quad S_2 = t_1 + t_2 = 1 + 3 = 4, \quad S_3 = t_1 + t_2 + t_3 = 1 + 3 + 6 = 10, \text{ and so on.}$$

This is called the sum sequence of the original sequence.

Notice that $S_2 = S_1 + t_2$, $S_3 = S_2 + t_3$, ... This property can be used to give an inductive definition for the sum sequence:

> For a given sequence u_i, the **sum sequence** $S_i = u_1 + ... + u_i$ is defined by $S_1 = u_1$ and $S_{i+1} = S_i + u_{i+1}$.

(If the original sequence begins with u_0 rather than u_1, the equation $S_1 = u_1$ in the definition is replaced by $S_0 = u_0$.)

Geometric sequences have especially important sum sequences. Here are four examples, each with first term $a = 1$:

(a) $r = 3$

u_i	1	3	9	27	81	243	729	...
S_i	1	4	13	40	121	364	1093	...

Table 14.2

(b) $r = 0.2$

u_i	1	0.2	0.04	0.008	0.001 6	0.000 32	0.000 064	...
S_i	1	1.2	1.24	1.248	1.249 6	1.249 92	1.249 984	...

Table 14.3

(c) $r = -0.2$

u_i	1	−0.2	0.04	−0.008	0.001 6	−0.000 32	0.000 064	...
S_i	1	0.8	0.84	0.832	0.833 6	0.833 28	0.833 344	...

Table 14.4

(d) $r = -3$

u_i	1	−3	9	−27	81	−243	729	...
S_i	1	−2	7	−20	61	−182	547	...

Table 14.5

The sum sequences for (b) and (c) are quite different from the others. You would guess that in (b) the values of S_i are getting close to 1.25, but never reach it. This can be proved, since the formula for the sum of the first n values of u_i gives, with $a = 1$ and $r = 0.2$,

$$\frac{1-0.2^n}{1-0.2} = \frac{1-0.2^n}{0.8} = 1.25(1-0.2^n).$$

Now you can make 0.2^n as small as you like by taking n large enough, and then the expression in brackets comes very close to 1, though it never equals 1. You can say that the sum tends to the limit 1.25 as n tends to infinity.

It seems that the sum in (c) tends to $0.833\,33\ldots$ (the recurring decimal for $\frac{5}{6}$) as n tends to infinity, but here the values are alternately above and below the limiting value. This is because the formula for the sum is

$$\frac{1-(-0.2)^n}{1-(-0.2)} = \frac{1-(-0.2)^n}{1.2} = \frac{5}{6}(1-(-0.2)^n).$$

In this formula the expression $(-0.2)^n$ is alternately positive and negative, so $1-(-0.2)^n$ alternates above and below 1.

The other two sequences, for which the sum formulae are (a) $\frac{1}{2}(3^n-1)$ and (d) $\frac{1}{4}(1-(-3)^n)$, do not tend to a limit. The sum (a) can be made as large as you like by taking n large enough; it is said to **diverge to infinity** as n tends to infinity. The sum (d) can also be made as large as you like; the sum sequence is said to **oscillate infinitely**.

It is the expression r^n in the sum formula $\dfrac{a(1-r^n)}{1-r}$ which determines whether or not the sum tends to a limit. If $|r| > 1$, then $|r^n|$ increases indefinitely; but if $|r| < 1$, then $|r^n|$ tends to 0 and the sum tends to the value $\dfrac{a(1-0)}{1-r} = \dfrac{a}{1-r}$. As long as $|r| < 1$, even if r is very close to 1, r^n becomes very small if n is large enough; for example, if $r = 0.9999$ and $n = 1\,000\,000$, then $r^n \approx 3.70 \times 10^{-44}$.

If $|r| < 1$, the sum of the geometric series with first term a and common ratio r tends to the limit $S_\infty = \dfrac{a}{1-r}$ as the number of terms tends to infinity.

The infinite geometric series is then said to be **convergent**.

S_∞ is called the **sum to infinity** of the series.

Example 14.3.1

Express the recurring decimal $0.296\,296\,296\ldots$ as a fraction.

The decimal can be written as

$$0.296 + 0.000\,296 + 0.000\,000\,296 + \ldots$$

$$= 0.296 + 0.296 \times 0.001 + 0.296 \times (0.001)^2 + \ldots,$$

which is a geometric series with $a = 0.296$ and $r = 0.001$. Since $|r| < 1$, the series is convergent with limiting sum $\dfrac{0.296}{1 - 0.001} = \dfrac{296}{999}$.

Since $296 = 8 \times 37$ and $999 = 27 \times 37$, this fraction in its simplest form is $\frac{8}{27}$.

Example 14.3.2

A beetle starts at a point O on the floor. It walks 1 m east, then $\frac{1}{2}$ m west, then $\frac{1}{4}$ m east, and so on, halving the distance at each change of direction. How far from O does it end up?

The final distance from O is $1 - \frac{1}{2} + \frac{1}{4} - \frac{1}{8} + \ldots$, which is a geometric series with common ratio $-\frac{1}{2}$. Since $\left|-\frac{1}{2}\right| < 1$, the series converges to a limit

$$\frac{1}{1 - (-\frac{1}{2})} = \frac{1}{\frac{3}{2}} = \frac{2}{3}.$$

The beetle ends up $\frac{2}{3}$ m from O.

Notice that a point of trisection was obtained as the limit of a process of repeated halving.

Exercise 14B

1 Find the sum to infinity of the following geometric series. Give your answers to parts (a) to (j) as whole numbers, fractions or exact decimals.

(a) $1 + \frac{1}{2} + \frac{1}{4} + \ldots$

(b) $1 + \frac{1}{3} + \frac{1}{9} + \ldots$

(c) $\frac{1}{5} + \frac{1}{25} + \frac{1}{125} + \ldots$

(d) $0.1 + 0.01 + 0.001 + \ldots$

(e) $1 - \frac{1}{3} + \frac{1}{9} - \ldots$

(f) $0.2 - 0.04 + 0.008 - \ldots$

(g) $\frac{3}{2} + \frac{3}{4} + \frac{3}{8} + \ldots$

(h) $\frac{1}{2} - \frac{1}{4} + \frac{1}{8} - \ldots$

(i) $10 - 5 + 2.5 - \ldots$

(j) $50 + 10 + 2 + \ldots$

(k) $x + x^2 + x^3 + \ldots$, where $-1 < x < 1$

(l) $1 - x^2 + x^4 - \ldots$, where $x^2 < 1$

(m) $1 + x^{-1} + x^{-2} + \ldots$, where $|x| > 1$

(n) $x^2 - x + 1 - \ldots$, where $|x| > 1$

2 Express each of the following recurring decimals as exact fractions.

(a) $0.363\,636\ldots$

(b) $0.123\,123\,123\ldots$

(c) $0.555\ldots$

(d) $0.471\,471\,471\ldots$

(e) $0.142\,857\,142\,857\,142\,857\ldots$

(f) $0.285\,714\,285\,714\,285\,714\ldots$

(g) $0.714\,285\,714\,285\,714\,285\ldots$

(h) $0.857\,142\,857\,142\,857\,142\ldots$

3 Find the common ratio of a geometric series which has a first term of 5 and a sum to infinity of 6.

4 Find the common ratio of a geometric series which has a first term of 11 and a sum to infinity of 6.

5 Find the first term of a geometric series which has a common ratio of $\frac{3}{4}$ and a sum to infinity of 12.

6 Find the first term of a geometric series which has a common ratio of $-\frac{3}{5}$ and a sum to infinity of 12.

7 In Example 14.3.2 a beetle starts at a point O on the floor. It walks 1 m east, then $\frac{1}{2}$ m west, then $\frac{1}{4}$ m east and so on. It finished $\frac{2}{3}$ m to the east of O. How far did it actually walk?

8 A beetle starts at a point O on the floor and walks 0.6 m east, then 0.36 m west, 0.216 m east and so on. Find its final position and how far it actually walks.

9 A 'supa-ball' is thrown upwards from ground level. It hits the ground after 2 seconds and continues to bounce. The time it is in the air for a particular bounce is always 0.8 of the time for the previous bounce. How long does it take for the ball to stop bouncing?

10 A 'supa-ball' is dropped from a height of 1 metre onto a level table. It always rises to a height equal to 0.9 of the height from which it was dropped. How far does it travel in total until it stops bouncing?

11 A frog sits at one end of a table which is 2 m long. In its first jump the frog goes a distance of 1 m along the table, with its second jump $\frac{1}{2}$ m, with its third jump $\frac{1}{4}$ m and so on.

(a) What is the frog's final position?

(b) After how many jumps will the frog be within 1 cm of the far end of the table?

14.4 Exponential growth and decay

Many everyday situations are described by geometric sequences. Of the next two examples, the first has a common ratio greater than 1, and the second has a common ratio between 0 and 1.

Example 14.4.1
A person invests $1000 in a savings bank account which pays interest of 6% annually. Calculate the amount in the account over the next 8 years.

The interest in any year is 0.06 times the amount in the account at the beginning of the year. This is added on to the sum of money already in the account. The amount at the end of each year, after interest has been added, is 1.06 times the amount at the beginning of the year. So

$$\text{Amount after 1 year} \ = \$1000 \times 1.06 = \$1060$$
$$\text{Amount after 2 years} = \$1060 \times 1.06 = \$1124$$
$$\text{Amount after 3 years} = \$1124 \times 1.06 = \$1191, \text{ and so on.}$$

Continuing in this way, you get the amounts shown in Table 14.6, to the nearest whole number of dollars.

Number of years	0	1	2	3	4	5	6	7	8
Amount ($)	1000	1060	1124	1191	1262	1338	1419	1504	1594

Table 14.6

These values are shown in Fig. 14.7.

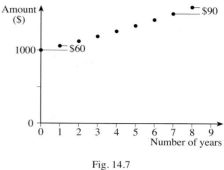

Notice that in the first year the interest is $60, but in the eighth year it is $90. This is because the amount on which the 6% is calculated has gone up from $1000 to $1504. This is characteristic of **exponential growth**, in which the increase is proportional to the current amount. As the amount goes up, the increase goes up.

Fig. 14.7

Example 14.4.2
A car cost $15000 when new, and each year its value decreases by 20%. Find its value on the first five anniversaries of its purchase.

> The value at the end of each year is 0.8 times its value a year earlier. The results of this calculation are given in Table 14.8.

Number of years	0	1	2	3	4	5
Value ($)	15000	12000	9600	7680	6144	4915

Table 14.8

These values are shown in Fig. 14.9.

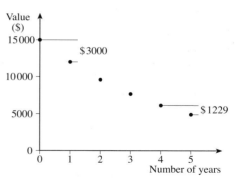

The value goes down by $3000 in the first year, but by only $1229 in the fifth year, because by then the 20% is calculated on only $6144 rather than $15000. This is characteristic of **exponential decay**, in which the decrease is proportional to the current value. Notice that, if the 20% rule continues, the value never becomes zero however long you keep the car.

Fig. 14.9

Notice that in both these examples it is more natural to think of the first term of the sequence as u_0 rather than u_1, so that $\$u_i$ is the amount in the account, or the value of the car, after i years. The sequence in Example 14.4.1 has

$$u_0 = 1000 \quad \text{and} \quad u_{i+1} = 1.06u_i \quad \text{for } 0 \leqslant i \leqslant 7.$$

From this you can deduce that $u_1 = 1000 \times 1.06$, $u_2 = 1000 \times 1.06^2$, and more generally $u_i = 1000 \times 1.06^i$. The sequence in Example 14.4.2 has

$$u_0 = 15000 \quad \text{and} \quad u_{i+1} = 0.8u_i \quad \text{for } 0 \leqslant i \leqslant 4.$$

In this case $u_1 = 15000 \times 0.8$, $u_2 = 15000 \times 0.8^2$ and $u_i = 15000 \times 0.8^i$.

These are both examples of exponential sequences. (The word 'exponential' comes from 'exponent', which is another word for index. The reason for the name is that the variable i appears in the exponent of the formula for u_i.) An exponential sequence is a special kind of geometric sequence, in which a and r are both positive. If the first term is denoted by u_0, the sequence can be defined inductively by

$$u_0 = a \quad \text{and} \quad u_{i+1} = ru_i,$$

or by the formula

$$u_i = ar^i.$$

If $r > 1$ the sequence represents exponential growth; if $0 < r < 1$ it represents exponential decay.

It may or may not be useful to find the sum of the terms of an exponential sequence. In Example 14.4.2 there would be no point in adding up the year-end values of the car. But many investment calculations (such as for pensions and mortgages) require the terms of an exponential sequence to be added up. This is illustrated by the next example.

Example 14.4.3

Saria's grandparents put $1000 into a savings bank account for her on each birthday from her 10th to her 18th. The account pays interest at 6% for each complete year that the money is invested. How much money is in the account on the day after her 18th birthday?

Start with the most recent deposit. The $1000 on her 18th birthday has not earned any interest. The $1000 on her 17th birthday has earned interest for one year, so is now worth $1000 \times 1.06 = \$1060$. Similarly, the $1000 on her 16th birthday is worth $1000 \times 1.06^2 = \$1124$, and so on. So the total amount is now $\$S$, where

$$S = 1000 + 1000 \times 1.06 + 1000 \times 1.06^2 + \ldots + 1000 \times 1.06^8.$$

Method 1   The terms of this series are just the amounts calculated in Example 14.4.1. The sum of the nine entries in Table 14.6 is 11 492.

Method 2   The sum is a geometric series with $a = 1000$, $r = 1.06$ and $n = 9$. Using the general formula in the alternative version for $r > 1$,

$$S = \frac{a(r^n - 1)}{r - 1} = \frac{1000(1.06^9 - 1)}{1.06 - 1} = 11\,491.32.$$

There is a small discrepancy between the two answers because the amounts in Table 14.6 were rounded to the nearest dollar. The amount in the account just after Saria's 18th birthday is $11 491.32.

Exercise 14C

1 Trudy puts $500 into a savings bank account on the first day of January each year from 2000 to 2010 inclusive. The account pays interest at 5% for each complete year of investment. How much money will there be in the account on 2 January 2010?

2 Jayesh invests $100 in a savings account on the first day of each month for one complete year. The account pays interest at $\frac{1}{2}$% for each complete month. How much does Jayesh have invested at the end of the year (but before making a thirteenth payment)?

3 Neeta takes out a 25-year mortgage of $40 000 to buy her house. Compound interest is charged on the loan at a rate of 8% per annum. She has to pay off the mortgage with 25 equal payments, the first of which is to be one year after the loan is taken out. Continue the following argument to calculate the value of each annual payment.

- After 1 year she owes $\$(40\,000 \times 1.08)$ (loan plus interest) less the payment made, $\$P$, that is, she owes $\$(40\,000 \times 1.08 - P)$.
- After 2 years she owes $\$((40\,000 \times 1.08 - P) \times 1.08 - P)$.
- After 3 years she owes $\$(((40\,000 \times 1.08 - P) \times 1.08 - P) \times 1.08 - P)$.

At the end of the 25 years this (continued) expression must be zero. Form an equation in P and solve it.

4 Fatima invests $100 per month for a complete year, with interest added every month at the rate of $\frac{1}{2}$% per month at the end of the month. How much would she have had to invest at the beginning of the year to have the same total amount after the complete year?

5 Charles borrows $6000 for a new car. Compound interest is charged on the loan at a rate of 2% per month. Charles has to pay off the loan with 24 equal monthly payments. Calculate the value of each monthly payment.

6 The population of Pascalia is increasing at a rate of 6% each year. On 1 January 1990 it was 35 200. What was its population on

(a) 1 January 2000,   (b) 1 July 1990,   (c) 1 January 1980?

7 The population of the United Kingdom in 1971 was 5.5615×10^7; by 1992 it was estimated to be 5.7384×10^7. Assuming a steady exponential growth estimate the population in

(a) 2003,   (b) 1981.

8 The population of Pythagora is decreasing steadily at a rate of 4% each year. The population in 1998 was 21 000. Estimate the population in

(a) 2002,   (b) 1990.

9 A man of mass 90 kg plans to diet and to reduce his mass to 72 kg in four weeks by a constant percentage reduction each day.

(a) What should his mass be 1 week after starting his diet?

(b) He forgets to stop after 4 weeks. Estimate his mass 1 week later.

10 A savings account is opened with a single payment of $2000. It attracts compound interest at a constant rate of 0.5% per month.

(a) Find the amount in the account after two complete years.

(b) Find, by trial, after how many months the value of the investment will have doubled.

11 The Bank of Utopia offers an interest rate of 100% per annum with various options as to how the interest may be added. Gopal invests $1000 and considers the following options.

Option A   Interest added annually at the end of the year.

Option B   Interest of 50% credited at the end of each half-year.

Option C, D, E, ...   The Bank is willing to add interest as often as required, subject to (interest rate) $\times$ (number of credits per year) $= 100$.

Investigate to find the maximum possible amount in Gopal's account after one year.

Miscellaneous exercise 14

1 In a geometric progression, the fifth term is 100 and the seventh term is 400. Find the first term.

2 A geometric series has first term a and common ratio $\dfrac{1}{\sqrt{2}}$. Show that the sum to infinity of the series is $a(2+\sqrt{2})$.   (Hint: $(\sqrt{2}-1)(\sqrt{2}+1)=1$.)

3 The nth term of a sequence is ar^{n-1}, where a and r are constants. The first term is 3 and the second term is $-\frac{3}{4}$. Find the values of a and r.

Hence find the sum of the first n terms of the sequence.

4 Evaluate, correct to the nearest whole number,
$$0.99+0.99^2+0.99^3+\ldots+0.99^{99}.$$

5 Find the sum of the infinite series $\dfrac{1}{10^3}+\dfrac{1}{10^6}+\dfrac{1}{10^9}+\ldots$, expressing your answer as a fraction in its lowest terms.

Hence express the infinite recurring decimal $0.108\,108\,108\ldots$ as a fraction in its lowest terms.

6 A geometric series has first term 1 and common ratio r. Given that the sum to infinity of the series is 5, find the value of r.

Find the least value of n for which the sum of the first n terms of the series exceeds 4.9.

7 In a geometric series, the first term is 12 and the fourth term is $-\frac{3}{2}$. Find the sum, S_n, of the first n terms of the series.

Find the sum to infinity, S_∞, of the series and the least value of n for which the magnitude of the difference between S_n and S_∞ is less than 0.001.

8 A geometric series has non-zero first term a and common ratio r, where $0<r<1$. Given that the sum of the first 8 terms of the series is equal to half the sum to infinity, find the value of r, correct to 3 decimal places. Given also that the 17th term of the series is 10, find a.

9 An athlete plans a training schedule which involves running 20 km in the first week of training; in each subsequent week the distance is to be increased by 10% over the previous week. Write down an expression for the distance to be covered in the nth week according to this schedule, and find in which week the athlete would first cover more than 100 km.

10 At the beginning of 1990, an investor decided to invest $6000, believing that the value of the investment should increase, on average, by 6% each year. Show that, if this percentage rate of increase was in fact maintained for 10 years, the value of the investment will be about $10 745.

The investor added a further $6000 at the beginning of each year between 1991 and 1995 inclusive. Assuming that the 6% annual rate of increase continues to apply, show that the total value, in dollars, of the investment at the beginning of the year 2000 may be written as $6000(1.06^5 + 1.06^6 + \ldots + 1.06^{10})$ and evaluate this, correct to the nearest dollar.

11 A post is being driven into the ground by a mechanical hammer. The distance it is driven by the first blow is 8 cm. Subsequently, the distance it is driven by each blow is $\frac{9}{10}$ of the distance it was driven by the previous blow.

(a) The post is to be driven a total distance of at least 70 cm into the ground. Find the smallest number of blows needed.

(b) Explain why the post can never be driven a total distance of more than 80 cm into the ground.

12 When a table-tennis ball is dropped vertically on to a table, the time interval between any particular bounce and the next bounce is 90% of the time interval between that particular bounce and the preceding bounce. The interval between the first and second bounces is 2 seconds. Given that the interval between the nth bounce and the $(n+1)$th bounce is the first such interval less than 0.02 seconds, find n. Also find the total time from the first bounce to the nth bounce, giving 3 significant figures in your answer.

13 An investment of $100 in a savings scheme is worth $150 after 5 years. Calculate as a percentage the annual rate of interest which would give this figure.

14 A geometric series G has positive first term a, common ratio r and sum to infinity S. The sum to infinity of the even-numbered terms of G (the second, fourth, sixth, … terms) is $-\frac{1}{2}S$. Find the value of r.

(a) Given that the third term of G is 2, show that the sum to infinity of the odd-numbered terms of G (the first, third, fifth, … terms) is $\frac{81}{4}$.

(b) In another geometric series H, each term is the modulus of the corresponding term of G. Show that the sum to infinity of H is $2S$.

15 An infinite geometric series has first term a and sum to infinity b, where $b \neq 0$. Prove that a lies between 0 and $2b$.

16 The sum of the infinite geometric series $1 + r + r^2 + \ldots$ is k times the sum of the series $1 - r + r^2 - \ldots$, where $k > 0$. Express r in terms of k.

17 A person wants to borrow \$100 000 to buy a house. He intends to pay back a fixed sum of \$C$ at the end of each year, so that after 25 years he has completely paid off the debt. Assuming a steady interest rate of 4% per year, explain why

$$100\,000 = C\left(\frac{1}{1.04} + \frac{1}{1.04^2} + \frac{1}{1.04^3} + \dots + \frac{1}{1.04^{25}}\right).$$

Calculate the value of C.

18 A person wants to buy a pension which will provide her with an income of \$10 000 at the end of each of the next n years. Show that, with a steady interest rate of 5% per year, the pension should cost her

$$\$10\,000\left(\frac{1}{1.05} + \frac{1}{1.05^2} + \frac{1}{1.05^3} + \dots + \frac{1}{1.05^n}\right).$$

Find a simple formula for calculating this sum, and find its value when $n = 10, 20, 30, 40, 50$.

19 Find the sum of the geometric series

$$(1-x) + \left(x^3 - x^4\right) + \left(x^6 - x^7\right) + \dots + \left(x^{3n} - x^{3n+1}\right).$$

Hence show that the sum of the infinite series $1 - x + x^3 - x^4 + x^6 - x^7 + \dots$ is equal to

$\dfrac{1}{1 + x + x^2}$, and state the values of x for which this is valid.

Use a similar method to find the sum of the infinite series $1 - x + x^5 - x^6 + x^{10} - x^{11} + \dots$.

20 Find the sums of the infinite geometric series

(a) $\sin^2 x° + \sin^4 x° + \sin^6 x° + \sin^8 x° + \dots$,

(b) $1 - \tan^2 x° + \tan^4 x° - \tan^6 x° + \tan^8 x° - \dots$,

giving your answers in as simple a form as possible. For what values of x are your results valid?

21 Use the formula to sum the geometric series $1 + (1 + x) + (1 + x)^2 + \dots + (1 + x)^6$ when $x \ne 0$. By considering the coefficients of x^2, deduce that

$$\binom{2}{2} + \binom{3}{2} + \binom{4}{2} + \binom{5}{2} + \binom{6}{2} = \binom{7}{3}.$$

Illustrate this result on a Pascal triangle.

Write down and prove a general result about binomial coefficients, of which this is a special case.

22 Make tables of values of $1 + x$, $1 + x + x^2$, $1 + x + x^2 + x^3$, $1 + x + x^2 + x^3 + x^4$ and $\dfrac{1}{1 - x}$ and use them to draw graphs of these functions of x for $-1.5 \le x \le 1.5$.

What do your graphs suggest about the possibility of using the polynomial

$1 + x + x^2 + x^3 + \dots + x^n$ as an approximation to the function $\dfrac{1}{1 - x}$?

15 Second derivatives

This chapter extends the idea of differentiation further. When you have completed it, you should

- understand the significance of the second derivative for the shape of graphs and in real-world applications
- be able to use second derivatives where appropriate to distinguish minimum and maximum points
- understand that at a point of inflexion the second derivative is zero.

15.1 Interpreting and sketching graphs

The results in Chapter 7, linking features of the graph of a function with values of the derivative, were restricted to functions which are continuous within their domains. These results used the idea that the derivative doesn't just measure the gradient at a particular point of a graph, but could itself be regarded as a function.

In this chapter a further restriction needs to be made, to functions which are 'smooth'; that is, functions whose graphs do not have sudden changes of direction. This means that, with a function such as $x^{\frac{2}{3}}(1-x)$ (from Example 7.2.3), you must exclude the 'awkward' point (the origin in this example) from the domain.

The 'smooth' condition means that the derivative, considered as a function, is continuous and can itself be differentiated. The result is called the **second derivative** of the function, and it is denoted by $f''(x)$. It is sometimes called the 'second order derivative'. If you are using the $\dfrac{dy}{dx}$ notation, the second derivative is written as $\dfrac{d^2y}{dx^2}$. (The reason for this rather curious symbol is explained in Section 15.5.)

Example 15.1.1
In the graph of $y = f(x) = x^3 - 3x^2$, identify the intervals in which $f(x)$, $f'(x)$ and $f''(x)$ are positive, and interpret these graphically.

$$\frac{dy}{dx} = f'(x) = 3x^2 - 6x, \quad \text{and} \quad \frac{d^2y}{dx^2} = f''(x) = 6x - 6.$$

Fig. 15.1 shows the graphs of the function and its first and second derivatives.

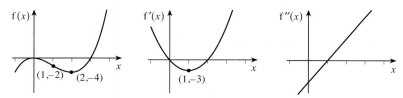

Fig. 15.1

Notice first that $f(x) = x^2(x-3)$, so that $f(x) > 0$ when $x > 3$. These are the values of x for which the graph of $f(x)$ lies above the x-axis.

Since $f'(x) = 3x(x-2)$, $f'(x) > 0$ when $x < 0$ or $x > 2$. In the graph of $f(x)$, the gradient is positive in these intervals, so that $f(x)$ is increasing.

Lastly, $f''(x) = 6(x-1)$, so that $f''(x) > 0$ when $x > 1$. It appears that this is the interval in which the graph of $f(x)$ can be described as bending upwards.

To make this idea of 'bending upwards' more precise, it is helpful to use the letter g to denote the gradient of the graph on the left of Fig. 15.1, so that $g = f'(x)$. Then $f''(x) = \dfrac{dg}{dx}$, which is the rate of change of the gradient with respect to x. In an interval where $f''(x) > 0$, the gradient increases as x increases.

This can be seen in the middle graph of Fig. 15.1, which is a quadratic graph with its vertex at $(1,-3)$. So the gradient of the graph on the left increases from a value of -3 at the point $(1,-2)$, through zero at the minimum point $(2,-4)$ and then becomes positive and continues to increase when $x > 2$.

Fig. 15.2 shows three curves which would be described as bending upwards, for which $f''(x) > 0$, and three bending downwards for which $f''(x) < 0$. The important thing to notice is that this property does not depend on the sign of the gradient. A curve can bend upwards whether its gradient is positive, negative or zero.

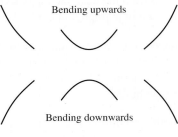

Fig. 15.2

Example 15.1.2

Investigate the graph of $y = f(x)$, where $f(x) = \dfrac{1}{x} - \dfrac{1}{x^2}$ with domain $x > 0$.

You can write $f(x)$ either as $\dfrac{x-1}{x^2}$ or, with negative indices, as $x^{-1} - x^{-2}$. So

$$f'(x) = -x^{-2} + 2x^{-3} = -\frac{1}{x^2} + \frac{2}{x^3} = \frac{-x+2}{x^3},$$

and $\quad f''(x) = 2x^{-3} - 6x^{-4} = \dfrac{2}{x^3} - \dfrac{6}{x^4} = \dfrac{2(x-3)}{x^4}.$

It follows that, in the given domain,

$\qquad f(x) < 0$ for $x < 1 \qquad$ and $\qquad f(x) > 0$ for $x > 1$;

$\qquad f'(x) > 0$ for $x < 2 \qquad$ and $\qquad f'(x) < 0$ for $x > 2$;

$\qquad f''(x) < 0$ for $x < 3 \qquad$ and $\qquad f''(x) > 0$ for $x > 3$.

So the graph lies below the x-axis when $0 < x < 1$ and above it when $x > 1$, crossing the axis at $(1,0)$. It has positive gradient when $0 < x < 2$ and negative gradient for $x > 2$, with a maximum point at $\left(2, \frac{1}{4}\right)$. And the graph bends downwards for $0 < x < 3$ and upwards for $x > 3$.

This is enough information to give a good idea of the shape of the graph for values of x in an interval covering the critical values $x = 1$, 2 and 3, but to complete the investigation it would be helpful to know more about the graph for very small and very large values of x. This suggests calculating, say,

$$\text{f}(0.01) = 100 - 10000 = -9900 \quad \text{and} \quad \text{f}(100) = 0.01 - 0.0001 = 0.0099.$$

So when x is small, y is a negative number with large modulus; and when x is large, y is a small positive number.

Try to sketch the graph for yourself using the information found in the example. If you have access to a graphic calculator use it to check your sketch.

The skill in sketching a graph is to work out the coordinates of only those points where something significant occurs. Example 15.1.2 draws attention to the point $(1,0)$, where the graph crosses the x-axis, and to the maximum point $\left(2, \frac{1}{4}\right)$. Another interesting point is $\left(3, \frac{2}{9}\right)$, where the graph changes from bending downwards to bending upwards. Notice that $\text{f}''(x)$ changes from $-$ to $+$ at this point, and that $\text{f}''(3) = 0$.

A point of a graph which separates a part of the curve which bends one way from a part which bends the other way is called a **point of inflexion** of the graph. If $(p, \text{f}(p))$ is a point of inflexion of the graph of a smooth function, $\text{f}''(p) = 0$.

15.2 Second derivatives in practice

There are many real-world situations in which second derivatives are important, because they give advance warning of future trends.

For example, the number of households possessing a computer has been increasing for a long time. Manufacturers will estimate the number of such households, H, in year t, and note that the graph of H against t has a positive gradient $\dfrac{\text{d}H}{\text{d}t}$. But to plan ahead they need to know whether this rate of increase is itself increasing (so that they should increase production of models for first-time users) or decreasing (in which case they might target existing customers to upgrade their equipment). So it is the value of $\dfrac{\text{d}^2 H}{\text{d}t^2}$ which affects such decisions.

Similarly, a weather forecaster observing the pressure p at time t may not be too concerned if $\dfrac{\text{d}p}{\text{d}t}$ is negative; but if she also notices that $\dfrac{\text{d}^2 p}{\text{d}t^2}$ is negative, it may be time to issue a warning of severe weather.

Exercise 15A

In this exercise try to sketch the graphs using information about the first and second derivatives. When you have drawn your sketch, check it from a graphic calculator or computer display if you have one available.

1 Consider the graph of $y = f(x)$ where $f(x) = x^3 - x$.

   (a) Use the fact that $f(x) = x(x^2 - 1) = x(x-1)(x+1)$ to find where the graph cuts the x-axis and hence sketch the graph.

   (b) Find $f'(x)$ and sketch the graph of $y = f'(x)$.

   (c) Find $f''(x)$ and sketch the graph of $y = f''(x)$.

   (d) Check the consistency of your sketches: for example, check that the graph of $y = f(x)$ is bending upwards where $f''(x) \geqslant 0$.

2 For the graph of $y = x^3 + x$

   (a) use factors to show that the graph crosses the x-axis once only;

   (b) find $\dfrac{dy}{dx}$ and $\dfrac{d^2 y}{dx^2}$;

   (c) find the interval in which the graph is bending upwards;

   (d) use the information gained to sketch the graph of $y = x^3 + x$.

3 Use information about $f'(x)$ and $f''(x)$ to sketch the graph of $y = f(x)$, where $f(x) = x^3 - 3x^2 + 3x - 9$. (Note that $x^3 - 3x^2 + 3x - 9 = (x-3)(x^2 + 3)$.)

4 Sketch the graphs of the following, giving the coordinates of any points at which

   (i) $\dfrac{dy}{dx} = 0$,   (ii) $\dfrac{d^2 y}{dx^2} = 0$.

   (a) $y = x^4 - 4x^2$ (b) $y = x^3 + x^2$ (c) $y = x + \dfrac{1}{x}$

   (d) $y = x - \dfrac{1}{x}$ (e) $y = x + \dfrac{4}{x^2}$ (f) $y = x - \dfrac{4}{x^2}$

5 (a) This graph shows prices (P) plotted against time (t).

         The rate of inflation, measured by $\dfrac{dP}{dt}$, is increasing. What does $\dfrac{d^2 P}{dt^2}$ represent and what can be said about its value?

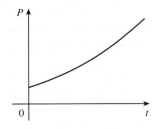

   (b) Sketch a graph showing that prices are increasing but that the rate of inflation is slowing down with an overall increase tending to 20%.

6 Write down the signs of f′(*x*) and f″(*x*) for the following graphs of *y* = f(*x*). In parts (e) and (f) you will need to state the relevant intervals.

(a)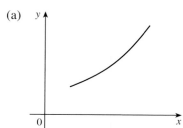

(b)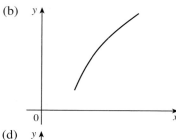

(c)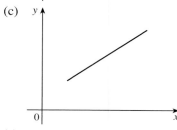

(d)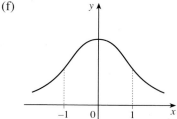

(e)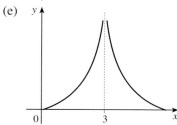

(f)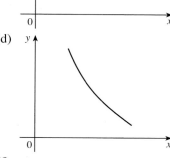

7 The graph shows the price *S* of shares in a certain company.

(a) For each stage of the graph, comment on $\dfrac{dS}{dt}$ and $\dfrac{d^2S}{dt^2}$.

(b) Describe what happened in non-technical language.

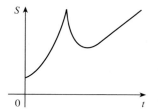

8 Colin sets off for school, which is 800 m from home. His speed is proportional to the distance he still has to go. Let *x* metres be the distance he has gone, and *y* metres be the distance that he still has to go.

(a) Sketch graphs of *x* against *t* and *y* against *t*.

(b) What are the signs of $\dfrac{dx}{dt}$, $\dfrac{d^2x}{dt^2}$, $\dfrac{dy}{dt}$ and $\dfrac{d^2y}{dt^2}$?

9 The rate of decay of a radioactive substance is proportional to the number, *N*, of radioactive atoms present at time *t*.

(a) Write an equation representing this information.

(b) Sketch a graph of *N* against *t*.

(c) What is the sign of $\dfrac{d^2N}{dt^2}$?

10   Sketch segments of graphs of $y = f(x)$ in each of the following cases.

(For example, in (a), you can only sketch the graph near the y-axis because you have no information for other values of x.)

(a) $f(0) = 3,$ $f'(0) = 2,$ $f''(0) = 1$ (b) $f(5) = -2,$ $f'(5) = -2,$ $f''(5) = -2$

(c) $f(0) = -3,$ $f'(0) = 0,$ $f''(0) = 3$

15.3 Minima and maxima revisited

In the last exercise you will sometimes have found that different pieces of information reinforce each other. This is especially true at points where a graph has a minimum or maximum. If you have identified a minimum from changes in the sign of $f'(x)$, you will also have found from $f''(x)$ that the graph is bending upwards.

The curves in Fig. 15.2 suggest a general result:

> If $f'(q) = 0$ and $f''(q) > 0$, then $f(x)$ has a minimum at $x = q$.
>
> If $f'(q) = 0$ and $f''(q) < 0$, then $f(x)$ has a maximum at $x = q$.

It is often simpler to use this instead of considering the change in sign of $f'(x)$ to decide whether a point on a graph is a minimum or a maximum. The procedure described in Section 7.3 can then be amended as follows.

> To find the minimum and maximum points on the graph of $y = f(x)$:
>
> **Step 1**   Decide the domain in which you are interested.
>
> **Step 2**   Find an expression for $f'(x)$.
>
> **Step 3**   List the values of x in the domain for which $f'(x)$ is 0. (If there are values where $f'(x)$ is undefined, use the old procedure, in Section 7.3.)
>
> **Step 4**   Find an expression for $f''(x)$.
>
> **Step 5**   For each value of x in Step 3, find the sign of $f''(x)$. If the sign is +, the graph has a minimum point; if −, a maximum. (If the value of $f''(x)$ is 0, follow the old procedure.)
>
> **Step 6**   For each value of x which gives a minimum or maximum, calculate $f(x)$.

Notice that there are two ways in which this procedure can break down.

First, the method only works for the graphs of smooth functions, so that it does not apply at points where $f'(x)$ is undefined.

Secondly, if $f'(q) = 0$ and $f''(q) = 0$, it is possible for $f(x)$ to have a minimum, or a maximum, or neither, at $x = q$. This can be shown by comparing $f(x) = x^3$ with $g(x) = x^4$ at $x = 0$. You can easily check that $f'(0) = f''(0) = 0$ and that $g'(0) = g''(0) = 0$. But $g(x)$ has a minimum at $x = 0$, whereas $f(x)$ has neither a minimum nor a maximum. (In fact the graph of $y = f(x)$ has a point of inflexion at the origin, since $f''(x) = 6x$, which is negative when $x < 0$ and positive when $x > 0$.)

You will also find later on that for some functions it can be very laborious to find the second derivative. In that case, it is more efficient to use the old procedure.

Example 15.3.1
Find the minimum and maximum points on the graph of $f(x) = x^4 + x^5$.

Step 1   The function is defined for all real numbers.

Step 2 $f'(x) = 4x^3 + 5x^4 = x^3(4 + 5x)$.

Step 3 $f'(x) = 0$ when $x = 0$ or $x = -0.8$.

Step 4 $f''(x) = 12x^2 + 20x^3 = 4x^2(3 + 5x)$.

Step 5 $f''(-0.8) = 4 \times (-0.8)^2 \times (3 - 4) < 0$, so $x = -0.8$ gives a maximum.

$f''(0) = 0$, so follow the old procedure. For $-0.8 < x < 0$, $x^3 < 0$ and $4 + 5x > 0$, so $f'(x) < 0$; for $x > 0$, $f'(x) > 0$. So $x = 0$ gives a minimum.

Step 6   The maximum point is $(-0.8, 0.081\ 92)$; the minimum point is $(0, 0)$.

Example 15.3.2
Find the minimum and maximum points on the graph of $y = \dfrac{(x+1)^2}{x}$.

The function is defined for all real numbers except 0.

To differentiate, write $\dfrac{(x+1)^2}{x}$ as $\dfrac{x^2 + 2x + 1}{x} = x + 2 + x^{-1}$.

Then $\dfrac{dy}{dx} = 1 - x^{-2} = 1 - \dfrac{1}{x^2} = \dfrac{x^2 - 1}{x^2}$, so $\dfrac{dy}{dx} = 0$ gives $x^2 - 1 = 0$, or $x = \pm 1$.

The second derivative is $\dfrac{d^2 y}{dx^2} = 2x^{-3} = \dfrac{2}{x^3}$. This has values -2 when $x = -1$, and 2 when $x = 1$. So $(-1, 0)$ is a maximum point and $(1, 4)$ is a minimum point.

The minimum value is greater than the maximum value. How can this happen?

▓▓▓▓▓▓▓▓▓▓▓▓▓▓▓▓▓ **Exercise 15B** ▓▓▓▓▓▓▓▓

Use first and second derivatives to locate and describe the stationary points on the graphs of the following functions and equations. If this method fails, then use the change of sign of $\dfrac{dy}{dx}$ or $f'(x)$ to distinguish maxima, minima and points of inflexion.

1   (a) $f(x) = 3x - x^3$ (b) $f(x) = x^3 - 3x^2$

      (c) $f(x) = 3x^4 + 1$ (d) $f(x) = 2x^3 - 3x^2 - 12x + 4$

      (e) $f(x) = \dfrac{2}{x^4} - \dfrac{1}{x}$ (f) $f(x) = x^2 + \dfrac{1}{x^2}$

      (g) $f(x) = \dfrac{1}{x} - \dfrac{1}{x^2}$ (h) $f(x) = 2x^3 - 12x^2 + 24x + 6$

2   (a) $y = 3x^4 - 4x^3 - 12x^2 - 3$ (b) $y = x^3 - 3x^2 + 3x + 5$

      (c) $y = 16x - 3x^3$ (d) $y = \dfrac{4}{x^2} - x$

      (e) $y = \dfrac{4 + x^2}{x}$ (f) $y = \dfrac{x - 3}{x^2}$

      (g) $y = 2x^5 - 7$ (h) $y = 3x^4 - 8x^3 + 6x^2 + 1$

15.4 Logical distinctions

You have seen that, for the graphs of smooth functions, it is true that

> if $(q, f(q))$ is a minimum or maximum point, then $f'(q) = 0$;

but the **converse** statement, that

> if $f'(q) = 0$, then $(q, f(q))$ is a minimum or maximum point,

is false.

You can show that it is false by finding a **counterexample**; that is, an example of a function for which the 'if …' part of the statement holds, but the 'then …' part does not.

Such a function is $f(x) = x^3$ with $q = 0$. Since $f'(x) = 3x^2$, $f'(0) = 0$, but $(0,0)$ is not a minimum or maximum point of the graph of $y = x^3$.

A similar situation arises with points of inflexion. For the graphs of smooth functions it is true that

> if $(p, f(p))$ is a point of inflexion, then $f''(p) = 0$;

but the converse, that

> if $f''(p) = 0$, then $(p, f(p))$ is a point of inflexion,

is false.

A suitable counterexample in this case is $f(x) = x^4$ with $x = 0$. Since $f''(x) = 12x^2$, $f''(0) = 0$, but $(0,0)$ is a minimum point on the graph of $y = x^4$, not a point of inflexion.

Much of advanced mathematics involves applying general theorems to particular functions. There are many theorems (such as Pythagoras' theorem) whose converses are also true. But if, as in the examples above, the converse of a theorem is false, it is very important to be sure that you are applying the (true) theorem rather than its (false) converse.

15.5 Extending $\dfrac{dy}{dx}$ notation

Although $\dfrac{dy}{dx}$ is a symbol which should not be split into smaller bits, it can usefully be adapted by separating off the y, as $\dfrac{d}{dx} y$, so that if $y = f(x)$, you can write

$$f'(x) = \frac{d}{dx} f(x).$$

This can be used as a convenient shorthand. For example, instead of having to write

$$\text{if } y = x^4, \text{ then } \frac{dy}{dx} = 4x^3$$

you can abbreviate this to

$$\frac{d}{dx} x^4 = 4x^3.$$

You can think of $\dfrac{d}{dx}$ as an instruction to differentiate whatever comes after it.

You may have seen calculators which do algebra as well as arithmetic. With these, you can input a function such as x^4, key in 'differentiate', and the output $4x^3$ appears in the display. The symbol $\dfrac{d}{dx}$, sometimes called the **differential operator**, is the equivalent of pressing the 'differentiate' key.

This explains the notation used for the second derivative, which is what you get by differentiating $\dfrac{dy}{dx}$; that is, $\dfrac{d}{dx}\dfrac{dy}{dx}$. If you collect the elements of this expression into a single symbol, the top line becomes $d^2 y$, and the bottom line $(dx)^2$. Dropping the brackets, this takes the form $\dfrac{d^2 y}{dx^2}$.

15.6* Higher derivatives

There is no reason to stop at the second derivative. Since $\dfrac{d^2 y}{dx^2}$ is also a function, provided it is smooth it can be differentiated to give a third derivative; and the process can continue indefinitely, giving a whole sequence of higher derivatives

$$\frac{d^3 y}{dx^3}, \quad \frac{d^4 y}{dx^4}, \quad \frac{d^5 y}{dx^5}, \quad \dots .$$

In function notation these are written as

$$f'''(x), \qquad f^{(4)}(x), \qquad f^{(5)}(x), \qquad \dots .$$

Notice that, from the fourth derivative onwards, the dashes are replaced by a small numeral in brackets.

These further derivatives do not often have useful interpretations in graph sketching or in real-world applications. But they are important in some applications, for example in finding approximations and for expressing functions in series form.

Exercise 15C*

1 Find $\dfrac{dy}{dx}$, $\dfrac{d^2y}{dx^2}$, $\dfrac{d^3y}{dx^3}$ and $\dfrac{d^4y}{dx^4}$ for the following.

    (a) $y = x^2 + 3x - 7$ (b) $y = 2x^3 + x + \dfrac{1}{x}$ (c) $y = x^4 - 2$

    (d) $y = \sqrt{x}$ (e) $y = \dfrac{1}{\sqrt{x}}$ (f) $y = x^{\frac{1}{4}}$

2 Find $f'(x)$, $f''(x)$, $f'''(x)$ and $f^{(4)}(x)$ for the following.

    (a) $f(x) = x^2 - 5x + 2$ (b) $f(x) = 2x^5 - 3x^2$ (c) $f(x) = \dfrac{1}{x^4}$

    (d) $f(x) = x^2\left(3 - x^4\right)$ (e) $f(x) = x^{\frac{3}{4}}$ (f) $f(x) = x^{\frac{3}{8}}$

3 Find $\dfrac{d^n y}{dx^n}$ for $y = x^n$ in the case where n is a positive integer.

4 Find an expression for $\dfrac{d^n y}{dx^n}$ for $y = x^{n+2}$ where n is a positive integer.

5 Find $\dfrac{d^n y}{dx^n}$ where $y = x^m$ in the case where m is a positive integer and $n > m$.

Miscellaneous exercise 15

1 Find the maximum and minimum values of $x^3 - 6x^2 + 9x + 6$, showing carefully how you determine which is which.

2 Find any maximum and minimum values of the function $f(x) = 16x + \dfrac{1}{x^2}$, indicating how you decide whether they are maxima or minima.

3 Find any maximum and minimum values of the function $f(x) = \sqrt{x} + \sqrt{30 - 5x}$, and give the corresponding values of x.

4 Find the coordinates of the maximum and minimum points on the graph of $y = \dfrac{1}{x} + \dfrac{1}{1 - 4x}$.

5 The rate at which Nasreen's coffee cools is proportional to the difference between its temperature, $\theta°$, and room temperature, $\alpha°$. Sketch a graph of θ against t given that $\alpha = 20$ and that $\theta = 95$ when $t = 0$. State the signs of θ, $\dfrac{d\theta}{dt}$ and $\dfrac{d^2\theta}{dt^2}$ for $t > 0$.

6 Aeroplanes in flight experience a resistance known as drag. For a particular aeroplane at low speeds the drag is equal to kS^2, where k is the (constant) drag coefficient and S is the speed of the aeroplane.

At high speeds, however, k increases with speed, and a typical graph of k against S is shown here. (The transonic region is commonly known as the 'sound barrier'.)

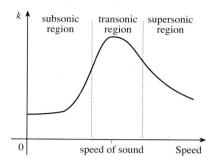

(a) Give the signs of $\dfrac{dk}{dS}$ and $\dfrac{d^2k}{dS^2}$ for each of the three sections of the graph and, in particular, say where each is zero.

(b) Where is k changing most rapidly?

(c) What does the graph imply about k at even higher speeds?

7 A window consists of a lower rectangular part $ABCD$ of width $2x$ metres and height y metres and an upper part which is a semicircle of radius x metres on AB as diameter, as shown in the diagram.

The perimeter of the window is 10 metres.

Find an expression in terms of x and π for the total area of the window, and find the value of x for which the area is a maximum. Use the value of $\dfrac{d^2y}{dx^2}$ to verify that the area is a maximum for this value of x.

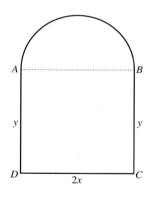

8 Investigate the maxima and minima of the following functions, where $a > 0$.

(a) $x^2(x-a)$ (b) $x^3(x-a)$ (c) $x^2(x-a)^2$ (d) $x^3(x-a)^2$

Make a conjecture about $x^n(x-a)^m$.

9 Find an expression for $f^{(n)}(x)$ where

(a) $f(x) = \dfrac{1}{x^3}$,   (b) $f(x) = \sqrt{x}$.

10* Find the coordinates of any points of inflexion on the curves with equations

(a) $y = x^4 - 8x^3 + 18x^2 + 4$,   (b) $y = x^2 - \dfrac{1}{x} + 2$.

16 Integration

Integration is the reverse process of differentiation. When you have completed this chapter, you should

- understand the term 'indefinite integral' and the need to add an arbitrary constant
- be able to integrate functions which can be expressed as sums of powers of x, and be aware of any exceptions
- know how to find the equation of a graph given its derivative and a point on the graph
- know how to evaluate a definite integral
- be able to use definite integrals to find areas.

16.1 Finding a function from its derivative

It was shown in Chapter 7 that some features of the graph of a function can be interpreted in terms of the graph of its derived function.

Suppose now that you know the graph of the derived function. What does this tell you about the graph of the original function?

It is useful to begin by trying to answer this question geometrically. Fig. 16.1 shows the graph of the derived function $f'(x)$ of some function. The problem is to sketch the graph of $f(x)$. Scanning the domain from left to right, you can see that:

For $x < 1$ the gradient is negative, so $f(x)$ is decreasing.

At $x = 1$ the gradient changes from $-$ to $+$, so $f(x)$ has a minimum.

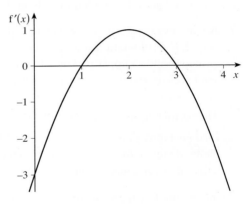

Fig. 16.1

For $1 < x < 3$ the gradient is positive, so $f(x)$ is increasing. Notice that the gradient is greatest when $x = 2$, so that is where the graph climbs most steeply.

At $x = 3$ the gradient changes from $+$ to $-$, so $f(x)$ has a maximum.

For $x > 3$ the gradient is negative, so $f(x)$ is again decreasing.

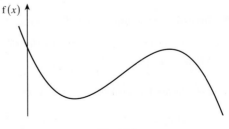

Fig. 16.2

Using this information you can make a sketch like Fig. 16.2, which gives an idea of the shape of the graph of $f(x)$. But there is no way of deciding precisely where the graph is located. You could translate it in the y-direction by any amount, and it would still have the same gradient $f'(x)$. So there is no unique answer to the problem; there are many functions $f(x)$ with the given derived function.

This can be shown algebraically. The graph in Fig. 16.1 comes from the equation

$$f'(x) = (x-1)(3-x) = 4x - x^2 - 3.$$

What function has this expression as its derivative? The key is to note that in differentiating x^n the index decreases by 1, from n to $n-1$. So to reverse the process the index must go up by 1. The three terms $4x$, $-x^2$ and -3 must therefore come from multiples of x^2, x^3 and x. These functions have derivatives $2x$, $3x^2$ and 1, so to get the correct coefficients in $f'(x)$ you have to multiply by 2, $-\frac{1}{3}$ and -3. One possible answer is therefore

$$f(x) = 2x^2 - \tfrac{1}{3}x^3 - 3x.$$

But, as argued above, this is only one of many possible answers. You can translate the graph of $f(x)$ in the y-direction by any amount k without changing its gradient. This is because the derivative of any constant k is zero. So the complete solution to the problem is

$$f(x) = 2x^2 - \tfrac{1}{3}x^3 - 3x + k \qquad \text{for any constant } k.$$

The process of getting from $f'(x)$ to $f(x)$ is called **integration**, and the general expression for $f(x)$ is called the **indefinite integral** of $f'(x)$. Integration is the reverse process of differentiation.

The indefinite integral always includes an added constant k, which is called an **arbitrary constant**. The word 'arbitrary' means that, in any application, you can choose its value to fit some extra condition; for example, you can make the graph of $y = f(x)$ go through some given point.

It is easy to find a rule for integrating functions which are powers of x. Because differentiation reduces the index by 1, integration must increase it by 1. So the function x^n must be derived from some multiple of x^{n+1}. But the derivative of x^{n+1} is $(n+1)x^n$; so to reduce the coefficient in the derivative to 1 you have to multiply x^{n+1} by $\dfrac{1}{n+1}$. The rule is therefore that one integral of x^n is $\dfrac{1}{n+1}x^{n+1}$.

But notice an important exception to this rule. The formula has no meaning if $n+1$ is 0, so it does not give the integral of x^{-1}, or $\dfrac{1}{x}$. You will find in P2 that the integral of $\dfrac{1}{x}$ is not a power of x, but a quite different kind of function.

The extension to functions which are sums of powers of x then follows from the equivalent rules for differentiation:

> The indefinite integral of a function made up of the sum of multiples of x^n, where $n \neq -1$, is the corresponding sum of multiples of $\dfrac{1}{n+1}x^{n+1}$, together with an added arbitrary constant.

Example 16.1.1

The graph of $y = f(x)$ passes through $(2,3)$, and $f'(x) = 6x^2 - 5x$. Find its equation.

The indefinite integral is $6\left(\frac{1}{3}x^3\right) - 5\left(\frac{1}{2}x^2\right) + k$, so the graph has equation

$$y = 2x^3 - \frac{5}{2}x^2 + k$$

for some constant k. The coordinates $x = 2$, $y = 3$ have to satisfy this equation, so

$$3 = 2 \times 8 - \frac{5}{2} \times 4 + k, \text{ giving } k = 3 - 16 + 10 = -3.$$

The equation of the graph is therefore $y = 2x^3 - \frac{5}{2}x^2 - 3$.

Example 16.1.2

A gardener is digging a plot of land. As he gets tired he works more slowly; after t minutes he is digging at a rate of $\dfrac{2}{\sqrt{t}}$ square metres per minute. How long will it take him to dig an area of 40 square metres?

Let A square metres be the area he has dug after t minutes. Then his rate of digging is measured by the derivative $\dfrac{dA}{dt}$. So you know that $\dfrac{dA}{dt} = 2t^{-\frac{1}{2}}$; in this case $n = -\frac{1}{2}$, so $n + 1 = \frac{1}{2}$ and the indefinite integral is

$$A = 2\left(\frac{1}{1/2}t^{\frac{1}{2}}\right) + k = 4\sqrt{t} + k.$$

To find k, you need to know a pair of values of A and t. Since $A = 0$ when he starts to dig, which is when $t = 0$, $0 = 4\sqrt{0} + k$ and so $k = 0$.

The equation connecting A with t is therefore $A = 4\sqrt{t}$.

To find how long it takes to dig 40 square metres, substitute $A = 40$:

$$40 = 4\sqrt{t}, \text{ so that } \sqrt{t} = 10, \text{ and hence } t = 100.$$

It will take him 100 minutes to dig an area of 40 square metres.

Exercise 16A

1 Find a general expression for the function $f(x)$ in each of the following cases.

(a) $f'(x) = 4x^3$

(b) $f'(x) = 6x^5$

(c) $f'(x) = 2x$

(d) $f'(x) = 3x^2 + 5x^4$

(e) $f'(x) = 10x^9 - 8x^7 - 1$

(f) $f'(x) = -7x^6 + 3x^2 + 1$

2 Find a general expression for the function $f(x)$ in each of the following cases.

(a) $f'(x) = 9x^2 - 4x - 5$ (b) $f'(x) = 12x^2 + 6x + 4$

(c) $f'(x) = 7$ (d) $f'(x) = 16x^3 - 6x^2 + 10x - 3$

(e) $f'(x) = 2x^3 + 5x$ (f) $f'(x) = x + 2x^2$

(g) $f'(x) = 2x^2 - 3x - 4$ (h) $f'(x) = 1 - 2x - 3x^2$

3 Find y in terms of x in each of the following cases.

(a) $\dfrac{dy}{dx} = x^4 + x^2 + 1$ (b) $\dfrac{dy}{dx} = 7x - 3$

(c) $\dfrac{dy}{dx} = 2x^2 + x - 8$ (d) $\dfrac{dy}{dx} = 6x^3 - 5x^2 + 3x + 2$

(e) $\dfrac{dy}{dx} = \frac{2}{3}x^3 + \frac{1}{2}x^2 + \frac{1}{3}x + \frac{1}{6}$ (f) $\dfrac{dy}{dx} = \frac{1}{2}x^3 - \frac{1}{3}x^2 + x - \frac{1}{3}$

(g) $\dfrac{dy}{dx} = x - 3x^2 + 1$ (h) $\dfrac{dy}{dx} = x^3 + x^2 + x + 1$

4 The graph of $y = f(x)$ passes through the origin and $f'(x) = 8x - 5$. Find $f(x)$.

5 A curve passes through the point $(2,-5)$ and satisfies $\dfrac{dy}{dx} = 6x^2 - 1$. Find y in terms of x.

6 A curve passes through $(-4,9)$ and is such that $\dfrac{dy}{dx} = \frac{1}{2}x^3 + \frac{1}{4}x + 1$. Find y in terms of x.

7 Given that $f'(x) = 15x^2 - 6x + 4$ and $f(1) = 0$, find $f(x)$.

8 Each of the following diagrams shows the graph of a derived function $f'(x)$. In each case, sketch the graph of a possible function $f(x)$.

(a)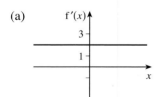

(b)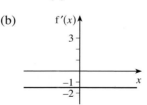

(c)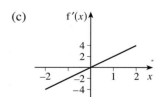

(d)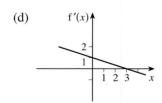

(e)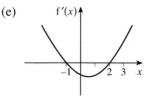

(f)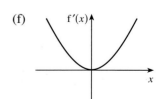

9 The graph of $y = f(x)$ passes through $(4,25)$ and $f'(x) = 6\sqrt{x}$. Find its equation.

10 Find y in terms of x in each of the following cases.

(a) $\dfrac{dy}{dx} = x^{\frac{1}{2}}$

(b) $\dfrac{dy}{dx} = 4x^{-\frac{2}{3}}$

(c) $\dfrac{dy}{dx} = \sqrt[3]{x}$

(d) $\dfrac{dy}{dx} = 2\sqrt{x} - \dfrac{2}{\sqrt{x}}$

(e) $\dfrac{dy}{dx} = \dfrac{5}{\sqrt[3]{x}}$

(f) $\dfrac{dy}{dx} = \dfrac{-2}{\sqrt[3]{x^2}}$

11 Find a general expression for the function $f(x)$ in each of the following cases.

(a) $f'(x) = x^{-2}$

(b) $f'(x) = 3x^{-4}$

(c) $f'(x) = \dfrac{6}{x^3}$

(d) $f'(x) = 4x - \dfrac{3}{x^2}$

(e) $f'(x) = \dfrac{1}{x^3} - \dfrac{1}{x^4}$

(f) $f'(x) = \dfrac{2}{x^2} - 2x^2$

12 The graph of $y = f(x)$ passes through $\left(\frac{1}{2}, 5\right)$ and $f'(x) = \dfrac{4}{x^2}$. Find its equation.

13 A curve passes through the point $(25, 3)$ and is such that $\dfrac{dy}{dx} = \dfrac{1}{2\sqrt{x}}$. Find the equation of the curve.

14 A curve passes through the point $(1, 5)$ and is such that $\dfrac{dy}{dx} = \sqrt[3]{x} - \dfrac{6}{x^3}$. Find the equation of the curve.

15 In each of the following cases, find y in terms of x.

(a) $\dfrac{dy}{dx} = 3x(x + 2)$

(b) $\dfrac{dy}{dx} = (2x - 1)(6x + 5)$

(c) $\dfrac{dy}{dx} = \dfrac{4x^3 + 1}{x^2}$

(d) $\dfrac{dy}{dx} = \dfrac{x + 4}{\sqrt{x}}$

(e) $\dfrac{dy}{dx} = \left(\sqrt{x} + 5\right)^2$

(f) $\dfrac{dy}{dx} = \dfrac{\sqrt{x} + 5}{\sqrt{x}}$

16 A tree is growing so that, after t years, its height is increasing at a rate of $\dfrac{30}{\sqrt[3]{t}}$ cm per year. Assume that, when $t = 0$, the height is 5 cm.

(a) Find the height of the tree after 4 years.

(b) After how many years will the height be 4.1 metres?

17 A pond, with surface area 48 square metres, is being invaded by a weed. At a time t months after the weed first appeared, the area of the weed on the surface is increasing at a rate of $\frac{1}{3}t$ square metres per month. How long will it be before the weed covers the whole surface of the pond?

18 The function $f(x)$ is such that $f'(x) = 9x^2 + 4x + c$, where c is a particular constant. Given that $f(2) = 14$ and $f(3) = 74$, find the value of $f(4)$.

16.2 Calculating areas

An important application of integration is to calculate areas and volumes. Many of the formulae you have learnt, such as those for the volume of a sphere or a cone, can be proved by using integration. This chapter deals only with areas.

12 The diagram shows the region bounded by $y = \frac{1}{2}x - 3$, by
$x = 14$ and the x-axis. Find the area of the shaded region by

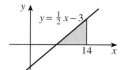

(a) using the formula for the area of a triangle,

(b) using integration.

13 Find the area of the region shaded in each of the following diagrams.

(a)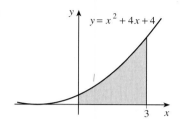

(b)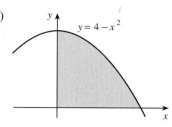

(c)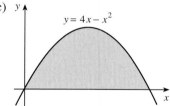

(d)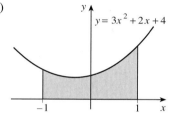

(e)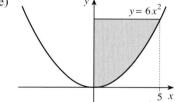

(f)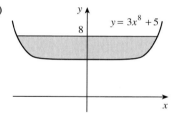

14 Find the following indefinite integrals.

(a) $\displaystyle\int \frac{1}{x^3}\,dx$

(b) $\displaystyle\int \left(x^2 - \frac{1}{x^2}\right)dx$

(c) $\displaystyle\int \sqrt{x}\,dx$

(d) $\displaystyle\int 6x^{\frac{2}{3}}\,dx$

(e) $\displaystyle\int \frac{6x^4 + 5}{x^2}\,dx$

(f) $\displaystyle\int \frac{1}{\sqrt{x}}\,dx$

15 Evaluate the following definite integrals.

(a) $\displaystyle\int_0^8 12\sqrt[3]{x}\,dx$

(b) $\displaystyle\int_1^2 \frac{3}{x^2}\,dx$

(c) $\displaystyle\int_1^4 \frac{10}{\sqrt{x}}\,dx$

(d) $\displaystyle\int_1^2 \left(\frac{8}{x^3} + x^3\right)dx$

(e) $\displaystyle\int_4^9 \frac{2\sqrt{x} + 3}{\sqrt{x}}\,dx$

(f) $\displaystyle\int_1^8 \frac{1}{\sqrt[3]{x^2}}\,dx$

16 Find the area under the curve $y = \dfrac{6}{x^4}$ between $x = 1$ and $x = 2$.

17 Find the area under the curve $y = \sqrt[3]{x}$ between $x = 1$ and $x = 27$.

18 Find the area under the curve $y = \dfrac{5}{x^2}$ between $x = -3$ and $x = -1$.

19 Given that $\displaystyle\int_0^a 12x^2\,\mathrm{d}x = 1372$, find the value of the constant a.

20 Given that $\displaystyle\int_0^9 p\sqrt{x}\,\mathrm{d}x = 90$, find the value of the constant p.

21 Find the area of the shaded region in each of the following diagrams.

(a)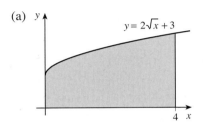

(b)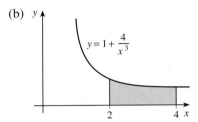

22 The diagram shows the graph of $y = 9x^2$. The point P has coordinates $(4,144)$. Find the area of the shaded region.

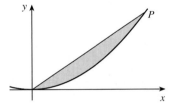

23 The diagram shows the graph of $y = \dfrac{1}{\sqrt{x}}$. Show that the area of the shaded region is $3 - \dfrac{5\sqrt{3}}{3}$.

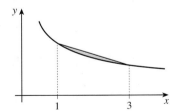

24 Find the area of the region between the curve $y = 9 + 15x - 6x^2$ and the x-axis.

16.4 Some properties of definite integrals

In definite integral notation the calculation in Section 16.2 of the area in Fig. 16.1 would be written

$$\int_1^3 (x-1)(3-x)\,\mathrm{d}x = \left[2x^2 - \tfrac{1}{3}x^3 - 3x\right]_1^3 = (0) - \left(-\tfrac{4}{3}\right) = \tfrac{4}{3}.$$

But how should you interpret the calculation

$$\int_0^3 (x-1)(3-x)\,dx = \left[2x^2 - \tfrac{1}{3}x^3 - 3x\right]_0^3 = (0) - (0) = 0\ ?$$

Clearly the area between the graph and the x-axis between $x = 0$ and $x = 3$ is not zero as the value of the definite integral suggests.

You can find the clue by calculating the integral between $x = 0$ and $x = 1$:

$$\int_0^1 (x-1)(3-x)\,dx = \left[2x^2 - \tfrac{1}{3}x^3 - 3x\right]_0^1 = \left(-\tfrac{4}{3}\right) - (0) = -\tfrac{4}{3}.$$

This shows that you need to be careful in identifying the definite integral as an area. In Fig. 16.1 the area of the region contained between the curve and the two axes is $\tfrac{4}{3}$, and the negative sign attached to the definite integral indicates that between $x = 0$ and $x = 1$ the graph lies below the x-axis.

The zero answer obtained for the integral from $x = 0$ to $x = 3$ is then explained by the fact that definite integrals are added exactly as you would expect:

$$\int_0^3 (x-1)(3-x)\,dx = \int_0^1 (x-1)(3-x)\,dx + \int_1^3 (x-1)(3-x)\,dx = -\tfrac{4}{3} + \tfrac{4}{3} = 0.$$

This is a special case of a general rule:

$$\int_a^b f(x)\,dx + \int_b^c f(x)\,dx = \int_a^c f(x)\,dx.$$

To prove this, let $I(x)$ denote the simplest integral of $f(x)$.

Then the sum of the integrals on the left side is equal to

$$\left[I(x)\right]_a^b + \left[I(x)\right]_b^c = \{I(b) - I(a)\} - \{I(c) - I(b)\} = I(c) - I(a) = \int_a^c f(x)\,dx.$$

Negative definite integrals can also arise when you interchange the bounds of integration. Since

$$\left[I(x)\right]_b^a = I(a) - I(b) = -\{I(b) - I(a)\} = -\left[I(x)\right]_a^b,$$

it follows that

$$\int_b^a f(x)\,dx = -\int_a^b f(x)\,dx.$$

You are not likely to use this in numerical examples, but such integrals may turn up if a or b are algebraic expressions.

16.5 Infinite and improper integrals

Example 16.5.1

Find the areas under the graphs of   (a) $y = \dfrac{1}{x^2}$,   (b) $y = \dfrac{1}{\sqrt{x}}$ in the intervals

(i) $x = 1$ to $x = s$, where $s > 1$,   (ii) $x = r$ to $x = 1$, where $0 < r < 1$.

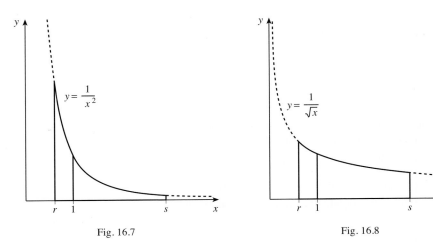

Fig. 16.7   Fig. 16.8

These areas are shown in Figs. 16.7 and 16.8.

The functions are (a) x^{-2} and (b) $x^{-\frac{1}{2}}$, so the simplest integrals are

(a) $-x^{-1} = -\dfrac{1}{x}$ and   (b) $2x^{\frac{1}{2}} = 2\sqrt{x}$.

(i) $\displaystyle\int_1^s \frac{1}{x^2}\,dx = \left[-\frac{1}{x}\right]_1^s = 1 - \frac{1}{s}$.

(ii) $\displaystyle\int_r^1 \frac{1}{x^2}\,dx = \left[-\frac{1}{x}\right]_r^1 = \frac{1}{r} - 1$.

(b) (i) $\displaystyle\int_1^s \frac{1}{\sqrt{x}}\,dx = \left[2\sqrt{x}\right]_1^s = 2\sqrt{s} - 2$.

(ii) $\displaystyle\int_r^1 \frac{1}{\sqrt{x}}\,dx = \left[2\sqrt{x}\right]_r^1 = 2 - 2\sqrt{r}$.

The interesting feature of these results appears if you consider what happens in (i) if s becomes indefinitely large, and in (ii) if r comes indefinitely close to 0.

Consider s first. By taking a large enough value for s, you can make $1 - \dfrac{1}{s}$ as close to 1 as you like, but it always remains less than 1. You can say that the integral (a)(i) 'tends to 1 as s tends to infinity' (written ' $\to 1$ as $s \to \infty$').

A shorthand for this is

$$\int_1^\infty \frac{1}{x^2}\,dx = 1.$$

This is called an **infinite integral**.

However, $2\sqrt{s} - 2$ can be made as large as you like by taking a large enough value for s, so the integral (b)(i) 'tends to infinity as s tends to infinity' (or '$\to \infty$ as $s \to \infty$'). Since 'infinity' is not a number, you cannot give a meaning to the symbol

$$\int_1^\infty \frac{1}{\sqrt{x}}\,dx.$$

In the case of r, the situation is reversed. The expression $2 - 2\sqrt{r}$ tends to 2 as r tends to 0. So you can write

$$\int_0^1 \frac{1}{\sqrt{x}}\,dx = 2$$

even though the integrand $\dfrac{1}{\sqrt{x}}$ is not defined when $x = 0$. This is called an **improper integral**. But in (a)(ii), $\dfrac{1}{r} - 1$ tends to infinity as r tends to 0, so you cannot give a meaning to the symbol

$$\int_0^1 \frac{1}{x^2}\,dx.$$

You can see from the graphs that, as you would expect, the cases where the integrals are defined correspond to regions in which the graph is very close to one of the axes. You can then say that the region has a finite area, even though it is unbounded.

16.6 The area between two graphs

You sometimes want to find the area of a region bounded by the graphs of two functions $f(x)$ and $g(x)$, and by two lines $x = a$ and $x = b$, as in Fig. 16.9.

Although you could find this as the difference of the areas of two regions of the kind illustrated in Fig. 16.5, calculated as

$$\int_a^b f(x)\,dx - \int_a^b g(x)\,dx,$$

it is often simpler to find this as a single integral

$$\int_a^b \big(f(x) - g(x)\big)\,dx.$$

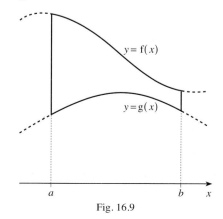

Fig. 16.9

Example 16.6.1

Show that the graphs of $f(x) = x^3 - x^2 - 6x + 8$ and $g(x) = x^3 + 2x^2 - 1$ intersect at two points, and find the area enclosed between them.

The graphs intersect where

$$x^3 - x^2 - 6x + 8 = x^3 + 2x^2 - 1,$$
$$0 = 3x^2 + 6x - 9,$$
$$3(x + 3)(x - 1) = 0.$$

The points of intersection are therefore $(-3, -10)$ and $(1, 2)$.

If you draw the graphs between $x = -3$ and $x = 1$, you will see that $f(x) > g(x)$ in this interval.

The area between the graphs is

$$\int_{-3}^{1} \left(f(x) - g(x) \right) dx = \int_{-3}^{1} \left(9 - 6x - 3x^2 \right) dx = \left[9x - 3x^2 - x^3 \right]_{-3}^{1}$$
$$= (9 - 3 - 1) - (-27 - 27 + 27) = 5 - (-27) = 32.$$

Notice that in this example, integrating $f(x) - g(x)$, rather than $f(x)$ and $g(x)$ separately, greatly reduces the amount of calculation.

Exercise 16C

1 Evaluate $\displaystyle\int_{0}^{2} 3x(x - 2)\, dx$ and comment on your answer.

2 Find the total area of the region shaded in each of the following diagrams.

(a)

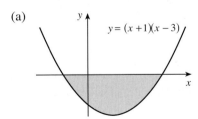

$y = (x + 1)(x - 3)$

(b)

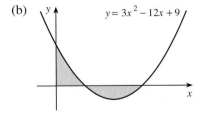

$y = 3x^2 - 12x + 9$

(c)

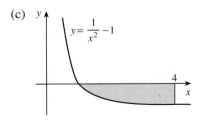

$y = \dfrac{1}{x^2} - 1$

(d)

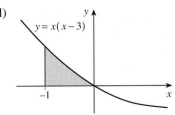

$y = x(x - 3)$

3 Find the values of the improper integrals

(a) $\displaystyle\int_{0}^{16} \frac{1}{\sqrt[4]{x}}\, dx$,

(b) $\displaystyle\int_{0}^{16} \frac{1}{\sqrt[4]{x^3}}\, dx$,

(c) $\displaystyle\int_{0}^{1} x^{-0.99}\, dx$.

4 Find the values of the infinite integrals

(a) $\displaystyle\int_2^\infty \frac{6}{x^4}\,dx$,

(b) $\displaystyle\int_4^\infty \frac{6}{x\sqrt{x}}\,dx$,

(c) $\displaystyle\int_1^\infty x^{-1.01}\,dx$.

5 Find an expression for $\displaystyle\int_1^s \frac{1}{x^m}\,dx$ in terms of m and s, where m is a positive rational number, $m \neq -1$ and $s > 1$. Show that the infinite integral $\displaystyle\int_1^\infty \frac{1}{x^m}\,dx$ has a meaning if $m > 1$, and state its value in terms of m.

6 Find an expression for $\displaystyle\int_r^1 \frac{1}{x^m}\,dx$ in terms of m and r, where m is a positive rational number, $m \neq -1$ and $0 < r < 1$. For what values of m does the improper integral $\displaystyle\int_0^1 \frac{1}{x^m}\,dx$ have a meaning? State its value in terms of m.

7 The diagram shows the graphs of
$y = 2x + 7$ and $y = 10 - x$.
Find the area of the shaded region.

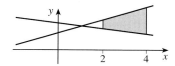

8 Find the area enclosed between the curves $y = x^2 + 7$ and $y = 2x^2 + 3$.

9 Find the area enclosed between the straight line $y = 12x + 14$ and the curve $y = 3x^2 + 6x + 5$.

10 The diagram shows the graphs of
$y = 16 + 4x - 2x^2$ and $y = x^2 - 2x - 8$.
Find the area of the region, shaded in the diagram, between the curves.

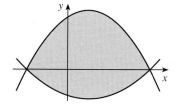

11 Find the area between the curves $y = (x - 4)(3x - 1)$ and $y = (4 - x)(1 + x)$.

12 Parts of the graphs of $f(x) = 2x^3 + x^2 - 8x$ and $g(x) = 2x^3 - 3x - 4$ enclose a finite region. Find its area.

13 The diagram shows the graph of $y = \sqrt{x}$.
Given that the area of the shaded region is 72, find the value of the constant a.

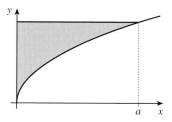

16.7 Integrating $(ax+b)^n$

You can also use the differentiation result in Section 12.1 in reverse for integration. For example, to integrate $(3x+1)^3$, you should recognise that it comes from differentiating $(3x+1)^4$.

A first guess at the integral $\displaystyle\int (3x+1)^3\,dx$ is $(3x+1)^4$. If you differentiate $(3x+1)^4$, you get $4(3x+1)^3 \times 3 = 12(3x+1)^3$. Therefore

$$\int (3x+1)^3\,dx = \tfrac{1}{12}(3x+1)^4 + k.$$

You can formalise the guessing process by reversing the last result from Section 12.1.

$$\int g(ax+b)\,dx = \frac{1}{a}f(ax+b) + k \quad \text{where } f(x) \text{ is the simplest integral of } g(x).$$

Applying this to the previous example, $g(x) = x^3$, $a = 3$ and $b = 1$. Then $f(x) = \tfrac{1}{4}x^4$, so

$$\int (3x+1)^3\,dx = \int g(3x+1)\,dx = \tfrac{1}{3}f(3x+1) + k = \tfrac{1}{3} \times \tfrac{1}{4}(3x+1)^4 + k$$

$$= \tfrac{1}{12}(3x+1)^4 + k.$$

Example 16.7.1
Find the integrals of   (a) $\sqrt{5-2x}$,   (b) $\dfrac{1}{(3-x)^2}$.

(a) **Method 1**   The first guess at $\displaystyle\int \sqrt{5-2x}\,dx = \int (5-2x)^{\frac{1}{2}}\,dx$ is $(5-2x)^{\frac{3}{2}}$.
Differentiating $(5-2x)^{\frac{3}{2}}$, you obtain $\tfrac{3}{2}(5-2x)^{\frac{1}{2}} \times (-2) = -3(5-2x)^{\frac{1}{2}}$. Therefore

$$\int (5-2x)^{\frac{1}{2}}\,dx = -\tfrac{1}{3}(5-2x)^{\frac{3}{2}} + k.$$

Method 2   Using the result in the shaded box, $g(x) = \sqrt{x} = x^{\frac{1}{2}}$, $a = -2$, $b = 5$.

So $f(x) = \dfrac{x^{\frac{3}{2}}}{\frac{3}{2}} = \tfrac{2}{3}x^{\frac{3}{2}}$, and $\displaystyle\int \sqrt{5-2x}\,dx = \tfrac{1}{-2} \times \tfrac{2}{3}(5-2x)^{\frac{3}{2}} + k = -\tfrac{1}{3}(5-2x)^{\frac{3}{2}} + k.$

(b) First write $\dfrac{1}{(3-x)^2}$ as $(3-x)^{-2}$. Then

$$\int \frac{1}{(3-x)^2}\,dx = \int (3-x)^{-2}\,dx = \tfrac{1}{-1} \times \tfrac{1}{-1}(3-x)^{-1} + k = \frac{1}{3-x} + k.$$

With practice you might find that you can write down the correct integral, but check your answer by differentiation, because it is easy to make a numerical mistake.

Example 16.7.2

Find the area between the curve $y = 16 - (2x+1)^4$ and the x-axis. (See Fig. 16.10.)

To find where the graph cuts the x-axis, solve the equation $16 - (2x+1)^4 = 0$. Thus $(2x+1)^4 = 16$, so $(2x+1) = 2$ or $(2x+1) = -2$, leading to the limits of integration, $x = \frac{1}{2}$ and $x = -\frac{3}{2}$.

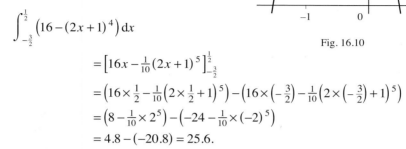

The area is given by

$$\int_{-\frac{3}{2}}^{\frac{1}{2}} \left(16 - (2x+1)^4\right) dx$$

Fig. 16.10

$$= \left[16x - \tfrac{1}{10}(2x+1)^5\right]_{-\frac{3}{2}}^{\frac{1}{2}}$$

$$= \left(16 \times \tfrac{1}{2} - \tfrac{1}{10}\left(2 \times \tfrac{1}{2} + 1\right)^5\right) - \left(16 \times \left(-\tfrac{3}{2}\right) - \tfrac{1}{10}\left(2 \times \left(-\tfrac{3}{2}\right) + 1\right)^5\right)$$

$$= \left(8 - \tfrac{1}{10} \times 2^5\right) - \left(-24 - \tfrac{1}{10} \times (-2)^5\right)$$

$$= 4.8 - (-20.8) = 25.6.$$

The required area is then 25.6.

Exercise 16D

1 Integrate the following with respect to x.

(a) $(2x+1)^6$

(b) $(3x-5)^4$

(c) $(1-7x)^3$

(d) $\left(\tfrac{1}{2}x+1\right)^{10}$

(e) $(5x+2)^{-3}$

(f) $2(1-3x)^{-2}$

(g) $\dfrac{1}{(x+1)^5}$

(h) $\dfrac{3}{2(4x+1)^4}$

(i) $\sqrt{10x+1}$

(j) $\dfrac{1}{\sqrt{2x-1}}$

(k) $\left(\tfrac{1}{2}x+2\right)^{\frac{2}{3}}$

(l) $\dfrac{8}{\sqrt[4]{2+6x}}$

2 Evaluate the following integrals.

(a) $\displaystyle\int_1^5 (2x-1)^3 \, dx$

(b) $\displaystyle\int_1^5 \sqrt{2x-1} \, dx$

(c) $\displaystyle\int_1^3 \dfrac{1}{(x+2)^2} \, dx$

(d) $\displaystyle\int_1^3 \dfrac{2}{(x+2)^3} \, dx$

3 Given that $\displaystyle\int_{1.25}^{p} (4x-5)^4 \, dx = 51.2$, find the value of p.

4 The diagram shows the curve $y = (2x-5)^4$. The point P has coordinates $(4, 81)$ and the tangent to the curve at P meets the x-axis at Q. Find the area of the region (shaded in the diagram) enclosed between the curve, PQ and the x-axis.

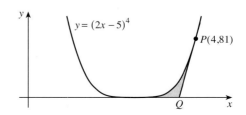

5 Find the area of each of the following shaded regions.

(a)

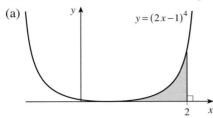

$y = (2x-1)^4$

(b)

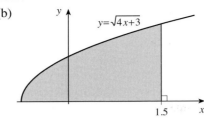

$y = \sqrt{4x+3}$

(c)

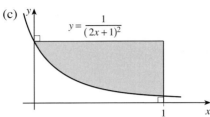

$y = \dfrac{1}{(2x+1)^2}$

(d)

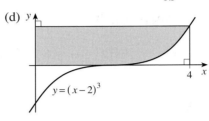

$y = (x-2)^3$

6 Find the area of the region enclosed between the curves $y = (x-2)^4$ and $y = (x-2)^3$.

7 The diagram shows the curve
$y = \left(\tfrac{1}{2}x - 2\right)^6 + 5$.

Find the area of the shaded region.

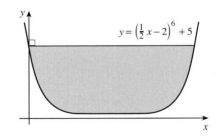

$y = \left(\tfrac{1}{2}x-2\right)^6 + 5$

8 The diagram shows a sketch of the curve
$y = \sqrt{4-x}$ and the line $y = 2 - \tfrac{1}{3}x$. The
coordinates of the points A and B where the curve
and line intersect are $(0,2)$ and $(3,1)$ respectively.
Calculate the area of the region between the line
and the curve (shaded in the diagram), giving your
answer as an exact fraction. (OCR)

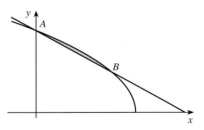

Miscellaneous exercise 16

1 Find $\displaystyle\int 6\sqrt{x}\,dx$, and hence evaluate $\displaystyle\int_1^4 6\sqrt{x}\,dx$. (OCR)

2 The diagram shows the graph of $y = 12 - 3x^2$.

Determine the x-coordinate of each of the points
where the curve crosses the x-axis.

Find by integration the area of the region (shaded in
the diagram) between the curve and the x-axis.

(OCR)

3 Evaluate $\int_0^{\frac{2}{3}} (3x-2)^3 \, dx$.   (OCR)

4 Find $\int_0^4 \sqrt{2x+1} \, dx$.   (OCR)

5 (a) Find $\int \left(\dfrac{1}{x^3} + x^3\right) dx$.   (b) Evaluate $\int_0^8 \dfrac{1}{\sqrt[3]{x}} \, dx$.   (OCR)

6 Find the area of the region enclosed between the curve $y = 12x^2 + 30x$ and the x-axis.

7 Given that $\int_{-a}^{a} 15x^2 \, dx = 3430$, find the value of the constant a.

8 The diagram shows the curve $y = x^3$. The point P has coordinates $(3,27)$ and PQ is the tangent to the curve at P. Find the area of the region enclosed between the curve, PQ and the x-axis.

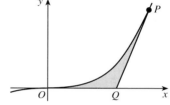

9 The diagram shows the curve $y = (x-2)^2 + 1$ with minimum point P. The point Q on the curve is such that the gradient of PQ is 2. Find the area of the region, shaded in the diagram, between PQ and the curve.

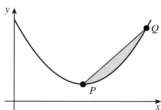

10 Evaluate $\int_0^2 x(x-1)(x-2) \, dx$ and explain your answer with reference to the graph of $y = x(x-1)(x-2)$.

11 (a) Find $\int x(x^2 - 2) \, dx$.

(b) The diagram shows the graph of $y = x(x^2 - 2)$ for $x \geqslant 0$. The value of a is such that the two shaded regions have equal areas. Find the value of a.   (OCR)

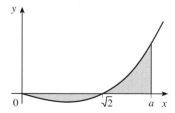

12 Given that $\int_1^p (8x^3 + 6x) \, dx = 39$, find two possible values of p. Use a graph to explain why there are two values.

13 Show that the area enclosed between the curves $y = 9 - x^2$ and $y = x^2 - 7$ is $\dfrac{128\sqrt{2}}{3}$.

14 The diagram shows a sketch of the graph of
$y = x^2$ and the normal to the curve at the point
$A(1,1)$.

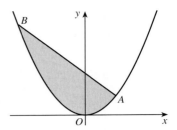

(a) Use differentiation to find the equation of
the normal at A. Verify that the point B
where the normal cuts the curve again has
coordinates $\left(-\frac{3}{2}, \frac{9}{4}\right)$.

(b) The region which is bounded by the curve
and the normal is shaded in the diagram.
Calculate its area, giving your answer as an
exact fraction.   (OCR)

15 Given that $f(x)$ and $g(x)$ are two functions such that $\displaystyle\int_0^4 f(x)\,dx = 17$ and $\displaystyle\int_0^4 g(x)\,dx = 11$,

find, where possible, the value of each of the following.

(a) $\displaystyle\int_0^4 \big(f(x) - g(x)\big)\,dx$

(b) $\displaystyle\int_0^4 \big(2f(x) + 3g(x)\big)\,dx$

(c) $\displaystyle\int_0^2 f(x)\,dx$

(d) $\displaystyle\int_0^4 \big(f(x) + 2x + 3\big)\,dx$

(e) $\displaystyle\int_0^1 f(x)\,dx + \int_1^4 f(x)\,dx$

(f) $\displaystyle\int_4^0 g(x)\,dx$

(g) $\displaystyle\int_1^5 f(x-1)\,dx$

(h) $\displaystyle\int_{-4}^0 g(-t)\,dt$

16 The diagram shows the graph of $y = \sqrt[3]{x} - x^2$.
Show by integration that the area of the region
(shaded in the diagram) between the curve and
the x-axis is $\frac{5}{12}$.   (OCR)

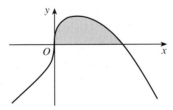

17 The diagram shows a sketch of the graph of the curve $y = x^3 - x$ together with the
tangent to the curve at the point $A(1,0)$.

(a) Use differentiation to find the equation of
the tangent to the curve at A, and verify that
the point B where the tangent cuts the curve
again has coordinates $(-2,-6)$.

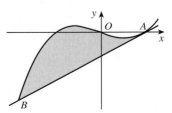

(b) Use integration to find the area of the region
bounded by the curve and the tangent
(shaded in the diagram), giving your answer
as a fraction in its lowest terms.   (OCR)

18 The diagram shows part of the curve $y = x^n$, where $n > 1$.

The point P on the curve has x-coordinate a. Show that the curve divides the rectangle $OAPB$ into two regions whose areas are in the ratio $n:1$.

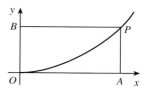

19 Find the stationary points on the graph of $y = x^4 - 8x^2$. Use your answers to make a sketch of the graph. Show that the graphs of $y = x^4 - 8x^2$ and $y = x^2$ enclose two finite regions. Find the area of one of them.

20 Using the same axes, make sketches of the graphs of $y = x^3$ and $y = (x+1)^3 - 1$. Then sketch on a larger scale the finite area enclosed between them.

Find the area of the region.

21 A function $f(x)$ with domain $x > 0$ is defined by $f(x) = \dfrac{6}{x^4} - \dfrac{2}{x^3}$.

(a) Find the values of $\displaystyle\int_2^3 f(x)\,dx$ and $\displaystyle\int_2^\infty f(x)\,dx$.

(b) Find the coordinates of
(i) the point where the graph of $y = f(x)$ crosses the x-axis,
(ii) the minimum point on the graph.
Use your answers to draw a sketch of the graph, and hence explain your answers to part (a).

22 The diagram shows the curve $y = (2x - 3)^3$.

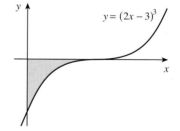

(a) Find the x-coordinates of the two points on the curve which have gradient 6.

(b) The region shaded in the diagram is bounded by part of the curve and by the two axes. Find, by integration, the area of this region. (OCR)

23 The diagram shows the curve with equation $y = \sqrt{4x + 1}$ and the normal to the curve at the point A with coordinates $(6,5)$.

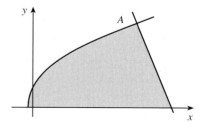

(a) Show that the equation of the normal to the curve at A is $y = -\frac{5}{2}x + 20$.

(b) Find the area of the region (shaded in the diagram) which is enclosed by the curve, the normal and the x-axis. Give your answer as a fraction in its lowest terms. (OCR)

17 Volume of revolution

This chapter is about using integration to find the volume of a particular kind of solid, called a solid of revolution. When you have completed it, you should

- be able to find a volume of revolution about either the x- or y-axis.

17.1 Volumes of revolution

Let O be the origin, and let OA be a line through the origin, as shown in Fig. 17.1. Consider the region between the line OA and the x-axis, shown shaded. If you rotate this region about the x-axis through $360°$, it sweeps out a solid cone, shown in Fig. 17.2. A solid shape constructed in this way is called a **solid of revolution**. The volume of a solid of revolution is sometimes called a **volume of revolution**.

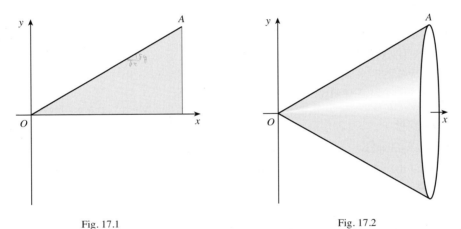

Fig. 17.1   Fig. 17.2

Calculating a volume of revolution is similar in many ways to calculating the area of a region under a curve, and can be illustrated by an example.

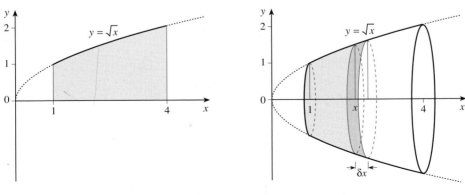

Fig. 17.3   Fig. 17.4

Suppose that the region between the graph of $y = \sqrt{x}$ and the x-axis from $x = 1$ to $x = 4$, shown in Fig. 17.3, is rotated about the x-axis to form the solid of revolution in Fig. 17.4.

The key is to begin by asking a more general question: what is the volume, V, of the solid of revolution from $x = 1$ as far as any value of x? This solid is shown by the light shading in Fig. 17.4.

Suppose that x is increased by δx. Since y and V are both functions of x, the corresponding increases in y and V can be written as δy and δV. The increase δV is shown by darker shading in Fig. 17.4. Examine this increase δV in the volume more closely. It is shown in more detail in the left diagram in Fig. 17.5.

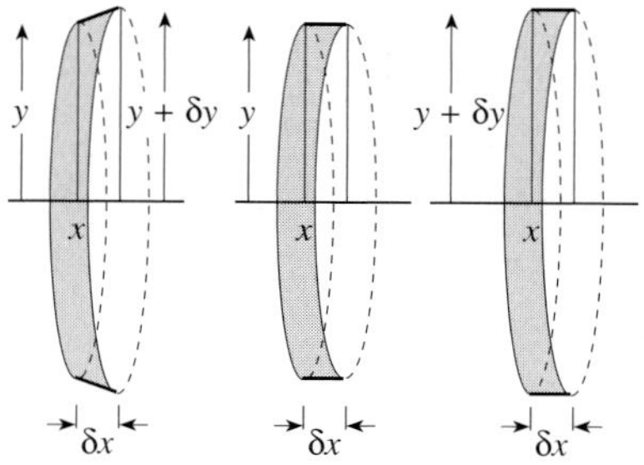

The increase δV in the volume is between the volumes of two disc-like cylinders, each of width δx and having radii y and $y + \delta y$. (These two cylinders are shown in the centre and right diagrams in Fig. 17.5.) So

Fig. 17.5

δV is between $\pi y^2 \delta x$ and $\pi (y + \delta y)^2 \delta x$

from which it follows that

$\dfrac{\delta V}{\delta x}$ is between πy^2 and $\pi (y + \delta y)^2$.

Now let δx tend to 0. From the definition in Section 7.4, $\dfrac{\delta V}{\delta x}$ tends to the derivative $\dfrac{dV}{dx}$. Also, δy tends to 0, so that $y + \delta y$ tends to y. It follows that

$\dfrac{dV}{dx} = \pi y^2$.

So V is a function whose derivative is πy^2, and since $y = \sqrt{x}$, $\dfrac{dV}{dx} = \pi x$. Therefore

$V = \frac{1}{2} \pi x^2 + k$

for some number k.

Since the volume $V = 0$ when $x = 1$, $0 = \frac{1}{2} \pi \times 1^2 + k$, giving $k = -\frac{1}{2} \pi$. Thus

$V = \frac{1}{2} \pi x^2 - \frac{1}{2} \pi$.

To find the volume up to $x = 4$, substitute $x = 4$ in this expression for V. The volume is $\frac{1}{2} \pi \times 4^2 - \frac{1}{2} \pi = \frac{1}{2} \pi (16 - 1) = \frac{15}{2} \pi$.

You can shorten the last part of this work by using the integral notation introduced in Section 16.3:

$$V = \int_1^4 \pi y^2 \, dx = \int_1^4 \pi x \, dx = \left[\tfrac{1}{2} \pi x^2 \right]_1^4 = \tfrac{1}{2} \pi \times 16 - \tfrac{1}{2} \pi \times 1 = \tfrac{15}{2} \pi.$$

Notice that the argument used at the beginning of the example was completely general, and did not depend in any way on the equation of the original curve.

> When the region under the graph of $y = f(x)$ between $x = a$ and $x = b$ (where $a < b$) is rotated about the x-axis, the volume of the solid of revolution formed is
>
> $$\int_a^b \pi \big(f(x)\big)^2 \, dx, \quad \text{or} \quad \int_a^b \pi y^2 \, dx.$$

Example 17.1.1

Find the volume generated when the region under the graph of $y = 1 + x^2$ between $x = -1$ and $x = 1$ is rotated through four right angles about the x-axis.

The phrase 'four right angles' is sometimes used in place of $360°$ for describing a full rotation about the x-axis.

The required volume is V, where

$$V = \int_{-1}^{1} \pi y^2 \, dx = \int_{-1}^{1} \pi \big(1 + x^2\big)^2 \, dx = \int_{-1}^{1} \pi \big(1 + 2x^2 + x^4\big) \, dx$$

$$= \Big[\pi \big(x + \tfrac{2}{3} x^3 + \tfrac{1}{5} x^5\big) \Big]_{-1}^{1}$$

$$= \pi \Big\{ \big(1 + \tfrac{2}{3} + \tfrac{1}{5}\big) - \big((-1) + \tfrac{2}{3}(-1)^3 + \tfrac{1}{5}(-1)^5\big) \Big\} = \tfrac{56}{15} \pi.$$

The volume of the solid is $\tfrac{56}{15} \pi$.

It is usual to give the result as an exact multiple of π, unless you are asked for an answer correct to a given number of significant figures or decimal places.

You can also use the method to obtain the formula for the volume of a cone.

Example 17.1.2

Prove that the volume V of a cone with base radius r and height h is $V = \tfrac{1}{3} \pi r^2 h$.

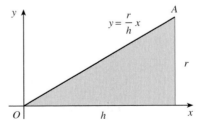
Fig. 17.6

The triangle which rotates to give the cone is shown in Fig. 17.6, where the 'height' has been drawn across the page. The gradient of OA is $\dfrac{r}{h}$, so its equation is $y = \dfrac{r}{h} x$.

Therefore, remembering that π, r and h are constants and do not depend on x,

$$V = \int_0^h \pi y^2 \, dx = \int_0^h \pi \left(\frac{r}{h} x\right)^2 dx = \int_0^h \pi \frac{r^2}{h^2} x^2 \, dx$$

$$= \pi \frac{r^2}{h^2} \int_0^h x^2 \, dx = \pi \frac{r^2}{h^2} \Big[\tfrac{1}{3} x^3 \Big]_0^h = \pi \frac{r^2}{h^2} \times \tfrac{1}{3} h^3 = \tfrac{1}{3} \pi r^2 h.$$

17.2 Volumes of revolution about the *y*-axis

In Fig. 17.7, the region between the graph of $y = f(x)$ between $y = c$ and $y = d$ is rotated about the *y*-axis to give the solid shown in Fig. 17.8.

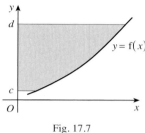

Fig. 17.7   Fig. 17.8

To find the volume of this solid of revolution about the *y*-axis, you can reverse the roles of *x* and *y* in the discussion in Section 17.1.

> When the region bounded by the graph of $y = f(x)$, the lines $y = c$ and $y = d$ and the *y*-axis is rotated about the *y*-axis, the volume of the solid of revolution formed is
>
> $$\int_c^d \pi x^2 \, dy.$$

You can only use this result if the inverse function $x = f^{-1}(y)$ is defined for $c \leqslant y \leqslant d$ (see Chapter 11). Remember that the limits in the integral are limits for y, not for x.

Example 17.2.1
Find the volume generated when the region bounded by $y = x^3$ and the *y*-axis between $y = 1$ and $y = 8$ is rotated through 360° about the *y*-axis.

Since the volume is given by $\int_1^8 \pi x^2 \, dy$, you need to express x^2 in terms of y.

The equation $y = x^3$ can be inverted to give $x = y^{\frac{1}{3}}$, so that $x^2 = y^{\frac{2}{3}}$. Then

$$V = \int_1^8 \pi y^{\frac{2}{3}} \, dy = \pi \left[\tfrac{3}{5} y^{\frac{5}{3}} \right]_1^8 = \pi \left(\tfrac{3}{5} \times 8^{\frac{5}{3}} \right) - \pi \left(\tfrac{3}{5} \times 1^{\frac{5}{3}} \right)$$

$$= \pi \left(\tfrac{3}{5} \times 32 \right) - \pi \left(\tfrac{3}{5} \times 1 \right) = \tfrac{93}{5} \pi.$$

The required volume is $\tfrac{93}{5} \pi$.

Exercise 17

In all the questions in this exercise, leave your answers as multiples of π.

1   Find the volume generated when the region under the graph of $y = f(x)$ between $x = a$ and $x = b$ is rotated through 360° about the *x*-axis.

(a) $f(x) = x$; $a = 3, b = 5$

(b) $f(x) = x^2$; $a = 2, b = 5$

(c) $f(x) = x^3$; $a = 2, b = 6$

(d) $f(x) = \dfrac{1}{x}$; $a = 1, b = 4$

2 Find the volume formed when the region under the graph of $y = f(x)$ between $x = a$ and $x = b$ is rotated through $360°$ about the x-axis.

   (a) $f(x) = x + 3$; $a = 3, b = 9$ (b) $f(x) = x^2 + 1$; $a = 2, b = 5$

   (c) $f(x) = \sqrt{x+1}$; $a = 0, b = 3$ (d) $f(x) = x(x - 2)$; $a = 0, b = 2$

3 Find the volume generated when the region bounded by the graph of $y = f(x)$, the y-axis and the lines $y = c$ and $y = d$ is rotated about the y-axis to form a solid of revolution.

   (a) $f(x) = x^2$; $c = 1, d = 3$ (b) $f(x) = x + 1$; $c = 1, d = 4$

   (c) $f(x) = \sqrt{x}$; $c = 2, d = 7$ (d) $f(x) = \dfrac{1}{x}$; $c = 2, d = 5$

   (e) $f(x) = \sqrt{9 - x}$; $c = 0, d = 3$ (f) $f(x) = x^2 + 1$; $c = 1, d = 4$

   (g) $f(x) = x^{\frac{2}{3}}$; $c = 1, d = 5$ (h) $f(x) = \dfrac{1}{x} + 2$; $c = 3, d = 5$

4 In each case the region enclosed between the following curves and the x-axis is rotated through $360°$ about the x-axis. Find the volume of the solid generated.

   (a) $y = (x + 1)(x - 3)$ (b) $y = 1 - x^2$

   (c) $y = x^2 - 5x + 6$ (d) $y = x^2 - 3x$

5 The region enclosed between the graphs of $y = x$ and $y = x^2$ is denoted by R. Find the volume generated when R is rotated through $360°$ about

   (a) the x-axis,   (b) the y-axis.

6 The region enclosed between the graphs of $y = 4x$ and $y = x^2$ is denoted by R. Find the volume generated when R is rotated through $360°$ about

   (a) the x-axis,   (b) the y-axis.

7 The region enclosed between the graphs of $y = \sqrt{x}$ and $y = x^2$ is denoted by R. Find the volume generated when R is rotated through $360°$ about

   (a) the x-axis,   (b) the y-axis.

8 A glass bowl is formed by rotating about the y-axis the region between the graphs of $y = x^2$ and $y = x^3$. Find the volume of glass in the bowl.

9 The region enclosed by both axes, the line $x = 2$ and the curve $y = \frac{1}{8}x^2 + 2$ is rotated about the y-axis to form a solid. Find the volume of this solid.

<hr>

Miscellaneous exercise 17

1 The region bounded by the curve $y = x^2 + 1$, the x-axis, the y-axis and the line $x = 2$ is rotated completely about the x-axis. Find, in terms of π, the volume of the solid formed.

                                                                   (OCR)

2 Explain why the coordinates (x,y) of any point on a circle, centre O, radius a satisfy the equation $x^2 + y^2 = a^2$.

The semicircle above the x-axis is rotated about the x-axis through $360°$ to form a sphere of radius a. Explain why the volume V of this sphere is given by

$$V = 2\pi \int_0^a \left(a^2 - x^2\right) dx.$$

Hence show that $V = \frac{4}{3}\pi a^3$.

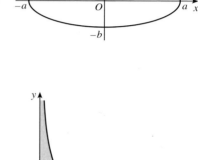

3 The ellipse with equation $\dfrac{x^2}{a^2} + \dfrac{y^2}{b^2} = 1$, shown in the diagram, has semi-axes a and b.

The ellipse is rotated about the x-axis to form an *ellipsoid*. Find the volume of this ellipsoid.

Deduce the volume of the ellipsoid formed if, instead, the ellipse had been rotated about the y-axis.

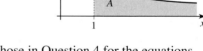

4 The diagram shows the curve $y = x^{-\frac{2}{3}}$.

(a) Show that the shaded area A is infinite.

(b) Find the shaded area B.

(c) Area A is rotated through $360°$ about the x-axis. Find the volume generated.

(d) Area B is rotated through $360°$ about the y-axis. Find the volume generated.

5 Investigate the equivalent areas and volumes to those in Question 4 for the equations
(i) $y = x^{-\frac{3}{5}}$,   (ii) $y = x^{-\frac{1}{4}}$.

6 Sketch the curve $y = 9 - x^2$, stating the coordinates of the turning point and of the intersections with the axes.

The finite region bounded by the curve and the x-axis is denoted by R.

(a) Find the area of R and hence or otherwise find $\displaystyle\int_0^9 \sqrt{9 - y}\, dy$.

(b) Find the volume of the solid of revolution obtained when R is rotated through $360°$ about the x-axis.

(c) Find the volume of the solid of revolution obtained when R is rotated through $360°$ about the y-axis.

7 The region R is bounded by the part of the curve $y = (x - 2)^{\frac{3}{2}}$ for which $2 \leqslant x \leqslant 4$, the x-axis, and the line $x = 4$. Find, in terms of π, the volume of the solid obtained when R is rotated through four right angles about the x-axis.   (OCR)

18 Radians

This chapter introduces radians, an alternative to degrees for measuring angles. When you have completed it, you should

- know how to convert from degrees to radians and vice versa
- be able to use the formula $r\theta$ for the length of a circular arc, and $\frac{1}{2}r^2\theta$ for the area of a circular sector
- know the graphs and symmetry properties of $\cos\theta$, $\sin\theta$ and $\tan\theta$ when θ is in radians
- know the meaning of $\cos^{-1}x$, $\sin^{-1}x$ and $\tan^{-1}x$, their domains and ranges
- be able to solve trigonometric equations with roots expressed in radians.

18.1 Radians

Suppose that you were meeting angles for the first time, and that you were asked to suggest a unit for measuring them. It seems highly unlikely that you would suggest the degree, which was invented by the Babylonians in ancient times. The full circle, or the right angle, both seem more natural units.

However, the unit used in modern mathematics is the radian, illustrated in Fig. 18.1. This is particularly useful in differentiating trigonometric functions, as you will see if you go on to unit P2 or unit P3.

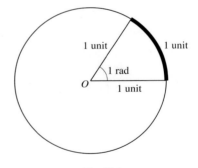

In a circle of radius 1 unit, radii joining the centre O to the ends of an arc of length 1 unit form an angle called **1 radian**. The abbreviation for radian is **rad**.

You can see immediately from this definition that there are 2π radians in $360°$. This leads to the following conversion rule for radians to degrees and vice versa:

Fig. 18.1

$$\pi \text{ rad} = 180°.$$

You could calculate that 1 radian is equal to $57.295...°$, but no one uses this conversion. It is simplest to remember that $\pi \text{ rad} = 180°$, and to use this to convert between radians and degrees.

You can set your calculator to radian mode, and then work entirely in radians.

You might find on your calculator another unit for angle called the 'grad'; there are 100 grads to the right angle. Grads will not be used in this course.

Example 18.1.1

Convert $40°$ to radians, leaving your answer as a multiple of π.

Since $40°$ is $\frac{2}{9}$ of $180°$, $40° = \frac{2}{9}\pi$ rad.

It is worthwhile learning a few common conversions, so that you can think in both radians and degrees. For example, you should know and recognise the following conversions:

$$180° = \pi \text{ rad}, \quad 90° = \tfrac{1}{2}\pi \text{ rad}, \quad 45° = \tfrac{1}{4}\pi \text{ rad}, \quad 30° = \tfrac{1}{6}\pi \text{ rad}, \quad 60° = \tfrac{1}{3}\pi \text{ rad}.$$

18.2 Length of arc and area of sector

Fig. 18.2 shows a circular arc, centre O and radius r, which subtends an angle θ rad at its centre. You can calculate the length of the circular arc by noticing that the length of the arc is the fraction $\dfrac{\theta}{2\pi}$ of the length $2\pi r$ of the circumference of the circle.

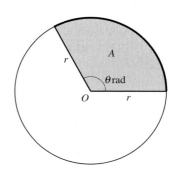

Let s be the arc length. Then

$$s = \frac{\theta}{2\pi} \times 2\pi r = r\theta.$$

Fig. 18.2

You can use a similar argument to calculate the area of a sector.

The circular sector, centre O and radius r, shown shaded in Fig. 18.3, has an angle θ rad at the centre.

The area of the circular sector is the fraction $\dfrac{\theta}{2\pi}$ of the area πr^2 of the full circle.

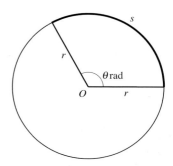

Let A be the required area. Then

$$A = \frac{\theta}{2\pi} \times \pi r^2 = \tfrac{1}{2}r^2\theta.$$

Fig. 18.3

The length of a circular arc with radius r and angle θ rad is $s = r\theta$.

The area of a circular sector with radius r and angle θ rad is $A = \tfrac{1}{2}r^2\theta$.

No units are given in the formulae above. The units are the appropriate units associated with the length; for instance, length in m *and area in* m^2.

Example 18.2.1

Find the perimeter and the area of the segment cut off by a chord PQ of length 8 cm from a circle centre O and radius 6 cm. Give your answers correct to 3 significant figures.

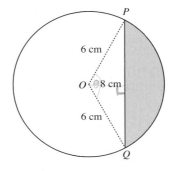

In problems of this type, it is helpful to start by thinking about the complete sector OPQ, rather than just the shaded segment of Fig. 18.4.

Fig. 18.4

The perimeter of the segment consists of two parts, the straight part of length 8 cm, and the curved part; to calculate the length of the curved part you need to know the angle POQ.

Call this angle θ. As triangle POQ is isosceles, a perpendicular drawn from O to PQ bisects both PQ and angle POQ.

$$\sin\tfrac{1}{2}\theta = \tfrac{4}{6} = 0.666\ldots \text{ , so } \tfrac{1}{2}\theta = 0.7297\ldots \text{ and } \theta = 1.459\ldots .$$

Make sure that your calculator is in radian mode.

Then the perimeter d cm is given by $d = 8 + 6\theta = 16.756\ldots$; the perimeter is 16.8 cm, correct to 3 significant figures.

To find the area of the segment, you need to find the area of the sector OPQ, and then subtract the area of the triangle OPQ. Using the formula $\tfrac{1}{2}bc\sin A$ for the area of a triangle, the area of the triangle POQ is given by $\tfrac{1}{2}r^2\sin\theta$. Thus the area in cm^2 of the shaded region is

$$\tfrac{1}{2}r^2\theta - \tfrac{1}{2}r^2\sin\theta = \tfrac{1}{2}\times 6^2 \times 1.459\ldots - \tfrac{1}{2}\times 6^2 \times \sin 1.459\ldots$$
$$= 8.381\ldots .$$

The area is 8.38 cm^2, correct to 3 significant figures.

It is worthwhile using your calculator to store the value of θ to use in the calculations. If you round θ to 3 significant figures and use the rounded value, you are liable to introduce errors.

In the course of Example 18.2.1, the notations $\sin\tfrac{1}{2}\theta = \tfrac{4}{6} = 0.666\ldots$, $\sin\theta$ and $\sin 1.459\ldots$ were used, without any indication that the angles were in radians. The convention is that when you see, for example, '$\sin 12$', you should read it as the sine of 12 radians. If it were the sine of $12°$ it would be written '$\sin 12°$'.

Example 18.2.2

A chord of a circle which subtends an angle of θ at the centre of the circle cuts off a segment equal in area to $\tfrac{1}{3}$ of the area of the whole circle.

(a) Show that $\theta - \sin\theta = \tfrac{2}{3}\pi$.

(b) Verify that $\theta = 2.61$ correct to 2 decimal places.

(a) Let r cm be the radius of the circle. Using a method similar to the one in Example 18.2.1, the area of the segment is

$$\tfrac{1}{2}r^2\theta - \tfrac{1}{2}r^2\sin\theta .$$

This is $\tfrac{1}{3}$ of the area of the whole circle if

$$\tfrac{1}{2}r^2\theta - \tfrac{1}{2}r^2\sin\theta = \tfrac{1}{3}\pi r^2 .$$

Multiplying by 2 and dividing by r^2 you find

$$\theta - \sin\theta = \tfrac{2}{3}\pi .$$

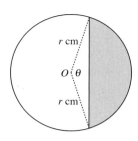

Fig. 18.5

(b) If you substitute $\theta = 2.61$ in the equation $f(\theta) \equiv \theta - \sin\theta$, you get $f(2.61) = 2.103\ldots$, which is very close to $\tfrac{2}{3}\pi = 2.094\ldots$.

This suggests that θ is close to 2.61, but it is not enough to show that it is '2.61 correct to 2 decimal places'. To do that you need to show that θ lies between 2.605 and 2.615.

It is obvious from Fig. 18.5 that θ lies between 0 and π, and that the shaded area gets larger as θ increases. So you have to show that the area is too small when $\theta = 2.605$ and too large when $\theta = 2.615$.

$$f(2.605) = 2.605 - \sin 2.605 = 2.093\ldots , \text{ and}$$

$$f(2.615) = 2.615 - \sin 2.615 = 2.112\ldots .$$

The first of these is smaller, and the second larger, than $\tfrac{2}{3}\pi = 2.094\ldots$.

It follows that the root of the equation is between 2.605 and 2.615; that is, the root is 2.61, correct to 2 decimal places.

Exercise 18A

1   Write each of the following angles in radians, leaving your answer as a multiple of π.

   (a) 90°   (b) 135°   (c) 45°   (d) 30°

   (e) 72°   (f) 18°   (g) 120°   (h) $22\tfrac{1}{2}^{\circ}$

   (i) 720°   (j) 600°   (k) 270°   (l) 1°

2   Each of the following is an angle in radians. Without using a calculator change these to degrees.

   (a) $\tfrac{1}{3}\pi$ (b) $\tfrac{1}{20}\pi$ (c) $\tfrac{1}{5}\pi$ (d) $\tfrac{1}{8}\pi$

   (e) $\tfrac{1}{9}\pi$ (f) $\tfrac{2}{3}\pi$ (g) $\tfrac{5}{8}\pi$ (h) $\tfrac{3}{5}\pi$

   (i) $\tfrac{1}{45}\pi$ (j) 6π (k) $-\tfrac{1}{2}\pi$ (l) $\tfrac{5}{18}\pi$

3   Without the use of a calculator write down the exact values of the following.

   (a) $\sin\tfrac{1}{3}\pi$ (b) $\cos\tfrac{1}{4}\pi$ (c) $\tan\tfrac{1}{6}\pi$ (d) $\cos\tfrac{3}{2}\pi$

   (e) $\sin\tfrac{7}{4}\pi$ (f) $\cos\tfrac{7}{6}\pi$ (g) $\tan\tfrac{5}{3}\pi$ (h) $\sin^2\tfrac{2}{3}\pi$

4 The following questions refer to the
  diagram, where

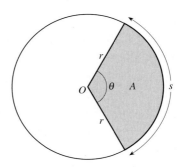

  r = radius of circle (in cm),

  s = arc length (in cm),

  A = area of sector (in cm^2),

  θ = angle subtended at centre (in radians).

  (a) $r = 7, \theta = 1.2$. Find s and A.

  (b) $r = 3.5$, $\theta = 2.1$. Find s and A.

  (c) $s = 12$, $r = 8$. Find θ and A.

  (d) $s = 14$, $\theta = 0.7$. Find r and A.

  (e) $A = 30$, $r = 5$. Find θ and s.   (f) $A = 24$, $r = 6$. Find s.

  (g) $A = 64$, $s = 16$. Find r and θ.   (h) $A = 30$, $s = 10$. Find θ.

5 Find the area of the shaded segment in
  each of the following cases.

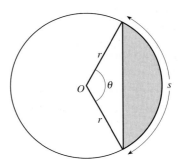

  (a) $r = 5$ cm, $\theta = \frac{1}{3}\pi$

  (b) $r = 3.1$ cm, $\theta = \frac{2}{5}\pi$

  (c) $r = 28$ cm, $\theta = \frac{5}{6}\pi$

  (d) $r = 6$ cm, $s = 9$ cm

  (e) $r = 9.5$ cm, $s = 4$ cm

6 Find the area of the segment cut off by a chord of length 10 cm from a circle radius 13 cm.

7 Find the perimeter of the segment cut off by a chord of length 14 cm from a circle radius
  25 cm.

8 A chord of a circle which subtends an angle of θ at the centre cuts off a segment equal in
  area to $\frac{1}{4}$ of the area of the whole circle.

  (a) Show that $\theta - \sin\theta = \frac{1}{2}\pi$.

  (b) Verify that $\theta = 2.31$, correct to 2 decimal places.

9 Two circles of radii 5 cm and 12 cm are drawn, partly overlapping. Their centres are
  13 cm apart. Find the area common to the two circles.

10 The diagram shows two intersecting
  circles of radius 6 cm and 4 cm with
  centres 7 cm apart. Find the perimeter and
  area of the shaded region common to both
  circles.

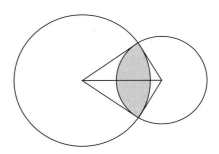

11 An eclipse of the sun is said to be 10% total when 10% of the area of the sun's disc is hidden behind the disc of the moon.

A child models this with two discs, each of radius r cm, as shown.

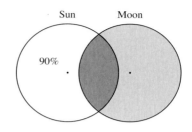

(a) Calculate, in terms of r, the distance between the centres of the two discs.

(b) Calculate also the distance between the centres when the eclipse is 80% total.

18.3 Graphs of the trigonometric functions

The graphs of $y = \cos\theta$, $y = \sin\theta$ and $y = \tan\theta$ when the angle is measured in radians have a similar shape to those for $y = \cos\theta°$, $y = \sin\theta°$ and $y = \tan\theta°$ which are drawn in Figs. 10.3, 10.4 and 10.5 on pages 139 and 140. The only change is the scale along the θ-axis.

The graphs of $y = \cos\theta$, $y = \sin\theta$ and $y = \tan\theta$, with θ in radians, are shown in Fig. 18.6, Fig. 18.7 and Fig. 18.8 respectively. These three graphs are drawn with the same scales on each axis.

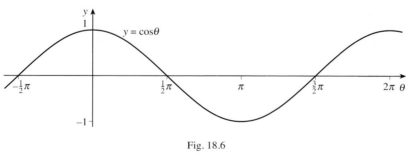

Fig. 18.6

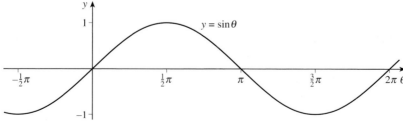

Fig. 18.7

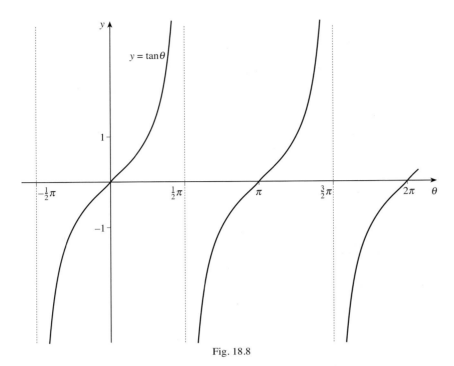

Fig. 18.8

If you were to draw the graphs in Section 10.1 and Section 10.2 with the same scales in each direction, they would be very wide and flat compared with the graphs shown here.

In fact radians are almost always used when you need to find the gradients of the graphs of $y = \cos\theta$, $y = \sin\theta$ and $y = \tan\theta$.

These graphs also have symmetry properties similar to those of the graphs of $y = \cos\theta°$, $y = \sin\theta°$ and $y = \tan\theta°$.

Periodic properties:	$\cos(\theta \pm 2\pi) = \cos\theta$	$\sin(\theta \pm 2\pi) = \sin\theta$	$\tan(\theta \pm \pi) = \tan\theta$
Odd/even properties:	$\cos(-\theta) = \cos\theta$	$\sin(-\theta) = -\sin\theta$	$\tan(-\theta) = -\tan\theta$
Translation properties:	$\cos(\theta - \pi) = -\cos\theta$	$\sin(\theta - \pi) = -\sin\theta$	
	$\cos(\pi - \theta) = -\cos\theta$	$\sin(\pi - \theta) = \sin\theta$	$\tan(\pi - \theta) = -\tan\theta$

Exercise 18B

1 Use the graphs of $y = \cos\theta$ and $y = \sin\theta$ to show that $\sin\left(\frac{1}{2}\pi - \theta\right) = \cos\theta$.

Use this property, and the symmetry properties of the sine, cosine and tangent functions in the box above to establish the following results.

(a) $\sin\left(\frac{3}{2}\pi + \theta\right) = -\cos\theta$

(b) $\sin\left(\frac{1}{2}\pi + \theta\right) = \cos\theta$

(c) $\cos\left(\frac{1}{2}\pi + \theta\right) = -\sin\theta$

(d) $\sin\left(-\theta - \frac{1}{2}\pi\right) = -\cos\theta$

2 With the same axes, sketch $y = \tan\theta$ and $y = \dfrac{1}{\tan\theta}$. Show that $\tan\!\left(\tfrac{1}{2}\pi - \theta\right) = \dfrac{1}{\tan\theta}$.

3 Find the least positive value of α for which

(a) $\cos(\alpha - \theta) = \sin\theta$,

(b) $\sin(\alpha - \theta) = \cos(\alpha + \theta)$,

(c) $\tan\theta = \tan(\theta + \alpha)$,

(d) $\sin(\theta + 2\alpha) = \cos(\alpha - \theta)$,

(e) $\cos(2\alpha - \theta) = \cos(\theta - \alpha)$,

(f) $\sin(5\alpha + \theta) = \cos(\theta - 3\alpha)$.

18.4 Inverse trigonometric functions

You have already met the notation $\sin^{-1}$, $\cos^{-1}$ and $\tan^{-1}$ a number of times. It is now time to give a more precise definition of the inverse trigonometric functions.

The functions $\cos x$, $\sin x$ and $\tan x$ are not one–one, as you can see from Section 18.3. It follows from Section 11.6 that they do not have inverses unless you restrict their domains of definition. The definitions given here assume that you are working in radians.

Fig. 18.9 shows how the domain of the cosine function is restricted to $0 \leqslant x \leqslant \pi$ to define the function $\cos^{-1}$.

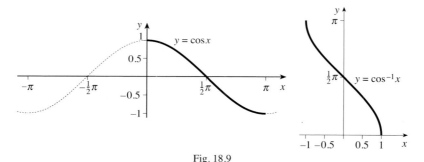

Fig. 18.9

Recall from Section 11.8 that if the graph of a function and its inverse are plotted on the same axes, then each is the reflection of the other in $y = x$. You can see that if the two graphs in Fig. 18.9 were superimposed, then the thicker part of the graph of $y = \cos x$ would be the reflection of $y = \cos^{-1} x$ in $y = x$, and vice versa.

Similarly Fig. 18.10 shows how the domain of the sine function is restricted to $-\tfrac{1}{2}\pi \leqslant x \leqslant \tfrac{1}{2}\pi$ to define the function $\sin^{-1}$.

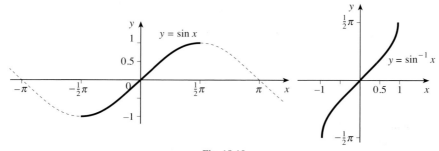

Fig. 18.10

Once again, the thicker part of the graph of $y = \sin x$ is the reflection of $y = \sin^{-1} x$ in the line $y = x$, and vice versa.

Fig. 18.11 shows the graph of the function $\tan^{-1}$, obtained by restricting the domain of the tangent function to $-\frac{1}{2}\pi < x < \frac{1}{2}\pi$.

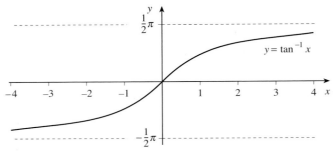

Fig. 18.11

$\cos^{-1}$ has domain $-1 \leqslant x \leqslant 1$ and range $0 \leqslant \cos^{-1} x \leqslant \pi$.

$\sin^{-1}$ has domain $-1 \leqslant x \leqslant 1$ and range $-\frac{1}{2}\pi \leqslant \sin^{-1} x \leqslant \frac{1}{2}\pi$.

$\tan^{-1}$ has domain $\mathbb{R}$ and range $-\frac{1}{2}\pi < \tan^{-1} x < \frac{1}{2}\pi$.

Exercise 18C

Do not use a calculator in Questions 1 to 5.

1 Find

(a) $\cos^{-1} \frac{1}{2}\sqrt{3}$,

(b) $\tan^{-1} 1$,

(c) $\cos^{-1} 0$,

(d) $\sin^{-1} \frac{1}{2}\sqrt{3}$,

(e) $\tan^{-1}\left(-\sqrt{3}\right)$,

(f) $\sin^{-1}(-1)$,

(g) $\tan^{-1}(-1)$,

(h) $\cos^{-1}(-1)$.

2 Find

(a) $\cos^{-1} \dfrac{1}{\sqrt{2}}$,

(b) $\sin^{-1}(-0.5)$,

(c) $\cos^{-1}(-0.5)$,

(d) $\tan^{-1}\left(\dfrac{1}{\sqrt{3}}\right)$.

3 Find

(a) $\sin\left(\sin^{-1} 0.5\right)$,

(b) $\cos\left(\cos^{-1}(-1)\right)$,

(c) $\tan\left(\tan^{-1} \sqrt{3}\right)$,

(d) $\cos\left(\cos^{-1} 0\right)$.

4 Find

(a) $\cos^{-1}\left(\cos \frac{3}{2}\pi\right)$,

(b) $\sin^{-1}\left(\sin \frac{13}{6}\pi\right)$,

(c) $\tan^{-1}\left(\tan \frac{1}{6}\pi\right)$,

(d) $\cos^{-1}(\cos 2\pi)$.

5 Find

(a) $\sin\left(\cos^{-1} \frac{1}{2}\sqrt{3}\right)$,

(b) $\dfrac{1}{\tan\left(\tan^{-1} 2\right)}$,

(c) $\cos\left(\sin^{-1}(-0.5)\right)$,

(d) $\tan\left(\cos^{-1} \frac{1}{2}\sqrt{2}\right)$.

6 Use a graphical method to solve, correct to 3 decimal places, the equation $\cos x = \cos^{-1} x$. What simpler equation has this as its only root?

18.5 Solving trigonometric equations using radians

When you have a trigonometric equation to solve, you will sometimes want to find an angle in radians. The principles are similar to those that you used for working in degrees in Section 10.5, but the functions $\cos^{-1}$, $\sin^{-1}$ and $\tan^{-1}$ will now have the meanings that were assigned to them in Section 18.4.

Example 18.5.1

Solve the equation $\cos\theta = -0.7$, giving all the roots in the interval $0 \leqslant \theta \leqslant 2\pi$ correct to 2 decimal places.

Step 1 $\cos^{-1}(-0.7) = 2.346\ldots$. This is one root in the interval $0 \leqslant \theta \leqslant 2\pi$.

Step 2 Use the symmetry property $\cos(-\theta) = \cos\theta$ to show that $-2.346\ldots$ is another root. Note that $-2.346\ldots$ is not in the required interval.

Step 3 Use the periodic property, $\cos(\theta \pm 2\pi) = \cos\theta$, to say that $-2.346\ldots + 2\pi = 3.936\ldots$ is a root in the required interval.

The roots of the equation $\cos\theta = -0.7$ in $0 \leqslant \theta \leqslant 2\pi$ are 2.35 and 3.94, correct to 2 decimal places.

Example 18.5.2

Solve the equation $\sin\theta = -0.2$, giving all the roots in the interval $-\pi \leqslant \theta \leqslant \pi$ correct to 2 decimal places.

Step 1 $\sin^{-1}(-0.2) = -0.201\ldots$. This is one root in the interval $-\pi \leqslant \theta \leqslant \pi$.

Step 2 Another root of the equation is $\pi - (-0.201\ldots) = 3.342\ldots$, but this is not in the required interval.

Step 3 Subtracting 2π gives $-2.940\ldots$, the other root in the interval $-\pi \leqslant \theta \leqslant \pi$.

Therefore the roots of $\sin\theta = -0.2$ in $-\pi \leqslant \theta \leqslant \pi$ are -2.94 and -0.20, correct to 2 decimal places.

Example 18.5.3

Solve the equation $\cos(3\theta - 0.1) = 0.3$, giving all the roots in the interval $-\pi \leqslant \theta \leqslant \pi$ correct to 2 decimal places.

Let $3\theta - 0.1 = \phi$, so that the equation becomes $\cos\phi = 0.3$. As θ lies in the interval $-\pi \leqslant \theta \leqslant \pi$, $\phi = 3\theta - 0.1$ lies in the interval $-3\pi - 0.1 \leqslant \phi \leqslant 3\pi - 0.1$ which is $-9.524\ldots \leqslant \phi \leqslant 9.324\ldots$.

The first part of the problem is to solve $\cos\phi = 0.3$ for $-9.524\ldots \leqslant \phi \leqslant 9.324\ldots$.

Step 1 $\cos^{-1}0.3 = 1.266\ldots$. This is one root in the interval $-9.524\ldots \leqslant \phi \leqslant 9.324\ldots$.

Step 2 Using the fact that the cosine function is even, another root is $-1.266\ldots$.

Step 3   Adding 2π to and subtracting 2π from $\pm 1.266\ldots$ gives $\pm 5.017\ldots$ and $\pm 7.549\ldots$ as the other roots.

Since $\theta = \frac{1}{3}(\phi + 0.1)$, the roots of the original equation are $-2.48, -1.64, -0.39, 0.46,$ $1.71, 2.55$, correct to 2 decimal places.

Example 18.5.4
Solve the equation $\tan\theta = \cos\theta$, giving all the roots in radians in the interval $0 \leqslant \theta \leqslant 2\pi$, correct to 2 decimal places.

If you have an equation like this it is usually a good idea to use the identity $\tan\theta \equiv \dfrac{\sin\theta}{\cos\theta}$ to replace $\tan\theta$. The equation then becomes $\dfrac{\sin\theta}{\cos\theta} = \cos\theta$, which, on multiplying both sides by $\cos\theta$, gives

$$\sin\theta = \cos^2\theta.$$

As it stands you cannot solve this equation, but if you use the identity $\cos^2\theta + \sin^2\theta \equiv 1$ to replace $\cos^2\theta$, you get the equation $\sin\theta = 1 - \sin^2\theta$, which you can rewrite as

$$\sin^2\theta + \sin\theta - 1 = 0.$$

This is a quadratic equation in $\sin\theta$, which you can solve using the quadratic formula in Section 4.4:

$$\sin\theta = \frac{-1 \pm \sqrt{1^2 - 4 \times 1 \times (-1)}}{2}, \text{ giving } \sin\theta = 0.618\ldots \text{ or } \sin\theta = -1.618\ldots .$$

One root is $\sin^{-1}0.618\ldots = 0.666\ldots$. The other root of $\sin\theta = 0.618\ldots$ in the interval, obtained from the symmetry of $\sin\theta$, is $\pi - 0.666\ldots = 2.475\ldots$.

The equation $\sin\theta = -1.618\ldots$ has no roots, as $\sin\theta$ has the property that $-1 \leqslant \sin\theta \leqslant 1$.

So the required roots are 0.67 and 2.48, correct to 2 decimal places.

Exercise 18D

1   Find in radians correct to 2 decimal places, the two smallest positive values of θ for which

(a) $\sin\theta = 0.12$,

(b) $\sin\theta = -0.86$,

(c) $\sin\theta = 0.925$,

(d) $\cos\theta = 0.81$,

(e) $\cos\theta = -0.81$,

(f) $\cos\theta = \sqrt{\dfrac{1}{3}}$,

(g) $\tan\theta = 4.1$,

(h) $\tan\theta = -0.35$,

(i) $\tan\theta = 0.17$,

(j) $\sin(\pi + \theta) = 0.3$,

(k) $\cos\!\left(\frac{1}{2}\pi - \theta\right) = -0.523$,

(l) $\tan\!\left(\frac{1}{2}\pi - \theta\right) = -4$,

(m) $\sin\!\left(2\theta + \frac{1}{3}\pi\right) = 0.123$,

(n) $\sin\!\left(\frac{1}{6}\pi - \theta\right) = 0.5$,

(o) $\cos\!\left(3\theta - \frac{2}{3}\pi\right) = 0$.

2 Find all values of θ in the interval $-\pi \leqslant \theta \leqslant \pi$ which satisfy each of the following equations, giving your answers correct to 2 decimal places where appropriate.

(a) $\sin\theta = 0.84$ (b) $\cos\theta = 0.27$ (c) $\tan\theta = 1.9$

(d) $\sin\theta = -0.73$ (e) $\cos\theta = -0.15$ (f) $4\tan\theta + 5 = 0$

(g) $4\sin\theta = 3\cos\theta$ (h) $3\sin\theta = \dfrac{1}{\sin\theta}$ (i) $3\sin\theta = \tan\theta$

3 Find all the solutions in the interval $0 < x \leqslant 2\pi$ of each of the following equations.

(a) $\cos 2x = \dfrac{1}{4}$ (b) $\tan 3x = 3$ (c) $\sin 2x = -0.62$

(d) $\cos 4x = -\dfrac{1}{5}$ (e) $\tan 2x = 0.5$ (f) $\sin 3x = -0.45$

4 Find the roots in the interval $-\pi < t \leqslant \pi$ of each of the following equations.

(a) $\cos 3t = \dfrac{3}{4}$ (b) $\tan 2t = -2$ (c) $\sin 3t = -0.32$

(d) $\cos 2t = 0.264$ (e) $\tan 5t = 0.7$ (f) $\sin 2t = -0.42$

5 Find the roots (if there are any) in the interval $-\pi < \theta \leqslant \pi$ of the following equations.

(a) $\cos\frac{1}{2}\theta = \frac{1}{3}$ (b) $\tan\frac{2}{3}\theta = -5$ (c) $\sin\frac{1}{5}\theta = -\frac{1}{5}$

(d) $\cos\frac{1}{3}\theta = \frac{1}{2}$ (e) $\tan\frac{2}{3}\theta = 0.5$ (f) $\sin\frac{2}{5}\theta = -0.4$

6 Without using a calculator, find the exact roots of the following equations, if there are any, giving your answers as multiples of π in the interval $0 < \theta \leqslant 2\pi$.

(a) $\sin\left(2\theta - \frac{1}{3}\pi\right) = \frac{1}{2}$ (b) $\tan\left(2\theta - \frac{1}{6}\pi\right) = 0$ (c) $\cos\left(3\theta + \frac{1}{4}\pi\right) = \frac{1}{2}\sqrt{3}$

(d) $\tan\left(\frac{3}{2}\theta - \frac{1}{6}\pi\right) = -\sqrt{3}$ (e) $\cos\left(2\theta - \frac{5}{18}\pi\right) = -\frac{1}{2}$ (f) $\sin\left(\frac{1}{2}\theta + \frac{5}{18}\pi\right) = 1$

(g) $\cos\left(\frac{1}{5}\theta - \frac{5}{18}\pi\right) = 0$ (h) $\tan(3\theta - \pi) = -1$ (i) $\sin\left(\frac{1}{4}\theta - \frac{1}{9}\pi\right) = 0$

7 Find the roots (if there are any) in the interval $-\pi < \theta \leqslant \pi$ of the following equations.

(a) $\tan\theta = 2\cos\theta$ (b) $\sin^2\theta = 2\cos\theta$ (c) $\sin^2\theta = 2\cos^2\theta$

(d) $\sin^2\theta = 2\cos^2\theta - 1$ (e) $2\sin\theta = \tan\theta$ (f) $\tan^2\theta = 2\cos^2\theta$

Miscellaneous exercise 18

1 The diagram shows a sector of a circle with centre O and radius 6 cm.
Angle $POQ = 0.6$ radians. Calculate the length of arc PQ and the area of sector POQ. (OCR)

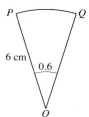

2 A sector OAB of a circle, of radius a and centre O, has $\angle AOB = \theta$ radians. Given that the area of the sector OAB is twice the square of the length of the arc AB, find θ. (OCR)

3   The diagram shows a sector of a circle, with centre O and radius r. The length of the arc is equal to half the perimeter of the sector. Find the area of the sector in terms of r.

(OCR)

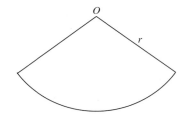

4   The diagram shows two circles, with centres A and B, intersecting at C and D in such a way that the centre of each lies on the circumference of the other. The radius of each circle is 1 unit. Write down the size of angle CAD and calculate the area of the shaded region (bounded by the arc CBD and the straight line CD). Hence show that the area of the region common to the interiors of the two circles is approximately 39% of the area of one circle.   (OCR)

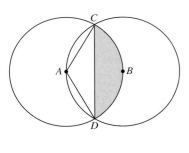

5   In the diagram, ABC is an arc of a circle with centre O and radius 5 cm. The lines AD and CD are tangents to the circle at A and C respectively. Angle $AOC = \frac{2}{3}\pi$ radians.

Calculate the area of the region enclosed by AD, DC and the arc ABC, giving your answer correct to 2 significant figures.

(OCR)

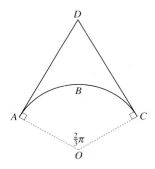

6   Find, either to 2 decimal places or an exact multiple of π, all values of x in the interval $-\pi < x \leqslant \pi$ satisfying the following equations.

(a) $\sin x = -0.16$ (b) $\cos x (1 + \sin x) = 0$ (c) $(1 - \tan x)\sin x = 0$

(d) $\sin 2x = 0.23$ (e) $\cos\left(\frac{3}{4}\pi - x\right) = 0.832$ (f) $\tan(3x - 17) = 3$

7   The electric current, c amperes, in a wire is given by the equation

$$c = 5\sin\left(100\pi t + \tfrac{1}{6}\pi\right),$$

where t denotes the time in seconds.

(a)   Calculate the period of the oscillation, and find the number of oscillations per second.

(b)   Find the first three positive values of t for which $c = 2$, giving your answers correct to 3 decimal places.

8   An oscillating particle has displacement y metres, where y is given by $y = a\sin(kt + \alpha)$, where a is measured in metres, t is measured in seconds and k and α are constants. The time for a complete oscillation is T seconds. Find

(a) k in terms of T,   (b)   the number, in terms of k, of complete oscillations per second.

9 The diagram shows a circle with centre O and radius r, and a chord AB which subtends an angle θ radians at O. Express the area of the shaded segment bounded by the chord AB in terms of r and θ.

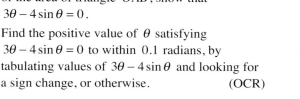

Given that the area of this segment is one-third of the area of triangle OAB, show that $3\theta - 4\sin\theta = 0$.

Find the positive value of θ satisfying $3\theta - 4\sin\theta = 0$ to within 0.1 radians, by tabulating values of $3\theta - 4\sin\theta$ and looking for a sign change, or otherwise. (OCR)

10 The diagram shows two circles, with centres A and B, which touch at C. The radius of each circle is r. The points D and E, one on each circle, are such that DE is parallel to the line ACB. Each of the angles DAC and EBC is θ radians, where $0 < \theta < \pi$. Express the length of DE in terms of r and θ.

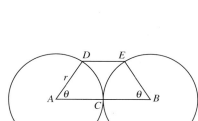

The length of DE is equal to the length of each of the minor arcs CD and CE.

(a) Show that $\theta + 2\cos\theta - 2 = 0$.

(b) Sketch the graph of $y = \cos\theta$ for $0 < \theta < \frac{1}{2}\pi$. By drawing on your graph a suitable straight line, the equation of which must be stated, show that the equation $\theta + 2\cos\theta - 2 = 0$ has exactly one root in the interval $0 < \theta < \frac{1}{2}\pi$.

Verify by calculation that θ lies between 1.10 and 1.11. (OCR)

11 The diagram shows an arc ABC of a circle with centre O and radius r, and the chord AC. The length of the arc ABC is s, and angle $AOC = \theta$ rad. Express θ in terms of r and s, and deduce that the area of triangle AOC may be expressed as

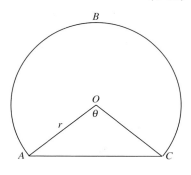

$$\tfrac{1}{2}r^2 \sin\left(2\pi - \frac{s}{r}\right).$$

Show, by a graphical argument based on a sketch of $y = \sin x$, or otherwise, that

$$\sin(2\pi - \alpha) = -\sin\alpha,$$

where α is any angle measured in radians.

Given that the area of triangle AOC is equal to one-fifth of the area of the major sector $OABC$, show that $\dfrac{s}{r} + 5\sin\left(\dfrac{s}{r}\right) = 0$.

12 By using a graphical method, or otherwise, establish the identities

(a) $\sin^{-1} x + \cos^{-1} x \equiv \frac{1}{2}\pi$,

(b) $\tan^{-1} x + \tan^{-1}\left(\dfrac{1}{x}\right) \equiv \frac{1}{2}\pi$ or $-\frac{1}{2}\pi$.

13 The diagram shows a sector of a circle with centre O and radius r, and a chord AB which subtends an angle θ radians at O, where $0 < \theta < \pi$.

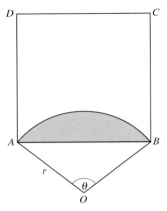

A square $ABCD$ is drawn, as shown in the diagram. It is given that the area of the shaded segment is exactly one-eighth of the area of the square. Show that

$$2\theta - 2\sin\theta + \cos\theta - 1 = 0.$$

Hence show that θ lies between 1 and 2, and use a tabulation method to find θ correct to 1 decimal place.

14 Give the domains and the ranges of the following functions.

(a) $2\sin^{-1} x - 4$ (b) $2\sin^{-1}(x - 4)$

15 Solve the equation $3\sin^2\theta + 4\cos\theta = 4$, giving all the roots, correct to 2 decimal places, in the interval $0 \leqslant \theta \leqslant 2\pi$.

16 Solve the following equations giving any roots in terms of π in the interval $-2\pi \leqslant 0 \leqslant 2\pi$.

(a) $2\cos^2\theta + \sin^2\theta = 0$ (b) $2\cos^2\theta + \sin^2\theta = 1$ (c) $2\cos^2\theta + \sin^2\theta = 2$

Revision exercise 3

1 Sketch the graphs of $y = 4 - x$ and $y = x^2 + 2x$, and calculate the coordinates of their points of intersection. Calculate the area of the finite region between the two graphs.

2 (a) Find the coordinates of the stationary points on the graph of $y = x^3 - 3x + 3$.

   (b) Calculate the coordinates of the point for which $\dfrac{d^2 y}{dx^2} = 0$.

   (c) Find the equation of the normal to the curve at the point where $x = -2$.

   (d) Calculate the area enclosed between the curve, the x-axis and the lines $x = 0$ and $x = 2$.

3 Without using a calculator, draw a sketch of $y = x^4 - x^5$, indicating those points for which $\dfrac{d^2 y}{dx^2}$ is positive and those for which $\dfrac{d^2 y}{dx^2}$ is negative.

4 Let n be a positive integer. Sketch the graphs of $y = x^n$ and $y = x^{\frac{1}{n}}$ for $x \geqslant 0$ and find the area of the region which they enclose.

5 A curve has an equation which satisfies $\dfrac{d^2 y}{dx^2} = 5$. The curve passes through the point $(0, 4)$ and the gradient of the tangent at this point is 3. Find y in terms of x.

6 The part of the curve $y = kx^2$, where k is a constant, between $y = 1$ and $y = 3$ is rotated through $360°$ about the y-axis. Given that the volume generated is 12π, calculate the value of k.

7 Find the value of $\displaystyle\int_1^3 \left(x^3 - 6x^2 + 11x - 6\right) dx$. Interpret your result geometrically.

8 The region R is bounded by the x-axis, the line $x = 16$ and the curve with equation $y = 6 - \sqrt{x}$, where $0 \leqslant x \leqslant 36$. Find, in terms of π, the volume of the solid generated when R is rotated through one revolution about the x-axis. (OCR, adapted)

9 Calculate the area of the region in the first quadrant bounded by the curve with equation $y = \sqrt{9 - x}$ and the axes.

10 (a) Draw a sketch of the part of the curve $y = \dfrac{1}{\sqrt{x}}$ from $x = 1$ to $x = 4$.

   (b) Calculate the area of the region R bounded by the curve, the x-axis and the lines $x = 1$ and $x = 4$.

11 The angle made by a wasp's wings with the horizontal is given by the equation $\theta = 0.4 \sin 600t$ radians, where t is the time in seconds. How many times a second do its wings oscillate?

12 Determine whether the point $(1,2,-1)$ lies on the line passing through $(3,1,2)$ and $(5,0,5)$.

13 The figure shows part of a circle with centre O and
radius r. Points A, B and C lie on the circle such
that AB is a diameter. Angle $BAC = \theta$ radians.

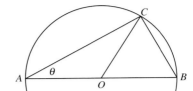

    (a) Find angle AOC in terms of θ, and use the
cosine rule in triangle AOC to express AC^2 in
terms of r and θ.

    (b) By considering triangle ABC, write down the
length of AC in terms of r and θ, and deduce
that $\cos 2\theta = 2\cos^2 \theta - 1$.   (OCR)

14 Sketch the graph of $y = \dfrac{9}{2x+3}$ for positive values of x.

The part of the curve between $x = 0$ and $x = 3$ is rotated through 2π radians about the
x-axis. Calculate the volume of the solid of revolution formed.

15 Differentiate each of the following functions with respect to x.

    (a) $\left(x^3 + 2x - 1\right)^3$ (b) $\sqrt{\dfrac{1}{x^2 + 1}}$

16 A teacher received a salary of £12 800 in his first full year of teaching. He models his
future salary by assuming it to increase by a constant amount of £950 each year up to a
maximum of £20 400.

    (a) How much will he earn in his fifth year of teaching?

    (b) In which year does he first receive the maximum salary?

    (c) Determine expressions for the total amount he will have received by the end of his nth
year of teaching, stating clearly for which values of n each is valid.

His twin sister chose accountancy as her profession. She started her career in the same year
as he did. Her first year's salary was £13 500, and she can expect her salary to increase at a
constant rate of 5% each year.

    (d) Select an appropriate mathematical model and use this to determine her annual salary
in her nth year as an accountant.

    (e) Show that she earns less than he in their 4th year of working.

    (f) Which is the first year after that in which he earns less than she?   (OCR)

17 A geometric progression has first term 6 and common ratio 0.75. Find the sum of the first
ten terms of this geometric progression, giving your answer correct to 2 decimal places.
Write down the sum to infinity of the geometric progression.

18 The vectors $\mathbf{a}$ and $\mathbf{b}$ are shown on the grid of unit
squares.

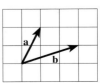

    (a) Calculate $|\mathbf{a} + \mathbf{b}|$.

    (b) Calculate $\mathbf{a} \cdot \mathbf{b}$.

    (c) Calculate the angle between $\mathbf{a}$ and $\mathbf{b}$.   (OCR)

19 A coin is made by starting with an equilateral triangle ABC of side 2 cm. With centre A an arc of a circle is drawn joining B to C. Similar arcs join C to A and A to B.

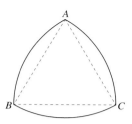

Find, exactly, the perimeter of the coin and the area of one of its faces.

20 Find the value of t such that the variable vector $\begin{pmatrix} 4 \\ 6 \\ 10 \end{pmatrix} + t \begin{pmatrix} -1 \\ 2 \\ 3 \end{pmatrix}$ is perpendicular to the

vector $\begin{pmatrix} 4 \\ 2 \\ -7 \end{pmatrix}$. Find also the angle between the vectors $\begin{pmatrix} -1 \\ 2 \\ 3 \end{pmatrix}$ and $\begin{pmatrix} 4 \\ 2 \\ -7 \end{pmatrix}$. Give your answer in

degrees correct to 1 decimal place.

21 Draw sketches of possible graphs for which the following data hold. Consider only the domain $0 \leqslant x \leqslant 5$, and assume that the graph of $y = \mathrm{f}''(x)$ is smooth.

(a) $\mathrm{f}(0) = 0$, $\mathrm{f}(2) = 5$, $\mathrm{f}'(2) = 0$, $\mathrm{f}''(2) < 0$, $\mathrm{f}(4) = 3$, $\mathrm{f}'(4) = 0$, $\mathrm{f}''(4) > 0$

(b) $\mathrm{f}(0) = 0$, $\mathrm{f}''(1) < 0$, $\mathrm{f}(2) = 5$, $\mathrm{f}'(2) = 0$, $\mathrm{f}''(3) > 0$, $\mathrm{f}(4) = 7$

(c) $\mathrm{f}(0) = 0$, $\mathrm{f}'(0) = -1$, $\mathrm{f}'(1) = 0$, $\mathrm{f}(3) = 0$, $\mathrm{f}'(3) = 2$, $\mathrm{f}''(3) = 0$, $\mathrm{f}''(4) < 0$

(d) $\mathrm{f}(0) = 1$, $\mathrm{f}'(0) = 1$, $\mathrm{f}''(0) = 1$ and $\mathrm{f}''(x)$ increases as x increases

(e) $\mathrm{f}(0) = 1$, $\mathrm{f}'(0) = 0$, $\mathrm{f}'(x) < 0$ for $0 < x < 5$, $\mathrm{f}(5) = \mathrm{f}'(5) = 0$

(f) $\mathrm{f}(0) = 3$, $\mathrm{f}'(0) = -2$, $\mathrm{f}''(x) > 0$ for $0 < x < 5$, $\mathrm{f}(5) = \mathrm{f}'(5) = 0$

22 The diagram shows a mass M suspended in a viscous liquid by an elastic spring with one end fixed to a beam. The mass has a natural position of equilibrium, and its displacement downwards from this position is given by x.

The mass is given a displacement d from its equilibrium position and is then given an initial velocity. Graph (i) shows x plotted against time t when the initial velocity is away from the equilibrium position. Graph (ii) shows x plotted against time when the initial velocity is small but towards the equilibrium position.

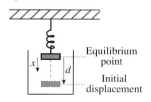

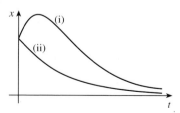

Make a sketch copy of the graph and add to it a sketch of x against t

(a) when the initial velocity is large and towards the equilibrium position, and

(b) when M is simply released at displacement d.

Describe the four graphs, (i), (ii) and your answers to (a) and (b), in terms of $\dfrac{\mathrm{d}x}{\mathrm{d}t}$ and $\dfrac{\mathrm{d}^2 x}{\mathrm{d}t^2}$.

23 The diagram shows the curve
$y = (1 - 4x)^5 + 20x$. The curve has a
maximum point at P as shown.

Show that the curve has a minimum point
which lies on the y-axis and calculate the
area of the region shaded in the diagram.

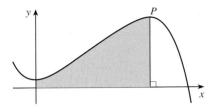

24 (a) Sketch the graphs of $y = x^2$ and $y = (x - 4)^2$, and find the coordinates of the point P
where they intersect.

(b) The region bounded by the x-axis between $x = 0$ and $x = 4$, the graph of $y = x^2$
between the origin and P, and the graph of $y = (x - 4)^2$ between P and the x-axis is
rotated through 2π radians about the x-axis. Calculate in terms of π the volume of
the solid of revolution formed.

25 A pyramid has a square base $ABCD$ of side 8 cm. The diagonals AC and BD of the base
meet at O. The point E is midway between O and A. The vertex V is at a height of 6 cm
vertically above E.

Calculate to the nearest tenth of a degree the angle between DV and BV.

26 The diagram shows the curve
$$y = \frac{1}{\sqrt[3]{4x + 3}}.$$

Find the area of the shaded region.

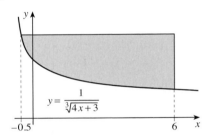

27 Use the methods of Exercise 6A to calculate an approximation to the gradient of the graph
$y = \sin x$ for $x = 0$ and $x = \frac{1}{4}\pi$. Use the symmetry properties of $y = \sin x$ to predict the
gradients at other values of x in the interval $0 \leqslant x \leqslant 2\pi$, and use your results to sketch a
graph of $\dfrac{dy}{dx}$ against x. Make a conjecture about the equation of this graph.

28 The diagram shows the region R, which is bounded by the
axes and the part of the curve $y^2 = 4a(a - x)$ lying in the
first quadrant. Find, in terms of a,

(a) the area of R,

(b) the volume, V_x, of the solid formed when R is rotated
completely about the x-axis.

The volume of the solid formed when R is rotated
completely about the y-axis is V_y. Show that $V_y = \frac{8}{15} V_x$.

The region S, lying in the first quadrant, is bounded by the
curve $y^2 = 4a(a - x)$ and the lines $y = a$ and $y = 2a$. Find,
in terms of a, the volume of the solid formed when S is
rotated completely about the y-axis.   (OCR, adapted)

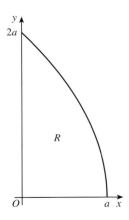

Practice examination 1

Time 1 hour 45 minutes

Answer all the questions.
The use of an electronic calculator is expected, where appropriate.

1 The 3rd and 4th terms of a geometric progression are 12 and 8 respectively. Find the sum to infinity of the progression. [5]

2 (i) Find $\int \left(\dfrac{1}{x^2} - \dfrac{1}{\sqrt{x}} \right) dx$. [4]

   (ii) A curve passes through the point $(1,0)$ and is such that $\dfrac{dy}{dx} = \dfrac{1}{x^2} - \dfrac{1}{\sqrt{x}}$. Find the equation of the curve. [2]

3 Points A and B have coordinates $(3,2)$ and $(-1,4)$ respectively.

   (i) Find the equation of the straight line which is perpendicular to AB and which passes through its mid-point. [4]

   (ii) Verify that the point C with coordinates $(0,1)$ lies on this line, and calculate the area of the triangle ABC. [3]

4 (i) Show that the equation $3\tan\theta = 2\cos\theta$ may be written in the form
$$2\sin^2\theta + 3\sin\theta - 2 = 0.$$
[3]

   (ii) Hence solve the equation $3\tan\theta = 2\cos\theta$, for $0 \le \theta \le 2\pi$. [4]

5 (i) Express the quadratic polynomial $x^2 + 6x + 3$ in completed square form. [2]

   (ii) Hence, or otherwise,

   (a) find the coordinates of the vertex of the graph of $y = x^2 + 6x + 3$, [2]

   (b) solve the inequality $x^2 + 6x + 3 < 0$, leaving your answer in an exact form. [3]

6 The functions f and g are defined by
$$\mathrm{f}: x \mapsto \frac{1}{x}, \qquad 0 < x \le 3,$$
$$\mathrm{g}: x \mapsto 2x - 1, \qquad x \in \mathbb{R}.$$

   (i) Using a graphical method, or otherwise, find the range of f. [1]

   (ii) Calculate $\mathrm{gf}(2)$. [1]

   (iii) Find an expression in terms of x for $\mathrm{g}^{-1}(x)$. [2]

   (iv) Sketch, in a single diagram, the graphs of $y = \mathrm{g}(x)$ and $y = \mathrm{g}^{-1}(x)$, and state a geometrical relationship between these graphs. [3]

7 (i) Solve the simultaneous equations

$$2x^2 + xy = 10,$$
$$x + y = 3.$$

[5]

(ii) Show that the simultaneous equations

$$2x^2 + xy = 10,$$
$$x + y = a.$$

always have two distinct solutions, for all possible values of the constant a.   [3]

8

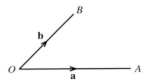

The diagram shows the origin O, and points A and B whose position vectors are denoted by **a** and **b** respectively.

(i) Copy the diagram, and show the positions of the points P and Q such that $\overrightarrow{OP} = 3\mathbf{a}$ and $\overrightarrow{OQ} = \mathbf{a} + \mathbf{b}$.   [2]

(ii) Given that $\mathbf{a} = \begin{pmatrix} 2 \\ 0 \end{pmatrix}$ and $\mathbf{b} = \begin{pmatrix} 1 \\ 1 \end{pmatrix}$, evaluate the scalar product $\overrightarrow{OQ}.\overrightarrow{BP}$.   [3]

(iii) Calculate the acute angle between the lines OQ and BP, giving your answer correct to the nearest degree.   [3]

9 A circle with centre O has radius r cm. A sector of the circle, which has an angle of θ radians at O, has perimeter 6 cm.

(i) Show that $\theta = \dfrac{6}{r} - 2$, and express the area A cm^2 of the sector in terms of r.   [4]

(ii) Show that A is a maximum, and not a minimum, when $r = \frac{3}{2}$, and calculate the corresponding value of θ.   [5]

10

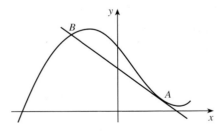

The diagram shows the curve $y = 4x^3 - 4x^2 - 10x + 12$ and the tangent at the point A where $x = 1$.

(i) Find the equation of this tangent.   [4]

(ii) Verify that this tangent meets the curve again at the point B with x-coordinate -1. [2]

(iii) Calculate the area of the region which lies between the curve and the tangent AB. [5]

8 $y = 0$

9 $y = -2x$

10 $12y = 12x - 17$

11 $x = 1$

12 $7y = -x + 64$

14 (a) $0.499\,875\ldots$ (b) $0.500\,012\ldots$
(c) $0.249\,968\ldots$ (d) $0.250\,015\ldots$
(e) $0.999\,999\ldots$ (f) $1.000\,001\ldots$

Exercise 6D (page 86)

1 (a) $3x^2 + 4x$ (b) $-6x^2 + 6x$
(c) $3x^2 - 12x + 11$ (d) $6x^2 - 6x + 1$
(e) $4x - 24x^3$ (f) $-3x^2$

2 (a) -10 (b) 6 (c) 58
(d) -1 (e) 8 (f) 12

3 (a) $-2, 2$ (b) $-\frac{4}{3}, 2$ (c) $-5, 7$
(d) 1 (e) $-1, -\frac{1}{3}$ (f) No values

4 (a) $\dfrac{1}{\sqrt{x}}$ (b) $\dfrac{1}{\sqrt{x}} + 1$ (c) $1 - \dfrac{1}{4\sqrt{x}}$

(d) $1 - \dfrac{1}{\sqrt{x}}$ (e) $1 + \dfrac{1}{x^2}$ (f) $2x + 1 - \dfrac{1}{x^2}$

(g) $1 - \dfrac{2}{x^2}$ (h) $1 + \dfrac{1}{\sqrt{x}}$

5 $y = 4x + 2$

6 $y = x + 2$

7 $4y = x + 4$

8 $4y = -x + 4$

9 $x = 1$

11 $y = -2x - 6$

12 $y = -a^2 x,\ y = 2a^2 x + 2a^3,\ y = 2a^2 x - 2a^3$

13 $\left(\frac{1}{2}, -2\right)$

14 (a) $-\dfrac{1}{4x^2}$ (b) $-\dfrac{6}{x^3}$ (c) 0

(d) $\dfrac{3}{4\sqrt[4]{x}}$ (e) $\dfrac{2}{3\sqrt[3]{x^2}}$ (f) $-\dfrac{2}{\sqrt{x^3}}$

(g) $-\dfrac{3}{x^2} - \dfrac{1}{x^4}$ (h) $10\sqrt{x^3}$ (i) $\dfrac{3}{2}\sqrt{x}$

(j) $-\dfrac{1}{6\sqrt[3]{x^4}}$ (k) $\dfrac{4-x}{x^3}$ (l) $\dfrac{3x-1}{4\sqrt[4]{x^5}}$

15 $3y - x = 4,\ y + 3x = 28$

16 $(0, 12),\ \left(\frac{3}{4}, 0\right)$

Exercise 6E (page 93)

1 $f'(p) = 3p^2$

2 $f'(p) = 8p^7$

3 $f'(p) = -\dfrac{2}{p^3}$

Miscellaneous exercise 6 (page 94)

1 $y = 13x - 16$

2 (a) -9 (b) $-\dfrac{19}{3}, 3$

3 $80y = 32x - 51$

4 $\left(-3, -\frac{1}{3}\right)$

5 2

6 $\left(-\frac{1}{3}, -4\frac{17}{27}\right),\ (2, 13)$

7 $x + 19y - 153 = 0$

8 13

9 $(2, 12)$

10 2

11 Both curves have gradient 12.

12 -183

13 $mn = -1$

14 $\left(\dfrac{11}{20}, \dfrac{4}{5}\right)$

15 $\left(\dfrac{67}{32}, \dfrac{5}{8}\right)$

7 Applications of differentiation

Exercise 7A (page 96)

3 (a) (b) (c) (d)

4 (a) (b)

Exercise 7B (page 103)

1 (a) $2x - 5,\ x \geqslant \frac{5}{2}$ (b) $2x + 6,\ x \geqslant -3$
(c) $-3 - 2x,\ x \leqslant -\frac{3}{2}$ (d) $6x - 5,\ x \geqslant \frac{5}{6}$
(e) $10x + 3,\ x \geqslant -\frac{3}{10}$ (f) $-4 - 6x,\ x \leqslant -\frac{2}{3}$

2 (a) $2x + 4,\ x \leqslant -2$ (b) $2x - 3,\ x \leqslant \frac{3}{2}$
(c) $-3 + 2x,\ x \leqslant \frac{3}{2}$ (d) $4x - 8,\ x \leqslant 2$
(e) $7 - 4x,\ x \geqslant \frac{7}{4}$ (f) $-5 - 14x,\ x \geqslant -\frac{5}{14}$

3 (a) $3x^2 - 12,\ x \leqslant -2$ and $x \geqslant 2$
(b) $6x^2 - 18,\ x \leqslant -\sqrt{3}$ and $x \geqslant \sqrt{3}$
(c) $6x^2 - 18x - 24,\ x \leqslant -1$ and $x \geqslant 4$
(d) $3x^2 - 6x + 3,$ all x
(e) $4x^3 - 4x,\ -1 \leqslant x \leqslant 0$ and $x \geqslant 1$
(f) $4x^3 + 12x^2,\ x \geqslant -3$
(g) $3 - 3x^2,\ -1 \leqslant x \leqslant 1$
(h) $10x^4 - 20x^3,\ x \leqslant 0$ and $x \geqslant 2$
(i) $3(1 + x^2),$ all x

4 (a) $3x^2 - 27, -3 \leqslant x \leqslant 3$

(b) $4x^3 + 8x, x \leqslant 0$

(c) $3x^2 - 6x + 3$, none

(d) $12 - 6x^2, x \leqslant -\sqrt{2}$ and $x \geqslant \sqrt{2}$

(e) $6x^2 + 6x - 36, -3 \leqslant x \leqslant 2$

(f) $12x^3 - 60x^2, x \leqslant 5$

(g) $72x - 8x^3, -3 \leqslant x \leqslant 0$ and $x \geqslant 3$

(h) $5x^4 - 5, -1 \leqslant x \leqslant 1$

(i) $nx^{n-1} - n$; $x \leqslant 1$ if n is even,
     $-1 \leqslant x \leqslant 1$ if n is odd

5 (a) $\frac{1}{2}x^{1/2}(5x-3); 0 < x < \frac{3}{5}$; $x \geqslant \frac{3}{5}$

(b) $\frac{1}{4}x^{-1/4}(3-14x); x \geqslant \frac{3}{14}; 0 \leqslant x \leqslant \frac{3}{14}$

(c) $\frac{1}{3}x^{-1/3}(5x+4); -\frac{4}{5} \leqslant x \leqslant 0$;

   $x \leqslant -\frac{4}{5}$ and $x \geqslant 0$

(d) $\frac{13}{5}x^{-2/5}(x^2-3); -\sqrt{3} \leqslant x \leqslant \sqrt{3}$;

   $x \leqslant -\sqrt{3}$ and $x \geqslant \sqrt{3}$

(e) $1 - \frac{3}{x^2}; -\sqrt{3} \leqslant x < 0$ and $0 < x \leqslant \sqrt{3}$;

   $x \leqslant -\sqrt{3}$ and $x \geqslant \sqrt{3}$

(f) $\frac{x-1}{2x\sqrt{x}}; 0 < x \leqslant 1; x \geqslant 1$

6 (a) (i) $(4,-12)$ (ii) minimum (iv) $f(x) \geqslant -12$

(b) (i) $(-2,-7)$ (ii) minimum (iv) $f(x) \geqslant -7$

(c) (i) $\left(-\frac{3}{5},\frac{1}{5}\right)$ (ii) minimum (iv) $f(x) \geqslant \frac{1}{5}$

(d) (i) $(-3,13)$ (ii) maximum (iv) $f(x) \leqslant 13$

(e) (i) $(-3,0)$ (ii) minimum (iv) $f(x) \geqslant 0$

(f) (i) $\left(-\frac{1}{2},2\right)$ (ii) maximum (iv) $f(x) \leqslant 2$

7 (a) $(-4,213)$, maximum; $(3,-130)$, minimum

(b) $(-3,88)$, maximum; $(5,-168)$, minimum

(c) $(0,0)$, minimum; $(1,1)$, neither

(d) $(-2,65)$, maximum; $(0,1)$, neither;
    $(2,-63)$, minimum

(e) $\left(-\frac{1}{3},-\frac{11}{27}\right)$, minimum; $\left(\frac{1}{2},\frac{3}{4}\right)$, maximum

(f) $(-1,0)$, neither

(g) $(-1,-2)$, maximum; $(1,2)$, minimum

(h) $(3,27)$, minimum

(i) none

(j) $\left(\frac{1}{4},-\frac{1}{4}\right)$, minimum

(k) $\left(6,\frac{1}{12}\right)$, maximum

(l) $(-2,17)$, minimum

(m) $(1,3)$, maximum

(n) $(-1,-5)$, minimum

(o) $(0,0)$, minimum; $\left(\frac{4}{5},\frac{256}{3125}\right)$, maximum

8 (a) $f(x) \geqslant \frac{3}{4}$

(b) $f(x) \geqslant -16$

(c) $f(x) \leqslant -2, f(x) \geqslant 2$

Exercise 7C (page 109)

1 (a) Gradient of road

(b) Rate of increase of crowd

(c) Rate of increase (or decrease if nega
    magnetic force with respect to distanc

(d) Acceleration of particle

(e) Rate of increase of petrol consumption
    respect to speed

2 (a) $\dfrac{dp}{dh}$, p in millibars, h in metres

(b) $\dfrac{d\theta}{dt}$, θ in degrees C, t in hours

(c) $\dfrac{dh}{dt}$, h in metres, t in hours

(d) $\dfrac{dW}{dt}$, W in kilograms, t in weeks

3 (a) $6t+7$ (b) $1 - \dfrac{1}{2\sqrt{x}}$

(c) $1 - \dfrac{6}{y^3}$ (d) $2t - \dfrac{1}{2t\sqrt{t}}$

(e) $2t+6$ (f) $12s^5 - 6s$

(g) 5 (h) $-\dfrac{2}{r^3} - 1$

4 (a) Velocity

(b) (i) Increasing (ii) Decreasing

(c) 9, occurs when velocity is zero and direction
    of motion changes

5 (a) $\dfrac{dx}{dt} = c$

(b) $\dfrac{dA}{dt} = kA$; A stands for the amount deposited

(c) $\dfrac{dx}{dt} = f(\theta)$; x stands for diameter, θ for air
    temperature

6 80 km h^{-1}

7 20 m

8 36

9 $4\sqrt{5}$

10 Greatest $V = 32\pi$ when $r = 4$,
     least $V = 0$ when $r = 0$ or $h = 0$

11 25

12 (b) 1800 m^2

13 $0 < x < 20$, 7.36 cm

14 20 cm

15 (b) $38\,400$ cm^3 (to 3 s.f.)

16 2420 cm^3 (to 3 s.f.)

Miscellaneous exercise 7 (page 110)

1 Maximum at $(-2,-4)$; minimum at $(2,4)$;
  y increases with x for $x \leqslant -2$ and $x \geqslant 2$

2 (a) $\dfrac{dn}{dt} = kn$ (b) $\dfrac{d\theta}{dt} = -k\theta$

  (c) $\dfrac{d\theta}{dt} = -k(\theta - \beta)$

4 $(20 - 4t)$ m s^{-1}, -4 m s^{-2}; for $0 \leqslant t \leqslant 5$

5 (a) 20 m (b) 6 s (c) 40 m s^{-1}

6 50

7 (a) $9\sqrt{2}$ cm (b) $40\frac{1}{2}$ cm^2

8 (a) $(-1,-7), (2,20)$
  (b) Graph crosses the x-axis three times.
  (c) $y = -5$ has three intersections with graph.
  (d) (i) $-20 < k < 7$ (ii) $k < -20$ and $k > 7$

9 $(-2,4)$, $(2,-28)$; $-28 \leqslant k \leqslant 4$

10 $\left(-\frac{2}{3}, \frac{4}{27}\right)$, $(0,0)$; $0 < k < \frac{4}{27}$

11 $(-1,5), (2,-22), (0,10)$;
  (a) $5 < k < 10$ (b) $-22 < k < 5$ and $k > 10$

12 $\left(\frac{1}{3}, \frac{4}{27}\right)$, $(1,0)$; $k < -\dfrac{2}{3\sqrt{3}}$ and $k > \dfrac{2}{3\sqrt{3}}$

13 (a) $P = 2x + 2r + \frac{1}{2}\pi r$, $A = \frac{1}{4}\pi r^2 + rx$
  (b) $x = \frac{1}{4}r(4 - \pi)$

14 Maximum at $\left(2, \frac{1}{4}\right)$
  (a) $\left(2, 5\frac{1}{4}\right)$
  (b) $\left(3, \frac{1}{2}\right)$; that is, when $x - 1 = 2$

16 (a) $1100 - 20x$ (b) $£x(1100 - 20x)$
  (c) $£(24\,000 - 400x)$;
  $£37.50$

17 (a) The gradient at P' is the negative of the gradient at P. So $f'(-p) = -f'(p)$. The derivative of an even function is odd.

8 Sequences

Exercise 8A (page 115)

1 (a) $7, 14, 21, 28, 35$ (b) $13, 8, 3, -2, -7$
  (c) $4, 12, 36, 108, 324$ (d) $6, 3, 1.5, 0.75, 0.375$
  (e) $2, 7, 22, 67, 202$ (f) $1, 4, 19, 364, 132\,499$

2 (a) $u_1 = 2, u_{r+1} = u_r + 2$
  (b) $u_1 = 11, u_{r+1} = u_r - 2$
  (c) $u_1 = 2, u_{r+1} = u + 4$
  (d) $u_1 = 2, u_{r+1} = 3u_r$
  (e) $u_1 = \frac{1}{3}, u_{r+1} = \frac{1}{3}u_r$
  (f) $u_1 = \frac{1}{2}a, u_{r+1} = \frac{1}{2}u_r$
  (g) $u_1 = b - 2c, u_{r+1} = u_r + c$
  (h) $u_1 = 1, u_{r+1} = -u_r$

(i) $u_1 = \dfrac{p}{q^3}, u_{r+1} = qu_r$

(j) $u_1 = \dfrac{a^3}{b^2}, u_{r+1} = \dfrac{bu_r}{a}$

(k) $u_1 = x^3, u_{r+1} = \dfrac{5u_r}{x}$

(l) $u_1 = 1, u_{r+1} = (1 + x)u_r$

3 (a) $5, 7, 9, 11, 13; u_1 = 5, u_{r+1} = u_r + 2$
  (b) $1, 4, 9, 16, 25; u_1 = 1, u_{r+1} = u_r + 2r + 1$
  (c) $1, 3, 6, 10, 15; u_1 = 1, u_{n+1} = u_r + r + 1$
  (d) $1, 5, 14, 30, 55; u_1 = 1, u_{n+1} = u_r + (r + 1)^2$
  (e) $6, 18, 54, 162, 486; u_1 = 6, u_{r+1} = 3u_r$
  (f) $3, 15, 75, 375, 1875; u_1 = 3, u_{r+1} = 5u_r$

4 (a) $u_r = 10 - r$ (b) $u_r = 2 \times 3^r$
  (c) $u_r = r^2 + 3$ (d) $u_r = 2r(r + 1)$
  (e) $u_r = \dfrac{2r - 1}{r + 3}$ (f) $u_n = \dfrac{r^2 + 1}{2^r}$

Exercise 8B (page 119)

2 (a) r (c) $1^3 = t_1^2 - t_0^2, 2^3 = t_2^2 - t_1^2,$
  $3^3 = t_3^2 - t_2^2, \dots, n^3 = t_n^2 - t_{n-1}^2$

3 (a) 5040 (b) 6720 (c) 35

4 (a) $\dfrac{8!}{4!}$ (b) $\dfrac{12!}{8!}$ (c) $\dfrac{n!}{(n-3)!}$

  (d) $\dfrac{(n+1)!}{(n-2)!}$ (e) $\dfrac{(n+3)!}{(n-1)!}$ (f) $\dfrac{(n+6)!}{(n+3)!}$

  (g) $8!$ (h) $n!$

5 (a) 12 (b) $22 \times 22!$
  (c) $n + 1$ (d) $n \times n!$

7 (a) $1, 5, 10, 10, 5, 1, 0, 0, \dots$
  (b) $1, 6, 15, 20, 15, 6, 1, 0, 0, \dots$
  (c) $1, 8, 28, 56, 70, 56, 28, 8, 1, 0, 0, \dots$

8 (a) $\dfrac{11!}{4! \times 7!}$ (b) $\dfrac{11!}{7! \times 4!}$ (c) $\dfrac{10!}{5! \times 5!}$

  (d) $\dfrac{12!}{3! \times 9!}$ (e) $\dfrac{12!}{9! \times 3!}$

10 $\dbinom{n}{r} + \dbinom{n}{r+1} = \dbinom{n+1}{r+1}$

11 The sum of the terms in the sequence is 2^n.

Exercise 8C (page 124)

1 (a), (d), (f), (h); 3, -2, q, x respectively

2 (a) $12, 2r$ (b) $32, 14 + 3r$
  (c) $-10, 8 - 3r$ (d) $3.3, 0.9 + 0.4r$
  (e) $3\frac{1}{2}, \frac{1}{2} + \frac{1}{2}r$ (f) $43, 79 - 6r$
  (g) $x + 10, x - 2 + 2r$ (h) $1 + 4x, 1 - 2x + xr$

3 (a) 14 (b) 88 (c) 36
  (d) 11 (e) 11 (f) 11
  (g) 16 (h) 28

4   (a)   610   (b)   795

    (c) -102 (d) $855\frac{1}{2}$

    (e) -1025 (f) $998\,001$

    (g) $3160a$ (h) $-15\,150\,p$

5   (a) $54, 3132$ (b) $20,920$

    (c) $46, 6532$ (d) $28, -910$

    (e) $28, 1120$ (f) $125, 42\,875$

    (g) $1000, 5\,005\,000$ (h) $61, -988.2$

6   (a) $a = 3, d = 4$ (b) $a = 2, d = 5$

    (c) $a = 1.4, d = 0.3$ (d) $a = 12, d = -2.5$

    (e) $a = 25, d = -3$ (f) $a = -7, d = 2$

    (g) $a = 3x, d = -x$ (h) $a = p+1, d = \frac{1}{2}p+3$

7   (a)   20   (b)   12   (c)   16

    (d)   40   (e)   96   (f)   28

8   (a)   62   (b)   25

9   (a)   \$76   (b)   \$1272

10   (a)   5050   (b) $15\,050$ (c) $\frac{1}{2}n(3n+1)$

11   \$1\,626\,000

Miscellaneous exercise 8 (page 125)

1   (a)   (i) $1, 2, 5, 14, 41$ (ii) $2, 5, 14, 41, 122$

       (iii) $0, -1, -4, -13, -40$

       (iv) $\frac{1}{2}, \frac{1}{2}, \frac{1}{2}, \frac{1}{2}, \frac{1}{2}$

    (b)   (i) $b = \frac{1}{2}$ (ii) $b = \frac{3}{2}$ (iii) $b = -\frac{1}{2}$

       (iv) $b = 0$

2   1444

3   (a) $3, 1, 3$; alternately 1 and 3

    (b)   All terms after the first are 2   (c)   2

4   (a)   Alternately 0 and -1; 1, then alternately 0 and -1; gets increasingly large

    (b) $\frac{1}{2}\left(1 \pm \sqrt{5}\right)$

5 $n(2n+3)$

6   168

7 -750

8 $2n - \frac{1}{2}$

9 $167\,167$; $111\,445$

10   40

11   (a)   991   (b) $50\,045.5$

12   (a)   18   (b) $2(2n+1)$

    (c) $a = 6, d = 4$, sum $= 2\,004\,000$

13 $71\,240$

14   (a)   47, 12 years left over   (b)   £345\,450

15 $a = \dfrac{10\,000}{n} - 5(n-1)$; 73

16   (a) $0, 1, 4, 9, 16; r^2$ (b) $0, 1, 2, 3, 4; r$

    (c) $1, 2, 4, 8, 16; 2^r$

9   The binomial theorem

Exercise 9A (page 130)

1   (a) $4x^2 + 4xy + y^2$

    (b) $25x^2 + 30xy + 9y^2$

    (c) $16 + 56p + 49p^2$

    (d) $1 - 16t + 64t^2$

    (e) $1 - 10x^2 + 25x^4$

    (f) $4 + 4x^3 + x^6$

    (g) $x^6 + 3x^4y^3 + 3x^2y^6 + y^9$

    (h) $27x^6 + 54x^4y^3 + 36x^2y^6 + 8y^9$

2   (a) $x^3 + 6x^2 + 12x + 8$

    (b) $8p^3 + 36p^2q + 54pq^2 + 27q^3$

    (c) $1 - 12x + 48x^2 - 64x^3$

    (d) $1 - 3x^3 + 3x^6 - x^9$

3   (a)   42   (b)   150

4   (a)   240   (b)   54

5   (a) $1 + 10x + 40x^2 + 80x^3 + 80x^4 + 32x^5$

    (b) $p^6 + 12p^5q + 60p^4q^2 + 160p^3q^3$
$$+ 240p^2q^4 + 192pq^5 + 64q^6$$

    (c) $16m^4 - 96m^3n + 216m^2n^2 - 216mn^3 + 81n^4$

    (d) $1 + 2x + \frac{3}{2}x^2 + \frac{1}{2}x^3 + \frac{1}{16}x^4$

6   (a)   270   (b) -1000

7 $1 + 2x + 5x^2 + 4x^3 + 4x^4$

8 $x^3 + 12x^2 + 48x + 64$;

    $x^4 + 13x^3 + 60x^2 + 112x + 64$

9 $72x^5 + 420x^4 + 950x^3 + 1035x^2 + 540x + 108$

10   7

11 $x^{11} + 11x^{10}y + 55x^9y^2 + 165x^8y^3 + 330x^7y^4$
$$+ 462x^6y^5 + 462x^5y^6 + 330x^4y^7$$
$$+ 165x^3y^8 + 55x^2y^9 + 11xy^{10} + y^{11}$$

12 $59\,136$

Exercise 9B (page 134)

1   (a)   35   (b)   28   (c)   126   (d)   715

    (e)   15   (f)   45   (g)   11   (h)   1225

2   (a)   10   (b) -56 (c)   165   (d) -560

3   (a)   84   (b) -1512 (c)   4032   (d) $-\frac{99}{4}$

4   (a)   3003   (b) $192\,192$

    (c) $560\,431\,872$ (d) $48\,048$

5   (a) $1 + 13x + 78x^2 + 286x^3$

    (b) $1 - 15x + 105x^2 - 455x^3$

    (c) $1 + 30x + 405x^2 + 3240x^3$

    (d) $128 - 2240x + 16\,800x^2 - 70\,000x^3$

6   (a) $1 + 22x + 231x^2$

    (b) $1 - 30x + 435x^2$

    (c) $1 - 72x + 2448x^2$

    (d) $1 + 114x + 6156x^2$

7 $1+16x+112x^2$; 1.17

8 $4096+122\,880x+1\,689\,600x^2$; 4220.57

9 $1+32x+480x^2+4480x^3$; 5920

10 $1-30x+405x^2$; 234

11   7

12 $2+56x^2+140x^4+56x^6+2x^8$;
2.005 601 400 056 000 2

13 $a=4, n=9$

Miscellaneous exercise 9 (page 135)

1 $27+108x+144x^2+64x^3$

2   (a) $1+40x+720x^2$ (b) $1-32x+480x^2$

3   (a) $-48\,384$ (b) $\frac{875}{4}$

4 $2187+25515x+127575x^2$; 2455

5 $256+256x+112x^2+28x^3$; 258.571

6 $256-3072x+16128x^2$; 253

7 $x^6+3x^3+3+\dfrac{1}{x^3}$

8 $16x^4-96x+\dfrac{216}{x^2}-\dfrac{216}{x^5}+\dfrac{81}{x^8}$

9 $2x^6+\dfrac{15x^2}{2}+\dfrac{15}{8x^2}+\dfrac{1}{32x^6}$

10   48

11   20 000

12   495;   (a) 40 095   (b) 7920   (c) $\dfrac{495}{16}$

13   30

14 $1+40x+760x^2$;
(a) 1.0408   (b) 0.9230

15 $1024-\dfrac{2560}{x^2}+\dfrac{2880}{x^4}$; 999

16   B, D

17 $\dfrac{7}{16}$

18   5376

19 $\dfrac{6435}{128}$

20 -2024

21 $1+12x+70x^2$; 1.127

22 $270x^2+250$; $\pm\frac{4}{3}$

23 $\pm\frac{5}{6}$

24   (a) $1+5\alpha t+10\alpha^2 t^2$ (b) $1-8\beta t+28\beta^2 t^2$;
$10\alpha^2-40\alpha\beta+28\beta^2$

25   (b) (i) 4 or 7   (ii) 3 or 13
(iii) 7 or 13   (iv) 17 or 28

27   (b) (i) $a=3, b=6, c=8$
(ii) $a=6, b=4, c=9$

29   1.005 413 792 056 807

30   (a) $217+88\sqrt{6}$ (b) $698\sqrt{2}+569\sqrt{3}$

31   (a) 568; 567 and 568   (b) 969 and 970

32 $2n(n+1)$

33 $a=-\frac{1}{6}, b=\frac{1}{2}, c=-\frac{1}{2}, d=\frac{1}{6}$

10 Trigonometry

Exercise 10A (page 141)

1   (a) (i) 0.9063   (ii) 0.4226   (iii) 0.4663
(b) (i) -0.5736 (ii) 0.8192   (iii) -1.4281
(c) (i) -0.7071 (ii) -0.7071 (iii) 1
(d) (i) 0.8192   (ii) -0.5736 (iii) -0.7002
(e) (i) -0.3420 (ii) 0.9397   (iii) -2.7475
(f) (i) 0.3843   (ii) 0.9232   (iii) 2.4023
(g) (i) -0.5721 (ii) 0.8202   (iii) -1.4335
(h) (i) -0.9703 (ii) -0.2419 (iii) 0.2493

2   (a) max 3 at $x=90$, min 1 at $x=270$
(b) max 11 at $x=180$, min 3 at $x=360$
(c) max 13 at $x=180$, min -3 at $x=90$
(d) max 4 at $x=90$, min 2 at $x=270$
(e) max 10 at $x=27\frac{1}{2}$, min 8 at $x=72\frac{1}{2}$
(f) max 5 at $x=90$, min 1.875 at $x=450$

3   (a) 160   (b) 320   (c) 240
(d) 50   (e) 220   (f) 340
(g) 40, 140   (h) 30, 330   (i) 70, 250
(j) 80, 100   (k) 160, 200   (l) 100, 280

4   (a) 160   (b) -40 (c) -120
(d) 50   (e) -140 (f) -20
(g) 40, 140   (h) 30   (i) $-110, 70$
(j) 80, 100   (k) ±160 (l) $-80, 100$

5   (a) $\frac{1}{2}\sqrt{2}$ (b) $-\frac{1}{2}$ (c) $-\frac{1}{2}$ (d) $\sqrt{3}$
(e) $-\frac{1}{2}\sqrt{2}$ (f) $\frac{1}{2}\sqrt{3}$ (g) -1 (h) $-\frac{1}{2}\sqrt{3}$
(i) $-\frac{1}{2}\sqrt{2}$ (j) 0   (k) 1   (l) $\frac{1}{2}\sqrt{2}$
(m) $-\frac{1}{2}$ (n) -1 (o) $-\frac{1}{2}$ (p) 0

6   (a) 60   (b) 240   (c) 120   (d) 30
(e) 30   (f) 135   (g) 210   (h) 90

7   (a) 120   (b) 60   (c) -90 (d) 180
(e) 60   (f) -30 (g) -45 (h) 0

8 $A=5, B=2.8$; 7.42 m

Exercise 10B (page 144)

3   (a) 90   (b) 45   (c) 180   (d) 30
(e) 360   (f) $11\frac{1}{4}$

Exercise 10C (page 148)

1   (a) 5.7, 174.3   (b) 237.1, 302.9
(c) 72.0, 108.0   (d) 36.9, 323.1
(e) 147.1, 212.9   (f) 35.3, 324.7
(g) 76.0, 256.0   (h) 162.3, 342.3
(i) 6.3, 186.3   (j) 203.6, 336.4
(k) 214.8, 325.2   (l) 161.6, 341.6

(m) 49.5, 160.5   (n) 240, 360
(o) 10, 70

2 (a) 53.1, 126.9   (b) ±75.5
(c) −116.6, 63.4   (d) −137.9, −42.1
(e) ±96.9   (f) −36.9, 143.1
(g) −128.7, 51.3   (h) ±45, ±135
(i) 0, ±60, ±180

3 (a) 35.3, 144.7, 215.3, 324.7
(b) 21.1, 81.1, 141.1, 201.1, 261.1, 321.1
(c) 108.4, 161.6, 288.4, 341.6
(d) 26.1, 63.9, 116.1, 153.9, 206.1, 243.9,
     296.1, 333.9
(e) 10.9, 100.9, 190.9, 280.9
(f) 68.3, 111.7, 188.3, 231.7, 308.3, 351.7

4 (a) ±16.1, ±103.9, ±136.1
(b) −125.8, −35.8, 54.2, 144.2
(c) −176.2, −123.8, −56.2, −3.8, 63.8, 116.2,
(d) ±37.9, ±142.1
(e) −172.3, −136.3, −100.3, −64.3, −28.3, 7.7
     43.7, 79.7, 115.7, 151.7
(f) −78.5, −11.5, 101.5, 168.5

5 (a) ±96.4   (b) −107.3, 162.7
(c) −56.0   (d) No roots in the interval
(e) 35.4   (f) −43.6

6 (a) 30, 90, 210, 270
(b) 22.5, 112.5, 202.5, 292.5
(c) 65, 85, 185, 205, 305, 325
(d) 110, 230, 350
(e) 85, 145, 265, 325
(f) 80
(g) No roots in the interval
(h) 45, 105, 165, 225, 285, 345
(i) 80

7 (a) −170.8, −9.2
(b) −90, 90
(c) −180, −135, 0, 45, 180
(d) −173.4, −96.6, 6.6, 83.4
(e) 11.3, 78.7
(f) −150.5, −90.5, −30.5, 29.5, 89.5, 149.5

8 (a) 27, 63, 207, 243
(b) 4, 68, 76, 140, 148, 212, 220, 284, 292, 356
(c) 20, 80, 140, 200, 260, 320

9 0, 60, 120, 180

10 For example,
(a) (i) $\sin 4\theta°$ (ii) $\cos 4\theta°$ (iii) $\tan 2\theta°$
(b) (i) $\sin 18\theta°$ (ii) $\cos 18\theta°$ (iii) $\tan 9\theta°$
(c) (i) $\sin \frac{15}{2}\theta°$ (ii) $\cos \frac{15}{2}\theta°$ (iii) $\tan \frac{15}{4}\theta°$
(d) (i) $\sin 3\theta°$ (ii) $\cos 3\theta°$ (iii) $\tan \frac{3}{2}\theta°$
(e) (i) $\sin \frac{1}{2}\theta°$ (ii) $\cos \frac{1}{2}\theta°$ (iii) $\tan \frac{1}{4}\theta°$
(f) (i) $\sin \frac{3}{5}\theta°$ (ii) $\cos \frac{3}{5}\theta°$ (iii) $\tan \frac{3}{10}\theta°$

11 (a) 120   (b) 180   (c) 90
(d) 540   (e) 720   (f) 720
(g) 120   (h) 90   (i) 360

12 (a) 0.986
(b) $A = 12, B = 6$, 6 hours 7 minutes
(c) Days 202, 345

Exercise 10D (page 152)

1 (a) (i) 11   (ii) $\frac{4}{5}, \frac{3}{5}, \frac{4}{3}$

(b) (i) 37.5   (ii) $\frac{15}{17}, \frac{8}{17}, \frac{15}{8}$

(c) (i) $\sqrt{13}$ (ii) $\frac{3}{13}\sqrt{13}, \frac{2}{13}\sqrt{13}, \frac{3}{2}$

(d) (i) 11   (ii) $\frac{5}{14}\sqrt{3}, \frac{11}{14}, \frac{5}{11}\sqrt{3}$

(e) (i) $17\sqrt{5}$ (ii) $\frac{22}{85}\sqrt{5}, \frac{31}{85}\sqrt{5}, \frac{22}{31}$

(f) (i) $12\sqrt{2}$ (ii) $\frac{1}{3}, \frac{2}{3}\sqrt{2}, \frac{1}{4}\sqrt{2}$

2 (a) $-\frac{11}{14}$ (b) $\frac{20}{29}$ (c) $\pm\frac{1}{2}\sqrt{3}$
(d) $0, \pm 78.5$ (to 1 d.p.)

4 (a) 30, 150, 210, 330   (b) 0, 180, 360
(c) 36.9, 143.1, 199.5, 340.5
(d) 0, 51.0, 180, 309.0, 360

5 −116.6, −26.6, 63.4, 153.4

Miscellaneous exercise 10 (page 152)

1 (a) 360   (b) 90

2 (a) $\cos x°$ (b) $-\cos x°$

3 (0, 1), (±180, 0)

4 (a) 21.8, 201.8   (b) 11.8, 78.2, 191.8, 258.2

5 24.1, 155.9

6 (a) Examples are $\tan x°$, $\sin 2x°$, $\cos 2x°$
(b) 10, 50, 130, 170

7 30, 270

8 (a) $2\sin 2x°$ (b) 105, 165, 285, 345

9 (a) 168.5   (b) 333.4   (c) 225   (d) 553.1

11 (a) 2, 0; 180, 90   (b) 9, 1; 240, 60
(c) 49, 9; 105, 45   (d) 8, 5; 90, 180
(e) 6, 3; 180, 360   (f) 60, 30; $7\frac{1}{2}, 52\frac{1}{2}$

12 (a) 0, 180, 360   (b) 0, 30, 150, 180, 360
(c) $67\frac{1}{2}, 157\frac{1}{2}, 247\frac{1}{2}, 337\frac{1}{2}$
(d) 30, 120, 210, 300

13 (a) 60   (b) 8.9, 68.9, 128.9
(c) (i) 51.1   (ii) 21.1

14 (a) $4.8 \pm 1.2\sin 15t°$ or $4.8 \pm 1.2\cos 15t°$
(b) $21\,500 \pm 6500\sin 36t°$ or
     $21\,500 \pm 6500\cos 36t°$
(c) $12 \pm 10\sin t°$ or $12 \pm 10\cos t°$

15 (a) 0.1 cm, 0.0009 seconds
(b) 0.0036 seconds
(c) 278   (d) 0.002 13 seconds

16 (a) 110 cm and 90 cm   (b) 0.36 seconds
(c) 0.72 seconds   (d) 0.468

17 (a) $k = \dfrac{360}{T}$ (b) $\dfrac{k}{360}$

18 (a) 7.2
(b) (i) $N - C$ (ii) $N + C$, after 37.5 weeks

19 (a) 30   (b) 3.25 m   (c) 27

20 $A = 0.5, B = 4.5, \alpha = 1, \beta = 12$

11 Combining and inverting functions

Exercise 11A (page 162)

1 (a) 121   (b) 4   (c) 676
2 (a) 17   (b) 8   (c) 152
3 (a) 1   (b) 4   (c) $\frac{1}{2}$
4 (a) 1   (b) 4   (c) $6\frac{1}{3}$
5 (a) 0   (b) 21
(c) $-3\frac{3}{4}$ (d) $x^2 - 4$
6 (a) 27   (b) 8
(c) $3\frac{3}{8}$ (d) $(\cos x° + 2)^3$
7 (a) 16   (b) 4
(c) 81   (d) $(2\sqrt{x} - 10)^2$
8 (a) $\times, 4, +, 9$ (b) $+, 9, =, \times, 4$
(c) square, $\times, 2, -, 5$ (d) $-5, =,$ square, $\times, 2$
(e) $\sqrt{\ }, -, 3, =,$ cube
(f) $\pm, 2, =,$ square, $+, 10, =, \sqrt{\ }$
9 (a) $\mathbb{R}, f(x) \geq 0$ (b) $\mathbb{R}, -1 \leq f(x) \leq 1$
(c) $x \geq 3, f(x) \geq 0$ (d) $\mathbb{R}, f(x) \geq 5$
(e) $x > 0, f(x) > 0$ (f) $\mathbb{R}, f(x) \leq 4$
(g) $0 \leq x \leq 4, 0 \leq f(x) \leq 2$
(h) $\mathbb{R}, f(x) \geq 6$ (i) $x \geq 3, f(x) \geq 0$
10 (a) 4   (b) -14 (c) -9 (d) 33
(e) 23   (f) -17 (g) 16   (h) 0
11 (a) 49   (b) 59   (c) 35
(d) $\frac{1}{16}$ (e) 9   (f) 899
12 (a) 7   (b) -19 (c) 1   (d) $\frac{1}{2}$
(e) $\frac{1}{2}$ (f) -1 (g) $3\frac{2}{3}$ (h) 2
13 (a) $x \mapsto 2x^2 + 5$ (b) $x \mapsto (2x + 5)^2$
(c) $x \mapsto \dfrac{2}{x} + 5$ (d) $x \mapsto \dfrac{1}{2x + 5}$
(e) $x \mapsto 4x + 15$ (f) $x \mapsto x$
(g) $x \mapsto \left(\dfrac{2}{x} + 5\right)^2$ (h) $x \mapsto \dfrac{1}{(2x + 5)^2}$

14 (a) $x \mapsto \sin x° - 3$ (b) $x \mapsto \sin(x - 3)°$
(c) $x \mapsto \sin(x^3 - 3)°$ (d) $x \mapsto \sin(x^3)°$
(e) $x \mapsto x - 9$ (f) $x \mapsto (\sin x°)^3$
15 (a) fh   (b) fg
(c) hh   (d) hg or ggh
(e) gf or fffg   (f) gffh
(g) fgfg or ffffgg   (h) hf
(i) hffg
16 (a) $x \geq 0, gf(x) \geq -5$
(b) $x \geq -3, gf(x) \geq 0$
(c) $x \neq 2, gf(x) \neq 0$
(d) $\mathbb{R}, 0 \leq gf(x) \leq 1$
(e) $\mathbb{R}, gf(x) \geq 0$
(f) $-4 \leq x \leq 4, 0 \leq gf(x) \leq 2$
(g) $x \leq -2$ or $x \geq 3, gf(x) \geq 0$
(h) $x < -2, gf(x) > 0$
17 (a) $-2\frac{2}{3}$ or 4   (b) 7   (c) 1
18 $a = 3, b = -7$ or $a = -3, b = 14$
19 $a = 4, b = 11$ or $a = 4\frac{1}{2}, b = 10$
21 (a) $t : r \mapsto \frac{1}{2}r(r + 1)$ (b) $f : r \mapsto a + (r - 1)d$
22 For p_r: (a) $\mathbb{N}$
(b) 2, 3, 5, 7, 11, 13, 17, 19, 23, 29, 31
(c) The set of prime numbers
For π: (a) $\mathbb{N}$
(b) 0, 1, 2, 2, 3, 3, 4, 4, 4, 4
(c) $\mathbb{N} \cup \{0\}$

Exercise 11B (page 169)

1 (a) $x \mapsto x - 4$ (b) $x \mapsto x + 5$
(c) $x \mapsto \frac{1}{2}x$ (d) $x \mapsto 4x$
(e) $x \mapsto \sqrt[3]{x}$ (f) $x \mapsto x^5$
2 (a) 10   (b) 7   (c) 3
(d) 5   (e) -4
3 (a) 4   (b) 20   (c) $\frac{7}{5}$
(d) 15   (e) -6
4 (a) 8   (b) $\frac{1}{8}$ (c) 512
(d) -27 (e) 5
5 a, d, f, g, k
6 a, c, e, f, g, h, j
7 (a) 0   (b) -1 (c) $\frac{2}{3}$
(d) 4   (e) -5 (f) -1
(g) $1\frac{1}{2}$ (h) 1   (i) 4
8 (a) $x \mapsto \frac{1}{3}(x + 1)$ (b) $x \mapsto 2(x - 4)$
(c) $x \mapsto \sqrt[3]{x - 5}$ (d) $x \mapsto (x + 3)^2, x > -3$
(e) $x \mapsto \frac{1}{5}(2x + 3)$ (f) $x \mapsto 1 + \sqrt{x - 6}, x \geq 6$
9 (a) $y \mapsto \frac{1}{6}(y - 5)$ (b) $y \mapsto 5y - 4$
(c) $y \mapsto \frac{1}{2}(4 - y)$ (d) $y \mapsto \frac{1}{2}(3y - 7)$
(e) $y \mapsto \sqrt[3]{\frac{1}{2}(y - 5)}$ (f) $y \mapsto \dfrac{1}{y - 4}, y \neq 4$

(g) $y \mapsto \dfrac{5}{y} + 1, y \neq 0$

(h) $y \mapsto \sqrt{y-7} - 2, y \geqslant 7$

(i) $y \mapsto \frac{1}{2}\left(3 + \sqrt{y+5}\right), y \geqslant -5$

(j) $y \mapsto 3 + \sqrt{y+9}, y \geqslant -9$

10 (a) $x \mapsto \frac{1}{4}x$ (b) $x \mapsto x - 3$

(c) $x \mapsto x^2, x \geqslant 0$ (d) $x \mapsto \frac{1}{2}(x-1)$

(e) $x \mapsto \sqrt{x} + 2, x \geqslant 0$ (f) $x \mapsto \frac{1}{3}(1-x)$

(g) $x \mapsto \dfrac{3}{x}, x \neq 0$ (h) $x \mapsto 7 - x$

12 (a) $y \mapsto \dfrac{2y}{y-1}, y \neq 1$ (b) $y \mapsto \dfrac{4y+1}{y-2}, y \neq 2$

(c) $y \mapsto \dfrac{5y+2}{y-1}, y \neq 1$ (d) $y \mapsto \dfrac{3y-11}{4y-3}, y \neq \frac{3}{4}$

13 (a) $\mathrm{f}(x) > -1$

(b) $x \mapsto 2 + \sqrt{x+1}, x > -1; \mathrm{f}^{-1}(x) > 2$

14 (a) $\mathrm{f}(x) > 3$

(b) $x \mapsto 2 + (x-3)^2, x > 3; \mathrm{f}^{-1}(x) > 2$

15 $k = -1$

(a) $\mathrm{f}(x) \geqslant 5$

(b) $x \mapsto -1 - \sqrt{x-5}, x \geqslant 5; \mathrm{f}^{-1}(x) \leqslant -1$

16 $a = \frac{1}{8}, b = \frac{3}{8}$

17 6

18 $x \mapsto \sqrt{x - 5\frac{3}{4}} - \frac{1}{2}, x > 6; \mathrm{f}^{-1}(x) > 0$

19 $x \mapsto 1 - \sqrt{-\frac{1}{2}(x+5)}, x < -5; \mathrm{f}^{-1}(x) < 1$

Miscellaneous exercise 11 (page 172)

1 (a) 29   (b) 61   (c) 2

(d) −3   (e) 290   (f) 497

2 (a) $\mathbb{R}, \mathrm{f}(x) \leqslant 4$ (b) $\mathbb{R}, \mathrm{f}(x) \geqslant -7$

(c) $x \geqslant -2, \mathrm{f}(x) \geqslant 0$ (d) $\mathbb{R}, \mathbb{R}$

(e) $\mathbb{R}, \mathrm{f}(x) \geqslant 0$ (f) $x \geqslant 0, \mathrm{f}(x) \leqslant 2$

3 (a) $x \mapsto (1-2x)^3$ (b) $x \mapsto 1 - 2x^3$

(c) $x \mapsto 1 - 2x^9$ (d) $x \mapsto 4x - 1$

(e) $x \mapsto \frac{1}{2}(1-x)$

4 (a) 48   (b) 3   (c) −1

(d) 4   (e) 4

5 (a) 12   (b) 27

6 $x \mapsto -3 + \sqrt{x-1}, x > 10$

7 $x \mapsto \sqrt[3]{\frac{1}{4}(x-3)}, x \in \mathbb{R}$; reflections in $y = x$

8 (a) $\sqrt{\frac{1}{3}(x+4)}$ (b) $3x^2 + 24x + 44$

9 (a) gf   (b) ff

(c) g^{-1} (d) fgh or fhg

(e) hfg   (f) f^{-1}

(g) g^{-1}fgh or g^{-1}fhg   (h) hf^{-1}

10 $\mathrm{f}^{-1}(x) = \sqrt{x-1}, x \geqslant 1$;

$\mathrm{gf}(x) = x^2 - 2, \mathrm{gf}(x) \geqslant -2$

11 $1 \pm \sqrt{3}$

12 $k = 1; x \mapsto 1 - \sqrt{x-6}, x \geqslant 6$

13 $a = -2, b = 11$ or $a = 2, b = -13$

14 (b) $-\sqrt{1-x}, x \leqslant 1$ (c) $-\frac{1}{2}$

15 (a) $x \mapsto \frac{1}{4}(x-5)$ (b) $x \mapsto \frac{1}{2}(3-x)$

(c) $x \mapsto -\frac{1}{8}(7+x)$ (d) $x \mapsto -8x - 7$

(e) $x \mapsto -\frac{1}{8}(7+x)$

16 (a) $x \mapsto \frac{1}{2}(x-7)$ (b) $x \mapsto \sqrt[3]{x+1}$

(c) $x \mapsto \sqrt[3]{\frac{1}{2}(x-5)}$ (d) $x \mapsto \frac{1}{2}\left(\sqrt[3]{x+1} - 7\right)$

(e) $x \mapsto 2x^3 + 5$ (f) $x \mapsto (2x+7)^3 - 1$

(g) $x \mapsto \sqrt[3]{\frac{1}{2}(x-5)}$ (h) $x \mapsto \frac{1}{2}\left(\sqrt[3]{x+1} - 7\right)$

17 (a) 3   (b) 7   (c) 3   (d) 7

18 (a) x (b) $\dfrac{x+5}{2x-1}$ (c) x

(d) x (e) $\dfrac{x+5}{2x-1}$

19 (a) $\dfrac{4}{2-x}$ (b) $\dfrac{4}{2-x}$ (c) x

(d) $\dfrac{2x-4}{x}$ (e) x (f) $\dfrac{2x-4}{x}$

12 Extending differentiation

Exercise 12A (page 174)

1 (a) $2(x+3)$ (b) $4(2x-3)$

(c) $-9(1-3x)^2$ (d) $3a(ax+b)^2$

(e) $-3a(b-ax)^2$ (f) $-5(1-x)^4$

(g) $8(2x-3)^3$ (h) $-8(3-2x)^3$

2 $na(ax+b)^{n-1}$

3 (a) $10(x+3)^9$ (b) $10(2x-1)^4$

(c) $-28(1-4x)^6$ (d) $15(3x-2)^4$

(e) $-12(4-2x)^5$ (f) $72(2+3x)^5$

(g) $10(2x+5)^4$ (h) $18(2x-3)^8$

Exercise 12B (page 176)

1 (a) $20(4x+5)^4$ (b) $16(2x-7)^7$

(c) $-6(2-x)^5$ (d) $2\left(\frac{1}{2}x+4\right)^3$

2 (a) $\dfrac{-3}{(3x+5)^2}$ (b) $\dfrac{2}{(4-x)^3}$

(c) $\dfrac{-6}{(2x+1)^4}$ (d) $\dfrac{-64}{(4x-1)^5}$

3 (a) $\dfrac{1}{\sqrt{2x+3}}$ (b) $\dfrac{2}{\sqrt[3]{(6x-1)^2}}$

(c) $\dfrac{-2}{\sqrt{(4x+7)^3}}$ (d) $\dfrac{-10}{\sqrt[3]{(3x-2)^5}}$

4 60

5 $(-6,125)$

6 $y = -\frac{3}{4}x - \frac{5}{4}$

7 $y = -3x + 48$

Exercise 12C (page 179)

1 (a) $30(5x+3)^5$ (b) $\frac{5}{2}(5x+3)^{-\frac{1}{2}}$

   (c) $\dfrac{-5}{(5x+3)^2}$

2 (a) $-20(1-4x)^4$ (b) $12(1-4x)^{-4}$

   (c) $\dfrac{-2}{\sqrt{1-4x}}$

3 (a) $15x^2(1+x^3)^4$ (b) $-12x^2(1+x^3)^{-5}$

   (c) $\dfrac{x^2}{(1+x^3)^{\frac{2}{3}}}$

4 (a) $24x(2x^2+3)^5$ (b) $\dfrac{-4x}{(2x^2+3)^2}$

   (c) $\dfrac{2}{\sqrt{(2x^2+3)^3}}$

5 $24x^3(3x^4+2)$

6 (a) $72x^8 + 72x^5 + 18x^2$ (b) $18x^2(2x^3+1)^2$

7 (a) $20x^4(x^5+1)^3$ (b) $48x^2(2x^3-1)^7$

   (c) $\dfrac{5}{2\sqrt{x}}(\sqrt{x}-1)^4$

8 (a) $8x(x^2+6)^3$ (b) $45x^2(5x^3+4)^2$

   (c) $28x^3(x^4-8)^6$ (d) $-45x^8(2-x^9)^4$

9 (a) $\dfrac{2}{\sqrt{(4x+3)}}$ (b) $12x(x^2+4)^5$

   (c) $-36x^2(6x^3-5)^{-3}$ (d) $3x^2(5-x^3)^{-2}$

10 (a) $-\frac{4}{25}$ (b) 0

11 $\frac{3}{8}$

12 (a) $6(x^2+3x+1)^5(2x+3)$ (b) $\dfrac{-3(2x+5)}{(x^2+5x)^4}$

13 $y = 12x - 25$

14 $x + 4y = 8$

15 $x + 6y = 23$

16 $6x(x^2-1)^{-\frac{1}{2}}(\sqrt{x^2-1}+1)^5$

17 $\dfrac{1}{\sqrt{(4x+3)(1+\sqrt{4x+3})}}$

18 $(0,3)$; minimum

Exercise 12D (page 182)

1 4500 per hour

2 0.622 °C per minute

3 (a) 4.8 cm s^{-1} (b) 24 cm^2 s^{-1}

4 (a) 240 mm^2 s^{-1} (b) 2400 mm^3 s^{-1}

5 942 mm^2 s^{-1}

6 0.25 m min^{-1}

7 0.0076 m s^{-1}

8 0.011 m s^{-1}

9 0.0040 cm s^{-1}

Miscellaneous exercise 12 (page 184)

1 $80(4x-1)^{19}$

2 $\dfrac{8}{(3-4x)^3}$

3 $40x^3(x^4+3)^4$

4 $24x + y = 49$

6 $-\frac{10}{27}$

7 $y = 20x + 11$

8 $\left(0,\frac{1}{4}\right)$

9 $3x + 4y = 18$

10 0.377 cm^2 s^{-1}

11 (a) $\dfrac{10}{\sqrt{\pi}}$ cm   (b) $\dfrac{1}{4\sqrt{\pi}}$ cm s^{-1}

12 $8x + 5y - 34 = 0$

13 $(2,-4)$; $(0,0),(4,0)$

   $(0,16),(4,-16)$; $(2,0),(2\pm2\sqrt{3},0),(0,16)$

14 $\dfrac{(1-1/x^2)}{2\sqrt{(x+1/x)}}$

15 4 m^2 s^{-1}

16 $y = 2x - 3$

17 $\dfrac{-12t}{(3t^2+5)^3}$

18 (a) $\dfrac{2-x}{\sqrt{4x-x^2}}$, $(2,2)$

19 (a) Minimum   (b) 20

20 $\dfrac{3}{20\pi}$ cm s^{-1}

21 0.052 m s^{-1}

22 $(-\sqrt{3},-4)$, minimum; $(-1,0)$, maximum;

   $(0,-4)$, minimum; $(1,0)$, maximum;

   $(\sqrt{3},-4)$, minimum

23 $\left(\frac{1}{2},\frac{1}{4}\right)$, maximum

24 $\left(2\frac{1}{2},6\right)$, minimum

Revision exercise 2
(page 187)

1 $9x - y = 16$

2 $(-1,7)$

3 $(1,0)$

4 $\left(-\frac{9}{4},\frac{81}{16}\right)$

5 $\left(-\frac{1}{4},\frac{1}{16}\right),\left(2\frac{1}{4},5\frac{1}{16}\right)$

6 $y + 2x = 3; \left(\frac{9}{4},-\frac{3}{2}\right)$

7 (a)　22.5 cm　　　　　(b)　45 cm , 15 cm
　　(c)　0.33, 3.67　　　　(d)　15

8 (a)　$4x^{-\frac{2}{3}}$; $y = x + 16$　　(b)　$23y - 22x = 360$
　　(c)　$(-8,8)$

9 $1 - \dfrac{1}{x^2}$; $\dfrac{1}{\sqrt{x}}$; $\dfrac{-3}{2x\sqrt{x}}$; $1 - \dfrac{1}{x\sqrt{x}} - \dfrac{2}{x^3}$

10 -4, maximum; -8, minimum

11 Maximum

12 (a)　$\pm 50.8, \pm 129.2$　(b)　$-150, -30$
　　(c)　$-166.7, -76.7, 13.3, 103.3$
　　(d)　$\pm 165, \pm 15$

13 (a)　$15, 75, 105, 165, 195, 255, 285, 345$
　　(c)　180; e.g., $(45, 1.5)$

14 $\dfrac{1}{2\sqrt{x}} - \dfrac{1}{2x\sqrt{x}}$; $1 - \dfrac{1}{x^2}$

15 3

16 $x \mapsto \dfrac{1-x}{1+2x}, x \in \mathbb{R}, x \neq -\frac{1}{2}$

17 $\frac{1}{2}(2n+1)$　　(b)　20

18 (a)　$x^8 - 8x^6 + 28x^4$　　(b)　216

19 $-(2x+3)^{-\frac{3}{2}}$

20 (a)　$(x-1)^2 - 2$; $-2 \leqslant \mathrm{f}(x) \leqslant 14$; not one–one
　　(b)　$x \geqslant 1$

21 (b)　22

22 (a)　5　(b)　$\frac{1}{2}$

23 (a)　$\mathrm{f}(x) \leqslant 4$　　　　(b)　Reflect in $y = 2$
　　(c)　$\sqrt{4-x}, x \leqslant 4$　　(d)　1.56

24 1215

25 21

26 (a)　$3\left(3x^2 + 2\right)\left(x^3 + 2x - 1\right)^2$
　　(b)　$-x\left(x^2 + 1\right)^{-\frac{3}{2}}$

27 (a)　$2\pi \times 10^{15}$ km^3 s^{-1}　(b)　$4\pi \times 10^9$ km^2 s^{-1}

28 (a)　360　　(b)　720　　(c)　240

29 (a)　89　(b)　\$1 341 600

31 $\left(\frac{1}{2}(p-q),\frac{1}{2}(p+q)\right)$, $\left(\frac{1}{2}(p+q),\frac{1}{2}(q-p)\right)$;

　　$\dfrac{p+q}{p-q}$ and $\dfrac{q-p}{p+q}$

13　Vectors

Exercise 13A (page 194)

2 (a)　$(4\mathbf{i}+\mathbf{j})+(-3\mathbf{i}+2\mathbf{j}) = \mathbf{i}+3\mathbf{j}$
　　(b)　$3(\mathbf{i}-2\mathbf{j}) = 3\mathbf{i}-6\mathbf{j}$
　　(c)　$4\mathbf{j}+2(\mathbf{i}-2\mathbf{j}) = 2\mathbf{i}$
　　(d)　$(3\mathbf{i}+\mathbf{j})-(5\mathbf{i}+\mathbf{j}) = -2\mathbf{i}$
　　(e)　$3(-\mathbf{i}+2\mathbf{j})-(-4\mathbf{i}+3\mathbf{j}) = \mathbf{i}+3\mathbf{j}$
　　(f)　$4(2\mathbf{i}+3\mathbf{j})-3(3\mathbf{i}+2\mathbf{j}) = -\mathbf{i}+6\mathbf{j}$
　　(g)　$(2\mathbf{i}-3\mathbf{j})+(4\mathbf{i}+5\mathbf{j})+(-6\mathbf{i}-2\mathbf{j}) = \mathbf{0}$
　　(h)　$2(3\mathbf{i}-\mathbf{j})+3(-2\mathbf{i}+3\mathbf{j})+(-7\mathbf{j}) = \mathbf{0}$

3 (a)　$\begin{pmatrix}1\\2\end{pmatrix}$　　(b)　$\begin{pmatrix}3\\0\end{pmatrix}$　　(c)　$\begin{pmatrix}-1\\1\end{pmatrix}$　　(d)　$\begin{pmatrix}4\\-3\end{pmatrix}$

4　$s = 2$

5　$s = 4; \mathbf{q} = \frac{1}{4}(\mathbf{r}-\mathbf{p})$

6　$2, 3$

7　$1\frac{1}{2}, -\frac{1}{2}$

8　$\begin{pmatrix}4\\-2\end{pmatrix}$ and $\begin{pmatrix}-6\\3\end{pmatrix}$ are parallel, $\begin{pmatrix}3\\1\end{pmatrix}$ is in a different direction; $\begin{pmatrix}-1\\2\end{pmatrix}$ is not parallel to $\begin{pmatrix}1\\1\end{pmatrix}-\begin{pmatrix}3\\4\end{pmatrix}$.

9　Any multiple of $1, -1, 2$

10 (a)　No　　(b)　$-2, 0$
　　$\mathbf{p}$ is parallel to $\mathbf{r}$, but $\mathbf{q}$ is in a different direction

Exercise 13B (page 197)

1 (a)　$(9,3)$　　　(b)　$(-1,-2)$　　(c)　$(2,-1)$
　　(d)　$(-8,-1)$　　(e)　$(10,5)$　　(f)　$\left(5,2\frac{1}{2}\right)$

2 (a)　$(-13,-23)$　(b)　$(-1,1)$

3　$\mathbf{c} = 2\mathbf{b} - \mathbf{a}$

4　$\frac{3}{7}\mathbf{a} + \frac{4}{7}\mathbf{b}$

6　$\mathbf{b} - \mathbf{a} = \mathbf{c} - \mathbf{d}$

7　$\frac{1}{2}(\mathbf{b}+\mathbf{c}-2\mathbf{a}), \frac{1}{4}(\mathbf{b}+\mathbf{c}-2\mathbf{a})$;　G is the mid-point of AD

8　$\mathbf{b} = \mathbf{a} + \mathbf{c}$, $\mathbf{m} = \frac{1}{2}(\mathbf{a}+2\mathbf{c})$, $\mathbf{p} = \frac{1}{3}(\mathbf{a}+2\mathbf{c})$;
　　O, P and M are collinear, and $OP = \frac{2}{3}OM$

9　$\mathbf{d} = \frac{1}{2}(\mathbf{b}+\mathbf{c})$, $\mathbf{e} = \frac{1}{4}(2\mathbf{a}+\mathbf{b}+\mathbf{c})$, $\mathbf{f} = \frac{1}{3}(2\mathbf{a}+\mathbf{c})$,
　　$\mathbf{g} = \frac{1}{4}(\mathbf{b}+2\mathbf{a}+\mathbf{c})$

10　$\frac{4}{15}\mathbf{b} - \frac{13}{15}\mathbf{a}$, $k = \frac{15}{13}$, $\mathbf{r} = \frac{4}{13}\mathbf{b}$;
　　R is on OB, with $OR{:}RB = 4{:}9$
　　S is on OA, with $OS{:}SA = 2{:}9$

Exercise 13C (page 200)

1 $\begin{pmatrix} 3 \\ 0 \\ 2 \end{pmatrix}$

2 (a) $\begin{pmatrix} 3 \\ -6 \\ -6 \end{pmatrix}$ (b) $3\mathbf{i} - 6\mathbf{j} - 6\mathbf{k}$

3 (a) *ABC* is not a straight line.
   (b) *ABC* is a straight line.

4 (a) $\begin{pmatrix} 1 \\ 2 \\ -7 \end{pmatrix}, \begin{pmatrix} -6 \\ 4 \\ -8 \end{pmatrix}, \begin{pmatrix} -2 \\ 0 \\ \frac{3}{2} \end{pmatrix}$ (b) $\left(-4, 7, -17\frac{1}{2}\right)$

5 $\mathbf{i} + \mathbf{j} - 6\mathbf{k}$, $\mathbf{i} + \mathbf{j} - 6\mathbf{k}$; it is a parallelogram

6 (a) $\begin{pmatrix} -3 \\ 6 \\ 1 \end{pmatrix}$ (b) $\begin{pmatrix} -2 \\ 4 \\ \frac{2}{3} \end{pmatrix}$ (c) $\begin{pmatrix} 2 \\ 3 \\ 2\frac{2}{3} \end{pmatrix}$

7 (a) $\begin{pmatrix} 2 \\ 2 \\ 1 \end{pmatrix}$ (b) $\begin{pmatrix} 2 \\ 2 \\ 1 \end{pmatrix}$

Exercise 13D (page 206)

1 -8, 11, 3

2 11, -3, 8

3 18, 0, 0; **r** is perpendicular to both **p** and **q**.

4 (a) and (d) are perpendicular; so are (b) and (c).

5 -4, -8, -12

6 (a) 5 (b) $\sqrt{5}$ (c) $\sqrt{5}$ (d) 1
   (e) 3 (f) 13 (g) 5 (h) $\sqrt{6}$
   (i) $\sqrt{5}$ (j) $\sqrt{13}$ (k) $\sqrt{30}$ (l) 2

7 $5, \begin{pmatrix} \frac{4}{5} \\ -\frac{3}{5} \end{pmatrix}$

8 $\begin{pmatrix} \frac{1}{3} \\ -\frac{2}{3} \\ \frac{2}{3} \end{pmatrix}, \frac{2}{3}\mathbf{i} - \frac{1}{3}\mathbf{j} + \frac{2}{3}\mathbf{k}$

9 (a) 45° (b) 167.3° (c) 180°
   (d) 136.7° (e) 7.0° (f) 90°

10 $\sqrt{(x_2 - x_1)^2 + (y_2 - y_1)^2}$; the distance between the points with position vectors $\mathbf{r}_1$ and $\mathbf{r}_2$.

11 172.2° (or 7.8°)

12 99.6° (or 80.4°)

13 70.5°

14 76.4°

15 48.2°

16 48.2°

Miscellaneous exercise 13 (page 207)

1 **a** and **b**, **a** and **c**, **b** and **c**, **b** and **d**

2 58.5°

3 (a) 7, 7 (b) −32 (c) 130.8°

4 (a) $\mathbf{d} = \begin{pmatrix} 9 \\ 4 \\ -5 \end{pmatrix}$ (b) $\begin{pmatrix} 3 \\ 3 \\ 0 \end{pmatrix}$ (c) 120.5°

5 (a) $x\mathbf{i}, -\frac{1}{2}x\mathbf{i} + \frac{1}{2}\sqrt{3}x\mathbf{j}, -\frac{1}{2}x\mathbf{i} - \frac{1}{2}\sqrt{3}x\mathbf{j}$
   (b) (i) $\overrightarrow{AP} = \overrightarrow{OP} - \overrightarrow{OA}$
       (ii) $-x\mathbf{i} + 30\mathbf{k}, \frac{1}{2}x\mathbf{i} - \frac{1}{2}\sqrt{3}x\mathbf{j} + 30\mathbf{k}$
   (c) $30\sqrt{2}$

6 $\dfrac{\mathbf{i} - 3\mathbf{j} - 2\mathbf{k}}{\sqrt{14}}, \dfrac{3\mathbf{i} + \mathbf{j} - 2\mathbf{k}}{\sqrt{14}}$, 73.4°

7 (a) 8.5°

8 (a) $\sqrt{29}$ (b) 119.9° (or 60.1°)

9 (a) $\begin{pmatrix} \frac{1}{2} \\ \frac{1}{2} \\ \frac{1}{2}\sqrt{2} \end{pmatrix}$ (b) 45°

10 (a) 60° (b) $\frac{3}{2}\sqrt{3}$

12 $\frac{4}{5}, \frac{9}{5}$; break up 4 Individual bags and 9 Jumbo bags, and use the fruit to make 5 King-size bags.

13 (a) $\begin{pmatrix} 14 \\ 2 \\ 5 \end{pmatrix}, \begin{pmatrix} -5 \\ 10 \\ 10 \end{pmatrix}$; (13, 14, 18)
   (b) $\frac{1}{3}, \frac{2}{15}$; the origin lies in the plane of the parallelogram.

14 (11.4, 3, 0) at 8.04 a.m.

14 Geometric sequences

Exercise 14A (page 213)

1 (a) 2; 24, 48 (b) 4; 128, 512
   (c) $\frac{1}{2}$; 4, 2 (d) −3; 162, −486
   (e) 1.1; 1.4641, 1.610 51 (f) $\frac{1}{x}; \frac{1}{x}, \frac{1}{x^2}$

2 (a) $2 \times 3^{i-1}$ (b) $10 \times \left(\frac{1}{2}\right)^{i-1}$ (c) $1 \times (-2)^{i-1}$
   (d) $81 \times \left(\frac{1}{3}\right)^{i-1}$ (e) x^i (f) $p^{2-i}q^{i+1}$

3 (a) 11 (b) 13 (c) 7
   (d) 14 (e) 6 (f) 13

4 (a) $3; 1\frac{1}{3}$ (b) $2; 1\frac{1}{2}$ or $-2; 1\frac{1}{2}$

   (c) $\frac{1}{3}; 531\,441$ (d) $\pm\sqrt{2}; 4$

   (e) $\pm 7; \dfrac{16807}{(\pm 7)^{n-1}}$

5 (a) $59\,048$ (b) $-29\,524$

   (c) 1.9922 (d) 0.6641

   (e) $12\,285$ (f) 8.9998

   (g) $\dfrac{x(1-x^n)}{1-x}$ (h) $\dfrac{x(1-(-x)^n)}{1+x}$

   (i) $\dfrac{x^{2n}-1}{x^{2n-3}(x^2-1)}$ (j) $\dfrac{x^{2n}-(-1)^n}{x^{2n-2}(x^2+1)}$

6 (a) 2047 (b) 683

   (c) $262\,143$ (d) $\frac{1023}{512}$

   (e) $\frac{29\,525}{39\,366}$ (f) $19.843\,75$

   (g) $\frac{341}{1024}$ (h) $2-\left(\frac{1}{2}\right)^n$

   (i) $\frac{1}{3}\left(64-\left(\frac{1}{4}\right)^n\right)$ (j) $\frac{1}{4}\left(243+\left(-\frac{1}{3}\right)^n\right)$

7 $2^{64}-1 \approx 1.84 \times 10^{19}$

8 $\$2\,684\,354.55$

10 (a) 2 (b) 8th

11 (a) 3 (b) 14th

12 (a) $\dfrac{p}{q}; n$ (c) (i) np^{n-1} (ii) $-np^{-(n+1)}$

Exercise 14B (page 217)

1 (a) 2 (b) $\frac{3}{2}$ (c) $\frac{1}{4}$ (d) $\frac{1}{9}$

   (e) $\frac{3}{4}$ (f) $\frac{1}{6}$ (g) 3 (h) $\frac{1}{3}$

   (i) $\frac{20}{3}$ (j) 62.5 (k) $\dfrac{x}{1-x}$ (l) $\dfrac{1}{1+x^2}$

   (m) $\dfrac{x}{x-1}$ (n) $\dfrac{x^3}{x+1}$

2 (a) $\frac{4}{11}$ (b) $\frac{41}{333}$ (c) $\frac{5}{9}$ (d) $\frac{157}{333}$

   (e) $\frac{1}{7}$ (f) $\frac{2}{7}$ (g) $\frac{5}{7}$ (h) $\frac{6}{7}$

3 $\frac{1}{6}$

4 $-\frac{5}{6}$

5 3

6 19.2

7 2 m

8 0.375 m east of O, 1.5 m

9 10 seconds

10 19 m

11 (a) Edge of table   (b) 8

Exercise 14C (page 221)

1 $\$7103.39$

2 $\$1239.72$

3 $40\,000 \times 1.08^{25} - P\left(1+1.08+\ldots+1.08^{24}\right) = 0$, $\$3747.15$

4 $\$1167.70$

5 $\$317.23$

6 (a) $63\,000$ (b) $36\,200$ (c) $19\,700$

7 (a) 5.83×10^7 (b) 5.65×10^7

8 (a) $17\,800$ (b) $29\,100$

9 (a) 85.1 kg   (b) 68.1 kg

10 (a) $\$2254.32$ (b) 139

11 $\$2718.28$

Miscellaneous exercise 14 (page 222)

1 $6\frac{1}{4}$

3 $a=3, r=-\frac{1}{4}; 2.4\left(1-\left(-\frac{1}{4}\right)^n\right)$

4 62

5 $\frac{1}{999}; \frac{4}{37}$

6 $\frac{4}{5}; 18$

7 $8\left(1-\left(-\frac{1}{2}\right)^n\right); 8, 13$

8 $r=0.917; a=40$

9 $20 \times 1.1^{n-1}; 17$

10 $\$56\,007$

11 (a) 20

   (b) The sum of the infinite series is only 80 cm.

12 $n=45, 19.8$ seconds

13 8.45%

14 $r=-\frac{1}{3}$

16 $r=\dfrac{k-1}{k+1}$

17 $\$6401$

18 $\$200\,000\left(1-\dfrac{1}{1.05^n}\right); \$77\,217, \$124\,622,$
$\$153\,725, \$171\,591, \$182\,559$

19 $\dfrac{(1-x)(1-x^{3n+3})}{1-x^3}; \; |x|<1;$

   $\dfrac{1}{1+x+x^2+x^3+x^4}, \; |x|<1$

20 (a) $\tan^2 x°, \; x \neq 90(2n+1), n \in \mathbb{Z}$

   (b) $\cos^2 x°, \; 180n-45 < x < 180n+45, \; n \in \mathbb{Z}$

21 $\dfrac{(1+x)^7 - 1}{x}$

$$1 \quad 2 \quad 1$$
$$1 \quad 3 \quad 3 \quad 1$$
$$1 \quad 4 \quad 6 \quad 4 \quad 1$$
$$1 \quad 5 \quad 10 \quad 10 \quad 5 \quad 1$$
$$1 \quad 6 \quad 15 \quad 20 \quad 15 \quad 6 \quad 1$$
$$1 \quad 7 \quad 21 \quad 35 \quad 35 \quad 21 \quad 7 \quad 1$$

$$\binom{r}{r} + \binom{r+1}{r} + \binom{r+2}{r} + \ldots + \binom{n}{r} = \binom{n+1}{r+1}$$

22 Possible if $|x| < 1$; within these bounds, the larger the value of n the better the approximation.

15 Second derivatives

Exercise 15A (page 228)

1 (a) At $x = -1, 0, 1$ (b) $3x^2 - 1$
    (c) $6x$

2 (b) $3x^2 + 1, 6x$ (c) $x \geqslant 0$

4 (a) (i) $(0,0), (\pm\sqrt{2}, 4)$ (ii) $\left(\pm\frac{1}{3}\sqrt{6}, -\frac{8}{9}\right)$
    (b) (i) $(0,0), \left(-\frac{2}{3}, \frac{4}{27}\right)$ (ii) $\left(-\frac{1}{3}, \frac{2}{27}\right)$
    (c) (i) $(\pm 1, \pm 2)$ (ii) None
    (d) (i) None   (ii) None
    (e) (i) $(2, 3)$ (ii) None
    (f) (i) $(-2, -3)$ (ii) None

5 (a) Rate of increase of inflation, positive

6 (a) $f'(x) +, f''(x) +$ (b) $f'(x) +, f''(x) -$
    (c) $f'(x) +, f''(x) \, 0$ (d) $f'(x) -, f''(x) +$
    (e) For $0 < x < 3$, $f'(x) +, f''(x) +$;
       for $x > 3$, $f'(x) -, f''(x) +$
    (f) For $x < -1, f'(x) +, f''(x) +$;
       for $-1 < x < 0, f'(x) +, f''(x) -$;
       for $0 < x < 1, f'(x) -, f''(x) -$;
       for $x > 1, f'(x) -, f''(x) +$

7 (a) Both positive, sudden change (drop in S),

     then $\dfrac{dS}{dt}$ is negative changing to positive

     with $\dfrac{d^2 S}{dt^2}$ positive.

    (b) Price rising sharply, sudden 'crash', price continues to drop but less quickly and then recovers to give steadier growth.

8 (b) $+, -, -, +$

9 (a) $\dfrac{dN}{dt} = -kN, k > 0$ (c) $+$

Exercise 15B (page 232)

1 (a) $(-1, -2)$, minimum; $(1, 2)$, maximum
    (b) $(0, 0)$, maximum; $(2, -4)$, minimum
    (c) $(0, 1)$, minimum
    (d) $(-1, 11)$, maximum; $(2, -16)$, minimum
    (e) $\left(2, -\frac{3}{8}\right)$, minimum
    (f) $(-1, 2)$, minimum; $(1, 2)$, minimum
    (g) $\left(2, \frac{1}{4}\right)$, maximum
    (h) $(2, 22)$, inflexion

2 (a) $(-1, -8)$, minimum; $(0, -3)$, maximum; $(2, -35)$, minimum
    (b) $(1, 6)$, inflexion
    (c) $\left(-\frac{4}{3}, -14\frac{2}{9}\right)$, minimum; $\left(\frac{4}{3}, 14\frac{2}{9}\right)$, maximum
    (d) $(-2, 3)$, minimum
    (e) $(-2, -4)$, maximum; $(2, 4)$, minimum
    (f) $\left(6, \frac{1}{12}\right)$, maximum
    (g) $(0, -7)$, inflexion
    (h) $(0, 1)$, minimum; $(1, 2)$, inflexion

Exercise 15C (page 234)

1 (a) $2x + 3, 2, 0, 0$
    (b) $6x^2 + 1 - \dfrac{1}{x^2}, 12x + \dfrac{2}{x^3}, 12 - \dfrac{6}{x^4}, \dfrac{24}{x^5}$
    (c) $4x^3, 12x^2, 24x, 24$
    (d) $\frac{1}{2}x^{-1/2}, -\frac{1}{4}x^{-3/2}, \frac{3}{8}x^{-5/2}, -\frac{15}{16}x^{-7/2}$
    (e) $-\frac{1}{2}x^{-3/2}, \frac{3}{4}x^{-5/2}, -\frac{15}{8}x^{-7/2}, \frac{105}{16}x^{-9/2}$
    (f) $\frac{1}{4}x^{-3/4}, -\frac{3}{16}x^{-7/4}, \frac{21}{64}x^{-11/4}, -\frac{231}{256}x^{-15/4}$

2 (a) $2x - 5, 2, 0, 0$
    (b) $10x^4 - 6x, 40x^3 - 6, 120x^2, 240x$
    (c) $-4x^{-5}, 20x^{-6}, -120x^{-7}, 840x^{-8}$
    (d) $6x - 6x^5, 6 - 30x^4, -120x^3, -360x^2$
    (e) $\frac{3}{4}x^{-1/4}, -\frac{3}{16}x^{-5/4}, \frac{15}{64}x^{-9/4}, -\frac{135}{256}x^{-13/4}$
    (f) $\frac{3}{8}x^{-5/8}, -\frac{15}{64}x^{-13/8}, \frac{195}{512}x^{-21/8}, -\frac{4095}{4096}x^{-29/8}$

3 $n(n-1)(n-2) \times \ldots \times 3 \times 2 \times 1$ (i.e., $n!$)

4 $(n+2)(n+1)n(n-1) \times \ldots \times 3x^2$

5 0

Miscellaneous exercise 15 (page 234)

1 Minimum 6, maximum 10

2 Minimum $32\frac{1}{4}$

3 Maximum 6 when $x = 1$

4 Maximum $\left(\frac{1}{2}, -\frac{1}{2}\right)$, minimum $\left(\frac{1}{6}, 9\right)$

5 $+, -, +$

6 (a) Subsonic: $\dfrac{dk}{dS}$ +, initially small then

increasing; $\dfrac{d^2k}{dS^2}$ +, decreasing to zero.

Transonic: $\dfrac{dk}{dS}$ + at first, zero at speed of

sound, then –; $\dfrac{d^2k}{dS^2}$ zero, –, zero again.

Supersonic: $\dfrac{dk}{dS}$ –; $\dfrac{d^2k}{dS^2}$ zero, then +.

(b) At the boundaries between the regions.

(c) Possibly levelling out, becoming constant again.

7 $10x - 2x^2 - \frac{1}{2}\pi x^2$, $\dfrac{10}{4+\pi} \approx 1.40$

8 (a) Maximum 0 when $x = 0$,

minimum $-\frac{4}{27}a^2$ when $x = \frac{2}{3}a$

(b) Minimum $-\frac{27}{256}a^4$ when $x = \frac{3}{4}a$

(c) Minimum 0 when $x = 0$,

maximum $\frac{1}{16}a^4$ when $x = \frac{1}{2}a$,

minimum 0 when $x = a$

(d) Maximum $\frac{108}{3125}a^5$ when $x = \frac{3}{5}a$,

minimum 0 when $x = a$

9 (a) $(-1)^n (n+2)(n+1)n(n-1) \times \ldots \times 3 x^{-(n+3)}$

(b) $(-1)^{n-1} \times \dfrac{3 \times 5 \times 7 \times \ldots \times (2n-3)}{2^n} x^{-\frac{1}{2}(2n-1)}$ if

$n \geqslant 3$

10 (a) $(1,15)$, $(3,31)$ (b) $(1,2)$

16 Integration

Exercise 16A (page 238)

1 (a) $x^4 + k$ (b) $x^6 + k$
   (c) $x^2 + k$ (d) $x^3 + x^5 + k$
   (e) $x^{10} - x^8 - x + k$ (f) $-x^7 + x^3 + x + k$

2 (a) $3x^3 - 2x^2 - 5x + k$
   (b) $4x^3 + 3x^2 + 4x + k$
   (c) $7x + k$
   (d) $4x^4 - 2x^3 + 5x^2 - 3x + k$
   (e) $\frac{1}{2}x^4 + \frac{5}{2}x^2 + k$
   (f) $\frac{1}{2}x^2 + \frac{2}{3}x^3 + k$
   (g) $\frac{2}{3}x^3 - \frac{3}{2}x^2 - 4x + k$
   (h) $x - x^2 - x^3 + k$

3 (a) $\frac{1}{5}x^5 + \frac{1}{3}x^3 + x + k$
   (b) $\frac{7}{2}x^2 - 3x + k$
   (c) $\frac{2}{3}x^3 + \frac{1}{2}x^2 - 8x + k$

(d) $\frac{3}{2}x^4 - \frac{5}{3}x^3 + \frac{3}{2}x^2 + 2x + k$
(e) $\frac{1}{6}x^4 + \frac{1}{6}x^3 + \frac{1}{6}x^2 + \frac{1}{6}x + k$
(f) $\frac{1}{8}x^4 - \frac{1}{9}x^3 + \frac{1}{2}x^2 - \frac{1}{3}x + k$
(g) $\frac{1}{2}x^2 - x^3 + x + k$
(h) $\frac{1}{4}x^4 + \frac{1}{3}x^3 + \frac{1}{2}x^2 + x + k$

4 $4x^2 - 5x$

5 $y = 2x^3 - x - 19$

6 $y = \frac{1}{8}x^4 + \frac{1}{8}x^2 + x - 21$

7 $5x^3 - 3x^2 + 4x - 6$

9 $y = 4x\sqrt{x} - 7$

10 (a) $y = \frac{2}{3}x^{3/2} + k$ (b) $y = 12x^{1/3} + k$
  (c) $y = \frac{3}{4}x^{4/3} + k$
  (d) $y = \frac{4}{3}x\sqrt{x} - 4\sqrt{x} + k$
  (e) $y = \frac{15}{2}\sqrt[3]{x^2} + k$ (f) $y = -6\sqrt[3]{x} + k$

11 (a) $-\dfrac{1}{x} + k$ (b) $-\dfrac{1}{x^3} + k$

  (c) $-\dfrac{3}{x^2} + k$ (d) $2x^2 + \dfrac{3}{x} + k$

  (e) $-\dfrac{1}{2x^2} + \dfrac{1}{3x^3} + k$ (f) $-\dfrac{2}{x} - \dfrac{2}{3}x^3 + k$

12 $y = -4x^{-1} + 13$

13 $y = \sqrt{x} - 2$

14 $y = \frac{3}{4}x^{4/3} + 3x^{-2} + \frac{5}{4}$

15 (a) $y = x^3 + 3x^2 + k$
  (b) $y = 4x^3 + 2x^2 - 5x + k$
  (c) $y = 2x^2 - \dfrac{1}{x} + k$
  (d) $y = \frac{2}{3}x\sqrt{x} + 8\sqrt{x} + k$
  (e) $y = \frac{1}{2}x^2 + \frac{20}{3}x\sqrt{x} + 25x + k$
  (f) $y = x + 10\sqrt{x} + k$

16 (a) 118 cm (to 3 s.f.)   (b) 27

17 17 months (to the nearest month)

18 192

Exercise 16B (page 244)

1 (a) $2x^2 + k$ (b) $5x^3 + k$ (c) $\frac{1}{3}x^6 + k$
  (d) $9x + k$ (e) $\frac{1}{18}x^9 + k$ (f) $\frac{2}{15}x^5 + k$

2 (a) 7   (b) 84   (c) 4
  (d) 4   (e) $\frac{1}{16}$ (f) 2

3 (a) $3x^2 + 7x + k$
  (b) $2x^3 - x^2 - 5x + k$
  (c) $\frac{1}{2}x^4 + \frac{7}{2}x^2 + k$
  (d) $\frac{3}{5}x^5 - 2x^4 + 3x^3 - \frac{1}{2}x^2 + 4x + k$
  (e) $\frac{2}{3}x^3 - \frac{3}{2}x^2 - 20x + k$
  (f) $\frac{1}{4}x^4 - 2x^2 + k$

4 (a) 22   (b) 22   (c) 36
    (d) $7\frac{1}{6}$ (e) 210   (f) 0

5 72

6 15

7 195

8 80

9 80

10 $10\frac{2}{5}$

11 18

12 16

13 (a) 39   (b) $5\frac{1}{3}$ (c) $10\frac{2}{3}$
    (d) 10   (e) 500   (f) $5\frac{1}{3}$

14 (a) $-\dfrac{1}{2x^2}+k$ (b) $\frac{1}{3}x^3+\dfrac{1}{x}+k$

    (c) $\frac{2}{3}x\sqrt{x}+k$ (d) $\frac{18}{5}x^{5/3}+k$

    (e) $2x^3-\dfrac{5}{x}+k$ (f) $2\sqrt{x}+k$

15 (a) 144   (b) $1\frac{1}{2}$ (c) 20
    (d) $6\frac{3}{4}$ (e) 16   (f) 3

16 $1\frac{3}{4}$

17 60

18 $3\frac{1}{3}$

19 7

20 5

21 (a) $22\frac{2}{3}$ (b) $2\frac{3}{8}$

22 96

24 $42\frac{7}{8}$

Exercise 16C (page 250)

1 -4; the graph lies below the x-axis for $0<x<2$.

2 (a) $10\frac{2}{3}$ (b) 8   (c) $2\frac{1}{4}$ (d) $1\frac{5}{6}$

3 (a) $10\frac{2}{3}$ (b) 8   (c) 100

4 (a) $\frac{1}{4}$ (b) 6   (c) 100

5 $\dfrac{s^{1-m}-1}{1-m}$; $\dfrac{1}{m-1}$

6 $\dfrac{1-r^{1-m}}{1-m}$; $m<1$, $\dfrac{1}{1-m}$

7 12

8 $10\frac{2}{3}$

9 32

10 108

11 $42\frac{2}{3}$

12 $4\frac{1}{2}$

13 36

Exercise 16D (page 253)

1 (a) $\frac{1}{14}(2x+1)^7+k$ (b) $\frac{1}{15}(3x-5)^5+k$

    (c) $-\frac{1}{28}(1-7x)^4+k$ (d) $\frac{2}{11}\left(\frac{1}{2}x+1\right)^{11}+k$

    (e) $-\frac{1}{10}(5x+2)^{-2}+k$ (f) $\frac{2}{3}(1-3x)^{-1}+k$

    (g) $-\frac{1}{4}(x+1)^{-4}+k$ (h) $-\frac{1}{8}(4x+1)^{-3}+k$

    (i) $\frac{1}{15}(10x+1)^{\frac{3}{2}}+k$ (j) $\sqrt{2x-1}+k$

    (k) $\frac{6}{5}\left(\frac{1}{2}x+2\right)^{\frac{5}{3}}+k$ (l) $\frac{16}{9}(2+6x)^{\frac{3}{4}}+k$

2 (a) 820   (b) $\frac{26}{3}$ (c) $\frac{2}{15}$ (d) $\frac{16}{225}$

3 2.25

4 9.1125

5 (a) $\frac{243}{10}$ (b) $4\frac{1}{2}$ (c) $\frac{2}{3}$ (d) 28

6 $\frac{1}{20}$

7 $438\frac{6}{7}$

8 $\frac{1}{6}$

Miscellaneous exercise 16 (page 254)

1 $4x\sqrt{x}+k$; 28

2 ±2; 32

3 $-\frac{4}{3}$

4 $8\frac{2}{3}$

5 (a) $-\dfrac{1}{2x^2}+\frac{1}{4}x^4+k$ (b) 6

6 $31\frac{1}{4}$

7 7

8 $6\frac{3}{4}$

9 $1\frac{1}{3}$

10 0; integrand is >0 for $0<x<1$, <0 for $1<x<2$

11 (a) $\frac{1}{4}x^4-x^2+k$ (b) 2

12 ±2

14 (a) $y=-\frac{1}{2}x+\frac{3}{2}$ (b) $2\frac{29}{48}$

15 (a) 6   (b) 67   (c) —   (d) 45
    (e) 17   (f) -11 (g) 17   (h) 11

17 (a) $y=2x-2$ (b) $6\frac{3}{4}$

19 $(0,0),(\pm2,-16)$; 32.4

20 $\frac{1}{2}$

21 (a) $\frac{1}{27},0$ (b) (i) $(3,0)$ (ii) $\left(4,-\frac{1}{128}\right)$

22 (a) 1,2   (b) $10\frac{1}{8}$

23 (b) $25\frac{5}{6}$

17 Volume of revolution

Exercise 17 (page 261)

1 (a) $\frac{98}{3}\pi$ (b) $\frac{3093}{5}\pi$

   (c) $\frac{279\,808}{7}\pi$ (d) $\frac{3}{4}\pi$

2 (a) 504π (b) $\frac{3498}{5}\pi$

   (c) $\frac{15}{2}\pi$ (d) $\frac{16}{15}\pi$

3 (a) 4π (b) 9π (c) 3355π

   (d) $\frac{3}{10}\pi$ (e) $\frac{648}{5}\pi$ (f) $\frac{9}{2}\pi$

   (g) 156π (h) $\frac{2}{3}\pi$

4 (a) $\frac{512}{15}\pi$ (b) $\frac{16}{15}\pi$

   (c) $\frac{1}{30}\pi$ (d) $\frac{81}{10}\pi$

5 (a) $\frac{2}{15}\pi$ (b) $\frac{1}{6}\pi$

6 (a) $\frac{2048}{15}\pi$ (b) $\frac{128}{3}\pi$

7 (a) $\frac{3}{10}\pi$ (b) $\frac{3}{10}\pi$

8 $\frac{1}{10}\pi$

9 9π

Miscellaneous exercise 17 (page 262)

1 $\frac{206}{15}\pi$

3 $\frac{4}{3}\pi ab^2$; $\frac{4}{3}\pi a^2 b$

4 (b) 3   (c) 3π (d) $\frac{1}{2}\pi$

5 (i) (a) Infinite   (b) $1\frac{1}{2}$

     (c) 5π (d) $\frac{3}{7}\pi$

   (ii) (a) Infinite   (b) $\frac{1}{3}$

     (c) Infinite   (d) $\frac{1}{7}\pi$

6 (a) 36 , 18   (b) $\frac{1296}{5}\pi$ (c) $\frac{81}{2}\pi$

7 4π

18 Radians

Exercise 18A (page 267)

1 (a) $\frac{1}{2}\pi$ (b) $\frac{3}{4}\pi$ (c) $\frac{1}{4}\pi$ (d) $\frac{1}{6}\pi$

   (e) $\frac{2}{5}\pi$ (f) $\frac{1}{10}\pi$ (g) $\frac{2}{3}\pi$ (h) $\frac{1}{8}\pi$

   (i) 4π (j) $\frac{10}{3}\pi$ (k) $\frac{3}{2}\pi$ (l) $\frac{1}{180}\pi$

2 (a) $60°$ (b) $9°$ (c) $36°$ (d) $22\frac{1}{2}°$

   (e) $20°$ (f) $120°$ (g) $112\frac{1}{2}°$ (h) $108°$

   (i) $4°$ (j) $1080°$ (k) $-90°$ (l) $50°$

3 (a) $\frac{1}{2}\sqrt{3}$ (b) $\frac{1}{2}\sqrt{2}$ (c) $\frac{1}{3}\sqrt{3}$ (d) 0

   (e) $-\frac{1}{2}\sqrt{2}$ (f) $-\frac{1}{2}\sqrt{3}$ (g) $-\sqrt{3}$ (h) $\frac{3}{4}$

4 (a) $s = 8.4, A = 29.4$

   (b) $s = 7.35, A = 12.8625$

   (c) $\theta = 1.5, A = 48$ (d) $r = 20, A = 140$

   (e) $\theta = 2.4, s = 12$ (f) $s = 8$

   (g) $r = 8, \theta = 2$ (h) $\theta = \frac{5}{3}$

5 (a) $2.26\,\text{cm}^2$ (b) $1.47\,\text{cm}^2$ (c) $830\,\text{cm}^2$

   (d) $9.05\,\text{cm}^2$ (e) $0.556\,\text{cm}^2$

6 $6.72\,\text{cm}^2$

7 $28.2\,\text{cm}$

9 $26.3\,\text{cm}^2$

10 $15.5\,\text{cm}$, $14.3\,\text{cm}^2$

11 (a) $1.61r$ (b) $0.32r$

Exercise 18B (page 270)

3 (a) $\frac{1}{2}\pi$ (b) $\frac{1}{4}\pi$ (c) π

   (d) $\frac{1}{6}\pi$ (e) 2π (f) $\frac{1}{16}\pi$

Exercise 18C (page 272)

1 (a) $\frac{1}{6}\pi$ (b) $\frac{1}{4}\pi$ (c) $\frac{1}{2}\pi$ (d) $\frac{1}{3}\pi$

   (e) $-\frac{1}{3}\pi$ (f) $-\frac{1}{2}\pi$ (g) $-\frac{1}{4}\pi$ (h) π

2 (a) $\frac{1}{4}\pi$ (b) $-\frac{1}{6}\pi$ (c) $\frac{2}{3}\pi$ (d) $\frac{1}{6}\pi$

3 (a) 0.5 (b) -1 (c) $\sqrt{3}$ (d) 0

4 (a) $\frac{1}{2}\pi$ (b) $\frac{1}{6}\pi$ (c) $\frac{1}{6}\pi$ (d) 0

5 (a) $\frac{1}{2}$ (b) $\frac{1}{2}$ (c) $\frac{1}{2}\sqrt{3}$ (d) 1

6 0.739; $\cos x = x$

Exercise 18D (page 274)

1 (a) $0.12, 3.02$ (b) $4.18, 5.25$

   (c) $1.18, 1.96$ (d) $0.63, 5.66$

   (e) $2.51, 3.77$ (f) $0.96, 5.33$

   (g) $1.33, 4.47$ (h) $2.80, 5.95$

   (i) $0.17, 3.31$ (j) $3.45, 5.98$

   (k) $3.69, 5.73$ (l) $2.90, 6.04$

   (m) $0.99, 2.68$ (n) $4.19, 6.28$

   (o) $0.17, 1.22$

2 (a) $1.00, 2.14$ (b) $-1.30, 1.30$

   (c) $-2.06, 1.09$ (d) $-2.32, -0.82$

   (e) $-1.72, 1.72$ (f) $-0.90 , 2.25$

   (g) $-2.50, 0.64$

   (h) $-2.53, -0.62 , 0.62, 2.53$

   (i) $-\pi , -1.23, 0, 1.23, \pi$

3 (a) $0.66, 2.48, 3.80, 5.63$

   (b) $0.42, 1.46, 2.51, 3.56, 4.61, 5.65$

   (c) $1.91, 2.81, 5.05, 5.95$

   (d) $0.44, 1.13, 2.01, 2.70, 3.58, 4.27, 5.16, 5.84$

   (e) $0.23, 1.80, 3.37, 4.94$

   (f) $1.20, 1.94, 3.30, 4.03, 5.39, 6.13$

4 (a) $-2.33, -1.85, -0.24, 0.24, 1.85, 2.33$
  (b) $-2.12, -0.55, 1.02, 2.59$
  (c) $-3.03, -2.20, -0.94, -0.11, 1.16, 1.99$
  (d) $-2.49, -0.65, 0.65, 2.49$
  (e) $-3.02, -2.39, -1.76, -1.13, \pm 0.51, 0.12,$
    $0.75, 1.38, 2.01, 2.64$
  (f) $-1.35, -0.22, 1.79, 2.92$

5 (a) $-2.46, 2.46$ (b) $-2.06, 2.65$
  (c) -1.01 (d) π
  (e) 0.70 (f) -1.03

6 (a) $\frac{1}{4}\pi, \frac{7}{12}\pi, \frac{5}{4}\pi, \frac{19}{12}\pi$

  (b) $\frac{1}{12}\pi, \frac{7}{12}\pi, \frac{13}{12}\pi, \frac{19}{12}\pi$

  (c) $\frac{19}{36}\pi, \frac{23}{36}\pi, \frac{43}{36}\pi, \frac{47}{36}\pi, \frac{67}{36}\pi, \frac{71}{36}\pi$

  (d) $\frac{5}{9}\pi, \frac{11}{9}\pi, \frac{17}{9}\pi$

  (e) $\frac{17}{36}\pi, \frac{29}{36}\pi, \frac{53}{36}\pi, \frac{65}{36}\pi$

  (f) $\frac{4}{9}\pi$

  (g) No roots

  (h) $\frac{1}{4}\pi, \frac{7}{12}\pi, \frac{11}{12}\pi, \frac{5}{4}\pi, \frac{19}{12}\pi, \frac{23}{12}\pi$

  (i) $\frac{4}{9}\pi$

7 (a) $0.90, 2.25$ (b) $-1.14, 1.14$
  (c) $-2.19, -0.96, 0.96, 2.19$
  (d) $-2.53, -0.62, 0.62, 2.53$
  (e) $-1.04, 0, 1.04$
  (f) $-2.36, -0.79, 0.79, 2.36$

Miscellaneous exercise 18 (page 275)

1 $3.6 \text{ cm}, 10.8 \text{ cm}^2$

2 $\frac{1}{4}$

3 r^2

4 $\frac{2}{3}\pi, \frac{1}{3}\pi - \frac{1}{4}\sqrt{3}$

5 17 cm^2

6 (a) $-2.98, -0.16$ (b) $-\frac{1}{2}\pi, \frac{1}{2}\pi$

  (c) $-\frac{3}{4}\pi, 0, \frac{1}{4}\pi$

  (d) $-3.02, -1.69, 0.12, 1.45$

  (e) $1.77, 2.94$

  (f) $-2.29, -1.25, -0.20, 0.85, 1.89, 2.94$

7 (a) 0.02 seconds, 50
  (b) $0.007, 0.020, 0.027$

8 (a) $k = \dfrac{2\pi}{T}$ (b) $\dfrac{k}{2\pi}$

9 $\frac{1}{2}r^2(\theta - \sin\theta), \ 1.2 < \theta < 1.3$

10 $DE = 2r - 2r\cos\theta$

11 $\theta = 2\pi - \dfrac{s}{r}$

13 1.4

14 (a) $-1 \leqslant x \leqslant 1, \ -\pi - 4 \leqslant y \leqslant \pi - 4$
  (b) $3 \leqslant x \leqslant 5, \ -\pi \leqslant y \leqslant \pi$

15 $0, 1.23, 5.05, \ 2\pi$

16 (a) No roots   (b) $-\frac{3}{2}\pi, \ -\frac{1}{2}\pi, \ \frac{1}{2}\pi, \ \frac{3}{2}\pi$
  (c) $-2\pi, \ -\pi, 0, \ \pi, \ 2\pi$

Revision exercise 3
(page 279)

1 $(-4,8), (1,3); 20\frac{5}{6}$

2 (a) $(-1,5), (1,1)$ (b) $(0,3)$
  (c) $9y + x = 7$ (d) 4

4 $\dfrac{n-1}{n+1}$

5 $y = \frac{5}{2}x^2 + 3x + 4$

6 $\frac{1}{3}$

7 0; between $x = 1$ and $x = 3$, there is the same area above and below the x-axis.

8 24π

9 18

10 (b) 2

11 $\dfrac{300}{\pi}$

12 The point does lie on the line.

13 (a) $\pi - 2\theta, \ 2r^2 + 2r^2 \cos 2\theta$ (b) $2r\cos\theta$

14 9π

15 (a) $3(3x^2 + 2)(x^3 + 2x - 1)^2$

  (b) $-x(x^2 + 1)^{-\frac{3}{2}}$

16 (a) £16 600   (b) Year 9
  (c) $\pounds(475n^2 + 12\,325n)$ for $0 \leqslant n \leqslant 9$;
    $\pounds(20\,400n - 34\,200)$ for $n > 9$
  (d) $\pounds 13\,500 \times 1.05^{n-1}$
  (f) Year 10

17 $22.65, 24$

18 (a) 5 (b) 5 (c) $\frac{1}{4}\pi$

19 $2\pi \text{ cm}, 2(\pi - \sqrt{3}) \text{ cm}^2$

20 $-2, 132.5°$

22 (i) $\dfrac{dx}{dt}$ is $+,0,-$ with $\dfrac{d^2x}{dt^2}$ $-,0,+$

   (ii) $\dfrac{dx}{dt}$ is $-$; $\dfrac{d^2x}{dt^2}$ is $+$

   (a) Graph dips below $x=0$ with a minimum, then tends to $x=0$. Hence

$$\dfrac{dx}{dt} \text{ is } -,0,+ \text{ with } \dfrac{d^2x}{dt^2} +,0,-.$$

   (b) $\dfrac{dx}{dt}$ is $0,-$ with $\dfrac{d^2x}{dt^2}$ $-,0,+$.

23 $2\frac{1}{2}$

24 (a) $(2,4)$ (b) $\frac{64}{5}\pi$

25 $80.9°$

26 $3\frac{1}{2}$

27 $1,0.71$

28 (a) $\frac{4}{3}a^2$ (b) $2\pi a^3$; $\frac{53}{240}\pi a^3$

Practice examinations

Practice examination 1 (page 283)

1 81

2 (i) $-\dfrac{1}{x}-2\sqrt{x}+k$ (ii) $y=-\dfrac{1}{x}-2\sqrt{x}+3$

3 (i) $y=2x+1$ (ii) 5

4 (ii) $\frac{1}{6}\pi$, $\frac{5}{6}\pi$

5 (i) $(x+3)^2-6$

   (ii) (a) $(-3,-6)$ (b) $-3-\sqrt{6}<x<-3+\sqrt{6}$

6 (i) $f(x)\geqslant \frac{1}{3}$ (ii) 0 (iii) $\frac{1}{2}(x+1)$

   (iv)

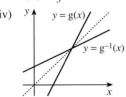

Reflections in $y=x$

7 (i) $x=-5$, $y=8$ or $x=2$, $y=1$

8 (i)

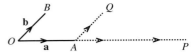

   (ii) 14

   (iii) $30°$

9 (i) $A=3r-r^2$ (ii) $\theta=2$

10 (i) $y+6x=8$ (iii) $\frac{16}{3}$

Practice examination 2 (page 285)

1 $81x^4+216x^3+216x^2+96x+16$

2 $\frac{1}{12}\pi$

3 (i) $y=3x-14$ (ii) $(5,1)$

4 (i)

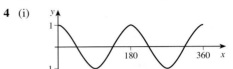

   (ii) $67.2, 112.8, 247.2, 292.8$

5 (i) $(-1,1)$ (ii) $\frac{32}{3}$

6 (i) $a+d, a+5d$ (iii) $660, 715\,827\,882$

7 (i) $f(x)\in\mathbb{R}$, $f(x)\neq1$; $g(x)\in\mathbb{R}$, $g(x)\geqslant-1$

   (ii) g is not one–one

   (iii) $f^{-1}:x\mapsto \dfrac{1+x}{3(1-x)}$, $x\in\mathbb{R}$, $x\neq1$

8 (i) 1.107 (ii) $4.02\ \text{cm}^2$

   (iii) $4.33\ \text{cm}^2$ (iv) $8.40\ \text{cm}$

9 (a) $\dfrac{1}{2\sqrt{x}}-\dfrac{2}{(2x+1)^2}$

   (b) (i) $3x^2-6x+12$

10 (i) $4\mathbf{j}+3\mathbf{k}$, 5

   (iii) The scalar product is non-zero.

   (iv) $101°$

Index

The page numbers refer to the first mention of each term, or the box if there is one.

PUBLISHED BY
THE READER'S DIGEST ASSOCIATION LIMITED
LONDON • NEW YORK • SYDNEY • MONTREAL

The most amazing places in Britain's countryside

More than 500 spectacular scenic wonders

Contents

Introduction

Britain is blessed with many spectacular scenic treasures – some to be found surprisingly near towns and cities, others off the beaten track. Wherever you go, you'll find inspiring, unspoiled countryside to explore and enjoy.

Stretching about 600 miles, from north to south, and around 300 miles across at the widest point, Britain is a small country, yet it offers a wide range of beautiful places to visit. It is a land of great contrasts – you can climb to the top of rugged mountains or stroll among gentle, rolling hills; battle the elements on windswept moors or warm your face on sunny downs; be calmed by the peace and tranquillity of a lakeside view or dazzled by waves breaking against a rocky shore.

The Most Amazing Places in Britain's Countryside will introduce you to both the more remote destinations that Britain has to offer, as well as spots that may be a little closer to home. You'll discover some unexpected natural wonders and learn more about the fascinating wildlife you may meet on the way. Interspersed throughout the book are features that take an in-depth look at aspects of the British countryside – from ancient chalk figures in the hillsides of southern England to the ever-changing coastline of East Anglia.

How to use this book

The book is divided by region into six chapters: South-west England, Southern England, Eastern England, Wales and the Welsh Borders, Northern England, and Scotland (see right). Each chapter is then sub-divided into areas of outstanding beauty and interest, such as Dartmoor or The Mendip Hills in the South-west England chapter.

At the beginning of each chapter you will find a map of the region, with the featured areas highlighted. The numbers within each area on the map correspond with the

SCOTLAND
256–311

NORTHERN
ENGLAND
202–255

WALES
and
THE WELSH
BORDERS
136–201

EASTERN
ENGLAND
116–135

SOUTHERN
ENGLAND
68–115

SOUTH-WEST
ENGLAND
8–67

numbered entries that make up each section, so when you are reading about a place you can easily find it on the map. If, for example, you want to visit Ashdown Forest, featured on page 109 in the Downland and Weald section of the Southern England chapter, turn to the map on pages 68–69 and look for number 6 in the Downland and Weald area to find its location.

Alternatively, if you want to explore a particular area, you can consult the map at the beginning of a chapter and turn to the relevant pages to locate the numbered entries.

Planning your trip

The book contains more than 500 entries for locations in 35 scenic areas across England, Scotland and Wales. At the end of each entry there is useful information on how to find the place described. Always double-check the details of your route before setting out.

All locations are accessible by car or on foot. Some places may be reached by a gentle ramble; others require a more strenuous hike. No matter what kind of walk you are taking, you should always be well prepared. Take an up-to-date map and a compass, wear proper walking boots and suitable weatherproof clothing, and always check the weather report before you set out.

Wherever your journey takes you through Britain, remember to enjoy the countryside responsibly and to leave the landscape as you find it, so others may be amazed at its beauty in their turn.

Useful websites

The following websites offer advice and information for anyone wanting to enjoy Britain's natural heritage:

www.countrysideaccess.gov.uk – information on access to the countryside and the Countryside Code; links will take you to the relevant Welsh and Scottish sites

www.ordnancesurvey.co.uk – mapping information

www.nationalparks.gov.uk – information on Britain's National Parks

www.aonb.org.uk – the National Association for Areas of Outstanding Natural Beauty in England and Wales

www.snh.org.uk – Scottish Natural Heritage

www.forestry.gov.uk – the Forestry Commission

www.metoffice.gov.uk – Met Office weather forecasts

www.ramblers.org.uk – the Ramblers Association

www.rspb.org.uk – the Royal Society for the Protection of Birds

www.wildlifetrusts.org – The Wildlife Trusts movement

Much of the British countryside is owned or controlled by heritage organisations. More information can be found at:

www.english-heritage.org.uk – English Heritage

www.cadw.wales.gov.uk – Cadw (Welsh Historic Monuments)

www.historic-scotland.gov.uk – Historic Scotland

www.nationaltrust.org.uk – The National Trust

www.nts.org.uk – The National Trust for Scotland

South-west England

Shaped by the power of the waves, England's south-western peninsula boasts dramatic coastal scenery with rugged cliffs, sandy coves and tranquil creeks, while inland lies a timeless landscape of wild moors, wooded combes and rolling hills.

EXMOOR and NORTH DEVON 31–41

CORNWALL'S COAST and MOORLAND 10–21

DARTMOOR 22–30

Isles of Scilly
Tresco
St Mary's

Ilfracombe
Barnstaple
Bideford
Bude
Okehampton
Launceston
Padstow
Bodmin
Tavistock
Liskeard
Newquay
Plymouth
St Austell
Truro
St Ives
Penzance
Helston
Falmouth
Exeter
Tiverton
Torquay
Dartmouth
Salcombe
Mineh

A39 · A361 · A386 · A37 · A30 · A390 · A38 · A380 · A385 · A394

Bristol

Weston-super-Mare

Bath

A38

A37

7

1

5 2

4 3

6

8

11

9

10

12 Frome

13

A361

THE MENDIP HILLS
49-55

Glastonbury

A361

Bridgwater

1

3 2

4 5

13

7

9

8

11 12

10

THE
QUANTOCK
HILLS
42-48

Taunton

A37

A303

A303

Yeovil

Shaftesbury

A30

2

1

A354

A350

3

Blandford
Forum

A37

Honiton

A35

4

Poole

A348

A338

Bournemouth

5

Lyme Regis

A35

6

A35

12

Swanage

DORSET
HILLS 58-67

19

18

17

16

Dorchester

11

9

7

Weymouth

8

13

14

10

15

CORNWALL'S COAST and MOORLAND

A spectacular coastline of rugged cliffs and sandy coves dominates the Cornish landscape. Wherever you are in the county – even on the highest point of Bodmin Moor – the sea is never more than 20 miles away.

❶ Henna Cliff

From the heights of Henna Cliff the Atlantic breakers below seem hushed almost to a murmur, for it plunges a sheer 140m (450ft) to the sea. Except for Beachy Head, this is the highest sheer drop of any sea-cliff in England.

Northwards you can see beyond Hartland Point and Lundy island to the blue haze of the Pembroke coast some 50 miles away. South-west there are views along 40 miles of the Cornish coast to Trevose Head, gnarled with headlands such as Tintagel. Gorse and heather cover the cliff-top, despite the battering of savage Atlantic gales. In summer the pink-flowering thrift grows here in profusion.

About a quarter of a mile south of Henna Cliff is Vicarage Cliff, owned by the National Trust, where a driftwood lookout hut built by the Rev. Robert Stephen Hawker is perched on the cliff-edge. From 1834 until 1875 Hawker was the vicar of nearby Morwenstow, which takes its name from the holy well of St Morwenna set in the steep face of the cliff.

Parson Hawker was noted for his help and compassion for the many victims of shipwrecks under the cliffs, but today he is best remembered as the writer of 'The Song of the Western Men', the famous Cornish ballad.

▶ *Henna Cliff is about ½ mile north-west of Morwenstow, where there is parking space by the church. Morwenstow is 4 miles north-west of Kilkhampton along minor roads off the A39.*

❷ Coombe Valley

A steep, wooded valley with a gentle stream comes as a surprise within a mile of the rugged, windswept coast of north Cornwall. Yet Coombe Valley is only half a mile from Steeple Point and the surfing beach of Duckpool. It stretches about 2 miles eastwards from the picturesque hamlet of Coombe – a cluster of cottages that once housed the miller and his men who worked the nearby water-mill, now disused. The cottages belong to the Landmark Trust.

Some of the stones used to build the mill in 1842 were probably taken from the old manor house that once stood in the valley – the family home of Sir Richard Grenville, immortalised in Lord Tennyson's poem 'The Revenge'.

Sir Richard, who was County Sheriff of Cornwall in 1577, commanded the *Revenge* in 1591 when it engaged single-handed a fleet of 53 Spanish warships near Flores in the Azores, having become separated from the main British fleet. The *Revenge* held off the Spaniards for 15 hours, until only 20 men survived; Sir Richard was mortally wounded and died aboard the Spanish flagship.

Today, Coombe Valley is as green and peaceful as it must have been when Sir Richard rode there over 400 years ago. A variety of nature trails and walks follow the stream among oak woods hung with honeysuckle and through Forestry Commission plantations of conifers.

Buzzards circle above the valley, great spotted woodpeckers and treecreepers may be seen feeding on the oaks, and tiny goldcrests live among the conifers. By the stream there are dippers, grey wagtails and occasionally a kingfisher. Butterflies abound in the woodland clearings in summer, including the pale yellow brimstone that lays its eggs on the damp-loving alder buckthorn.

▶ *Coombe Valley is 4 miles north of Bude, and can be reached along minor roads north-west off the A39 via Stibb and Stowe Barton. A nature trail starts at the car park near Coombe Cottages.*

DUCKPOOL

❸ High Cliff

As you look down from High Cliff, the highest point on the Cornish coast, the silver-grey expanse of sea 200m (700ft) or more below seems remote and unreal, although the strong onshore winds dispel any sensation of dreaminess. The cliff is not sheer; two hummocks interrupt its slope to the sea.

Just to the north, towards the headland of Cambeak, is the jagged cliff known as the Voter Run, which produces a strange roaring when wind and tide are at a certain strength. Beyond Voter Run lies the treacherous reef of The Strangles, a reminder that, despite the shimmering beauty of the sea from this vantage point, this is a dangerous coast where many sailing ships have come to grief in times past. There is little or no shelter along these cliffs for miles, save for the narrow Boscastle harbour to the south.

Samphire Rock just beyond The Strangles recalls another hazardous undertaking of past times – the collection of rock samphire. Cornishmen once regularly climbed down the cliffs to collect this plant from the rock clefts; its fleshy leaves were pickled and eaten and considered a delicacy. Samphire pickers were in danger of falling to their deaths, should they miss their footing on the steep and slippery slopes, or of falling victim to one of the landslips to which the soft shale cliffs are very susceptible.

▶ *To reach High Cliff, leave the A39 Camelford-Stratton road at Tresparrett Down, and follow a minor road north-west for about 1½ miles.*

❹ Beeny Cliff

One thing sets Beeny Cliff apart from the other rugged and beautiful headlands of Cornwall's north coast – it is the only headland carved from chert, a tough, black flint-like rock. Because of this the cliff-face is easy to recognise against the slate-grey of the headlands around.

From the cliff-top there are magnificent views out to sea beyond the wave-lashed reef known as the Beeny Sisters, and grey seals can sometimes be seen basking on the rocks below. South-westwards you can see the land-locked harbour of Boscastle, and north-east the towering High Cliff. Below the southern tip of Beeny Cliff is Pentargon waterfall, where a local stream plunges more than 30m (100ft) into the ocean down a deep chasm cut into the cliff by the Atlantic.

▶ *Beeny Cliff is ½ mile west of the hamlet of Beeny, which is west off the B3263 about 1½ miles north-east of Boscastle.*

11

❺ Bodmin Moor

Bodmin Moor is crowned by stark and spectacular tors, castle-like columns of balanced granite boulders that stand above the moorland tracts, with wonderful views from their summits. Two of the highest peaks in Cornwall rise above the northern moor – Brown Willy (420m (1,377ft)) and Rough Tor (400m (1,311ft)). Looming large on the south-east moor are Kilmar Tor, overlooking Twelve Men's Moor, and Stowe's Hill, with the strange rockpile known as the Cheesewring on its western slopes.

Hauntingly poignant among the moorland wastes are standing stones, the countless relics of forgotten times. In the ghostly atmosphere of Bodmin Moor they cast a strange enchantment over the grey-green grassland. The moor was the most heavily populated part of Cornwall in prehistoric times, but in later centuries the population dwindled away. By the 13th century, however, Cornwall's swelling population had begun to look for new pastures, and people turned once again to the upland moor. Peasant cattle farmers built their granite homes near running water in hollows sheltered from the moorland winds.

In the 18th century Bodmin Moor saw a mining boom. It lasted 100 years and, in their heyday, the Caradon copper mines were among the richest in the world. Today, the gaunt stacks of the engine-houses stand as silent monuments to those prosperous times.

The rainfall on Bodmin Moor is heavy – up to 2,032mm (80in) a year. Bogs and marshes have formed in those areas where the water has been unable to find an easy path away from the impervious underlying granite. This has happened at Dozmary Pool, where the water has gathered to form a lake – a rarity in Cornwall. Local legends claimed it was bottomless but, in fact, it is quite shallow and has been known to dry up. Elsewhere, reservoirs like Crowdy attract water-fowl and other birds, such as golden plovers, lapwings, grebes and hen harriers.
▶ *Bodmin moor lies on either side of the A30 running between Launceston and Bodmin.*

❻ Pentire Point

At the western tip of a square headland that juts into the Atlantic, Pentire Point is an 80m (260ft) high block of solidified lava known as pillow lava, for it was poured out in pillow-like masses from a submarine volcano millions of years ago. On all sides, the views are impressive. A wide sweep of the grey Atlantic stretches to the west, north and north-west. To the north-east you can see beyond Boscastle and Cambeak to the long line of cliffs near Bude, and again beyond, some 35 miles distant, to the great mass of Hartland Point on the North Devon coast.

South-westwards, Stepper Point guards the opposite, western shore of the River Camel estuary, and beyond is Trevose Head and its lighthouse. Southwards from Pentire Point, you can look down the river to the great sandbank known as The Doom Bar. This bar has blocked the mouth of the Camel for 150 years or more, reducing the river to a narrow channel and ending Padstow's prosperity as a busy port and harbour. According to legend, the bank built up because of a mermaid's curse, made after she had been fatally wounded by a Padstow fisherman who shot her with a bow and arrow in mistake for a seal. Nearly 300 ships have been driven on to the treacherous bar to be wrecked or stranded, with considerable loss of life.

The rocky islets of Newland and The Mouls that lie north-west and north-east off the Pentire

ROUGH TOR ON BODMIN MOOR

headland are a haven for grey seals and puffins. The Mouls lies off Rumps Point at the eastern tip of the headland, a Y-shaped promontory crowned by an Iron Age fort known as The Rumps. Some 2,000 years ago a small Celtic community lived here in round thatched huts, guarded from invaders by three banks and ditches whose outlines can still be seen across the neck of the promontory. Scraps of pottery found on the site show that they may have come from Brittany in north-west France, and that they drank wine from the Mediterranean.

You can walk right round the headland, which is owned and farmed by the National Trust. Many of the cliffs are covered with bracken that glows warm brown in autumn, and in summer foxgloves and red campion are among the flowers that line the way. At Pentireglaze on the south of the headland there are remains of a mine that was worked for silver and lead ore in the 18th and 19th centuries.

▶ *Pentire Point is 6 miles north-west of Wadebridge. Leave the town by the B3314 and after 4 miles, at Plain Street, turn north-west along a minor road towards Pentire Farm, where there is a car park.*

❼ Bedruthan Steps

Huge, irregular rock stacks shaped by the Atlantic, Bedruthan Steps are a magnificent sight at any time of the year – whether surrounded by vast stretches of sand at low tide in summer, or pounded by mountainous winter waves. Said to be stepping-stones to the 60m (200ft) cliff used by the legendary Celtic giant Bedruthan, they are formed of slate, like the cliff itself. A number of rocky arches at the cliff base will in time probably collapse under the relentless onslaught of the sea to form more steps.

One of the rock stacks is known as the Queen Bess Rock because it is said to look like Elizabeth I in profile. Another is called the Samaritan Rock – a name that recalls the wreck of the *Good Samaritan*, an East Indiaman from Liverpool, that was smashed on to the shore by a savage Atlantic storm in 1846. Although a tragedy for the crew, the wreck was a windfall for the impoverished locals, many of whom added to their meagre living by salvaging the goods from wrecks.

About 1½ miles from the cliffs is the isolated Church of St Uvelos at St Eval, its tall tower a landmark by day to guide ships away from the rocks. It was so valued by seamen that in 1727 Bristol merchants paid for the tower's repair.

The South West Coast Path follows the top of the cliff, in summer bright with the yellow of gorse and kidney vetch and heavy with the scent of burnet rose. There are 120 steps leading down to the beach, a restored stairway that was originally cut by smugglers and wreck robbers who probably stored their loot in caves at the cliff bottom. The caves include one known as the Great Cavern.

▶ *Bedruthan Steps lie west of the Newquay-Padstow road (B3276) about 1 mile north of Trenance. There is a large car park at the top of the cliff. It is managed by the National Trust, under the name of Carnewas and Bedruthan Steps. The cliff staircase is closed in winter.*

❽ St Agnes Beacon

One of the north Cornish coast's finest scenic grandstands, St Agnes Beacon, 192m (630ft), gives not only superb coastal views stretching from Trevose Head and Newquay south to St Ives, but also views inland to the heights of Bodmin Moor and across the peninsula to Falmouth and St Michael's Mount.

Around the beacon itself, the hillsides are dotted with the remains of the local mining industry that flourished in the 19th century, when St Agnes was a great centre of tin and copper mining. Gaunt, ruined engine-houses with their tall chimneys – Cornish castles – are scattered along the cliffs.

A 3 mile walk from Chapel Porth round St Agnes Head to Trevaunance Cove takes in not only the fine cliff scenery but also Wheal Coates – *wheal* is a Cornish word for 'mine'. The ruins are perched partway down the cliffs below the west slopes of the beacon, and are now owned by the National Trust. If you go in late spring or early summer, you will find the cliffs bright with wild flowers such as the pale blue, star-like spring squill, the yellow kidney vetch and the golden prostrate broom. In late summer and autumn they are aglow with the purple of heather and the gold of western gorse.

Trevaunance Cove shelters below the eastern side of St Agnes Head, and was once the harbour where tin and copper were exported. No signs of the quays remain today. They were very difficult to construct in this rock-girt cove, and four attempts between 1632 and 1736 were swept away by the sea. The narrow, rocky Trevellas Porth adjoins Trevaunance Cove, and from here you can walk beside the stream up the lovely combe known as Trevellas Coombe to Trevellas and Harmony Cot, about a mile north-east of the valley.

▶ *St Agnes is 6 miles north of Redruth via the A30 and B3277. The beacon is found 1 mile south-west of the village.*

SOUTH-WEST ENGLAND

❾ Zennor Head

Backed by the bleak heather moors of Penwith, Zennor Head is a grand, lonely spot overlooking the Atlantic, with a narrow gorge known as the Horse's Mouth cutting into the headland. It is a good place for viewing a 'green flash' – a phenomenon that sometimes occurs over the sea while the sun is sinking or rising, when a green light momentarily floods the sky.

On a calm summer day the view from the 90m (300ft) headland can be deceptively gentle, but when an Atlantic gale is blowing, mountainous seas can be heard hurling huge boulders over the rocks below. From The Carracks – rocky, seal-haunted islands 2 miles north-east – down to Pendeen Watch, 5 miles south-west beyond Gurnard's Head, this coast has been the scene of many shipwrecks.

Zennor village shelters in a hollow about half a mile inland from Zennor Head, and about half a mile south-east of the village is Zennor Quoit, a chambered tomb dating back some 5,000 years to the Stone Age. Its huge stones, including a 5m (15ft) wide slab capstone, form a rectangular enclosure once covered by an earthen mound. Some of the support stones were taken by a 19th-century farmer for building, and another damaged the tomb by blasting in an unsuccessful treasure hunt.
▶ *Zennor is 4 miles west of St Ives on the B3306, and the headland is ½ mile north-west from the village.*

❿ Cape Cornwall

The lonely stack of a deserted mine marks Cape Cornwall, where the turbulent Atlantic beats against the granite moors of the Penwith peninsula just north of Land's End. Such is the force and persistence of the breakers that parts of the cliff have worn away to leave the windswept cape almost an island.

Heather and gorse dapple the headland, and primroses and squill splash the cliffs with colour in the spring. In summer, clusters of thrift, or sea pink, are scattered among the rocks and clefts. Some of the clefts are relics of the headland's mining days; such clefts – in Cornish 'zawns' – were man-made when miners removed the rocks to get at the seams of copper and tin. For hundreds of years, Cornish miners descended the zawns to underground workings on ladders, their only light underground coming from the candles fixed with clay to their hard felt hats. Tin streaming was known in Cornwall in prehistoric times, but tin mining first began in the 1500s, with copper mining 200 years later.

Cape Cornwall and the surrounding area was once a thriving mining centre. Much of the world's tin and copper was produced in Cornwall but in the late 1800s discoveries in places such as Africa and Australia caused the collapse of the Cornish mining industry. No pounding pistons or thudding hammers compete with the roar of the sea and wind now; the silent stack at Cape Cornwall looks out across the grey Atlantic and to where a seething line of surf marks the dangerous Brisons rocks.

The Cape Cornwall mine was abandoned in the late 1870s and the mines at nearby Botallack in 1895 (except for a brief re-opening in the early 1900s). Now only the ruins of engine-houses remain, chimneyed buildings which once housed the steam-engines that pumped away water – the miners' constant peril – from the workings. The National Trust owns Botallack and the restored Count House features displays on the history of local mining. The tin mine at Geevor, near Trewellard about 2 miles north-east of Cape Cornwall, has a visitor centre and tin-mining museum.
▶ *Cape Cornwall lies 1½ miles west of St Just in Penwith, along a signposted minor road.*

⓫ Chysauster

It is probably 1,800 years since the Iron Age villagers of Chysauster abandoned their courtyard homes high on the Guval Downs north of Penzance, yet the dry-stone walls still stand about 1m (3ft) high in places, and you can still distinguish the outlines of their walled and terraced gardens. The village was inhabited from about 100 BC until the 2nd century AD, and here the Celtic occupants tilled their fields on the terraced green hillsides and streamed for tin in the valley below.

Castle-an-Dinas, an Iron Age hill-fort, and Roger's Tower, an early 19th-century folly, overlook the village from the 233m (760ft) summit about a mile to the east. The village itself is about 180m (600ft) above sea-level, with magnificent views south to Mount's Bay.

The remains of nine houses are visible in Chysauster, eight of them in two rows of four on each side of a narrow lane. All the main entrances faced north-east, away from the prevailing south-west winds. Roughly oval in shape and nearly 30m (100ft) across, the houses had thick walls enclosing circular rooms that opened on to a central courtyard. In each house, a long, narrow passage with stone-faced earthen walls led to the courtyard; recesses in the courtyard walls may have been cattle byres. The main room of each house, opposite the passage

PRUSSIA COVE

entrance, contains a central stone with a socket for a roof-post, which probably supported a thatched or turved roof.

Most of the floors are paved and have drainage channels, and some of the side chambers have a sump. Granite mortars and hand grindstones have been found in the village, and to the south of the houses there is a fougou – an underground chamber that was probably used as a food store by the whole community.

▶ *To reach Chysauster, turn north-west at Badger's Cross on the Penzance-St Ives road, the B3311. The village lies about 1½ miles along a signposted minor road. There is a small car park near the site. Chysauster is an English Heritage site and there is a charge for admission.*

⑫ Prussia Cove

A narrow inlet in the slate rocks of Bessy's Cove in Mount's Bay, Prussia Cove takes its name from a notorious smuggler, John Carter, whose nickname was the King of Prussia. No one knows for sure whether this was because he looked like Frederick the Great, or because that king was his hero. Bessy's Cove is named after the keeper of an alehouse that once stood on the cliffs above.

In the late 1700s, John Carter, from Breage, made the cove his headquarters for the landing and storing of contraband such as brandy, tobacco and bales of silk. The only landward approach was by a steep path down the cliff. Once, when one of his cargoes was discovered and seized by Customs men, Carter raided the Penzance Customs House the following night in order to retrieve it. The captive goods were promised to customers and Carter never broke his word. He became so bold that he ringed the cliffs above the cove with cannon as a means to keep away the Customs cutters.

The rugged, picturesque coves are more peaceful today, along with the adjoining Piskies Cove. The caves that the smugglers found so useful were worn from the rocks by the pounding sea, and Piskies Cove in particular has been much eroded. When the seas run high, the immense clouds of spray that rise among the rocks are a spectacular sight. The climate here is generally mild, allowing a profusion of flowers such as thrift, and evergreen tamarisk shrubs line the cliff-top.

▶ *Prussia Cove is 5 miles east of Penzance, and is signposted south off the A394 Penzance-Helston road at Rosudgeon. Cars can be parked in a field on the cliffs above the cove.*

15

⑬ Loe Pool

Cornwall's largest natural lake, Loe Pool, lies at the mouth of the River Cober, dammed from the sea by a 180m (600ft) wide ridge of shingle known as Loe Bar. Local legend says the bar was formed when Jan Tregeagle, a notorious folk-figure, was forced to clear Berepper beach of sand by the Devil. During his labours he dropped a sack of sand across the Cober estuary when a spiteful demon tripped him up. The lake is also said to be the place where King Arthur's sword Excalibur was thrown after the king was mortally wounded at the battle of Camlamm. Peaceful woods of sycamore, oak and pine stretch down to both shores of the narrow, mile-long lake. Rhododendrons make a vivid splash of colour in early summer, and there are white water lilies floating on the water. Grey herons hunt among the reeds, and mallards and swans frequent Carminowe Creek, which runs into the lake at its seaward end.

At one time, the Helston residents regularly had to cut a channel for the water through the shingle bar to prevent flooding in the lower part of the town, but today there is a permanent water outlet. The sandy beach on the seaward side of Loe Bar is popular with holidaymakers, but it has not always been the scene solely of leisure.

A naval frigate, HMS *Anson*, was wrecked on the bar in December 1807, and 100 lives were lost. One man who witnessed the tragedy was Henry Trengrouse, a cabinet-maker from Helston, who was appalled to see so many drowned so close to land. It led him to spend a great deal of his time and money on devising a means of rescue, and he was the originator of the line-carrying rocket that enabled a breeches buoy to be rigged to transfer people ashore. This device has since saved many lives.

The lake is part of the Penrose estate, owned by the National Trust. A number of small car parks have been established, set well back from the water. These are linked by a network of footpaths which provides some of the most beautiful walks in the county (no dogs are allowed).

▶ *Loe Pool can be reached from Porthleven, 2½ miles south-west of Helston on the B3304. Park on the south-east side of the town above Porthleven Sands, from where there is a path south-eastwards to Loe Bar and Pool. Alternatively, minor roads and tracks lead south from the B3304 to Loe Pool.*

⑭ Kynance Cove

Some of Cornwall's loveliest scenery lies along the 6 mile stretch of coast between Mullion Cove and Lizard Point, particularly at Kynance Cove where the cliffs sweep down to weathered serpentine rocks lapped by a surf-fringed azure sea, with pale golden sands revealed at low tide.

Apart from their idyllic setting, the Kynance rocks are spectacular because of their colours and shapes. The mottled grey-green or red-brown serpentine rock – named for its resemblance to snake skin – glows with streaks of red, white, yellow and black, especially in the caves at the foot of the cliff, which have names like the Parlour and the Ladies' Bathing Pool.

The cove is scattered with wild-shaped rocks, worn by the sea, such as the tall Steeple Rock and the Bishop's Rock that looks something like a mitred head. In the weird Devil's Letterbox and Bellows in the side of Asparagus Island, the incoming tide is sucked through a narrow hole with a massive roar, then spewed out in a shower of spray. Asparagus Island is named for the wild asparagus that grows on its slopes.

Wild flowers grow in profusion all along these cliffs, including blue-flowering spring squill from April to June, and in summer the exotic Hottentot-fig, the Cornish heath (a feature of the Lizard peninsula), pink thrift, buttercups, foxgloves, tormentil, heath milk-wort and blackthorn. A Victorian naturalist the Rev. Charles Johns, author of *A Week at the Lizard* (1848), claimed to have found 12 wild plants within the area covered by his hat.

The Lizard has seen the return of the chough, a distinctive member of the crow family with glossy black plumage and bright red legs and beak. Extinct in Cornwall since the 1970s, a breeding pair of wild birds arrived on the Lizard in 2001, probably from Brittany. They nested successfully in 2002 and numbers have increased every year since. Grassy cliff-tops that have been cropped by rabbits and grazing livestock are the ideal environment for choughs, who feed on insects living in the soil and among dried animal droppings. A change in farming methods saw a reduction of suitable habitats in the 20th century but efforts to provide areas where choughs might thrive have paid off and these striking birds may now be seen again in Cornwall.

SCATTERED WITH WILD-SHAPED ROCKS
KYNANCE COVE

Mullion Cove is a walk of about 4 miles along the cliff-tops from Kynance. Hemmed in by lichen-covered cliffs, it has a stone-jettied harbour where fish were once landed. Lizard Point is about 2 miles south from Kynance, its lighthouse the most southerly point on the English mainland. The Lizard's strange name is derived from the Cornish *lis*, a court or palace, and *arth*, meaning high or holy.

▶ *Kynance Cove is signposted off the A3083 Helston–Lizard road, from where a toll-road leads to the car park.*

⓯ Croft Pascoe

Still, silent pinewoods within sight of the sea are unusual along the Cornish coast.

The Croft Pascoe pine plantation on Goonhilly Downs, only about 2 miles from the southern cliffs of the Lizard peninsula, was planted by the Forestry Commission in 1955 as an experiment in tree-growing on the thin clay soil overlying the serpentine rock. Coastal lodgepole and Monterey pines proved to be the most successful.

Trees and surrounding heathland have provided a happy nesting and hunting ground for the buzzards to be seen circling overhead, and the drumming of great spotted woodpeckers among the pines mixes with the trilling of soaring skylarks on the downland. Close by the plantation, Croft Pascoe Pool is a refuge for moorhens and many kinds of wildfowl.

In spring the flat, open heathlands of Goonhilly Downs are heady with the scent of gorse, its golden glow broken in places by the white flowers of blackthorn, which appear before the leaves. In late summer, by the time the blackthorn sloes are beginning to swell, the gorse flowers have given way to the purple of heather, particularly the pale pink or lilac of Cornish heath found on the Lizard.

The highest point on Goonhilly Downs, 113m (370ft), is at Dry Tree, about a mile north from Croft Pascoe, near the huge dish aerials that were once part of Goonhilly Satellite Earth Station. The name Goonhilly is a corruption of the old Cornish *gun helghy* – meaning 'hunting downs'. There are many burial mounds and some hut circles and standing stones, including the 3,000-year-old 5m (15ft) standing stone near Dry Tree, once fallen but now re-erected. Until about 200 years ago there are said to have been wild ponies derived from Celtic stock, known as 'goonhillies', roaming the downs.

▶ *Croft Pascoe is off the B3293 Helston-St Keverne road, along a minor road about ½ mile south from Traboe Cross.*

SOUTH-WEST ENGLAND

⓰ Rosemullion Head

Sheltered by the Lizard peninsula from the full fury of the Atlantic gales, the corner of Cornwall north of the Helford River is a comparatively gentle, richly wooded area with leafy lanes and lovely creeks, and sandy beaches where it is safe to bathe. Perched on the cliff overlooking the rivermouth and Parson's Beach is 15th-century Mawnan Church. From it, a flower-lined footpath leads to Rosemullion Head about a mile to the north-east, a low promontory overlooking the western side of Falmouth Bay.

A tranquil spot where the sea laps lazily against the rocks, the headland is sea-girt on three sides, with a pathway to the south leading down to a sand and shingle beach with numerous rock pools in the wave-cut platform. Thickly covered with gorse and bracken, Rosemullion Head climbs gently inland to a height of 67m (220ft). More than half-a-dozen headlands come into view, including Pendennis Point with its Tudor fortress guarding the western side of Falmouth harbour, and Zone Point and the pine-clad St Anthony Head on the other side of Falmouth Bay.

St Anthony Head is distinguished by the white lighthouse at the foot of the cliff, which throws a beam of light across the harbour entrance, and also sends a red light flashing south-west to the dangerous Manacles reef. Looking south from Rosemullion Head you can see Nare Point on the south shore of Helford rivermouth and beyond it Manacle Point which is north-west of The Manacles.

Nare Point was the scene of a savage shipwreck in the terrible West Country blizzards of March 1891, when the *Bay of Panama*, a clipper carrying jute from Calcutta, was hurled against its cliffs. The survivors clung to the rigging all night, some freezing to death; those still left alive were taken off by breeches buoy next morning. Even then, the horse-bus taking them to refuge in St Keverne was caught in a snow-drift and had to be abandoned. Seventeen of the crew of 40 survived.

▶ *Rosemullion Head, owned by the National Trust, is 3 miles south of Falmouth along minor roads via Mawnan Smith and Mawnan. There is a car park by Mawnan Church, from where a path leads about a mile to the headland.*

⓱ Froe Creek

A finger of water lined in parts by centuries-old woods, Froe Creek flows between rocks into the Percuil River just north of its confluence with the famous anchorage of the Carrick Roads that opens into Falmouth Bay. Pines, beeches and scrub oaks, rising from both banks, make a wonderful canopy of varying shades of green in summer. The half-mile long creek is a haven for moorhens, mallards, mute swans and grey herons, and only the rustle of the reeds and the occasional splash of a diving kingfisher disturb the peace.

There is a dam at the head of the creek, once the mill-pond of a tide-mill now pulled down. The head of the creek is the starting point for a 6½ mile circular walk round the peninsula of St Anthony-in-Roseland; a field path leads first to Towan Beach, from where the route follows the coast path south-west to Porthmellin Head, and on to Zone Point and St Anthony Head. It then turns north past Carricknath Point and St Anthony and back through National Trust pinewoods to Froe Creek.

A shorter walk of 3½ miles takes you direct from Porthmellin Head westwards to St Anthony, cutting out the headland. Zone Point and St Anthony Head (also owned by the National Trust) can, however, be reached by road. They lie about 2 miles south-west of Froe Creek, and give sweeping views of Falmouth Bay.

▶ *To reach Froe Creek, turn south off the Tregony-St Mawes road, A3078, at Trewithian. Froe is 2½ miles south via Gerrans and Trewince.*

⓲ Nare Head

All the sights that are typical of the Cornish coast can be enjoyed at Nare Head, a quiet spot overlooking Veryan Bay to the east and Gerrans Bay to the west. The flat cliff-top, 100m (330ft) high, is bright with the chatter of birds above the dull pounding of the surf on the rocks below, and sweet with the scent of bell heather stirred by the stiff sea breezes. On Gull Rock, offshore to the south-east, cormorants can be seen sitting with wings outstretched to dry.

The constant pounding of the waves has eaten away the slate cliffs, leaving the headland as a narrow point at its seaward tip. It broadens out inland, where hedgerows are bright with foxgloves and red campion in summer. Cornfields cover the slopes on the headland and a pathway leads down past a derelict fisherman's hut to the sandy coves below. On the west side of the headland a small stream runs through a bracken-covered valley to the sandy Pendower Beach.

Carne Beacon, a hill with magnificent views a mile north of Nare Head, can be reached by a public footpath from the hamlet of Carne. The easiest approach is from its north-west side, and once on top there are breathtaking views of the surrounding countryside. The gorse-covered mound on the summit with its gnarled old lilac tree is a round barrow – a Bronze Age burial mound more than 3,000 years old. But legend assigns it as the grave of Gerennius, a king or saint who died some 1,400 years ago.

This semi-legendary king – who may have been the Geraint of King Arthur's Round Table – gave his name to Gerrans Bay and the village of Gerrans round the bay to the west. Believed to have been a Celtic prince who took refuge in this part of Cornwall after being driven from Wales by the Saxons, he is said to have lived at Dingerein Castle, now only an earthen mound north of Gerrans. On his death, according to legend, Gerennius was rowed across Gerrans Bay in a golden boat with silver oars, and his boat buried with him in the Carne mound. But no boat was found when the mound was excavated in 1855.

▶ *Nare Head and Carne Beacon are both owned by the National Trust. Take the Veryan turning east off the A3078 St Mawes-Truro road and follow signposts to Carne, where cars can be parked.*

⓳ Dodman Point

From the prominent heather-covered headland of Dodman Point, 114m (373ft) above the English Channel, the eye can sweep, in clear weather, across a 95 mile curve of coastline from Black Head on the Lizard peninsula some 20 miles to the south-west, to Bolt Head in Devon some 45 miles to the east.

Dodman Point is marked by a tall granite cross, erected as a landmark for ships in 1896 by a local clergyman. Sailors called the point the Dodman, an old English word for a snail, but its name is probably a corruption of Dead-man Point, for there are treacherous currents around the grey slate cliffs of the headland, where there have been many shipwrecks.

A pleasant pathway leads up to the point from Penare, between hedgerows banked with bluebells and primroses in spring, and with skylarks singing overhead. From Dodman Point, the South West Coast Path leads northwards to Maenease Point and down to the fishing village of Gorran Haven.

▶ *Dodman Point is a ½ mile walk south from Penare, where there is a car park. Penare is about 3 miles south of Mevagissey along minor roads.*

⓴ Pont Pill Creek

Although it opens into Fowey harbour right opposite the town itself, Pont Pill Creek is a quiet, beautiful backwater that gives the impression it is miles from anywhere. Time seems to stand still here, but not the tide, which ebbs and flows along the narrow, mile-long creek twice daily. Woods of oak, chestnut, sycamore and hazel line the north bank, sweeping down to the water's edge, near the creek head at the hamlet of Pont, where a tiny stream filters in.

A tranquil spot where herons haunt the reeds below the leafy bank, the creek was not always so peaceful. Once it was part of the port of Fowey (pronounced 'foy'), and less than a century ago boats came regularly to the quays at Pont to collect cargoes of grain, timber, coal and sand. The quays and footbridge have been restored by the National Trust, which owns land on both shores of the creek.

At the mouth of the creek, at Pentleath Point on the north shore, there is a memorial to Sir Arthur Quiller-Couch, the writer known as 'Q', who died at Fowey in 1944; this is a good place for views of the town. Sir Arthur's home, The Haven, overlooks the harbour. Fowey was the setting for his novel *Troy Town*. It was also 'the little grey sea town' with 'flights of stone steps over-hung by great pink tufts of valerian' described by Sea Rat in Kenneth Grahame's *The Wind in the Willows* written in 1908. Grahame, a friend of Sir Arthur, was married at Fowey in 1899 and often visited the town.

From Fowey you can make a round trip along both shores of Pont Pill Creek, walking for some 3 miles along the National Trust's Hall Walk, which starts at Bodinnick ferry across the river from Fowey. It leads eastwards along the north bank of the creek and westwards along the south bank to Polruan, where there is another ferry back to Fowey.

The start of the walk leads down to the 'Q' memorial, along what was once a promenade of the old mansion of Hall, the home of the Mohun family; all that remains is the old chapel, now part of the farm buildings of Hall Farm. It was on this promenade in 1644 that Charles I was almost killed by a shot fired from a cannon at Fowey, where Parliamentarians led by the Earl of Essex were under siege.

▶ *Fowey is on the A3082, 7 miles east of St Austell. Pont Pill Creek can also be reached along minor roads west from Polperro (signposted Bodinnick) to Pont, where there is a car park.*

㉑ Pencarrow Head

One of the most attractive headlands in Cornwall, Pencarrow Head combines the intimacy of its greenery, its flowers and its birdsong with the exhilaration of its wide-ranging views – sunswept fields, sandy bays, and silent promontories reaching down to the sea.

Buzzards soar overhead while yellow-hammers chirp busily in the thickets below, and in summer the bright pink of lesser and greater centaury and the occasional vermilion gleam of scarlet pimpernel contrast with the green of grass and bracken. Rabbits abound, prey to the circling buzzards as well as the many foxes and weasels that make their home here.

From the 136m (447ft) summit of the headland on a clear day you can see eastwards as far as Rame Head, 20 miles away, or sometimes beyond to Bolt Head in Devon. About 15 miles south-west, the Dodman juts out into the Channel and beyond it in a blue haze is the Lizard coast around St Keverne. Inland and a mile north-west from Pencarrow Head, the 14th-century tower of St Willow, the parish church of Lanteglos by Fowey, rises above its bower of trees.

Some 60m (200ft) below Pencarrow's sloping summit, the South West Coast Path curves right round the headland, and stretches away on either side along the cliffs above the bays of Lantic to the west and Lantivet to the east. Fields slope gently down to the jagged rocks that overhang the semicircular bays, which can both be reached from the coastal path. Even in high summer you may find their sandy beaches uncrowded, and delight in the rock pools and the small coves that may have been the haunt of 18th-century smugglers. In high summer, too, the blue and mauve flowers of sea holly and the pink, white-striped flowers of sea bindweed glow among the shingle.

▶ *Pencarrow Head can be reached along the unclassified Lansallos-Polruan road west from the A387 at Polperro. After about 4 miles there is a large car park beside the road, from where a path leads to the headland, owned by the National Trust.*

㉒ Rame Head

The heavy seas of the English Channel beat against the grey slate rocks of Rame Head on three sides for only a narrow neck of land links it to the mainland. It is majestic and remote, its bracken-covered slopes stretching steeply to the sea from its 90m (300ft) summit. Rame Head is at the western tip of the headland that guards the Cornish side of Plymouth Sound, with Penlee Point 1½ miles to the east.

Gulls mewing above the roar of the sea on the rocks are the most constant sounds reaching this high vantage point, which is rich with wild flowers in summer. There are magnificent views of the Channel and its shipping, and of ships heading in and out of Plymouth Sound. On clear days it is sometimes possible to pick out the Lizard on the horizon some 50 miles to the south-west, and nearer at hand 9 miles out to sea is the 40m (133ft) Eddystone Lighthouse. It was near this point, on July 20, 1588, that the English fleet first engaged the Spanish Armada.

The first lighthouse was begun on the Eddystone reef in 1696, taking nearly four years to complete. In June 1697 its designer, Henry Winstanley, was carried off by a French privateer while at work on the reef, but the Admiralty negotiated his release a month later. Only four years after its completion, the timber structure was swept away in a severe gale on November 26, 1703, and along with it its keepers and Henry Winstanley, who had gone there to supervise repairs. The second lighthouse, built by John Smeaton in 1759, was dismantled in 1877 and now stands on Plymouth Hoe.

On the summit of Rame Head there are remains of a slate-built chapel dedicated in 1397 to St Michael, the patron saint of Cornwall, and rebuilt in the 1880s. In the Middle Ages, men were paid by the Plymouth authorities to keep watch from this point and give warning of the approach of pirates or privateers. They also lit and tended beacons as a guide to ships. When gales whip up the waters of the Channel, this is a dangerous coast, particularly for sailing ships. Those sunk directly beneath Rame Head include the *Friends Endeavour*, a sloop from Fowey, in January 1811, and the *Deptford*, a brig from Sunderland, in January 1818.

▶ *Rame Head is about 3 miles south of Millbrook. Turn off the B3247 at Coombe Farm along a minor road leading south beyond Rame village to the former Coastguard Station, where there is a car park. Rame Head is a ½ mile walk from there.*

㉓ Isles of Scilly

Set like stepping-stones into the Atlantic, the southernmost fragment of Britain has the most gentle climate in the kingdom — warm summers followed by winters that are so mild that daffodils bloom in December. Yet there are extremes — one day the land cowers beneath fierce Atlantic gales, and the next day it is bathed in sunlight of startling clarity.

Lying some 28 miles west of Land's End, the low-lying, flat-topped granite islands rarely rise above 30m (100ft). The 200 or so islands, islets and named rocks — of which only five are inhabited — are the remnants of a granite mass formed at the same time as Dartmoor, Bodmin Moor and Land's End. Straddling one of the busiest approaches to Britain's south-western ports, the archipelago has been the graveyard of hundreds of ships — on one night alone in 1707, four ships and 2,000 men of Sir Cloudesley Shovell's Mediterranean Squadron were lost.

In folklore, the Isles of Scilly are said to be part of the legendary lost Cornish kingdom of Lyonesse that was engulfed by the sea as a punishment for the dissolute life of its inhabitants. There are similarities between the islands and the mainland that suggest that they were once linked — perhaps some 300,000 years ago. For example, there is a striking resemblance between the granite formations at Peninnis Head on St Mary's and those at Treen Cliff on the mainland 4 miles south-east of Land's End.

The islands were probably first colonised by Bronze Age people from the southern Iberian peninsula. They arrived around 2000 BC and settled extensively throughout the archipelago — there are three times as many prehistoric tombs there as in the rest of Cornwall. Two fine examples exist on St Mary's, one at Porth Hellick Point and the other — Bant's Carn — in the island's north-west.

Later visitors included the Phoenicians, who are believed to have discovered the Isles of Scilly while seeking tin in Cornwall. The Romans never settled there but used the islands as a place of banishment for wrongdoers. Danish raiders found them a convenient base for raids on the Bristol Channel. Later, the islands became a centre for smuggling, but by the early 19th century even this source of livelihood had slumped. It was not until the 1880s that the economy revived with the introduction of the early flower trade.

Today, the islands are a popular destination for tourists and bird watchers. Many different birds can be seen and rare migrant species often stop off at the Scillies, particularly in October.

▶ *St Mary's, the largest of the islands, can be reached by air from some airports in the south of England and by helicopter from Penzance. There is also a summer ferry service from Penzance.*

THOMAS PORTH ON ST MARY'S ISLAND

DARTMOOR

Dartmoor is crowned with tors, granite outcrops that rise above the bleak moors, and the remains of ancient settlements. Fast-flowing rivers run down from upland bogs and cut through steep valleys.

❶ Dunsford Nature Reserve

This delightful stretch of woodland runs for 2 miles along the north bank of the River Teign, from Clifford Bridge downstream to Steps Bridge, with ash, alder, oak, birch and hazel, as well as open areas of scrub with saplings, low bushes and bracken. For the geologist, the reserve is chiefly interesting because the underlying rocks are shale, slates and sandstones, not the typical Dartmoor granite.

For the naturalist, its delights include many woodland birds, as well as wagtails and dippers along the river banks, and the occasional kingfisher flashing over the surface. The area also has more than 20 species of butterflies, including the easily recognised red admiral, painted lady, common blue and orange tip, and the rarer pearl-bordered, high-brown and silver-washed fritillaries. The reserve is also home to the wood cricket, a species rarely found outside the New Forest.

▶ *One entrance to the reserve, managed by the Devon Wildlife Trust, is at Steps Bridge on the B3212 between Moretonhampstead and Exeter. There is a large car park near the entrance. The other, at Clifford Bridge, is on the minor road between Dunsford and Drewsteignton.*

❷ Bridford Wood

On a hillside above the River Teign lies the glorious confusion of Bridford Wood, a wilderness of ash, alder, oak, silver birch and many other species of tree. A great variety of woodland birds can be found here, including blue and long-tailed tits, finches, thrushes, wrens, woodpeckers and, overhead, the occasional buzzard, sparrowhawk and raven. In summer the song of blackcaps and other warblers and the cooing of wood pigeons can be heard. A pleasant walk leads up through the wood to the top of the hill, and then to Heltor Rock, about 1½ miles away. The route leads through Burnicombe Farm and then on to the road. Turn right to reach the stile leading up to the rock. The approach to the tor is not easy; the overgrown path leads through foxgloves, brambles and gorse. It is well worth persevering to the top, however.

The massive granite outcrop of Heltor Rock stands austerely defiant of wind and rain in the north-east corner of Dartmoor, and everything about it seems raw and revealed, as if the rock was the bones of the earth laid bare. The surrounding countryside heightens this impression, for the view is unlike that from most other Dartmoor tors, where granite-strewn peaks and wild, open moorland stretch as far as the eye can see. The countryside around Heltor Rock is as gentle on the eye as the tor itself is bleak and unyielding, a panorama of green pastureland and, in summer, fields rippling with golden corn.

▶ *Bridford Wood is on the B3212 opposite the entrance to Dunsford Nature Reserve at Steps Bridge, 4 miles north-east of Moretonhampstead. There is a large car park near the entrance.*

❸ Fingle Bridge

Snaking west to east across the north moor the River Teign enters a deep gorge at Hunter's Tor, and for the next 5 miles flows through some of the loveliest scenery on Dartmoor. Thickly wooded slopes tower 120m (400ft) above the sparkling river, here swirling around massive water-smoothed boulders as it races towards Fingle Bridge.

The bridge dates from the 16th or 17th centuries and was part of a pack-horse track. Its three, buttressed, granite arches span the river where brown trout leap to take an unwary fly. Occasionally salmon may be seen. High above the bridge, on the north bank, stands Prestonbury Castle, an Iron Age hill-fort with three widely spaced ramparts. Across the gorge lies Cranbrook Castle, another Iron Age hill-fort. Between them, the two forts commanded the valley below.

There are walks along the river bank from Fingle Bridge, and following the river eastwards the path leads to Clifford Bridge and Steps Bridge and passes oak woodlands and conifer plantations. In the woods above the river near Clifford Bridge is found Wooston Castle, another Iron Age fort, this one built on a slope just below the hilltop.

▶ *Fingle Bridge is about 6 miles north of Moretonhampstead by road. Leave the A382 at Sandypark for Drewsteignton 2 miles north-east. The only access to the bridge is along a minor road east of Drewsteignton.*

❹ Scorhill

A prehistoric stone circle on wild, heather-covered moorland; a primitive clapper bridge over a swiftly flowing stream; the ruins of a Norman castle in a remote village which time seems to have passed by; all the most powerful and mysterious qualities of Dartmoor can be found within easy reach of Scorhill. And the wild moorland landscape is made wilder still by the impressive views north to the agricultural lowlands of Devon, and west to the granite massif of Dartmoor proper.

Scorhill stands above Gidleigh, a remote village on the northern edge of the moor, notable for its early 16th-century church and the ruins of Gidleigh Castle, a late Norman fortified house. The Scorhill stone circle, some 3,000 years old, stands just west of the path leading over the moor from the hamlet of Berrydown. Beyond the circle the path drops down to the Walla Brook, just below the point where it joins the North Teign river, crossed by a clapper bridge of great but uncertain age.

The bank of the river is well wooded with conifers, and in the more sheltered parts foxgloves and tormentil grow. In late summer and autumn the moor blazes with the pink and purple flowers of both common and bell heathers and cross-leaved heath. Milkwort, whortleberry and the white, sweet-smelling heath bedstraw can also be found.

To the north of Scorhill is Buttern Hill, with the foundations of Bronze Age hut circles.

▶ *Take the A382 north-west out of Moretonhampstead, and after 3 miles turn left to Chagford. Gidleigh is about 2 miles west of Chagford, and Scorhill is 1 mile south-west of the village. Parking space is limited.*

❺ Fernworthy

The forest and reservoir of Fernworthy are set against the majestic backdrop of some of Dartmoor's highest peaks; and the fact that both are man-made in no way detracts from the natural beauty of the scene. The reservoir is fed by numerous streams tumbling down from the granite heights, and it stretches for about a mile to the forest at its south-west end. There are some 570ha (1,400 acres) of woodland – mainly plantations of Norway and Sitka spruce – and a delightful, 4 mile long nature trail running through the forest.

Along the trail the yellow flowers of tormentil and the blue of milkwort, along with vetches and herb Robert light up the undergrowth in summer. The banks are cloaked with bilberry patches, and lichens thrive among the boulders and on the tree stumps and felled branches. There is also a group of prehistoric hut circles, which were inhabited some 4,000 years ago by the Beaker People, so called because of their characteristic pottery. Roe, red and fallow deer can sometimes be glimpsed between the trees. The forest is also home to crossbills and the elusive nightjar, whose 'churring' song can sometimes be heard around dusk in early summer.

At intervals along the trail there are views across the moor, to the ragged northern skyline of Cawsand Beacon, Shovel Down, Thornworthy Tor and Kestor Rock.

▶ *Follow the A382 north-west out of Moretonhampstead, and after 3 miles turn left at Easton to Chagford. Fernworthy Reservoir and Forest are signposted from here. There are car parks at the reservoir, and the start of the nature trail.*

STONE CIRCLE AT SCORHILL

⑥ Lydford Gorge

Four centuries ago, so the story goes, no name was more feared on Dartmoor than that of Gubbins. This was the name of a wild gang of outlaws, as renowned for their red beards as for their ruthless pillaging of local farms and cottages. They lived like animals in the dark caves of Lydford Gorge.

But today the National Trust owns the gorge, and the dramatic scenery and abundant wildlife inspire delight, not terror. The River Lyd roars down the well-wooded valley, and crashes over 30m (100ft) high White Lady Falls. By the river, grey herons wait patiently for fish, while dippers plunge into the water in search of water beetles and other aquatic insects. Great spotted woodpeckers can sometimes be heard drumming on dead boughs in the woods, and in the shadow of the trees there are many ferns and plants such as herb Robert and meadowsweet.

▶ *Lydford is situated just off the A386 between Okehampton and Tavistock. Follow the road through the village to the car park beyond the church, where the walk along the gorge starts.*

⑦ Brent Tor

The conical peak of Brent Tor, 344m (1,130ft) high, dominates the western side of Dartmoor and draws the eye from miles around. The wonder of the tor lies not simply in the power of its appearance. Unlike the granite peaks around it, Brent Tor owes its character to volcanic action and also to the medieval Church of St Michael on its top. Legend claims that the church was built by a merchant saved from shipwreck on the stormy Devon coast — he swore that if he ever regained the shore, he would have a church built on the highest peak he could see. In fact, the present church was built under contract from nearby Tavistock Abbey and dedicated in 1319. It was built on the site of an earlier church, called St Michael on the Rock, dating from the middle of the 12th century.

The easiest approach to the summit is by the path that climbs gently through the gorse on the south-west side of the hill.

▶ *A signposted minor road leads from Tavistock to Brent Tor, 4 miles to the north. There is a small car park at the bottom of the hill.*

THERE CAN BE FEW MORE BLEAK SPOTS ON DARTMOOR
GRIMSPOUND BRONZE AGE SETTLEMENT

❽ Warren House Inn

There can be few more bleak spots on Dartmoor than Warren House Inn, a solitary public house on the high moorland road between Moretonhampstead and Two Bridges. The inn was built for the miners who, daily during the 19th century, trudged down the path 180m (200yd) north of the inn to work in the Dagger valley below. The inn takes its name from one of the extensive warrens, or game preserves, on medieval Dartmoor – in this instance, Headland Warren on the hill slopes to the east.

At the foot of the hill, on the valley floor, the stacks of the ruined mine buildings can still be seen. A stream threads its way through the valley, and the place has the atmosphere of a ghost town. Sheep graze the moorland turf, and along the stream gnarled oaks and hawthorns stand in ancient and splendid isolation. To the south the bracken and heather-covered moorland stretches away to a stately stand of conifers. The yellow-breasted grey wagtail can often be seen flitting over the stream in search of insects, and occasionally a buzzard soars above. Nearby is Hameldown Tor and Grimspound, the prehistoric settlement where Sherlock Holmes was supposed to have hidden while investigating the phantom hound of the Baskervilles.

A century ago Warren House Inn was the home of Jonas Coaker, who liked to describe himself as 'the poet of the moor'. It was Jonas who moved the pub from its original site on the opposite side of the road – a move strangely lacking in business sense. The original pub stood on common land and was therefore free. When he crossed the road Jonas moved on to land owned by the Duchy of Cornwall and ended up paying rent.

From the A382 at Moretonhampstead take the B3212 south west towards Two Bridges. Warren House Inn is on the right after 6 miles. There is a car park at the inn and a smaller one by the footpath to the Dagger valley.

❾ Gibbet Hill

The criminal's body hanging in chains on Gibbet Hill can have done little to enhance the magnificent views east over Dartmoor and west to the Church of St Michael on Brent Tor. And even today when the mists descend on the hill, and draw a veil over the views, they seem to bring with them brooding memories of those long-forgotten dead men, and of Lady Howard from Tavistock, who was allegedly burned here as a witch in the 17th century after murdering all four of her husbands. The flames were not hot enough to rid the moor of Lady Howard, whose ghost is still said to ride from Okehampton to Tavistock on wild Dartmoor nights, in a coach made of bones, drawn by a team of headless horses and preceded by a black hound.

Gibbet Hill is a true moorland summit, the highest point of Black Down, the focal point of a bleak, open, bracken-covered landscape where no trees grow. The shrill calls of stone-chats and wheatears carry far across the moor, and high overhead buzzards wheel lazily on the wind. At the bottom of the hill, on the east side of the road, stands the ruined stack of the Wheal Betsy silver and lead mine – abandoned around the beginning of the century when the workings became exhausted. The mine was acquired by the National Trust in 1967 as a memorial to the mining industry of Dartmoor.

▶ *Gibbet Hill is about 1 mile north of Mary Tavy on the A386. A track leads westwards from the main road to the summit. Cars can be parked on the roadside.*

❿ Wistman's Wood

Mystery and legend are wrapped in the gnarled and twisted branches of this ancient forest – now a National Nature Reserve. How ancient nobody knows, that is the mystery, but the stunted, grotesque oaks are several centuries old and the woodland itself is probably a remnant of the original native woods.

Age and mystery, as always, lead to legend, and it is said that Wistman's Wood was a sacred grove of the Druids. There is no evidence to support the belief, but it is not hard to imagine the mystic rituals taking place in such a bizarre and almost nightmarish setting. Lichen-covered boulders are strewn among the dense undergrowth of ferns, and mosses cling to the trees, cladding the misshapen trunks and branches in a velvet mantle. The air of remoteness and solitude is heightened by the silence, broken only by birdsong and the sound of a stream in the valley.

Wistman's Wood covers only 3.2ha (8 acres) and lies on a hillside 2 miles north of Two Bridges. It can be reached by following the footpath which leads up the valley from a parking area opposite the Two Bridges Hotel on the B3357.

▶ *Two Bridges is 8 miles east of Tavistock on the B3357.*

A SACRED
GROVE OF
THE DRUIDS
WISTMAN'S WOOD

⑪ Yarner Wood

On a still summer's day only the singing of the birds and the tinkling of the stream threading its way among the trees disturb the quiet of Yarner Wood National Nature Reserve. This marvellous 150ha (372 acre) oak woodland spreads across two small valleys and the spur of land between them, on the eastern fringe of Dartmoor. Sessile oak, the type in which the acorn sits directly on the twig, without a stalk, is the most common tree. But there are also birch, rowan and holly. The birdlife includes all three British species of woodpeckers – the great spotted,

the lesser spotted and the green – as well as wood warblers, nuthatches, pied flycatchers and redstarts.

Yarner Wood was not always so quiet. In the mid-19th century it rang with the sounds of a copper mine in full production. Between 1858 and 1867, 2,300 tonnes of copper ore were extracted at Devon Wheal Frances, as the mine was known; and the old mine building still stands today, now as silent as the woods around it.

▶ *Yarner Wood is about 3 miles west of Bovey Tracey, off the minor road to Manaton. There is a car park at the entrance at Reddaford Water. To avoid disturbing wildlife, visitors are asked to keep to the waymarked Woodland Walk.*

⑫ Buckland Beacon

The view from the top of Buckland Beacon is one of the finest on the moor. To the east the River Teign winds through delightful countryside to the South Devon coast; to the south the view extends over the wide, green canopy of the Dart valley; and 10 miles to the west North Hessary Tor, marked by an unsightly television mast, stands above Princetown. The beacon itself is bare and exposed; but in summer and autumn there is no shortage of colour, with the vivid yellow of the gorse and the rich purple of the ling. In 1928 the words of the Ten Commandments were carved on the rocks crowning Buckland Beacon, on the instructions of a former lord of the manor; and the carving aptly emphasises the Old Testament atmosphere of the scene.

A 5 mile drive north from Buckland Common to Manaton leads through the countryside that was the setting for Conan Doyle's story *The Hound of the Baskervilles*. Some 2 miles south-west of Manaton, where the road forks three ways, a path leads south-east to the fang-like rocks crowning Hound Tor, the haunt of the phantom hound.

▶ *Buckland Beacon is 2½ miles north-west of Ashburton on the A38. Minor roads lead from Ashburton to Buckland in the Moor – the beacon is 1 mile east of the village. A path to the top starts just north of the cattle-grid on the road between Ausewell Cross and Cold East Cross.*

⑬ Dartmeet

A simple stone beside the road about half a mile east of Dartmeet symbolises perfectly the harsh side of life as it used to be lived on Dartmoor. The stone was a resting place in the days when men had to carry their dead across the moor for burial at Widecombe. Here they rested the coffin, while mourners gathered to sing praises and murmur prayers, before the long climb ahead. On the stone they sometimes carved the initials of the deceased. Among the lichen which surrounds the stone today, five crosses and sets of initials can still be seen.

At Dartmeet itself the East and West Dart rivers join, and here is the best of both worlds of Dartmoor. Above lies dramatic moorland; spread out below lie densely wooded valleys. There are many delightful walks in the area – north up the East Dart valley to Babeny, south-east to the reservoir on Holne Moor and west to Huccaby.

The path to Huccaby – just under a mile away – climbs up through pleasant pastureland to the wind-blown heights of the open moor, before dropping down again to the village. The top of the moor is a particularly marvellous sight in summer, when it is cloaked with the vivid yellow of gorse and tormentil; and in autumn, when it glows with a thick, golden cover of bracken.

▶ *Dartmeet is on the B3357, some 6 miles north-west of Ashburton.*

⑭ Sampford Spiney

The few houses and the church that make up the tiny moorland hamlet of Sampford Spiney seem remote and isolated in time as well as location, as if the centuries pass more slowly here than elsewhere, and the 21st century is still far off in the future. Pigs and sheep graze the common as they have always done since man first came here, wheatears breed among the boulders strewn across the harsh, unchanging landscape, buzzards wheel and call over the valley by the church.

Overlooking the hamlet and the nearby oakwoods above the Walkham valley – some of the loveliest in Devon – stands the impressive peak of Pew Tor. It is impressive not so much for its height, since it is only 320m (1,050ft) above sea-level, as for its commanding position. From the summit there are sweeping views west across Tavistock to Bodmin Moor and east Cornwall, and south to Plymouth.

▶ *Sampford Spiney can be reached by turning south off the B3357, 2 miles east of Tavistock at Moorshop. Follow the signs to the hamlet. Cars can be parked on the roadside. Pew Tor is ½ mile north of the village.*

⓮ Double Waters

There are many beautiful trees at Double Waters, where the rivers Tavy and Walkham meet, and they give no impression that only about 100 years ago this was an industrial area, for a copper seam lies in the ground below. Once the copper made Double Waters one of the most important mining centres in Devon, with some 200 people working at the mine. But today the only reminder of the area's industrial past is the ruined stack of the mine's engine-house.

Double Waters lies at the end of a gentle 2 mile walk from Horrabridge, a village on the River Walkham. The walk follows the course of the river downstream and crosses a bridge to the opposite bank. Sycamore, alder and ash are among the trees which grow in profusion along the river; and beneath the green canopy of trees there are wood sorrels and wood anemones, whortleberries, blackberries and many other plants and flowers. In springtime the grassy banks are thickly carpeted with bluebells. It's a good place to see grey wagtails and dippers. At any time of the year it is a pleasant and picturesque spot, and down by the water where the rivers join it seems a world away from the more typical, bleak, open landscape of Dartmoor.

▶ *Horrabridge is 4 miles south-east of Tavistock, on the A386. Double Waters lies to the west of the village.*

THE MOOR NEAR PEW TOR

🔟 Harford Moor

The earliest inhabitants of Dartmoor found much that was attractive to them on Harford Moor in the upper Erme valley, as the many cairns, stone rows, enclosures, hut circles and other Bronze Age antiquities indicate. The area is noted for its stone rows – mostly single lines of stones, one more than 2 miles long, leading to burial cairns. A fine example can be seen high on Stall Moor across the Erme.

In the Middle Ages and afterwards, the tin-miners were drawn to the place by the riches below ground. Today it is the wildness of the moor that attracts, with the rolling moorland stretching as far as the eye can see, interspersed with bogs and divided by numerous streams.

Harford Church, from which a track climbs up to Piles Hill and then on to the moor, is famous for its medieval cross, one of many similar pale granite stones which once served as signposts for travellers crossing the moor.

▶ *Harford Moor can be reached by turning north off the A38 Plymouth-Exeter road at Ivybridge. There is a small car park above Harford Church, from where a footpath leads north-east on to the moor.*

🔟 Upper Plym Valley

It is a 5 mile walk from Cadover Bridge to the bogs east of Eylesbarrow where the River Plym rises at Plym Head, but it is easy walking country and there is much of interest along the way. There are stone circles, huts and many other relics of the prehistoric inhabitants of the moor; spoil-heaps from tin mines abandoned less than a century ago; spectacular views, and wild, invigorating scenery. The river flows south-westerly off the moor, and is fed by numerous tributaries with strange and evocative names, including Calves Lake, Evil Combe Water, Shavercombe Brook, Drizzlecombe, Meavy Pool and Leggis Lake. From the moorland above Ditsworthy Warren House, 2½ miles north-east of Cadover Bridge, it is possible to see as far as Plymouth in the south-west, while Cornwall lies far away to the west, beyond the Tamar.

From Ditsworthy Warren House, a path leads north-west to the village of Sheepstor and Burrator Reservoir. The lake, in the shadow of Sheeps Tor, is a popular beauty spot, fringed by woodland that holds many songbirds and which teems with wildfowl in winter.

▶ *Cadover Bridge is 4 miles south-east of Yelverton on a minor road off the A386, signposted to Cornwood. Parking is possible beside the road near the bridge.*

🔟 Abbot's Way

This romantically named track across the southern part of the moor is said to have been used by abbots travelling between Buckland Abbey and Buckfast Abbey. Since the track traceable today goes nowhere near Buckland it seems an unlikely story – more probably it was a wool-trader's packhorse route from the Plym valley to the Dart, dating from early medieval times.

Whatever its origin, Abbot's Way provides a challenging and rewarding walk from Cross Furzes to Princetown through wild, open countryside, past copses and over ancient clapper bridges, across moorland bogs and by rivers and streams. On either side of the track are the signs of man's activities, from the cairns and hut circles of the Bronze and Iron Ages to the modern Avon Dam reservoir below Dean Moor. Medieval granite crosses such as Huntingdon Cross and Nun's Cross were waymarks, often placed where tracks crossed.

Near the source of the River Erme, which flows southwards across the moor, another track heads north for about half a mile to the remains of a smelting-house, or blowing-house. More than 70 of these buildings are scattered across Dartmoor, dating from between the 15th and 17th centuries.

Water-wheels were used to power the furnace bellows, and some had water-powered millstones for crushing the tin ore – knocking mills for coarse crushing and crazing mills for finer grinding of the stone.

▶ *Abbot's Way starts at Cross Furzes, 2½ miles west of Buckfastleigh on the A38. It fords the upper reaches of the River Plym, then heads northwards through Nun's Cross Farm and on to Princetown.*

EXMOOR and NORTH DEVON

Behind the rocky shores of the North Devon coast lie the hills of Exmoor. Its rugged heathland is home to wild ponies, while red deer hide in the deep wooded combes.

❶ Braunton Burrows

The gently undulating landscape of Braunton Burrows has a Sahara-like quality about it; acre upon acre of sand-dunes stretching for 4 miles along the north side of the Taw and Torridge estuaries. This is one of the finest stretches of dunes in the south-west and is rich in unusual plants, as well as sea and marsh birds.

Braunton Burrows consists of two parallel groups of dunes, rising in places to 30m (100ft) above the sea. In spring and autumn, large flocks of waders use the dunes as a resting place during migration. In winter, merlins, harriers and short-eared owls are among the birds of prey which hunt for voles, shrews and other small mammals. Resident here all the year round are grey herons, which stand like sentinels along the water's edge at low tide, and rabbits which breed among the dunes. In summer, shelduck and wheatears often nest in disused rabbit burrows.

Several interesting species of moss grow here – *Tortula ruraliformis*, for example, which takes on a golden-green colour after rain – as well as the rare round-headed club-rush and sand toadflax.

▶ *Part of Braunton Burrows, which is situated off the B3231 Braunton-Croyde road, is a National Nature Reserve. The area is used from time to time by the military, but the footpaths can be followed except when the red flag is flying. Car parking is available.*

❷ Morte Point

The glistening, razor-sharp slates of Morte Point are as dangerous as they are beautiful. For centuries this jutting headland west of Ilfracombe, and the deadly reef extending beyond it, have made the surrounding waters among the most treacherous off the North Devon coast.

Many a ship has come to grief at Morte Point. In the winter of 1852, no fewer than five ships ran aground there, and in the 18th century the point was a favourite place for wreckers. It is said that they tied lanterns to the horns of cows so that sailors would mistake them for the lights of Ilfracombe.

In calm weather, however, there is a beauty and serenity about the Morte Point and its surrounding coastline which belies its reputation as a graveyard for shipping. The view south takes in the long, golden sweep of surf-washed Woolacombe Sand; and the South West Coast Path leads north-east across the cliff-top to Bull Point, where a lighthouse flashes out its warning to shipping in the Bristol Channel. The lighthouse standing on the headland today replaced an older one built in 1879, which gradually slipped down into the sea because of coastal erosion.

▶ *Morte Point is about 1 mile west of Mortehoe, which is 1 mile north of Woolacombe on the B3343.*

BRAUNTON BURROWS

❸ Torrs Park

For 2 miles the cliffs rise and fall between Torrs Park, on the outskirts of Ilfracombe, to the woods around Lee Bay. The South West Coast Path leading across them offers splendid walking, with many marvellous views and frequent opportunities for bird-watching.

The path is steep as it leaves Ilfracombe, and very slippery after rain; but soon it levels out, and the going is then much easier all the way to Lee. One of the finest views is from Brandy Cove Point – out across the Bristol Channel to Lundy island and South Wales, back to Ilfracombe slumbering in the lee of the point, and along the line of hog-backed cliffs stretching eastwards to Combe Martin Bay. Gorse and brambles cling to the steep slopes of the cliffs; further back, sheep graze on pastureland as green as any found in Exmoor's famous combes. Razorbills, guillemots and fulmars are among the many sea-birds to be seen beneath the cliff-tops.

At Lee, the path descends to a tiny cove of rocks and sand, and a cleft in the rocks leads to another sandy bay to the west. A path leading inland follows a valley abundant with fuchsias.

▶ *A steep road on the western side of Ilfracombe leads to Torrs Park. There is a small National Trust car park near the entrance to the park.*

❹ Little Hangman and Great Hangman

A steep climb north-east up the cliff path from Combe Martin leads to a craggy headland with two massive bluffs known as Little Hangman and Great Hangman.

The Little Hangman, which rises 218m (716ft) above the sea, offers spectacular views in all directions: north to Wales and west to Lundy island, east and west along the towering hog-back cliff-tops, and south to the green, rolling hills of lowland Devon. The hill is at its most colourful in early autumn, when the cliff-top vegetation takes on every shade of green, red and brown. Far below, the sea surges incessantly against the rocks, and in the up-draughts off the cliff many different species of sea-bird can be seen wheeling and swooping.

The Great Hangman towers 318m (1,043ft) above Blackstone Point, with the delightful Sherrycombe Water tumbling through a wild valley below. According to legend, the hills were named after a sheep-stealer who carried a heavy carcass on a rope over his shoulder and took a rest against a stone. Setting the carcass on the stone, he fell asleep with his back to the rock. As he slept,

the carcass slipped off the rock and pulled the cord tight around his neck, strangling him to death.

The whole area is rich in scenic beauty and wildlife, and also in minerals. At Wild Pear Beach, below the Little Hangman, iron ore was discovered in the late 18th century, and soon it was being mined and shipped across the Bristol Channel to South Wales. From the 13th century to the late 19th century, silver and lead were mined in Combe Martin, and the silent stack of a deserted engine-house can still be seen standing close to the church.

▶ *Combe Martin is on the A399, 4 miles east of Ilfracombe.*

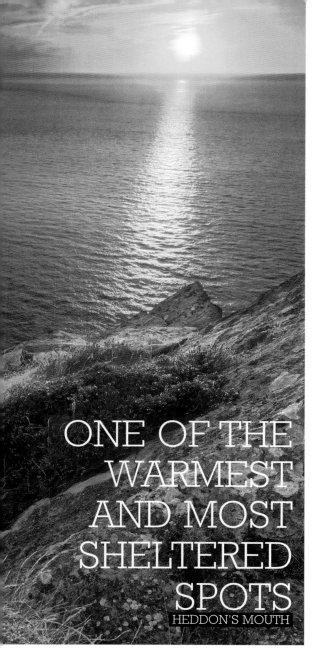

yellow of gorse blends with the green, red and brown pastel tints of waning foliage. Walk down the valley floor to Heddon's Mouth, along the tiny footpath leading from Hunter's Inn, and a more gentle view unfolds. The path follows the east side of the river, as it dashes over rapids and slides through crystal-clear pools to the Bristol Channel; lovely woods of oak, sycamore, poplar and fir overhang the banks and cling to the steep sides of the valley. Wagtails dart among the boulders and dippers dive under the water in search of food. Grey herons wade through the water, or stand silently watching for the silver glint of fish.

▶ *Heddon's Mouth is 4 miles west of Lynton. Turn west off the A39 just north of Parracombe on to a minor road, then walk from Hunter's Inn about 2½ miles further down the road.*

❻ Woody Bay

At the end of the 19th century a London solicitor planned to develop Woody Bay as a rival to Lynmouth, hoping to attract holidaymakers to travel by paddle-steamer from Weston-super-Mare, Ilfracombe and South Wales, to take tea in the shade of some of North Devon's most spectacular cliffs. But the plan misfired because of lack of financial support, and so the seclusion of Woody Bay remained delightfully undisturbed, as it still does to this day.

From the car park above this aptly named bay, a path runs westwards along the cliff-top, over the headlands of Wringapeak and The Cow and Calf to Highveer Point. The cliffs are topped with bracken, gorse and heather, and offer magnificent views over the wooded valleys, down the coast and out across the Bristol Channel to Lundy island and Wales. Another path drops down steeply through dense woodland of oaks, sycamores, beeches and conifers, to the tiny shingle beach at the bottom set in a wooded amphitheatre of oak trees. The ruined limekiln on the beach is a relic of the days when local farmers burned limestone here, and then hauled it up the cliff to spread on their fields.

▶ *Woody Bay, 3 miles west of Lynton, is reached by the coast road from Lynton, passing through The Valley of the Rocks and then continuing along the toll road.*

ONE OF THE WARMEST AND MOST SHELTERED SPOTS
HEDDON'S MOUTH

❺ Heddon's Mouth

The ravine which the River Heddon has carved on its way to the sea is cut so deep – the sides are some 210m (700ft) high – that it is always one of the warmest and most sheltered spots on the North Devon coast. Yet seen from the headland of Highveer Point, at the eastern end of Heddon's Mouth, it can look uncompromisingly bleak and desolate. A giant expanse of grey scree covers the western cliff, and little grows on it except the odd clump of gorse or heather. There is more colour on the eastern side, especially in autumn when the blazing

7 Waters Meet

In the spectacular gorge at Waters Meet, the combined Farley Water and Hoaroak Water meet the East Lyn river, and the hurrying waters tumble loudly over the boulders lining the river-bed, flowing on towards the sea at Lynmouth. The best approach is from Hillsford Bridge (where the Farley Water and Hoaroak Water combine), from where a path follows the Farley Brook to Waters Meet, three-quarters of a mile away.

The sides of the gorge are steep and well wooded, a tousled array including oak, beech and sycamore clinging precariously to the slopes and spilling down to the water's edge. Wild flowers are abundant, especially in spring when the bright colours of bluebells and primroses are set against the luxuriant green of young ferns. In spring, too, birdsong fills the woods, the sound mingling with the incessant roar of the stream. In the wild, rushing water the aquatic dipper may be seen plunging from a rock to walk along the bottom in search of food. But in winter, when snow is melting on the uplands where the rivers rise, or heavy rain is falling, the roar of the river rises to a crescendo, drowning all other sounds, dominating all other signs of life.

During the summer, Waters Meet is a popular spot for holidaymakers.

▶ *A pleasant ½ mile walk leads to Waters Meet from Hillsford Bridge on the A39, some 1½ miles south-east of Lynmouth, where there is a small car park. The National Trust own Watersmeet House, a 19th-century fishing lodge, now shop, tea room and information centre.*

8 Countisbury Common

The common, known locally as Barna Barrow, lies wedged between the hog-backed cliff of Foreland Point – topped by a lighthouse overlooking the Bristol Channel – and the road dropping down into Lynmouth. There are spectacular views near Countisbury Church, with its low tower and grey walls scoured by wind and rain. The panorama stretches north across the Bristol Channel to the coast of Wales, and west to where Lynton smudges the headland on the far side of Lynmouth Bay. A footpath threads its way along the cliff-top through acres of crisp bracken, gorse and scrub; nothing disturbs the silence save the call of the wind, the distant pounding of the waves and the cries of sea-birds.

In 1899, during a savage, north-westerly gale, the wild moorland of Countisbury Common was the scene of extraordinary endeavour. A dozen horses and 100 men dragged the lifeboat from Lynmouth 13 miles across the common and over the 302m (991ft) high Countisbury Hill to Porlock. A ship was sending up distress signals off Porlock Weir, but the heavy seas at Lynmouth made it impossible to launch the lifeboat there. Mile after gruelling mile the boat was hauled on a cart, up a 1-in-4 lane and on to the common. When the cart lost a wheel they dragged the boat bodily over skids. Ten hours later, after the long, back-breaking journey, the lifeboat was launched from Porlock Weir, and the ship's crew was rescued.

▶ *Countisbury Common is north of the A39, about 2 miles east of Lynmouth. There is a small car park off the main road, about ½ mile east of the Blue Ball Inn.*

9 Brendon Common

The rolling heights of Brendon Common are as fine an example of open moorland as can be found in England today. Look out across the moor to its southern ridge, standing silhouetted against the sky; or stand in autumn sunshine on Withycombe Ridge and survey the purple heather all around, set off against the sombre browns of dying bracken. It is hard to say which response is the stronger, the sense of desolation or of the freedom that such plain, austere landscapes always inspire.

The only signs of life are the sheep that graze the common – local farmers still retain common grazing rights here – the tough, little Exmoor ponies that gallop off when a stranger approaches, or perhaps a buzzard slowly turning on the wind, searching for voles, mice or rabbits hidden in the heather. But here the elements, too, seem alive: the mist that suddenly descends, cutting off the common from the outside world; the sweeping wind that carries with it all the unmistakable moorland scents; and the rain that varies from the soft drizzle that seems to hover in the air to the drenching torrents slashing and cutting across the waste with stinging ferocity.

▶ *Brendon Common is about 5 miles south-east of Lynton on the eastern side of the B3223.*

⑩ Simonsbath

Lying at the centre of the ancient forest of Exmoor, Simonsbath provides a good starting point for exploring the valley of the River Barle as it flows south-east between steep, grassy hills towards Dulverton, swelled by numerous tributary streams where trout and dippers haunt.

South-east from the village, opposite the hotel, the Two Moors Way leads through the beechwood planted by John Knight, who lived at Simonsbath Lodge and who developed much of the surrounding land in the mid-19th century. The path follows the River Barle downstream, and about half a mile south-east of Simonsbath a ruined cottage stands beside the river. This is all that remains of the Wheal Eliza copper and iron mine, which John Knight's son Sir Frederic and other businessmen tried to develop between 1846 and 1860. But the veins of iron ore proved too thin to be profitable.

About a mile beyond the mine stands Cow Castle, an Iron Age hill-fort on a spur overlooking the river. The river can be forded a few hundred metres below the fort and the walk returns to Simonsbath along a farm lane to Blue Gate and then by a minor road running towards the north-east.

▶ *Simonsbath is 11 miles south-east of Lynmouth at the junction where the B3358 meets the B3223.*

⑪ Badgworthy Water

The lovely valley of Badgworthy (pronounced 'Badgerry') Water lies at the east end of two large combes – Lank and Hoccombe. In its upper reaches it passes between steep hillsides covered with heather, bracken and gorse; lower down it has a gentler aspect, with a profusion of oak, ash and fir rising from the valley floor. It is the contrast between upland and lowland scenery that gives it its special charm, and adds weight to the claim that it is the most beautiful of all Exmoor's valleys.

But it is not only for its beauty that Badgworthy Water is renowned; it is also the heart of Doone country, the area of Exmoor which R. D. Blackmore immortalised in his novel *Lorna Doone* as the stronghold of the murderous outlaws, the Doones. It was in the old village of Badgworthy, which lies in Hoccombe Combe, that the outlaws are supposed to have lived, in fact as well as fiction. For Blackmore based his story on long-established Exmoor legends, which had grown out of the true exploits of a gang of desperadoes who settled in Badgworthy in the 17th century.

Little remains of the old village, which may have originated as early as Saxon times. The stonework is crumbled to the ground and lies overgrown by grass and brambles; the ruins further up the valley, known as Lorna's Cot, are actually what remains of a 19th-century shepherd's cottage, and have nothing to do with the original settlement.

▶ *The easiest approach to Badgworthy Water is from Malmsmead, on the road between Brendon and Oare, off the A39 between Lynmouth and Porlock. There is a car park, and the walk to Badgworthy, easy going on level ground, is about 3½ miles.*

⑫ Culbone Coombe

There is only one way to reach the secluded cluster of buildings beneath Culbone Hill, and that is on foot. A footpath leads from the toll-gate at Worthy, about 1½ miles away, following the steep face of the coast through a splendid confusion of oak, beech and alder. The sound of the sea can be heard below, and sometimes a sparkle of waves can be glimpsed through the trees that cling to the slopes. On sunny days shafts of light strike down through the trees, illuminating the tiny brook that flows down to the coombe, and the dense banks of rhododendrons that overhang it.

When the path emerges at Culbone Coombe, one of the great treasures of Exmoor lies ahead – Culbone Church, only 11m (35ft) long and said to be the smallest parish church in England. The church dates from the 12th century and is dedicated to St Beuno, renowned for his skill as a healer in the 6th century.

▶ *Worthy is on the toll road west of Porlock Weir, which lies on the B3225, north-west of Porlock.*

SOUTH-WEST ENGLAND

⑬ Porlock Bay

The graceful sweep of Porlock Bay, stretching for some 3 miles from Gore Point in the west to Hurlstone Point in the east, enjoys the mildest climate on Exmoor. On three sides it is enclosed by the moorland heights – the name Porlock means a land-locked port, but the village of Porlock is a port no longer, for the sea receded in the 11th century. Porlock Weir, at the western end of the bay, was a busy little port in the 17th century, with coastal vessels loading timber and barley and unloading limestone from Wales at the stone jetty.

During the summer months, the breezes that blow from the Bristol Channel keep the bay pleasantly cool; in winter they prevent frosts, making this area a perfect haven for less-than-hardy plants. Among the wild flowers that can be found growing around the bay are the scarce silver ragwort along the shingle beach, and New Zealand willowherb.

The bay is as peaceful as it is mild: most of the time the only sounds that can be heard are the gentle lapping of sea on shore, and the plaintive cries of sea-birds. This is a perfect place for bird-watching. Great black-backed gulls, fulmars and, occasionally, Manx shearwaters can be seen along the coast. In winter, herring gulls, black-headed gulls and oystercatchers gather on the shingle looking for food, while immediately inland the reed-beds of Porlock Marshes hold wintering wildfowl such as mallard, teal, wigeon and shoveler. The reed-beds also attract flocks of migrating waders in spring and autumn.

▶ *Take the Bossington turning off the A39 east of Porlock. At Bossington a rough track leads down to the beach.*

THE BAY IS AS PEACEFUL AS IT IS MILD
PORLOCK BAY

⑭ Horner Wood

The Horner Woods are warm, damp and still, and yet they are always full of sound: the rushing of Horner Water as it flows down from the uplands towards the Bristol Channel at Porlock Bay; the screech of jays, the shrill, piercing song of wrens, the musical trilling of warblers and the noise of other woodland songbirds. Sometimes the loud, laughing call of the green woodpecker can be heard echoing among the oak trees – the call that earned the bird its country name of yaffle – or else it may be seen moving in ungainly hops across a clearing, feeding on ants in the grass. Horner Wood is one of Exmoor's most extensive red deer coverts, and there is always a chance of seeing them slipping among the trees in the early morning or evening.

The stream flows gently through the woods in summer; but in winter, after heavy rain or snow, it can become a wild, roaring torrent. It is said that a horse once threw its rider into the river near Horner, when the water was high. Such was the force of the current that the drowned man's body could not be recovered before Bossington, 2 miles downstream. But in summer there is no such danger, just a lovely stream passing through one of Exmoor's most memorable stretches of woodland, with quiet paths leading along its banks and wild flowers all around.

Above the valley the woods give way to the bold summit of Ley Hill, where the view extends across the roof-tops of Porlock to the sea.

▶ *To reach Horner Wood, take the Luccombe turning off the A39, ½ mile east of Porlock. There is parking in the village of Horner, from where paths following the Horner Water lead into the wood.*

TARR STEPS

⓯ Tarr Steps

Some experts believe that the ancient bridge across the River Barle, called Tarr Steps, is prehistoric; others claim that it is medieval, perhaps dating from the 13th century. Whatever its age, it is one of the best-preserved clapper bridges in England, a series of immense stone slabs supported on piers. The bridge is about 55m (180ft) long from end to end and stands only 1m (3ft) above the rippling water. The bridge links the ancient trackways on either side of the Barle, where numerous remains show that the area was well populated during prehistoric times. It is to this day, and is best visited on weekdays or out of season, since it is a favourite spot for visitors.

However, to find solitude there is a footpath that leads upstream on the east side of the river to Withypool, about 4 miles away. This is one of the loveliest walks on Exmoor. At any time of year the mixture of woodland and water is delightful; and the birds which may be seen include grey herons, kingfishers, grey wagtails and dippers along the river bank, and pied flycatchers, wood warblers and redstarts in the woods. But the most stirring sight of all in this wild, romantic setting is when red deer emerge suddenly from among the shadows of the trees, and break away in full flight through the undergrowth.

▶ *To reach Tarr Steps turn south-west off the B3223 at Spire Cross, about 6 miles north-west of Dulverton. Follow this road for 1½ miles to the large car park about ½ mile from the Steps.*

A ROCKY BEACH BELOW BLUE-GREY CLIFFS

BEACH BELOW KILVE PILL

❷ Beacon Hill

Just about every range of hills in England has its Beacon Hill – and sometimes more than one – where great fires were lit to serve as warnings of the approaching Spanish Armada in 1588. All these Beacon Hills have one thing in common – they can be seen for miles and miles, and are within view of other hills with beacons. For the men who stood watch on the Beacon Hill in the Quantocks, the red glow on Crowcombe Fire Beacon and Hurley Beacon to the south-east would have been the signal to set ablaze their fiery warning. That warning would have been seen as far away as Dunkery Beacon on Exmoor and the Brecon Beacons across the Bristol Channel.

It was in the summer that the Spaniards came, and on any clear summer's day those far-off beacon hills can still be seen from the 310m (1,018ft) summit of this Beacon Hill – and in between lie far-sweeping panoramas of neat patchwork fields, heavily wooded combes, bright gorse and purple heather-covered slopes and the silver-grey sea.

To reach Beacon Hill, take the road from West Quantoxhead to Bicknoller. The first turn on the left at Staple Farm (opposite the road to Williton and Minehead) leads to a parking place on the hills. From here there is a fine walk to the summit of the hill.

Beacon Hill is the last point in the Quantocks higher than 305m (1,000ft) before the hills drop away to the shores of Bridgwater Bay. The summit is crossed by the prehistoric track coming up from the south-east, and marks the end of the Ridgeway, or Pack Way, for walkers setting out from Lydeard Hill 6 miles to the south-east.

▶ *West Quantoxhead, just over 1 mile north-west of Beacon Hill, can be found on the A39 between Kilve and Williton.*

❸ Staple Plantation

This pocket-sized patch of Forestry Commission woodland lying at the foot of Beacon Hill is barely half a mile square. It lies in an easily accessible corner of the Quantocks on their north-western fringe, where the ancient Devonian sandstone rocks give way to the lush farmland of West Somerset. From the car park at Staple Plain, above West Quantoxhead, a pathway drops down between silent stands of conifers, with westward views over the Brendon Hills, and Exmoor's lofty Dunkery Hill a purple mound in the distance.

Staple Plantation is at its best in autumn, when the beech and sweet chestnut turn to copper and gold against the never-changing green of the conifers. Beyond the woodland, Weacombe Combe runs east to Bicknoller Post, its flanks of bracken providing perfect camouflage for red deer which occasionally venture from the heights to raid the orchards and gardens in the hamlet of Weacombe. The hamlet lies at the bottom of the path from Staple Plain, at the south-west end of the plantation.

▶ *To reach Staple Plantation, turn south off the A39, ½ mile west of West Quantoxhead, and follow the road which leads to the car park at Staple Plain.*

❹ Bicknoller Hill

A pathway climbing up through a beech-lined combe leads to Bicknoller Hill, one of the most impressive points in the Quantocks. The route, particularly on a crisp autumn morning, provides a fusion of pastel colours, with the beeches, oaks and limes in the combe giving way to brambles and bracken as the hill is climbed. Red deer may be seen here, or may be heard in November when the throaty bellow of the stag's rutting call echoes through the woods.

Iron Age man settled on Bicknoller Hill, not on the top but on the south-western slope, and the remains of the encampment – Trendle Ring – are still visible. Its builders obviously chose the site for its wide views, and we can appreciate it today as one of the best vantage spots in the Quantocks. About 4 miles to the west are the Brendon Hills and, beyond them, the dark shape of Exmoor; 8 miles to the south lies the wide Vale of Taunton Deane and the town of Wellington, with the Black Down Hills rising behind the town. On a clear day Wellington's Monument can be seen 14 miles away on the northern edge of the hills, its narrow finger prodding the fluffy clouds above Wellington Hill. The obelisk commemorates the Iron Duke, the victor at Waterloo.

▶ *Bicknoller Hill can be reached by turning off the A358 just south of Bicknoller village, at Chilcombe Lane. There are several parking places at the lane end.*

❺ Longstone Hill

There are two good reasons for visiting Longstone Hill – the view from the top and the views on the way up. The climb is easy, a gentle stroll from the village of Holford along a bridle-path that leads through a magnificent tunnel of windswept beeches and oaks arching across the broad path. Between the trees the dignified, whitewashed Alfoxton House is visible. Today a hotel, it was for a year the home of William Wordsworth and his sister Dorothy, who moved there in 1797 to be near the poet Samuel Taylor Coleridge living at Nether Stowey.

Higher up the hill the beeches and oaks give way to more open ground, with bracken and clumps of gorse. Now other and more distant views attract the eye. To the south-east is Hodder's Combe, lying invitingly among the trees with a stream rushing through. Beyond it lies Holford Combe, where Wordsworth composed his poem 'Lines Written in Early Spring': '… through primrose tufts in that green bower, the periwinkle trailed its wreaths…'.

The summit of Longstone Hill is 305m (1,000ft) above sea-level, one of the highest points at the northern end of the Quantocks. To the south-east the hills and combes roll away into the distance; to the north the Bristol Channel is a glistening seascape, with the South Wales mountains making occasional hazy appearances when the sea mists clear.

▶ *Holford is on the A39, 11 miles north-west of Bridgwater. The bridle-path to Longstone Hill starts from the north-west side of the village, where there is a car park.*

ONE OF THE BEST VANTAGE
SPOTS IN THE QUANTOCKS
THE HILLS NEAR BICKNOLLER POST

❻ Dowsborough

Between Nether Stowey and Crowcombe lies a magnificent winding scenic drive, with plenty of stopping places of interest along its route. It is called the Coach Road, and runs past Walford's Gibbet, Five Lords Combe, Dowsborough hill-fort, Dead Women's Ditch, and then to a viewpoint at Crowcombe Park Gate where the road plunges down a wooded valley into Crowcombe village.

The Old Coach Road is signposted south about a mile west of Nether Stowey on the A39. Thick woods crowd in on the right-hand side of the road for about half a mile, where a sharp right turn takes the road up past Five Lords Combe. From this corner, a path leads across a field to a small quarry – a place with the sinister-sounding name of Walford's Gibbet.

On a clear day, there are magnificent views across the Bristol Channel to Wales. Birds sing in the hedges, and on fine summer evenings the shy deer come down from the neighbouring woods to drink at the stream.

The Old Coach Road continues past Five Lords Combe on the left – a splendid Quantocks woodland of mixed oak and beech. At the top of the combe the road turns sharp left to run across open moorland. At this turn, on the right-hand side, a path leads up through the woods to the hill called Dowsborough. Some local people call it Danesborough, though the fort on top is actually Iron Age and has no connection with Scandinavian invaders.

The oval, 3ha (7 acre) fort occupies the higher end of the narrow ridge. Its defensive banks and ditch follow the natural contours of the land. The ditch is now full of scrub oak and the ramparts are crowned with heather. Like all Iron Age sites, little is known about the people who lived here some 2,000 years ago. This air of mystery adds to the character of Dowsborough, with its superb views across the Bristol Channel.

From below Dowsborough, the road continues to a junction at which stands a signpost with the name Dead Women's Ditch. However, there is nothing morbid about this place; many pleasant walks lead off in all directions into the hills and combes round about, and there is adequate roadside parking.

About a mile beyond the road junction is Crowcombe Park Gate, which lies at the top of the combe above Crowcombe village. From this point, there are superb views of Fire Beacon hill, half a mile to the south, and Wills Neck – the highest point in the Quantocks – 2 miles to the south-east. The drive down the combe to the village is beautiful, with wooded banks on either side which are bright with bluebells in late spring and clothed in ferns and wild flowers in summer.

▶ *Nether Stowey, the starting point for the drive, lies on the A39, 7 miles west of Bridgwater.*

❼ Quantock Forest

Though large areas of Quantock Forest are now conifer plantations belonging to the Forestry Commission, the woodland dates back as far as Saxon times and was a royal hunting ground. Ash trees formed much of the old forest – the nearby village of Aisholt takes its name from them – and there are parts of the forest where they still grow, along with oaks, beeches and cedars.

A forest walk of about 5 miles starts from Triscombe Stone, the highest point at 319m (1,047ft) above sea-level. The lowest point on the walk is at Pepper Hill Farm, some 180m (600ft) below. Although the route takes in some beautiful broad-leaved woodland as it passes through the parkland round Pepper Hill Farm, much of it is through conifers, which are not to everyone's taste. There is no denying, however, the magnificence of stately Douglas fir, Sitka spruce, Japanese larch and Scots pine – especially on a warm, summer's day when sunlight shafts through the trees and the scent of pine is heavy on the air.

There is another walk through Quantock Forest, starting at Seven Wells, where streams threading their way off the heights attract grey herons, dippers, kingfishers and grey wagtails. At Adscombe Farm, on the fringe of the forest, are the remains of a chapel built in the 10th century by the monks of Athelney Abbey.

▶ *Triscombe Stone and Seven Wells can both be reached by driving along minor roads from Nether Stowey, on the A39. There are car parks at both places.*

❽ Aisholt Common

This is the heart of the Quantocks, a high moorland plateau fringed by the dark green edge of Quantock Forest and dropping away to a deep valley which the poet Samuel Taylor Coleridge called 'a deep romantic chasm … down a green hill'. Below lies the village of Aisholt, so remote that even the solitude-seeking Coleridge rejected it as a place to settle, for fear that it would be too lonely a place for his wife. The village takes its name from the ash trees of the Quantock Forest where the Saxons settled.

The common is best seen by walking around it, using the 5½ mile trail laid out by the Somerset Wildlife Trust. The walk starts from Birches Corner. Cuckoos, buzzards and stonechats can be seen flying low above the gorse, bracken and heather, with an occasional glimpse of red deer. And along the trail there are ever-changing views as the path, starting at 305m (1,000ft), drops to 120m (400ft) as it passes through the village of Aisholt, and then follows the edge of the Quantock Forest, finally climbing to 384m (1,260ft) at Wills Neck, the highest hill in the Quantocks. At one point it is possible to see three National Parks – Brecon Beacons, Exmoor and Dartmoor.

Aisholt is an attractive village of thatched cottages, oak barns and a 14th-century church. The poet Henry Newbolt lived here in the 1930s – his best-known poem is 'Drake's Drum'. A short detour north from the village leads along the side of Aisholt Wood and follows a small stream. You may be lucky enough to see red deer sheltering under the beech and ash trees.
▶ *To reach Aisholt Common, take the road which climbs steeply east from West Bagborough to Birches Corner, where there is a car park. West Bagborough is 9 miles north-west of Taunton, east off the A358.*

❾ Hawkridge Reservoir

One of the reservoirs that serves Taunton and Bridgwater, Hawkridge Reservoir is little more than 805m (880yd) long and about 137m (150yd) wide. Its small size, however, adds to its charm and there is little to suggest that this is a man-made lake. At the western end the neat, rounded hills of the eastern Quantocks reach down to the water.

Hawkridge Reservoir was completed in 1961, and has become 'naturalised' with remarkable speed. Meadowsweet and cuckoo flowers grow in the damp ground, and at the water's edge the golden marsh-marigold can be seen in spring.

Water birds lost little time in taking advantage of the reservoir, particularly coots and moorhens; they are relatively new to the Quantocks since there is no other stretch of inland water in the area apart from a reservoir on the outskirts of Bridgwater. In the dense vegetation away from the water's edge, the songs of reed warblers and sedge warblers can be heard in summer.
▶ *There are plenty of parking spaces around the reservoir, which can be reached by several roads leaving the A39 west of Bridgwater. The road from the village of Spaxton, 1 mile to the north-east of the reservoir, follows the southern shore.*

❿ Wills Neck

From the 384m (1,260ft) summit of Wills Neck, the patchwork quilt of the west Somerset countryside unfolds in all its splendour. To the west, the Brendon Hills and the distant purple dome of Exmoor loom on the horizon; to the north, beyond the sheen of the Bristol Channel, the South Wales mountains are visible on a clear day.

Wills Neck lies on a ridge – the name is derived from Old English and means 'Ridge of the Welshmen', referring to the Celtic tribe who probably fought a battle with the Saxons here; *walh* or *wealh* was an Anglo-Saxon word for foreigners or Welshmen. All around there is open moorland, dotted with clumps of gorse and bilberries rising from a carpet of bracken and heather. Sheep and ponies roam the paths, buzzards wheel overhead and, on sunny days in April and May, the emperor moth can be seen flitting over the heather, or in July and August the oak eggar moth.

On the south side of the hill the land falls away sharply to the tiny village of West Bagborough. In 1841, William Wordsworth and his wife, Mary, stayed as the guests of the Popham family at Bagborough House, a white, five-bayed Georgian house whose lawns are frosted with snowdrops in spring.
▶ *The easiest approach to the top of Wills Neck is from Triscombe Stone, which can be reached by taking the road from Nether Stowey (on the A39) south-west through Cockercombe in Quantock Forest. There is a car park at Triscombe Stone, from where a footpath leads to Wills Neck.*

SOUTH-WEST ENGLAND

⑪ Cothelstone Hill

The road climbs steeply from Cothelstone village to the crossroads on the hill. To the right a clump of wind-ravaged beeches shares the summit, known locally as Cothelstone Beacon, with the ruins of a folly tower. Perhaps Lady Hillsborough, who built the tower about 1770, used it as a point from which to enjoy the view. It is said that several counties can be seen from here on a clear day, but at any time the view is captivating with ash and beech woods cladding the slopes, and the fields and meadows of the Vale of Taunton Deane spread out below.

The left turn at the crossroads leads to Lydeard Hill, where there is a car park, and passes through mixed oak and beech woodlands with picturesque names, such as Paradise, Badger Copse and Much Care Wood.

At the foot of Cothelstone Hill, near Cothelstone Church, are the grounds and buildings of Cothelstone Manor, a skilfully restored Elizabethan house of pink sandstone with its original gatehouse. There are memories here of the infamous Judge Jeffreys, who hanged two of the Duke of Monmouth's followers in the gateway after the duke's defeat at Sedgemoor in 1685. The village itself is charming, with red-sandstone cottages and a holy well. The well, called St Agnes's Well, lies hidden in greenery in a field a little way up the hill.

▶ *Cothelstone village is sign posted along minor roads from Bishops Lydeard just off the A358. There is roadside parking on Cothelstone Hill, reached by following the road through the village.*

IN SPRING AND SUMMER THE WOODS COME ALIVE
FIVE PONDS WOOD

⑫ Five Ponds Wood

The five ponds from which this wood takes its name were dug in the 19th century, probably to enhance the grounds of nearby Fyne Court. The ponds have long since disappeared, and the wooded valley where they once lay is now a nature reserve with a trail laid out by the Somerset Wildlife Trust.

The woodland is only 550m (600yd) long and 64m (70yd) wide. The trail follows the course of a stream that runs through the valley, where native trees mingle with introduced species, planted about the same time as the ponds were dug. Most prominent of the planted trees are beeches, in a line topping a bank along the wood's southern edge, which were originally part of a hedge; some have now grown to an enormous size. Sycamores and poplars have been added to the wood in more recent years, to join the laurels, snowberries and rhododendrons so favoured by the Victorians.

In spring and summer the woods come alive with the colours of bluebells, red campions, snowdrops and primroses, and beside the stream the banks are speckled with the gold of kingcups and saxifrages.

▶ *Fyne Court, from where the trail starts, has a National Trust visitor centre. It is close to the village of Broomfield. The most direct route is sign posted west from North Petherton, which lies 5 miles to the east on the A38.*

⑬ Walford's Gibbet

What is today a pleasant spot on a hillside, was the scene of a grisly murder more than 200 years ago. John Walford was a well-liked local charcoal-burner whose true love was Ann Rice, but he married half-witted Jane who visited him in the woods, and whose two children he fathered.

One night in 1789 as the couple were going from their cottage above Bin Coombe to buy cider at the Castle of Comfort Inn, they quarrelled. Walford struck and killed Jane with a fence stake, then, panic-stricken, left her body in a ditch. He was arrested, tried and found guilty. On his way to be hanged, Walford was allowed to make a final farewell to Ann. As was the custom, his body was gibbeted at the scene of the crime.

▶ *A mile west of Nether Stowey on the A39 turn south onto the Old Coach Road. After ½ mile, Walford's Gibbet can be reached along a path leading from a sharp right hand bend.*

The MENDIP HILLS

Many millennia ago, ancient rivers hollowed out the limestone rocks of the Mendip Hills to form chasms and caverns. Once home to prehistoric Britons, today they draw many visitors to the region.

❶ Burrington Ham

In summer and at weekends, Burrington Combe attracts many visitors, but a short drive to the top of this miniature Cheddar Gorge leaves the crowds behind and leads to Burrington Ham, one of the great delights of the Mendip Hills.

From the ridge, only a few metres from the car park, there is a view over North Somerset and as far as South Gloucestershire, providing an inspiring panorama. The view is north-east over Blagdon Lake and Chew Valley Lake to the point where, 7 miles from the Bristol Channel, Bristol nestles comfortably in and around the Avon Gorge. On a clear day, the unmistakable outline of the Welsh hills looms on the north-eastern horizon, on the other side of the murky waters of the Bristol Channel.

Burrington Ham represents the softer face of the Mendips. A bridleway drops gently down between brambles and bracken, a marvellous sea of brown in the soft light of autumn, to the village of Burrington, lying in the lee of the steep north-facing edge of the hills. There is an Iron Age oval earthwork, Dolebury Camp, on the hillside above the combe – another good vantage point – and close by is the rocky cleft in which the Blagdon curate Augustus Toplady is said to have written the hymn 'Rock of Ages' while sheltering from a storm.

▶ *The B3134 runs through Burrington Coombe, which starts just south of the point where the road joins the A368. The parking area for exploring Burrington Ham is on the north side of the road at the top of the combe.*

❷ Black Down

The highest peak on the Mendip Hills is also, without doubt, the loneliest. This long, seemingly unending hill rises above the limestone plateau like a giant tortoise, gaunt and forbidding against the soft countryside around.

It is not surprising that Black Down presents a different appearance to the rest of the Mendip range, for the 325m (1,067ft) peak is sandstone, not limestone. The different rock structure is apparent in the vegetation: the thin, peaty soil is covered with whortleberries, rough grass, ling and heath which, in the depth of winter, take on a black appearance, believed to be the reason for its name.

The best way up Black Down is to take the footpath that leads from beside Ellick House, which is at the top of Burrington Combe on the B3134, just a few metres beyond the Burrington Ham parking area. A series of tracks leads to the summit, which can be reached comfortably in less than 30 minutes.

The hill is crowned by the Beacon Batch Bronze Age barrows, and a line of what appear to be molehills – these were wartime defences to prevent aircraft from landing on the summit. On a clear day the views from the top are truly memorable: north over the soft folds of the hills to Bristol and beyond; west to Flat Holm and Steep Holm out in the Bristol Channel; south over the Somerset Levels to Glastonbury Tor.

▶ *Black Down is 1½ miles south of Burrington just off the A368. Ellick House is 2 miles along the B3134, which heads south from the A368 about 180m (200yd) west of Burrington.*

SOUTH-WEST ENGLAND

❸ Charterhouse

This lonely village sits high on a hill in a flat, windswept landscape but it is assured for ever of its place in history. It was here, some 2,000 years ago, that the Romans launched Britain's earliest lead-mining industry. Six-thousand people lived here then; today Charterhouse's population can be counted almost on the fingers of one hand.

Little evidence of the Roman occupation remains, but wildlife thrives. A nature reserve has been established in the patches of furrowed land containing the overgrown remains of filled-in mine-shafts and other lead workings. Here alpine penny-cress and spring sandwort are found beside sheep's fescue, sea campions and other wild flowers. There are also many butterflies, such as marbled whites and dark green fritillaries.

There is an almost eerie stillness about Charterhouse, with few sounds apart from the gentle rustle of the wind in the leaves of the trees. Beeches, sycamores, alders, oaks and ash trees grow in isolated stands, alongside the scrub layer of hawthorns, elders and dogwood, just as they must have done before the Romans came.

▶ *Charterhouse is 2½ miles north-east of Cheddar and lies 1 mile from the B3134 from Burrington Combe, along a minor road.*

❹ Black Rock

Less than 2 miles from Cheddar lies Black Rock, a place so quiet, so unspoiled, that it could be miles from any tourist spot. It was once part of the medieval Mendip Forest, a royal hunting preserve, and is at the north-eastern end of Cheddar Gorge. Here the gorge opens out into two valleys, one of which runs north-eastwards and then north to Long Wood. Just south of Long Wood, the path splits again, and heads north-east along another valley. This is a historic trail; almost 2,000 years ago it was a track leading to Roman mines at Charterhouse, 2 miles away through Velvet Bottom. In the valley itself, man once quarried the limestone.

Even on the roughest days, Black Rock is sheltered. It has a wide range of trees, typical of those found in limestone areas – mostly ashes and yews – but on the hillside above, larches and Scots pines also grow. In spring, before the trees are in leaf, dog's mercury and bluebells flower, and along the dry-stone walls there are lime-loving plants, notably common spleenworts and liverworts.

▶ *The valley can be reached by parking at Black Rock Gate, which is on the B3135 at the top end of the Cheddar Gorge. There are one or two parking places on the side of the road.*

❺ Long Wood

The subterranean mysteries of the Mendips meet the surface beneath a glorious canopy of green at Long Wood. Shortly after the end of World War II a network of water holes – called swallets – was unearthed in the middle of this unspoiled stretch of woodland, leading to a complicated labyrinth of underground passages and caves. Today the entrances to the swallets are closed because of the dangers they present to inexperienced explorers.

The wood contains much wildlife, which can be seen from the 2½ mile nature trail established by the Somerset Wildlife Trust. Here you can find ancient stands of beech, some of which were planted 150 years ago, along with other trees associated with limestone – such as yews, elders and ashes. Blackberries grow profusely and, in the clearings between the trees, there are rosebay willowherb, hemp agrimony and the rarer herb paris. In the moister areas, fungi such as the uncommon amethyst agaric and the deadly deathcap toadstool occur.

At one point along the trail a blowhole can be seen. This was formed in 1968 when the underground stream burst through to the surface. The thickets are the home of song thrushes, wrens and the green and lesser spotted woodpeckers. In spring, the air is filled with the sound of migrant birds – the willow warblers, blackcaps and redstarts – all competing for territory. Roe deer, badgers, foxes, squirrels, shrews and weasels are common, and adders and grass snakes can also be seen occasionally. Care should be taken when wandering along the paths, particularly during warm weather, so as not to disturb the poisonous adder, recognisable by its zigzag markings.

▶ *Long Wood can be reached by following the path from Black Rock Gate, 1½ miles north-east of Cheddar on the B3135. The entrance to the wood is at the northern end of the gorge, ½ mile from Black Rock Gate.*

❻ Crook Peak

A stiff climb up a bridleway from the minor road skirting the western flank of the hill leads to the top of Crook Peak. There is also a more gentle approach from the village of Compton Bishop, three-quarters of a mile to the south-east of the summit.

The limestone strata slope gently south to the green Somerset plain, across which, 10 miles away, runs the low east-west ridge of the Polden Hills. On clear days, far away to the south-west, the purple-clad slope of Dunkery Hill on Exmoor can be seen.

The peak, which takes its name from the ancient British word *cruc*, meaning 'a pointed hilltop', is well named. It stands 191m (628ft) above sea-level, its limestone head worn to a jagged edge by centuries of erosion by the elements. The limestone contains many marine fossils from the time when the area was covered by the sea.

On the southern slopes, where erosion of the rocks has produced a limestone-pavement effect, there are common rock-roses, wild thyme, quaking grass, tormentils and rarer species, such as the spring cinquefoil, the delicate bee orchid, autumn lady's tresses, slender thistles, honewort, dropwort, Somerset hair grass and white horehound. Badgers have their underground setts in cracks in the rocks. They appear at dusk to feed on worms, beetles, blackberries and other food found on the hill.

The open downland is a nesting place for skylarks and meadow pipits, while linnets make their nests in dry-stone walls. Thirty species of butterflies occur annually, notably marbled whites, common blues and small pearl-bordered and dark green fritillaries.

A walk east along the crest of the ridge, following the dry-stone wall, leads to Compton Hill, Wavering Down and King's Wood. The wall forms the boundary between Somerset and North Somerset. However, the line it follows is much older – it divides the parishes of Compton Bishop and Winscombe, and was defined as long ago as Saxon times when it was an important estate boundary.

▶ *Crook Peak is 2½ miles west of Axbridge. A minor road skirts the western foot of the hill, and there is a small parking area close to the start of the bridleway.*

A NESTING PLACE FOR SKYLARKS AND MEADOW PIPITS
CROOK PEAK

❼ Bleadon Hill

The pathway which leads up from the centre of Loxton village to the top of Bleadon Hill offers magnificent views in all directions. To the south is the solitary stack of Brent Knoll, an island of limestone rising 137m (450ft) above the marshes of the Somerset plain; east is the main bulk of the Mendips. From the ridge of the hill is a marvellous vista of the Bristol Channel, Brean Down, the islands of Steep Holm and Flat Holm and, on clear days, the hills of South Wales.

In its early stages the path, the West Mendip Way, climbs steeply. Clumps of oak and beech line the pathway before the upper reaches of the hill are reached, where the vegetation becomes more sparse, and bracken and brambles predominate. Beyond Christon Plantation, the scenery becomes well wooded again and here you are likely to startle a pheasant into laborious flight. In wet weather the path at this point is very sticky, so sturdy footwear is recommended.
▶ *Loxton is 5 miles south-east of Weston-super-Mare just off the Bleadon-Axbridge road, on the west side of the M5. The path over Bleadon Hill starts from the centre of Loxton, opposite the rectory.*

❽ King's Wood

Just below Shute Shelve Hill, and on the eastern side of Wavering Down, lies one of the unexpected pleasures of the Mendips. King's Wood, which stretches for about half a mile, is a marvellous place to be at any time of the year – especially in autumn, when the dying leaves provide a spectacular canopy of colour.

Yet this has not always been a pleasant spot. In the 17th century, Shute Shelve was the site of a gibbet, and travellers on the old Bristol to Exeter road, which passes close to the wood, would have heard the clank of chains as the grisly remains of the unfortunate victims swung in the wind.

The soil in King's Wood is deeper than on the other side of Wavering Down, so a wide range of trees grows here: oaks, ashes, beeches, cherries, maples, small-leaved limes and Scots pines. This beautiful stretch of woodland also has many wild flowers, especially in early spring. Then the wood is a riot of colour with bluebells, primroses, dog's mercury, wild arums and wood anemones growing in large numbers. The rarer herb paris also grows here, as do the hart's-tongue fern and common polypody.
▶ *King's Wood is 1 mile north-west of Axbridge. A minor road west from the A38 leads to it. The entrance to the wood is about 45m (50yd) along on the south side of the road, and there is a small parking area.*

❾ Ebbor Gorge

About 270 million years ago, enormous pressure from inside the earth's crust pushed down a strip of Millstone Grit beneath the limestone to form an impermeable floor, over which a river once ran. The result of this transformation of the landscape was Ebbor Gorge, a wooded chasm which is now part of a 47ha (116 acre) nature reserve managed by Natural England. It is claimed to be the loveliest and most unspoiled gorge in the Mendips. Here ashes, pedunculate oaks, wych elms and other

A GREENERY UNMATCHED ELSEWHERE

NEAR EBBOR GORGE

trees grow in dense and glorious confusion, providing a greenery unmatched anywhere elsewhere in this area.

The damp woodland in the gorge is rich in mosses, fungi and ferns; here you will also find dog's mercury, hart's-tongue fern and enchanter's nightshade. Badgers live in the woods, and the entrance to a sett – the badger's underground home – can be seen close to one of the paths through the gorge.

Caves and fissures worn by rainwater provided shelter for New Stone Age man, who lived in the gorge about 3000 BC, and his bones, tools and ornaments have been found there. In Bridged Pot Shelter, at the head of the gorge, a superb axe of highly polished greenstone was found; it is now in the museum at Wells. Remains of animals such as bears, reindeer and lemmings have also been uncovered. Today the caves are an important habitat for wildlife, most notably greater and lesser horseshoe bats and cave spiders.

▶ *The gorge is situated about 1½ miles north-east of Easton on the A371 between Wells and Cheddar. The property, owned by the National Trust, has a car park, from where two nature trails start.*

⑩ Pen Hill

A walk of about 3 miles, from Pen Hill to Rookham, follows the south-western face of a ridge above the Somerset plain. Following the bridleway down the side of the hill, the view takes in Queen's Sedge Moor and Glastonbury Tor, the steep hill crowned by the 14th-century tower of St Michael, looming above the town. Beyond are the Black Down Hills and the Quantocks. On a clear day, Dartmoor can also be seen, its outline rising darkly on the horizon. Immediately beneath the hill lies the ancient city of Wells, crowned by the delicate square towers of the cathedral and St Cuthbert's Church.

On Pen Hill, the Old Red Sandstone has broken through the limestone layer covering the Mendip plateau, resulting in a landscape that is pastoral and well wooded. Ashes and oaks mingle among the stately stands of conifers, and pheasants scuttle in and out of the woods which line the bridle-path.

▶ *Pen Hill is about 3 miles north-east of Wells along the A39. There is a small parking area near the entrance to a television transmitter station which crowns the hill. The bridle-path runs off south-west from the parking area. After about ½ mile, it bears west beneath Pen Hill Farm.*

⑪ Ashen Hill Barrows

A gentle walk of about a quarter of a mile over upland pasture leads to Ashen Hill, a Bronze Age barrow cemetery. Like many prehistoric sites, it is in an austere setting. The scattered community of Priddy is situated high up on the limestone plateau, about 240m (800ft) above sea-level, and is exposed to the cruel ravages of the winter winds. Centuries of trampling by human and animal feet – to say nothing of the work of rabbits – has reduced the barrows to a fraction of their original size. But they and their prehistoric neighbours a short distance south on North Hill, Priddy Nine Barrows, form a landmark which can be recognised for many miles around. In the 19th century some of the Priddy Nine Barrows – there are only seven, in fact – were excavated.

LIKE MANY PREHISTORIC SITES, IT IS IN AN AUSTERE SETTING

PRIDDY NINE BARROWS

They were found to contain burned bones and, in one case, beads similar to those found in Egyptian tombs.

Half a mile to the north, over the B3135, lie the four Priddy Circles. Each of these is 180m (600ft) in diameter – their significance is not known but it is believed they are connected with religious ceremonies associated with the group of barrows to the south.

Stands of beeches and firs dot the hillside, adding colour and variety to the landscape. There is plenty of wildlife, including badgers in the neighbouring woods. Badgers are plentiful in the Mendip woods, but are seen only at dusk.

▶ *Priddy is 5 miles east of Cheddar. It is reached by turning south off the B3135 at Townsend, 2 miles from the junction with the B3371. Turn left down Nine Barrows Lane in the village. The barrows lie east, about 1 mile along the lane.*

⑫ Babington Wood

A short walk across open fields on a public footpath from the village of Kilmersdon leads to Babington Wood. The wood, with a bubbling stream – a tributary of the Somer – running through the centre of it, is a marvellous retreat, and pleasantly secluded.

There is a wild beauty here which is hard to find elsewhere in the Mendips. The trees – hazels, oaks, Douglas firs, ashes, limes and maples – reach skywards in haphazard fashion, and in autumn, when the sun slants through the dying foliage, the wood is a wonderland of colour, with every shade of green, red and brown. There are riches, too, in the undergrowth, seen at its best in spring. Flowering bluebells, periwinkles and wood anemones provide an early splash of colour before the wild rhododendrons, overhanging the bank of the stream, burst into bloom in May.

The public path threads its way through the wood, crossing the stream by a simple bridge and then continuing for about 450m (500yd) to Babington Church, a delightful little Georgian building which stands like a private chapel within the grounds of Babington House.

▶ *Kilmersdon is 2 miles south of Radstock. Babington Wood can be reached by parking on the B3139, just east of Kilmersdon. The public footpath leads up from the south side of the road, west of the bridge over the stream.*

⑬ Maesbury Castle

For many people, Maesbury Castle is the most exhilarating spot on the whole of the Mendip Hills. This impressive Iron Age fort crowns a hill on the southern side of the plateau, and from it there are compelling views of the Somerset countryside, with the main ridge of the hills rising to the north-west.

Maesbury would have been a difficult place to conquer in those prehistoric days, situated as it was in such a commanding position. Today it is rather easier to tackle; by simply walking across a field from the road which runs along the hill. The outline of the original fortifications which encircle the top of the hill can still be seen in the oval-shaped mound, now covered with grass.

▶ *Maesbury Castle lies 4 miles east of Wells. The road to it is signposted off the B3139, between Wells and Chilcompton.*

In the cider shed

Among the apple orchards of Somerset, you'll find a thriving local industry that's still making cider the traditional way.

It is a slow, drowsy afternoon on the Somerset Levels, and nowhere is slower or drowsier than Roger Wilkins's cider shed. The Wilkins family has been making and selling good cider at Land's End Farm in the hamlet of Mudgley, perched among apple trees a little above the flatlands of the Levels, since time out of mind. There is something restful about this dark, creaky shed where a handful of men sit well back in plastic garden chairs, ruminating and sipping. The air is full of the heady, sweetly fermented smell of cider, a drink that does for its component element what wine does for grapes or poteen for potatoes, transforming humble produce into liquid magic. In the small glasses over which the purchasers are humming and hawing, the cider has a milky hue, an absinthe shade with a faint greenish

There are two big dark oak barrels at one side of the shed, sweating slightly in the summer heat. They smell of sawdust, a faint whiff of wood resin and a tarry tang of former ciders.

tint. Farm cider and absinthe have quite a lot in common, in fact: they both carry a great weight of myth, they are both very much a drink for specialists, not to say connoisseurs, and over-indulgence in either packs a weird psychological punch which has little to do with the well-known effects of alcohol.

There are two big dark oak barrels at one side of the shed, sweating slightly in the summer heat. They smell of sawdust, a faint whiff of wood resin and a tarry tang of former ciders. One holds the sweet (not that the uninitiated palate would find it so), the other the dry. The trick is to mix the two – a trickle from this, a smidgeon from the other – until you have exactly the taste that suits you. That can vary. A few weeks on the sweet side can sicken a devotee. Only a counter-blast of proper cheek-sucking dry will restore palate balance. Most purchasers are content to let Roger mix them a medium blend, enough dry to get the cidrous tang, enough sweet to ease it past the gullet.

TRIED AND TESTED

Most of the point of an afternoon in the Wilkins cider shed is to soak up the timeless atmosphere. If anyone wants to know how the world outside is wagging there's usually a newspaper about, generally the local rag, and one of the customers will be hunched over that, glass in hand, stertorously breathing, perhaps reading, probably not. Mostly people chat from their chairs, or propped up by the crook of an arm against the barrels or a wooden beam – lazy talk, inconsequential and purely local, but sometimes digging down to the pips of Levels scandal. Everyone sips as the talk goes round. Cheeks get a little redder, laughter a little thicker. These are moderate consumers: a couple of local young men, a farmer friend of Roger Wilkins, a chap down from Bristol to buy a gallon for a party he's having in his city garden tonight. Roger himself could put away a couple of gallons a day when he was younger. He has slowed down a lot since then, and says cider has never done him any harm.

The Wilkins method of making cider is the old one, and the best. Roger grows and hand-picks his own apples, and buys locally what the Land's End trees can't produce. He looks for a good balance of bitter sharp and bitter sweet. The apples are crushed in a big hydraulic press to make pomace, traditionally a process done by piling up a 'cheese' with alternative layers of straw or sacking and apples. The apple juice runs down the outside of the 'cheese' in streamlets and trickles, to be collected, fermented and stored in the big barrels until the old

oak, the apple juice and the slow concentration by sweating produces a drinkable, and then a delectable, cider. The wrung-out pomace goes to the pigs and cows. Nothing's wasted here.

You'll sometimes find the term 'scrumpy' used to describe this kind of home-made cider. As a generally accepted term for farm-produced cider with no added sugars or colourings, that is fair enough. Others call it 'rough cider', a term that conjures up a palate-curdling brew with a vinegary savour and a kick like a mule.

The kind of cider produced by Roger Wilkins and other small-scale West Country cider-makers is nothing like that at all. It is not exactly smooth, but it's very far from rough. It doesn't slip down without touching the sides; instead, there is a faintly but pleasantly abrasive effect along the gullet, and a sharp after-tang on the palate that dissolves almost instantly to release a burst of intense apple savour. A glass of this cider is not clear, as a commercially-produced sparkling cider is see-through clear, but its distinctive cloudiness is not of the 'nasty floating bits' type; it is more of a thick haze, of the type seen on hot summer afternoons such as this one, hanging just above the water-filled ditches and damp meadows of the Somerset Levels – an indicator of lushness rather than of corruption. Hold a glass of Wilkins's cider up to the light and you will see a diffuse glow, as though looking up through deep water at the sun.

HONOURING THE APPLE

In times past the cider-maker might chuck a handful of raw beef – some say it was a skinned rat – into the vat to give the cider a bit of body. If Roger follows that tradition, he's not saying. One old custom he does keep up, though, is the wassail on a Saturday evening in January. If you don't honour the trees with a wassail, they won't produce for you. You drink, you dance, and you sing:

Old apple tree, we wassail thee,
And hoping thou wilt bear
For the Lord doth know where we shall be
Till apples come another year.
For to bear well, and to bear well
So merry let us be;
Let every man take off his hat,
And shout to thee, old apple tree!
Old apple tree, we wassail thee,
And hoping thou wilt bear
Hatfuls, capfuls, three bushel bagfuls –
And a little heap under the stairs!
Hip! Hip! Huzzah!

The DORSET HILLS

The Dorset countryside is one of broad chalk downs and untamed heathland. The sweeping bays, dramatic cliffs and rock formations of the county's coast form part of England's only natural World Heritage site.

❶ Cranborne Chase

It is easy to pass by Cranborne Chase without realising it is there, for the forest laws that protected it for a thousand years as a hunting ground for the privileged – including King John when he was Earl of Gloucester – have set it apart from the surrounding countryside. The roads that lead into it are few and narrow, and its villages are hidden haphazardly in clearings.

The chalk uplands of Cranborne Chase straddle the A354 between Salisbury and Blandford Forum. Its boundaries have varied, but at their fullest they enclosed nearly 320,000ha (800,000 acres) within a 100 mile perimeter. The oldest part, with hunting rights dating back to Saxon times, is the Inner Chase – an area 10 miles by 3 miles to the north-west of the A354, centred around the hamlet of Tollard Royal. Win Green hill in Wiltshire, at 277m (910ft) the highest point, is now owned by the National Trust. Its tree-crowned summit is a perfect place from which to survey the wide sweep of the Chase.

Deer-poaching is as old as the Chase itself. At Sixpenny Handley, carcasses were hidden in an old tomb; the tomb cover – now inscribed – is still in the churchyard. For centuries the Chase was a battleground between an army of keepers and local farmers and poachers. Farmers put up fences to save their crops from deer; keepers tore them down. Murderous affrays became so commonplace that keepers and some poachers, 18th-century 'bloods', even wore protective clothing – straw-lined, beehive helmets and padded jackets. But the sporting ardour of the 'bloods' cooled after 1736 when the penalty for a second poaching conviction was transportation.

Hunting rights ended in 1828, and much of the ancient forest – described by Thomas Hardy as the oldest wood in England – was eventually cut down. One of the loveliest parts that still remains is Chase Wood, which can be reached by road (to New Town) or by a track across Handley Common.

▶ *To reach Win Green hill turn north off the B3081, 4 miles south-east of Shaftesbury. Handley Common is also off the B3081 just north-west of Sixpenny Handley, and New Town is along a minor road north off the B3081 at Sixpenny Handley.*

❷ Ashmore

Its pond is the pride of Ashmore, for the village is the highest in Dorset, 217m (711ft) above sea-level, and on the hilltops open water is a rare curiosity. The pond lies at the centre of the village, a huge circular mirror 12m (40yd) across and 5m (16ft) deep in the middle. Mallard and Muscovy ducks dabble on its surface, and reflected in its placid waters are an old stone barn, thatched cottages of stone and flint, the Georgian Old Rectory with its spreading cedar, and the wide downland sky.

No one knows how long the pond has been there, but it probably existed in pre-Saxon times, despite the Saxon name of the village recorded in the Domesday Book – Aisemare, meaning 'the pond by the ash tree'. In the last half century the pond has rarely dried out; sometimes, in fact, the water rises even when there has been no rain – a phenomenon characteristic of chalk country, where rain drains away through the upper layers of rock and collects in underground reservoirs. Each year around Midsummer Day the villagers honour the pond in a ceremony, called Filly Loo, of uncertain origin. A band plays from a platform in the middle of the pond and Morris Men dance on the shore.

There are fine views across the downs and combes from the ridgeway road which leads to the village from Shaftesbury.

▶ *To reach Ashmore take the B3081 south-east out of Shaftesbury towards Tollard Royal, but after 4½ miles, turn right along a minor road; Ashmore is 1 mile further.*

3 Hod and Hambledon Hills

Two Iron Age hill-forts confront each other across the narrow valley where the road winds from Child Okeford to Stepleton House. On one side looms Hambledon Hill, grim and bare and over 180m (600ft) high; on the other, slightly lower, stands Hod Hill. Both hills have been the scenes of local stands against invaders – both unsuccessful.

On Hod Hill in AD 43, a band of Dorset people – Durotriges Celts – tried to halt the Roman advance through southern Britain. The 2nd Augustan Legion under the Roman general Vespasian poured a deadly rain of ballista bolts on the defenders and quickly took the fort. The Romans used a corner of the 20ha (50 acre) hill-fort – the largest in Dorset – to construct their own smaller fort. Behind the ramparts they built barracks for 850 legionaries and horsemen, and a house for the commander; and they cut water tanks in the chalk large enough to hold 9,000 litres (2,000 gallons), lining them with clay.

On Hambledon Hill in 1645, during the Civil War, some 2,000 villagers made a stand against Cromwell. They belonged to a group known as the Clubmen, because of their primitive weapons; these men were sick of war and damage to their property and crops, and resisted both Royalists and Roundheads. But they were routed by 50 Roundhead dragoons, who locked some of them in Shroton Church.

South-east from Hambledon's Iron Age hill-fort are remains of a much older causewayed camp enclosing about 8ha (20 acres). Excavations in the late 1970s show that this was just part of a large Stone Age settlement on the hill where, some 4,500 years ago, men lived and kept herds of milk cattle within a defensive timber-faced earthen rampart and ditch. That they were subject to attack is evident from the discovery of a skeleton with an arrowhead embedded in the chest, and signs of fire damage to the defences.

Both Hod and Hambledon hills are privately owned and farmed, but there are public bridle-paths, one on the west side of Hod Hill, one across the Hambledon summit and by the Stone Age camp, and one on the north side of Hambledon Hill up to the hill-fort.

▶ *To reach Hod and Hambledon hills, take the A350 Shaftesbury road from Blandford Forum, and 3 miles north turn left towards Child Okeford. After ½ mile, an iron swing-gate (hidden by rising ground) in a clump of beeches on the left marks the bridle-path to Hod Hill. One mile further, a stile on the right leads to the summit of Hambledon Hill. For the hill-fort, continue on the A350 and take the turning to Iwerne Courtney or Shroton, then the path from the village.*

BLACKMOOR VALE FROM HAMBLEDON HILL

❹ Cerne Abbas

The wild, aggressively masculine figure of a giant, 55m (180ft) tall and brandishing an immense club in his right hand, is outlined in the chalk hillside above the quiet village of Cerne Abbas. Who carved the image and why remains a mystery.

Some suggest that the giant is about 2,000 years old, representing a pagan fertility god, and that he was an idol at the centre of Celtic religious ritual. But another theory is that the figure portrays the Roman god Hercules, and was carved perhaps 1,700 years ago.

The pagan figure overlooks the few but impressive ruins of an abbey half-hidden among beech trees just to the north of Cerne Abbas village. A path from the village leads to the sheep-grazed slopes of Giant Hill, but the stiff climb up the hill yields only glimpses of the 60cm (2ft) deep by 60cm (2ft) wide trench that forms the giant's outline, maintained by the National Trust. From the hillside there are fine views of Cerne Abbas in its bowl of green hills.

Above the giant's head lies the Trendle, or Frying Pan, a square Iron Age earthwork on the hilltop thought to have been used for Celtic ritual. Until recent times, the villagers used to set up a maypole here on May Day – a strange echo of the fertility cult that the giant may represent. According to folklore, couples who visit the giant at night can expect a fruitful marriage.
▶ *Cerne Abbas is 7 miles north of Dorchester on the A352 Sherborne road. The best view of the giant is from the lay-by on the A352, just north of the village.*

❺ Marshwood Vale

A network of meandering, high-banked lanes wanders through Marshwood Vale, the valley of the River Char which winds down to Lyme Bay at Charmouth. Hidden among the lanes, villages of tawny sandstone patterned with grey-green lichen shelter below heavily wooded hills such as Wootton and Lewesdon, some of them crowned with ancient hill-forts such as Lambert's Castle. The capital of the Vale is the small hillside village of Whitchurch Canonicorum, so called because its parish tithes

were split between the canons of Wells and Salisbury cathedrals. In the mainly Early English church there is a rare healing shrine, a 13th-century stone tomb containing the relics of St Wite, a Saxon saint; the three oval holes in its side were where pilgrims in hope of miracles once placed their crippled limbs.

Three miles to the north-west lies Wootton Hill, where the road climbs through tunnels of beeches to a Forestry Commission car park in the shelter of tall Monterey pines. A gentle walk leads through Charmouth Forest, on the crown of the hill, where roe deer emerge from cover at dawn and dusk.

The forest road joins the B3165 which, a mile to the north-east, skirts the towering sides of Lambert's Castle, an Iron Age earthwork on the frontier between the territories of the Durotriges of Dorset and the Dumnovici, who gave their name to neighbouring Devon. From the south-west side the ascent is easy. The top is so spacious that horse races used to be run there in the 18th and 19th centuries. Now it is National Trust property, with superb views over the Vale and north-east to the distinctive Pilsdon Pen; at 277m (909ft), it is the highest hill in Dorset and is crowned by another hill-fort.
▶ *Whitchurch Canonicorum is 4 miles north-east of Lyme Regis. A turning to the left from the A35 just east of Charmouth leads to the Vale.*

❻ Golden Cap Estate

When Golden Cap hill glistens in the sun, it is one of those landmarks so unforgettable that whole regions revolve around them. A flat-topped band of orange sandstone, the hill crowns the highest cliff on England's south coast, overlooking Lyme Bay. It forms part of the Jurassic Coast: England's only natural World Heritage site, this runs for 95 miles from Exmouth, in Devon, to Studland, in Dorset. The National Trust has made Golden Cap the focal point of a miniature national park, which spans 5 miles of colourful coastline from Eype's Mouth westwards to The Spittles rocks near Lyme Regis, with beaches, woods, two rivermouths, two cliff peaks and miles of downland slopes and combes. The South West Coast Path runs right along the estate coastline.

A narrow lane winds down to Eype's Mouth, lying south-west of Bridport. At Seatown the River Winniford twists down a long combe to end in a small pool on the inland side of the pebble shore; here, the cliffs to the east are a subtle blend of green and grey, merging above into a tawny yellow.

The coast path crosses Seatown beach after descending westwards over Doghouse Hill from the green, 155m (507ft) high Thorncombe Beacon; then it climbs steeply westwards to the 191m (626ft) high summit of Golden Cap. Another, easier route to the cliff-top starts from the Langdon Hill car park west of Chideock (the only car park on the east side of the estate), and leads south through woods to the downs before finally climbing to the summit, topped with gorse and heather.

Out to sea the views from Golden Cap stretch from Start Point in Devon to the white cliffs of Bill of Portland, and inland to the west the long ridge of Stonebarrow Hill drops to the sea at the sombre cliffs called Cain's Folly. Beyond Charmouth are the tumbled landslips of Black Ven, a favourite haunt for fossil hunters.

▶ *Golden Cap is 4 miles east of Lyme Regis. A number of narrow lanes lead south from the A35 Lyme Regis–Bridport road to Golden Cap Estate. Stonebarrow Lane, at the eastern end of Charmouth, leads to Stonebarrow Hill where there is a National Trust information centre and car park.*

❼ Black Down

Gorse and heather cover the summit of Black Down, 237m (777ft) above the sea and surmounted by a monument to Vice-Admiral Sir Thomas Masterman Hardy, Nelson's flag-captain at Trafalgar. The monument was erected by public subscription in 1846, and quickly became a familiar part of the Dorset landscape. The 21m (70ft) high, octagonal stone stack captures the eye from far and wide, and from its base there are magnificent sea views across to the Isle of Wight, to Golden Cap and to Start Point, almost 60 miles south-west in Devon. A bridle-path winds down from the summit of Black Down to Portesham where the admiral lived as a boy, in a modest Georgian stone house which still stands.

The downs in this area are rich in prehistoric burial mounds and standing stones. About a quarter of a mile west of the path, on the hill above Portesham, there is a partly reconstructed New Stone Age chambered tomb called the Hell Stone. At the end of the Valley of Stones, in a field 1½ miles north-west of Portesham, remains of another New Stone Age tomb known as The Grey Mare and her Colts can be seen over the hedge; a Bronze Age stone circle stands a mile to its south-east near the footpath to Portesham Hill. To the north of Black Down, the outline of ancient fields can be traced in the grass.

▶ *Black Down is 5 miles from Dorchester. Take the A35 west from Dorchester and turn south to Portesham at Winterbourne Abbas. Black Down is to the east of the minor road; there is a car park near the monument.*

❽ Abbotsbury

Nearly 470 years after the dissolution of Abbotsbury's ancient Benedictine abbey, the monks' great swannery still flourishes on the Fleet, a brackish lagoon that lies behind Chesil Beach. The waters are rich in eel-grass and other vegetation on which the swans feed, and in April the meadow at the Fleet's end provides them with perfect nesting sites. It is in May, when the birds are incubating their eggs, that they show themselves to be every bit as wild as they are graceful in their aggressive defence of their territories.

Many of the cottages in Abbotsbury were built with stones taken from the demolished abbey, and the enormous stone-built tithe barn – 83m (91yd) long, massively buttressed and with a cart-high porch – hints at the abbey's former riches. South-west of the village on Chapel Hill, overlooking the sea, the 14th-century St Catherine's Chapel still captures the eye. It was probably spared from destruction by Giles Strangways, Henry VIII's Dissolution Commissioner, because it was a landmark for mariners. From the chapel there are magnificent views out to sea and along the coast.

▶ *Abbotsbury is 8 miles north-west of Weymouth on the B3157. The swannery is 1 mile south of the village, reached from New Barn Road where there is a car park.*

SOUTH-WEST ENGLAND

9 Maiden Castle

The Celtic tribe who gave their name to Dorset – the Durotriges – made Maiden Castle their hilltop capital. But the fort, whose mighty multiple ramparts wind sinuously around a hill outside Dorchester, was many centuries in the making.

Hardly discernible now is the New Stone Age camp that crowned the eastern summit long before 2000BC; but a crudely shaped chalk idol, dating from this period and possibly the image of a mother-goddess, was found on the hilltop and can now be seen in the County Museum in Dorchester. Largely lost, too, is the enormous New Stone Age long-barrow burial mound that ran one-third of a mile along the top.

The first Celtic inhabitants, who arrived about 300 BC, fortified their single rampart with timber. It enclosed about 6ha (16 acres), and within its protection they lived in timber huts, laid out in streets, and stored their corn and water in large circular pits. The enclosure was enlarged to its present size of 19ha (47 acres) – making it a small town – after 250 BC.

Maiden Castle as it is today dates from later Celtic times, largely from the 1st century BC, and was a response to the threat of a new weapon, the sling-shot, that could kill at 90m (100yd) against the 27m (30yd) of primitive arrows. Extra lines of ramparts were added – and were raised as high as possible. You can still walk round an inner rampart that rises 15m (50ft) above its ditch.

But none of these fortifications offered adequate defence against the *ballistae* – or giant crossbows – of the Roman 2nd Legion, which attacked in AD 43. The Durotriges were routed and suffered heavy losses.

By AD 70 the fort was completely deserted, and the survivors driven down into the new Roman town of Durnovaria, now the modern town of Dorchester. Around AD 380, the hilltop was re-occupied by the people who built the mysterious Romano-British temple whose foundations can be seen there today. Nearly 300 years later, in around AD 635, a sacrificial victim with a hole cut in his skull was buried in the bank-barrow. By whom and for what reason is unknown.

▶ *Maiden Castle is 2 miles south-west of Dorchester. At the southern end of the town, a signposted minor road leads south-west off the A354 Weymouth road; there is a car park at the end of this road.*

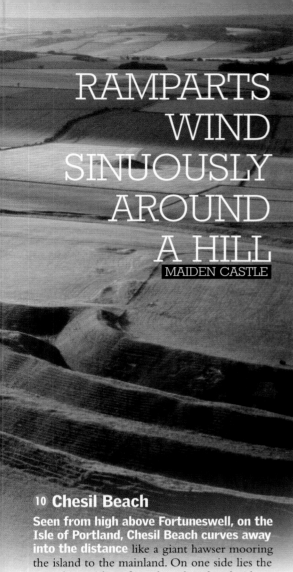

RAMPARTS WIND SINUOUSLY AROUND A HILL

MAIDEN CASTLE

10 Chesil Beach

Seen from high above Fortuneswell, on the Isle of Portland, Chesil Beach curves away into the distance like a giant hawser mooring the island to the mainland. On one side lies the sea, white with surf; on the other the placid waters of the Fleet, a lagoon bordering the great bank of pebbles for half of the 16 miles to its anchorage in the tawny cliffs near Burton Bradstock. And all along the beach there is a deep and continuous hiss and roar as the waves suck back then hurl forward millions of pebbles.

About 180m (200yd) wide and 12m (40ft) high at the Portland end, the beach changes shape with the sea's moods. Fishermen judge their position along the beach by the size of the pebbles, which the tide has graded in size from west to east; at Portland they are the size of a man's fist, at Burton Bradstock they are no bigger than raisins.

Chesil Beach was the scourge of sailing ships when strong south-westerly winds swept across Lyme Bay. Many a good ship has been battered to pieces on the seething pebbles. Casualties include seven ships of the line in November 1795, with the loss of more than 200 men and women. They were part of a fleet commanded by Rear-Admiral Sir Hugh Christian, on his way to the West Indies to become Commander-in-Chief. In 1824 two West-Indiamen, *Carvalho* and *Colville*, met their fate here with all hands drowned, and the sloop *Ebenezer* was flung almost into the Fleet, in which it was later re-floated.

The gales of 1824 claimed not only ships but also the village of Fleet near the eastern end of the lagoon, swept away when a freak tide roared over the bank. Only the chancel of the old village church survives.

▶ *To reach Fortuneswell, take the A354 Portland road south out of Weymouth, and cross the causeway. There is a car park in Fortuneswell.*

⑪ The Bockhamptons

The heart of Thomas Hardy lies buried in Stinsford churchyard, not far from the swift-flowing River Frome. His ashes are interred in Westminster Abbey. From the foot-bridge across a stream, a path leads westwards through old water-meadows to Grey's Bridge and Dorchester. Eastwards it runs alongside the stream, starred with the white flowers of river water crowfoot and alive with serpentine strands of waving weed, to the stone-and-thatch village of Lower Bockhampton, where Hardy went to school.

About a mile's walk or drive northwards across the downs is Higher Bockhampton, and the wildlife sanctuary of Thorncombe Wood. From there a nature trail about 1½ miles long leads through a magnificent collection of sweet chestnuts, beeches and oaks, and on the eastern side of the wood through 8ha (20 acres) of black heath, a tangle of furze, birch saplings, holly, heather and rhododendrons.

A track leads from the trail up the hillside to Hardy's cottage birthplace. Where the Great Heath once swept down to the little barred back window there are now the dark conifers of the Forestry Commission's Puddletown Forest. Along the 2½ mile Forest Walk you may glimpse Sika deer and see badger tracks.

▶ *Stinsford is just off the A35, 1½ miles east of Dorchester. Higher Bockhampton and Thorncombe Wood car park are about 1 mile north-east along minor roads.*

SOUTH-WEST ENGLAND

⑫ Cull-peppers Dish

On Affpuddle Heath a tall tree grows from the 15m (50ft) depths of a smooth-sided crater measuring 46m (150yd) across. The tree and crater resemble a huge mortar and pestle, and may have been named after the 17th-century herbalist Nicholas Culpeper. Once thought to be a prehistoric temple, the crater is now recognised as a swallow-hole – one of 200 or so on the heath – a subsidence caused by underground streams eroding sand and chalk.

In the northern part of the heath, the many little bridges and decaying sluice gates tell of the once-intricate system of water-meadows around the River Piddle. The controlled flooding of these meadows early in the year resulted in early grazing for stock, because the incoming water, warmer than the soil, advanced grass growth.

To the south, tracks lead down from the heath through Forestry Commission conifers and past Rimsmoor Pond to the bridle-path to Clouds Hill. Here the National Trust maintains the cottage that was the home of Lawrence of Arabia from 1923. He rented it while, as Private Shaw of the Royal Tank Corps, he was stationed at nearby Bovington Camp. Later he transferred to the RAF, and on his discharge in 1935 returned to live at Clouds Hill, which he had bought, until his death a few months later. Lawrence described the cottage, which lies concealed in a riot of rhododendrons, as 'earthly paradise'.

▶ *Cull-peppers Dish is 8 miles east of Dorchester. Take the A35 eastwards and turn on to the B3390 towards Affpuddle; the signpost and car park are east of the road about 1 mile south of the village.*

⑬ Ringstead Bay

The massive chalk headland of White Nothe, called Nose locally, protects Ringstead Bay to the east. On the south-west side, the formidable stone rampart of the Isle of Portland shelters both Ringstead and Weymouth bays.

The deserted medieval village of Ringstead lies around a mile east of Osmington Mills, the place where John Constable painted his picture of Weymouth Bay. The village is now no more than a collection of grassy mounds and the ruined fragment of a church. Why it was deserted local records do not say. It's possible that the villagers may have succumbed to the Black Death. A more likely story, however, is that they were the victims of French raiders in 1420, during the Hundred Years' War.

A coastal path climbs eastwards for about 2 miles to White Nothe, across sloping downland overlooking a long sweep of pebbled beach, sheltered in places by ledges of rock running into the sea. Even the chaotic, tumbled layers of the Burning Cliff in no way disrupt the bay's idyllic and tranquil atmosphere. The Burning Cliff is so called because the dark, sulphurous oil-shale – or Kimmeridge coal – of which it is composed, ignited spontaneously in 1826 and smouldered for four years.

The approach to towering White Nothe is through wooded gullies bright with red campion in summer. The final climb is very steep, but for those who make it there are superb views.

▶ *Ringstead Bay is 5 miles east of Weymouth. For Ringstead car park take the Upton turning (a toll-road) south from the A353 Weymouth-Wareham road.*

⑭ Worbarrow and Kimmeridge Bays

A rich underwater life, flourishing on the low ledges of clay and shale that shelve into the sea, is one of the few qualities the neighbouring Worbarrow and Kimmeridge bays have in common, together with the fact that they are both part of the Purbeck Marine Wildlife Reserve. Otherwise they contrast dramatically.

Worbarrow Bay is flanked on the east side by the towering limestone pyramid of Worbarrow Tout; to the west – across almost 2 miles of glistening water – is Mupe Bay and the tumbling Mupe Rocks. In between, the waves have cut back the softer disarray of rock to form cliffs that are green, grey, pink or ochre, and are broken in the middle by the shining white cove of Arish Mell, where the Purbeck-chalk range drops to the sea. A wooded gully leads to Worbarrow Bay, running down to the sea from the deserted village of Tyneham.

Kimmeridge Bay is less dramatic, backed by low green downland and with modest cliffs whose crumbly, tawny rocks alternate with dark grey shale and clay. On the bay's eastern arm is a tower commemorating Sir William Clavell of nearby Smedmore House; in the 1600s he came close to ruin trying to develop the commercial potential of the local sulphurous oil-shale, using

THE GREEN UNDERCLIFF,

it as fuel first for producing alum, then for a glass works. The Celts were more successful with their use of the shale well into Romano-British times, and their bangles and ornaments made from hardened Kimmeridge oil-shale have been found as far away as Hadrian's Wall

Worbarrow Bay is within an army firing range, but it is open to the public most weekends and public holidays. Dates are given in the local press and on the army road boards. Marked paths lead to the bay from Tyneham car park, and it is essential to keep to the paths in case of unexploded shells.

▶ *Kimmeridge and Worbarrow bays are 8 and 10 miles west of Swanage. To reach both bays, turn off the A351 Swanage-Wareham road at Corfe Castle for Church Knowle. Just beyond Church Knowle, a turning south leads about 2 miles to Kimmeridge, from where a toll-road leads to the bay car park. For Worbarrow Bay, pass the Kimmeridge turning and continue about 4 miles via Steeple to Tyneham, where there is a car park.*

⑮ St Aldhelm's Head

The grey wall of rock that sweeps westwards from Swanage reaches its climax at St Aldhelm's Head, a towering 100m (350ft) cliff thrusting boldly out into the Channel. A few metres back from the cliff-edge a small Norman chapel dedicated to the evangelist St Aldhelm (c.640–709), a Saxon Bishop of Sherborne, stands solitary on the windswept grassy plateau, heavily buttressed against the gales. Where a stone cross now stands on its roof, there was originally a fire basket whose bright glow warned sailors of the tide-race off the headland.

Westwards from the cliff the rock collapses in spectacular disarray, and strangely fretted towers and pinnacles rise from the green undercliff, wreathed in wild flowers. The South West Coast Path follows near the cliff-edge to Emmetts Hill overlooking Chapman's Pool, a quiet cove in a deep cleft bordered on the west by Houns-tout Cliff. A path leads to Chapman's Pool but care should be taken as landslips and erosion have made some areas unsafe. Keep away from the cliff-edge.

▶ *St Aldhelm's Head is 5 miles south-west of Swanage. From Worth Matravers (off B3069 west of Swanage), a pot-holed road runs westwards to Renscombe Farm, then turns south from the farmyard to St Aldhelm's Head, 1½ miles further on.*

⑯ Durlston Head

The rock formations of the Isle of Purbeck are nowhere more dramatic than in the great grey cliffs of Portland stone that rise from the waves at Durlston Head. And in the park above the cliffs is a man-made rock formation – the Great Globe, a chart of the world cut from 40 tonnes of Portland stone and surrounded by stone slabs carved with cosmic information and quotations from the poets. It was carved in the 1880s by George Burt, a local quarryman who made his fortune supplying paving stones for Victorian London.

The Dorset County Council's Country Park here has a 'stone trail', a nature trail and geological models that tell the story of the local rocks. A path leads down through holm oaks and tamarisk to a cliff-edge sea-bird sanctuary, and then strides on towards the Anvil Point Lighthouse, descending into the gully where the Tilly Whim Caves emerge. Rock falls have forced the closure of these old quarry workings, but the great wall of Portland stone, divided into gargantuan blocks by natural joints, remains awe-inspiring. There are other impressive quarry caves at Winspit, a few miles to the west. This is an idyllic spot on a sunny day, with its great stone stacks and the sea dancing over the ledges from which generations of quarrymen winched their stone into the barges waiting below. The Country Park is one of the best places in Britain to see butterflies and supports over 250 species of bird.

▶ *Durlston Head is 1 mile south of Swanage, reached by the road climbing southwards just east of Swanage pier; there is a car park just before the castle. Winspit is 4 miles west of Durlston Head, along a 1½ mile track south from Worth Matravers, which has a car park on the Corfe road.*

SOUTH-WEST ENGLAND

WREATHED IN WILD FLOWERS

ST ALDHELM'S HEAD

⑰ Ballard Down

The Dorset chalklands begin dramatically at Ballard Down, where the hills of the Isle of Purbeck meet the sea. Below Studland's small Norman church, a fingerpost indicates two paths. One climbs straight ahead, first by a lane, then through blazing gorse and stone-strewn cornfields south to the crest of Ballard Down. About a mile west is Nine Barrow Down with views of Corfe Castle, 4 miles westwards. The other path descends east towards the beach then turns to climb through Studland Wood, and finally emerges on the springy turf of the cliff-top. Do not go near the edge, for these cliffs are dangerous.

Far below, chalk stacks rise dazzlingly from the sea. The great cliffs of The Foreland, a mile east of Studland, are penetrated by wave-pierced arches, and beyond lies Old Harry rock and, now just underwater, Old Harry's Wife. Old Harry is a synonym for the Devil, and the area on the cliff-top is known as Old Nick's Ground. But on a sunny afternoon the place is nothing if not heavenly. Gulls circle lazily around the soaring white pinnacles, and the yellow spikes of wild cabbage brighten the cliff-edge.

The path continues along the cliff, with the green down to the right. At Ballard Point, a mile south-west of The Foreland, two seas come into view – to the north the great sweep of Studland Bay to Poole Harbour, and to the south the graceful crescent extending to Swanage and Peveril Point. The path then winds into Swanage.

▶ *Ballard Down, owned by the National Trust, is 1½ miles north of Swanage. It can be reached from Swanage by taking the Studland road to New Swanage, where the southern end of the downland path starts from Ballard Way.*

⑱ Studland Heath

The ancient wilderness of Dorset's heathland, glowing with gorse and heather, butts up against the sparkling creeks and inlets of Poole's vast, landlocked harbour. At Studland, 635ha (1,570 acres) of the heath are under the protection of the National Trust, and east of the toll-road to the South Haven Point–Sandbanks chain-ferry there are two nature trails starting from the Knoll car park. One leads over the beach and sand-dunes, the other through woodland and swamp.

The sand-dunes trail first follows the superb crescent of Studland's beach, well sheltered and with wide white sands, one of the finest bathing beaches in Britain. Shells to be found along the waterline include Pandora shells, about 3cm (1½ in) long and with a mother-of-pearl sheen; they are rare in Britain and are found here and elsewhere along the Dorset coast, as well as in a few other spots on the South Coast, and in the Channel Isles. From the beach the trail turns inland over three lines of dunes which grow greener the further they are from the sea. These sand-dunes demonstrate how the peninsula has been built up over 250 years from a small spit of land – the wind sweeping sand inshore and plants gradually colonising and anchoring the newly created dunes.

The most seaward dune is known as the Zero Ridge. The centre one is called the First Ridge, because it was the nearest dune to the sea when the area was surveyed in the 1930s. The third, innermost, ridge dates from the 18th century.

The woodland trail passes close to the south end of Studland's Little Sea, a mile-long freshwater lake edged with sallow, reedmace, yellow flag and bog bean. Until 350 years ago it was a coastal bay, but developing sand-dunes have now completely cut it off from the sea, and drainage from inland streams has gradually replaced the salt water.

A wooden hide, reached along a short path from the ferry road, overlooks the lake, where in winter many wildfowl, such as wigeon, pochard, goldeneye and shoveler, may be seen. Summer visitors include sedge and reed warblers, which can be heard singing in the reed beds. Britain's

three lizard and three snake species are all found on the reserve. Nearby is the Arne RSPB Nature Reserve, situated on a peninsula in the south-west corner of Poole harbour; it is one of the best places to see Dartford warblers.

▶ *Studland Heath is 4 miles north of Swanage. There are frequent ferries to the heath from Sandbanks to the north, although long queues of cars may form in summer. An alternative approach is through Wareham and Corfe via the A351 and B3351 roads. The Knoll car park is about ½ mile north of Studland along a toll-road.*

⑲ Brownsea Island

A castle overlooking the landing-stage, fields ablaze with daffodils in spring, a quarter-mile-long tunnel of rhododendrons, and a woodland path descending to a gently shelving beach, all give Brownsea the air of a paradise island. Herring gulls nest in scores along the cliff paths, rising in shrieking protest as visitors approach. Little egrets and grey herons nest in the island's heronry. Canada geese marshal their young to grassy feeding spots, red squirrels can be seen in the pinewoods, and the island echoes with the sharp cries of peacocks in the trees or vibrating their dazzling tails in the pathways.

From the southern cliffs there are wide views across the shimmering waters of Poole Harbour to Old Harry rock and Corfe Castle tucked into its cleft in the Purbeck Hills. Near by, a chunk of Portland stone commemorates the first, experimental Boy Scouts' camp, arranged here by Baden-Powell in 1907 – only scouts and guides can camp on the island.

From a lookout hut at the start of the island nature trail you can see cormorants resting on the shingle strip, and common terns nesting on the islands built for them. A 101ha (250 acre) nature reserve occupies the north side of the island, and includes one of the largest heronries in England. There are free guided walks every day and a self-guided trail arranged by Dorset Wildlife Trust.

▶ *Brownsea Island, owned by the National Trust, is reached by boat from Poole Quay, Sandbanks Jetty, Bournemouth Pier and Swanage Pier. No dogs are allowed on the island.*

SOUTH-WEST ENGLAND

THE COTSWOLD HILLS 70-78

THE CHILTERN HILLS 79-84

THE NORTH WESSEX DOWNS 85-95

THE NEW FOREST and ISLE OF WIGHT 98-105

Evesham
Banbury
Bedford
Milton Keynes
Luton
Bicester
Cheltenham
Stow-on-the-Wold
Gloucester
Witney
Wendover
Tring
Watford
Oxford
High Wycombe
Stroud
Cirencester
Reading
Slough
London
Tetbury
Swindon
Woking
Croydon
Marlborough
Hungerford
Newbury
Devizes
Basingstoke
Aldershot
Guildford
Dorking
Godalming
Warminster
Alton
Haslemere
Horsham
Salisbury
Winchester
Petersfield
Midhurst
Southampton
Chichester
Worthing
Brighton and Hove
Ringwood
Lymington
Portsmouth
Christchurch
Cowes
Ryde
Newport
Yarmouth
Ventnor

Romford

M25
M20
M20
M2
A299
Ramsgate
A28
Sevenoaks
A26
Maidstone
Canterbury
8
M20
A2
9
Ashford
Dover
A2070
M20
Folkestone
7
A229
Tunbridge Wells
A21
10
A259
A26
DOWNLAND
and WEALD
106–115
A21
Rye
A22
A259
Hailsham
Hastings
A27
14
13
12
Eastbourne
11

Southern England

Away from its teeming towns, the South of England is home to many scenic wonders. Nestled among its gentle hills, majestic downs and patchwork fields are ancient mounds and monuments, reminders that man has been making his mark here for many centuries.

The COTSWOLD HILLS

The Cotswolds form the highest and widest part of a belt of limestone that stretches from Dorset to the Humber. Towns and villages built from this honey-coloured stone nestle among the Cotswold hills and vales.

❶ Bredon Hill

The isolated limestone outcrop of Bredon Hill rises between the gentle vales of Evesham and Gloucester. At 294m (961ft), it is not quite the highest point in the Cotswolds, but it seems like it. From the windy summit, on which Iron Age men built a great fort, at least eight counties can be seen. In his poem 'Bredon Hill' the poet A. E. Housman called them 'the coloured counties' – a reference to the differing lines of the patchwork countryside. The Malverns, the Welsh hills, the gleam of the Severn estuary and that fruitful lap of England, the Vale of Evesham, spread away in an immense cloud-smudged pattern of fields and orchards as if the Industrial Revolution had never happened.

Bredon Hill is like a giant layer cake, with strata of limestone clays topped at the summit by the true Cotswold stone – a hard, creamy-yellow limestone. At the highest point, near the Iron Age hill-fort known locally as Kemerton Camp, the Cotswold-stone layer is about 30m (100ft) thick. A large chunk of stone, the Banbury Stone, once stood on the edge of a cavity near the outer rim of the hill-fort. About 120 years ago, a landslip brought the stone crashing down into the cavity where it split into large pieces. One is known as the Elephant Stone because it resembles a kneeling elephant with its trunk extended.

About 2 miles south-east of the summit hill-fort is Conderton Camp, a much smaller Iron Age earthwork. It was probably built in the 2nd century BC as a cattle enclosure. Some time in the 1st century BC, it was developed as a small settlement. The northern end was enclosed by a bank and a dry-stone wall, within which was built a small village of huts and storage pits.

The area is rich in fossils. The remains of a type of oyster with a thick, curved shell, known locally as 'Devil's toenails', are found in fields. Also common are belemnites – long, cylindrical shells with a pointed end, nicknamed 'bullets' – and snail-like ammonites. In the Cotswold stone are brachiopods, or 'lamp-shells'; starfish-shaped crinoids known as 'star-stones', and the remains of primitive sea-urchins.

▶ *Bredon Hill is 6 miles south-west of Evesham. Minor roads from the A46, B4079, B4080 and B4084 lead to the villages below the hill. Paths from these villages lead to the top of the hill.*

❷ Stanton and Stanway

The villages of Stanton and Stanway, tucked under the western escarpment of the Cotswolds, are perhaps at their loveliest in the evening light. A short, easy stroll out from Stanway's avenue of oak trees, called The Liberty and a favourite haunt of nuthatches and owls, leads to a footpath to Stanton, one of the most perfect Cotswold villages. The path heads north across open fields at the foot of the steep escarpment. The walk from Stanway passes a fine Tudor house, with a Jacobean gateway, and a medieval tithe barn. Stanton, which is not on the road to anywhere, is a meandering, many-gabled street of Elizabethan and 17th-century cottages with a wayside cross and a Gothic manor house.

A footpath and bridleway climb steeply out of Stanton up to Shenberrow Hill and its airy, ramparted Iron Age fort standing in the lee of the lofty ash trees on the ridge above. The path crosses farmland as it climbs, following the contours of the curving hill, and views drop away behind to Bredon, Dumbleton Hill and the Malverns. Sheep graze on the hill, and kestrels can sometimes be seen hovering.

The circuit uphill and down round the fort is not clearly marked and it is easy to stray from the path here, but the descent from the fort is well trodden and the path emerges at the eastern end of the village.

▶ *Stanway is on the B4077, 3½ miles north-east of Winchcombe; Stanton is 1½ miles north of Stanway on a minor road.*

❸ Broadway Hill

This is among the highest points in the Cotswolds – 312m (1,024ft) above sea-level – and has a magnificent view across the Vale of Evesham to the great whaleback of Bredon Hill and the Malverns, the Black Mountains in Wales and even the Shropshire Wrekin. In spring, the Vale of Evesham froths with blossom. Footpaths drop down to Broadway and pass through neighbouring woods of planted beech, larch, spruce and Scots pine. The woods are the haunt of badgers, grey squirrels, and many birds, moths and butterflies. Among the shrubs there are hawthorns and wild roses. Wild flowers are plentiful, and include dog's mercury in spring and rosebay willowherb in late summer.

Broadway Tower is a folly – a mock castle designed by the architect James Wyatt at the end of the 18th century for the Earl of Coventry. It stands on Broadway Hill – known locally as Broadway Beacon – and up to 13 counties can be seen from its rooftop gallery. Traditionally the hill was used for beacon fires to communicate special happenings to other parts of the country. The land was owned by the Earl and legend tells that his wife, wondering whether the summit could be seen from their mansion near Worcester, had a large bonfire lit. This was seen clearly, and she persuaded her husband to build the folly to mark the summit.

Buckle Street, the minor road leading off the main A44 from Broadway to Chipping Norton, which skirts around Broadway Hill, is part of the ancient Buggildway along the ridge to Bourton-on-the-Water.

▶ *Take the A44 east out of Broadway and after 2 miles turn south on to Buckle Street. The tower is ½ mile along the road. Alternatively, park in Broadway and follow the footpaths south-east from the village.*

BROADWAY TOWER

❹ Condicote

This is upland country where remote stone villages sit snugly in summer and doggedly in winter. From the village of Condicote the Roman Ryknild Street runs south-east and straight across the top of the high downland. It forms a clear track from here to the A436. North-east of Condicote is Eubury Camp, an Iron Age fortification of high bank-and-ditch construction on the north side of a minor road running from the village to the A424, it is clearly visible from the road. A closer look can be taken from the path over private land that winds round the valley bottom past a water-tower.

On the same minor road, almost in Condicote itself, a large triangle of grassland on the south side of the road marks the site of a prehistoric henge – an enclosure marked by stone or timber – built for some unknown purpose about 2500 BC.

From a minor road leading south-east from Condicote and then east to join the A424 there is a fine view of the lake by the brewery, from which the River Dikler rises to wind past the villages of Upper and Lower Swell. It is one of the most enchanting valleys in the Cotswolds.

▶ *Condicote is 3 miles north-west of Stow-on-the-Wold between the B4077 and A424.*

❺ Salt Way and Salter's Hill

Salt was an essential meat preservative in medieval times, when people had to slaughter their livestock in autumn because there would not be enough feed for the animals during winter. Salt became an important commodity and for centuries packhorses loaded with it travelled along roads and paths throughout England from the coastal saltpans or inland mines. One of the 'salt ways' runs across a high ridge of the Cotswolds on what was probably a prehistoric path. Remote, windy and sunny, the narrow road that skirts the vale of Sudeley to the west and the gentle Windrush valley to the east is still called the Salt Way. Salter's Hill lies 2 miles east of Winchcombe on the northern section of the Way.

On the west slope of the ridge above the vale of Sudeley there is a planted woodland of conifers. Along the path through the wood the grassy banks are vivid with rock-roses and bright blue tufted vetch. The path starts on the west side of the Salt Way 3 miles north of the A436. From it, swallows can be seen swooping and diving in the air over Winchcombe, the valley of the River Isbourne, wooded Sudeley Castle and the blue reaches of Cleeve Common far beyond.

At its northern end, the Salt Way is a footpath and leads to Salter's Hill. Beyond the hill the path dips down to Salter's Lane and into a precipitous valley. From the path there is a rare view of the ruins of Hailes Abbey, owned by the National Trust and built in the 13th century for the white-robed Cistercian monks.

▶ *This section of the Salt Way lies north of the A436, and starts some 2½ miles east of Andoversford. It leads northwards for 7 miles, and ends just beyond Hailes Abbey, where it then meets the B4632 north of Winchcombe.*

❻ Cleeve Hill

At 330m (1,083ft) above sea-level, the ridge 1½ miles south-east of Cleeve Hill is the highest point of the Cotswolds. This airy upland remains one of the most breathtaking viewpoints anywhere in England. Herefordshire Beacon is 16 miles north-west, while Tewkesbury Abbey, in the same direction, seems close enough to touch. The Sugar Loaf mountain, 45 miles to the west in the Brecon Beacons, is clearly silhouetted against the distant horizon.

Just over 2 miles east of Cleeve Cloud, the west-facing ridge below Cleeve Common, is a long barrow, Belas Knap, a green-turfed hump on the wooded escarpment above the vale of Sudeley. The barrow was built by New Stone Age men about 5,000 years ago, and is some 55m (180ft) long and 18m (60ft) wide. It contains four burial chambers in which the remains of more than 30 people have been found. It is superbly built, in the same manner as Cotswold masons still construct dry-stone walls today. Its name comes from the Anglo-Saxon for a beacon on a hill.

Belas Knap can be reached on foot from Cleeve Hill by following the path south-east over Cleeve Common, past the radio mast, and east to Wontley Farm. From there turn north-east along a track and footpath to the barrow.

The walk from Cleeve Hill to Belas Knap and back takes about three hours. Alternatively, to reach the barrow, drive north on the B4632 and just before Winchcombe turn south on to a minor road to Charlton Abbots. A mile beyond the junction a steep lane branches south-west, signposted to Corndean. Either take this lane and join the path from Cleeve Cloud just past a small farmyard, or drive on half a mile to a lay-by and walk up a steep, signposted path through woodland on the west side of the road to Belas Knap above.

▶ *Cleeve Hill is 3 miles north-east of Cheltenham. Take the B4632 from Cheltenham to Cleeve Hill Golf Club. There is a car park just beyond the club.*

❼ The Windrush Valley

In summer the Windrush is a beguiling little stream on its upper reaches, but in winter it has been known to flood, and so gave the name Guiting – from the Anglo-Saxon *gute* for 'flood' – to two of the villages lying in its valley; Temple Guiting and Guiting Power. South of Temple Guiting lies Leigh Wood – a cool and shady place to explore. The woods are owned by Christchurch College, Oxford, and a Tudor manor at Temple Guiting was probably built as a summer residence for the Bishops of Oxford.

At Kineton, a mile south of Temple Guiting, a steep lane at the north end of the hamlet leads down eastwards through the cottages, and is marked 'Not Suitable for Motorists'. It leads to a clear, gravelly ford and a narrow, high-hedged lane lying in the shadow of Leigh Wood. Further along the lane a track dips away to the south and crosses the Windrush again at another ford – sun-dappled under ancient trees, with a medieval packhorse bridge to make the crossing easier in flood.

A footpath winds south through the lush, wooded water-meadows at this spot, where the hills drop to create a still and sunlit place that feels strangely secret. The footpath is entangled in cow parsley, elder trees, hawthorns and blackthorns. In summer there are creamy curds of elder; in spring cowslips dapple the grassy banks; in autumn there are red hawthorn berries and sloes.

Deep within the watery woodland a narrow foot-bridge – a slab of ancient stone – crosses the chuckling Windrush. Grey wagtails flash their yellow chests as they dance in the air to take insects in flight, and warblers and thrushes nest in the willows, hazels and ash trees.

Guiting Power, 1½ miles south of Kineton, is a classic Cotswold village with a sloping, triangular green, and honey-coloured stone houses. A footpath leads southwards past the church and then across open fields. The land is private, so keep to the public footpath. From it there are extensive views down the Windrush valley. Wild flowers and grasses cover the warm slopes where the occasional ancient oak tree stands sentinel.

After crossing a small tributary of the Windrush, the path continues on down the valley, partly by way of a minor road, to Naunton. The river here ambles behind the old stone cottages that line the street through this delightful backwater village.

Further down the valley, across the A429 at Bourton-on-the-Water, the atmosphere becomes more formal and self-conscious – and there are many more visitors.

▶ *The Windrush valley is 6 miles west of Stow-on-the-Wold. Temple Guiting is on a minor road south of the B4077.*

SUN-DAPPLED UNDER ANCIENT TREES
THE WINDRUSH RIVER

❽ Birdlip Hill and Crickley Hill

These commanding and ancient peaks overlook the whole of the Vale of Gloucester to the Welsh hills. Birdlip Hill has cool beechwoods and a windy, bare turf peak with views south-west to the enfolding Witcombe Wood, curving round the escarpment to Buckholt Wood and Cooper's Hill. The woods are private, and visitors should keep to the public footpaths that give access to the wealth of mixed woodland, birds and forest plants. The Roman Ermin Way runs east from the village of Birdlip, perched above its precipitous hill, and from the Iron Age burial mound at Barrow Wake – just north of the village – came the bronze Birdlip Mirror now in Gloucester City Museum.

Crickley Hill, a Country Park, has traces of both a New Stone Age settlement and an Iron Age promontory fort. The site was abandoned early in the Iron Age, but reoccupied during the 6th century AD. The sides of the promontory are steep and rugged, and modern quarrying has exaggerated them. Traces of quarrying can be found all over the hill, which has resulted in fascinating exposed geological formations. There is a nature trail on Crickley, together with geological and archaeological trails, and there are superb views to the Malverns and across nearby Cheltenham.

Both of the hills can be reached by road off the A417, and there are several good footpaths. Not far from the road stands a monument to a young geologist, Peter Hopkins, that clearly shows the geological formation so vividly characterised here by the twin escarpments of the Malverns and Cotswolds. Describing 'over 500 million years of Britain's history', the monument is made from sandstone, blue lias limestone, and Malvern gneiss found on the twin escarpments, as well as the 150-million-year-old pea grit and oolite limestone to be seen virtually underfoot in this area.

▶ *The hills lie 6 miles south-east of Gloucester; Birdlip Hill is ½ mile north-west of Birdlip on the A417 and Crickley Hill is ½ mile west of the junction of the A417 and A436.*

❾ Leckhampton Hill

Part of Leckhampton Hill's dramatic quality lies in its bare, spectacular limestone cliff and the teetering rock column called the Devil's Chimney which seems to hang in space over the Severn vale below. It was from the quarries on this hill that the stone for Regency Cheltenham was cut. A steep footpath climbs up from the car park on the minor road at the northern foot of the hill and divides. The route to the west goes round the hill below the summit and provides the most impressive view of the Devil's Chimney set in the cliff below the summit; the other path leads to the summit from which there are views south-west to the Forest of Dean and west to the Black Mountains in Wales.

On the summit, above the Devil's Chimney, is the grassy site of an Iron Age fortification, where coins have been found revealing later Roman and Saxon occupation. A path leads east and, initially, takes a wide, meandering course over the plateau of Leckhampton Hill. It eventually turns south-east through fields to join a minor road leading west past a quarry. East of the quarry, a path leads north to join the footpath below the summit, and so provides a circular route round the hill. Leckhampton Hill is carpeted with wild flowers – the vivid pink buds and blue petals of viper's bugloss, blue tufted vetches, pink sainfoin, ox-eye daisies, common rock-roses and woody nightshade. Pink and white dog-roses abound, and in autumn the sloe berries with their blue bloom appear on the blackthorn bushes.

Flocks of goldfinches and, in winter, long-tailed tits, visit Leckhampton Hill. The common blue butterfly and the meadow brown are often seen, and the chalkhill blue can be found where there is horseshoe vetch. Yellow charlock and pink field bindweed grow in the cornfields.

▶ *Leckhampton Hill is 2½ miles south of Cheltenham. Leave the A46 and follow minor roads to the south of Leckhampton where there is a car park on the north side of the hill.*

❿ Cooper's Hill

A celebrated and distinctly dangerous cheese-rolling ceremony is held each Whitsuntide on Cooper's Hill, when those prepared to risk life and limb chase a whole cheese down a precipitous slope below the cockerel-crowned maypole on its northern rim. But for the rest of the year the hill is a peaceful nature reserve of some 55ha (137 acres), now in the care of Gloucestershire County Council.

Cooper's Hill was once one of the largest Iron Age fortifications in the Cotswolds, probably also known to Bronze Age predecessors, but it has been common land since well before the 10th century. Local property owners still have commoners' rights such as pannage, the right to let pigs loose to feed on beechmast, or estovers, the right to gather wood for fuel. The cheese-rolling ceremony is thought to have its origin in ancient prehistoric ceremonies concerning sun worship – it used to be held on Midsummer Day. The cheeses may have represented the sun.

Views from Cooper's Hill are very fine, looking out over the Vale of Gloucester with the Severn Bridge just visible to the south-west and Bredon Hill and the Malverns to the north. There are exposed limestone scarp slopes on the western edge, with some handsome beechwoods.

▶ *Cooper's Hill is 6 miles south-west of Cheltenham. Steep paths lead up the hill from a signposted car park below its western flank on the A46. Alternatively, a minor road east off the A46, half a mile to the north, ends in a grassy car park. From it, a path winds up through ancient beechwoods immediately below the cheese-rolling slope.*

CRICKLEY HILL

⓫ The Churn Valley

The River Churn is one of the most westerly tributaries of the Thames, and lays disputed claim to be its source. The Churn rises at the village of Seven Springs near the junction of the A435 and A436, and its springs have never been known to run dry.

Narrow, wooded and winding, the Churn valley is spanned by several interesting villages and fine houses, so that although the main A435 from Cheltenham to Cirencester follows it south, it has a secret and peaceful air. Turn west off the A435 towards Cowley, with its 17th-century manor and chain of lilied lakes, and cross the Churn at Marsden Manor. Look for dippers here, strange little birds that plunge into the shallow river and run along the bottom searching for food among the pebbles. There are pied and grey wagtails, too, and sometimes grey herons.

Further downstream is North Cerney, with a fine church incorporating Norman and medieval work. To the south-west of North Cerney is the village of Bagendon, where the British tribe of the Dobunni had an important settlement associated with metalworking. Bagendon may have been the forerunner of the Roman town of Cirencester (Corinium), which became the new tribal capital – a new market and administration centre for the Dobunni. Excavations at Bagendon have yielded precious objects such as jewellery, pottery, glass and coins, establishing these pre-Roman people as prosperous and unexpectedly civilised farmers, merchants and manufacturers. Nor is there any evidence of fighting here: Romans and local people seem to have lived together peaceably.

Up on high and windy North Cerney Downs the ancient track called the White Way, an extension of the old Salt Way, runs south to Cirencester and the Foss Way. There is a long but lonely walk east from North Cerney up to these downlands and woods. The lane crosses the White Way to the perfect little hamlet of Calmsden with its row of tiny stone cottages with long, narrow gardens.

▶ *The Churn valley follows the A435 between Cheltenham and Cirencester. Seven Springs, on the A435, is 4 miles south of Cheltenham.*

⓬ The Duntisbournes

The tiny, unhurried stream of the Duntbrook meanders south-east through two exquisite little villages, two hamlets and four fords in the space of about 2 miles. This is one of the most charming and timelessly gentle landscapes anywhere in England. Eastwards on the ridge above, the Roman Ermin Way takes the A417 arrow-straight to Cirencester: westwards, the valley rises gently to parkland and downs, then falls away steeply into the heavily wooded valley of the River Frome.

At Duntisbourne Abbots, the larger of the two villages, the Duntbrook becomes part of the old cobbled road, with high walls and a raised pavement on either side. Carters washed their horses' feet and cleaned their wagons here, and villagers resist all attempts to culvert the sometimes swift-flowing stream. The village water supply still trickles into a stone pool here, though the pool is mossy now and planted in summer with delicate primulas and mimulus.

At Duntisbourne Leer and Middle Duntisbourne, barns and farms drowse in the sun by their fords. The tiny hamlet of Duntisbourne Leer was once owned by the abbey of Lire in France. Further down the open, green valley the tiny Saxon and Norman church at Duntisbourne Rouse perches on a slope above its own stretch of the Duntbrook.

▶ *The Duntisbournes lie west of the A417 and about 4 to 5 miles north-west of Cirencester.*

CHARMING AND TIMELESSLY

⑬ Haresfield Beacon and Standish Wood

This area of high, open grassland and mixed woodland owned by the National Trust contains a much-loved local beacon with the finest of all viewpoints on the south-western edge of the Cotswold escarpment. Gloucester lies below with its limestone outlier of Robins Wood Hill; the Severn is a wide swathe of often muddy silver to the south-west, and beyond the Forest of Dean are the distant peaks of Welsh mountains.

Haresfield Beacon is a natural promontory fortification, 217m (712ft) high, and lies secluded above swathes of dark woodland that clothe the slopes on either side of it. Many people have used this perfect military site to their advantage, including the Romans who had a large camp here after the Iron Age settlement. In 1837 some 3,000 Roman coins were unearthed on Haresfield Beacon.

The beacon lies on the Cotswold Way, and the National Trust has way-marked the footpaths from the spot. In one direction, the Way leads north-east for three-quarters of a mile to Cromwell's Siege Stone. It is dated 1643 and commemorates the successful defence of Gloucester against Charles I and the Royalists. About a mile further on is an unusual hexagonal-shaped farmhouse.

In the other direction, the Cotswold Way follows the deeply indented ridge southwards, past a topograph (a direction finder) overlooking the Severn valley, and then into beautiful Standish Wood.

In summer, local people fly kites and model aeroplanes from the beacon's steep rim, but despite the distant murmur of the M5 motorway far below in the Severn vale the National Trust's 140ha (348 acres) allow plenty of room for space, peace and solitude. Kestrels hover, treecreepers, nuthatches and woodpeckers frequent the woods, there are primroses and bluebells in spring and dog-roses everywhere in summer.

▶ *Haresfield Beacon is 6 miles south of Gloucester. To reach the beacon there is a narrow and pleasant road from the village of Edge on the A4173.*

⑭ Uley Bury Fort

Beechwoods flank the hills around the village of Uley, above which stands a massive Iron Age hill-fort enclosing 13ha (32 acres) of the lofty heights. Only the banked ditches of the outer rim are clear to walkers, the plateau top being used for arable crops. But the views from the summit are immense and give a sense of just how awesome this great fortress must have been when first constructed. Those masons and labourers must have themselves looked out at the dark curve of Stinchcombe Hill to the west and the lowland beside the Severn estuary. The spirit of ancient Britons lingers on among the ramparts; on a day when rain marches over that lowland, the fort seems to come strangely alive.

Just north of the fort is Hetty Pegler's Tump, a Neolithic long barrow almost as fine as Belas Knap near Cheltenham. The barrow is 37m (120ft) long and 25m (82ft) wide, and its walls and ceiling are made of large stone slabs filled in with areas of dry-stone work. In the barrow, torches are needed to illuminate the burial chambers while crouching inside. Each of the four chambers is reached by a short passage. More than 20 skeletons were discovered in them in the 19th century. The barrow was named after the wife of a local landowner, but no one knows why; only that there was a Hester Pegler who lived locally in the 17th century.

▶ *Hetty Pegler's Tump is signposted and reached by a narrow field path from the B4066, 1 mile north of Uley. Uley is on the B4066, 2 miles east of Dursley.*

SOUTHERN ENGLAND

GENTLE LANDSCAPES
THE DUNTISBOURNES

⑮ Golden Valley

Magnificent and solitary woods enfold the River Frome in Golden Valley, which in autumn is gilded by beech, oak and ash. Here the old Thames and Severn Canal runs beside the river; ancient backwater villages mark the canal's hidden path from steep and twisting Chalford to golden-stoned Sapperton. At Daneway the canal is dry, and has become a garden of willow, whitebeam and sedge. The old towpath rises to Sapperton Tunnel, almost 2½ miles long and closed since 1911.

Chalford and Sapperton are ancient villages, each with a sturdy character of its own. Chalford, with its heritage of mills and fortunes made by the wealthy clothiers, terraces the precipitous hillside of the River Frome and has been nicknamed 'the Alpine village'. Its parish embraces hilltop villages and hamlets such as Bussage and Oakridge. Sapperton was first recorded in Anglo-Saxon times. Its name means 'soap-makers' farmstead' – soap, however, may have meant fullers' earth which was used for 'fulling', or cleaning wool, not for washing.

▶ *Chalford is 3 miles south-east of Stroud. Turn north off the A419 in Chalford to follow the course of the River Frome. Follow all the paths and lanes along Golden Valley: all are worth investigating.*

⑯ Westonbirt Arboretum

The owners of Westonbirt House, the Holfords, planted the arboretum in 1829 with hardy native and evergreen species such as oaks, Scots pines, beeches, yews and laurels, giving shelter to subsequent plantings of more exotic species.

Westonbirt may be artificial, but over time it has become so established that it appears almost natural. Trees simply like growing there. Many are the largest of their species anywhere in Britain, including maples, whitebeams and Caucasian oaks. There is now a Cherry Glade, glorious in spring; a collection of native British species (which number 25 only – Britain's wealth of tree species have almost all been imported); and a collection of willows. In autumn the maples set parts of Westonbirt ablaze with flame-red. In late spring the rhododendrons and azaleas are magnificent.

▶ *There is complete freedom to walk anywhere in the woods and the rides and paths are clearly marked by the Forestry Commission which owns the site. Westonbirt is the National Arboretum, and is open to the public all year round. It can be found on the north side of the A433 about 3 miles south-west of Tetbury.*

⑰ The Bottoms

These deep combes and valleys that lie along the edge of the Cotswold escarpment, around the suitably named Wotton-under-Edge, include some of the most secret and beautiful landscapes anywhere in England.

Above and north of Wotton-under-Edge is Westridge Wood and the wooded Iron Age fort of Brackenbury Ditches. South of the fort, on the curving ridge of Wotton Hill, owned by the National Trust, are the remains of strip lynchets, ploughed terraces of Anglo-Saxon origin.

North-east of Westridge Wood is Waterley Bottom, high-edged and lonely, in which the motorist may see nothing beyond the immense lane banks. North-east of Wotton, reached by a narrow lane and the drive of a private house, is a footpath up Tyley Bottom into the narrow wooded head of the valley.

Most beautiful of all, and reached only on foot, is the head of Ozleworth Bottom, named after the Anglo-Saxon word for blackbird – and they are among the many birds found here. A narrow lane runs for 2 miles from the hamlet of Wortley to two cottages that span the stream below Ozleworth Park. From this shadowy bridge a muddy track on the south side of the stream climbs under trees to a field gate. There, a pathway climbs through grassy fields, streams, shady glades and warm, silent banks towards Boxwell. Orchids, wild forget-me-nots, pink hedge parsley and honeysuckle grow here and attract numerous butterflies.

Meandering lanes then wind northwards from Ozleworth to footpaths that circle over lonely turf west through Newark Park and Tor Hill, and back south through Wortley to Alderley, Hillesley and Lower Kilcott – all enchanted valleys. Finally, the route emerges through Midger Wood Nature Reserve (managed by Gloucestershire Wildlife Trust) and up on to the suddenly 21st-century A46 – relieved only by the abrupt sight of Nan Tow's Tump, one of the largest and most mysterious Bronze Age round barrows in the Cotswolds. About 3m (9ft) high and some 30m (100ft) in diameter, crowned with trees, the barrow is believed to contain the skeleton of Nan Tow – a local witch who was buried upright.

▶ *The starting point for exploring The Bottoms is Wotton-under-Edge, which is on the B4058, 7 miles south-west of Nailsworth.*

The CHILTERN HILLS

The grassy downland and beech-clad hills of the Chilterns curve around the London Basin to the north-west. A prehistoric route more than 4,000 years old, the Icknield Way strides across the landscape.

❶ Sharpenhoe Clappers

A range of low hills shaped like an inverted question-mark stretches from east to west across the Bedfordshire plain for about 3 miles. This is Sharpenhoe Clappers, the last remnant of the Chilterns before the landscape levels to the Midland plain. The most northerly point of the hills stands above the village of Sharpenhoe, surmounted by Clappers Wood and an Iron Age hill-fort. In summer leafy beeches cushion the hill crest, but in winter the bare trees stand out like spines along the ridge.

From Sharpenhoe, a minor road climbs south to the National Trust car park from where footpaths wind east along the ridge. They lead first through a wooded glen of beech and rowan. Beyond, the paths are through hedgerows where chalk-loving plants can be found. Musk thistle, with its purple flowers, is predominant. In addition, there are common rock-roses, tall-growing tansies and old man's beard.

Suddenly the hedgerows give way to grassy downland, with a full view across a plain plumed with Lombardy poplars. In summer, the downs are speckled with the yellow bird's-foot trefoil and purple self-heal. In spring they are the home of the rare pasque flower. Where the ridge ends, beeches cling precariously to the steep slope, nevertheless maintaining their stately dignity.

▶ *Sharpenhoe is 6 miles north of Luton, and can be reached along minor roads west off the A6 at Streatley or Barton-le-Clay.*

❷ Dunstable Downs

The view stretches for miles from the humped, grassy shoulders of Dunstable Downs, which loom over the flatness of the Vale of Aylesbury. The feeling of space and distance is almost intoxicating. There are few trees on the downs, apart from the land owned by the National Trust; the wide stretches of grassland fall quickly away to the valley floor where the ancient Icknield Way (now a modern road) starts to pick its course along the Chilterns. At the northern tip of the downs it passes the Five Knolls barrow cemetery, where relics of the New Stone Age and Bronze Age have been found. South-westwards it continues to Ivinghoe Beacon (also known as Beacon Hill), rising to 230m (756ft) on the skyline and marking the start of the main Chiltern ridge that stretches down to the Thames valley.

From the top of the downs, lanes lead south-east to Whipsnade Heath, a grassy expanse in a sheltered dell that lies east of the B4541 and north of the B4540. Here man and nature have combined to shape a Tree Cathedral, the inspiration of a local landowner Edmund Kell Blyth. He planted a variety of trees during the 1930s, setting them out to form a nave, transepts, cloisters and chapels. Now the trees have matured to give the effect of a cathedral, with a dew-pond in the position of the altar.

▶ *Dunstable Downs border the western side of the B4541 Whipsnade road 2 miles south of Dunstable.*

DUNSTABLE DOWNS

3 Ashridge and Ivinghoe

The woods at Ashridge are the last of the ridge-top forest at the north-east end of the Chilterns, giving way to grassy downland towards Ivinghoe Beacon, marked as Beacon Hill on Ordnance Survey maps. Two square miles of mainly beechwoods sweep up from Aldbury Common. Overlooking the hillside above Aldbury village, the 33m (108ft) high Bridgewater monument peeps over the tree-tops. From it a broad avenue leads through the beechwoods to the Berkhamsted-Dagnall road.

The monument was erected in 1832 in memory of the 3rd Duke of Bridgewater, pioneer of Britain's canal system, who once lived at nearby Ashridge House. For those who climb the 172 muscle-dragging steps to the top, there are fine views over the 1,600ha (4,000 acre) Ashridge estate, owned by the National Trust.

A nature trail of 1½ miles starts from the monument, winding its way northwards at first between a forest of silver-grey trunks. There is little undergrowth where the beeches hold sway, their fallen leaves covering the ground with a sea of burnished copper for most of the year. Where there are other trees – oaks, sycamores and birches – there is enough light to encourage wild flowers such as wood anemones and wood sorrel. Various species of tits feed on birch seeds, and grey squirrels also strip the bark from these trees and often kill the branches.

Where there is thick undergrowth, particularly bracken, there are fallow and muntjac deer. They are best seen at dawn or dusk, when they come out of cover to feed. After mid-August you may see a fallow buck with his full spread of antlers, and at the end of October you

A SEA OF BURNISHED COPPER

ASHRIDGE FOREST

may hear his belching snort as the rutting, or mating, season approaches.

Ivinghoe Beacon lies about 2½ miles north of the Bridgewater monument. The hillside is almost bare of cover, only a few thorn bushes breaking its bold outline. There are paths to the summit – white trails worn in the chalk – and the wild flowers there are lime-lovers, such as thyme and common rock-roses. From the summit there is a panorama of the vale below, and to the east you can see the hill-figure of a white lion cut in the chalk of Dunstable Downs, advertising the presence of Whipsnade Zoo.

▶ *Ashridge is on the B4506 between Berkhamsted and Dagnall. It can also be reached from the village of Aldbury, 2½ miles east of Tring. From there, a minor road climbs steeply up the hillside to join the B4506, giving fine views on the way. Ivinghoe Beacon is south of the B489, 1 mile north-east of Ivinghoe.*

❹ Tring Reservoirs

The sound of rushing water greets you as you leave the car park, and within a few steps you are standing by the tumbling waters of a weir. This is a backwater of the Grand Union Canal, half hidden among overhanging trees, where the shallow, crystal-clear water swarms with minnows and sticklebacks. Beyond the weir is the canal itself, sweeping in a wide arc lined with patient anglers.

To the south of the canal, a bank hides the waters of Startop's End Reservoir, one of the group of three that comprise the Tring Reservoirs National Nature Reserve. Climb the bank and you will see that Startop's End looks the most man-made of the three – angular and featureless – but the bank provides a good view of the canal curving away into the distance and Ivinghoe Beacon jutting on the skyline to the north-east.

Beyond the canal bend is the first of a flight of six locks, known as Tring Steps, that lift the canal to a height of almost 120m (400ft) as it cuts through the Chilterns. The lock is dated 1865, and its wooden-framed gates are overgrown with grass and nettles. On summer days it is constantly in use as boats pass to and fro, but in the quiet of the evening you may see a kingfisher using the gates as a diving board.

South of the canal, opposite the lock, lies reed-fringed Marsworth Reservoir. Among the waterbirds that bred here are great crested grebes, grey herons, common terns, mallards and coots; around the reservoir live whitethroats, sedge warblers, reed buntings and many others. A wide range of ducks, including teal, wigeon, gad-wall, goldeneye and goosander, visit in winter and bitterns overwinter in the reedbeds. Among the most fascinating of the birds at Tring are the great crested grebes. Between December and May, watch out for their stately courtship displays, especially the dance when they dive for weeds, surface and swim towards each other, then rise breast to breast with feet paddling and necks swaying.

A bank divides Marsworth and Startop's End reservoirs, and a footpath across the top leads to Tringford Reservoir, passing close to a heronry identified by the bundles of twigs in the branches of dead trees. At the far end of Tringford Reservoir there is a public hide. In autumn, when the water level is low, you may see common, green or wood sandpipers, redshanks, greenshanks, snipe and ringed plovers feeding in the mud.

▶ *Tring Reservoirs can be reached from the A41 Aylesbury-Tring road. Turn north on to the B489 towards Ivinghoe. The reservoirs border the east side of the B489, and the car park is on the right-hand side just before the bridge over the canal.*

❺ Wendover Woods

Wendover nestles at the mouth of a narrow gap in the Chiltern ridge with Coombe Hill rising to the south-west. To the north-east Wendover Woods, part of the Chiltern Forest, blanket the steep ridges of Boddington Hill, Haddington Hill and Aston Hill. These woods are the highest part of the Chilterns, the summit (267m (876ft)) on the edge of Halton Wood being marked by a cairn.

A minor road winds up from the Upper Icknield Way through overhanging trees to a small car park on Aston Hill, one of the starting points for a number of waymarked walks and trails through the woods. From the hill there is an uninterrupted view across the flat farmlands of the Aylesbury plain, stretching for miles far below. The Tring Reservoirs can be picked out to the north-east, the sky mirrored in their shimmering waters.

A forest walk, the quaintly named Daniel's Trudge, starts just below the car park; this name derives from the Old English *denn* (a pasture) and *hol* (a deep place). A trudge it may be, certainly on its second half, for all but the energetic. The path descends the steep ridge through woodlands, then climbs to the top again by a zigzag route, finally leading among ancient cultivation terraces known as lynchets.

There are four other forest walks, all starting from the Cedar Car Park which lies about 2 miles south on the same minor road. Aston Hill Ramble leads through beechwoods and a yew glade; the Beech Hangings is a walk through typical Chiltern hanging beechwoods on the side of a steep slope; Boddington Banks walk follows the line of ancient Iron Age earthworks, and Hale View walk climbs to a viewpoint above the Wendover Gap.

▶ *Aston Hill and the Cedar Car Park are 2 miles north-east of Wendover. Turn sharply south from the B4009 between Wendover and Tring following signs to Wendover Woods.*

❻ Coombe Hill

One of the highest points in the Chilterns, Coombe Hill (260m (852ft)) thrusts out into the landscape to give magnificent views of its neighbouring ridges and the Vale of Aylesbury spread out below. A tall granite monument perched on the hillside commemorates the Buckinghamshire men who died in the Boer War, and its stepped base makes a good vantage point.

Chequers, the country house of Britain's prime ministers, can be glimpsed among the trees to the south-west, and westwards behind Ellesborough, marked by its church tower, lies Cymbeline's Mount, or Castle. The mound's history is shrouded in the mists of time, but it is said to be the place where the sons of the Celtic King Cunobelinus were killed in a battle with the Romans. The villages of Great and Little Kimble to the west of the mound probably derive their names from it. To the north-east lies Wendover, with the tree-clad ridges of Wendover Woods climbing behind its rooftops.

Coombe Hill, with 43ha (106 acres) owned by the National Trust, is on the route of the Ridgeway National Trail. Heather and gorse are scattered over the summit, and below the northern end of the ridge the steep slopes are thick with lime-loving scrub and trees such as the spindle and the wayfaring tree. There are sometimes sheep on the hill – they help to keep down the scrub. Some of the rams have as many as six horns; these are Joseph's sheep, thought to be the 'sheepe with the little spots and great spots' mentioned in the Book of Genesis in the 1599 edition of the Bible.

▶ *Coombe Hill can be reached along a minor road south off the A4010 at Butler's Cross, 1½ miles west of Wendover. Take the sharp left turn towards Dunsmore that climbs between gnarled beeches to a parking area beneath overhanging trees, where the road bends. A gate leads to the hill, which is only a gentle stroll away. It can also be reached by a fine 1½ mile walk along the ridge from Wendover; the path (The Upper Icknield Way) starts at a sharp bend in Ellesborough Road which heads west out of Wendover just past the railway station.*

RED KITES CIRCLE LAZILY IN THE AIR OVER THE CHILTERNS
ASTON ROWANT

⑦ Whiteleaf Hill

A huge white cross is cut in the chalk on the side of Whiteleaf Hill, a mile north-east of Princes Risborough. This 24m (80ft) cross overlooks the Upper Icknield Way, and rises from the roadside on a pyramid about 90m (300ft) across at its base.

No one knows who cut the cross or why – theories suggest it to be a Christianised fertility symbol, a signpost at the crossing of ancient trackways, an acclamation of faith by medieval monks or Cromwellian troops, or just a 17th or 18th-century folly. There is a similar cross, but without a pyramidal base, cut in the chalk of Bledlow Ridge a few miles to the south-west.

Remains of some New Stone Age long barrows can be seen on the summit of the hill, from where there are fine views of the Berkshire Downs to the south-west. A car park at the top of the hill is a good starting point for walks through some pleasant woods.

▶ *To reach Whiteleaf Hill car park, turn south-east off the A4010 Princes Risborough-Stoke Mandeville road on to a minor road at Monks Risborough.*

⑧ Goring Gap

At Goring Gap, the River Thames breaks through the chalk hills to separate the Berkshire Downs from the Chiltern Hills. Goring is the meeting place of the ancient Berkshire Ridge Way and the Chiltern Icknield Way. For centuries from prehistoric times, travellers forded the river there on their journey north-east to the farmlands and flint mines of East Anglia, or westwards to the great stone circles of Avebury and Stonehenge.

Today, Goring is a charming Georgian town where trees slope down to the riverside. Here the gentle waters of the Thames become turbulent for a while as they stream over the weirs close to the double bridge Southwards across the river, on the Berkshire side, lies Basildon Park, where fine parkland surrounds a splendid Georgian mansion owned by the National Trust.

Goring is at the south-west tip of the Chilterns, and 4 miles east of the town lies Goring Heath, where the Chiltern beechwoods begin. Cool and spacious with little undergrowth, they are made for easy wandering. But since the woods are deep, and one beech tree looks very much like another, it is as well not to wander too far.

▶ *Goring is 8 miles north-west of Reading at the B4526 and B4009 junction.*

⑨ Aston Rowant National Nature Reserve

Typical Chiltern countryside – grass downland, scrub and beechwoods – is all preserved in the 104ha (258 acre) Aston Rowant National Nature Reserve, which includes the steep slopes of Beacon Hill, at 244m (800ft) one of the highest points of the Chilterns. Like its sister ridges, it gives fine views over the Vale of Aylesbury below, with the Cotswolds visible on a clear day. The Beacon Hill nature trail, peaceful and undisturbed despite the hum of motorway traffic below, explains the landscape and wildlife of the area.

This countryside is rich in woods and wildlife. Aston Wood, 42ha (104 acres) of mixed woods owned by the National Trust, borders the reserve to the north, and south-westwards is Cowleaze Wood, part of the Chiltern Forest managed by the Forestry Commission. There are car parks, a picnic area and waymarked walks in the depths of the conifer and deciduous forest. In summer, willow warblers dart elusively in the branches overhead, easy to hear but difficult to see. The woods are a good vantage point from which to watch red kites circle lazily in the air over the Chilterns. They were successfully reintroduced into the area in the 1990s.

Muntjac and fallow deer may be seen in the woods, and there are foxes and badgers. Jays and magpies swoop among the trees, woodpeckers drum in the woodland depths, and kestrels may be seen hovering above scrub and grassland. Plants include nightshades, wood anemones, woodruffs, bluebells and various kinds of orchid.

South-westwards from the reserve, a minor road leads to Christmas Common. It gained its name in 1643, during the Civil War, when Parliamentarians held the valley and Royalists the ridge above. They called a truce at Christmas and met on the common.

From the road junctions to the east of the common, the north-west road descends Watlington Hill, another National Trust property, with chalk downs, copses and a natural yew wood. The south-east road plunges into a tunnel of beech trees and mossy banks to wind down to Turville, Fingest and Hambleden.

▶ *Aston Rowant National Nature Reserve is 10 miles north-west of High Wycombe. It can be reached along a minor road off the A40 about 1 mile north-west of Stokenchurch, signposted Christmas Common. Beacon Hill nature trail car park is along a right turn on the minor road, ⅓ mile from the A40 junction. Aston Wood lies 1½ miles north-west of Stokenchurch and straddles the A40.*

SOUTHERN ENGLAND

83

⑩ Marlow Reach and Cliveden Reach

Some of the loveliest Chiltern scenery lies along the winding loop of the River Thames between Marlow and Maidenhead. Winter Hill, high above Marlow on the south side of the river, gives superb views of Marlow Reach and the softly contoured hills to the north. Early in the year when the winds are high, Winter Hill is well named; but in summer, warm breezes temper the air and send hundreds of bright-sailed yachts scudding across the river below. There are fine beechwood walks through Quarry Wood, below the west-facing upper slopes of the hill.

Cookham, with its many pleasant Georgian houses, lies within the loop of the river. Footpaths lead from the village to the river bank and beside the backwaters that join the river at Cliveden Reach. From Cookham Lock to Boulter's Lock, beechwoods sweep down to the water's edge on the eastern side – a lovely sight at any time, but glorious in autumn when the woods are ablaze with tints of russet and gold.

High above the river is Cliveden House. The present mansion in 16th-century Italian style was built in 1850, designed by Sir Charles Barry for the Duke of Sutherland. Later it was the home of Lord and Lady Astor, and is now owned by the National Trust. Its grounds provide fine views of the Thames.

▶ *Marlow is 4 miles south of High Wycombe on the A404, Cookham 3 miles north of Maidenhead on the A4094. Winter Hill (National Trust) is reached from Cookham Dean, west of Cookham. Cliveden is found via minor roads north of the A4 about 1 mile east of Maidenhead; the entrance is opposite the Feathers Inn.*

⑪ Burnham Beeches

Ancient pollarded beeches of massive girth, their gnarled and stunted trunks bent and twisted into grotesque shapes, are the patriarchs of Burnham Beeches. Their crowns were cut when they were about 2m (6ft) high to produce poles for firewood. Their fascinating misshapenness is the result of regular lopping and re-growth until the early 1800s, when coal became more common. Now several centuries old, these ancient beeches are gradually dying.

An area of nearly 200ha (500 acres) of woods and commons, Burnham Beeches is owned by the City of London authority who bought about 160ha (400 acres) for the benefit of the public in 1879. The name Burnham is after Viscount Burnham, who donated the 36ha (88 acres) of Fleet Wood in 1921. On the northern fringe are Egypt Woods, which got their name because of an association with gypsies who once lived in the forest. The first wandering bands of gypsies who arrived in Britain early in the 16th century were known as 'Dukes of Little Egypt' a name that was turned into 'gypsies'.

Although beeches abound, there are many other trees in the woods. Silver birches add a lighter touch; holly, pines and firs provide all-year-round greenness; and lovely rhododendrons bloom in some of the dells. Patches of heathland break up the wooded areas, dotted with bright yellow gorse in summer. There are numerous criss-crossing footpaths and bridle-paths, and a number of metalled roads, ramped to restrict speed, give access to various parking areas.

▶ *Burnham Beeches lies to the south of Beaconsfield and north of Slough, to the west of the A355.*

The NORTH WESSEX DOWNS

The wide, sweeping slopes of the North Wessex Downs are dotted with stone circles, hill-forts and burial mounds – historic landmarks left behind by our distant ancestors.

LAMBOURN DOWNS

❶ Whitehorse Hill

The White Horse of Uffington has been galloping across the Berkshire Downs for centuries; no one knows how many – some say it was carved to celebrate a victory over the Danes by King Alfred, others believe that it dates from the Iron Age and represents the goddess Epona, protector of horses. Whatever its origins, the Uffington horse is impressive and beautiful.

Whitehorse Hill is crowned by Uffington Castle, a circular Iron Age fort. The ramparts are windswept, but it is worth the buffeting to climb to the top and look down into the valley with the thatched roofs of farms and cottages embedded among dark green clumps of trees.

Below the White Horse is Dragon Hill, a small, almost insignificant mound where St George, the patron saint of England since the 14th century, is said to have killed the dragon. To give credence to the story, a patch of ground on the hill where grass never grows is supposed to have been poisoned by the dragon's blood.

Legends abound in this area and another concerns Wayland's Smithy, south-west of Whitehorse Hill. There is nothing legendary about its origin; it is a chambered long barrow dating from about 3000 BC. It has two chambers, entered beneath a massive sandstone lintel. The Saxons believed that Wayland, smith to their gods, lived here, and that if a horse was left by the entrance he would shoe it, provided a coin was left on the lintel stone. Wayland's Smithy is a pleasant 1½ mile walk, south-west along the Ridgeway Path from Uffington Castle.

▶ *Whitehorse Hill is 6 miles west of Wantage, just south of the B4507. Two signposted roads climb from the B4507 to a car park at the top of the hill.*

❷ Lambourn Downs

The broad shoulder of Lambourn Downs rises to the north of Lambourn, and can be climbed using a path across Pit Down; an easy, ten-minute walk up to downland caressed by fresh breezes that bend the long grass in rippling swathes. In spring, the rare pasque flower blooms here. And at any time of the year there are horses; not the chalk figures seen further west but thoroughbreds from the Lambourn stables out for a training gallop. They make a thrilling sight, with their tails streaming in the wind.

In the valley west of Pit Down are Lambourn Seven Barrows, a group of 40 ancient burial mounds. They date from the Wessex Bronze Age, which flourished some 4,000–2,500 years ago, and appear to be contemporary with later building phases of Stonehenge. A little to the north of the group is a chambered long barrow of the New Stone Age.

The Ridgeway Path skirts the north side of the Lambourn Downs where it crosses Blowingstone Hill. About half a mile north is the strange stone from which the hill takes its name. It is a massive hollow boulder which will produce an eerie, hornlike sound if blown into through one of its holes. It is said that King Alfred used the Blowing Stone to summon his troops to battle, an interesting but unlikely story. The stone is at the bottom of the hill, just off the B4507, and stands beneath an elm in the garden of a cottage that was once a smithy.

▶ *The B4001 runs north from Lambourn across Lambourn Downs; a westward fork some 1 mile north of Lambourn leads to the Seven Barrows (the start of the Pit Down path) and to Blowingstone Hill and the B4507.*

❸ Liddington Castle

In the fading light of evening, the bold outlines of Liddington Castle are dramatic. The earthen ramparts jut out against the sky, and long shadows pick out the faint outlines of wide ditches curling round the southern side. This was an Iron Age hill-fort, a rough and hummocky expanse covering more than 3ha (7 acres) and sprawling across the brow of a 277m (910ft) high hill.

The path to the castle is lined with aromatic clusters of purple marjoram and lesser bindweed twines its white and pink cups among the hedgerows. The banks of the castle are clad in lush green grass dotted with yellow carline thistle – a plant that can withstand the attention of grazing cows. A dip in the bank on its north-western side was probably an entrance to the fort, and the best views of the surrounding countryside are from the top of this bank.

Ignoring the grey swathe of the M4 motorway to the east – it is decently buried in a cutting to the north – the view takes in the western end of the Vale of White Horse and the Cotswold Hills rising mistily beyond the redbrick sprawl of Swindon.

▶ *Liddington Castle is 4 miles south-east of Swindon, just south of the Ridgeway Path – a road at this point – and about ¾ mile west of the B4192.*

❹ The Ridgeway Path

There is no better way to appreciate the beauty of the Marlborough Downs than to take a stroll along a small section of this prehistoric track, which stretches for 87 miles through the North Wessex Downs and Chilterns. It starts at Overton Hill, and climbs steeply over downland, rising to 202m (663ft) in the first half mile. Sarsen stones litter the fields and the humps of round barrows come into view like small islands – the lonely graves of Bronze Age people who lived here about 3,000 years ago. To the west the great mound of Silbury Hill and the stone circle at Avebury are further reminders that this was the country of ancient people whose culture is still not fully understood.

The path climbs steadily to Hackpen Hill, 272m (892ft) at its highest point, and the view broadens to take in the sweep of rippling hills and downlands. Here and there, copses of beech break up the otherwise treeless contours. The trees were planted to make windbreaks during the 18th century and are now a natural part of the landscape.

The distance from Overton Hill to Hackpen Hill is about 4 miles and although the return journey is along the same route, it provides a chance to see some of the wild flowers which may have been missed on the way – the yellow common rock-rose, the blue, white or pink flowers of common milkwort and possibly a fragrant or pyramidal orchid.

▶ *The start of the Ridgeway Path, at Overton Hill, is on the north side of the A4, 4 miles west of Marlborough.*

SILBURY HILL

➎ Barbury Castle

This Iron Age fort is one of the best known in southern England. Perched on the 260m (850ft) high northern rim of the Marlborough Downs, the fort overlooks the Ridgeway Path and gives sweeping views of the surrounding countryside. To the west lies a vast sprawl of rolling chalkland, a patchwork of green fields and a sprinkling of trees with hills rising like smoke in the distance. Half a mile to the north lies the battlefield of Beranburh where the Saxon chief Cynrie and his son Ceawlin defeated the Britons in a bloody massacre. It established the Saxons as overlords of southern England and later, in AD 560, Ceawlin became King of Wessex.

Barbury Castle is a well-defined oval of about 5ha (12 acres), with entrances at the eastern and western sides passing through the towering double ramparts. Finds from inside are now in the Wiltshire Heritage Museum in Devizes, and include fittings for chariots. Below the fort on the eastern side can be seen the angular outlines of more ancient field systems, probably dating from the Iron Age. They stand out clearly against the softer contours of the surrounding landscape.

The path down from the castle's western entrance joins the Ridgeway Path, and there is a pleasant 30 minute walk along it eastwards to Burderop Down and back to the car park. The deeply rutted track winds downhill, with pink and white hawthorns lining the path and yellow honeysuckle scenting the air.

▶ *Barbury Castle lies 5 miles south of Swindon. Take the A4361 out of the town and at Wroughton turn on to the B4005. A mile east, an unclassified road runs south to Burderop Down and ends at a large car park. The fort is ½ mile west along a footpath across a field.*

➏ River Marden

One of the best ways of appreciating the beauty of the gently flowing River Marden is to walk along the old railway route that runs through a shallow valley of woods and meadows between Calne and Chippenham. There is an entry to the route at the old stone bridge half a mile north-east of Studley, where steps lead down to a cutting which has been planted with young larch trees.

The walk westwards leads into Great Bodnage Copse, a small wood of ash, elm, conifers, great sallow, hazel, blackthorn and hawthorn. The trees arching over the track provide an ideal site for such woodland plants as anemones, bluebells, primroses and violets, and wild strawberries grow among the stones that were the ballast for the railway sleepers. Further along the track the river comes into view, moving sluggishly between the meadows where grey herons fly on slow-beating wings and occasionally there is a flash of blue from a kingfisher. To avoid leaving the footpath and walking along a minor road, turn back at the remains of Stanley Abbey, a former Cistercian abbey founded by Henry II in the 12th century.

The walk south-eastwards from the bridge ends at Black Dog Hill before it meets the A4. To the left are water-meadows bright with red campions and ox-eye daisies in late spring, with patches of blue speedwells and purple vetch. Some areas of meadow and woodland are marshy, so the plants that thrive here include marsh marigolds, reeds, sedges and mosses. Towards the end of the walk there are laurels, rhododendrons, laburnums and dogwood.

▶ *Studley is 2 miles west of Calne, along a minor road north off the A4.*

THIS WAS THE COUNTRY OF ANCIENT PEOPLE
RIDGEWAY PATH

SOUTHERN ENGLAND

AS THE SUN RISES THE STONES TRANSFORM

AVEBURY STONE CIRCLE

⑦ Avebury

On an autumn morning with a light mist rising from the meadows, the great stone circle of Avebury takes on an air of fantasy, almost as if the brooding stones might fade like ghosts in the full light of day. But as the sun rises the stones transform and become real again, fantasy gives way to mystery; how did the stones get there, and what was their purpose?

Archaeologists know the answer to the first question. The stones were hauled from the Marlborough Downs in the late Stone Age, around 2000 BC, probably by the Beaker People. This group of settlers from the Low Countries take their name from the sophisticated pottery they made and often buried with their dead. As to the purpose of the stones, no one knows – a temple for sun worship perhaps, or a centre for pagan rituals. It is easy to understand how the circle was built, but less easy to fathom the minds of its creators.

The circle stands inside a great earth bank, 430m (1,400ft) in diameter, and encloses the remains of two smaller circles. Only 27 of the original stones remain, though concrete posts replace the missing stones to show the original layout. Unlike Stonehenge, Avebury's stones are unhewn. Their natural shapes – some tall and slender, others broad and squat – may be representations of male and female figures.

Avebury village is a quiet and pleasant place built within the outer ring of stones. There are easy downland walks from the village to other ancient sites, such as Windmill Hill 1½ miles to the north-west. On it stands a fortified camp dating from about 2900 BC, and a Bronze Age burial site of about 1700–1400 BC. It is believed that the camp served as a rallying point, or fair, where Stone Age farmers gathered at certain seasons for barter and perhaps for worship.

▶ *Avebury lies just north of the A4, 6 miles west of Marlborough, and can be reached by the B4003 or by the A4361 which crosses the A4, 1 mile south-west of the village.*

⑧ Fyfield Down

To reach Fyfield Down, make a diversion eastwards from the Ridgeway Path, about 2 miles north from its start at Overton Hill on the A4. This pleasant 30 minute walk leads to a stretch of natural downland, strewn with thousands of sarsen stones, the largest naturally deposited collection of these stones in the country. The half-buried boulders of sandstone

look, from a distance, like flocks of grazing sheep. For this reason they are sometimes known as 'grey wethers', the word 'wether' coming from the Old English for 'sheep'.

Fyfield Down is a nature reserve on which visitors should not wander. Only the paths across it are rights of way. But there is plenty to see without leaving the paths, such as the plants growing close to the stones. Heath bedstraw and sheep's sorrel grow here, living in the pockets of acid soil formed by the sandstone. These plants could never flourish in the surrounding chalk. In autumn a violet haze of gentians softens the cold grey of the stones. A significant collection of rare and important lichens can be found growing on the stones themselves.

An alternative approach to Fyfield Down is to take the path from Avebury that climbs east over Avebury Down to meet the Ridgeway Path, and join the diversion north of Overton Hill. On old maps it is called a 'herepath', a name that comes from the Old English *here* meaning an army or multitude. It suggests that this may have been a route taken by marauding Saxons as they invaded Wessex.

▶ *Fyfield Down is 2½ miles east of Avebury. The Ridgeway Path from Overton Hill starts on the north side of the A4, 4 miles west of Marlborough.*

❾ Snelsmore Common

Few trees are so instantly recognisable or so attractive as birches, with their slender, silver-grey trunks. At Snelsmore they dominate the woodlands, standing in groves like collections of antique silver pieces.

Snelsmore Common Country Park is the largest single tract of open heathland in Berkshire, and the public are free to roam here. There is much to see for the heath and woods are full of wildlife. In the summer grasshopper warblers, tree pipits and dusk-flying nightjars can be seen, and all-year residents include woodcocks and woodpeckers. The heathland vegetation is mainly gorse, heather and bracken, providing a retreat for deer, foxes, stoats and weasels as well as common lizards, adders and grass snakes.

The valley bog areas support plants which are rare in many other parts of the country, such as bogbean with its pink and white flowers, and the golden-coloured bog asphodel. Here, too, grows the insect-eating round-leaved sundew, its spoon-shaped leaves and their glistening red tentacles spread invitingly to entice its victims.

▶ *Snelsmore Common Country Park is 2½ miles north of Newbury and lies to the west of the B4494 between Newbury and Wantage.*

⑩ Bucklebury Common

In western Berkshire lies an area of woods and commons that was once part of a royal hunting ground. It was recorded in the Domesday Book as Borgeldeberie Hundred – the land of Burghild's fort; today it is Bucklebury Common, a peaceful backwater of rural Berkshire at its very best.

The common lies between the rivers Pang and Kennet. An unclassified road parallel to the rivers crosses it, running from the village of Upper Bucklebury to the hamlet of Chapel Row and passing between woodlands streaked with the pearly grey of silver birches and darkened here and there with Scots pines. Every 350m (400yd) or so along the road, tracks dive into green tunnels of trees, and there are hard-standings for cars from where paths disappear into the ferns and brambles.

Bucklebury claims to have more footpaths than any other parish in England. More than one leads to the two fishponds, north-east of the crossroads on the common, that were created in the 12th century by the Abbot of Reading to provide fish for his table. Today, small boys netting newts and tadpoles have replaced the abbot's monks as fishermen. Apart from the small boys, the still waters, emerald-green with pond-weed, are disturbed only by skimming water-boatmen and the occasional leaf falling from overhanging trees.

East of Chapel Row, the road becomes The Avenue, flanked by wide grass verges and rows of stately oaks in the manner of a processional way leading to some great house. The trees give Chapel Row an air of formality and they were planted to commemorate the visit of Elizabeth I to the home of John Winchcombe, lord of the manor in the 16th century.

▶ *Bucklebury Common lies some 5 miles east of Newbury. The road across Bucklebury Common is just north of the A4 between Thatcham and Woolhampton. Roads north from either of these two villages lead to the common.*

⑪ Savernake Forest

In the Middle Ages, Savernake was a wilderness of bracken and heathland that had been a royal hunting ground from before the Norman Conquest. In 1540 it was acquired by the Protector, the Duke of Somerset. It thus became an oddity – a forest in private hands. It still remained hunting land with small coppices providing shelter for the deer and their 'vert', or winter feed. Timber was a by-product but there was no systematic replanting. By 1675, the trees were so decayed that a Navy Surveyor found only three or four fit for use. A few of these ancient trees survive – the big-bellied oak on the A346 Salisbury road is the easiest to see.

In the 18th-century, landscape gardener Capability Brown devised a 4 mile long Grand Avenue that ran arrow-straight through the forest. About halfway along its length he created a 'circus' from which radiated eight walks.

Brown's Grand Avenue may have been as formal as a processional way when it was created, but time has given it an air of informality. The road is narrow, and although the great beeches climb like columns in a cathedral nave they have been joined by new trees that crowd the road edge and arch in leafy tunnels. Occasionally the

SAVERNAKE FOREST

grandeur returns, especially at the circus where tall pines intermingle with the beeches and the young intruders are held at bay. Once again the atmosphere cathedral-like, with the sun filtering through windows mullioned by slender branches.

Informality can be found, too, in the many other walks and drives in the forest, especially in the Postern Hill Walk which is a 2 mile nature trail. Here the venerable beeches give way to a trim, 30-year-old plantation of oaks, young beeches and rowan trees. Bluebells carpet the woods in early summer, when chiffchaffs, willow warblers and whitethroats arrive. Another drive – Long Harry – has trees 27m (90ft) tall, where rooks and jackdaws add their raucous calls to the fluting notes of blackbirds and thrushes.

You may catch a glimpse of a fallow deer, with fan-shaped antlers and spotted summer coat, as it slips silently into a thicket. And a fluster of brightly coloured feathers across a forest path marks the scurrying retreat of a pheasant.

▶ *Savernake Forest is ½ mile south-east of Marlborough, between the A4 and A346. The Grand Avenue starts at Forest Hill, on the A4, and cuts diagonally through the forest in a north-west to south-east direction. The Postern Hill nature trail starts at the picnic site just off the A346 at the western end of the forest.*

⑫ West Kennett

A half-mile walk along a footpath from the A4 leads to the 4,500-year-old West Kennett Long Barrow, the largest chambered tomb in England. The walk to the long barrow is a pleasant stroll which crosses the slow-moving River Kennet, passes through a kissing-gate and climbs a gentle hill to a semicircular forecourt at the entrance to the tomb.

The entrance is startling. Massive standing stones guard the narrow passageway, but it is just possible to sidle past the largest and enter the chamber. Inside are five burial chambers, two on each side and one at the far end, where the remains of some 20 adults, one youth and at least a dozen children were found when the barrow was excavated in 1956. Because of its size – the barrow is 100m (330ft) long, 24m (80ft) wide and 3m (10ft) high – it is thought that it served as a mausoleum for something like 1,000 years.

On the return walk the view of the landscape is dominated by the great, green cone of Silbury Hill. It is the largest man-made prehistoric mound in Europe and stands 40m (130ft) high. Its flat top could comfortably accommodate the giant circle of Stonehenge, and its purpose may have been to serve as a plinth for a similar stone circle. Recent excavations have shown that it was built in four stages, between the period 2145 BC and 95 BC. But that is all that is known for certain, and Silbury Hill remains one of the great archaeological mysteries – and all the more enchanting for it. The mystical stones of Avebury lie to the north, with the stone-lined West Kennett Avenue stretching south-east from them, and all around are the green hills and vales of Wiltshire.

There is another long barrow at East Kennett, about 2 miles south-east of Silbury, but this one has not been excavated. It lies in farmland, and its distinctive hump is crested with tall trees. It looks, and is, a lonely place, and whoever sleeps within it, sleeps undisturbed.

▶ *Silbury Hill and the start of the footpath to the West Kennett Long Barrow are north and south respectively of the A4, 6 miles west of Marlborough. There is a lay-by for limited parking.*

⑬ The Wansdyke

No journey of discovery into Berkshire and Wiltshire would be complete without a look at this impressive earthwork. It is thought to date from the 5th century AD, and originally ran from the Bristol Channel to the Vale of Pewsey. No one knows who built it, though its function was clearly to keep out invaders from the north. It has been suggested that it was the work of Ambrosius Aurelianus, the last of the Romano-British generals, to keep out invading Saxons who were hard on the heels of the departing Romans.

In places the Wansdyke can be seen much as it was when it was built; a massive bank about 8m (25ft) high with a deep ditch on the northern side. A 2 mile walk along the Ridgeway Path, south from East Kennett village, leads to the point where the earthwork rides high on the back of Pewsey Downs before plunging into a valley where the ditch becomes lost in a tunnel of thickly woven trees in West Woods. The tangle of trees and undergrowth is almost impenetrable here, and there is an eerie silence save for the sighing of the wind in the tall trees.

▶ *East Kennett is 5 miles west of Marlborough, ½ mile south of the A4 at Overton Hill. West Woods lie just south of Lockeridge, south off the A4, 3 miles west of Marlborough. There is also an entrance near Park Farm on a minor road west off the A345, 3 miles south-west of Marlborough. About 360m (400yd) along the wide track skirting the southern edge of the woods, a path branching south follows the Wansdyke westwards.*

⑭ Vale of Pewsey

Running between Devizes and Pewsey is the village-dotted Vale of Pewsey. On its northern edge, a ridge of hills lies like a ribbon of fresh green paint, the treeless slopes softly rounded as they sweep down to the valley floor where hamlets and farms are shielded from the north winds by this 270m (900ft) high arm of the Marlborough Downs.

From the road along the north side of the valley there are distant views of Bishop's Cannings Down, then Easton and Horton downs. But at Allington they begin to loom larger – Clifford's Hill, Tan Hill and Milk Hill have their lower slopes close to the road, and footpaths to their summits.

At Alton Barnes crossroads the northbound road climbs almost to the summit of Walker's Hill. A path from the roadside provides a stiffish but short climb to a long barrow called Adam's Grave, from which there are fine views across the valley and along the Downs. On the slopes of Milk Hill there is, inevitably, the figure of a white horse, carved in 1812. Northwards the view takes in Silbury Hill.

Just below the brow of Walker's Hill, on the northern side, a footpath from the road leads to a New Stone Age camp on Knap Hill and to the steep slopes of Golden Ball and Draycot hills.

▶ *A minor road leads through the Vale of Pewsey from the A361 in the west, 1½ miles north-east of Devizes, to the A345 in the east, 1½ miles north of Pewsey.*

⑮ Inkpen Hill and Walbury Hill

A great surge of hills sweeps across the southern border of Berkshire, with Inkpen and Walbury thrusting up to almost 300m (1,000ft) – the highest chalk hills in England. Seen from afar the bare hills have changing moods; dark and brooding on grey days, green and pleasant under a cloudless sky but always benevolent like lofty guardians of the wide Kennet valley below.

Roads climb steeply up the northern slopes of the hills, and the views from the summits are magnificent. From Walbury, looking back into the Kennet valley, the patchwork of fields and meadows is laced with the dark threads of hedgerows and strewn with the irregular shapes of woods and copses. Looking southwards on a clear day it is possible to see St Catherine's Hill south of Winchester, 23 miles away; to the west are the Wiltshire Downs; to the north-east the slopes of the Berkshire Downs roll away to the valley of the Thames.

Iron Age Celts built a 33ha (82 acre) fort on the summit of Walbury Hill. About a mile to the west, on Inkpen Hill, there is a grim reminder of more recent times. Here a gibbet looms stark against the skyline. Justice was swift and severe during the days of highwaymen and cut-throats, and after being hanged the corpse of any miscreant was strung up on the gibbet as a warning to others. The present gibbet is a replica of one built in 1676, when a man and wife who had murdered two of their children were hung from its two arms.

A path runs along the entire length of the ridge, providing an easy stroll between the two hills with hawthorn, dogwood, wild roses and wild cherry to brighten the way.

▶ *Inkpen and Walbury hills are about 5 miles south-east of Hungerford. The road leading to the top of Walbury Hill starts at the village of Inkpen, on minor roads 3 miles south-east of Hungerford. Follow the signs to Combe. There is a car park on the crest of Walbury Hill.*

⓰ Beacon Hill

A steep, straight path leads from the A34 to the top of Beacon Hill, a daunting climb but worth the effort for the scenery on the way and for the view from the 261m (858ft) summit. Buttercups and dropwort speckle the green turf on the lower slopes of the hill, with gorse gilding the crest.

Not surprisingly, there is a superb Iron Age hill-fort on the summit but a modern grave comes as an unusual discovery. It is the burial place of the 5th Earl of Carnarvon, who led the 1922 expedition to open Tutankhamun's tomb in Egypt and died during the course of the excavations in the Valley of the Kings. His death at the age of 57 was due to an infection that developed after he had been bitten on the cheek by a mosquito. This gave rise to the superstitious fear that he had fallen a victim to a curse associated with the tomb.

It was his wish that he should be buried on Beacon Hill, which overlooks his birthplace, Highclere Castle, to the north-west. The Elizabethan-style mansion is a noble landmark, set in a wooded park ablaze in spring with rhododendrons and azaleas.

To the east beyond the earthworks on Ladle Hill is another landmark, best known for its fictitious family of rabbits – Watership Down of Richard Adams's novel. Lying between Ladle Hill and the more distant White Hill, Watership Down is one of the high ridges that catch the eye and lead on to the great open scarp of the north Hampshire Downs riding away into the distance.

To the west, the heavily wooded Sidown Hill contrasts sharply with the almost treeless surrounding hills. In the valley between Sidown Hill and Beacon Hill are fields that are thick with oilseed rape in summer, their bright yellow standing out vividly against the dark green of meadows and downland.

The Beacon Hill fort, built between 200 and 150 BC, is hour-glass in plan, and encloses about 5ha (12 acres). Dotted about within the camp are the outlines of circular huts, which suggest the camp was permanently occupied. Its southern entrance overlooks the outlines of a Celtic field system.

▶ *Beacon Hill is ½ mile west of the A34, 6 miles south of Newbury. Watership Down is 2 miles south-west of Kingsclere, which is on the A339, 7 miles south-east of Newbury.*

BEACON HILL

⑰ Roundway Hill

A beechwood crowns Roundway Hill, its majestic trees standing sentinel-like over verdant downland. Clover springs from the long grass, and there are wild flowers such as blue speedwells and yellow goat's beard. Here, the walker can relax beneath the trees or take in the views of the Marlborough Downs to the north-east, where they sweep down to the meandering River Kennet and extend beyond to the Vale of Pewsey.

Roundway was the scene of a Civil War battle on July 13, 1643, when Prince Maurice, brother of Prince Rupert, led a Royalist force to victory against the Roundheads. The battlefield, on Roundway Down, is out of sight from the top of the hill, tucked away in a fold of the Downs about a mile north of the car park at the foot of Roundway Hill. Legend tells that, on the anniversary of the battle, the dead cry out from the nearby ditch where they were buried.

▶ *Roundway Hill is about 1 mile north-east of Devizes, along a minor road that forks northwards from the A361.*

⑱ Westbury Hill

A road leads all the way to the top of Westbury Hill, where Salisbury Plain ends its westward sweep in a climb to 230m (755ft) before falling away dramatically to the Bristol Avon valley. The view here is tremendous, with the steep, chalk slope dropping precipitously into a valley criss-crossed with roads and hedgerows and dotted with farmsteads and villages.

These are commanding heights indeed, which Iron Age men must have recognised when they built Bratton Castle on the summit. The fort spreads over 10ha (25 acres) of the flat plateau, with its ramparts along the edges. Cut into the side of the hill is Wiltshire's oldest and best-known white horse, measuring 53m (175ft) long and 33m (107ft) high with its head just below the castle's upper rampart. The Westbury horse dates from the 18th century, but it replaces an earlier figure said to have been carved to commemorate King Alfred's victory over the Danes at the Battle of Ethandun in AD 878.

The wide downland on the summit provides plenty of space for visitors to roam freely. In spring and summer, harebells and bee orchids strew the grass, and the yellow splash of bird's-foot trefoil attracts the chalkhill blue butterfly to lay its eggs.

▶ *Westbury is 4 miles north of Warminster on the A350. Westbury Hill is 2 miles east of Westbury, south-west off the B3098 from Bratton village.*

⑲ Kennet and Avon Canal

West of Devizes the land falls away into a shallow valley, dropping more than 60m (200ft) in 2 miles. But to the Georgian engineer John Rennie, whose Kennet and Avon Canal had to cross the valley, this was no problem. He built locks, 29 of them, and 170 years later they are still there for all but the unimaginative to wonder at.

Four steps down from the main road out of Devizes lead to the canal; wide at this point with deep, dark and still waters. Reeds and water-lilies fringe the banks; ducks, little grebes and moorhens nibble at the weeds and patient anglers nibble at their sandwiches. To the north-east, the western escarpments of the Marlborough Downs edge the skyline like pale green clouds.

A walk westwards along the gravel towpath brings the first of a series of locks into view at Caen Hill. The locks descend like a giant staircase, with little more than a narrowboat's length between them. When the Kennet and Avon Canal was a vital part of Victorian England's waterways, this area bustled with activity as the bargees sweated and strained to work their laden craft through the 29 locks – each double-gated. No wonder it took half a day, and no doubt those eastward bound paused at the Black Horse inn where today you are more likely to find narrow boats and cruisers used purely for pleasure for, after being dry for many years, the canals and locks have been restored to full-working order.

▶ *There is access to the canal from the A361 west of Devizes, about 23m (25yd) west of the place where it crosses the canal, opposite Avon Road, where parking is possible.*

⑳ Yarnbury Castle

Few Wiltshire guidebooks mention Yarnbury, perhaps because its neighbour, Stonehenge, is better known. But Yarnbury Castle offers a haven of tranquillity, away from the crowds that flock to the great stone circle. It is an Iron Age hill-fort dating from the 2nd century BC, with three grassy banks and three ditches enclosing an area of 11.5ha (28½ acres). In its centre are the just discernible traces of an earlier earthwork built between the 7th and 5th centuries BC, which was overlaid with sheep-pens in the 18th century.

Sheep still graze there, cropping the grass short and pausing only to stare indignantly at intruders who come up the short path from the A303 and climb the steep banks. This is an ideal place to rest awhile; to stretch out on the close-cropped grass and still be able to see the sweeping countryside in all directions. To the south the landscape is soft and gentle, for this is the southern edge of Salisbury Plain where it descends into the Wylye valley. To the north, east and west are the rolling uplands of the plain, the broad cornfields stretching to the horizon reminiscent of the American prairies.

▶ *Yarnbury Castle lies north of the A303, 3 miles west of Winterbourne Stoke. The only access path runs from the northern half of the dual-carriageway. There is no break in the central reservation at this point; if approached from the east, it is necessary to travel about 1 mile further on to leave the A303 at the next junction and return on the westbound carriageway.*

㉑ Woodford Valley

The course of the River Avon, flowing south across Salisbury Plain, is diverted suddenly by the broad shoulder of Amesbury Down. Here the Avon makes a hairpin turn before entering the lovely Woodford valley. From West Amesbury a road winds southwards through the valley, following almost every twist and turn of the west bank of the river and passing through straggling, picturesque villages of thatch and chequered stonework that shelter in the lee of downland slopes.

Sometimes the road climbs the valley side to give glimpses of water-meadows below with rows of weeping willows marking the river's course. Elsewhere, the road and river almost touch, as at Middle Woodford where only a narrow grassy bank divides them. The Avon here is wide, shallow and fast-flowing with green streamers of waterweed fanning out in the rippling current. Watercress grows at the river's edge and rows of willows curve away as the river meanders yet again on its way to Lower Woodford and Avon Bridge.

From Avon Bridge a road leads back up the valley, following the Avon's eastern bank for 4 miles to Great Durnford where there are riverside walks and a restored mill. The Durnford road passes Upper Woodford, which has the only road bridge across the river in the 7 mile stretch between West Amesbury and Avon Bridge. After Great Durnford the east bank road turns north-east, and passes Ogbury Iron Age camp before climbing to Amesbury Down.

▶ *The Woodford valley can be explored either by starting at West Amesbury, 1 mile west of Amesbury and just south of the A303, or by leaving Salisbury north on the A345 and turning west at the road signposted Stratford sub Castle.*

A HAVEN OF TRANQUILLITY AWAY FROM THE CROWDS
YARNBURY CASTLE

SOUTHERN ENGLAND

Figures in the chalk

Monumental works of art, the chalk figures of southern England stand out clear and white against the rolling hills.

It is the summer of 2002 and Dave Grafton is sitting on the gracefully arched neck of the Cherhill white horse, his boots, trousers and hands plastered white with chalk dust. Bags of newly dug chalk go whistling down a builder's chute not far away. Fellow workers are tamping chalk into place across the horse's belly. The enormous figure in the turf of Cherhill Down is being restored to the original shining whiteness of fresh-cut chalk that the 'mad doctor' Christopher Alsop of Calne had in mind when he first caused the horse to be cut on this Wiltshire escarpment in 1780.

Wiltshire with its abundance of billowing chalk downs is white horse country par excellence. There are 21 white horse hill carvings in Britain, and Wiltshire possesses 13 of them. Five are now overgrown beyond recognition, and the eight that remain exposed to view need regular maintenance. Hence the formation of the Cherhill White Horse Restoration Group, the raising of some £18,000, and the hard work in the summer of 2002 to restore the jaded old nag on the hill to its former glory.

BRONZE AGE BEAST

Contrary to popular belief, the chalk-cut white horses of Britain are not figures of great antiquity. By far the oldest of them all is the magnificent Bronze Age horse above Uffington (see right), in Oxfordshire, just across the Wiltshire border. This is a splendid, cavorting, disjointed beast-god, at least 3,000 years old and as stirring to the modern mind as it must have been to its creators. The Wiltshire horses, however, are mostly 18th and 19th century creations. Some were patriotic figures celebrating coronations; others seem to have been cut just for the hell of it.

These Wiltshire horses are enormous beasts. When freshly scoured and rechalked they shine like beacons from their escarpments. Yet only a few years' neglect sees scrub encroaching, the chalk layers weathering to grey and the outlines crumbling. Five of Wiltshire's 13 horses have completely disappeared over the years; a sad fact, though it is somehow pleasing to think of these five beasts still there in outline, trotting or galloping for ever under the turf of their hills.

Of the eight Wiltshire white horses that remain exposed to view, the oldest and best known is the Westbury horse. The original may have been Saxon or even older. It stands, beautifully placed, gazing sleepily off into space at the edge of Bratton Down; a calm horse in a static pose. Others include the horse

at Cherhill, cradled in a steep fold of National Trust downland above the Avebury-to-Calne road; the horse at Broad Town, trotting energetically north on a very steep slope above the village, one forefoot raised, head erect, tail streaming out behind; the spindly-legged but handsome beast on Hackpen Hill, below the Ridgeway ancient trackway; and Alton Barnes, cut in 1812, a big horse with a long, giraffe-like neck shown quietly walking along the south-facing escarpment of Milk Hill.

White horses are not the only expressions of chalk turf art in the South of England. The Long Man of Wilmington stares blankly from a steep hillside near Eastbourne, clutching two enormous staves and turning his feet eastwards as if about to cross East Sussex in a few enormous strides. No-one knows the age of the Long Man, nor who first outlined his tall figure in the chalk of Wilmington Hill. He has certainly changed shape in the three centuries since people began to sketch and make notes about him; gone now is the helmet he wore, along with the features of the face that once stared out from beneath it.

By contrast, the regimental badges that were cut into the downs above Fovant in Wiltshire during the 20th century have been thoroughly documented in photographs – the Prince of Wales' feathers of the Royal Wiltshire Yeomanry, the speeding Mercury of the Royal Corps of Signals, the Maltese Cross of the Post Office Rifles and many others, most of them cut during the First World War, with others added after the Second.

MODERN DESIGNS

Times have changed since Dr Christopher Alsop of Calne created the Cherhill white horse. When plans were unveiled around the Millennium to cut a giant Kentish white horse on Cheriton Hill at Folkestone, they fell foul of conservationists opposed to the disturbance of rare plant and butterfly habitats. Alsop would probably have horsewhipped such objectors from the downs. As it was, patient negotiation saw the Millennium horse 'launched' in May 2003.

And what a horse was revealed on the green slope above the Channel Tunnel – no stolid, chunky workhorse, but a joyous beast leaping like a steeplechaser, muzzle lifted to the skies, mane and tail flying free. As a nod to the New Age, the horse's eye was sited exactly over a 'powerful positive earth energy point'. What more apt expression of hope and optimism could there be to welcome strangers at the threshold of these islands and of a new millennium?

By far the oldest of them
all is the magnificent Bronze
Age horse above Uffington ...
a splendid, cavorting, disjointed
beast-god, at least 3,000 years old
and as stirring to the modern mind
as it must have been to its creators.

The NEW FOREST and ISLE OF WIGHT

Created by William the Conqueror as a royal hunting ground, the New Forest sweeps down to the sea. Across the Solent lies the Isle of Wight, favoured as a resort by a later monarch, Queen Victoria.

❶ Breamore Down

The Avon valley separates Breamore Down from the New Forest at its north-western edge, and here the scenery changes from woodlands and plains to chalk downland, with small copses of ancient yew trees and paths decked with flowers of the chalk. From behind the Elizabethan manor house half a mile north-west of Breamore village a path climbs steeply north-west through Breamore Wood to the Mizmaze, a turf labyrinth surrounded by yews and set in a small clearing of conifers.

The Mizmaze is one of half a dozen surviving in England. Channels cut in the chalk, with grass strips between, lead tortuously in a complex circular pattern of whorls to a grass-covered podium or hub in the centre, which is said to symbolise Paradise. The design measures 27m (87ft) across, and how it came to be there is an unsolved mystery. It may have been connected with a pagan rite, or devised as a symbol of morality by monks from the priory below. Alternatively, it could have been the setting for a medieval May Day dance. Certainly it has Celtic echoes, and Britons lived on Breamore Down at least until AD 519, when thousands died in a battle with the invading Saxons under their leader Cerdic. A few hundred metres to the south-west is a 55m (180ft) long barrow, called the Giant's Grave, where the Celtic leader King Natan-Leod is said to be buried.

Three-quarters of a mile north-west of the barrow is Grim's Ditch, a double-banked Iron Age earthwork. Although obscured in summer by crops and vegetation, its south-west to north-east course can be traced for about 4 miles. It forms one boundary of what was once a roughly rectangular enclosure containing some 16 square miles. It is believed that the enclosed land was once a great stock ranch, dating from about 1000 BC and owned by a single tribe.

▶ *Breamore is on the A338, 7 miles south of Salisbury. The path to the Mizmaze runs north from Breamore House.*

❷ Ashley Walk

A 'walk' in New Forest parlance is an area which was once the 'beat' of a forest keeper, in the days when deer reigned supreme. There are 15 of them, and Ashley Walk is one of the wildest and most desolate. It lies in the north-west corner of the forest, where windswept heathland rolls away on either side of a road called Deadman Hill. These forest 'highlands' were once likened to the Scottish moors by the novelist Sir Walter Scott, and from any point along the road there are views of treeless ridges and heather-clad valleys laced with brooks and streams. The dense woodlands are away to the south – a distant vista of blue-black and dark green against the sky.

Deadman Hill follows a ridge, and to its north the deep valley of Millersford Bottom opens up like a vast crater in the landscape, with clumps of gorse clinging to its sides. To the south, tracks lead down to Black Gutter Bottom and Stone Quarry Bottom and the rippling Ditchend Brook. The tracks continue over Cockley Hill to Little Cockley Plain, scattered with isolated holly trees and the domain of ponies and grazing cattle.

Where the route begins to descend to Godshill, a road turning off north by the Fighting Cocks public house leads to Castle Hill, an undated Iron Age hill-fort with ramparts and ditches overlooking the Avon valley. The earthworks are overgrown with trees and are hard to make out, but as the road climbs to a ridge a magnificent view begins to unfold in the valley below. Here the Avon snakes across the valley, through water-meadows and passing a red-brick mill by a stone bridge. Then the river makes another turn and disappears from view as it runs close to the western foot of the hill.

▶ *Ashley Walk is crossed by the B3078 between Cadnam and Fordingbridge, and includes Deadman Hill which leads to Godshill Ridge as the road descends to Godshill. The road leading to Castle Hill is 1½ miles east of Fordingbridge.*

❸ Eyeworth Pond

A narrow lane runs from the tiny hamlet of Fritham and passes through woodland of oaks, beeches and holly before descending to a shallow valley of heath and beechwoods, and the glistening water of Eyeworth Pond. The wedge-shaped stretch of water lies half surrounded by the beeches of Eyeworth Wood which spread down to the water's edge. A green apron of reeds covers almost half the pond, at its narrow end, but in the clear end are water-liles and artificial islands for coots, moorhens, mallard ducks and, most notably, mandarin ducks, which make their home in tree holes and special nesting boxes.

Through the valley runs the Latchmore Brook, and it was by damming this in the 19th century that the pond was formed. Its purpose was to supply water power for a gunpowder factory, and the pond still brims over a weir, near where the factory once stood. At the far end of the pond, the brook rises from a spring which was once a medicinal 'iron well', and the water is still tinged a rusty red.

▶ *Fritham lies 5 miles east of Fordingbridge and to the west of an unclassified road running between the A31 and B3078. Eyeworth Pond is not signposted in Fritham, and the lane to it starts from the end of a No Through Road which runs west from the hamlet.*

❹ Canterton Glen

In this narrow, green valley of oaks and tall beeches the Rufus Stone marks the spot where William II, called Rufus because of his red hair, died in a hunting accident. The death of Rufus is one of history's great mysteries, but certainly the arrow fired from Sir William Tirel's bow brought short the reign of a king who had many enemies. Legend has embroidered the tale, and Ocknell Pond, 2 miles to the west, is pointed out as the place where Tirel paused to wash the blood from his hands. The pond is said to redden on each anniversary of the deed, which took place on the morning of August 2, 1100.

The village of Minstead, a mile south-east of Canterton Glen, is a typical New Forest settlement with thatched cottages and a small green. On the western edge of the village stands Castle Malwood, now only an earthwork crowning a wooded knoll but believed to be where William Rufus spent the night before his death. Fittingly, this village bound in with one of history's puzzles is the burial place of the master of mysterious tales, Sir Arthur Conan Doyle. His grave is in Minstead churchyard.

▶ *The road through Canterton Glen runs between the A31 and B3079, 2 miles west of Cadnam. The road to Minstead runs south-east from the A31.*

FALLOW DEER IN THE NEW FOREST

❺ Bolderwood Grounds and Mark Ash Wood

There are three walks laid out by the Forestry Commission in these woods, all of which start at Bolderwood Green, south of the A31. The walks take in some of the finest woodland scenery in the forest and provide the best chance to see deer. There might also be an opportunity to see all three British species of woodpecker – the green, great spotted and lesser spotted – as well as redstarts, firecrests, wood warblers and crossbills.

The Radnor Trail is a short stroll among Douglas firs dating from 1860. There is a flavour of the Canadian timber forests here, with slender trunks climbing ruler-straight to a height of almost 30m (100ft), and the delicate evergreen foliage contrasting harmoniously with the paler green of the ferns below. In a green glade is the memorial to the 7th Earl of Radnor, who was a Forestry Commissioner from 1942 to 1963. The memorial is carved from Westmorland slate and is sculpted with figures depicting the wildlife of the forest.

The Jubilee Walk is another short trail which passes through the lofty avenues of an arboretum, where about 40 different species of trees are numbered and labelled for easy identification. This is a wonderland of greens, reds and browns, with the sweet scent of pine heavy on the air. There are redwoods from California, Japanese cedar, Italian poplar, Norway spruce, Chinese fir and Corsican pine. At one point the walk diverges through tall beeches to an observation platform which overlooks a rough meadow preserved as a deer sanctuary.

The walk through Mark Ash Wood, though no more than a 3 mile circular stroll, plunges deep into one of the oldest parts of the forest, where ancient beeches cast a deep shade and the branches of some old trees are so close that they have actually become joined. This 'inosculation', as it is called, occurs frequently between trees of the same species, but in the Knightwood Inclosure, a mile to the south-east of Mark Ash Wood, a beech and an oak have joined together. Here, too, is the New Forest's oldest pollarded oak, a survivor of the days when trees were lopped to provide young shoots for deer to eat. The Knightwood Oak, 7m (22ft) around at shoulder height, is one of the New Forest's institutions – like the deer and the ponies.

▶ *The start of the Radnor, Arboretum and Mark Ash Wood walks is at the north-western end of the Ornamental Drive which runs north from the A35, 2½ miles south-west of Lyndhurst, towards the A31. The Knightwood Oak car park is ½ mile along the Ornamental Drive from the A35.*

❻ Ridley Wood

From the Vereley Hill car park, north-west of Burley on the western edge of the forest, a path leads into Ridley Wood – a path trodden more than 250 years ago by the New Forest smugglers who set up their 'market' beneath the dark canopy of beech trees for the distribution of tea, brandy, silks and lace brought up from the coast.

The favourite place for the landing of smuggled goods was Chewton Bunny, a small gorge at Highcliffe on Christchurch Bay. From there, packhorses and wagons travelled over moors and forest tracks along the smugglers' road to Ridley Wood and beyond. Still remembered in Burley is a woman smuggler, Lovey Warne. When she became too old to handle the heavy crates and kegs, she became a look-out for the gang and would stroll across Vereley Hill wearing a bright red cloak whenever the revenue men were in the area. She could be seen for miles – as anyone similarly dressed would be today.

▶ *Vereley Hill is 3 miles east of Ringwood and ½ mile south of Picket Post, on the A31.*

❼ Tall Trees Trail

This is possibly the most beautiful and awe-inspiring part of the whole of the New Forest. The conifers here were planted in 1859, and anything less than 18m (60ft) tall is a mere stripling. There are 20 species represented. They form an avenue of timber giants, among which a mighty redwood is outstripped by a pair of soaring Wellingtonias.

The redwood and a white spruce, a red spruce, a Spanish fir and a Lawson cypress are the tallest of their species in England. But it is not only the sheer height of these noble trees that makes the 1½ mile Tall Trees Trail so enjoyable, for the avenue has been carefully planned so that the trees can be properly admired, and more than 50 of them have been labelled for easy identification. Many need no labels; it is not difficult to spot the rich red bark of the redwood or the pale needles of silver fir. Nor is it hard to recognise the green pyramid of a Norway spruce, the traditional Christmas tree.

At its northern end, the walk runs through a plantation of sedate oaks, grown for timber production and almost branchless, unlike the traditional English oak of greenwood and village green. Here, too, is Vinney Ridge, the first of the forest's inclosures dating from 1700. Originally it was enclosed by a 1.5m (5ft) ditch and a 2m (6ft) high bank topped by an oak fence, and a short section has been reconstructed along the walk.

A diversion from Tall Trees Trail leads to Brock Hill, where beeches and oaks stand in a 150-year-old grove crowning a knoll. *Broc* is Old English for 'badger', and on the hill the New Forest's shyest creatures build their setts in the widespreading roots of the beech trees. Badgers are mostly nocturnal animals, and are unlikely to be seen except possibly at break of day or late evening. The walk in this typically English woodland of shaded glades makes an interesting contrast to the North American-style grandness of the tall timbers.

From the car park at the southern end of Tall Trees Trail, a path leads to the Blackwater. The path crosses the stream by a wooden bridge and then follows the bank among plantations of young conifer and broad-leaved trees.

▶ *Tall Trees Trail consists of two avenues running parallel to the Rhinefield Ornamental Drive. The drive is a turning south off the A35, 2½ miles south-west of Lyndhurst. There are car parks at Brock Hill, about ½ mile along the drive, and at Blackwater, 1 mile further south.*

❽ Ober Water

The Forestry Commission has laid out two walks by the Ober Water which, it says, 'show within a short distance some of the secrets of the New Forest'. Both walks are easy strolls through typical forest scenery, with the added attraction of a peat-stained stream wending its way between the trees.

The walks follow the stream closely for part of the way, along banks thick with bog myrtle and sphagnum moss. In places the stream twists so tortuously that it has formed loops which became cut off when the ends met, leaving horseshoe-shaped pools called 'ox-bows'. There are brown trout in the deep water, though they are difficult to spot and much less noticeable than the shoals of minnows in the shallows.

At one point the pathway passes briefly through the Aldridge Inclosure of oaks, originally planted in 1775. Here, young oaks are growing beneath the protection of self-sown Scots pine. Any dead pines left standing are peppered with the bore-holes of longhorn beetles; their larvae provide food for woodpeckers whose staccato tattoo is often heard echoing through the forest.

▶ *The Ober Water walks start at either Putties Bridge or Whitefield Moor, both on the Rhinefield road 2 miles west of Brockenhurst. There are car parks at both places.*

❾ Queen Bower

The Ober Water flows into the Lymington River at Bolderford Bridge, a narrow wooden bridge which carries a forest track over the river. The track from the Beachern Wood car park winds through oaks and beeches that border the Ober Water. Here and there, openings lead into green glades where the peace is broken only by the hammering of woodpeckers. Fallen trees, dead or uprooted, lie across the stream whose rusty-brown, peat-stained waters are sun-dappled in luminous patterns of brown and grey. After about a mile, the path emerges at Bolderford Bridge. Here, just north-west of the bridge, is Queen Bower, a magical glade where gnarled oaks and beeches dip their bare roots into the water, and the mossy banks are vivid green in the sunlight shafting through the trees.

The queen who loved this place was Eleanor, wife of Edward I, and its majestic beauty is certainly fit for a queen; but after a heavy rainfall Queen Bower is not only beautiful, it is awe-inspiring. Then the swollen Ober Water and Lymington meet in a head-long rush, and their waters become a creamy torrent, racing beneath the bridge, surging over the banks and swirling among the trees. As the water-level rises, seeking out every tiny dell, the glade becomes a swampland of red-brown pools and green islands.

▶ *The forest track to Bolderford Bridge and Queen Bower starts at the Beachern Wood car park on the Rhinefield road on the western fringe of Brockenhurst. There is also a footpath to Queen Bower from Balmer Lawn, just north of Brockenhurst beside the A337.*

OAKS AND BEECHES DIP THEIR BARE ROOTS INTO THE WATER
QUEEN BOWER

⑩ Bucklers Hard

A broad, grass-verged street leads down past red-brick cottages then, suddenly, there is a glimpse of water and the tang of the sea. The water is the Beaulieu River, swinging in a great lazy circle around an island of reeds and mud, with dark woods rising behind.

The old rubs shoulders with the new at Bucklers Hard, for close to the marina where sleek-hulled sailing cruisers ride are the remains of slipways where 18th-century warships were built from New Forest oaks. Nelson's 64-gun HMS *Agamemnon* was launched here in 1781.

Boats are still built on the banks of the Beaulieu, in the Agamemnon Boatyard where a 2 mile riverside walk to Beaulieu starts. With the return journey, it takes about two and a half hours at a leisurely pace. The walk is waymarked,

and the first section begins at a tall Scots pine known to be about 200 years old. The footpath leads through a copse and crosses a salt-marsh carpeted with sea lavender and sea purslane.

The walk ends by a 16th-century corn-mill, and beyond the mill-pond stands a gateway which is now part of Beaulieu Palace House.
▶ *Bucklers Hard is 2 miles south-east of Beaulieu village and is signposted from the B3054. There is a car park at the top of the village street for visitors.*

⑪ Beaulieu Heath

In the south-east corner of the New Forest the vast, gently undulating vistas of Beaulieu Heath stretch almost from Southampton Water to Lymington. In spring and early summer the eastern part of the heath is ablaze with gorse, massed in great clumps, and

westward roll dark seas of heather that turn to purple as autumn approaches. Near the centre of the heath lies the crescent-shaped Hatchet Pond, one of the forest's largest expanses of water. It is close to the junction of the B3055 and B3054, and there are car parks along its banks.

Although little of this sandy heath is more than 30m (100ft) above sea-level, there are often exhilarating views across The Solent to the Isle of Wight. Round barrows scattered over the heath are a reminder that Bronze Age men settled here, when the sea-level was lower than it is now and The Solent was a fertile river valley.

The Beaulieu River cuts a meandering channel across the heath, and widens between grassy banks and mudflats to become tidal at Beaulieu village.

▶ *The B3054 Hythe-Lymington road cuts across Beaulieu Heath in a north-east to south-west direction.*

BUCKLERS HARD

⑫ Hengistbury Head

Heath, woodland, marsh and meadow are packed into the mile-long Hengistbury Head, a wild and windswept promontory curling like a bent finger around Christchurch Harbour. It is a tiny world in itself, with a history of human activity spanning 11,000 years. Paths run to Warren Hill, at the southern side of the Head, passing an Iron Age double dyke with a 4m (12ft) high rampart on the way and then crossing short-grassed meadowland. At the foot of the hill the promontory is almost cut in two by a deep gully, which was an ironstone quarry during the 19th century.

The summit of Warren Hill forms a broad plateau ending in tawny sand-cliffs plunging to the sea. A constant wind scything in from the sea keeps the clumps of ling, heather and gorse low-growing, and the turf is thin and patchy. But in the lee of the hill are woodlands, scrub and marshes bordering the harbour, and a lily-pond where dragonflies skim the water in summer.

About 11,000 years ago, when Britain was still joined to the Continent, Stone Age men built a camp on Warren Hill, and flint tools from that period have been found there. During the Iron Age, some 8,500 years later, Hengistbury was a busy port. It remained so under the Romans but was abandoned when they left. It did not attract the invading Saxons, who built their village on the other side of the harbour, and Hengistbury reverted to desolate heathland – until the quarry-men came to dig for ironstone.

Hengistbury Head is one of the finest vantage points on the south coast. Christchurch Harbour, held in the crook of a sand-spit curving round from the Head, is almost a lake; the harbour's outlet to the sea is a 27m (30yd) gap – the Avon Run – between the sand-spit and Mudeford Quay.

At Christchurch, a greystone jewel set at the water's edge, the River Avon meets the Stour, and the green apron of Stanpit Marsh divides the harbour into muddy channels. To the east of the harbour, across Christchurch Bay, are the bulky outlines of the Isle of Wight, with the gleaming Needles rocks and the coloured cliffs of Alum Bay easily visible on a clear day.

Westward the land curves around the broad sweep of Poole Bay and the misty Purbeck Hills loom above the chalk cliffs of Ballard Down.

▶ *The Hengistbury Head car park can be reached by taking the Southbourne road from Christchurch and then following the signposts shortly after crossing Tuckton Bridge. A land train runs from here to the Head. There are also boat trips to the Head from Christchurch and Mudeford Quays.*

ISLE OF WIGHT

⑬ Tennyson Down

Above the Needles, white cliffs rise sheer from the sea to Tennyson Down, named after the poet who loved to walk there. The finest approach starts from west of Freshwater Bay, past a thatched church, and is clearly signposted 'Tennyson Down and the Needles'. The fairly long walk climbs to 150m (500ft), and provides magnificent views south-east along the foam-fringed coastline curving sinuously away to St Catherine's Point. To the north-west lies the Hampshire coast, while on the north side of the down the white chalk gives way to multi-coloured sandstone cliffs at Alum Bay.

▶ *There are several footpaths over Tennyson Down; the Coastal Path can be picked up at Freshwater Bay, just off the A3055.*

⑭ Brighstone Down

Halfway along the minor road between Calbourne and Brighstone is an area of outstanding walking country. To the west of the road lies a forest trail which rises to Westover Down – crowned by five burial mounds – from which there are sweeping views of the island. To the east of the road, a downland trail leads along a gradually climbing path that slowly yields spectacular views of the island from Culver Cliff to Freshwater. At the summit, a wide path beyond a gate leads through woods to Callibury Hump – the remains of a Bronze Age burial mound.

▶ *The road from Brighstone to Calbourne heads north from the B3399. There is a car park near the top of the down.*

⑮ St Catherine's Hill

At the island's southern end, St Catherine's Hill provides the best vantage point for viewing both the south-eastern and south-western coasts. The Needles can be seen in one direction and the Foreland in another. The hill is reached by a short climb from the A3055, just above Blackgang Chine. Crowning the hill are the remains of two former lighthouses. One is St Catherine's Oratory, an octagonal tower built in 1328, the other is a building started in 1785 but never completed. The two ruins are popularly called the Pepper Pot and the Salt Cellar.

▶ *There is a car park to the south of the A3055, east of Blackgang, the footpath to St Catherine's Oratory begins on the other side of the road.*

WHITE CLIFFS RISE SHEER FROM THE SEA

TENNYSON DOWN FROM FRESHWATER BAY

16 St Boniface Down and The Landslip

The highest point on the island is St Boniface Down. Though cluttered by the aerials of a radar station, the 235m (771ft) summit is a superb vantage point from which to see the whole 6 mile sweep of the south-east coast round to the white face of Culver Cliff.

There are fine walks northwards, over the springy-turfed downs stretching away under huge skies. One starts just north of the approach to the car park on St Boniface Down. Pass through a gate and follow the trail signposted 'Bridle Path to Shanklin'. The walk, over grassy slopes patterned by patches of gorse, leads to Shanklin Down and St Martin's Down.

Below St Boniface Down is The Landslip, a wooded wilderness of fallen rocks brought about by landslides in 1810 and 1928. There is an eeriness in this strange twilight world, with the twisted branches of ash, beech and oak intertwining above a path that winds through fallen boulders.

The footpath leads through The Landslip to Luccombe Chine, where huge hydrangeas embower the path in summer in a mass of pink blossom. Small waterfalls gush from the rock face and form streams that run down to the sea – a distant whisper below.

▶ *The car park for St Boniface Down is reached via a minor road off the B3327 just above Ventnor. There is a car park for The Landslip and Luccombe Chine just to the east of Bonchurch, on the A3055.*

105

DOWNLAND and WEALD

The south-east corner of England is dominated by the North and South Downs, which run from Hampshire to the east coast. Between these two chalk ridges lies the softer, gentler landscape of the Weald.

❶ Ranmore Common

Wooded Ranmore Common, lovely and unspoiled, lies on a ridge of the North Downs that looks eastwards across the River Mole valley as it cuts through the hills below the western slopes of Box Hill. If you climb to the common from the steep southern slopes above Dorking, you can look back on marvellous views across the Tilling Bourne valley south-west and south-east to the woodlands of the Weald, ever-widening as you ascend the slope.

Pleasant walks across the 191ha (472 acre) common, owned by the National Trust, take you through beech and oak woods where the glades are a mass of bluebells in spring, and where foxgloves stand in purple ranks in summer. Some footpaths are waymarked, and one circular walk through woods and fields includes a spectacular avenue of yews. Wood anemones, red clover, celandines and rosebay willowherb can be found along the way, and occasionally there are deer to be seen – especially in winter when the trees are bare and views less restricted.

▶ *Ranmore Common is 2 miles north-west of Dorking. The circular walk starts from the Stonyrock Road car park, one of several on the common, which can be reached along a minor road west from Dorking.*

❷ Friday Street

Today, Friday Street is a peaceful hamlet hidden in the heart of the Surrey Weald, but 300 years ago it was a stronghold of the flourishing Wealden iron industry. Its hammer-pond, dammed from the Tilling Bourne, is one of the most attractive in the area, with pine trees crowding down to the water's edge. The best way to enjoy this beautiful part of Surrey is to start from the hamlet of Wotton and follow the Tilling Bourne stream south to Friday Street and then go on to Abinger Bottom – a 2½ mile walk through unforgettable scenery.

From the Wotton Hatch Inn the footpath leads across a field into woods, and then over a stream where dragonflies skim the water. At Friday Street the stream widens out to the mirror-flat surface of the hammer-pond, with redbrick cottages reflected in its waters. Coots, moorhens and mallards glide among the vivid green patches of duckweed.

The timber-framed Stephan Langton Inn was named for King John's Archbishop of Canterbury, who was born in Friday Street in 1150. Beyond the inn a footpath heads along a valley shaded by Scots pines; they were planted by John Evelyn, the 17th-century diarist and author on tree culture, on his brother's Wotton estate. The tinkling chatter of tiny streams provides a cheerful accompaniment all the way to the pretty cluster of houses at Abinger Bottom.

▶ *Friday Street is 3½ miles south-west of Dorking, and Wotton is on the A25 north of Friday Street.*

❸ Hydon's Ball

Woods, hills and valleys sprawl in a pleasant jumble below Hydon's Ball, a wooded, conical hill on Hydon Heath north-east of Hambledon in the north-west Weald. The views come and go with the mist, sometimes stretching eastwards as far as Leith Hill, or south across the Weald to the South Downs.

The heath is sandy and pitted with rabbit warrens, and early in the morning the musky scent of a fox is easily picked up. In the 13th century the local sand was used for glass-making, an industry introduced by the Normans. Charcoal from the woods fired the furnaces and for four centuries the industry thrived, with the village of Chiddingfold its centre. In 1615, because of the danger of deforestation, the use of wood as fuel for glass-making was banned. The industry moved to coal-producing areas, and the sandy heaths became quiet open stretches of heather and bracken.

Hydon's Ball and 50ha (125 acres) of the surrounding woods and heaths belong to the National Trust. On the summit of the hill there is a memorial to Octavia Hill (1838–1912), a social reformer who was one of the founders of the Trust, formed in 1894 to preserve places of natural beauty or historical significance. About 1½ miles north-east is Winkworth Arboretum, 41ha (99 acres) of woods particularly noted for its rare maples and whitebeams. It is thickly carpeted with bluebells in spring, and ablaze with azaleas in summer.

▶ *Hydon Heath is 3 miles south of Godalming, reached along minor roads west from the B2130. Winkworth Arboretum is 2 miles south-east of Godalming, east of the B2130.*

❹ Holmbury Hill

Wealthy Victorians developed the village of Holmbury St Mary, its houses dotted amid pines on the sandy slopes of a narrow, steep-sided valley about 3 miles south of the North Downs. George Edmund Street, the architect, built the Neo-Gothic church in 1879, at his own expense. Holmbury Hill, 261m (857ft), guards the western side of the valley where it opens out at its southern end. Leith Hill slopes away on the eastern side. Both hills provide magnificent views across the hills and woods of the Weald, patterned like a chessboard, that stretches southwards to the distant South Downs.

Wild, picturesque country surrounds Holmbury Hill, excellent walking country where foxes may be seen on the hillside and where roe deer browse among the brambles. Jays and magpies swoop through the trees, tree pipits fly up from the bushes in spring and early summer and nightjars are sometimes heard uttering their strange churring songs after dusk. In dry, open spots a poisonous, zigzagged adder may sometimes be seen basking in the sun. Almost hidden among the bracken and brambles are the double ditches and banks of an Iron Age hill-fort, around 3ha (8 acres) in extent, that was in use about 2,000 years ago. The remains of 20 stones used for hand-grinding corn were found there in the 1930s.

Leith Hill, 294m (965ft), is the highest point in south-east England. The 20m (64ft) tower on its summit, built in 1766 by Richard Hull of Leith Hill Place, increases its height to more than 305m (1,000ft), and it is worth climbing to the tower top for the splendour of the view, said to take in 13 counties. South-westwards, Black Down, 280m (919ft), the highest point in Sussex, juts out into the Weald.

▶ *Holmbury Hill, 6 miles south-west of Dorking, can be reached from Peaslake, south of Gomshall on the A25; from the village a minor woodland road opposite the Hurtwood Inn leads to a car park less than 1 mile from the summit. For Leith Hill, follow the A29 south from Dorking, turn west along the B2126 and after about 1 mile turn north; after 1 mile bear left to the car park on the west side of the hill, from where the climb is comparatively easy. There are other car parks around the hill but the climbs from these are steeper.*

LEITH HILL

❺ Black Down

The highest point in Sussex, Black Down, rears up dramatically from the Weald to a height of 280m (919ft) – a sandstone ridge clothed mainly in Scots pine, black fir and birch. Rhododendrons burst into flower in early summer, and everywhere there is a golden sea of gorse dappled with the pink and purple of heather. Meadow pipits, linnets, wrens and yellowhammers can sometimes be seen.

There was already a beacon on Black Down by the 16th century, and it was probably used to pass news of the Armada sailing up the channel. Later, in 1796, the Admiralty installed a telegraph system between Portsmouth and London: the Black Down station was sited on a projecting knob of land, known locally as Tally Knob, to the south-east of the Temple of the Winds.

The view he loved is little changed – green Sussex countryside sweeping across the Weald to the bare ridge of the South Downs, marked by tree-crowned Chanctonbury Ring. Beyond lies the silver-grey of the sea fusing with the hazy blue of the sky.

The best view is to be had from the Temple of the Winds, a group of firs that lies at the southern end of Black Down. It can be reached along the 1½ mile nature trail that leads from the upper car park through beechwoods and pine plantations, and by the site of a Stone Age settlement of about 6000 BC. Stopping points along the way give long, lingering views to the west, east and south.

▶ *Black Down is 2½ miles south-east of Haslemere. To reach the National Trust car parks, turn south off the B2131 at Haste Hill to follow Tennyson's Lane, a minor road leading south-east.*

❻ Ashdown Forest

From the ridge at King's Standing, you can look down on one of Britain's most heavily wooded areas – great stretches of heath and woodland that 2,000 years ago were part of the impenetrable forest the Romans called Silva Anderida, 'the Forest of Anderida'. Ashdown Forest in the High Weald stretches for 8 miles, from Maresfield in the south to Forest Row in the north, and covers some 5,700ha (14,000 acres) it is still wild and wooded, with a great variety of trees at every stage of growth.

Ashdown Forest became a medieval hunting ground, and many of the clumps of trees on high ground mark the spot where an English king stood and watched the chase; King's Standing was a vantage point for both Edward II and Edward III. In the 14th century the area was fenced in as a deer preserve for the Dukes of Lancaster. Place names such as Chuck Hatch Gate and Friar's Gate mark the boundaries. In Tudor and Stuart times, hunting declined and the forest was thick with ironworks, such as at Newbridge and Crowborough Warren. Near Hartfield is the Poohsticks Bridge, believed to be the place where A. A. Milne first played the game with his son, Christopher Robin, in the 1920s.

A drive along the road between Hartfield and Maresfield (B2026) gives some idea of the forest's extent. Paths lead everywhere, and heather and bracken, dappled with the yellow splashes of gorse, line the road edges. Swallows and swifts wheel in the summer sky, and the air is filled with the rich song of woodlarks and linnets. And high above, the hook-beaked hobby soars in pursuit of swallows, swifts and skylarks.

▶ *King's Standing is 3½ miles south of Hartfield on the B2188, close to its junction with the B2026.*

❼ Horsmonden

In an idyllic setting amid the Kentish orchards, Horsmonden village was once a busy centre of the Wealden iron industry. About half a mile north-west of the village is Furnace Pond, one of the finest of the old hammer-ponds, more than a quarter of a mile long. Its dammed water once turned the wheels that worked bellows for the furnaces and trip-hammers in the forges. The pond glowed from the flames of the furnace fires, and the valley echoed to the thudding of the hammers.

Now the waters reflect only the blue sky and passing clouds, and the stillness is disturbed only by the hunting dive of a kingfisher or the quiet plop of a rising fish. There is a footpath to the pond starting half a mile west of Horsmonden village from Furnace Lane. The village is grouped round a triangular green above the valley of the River Teise, a tributary of the River Medway. With the rise of the 16th-century iron industry, the villagers left the old settlement 1½ miles south to be nearer the scene of their labours. This is why Horsmonden's 14th-century church is so far from the village centre.

Reached along narrow lanes heavy with apple blossom in spring, the sandstone church, with its buttressed and battlemented tower, stands on a hill slope near the hamlet of Elphicks. Eastwards across the Teise valley, with its patchwork of hop-fields, water-meadows and orchards, stands the picturesque hill-top village of Goudhurst, where the squat church tower gives fine views across the Weald.

▶ *Horsmonden is 7 miles east of Tunbridge Wells on the B2162.*

THE POOHSTICKS BRIDGE

SOUTHERN ENGLAND

❽ Challock Forest

Hop poles for supporting the climbing hop plants are an inseparable part of the Kentish scenery. Many of them are grown in Challock Forest in the Kentish North Downs, where there are coppices of sweet-chestnut trees. The trees are cut off at ground level and the new shoots that spring from the stumps grow into poles after about 15 years, when they can be cut for fencing stakes or props as well as hop poles.

King's Wood, in the heart of Challock Forest, was once part of the vast Eastwell Park, the former estate of the Earls of Winchelsea. Here, sweet-chestnut coppices are intermingled with glades of beech and conifers such as Scots and Corsican pines and Norway spruce – the Christmas tree. The Forestry Commission has laid out a 2½ mile forest walk through King's Wood, where crossbills can sometimes be seen feeding on the pine cones. There are fallow deer here, too, seldom seen except at dusk, when the silence of the woods may be broken by the churring call of a nightjar.

Park Wood, in the north-east corner of the forest, is another oasis amid the tall conifer plantations. It is light and airy, with sunlight filtering through groves of oaks, beeches and hornbeams, and here in summer you may see blackcaps, chiffchaffs and willow warblers.

Soakham Downs lie to the south of King's Wood, a velvety stretch of sheep-grazed downland overlooking the Great Stour valley. There are fine views south-west to the bare sweep of the South Downs – a hazy line on the horizon.

▶ *Challock Forest is 5 miles north of Ashford. King's Wood Forest Walk starts on the A251 about ½ mile south-east of Challock crossroads (A251/252). There is a car park on the minor road that forks off to Wye, also leading to Soakham Downs. Park Wood is on the A252 about 2 miles north-east of Challock crossroads.*

❾ Wye and Crundale Downs

According to medieval superstitions, the Devil shaped much of the English landscape. On the North Downs he is credited with the Devil's Kneadingtrough, a steep-sided valley that cuts 60m (200ft) deep into the ridge of the Wye and Crundale Downs. In reality, it was probably formed by water erosion during a massive thaw about 8000 BC, after the last Ice Age.

The Devil's Kneadingtrough is within the 133ha (329 acre) Wye National Nature Reserve, and there is a nature trail about three-quarters of a mile long through some of the finest stretches of chalk grassland and woodland on the North Downs. Wonderful views from the crest of the Downs, over 170m (550ft) above sea-level, take in the farmlands of the Great Stour valley to the west and the Weald beyond, stretching some 40 miles away to Ashdown Forest.

Blackcaps, willow warblers, yellowhammers and nightingales nest in the scrub at the woodland edges, and in the woods – mainly ash with hazel scrub – there are nuthatches, treecreepers, chiffchaffs and garden warblers. The call of the green woodpecker echoes among the trees and there are badger setts, recognised by the chalky rubble thrown up by their burrowing.

▶ *The nature reserve is 4 miles north-east of Ashford between Wye and Hastingleigh, reached by minor roads east from the A28 or north-east from the A20.*

❿ Romney Marsh

Reclaimed from the sea, Romney Marsh today is a marsh in name only, where longwool sheep graze fertile pastures and reed-lined dykes carve across the flat landscape. Most of the area is barely above sea-level, and village churches, such as St Mary in the Marsh and St Thomas a Becket, in Fairfield, are conspicuous landmarks. When sea mists drift in, the marsh becomes an eerie place where only the mournful sounds of ships' foghorns and the croaking of marsh frogs break the silence. On clear days, however, there are splendid sunrises and sunsets, streaking the sky with fingers of light.

The first attempts to reclaim the marsh were made in prehistoric times by Belgic tribes, already skilled in keeping out water from the Low Countries. The Romans built a paved road from Canterbury down on to the marsh at

Lympne, and the Saxons built a wall – the Rhee Wall, which is now the line of the road from Old Romney to Appledore – and thereby reclaimed several thousand acres. Most reclamation, however, took place in medieval times and was completed by the 1660s. Local landowners still pay for the upkeep of the dykes.

The other major change to the landscape came in 1840, when the Royal Military Canal was built as a defence line during the Napoleonic Wars. The 23 mile long canal, from Hythe to Rye, makes Romney Marsh virtually an island.

Its closeness to the sea and the Continent made the marsh an ideal haven for smugglers; local men who knew every lane and dyke and who could easily outwit their pursuers. The smugglers, known as 'owlers' because of their nocturnal activities, took wool to the Continent to get a better price, and brought in tobacco and brandy. Sometimes churches were used to hide the contraband. In the 13th-century St Dunstan's Church at Snargate, a sealed-off part of the south aisle was said to be a smugglers' den, and 18th-century Excisemen recovered tobacco from the belfry and gin from the vestry.

▶ *Romney Marsh lies south-east of Ashford mainly east of the A2070. The church of St Mary in the Marsh is 2 miles south-east of Dymchurch along minor roads off the A259. Snargate is on the B2080, 1½ miles north-west of the junction of the A259 and the A2070.*

⑪ Beachy Head

White cliffs rise sheer from the sea to 163m (534ft) of rugged grandeur at Beachy Head, with a rousing seascape of pounding waves, blown spume, and shrieking gulls wheeling on the wind. Offshore, the red-banded lighthouse looks like a tiny toy, but its powerful beam can be seen 16 miles across the English Channel.

The South Downs Way begins its westward route at Eastbourne, less than a mile north-east of Beachy Head. The 3 mile walk along this part of the pathway towards the Seven Sisters takes in magnificent coastal scenery. The views stretch eastwards as far as Dungeness, and west to the Isle of Wight. West from Beachy Head the path drops down and passes the remains of the old Belle Tout lighthouse, built of granite in 1831.

The frowning brows of the Seven Sisters cliffs soon come into view, rising and falling like a roller-coaster track that ends at Cuckmere Haven. The dips were once the valleys of ancient rivers. An additional 3 mile walk along the switchback path leads to Haven Brow and views of the Cuckmere River winding through its valley to the sea, where the shingle bar lies piled up at its mouth. Viewed from afar, and even more obvious to the walker, the Seven Sisters clearly number eight. Their name owes more to romantic alliteration than to accuracy.

▶ *The B2103 leads south from Eastbourne; a signposted road leads to Beachy Head.*

THE MARSH BECOMES AN EERIE PLACE
CHURCH OF ST THOMAS A BECKET ON ROMNEY MARSH

⑫ Friston Forest

A few miles inland from Seven Sisters cliffs, beyond the bare, windswept ridge of the South Downs, is Friston Forest, a superb beechwood around 80 years old. When the Forestry Commission began planting the forest in 1927, they used fast-growing Scots and Corsican pines as 'nurse trees' to protect the young beeches until they were fully established.

The pines have done their job, and many have been felled to leave the glorious beeches in full view, with the sun filtering through the leaves in great, golden shafts. The forest is a light and cheerful place, with plenty of space to wander at will, or to follow the two waymarked walks, one nearly 3 miles long, the other about half that. Fallow and roe deer both inhabit the forest and butterflies, such as the White Admiral, can be seen in open spaces between the trees.

From Exceat Bridge on the Eastbourne-Seaford road (A259), there are fine views of the lovely Cuckmere River as it winds its way through water-meadows to the sea. This peaceful place is part of the Seven Sisters Country Park, where there are nature trails and hides by the river for watching wildlife.

▶ *Friston Forest is north of the A259 Eastbourne-Seaford road. The entrance and car park are on a minor road about 2¼ miles west of Friston.*

⑬ Windover Hill

On the steep northern slope of Windover Hill, early man has left a lasting but mysterious mark. A chalk figure known as the Long Man – holding a stave in each hand – towers above the village of Wilmington.

His origin is unknown. Does he date back some 3,500 years to the Bronze Age, those staves representing the gates of dawn being opened by the god Baldur? Or is he a 1,700-year-old Romano-British figure; some Roman coins bear the figure of Woden in a similar stance. Could he be a 1,000-year-old Saxon image of a king carrying a spear in each hand? There is a similarity to figures found on the helmet in the 7th-century Saxon ship uncovered at Sutton Hoo in 1939. Other relics of early man on the hill are a Bronze Age ditched bowl-barrow and a Stone Age long barrow on the highest point.

North-wards from the crown of Windover Hill lie the fields and forests of the Weald, and westwards you can see across the Cuckmere valley to Firle Beacon and in the distant haze the beech-crowned Chanctonbury Ring.

▶ *Wilmington is 6 miles north-west of Eastbourne and just south of the A27, 2 miles west of Polegate on the A22. About ½ mile south-west of Wilmington a path from the minor road leads to Windover Hill, linking up with the South Downs Way.*

MAGICAL VIEWS OVER THE COUNTRYSIDE
DITCHLING BEACON

⑭ Firle Beacon

In the summer of 1588, Firle Beacon was part of England's early warning system, when beacons blazed along the coast to signal the approach of the Spanish Armada. At 217m (713ft) it was a natural choice; the highest point of the eastern South Downs and a prominent landmark even without its crest of fire.

The South Downs Way skirts the hill, but a short detour to the summit is worth the effort. It can also be reached by road from the village of West Firle, followed by a mile walk. Either way the walk is easy, across springy turf and clover and with constantly widening views southwards of the coastline. To the north-west the River Ouse winds sleekly round the heights on which stands Lewes Castle.

The Stone Age custom of burying the dead in high places is evident on the summit of Firle Beacon, where there is a long barrow measuring 30m (100ft). Bronze Age round barrows are also dotted around the area, and a group of them, called Lord's Burghs, can be seen on a spur to the south-west. Iron Age Celts farmed the southern slopes, where the outlines of their cultivation terraces (lynchets) can still be seen.

▶ *West Firle is 3½ miles south-east of Lewes, south of the A27. The road from the village to the Beacon is signposted, and there is a car park at the end.*

⑮ Ditchling Beacon

Wonderful downland surrounds the 248m (813ft) summit of Ditchling Beacon, on the South Downs north of Brighton. There are magical views over the countryside, with the Hog's Back, 31 miles away, visible on a clear day.

A footpath, the South Downs Way, runs westwards along the ridge, passes the ramparts of an Iron Age fort and then skirts a dew-pond, a reminder of the days when sheep were a familiar sight on the South Downs. Dew-ponds, from which the sheep drank, were built by shepherds, who lined a hollow with clay to catch the moisture from the heavy mists sweeping in from the English Channel.

Beyond another dew-pond, the path begins to descend towards the village of Clayton, and the sails of two 19th-century windmills – called Jack and Jill – come into view. Jill is a white post-mill whose entire body could be turned to face the wind. Jack is a brick-built tower-mill with a revolving cap which carries the sails.

▶ *Ditchling Beacon is 6 miles north of Brighton. A minor road from Brighton to Ditchling village crosses the Downs just below the summit. From Brighton in the south there is a long, steady climb; from Ditchling to the north the road snakes upwards with sharp bends and steep inclines. Clayton is on the A273 near the B2112 junction.*

⑯ Chanctonbury and Cissbury Rings

When Celtic warriors strode the South Downs 2,000 years ago, Chanctonbury Ring was a bare hilltop commanded by the low earthen bank and ditch of an Iron Age hill-fort. Today, a graceful grove of trees, mostly beeches, stands tall and slender within the encircling earthworks, and is a well-loved landmark for miles around. The trees were planted in 1760 by Sir Charles Goring while he was still a boy. In the centre of the ring, among the trees, there are traces of the foundations of a Romano-British temple of the 1st century.

The South Downs at Chanctonbury, 238m (779ft) above sea-level, are wide and open, and on a breezy day the noise of the wind is dramatically magnified as it gusts through the branches. There are superb views from the summit. North-west below the hill lies the charming village of Washington, and to the north-east is wooded Wiston Park and its mansion, once the home of Sir Charles Goring and now a conference centre. Far away to the north, the flanks of Leith Hill emerge as a blur.

Cissbury Ring lies just over 2 miles south of Chanctonbury, a far larger Iron Age hill-fort with mile-long double ramparts enclosing some 26ha (65 acres). It is one of the largest and most impressive hill-forts in Britain, with probably 60,000 tonnes of chalk rubble forming its ramparts, which, when originally built about 250 BC, were faced with timber stakes. From the ramparts there are views along the coast to Beachy Head, 30 miles eastwards, and to the south-west, beyond the sheen of The Solent, lies the dark line of the Isle of Wight.

At the south-west end of the fort, within and without the ramparts, bushes now overgrow the dips and furrows that mark the site of flint mines worked by men of the New Stone Age over 4,000 years ago. The many mine-shafts through the flint seams, dug out with antler picks, went as deep as 12m (40ft). Nineteenth-century investigators discovered in one of them the skeleton of a woman who had evidently fallen to her death – or whose body had been thrown down – at a date unknown.

▶ *Chanctonbury and Cissbury rings are 6 miles and 4 miles north of Worthing. Chanctonbury Ring can be reached along a footpath south-east from Washington, just off the A24 – a stiff 1½ mile climb. For Cissbury Ring, a well-marked minor road leads 1½ miles east from Findon village, also just off the A24. There are footpaths up to the fort from the minor road. Both rings are linked by a footpath, and Chanctonbury Ring is also on the South Downs Way.*

⑰ Stane Street

A major Roman road stretching 57 miles between London and Chichester – then called Noviomagus, capital of the Regni tribe – Stane Street once echoed to the tramping feet of Roman legions and the heavy rumbling of ox-carts. Not much of it remains today, but there is one stretch that can still be followed through a picturesque part of the South Downs on the National Trust's Slindon Estate.

The Saxons gave the road the name of Stane – or stone – Street, for the 9m (30ft) wide embankment, bordered by wide ditching, was surfaced with a 60cm (2ft) layer of gravel and flint on top of rammed chalk. Today, the 3½ mile stretch from Eartham Wood north-east to Bignor Hill is a peaceful, tree-lined bridle-path.

Beech trees grow thickly in Eartham Wood, and there are groves of silver birch and sycamore trees where the sun slants through the branches in dusty shafts. Beyond the wood, the road climbs between a line of trees to the 225m (737ft) summit of Bignor Hill to give breathtaking views of the wooded Weald to the north, on a clear day as far as the distant pine-covered slopes of Black Down. At Bignor, below the northern slope, there are remains of one of Britain's largest Roman villas, noted for its fine mosaic floors.

▶ *Eartham and Bignor lie 5 miles and 9 miles respectively north-east of Chichester on minor roads between the A285 and A29. Eartham Wood is about ½ mile north of Eartham village.*

⑱ Beacon Hill

Near its western end, the South Downs Way skirts the southern slopes of Beacon Hill, at 242m (793ft) one of the highest points along the ridge of the South Downs. You can join the long-distance footpath at Harting Downs and follow it eastwards for about a mile before leaving it to reach the summit of the hill.

From the very start of the walk there are exhilarating views of the Weald to the north, with the bright green spire of South Harting Church spiking through the trees just below the ridge. As you climb to the summit of Beacon Hill, the silvery creeks of Chichester Harbour come into view to the south, and the slender finger of Chichester Cathedral's tapering spire probes the skyline. Around the summit of the hill, the rectangular ramparts of an Iron Age hill-fort, over 2,000 years old, are clearly defined.

South-east from Beacon Hill are the Devil's Jumps, a line of six rounded mounds that are Bronze Age bell-barrows – warriors' graves of some 3,500 years ago. One of the central barrows is 5m (16ft) high and 43m (140ft) in diameter, the largest in Britain. To visit them adds another 1½ miles to the walk. From Beacon Hill, you can rejoin the South Downs Way as it dips and climbs eastwards across Pen Hill, then turns south-eastwards towards Buriton Farm.

Here the path is dotted with wild flowers – yellow cowslips in spring, and rough hawkbit, common ragwort and spiky common toadflax continuing the yellow theme into early autumn; small scabious and greater knapweed add a touch of lilac and purple in summer. The path to the barrows is a turning east from the South Downs Way up the slopes of Treyford Hill. They lie beyond a beechwood, half hidden in the scrub.

▶ *Harting Downs, where the South Downs Way crosses the B2141, lie 5 miles south-east of Petersfield. There is a car park and picnic site close to the road.*

⑲ Kingley Vale

Yew woods are rare, but on the slopes of Bow Hill – a southern outlier of the South Downs – stands the finest yew wood in Europe. The hill is appropriately named, for until the reign of Elizabeth I the evergreen yew was protected, as its wood was used for making longbows, the main military weapon of the day. It is said that a yew grove was planted here in AD 859 to commemorate a victorious battle fought by the men of nearby Chichester against marauding Vikings.

Many of the trees at Kingley Vale are at least 500 years old. Today the Vale is a 150ha (370 acre) National Nature Reserve, and a fascinating 1½ mile nature trail among the haunts of blackcaps, common rock-roses and bee orchids, takes in the yew groves. The oldest trees are at the foot of the hill in Kingley Bottom; age has gnarled and twisted their huge trunks, and one or two have bowed branches whose tips have rooted in the ground to form another ring of trees. Younger trees about 90–120 years old – the seeded offspring of the older trees – fan out up the slopes. The dense foliage of these closely growing younger trees blots out sound and most of the light, and in this eerie twilight no other plants can grow. The few birds seen among the branches include robins, blackbirds, great tits and coal tits.

Mixed woods that include oaks, ashes, whitebeams, hawthorns and dogwood also thrive on the chalk soil. On the higher slopes the woods give way to chalk turf where the orchids grow, and the thin clay layer on the summit supports heather in profusion. More than 50 species of birds breed in Kingley Vale, including green woodpeckers and treecreepers. In autumn, flocks of fieldfares and redwings arrive for the winter, and gorge for a month on the red yew berries, scattering the pips and so propagating the trees.

The Devil's Humps – four round Bronze Age burial mounds some 3,000 years old – crown the summit of the hill, two of them half hidden by trees. There are glorious views southwards of the four arms of Chichester Harbour, especially at sunset when the deepening rays turn the waters red.

▶ *Kingley Vale is 4 miles north-west of Chichester. The nature-trail car park is at West Stoke, which is on a minor road north from the B2178 to Funtington.*

⑳ Queen Elizabeth Country Park

At the western end of the South Downs, Butser Hill, 270m (888ft), and War Down stand west and east respectively of a deep valley where the Portsmouth road cuts through. In 1953, the coronation year of Elizabeth II, they were combined to become the 546ha (1,350 acre) Queen Elizabeth Country Park.

The long, curved summit of Butser Hill juts out boldly above a ravine thickly wooded with yew trees. This is fine walking country through some of the most scenic parts of the Downs, with paths radiating in all directions, many of them ancient tracks. On Ramsdean Down to the north, there are three Bronze Age round barrows, and several lynchets – the outlines of Celtic fields. The views stretch eastwards across the Weald and southwards as far as Portsmouth Harbour with the faint outline of the Isle of Wight in the distance.

On War Down the scenery changes from the wide open spaces and springy turf of Butser Hill to groves of beeches, alders and Scots pines in Queen Elizabeth Forest. A waymarked forest walk lasting about an hour and a half leads through sun-splashed glades and leafy avenues, and gives occasional glimpses of Hayling Island, The Solent and the Isle of Wight. There are roe and fallow deer in the forest and the rare Duke of Burgundy fritillary butterfly has been known to breed in the park.

▶ *Queen Elizabeth Country Park is 3 miles south of Petersfield on the A3, with the park centre at Gravel Hill near the south end of the forest. There are several car parks. The forest walk starts at Buriton, 1 mile east of the A3. At the southern end of the park, a minor road west from the A3 leads to Butser Hill.*

SOUTHERN ENGLAND

THE LINCOLNSHIRE
WOLDS and MARSHES
118-122

NORFOLK and the
CAMBRIDGE FENS
123-129

THE SUFFOLK
COAST and
HEATHLANDS 132-135

Scunthorpe
Grimsby
Market Rasen
Louth
Alford
Lincoln
North Hykeham
Horncastle
Skegness
Boston
Grantham
Spalding
Stamford
Peterborough
Wisbech
Chatteris
Ely
Huntingdon
St Neots
Cambridge
Newmarket
Hunstanton
Wells-next-the-Sea
King's Lynn
Swaffham
Norwich
North Walsham
Great Yarmouth
Lowestoft
Brandon
Thetford
Diss
Halesworth
Southwold
Bury St Edmunds
Stowmarket
Woodbridge
Ipswich
Felixstowe
Sudbury
Colchester

Eastern England

From the misty vales of Suffolk's Constable country
to the shifting salt-marshes of the Lincolnshire
coast and from the watery fens of Cambridgeshire
to the reed-fringed broads of Norfolk, the landscape
of Eastern England is surprisingly rich and varied.

The LINCOLNSHIRE WOLDS and MARSHES

The tranquil Lincolnshire Wolds shelter wide pastures and rippling cornfields. These chalk-tipped hills slope gently down towards the North Sea where dunes and salt marshes are rich in wildlife.

❶ Tetney Haven

Sea-birds wheel and cry above the lonely expanse of mud-flats and salt-marsh, bright with sea asters in summer, that surrounds Tetney Haven on the North Sea coast. Silent oil tankers wait to discharge at the deep-water monobuoy, or pass upriver to Immingham, and Grimsby trawlers pass by in the estuary beyond the Haile Sand Fort – a remnant of First World War defences.

Once, the haven sheltered ships that were waiting for the tide to carry them through the narrow channel leading to the Louth Navigation, a canal extension of the River Lud by which ships of up to 30 tonnes could go 12 miles inland south-west to the Riverhead warehouses at Louth. They brought in coal and timber and took out wool and corn. Opened in 1770, the canal thrived until the East Coast railway arrived in 1848. It was disused by 1915, and was closed in 1924. Now it is a land drain. The old lock gates have gone and new sluice gates have been built nearer the sea. It also serves as a collector to feed the 88ha (218 acre) Covenham Reservoir, Lincolnshire's largest lake.

The steep banks of the canal cutting keep the water strangely calm, disturbed only by the floats of the lone anglers strung along the canal side, fishing for pike and perch. From the bridge at Tetney Lock hamlet, 1½ miles south-west of Tetney Haven, a path follows the canal on its southern side for the last mile or so seawards.

Tetney Marshes is a nature reserve managed by the Royal Society for the Protection of Birds, found on the foreshore and saltings near Tetney Haven. Little terns nest there in summer, while later in the year many waders and flocks of brent geese winter there. It is unwise to wander on to the saltings, for it is dangerous underfoot, with deep channels hidden by undergrowth. Access to the reserve is restricted but it can be viewed from paths along the edge and from the car parks at Humberston Fitties and Horse Shoe Point.

▶ *Tetney Lock is 5 miles south-east of Cleethorpes, and reached by a minor road off the A1031 at Tetney.*

❷ Nettleton Beck

Rising in the Wolds to the south-east of Nettleton village, the Nettleton Beck winds its way down to the foot of the Wolds, and on to the Ancholme valley. Its lower reaches are bordered in summer by breeze-rippled wheatfields fringed with poppies. A grassy footpath – part of the Viking Way – starts from a point half a mile south-east of the village and follows beside the beck to its source about 2 miles upstream.

Near the start of the beckside path, a public bridleway climbs to the east through a cattle meadow, and from the barn on its slope there is a good view of the valley below. Nettleton Hill – known locally as Nettleton Bump because of its modest height (114m (374ft)) – rises above the west side of the valley; and to the north are the red and grey rooftops of the small market town of Caistor, a mile away.

Return from the bridleway to the beckside path, which ascends gradually upstream beside the beck, passing the scars of old mine workings that, until they became uneconomic in 1969, produced Claxby ironstone, named after a village to the south. As you leave the valley and breast the brow of the hill 2 miles from the start of the path, a short distance ahead, some of the most spectacular views in Lincolnshire stretch across the valley to the north-west, where the Ancholme river flows on its way to the Humber.

After it leaves the valley, the path dips and rises to reach the road that runs from Nettleton to Normanby le Wold almost opposite Acre House. The hamlet of Normanby, between 140–150m (450–500ft) above sea-level, is just below the highest part of the Wolds. It stands on a very steep slope, and from here the plain below is dramatically revealed.

▶ *Nettleton is on the A46, 1 mile south-west of Caistor. To reach Nettleton Beck footpath, take the Normanby road south from the village, and just before the end of the village, turn south-east on to the lane marked by a Viking Way sign. The beck is ¼ mile along this lane.*

❸ Saltfleetby and Theddlethorpe Dunes

Stretching for nearly 5 miles along the seashore, the Saltfleetby-Theddlethorpe Dunes National Nature Reserve is shielded on its landward side by a scrub of sea buckthorn, interspersed with elder, blackthorn, hawthorn, dog rose and some willow. There are sandy paths to the foreshore but do not attempt the walk to the sea at low tide – when the tide turns it comes in fast, and sandbanks soon become islands cut off from the shore.

This is a good place to observe how the eastern coastline is gradually creeping seawards, with marram-clad dunes trapping wind-blown sand. The mature salt-marsh on the foreshore gradually fades to patches of glasswort, or samphire, towards the sea. Dewberry is abundant on the older dunes, which are some 700 years old and the highest on the Lincolnshire coast. Apart from the many common brown or blue grassland butterflies that are abundant in summer, you may occasionally see a dark green fritillary.

Swallows wheel above the scrub and swoop over the saltings; skylarks, linnets, yellowhammers, white throats and dunnocks nest in the dense scrub or long grass; and reed buntings and a few sedge warblers favour freshwater marshes. Britain's rarest toad, the natterjack, also breeds among the sandbanks, and grey and common seals may sometimes be seen at low tide.

Part of the reserve lies within RAF firing ranges. Do not enter areas marked by red flags or danger signs. Safety regulations are on display.

▶ *The dunes lie to the east of the A1031 between Saltfleet Haven and Theddlethorpe St Helen. There are seven car parks around the edge of the reserve.*

❹ The River Bain

Attractive but elusive, the River Bain flows for 20 miles or so below the western edge of the Wolds, dawdling southwards through meadows and fields, and the occasional wood, to meet the River Witham just south of Tattershall. Rising in the Wolds west of Ludford, the river is cradled by hills as far as Donington on Bain.

The banks of the Bain are not easily accessible, except at Donington where there is a picturesque, old water-mill by the weir. From here you can walk along part of the Viking Way through farm and parkland and the sites of lost villages, following the river upstream for part of the way. The Viking Way is a way-marked long-distance footpath between Oakham, in Leicestershire, and the Humber Bridge, and it runs for some 40 miles through the Wolds.

Biscathorpe House, an early Victorian mansion, stands about a mile north of Donington amid parkland that sweeps down to the Bain. North of the A157 are the grounds of Girsby Manor – known locally as the Grange, the house is no more than a ruin. Beyond Girsby the river winds to Wykeham Hall and the sites of the lost villages of East and West Wykeham.

To follow the Viking Way through lovely country between Donington on Bain and Girsby Top above Wykeham Hall, a walk of about 5 miles, turn into Welsdale Lane by Donington Mill, just north of the village. A horned-helmet sign marks the route across fields and beside Biscathorpe House, across a minor road and the River Bain, and eventually on to a minor road which joins the A157. Across the A157, the Way follows a wide track between cornfields that turns west towards Wykeham Hall and then south and west to Girsby Top.

▶ *Donington on Bain lies on a signposted minor road 6 miles west of Louth.*

GREY SEALS NEAR SALTFLEETBY

❺ Red Hill

A brick-red gash in the hillside marks the site of a disused chalk quarry on the steep side of Red Hill, now a nature reserve. Like a large cutaway model from a geological museum, the scar reveals the rocks that form the Wolds. A band of rust-coloured sandstone, called carstone, is topped by a thick layer of red chalk, which lies below a layer of white chalk. Red chalk, its colour resulting from the presence of iron, stretches roughly from South Yorkshire to North Norfolk, underlying the Wolds.

Hawthorn bushes line the top of the scar and cluster at its foot. A worn pathway descends beside it, but it is now dangerous to climb the rock face. There is a car park at the top of the steep hill, and from it you can walk across downland to the grassed-over workings behind the scar. Tread carefully in the long grass, however, for this is one of the few places in the Wolds where the meadow pipit breeds, making its nest in grass tussocks.

Because of its steepness, the hillside has never been used for farming, like the gentler slopes near by, so has been undisturbed perhaps for centuries. The result is a profusion of wild flowers: autumn gentians, yellow-wort, felwort, kidney vetch, common rock-rose and the purple-flowered pyramidal orchid.

From the summit of Red Hill, which is on the steeper western edge of the Wolds, the view of the valley below is, on a clear day, like looking at the landscape from an aircraft − remote, tranquil and astonishing in its clarity and extent.
▶ *Red Hill is 2½ miles south-east of Donington on Bain, east of the road from Donington to the A153. Follow this road to Manor Farm, then turn north-east − the quarry can be clearly seen from the road. The road from Donington passes another Red Hill which lies 1½ miles north-west of the nature reserve and is topped by radar dishes.*

❻ The Bluestone Heath Road

Sweeping along the crest of the Wolds, the Bluestone Heath Road winds for 14 miles between cornfields and woods that dip away on either side. There are no villages along the road, only wide verges, low hawthorn hedges and occasional lines of trees. To the west, there are magnificent panoramas of Lincoln Heath.

The downland turf verges that line the road are reminders that once much of the Wolds was rolling grassland that supported thousands of sheep. Today, modern farming methods and fertilisers have turned most of the slopes from pasture to plough.

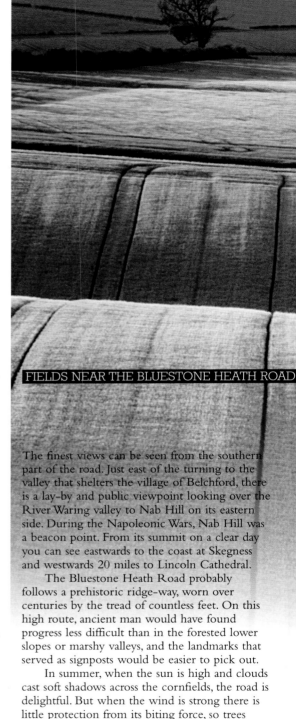

FIELDS NEAR THE BLUESTONE HEATH ROAD

The finest views can be seen from the southern part of the road. Just east of the turning to the valley that shelters the village of Belchford, there is a lay-by and public viewpoint looking over the River Waring valley to Nab Hill on its eastern side. During the Napoleonic Wars, Nab Hill was a beacon point. From its summit on a clear day you can see eastwards to the coast at Skegness and westwards 20 miles to Lincoln Cathedral.

The Bluestone Heath Road probably follows a prehistoric ridge-way, worn over centuries by the tread of countless feet. On this high route, ancient man would have found progress less difficult than in the forested lower slopes or marshy valleys, and the landmarks that served as signposts would be easier to pick out.

In summer, when the sun is high and clouds cast soft shadows across the cornfields, the road is delightful. But when the wind is strong there is little protection from its biting force, so trees have been planted on more exposed parts.
▶ *The northern section of the Bluestone Heath Road joins the A157 about 5 miles west of Louth. The southern section joins the A16 east of Calceby.*

A Norman doorway from Calceby Church is now incorporated in the south aisle of the church at South Ormsby village, tucked away in tree-shaded surroundings a mile westwards. Calceby and South Ormsby lie in a lovely, little-known area of secluded villages and wooded parkland. Southwards from Calceby, a field footpath leads to the cul-de-sac hamlet of Driby, and onwards to the south-west there is a bridle-path to Brinkhill.

Northwards from South Ormsby, the wooded parklands of Ormsby Hall (not open to the public) border the west side of the road. The Great Eau (from the Old English *ea*, 'a stream'), which rises high in the Wolds beyond, powered the old water-mill at Ketsby further north. It stands just off the minor road, its water-wheel still in position.

▶ *All the villages can be reached along minor roads that lead south from the A16 between Burwell and Ulceby Cross.*

❽ Somersby

Narrow, leafy lanes, cool even in strong sunshine, approach the village of Somersby, which lies at the foot of Warden Hill. South-east from the village, a lane winds between tall trees to Bag Enderby and Harrington.

Peaceful and pastoral, this countryside was the boyhood haunt of the poet Alfred, Lord Tennyson, the 'silent woody places' he mentions in his poem 'Maud'. His father was the rector of Somersby and Bag Enderby, and the poet was born in 1809 in Somersby rectory (now Somersby House, not open to the public).

At Bag Enderby, a side lane loops off the main way, passing the greenstone 'Tennyson Church' (the 15th-century St Margaret's) where services in memory of the poet are still held every other year in alternation with St Margaret's in Somersby. Oaks, beeches and other tall trees stand protectively over the sleepy cottages.

The straggling hamlet of Harrington is about a mile east of Bag Enderby. At its western end you pass a neat and whitewashed thatched cottage backed by conifers, with a delightful garden. The manor house of Harrington Hall, built mainly in the reign of Charles II but partly Elizabethan, is at the east end of the hamlet: its gardens are open to the public in summer. The young Tennyson was often a visitor here and it is said that he was inspired to write the poem which opens with the line 'Come into the garden, Maud' while on the terrace overlooking the front gardens.

▶ *Somersby is 6 miles east of Horncastle, and can be reached along minor roads north off the A158.*

❼ Calceby

Near the south end of the Bluestone Heath Road, an ivy-covered chalk-stone ruin on a hilly outcrop springs dramatically into view. This is all that remains of the parish church of Calceby, a lost village of the Wolds.

Turn into the road leading north to the A16; from the field gate opposite a red-brick Georgian farmhouse the mounds that mark the village site can be clearly seen. As the '-*by*' in its name indicates, Calceby was probably founded by Danish settlers, some time during the 9th or 10th centuries. In medieval times, it was a busy community. According to the Domesday Book, it received income, with four other villages, from salt-pan holdings on the coast.

Why the village was deserted remains uncertain. The community survived for some 200 years after the Black Death. There were still 18 families living there in 1563, but with the death of the last vicar in 1621 the village dwindled to the present farmhouse and a handful of scattered cottages.

EASTERN ENGLAND

⑨ Snipe Dales

Stony streams chatter among the steep-sided grassy valleys of Snipe Dales, a 48ha (120 acre) nature reserve in the southern Wolds. In the damp valley bottoms, below the spring line where the sandstone slopes meet the clay below, marsh marigolds glow yellow among green ferns in spring and early summer, and later meadowsweet and ragged robin stand tall above the grasses. Long-billed snipe are now a rare sight and may come out mainly at dusk to probe in the mud for food, but herons, kestrels and short-eared owls live here too.

Once, the Snipe Dales area was more wooded. Oak and ash grew on the slopes where today bluebells and primroses still flower in spring. The valleys were thick with willow and alder, as names such as Isaac's Holt — meaning Isaac's wood or copse — recall. Woodland is to be restored to the Dales by the Lincolnshire Wildlife Trust. Oak, ash and beech will be planted on the slopes, and alder carr — a name of Scandinavian origin meaning 'fen woods' — in the valleys.

Little now disturbs the peace of Snipe Dales, but on an autumn day 300 years ago, its valleys were jarred by the rattle of muskets, the clash of steel and the chant of psalms, for Slash Hollow, just to the west where the main roads converge, was a scene of conflict in the Civil War.

Here at the Battle of Winceby on October 11, 1643, Parliament troops led by Sir Thomas Fairfax and Colonel Oliver Cromwell lined up against a Royalist force under the Marquis of Newcastle, on its way to relieve the garrison at Old Bolingbroke Castle 3 miles south-east. The Royalists were routed, and afterwards the castle, once owned by John of Gaunt, was destroyed; only grassy mounds remain.

▶ *Snipe Dales is 4½ miles east of Horncastle, north of the B1195 Spilsby road. There are car parks, with picnic sites, in Winceby and at the Country Park entrance 1 mile to the east.*

⑩ Gibraltar Point

Where the North Sea coast turns inwards to form the north side of the 12 mile wide mouth of The Wash, Gibraltar Point looks out across some of the most extensive salt-marshes in Europe. A lonely but peaceful spot, steeped in the salty tang of the sea air and lulled by the constant lap of the tides, it is the southernmost tip of a 430ha (1,062 acre) nature reserve rich in a variety of wildlife and managed by the Lincolnshire Wildlife Trust.

Gibraltar Point in spring resounds with the warbling songs of skylarks and, in summer, little terns and ringed plovers nest on the shingle. In autumn, vast flocks of waders — oystercatchers, knots, dunlins and godwits — visit the reserve on passage or to spend the winter. As the tide comes in, they rise in their thousands to seek higher ground. Common and grey seals bask on the sandbanks about a mile offshore, and in summer, seal pups are often born there, ready to swim off with their mothers at high tide.

Sharp-spined sea buckthorn grows on the East Dunes, its bright orange berries providing autumn and winter food for migrant birds, especially large flocks of fieldfares. Small birds such as yellowhammers and whitethroats nest in the buckthorn and elder scrub, and the older dunes in summer are bright with flowers such as cowslips and lady's bedstraw, or the deep blue of tall viper's bugloss. From Mill Hill, the sand-dune that is the highest part of the reserve, you can see north-west to the Wolds, and south on a clear day across The Wash to the Hunstanton cliffs on the Norfolk coast.

In the new salt-marsh, covered by the sea at high tide, are marsh samphire, rice grass, sea blite, sea aster, sea purslane and sea meadow-grass — all plants that can survive long periods in sea water. The older salt-marsh is covered with a lilac carpet of sea lavender in summer, and reed buntings nest among the sea couch grass.

Freshwater marshes as well as salt-marshes lie within the reserve, and there is a public hide for watching birds that visit the freshwater Mere, half a mile north of the Visitor Centre. From the hide you may see waders and ducks, as well as grey herons and perhaps kingfishers.

▶ *Gibraltar Point lies 3 miles south of Skegness along an unclassified road.*

STEEPED IN THE SALTY TANG OF THE SEA
GIBRALTAR POINT

NORFOLK and the CAMBRIDGE FENS

Some of the finest beauty spots in East Anglia are found where land and water meet. Broads and fens thread through the countryside while shimmering expanses of sand and shingle line the coast.

❶ Sandringham Country Park

The best time to visit Sandringham Country Park is in early summer, when woods and roadsides are swamped with the rich purples, blues and crimsons of rhododendrons in bloom. They pile up in great masses of colour among the pines, cedars and silver birches, almost overpowering in their splendour and compelling the eye at every turn of the road. There are footpaths through the woods, dipping into steep-banked glens where the rhododendrons cluster 6m (20ft) above and brightly coloured jays swoop among the tree-tops.

Sandringham Country Park is part of the 2,800ha (7,000 acre) Sandringham estate, bought by Edward VII when he was Prince of Wales, and since then a favourite royal retreat. From the large, red-brick house and its grounds the estate spreads westwards in a green apron of well-kept woodland and trim lawns. The Country Park lies east of the A149, an area of natural woodland and heath which few places can surpass in loveliness.

To the west of the Park lies the village of Wolferton. Its Edwardian railway station was once used by the royal family on their visits to Sandringham. About 2 miles south of the Park is Castle Rising. It was a port on the Babingley river until the 15th century, when ships became too large to navigate the river. Later, the river silted up and the sea retreated. As a result, the trade went to King's Lynn.

The village is dominated by the Norman castle (maintained by English Heritage), built in 1150 by William de Albini. According to legend, the ghostly screams of Queen Isabella echo through the keep where she was banished by her son, Edward III, after her part in the murder of her husband, Edward II. Beyond Wolferton and Castle Rising, reclaimed marshes stretch to the shores of The Wash.

▶ *Sandringham Country Park is 6 miles north-east of King's Lynn, to the east of the A149.*

❷ Scolt Head Island

Only a narrow tidal creek separates this wild and lonely island from the Norfolk mainland, a creek that winds among salt-marshes where countless tiny channels spread like veins across the desolate mud-flats. The island stretches for 3½ miles from Brancaster Harbour to Burnham Harbour, its sand-dunes, shingle banks, marshes and salt-marshes forming an isolated segment typical of the whole North Norfolk coastline.

Owned jointly by the National Trust and the Norfolk Wildlife Trust, the island is managed by Natural England whose aim is to ensure that natural development continues with the least possible human interference. Visitors to the island are invited to use a nature trail about three-quarters of a mile long, which takes in some of the most interesting and scenic areas, and gives an opportunity to see the rich variety of plant and wildlife. Boats to the island leave from Burnham Overy Staithe an hour or two before and after high water.

Near the island landing point is the ternery, where 1.5ha (4 acres) of shingle and sand are a breeding ground for common terns and Sandwich terns. Further along the trail, marshland vegetation includes sea asters, sea lavender and sea pinks, bright with flowers in summer. Waders such as oystercatchers, ringed plovers and redshanks can all be seen. There are many shelduck, recognised by their chestnut belts, which often nest in deserted rabbit burrows. The many moths and butterflies include the hummingbird hawk moth, and the sand dart and rosy minor moths.

▶ *Burnham Overy Staithe is on the A149, 5 miles west of Wells-next-the-Sea.*

EASTERN ENGLAND

❸ Holkham Gap

A vast, sweeping cove with a beach so flat it looks as though it has been rolled; grassy dunes of soft sand; pine trees growing almost to the water's edge – yes, this is Norfolk, despite the Mediterranean flavour.

Holkham Gap is as beautiful and unspoiled as anywhere on the Norfolk coast, but its uncharacteristic scenery is not the work of nature alone. About 100 years ago, Corsican pines were planted to stabilise the sand, and since 1967 it has been part of a National Nature Reserve managed by Natural England.

The reserve stretches for about 10 miles along the coast, except for a narrow strip at Wells. It is mainly dunes and salt-marshes, some reclaimed for agriculture, but at Holkham there is a driveway from the A149, Lady Ann's Drive, which leads to a point near the beach where a short walk brings the panorama of the cove into view.

At the seaward end of the drive there are evergreen holm oaks, introduced from the Mediterranean, and a few maritime and Monterey pines. In places the pines form a canopy, blotting out the light, and there are large numbers of fungi. Beneath some of the pines grow creeping lady's tresses – rare plants in the southern half of Britain.

Marram grass and sand sedge are common on the dunes, and there are also flowering plants such as common ragwort with its yellow, daisy-like flowers, sea bindweed, creeping thistle and sea holly.

Britain's smallest bird, the minute goldcrest, nests among the pines. These trees are also a home to most species of tits, particularly coal tits, blue tits and great tits. Colourful green woodpeckers and occasionally crossbills may also be seen.

▶ *Holkham lies on the A149, 1½ miles west of Wells-next-the-Sea.*

GRASSY DUNES
OF SOFT SAND
DUNES AT HOLKHAM GAP

❹ Blakeney Point

A vast spit of shingle and sand, Blakeney Point embraces the villages of Blakeney and Morston. Whether shimmering under blue skies or lying dully beneath lead-grey clouds, it has a compelling beauty.

Blakeney Point's 'spine' is a ridge of shingle running along its entire length on the seaward side. On the landward side there are sand-dunes, salt-marshes and mud-flats. Seals may be seen basking on the sandbanks, and there is also plenty of vegetation and other wildlife.

Marram grass and red fescue grass are common on the dunes, along with such flowering plants as sea bindweed, ragwort, scarlet pimpernel and yellow stonecrop. Two sea lavenders grow on the salt-marshes – common sea lavender and lax-flowered sea lavender. Sea asters are also common; their lilac outer petals soon fall, leaving the bright yellow centre.

Because of its extreme northern position on the Norfolk coast, Blakeney makes a good landfall for migrating birds, particularly in autumn. Visitors include warblers, wheatears, whinchats, pied flycatchers and rarer migrants such as bluethroats and wrynecks. Perhaps the most delightful visitors are the Sandwich, common, Arctic and little terns, distinguished from the black-headed gulls by their forked tails and long, swept-back wings that give them the appropriate alternative name of sea swallow.

About 580ha (1,435 acres) of Blakeney Point are managed as a nature reserve by the National Trust. Part of the reserve can be reached on foot by following the shoreline westwards from Cley Beach Road car park.

▶ *Blakeney lies on the A149, 7 miles east of Wells-next-the-Sea.*

❺ Cley next the Sea

Just over half a mile of marshland now lies between Cley (pronounced 'Cly') and the sea, so 'Cley not far from the sea' might be a better name. A busy port in medieval times, the harbour was destroyed when marsh reclamation began in the 17th century, and meadows now lie where ships once rode at anchor. But the magnificent 14th and 15th-century church and the narrow streets of flint houses still give the place something of a medieval air.

In 1926 some of the reclaimed marshes were established as one of Britain's first nature reserves. Now managed by the Norfolk Wildlife Trust, the reserve has a number of trails and hides. From the road edging the marshes, there are views across the broad, flat landscape criss-crossed by dykes and dotted with pools and shallows. To the west the River Glaven bends sharply westwards to flow into the channels north of Blakeney.

Cattle graze on the marshes in summer, but mostly they are the home of wildfowl and sea-birds. Many rare migrant birds appear each year, and bitterns, marsh harriers and avocets breed here. At Salthouse, 2 miles east of Cley, a wide ditch runs close to the roadside, and several species of wildfowl can be seen, including greylag and Canada geese, tufted ducks, coots, mallards and shelduck.

The marshland road at Cley, and another at Salthouse, leads to the shingle beach from where there are good views across the marshes and along the unbroken shoreline.

▶ *Cley and Salthouse are on the A149 Cromer-Wells-next-the-Sea road.*

❻ Pretty Corner

Nowhere in Norfolk is there a place more aptly named, and nowhere a place that so thoroughly dispels the widely held notion that Norfolk is flat and featureless. Just over a mile from the beaches of Cromer and Sheringham, the land rises to a ridge running parallel to the coast, reaching over 30m (300ft) in places.

The ridge is thickly wooded with birch, beech, ash, rowan, pine and fir trees, below which is a tangled undergrowth of brambles and rhododendrons. At Pretty Corner car park, signposted from the A148 that runs along the ridge, there are several paths leading into the woods. The scenery changes in character every few metres. From glades of gnarled beeches the ground may drop steeply among tall pines into a sunless dell. Jays swoop among the trees, tits and finches flit among the lower branches, and grey squirrels scurry across the paths.

About a quarter of a mile west of the car park, on the A1082 out of Sheringham, a rough track that can be used by cars leads up into the woods. Side-roads branch off the track and make it possible to drive a considerable distance in all directions among the trees. Along the side-roads are vantage points that give magnificent views across the ridge and out to the North Sea.

About 2 miles east of Pretty Corner car park, a north turn off the A148 signposted 'West Runton' leads to the Roman Camp, another thickly wooded area from which there are splendid walks westwards over Beacon Hill and down to Row Heath and Beeston Regis Heath. The Roman Camp, owned by the National Trust, is the highest point in Norfolk.

▶ *Pretty Corner is 1½ miles south of Sheringham, to the east of the A1082 at its junction with the A148.*

EASTERN ENGLAND

❼ Felbrigg Great Wood

Mostly natural woodland of sycamores, old beeches, sweet chestnuts, oaks, birches and rowan, Felbrigg Great Wood is part of a belt of trees that extends along the Cromer Ridge. It is believed that there have been beechwoods on the site since the end of the last Ice Age, and that some of the ground has never been cultivated.

The wood adjoins Felbrigg Hall, owned by the National Trust. The estate dates back to Norman times, and was owned by the Windham, or Wymondham, family from the 15th century until 1969. The present house was built between 1616 and 1627. William Windham I, who inherited the estate in 1665, extended the house and founded the Great Wood that shelters it from the North Sea, planting new trees to unify existing scattered woods into the 200ha (500 acre) wood. His great-grandson, William Windham III, was an outstanding 18th-century politician who was Secretary at War in William Pitt's government from 1794 until 1801.

A waymarked walk of about a mile takes in much of the Great Wood, and includes a plantation of Douglas firs, Scots pines and Norway spruce, and also a strip of heathland where silver birches and young beeches have been planted along the edge. Stoats may be glimpsed in the undergrowth of brambles and bracken. Great spotted woodpeckers, redstarts and nuthatches are also likely to be seen.

The lake, in another part of the grounds, is the home of herons, Canada geese, swans, coots and mallard, and there is a lakeside walk. The lake is fed by small streams spanned by three iron bridges, made by a blacksmith whose smithy and cottage are close by.

▶ *Felbrigg Great Wood is 2 miles south-west of Cromer off the A148. From this road, branch south-east on to the B1436. After ½ mile, a signposted west turn leads to Felbrigg Hall. The estate grounds are open from dawn to dusk all year.*

❽ Bacton Wood

A short way south of the coastal village of Bacton stand the ruins of the 12th-century priory of Broomholm. Today deserted and forgotten, in medieval times it was a popular place of pilgrimage, for one of its relics was believed to be a piece of the true cross. In Chaucer's *Canterbury Tales*, the Reeve tells how the startled miller's wife screamed 'Holy cross of Bromeholme keep Us!'

The ruins stand within sight of the sea beside the B1159 road. South-west along the same road, barely 3 miles inland, lies Bacton

Wood, tucked away in a pocket of land that dips into a shallow valley. Part of the Forestry Commission's scattered Wensum Forest, it is also known locally as Witton Wood. Some 30 kinds of trees grow here – old-established species such as sweet chestnut and birch, and others from Japan, northern Europe, Corsica and the north-west coast of America. The imported trees have replaced those felled during the Second World War, so that Bacton Wood is a relatively young forest, although the area was probably wooded in Saxon times.

From the small car park in a dell on the eastern edge of the woods, there is a 1½ mile trail that leads first along a ridge and then into a valley. Rosebay willow-herb, gorse and young birch trees border the trail as it runs along the ridge, softly contrasting with the dark background of closely set conifers, which blot out the light on even the sunniest day.

The scene changes on the valley slopes, splashed with many shades of green – the deep green of Scots pines, the light green of larches, the bronze-green of western red cedars and the blue-green of grand firs. Goldcrests and, in summer, warblers can be found in the larch woods, and blue tits are seen everywhere.

▶ *Bacton, or Witton, Wood lies about 2½ miles east of North Walsham on the minor road running from Honing to Edingthorpe.*

HIDDEN
BEHIND TREES
AND REED-BEDS

HICKLING BROAD

9 Hickling Broad

A small sign at the Hickling Heath crossroads reads 'To the Broad' – a modest introduction to the largest and least spoiled of Norfolk's unique waterways. Indeed, this vast expanse of water can easily be missed by the motorist following the sign, for it is hidden behind trees and reed-beds, and comes into view only briefly at Hickling Staithe, where craft are moored at the quay by the Pleasure Boat Inn.

Like most of the broads, Hickling can be fully appreciated only from the water. Boats can be hired at the nearby boatyard, and the Norfolk Wildlife Trust operates water-trail boat trips daily in peak season.

The whole of Hickling Broad is part of a 600ha (1,400 acre) National Nature Reserve maintained by the Norfolk Wildlife Trust, and there are wader pools where birds such as spotted redshanks, black terns and sometimes spoonbills can be seen. Among the reeds there are reed and sedge warblers, reed buntings and bearded reedlings – also known as reed pheasants. The broad is also a home of Britain's largest butterfly and a broadland speciality, the swallowtail, with an 8cm (3in) wingspan.

▶ *Hickling Broad, 11 miles north-west of Great Yarmouth, is best approached by the A149. Follow the signposted road 1 mile north of Potter Heigham.*

10 Ranworth Broad

Between Wroxham and Thurne, the River Bure winds a serpentine course through the heart of the Broads. Some, such as Hoveton Great Broad, have nature trails that can be reached only by boat. At Ranworth is the Broadland Conservation Centre, founded in 1976 and now run by the Norfolk Wildlife Trust.

Ranworth Broad nature trail leads through woodland before crossing the marshes. The trail here is over duck-boards that span the black, almost liquid mud, said to be 9m (30ft) deep beneath a covering of bog mosses and marsh plants. Later the scene changes to reed-beds; the trail ends at near the Conservation Centre.

A permanent exhibition on the ground floor illustrates the natural life of the broads. Many kinds of birds can be seen from the viewing gallery. Diving ducks, common terns, coots and black-headed gulls can come quite close, and often a grey heron lands among the reeds near by. The elegant great crested grebe can be seen as it dives for food, and there is always a chance of seeing a rare migrant such as an osprey.

▶ *Ranworth is 9 miles north-east of Norwich and lies along a signposted road from the B1140 at South Walsham. The entrance to the Conservation Centre is along a lane leading north past the church; cars must be parked in the car park opposite the staithe, or quay.*

⑪ Wicken Fen

Wild and lonely Wicken Fen is one of the few areas of undrained fenland left in Britain – just over one square mile of the treacherous marshland that once covered some 15,000 sq miles of East Anglia. The Romans were the first to try draining the fens, but it was a Dutch engineer, Vermuyden, who devised a workable drainage scheme in the 17th century. Employed by the 4th Earl of Bedford, Vermuyden dug the Old Bedford River and the New Bedford River, and made a large area of fenland fit for pasture. In the 18th century the landscape was dotted with windmills driving huge pumps, but in time they gave way to the steam-engine, then to today's diesel and electric pumps.

One windmill is still at work in Wicken Fen. Today, however, it is pumping not to drain the fen but to bring water in to keep it a wetland, for the fen is now a nature reserve maintained by the National Trust.

Before the fen became a reserve, it was strip-farmed for sedge and peat by local villagers; they used the sedge for thatching, kindling and animal litter, and the peat for fuel. When this work was

WICKEN FEN

abandoned and the surrounding water-level had fallen, scrub began to choke the sedge-beds. Now that much of it has been cleared and the water-level raised, the fen is once again rich in sedge, and supports many kinds of plant and animal life.

Footpaths across the fen start from the National Trust building near to Wicken Lode, one of the old man-made waterways that controlled water-levels and were used as barge roads to fen villages. A walk of about 2 miles gives an opportunity to see many different birds, plants and butterflies.

The Wildfowl and Wetlands Trust has a Wetland Centre at Welney on the Ouse Washes, a strip of land between the canals known as the Old and New Bedford rivers; waders, ducks, swans and geese can be watched from here. The Royal Society for the Protection of Birds also has a reserve on the Ouse Washes at Welches Dam on the Old Bedford River.

▶ *Wicken Fen is 9 miles north-east of Cambridge, signposted from Wicken village on the A1123. The Welney Wetland Centre is 4 miles north of Littleport on the A1101. The Ouse Washes RSPB reserve is 5 miles east of Chatteris and signposted on a minor road south of the village of Manea on the B1093.*

⑫ East Wretham Heath

On the eastern edge of Thetford Forest, the regimented rows of pine trees give way to natural woodland, scrub and heath. This is the true Breckland – wild, desolate and mysterious, its reed-fringed meres sometimes gleaming pools, sometimes only dry hollows in the turf.

Wildfowl make their home on the meres. Tufted ducks may be seen feeding in pairs or performing a graceful water ballet as they dive and surface again in perfect rhythm. They are often accompanied by pochards; the drakes can be recognised by their chestnut-red heads. Waders visit the meres from time to time.

Several meres are within nature reserves. Ring Mere is on the west side of the A1075 between Thetford and East Wretham and a rough track across the heath a quarter of a mile north passes 137m (150yd) south of Lang Mere, lying in a shallow bowl of emerald-green turf and rimmed with heather and clumps of hawthorn.

In spring and summer the short Breckland turf is flecked with flowers such as yellow and blue forget-me-nots, speedwell and thyme. Many Breckland wild flowers are rare in other parts of Britain, and some, like Spanish catchfly and field wormwood, grow only in this area.

▶ *East Wretham Heath is 4 miles north-east of Thetford on the A1075. Visitors to the nature reserve can park near the Warden's Office.*

⑬ Santon Downham

In 1668 wind-blown sand from the surrounding Breckland wastes swept through the village of Santon Downham, swamping houses and temporarily blocking the Little Ouse river. John Evelyn, the diarist, who visited the area nine years later, described the event as: 'Travelling sands, about ten miles wide and like the sands in the deserts of Libya.'

Today tree roots anchor the light sandy soil, and Santon Downham stands at the heart of Thetford Forest. A pleasant, varied forest trail leads from the Forestry Commission Information Centre, where there is a large car park. Much of the forest is coniferous, with Scots and Corsican pines and Douglas firs planted for commercial use, but there are also oaks, sycamores, beeches, birches, and at one point an avenue of 100-year-old limes. Roe deer live in the forest, shy creatures that stay in the dense undergrowth of snowberry unless disturbed.

If riverside walks are to your liking, there are few to compare with a gentle stroll downstream along the banks of the Little Ouse. It flows through a shallow valley, and steps lead down to the riverside from the far side of the road bridge about 180m (200yd) from the car park. Alders, birches and willows fringe this peaceful stream, which here forms the boundary between Suffolk and Norfolk. The river is crystal clear, with long, trailing weeds on the riverbed combed out like tresses by the slow-moving waters. Swallows skim over the river to scoop up gnats and midges.

A white-painted footbridge, arching across the river like a bow, adds a picturesque element to the scene. It leads to a footpath on the south bank that links up with the forest trail, which can then be followed back to the car park. There is also a car park and picnic site, St Helen's, on the north bank only a short distance from the river and footbridge. Go north-east out of the village, cross the road bridge and after 270m (300yd) turn right just before the level-crossing. St Helen's car park is about three-quarters of a mile along this road.

▶ *Santon Downham lies 4 miles north-west of Thetford. It can be reached by three unclassified roads, one from the A134 Thetford to Mundford road, 3 miles south-east of Mundford, and the other two from the B1107 Thetford to Brandon road, 1 mile and 2½ miles east of Brandon.*

EASTERN ENGLAND

Bending the coast

England's eastern shores are undergoing a transformation – sea levels are rising while the coast is sinking – and new ways of managing sea defences are having a profound effect.

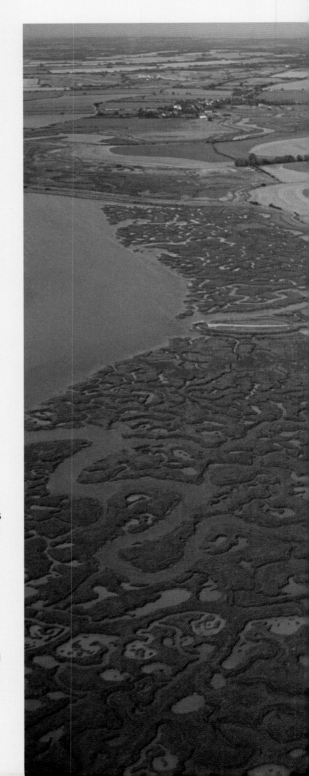

The sinking effect experienced along this country's eastern coastline is only measurable in terms of a few millimetres a year, but those millimetres soon add up. The same applies to rising sea levels. Current estimates are that the average height of the sea could rise by up to 90cm (3ft) during the 21st century – an increase that would find the sea moving 90m (300ft) inland in some places.

Sand, shingle and mud, the natural materials of the east coast, make very efficient natural defences against the sea. Mud banks spread the force of the tide, while the complex, maze-like channels among the pebbles of a shingle beach or between a dense tangle of saltmarsh plants absorb and dissipate incoming waves. At the opposite end of the scale are the rigid sea defences that man creates – tall concrete walls with steep slopes, clutters of huge stone blocks, baulks of timber.

Coastal settlements, ports and docks, factories, farms and agricultural land all need protection from flooding by the tides; but hard, man-made defences can only keep the sea at bay at the expense of shingle beaches, marshes, mud flats and sand banks. These soft and gradual natural barriers, and their rich and specialised wildlife, become squeezed and eroded between the hard artificial flood defences erected on their inland margins and the advancing, rising tide on their seaward edge.

NATURAL SOLUTIONS

Contemporary thinking on coastal defence by the Environment Agency and by Natural England is moving away from maintaining rigid traditional defences all along our shores. It is too expensive, and ultimately futile in the face of rising sea levels and a dipping coast. Now strategy is leaning towards what is called 'managed realignment' – in other words, making hard-headed choices about what to preserve from the sea, and what to relinquish to its natural processes. Coast dwellers protest as maintenance is withdrawn from the sea defences that guard their favourite piece of coast or much-loved building. Yet there are counterbalancing voices, too, with the realisation that the new strategy will result in the creation of a whole new order of wildlife havens and habitats.

Three places along the coast of Eastern England are seeing the effects of the new policy. The Humber estuary is lined with industrial stretches, with ports and docks, oil installations, villages and towns –

Grimsby, Immingham, Hull – where full protection is being maintained. But managed realignment has already been initiated elsewhere along the estuary. At Paull Holme Sands, a few miles downriver of Hull, a new sea wall has been built up to 500m (1,500ft) inland of its now breached predecessor. The

The former fields lie under new marsh and mud, with brackish tidal water pushing in and draining out with the tide.

abandoned land, flooded twice every 24 hours, is already thick with mud banks and greening over with developing saltmarsh. Meanwhile, far upstream of Hull, 440ha (1,100 acres) of low-lying agricultural land at Alkborough Flats has been similarly opened to the tides through deliberately created gaps in the sea defences. The former fields lie under new marsh and mud, with brackish tidal water pushing in and draining out with each tide.

Further south on the Essex coast, the Essex Wildlife Trust has bought the 284ha (700 acre) arable farm of Abbotts Hall (see left) at Great Wigborough on a creek of the River Blackwater south of Colchester. Half is now being farmed in a wildlife-friendly way, while the seawall has been breached to allow the other half of the land to flood, creating areas of new saltmarsh. And further south again an even bigger pioneering experiment in managed realignment is taking place under the auspices of the Royal Society for the Protection of Birds in a region unvisited and unknown by the vast majority of people.

TIME AND TIDE

Out beyond Southend-on-Sea, beyond Rochford and Great Stambridge and many other Essex villages, lies a maze of flat islands separated only by narrow muddy creeks. Potton Island, Havengore Island, Wallasea, Foulness – the curves of their shores fit so closely together that from the air they resemble a broken china plate. Along the northern edge of Wallasea and Foulness washes the mud-charged River Crouch and since 2006, when the Wallasea sea wall was breached, the river penetrates deep into the island's interior on every high tide. Intensively farmed fields, themselves reclaimed from the sea only a few centuries ago, have reverted to tidal land, carefully managed and controlled with sluices, artificial banks and 'islands' to create a mosaic of shallow pools, saltmarsh, mud flats and brackish lagoons. Already numbers of birds have soared upwards, with increased sightings of peregrines and marsh harriers, over-wintering wigeon and brent geese, blue-legged avocet and many other species.

This new tidal wetland occupies about a fifth of Wallasea's land. Most of the rest will now be opened to the sea in the same way. Not only will it add to the already augmented habitat for coastal birds; it will also relieve flood pressure on nearby 'hard' defences such as those that protect Burnham-on-Crouch, just across the river. The experiment of managed realignment has earned a cautious thumbs-up so far. The familiar shape and character of Eastern England's dynamic, flood-prone coast seem set for big changes in the not too distant future.

The SUFFOLK COAST and HEATHLANDS

Where the North Sea beats against its coast, the landscape of Suffolk has been shaped by the waves. Inland lies rugged heathland, the remains of ancient forests and the tranquil farmland that once inspired an artist.

❶ Covehithe

A ten-minute walk along a footpath from Covehithe leads to one of the most rewarding views on the Suffolk coast. Low cliffs topped with gorse and broom-dappled heathland shelter a beach that stretches to a point where sand, sea and sky dissolve into a soft, indefinable horizon.

A short distance from the end of the footpath, the cliffs slope down among sand-dunes to give access to the beach. Here the sands are backed by a lagoon, where shelduck and grey herons are seen. At low tide oystercatchers, ringed plovers and other waders probe the sands.

In Covehithe the gaunt ruin of St Andrew's Church dominates. It was originally built in the 15th century, but in 1672 parishioners found that they could no longer afford it. They were given permission to build a new church using the fabric of the old. They constructed it, with a thatched roof, inside the shell of the partly demolished building, retaining the original tower.

▶ *Covehithe is 7 miles south of Lowestoft, along a signposted lane from Wrentham on the A12. The footpath to the beach starts at a field entrance, 90m (100yd) west of the church.*

❷ Westleton Heath

In medieval times Suffolk was wool country, and Westleton Heath is one of the last-surviving examples of the east Suffolk heaths where sheep once grazed. Close by is Dunwich Forest, its natural disorder of bracken, heather and stands of silver birch growing in pleasant contrast with the neatly arrayed pine trees of the Forestry Commission plantation.

Today the heath encloses a nature reserve, and the whole area is splendid for walking and exploring. The sandy soil supports gorse, heather and broom as well as rarer wild flowers such as the heath spotted orchid. In summer, yellowhammers, whitethroats and linnets flit among the bushes, and from just after dusk there is a chance of hearing the strange mechanical sounding churring song of the nightjar – most common from late May to July. Rabbits are plentiful, and there are a few hares. Westleton Heath is also a home of the adder, Britain's only poisonous snake, which is sometimes found basking on sun-baked footpaths.

▶ *To reach Westleton Heath, take the signposted lane from Westleton village, which is on the B1125, 6 miles south-west of Southwold.*

OPEN TRACTS OF FRAGRANT HEATHER
DUNWICH HEATH

❸ Dunwich Village

Nowhere is the Suffolk coast's never-ending battle with the sea more dramatically illustrated than at Dunwich, where a once-proud town vanished beneath the waves. Terror came to Dunwich in January 1326, when a violent storm plucked 400 houses and three of the nine churches from their crumbling foundations and hurled them into the sea. It was the beginning of the end for the town that had been founded in AD 632 by St Felix of Burgundy, who crossed the Channel to convert the heathen East Anglians to Christianity.

With only low, sandy cliffs forming a fragile barrier, Dunwich stood no chance against the remorseless attack of the sea. Year after year, century after century, streets and buildings toppled from the cliffs, and in 1677 the waves were lapping at the doors of the houses in the town's market-place.

By the 19th century the medieval Church of All Saints, which had probably once stood in the middle of the town, was on the cliff-edge. In 1904 part of the church went into the sea, followed by the tower in 1919.

What remains of Dunwich is only a small village. It is said that at times the submerged church bells can be heard, warning of an approaching storm. The legend persists, though there would have been plenty of time to remove the bells before the church was engulfed by the sea. But perhaps by then, nobody cared.

▶ *Dunwich is 3 miles south-east of Blythburgh on the A12. It lies along a minor road, south-east off the B1125.*

❹ Dunwich Heath

The Sandlings Heathland is made up of open tracts of fragrant heather and gorse, punctuated with woodland and fringed by sandy cliffs and beaches. Dunwich Heath is one of the few surviving remnants of an area of lowland heath that once stretched for miles along the Suffolk coast.

An air of mystery hangs over Dunwich Heath, especially when viewed from Minsmere Cliffs on its eastern side. From here you can see a mile-long stretch of beach, shingle and sand backed by grassy dunes that separate the ever-encroaching sea from the marshes. With their reed-beds, streams and patches of dense woodland, the marshes are a shelter and breeding ground for many species of rare bird. Along the River Minsmere to the south, the marshes are kept as a nature reserve by the Royal Society for the Protection of Birds.

Marsh harriers may be found here, gliding above the reed-beds in search of prey, or sparrow-sized bearded reedlings jerking among the reeds after seeds or insects. Little terns and avocets are among the visitors.

Marram grass has been planted along the sand-dunes, its fibrous roots helping to hold them together as a barrier against the sea. Spiky blue-green sea holly may also be found there, as well as bird's-foot trefoil and restharrow in dry, grassy spots.

▶ *To reach Dunwich Heath, turn off the Westleton to Dunwich road at the Minsmere signpost, or follow signposts from Dunwich village. A footpath leads from Minsmere Cliffs down to the beach and the marshes.*

❺ Tunstall Forest

Rendlesham, Dunwich and Tunstall forests together form the Sandlings Forests, located in the heathland of the same name that lies behind Suffolk's coastline. Each of the three areas of woodland has a distinctive beauty and character; Tunstall's charm is its airiness and diversity. Well-spaced Corsican pines, larches and Scots pines rise from the forest floor and its carpet of pine needles and cones, and on a bright day the sun slants through the branches to bathe the undergrowth in a soft light.

Tunstall lost around 300,000 trees during the Great Storm of 1987 and when the Forestry Commission replanted, it left more open areas in the forest. These clearings have proved to be havens for wildlife. Most common woodland birds can be seen, as well as typical coniferous-forest birds such as crossbills, which frequent the tree-tops. Nightjars inhabit heathland areas. There are also fallow and roe deer, and red deer are occasional visitors.

At the forest edge, the deep green of the conifers is relieved in spring by flowering trees and shrubs – gorse, hawthorn and flowering currants – which dapple the roadside hedgerows with splashes of yellow, white and red. In some parts of the forest the conifers give way to beech and the occasional oak, and rhododendrons line the roadside verges.

▶ *Tunstall is 7 miles north-east of Woodbridge via the A1152 and B1069. Tunstall Forest straddles the B1078 between Tunstall village and the B1084.*

EASTERN ENGLAND

133

❻ Havergate Island

A small island in the River Alde (or Ore) estuary, Havergate is owned by the Royal Society for the Protection of Birds. Its 110ha (280 acres) of salt-marsh were one of the two British breeding grounds of the avocet, which returned here to nest in 1947 after being absent from Britain for 100 years. Drainage of the fens had reduced their numbers in the 18th century, and the birds that were left were shot for their feathers to make fishing flies, and their eggs were stolen for cooking.

Tall, elegant birds with patterned black-and-white plumage and upturned bills, the avocets arrive early in March to begin breeding, and then usually leave in June or July for their African wintering grounds. The island is also noted for migratory waders such as the curlew-sandpiper, black-tailed godwit and spotted redshank which pass through in spring and autumn. The day-flying short-eared owl also breeds here.

Havergate Island can be visited by boat from Orford Quay with the trip lasting from 10am until 3pm. Bookings should be made through the RSPB Minsmere visitor centre.
▶ *Orford is 10 miles east of Woodbridge on the B1084. There is a large car park about 90m (100yd) before the quay.*

❼ Rendlesham Forest

Though scarcely 2 miles from Tunstall Forest, Rendlesham is subtly different in character. Here the forest is denser and its beauty more sinister, with a silence that makes a twig breaking underfoot sound like a pistol shot. Where the pines are thickly set, there is no undergrowth, only a soft carpet of moss scattered with cones and needles. Few birds penetrate the densest woodland, although the cries of jays and magpies may be heard, or the song of goldcrests.

Rendlesham Forest is the oldest and largest of the woodland areas found in the Sandlings. It began with the planting of 1,030ha (2,544 acres) in 1920 and now covers almost 1,620ha (4,000 acres). Previously most of the land was heath used for sheep grazing, and some patches of heathland have survived, such as Upper and Lower Hollesley commons on the south-western edge. Rendlesham suffered severe damage during the storm of 1987; it is reckoned that Suffolk lost around a million trees in one night. The Forestry Commission are leaving some parts of the forest to revert to heath to encourage those creatures, such as woodlarks and nightjars, that prefer habitats found in sandy heathland.

During the Second World War, Woodbridge airfield was cut out of the forest, and it is still a military base.
▶ *The B1084 Woodbridge to Orford road cuts through the forest. A large open area on the northern side of the road has been set aside for car parking.*

❽ Kyson Hill

At the ancient town of Woodbridge, the Deben becomes a river worthy of the name – broad and fast-flowing, with the salty tang of the sea borne on the breezes coming up from the estuary some 8 miles away. South of the town is Kyson Hill, a finger of land projecting into the Deben where the river makes a brief incursion into Martlesham Creek and then heads for the sea; an area of the hill belongs to the National Trust.

From the aptly named Broom Heath on the southern slopes of Kyson Hill, ablaze with yellow in the spring, there are fine views across the valley, though the river hides coyly in the tree-clad folds of the land. But a footpath leading down between hedgerows and tall trees soon brings the broad mud-flats and foreshore of the Deben into view. Yachts rest at anchor in the creek, or perch on the mud at low tide, and the

DEDHAM VALE

stranded pools and river's edge are a meeting place for sea and freshwater birds. Shelduck and oystercatchers probe the mud, black-headed gulls wheel above, and out in the deeper water the surface may be rippled by diving cormorants.

At the bottom of Kyson Hill, a footpath follows the river bank back to Woodbridge, skirting a narrow backwater where tall reeds grow. On the quayside at Woodbridge stands a restored 18th-century mill whose wheel was once driven by the tides.

▶ *There is a small car park on Broom Heath, reached from Sandy Lane, a turning off the Ipswich road (B1438) in Woodbridge.*

❾ Shingle Street

On this astonishing strip of the Suffolk coast the River Ore, having run parallel to the sea for about 10 miles and changed its name from the Alde, finally flows into Hollesley Bay at Orford Haven. A high bank of shingle hides the sea from the road, and from the top of the bank the view is of yet more shingle – to the south, to the north and across the river on Orford Beach. A natural landscape undoubtedly – desolate, featureless and yet with a tranquillity that beguiles the visitor to linger. Many a yachtsman has spent an enforced stay here – stranded through a misjudgment of the tide.

Only the hardiest of wild flowers flourish here: the bright green, low-growing sea pea, bright with purple flowers in June and July, the yellow horned poppy and the dark green sea beet, its leaves red-tinged. Hollows in the shingle enclose lagoons left by the high tides, sheltered pools for oyster-catchers and black-headed gulls.

▶ *Shingle Street is 7 miles south-east of Woodbridge and reached by a signposted lane from Hollesley village, which is off the B1083. The lane ends at the Martello tower, but where it runs along parallel to the shingle bank there is a concrete roadway almost to the water's edge.*

❿ Flatford and Dedham Vale

Constable immortalised Flatford in 1817, when he captured forever the beauty of this stretch of the River Stour and its mill. After descending between high, ivy-clad banks, the road leads to the riverside where a thatched, pink-washed 16th-century cottage stands by a small wooden bridge. A left turn beyond the bridge leads past a small lock, and then Flatford Mill comes into view, the waters of its mill-pond tumbling over weirs into a wide expanse of river.

Across the bridge, a footpath winds beside the river, fringed with gnarled willows. It leads about 1½ miles upstream, across water-meadows, to Dedham Mill, where weeping willows bend low over the mill-pond. The meadows are home to many wild flowers, such as rare oxlips and marsh-mallows, and in summer the yellow-brown Essex skipper butterfly may be seen.

Essex and Suffolk share Dedham Vale, which borders the River Stour from Flatford to Nayland, but it was John Constable who brushed out the county boundary through his landscapes. This part of England has become known simply as 'Constable country'. The artist was born at East Bergholt in 1776. His father owned both water-mills, at Flatford and at Dedham, and these were the subjects of his earlier works. He also painted many scenes along the banks of the Stour and the surrounding countryside. He wrote: 'The sound of water escaping from mill dams, willows, old rotten planks, slimy posts and brickwork … these scenes made me a painter.' The landscape he painted is still enchanting: unchanged and unchanging, Constable country remains much as the painter saw it.

▶ *Dedham Vale lies north of Colchester and can be reached by either the A12 or the A134. Dedham is 6 miles north-east of Colchester via the A137 and B1029. Flatford is reached by a signposted lane from East Bergholt, which is on the B1070 about 1 mile south-east of the A12.*

ANGLESEY and the
LLEYN PENINSULA
180-184

Holyhead

Llandudno

Colwyn
Bay

Bangor

Caernarfon

Ruthin

Wrexham

Llangollen

Betws-
y-Coed

Oswestry

SNOWDONIA'S
PEAKS and
VALLEYS 170-179

Porthmadog

Pwllheli

Y Bala

Dolgellau

Shrewsb

Welshpool

Machynlleth

Montgomery

Newtown

Bishop's
Castle

Aberystwyth

Llanidloes

Knighton

Lu

THE CAMBRIAN
MOUNTAINS
163-167

Leomins

Kington

Llandrindod
Wells

Cardigan

Lampeter

Llanwrtyd
Wells

Builth Wells

Hay-on-Wye

Here

Fishguard

Llandovery

Her

St David's

THE PEMBROKESHIRE
COAST 153-162

Llandeilo

Brecon

THE BRECON
BEACONS
138-146

Abergavenny

Mor

Haverfordwest

Carmarthen

Milford
Haven

Merthyr
Tydfil

Abertillery

Usk

Tenby

Pontypool

Che

Rhondda

Caerleon

Swansea

Pontypridd

Caerphilly

Newport

THE GOWER
PENINSULA 147-152

Bridgend

Cardiff

Penarth

Wales and the Welsh Borders

Sculpted by ice, mountains rear up from the green valleys of Wales, probing the sky with their highest peaks, while the tranquil hills of the Welsh borderland offer a gentle rural life, their fortifications the only reminder of a history of bitter warfare.

A41

A518

M54 A41

A442

uch
enlock   A454

dgnorth   A442

1
ard   2   3

4   Great
Malvern

dbury   5   7
9   8   10
11

A449

e

5
A40   A417

A48

M5

The BRECON BEACONS

The sandstone mountains of the Brecon Beacons loom large over windswept moors and wooded valleys. Between the cliffs and crags lie myriad lakes – created by both man and nature.

❶ Hay Bluff

Nothing surpasses the breathtaking prospect spreading in all directions from the tip of Hay Bluff. South-west runs the edge of the Black Mountains and the Brecon Beacons, North-west the crests and valleys roll over the heart of Wales towards Snowdon, northwards lie the hills of Shropshire, and eastwards is the long, hump-backed line of the Malvern Hills.

The 677m (2,220ft) high summit of the Bluff, no more than 275m (300yd) from the border between Wales and England, is one of the most accessible peaks in the Black Mountains. Only a steep half-mile walk is needed up the western slope from the small car park 542m (1,778ft) up on the narrow Gospel Pass road between Hay-on-Wye and the Vale of Ewyas. Even from the road the panorama is almost as vast. Along the eastern side of the long triangle of land mounting to the summit runs the Offa's Dyke long-distance footpath, another magnificent vantage point overlooking the lush farmlands of Herefordshire.

In the foreground down below the Bluff is the town of Hay-on-Wye, with its narrow medieval streets and traces of old wall and castle. Just a mile north-west of Hay is Clyro, where Francis Kilvert was curate from 1870–9. His diaries bring vividly to life the countryside round Hay where he loved to walk.

A good walk of just over 2 miles runs south-westwards from Hay Bluff along the escarpment, crosses the Gospel Pass road and finally climbs to the 690m (2,263ft) high summit of Twmpa. From this summit a 3½ mile path descends first south-west into the Nant y Bwch valley and then down the steep, stream-cut valley to the tiny hamlet of Capel-y-ffin on the River Honddu in the upper Vale of Ewyas.

▶ *Hay Bluff is 4 miles south of Hay-on-Wye. The minor road leading up to the car park on the hillside leaves the B4350 just west of the town.*

❷ Pen-y-crug

Five ramparts and ditches encircle the conical tip of Pen-y-crug. Although worn down by 2,000 years of erosion, the earthworks are still clearly visible. They enclose an area more than 460m (500yd) across at the 331m (1,087ft) summit of the hill.

The warlike Celtic immigrants who came to Britain from northern France in around 300 BC were fine judges of a strategic site. Hilltops were their choice. Pen-y-crug commands the valleys radiating from present-day Brecon. Its views reach south over wooded valleys to the Brecon Beacons and north to the upland wilderness of Mynydd Eppynt. It gave the Celts a lookout point and a safe refuge – for themselves and for the cattle and horses they reared – when marauding bands from other tribes came raiding.

The strategic importance of the area attracted the Romans too in their push into Wales about AD 75. Two miles west of Pen-y-crug is the 2ha (5 acre) site of Y Gaer, the largest in Wales of the forts that were built between the huge legionary fortresses, such as Caerleon, to control the interior of the conquered territory. Y Gaer could accommodate 1,000 auxiliaries drawn from the conquered tribes of the empire. Originally it had a timber-palisaded bank protected by two ditches, and the buildings inside were of wood. During the 2nd century the ramparts were rebuilt in stone. Later that century the fort was badly damaged by the Celts, but it was repaired and occupied on and off until the Romans left Britain about AD 450. Sir Mortimer Wheeler excavated the site in 1924.

Danewort, the rare, wild dwarf elder, grows in the fields round the fort and scents the air of early summer with its creamy flowers.

▶ *Pen-y-crug is 1 mile north-west of Brecon along a marked minor road off the B4520. A marked footpath leads to the summit. Y Gaer is signposted from the A40, 4 miles west of Brecon.*

❸ Mynydd bach Trescastell

Stone circles high on the moorland of Mynydd bach Trescastell suggest that Bronze Age people pioneered a route along the ridge between Trecastle and Llandovery almost 4,000 years ago. Generations of travellers followed them on the track until the early 1800s, when the road that is now the A40 replaced it.

The old road is tar-sealed for more than 2 miles west of Trecastle. It then becomes a grassy track, perfect for walking or pony-trekking. The broad ridge along which it runs rises between the headwaters of the River Usk and the wooded gorge of Cwm Dwr. Just north of the track at the highest point on the ridge are the banks that outline the two superimposed Roman camps of Y Pigwn.

South of the track, woodlands shelter the Usk Reservoir. The road to the reservoir swings south through the woods and joins a road that leads to a delightful spot, Pont ar Wysg. Here the Usk is only 3 miles down from its source. The Glasfynydd Forest lines one bank, and from the other rises airy open moorland.

▶ *A minor road running west from Trecastle leads to the reservoir, where there is a car park. For Mynydd bach Trescastell, take the fork to the right 640m (700yd) from the start of the minor road.*

❹ Carn Goch

Above ferny lanes dotted with foxgloves stands the long mass of Carn Goch, crowned by the rugged silhouette of its ancient Iron Age hill-fort. The tumbled, pale grey ramparts of loose stones guard the two highest points of the hill. The builders of this largest hill-fort in Wales chose their site well and made the most of its natural defences. The ridge is 210m (700ft) high and commands sweeping views of the surrounding countryside. Any attackers would have had to advance up the steep slopes under a hail of slingshots from warriors manning the ramparts.

The power of the fort shows best not from within it but from the village of Bethlehem, to the north at the foot of the hill. In spring the ramparts stand out from the green hillside unmasked by the brackens that thrust up later.

Just west of Bethlehem Church a grassy footpath mounts the hill and passes through the fort. The climb is worth it for the views from the summit. Below and to the north-west the winding River Towy loops between the meadows. Llandeilo, set on a hill, is a major landmark to the south-west.

▶ *Carn Goch is 3 miles south-west of Llangadog, along a minor road that branches west off the A4069.*

GOSPEL PASS

❺ Carreg Cennen Castle

Perched on the brink of a lofty limestone crag, Carreg Cennen Castle stands 90m (300ft) above the narrow valley of the River Cennen, which winds its way beneath the bare north-west slopes of the brooding Black Mountain. Jackdaws and kestrels nest on the cliff-face below the castle, above the green blanket of ash, elm, yew and hawthorn that clothes the lower face. Across the valley, broad-winged buzzards circle high above the mountain slopes.

In the castle courtyard opposite the ruined gatehouse is the entrance to a 70m (230ft) long passage cut through the rock, with valley views from a number of loopholes along its length. It leads to a natural limestone cave in the cliff – perhaps the first stronghold occupied at the site. Because of its fine defensive position, the cliff-top has probably been fortified for at least 2,000 years; Roman coins of the 1st and 2nd centuries have been found on the site. The first stone defences were built there in the 12th century by Rhys ap Gruffydd, ruler of the South Wales kingdom of Deheubarth.

The crumbling walls and towers of the existing castle date from the 13th and 14th centuries. Their stones last rang to the sound of conflict in 1462 during the Wars of the Roses. The defending Red Rose Lancastrians finally agreed to surrender to the attacking White Rose Yorkists, who later set 500 men to smash the castle foundations.

The best views of the castle, in its spectacular cliff-top setting against a background of high, rolling hills, are from the other side of the Cennen valley. Southwards from the castle, a public footpath leads over the river and across streams and fields to climb to a cave that shelters the source of the River Loughor.

Not far north-east of the Loughor cave, near a minor road, there are some long, low, grass-covered 'pillow' mounds. The place is called Beddau'r Derwyddon, or the Druids' Graves. But despite the romantic name, the mounds are really man-made rabbit warrens, built in medieval times for breeding and rearing rabbits to add to the meat supply. From the mounds, a track leads back across fields to the castle. The walk from the castle and back covers about 5 miles.

▶ *Carreg Cennen Castle can be reached from Trapp, which lies 3 miles south-east of Llandeilo along a minor road branching east from the A483 about 550m (600yd) south of Llandeilo Bridge. The castle car park is 1 mile east of Trapp.*

❻ Black Mountain

Scattered peaks soaring above a wilderness of jagged rocks, bogs, prehistoric burial chambers and long-abandoned quarries are the reality of Black Mountain – for, despite its name, it is a range of mountains, triangular and widening from Ammanford at the south-western corner to a long scarp over the Tawe valley at the eastern end. The whole area is the home of curlews, snipe, ring ouzels and buzzards, and of hardy sheep that are sometimes rounded up by shepherds for shearing or dipping.

Treeless moorland riven by dark, peaty valleys slopes up from the south to reach the highest summits in the north-east corner. Here the steep, cliff-topped scarp of Fan Foel juts out in an immense tongue. Bannau Brycheiniog, Fan Foel's highest point at 802m (2,630ft), towers over great banks of scree on the Fan's north-east face with Llyn y Fan Fawr, 'Big Lake of the Fan', tucked below. The summit gives an enormous view – south as far as Exmoor, west to Mynydd Preseli (the Preseli Mountain) and north to Cadair Idris.

The Fan's north-west face is the dramatic red cliff of Bannau Sir Gaer, 749m (2,460ft) high and curving to enclose the secret, dark water of Llyn y Fan Fach, 'Little Lake of the Fan', 150m (500ft) below.

The lake was the legendary home of a beautiful water fairy who fell in love with Rhiwallon, a farmer from the Sawdde valley, and married him on condition that he would never touch her with iron. Accidentally he broke the pledge after years of marriage and she returned to the lake, taking back her dowry of cattle but leaving behind her three sons. She met the sons later and taught them her secret herbal cures. The sons became physicians at Myddfai, a village some 6 miles to the north. Their descendants were still physicians in the 19th century.

A glorious 3 mile walk starts at Llyn y Fan Fach, climbs to the top of the scarp, and follows it out to the tip of Fan Foel's tongue and round to the summit of Bannau Brycheiniog.

▶ *A 2½ mile track leading east from the village of Llanddeusant leads to Llyn y Fan Fach. Llanddeusant is 3 miles along a minor road that branches east from the A4069, 3 miles south-east of Llangadog.*

❼ Pont Melin-fâch

Smooth natural platforms of grey rock hang over seething misty cauldrons where the upper waters of the River Neath roar over waterfalls into the deep pools beneath. A footpath from Pont Melin-fâch, 'Bridge by the Little Mill', follows the western side of the river downstream on a marvellous, but not easy, course – now on a ledge where the sheet of water rolls off the edge, now scrambling down a steep ravine to a shelf beside the pool below.

In the cool, damp world under the ash trees, alders, oaks and wych elms are mossy rocks, and among them the vivid green of hart's-tongue ferns, shield ferns and bladder ferns. Close to the bridge there is a beautiful and secluded picnic place, and running upstream from it is another path which runs a good 2 miles, crossing the river once, to Pwll-y-rhyd.

This is near the edge of the soft limestone outcrop into which the river has cut so deeply to make the fairytale cascades and gorges. At Pwll-y-rhyd the river has worn a chasm so deep and narrow that the water has disappeared; it rumbles far below the boulder-strewn surface. Caves and tunnels writhe beneath the rocks – but these are accessible only to experienced cavers.

▶ *Leave the A465, 10 miles west of Merthyr Tydfil, and take the B4242 to Pontneddfechan. Take the minor road north towards Ystradfellte and after 2 miles a road branches left to Pont Melin-fâch. There is a car park near the picnic site.*

MOORLAND RIVEN BY DARK, PEATY VALLEYS
BLACK MOUNTAIN

❽ Ystradfellte

Romantic wooded gorges and the exciting plunge of foaming cascades make the walk down the Mellte valley one of rare enchantment. The path starts from Porth yr Ogof, 'Entrance to the Cave', less than a mile south of Ystradfellte, but it does not follow the river for long. The water suddenly vanishes into the wide cavern below a towering cliff into a long stretch of limestone caves – whose exploration is strictly for the experts – to emerge dancing and bubbling from its rocky arch a little further on and rush down the valley to its three beautiful waterfalls.

At the horseshoe-shaped middle fall you can stand on the flat shelf beside the wide crescent of water as it rolls over the brink and see it frothing down the rocks and through the dappled green valley. The path which has scrambled with difficulty alongside the stream cuts across the woodland from the lower fall to the Mellte's main tributary, the Hepste. Here the Sgwd yr Eira, 'Fall of Snow', makes a spectacular leap of 12–15m (40–50ft) into a deep plunge pool while behind its sparkling, hissing curtain there runs a broad path – so broad that farmers used to drive their stock along it.

Alternate bands of hard sandstone and soft shales have created the falls. The sandstone has resisted erosion but the soft shales have been worn away by the water until they now lie far below the level of the sandstone.

The area is a favourite haunt of dippers, small blackish brown birds with white bibs. They sit bobbing on the rocks or walk in the shallows, often against the stream, with heads below water looking for food.

North of Ystradfellte, a road follows the stream of the Llia towards its source in the wilderness of Fforest Fawr, a tract of open moorland that was a royal hunting ground in medieval times. Near the road's highest point, some 430m (1,400ft) above sea-level, is the huge megalith of Maen Llia. Erected during the Bronze Age, perhaps as a memorial, it has been used through the ensuing centuries as a marker for the routes over the moor. The stone is 3.6m (12ft) high, 2.7m (9ft) wide, and almost 1m (3ft) thick. From just north of the stone there are beautiful views down the Senni valley, where a patchwork of fields nestles among mountains rising to more than 600m (2,000ft).

▶ *Ystradfellte is 6 miles north of Hirwaun, and can be reached by a minor road which leaves the A4059, 4 miles north of Hirwaun.*

Wales and the Welsh Borders

❾ Pen y Fan

The long wave of red sandstone that swells up gradually from the South Wales coalfield reaches its crest at the steep, scalloped rim of crags facing north to Brecon. These are the unmistakable outlines of the Brecon Beacons – five great flat-topped noses jutting out between the four deep round-headed valleys or cwms.

The highest of the jutting noses is Pen y Fan at a height of 886m (2,906ft); the nearby Corn Dû is 873m (2,863ft). Both of these crags are capped by hard bands of rock known as plateau beds which have remained steeper and less weathered than the other summits. Pen y Fan's 180m (600ft) high band is layered so uniformly that it looks as if the rocks were laid on by human hand. The slopes and summits are too barren to attract many animals, but buzzards and ravens nest on them.

In the cwms, where the sun could not reach, the Ice Age glaciers became deepest and stayed longest. They bored down at the base and, when they finally retreated, left heaps of rocks and rubble over which the valley streams now dimple and bubble. Below Pen y Fan the rubble formed a dam behind which the small lake, Llyn Cwm Llwch, was trapped. The most attractive approach to the mountain is up a 3 mile path that runs upstream to the lake, climbs the steep crag behind it to mount the ridge, and then turns east towards Pen y Fan.

From the summit immense views look over Brecon to Cadair Idris, over the fields of Hereford to the Malverns, and over the Bristol Channel to the hills of Somerset and Devon.

▶ *To reach the summit, turn east from the A470, 3½ miles south-west of Brecon on to a minor road at Tai'r Bull; follow this for ¾ mile and, where the road turns sharp left, carry straight on along the track and path.*

CORN DÛ FROM PEN Y FAN

⑩ Craig Cerrig-gleisiad

The high, brooding crags of Craig Cerrig-gleisiad sweep round in a half-circle of steep smooth walls scattered with rowans and enclosing an empty valley. Ravens soar from their nests on the cliff-face to hang lazily above, dipping and swaying gracefully as unseen currents change their course.

The crag is awesome evidence of how Ice Age glaciers carved a hollow into the soft face of the Old Red Sandstone. The whole three-quarter mile crescent swinging west and north is part of a National Nature Reserve, for it marks the southern limit of arctic-alpine plants.

The grandeur of the crags is best seen from a footpath that leads across the hollow below them (walkers are asked to keep off the crags to protect the wild flowers that grow there). The path continues beyond the hollow, following paths and bridleways for 4 miles until it reaches the National Park's Mountain Centre on the edge of Mynydd Illtud Common. In a hollow on the common are two huge mossy stones, hidden among bracken, that mark the burial place of Illtyd, a 5th-century Christian missionary to Wales. Beyond the grazing sheep and ponies, in the north-east corner of the common, are the ditch and rampart of an Iron Age hill-fort where tribesmen took refuge during local skirmishes.

On the road south of Craig Cerrig-gleisiad the pass at Storey Arms is only a mile away. A bridleway starts there and leads north towards Brecon along the east side of the Tarell valley. Until early in the 19th century, when a road was built between Brecon and Merthyr Tydfil, this was the main drove road over the mountains. It was etched into the landscape by generations of cattle and sheep as they were driven northwards to graze on the Usk valley pastures.

▶ *The footpath to Craig Cerrig-gleisiad leads from the A470 at a point 7 miles south-west of Brecon and just 320m (350yd) south of a marked picnic site.*

⑪ Taf Fawr Valley

Under open skies and bare, smooth moors is the silken sheen of a lake reflecting the dark forests at its fringes or suddenly ruched by a stir of wind. This glorious scene is there to relish three times on the drive south down the Taf Fawr valley from its head at the 400m (1,400ft) pass over Storey Arms until it narrows at the southern end beneath the crags of Daren Fach, where sandstone suddenly gives way to limestone. The road over the pass was originally a turnpike road. It was used in the 19th century by carts carrying farm produce to the industrial south.

The three stretches of water and the forests are man-made, but they have added life, variety and beauty to the barren moors. The reservoirs were built between 1892 and 1927 to supply water for Cardiff, and most of the trees have been planted since 1950. The varied golds and ambers of oak, rowan, sycamore, birch and willow enrich the forest in autumn, for these trees have planted themselves in the valley. In spring, too, their fresh leaves – and the new, delicate green fronds of the larches – enliven the darker evergreen conifers.

Just above the head of the southern reservoir, a road branches west to the Garwnant Visitor Centre, housed in a former farm on a wooded slope overlooking the water. Waymarked walks and a cycle trail start from the centre and wind among the glades. The forest, the water and the surrounding moorland give food and shelter to a wide range of creatures, among them foxes, hares, grass snakes, sparrowhawks and forest songbirds, including the tiny goldcrest.

▶ *The road from Storey Arms is the A470. At the south of the valley, 8 miles from Storey Arms, it connects with the A465, just outside Merthyr Tydfil.*

⑫ Taf Fechan Valley

The sylvan beauties of the Taf Fechan valley as it is today had a miserable start. A cholera epidemic in Merthyr Tydfil in 1854 demonstrated tragically the need for an unpolluted water supply. The town's health authority got permission to make a reservoir in the valley, and work was completed on it by 1859. Three more reservoirs were created between 1884 and 1927, and now the chain of man-made lakes runs down the valley for 5 miles, sheltered beneath the huge conifer forests that protect the hillsides from erosion.

Miles of waymarked woodland trails thread through the forest in the shady green avenues on a soft, silent carpet of amber needles. It is difficult to believe that the forest starts only 4 miles from the industrial hubbub of Merthyr Tydfil. The trails start from the car parks that are on the road running through the woods on the western side of the lower reservoirs. From the furthest car park a track runs north above the eastern side of the upper reservoirs to the very edge of the Beacons crest only 2½ miles away. Here an immense view stretches north over the Usk and Brecon towards Cadair Idris. From the crest the track plunges down Cwm Cynwyn in the direction of Brecon, following the old bridleway that once went from Merthyr to Brecon.

▶ *The road up the Taf Fechan valley is marked from the A465 (Heads of the Valleys Road) on the northern outskirts of Merthyr Tydfil.*

⑬ Talybont Forest

The irresistible music of waterfalls, tumbling down cliffs of dark red sandstone, fills the air in the western crescent of Talybont Forest. Nine cascades, some making spectacular leaps, some splashing gently, glint through the trees along the tracks west of Pont Blaen-y-glyn. They are on the course of the Nant Bwrefwr and its parent the Caerfanell, which flow from the lofty moors to be caught in Talybont Reservoir before joining the Usk.

Waymarked trails start from Pont Blaen-y-glyn and wind through the forest. High up the southern slope a green strand lies between the vast stretches of pine, larch and spruce, all planted since 1950 between the few stands of native oak, ash and alder. The strand follows the course of the old railway that ran beside the quarries on the hillside and looped round to Merthyr Tydfil. Before the railway was built, ponies used to drag sledges laden with stone down to Merthyr.

The eastern arms of Talybont Forest embrace Talybont Reservoir, keeping its water sheltered and still. Large colonies of wildfowl and other water birds are attracted to it in winter – coot, teal, pochard, mallard, tufted duck, goldeneye, goosander, wigeon, shoveler, whooper swan, grey heron, great crested grebe and cormorant all congregate on the waters and the marshy southern shore.

The reservoir was completed in 1938 to provide water for Newport. It has a capacity of 12,000 million litres (2,567 million gallons) and a dam 30m (97ft) high. Rhododendrons bloom at the dam in colourful profusion during the early summer months.

▶ *From the A40, 6 miles south-east of Brecon, a minor road branches south-west at Llansantffraed to cross the Usk to Talybont. From the village the road runs down the western side of the reservoir to Pont Blaen-y-glyn. There are car parks at the reservoir, at Pont Blaen-y-glyn, and at the western edge of the forest, 6 miles beyond Talybont village.*

⑭ Bwlch

Scant fragments of purple stone wall, a tumbledown tower and a sycamore-clad mound within a silted ditch are all that remain of the Norman stronghold of Castell Blaenllynfi half a mile north of Bwlch. It was built to command the valleys of the Usk and the Llynfi when Brecon was a Norman lordship.

The village, a borough in Norman times, is set in the high gap between Buckland Hill and the southern tips of Allt yr Esgair and Cefn Moel. Roman soldiers marched through here from their fort at Pen-y-gaer, 1½ miles to the east, towards Brecon. The Roman road heaved up over the pass – the Welsh *bwlch* means 'pass' – as the modern road does now.

The castle that is now barely a skeleton was a formidable stronghold when Llewelyn the Great was fighting for Welsh independence from King John in 1214. It was one of the castles that Llewelyn and his Norman son-in-law Reginald de Braose recaptured for the de Braose family. It had belonged to Reginald's father, William, most powerful of the Marcher lords and a friend of King John until a fierce quarrel in 1207. William was declared an outlaw and had to flee to France, losing all his Welsh possessions.

The most delightful of many walks from the village climbs the wooded ridge of Buckland Hill to 316m (1,038ft), then drops down to the Usk where the water winds beneath the great hills. A lower path returns past the broad-leaved Lower Cilwich Wood and round the foot of Buckland Hill to complete the circuit.

▶ *Bwlch is on the A40, 8 miles south-east of Brecon.*

⑮ Llangattock

Behind the village of Llangattock looms the great mountain mass of Mynydd Llangatwg, divided from the village below by rugged limestone crags. Old quarries are strung along the cliff-face, linked now by the grassy track that was once a tramway for carrying stone to the ironworks of Nantyglo. Cottages once occupied by quarrymen still dot the steep slopes.

One stretch of the crag is the Craig y Cilau National Nature Reserve. The large and the small-leaved limes grow here, and the rare lesser whitebeam. Alpine enchanter's nightshade, hawkweeds and Solomon's seal cling to the rocky ledges. The scree and rock faces are dangerously loose; binoculars used from the tracks give safe views. Caves and passages tunnel inside the mountain. The surface is pitted with swallow-holes where the soft rock has collapsed into a cavity beneath. Within the reserve is the entrance to Agen Allwedd, 'The Keyhole', a 12 mile labyrinth of caves and tunnels: only experienced cavers with permits are allowed to enter.

Down in the attractive village of Llangattock, stone-built weavers' cottages stand beside the lanes, and pretty stone bridges cross the streams and the winding Monmouthshire and Brecon Canal. The Church of St Catwg has the old stocks and whipping-post inside it – fixtures where misdemeanours were punished.

On the south-western edge of the village the lane forks. The left fork passes Llangattock Park House and joins a path leading to the crags and the old tramway. The right fork connects after 3¼ miles with the B4560, the only road over Mynydd Llangatwg. It gives beautiful views back over the Usk valley to the Black Mountains with Table Mountain and Pen Cerrig-calch notable landmarks behind Crickhowell.

▶ *Llangattock is ½ mile across the Usk from Crickhowell, which is on the A40, 6 miles north-west of Abergavenny.*

⑯ The Sugar Loaf

The unmistakable cone of the Sugar Loaf mountain stands neat and distinct to the north-west of Abergavenny. Its graceful ridge, rising above three great shoulders, makes it by far the most outstanding feature in the landscape, though it possesses little of the steepness usually associated with the sugar-loaf shape. Its green flanks are gashed with red sandstone, patched with bracken, splashed with gorse, and – in early autumn – covered with the ground-hugging dwarf shrubs that conceal powdered purple bilberries beneath every leaf.

Bulky shoulders buttress the lower slopes of the mountain and ridge tracks surmount them to lead to the 596m (1,995ft) summit. This is surprisingly spacious – not pointed but a tilted sheet of rock and grass. Now the full and varied panorama opens below: Ysgyryd Fawr, the Malverns, and the Cotswolds to the east, the Black Mountains to the north, the gentle Usk skirting the Brecon Beacons to the west, and to the south, a glimpse of the Severn.

The many paths to the summit involve some stiff walking. From the parking place on the southern approach, a 2 mile grassy track winds upwards – and on the way crosses other, steeper ascents. The car park itself is at a magnificent viewpoint 345m (1,132ft) above the Usk.

Lying below the car park, to the east, is St Mary's Vale twisting through a lovely deciduous wood. In the bracken-thick glades are handsome oaks, while alders line the stream and massive beeches make dense pools of shade. A nature trail is laid out in the wood and takes about one and a half hours of leisurely walking to complete.

▶ *The car park and viewpoint are 1½ miles off the A40 on the western outskirts of Abergavenny, and reached by a turning marked at Pentre Road. The car park for St Mary's Vale is found at the end of Chapel Lane, north of Abergavenny town centre.*

TALYBONT RESERVOIR

wales and the Welsh Borders

🔟 Vale of Ewyas

Far beneath the long steep ridges that guard it, runs the beautiful sheltered valley of the Honddu. The ridges are more than 610m (2,000ft) above sea-level for much of their length, thrusting forward to narrow the valley as it twists beneath them. Trees hang above the water in the lower stretches but upstream great purple cliffs rise, and near the source only a few thorns cling to the red-gashed slopes. Wood warblers, redstarts, woodpeckers and pied flycatchers are noisy in the woods while buzzards, kestrels, ravens and ring ouzels haunt the crags, and red grouse breed up on the moors.

Numerous marked footpaths and bridleways climb the slopes from the valley and make it ideal for walks of different lengths. A minor road also runs north through the valley and over the 550m (1,800ft) Gospel Pass at the head. There are spectacular expanses north from the road into the heart of Wales and west along the crests of the Black Mountains as the road drops down towards Hay-on-Wye. Offa's Dyke long-distance footpath runs along the top of the ridge at the east of the valley, marching along with the boundary of the National Park and the border with England.

Llanthony Priory is 6 miles up the valley; now only lovely fragments of the 12th-century towers, high walls and pointed arches remain. Giraldus, the 12th-century chronicler, wrote after visiting the priory: 'Here the monks, sitting in the cloisters, enjoying the fresh air, when they happen to look up towards the horizon behold the tops of the mountains touching the heavens and herds of wild deer feeding on their summits.'

A much later religious foundation still stands 4 miles upstream from the priory at Capel-y-ffin. The brick pseudo-Gothic monastery was the enterprise of an Anglican deacon, Joseph Leycester Lyne, who called himself Father Ignatius. He attracted passionate adherents by his fiery preaching and repelled equally passionate opponents by his showmanship. His community broke up soon after his death in 1908.

Eric Gill bought the monastery in the 1920s and lived there with a group of other artists and their families. Gill's sculptures, type-face designs and wood engravings displayed his artistic versatility. The monastery is the subject of some of his engravings.

▶ *The minor road through the Vale of Ewyas branches off the A465 at Llanfihangel Crucorney, 4 miles north of Abergavenny.*

🔟 Grwyne Fawr Valley

Cutting through the heart of the Black Mountains is the long, narrow valley of the Grwyne Fawr. The river's head lies at 670m (2,200ft), above the steep north-west scarp of the mountains. The river rushes through its high moorland valley below the barren summits of the 811m (2,660ft) Waun Fach and the 800m (2,624ft) Pen y Gadair Fawr, the two highest points in the Black Mountains. Their steep slopes are reflected in the small Grwyne Fawr Reservoir, where the river is checked before it rushes on again to enter the shady mixed woodland of Mynydd Du Forest. Towards the southern end of the forest, just above Pont Cadwgan, there is a forest trail which takes about one and a half hours to walk. It passes one of several deserted farmsteads in the valley, a poignant reminder of the days when people had to move south to make a living in the coalfields.

It is a long but exhilarating walk to the very source of the river up the 6 mile track that continues beyond the forest trail. Downstream from Pont Cadwgan there is another enjoyable but quite different walk. The river winds through beautiful oakwoods. Hidden in a narrow lane up the hillside west of the river is probably the valley's greatest treasure, the 11th-century Partrishow Church.

▶ *From Glangrwyne on the A40, 4 miles west of Abergavenny, follow the minor road through Llangenny, past the turn-off to Llanbedr, and a further 3 miles to a left take a turn marked Partrishow and Mynydd Du Forest. The forest trail starts from a car park 3 miles up this road.*

The **GOWER PENINSULA**

The sea can be glimpsed from most places in Gower, breaking over vast beaches or crashing onto rocky shores. A ridge of hills inland offers panoramic views over the entire peninsula.

❶ Burry Holms

Memories of medieval monks cling to this tiny island at the northern end of Rhossili Bay. On the landward side are the remains of a small religious settlement first mentioned in 1195. It was dedicated to St Cenydd, who founded a monastic community at Llangennith in the 6th century. Cenydd is said to have been the illegitimate son of one of King Arthur's knights. According to legend he was born with a deformed leg, as a punishment for the sins of his parents, and cast adrift on the Loughor estuary in a cradle. This drifted out beyond Whiteford Point but the baby was rescued by sea-birds, taken to Worms Head – at the southern end of Rhossili Bay – and looked after by angels.

The limestone island is cut in half by a ditch believed to have been hacked out by Iron Age dwellers about 2,000 years ago. At that time, Burry Holms may have been a headland rather than an island. Later, this fortification may also have been used as a base by Viking raiders; 'holms' is derived from an Old Norse word meaning 'island'. The island is now joined to the mainland for just over two hours on either side of low water. Tide times should be obtained from the coastguard station by the car park at Rhossili.

Although it covers only 6ha (15¼ acres), The Holms, as it is known locally, has plenty of atmosphere, and is the haunt of sea-birds and waders. Birds likely to be seen on and near the island include fulmars, gannets, cormorants, oystercatchers, dunlins and purple sandpipers.

▶ *From Llanrhidian, at the intersection of the B4271 and B4295, follow the signposted minor road to Llangennith. Follow the lane to Llangennith Burrows (where there is limited parking).*

❷ Whiteford Burrows

Sweeping northwards to Whiteford Point, this desert of wind-sculpted sand-dunes overlooks one of Gower's largest and loneliest beaches. Reached on foot from either Llanmadoc or the neighbouring hamlet of Cwm Ivy, the dunes are included within a 1,200ha (3,000 acre) National Nature Reserve leased to the Countryside Council for Wales by the National Trust.

Rich in lime and relatively undisturbed, the dunes have many damp hollows – known as 'slacks' – where a great variety of insects, including froghoppers, leafhoppers, spiders, wasps, soldier-flies and beetles, live among the creeping willow, mosses, liverworts and orchids. A plantation of conifers, planted to help stabilise the dunes, contrasts with the huge expanse of slender marram grass.

To the south, beyond the limestone cliffs of Hills Tor, there are walks over the dunes or along the shore to Broughton Bay and Bluepool Corner, accessible only on foot. This part of the coast is scoured by strong tides that sweep in and out of the Loughor estuary. Sixteen ships, outward bound from Llanelli, were wrecked between the Burry Inlet and Broughton Bay in a single night in 1868. The chief cause of the disaster was a heavy onshore swell, resulting from an earlier storm, combined with a lack of wind to fill the sails. Four of the vessels were lost with all hands, and in the morning the sands down the north-west Gower coast were strewn with lost cargoes, shattered wrecks and corpses.

▶ *The village of Llanmadoc is signposted along minor roads from the intersection of the B4295 and B4271 at Llanrhidian.*

Wales and the Welsh Borders

147

❸ Llanmadoc Hill

Reached by footpaths from Llanmadoc, Cheriton and Llangennith, this steep-sided, flat-topped hill dominates the north-west corner of Gower and is one of the peninsula's most rewarding viewpoints. Weobley Castle is a major landmark, perched on a steep slope above the green wilderness of Llanrhidian Marsh where streams known locally as 'pills' wriggle towards the sea like silver snakes.

The summit of the hill is 186m (609ft) above the nearby sea, and shares with Cefn Bryn the distinction of being the second highest point on the Gower peninsula. The highest, The Beacon on Rhossili Down, is just over 2 miles away to the south.

Sheep and ponies wander over the slopes, grazing on the springy upland turf that grows between thick carpets of bracken, gorse and heathers. The top of the hill forms a mile-long ridge whose eastern end is notable for a fine Iron Age earthwork known as The Bulwark. Although not easy to discern from the foot of the hill, the complexity of the enclosure's defences is obvious to walkers. On the western side there are no fewer than six banks and five ditches to protect what was probably a refuge in times of trouble rather than a permanent community. Cairns of tumbled stones elsewhere on the ridge are the remains of Bronze Age burial sites.

▶ *Llangennith, Llanmadoc and Cheriton lie on signposted minor roads to the west of Llanrhidian, at the junction of the B4295 and B4271.*

❹ Cefn Bryn

The Gower Peninsula is famed for its spectacular coastal scenery, but visitors who ignore inland Cefn Bryn are missing one of the peninsula's most interesting and attractive features. Formed of Old Red Sandstone, the heather, gorse and bracken-clad ridge is the 'backbone' of Gower and runs north-westwards from Penmaen towards Burry Green. It reaches 186m (609ft) – about the highest point on Gower after Rhossili Down – and can be walked from end to end following Talbot's Way, a green road named after a 19th-century occupier of Penrice Castle. Walkers share the ridge with free-roaming sheep and ponies.

There are superb views from the road that runs eastwards from Reynoldston. The Brecon Beacons, Mynydd Preseli, Lundy island and parts of Somerset and Devon are clearly visible in good conditions. Oxwich Point and Rhossili Down are major landmarks on Gower itself.

From the point where the road from Reynoldston crosses the crest there is a short walk westwards to Arthur's Stone. Despite its name, this Bronze Age burial chamber dates from about 2500 BC and was old long before the time of the legendary warrior-king.

A mile north-east of Arthur's Store, near the point where the Reynoldston road joins the B4271, lies Broad Pool. This large expanse of water was formed when glacial clays lined a large hollow, or sink, carved out of Gower's underlying limestone by acidic water. The attractive pool, in which water-lilies grow, has been made a nature reserve which is owned by The Wildlife Trust of South and West Wales. Birds on and around the pool include mute swans, little grebes and grey herons. Five minutes' walk to the north-east is another massive sink, 9m (30ft) deep, called Moor Mills. Several streams drain into it and vanish because there is no glacial clay to retain the water.

▶ *Penmaen, on the A4118, lies at the eastern end of Cefn Bryn and is a good starting point for walks. Several minor roads off the A4118 west of Penmaen lead north on to the ridge.*

❺ Llanrhidian

Built on a steep slope above the Loughor estuary, Llanrhidian overlooks a vast wilderness of tidal salt-marsh, beyond which are immense sandbanks where local people have harvested cockles for hundreds of years. Just over 4 miles to the north-west, the abandoned lighthouse off Whiteford Point marks the seaward end of the estuary where huge expanses of muddy sand, carved by deep and steep-sided channels, glisten and shimmer at low tide.

The marsh itself is formed from tidal mud that has been trapped and stabilised by plants such as glasswort and cord-grass. On this has spread a sprawling growth of sea manna-grass, sea lavender, creeping fescue and marsh mallow which now provides grazing for sheep and ponies. Birds likely to be seen include mallard,

A VAST WILDERNESS

wigeons, teal, brent geese, white-fronted geese, oystercatchers, curlews, snipe, dunlins, sanderlings and golden, grey and ringed plovers.

Cars may be parked along the lane between Llanrhidian and Crofty, but you should take advice before venturing on to the marsh. Walkers can easily be trapped by fast-rising tides. Also, it is advisable to keep to the paths as this area was a military firing range during the Second World War and there is still the risk of unexploded missiles off the beaten path.

Less than a mile east of Llanrhidian, the summit of Cilifor Top is crowned with an Iron Age fort dating from the 1st century BC; it is the largest enclosure of its type on Gower. From within the three great ramparts and ditches that enclose the steep-sided hill, the Silures – the dominant Celtic tribe in Iron Age South Wales – were able to delay the Roman conquest of the area until late in the 1st century AD.

To the west of Llanrhidian, the lane that runs towards Cheriton and Llanmadoc passes Weobley Castle which, despite its name, was never much more than a fortified manor house. Between the 13th and 20th centuries, it was only once involved in a battle, and that was in Owain Glyndwr's revolt of 1400. Otherwise, it gently deteriorated into a farm and then to a barn and a storeroom; now it is a ruin, and the only warlike notes it hears are the distant bangs of huntsmen's guns – in season – from the marshes.

▶ *Llanrhidian lies at the junction of the B4295 and B4271 on the north coast of Gower.*

❻ Park Woods

Green Cwm, the valley that runs through the heart of Park Woods, was carved by a stream that now flows beneath the limestone for more than a mile before emerging above Parkmill. Its course is followed by a Forestry Commission road, open only to walkers, which passes the Parc le Breos burial chamber. Known locally as the Giants' Grave, the tomb is covered by a 20m (70ft) long mound of stones, and is one of Gower's best-preserved prehistoric sites. Skeletons dating from about 4,500 years ago were found here when the tomb was opened in 1869.

Cathole, a cave where the remains of prehistoric animals have been found, is on a steep slope about 180m (200yd) higher up the valley.

The walk can be continued to Llethrid, on the B4271 between Upper Killay and Llanrhidian, where the stream commences its underground journey. Llethrid Swallet, a limestone cavern near the road bridge, has beautiful stalactites and stalagmites, but should only be explored by experienced cavers.

▶ *Parkmill lies just north of the A4118, 2 miles east of Penmaen.*

❼ Pwlldu Bay

A stream bustles southwards from Bishopston, curling through a valley dark with trees, then runs to meet the sea in this lovely little bay. Two isolated, whitewashed cottages overlook a beach where a storm-raised bank of shingle leads to a broad expanse of low-tide sand. To the west lies Pwlldu Head, the highest point on the entire Gower coast.

The rocks below the headland are known as Graves End, in memory of some 70 sailors who were buried there after a shipwreck in 1760. The vessel was almost certainly the *Caesar*, carrying munitions and a number of recently impressed men battened below hatches. No doubt it was these unfortunates who accounted for the high rate of casualties.

From the headland, and from the lower cliffs on the opposite side of the bay, there are superb views across the Bristol Channel to Somerset and Devon. The cliff-top path east of Pwlldu leads to Brandy Cove, a tiny bay once used by smugglers.

Like many of Gower's most attractive beaches, Pwlldu can be reached only on foot, but lanes and footpaths converge on it from Pennard, Pyle and Bishopston.

▶ *Bishopston lies on the B4436, which runs between the A4118 and the A4067.*

OF TIDAL SALT-MARSH
LLANRHIDIAN

HIGH, SANDY SLOPES
CLAD WITH BRACKEN
THREE CLIFF BAY

❽ Three Cliff Bay

High, sandy slopes clad with bracken form a natural amphitheatre behind this handsome bay whose beach is bisected by the waters of Pennard Pill. The bay is named from the three triangular crags of limestone, pierced by a natural arch, that mark its eastern boundary. To the west, Great Tor overlooks Oxwich Bay.

Reached by footpaths from Southgate, Parkmill and Penmaen, Three Cliff Bay embraces considerable, if fading, evidence of early occupation by man. On the high ground behind Great Tor there is a prehistoric tomb, traces of a 12th-century Norman castle, and a few stones marking the site of a medieval church.

On the opposite side of the bay, about half a mile inland, the remains of Pennard Castle stand upon a steep slope high above the river. Built in the 13th century it was said to have been the home of Rhys ap Iestyn. For his churlish behaviour towards the Little Folk – he refused to let them join in his wedding revels – Lord Rhys, his castle and all his people were overwhelmed by sand on the same night. Whatever the truth of the story, Pennard Castle was described as 'desolate and ruinous' as long ago as 1650.

▶ *Parkmill and Penmaen lie on the A4118.*

❾ Oxwich Bay

One of Gower's best-loved features is Oxwich Bay, which lies halfway along the southern coast. It is best seen from the top of Oxwich Point, which towers 85m (280ft) above the sea; from there, the graceful crescent of sand sweeps round to Great Tor, Three Cliff Bay and the battered ramparts of silver-grey limestone that rise to a dramatic climax at Pwlldu Head, 4 miles to the east.

Behind the beach are sand-dunes, a salt-water marsh, a freshwater marsh and reedy pools, some of which are man-made and were stocked with fish early in the 19th century. This profusion of greenery is threaded by the Nicholaston Pill stream that flows beneath hanging woodlands to the sea. Much of the area has been a National Nature Reserve since 1963, to which access is limited; however, there are two excellent nature trails. One explores the dunes and offers a vantage point with views over the wilderness where grey herons, coots, moorhens, reed warblers and many other birds live amid water-lilies and willows.

The woodland walk along the steep flanks of Oxwich Point takes up to three hours to complete. It starts by St Illtyd's Church, whose tiny chancel is thought to have been the cell of a Celtic monk. At the landward end of the headland, a steep lane climbs through a tunnel of trees to reach ruined Oxwich Castle, a fortified manor house, which dates from the middle of the 16th century. Its first owners were the Mansels, one of whom, Anne, was killed outside the gatehouse in 1557, when her family came to blows with some Swansea men over the ownership of a cargo from a French ship wrecked in Oxwich Bay. From the castle there are extensive views over the bay towards Pwlldu Head.

▶ *Oxwich, a focal point for walks round the bay, is signposted off the A4118, 1½ miles west of Penmaen.*

❿ Port-Eynon

The road that plunges down into this compact and colourful village passes a poignant reminder that the seas about Gower are not always tranquil. In a corner of a churchyard stands the statue of Billy Gibbs, the coxswain of the local lifeboat, who died with two of his crew while trying to reach a ship in distress off Pwlldu Head in 1916.

The road ends in a car park above the long, dune-backed sweep of Port-Eynon Bay. This is sheltered by a rugged headland where limestone was quarried in the 19th century and shipped out across the Bristol Channel. On the 2¾ mile nature trail climbing the headland there is a chance of seeing ravens, kestrels, Manx shearwaters, fulmars, gannets and cormorants, as well as various species of gulls and auks.

The coves and caves along the rugged coast made Port-Eynon a smuggling base until the end of the 18th century. The most notorious local smuggler and wrecker was John Lucas who, during the 16th century, acquired something of a Robin Hood reputation in the area. He lived in the Salt House on Port-Eynon Point, where its remains can still be seen – or rather, those of two cottages built out of the ruins after the house was destroyed by a storm in 1703

Just beyond the point, and accessible only at low tide, is Culver Hole, a deep gully fronted by an extraordinary 18m (60ft) high wall, pierced by openings for doors and windows. Who built this structure, and why, is unknown. Legend says that Culver Hole was a gigantic store-room for John Lucas's loot; or more prosaically, it could have been an elaborate dovecot, built to provide local people with fresh meat in winter.

▶ *Port-Eynon is at the end of the A4118, the main road through Gower.*

⑪ Rhossili

Hang-gliders are launched from the slopes of Rhossili Down and are often seen floating like colourful pterodactyls above Gower's most westerly village. Rhossili, lashed by winter storms, stands on a cliff 75m (250ft) above the sea, and from here a footpath runs down to the vast, surf-pounded beach that sweeps northwards to Burry Holms. At low tide, the oak ribs of the *Helvetia* – a coaster driven ashore by a gale in 1887 – are clearly visible on the sands below the village. All hands were saved, but her cargo, 500 tonnes of timber, was scattered all over the beach. The villagers 'rescued' it with horse and cart and sold it cheap to South Wales timber merchants.

Somewhere near by, Gower's most famous shipwreck lies. No one knows her name, or where she came from, and she is simply known as 'The Dollar Ship', from the gold moidores and doubloons found from time to time in the sand. The coins date from the 17th century, so she had nothing to do with the Armada. One story says that the vessel was carrying a Spanish lady's dowry to her English husband, but this is probably Gower romanticism. Sadly, no coins have been reported for about a century, but it might be worth keeping your eyes open as you walk along the beach.

There is a splendid walk northwards from the village over the whaleback ridge of Rhossili Down, which rises to 193m (632ft) – the highest point on Gower. Neolithic burial chambers near the summit are known as Sweyne's Howes. According to legend, they mark the grave of a Viking chief named Sweyne, who may have given his name to Swansea – 'Sweyne's-ey', or island.

From Rhossili Down, on days when the frequent Welsh hazards of haze, drizzle or mist are absent, it is possible to see Hartland Point, 40 miles away on the Devon coast, and St Govan's Head on the edge of Pembrokeshire.

▶ *Rhossili lies at the western end of the B4247, which branches off the A4118 about 2 miles north of Port-Eynon.*

⑫ Worms Head

One mile long, but nowhere more than a few hundred metres wide, Worms Head is one of Gower's most spectacular natural features. Reached after a walk of 15–20 minutes along the cliff-top from Rhossili, the promontory is joined to the mainland by a rocky causeway that is submerged at high tide and passable only for about two and a half hours on either side of high water. Times when it is safe to cross are posted outside the coastguard station and at the National Trust Visitor Centre in Rhossili. It is essential to heed the notice, and to keep a close eye on the clock: if you do not leave Worm – as it is called locally – at least three and a half hours before high water you will be trapped.

Worms Head is derived from *wurm* – the Old English word for 'dragon' – and the headland does indeed resemble an immense sea monster, particularly from the air and from the Bristol Channel. Near its seaward end is a natural arch known as the Devil's Bridge, while a narrow cleft through which wind and water hiss and thunder is called the Blow Hole.

Worms Head is part of a nature reserve that includes the Limestone Nature Trail, which starts and ends in Rhossili. Along the way you can see the ribs of the wrecked *Helvetia* (see left) and the remains of an Iron Age fortified village, the Rhossili Vile – a rare Saxon open-field system still in use – and, in spring, the nests of guillemots and razorbills on Worms Head cliffs.

▶ *Take the B4247 to Rhossili, where there is a car park. The National Trust Visitor Centre is 45m (50yd) from the car park.*

The PEMBROKESHIRE COAST

The coast of the Pembrokeshire peninsula is lined with towering cliffs, craggy islands and shingle coves. Inland stand mountains of volcanic rock, glowering over a landscape of patchwork fields.

❶ Cemaes Head

Dramatic cliffs made up of layers of rock, contorted into fantastic folds, rise almost 170m (550ft) from the sea at Cemaes Head. Layers of sand and mud deposited on the sea-bed 500 million years ago were compressed into rock, then subjected to immense sideways pressure that made them buckle into the present folds. The formations show best in the high cliff and at Pen yr Afr, 1½ miles south-west of Cemaes Head. The path along the cliff-top brings them into view as it winds back and forth: parts of the path are steep and become slippery in wet weather. From the highest point there are views across Cardigan Bay to Snowdonia and the peaks of Yr Eifl, 60 miles away on the Lleyn Peninsula.

Below the eastern edge of Cemaes Head lies the broad, sheltered estuary of the River Teifi. Poppit Sands stretch out into the estuary at low tide and at the northern tip is Cardigan Island. Puffins nested there before rats overran the island, but now the rats have gone and it is hoped the puffins will return.

▶ *Cemaes Head is 4 miles north-west of Cardigan. The B4546 from Cardigan runs beside the estuary for 3 miles to Poppit Sands. From there a narrow lane continues for almost 2 miles to the path.*

❷ Dinas Island

An immense table of rock forms the headland called Dinas Island. It really was an island about 10,000 years ago – very recently in geological terms – when melt-water from Ice Age glaciers flowed through the flat-bottomed, wooded valley that still marks the 'island's' southern edge.

The table of rock tilts from the 142m (465ft) cliffs at Dinas Head in the north down to the valley. A path runs across the valley between the two delightful beaches – at Pwllgwaelod and Cwm-yr-eglwys. The remains of a small and ancient church stand just above the beach at Cwm-yr-eglwys, a poignant reminder of the sea's awesome power. On October 25, 1859, the church was smashed by a hurricane which also wrecked 114 ships on the coasts of Wales.

A footpath runs right round the headland, overlooking cliffs and stacks where black-backed gulls, fulmars, shags, razorbills and guillemots breed. On the landward slope, sheltered from Atlantic storms, wild flowers attract red admirals, peacock butterflies and the small blue.

▶ *Off the A487, east from Fishguard, there are three minor roads. The first two lead to Pwllgwaelod, the third leads to Cwm-yr-eglwys,.*

THE VIEW FROM DINAS ISLAND

❸ Pen Caer

This rugged, windswept peninsula juts sturdily northwards, sheltering Fishguard Bay which stretches below its eastern slope. Across the bay, a tumble of cliffs running up to Dinas Head makes a gaunt backdrop to the serene waters, ruffled now and then as the ferry boats leave Fishguard for Ireland. The wild and craggy Strumble Head is the most northerly point of the peninsula. It is a fine viewpoint for surveying the whole of Cardigan Bay, and is reached after an exhilarating walk across a remote stretch of bracken, heather and broom, where gulls, choughs and ravens wheel above.

Pen Caer is only the tip of an immensely thick layer – over 1,000m (3,500ft) deep – of hard volcanic rock. Its highest cliffs tower up 120m (400ft) and are at their most impressive at Pwll Deri on the western rim of the promontory. Here, seals roll in the water far beneath the summit. Pen Caer is crowned by an Iron Age hill-fort with several rows of stone ramparts linking the natural outcrops of rock.

A solitary stone on Carregwastad Point, east of Strumble Head, commemorates the last invasion of Britain. It took place in February 1797, when more than 1,200 Frenchmen – mainly ex-convicts rather than disciplined troops – landed under the leadership of an American, William Tate. They sacked local farms before surrendering at the end of two days of minor skirmishes. Local folklore claims that the invaders mistook the numerous red shawls of Fishguard's ladies for the red coats of a crack British regiment, and yielded before this superior force. Twenty invaders lost their lives and there were two Welsh casualties.

▶ *From Goodwick on the A40 a minor road curves through the hamlet of Llanwnda and round the peninsula about ½ mile from the coast. Tracks lead from the road at various points to Carregwastad Point, Strumble Head and Pwll Deri. The coastal-path walk from Carregwastad Point to Pwll Deri is about 6 miles. There is a car park at Pwll Deri.*

❹ Cwm Gwaun

Carved by a clear river in which swim salmon and sea trout – known as sewin in Wales – the gentle beauty of the deep, wooded valley with its narrow, tree-flanked lanes seems a world apart from the savage grandeur of the nearby coast. Instead of gorse-clad cliffs there are lush groves of oak, sycamore and hazel, thickly carpeted with woodruff, celandines, primroses, bluebells and wood anemones. Instead of the aggressive screams of sea-birds, the sweet songs of warblers and dippers, and the sharp, high-pitched calls of grey wagtails are gentle accompaniments to the rippling stream.

Waymarked walks start from two Forestry Commission picnic places in the valley above Cilrhedyn Bridge. The lane that climbs steeply from Llanychaer Bridge swings right on the valley's rim and passes Parc y Meirw – 'Field of the Dead' – a 40m (140ft) row of eight Bronze Age megaliths, four of the huge stones still upright. A lady dressed in white haunts them on dark nights – according to local belief. People in Cwm Gwaun's scattered hamlets and farms still celebrate New Year's Eve on January 12, cheerfully ignoring the fact that the Gregorian calendar was changed in 1752 to bring the country into line with the rest of Europe.

Lower Town, where Cwm Gwaun meets the sea, is a picturesque village where *Moby Dick* and *Under Milk Wood* were filmed.

▶ *Llanychaer Bridge is 2¼ miles south-east of Fishguard on the B4313. About 1 mile further on is a lane that branches left and winds up the valley.*

❺ Carningli Common

Local legends maintain that St Brynach, one of St David's contemporaries in the 6th century, used to climb to Carningli's rocky summit to talk with the angels. It is certainly a wonderful vantage point, 347m (1,138ft) above Newport Bay, from which to admire the wide-ranging views north-east over Cemaes Head and across Cardigan Bay, and west over Fishguard to the cliffs of Strumble Head. Just south is Mynydd Preseli, rising above Cwm Gwaun.

The common, carpeted with heather and gorse, rises steeply to a rough peak whose tumbled rocks are mottled with lichens. Iron Age men used the stone to build the defensive wall that encircles the summit. Plain to see inside the wall are the stone foundation circles of the beehive-shaped huts where they lived.

Numerous paths cross the common; the most direct way to the summit starts from the narrow lane that runs south-east from Newport towards Cilgwyn. Short but steep, the path at first follows the arrow-straight line of a tramway, long since vanished, which transported stone from a small quarry. The stone supports for the winding gear that used to haul wagons up the slope are still standing.

Away below the common is the delightful tangle of Newport's narrow streets and colour-washed buildings, huddling round the ruins of the medieval castle. The bay at Newport was once busy with sailing-ships coming to trade or for repair in the shipyard. Square-rigged vessels and schooners were built in the yard during the 19th century. The port was used by trading coasters until the 1930s, but now the harbour has silted up.

▶ *From Newport, on the A487, a minor road runs south-east to Cilgwyn. The path up Carningli Common starts from this minor road, at New England, just over 1 mile from Newport.*

TUMBLED ROCKS ARE MOTTLED WITH LICHENS
CARNINGLI MOUNTAIN

❻ Mynydd Preseli

Smooth but steep, Mynydd Preseli – the Preseli Mountain – rises to peaks of shattered rock striding west from Crymych towards the sea. An ancient ridge way rises and dips from one summit to the next, giving marvellous views. Foel-cwmcerwyn, the highest point, lies just south of the ridge way. From its 536m (1,760ft) top, there is a view of Pembrokeshire's tiny patchwork fields, held in a sweep of the sea and probed by the fingers of Milford Haven. Beyond the encircling sea the Lleyn Peninsula rises in the north, and Devon's rocky coast is seen far away in the south.

The ridge track forms part of a prehistoric route used by travellers from Salisbury Plain to Whitesands Bay who then sailed to Ireland to barter for copper and gold. Bronze Age burial cairns and Iron Age defences and hut circles are scattered over the slopes.

Carnmenyn was the source of the massive bluestones that were used to build Stonehenge. Over 4,000 years ago, more than 80 huge stones weighing a total of about 250 tonnes were prised from the hillside. Hewing and transporting such monoliths would have been a formidable task for men without sophisticated machinery and transport. Our ancestors must have used simple sledges, rollers and rafts to take their precious cargoes down to the tidal waters above Milford Haven, out into the open sea, along the Bristol Channel, and then presumably up the rivers of south-west England to Salisbury Plain.

▶ *Crymych is on the A478, 8½ miles south of Cardigan. Just south of the village a lane turns west and after a mile reaches the ridge way. Cammenyn is 1½ miles west along the ridge way and lies just south of it. Foel-cwmcerwyn is a further 3 miles west and lies ½ mile south of the track; it can also be approached by a 2 mile walk east from the B4329.*

❼ Abercastle

An old lime-kiln and the ruins of two small warehouses are reminders that this rocky inlet – a safe haven on a treacherous coast – flourished as a little port when the sea was Pembrokeshire's main link with the outside world. Records of coastal trading here date back to Tudor times. In the 19th century sloops plied from the harbour to Liverpool and Bristol, carrying out cargoes of corn and butter and bringing back goods from the shops. Exports of oats and imports of coal did not cease until the 1920s. Now a few private craft shelter in the narrow harbour, overlooked by cottages and resting on the greyish sand that appears at low tide beyond the pebbles. The harbour is a natural one formed in a 'drowned' valley where the sea-level rose as the glaciers of the Ice Age melted.

A splendid cliff-top walk runs eastwards to the secluded, shingle-backed bays of Aber Mawr and Aber Bach, 2½ and 3 miles away. Beyond, the cliffs of the Pen Caer peninsula rise dramatically to more than 120m (400ft) above coves where seals breed.

A much shorter stroll on the opposite side of Abercastle's inlet leads to Carreg Samson, a Neolithic burial chamber 3,000 years old. Its capstone is 5m (16ft) long and still rests on three of the original seven uprights. The story goes that Samson lifted the capstone into place with his little finger; the finger is supposed to have been buried on the rocky promontory of Ynys y Castell, which shields the harbour from the north. Here you can look back at Abercastle's inlet and the great table of Carreg Samson.

▶ *Six miles south-west of Fishguard along the A487 a minor road branches north-west through Mathry to Abercastle, which is 2½ miles off the main road.*

❽ Porthgain

Porthgain, a village in a narrow cleft in northern Pembrokeshire's spectacularly wild coast, has an unexpected and individual character. The village is little more than a few 19th-century cottages and a pub – but its snug harbour is overlooked by huge, bramble-wreathed ruins. Here, stone from quarries on the western side of the creek was crushed and stored in bins beside the quay to await loading on to schooners and, later, steamships.

The stone – volcanic, blue-grey and very hard – was used for roadstone from Victorian times until the quarries closed in 1931. In its heyday the village produced 40,000 tonnes a year to ship to ports as far off as London, Whitstable and Belfast, as well as to local destinations. Tramways linked the quarries, the crushing plant and the quayside loading areas. Old mooring chains and seaweed-draped ladders set into the harbour walls are additional reminders that this was once a bustling, thriving port. The pillars that guided ships into Porthgain's rocky inlet still stand on the embracing headlands.

A path running west along the cliff passes the old quarry workings on its way to the sandy beach at Traeth Llyfn. It is a magnificent walk over the empty, gorse-clad headlands with the sea foaming against the adamant fingers of rock and lapping quietly into the sandy inlets.

▶ *Porthgain is at the end of a minor road that turns north-west off the A487 at Croesgoch, 9 miles south-west of Fishguard.*

ST DAVID'S HEAD FROM PENBERRY

⑨ St David's Head

This exposed, rocky headland stretches out into the Atlantic, superbly wild crags lining its northern rim and the pretty little cove of Porthmelgan tucked under its southern edge. Thrift, sea campion and heathers smother the rocks in surprising profusion.

From the path above the crags you can see the waves foaming over the treacherous offshore rocks known as the Bishops and Clerks, and then rolling in to break as crashing surf on the long, sandy stretch of Whitesands Bay south of the headland. The best vantage point of all is Carn Llidi, the steep-flanked hill whose rocky summit rises 181m (595ft) above the nearby sea. The hills of Ireland, 85 miles away, are visible on the best days, and there are few better places from which to gaze spellbound at the glory of a summer sunset.

The western tip of St David's Head was used as a fortress during the Iron Age, sealed off by a stone barrier, now tumbled, which later generations dubbed the Warriors' Dyke. Within its protection, boulders embedded in the turf mark the bases of circular huts where Iron Age tribesmen lived almost 2,000 years ago. Near by, on Carn Llidi's north-west slopes, the stone walls that enclosed their small fields still show each year before the bracken grows too high.

Whitesands Bay was the western end of a Bronze Age trade route that started at Salisbury Plain. Primitive craft set out from the bay to sail to Ireland in continuation of the trade route. Copper and gold was the lure that made them undertake the voyage. St Patrick is said to have sailed from Whitesands on his last voyage to Ireland, and an inscribed stone marks the site of an ancient chapel dedicated to him.

▶ *Signposted lanes lead from the city of St David's to Whitesands Bay, 2 miles to the north-west. There is a car park at the bay, and a path leads from it to St David's Head, 1 mile away.*

⑩ Ramsey Island

Sea-scoured caves and cliff-flanked coves beyond the reach of man make Ramsey an ideal breeding ground for grey seals. These creatures love the caves and rocky beaches all around the island, and gather there to give birth to their pups from late August to November.

The island's 2 mile length changes from fertile growth in the north and east to heathland on the thin soils that cover the hard, volcanic rocks of the south and west. Vast numbers of rabbits graze the land, along with sheep, goats and a herd of red deer imported from the mainland. Choughs, kittiwakes, razorbills and guillemots line the cliffs in summer.

The cliffs rise to 90m (300ft) and are so formidable that there is only one landing point for boats. It did not exist until 1935, when, with great difficulty, a wall was built between Ramsey's edge and a vast hump of rock close beside it. This kept out the ferocious waters that had surged between them, and it created a quiet haven in its lee.

St Justinian is credited with making Ramsey an island, in the 6th century. Seeking complete solitude, this stern disciplinarian left his self-indulgent colleagues at St David's monastery and strode off to Ramsey. As he went along he smote with his axe at the narrow neck of rock that linked the mainland and Ramsey. All that he left of it was the cruel reef called The Bitches and Whelps – now usually shortened to The Bitches – through and over which the high tides race at 8 knots. Justinian's austere ways eventually alienated those who had followed him, and they cut off his head. It is said that he walked back to the mainland carrying his own head, and was buried at the chapel whose ruins still stand near St Justinian's on the mainland.

Ramsey has not been inhabited since the 1960s but it is possible to visit the island, and enquiries regarding boat times should be made at the tourist office in St David's.

▶ *Ramsey is reached by boat from St Justinian's, which is 2 miles west of St David's along a marked minor road. There is a car park at St Justinian's.*

⑪ Skomer Island

Birds are the reason for visiting Skomer National Nature Reserve. There are hundreds of thousands, crowded clamorously on the cliffs that surround the 290ha (720 acre) island. Razorbills, guillemots, kittiwakes, shags, fulmars, great black-backed gulls and herring gulls pack the ledges. Puffins breed on the island, either in abandoned rabbit burrows or in those they have excavated themselves.

The puffins' burrows are heavily outnumbered by those of the Manx shearwaters. Skomer is the main breeding site for this species and home to more than 100,000 pairs, making them the largest group of birds by far on the island. But there is no sign of them; these black-and-white petrels spend their days at sea or in their burrows, emerging only late at night.

However, Skomer is far from being simply a bird-thronged island. On the contrary, it is like a vast rock garden in spring and summer. Sea campions, blue squills, pink thrift and yellowish-green rock samphire drape the hard, dark grey volcanic cliffs and spread on to the island top among the bluebells, red campions and fresh green bracken.

Birds, rabbits and the Skomer vole have taken complete possession of Skomer now, but 2,000 years ago Iron Age field enclosures and cultivation strips – lynchets – covered the surface. They are still visible, along with the foundations of circular huts.

From the cliff-tops you can look down on the grey seals sprawling on the rocks or gliding sinuously through the waters. Two miles to the south is the red-sandstone mass of Skokholm, another island sanctuary for sea-birds, with only limited access for visitors at present. Like Skomer it has a Norse name, not a sign of Norse occupation but of the supremacy of the Norsemen over these seas in the Dark Ages.

▶ *Boats cross to Skomer between April and September from Martin's Haven. This is 3 miles beyond a marked turning off the B4327, 11 miles south-west of Haverfordwest. There is a landing fee. A 4 mile marked nature trail circles the island.*

LIKE A VAST ROCK GARDEN IN SPRING AND SUMMER
SKOMER ISLAND

⑫ Martin's Haven

The steep-sided valley between the pebbled cove of Martin's Haven and the sandy little beach at Renny Slip offered a natural basis on which an Iron Age tribe made a defensive earthwork. This cut off the square promontory to the west of the valley and made it a secure site for their settlement. Now the promontory lies behind a disintegrating stone wall and is known as the Deer Park. It was intended to improve the estate of the great landowning Edwardes family, but no deer were ever introduced.

The 1½ mile walk round the Deer Park has a beauty out of all proportion to its modest length. Over the broad expanse of gorse, heather, bracken and brambles, flickering with butterflies, there are kestrels hovering, ravens soaring, stonechats dancing, and those rare red-legged, red-billed crows, the choughs, giving dazzling aerobatic displays. Below in the creaming waters grey seals play, and in the little bays their round-eyed silvery pups bask in October.

There is a wonderful scene from the highest point of the walk, where a coastguards' lookout stands almost 60m (200ft) above sea-level. Martin's Haven lies below, bustling now and again when a boat sets off for Skomer. The view sweeps round St Brides Bay, past the 2 mile stretch of Newgale Sands to the opposite end of the bay. There, violet-coloured cliffs rise just south of St David's, and at the very tip Ramsey Island lies across its narrow, wicked sound. The Deer Park's furthest spot is Wooltack Point, where the cliffs are high; you can look across the racing waters of Jack Sound to the bright floral carpet laid out on Skomer above its cliffs that quiver with sea-birds.

▶ *Martin's Haven is 12 miles south-west of Haverfordwest, 3 miles along a marked minor road that turns west off the B4327. There is a car park.*

⑬ St Brides Haven

Every bit as beautiful and tranquil as its name suggests, St Brides Haven was a welcome refuge for sailors for many hundreds of years. A few lengths of old mooring chain and the remains of a red-stone lime-kiln are relics of the coastal trade that flourished here until the late 19th century. Limestone was shipped in, burned in the kiln and used to fertilise the fields of local farms.

The ruined kiln now looks out over a snug inlet of red-speckled sand where the tide creams in between tilted tables of purple-red rock. Paths, ploughed fields, beach and cliffs all glow a rich crimson colour – unforgettable when a rosy sunset lights them. From the beach and the neighbouring cliffs there are wide-ranging views across St Brides Bay, which takes its name from the haven, towards St David's peninsula.

The St Bride who is remembered here was the glad-hearted Brigid of Kildare, whose feast day is February 1. She lived about AD 450–525 and was the first abbess to have authority over both a nunnery and a monastery. Brigid never left Ireland, but her adherents travelled widely throughout Europe spreading her fame. Churches are dedicated to her in Cornwall, Brittany, Italy and Belgium.

The church just above the beach at St Brides Haven dates from Norman times, but is only the replacement for a much earlier building which was devoured by the hungry sea. The sea is continually eroding the cliff, and just to the north of the lime-kiln, a number of small stone coffins from the 6th and 10th centuries have been exposed.

The waters lash below the open, attractive cliff walks on either side of the haven. On the eastern side are remote bays with names such as Dutch Gin and Brandy Bay, recalling the smuggling days of long ago. In the other direction there is wild Nab Head, where skilful Stone Age workers had a flint 'factory' 10,000 years ago to chip tools and weapons from the rocks. Down the western side of the headland the sea has worn a blow-hole through the rock, and bursts through it like a vast fountain in rough weather.

▶ *St Brides Haven is 2 miles along a marked minor road that turns right from the B4327, 8 miles south-west of Haverfordwest.*

THOUSANDS
OF WHITE
WATER-LILIES
BOSHERSTON LILY PONDS

⑭ Marloes

Pembrokeshire is richly endowed with enticing beaches, but few can rival Marloes Sands. The long stretch of sand is backed by boulders and rock pools. Behind them tower cliffs whose strata were contorted and tilted by violent earth movements about 400 million years ago. Constant attacks by the sea have left great mounds of rock on the beach, and worn an arch right through the rock at one point.

A 2 mile nature trail starts from the village car park and runs north-west along the cliffs. Gateholm Island, at the western end of the beach, is a craggy outcrop of Old Red Sandstone cut off from the mainland only at high water. From this outcrop there is a fine view of the sea-birds circling the cliffs of Skomer and Skokholm. Gateholm, a fine natural fortress, has traces of more than 100 huts arranged round three sides of a square: perhaps they were an Iron Age village or an early Christian monastic settlement.

Albion Sands, the beach just on the western side of Gateholm, is named after an early paddle-steamer wrecked there in the 1840s. The gaunt skeleton of the wreck projects from the sands at low tide. Musselwick Sands, reached on foot north from the lane between Marloes and Martin's Haven, is another superb and secluded beach, sheltered by sheer black cliffs and looking out across St Brides Bay.

▶ *Marloes village is 1 mile along a marked minor road that branches west from the B4327, 11 miles south-west of Haverfordwest. There is a car park 1 mile west of the village, and a path leads from there to the beach ¾ mile away.*

⑮ Minwear Wood

Far up the tidal reaches above Milford Haven are many narrow lanes and footpaths leading to lonely creeks rich in birdlife. Near the tidal limit of the Eastern Cleddau at Canaston Bridge is Minwear Wood, where plantations of American red oaks flash bright green in summer and glow in autumn among fast-growing conifers. Here, mallards and swans dip into the river, and badgers roam after dark.

Blackpool Mill stands at the north-east corner of the wood. Minwear Wood used to provide fuel for an ironworks at Blackpool, but demand eventually exceeded supply and the works was replaced by the flour-mill powered by the tidal water. From the mill, paths lead east through Canaston Wood, north-west into Pickle Wood across the river, and into Minwear Wood, where a circular walk has been marked by the Forestry Commission.

The Eastern Cleddau flows down to Minwear from Mynydd Preseli. It is very likely that the great bluestones used to build Stonehenge passed by Minwear Wood over 4,000 years ago – when it was a natural forest of native oaks. The stones were probably dragged on sledges down the slopes to the tidal creek just above Minwear, and there may have been slung between rafts for a river journey down to the coast and up the Bristol Channel on their way to Salisbury Plain.

▶ *The A40 east from Haverfordwest crosses Canaston Bridge after 7 miles. The A4075 runs south from the bridge and in 275m (300yd) a minor road goes to the west towards Blackpool Mill and Minwear Wood. There is a car park at the wood.*

⑯ Bosherston

Thousands of white water-lilies bloom in summer on the large freshwater pools lying east of the little village of Bosherston. From woodland paths beside the pools you can see the flowers – at their best in June – and watch the hovering dragonflies, the elegant swans, haughty herons and darting kingfishers. At the seaward end of the pools an expanse of 'young' dunes, formed during the last 200 years, leads to the sandy shore of Broad Haven. A lane from the village also leads more directly to the beach.

Fascinating contortions of rocks lie below the 5 mile cliff-path that works westward from Broad Haven to Elegug Stacks – but look for the notice in the village post office indicating when the path is open, for the area is a military training ground. About a mile from Broad Haven is the astonishing St Govan's Chapel. Built in the 13th century on the site of a Celtic hermit's cell, the tiny church is wedged deep in a rocky cleft where waves thunder over huge boulders.

A little further along the path is Bosherston Mere, a great cleft from which the sea spouts up 12m (40ft) or more in rough weather. Here is the Huntsman's Leap, where a rider leaped over the narrow gap, but died of shock when he realised that the chasm was 40m (130ft) deep.

At the end of the cliff-path are Elegug Stacks, standing just off shore. The two huge, sheer pillars of limestone are crowned by tree mallow, and in summer their faces are packed with the chocolate-brown, grey, black and white of guillemots, razorbills, fulmars and kittiwakes nesting in the cracks and on the narrowest of ledges. Elegug is the local name for the guillemot. Opposite the western stack, the pounding water has worn away a superb arch through the cliff called The Green Bridge of Wales.

▶ *Bosherston lies along a minor road south of the B4319, 4 miles south of Pembroke.*

⑰ Stackpole Quay

The Old Red Sandstone cliffs that run west from Manorbier suddenly give way to ramparts of vertical limestone at Stackpole Quay. The division is clearly defined in the rocks immediately east of this enchanting little cove at the mouth of a wooded valley. Grey and flat-topped, the cliffs sweep south to Stackpole Head, while to the north-east the worn and undulating sandstone glows warmly. The cove is artificial, carved from an old limestone quarry and guarded by a short, sturdy breakwater. Stone from the quarry was burned in the rectangular kiln beside the lane above the cove.

A broad expanse of beautiful sand backed by a wilderness of dunes clad with marram grass and shrubs is at Barafundle Bay, only a ten-minute walk away south along the cliff path. Steps cut into the cliff lead down to the beach. At the southern end of the beach, below the cliffs of Stackpole Head, the sea has worn away arches through the jutting rocks. On the far side of the headland, caves carved deep into the cliffs by the persistent sea have collapsed and left blowholes through the rock; water comes bursting up from them when there are heavy seas. From the lonely walk along the cliff path round the headland, miles of the Bristol Channel stretch away uninterrupted as far as the Gower peninsula in the east and Lundy island backed by the Devon coastline in the south.

▶ *Stackpole village is signposted from the B4319 along lanes that branch off 2½ and 3½ miles south of Pembroke. Half a mile east of the village a lane runs to the cliffs above Stackpole Quay; there is a car park.*

⑱ Manorbier

A mighty castle dominates the tongue of high ground in the green valley that runs down to Manorbier's sandy beach. Footpaths climb the Old Red Sandstone headlands that flank the bay, and join the track that runs along the cliff-top. Only a mile to the west along the cliff, after a walk that surveys the dramatic cliff scenery round to St Govan's Head, you can enjoy the beach at Swanlake Bay.

The King's Quoit rears up on the headland to the south of Manorbier Bay. It is a burial chamber about 5,000 years old, with a massive 4.5m (15ft) capstone resting on the ground at one end and supported by two upright stones at the other. From the path that leads a short distance to the east you can look across to the beautiful low dome of Caldey Island, resting on its platform of red-sandstone cliffs at the far end and white limestone near the mainland.

Manorbier Castle is impressive enough in itself, but has an extra claim to attention as the place where Gerald de Barri was born about 1146. The son of a Norman knight and a Welsh princess, he went into the Church and became known as Giraldus Cambrensis – 'Gerald of Wales'. Gerald never achieved his ambition to become Bishop of St David's, but won enduring fame for his *Journey through Wales*, a vivid picture of the country written after Gerald had travelled through Wales with Archbishop Baldwin of Canterbury in 1188, raising support for the Third Crusade.

▶ *Manorbier is 4½ miles west of Tenby on the B4585, which leads off the A4139.*

⑲ Caldey Island

The dark-robed Cistercian monks who farm Caldey and make perfume from its golden abundance of gorse flowers form a link with the legend-laced Age of Saints, when Celtic holy men sought refuge and solitude on several islands off the Welsh coast. The present community was founded in 1929, but Caldey has been a religious centre since the 6th century.

The smooth, high table of land slopes up gently from the limestone cliffs nearest the mainland to the red-sandstone cliffs at the southern end. Small sandy bays nestle under the cliffs. Quiet lanes thread beneath the trees and between the fields marked out by stone walls.

A footpath from the quay at Priory Bay leads up to the abbey, built in 1910 and designed by John Coates-Carter, whose white-washed walls, weathered red roofs, arches, turrets and pinnacles create an exotic atmosphere more Mediterranean than Welsh. A leafy lane runs south from the abbey to a lighthouse built in 1829 and standing almost 60m (200ft) above sea-level. From this highest part of the island there is a lovely view, across the neatly chequered island itself, and also across the sweep of Carmarthen Bay to the Gower Peninsula in the east and St Govan's Head to the west. Beyond the waters of the Bristol Channel the rocky coastline of North Devon rears up.

A little way on from the lighthouse are the old priory buildings on the site of the first monastery. It was set near the spring of fresh water, which is still the island's water source. Farm buildings surround the sturdy-walled priory church which was a place of refuge when the island was attacked by Vikings and other marauders. Now it shelters an ancient stone carved with ogham characters – ancient Celtic script – some 1,400 years ago.

▶ *Caldey Island is reached by boat from Tenby throughout the summer months. Tenby is at the southern end of the A478.*

The CAMBRIAN MOUNTAINS

Lakes, streams and waterfalls carve through these steep but smooth mountains of central Wales and major rivers – including the Severn, Wye, Teifi and Tywi – spring from their slopes.

❶ Furnace

The Afon Einion rushes down its wooded valley to join the River Dovey, and when it reaches Furnace it suddenly cascades over mossy, fern-flanked rocks sheltered by a grove of slender trees. The enchanting waterfall is overlooked by a sturdy stone building of the 18th century. Clinging to one wall is a great wheel that dips into a channel cut to let water from the river race through. The wheel powered the bellows of an iron-smelting furnace – from which the hamlet got its name.

The once-rampant native woods are less widespread in the district now, but Cwm Einion, the ravine down which the water hastens, still has a few oaks clinging to its steep sides. A lane climbs steeply alongside the water into Cwm Einion, and from it a waymarked walk of about a mile winds through the woods.

West of the main road through Furnace, fields and heath run down to the shore of the Dovey estuary. The Royal Society for the Protection of Birds has a reserve here, at Ynys-hir.
▶ *Furnace is 11 miles north-east of Aberystwyth, on the A487.*

❷ Dylife

A wild, high tract of uninhabited country lies between Plynlimon and the valley of the Dovey. The drive north-west across it from Staylittle to Machynlleth winds through the hills giving an ever-changing view of them, and a distant, unchanging prospect of Cadair Idris's towering line of crags and Aran Fawddwy's peak.

Before the road begins its climb, it runs beside the infant Afon Twymyn and sees the water plunge 43m (140ft) down Ffrwd Fawr, one of the highest falls in Wales. The river drops over the cliff-edge of Craig y Maes, then turns and runs beneath the cliff through a narrow valley.

After the road has passed through Dylife, a once-flourishing village that was a centre for lead-mining, it climbs steeply and from the highest point a broad track runs south-west. It is a bracing walk along it, passing the small lake of Glaslyn and then on to the foot of the crags of Taren Bwlch-gwyn.
▶ *The 11 mile minor road through Dylife to Machynlleth leaves the B4518 about 1 mile north of Staylittle. Staylittle is 7 miles north-west of Llanidloes on the B4518.*

FURNACE FALLS

❸ Llyn Clywedog

Fed by streams hurtling down steep, rocky slopes, the Afon Clywedog used to be one of the main causes of flooding in the Severn valley. The towns of Llanidloes, Newtown, Welshpool and Shrewsbury knew that they could expect trouble when heavy rain fell on the hills above the Clywedog.

But the turbulent, troublesome river was tamed when Llyn Clywedog was created. Its 72m (237ft) high dam, the tallest in Britain, was completed in 1968 at the southern end of a 6 mile long reservoir, winding between the jutting snouts of the hills. The water-level is allowed to fall during the summer to give plenty of spare capacity to absorb the fury of winter storms. Sailing boats scud over the reservoir, their sails adding bright dashes of colour to the scene of green hills and woodlands.

Now the energetic rivulets tumbling down the dingles of birches, hawthorns, rowans and hazels add to the interest of the shores. From the southern end of the reservoir a long, wooded peninsula curves out across the water. A scenic trail of 2½ miles, which can be cut short to a mile, loops round it. The trail crosses mixed woodland and leads through conifer woods – the habitats of a variety of birds – and then by grassy banks haunted by vivid butterflies. Wild thyme, tormentil, harebells and heather sweeten the air in their seasons.

A road that runs to the west of the lake climbs and dives over hills and valleys with the glistening waters almost constantly in view, then skirts the water's edge for a while before curving away into Hafren Forest. The forest, 17 sq miles of conifers planted by the Forestry Commission since 1937, takes its name from the Afon Hafren – more widely known as the Severn, which rises a few miles to the west and flows through the woodland for 5 miles. On its way, the young river gathers in the water from the streams and rivulets that hurry down from the hills along boulder-strewn gullies and over gushing waterfalls.

Several marked walks explore the glades and hollows beside the streams. The longest walk, of 8 miles, follows the Severn back to its source 610m (2,000ft) up on the slopes of Plynlimon. A shorter, but strenuous, walk of 3½ miles leads past the waterfall of Hafren-tori-gwddf – 'Severn-break-its-neck' – and the Cascades Trail passes a picturesque waterfall that drops into a deep pool once used for sheep-washing.

▶ *The minor road that skirts the western side of Llyn Clywedog branches west from the B4518, 2 miles north-west of Llanidloes. The Hafren Forest car park is 9 miles along this minor road.*

❹ Ponterwyd

The majestic bulk of Plynlimon soars upwards to the north of the village of Ponterwyd, gathered around a craggy gorge above the Afon Rheidol. Plynlimon (or Pumlumon Fawr) is a long cluster of smooth-sided hills that merges into one extensive whalebacked mountain. Just north of its highest point, rocky outcrops round a small tarn give it a more conventionally mountainous look.

Plynlimon's moist, peaty slopes are the source of the rivers Severn, Wye and Rheidol. The minor road coming north from Ponterwyd on the western slope, above the Rheidol, is the best start for a climb up the mountain. A track turns north-east from the road 2 miles north of Ponterwyd, mounts a shoulder of hill topped by woodland and joins a path that runs north to the summit. From here you can see the mountains of North and South Wales, and look north-westwards across the dark green expanse of the Rheidol Forest to Cardigan Bay.

Just south of Ponterwyd is Ysbyty Cynfyn. Its present church, built in 1827, stands on ground where people have worshipped for about 4,000 years. Five prehistoric monoliths now form part of the churchyard wall. The first Christian church at Ysbyty Cynfyn was probably built almost 1,500 years ago by Celtic monks. The 'new' religion often took over ancient pagan sites.

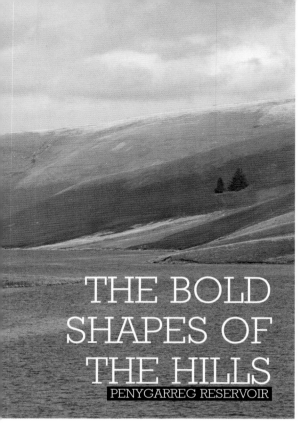

THE BOLD SHAPES OF THE HILLS

PENYGARREG RESERVOIR

From the churchyard there is a short walk to Parson's Bridge. The path zigzags down the slope to the bridge that spans the most dramatic part of the Rheidol Gorge. Far below it the river, which has raced south from Ponterwyd between crags and steep banks, seethes and roars among the rocks and holes it has sculpted and smoothed. Then it hastens on again through the tree-hung slopes towards Devil's Bridge.

▶ *Ponterwyd is 12 miles east of Aberystwyth, on the A44. Ysbyty Cynfyn is 1½ miles south on the A4120.*

❺ Vale of Rheidol

The Afon Rheidol is one of the most energetic rivers in Wales. It follows a 25 mile course from its source on Plynlimon to the sea at Aberystwyth. From the lanes that dip into the valley, or from the Vale of Rheidol steam railway that runs up from Aberystwyth, you might see grey herons visiting from the Dovey estuary. Blackthorn thickets spread across the ungrazed land, numerous sand martins are attracted to the still backwaters where insects breed, and occasionally you may see the brilliant turquoise flash of a kingfisher darting across the water. As the valley becomes narrower and steeper, the sides are clothed with sessile oaks, birches, beeches, sycamores and rowans. Pied flycatchers, nuthatches and redstarts breed here. Higher still, old lead workings have left their marks on the slopes.

Now the valley becomes even deeper and more confined, until it is a gorge 245m (800ft) deep. The scenic climax comes at a sharp bend where the Rheidol, thundering south from its craggy cleft, is joined by the Mynach flowing from the east on a course higher by 120m (400ft).

Tumbling down to join the Rheidol, the Mynach produces one frothing silver cascade after another, hissing noisily over the rock walls. Three bridges span the gorge. The medieval arched bridge lies at the lowest point – and is unaccountably named Devil's Bridge, although it was built for the monks from Strata Florida. The 18th-century bridge is much higher, and the 19th-century one is highest of all.

▶ *From Aberystwyth the A4120 runs south of the Vale of Rheidol, and the A44 runs north; lanes from them lead down to the valley, but no road runs along its full course. The A4120 reaches Mynach Falls 12 miles east of Aberystwyth.*

❻ Rhayader

The Afon Elan threads its way south through a world of heath-topped hills where ravens, skylarks and meadow pipits abound. More than 60 rivulets and streams run down the steep, grassy folds between the hills to mingle in its waters. Four reservoirs are strung along the Elan – Craig Goch, Penygarreg, Garreg-ddu and Caban-coch – all of them long and narrow.

Rhayader, the gateway to the valley, stands on the River Wye a mile or two north of the spot where the Elan joins it. It is a small town of colour-washed buildings clustered round a crossroads. A Victorian 'Gothic' suspension-bridge spans the river. Beyond the bridge, the road skirts Caban-coch Reservoir, crosses the dam and then follows the Afon Claerwen as it flows beneath lofty crags and thunders over a boulder-strewn waterfall. The road comes to an end on the Claerwen Reservoir dam, completed in 1952.

A drive up the four Elan reservoirs passes through 9 miles of lakeland, with the reflections of trees, crags and sky mirrored in the shining waters. But the uplands between the Elan valley and the Claerwen Reservoir are for those walkers who love to see the bold shapes of the hills in all their grandeur. There is a 6 mile track along the north bank of the Claerwen Reservoir, and in another mile it joins a track called Ancient Road. This strides north-east across the hills for 7 miles until it strikes the road at the head of the Elan reservoirs.

▶ *Rhayader is on the A470, 13 miles north-west of Builth Wells. The B4518 runs south-west along the Elan valley from Rhayader for 3 miles, then becomes an unclassified road skirting the reservoirs.*

❼ Strata Florida

Hidden away in a green and peaceful valley that gathers the upper waters of the Afon Teifi are the ruins of Strata Florida Abbey. Steep hills patched with stands of trees look down on the abbey that was once a centre of learning, religion and business. It was in 1164 that Cistercian monks first settled in Ystrad Fflur, the 'vale of flowers'; Strata Florida was their Latin version of the name. A large Norman church and abbey were built for them 2 miles from the first site, on land given by Robert Fitz-Stephen, a Norman baron. Local stone was the main material, but it was clad with sandstone, which must have been brought in, for there is none found locally.

Many a famous gathering met at the abbey. Llywelyn the Great summoned the Welsh princes there to swear allegiance to his son Dafydd in 1238, and noblemen from far away chose to be buried at Strata Florida. The abbey not only attracted the rich, but also became rich itself by trading in sheep, wool and lead. It owned large areas of land, stretching right to the coast 15 miles away. On the shore at Llanon there are the remains of curved stone fish-traps that were first built by the monks.

The contemplative life was interrupted by natural and political disasters, as well as by ceremonies and commerce. Lightning struck the abbey in 1285 and caused great damage. Ten years later, Edward I set fire to it because it was a stronghold of Welsh nationalism. It suffered further damage when it became a garrison for Henry IV's troops early in the 15th century during Owain Glyndwr's rebellion.

More than 460 years have passed since Strata Florida was closed by order of Henry VIII. Only the outline of the ground plan and an arch at the west door remain, but in their tranquil setting the crumbling lines of stonework gently evoke the days when monks toiled and prayed here.

▶ *The B4340 to Pontrhydfendigaid branches south-east off the A487, 1 mile south of Aberystwyth. From Pontrhydfendigaid, a minor road leads to Strata Florida, 1 mile to the south-east.*

❽ Tregaron

Stretching north from the town of Tregaron lies a wilderness of wetland. Thousands of years ago a glacier melting at the end of the Ice Age dropped debris that blocked the course of the Afon Teifi. The river spread behind the barrier and formed a large, shallow lake. Gradually the lake filled with sediments and wetland vegetation, which eventually formed successive layers of peat. The accumulating peat formed a convex shape, with its highest points some 6m (20ft) above the river that now meanders across it.

More than 3 square miles of Tregaron Bog – Cors Caron or Cors-goch Glan Teifi – now form Cors Caron National Nature Reserve, managed by the Countryside Council for Wales. An observation building provides extensive views over the wetland.

The moist, acid soil nurtures round-leaved sundew, bog rosemary, bog asphodel, crowberry and cranberry. In high summer the bog is white with the downy heads of cotton-grass, and in autumn it is rusty red with their dead stalks. Curlews, lapwings, sedge warblers and reed buntings are among the marsh birds that breed there, and among the scarce predators that visit the bog are hen harriers, merlins and red kites. It is also a summer hunting ground for polecats.

From Tregaron, the 'Mountain Road' runs south-east some 15 miles to the hamlet of Abergwesyn. The road, narrow and very steep in places, climbs to almost 500m (1,600ft) as it rises and drops across the wild, windswept tracts cut by deep, steep-sided valleys. This road was only the beginning of a journey for the drovers who used the mountain track from medieval times until the end of the 19th century. They would set out from Tregaron with cattle, sheep, pigs and even geese and turkeys to walk to markets as far away as Kent and Essex. The fowls had their feet coated with tar to save them from damage on the long trek. The drovers were accompanied by corgi dogs which were trained to keep the livestock together in open country. The dogs often made their own way home, arriving several days before their masters.

▶ *Tregaron is 9 miles north-east of Lampeter on the A485. Access to the Cors Caron reserve is from the B4343, 3 miles north of Tregaron.*

9 Llyn Brianne

An increased demand for water lead to one of the wildest and most remote parts of Wales being opened up. To supplement Swansea's water supply the reservoir of Llyn Brianne was created by damming the Afon Tywi; work was completed in 1973. Now the long, narrow stretch of water lies beneath steep hills and probes four sinuous tentacles into the conifer spread of the Tywi Forest. The lane that once ended at the isolated village of Rhandirmwyn, 4 miles below the dam, now goes on up the Tywi valley and above the lake's eastern shore.

A mile south of the dam, in the Dinas reserve run by the Royal Society for the Protection of Birds, a nature trail through colourful oakwoods curls round a steep, crag-topped hill. The 2 mile trail first runs beside the Tywi as it races through a spectacular gorge, and then climbs through the trees to Twm-Shon-Catti's Cave. It was a hideout of Catti, a 16th-century outlaw and highwayman whom folklore has turned into a Welsh Robin Hood.

The woodland scenery is a delight of unblemished green – and busy with redstarts and pied flycatchers in spring. A bonus for walkers is the occasional sight of a red kite circling effortlessly for hour after hour. The rust-coloured hunter, with its forked tail and wings bent sharply back, was so common in Britain 300 years ago that it scavenged even in the streets of London. Once scarce, they are now making a comeback in several parts of Britain.

▶ *Llyn Brianne is about 10 miles north of Llandovery and reached by minor roads branching off the A483 at Cynghordy.*

10 Pumsaint

Gold for the coffers of ancient Rome was once mined on the slopes rising steeply above the Afon Cothi. Where the village of Pumsaint now stands, the Romans built a fort covering 2ha (5 acres). Iron Age men had already dug there for the yellow metal before the Romans came, but from about AD 75 the Romans exploited the deposits much more methodically than earlier miners. The Dolaucothi mines were probably worked by the Romans for some 250 years and have been reworked at various periods since.

Three waymarked National Trust paths of 1, 3 and 5 miles explore the old workings. The paths climb through groves of mossy-limbed oaks and across sheep-grazed fields that give wide views over a landscape of rounded hills, deep valleys, woodlands and small farms.

The Romans built a 4 mile aqueduct from the Afon Annell, and a 7 mile aqueduct from the Cothi. Holding-tanks and sluice gates were built into the system. Around 14 million litres (3 million gallons) of water a day was delivered in powerful streams that washed away the topsoil and exposed the gold-bearing ore. When all the gold near the surface had been extracted, shafts and tunnels were dug to reach the ore.

Extracted ore was pounded and washed before being sent to the mint. Carreg Pumsaint, the 1m (3ft) high stone which stands in the grassy clearing where the marked walks start, was almost certainly used for the pounding of ore. But folklore has a more romantic explanation for the hollows that pit its surface. Five saintly brothers are said to have sheltered beside the stone during a blizzard. As the brothers – Gwyn, Gwyno, Gwynoro, Celynin and Ceitho – huddled against the stone, their shoulders made the round depressions in it. The name Pumsaint recalls the brothers, for it means 'five saints'. The stone is in fact diorite, a hard rock which is not found locally, and was probably brought in specially for the ore-crushing.

▶ *Pumsaint is on the A482, 7 miles south-east of Lampeter. The Dolaucothi Gold Mines are about ½ mile east of the village along a marked minor road.*

CLIMB THROUGH GROVES OF MOSSY-LIMBED OAKS

PUMSAINT

The scars of industry

The hills and valleys of Wales have been marked by centuries of heavy industry. Today, these past scars are being healed and the landscape, where wildlife thrives once more, is being reclaimed.

Down in Ebbw Vale, a wide stretch of flat ground lies beside the Ebbw River. The black slag heaps of the former Marine Colliery have been smoothed into green hillsides, and the pit wheels are sunk up to their hubs in the ground as memorials to the South Wales mine, closed in 1989 with the loss of 648 jobs.

'I worked 26 years here,' says Richard Smith, a former miner, 'and my father before me for 56 years. I was opening up new faces for the cutters – good work, it was. I don't like to see her closed. But they've made a beautiful job of this walkway, haven't they? The Ebbw's running clear, too, have you noticed? It's been a black river all my life, dead as a stone, so I'm glad to see that.'

The Welsh valleys tend to be written off by those who have never been there, discounted as a landscape worth looking at. It's assumed that the disappearance of the iron and coal industries at the end of the 20th century has left them irreparably scarred. Any explorer with open eyes and mind, however, finds exactly the opposite: a resilient countryside undergoing regeneration.

INDUSTRIAL EXPANSION

The valleys of South Wales are rich in minerals – particularly coal and iron, the basic materials that fed the Industrial Revolution. In the late 18th century the harnessing of the power of water, and later of steam, opened the whole treasure chest of Britain's mineral wealth. In the valleys the effects were galvanic. A population of around 3,000 swelled to half a million. Merthyr Tydfil's Dowlais Ironworks became the greatest ironworks in the world, its production soaring to 100,000 tonnes a year. In the parallel valleys of Rhondda Fach and Rhondda Fawr a population which barely topped 3,000 in the 1860s exploded to 160,000 within 50 years, while annual coal production jumped in the same period from a million to around 9 million tonnes.

Over in the western valleys above Swansea it was the processing of ores brought in by sea that dominated industry in the area. By the early 19th century Swansea was known as 'Copperopolis' and 90 per cent of the world's copper was smelted here, along with silver, brass and zinc. Landowners such as the Marquesses of Bute, owners of ironworks, coal mines, and the docks at Cardiff through which the iron and coal were exported, grew fabulously rich. Meanwhile, the workers, housed in damp, dark, insanitary dwellings, slaved at their dangerous, debilitating jobs.

The consequences for the landscape of the Valleys of these enormous population jumps, these vast diggings and delvings, were profound. Every crevice and scrap of spare ground became crammed with terraced housing for miners, steel workers and smelters. Pithead buildings, pit wheels and sheds proliferated. Huge black slag heaps rose like dark mountains until they towered over the pit villages and iron-mining towns. Hillsides disappeared or were chopped into raw rock galleries. Coal smoke hung like a pall over Cwm Rhondda and Ebbw Vale. Fouled rivers ran red with iron ore, or black with coal dust. In the Lower Swansea Valley the River Tawe rolled sluggishly in mineral streaks of yellow, green and grey, while copper smoke stunted trees, blighted grasslands and poisoned people with sulphur and arsenic.

The valleys of South Wales were not the only Welsh landscapes to be grossly degraded by the mineral demands of the Industrial Revolution. Up in Snowdonia, in the north-west corner of Wales, slate quarries ate away enormous quantities of mountainside, some all too visible, others digging far into the bowels of the hills in caverns as large as cathedrals. Blaenau Ffestiniog and Dinorwig, Glodfa Ganol and Llechwedd roofed the world, or a huge proportion of it, leaving pits 60m (200ft) deep, galleries hundreds of miles in length, Brobdingnagian slopes of industrial scree and green and turquoise pools of poison. Massive industrial buildings were erected to serve the quarries, like the Ynys y Pandy slate mill near the Gorseddu quarry (see right), built in 1855 and now a roofless shell

BACK TO NATURE

These black slate quarries of Snowdonia will take more than a few decades to seem anything other than tortured ground. But down in the valleys it is a different story. Some of the former coal-mining and steelworking landscapes have re-clothed themselves astonishingly quickly in grass, in trees, in clean air, clean water and the uninterrupted sounds of nature. Silent Valley, high in the side cleft of Cwm Merddog above Ebbw Vale, is a place of quiet beechwoods and birdsong, where warblers and flycatchers nest and old-man's-beard lichens trail from the trees,

... slate quarries ate away enormous quantities of mountainside, some all too visible, others digging far into the bowels of the hills in caverns as large as cathedrals.

betokening unpolluted air. Chips of coal still glint through the grass and heather, though, as a reminder of how things used to be.

Other places have benefited from man's helping hand. Flooded limestone quarries near Penarth have become Cosmeston Lakes Country Park, a place for fishing, for quiet walking, for swimming and birdwatching. Much the same has been done with the former ironworks feeder pond at Cwm-Celyn near Abertillery. In Cwm Rhondda and the Rhymney Valley giant slag heaps are greening over, planted with trees or seeded with grasses and wild flowers. Former railway lines and canal towpaths have been converted into a great footpath and cycleway from Cardiff, the Taff Trail. As for the Lower Swansea Valley, so polluted by the 1960s that some people

thought it could never recover, the poisoned ground has been cleared to a great depth and replanted with trees and flowers. Settling ponds are now fishing lakes, mineral railways are footpaths – much of this work carried out by local volunteers whose reward has been to see wildlife return and their own environment change hugely for the better.

Under the skin of the landscape, however, those with eyes to see continue to spot the bones of the past: a conical hill that was once a coal-mine slag heap, the sluice gates in the lake, the railway embankment that now carries the cycle path. Such strong industrial shadows cannot soon be edited out of the landscape. Nor should they be, if only to pay homage to generations of hard-working men, like Richard Smith of Ebbw Vale's Marine Colliery.

SNOWDONIA'S PEAKS and VALLEYS

The mountains of Snowdonia offer some of the most remarkable and far-reaching views in Britain; indeed, every country that makes up these islands can be seen from its lofty peaks.

❶ Abergwyngregyn

A far-off murmur of falling water swells to a mighty crescendo, drawing the walker along the path that accompanies the busy, swirling Rhaeadr-fawr river on its 2 mile course through the Coedydd Aber National Nature Reserve. At the head of the valley, the river bursts through a cleft in the high cliffs to fall in a long white skein to the glistening rocks below.

The falls provide a suitably dramatic ending to a lovely walk. The valley's steep sides are clothed with ash, oak, alder and birch, and high above them again are the wooded slopes of Maes y Gaer, whose 223m (731ft) summit is crowned by an Iron Age fort. The river, driven on by the impetus of its tumble, swirls and eddies around boulders and fallen trees.

Abergwyngregyn stands at the valley mouth beside a motte – the mound of a Norman castle that once stood here. For centuries, the village was a starting point for travellers to Anglesey, who crossed the Lavan Sands at low tide. At Bont Newydd, about three-quarters of a mile along the valley, the river is crossed by a stone bridge. Beyond, a rough track which is actually a Roman road leads to the Vale of Conwy.

▶ *Abergwyngregyn is situated on the A55, between Bangor and Llanfairfechan.*

❷ Rowen

The Romans came to this part of Britain in the 1st century AD. Undeterred by the inhospitable countryside, they drove their roads across hills, moors and rivers to link settlements with forts and forts with mines. One such road joined Chester and Caernarfon and traces of it can still be seen around Rowen, which actually stands on the route.

West of the village, the Roman road climbs to 425m (1,400ft) and crosses mountains scattered with burial chambers and standing stones that were ancient before the legions came. One burial chamber is called Maen-y-Bardd – the 'Bard's Stone' – and consists of a massive capstone resting upon four uprights. After a while, the metalled road peters out into a broad,

well-defined track which links up with a lane leading down to the coast at Abergwyngregyn. This is walking country, with views across the Lavan Sands and the Menai Strait to Anglesey.

The Roman road crossed the Conwy south-east of Rowen, at Caerhun, where the grass-covered outline of a fort can still be seen. Called Canovium, it was built about AD 78.

▶ *Rowen is 4 miles south of Conwy, and lies just to the west of the B5106 to Betws-y-Coed.*

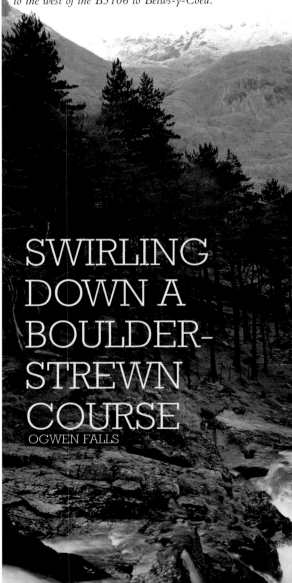

SWIRLING DOWN A BOULDER-STREWN COURSE
OGWEN FALLS

❸ Llyn Ogwen

The great cloud-capped forms of Y Garn, Glyder Fawr, Glyder Fâch, Tryfan and Pen yr Ole Wen stand watch over the mile-long, shallow waters of Llyn Ogwen. Tryfan is said to be the burial place of Sir Bedivere, the last of King Arthur's knights, and Ogwen one of the possible lakes into which he might have thrown Excalibur. From Tryfan, too, many years ago, a great landslide fell into Ogwen, apparently burying a cave containing a fabulous treasure. A phantom coach has occasionally been reported among the tumbled rocks, and a ghostly passenger who descends from it and disappears into a cleft is said to be the Devil himself.

The most glorious approach to Llyn Ogwen is up the Nant Ffrancon Pass from Bethesda, following the road that Thomas Telford drove through the mountains in the early 19th century.

Steep screes plunge down to the roadside, and across the valley great ramparts of rock are streaked with the white threads of waterfalls.

The Afon Ogwen throws itself over the head of the pass in a 60m (200ft) cataract, swirling down a boulder-strewn course to cascade beneath the A5 at Roman Bridge. Part of the original bridge – not Roman, but medieval – can be seen beneath the modern structure. Beyond the bridge is Llyn Ogwen, with Pen yr Ole Wen sweeping down to the northern shore, and the Glyders and Tryfan to the south, towering above the valley of Cwm Idwal.

There is a 2 mile nature trail round the floor of the cwm which passes the Devil's Kitchen, an awesome cleft. It goes on to encircle the mountain-shadowed Llyn Idwal, which has its own legend. It is said that 800 years ago a prince of Gwynedd was drowned in the lake, and all the birds fled in sorrow, never to return. But they must have recovered their spirits in more recent times, since grey herons, gulls, cormorants and ducks all visit the shores.

▶ *Llyn Ogwen lies along the side of the A5, 9 miles south-east of Bangor.*

❹ Llyn Crafnant

This enchanting lake, darkly set among trees and high hills, lies 2 miles south-west of Trefriw, a tiny spa town with a pump-room and baths. The narrow road to the lake climbs steeply at first, following the rushing Afon Crafnant to a Forestry Commission car park, from which a short, steep walk through the trees brings the near-mile-long sweep of water into view. Whether glittering like polished silver under a bright sky, or pewter-grey beneath lowering clouds, Llyn Crafnant is beautiful. The hills all around sweep down from grey crags to tree-clad slopes that tumble down to the shores. Barely a ripple disturbs the still water, and only a few boulders, like stepping-stones, break the untroubled surface.

Away in the distance, the white-washed walls of an isolated farmhouse stand bright beneath the 548m (1,798ft) crags of Craig-wen. Serious walkers can take a footpath that skirts the peak and crosses open moorland before dropping down to Capel Curig.

The lake was formerly a reservoir for the market town of Llanrwst, whose chief claims to fame are a bridge and a chapel attributed to Inigo Jones. The huge stone coffin in the chapel is said to be that of Llewelyn the Great.

▶ *Trefriw is on the B5106, 9 miles south of Conwy. Llanrwst lies on the opposite side of the Vale of Conwy, on the A470.*

Wales and the Welsh Borders

5 Penmachno

This little village on the banks of the Afon Machno is a good starting place from which to sample the contrasts of Snowdonia. South of the village the road follows the river upstream, and a turning to the right loops into Cwm Penmachno, a mile-long shallow valley of pine-covered slopes where the river trickles merrily over grey rocks between banks tufted with ferns and heather. Back on the road from Penmachno, and continuing south, the scenery changes suddenly. The road climbs almost 500m (1,600ft) to wild moorlands. On the skyline is Arenig Fâch, towering above bogs, streams and small lakes; in a fold of the land, and reached by a three-quarters of a mile long track, is Llyn Conwy, the source of the Afon Conwy.

Two miles to the north-west of Penmachno is the Bishop Morgan Trail, an easy stroll through forest and upland farming country. It concludes at Ty Mawr, the farmhouse birthplace of William Morgan, Bishop of St Asaph, who translated the Bible into Welsh in the 16th century, so laying the foundations of Welsh Protestantism, and of Welsh as a written prose language. The house, owned by the National Trust, is open to the public and contains a number of Bibles as well as typical Welsh farmhouse furnishings.

▶ *Penmachno is 4 miles south of Betws-y-Coed, and is reached by taking the B4406 from the A5.*

6 Dolwyddelan

The spectacularly lovely road between Betws-y-Coed and Blaenau Ffestiniog follows the winding Afon Lledr and comes to the village of Dolwyddelan, frowned over by the crags of Moel Siabod. The mountain's boulder-strewn slopes and shattered pinnacles, reaching up to 872m (2,860ft), look like the debris of some titanic explosion at the world's beginning.

West of the village, appearing as though it has grown from the crag on which it stands, is a mighty castle. Its great tower dates from the 12th century, and is one of the oldest of its kind in Britain. Here, almost certainly, Llewelyn the Great was born in 1173, and later the castle played an important role in his grandson's struggles against Edward I; it finally fell to the English in 1283. The savage terrain round about can have changed little since those tumultuous days, and you can see it from a Welsh man-at-arm's viewpoint by climbing up to the ramparts.

But should you wish a more intimate glimpse, you should take the path that runs northwards from the village through the woods for about 1½ miles until it breaks into open country just short of Llyn y Foel. There, by the deep, cold lake beneath the tumbled wildness of Moel Siabod, is the loneliness and majesty of Snowdonia in microcosm. A further scramble, up a fairly hard climb to the north-east shoulder of the mountain, gives you the entire National Park – Snowdon itself to the west and, all about, the mountains, forests and lakes of one of the few wildernesses left in Europe.

▶ *Dolwyddelan is on the A470, some 5 miles north-east of Blaenau Ffestiniog.*

7 Nantgwynant

Celtic legends mingle with memories of mountaineering heroes in this long and lovely valley overlooked by Snowdon and the rocky peaks of Glyder Fawr and Glyder Fâch. The Pen-y-Gwryd Hotel, 6 miles north-east of Beddgelert, is so famous among mountaineers that it is practically an extension of the Alpine Club. Here it was that John Hunt – later Lord Hunt – and his team planned their successful 1953 assault upon Everest.

From the upper part of the valley, where noisy streams thrust through groves of trees greyed with lichen, the Snowdon range, known as Eryri in Welsh, or the 'High Lands', stretches ahead. This great horseshoe of naked rock rises to the summit of Snowdon itself – known as Yr Wyddfa, 'the tumulus' or 'tomb', supposedly the grave of a giant slain by King Arthur.

The lower part of the glacier-gouged valley cups two surprisingly tranquil lakes, Llyn Dinas and Llyn Gwynant. You should come to Gwynant at sunset, when the high terraces of Snowdon flare briefly into old gold and ochre; but spare a glance for Dinas, where the ancient throne of Britain is said to be concealed, awaiting a youth who will one day rediscover it and restore the Celtic kingdom. A waymarked walk, which takes about an hour to complete, climbs steeply from the roadside at the southern end of Llyn Gwynant. The Watkin Path, one of the classic routes up Snowdon, starts from Pont Bethania, a bridge on the A498 just east of Llyn Dinas.

Between Beddgelert and Llyn Dinas, a tree-clothed crag overhangs the road. This is Dinas Emrys, to whose summit clings the remains of strongholds dating from the Iron Age to the Middle Ages. Legends link the place with Merlin, and with Vortigern, the 5th-century British king who, having called in Danish mercenaries to help him in his struggles against the Scots, was unable to pay them. So they took his kingdom instead.

▶ *The A498 runs through the Nantgwynant valley, entering it at Beddgelert before running north-east to meet the A4086 at the start of the Pass of Llanberis.*

⑧ Snowdon

Given the blessing of ideal conditions, large portions of the British Isles can be seen from Snowdon's 1,085m (3,560ft) stony summit. The earliest recorded person to enjoy the view was Thomas Johnson, an intrepid botanist who made the ascent in 1639. But he could hardly have been the first, since Welsh folklore abounds with tales of heroes, giants and dragons that once cavorted among the crags.

Snowdon is a massif of volcanic and sedimentary rocks, scarred by Ice Age glaciers – glaciers that carved the cliffs overhanging the lake of Glaslyn. It is said that a monster, who terrorised the Vale of Conwy, was hurled into the lake from the top of the cliffs after being hauled over the mountains by the two biggest oxen in Wales. Another Snowdon legend was Rhita Fawr, a giant who wore a cloak woven from the beards of the kings he had slain. He met his match in King Arthur, however, and now lies beneath the summit, still called Yr Wyddfa – 'the tomb'.

Snowdon's beauty can be appreciated from spots along the A498, but if you wish to know it properly, you must walk. There are several routes to the summit, none of them really difficult except in bad weather, which can descend with terrifying swiftness. Walkers must be properly equipped; those who are not risk life and limb – their own, and those of the Mountain Rescue teams. And remember to allow enough time before night falls; it will take at least five hours to the summit and back, whichever route is chosen.

The walk from Llanberis runs roughly parallel to the Snowdon Mountain Railway, Britain's only rack railway, that runs to within 20m (67ft) of the summit. This walk is the longest but easiest. The Pyg Track starts from the 357m (1,170ft) high Pass of Llanberis, and is therefore the shortest route in terms of vertical effort. It looks down Llyn Llydaw and Glaslyn, but there is a steep zigzag scramble up a scree slope before you reach the top. Alternatively, the old Miners' Track may be followed to Glaslyn where another steep path reaches up to join the Pyg Track.

Though it involves a climb of about 1,000m (3,300ft), the Watkin Path is perhaps the most interesting route. Opened in 1892, it starts in Nantgwynant, passes waterfalls, old copper mines and slate workings before its final slippery zigzag to Yr Wyddfa. The Rhyd Ddu and Snowdon Ranger paths climb the mountain's western slopes from the Beddgelert-Caernarfon road. Both offer relatively easy walking but it should be emphasised that no walk up Snowdon should be taken lightly.

▶ *Snowdon, a National Nature Reserve, is best reached by the A4085 or A4086 from Caernarfon.*

TOWARDS SNOWDON FROM GLYDER FÂCH

❾ Vale of Ffestiniog

Behind the church at Llan Ffestiniog there is a 210m (700ft) crag from whose easy-to-climb summit you can see all of this lovely valley – its quiet river and rich alluvial pastures; its framing of lofty mountains, whose lower slopes are draped with hanging woods; its distant ending in the broad gleam of the Dwyryd estuary, where it meets the flats of the Traeth Bach – the 'Little Sands'.

South of the church, a path goes down to Rhaeadr Cynfal, a fall whose waters plunge tumultuously into a 60m (200ft) ravine. A pillar of rock above the fall is called Huw Lloyd's Pulpit, Huw Lloyd being a 17th-century poet, warrior and wizard who used to summon up his demons from here.

The churchyard at Maentwrog, in the heart of the valley, contains an enormous boulder, hurled over the hills by St Twrog in the 6th century to destroy a pagan altar. And even if geologists say that it was probably deposited there by a melting glacier, the deed is remembered still in the village name, which means Twrog's Stone.

The road that leads from Maentwrog to Harlech looks across the estuary to the old quays where slate from the quarries at Blaenau Ffestiniog was once loaded into sailing ships. In 1836, a narrow-gauge railway was built to transport the slate down to Porthmadog, but it now carries passengers between Porthmadog and Blaenau Ffestiniog.

▶ *Llan Ffestiniog is on the A470, 3 miles south of Blaenau Ffestiniog, and Maentwrog is 3 miles west, at the junction of the A496 and A487.*

THE VALE OF FFESTINIOG FROM CEINEWYDD

⑩ Trawsfynydd

Looking westwards from the churchyard to the Rhinog mountains, the countryside is a splendid wilderness, lightened a little by the placid waters of Llyn Trawsfynydd in the foreground. The shepherd poet, Ellis Humphrey Evans – better known as Hedd Wyn – was born in Trawsfynydd in 1887, and much of his poetry was inspired by what he saw about him. He was awarded the Bardic Chair at the National Eisteddfod in 1917, but never lived to be enthroned since he was killed in Flanders a few days before the ceremony was due to take place. There is a statue to his memory in the village.

He wrote of the surrounding mountains and valleys, but references to Llyn Trawsfynydd are missing from his works since it did not exist before the 1920s, when it was created to power a hydroelectric scheme. More than 80 years later, and the 3 mile lake looks as though it has been part of the landscape for ever, and now serves a nuclear power station, which is in the process of being decommissioned, tucked unobtrusively away on the northern shore.

A narrow, gated road signposted Aber-Geirw leaves the A470 just south of Trawsfynydd, then after 2 miles turns eastwards to cross some of the wildest country in Wales. To the south there are glimpses of Cadair Idris, framed by the wooded Gain valley; then the road climbs to over 500m (1,700ft) – one of the highest roads in Wales. Just about the point where it drops down to join the A494, there are fine prospects of the waterfalls above Llanuwchllyn.

▶ *Trawsfynydd is just off the A470, 11 miles north of Dolgellau.*

⑪ Bala Lake

Standing on the tiny promenade in Bala village and gazing down the 4 mile length of Llyn Tegid, or Bala Lake, to the ramparts of Aran Benllyn, Aran Fawddwy and Cadair Idris at the far end, the valley appears as though it had been created by gigantic hands that had gripped the mountains on either side and torn them apart to form the water-filled gash that is the largest natural lake in Wales.

Though barely a mile wide, its cold, dark waters reach abruptly down to a depth of 45m (150ft), providing a home for the gwyniad, a trout-like fish found nowhere else in Britain. Less certainly, they also cover a palace, a prince and all his people who were drowned as a punishment for their wickedness. The only survivor was a harpist, who had been given timely warning of the approaching cataclysm by a small bird.

The A494 from Dolgellau follows the line of a Roman road that ran to Caer Gai fort, about half a mile from the south-west corner of the lake. During the 1st century AD, this was occupied by the First Cohort of Nervii, auxiliary infantry from what is now Belgium. The fortifications they left are still impressive, but permission to see them should be sought from the nearby farm.

Roads run down both sides of the lake, the views are glorious, and there are plenty of paths leading down to the pebbled shore. The Afon Dyfrdwy, flowing from its source on the high moors, enters Bala Lake at its southern end and exits at the northern end where it becomes the Dee. Local tradition has it that the river waters run straight through those of the lake without ever mingling.

▶ *Bala Lake lies beside the A494, some 15 miles north-east of Dolgellau.*

⑫ Cwm Hirnant

The tiny village of Rhos-y-gwaliau is the northern gateway to Cwm Hirnant. The narrow road plunges into the valley, dark with the conifers of Aberhirnant Forest, and follows a crystal-clear stream before climbing 500m (1,600ft) into the Berwyn mountains. Keep an eye open for the enchanting picnic place carved out beside the stream.

The summit of the road looks down upon Lake Vyrnwy, a mile across by 5 miles long and with a perimeter of 11 miles, appearing entirely natural in its dark green framing of mature conifers. In fact, it was created in 1881 to supply Liverpool with water, and is a fine example of what Victorian engineers could do when resolved upon a blending of the works of man and nature. The 44m (144ft) high dam, faced with 12 tonne blocks of stone, looks like a medieval fortification, while the jaunty little tower on the eastern shore could have been transported straight from the banks of the Rhine or the Loire. Actually, it marks the beginning of a 75 mile pipeline that carries water to Liverpool.

The road crosses the dam and runs right round the lake. This is a pleasant enough drive, but if you wish for further adventures then take the road that runs off the western shore and climbs up over the desolate moors to Bwlch y Groes. At 545m (1,790ft), this is the highest stretch of mountain road in Wales.

▶ *Rhos-y-gwaliau lies about 1 mile south-east of Bala on a minor road off the B4391. The road that runs around Lake Vyrnwy is the B4393.*

⑬ Llanfachreth

Despite its awesome name, the Precipice Walk near Llanfachreth is an easy 3 mile ramble with little climbing involved since, throughout its circular course, the path sticks fairly constantly to the 240m (787ft) contour, with the steep flank of Foel Cynwch rising a further 86m (282ft) on one side and an airy drop on the other.

The path, which follows the edge of a precipice, was probably an ancient sheep-track before it was widened and opened to the public in 1890. Its winding course, which loops around the elongated summit of Foel Cynwch before dropping gently down to the shores of Llyn Cynwch, is a gallery to all of Snowdonia. To the north are Snowdon and the Moelwyn range, to the north-west the peaks of Rhinog, to the south Cadair Idris, and to the east and north-east the high ranges of Aran and Arenig respectively.

In the valley below Foel Cynwch's south-westerly slope, the remains of a 13th-century Cistercian monastery, Cymer Abbey, stand surrounded by sheep-cropped grass. It was never completed, largely because at the time of its building it was in the path of opposing English and Welsh armies, a situation unsympathetic to the contemplative life.

▶ *The Precipice Walk begins near Saith Groesffordd, about 1 mile south-west of Llanfachreth at the junction with the Ty'n-y-groes road. Llanfachreth lies 4 miles north-east of Dolgellau and can be reached, eventually, by a number of minor roads running off the A494.*

⑭ Coed y Brenin

The King's Forest – Coed y Brenin – was so named to commemorate the Diamond Jubilee of King George V in 1935, and a royal place it is indeed, all 9,000ha (22,000 acres) of it, embracing farmlands and rapids, mountain views and gold mines, and mile upon mile of forest trails along which there is at least a chance of glimpsing otters and polecats, as well as more easily seen buzzards and fallow deer.

Of all these pleasant things, the only one to have passed away is gold, and it is hard to believe now that in the 1840s people dug into the Mawddach valley in search of the metal with a fervour exceeded only by that of the Californian miners of the same period. Results were not comparable, however. During the decade some 24 mines were opened and 150 shafts sunk, but almost all these ventures were abandoned since the value of the gold found did not equal the cost of getting it out of the ground. One mine, the Gwynfynydd, did struggle on until 1938, but now it, too, stands derelict along the 'Gold Road' footpath that starts near Ganllwyd.

The remains of the ore-crushing mill stand on a triangle of land between Pistyll Cain and Rhaeadr Mawddach, two splendid waterfalls flanked by trees that flare into glorious colour during early autumn. The voice of Rhaeadr Mawddach, the falls that powered the mill, can be heard far down the valley, while a bridge at the foot of Pistyll Cain offers a fine duck's-eye view of that tumbling cascade.

The forest's many miles of footpaths include waymarked trails that start from Pont Dolgefeiliau, a bridge where drovers paused to have their cattle shod before beginning the trek over the mountain to the markets of England. One of the trails follows a section of Sarn Helen, a Roman road built to link North and South Wales, while another, between Ty'n-y-groes and Llanfachreth, runs through a pretty little arboretum, the ideal place for a short and not too energetic stroll.

▶ *Pont Dolgefeiliau is on the A470, 6 miles to the north of Dolgellau. There is a visitor centre ½ mile off the road which houses an exhibition of restored gold-mining equipment.*

⑮ Llanbedr

The little village of Llanbedr stands between the mountains and the sea, looking west across the salt-marshes and the dunes to Cardigan Bay and east to the mouths of two valleys that run deep into the heart of the lonely Rhinog range. One narrow road, edged by lichen-clad trees, ends at Cwm Bychan, a vast, rocky amphitheatre with a jewel-like lake set at its centre. An easy walk from here through a magical wood leads to the Roman Steps, a paved route now generally, if reluctantly, conceded to be a medieval packhorse way rather than the work of the legions. But to be fair, such tracks were often constructed on paths already established, and it is not unlikely that the Romans did come this way in search of minerals. Whoever it was that built the track, its fine,

MILES OF LONELY FOOTPATHS

DYFFRYN ARDUDWY

sensible course climbs up to the wild pass of Bwlch Tyddiad before curving down again to join the Dolgellau-to-Ffestiniog road.

The twisting road up neighbouring Cwm Nantcol takes in two nature trails before petering out at a gate overlooked by the peaks of Rhinog Fawr and Rhinog Fach. They stand at 720m (2,362ft) and 712m (2,333ft) – modest edifices by local standards – but their jagged crags and pinnacles give them a stark dignity all their own.

The pass between them is called Drws Ardudwy – the 'Door of Ardudwy' – and was a gateway to the coastal plain long before today's roads were built.

▶ *The roads into the valleys start just east of Llanbedr, which is 3 miles south of Harlech on the A496.*

⑯ Dyffryn Ardudwy

The golden hem of sand that runs from Barmouth to Harlech is bucket-and-spade country, but behind Dyffryn Ardudwy village, miles of lonely foot-paths and ancient tracks run off into the wild hinterland of the Rhinog mountain range. One track leads to Llyn Bodlyn, the remote source of the Afon Ysgethin which on its curling 5 mile course runs around Craig y Dinas, with its Iron Age hill-fort, before coming to the sea beyond Tal-y-bont.

That the area was not always lonely is apparent in the great number of prehistoric remains – cairns, standing stones and stone circles – scattered about the hills. Most impressive perhaps are the Neolithic twin burial chambers near the village. The stones surrounding them are the remains of their covering cairn which, when originally built, was some 30m (100ft) long and 15m (50ft) across.

Evidence of the drowned city of Cantref-y-Gwaelod that lies beneath the waters of Cardigan Bay is less tangible. Its story is about the dissolute prince who neglected his sea defences in favour of persistent carousing until, one stormy night, the city and all its inhabitants were overwhelmed by the waves. A causeway called Sarn Badrig can be seen at low tide running out into the sea just north-west of Dyffryn Ardudwy, which is often pointed out as part of the lost city's sea wall. Unimaginative geologists, however, declare it to be a natural reef.

▶ *Dyffryn Ardudwy is 5 miles north of Barmouth on the A496.*

⑰ Mawddach Estuary

The Mawddach river rises in the mountains south-west of Bala, and races white-flecked through tree-stepped gorges until it is braked by the tide at Llanelltyd. Here it is joined by the Wnion, a little downstream from Dolgellau, and the united rivers broaden out into a ragged-shored estuary that must surely be one of the loveliest in Britain. Finally, the Mawddach meets the sea at Barmouth.

John Ruskin, the Victorian art critic, said that he knew of only one walk that excelled that from Dolgellau to Barmouth, and that was the one from Barmouth to Dolgellau. A little ponderous, perhaps, but a hint worth taking for all that, even if Ruskin's preferred route along the north shore is now occupied by the A496. However, it is still a most spectacular drive between the peaks of Rhinog to the north and the regal massif of Cadair Idris, rearing its 893m (2,927ft) bulk to the south, on the other side of the estuary. The road passes through Bontddu, a pretty little village, behind which is St David's gold mine, which finally closed in the 1990s. When it was still a working mine, it was part of the gold fever that gripped this part of Wales in the middle of the 19th century.

If you prefer to walk, you can cross the river by the Victorian railway bridge at Barmouth, built high over the water to permit passage to sailing ships, or by the bridge at Pen-y-bryn, 2 miles west of Dolgellau. The southern shore provides walks of sufficient delight to mollify even Ruskin for the loss of his northerly path – sandbanks and pastures, a bird sanctuary and banks of rhododendrons, all embraced between the great arms of the mountains.

From Arthog village, about a mile north-east along the shore from the southern end of the railway bridge, a steep, twisting little lane leads up on to the moors, presenting an ever-widening panorama of the estuary and the mountain bastions to the north. The lane leads to Llynnau Cregennen – 'Cregennen Lakes' – two dark pools set in a rough moorland plateau. There is an ancient trackway here, marked by standing stones, and known as Ffordd Ddu, the 'Black Road'. It is an old drovers' road, but its course may have been first marked out by the Romans.

▶ *The A496 runs along the north of the estuary; the A493 is to the south.*

AND ANCIENT TRACKS

A GREAT ROLLING HEAVE OF VOLCANIC ROCK

LLYNNAU CREGENNEN AND CADAIR IDRIS

⑱ Cadair Idris

Wherever you go in Snowdonia, Cadair Idris is there too. This quiet dominance is due not so much to the height of the range – the highest point is only 893m (2,927ft) – as to its extent, a great rolling heave of volcanic rock that runs for some 10 miles across north-west Wales, dividing the old territory of Gwynedd from the land of Powys. It rises sharply above Dolgellau and descends in craggy steps to the sea at Llwyngwril, and everywhere there are the scars of the Ice Age – beetling cliffs 300m (1,000ft) high and deep, stilly, water-filled hollows.

The summit ridge of frost-shattered boulders is called Penygadair, and is best reached by way of the Pony Path which begins at Ty Nant, south-west of Dolgellau. It is a long climb, taking some two or three hours, but the view from the top is among the best in Britain. Far off to the east are the hills of the English border, and to the west, across the Irish Sea, the mountains of Wicklow. Immediately below to the north-west is Llyn y Gadair, like a sheet of blue-grey slate held in a clasp of rock. Further west lie the lovely twin lakes, Llynnau Cregennen, and to the south-east the reputedly bottomless pool of Llyn Cau, dark and still below its protecting rim of volcanic cliffs. A monster lives here, so it is said, its presence confirmed by a rash youth in the 18th century who, bathing in the lake for a dare, abruptly disappeared beneath the surface, never to be seen again. Another legend of the same period says that if you sleep by Llyn Cau, you will awake blind, mad or a poet.
▶ *The Pony Path can be picked up at Ty Nant, 3 miles south-west of Dolgellau, along a minor road that leads past Llyn Gwernan.*

⑲ Castell y Bere

The Dysynni river flows from Tal-y-llyn Lake in the shadow of Cadair Idris, then makes a sudden right swerve between the mountain peaks to enter a broad, fertile valley. Here, the fields are lush green and trimly hedged; the mountains no longer crowd in, but are instead misty slopes rising gently from the valley floor.

About half a mile short of the head of the valley there is a rocky headland on which stand the remains of Castell y Bere. The last Welsh stronghold to fall in Edward I's conquest of Snowdonia, its garrison of 49 men surrendered to the Earl of Pembroke's army after a ten-day siege in 1283, a year after the death of Prince Llywelyn ap Gruffydd. The castle's custodian was Dafydd, the prince's unruly brother, who managed to escape before the surrender, only to wander as a fugitive among the crags of Cadair Idris. His presence there was betrayed by his own countrymen, and he was captured and taken to Shrewsbury where he was tried on a number of charges ranging from blasphemy to murder. Verdict and sentence were a foregone conclusion. He was hanged, drawn and quartered and his head sent to decorate the Tower of London beside that of his brother.

Now the only tangible memory of those last stormy hours of Welsh independence is the jagged grey walls of Castell y Bere that appear almost as one with the lichen-covered rocks of the ridge. Worn and weathered steps lead up to the broken ramparts that look high over the valley to the boulder-strewn hillsides, where ravens and buzzards soar.
▶ *The B4405 runs up the Dysynni valley from Llanegryn, which is situated just off the A493, 3 miles north of Tywyn.*

⑳ Dinas-Mawddwy

It used to be said of Dinas that its earth is blue and its sky is water, emphasising the aloofness of the place from the rest of Wales. True enough, lead and slate have been its industries, and the smooth, steep mountains that ring the village attract more than their fair share of storms and mist. But what really makes Dinas different is its inhabitants, who for centuries have been aware that they are not quite like the rest of the Welsh. In South Wales people tend to be dark, and in Anglesey fair, but in Dinas there is and always has been a strong preponderance of red-headed folk, and it has been suggested that they are in fact descendants of long-ago Scots colonists from Ireland or northern Britain.

It is not unknown for red hair and a spirit of independence to go together, and perhaps it was this that led to the formation of the Red Brigands in the 16th century. Whether they were really thieves or a band of red-haired men with a violent dislike of outsiders is uncertain, but at any rate they terrorised the district until they were suppressed with sword and rope in 1554. Their only monument is a pub called The Brigands' Inn, and today Dinas is a peaceful, single-street village of considerable charm and character. Just north of it, a narrow lane curves around the foot of Foel Benddin and into the Cywarch valley to end beneath the spectacular 670m (2,200ft) high crags of Craig Cywarch. The track beyond the lane leads into the heart of the lonely Aran mountains, which reach their climax at the 905m (2,969ft) summit of Aran Fawddwy.
▶ *Dinas-Mawddwy lies on the A470, 8 miles to the east of Dolgellau.*

ANGLESEY and the LLEYN PENINSULA

In the north-west corner of Wales lies the isle of Anglesey, overlooked from the south by the Lleyn Peninsula. Their spectacular coastlines encircle remote hills and stretches of wild heathland.

❶ Cemlyn Bay

A long arm of shingle cast up by storms separates the tidal waters of Cemlyn Bay from a large, brackish lagoon whose level is controlled by a weir. The lagoon is a breeding ground and sanctuary for many birds, including the remarkable Arctic tern, whose migration covers up to 13,000 miles a year, to the Antarctic and back. The reserve, which is managed by the North Wales Wildlife Trust for the National Trust, can be seen from the road, and more closely from the bank of sea-smoothed shingle. However, visitors are asked not to walk along the bank between April and July when the birds are breeding. The terns are quite likely to attack anyone who ventures too close to their nests.

A blustery, rugged promontory to the east separates Cemlyn Bay from Cemaes Bay, where three alluring sandy beaches snuggle into the lee of twin headlands. There is fine walking on the promontory, looking across a noble seascape in which there are always large ships in view.

The little fishing village of Cemaes in the deepest recess of the bay has a small tidal harbour that was an important port before nearby Amlwch was developed. Shipbuilding and trading thrived there in the 19th century – and smuggling too, in the hidden coves.

Towards the eastern tip of Cemaes Bay is Llanbadrig, where an ancient church teeters on the brink of a precipitous cliff. It is said to have been founded in the 5th century by St Patrick in thanksgiving for having survived a shipwreck on the Middle Mouse, a wicked reef a mile offshore. The church's simple rendered walls give no hint of its astonishing interior, where tiles and cusped arches gleam in the blue light filtering through the stained-glass window. The church was restored in 1884 by the 3rd Lord Stanley, a local landowner who had embraced the Islamic faith. He financed the restoration on condition that the new interior resembled that of a mosque.

▶ *The A5025, which circles northern Anglesey, reaches Cemaes 22 miles north-west of Menai Bridge. A marked minor road 1 mile further on branches right to Cemlyn Bay, which is 1½ miles away.*

❷ Holyhead Mountain

A craggy fist of rock rising 220m (720ft) above the sea, Holyhead Mountain is the highest point in Anglesey. On a clear day the views are tremendous, taking in the Wicklow Mountains and the Mountains of Mourne in Ireland; the Isle of Man; Snowdon in the south-east; and, to the south across Caernarfon Bay, a glimpse of Bardsey Island at the tip of the Lleyn Peninsula. Dwarfed to toy-town proportions below is Holyhead, protected by its 1¾ mile breakwater – the longest in Britain.

Snaking round the summit are the stone ramparts of an Iron Age fort. Caer y Twr, 'the Fortress of the Tower', was probably a refuge for people of the coastal villages when they were threatened by raiders from across the Irish Sea. The fort was abandoned in the 4th century AD. Some 1,500 years later, Liverpool ship-owners established a signal station on the site in order to capture the earliest possible intelligence of ships inward bound from the New World.

Paths from Holyhead lead up and over the mountain – a rough, breezy walk above the rocky slopes plummeting down to Gogarth Bay. Grey seals breed in the sea caves here, and can often be seen in the surf. At the southern end of the bay a long flight of steps leads down to South Stack lighthouse. If you look back at the cliffs from the lighthouse you will see ledges crowded with guillemots, razorbills, fulmars and puffins. The collective cacophony of their cries can drown out even the boom of the sea. Ravens and choughs also nest nearby. South Stack and the cliffs are managed by the RSPB as a reserve.

Half a mile inland from South Stack are the remains of a 2nd-century settlement called Cytiau'r Gwyddelod, 'the Huts of the Irish', reputedly once occupied by Irish metal-workers. Although their thatched roofs have gone, the lower parts of the houses still contain hearths and stone seats or beds, reminders of the simple life-style of the folk who once lived here.

▶ *Holyhead town lies at the western end of the A55. From here, a minor road skirts Holyhead Mountain, giving access to footpaths to the summit.*

❸ Mynydd Bodafon

Heather, bracken, gorse and springy turf carpet the rocky ridge of Mynydd Bodafon, whose numerous paths and tracks make it a delightful place for gentle strolls. Rising steeply to 178m (584ft), the hill commands a superb panorama which takes in the whole of Anglesey, mile after mile of the mainland coast and, behind the coast, the serried summits of Snowdonia. The narrow road crossing the hill skirts a small, tranquil pool overlooked by cottages and farm buildings, before climbing to the summit.

Below to the east is the coastal village of Moelfre, looking more Cornish than Welsh. Across its pebbly beach there is a magnificent prospect of sea, cliffs and distant mountains which can be seen even better from the mile-long walk along the top of the low cliffs to sandy Lligwy Bay. A short distance along the minor road leading south-east from the beach, a waymarked footpath crosses an open field and runs through a grove of ivy-clad trees to reach Din Lligwy, the well-preserved remains of a fortified village. A 1.5m (5ft) thick wall surrounds the ruins of nine substantial stone buildings. Almost certainly, this was the palace of Celtic chiefs or lords. To judge by coins and a silver ingot discovered when the site was excavated in 1905, it was abandoned in the 4th century.

▶ *Mynydd Bodafon is 1 mile along minor roads leading west from the A5025, 10 and 11 miles north of Menai Bridge.*

❹ Penmon

Superb views reward walkers who take any one of the routes radiating from the pretty village of Penmon, set on its rocky spur at Anglesey's eastern tip. Across the Menai Strait are the great bastions of Snowdonia; to the east over Conwy Bay is Great Ormes Head, a massive limestone headland above Llandudno; and less than a mile offshore is the craggy lozenge of Puffin Island. A toll-road, free to walkers, runs for three-quarters of a mile to Trwyn-du (or Black Point), where a coastguard station overlooks the island, whose only inhabitants are the birds that gave the place its name. They are less numerous now than they used to be. A main cause of the decline in population was a taste – now fortunately abandoned – among French and English gourmets in the 19th century, for pickled puffins. To satisfy it, thousands of boned carcases were exported annually in barrels of spiced vinegar. Among the birds' other enemies were rats, which lived on the island, robbing the puffin burrows of eggs and young.

Penmon's saint was Seiriol, who in the 6th century established a community here. The remains of his cell and baptismal well can still be seen among the ruins of a 12th-century Augustinian priory dedicated to him. So, too, was the early medieval monastic settlement on Puffin Island; here the Augustinians were buried, and there are fragments of a Norman tower.

If you walk towards Holyhead, you are treading where the saints have trod. St Seiriol the White, as he was called, and his friend, St Cybi the Yellow, who had established a monastery at Holyhead, used to walk daily the 25 miles between the opposite tips of Anglesey to meet and discuss matters spiritual. Seiriol, who had to walk west in the morning and east in the afternoon, always had his back to the sun and so remained pale. Cybi, on the other hand, was always facing the sun and so acquired a tan.

▶ *Penmon is 3 miles north-east of Beaumaris, and is reached via marked minor roads from the B5109. Puffin Island is privately owned and landing is not allowed without permission. Boat trips around the island are available during summer.*

TRWYN-DU LIGHTHOUSE

❺ Aberffraw

The village is a gathering of sturdy, greystone cottages set among close-cropped grass by the side of the shallow, tidal Afon Ffraw, which glides beneath the hump-backed packhorse bridge to disappear in the wilderness of sand-dunes that rolls for nearly a mile down to the sea's edge. Beyond the dunes, the unmistakable prongs of Yr Eifl soar above the Lleyn coastline.

For 700 years, until about 1300, Aberffraw was the home of Welsh princes. No trace of their palace remains, apart, perhaps, from an arch built into the village church.

A footpath from Aberffraw follows the coast westwards along the cliff-tops overlooking Aberffraw Bay and then northwards to Porth Cwyfan, a lonely little bay sheltering an islet on which the 7th-century Church of St Cythan stands high on a mound. The island is linked to the shore by a cowrie-scattered causeway which is covered by the sea at high tide. When the church was in regular use, the length of services depended to a great extent on the weather. No matter how eloquent the sermon, the congregation would beat a hasty retreat to the mainland if strong westerly winds threatened to maroon them.

▶ *Aberffraw is on the A4080, 13 miles west of Menai Bridge.*

❻ Bryncelli Ddu

Whitewashed cottages, low farm buildings, fields divided by turf walls draped with red and white valerian – that is the smiling face that the present-day Anglesey shows to its visitors. But look closely, and you will see that once it was very different, a place of great religious significance where a people long forgotten worshipped gods now unknown.

One such reminder is Bryncelli Ddu – 'the Mound in the Dark Grove' – though in fact it stands nowadays in an open field. Constructed some 4,000 years ago, it is the finest passage grave in Wales, concealing in its heart a 2.4m (8ft) wide burial chamber walled and roofed over with enormous slabs. This has remained as its builders left it; and so has most of the 8.2m (27ft) long stone-lined passage that leads beneath the mound to the chamber.

When the chamber was opened, it was found to contain a slab incised with elaborate wavy patterns, which covered a pit containing cremated human bones. A cast of the slab can still be seen, but the original is now in the National Museum in Cardiff. Outside the entrance to the passage, in a kind of forecourt, were discovered the bones of an ox, perhaps offered as a sacrifice when the burial chamber was sealed.

The site was sacred long before the tomb was built, since it was originally occupied by a henge monument – a circle of standing stones surrounded by a broad, deep ditch; this ancient temple has now been most lovingly restored.

▶ *A signposted path branches west from the A4080, 2½ miles south-west of Menai Bridge, and leads to Bryncelli Ddu, ½ mile away, where there is a car park.*

❼ Newborough Warren

Medieval farms and the lost village of Rhosyr lie beneath this wilderness of dunes and the damp hollows known as slacks. Possession of this, the south-west corner of Anglesey, has been contended between man and nature ever since Newborough itself was founded by order of Edward I at the end of the 13th century. Trees were felled then to create farmland, but their removal permitted vast quantities of sand to be swept inland by storms, engulfing houses and choking the anchorage at Abermenai Point. During Elizabeth I's reign, a law was passed forbidding the cutting of marram grass, whose roots help to stabilise sand-dunes. All the same, Newborough later became a centre for marram-weaving. The dunes were a breeding ground for rabbits: as many as 100,000 were trapped every year until their numbers were reduced drastically by myxomatosis in 1954.

Tree planting by the Forestry Commission began in 1948, and now a waymarked trail and several public footpaths wind through both the new pine forest and the warren. Herring gulls, oystercatchers, curlews, skylarks, swans and many other birds feed among the dunes and on the Cefni estuary's salt-marsh. A bird-watchers' hide is tucked away at the edge of Llyn Rhos-ddu, a small, reed-fringed lake on the back edge of the warren. The warren is a National Nature Reserve managed by the Countryside Council for Wales, and permits are required to visit some parts of it.

A narrow isthmus juts out from the forest, connecting it to the lovely little island of Llanddwyn. As you walk south down the island there is a magnificent prospect of the three cones of Yr Eifl rising straight from the sea, and to the east of them the blue mass of Snowdonia. At the tip of the island a 200-year-old tower, built as a landmark for sailors, overlooks rocks where shags and cormorants breed.

▶ *Leave the A55 just after it crosses the Menai Strait and follow the A4080 westwards to reach Newborough after 11 miles. It is a 3 mile walk from Newborough to the very tip of Llanddwyn Island.*

⑧ Tre'r Ceiri

Like a sturdy trident thrusting up from the sea, Yr Eifl dominates the skyline of the Lleyn Peninsula. The name for the three sharply pointed summits is very apt, it means 'the fork' in Welsh. Their English name, for once more poetic, is The Rivals.

All three peaks are scattered with boulders and rocky outcrops, in harsh contrast with the gentle green lands below. It is only on climbing the steep path up the most easterly prong of the fork that you can see that people once lived here, turning inaccessibility into safety. At almost 500m (1,600ft) on the windswept hilltop is Tre'r Ceiri, 'the Giants' Town'. Massive stone walls, 4.5m (15ft) thick and almost as high in some places, link up natural rocky heights to encircle the remains of an Iron Age hill-fort with around 150 circular, stonewalled dwellings.

The view is tremendous. On the best days it covers parts of the Isle of Man and Ireland, the whole of Anglesey, Snowdonia's peaks, Cadair Idris, the mountains of central Wales, and part of the Pembrokeshire coast, almost 70 miles away across Cardigan Bay. Certainly, the 300 or 400 people who lived in Giants' Town could never have been caught unawares – and perhaps this is why the settlement flourished during most of the Roman occupation.

▶ *Tre'r Ceiri is 1 mile west of Llanaelhaearn, which is near the junction of the A499 and B4417. Paths climb Tre'r Ceiri from 1, 2 and 3 miles along the B4417 from Llanaelhaearn.*

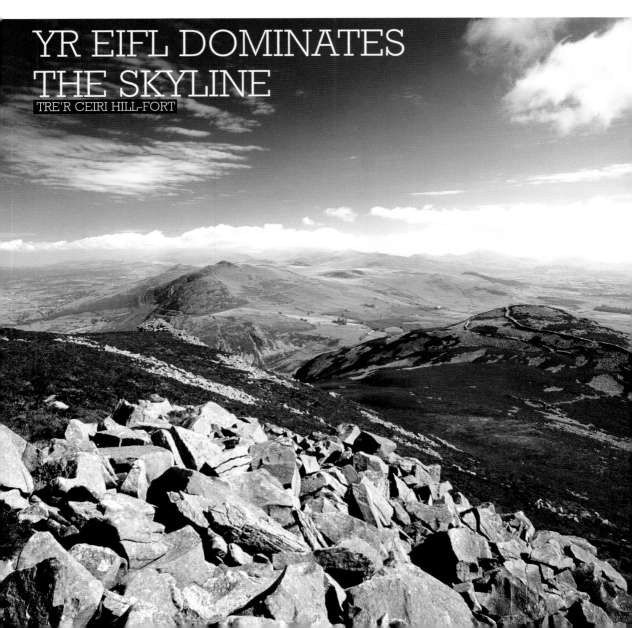

YR EIFL DOMINATES THE SKYLINE
TRE'R CEIRI HILL-FORT

⑨ Mynydd Mawr

Standing guard at the very tip of the Lleyn Peninsula is Mynydd Mawr, a steep, heathery, bracken-clothed hill sitting on top of sheer, black cliffs. A number of charming tracks and lanes, bright with celandines, violets or foxgloves, climb over and spread out from the hill to explore the craggy shore, with its secret bays and rocky coves. One of them, Porth Oer, is known as Whistling Sands; and in warm, dry weather the sands do at least squeak as you walk over them. The cause is said to lie in the unusual shape of the particles, which make a noise when rubbed together.

Mynydd Mawr is only 160m (524ft) high, but because it sits right on the rim of the land, it makes a magnificent vantage point. The huge, graceful curve of Cardigan Bay stretches away to the south, and to the north-east are the blue peaks of Snowdonia. Closer at hand Aberdaron sits on its pale, windy beach, and south-west across the choppy water is Bardsey Island.

This little strip of land, with rock-strewn fields and a green hump rising to 167m (548ft) at one end, is not always easily reached. There is a fearsome tide-race through Bardsey Sound, and quite often the island is cut off for several days at a time. Nevertheless, in the early Middle Ages, Bardsey was thought to be 'the gate of Paradise', and three pilgrimages to its abbey – now a ruin – were considered, for the soul's health, to be the equivalent of one journey to Rome. The dust of 20,000 Celtic saints is said to mingle with the island's soil.

Now only a handful of people reside among the thousands of birds that attract ornithologists to Bardsey between April and October. Choughs wheel overhead, colonies of razorbills, guillemots and kittiwakes clamour on the cliffs, and young Manx shearwaters wait silently in their burrows until dead of night, when their parents return to them with food from the sea.

▶ *At Llanbedrog, almost 4 miles south-west of Pwllheli along the A499, the B4413 branches right to Aberdaron which is 12 miles further west. A marked minor road from Aberdaron continues west to within ½ mile of the summit of Mynydd Mawr. Porth Oer is 2½ miles north of Aberdaron, near Methlem. Boats for Bardsey Island sail from Porth Meudwy, near Aberdaron, and from Pwllheli.*

⑩ Porth Neigwl

Lofty headlands frame Porth Neigwl's 3½ miles of sandy beach, idyllic on a calm, sunny day, but when south-westerly gales drive snarling waves on to the shore it is easy to understand why, in the days of sail, the bay acquired the name of Hell's Mouth. Many ships were devoured by its relentless breakers.

Less than a mile behind the beach, near its eastern end, is the tiny village of Llanengan, gathered about the twin-naved church that St Einion, King of Lleyn, founded in the 6th century. The lane south of the village loops round to the beach, while north it runs beside the slow, winding River Soch. Swans live by the quiet pools, herons stalk beside the stream, and ponies run free over the flat, wet lands of the valley. A lane swings 3 miles east and south from the village to mount the grassy promontory of Mynydd Cilan which forms the lower jaw of Hell's Mouth. Beyond the bright gorse and the deep pink valerian that spills from every cranny in the rocks, all Cardigan Bay stretches away to the south.

The upper jaw of Hell's Mouth, Mynydd Penarfynydd, is much steeper and craggier. On its other side is Porth Ysgo, a cliff-backed bay whose sandy beach is generally ignored by the crowds. A stream cascades down to the sea in a series of small waterfalls, through a valley of ferns, gorse and foxgloves. But Porth Ysgo, like its notorious eastern neighbour, becomes a boiling cauldron when gales drive in from the south-west. Behind the headland rises the whaleback ridge of Mynydd Rhiw. There is a 2 mile walk along the ridge path that rises to almost 300m (1,000ft), with the rocky slopes of 372m (1,217ft) Cam Fadryn dominating the view ahead and the long stretch of Hell's Mouth below.

▶ *Llanengan is on a minor road 1½ miles south-west of Abersoch, which is on the A499, 6 miles south-west of Pwllheli. Porth Ysgo, Mynydd Penarfynydd and Mynydd Rhiw are reached by lanes from Rhiw, which is on a minor road at the western end of Porth Neigwl, 7 miles south-west of Llanbedrog.*

The SHROPSHIRE HILLS

An ancient border runs through Shropshire – once a buffer zone between warring Celtic Wales and Saxon England – but today Offa's Dyke looks down on a peaceful landscape of fields and forests.

❶ The Wrekin

The sombre hump of The Wrekin stands out like some giant geological pimple on the smooth face of the Severn Plain. It rises abruptly between the Shropshire hills to the south and the flat, northern lands. Visible for miles around, The Wrekin is formed from some of the oldest rocks in Britain – lava, ashes and debris disgorged from a volcanic cleft 900 million years ago. Though it has the appearance of an extinct volcano, it is not one.

According to legend, however, its formation was quite different. Two giants are supposed to have fashioned the mound from mud dug from the Severn. But during a quarrel, one struck at the other with his spade, missed, and cleft the rock now called the Needle's Eye. His next blow was thwarted by a raven pecking at his eyes, and the tears he shed formed the pool known as the Raven's Bowl, which has never run dry since. The aggressor's third blow was successful, and he buried his unconscious adversary beneath the nearby hill, called The Ercall, from where his groans can still be heard at dead of night.

Two-thousand years ago, the earthworks on the summit were the ramparts of the tribal capital of the Cornovii. Now almost obliterated by time and weather, the remains stand as a reminder of the fiercely fought resistance of the British tribes to the Roman expansion from the east. Hut floors, post holes, gutters and storage pits have been found inside the main fort, which was probably built later when local wars and land-hunger among neighbouring tribes made it necessary to fortify the site.

To tread the broad tracks and paths that wind up to the summit through oak, birch, holly, yew and upland bracken is to tread the paths that our ancestors followed. Nature's gently changing seasons add to the timeless character. Bluebells carpet the woods in spring, and on the lonelier southern slopes there are primroses; in summer, foxgloves and rosebay willowherb flourish. Green woodpeckers may be seen searching for ants on the ground, treecreepers dart up the oak trunks and tits flock among the branches.

Though now crowned by a television transmission mast, the wild and windy summit is magnificent. The inner and outer entrances to the hill-fort are known as Heaven Gate and Hell Gate. A topographic stone map identifies the surrounding heights: west to Wales; north to the flat plains; east to Staffordshire and the Black Country; and south into the main mass of the Shropshire hills – a remote and misty landscape of crags, sharp peaks and whaleback ridges.

▶ *The Wrekin is 2½ miles south-west of Wellington. The path to the summit via Hell Gate and Heaven Gate starts at the car park on the east side of the hill, on the minor road from Wellington to Little Wenlock.*

❷ Earl's Hill

A narrow lane leads to one of the most enchantingly varied fragments of wild countryside in Shropshire. Iron Age settlers built a fort on the craggy summit of Earl's Hill; perhaps they, too, appreciated the beautiful lap of the Habberley valley to the south. Buzzards circle, swifts dart and dive; delicate blue harebells quiver in the grass and dwarf dandelions, wild thyme and gorse grow on the thin soil.

Earl's Hill is in the care of the Shropshire Wildlife Trust, which has laid out a nature trail leading to the summit of the hill. Its course runs through ash and oak woods, across upland meadows and along a stream in a deep valley. A walk here reveals places where mosses and yellow stonecrop thrive; where the hummocks built by yellow ants provide tiny gardens of clover, speedwell and forget-me-not; and where cowslips grow in the long grass.

Dippers and grey wagtails can be seen by the brook, where rare alpine enchanter's nightshade grows on the banks. Woodpeckers, tree pipits, pied flycatchers, redstarts, tits and warblers live in the woods; ravens and buzzards wheel overhead. Butterflies are abundant: peacocks, small tortoiseshells and commas emerge from winter hibernation in late March, and in spring and summer the grizzled and dingy skippers, the green hairstreak, the common blue and the pearl-bordered fritillary can also be seen.

The paths on and around Earl's Hill sometimes call for a breathless scramble, but so much is seen and learned along the way that the two or three hours needed are well worth while.

▶ *Earl's Hill lies 7 miles south-west of Shrewsbury along the A488. Just after Pontesford a lane leads south to the reserve. There is a Forestry Commission car park.*

Wales and the Welsh Borders

❸ The Stiperstones

When all around is sunshine, the chances are that there will be a dark cloud smudging the bleak and ragged ridge of the Stiperstones, at 536m (1,762ft) the second highest hills in Shropshire. Even the most unimaginative feel a sense of desolation and unease when in the shadow of the Stiperstones, or on their grim, rock-strewn summit. One of the curious rock formations is called the Devil's Chair, and it is said that when cloud hides the Stiperstones, the Devil has taken his seat. According to legend, witches and demons have met here for centuries.

The Stiperstones lie 5 miles north-west of the great moorland back of The Long Mynd. The rocks were formed about 500 million years ago, when shales and sandstones were laid down under a shallow sea. Later folding of the rock brought the Stiperstones quartzite, hard white sandstone, to outcrop at a steep angle. During and after the last Ice Age, frost shattered the quartzite into the jagged tors and tumbled screes that cover the summit today. Because of their geological interest and vegetation – a transition between the southern heaths and the northern moors – the Stiperstones were bought by the Nature Conservancy Council (now Natural England) in 1981 to become a 448ha (1,015 acre) National Nature Reserve.

There are several paths up to the Stiperstones, and the views, should the day be clear, are magnificent, looking west into Wales and south-east to The Long Mynd. The easiest path leads off the single track road that leads north-west from the village of Bridges, on the eastern side up to The Bog.

▶ *The Stiperstones are about 7 miles north-east of Bishop's Castle. Take the A488 to Lydham, turn east on to the A489 and at Eaton take the minor road north through Wentnor to Bridges.*

❹ Clun Forest

This great border landscape was once a royal hunting forest, although probably never heavily wooded. Many of the woods that stand here now have been recently planted, and most of them lie to the east of the peaceful little town of Clun.

Today the area is one of the most remote in Shropshire. Studded with lonely farms and bracken-covered uplands where buzzards and ravens sweep, it has a turbulent history and the town was continually fought over and sacked by both Welsh and English for centuries. Now Clun sheep, a famous breed, safely graze these once violent Welsh Marches.

East of Clun and south of the meandering River Clun stands Sowdley Wood. A narrow lane signposted Woodside, just past the parish church, leads to an unmarked track which hugs the edge of the wood. The first part of the path skirts an oakwood, full of mosses, ferns, lichens and sunshine. In autumn, puffballs and scarlet-lacquered toadstools sprout from its moist turf.

Between Clun and Bishop's Castle are wooded hills and swathes of valleys, golden with corn in late summer. A beautiful walk over these upland fields starts from Clun, near the youth hostel on a minor road north-east of the town. The path heads north-east between Radnor Wood and Steppleknoll to skirt the ramparts of Bury Ditches, an Iron Age hill-fort. This is Forestry Commission land, and several tracks lead to the fort. On the eastern side, on a minor road, there is a car park and picnic site where three walks and a cycle trail head into the forest. The Forestry Commission also signpost access through Mortimer Forest, a remnant of an ancient Saxon hunting forest, lying to the west of the B4361, just south of Ludlow.

▶ *Clun lies on the A488, 6 miles north of Knighton and 5 miles south of Bishop's Castle.*

THE LONG MYND

❺ The Long Mynd

The great 6 mile range of hills known as The Long Mynd is a world of its own. It includes wild moorland where red grouse whirr out of the heather, waterfalls cascade into half-hidden narrow valleys, and springs rise icy clear through bog moss and pink bog pimpernel onto bracken-covered hillsides and into sunlit streams.

The best way to explore The Long Mynd is on foot, from one of the villages along its eastern flanks. The Burway, a single track, climbs steeply up out of Church Stretton and gives spectacular views of the surrounding Shropshire hills. The springs that rise on The Long Mynd have carved deep valleys known as 'hollows', or 'batches', the most famous being Cardingmill valley with the Light Spout waterfall at its head. Much less frequented and almost equally lovely is Ashes Hollow, reached from the black-and-white village of Little Stretton where a brook chuckles down between the houses. From here, too, can be found Callow Hollow, over an intervening hillside. Further south is Minton Batch. Minton village is secluded and charming, and from Priors Holt in the lee of woodland there is a walk north through the trees and up The Long Mynd slopes to the Port Way, a 3,500 year old track that runs along the top.

Almost in Church Stretton itself is Rectory Wood, 7ha (17½ acres) of mixed woodland with a yew-shadowed pool, fine views of the Stretton valley and delightful meandering paths. Native and exotic trees mingle here, and are cared for by Shropshire County Council. It is not easy to find: the stile entrance is along a path that leads away south from the cattle-grid start of the Burway, west out of Church Stretton.

▶ *The Long Mynd ridge is about 3 miles west of Church Stretton on the A49. Minor roads from the B4370 lead west to footpaths that climb to the moorland on The Long Mynd.*

❻ The Stretton Hills

Across the narrow Stretton valley, to the east of The Long Mynd, is the miniature mountain range of the Stretton Hills. The valley itself follows an enormous fault, a break in the earth's crust, and separates the rounded whaleback of the pre-Cambrian Long Mynd from the even older and craggier summits of Caer Caradoc, The Lawley and Ragleth Hill.

The Stretton Hills encompass shady trackways, pebbled streams, bracken-covered slopes and high, invigorating summits. Caer Caradoc is the highest peak at more than 450m (1,500ft). It can be reached either from the crossroads in the hamlet of Comley at its northern foot, or by way of a lane and track leading from Cardington. These ancient tracks and paths link Cardington with Church Stretton, winding through farm and moorland under the crags of Caer Caradoc and the Gaer Stone. The climbs up to the windy summits are not difficult, and yield immense views.

On the summit of Caer Caradoc is a high and precipitous Iron Age hill-fort, enclosing some 2.4ha (6 acres) with well-defined double ramparts. It is said that the British chief Caratacus made a stand here against the invading Roman army – although such claims are made for several other parts of England. Heather and bracken grow on the hill and in early summer the bilberry – sometimes known as the whortleberry – flowers pink over its slopes.

Beyond Caer Caradoc is the gentler Lawley to the north, and the more wooded hills of Helmeth and Ragleth to the south above Church Stretton.

▶ *From Church Stretton on the A49, the B4371 heads eastwards across the Stretton Hills. Tracks lead north and south from the road into the hills, and a minor road from Wall under Heywood leads north to Cardington and Comley.*

WOODS THAT LIE IN FOLDS DOWN THE STEEP SLOPE
THE WREKIN FROM WENLOCK EDGE

⑦ Wenlock Edge

Wenlock Edge runs straight for 16 miles across Shropshire from north-east to south-west and, though distinct from a distance, it is strangely elusive when approached. The only main road to cross it is the A458 at the north-east end, but a good secondary road runs along the northern half. From remote black-and-white half-timbered villages along its slopes, many tracks and paths cross open farmland and deep woods to climb up to its unexpectedly level plateau. At Rushbury the Romans had an outpost, commemorated in the hill lane called Roman Bank. In many places, almost forgotten, are the mounds of an early medieval motte-and-bailey castle or an Iron Age earthwork.

In the northern half of the Edge lie many quarries, for the limestone was once used as a building material and is today used as aggregate. Ippikin's Rock is opposite Lilleshall Quarry, now disused, beside the B4371 north-east of Easthope. A projecting crag of hard, weathered rock, it gives a view across Ape Dale towards the Stretton Hills. Legend tells that the crag was named after a notorious robber who lived in a cave in the cliff. Ippikin's stolen hoard was buried by a landslide and his ghost still stands guard, ready to push over the cliff anyone nearing the treasure.

Major's Leap, near Stretton Westwood, owes its name to a Royalist officer, Major Thomas Smallman, who rode his horse over a cliff to evade Roundheads. His horse was killed, but his fall was broken by a tree and he escaped safely. His family home, the 16th-century Wilderhope Manor, stands just below the Edge and belongs to the National Trust.

Wolverton Wood, west of the point where the minor road from Harton crosses the Edge, contains a secluded nature reserve with a shadowy entrance in the woods that lie in folds down the steep slope. At another point on the Edge, there is an old quarry and lime-kiln. This is one of the places where farmers produced lime, used as a dressing on their fields. Near the kilns there are lime-loving plants such as common spotted orchids and spindle trees, whose wood was once used for making wool spindles.

▶ *Wenlock Edge can be reached along minor roads north-west from the B4368 and B4378 between Craven Arms and Much Wenlock, or from the B4371 between Church Stretton and Much Wenlock.*

❽ Brown Clee Hill

Highest of the Shropshire hills is Brown Clee Hill at almost 550m (1,800ft). Coal and ironstone were once mined here and the old shallow-shaft workings have left a hillocky summit now invaded by bracken.

Many people around the slopes of Brown Clee had common rights for grazing and gathering wood on the hill, and those who lived further away, 'the out-commoners', used old tracks called 'driftways', 'straker ways' or 'outracks' to climb to the grazing areas on the hillsides or carry iron ore and coal down. Many of the driftways still exist as sunken tracks, and the name Outrack is still given to a sunken road in Ditton Priors leading to Brown Clee. The commoners were granted these rights when Brown Clee was part of the Clee Forest – a royal hunting preserve until medieval times. By the 16th century, local people had encroached into the forest and their villages and fields had eaten into the wild land.

Just above one of these 'squatter' villages, the hamlet of Cockshutford on the western slopes of Brown Clee, is Nordybank Iron Age hill-fort. It is well preserved with clear ramparts and ditches, and provides a fine vantage point amid wide grass rides and bracken-covered slopes.

On the eastern side of Brown Clee, just out of the village of Cleobury North, lies Brown Clee Forest Trail climbing up open sunny hillsides to private woodlands. This trail winds through woodlands of Norway and Sitka spruce and pine, although there are some fine deciduous trees including sweet chestnuts, sycamore and birch. The trail diverges from the public footpath in the woods, but if the footpath is followed to Abdon Burf there are immense views.

▶ *Brown Clee Hill is 9 miles south-west of Bridgnorth. Cleobury North lies on the B4364 from Bridgnorth. A minor road from the village circles northwards round the hill to Cockshutford.*

❾ Hopesay Common

Two miles to the west of Craven Arms lies Hopesay Common, owned by the National Trust. From its hedged and narrow-laned western foot, just north of the village of Hopesay, a path climbs steeply up to the sparse pines on the crest of Hopesay Hill. Another track east of the hamlet of Round Oak makes a wide grassy swathe southwards through bracken along the lofty summit of the hill.

Nowhere is so airy and peaceful as Hopesay on an early morning in late summer, when mists hang in the valleys all the way to The Wrekin in the north-east. Yet this border country, with

Wales only 7 miles away, has been fought over for centuries. To the north the bare peak of Wart Hill rises above dark Forestry Commission conifers. It is capped by an Iron Age hill-fort. So, too, is the green cone of Burrow, 2 miles to the south-west, its centuries-old fortifications sharply defined in the morning sun.

On Hopesay it is possible to see how these hill-forts mark a clear line across Shropshire, each one backed up by the next. Caer Caradoc's ramparts stand out crisp against the sky. There is a sense of watchfulness here, and of great age. Even the trees that brood over the scene are old: ancient hollies, hawthorn, ash and Scots pine.

▶ *Hopesay Common is 2 miles to the west of Craven Arms. Take the B4368 westwards, and at Aston on Clun turn north along a minor road to Hopesay. A turning east in the village leads to the common and Round Oak. Long Lane, a minor road west off the A49 at Craven Arms, leads direct to Round Oak.*

❿ Bringewood Forge

Although only a few miles west of Ludlow as the crow flies, this stretch of the River Teme is one of the wildest and most secluded in the area. It twists north through a steep-sided valley at the village of Downton on the Rock, then winds north-east to Bromfield, whose history goes back to the Bronze Age. In places the valley is a narrow gorge, and rock strata are clearly visible along its sides.

At Bringewood Forge, reached down a narrow, little-used lane that heads east beyond the main entrance to Downton Castle, great charcoal furnaces once smelted over 500 tonnes of iron a year. By the end of the 18th century, coal had supplanted timber and Bringewood Forge was shut down. All that remains are ancient crumbling buildings and a magnificent, lonely 18th-century stone span of bridge, a great high arch over the Teme, standing as a monument to those early ironmasters.

Footpaths lead west through the wild parkland of Downton Castle, built in the 19th century by the Knight family whose wealth came from the iron. Northwards, through tangled woods, past overgrown streams and lakes crowded with wildfowl, the paths lead to Bromfield. The village is close to the site of one of the biggest Bronze Age settlements in the west of England and, to the north, is the site of a Roman fort that once stood guard at this junction of the rivers Teme and Onny.

▶ *Downton on the Rock is 5½ miles west of Ludlow. Take the A49 north to Bromfield, then turn west on to the A4113. After 2 miles a signposted minor road leads south-west to Downton on the Rock.*

⑪ Stow Hill

Two miles north-east of the Welsh town of Knighton, the great curved upland of Stow Hill guards the valley of the Teme. It is 424m (1,391ft) high and an ancient 'green lane', a track that may have been used as long ago as the Bronze Age, spans the length of it.

South from Clun, on the main A488, is the quaintly named New Invention. Legend has it that the hamlet earned its name when Dick Turpin stopped here and had his horse shod back to front, in order to confuse his pursuers. South up the hill from New Invention is Five Turnings, aptly named because here the green lane crosses the road, and another way turns north-east to skirt Caer Caradoc. This should not to be confused with Shropshire's other Caer Caradoc, lying further to the north, in the Stretton Hills.

The green lane passes through Five Turnings Farm and begins a long and gentle climb to the east up Stow Hill. Vetches, hawkweeds, hedge parsley, thistles and lesser celandines grow in the sunny ditches. Further along, the lane opens on to high pasture. From here it is possible to look north and see, just across a deep stream valley, the bracken-covered summit of Caer Caradoc – and beyond it, in the far distance, the other Caer Caradoc of the Stretton Hills. Both bear the ramparts of Iron Age hill-forts, and both are associated with the story of the British chief Caratacus making his last stand on their summits against the invading Romans.

Higher still, the views grow broader at every step: south into Herefordshire to the Welsh borders, west into Wales, east to the Clee Hills, north to The Long Mynd. The lane drops down north-eastwards between stands of conifers on high grasslands. There are dew-ponds here, and buzzards and ravens circle in the sky above. Over the southern edge of the hill, steep rocky slopes fall away to the Teme winding below. At the end of the trackway is the river Redlake, meandering cheerfully over pebbles through a charming valley and under a small wooden bridge. The lane here winds round to Chapel Lawn from which a footpath leads to the summit of Caer Caradoc. It is a high, remote, delightful three-hour walk.

▶ *Five Turnings, from where the walk across Stow Hill starts, is 4 miles south of Clun and 2 miles north of Knighton along the A488.*

⑫ Bircher Common

This high open grassland, rising to 275m (900ft), is part of the Croft Castle estate, just over the Herefordshire border. The castle is National Trust property and includes not only the common, with its bracken, gorse and small woodlands, but also a landscaped stream valley, parkland and an Iron Age hill-fort on the crest of a steep limestone ridge.

The Croft family are thought to have come to England from Normandy even before the Norman Conquest, and still occupy the castle, forming one of the oldest territorial links in Britain. Their castle is set in classic parkland with huge oaks and avenues of Spanish chestnuts thought to be more than 350 years old.

There is a walk up past the Spanish chestnuts through Forestry Commission woodland to the windy and bracken-covered summit of Croft Ambrey, a hill-fort with views to Wales and south-east to the Cotswolds. Fourteen counties, it is said, can be seen on a clear day. The hill-fort is impressive, with 15ha (38 acres) enclosed behind massive ramparts and a precipitous natural drop on the north side. It is known to have been occupied from about 400 BC until the defeat of Caratacus in AD 50.

There are fine trees on the Croft estate, including giant Wellingtonias. Wild flowers include herb robert and dove's-foot cranesbill with its tiny purple flowers. Also seen are butterflies – holly blues, ringlets, commas, small tortoiseshells and dark-green fritillaries – and there have been sightings of one of Britains most threatened species, the high brown fritillary.

▶ *Bircher Common is 6½ miles south-west of Ludlow. Take the A49 from Ludlow, and at Woofferton turn west on to the B4362. The common and Croft Castle are on minor roads north after Bircher.*

BUZZARDS AND RAVENS CIRCLE IN THE SKY
STOW HILL

The MALVERN HILLS

Although as English as Elgar, who lived in their shadow, the Malvern Hills are the last vestiges of Welsh rock to encroach into England. Their very name is Celtic in origin, derived from *moel*, or bald, and *bryn*, or hill.

❶ Bromyard Downs

Bromyard, a small market town 10 miles north-west of Malvern, was recorded in the Domesday Book of 1086 as one of the most important towns in the country, but today it slumbers contentedly among apple orchards and hopfields. The layout of its streets remains medieval and it boasts several fine black-and-white timbered houses.

Above the town to the east are Bromyard Downs, steep sheep-grazed common land with clear views westwards to Wales and south-east to the Malvern Hills. Delicate blue harebells grow there in summer, particularly on the crest of the Downs in Warren Wood, which is owned by the National Trust.

Deep in the heart of a secluded valley on the other side of the Downs is Lower Brockhampton, one of the most perfect medieval manor houses in England. Built in about 1400 for a local squire, it has survived almost untouched, complete with a gatehouse dating from the late 15th century and a moat fringed with pink-flowered water mint. It, and the surrounding Brockhampton Estate, is also owned by the National Trust.

There are four circular walks that wind through the estate, ranging in length from 1 to 4½ miles. They meander through mixed woodland that includes ancient oaks planted in the time of Henry VIII, and through fragrant orchards. Here, the fruit trees offer shelter to a wide variety of wildlife, with woodpeckers, redstarts and little owls making nests among their boughs. Ravens and buzzards fly high above the trees, while far below, in the thick undergrowth, lurk dormice. These tiny creatures are mainly nocturnal but they are sometimes glimpsed at dusk, in summer, as they emerge from hiding to look for nuts, berries and small insects. Also out hunting at this time are pipistrelle bats and you may be lucky enough to see them just as the estate is closing for the day.

▶ *Bromyard Downs, Warren Wood and Brockhampton Estate lie just north of the A44, 1 or 2 miles to the east of Bromyard.*

❷ Ravenshill Woodland Reserve

An enchanting survival of the woodland that once stretched from Malvern Chase to the Wyre Forest, Ravenshill Woodland Reserve is privately owned and managed for conservation using traditional methods. Parts of the reserve were planted with various species of conifer in the 1930s and some 30 kinds of native tree, including oak, ash, wild cherry, yew and spindle flourish there. Coppicing, an ancient system of woodland management, is carried out. This involves lopping the main stem of a tree back to a stump. Fresh shoots spring from the stump and provide a crop of poles, which are cut every 7–20 years, depending on the species of tree. Further shoots sprout to provide a new crop.

More than 170 different plants have been recorded in the reserve, including the locally rare herb paris, the bird's-nest orchid, and the creamy-pink spikes of the broad-leaved helleborine. In spring there are bluebells and wild daffodils, primroses and wild violets.

There are badger setts in the wood, and it is not unusual to smell the musky scent of a fox that has just slipped across the path. Buzzards and three species of woodpecker are occasionally seen. Evidence of ancient ridge-and-furrow farming methods can also be found.

The paths in the reserve are clearly marked, and from the highest point there are fine views of the Malverns, Worcester Cathedral, and the Severn plain. Despite the detailed management, the woods retain an atmosphere of intimacy and hushed seclusion.

▶ *Alfrick lies south of the A44 on a minor road 7 miles west of Worcester. The reserve is about 1 mile along the road leading north-west out of the village, opposite Lulsley Lagoon.*

Wales and the Welsh Borders

❸ Leigh Brook

The northern foothills of the Malverns that drop to the valley of the River Teme and its tributary, the Leigh Brook, are wild, wooded and remote. Although the towns of the Malverns are only a few miles away, they are concealed beyond the lofty summits.

Leigh Brook winds through a secluded valley of which 24ha (60 acres) are managed as a nature reserve by the Worcestershire Wildlife Trust. The Knapp and Papermill Nature Reserve is reached by way of a cottage garden where a meandering lane crosses the brook. Dippers and kingfishers nest along the banks. Further on are old coppiced woodlands and permanent meadows where wild daffodils and early purple orchids grow.

Rising from the valley of the Leigh Brook to the 204m (670ft) peak called The Beck is Old Storridge Common, where ancient tracks – paved in places – lead up through birch woodland, ash trees, oaks and bracken. Here the low evening sun turns the dark slopes into a strangely foreign world: looking back on the climb, the rosebay willowherb is turned to purple fire, and there is neither roof nor chimney-pot visible anywhere.

Local legend says that St Augustine once conferred with the Celtic clergy from Wales on the sparsely wooded cone of The Beck and in Anglo-Saxon times, the spot was called Augustine's Oak. It is a superb viewpoint with unparalleled views of Wales from its summit.

Beyond The Beck is the hamlet of Birchwood, where the English composer Sir Edward Elgar spent the summer of 1900 and wrote the oratorio *The Dream of Gerontius*. He wrote then: 'I don't like to say a word about these woods for fear you should feel envious, but it is godlike in the shade with the snakes and other cool creatures.'

Snakes do abound here, particularly the grass snake, and Old Storridge Common is noted for bees and butterflies, including the dark green fritillary, the holly blue and the speckled wood.
▶ *The Leigh Brook valley lies 6 miles west of Worcester, north of the A4103. The nature reserve is 1 mile south of Alfrick, which lies on minor roads between the A4103 and A44.*

❹ North Hill

North Hill is the most northerly of the Malverns, rising to 397m (1,307ft). Although not the highest, it is wilder and less trodden than its neighbour, Worcestershire Beacon. The path begins from a car park just below the brick Clock Tower in Great Malvern, passing a gaunt quarry face before curving on to the precipitous slopes of the east escarpment. There are other routes, but this gives magnificent views of Great Malvern – from here it is possible to see how closely it clings to the rock face. Through the shrub and woodland the pink and buff stone of Malvern Priory stands out clear against the Severn plain beyond.

The path winds past Ivy Scar Rock as it levels a little. Younger than the pre-Cambrian rocks which make up most of the Malvern Hills, this great lichen-covered rock face is dark and fine-grained. The succulent wall pennywort grows on its surface, and an ancient oak wrests its way out of a fissure.

After curling round the hill, the path drops into woodland and then climbs the broad track of Green Valley, once part of the old way across the hills from Great Malvern. At some points, the ancient paving stones thrust their way through the turf. The ancient track was planted with an avenue of sycamores some 60 years ago.

The summit of North Hill is grazed by sheep and is bare of the bracken, rowan trees and gorse found lower down. Only thin fescue grass and wild thyme grow here. Skylarks nest among the grasses close to the sharp peak. Not far below, the sound of traffic and even human speech or the bark of a dog rise with startling clarity from the town, but up here there is only the sound of the wind. The view encompasses the wooded northern foothills rolling down to Old Storridge Common and then as far as the Shropshire Wrekin. West are the Welsh borders, east the Severn plain and Bredon Hill, and, to the south, Worcestershire Beacon and the Malverns.
▶ *North Hill lies ½ mile outside Great Malvern, to the west of the A449.*

❺ Herefordshire Beacon

On Herefordshire Beacon stands one of the finest earthworks in Britain, an ancient fortified settlement built 338m (1,109ft) above sea-level on this windy summit. The earliest structure dates from about the 3rd century BC. It is reached from the busy hub of the Malvern ridge walk, a car park opposite the Malvern Hills Hotel on the A449. British Camp, as the hill-fort is called, is well marked. Almost too well: so many walkers climb up to it that the Malvern Hill Conservators, who look after the hills, have been obliged to build tarmac paths. Yet the fortification itself, once reached, is so immense, so indifferent to the tramp of human beings upon it, that it entirely retains its quality of endurance and mysterious pre-history.

It stretches away along the ridge to the south. Its broad level centre is the earliest part, surrounded by a bank and ditch – the ramparts were drystone walled. It is thought that in the 12th century a castle keep was built within this flat summit, and according to legend Owain Glyndwr, prince of Wales, made an unsuccessful attempt to defeat the English somewhere in the vicinity early in the 15th century.

From the centre of the fort the successive banks and ditches, built at later dates, widen like ripples in the great grassy hill. There are several entrances, and an ancient track climbing up from the west. One of a line of such forts extending from the Dorset coast into northern Wales, British Camp is one of the largest and most impressive. This is one of the many spots where it is claimed that the British chief Caractacus made his last, and unsuccessful, stand against the invading Roman army.

The views from Herefordshire Beacon are magnificent, and in its grasslands grow wild mignonette and harebells, with heather on its southern slopes. Yet the past is most important here. Archaeologists suggest that 1,500 to 2,000 people may once have lived here, although it is strange that there is no natural water supply inside the fort's defensive ramparts. John Masefield, born 3½ miles away in Ledbury, wrote after a childhood visit: 'People there had made the earth their father and protection; and the earth remembered that, and they, as parts of the memory of the earth, could still impress and terrify. Often they have terrified me.'

▶ *Herefordshire Beacon is ¼ mile south of the A449 just west of Little Malvern.*

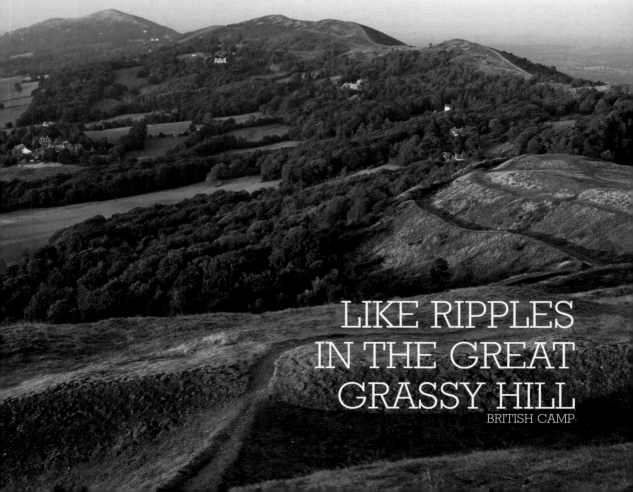

LIKE RIPPLES IN THE GREAT GRASSY HILL
BRITISH CAMP

❻ Worcestershire Beacon

A clear day is desirable for climbing the 425m (1,395ft) to the summit of the Worcestershire Beacon, the highest point of the Malvern Hills. The views are extraordinary; a direction indicator, or toposcope, set on the peak to commemorate the reign of Queen Victoria, clearly confirms that they stretch north from the Wrekin in Shropshire to the Mendips of Somerset in the south, beyond the Severn Estuary, and from Plynlimon in Wales to Bardon Hill above Leicester to the north-east. From here, too, can be seen vividly the three great cathedrals of Gloucester, Hereford and Worcester, as well as six battlefields of England's warring past – Evesham (1265), where Simon de Montfort was defeated by Prince Edward, later Edward I; Shrewsbury (1403), the scene of the defeat of Henry Percy by Henry IV; Mortimer's Cross (1461) and Tewkesbury (1471), in the Wars of the Roses; and Edgehill (1642) and Worcester (1651), where Parliamentarians and Royalists clashed in the Civil War.

Evidence of Bronze Age cremations more than 3,500 years ago has been found on the summit, and it has been used as a beacon site for at least 400 years. According to the poet Lord Macaulay, when beacons were lit throughout England to warn of the approach of the Spanish Armada, 'twelve fair counties saw the blaze from Malvern's lonely height'.

Worcestershire Beacon is much trodden and encircled with paths. A cafe (now gone) on the summit was opened in 1878 and it was visited, among others, by Edward VII who drove up most of the way – along one of the Victorian gravelled carriage routes – in his Daimler.

▶ *Worcestershire Beacon lies ½ mile outside Great Malvern, west of the A449.*

ALONG ITS PATHS ARE MANY WILD FLOWERS

LEDBURY

❼ Broad Down and Castlemorton Common

Below Herefordshire Beacon the Malvern Hills become gentler, and Broad Down immediately to the south-east is, as its name implies, a wide round hill with steep woods owned by the National Trust. There is a 19th-century reservoir at its northern edge, from which Turkey oaks, sweet chestnuts and rowan trees have spread uphill. Rare red-backed shrikes were once known to nest here, but have not been recorded since 1969.

On the western side of Broad Down is a small man-made cave cut from the basalt rock called Giant's or Clutter's Cave. It is said that the cave was once occupied by a hermit. Legend also links it with the Welsh prince Owain Glyndwr, who hid in it after fleeing from a battle against the English on Herefordshire Beacon in about 1405. Another story claims that the fugitive Lollard leader, Sir John Oldcastle, sheltered here after plotting against Henry V. Once a boon companion of the king, Sir John was the model for Shakespeare's Falstaff in *Henry IV*. It is more likely that the small hollow – conveniently close to the ancient spring of Walm's Well – was probably carved out as a shelter by one of the lonely medieval shepherds or swineherds who had to spend weeks on the hills.

East of Broad Down, on the edge of the Severn plain below the Malvern escarpment, is Castlemorton Common. It is one of the many areas of common land in the Malverns saved from enclosure in the 18th and 19th centuries by the resistance of local people. So valuable are Castlemorton's 240ha (600 acres) of ancient and unimproved rough-grazing land that 80ha (200 acres) have been designated by the Natural England as a Site of Special Scientific Interest.

Marshy, with streams and patches of gorse, Castlemorton Common supports at least 200 species of plants, including cowslips, harebells, marsh pennywort, ivy-leaved crowfoot, devil's-bit scabious and ragged-robin. It is well known for fungi, with almost 100 recorded species, and for the 60 pollarded native black poplars which are now rare in Britain.

Yellowhammers, linnets and stonechats flit through the gorse wilderness of Castlemorton, and even the sheep and cattle that graze unfenced along the single minor road that crosses the common have about them an untamed look.

▶ *Broad Down is ½ mile south of Little Malvern on the A449. Castlemorton Common lies south of the A4104 between Little Malvern and Welland.*

⑧ Midsummer and Hollybush Hills

The southern summits of the Malverns are lower and more densely wooded than those to the north. Here on the twin peaks of Midsummer and Hollybush hills the men of the Iron Age built a great defensive settlement in about 400 BC. Owned by the National Trust, the hill-fort can be reached either along the Malvern ridge or up a long track from Hollybush Pass below, where the A438 curves over the hills from east to west. It is not easy to see from below, but the track turns into a sharp twist of footpath at the top of the ridge and emerges through woodland to the bare turfed summit.

Excavations were made at Midsummer Hill between 1965 and 1970, and revealed pottery and metalwork linking it with a similar massive hill-fort on Bredon Hill, a northern outpost of the Cotswolds. Drystone faced ramparts and 17 timber gateways enclosed some 8ha (19 acres), including both Midsummer and Hollybush summits. Within the walls is a natural spring and evidence of some 250 hut sites: it is believed that as many as 1,500 people lived here before the Romans invaded in about AD 55.

Dusk is a ghostly time here because of the pale green lights of the glow-worms that inhabit the grassy slopes. Midsummer Hill is one of the few places where this dwindling species of beetle can still be found.

Just to the south of the hamlet of Hollybush is a deep ditch and bank, part of the Shire Ditch which runs from north to south along the Malvern ridge. It was built by Gilbert de Clare, red-headed Earl of Gloucester and the owner of Malvern Chase, in the 13th century. After a violent dispute with the Bishop of Hereford about where their common boundary lay, the line was finally agreed. The Red Earl is said to have so constructed the ditch and fence that although the bishop's deer could easily jump downhill on to his land they could not leap back uphill on to the bishop's side.

▶ *Midsummer and Hollybush hills lie north of the A438 at Hollybush, 9 miles north-west of Tewkesbury.*

⑨ Ledbury

Just 7 miles south-west of Malvern, in one of the most fruitful corners of Herefordshire, is the unspoiled little market town of Ledbury. For centuries Ledbury has flourished on the hops, fruit and Hereford cattle that have been bred here since the 17th century, and its comfortable citizens have bequeathed it a wealth of black-and-white timbered houses. There is a 17th-century market cross, a cobbled lane with overhanging gables, almshouses and many Elizabethan buildings.

There are several walks from the town. Cobbled Church Lane leads to the charming little woodland of Doghill, and the path continues across a lane up to Frith Wood. A mixed broadleaved woodland on a steep west-facing hillside, it is owned by the Forestry Commission. Along its paths are many wild flowers, including the rare violet helleborine and herb paris. It is a good place to see moths and butterflies, including the alder kitten moth.

North of Frith Wood an unmarked path leads across Wellington Heath, east of the village of the same name. The path continues past rising woodland to Oyster Hill, a bare summit giving fine views. Below Oyster Hill is Hope End, the childhood home of the 19th-century poet Elizabeth Barrett Browning. She lived there for about 20 years and wrote lovingly of its beautiful and secluded valley:

'Dappled very close with shade,
Summer-snow of apple-blossoms,
running up from glade to glade.'

Only the stables – now a hotel – survive, and still have the minarets that were part of the original oriental design of Hope End in 1809.

East of Frith Wood, across a lane, is the low rise of Kilbury Camp. Not easy to spot but easily reached across a field, it is a thistly coppice of ancient crab-apple and thorn trees, and on its wild little summit the earthworks are clearly visible. From here the hill-fort on Herefordshire Beacon to the east looks startlingly close.

Also within easy walking distance from Ledbury itself, off the Tewkesbury road just past the church, is Coneygree Wood – the name probably comes from Coney Garth, meaning rabbit warren. In medieval times rabbits were carefully protected by landowners to provide an additional source of meat. Coneygree Wood is natural woodland, with small quarries in which many fossils have been found.

▶ *Ledbury is on the A449, at the junction with the A438 and A417. Frith Wood is to the north of the town and Kilbury Camp is to the north-east, about 1 mile along the A449.*

Wales and the Welsh Borders

CHASE END HILL

⑩ Raggedstone Hill and Golden Valley

According to legend, this dark double peak of the Malverns – bleak, bare and jagged from almost any viewpoint – has a menacing shadow. In medieval times a young monk from Little Malvern Priory is said to have fallen in love, and as a penance for breaking his vow of chastity was ordered to crawl each day on his hands and knees the 2½ miles from the priory gate to pray on the summit of Raggedstone Hill. One day, exhausted and bitter, he reached the peak but instead of praying he called down a curse on all those on whom the shadow of Raggedstone might fall. Cardinal Wolsey, the powerful chancellor of Henry VIII, once lived at nearby Birtsmorton Court, and one afternoon fell asleep in the garden: the shadow of Raggedstone passed over him and his downfall began from that moment.

On the marshy eastern levels below Raggedstone Hill is Golden Valley, from where the hill looks sinister enough, but remote. Golden Valley is another stretch of the wild Malvern sheep-grazed common land, covered with yellow gorse, thorn and oaks, turf and bracken. Magnificent sedge, irises and bulrushes fringe its wide old mill-pond. A short drive down a track from the B4208 leads to gentle walks and a picnic spot.

▶ *Raggedstone Hill lies just south of Hollybush on the A438.*

⑪ Chase End Hill

This is not only the southern tip of the Malvern Hills and the chase, or hunting territory, it also marks the last spot where the Cambrian rocks of Wales appear in England. To the north the Malverns look like sleeping hounds, hunched against each other for warmth; to the west lie the blue hills of Wales. But south and east a pageant of plump and fruitful fields stretches across the Severn plain to the golden Cotswolds and the Vale of Evesham.

Yet Chase End Hill and the hamlet of Whiteleaved Oak at its foot form one of the most wild and romantic parts of the Malverns. In summer, wild flowers bloom and flourish here and in autumn there is a bounty of hazelnuts and elderberries, and a tangle of blackberries. Woodpeckers, skylarks, pipits and warblers sing in its woodlands and buzzards circle its windy summit. It is known for butterflies, such as the grizzled skipper and the green hairstreak.

The tiny hamlet of Whiteleaved Oak, tucked into the narrow lonely pass between the hills of Raggedstone and Chase End, is believed to have acquired its name from a variegated oak which once grew there. Sheltered in a green bowl of the wooded and bracken-covered hillsides, the perfect timbered cottages of this secluded place seem to belong to a past century, where sheep wander still over a tiny green and grassy verges.

▶ *Chase End Hill lies 1 mile south of the A438, 2 miles east of Eastnor.*

196

The WYE and SEVERN VALLEYS

The waters of the rivers Wye and Severn rise on the barren slopes of Plynlimon, in the Cambrian Mountains, and then flow through Wales and on into England before meeting again in the Severn Estuary.

❶ Radnor Forest

Despite its name and its closeness to the woods of western Hereford, this is not a forest in the modern sense. It was a Norman forest – an extensive tract of country with or without trees set aside for hunting. Though many trees have been planted by the Forestry Commission in recent years, most of the land is still open grazing roamed by huge flocks of hardy mountain sheep.

From a haphazard framework of valleys the forest plateau rises on steep, smooth flanks seamed by many rivulets. One dashing stream suddenly plunges 22m (75ft) into a wooded gorge. After a wet spell of weather this waterfall vividly fulfils its name, Water-break-its-neck. From here a walk follows the plateau's western rim and gives fine views over the Ithon valley to the heart of Wales.

No roads suitable for cars cross the forest, but its footpaths, ancient track-ways and open spaces make it ideal country for pony-trekkers and determined walkers – but not when clouds come down and conceal the landmarks. The highest point in the forest is 660m (2,165ft) – high enough to be very bleak in bad weather – and much of the land is above 480m (1,600ft). The quaintly named conical peak of the Whimble, near the forest's southern edge, is almost 600m (2,000ft). It is a brisk but rewarding walk from New Radnor up the zigzagging path to the summit, which looks south over the layers of hills towards Hay Bluff, 15 miles away.

New Radnor fits neatly into the landscape. Grassy, hedge-topped banks mark the line of medieval town walls and partially enclose the village, whose rectangular street pattern has survived since the 13th century. The layout is seen best from the steep hill above the church. Hummocks on the grassy hill are all that remain of New Radnor's once mighty castle.

▶ *New Radnor is on the A44, 6½ miles north-west of Kington. The path to Water-break-its-neck leaves the A44 1½ miles south-west of New Radnor, and continues round Radnor Forest's western edge. The A488, 5 miles south-west of Knighton, runs along the forest's northern edge.*

❷ Kington

High, rounded hills encircle the ancient market town of Kington, giving it a backdrop of great beauty whichever way you look. From their summits the hills survey glorious scenes. Kingswood Common, 2 miles south of the town, looks down to the Wye meandering gently to and fro across a wide, fertile valley, with wooded slopes beyond it. Smooth, small hills lie to the east, but in the south the Black Mountains loom dark and bold. On the other side of the town, Bradnor Hill rises sharply. A strenuous 2 mile walk from Kington Church climbs the hill to a magnificent 391m (1,282ft) viewpoint which scans line upon line of hills as far as the majestic peaks of the Brecon Beacons. Just to the north are well-preserved sections of Offa's Dyke.

From Kington Church a lane climbs west up the shoulder of Hergest Ridge to a lofty, turf track that marches for 2 miles along the crest at almost 430m (1,400ft) – a heady, open walk between patches of gorse and bracken. All this territory was once owned by the Vaughan family, the great landowners of the region. Their house, Hergest Court, lies on the south side of the ridge. The most notorious of its residents were Thomas Vaughan, known as Black Vaughan, and his wife Ellin, who for some unknown reason was known as Gethin the Terrible.

This vengeful lady dressed as a man to attend an archery contest where one of the competitors was a relative who had killed her brother. When her turn came, she shot her arrow at the assassin and killed him, escaping in the resulting confusion. Thomas was killed in the Wars of the Roses, but his ghost haunted the lanes until 12 parsons armed with 12 candles lured the ghost into a silver snuff-box and cast it into Hergest Pool. Effigies of the wicked couple, with deceptively placid faces, lie on their tomb in Kington Church.

▶ *Kington is 14 miles west of Leominster along the A44.*

Wales and the Welsh Borders

❸ Golden Valley

Rich, fat and fertile, the Golden Valley lies between Hereford and the dark line of the Black Mountains. Red-gold with Herefordshire cattle, ripening apples and fields of corn it seems aptly named, but the name probably arose only from a confusion of languages. The Welsh referred to the valley's river as *dŵr*, meaning 'water', but the Normans mistook this for *d'or*, the French for 'golden', and so the River Dore flows through the Golden Valley, not to be confused with those valleys of the same name in the Malverns and Cotswolds.

Standing sentinel at the northern end of the valley is Merbach Hill, swelling steeply to 318m (1,044ft). The river rises on its southern slope and slides gently through the tranquil charm of Dorstone, Peterchurch, Vowchurch and Abbey Dore. It mingles with the Monnow at Pontrilas. All the way down, the dramatic natural rampart of the Black Mountains dominates the western view, its rim towering above the mosaic of fields at its feet. Wooded slopes make a softer horizon to the east.

During the long years of border warfare, the valley was a favoured route for Welsh raiders coming in to harry Norman estates. A castle was built at Snodhill, south of Dorstone, to command the valley and deny the raiders entry. Now only scanty remains of the stronghold are left. Just over half a mile to the north of the village is Arthur's Stone, one of the few Neolithic tombs in the area. The enormous capstone on ten uprights covers a chamber 6m (20ft) long.

Down the valley at Abbey Dore there is a fine, large, Early English church, once part of the great Cistercian abbey of the 12th century and restored and re-roofed as a parish church by Viscount Scudamore in the 17th century. His family had become wealthy and powerful on spoils from monasteries after the Dissolution – a deed that lay heavy on the viscount's conscience. He compensated for it by endowing half-a-dozen churches, supporting unemployed clergy, and leaving sums of money to maintain schools for Hereford's poor.

▶ *Dorstone is on the B4348, 6 miles east of Hay-on-Wye. Pontrilas is on the A465, 11 miles south-west of Hereford.*

GOLDEN VALLEY

❹ Mordiford

The wooded hills that spread east from Mordiford are laced with a tangled skein of narrow lanes, delightful and bewildering to the stranger. The lanes in turn are interwoven with many miles of footpaths and bridleways.

Mordiford stands on the River Lugg – a fine river for grayling – just above its junction with the Wye. Despite its plain name, the Lugg is a beautiful river, winding as sinuously as the Wye through rich farmland and orchards, and between lush water-meadows dotted with pale willows. At Mordiford the river glides beneath the nine arches of the 600-year-old bridge. Each time the king rode over this bridge in medieval times the lords of Hereford had to give him a pair of silver spurs; that was their payment in return for the manor of Mordiford. From Backbury Hill, reached by a path leading north-east from the town, you can look down on the river, the town, and beyond to Hereford's sandstone cathedral and even the distant mountains of Wales.

Haugh Wood flanks the lane between Mordiford and Woolhope, and has two butterfly trails, waymarked by the Forestry Commission. It makes a tranquil interlude to wind among the dappled glades, with glimpses through the oaks from the high ground to the fat land outside the woods. A winter and early spring visitor, attracted by the conifers, is the vivid little siskin, yellowy-green with a black bib, creaking and twittering in its jerky, bounding flight.

A delightful drive south from Mordiford towards Ross-on-Wye passes through some of the Wye valley's most attractive scenery. The road from Fownhope to Brockhampton is particularly lovely as it climbs through Capler Wood, where trees frame vistas of the river's graceful curves.
► *Mordiford is 4 miles south-east of Hereford along the B4224.*

❺ May Hill

The breezy summit of May Hill is a perfect spot for short but rewarding walks. For miles around, the topknot of dark trees on its broad dome is an easily spotted landmark. Tracks criss-cross the hill, mounting gradually up the springy turf between the bright splashes of gorse and the bracken fronds towards the crowning cluster of tall pines. The trees were planted to commemorate Queen Victoria's Golden Jubilee in 1887. In 1977, and again in 1980, there were further plantings; the first, to commemorate the Silver Jubilee of the Queen, and the second to mark the 80th birthday of the late Queen Mother.

The hilltop, at almost 305m (1,000ft), is a superb viewpoint. Green waves of wooded hills roll westwards to merge with the mountains of Wales. To the east, the long line of the Cotswolds rises suddenly from the broad Vale of Gloucester, where the Severn meanders seaward through a fertile landscape of farms and villages. The Forest of Dean lies to the south-west, but what catches the eye most is a huge silvery loop of water where the Severn curls around.

Newent Woods cover the north-east side of the hill. They are sunny with drifts of daffodils in spring and then sweet with perfume from the thick carpet of bluebells in early summer. By ancient custom, rival parties of young folk from Newent village used to walk up through the woods to the top of the hill on May Day and there do battle, summer's supporters against winter's. Summer's friends were always victorious, and triumphantly took fresh summer greenery back to the village.
► *May Hill is 1 mile along a marked minor road that turns north off the A40, 7 miles east of Ross-on-Wye.*

❻ Goodrich Castle

Towers and walls of rich red sandstone, springing from a dry moat cut deep into solid rock, create the impression that Goodrich Castle grew magically from its rock foundations rather than being built upon them.

The castle, whose name originated as Godric's Castle, stands high above the meandering Wye on a beautifully wooded spur. The oldest part, the three-storey keep, was built about 1160 for Godric Mappestone. Its purpose was to guard a river crossing during the turbulent period when the Wye was a river of considerable military importance. No better position could have been chosen, for the view over the river and the surrounding countryside is superb – a military advantage in the 12th century and a scenic one now.

The castle was impregnable during border warfare, and in the Civil War it was the last Herefordshire castle to fall to the Roundheads. It surrendered in 1646 after Colonel John Birch's artillery had battered the defences with 'Roaring Meg', a huge siege gun that can now be seen on Castle Green in Hereford.

During the fighting, the colonel's niece Alice ran away with her lover, Charles Clifford, but the pair were drowned when they attempted to cross the Wye. Their ghosts are supposed to haunt the river, trying to cross it on a phantom horse.
► *Goodrich is 4 miles south-west of Ross-on-Wye, just off the B4229, which connects the A40 and B4234. The castle is 150m (500yd) from the village.*

Wales and the Welsh Borders

199

❼ Highmeadow Woods

A vast woodland of oak and larch, beech and cedar, ash and elder, chestnut and spruce sprawls over the high ground across the river from Monmouth. Beneath the varied canopy, you can follow a waymarked trail northwards for almost 2 miles from the Staunton road to the Wye. On the way, the path passes the Suck Stone – 18m (60ft) long and 12m (40ft) wide – broken off from the hill above and thought to be the largest boulder in the country.

Where the path reaches the Wye, a suspension bridge for walkers spans the water, and on the other side you can take leisurely strolls either way along the towpath. The path leading west runs below the Seven Sisters Rocks and mounts one of them to give a wonderful view down the river. Then it climbs to King Arthur's Cave, occupied by human and animal hunters in prehistory; bones of mammoth, bear, rhinoceros and bison have been found in it.

Instead of crossing the footbridge you can follow the path eastwards above the river for 1½ miles, to an unsurpassed view from the most impressive vantage point on the Wye's 130 mile course. Symond's Yat Rock stands 154m (504ft) above sea-level on a narrow neck of land almost cut off by a great ox-bow loop in the river. The fields far below roll away to the north, while trees cling tenaciously to the steep slopes.

On the south side of the Staunton road the waymarked path leads to the Buck Stone, which may have been a pagan sacrificial altar. It used to be a rocking stone until a band of itinerant actors rolled its massive weight down the hill in 1885. It was replaced with great difficulty, but could not be made to balance again and is now pinned and cemented in place. The stone tops a steep hill, which is worth the climb for the wide view it gives over the woods.

Further west from Staunton another path strikes west up the Kymin, a steep 244m (800ft) hill that looks over Monmouth, the Wye and the Monnow valley, and across the border lands to the Black Mountains. On its crest is the Round House, a folly built in 1794 by Monmouth's leading gentry so that they could admire their surroundings through a telescope presented by the local MP. In 1800 the folly was joined by the pagoda-like Naval Temple, with its coloured plaques commemorating the victories of Nelson, Rodney, Hawke, Howe, Duncan and other contemporary naval heroes.

▶ *The waymarked path leading south to the Buck Stone and north into Highmeadow Woods crosses the A4136 just over 2 miles east of the bridge at Monmouth. The Kymin path starts 1 mile west.*

❽ Forest of Dean

A sense of life as it was hundreds of years ago pervades the Forest of Dean. Secret and wild it seems, stretching on and on whichever way you turn. But then the green glade widens and you can see out over undulating blue-green tree-tops to cultivated fields, distant hills and shimmering curves of river.

In reality the forest is far from wild. Replanting has gone on over the centuries and does today, making the mixture of trees very different from what it was in the forest the Normans knew. Now the oaks mingle with beech, birch, ash and sweet chestnut – and foreign softwoods outnumber these. Spruce, larch and fir are the fast-growing crop of the modern working forest; all the conifers are nursed and thinned over the great triangular spread of forest that lies between the Wye and the Severn.

Ferns and mosses, lichens and liverworts carpet the ground. You can glimpse shy deer and swift squirrels, and hear the busy drilling of woodpeckers. Deer were the quarry of the royal huntsmen who, from the 11th century, held this vast domain as their preserve. King Canute set up the Court of Verderers to be responsible for anything that grew or lived in the forest. The court still meets at the 11th-century Speech House deep in the heart of the woodlands.

Today, most people come to the Forest of Dean for leisure and quiet enjoyment. It was very different in previous centuries, for the forest, with its natural resources of coal and iron ore as well as timber, played an important role in England's economy for hundreds of years. The iron was mined from before Roman times until the Industrial Revolution. In medieval times the forest supplied timber for shipbuilding, and was so vital to British naval power that its destruction is said to have been an objective of the Spanish would-be invaders in 1588.

During the Victorian era, the forest was a coalfield producing a million tonnes of coal each year. After a decline in the 1930s, open-cast mining has been resumed in some areas. A few seams are exploited by 'free' miners. Their rights are a reward granted by Edward I: in 1296, when Berwick-upon-Tweed was under siege, the king enlisted miners from the Forest of Dean to tunnel under the city walls.

There are miles of forest walks laid out by the Forestry Commission, and numerous marked nature trails and leafy lanes.

▶ *The A4136 east from Monmouth crosses the northern part of the Forest of Dean. The B4234 runs north-south with the B4226 crossing the central area. There are car parks within the forest on all the roads.*

THE FOREST OF DEAN

❾ Llandogo

When timber, coal and iron ore made this one of the most valuable industrial areas in Britain, ships sailed from Llandogo to Bristol and the far corners of the world. When the railway came in the 1870s and its shipping trade died Llandogo became a beautiful, sleepy village.

You can walk beside the river to Bigsweir Bridge, a mile upstream, and beyond, if you like, towards Monmouth, with green woodlands tumbling down the western banks and, across the water, steep banks topped by Offa's Dyke. The mounted Saxons who patrolled the top of the dyke must have been a daunting sight for anyone planning to encroach into Mercia.

Behind Llandogo, paths climb north to Beacon Hill, which looks westwards over Trelleck towards the Brecon Beacons. Another lane from the village climbs south into the heart of Bargain Wood, where marked walks from the car park lead to superb, sweeping views of the river.

Llandogo is named after St Oudoceus, a 6th-century saint who was given the land by the Welsh Prince Ennion to build a monastery – though at a price. The tale is that the two men met when hunting, and argued about the stag they were pursuing. Finally they agreed that Oudoceus could have all the ground that the stag had covered that day in return for ensuring Ennion a place in Heaven.

▶ *Llandogo lies on the A466, some 7 miles south of Monmouth.*

❿ Tidenham Chase

Just 4 miles north of Chepstow and sprawling along the eastern bank of the Wye is Tidenham Chase, once the exclusive hunting preserve of the lords of Chepstow. The road that runs through the Chase from Chepstow offers some breathtaking viewpoints. Wintour's Leap towers 60m (200ft) above the Wye, a massive grey crag over water that sweeps sharply round in a hairpin bend after encircling the Lancaut peninsula. The backwash has worn away the tongue of land and made a hook at its tip. The leap is named after Sir John Wintour (or Winter), a Civil War hero who is said to have galloped his horse over the edge and swum across the river to escape from the Roundheads.

Offa's Dyke Path turns west from the road after a further half mile and follows the original Dyke. Striding along the steep, wooded slope, you can admire the line chosen for the 8th-century boundary between Mercia and Wales. The view of the river, and of the Welsh borders beyond it, is superb. The Devil's Pulpit is 2 miles along the path. Below this natural rock platform and across the river lies the ruins of Tintern Abbey. According to legend, the Devil used to visit the platform to shout insults at the Cistercian monks.

▶ *The B4228 turns off the A48 just east of Chepstow and runs past Wintour's Leap and across Tidenham Chase towards St Briavel's. Wintour's Leap is ½ mile north of the turn-off.*

wales and the Welsh Borders

Berwick-upon-Tweed

NORTHUMBERLAND'S COAST and HILLS 248-255

Alnwick

Newcastle upon Tyne

Hexham

Carlisle

THE LAKE DISTRICT 229-239

Keswick

Penrith

Sunderland

Durham

Darlington

Middlesbrough

Whitby

THE NORTH YORK MOORS 214-221

Richmond

Windermere

THE YORKSHIRE DALES 204-213

Scarborough

Ripon

Lancaster

Harrogate

York

Skipton

THE FOREST of BOWLAND 224-228

Bradford

Leeds

Kingston upon Hull

Preston

Wakefield

Salford

Manchester

Sheffield

Macclesfield

THE PEAK DISTRICT 240-247

Derby

Northern England

Dark peaks, lonely fells and remote moors tower over the deep valleys and dales in this land of highs and lows. Time-worn tracks and ancient pathways criss-cross the countryside, leading the traveller into the heart of Northern England.

The YORKSHIRE DALES

Dramatic steep-sided valleys, or dales, give this part of Yorkshire its name; valleys divided by weather-beaten drystone walls and overlooked by towering peaks and desolate moors.

❶ Arkengarthdale

Despite the sparkling clarity of its moorland setting, and its toy-town hamlets, there is a touch of harshness about Arkengarthdale. The medieval cattle marauders are still on the edge of memory, and the scars left by centuries of lead-mining are all too apparent. Long ago, this was a famous hunting forest, but now the area's main attraction is the wild, silent moors, where a curlew's cry seems to carry for ever.

From the lofty heights of Tan Hill, the moorland sweeps down to the banks of Arkle Beck, a tributary of the River Swale. Beside the sparkling waters of the beck are a string of tiny villages, some of them little more than clusters of farms. Their names – Whaw, Langthwaite, Arkle Town, Booze, Reeth – are as ancient as the name of the dale itself. Booze, rather disappointingly, is a corruption of the Old English word *bowehouse*, meaning 'house by the curve' – the village stands on a hillside above a bend in the river.

Reeth is the best touring centre for the dale. Starting from the stile by the east end of the bridge in the village, a footpath leads along the east bank of Arkle Beck all the way to Whaw, a distance of some 6 miles.

An easier walk is the short circular route north from Langthwaite, starting on the road up the west side of the beck. After three-quarters of a mile, turn right at the road junction on to the Barnard Castle road. In the 18th century, packhorses used the road to carry lead from the mines near Langthwaite to Barnard Castle, some 10 miles away, and relics of the old mining days can be seen everywhere.

The 3 mile circular walk is completed by following the Barnard Castle road across the bridge over the beck, turning right and following the riverside footpath back to Langthwaite.

▶ *Reeth is on the B6270, 9 miles west of Richmond. A signposted road from Reeth leads into Arkengarthdale and up the valley to Langthwaite and Whaw.*

THE MOORLAND SWEEPS DOWN
CASTLE FARM, ARKENGARTHDALE

❷ Tan Hill

One of the loneliest places in the Dales, the 536m (1,758ft) high summit of Tan Hill is often capped with ragged cloud or racked by harsh winds. But it is when the clouds clear that it takes on a wild beauty and the glorious fell scenery stretches out before the eye in every direction. To the south lie the jagged contours of Stonesdale Moor, to the east the bleak uplands of Arkengarthdale Moor, and to the north a vast stretch of empty moorland outside the National Park, which culminates in the massive bulk of Mickle Fell. The 790m (2,591ft) hill lies just inside County Durham.

Red grouse and a few hardy Swaledale sheep are the main inhabitants of the area. The drovers who once used this summit as a stopping place on the way south from the Scottish borders lodged in the remote Tan Hill Inn. This unassuming 18th-century building, lying on a crossing point of drovers' roads, is the highest inn in England. It was once known as the King's Pit House, and its licensing hours were dictated by need rather than by law – 'Refuse no-one at Tan Hill', the justices ordered one landlord.

Today, however, normal licensing hours apply, though the rigours of the countryside around it remain unchanged. Unmarked mine shafts provide a hazard for walkers, so it is essential to keep to the footpaths.

▶ *Tan Hill is 9 miles south-east of Brough. It can be reached by a well-signposted minor road off the B6270 just west of Keld, or through Arkengarthdale.*

❸ Kisdon Gorge

The steep, narrow and thickly wooded gorge is never silent. Its voice is that of the River Swale that tumbles through the glen from one limestone ledge to another. See it especially on an autumn evening when Kisdon Force, near Keld, is little more than a bass rumble in the darkling gorge, superbly overstating the flaming gold of the bracken above. Only a short distance along the river are Catrake Force, Currack Force, Rainby Force and the wild, swirling Wain Wath Force. Flowing close by are enchanting Stonesdale, Sleddale, Whitsundale and Hind Hole becks; and rearing high above, the lonely expanses of Great Shunner Fell, Rogan's Seat, Nine Standards Rigg and Water Crag.

Keld village – originally Appletreekeld, 'the spring of the apple tree' – was a lead-mining centre 100 years ago, and the tattered remains of the industry are scattered across the countryside. Nowadays, the village is best known as a stopping-off place on the Pennine Way. The green track of nearby Kisdon Road forms part of it, and is, too, a section of the old Corpse Way, the path along which the dead were carried in wickerwork coffins to the graveyard at Grinton, 11 miles down-river. The lightness of the coffin notwithstanding, the burden was a heavy one; this is why some kindly soul provided a coffin stone at the northern end of the pack-horse bridge at Ivelet, so that the bearers might rest their load on the long journey to Grinton.

A shorter walk from Keld, and one with less melancholy associations, leads along the riverside path, across the Swale, east of Crackpot Hall and then north to Swinner Gill. It is a tour of 2½ miles, and includes the best of both river and moorland scenery.

▶ *Keld is on the B6270, from Richmond to Kirkby Stephen, 4 miles north-west of Gunnerside.*

❹ Semer Water

Some 10,000 years ago, at the end of the Ice Age, the Yorkshire Dales were a Lake District in miniature – Coverdale was a 6 mile long lake, and there were many other stretches of water, both large and small, especially in Wensleydale around Hawes and Aysgarth. Today, Semer Water and Malham Tarn are the only survivors of the Ice Age lakes, all the rest having long drained away. Semer Water and its 1½ miles of shore are the focal point of many of the Dales' most beautiful views – from Stalling Busk, for example, less than a mile to the south on the slopes below Stake Moss; or in the late afternoon, from the hillside just below the farming hamlet of Countersett, north of the lake.

For more than 2,000 years farmers have worked the countryside around Semer Water. There are Celtic remains in the area, and the traces of Romano-British cattle enclosures on the fell east of Stalling Busk. An Iron Age village looked down over Wensleydale from close to the summit of Addlebrough; and the remains of Iron Age lake villages have been discovered by the shores. Perhaps it was one of these that gave rise to the legend that an ancient city lies drowned in the depths of Semer Water.

The lake gives birth to England's shortest river – the River Bain, which tumbles some 2 miles into Bainbridge where it joins the River Ure. Whatever the season, Semer Water mirrors the Dales' moods. It can seem serene and placid in its deep hollow, with cattle wading far out into the water; or grey and threatening, its waters lashed by blustery winds. In winter it sometimes puts on a sparkling mantle of ice.

▶ *Two minor roads lead from Bainbridge, 4 miles east of Hawes on the A684, to Semer Water.*

NORTHERN ENGLAND

❺ Dentdale

Bisected by the Dee, at this point a brawling, tumbling infant of a river, Dentdale is the smallest of the Yorkshire Dales and arguably the loveliest. Certainly, the variety of its scenery is extraordinary; west of handsome little Dent town, the geological phenomenon of the Dent Fault slashes through the valley. It could be said that along this line, the Yorkshire Dales come to an end and the Lake District begins, since to the east of the fault the landscape is one of smoothly swooping limestone fells, while to the west it is the weathered, craggy slate of the Lake District.

Barkin Beck, which rises about a mile west of Dent, follows the line of the fault, dividing the slate from the limestone. The change is abruptly emphasised just above the beck by the slate amphitheatre of Combe Scar.

The flat and once-swampy mouth of the valley kept Dentdale in isolation for centuries – so much so that it is said that the southward-raiding Scots never found the place.

Above the town of Dent, the dale narrows into a limestone gorge, and there is a fine hike from Lea Yeat, east of Dent, over to Great Knoutberry Hill (672m (2,203ft) high) in the Widdale Fell, along part of an old drovers' road. Around Dent itself there are a number of delightful riverside walks, and at the eastern end of the dale a road leads up the gorge under the railway and down to the B6255, giving good views of Dentdale.

▶ *Dent is reached by a minor road from the A65, just west of Ingleton. Another minor road enters the dale from Sedbergh, on the A683.*

❻ Whernside

The craggy bulk of Whernside – at 736m (2,419ft) it is the highest peak in the National Park – separates Dentdale, Kingsdale and Little Dale. A long ridge slopes up from the south, with a dry-stone wall along the crest, while the northern slopes are more gentle, with newly planted forests on the lower reaches. The 50m (165ft) high Ribblehead Viaduct runs along the foot of the hill. Its building in the 19th century cost the lives of more than 100 navvies, mostly to smallpox and accidents. There are outcrops of Millstone Grit to the east, and it is to this rock that the peak owes its name. 'Whernside' derives from the Old English *cweorn* meaning 'millstone', and this was the hillside where the rock for millstones was found.

The area is popular with potholers, but for walkers there are magnificent views of Pen-y-ghent and Ingleborough – the other two of the so-called Three Peaks of north-west Craven – and of Howgill Moss to the north.

There are several routes up on to the peak, including one from near Ribblehead and another – the easiest – by a well-marked footpath from Chapel le Dale. To reach the top of Whernside, break away from the footpath for the final steep mile to the summit. The footpath itself continues around the hill to Whernside Manor, on the north-western side of the peak.

Peregrine falcons can sometimes be seen hunting over the hills and dippers haunt the streams, particularly Gastack Beck on the lower, north-west slopes.

▶ *Chapel le Dale is on the B6255, 4 miles north-east of Ingleton.*

RIBBLEHEAD VIADUCT

❼ Ingleton Glens

Two rivers, the River Twiss and the River Doe, drop down through small valleys to Ingleton, where they converge and become the River Greta. Both rivers can be explored on a 4 mile walk that starts from Ingleton, which includes some spectacular waterfalls and fine woodland scenery.

The first half of the walk, beside the River Twiss, involves much clambering over boulders before it reaches Pecca Falls, which are the most dramatic waterfalls on the route. The path then climbs up past the magnificent Thornton Force waterfall, before joining Twisleton Lane, an old drovers' route that runs across the southern tip of Scales Moor.

From Twisleton Lane, the footpath drops down past Beezley Falls into the wooded valley of the River Doe, and continues back towards Ingleton through the deep gorge which contains the Snow Falls.

A short footpath from Beezley Falls leads across stepping-stones and up to White Scar Cave, which can also be reached from Ingleton by a well signposted road. It is something of a tourist attraction in the height of summer, but this detracts little from its dramatic impact. The cave reaches for about half a mile under Ingleborough, the major peak in the area, and contains some wonderful stalactite formations, as well as a river and two waterfalls. In persistent wet weather White Scar Cave is liable to flooding and may be closed.

▶ *Ingleton and White Scar Cave are both on the B6255, just off the A65, some 7 miles south-east of Kirkby Lonsdale.*

❽ Ingleborough

A steep, 2½ mile footpath climbs to the highest point of Ingleborough, which commands extensive views north to the Cumbrian fells and, on a clear day, north-west across to the Lake District fells. Ingleborough is not one peak but a series of them, a mass of high hills dominating the scenery between Chapel le Dale, Ribblesdale and Ingleton. Ingleborough Hill is the summit of the massif, and at 723m (2,373ft) it is the second highest peak in Yorkshire. An Iron Age hill-fort spreads across the square summit, enclosed by a 900m (3,000ft) long rampart containing at least 19 hut circles.

The flanks of the massif are well known to potholers, and Gaping Gill, on the south-eastern slopes, is the largest and one of the best-known potholes in Britain. The waters of Fell Beck plunge into its dark depths through a hole near by, and intrepid visitors are sometimes lowered by winch down to the 104m (340ft) deep floor of the hole itself. There, the pothole opens out into the Main Chamber, the second largest limestone cave in Britain; so large, it is often said, that York Minster would fit inside it. At the far end of the cave, you once again encounter the Fell Beck, falling in a misty torrent from the dim roof high above. Obviously, it is not advisable to explore Gaping Gill without expert assistance.

For overland explorers, a hard 2½ mile walk along a badly defined path leads from Ingleborough Hill to Simon Fell and Park Fell, where there is a chance of seeing peregrine falcons and buzzards.

▶ *Ingleborough can be reached by footpaths from Ingleton or Chapel le Dale, both on the B6255.*

NORTHERN ENGLAND

❾ Norber Boulders

Ice Age glaciers tore the massive Norber Boulders from Crummack Dale and Ribblesdale, and deposited them on the limestone on the southern flanks of the Ingleborough massif. Aeons of wind and rain eroded the countryside, all except the small portions of it protected by the boulders. The result is that the massive blocks of Silurian slate – some of them weighing 20 tonnes and more – are now perched on limestone pedestals some 60cm (2ft) above their surroundings. These famous curiosities may be visited by walking from the village of Clapham up the bridleway called Thwaite Lane. After 1½ miles, take the footpath that leads north across the fields.

Clapham village is set at the entrance to a small valley, found on the side of the Ingleborough massif. The stream which flows down the valley, Clapham Beck, feeds The Lake, just north of the village, around which there are several nature trails. Above The Lake, Ingleborough Cave is full of fantastic and fantastically named stalactite formations whose strange images are faithfully repeated in the still waters of the Pool of Reflections.

▶ *Clapham is on the B6480, just off the A65, 6 miles north-west of Settle.*

❿ Stainforth

Steep fells separate Ribblesdale from Littondale, and Stainforth is a good centre from which to explore them. The village itself stands on the River Ribble, which is crossed by a 17th-century packhorse bridge, part of the old route from Lancaster to Ripon. Just outside the village the river rushes over Stainforth Force, a series of cascades where salmon leap.

A minor road called Goat Lane leads north-east out of Stainforth, then forks left to Halton Gill or right to Arncliffe. Taking the left fork, the road follows part of the Pennine Way to the foot of Pen-y-ghent and Giant's Grave, a New Stone Age round barrow containing the remains of two stone burial chambers and probably dating from about 2000 BC. The barrow and other archaeological finds in the area suggest that by this time some early settlers had begun to leave the uplands and move to the lower slopes and into the river valleys.

From Giant's Grave the moorland road follows Pen-y-ghent Gill down into Halton Gill, with fine views of upper Littondale from Hesleden Bergh. Ring ouzels and golden plovers break from the paths that criss-cross the moor, and there is a seasonal parade of primroses, dog's mercury, wood-sorrel and shining cranesbill.

The right-hand fork on Goat Lane skirts Malham Tarn on the way to Arncliffe. The tarn is the largest lake in the National Park and the highest in England, and was a source of inspiration for Charles Kingsley's book, *The Water Babies*. It is also one of the Dales' most important bird-watching centres and its fishing has always been famous for centuries.

▶ *Stainforth lies on the B6479, 3 miles to the north of Settle.*

PEOPLE HAVE LIVED HERE SINCE TIME IMMEMORIAL
AIREDALE HEAD

⑪ Langcliffe Scar

Steep, narrow roads enclosed by dry-stone walls lead over the craggy limestone headlands of Langcliffe Scar, part of a Craven Fault above Settle and Langcliffe. The scar is riddled with caves, of which the most famous is the Victoria, which was discovered in the Coronation year of 1838 by one of those rabbiting terriers to whom archaeology owes so much. The floor was excavated layer by layer down to one formed when the cave gave shelter to hyenas who brought home the bones of such creatures as the straight-tusked elephant and the woolly hippo. Above these were the bones of Ice Age animals – arctic fox, reindeer and badgers – and above these again the spearhead of a Stone Age hunter. The uppermost level revealed Roman coins, Celtic weapons and splendid Celtic jewellery in silver and bronze. Presumably the cave had been a place of refuge during the troubled early years of the Roman occupation. Similar stories were unfolded at nearby Attermire and Jubilee caves.

A 4 mile moorland walk leads from Langcliffe to the scar, south along its foot, past Victoria Cave and Attermire Cave, before turning west towards Settle. About three-quarters of a mile north of the scar lie the Winskill Stones, great masses of slate, which have been transported from the dale floor by Ice Age glaciers and deposited on the limestone. Protected by the slate, the limestone on which they stand eroded more slowly than the surrounding countryside, leaving the stones to stand on limestone pedestals, like the Norbert Bolders. A further half mile north, Catrigg Beck meets Cowside Beck, and the stream tumbles over Catrigg Force – a favourite spot of the composer Elgar – on its way to join the River Ribble in Stainforth.

▶ *Settle is reached by the B6480 from the A65 which runs between Kirkby Lonsdale and Skipton. Langcliffe lies on the B6479.*

⑫ Airedale Head

The 5 mile cul-de-sac valley of Upper Airedale is the 18th-century Landscape Movement dream translated into limestone and turf. From the scars along the line of the North Craven Fault, springs and streams leap joyously to combine in the River Aire around Malham, the village which has donated the valley's alternative name of Malhamdale. Less than a mile to the north of the village are the 70m (240ft) high, bare limestone walls of Malham Cove; to the north-east, crags and gentle hills enfold the savagery of Gordale Scar. From Malham, walled roads climb steeply to the north, the only means of escape from the valley's blunt ending.

People have lived here since time immemorial – Stone Age hunters, Bronze and Iron Age farmers and cattlemen. Much later, in the century or so before the Norman Conquest, Scandinavian settlers carved out smallholdings on Malham Moor. After the Conquest, the land was held by the Percys and other great Anglo-Norman families, who, for the good of their souls, presented vast acreages to Fountains Abbey and Bolton Priory. The monks made fine use of the gift, and reared cattle and sheep on a grand scale. The long-wooled Dalesbred sheep – dark-faced with a splash of white on either side of the nostrils – may well be the monks' legacy.

About half a mile east of Malham, on the twisting road to Gordale Bridge, a footpath to the right leads to Janet's Cave, while a little further upstream is Janet's Foss, a waterfall that drops into a deep pool. Both are named after a fairy of local legend.

On the opposite side of the road, a three-quarters of a mile walk north following the course of the stream leads to the gorge where the Gordale Beck tumbles over the 120m (400ft) cliffs at Gordale Scar. The scar can be climbed by the surefooted, though with a final scramble through rocks to reach the top. The path leads north-west for a mile and joins a minor road that returns south to Malham village.

An alternative walk from the village follows the road north out of Malham for half a mile to where the Pennine Way breaks off to the right. The path leads to the greeny-white amphitheatre formed by the cliffs of Malham Cove. The Pennine Way leads up the western side of the cove, skirts round the top and then heads south-east. At the point where the way turns sharply north, a footpath on the right returns the walker to a minor road that heads south to Malham.

▶ *Malham lies 5 miles north along a minor road from Coniston Cold on the A65.*

NORTHERN ENGLAND

⑬ Trollers Gill

Sir Arthur Conan Doyle is said to have written *The Hound of the Baskervilles* after hearing the story of Trollers Gill, a spectacular limestone ravine below Barden Fell, close to the village of Skyreholme. But this may be Yorkshire patriotism, since similar literary claims are made for Herefordshire and, of course, Dartmoor.

Nevertheless, the place is said to be haunted by a spectral hound, known as a bar-guest; it is even reputed to have appeared one night to Troller, the lead-miner after whom the gill is named, on his way home from work. There is certainly a sense of eeriness about the place, and a touch of melancholy added by the disused lead mine at the end of the ravine. But it takes only a few minutes to walk out from Skyreholme to discover for yourself whether or not Troller's hound is still loose.

▶ *Skyreholme is reached by a minor road off the B6265, about 5 miles west of Pateley Bridge.*

⑭ Stump Cross Caverns

Probably the first human beings ever to enter these wonderful caverns were the lead-miners who accidentally discovered them in 1858. But they were by no means the last, for these natural catacombs are among the most popular attractions of the Dales. The entrance is 389m (1,275ft) up on Craven Moor, from which a stairway leads down into the network of limestone caves. Beneath their low roofs, the caves are lined with formations of stalactites and stalagmites, whose weird shapes have given rise to their names – The Jewel Box, The Sentinel, The Hawk, The Wedding Cake and many others. Part of a reindeer skeleton which was discovered in the caves is on display in the tea rooms outside the entrance. How the creature got into the caverns is something of a mystery.

The surrounding moorland is dotted with the spoil-heaps of ancient lead mines from which mineral specimens, such as galena, barytes, fluorspar and calcite, may be picked up. And the gritstone boulders of High Crag immediately behind the cave entrance are well worth climbing for the extensive views from the top.

▶ *Stump Cross Caverns are next to the B6265, 4½ miles west of Pateley Bridge.*

15 Middle Wharfedale

The scenery of Wharfedale is at its loveliest between Ilkley and Grassington. The valley becomes narrower here than it is lower down, more like the perfect picture of a dale; but even so, it is still broader, more gentle and less isolated than the upper reaches above Kettlewell. Homely greystone villages nestle among the fells, crags and waterfalls, and many of them, including Grassington, make ideal bases from which to explore the area.

About a mile north of Grassington lies one of the most outstanding Romano-British field systems in the Dales. The land is privately owned but a footpath skirts the site, where Celtic fields are clearly divided into squares and rectangles by stone banks. Among the fields are indications of a settlement, for circular outlines of hut foundations, perhaps part of prehistoric farmsteads, have been traced.

South-west from Grassington lies the village of Linton, just across the wide, shallow River Wharfe. Here it is possible to cross the river by clapper bridge, packhorse bridge, ford or stepping-stones. The stepping-stones are particularly adventurous and need a springy stride if the traveller is to have a dry crossing. They are situated behind the church, half a mile north-east of the village. A walk leads back through the fields to Grassington.

▶ *Grassington is on the B6265, 8 miles to the north of Skipton.*

16 Mastiles Lane

In the Middle Ages monks used this 5 mile drovers' track across Kilnsey and Malham moors, marking the way with crosses. The bases of some of the crosses still survive. Later, in the 18th and 19th centuries, lead was transported along the track from the moorland mines to Malham and Settle.

The path is well marked. From Malham Tarn it drops down into the valley drained by Gordale Beck, climbs up on to the moorland, then crosses another valley below Kealcup Hill. From High Long Ridge it crosses Kilnsey Moor before descending into Kilnsey itself, passing Kilnsey Crag, a 703m (240ft) high limestone rock overhanging the main road.

Malham Moor is a wide, wild, airy place whose horizons dance in the heat of summer and whose winter winds have an edge like a knife. It seems as lonely today as it was in the Middle Ages when the monks' herdsmen used to milk the cattle, with sword or stave lying beside them. The dozen or so farms on the moor are of astonishing age, much older than the farm buildings themselves. Norsemen, monks and dalesmen inhabited them in turn, watching over their herds. Great Close, beside Malham Tarn, was the scene of cattle fairs in the 18th century, with a turnover of up to 5,000 head of cattle, mostly driven down from Scotland.

▶ *Malham Tarn is reached by a minor road leading north off the A65 at Coniston Cold. Kilnsey is on the B6160, about 3 miles south of Kettlewell.*

THE PLACE IS SAID TO BE HAUNTED BY A SPECTRAL HOUND

TROLLERS GILL

NORTHERN ENGLAND

⑰ Littondale

It is for its short, spectacular walks that the quiet valley of Littondale is chiefly famed. It is separated from Wharfedale by three fells – Firth Fell, Moor End Fell and Hawkswick Moor. At least three paths cross this wedge of land, which is never more than 2 miles wide.

The longest walk – about 3½ miles – starts at the village of Litton, and climbs past waterfalls and across the steep ravine which has Crystal Beck in its depths, to Ackerley Moor and Firth Fell. The bridle-path is clearly marked, and leads to Buckden in Wharfedale. A less obvious bridle-path climbs steeply from Arncliffe and crosses Old Cote Moor before descending through woodlands to Starbotton. A third route follows a rough footpath from Hawkswick, across Hawkswick Moor and down over the scars to Kettlewell. The climb is steep at the start, and further on it provides fine views of Kettlewell and Wharfedale.

Mining and industry largely passed Littondale by, and the marks of human affairs it bears belong to periods earlier than is common in the Dales. There are traces of 1,000-year-old lynchets – terraced cultivated strips – on the fellsides; and high above are the remains of Iron Age farmsteads and enclosures.

Perhaps it is the lack of later development that makes Littondale a naturalist's paradise. At the head of the dale, where valley and woodland meet, there are redstarts, pied flycatchers, golden plovers and curlews. In the wooded lower reaches of the dale, snowdrops and monkshood grow beside the river in spring, and later in the year there is a chance to find bloody cranesbill and the rare mountain avens, growing here at the most southerly limit of its range in England.

▶ *Kettlewell, Starbotton and Buckden are on the B6160 which runs from the A684 at Aysgarth to the A59. A minor road runs through Littondale, joining the B6160 at Amerdale Dub.*

⑱ Great Whernside

From the magnificent, cloud-touching bulk of Great Whernside, above the village of Kettlewell, there are wide views of the northern hills and eastern moorland. There are several approaches to the 704m (2,310ft) high summit. A track leads out of Kettlewell to Hag Dike, or a more southerly footpath strikes across country. The easiest but longest route is by the Coverdale road to the Tor Dyke earthworks – probably constructed by the Brigantes at about the time of the Roman invasion – and then across the upper slopes of the hill.

The area's story is one typical of the Dales. The legions came here, marching along the road that connected the forts at Bainbridge and Ilkley. Later, there was the Norseman, Ketel, who gave his name to the village; and later still, land-hungry Norman barons and the monks of Bolton, Coverham and Fountains squabbled over the acres that remained. One of the monks' boundary markers, Hunter's Stone, can still be seen below Great Whernside to the north-west.

Forestry, smallholdings, lead-mining and cotton-weaving down the centuries have all left their mark upon the land, telling of prosperous times long gone. A hundred years ago the mines closed, people departed and the smallholdings fell into ruin. In our own time, Kettlewell has been saved by holiday-makers, but Great Whernside itself stands as a lonely summit – hospitable only to those who love its windswept heights.

▶ *Kettlewell lies on the B6160, 16 miles to the north of Skipton.*

⑲ Coverdale

Coverdale is a secluded, secret sort of place. Yet from earliest times it was a famous through-route across the country. Drovers, packmen, monks, miners and Yorkist soldiers passed this way and, earlier still, Iron Age men fortified the summits above Park Rash and Red Beck Gill to hold the way against some long-forgotten southern foe.

Even today the ancient winding lanes and steep moorland roads seem to be penetrating a private world. Its secrets, however, are most gloriously revealed from the top of Flamstone Pin. The view from here is a splendid medieval tapestry of castles – Middleham and Bolton – the abbey of Coverham, ancient churches and great estates set against a dark green backdrop. In such a landscape, racehorses at exercise from the stables at the lower end of the dale might easily be taken for the outriders of a medieval army.

Winding lanes lead into Coverdale from Leyburn, but the most dramatic route is the minor road from Kettlewell in Wharfedale. It climbs steeply out of Kettlewell village, and becomes even steeper at Park Rash, below the Iron Age earthworks at Tor Dyke. On the exposed and frequently misty high moorland of Cow Side, the road is often gated; but before dropping down into Carlton it passes through more sheltered scenery. The sense of remoteness ends at Carlton, for beyond it lies a string of villages. But a picturesque lane leads from Carlton across the River Cover to West Scrafton.

▶ *Kettlewell is on the B6160; Leyburn is at the junction of the A684 and the A6108.*

20 Buckden Pike

From the high peaty solitude of Buckden Pike, magnificent views stretch in every direction. To the west lies the massif of Langstrothdale Chase, the old hunting ground of which Buckden was the centre, and the central wilderness of the Dales, while the proverbial clear day reveals the hills around Morecambe Bay. At the foot of the pike lie the beautiful upland valleys of Langstrothdale and Wharfedale.

There are two routes to the summit of Buckden Pike. A 2½ mile bridle-path known as Walden Wood, running alongside Cam Gill Beck, begins from Starbotton. A shorter, steeper ascent starts from the centre of Buckden, climbs up through Rakes Wood, along the course of the old Roman road to Bainbridge, forks right after three-quarters of a mile and then leads straight on to the shoulder of the pike. The left-hand fork on this footpath leads to Cow Close, a hillside above the village of Cray with some lovely waterfalls. A track beyond Cray crosses Kidstones Fell and Stake Moss to Bainbridge in Wensleydale, but this is for experienced walkers only, as it is a lonely and exposed 8 mile trek.

The steep, wooded Langstrothdale is a quiet and pretty valley at the head of Wharfedale. A minor road leads up the dale from Buckden to Yockenthwaite, with its Bronze Age circle of 20 standing stones.

▶ *Buckden is on the B6160, near Wharfedale.*

The NORTH YORK MOORS

Bare hills and rocky outcrops break through the heather-clad uplands of the North York Moors while gentle dales and lush fields soften the lowland landscape.

❶ Roseberry Topping and Highcliff Nab

Standing apart from the rest of Cleveland like a wary old bull guarding its herd, Roseberry Topping is so dramatic a landmark that in Viking times it was regarded as a sacred hill, the abode of the war-god Odin. No hill in Yorkshire looks out on a prospect more sweeping, or wears a face more battered and scarred by man and time.

From its 320m (1,051ft) summit there are views to the west across the Leven-Tees valley with its pastures, woods, cornfields and towns stretching into misty distance where the Pennines rise. To the south, only a few miles away, there swells the much-quarried scarp face of the Cleveland Hills. Towards the north-east the crags of Highcliff Nab jut forward aggressively from conifer-clad slopes. To the north-west, beneath a perpetual haze, stretches industrial Teesside, an immense and impressive factory landscape.

The scars on Roseberry Topping, and the final touches to its distinctive shape, are the result of man's activities. Over the centuries the hill has been quarried and mined for sandstone, alum, coal, iron and jet.

Fossilised shells, leaves and ferns have been found high on the slopes of Roseberry, but the commonest fossil of all is jet, formed from the remains of swamp trees that died 180 million years ago.

Another spectacular viewpoint in this lovely tract of country is Highcliff Nab, an outcrop of crags about 2 miles north-east of Roseberry Topping, towering out of the wooded hillside above Guisborough. To reach the crags, follow the path east from the summit of Roseberry. The path follows the edge of woods first, then enters them. As the path winds among the conifers, Highcliff Nab appears and disappears through the trees. A final steep climb leads to the impressive viewpoint, looking out over woods and toy-town-like Guisborough at its foot.

▶ *Roseberry Topping is 2½ miles south-west of Guisborough. One of the best starting points for climbing the hill is from the car park on the A173 about 1 mile north-east of Great Ayton, just south of the village of Newton under Roseberry.*

ROSEBERRY TOPPING

❷ Danby Rigg

More than 2,000 years ago, a race speaking in a long-forgotten tongue left their mark on Danby Rigg in the form of defensive dykes and some 800 cairns. Nothing has been found beneath any of these piles of stones, so their purpose is a mystery, like so much on the moors.

The rigg lies like a long arm of high ground, pointing from the moors to the Esk Valley. The views are immense. To the north-west are Captain Cook's Monument, stabbing the sky from the gentle swell of Easby Moor, and the triangular outline of Roseberry Topping. To the west and south, the moor sweeps round in a great purple arc. Bronze Age men built a primitive stone circle on the rigg, as well as raising earthworks and cairns. Now only one stone of the circle remains.

A 4½ mile circular walk from the car park at The Moors National Park Centre near Danby leads across the rigg. Take the path that leads across a field to a footbridge over the Esk. Take care at the level-crossing, where the path crosses the Esk Valley railway. Turn east at the road and follow it to Danby Castle, now a farm, with only the romantic ruins of the tower remaining.

The road runs alongside the rigg past Crossley Gate Farm, reaching a junction about three-quarters of a mile further on. At this point take the steep bridleway north-west up the rigg, following the signpost to Ainthorpe. The first upright stone at the top of the rigg is a marker post. A detour along a footpath to the left near the marker stone leads after about 140m (150yd) to the remains of a Bronze Age dyke. After passing some disused quarries on the left, the path starts to descend. Turn left at the road and carry on through Ainthorpe village, back to Danby and the car park.

▶ *Danby is on a minor road south of the A171 from Whitby to Guisborough, signposted 2 miles west of Scaling Reservoir, and 8 miles east of Guisborough. The Moors Centre is ½ mile east of the village centre.*

❸ Glaisdale and Egton Bridge

Near the railway arches just to the east of Glaisdale is Beggar's Bridge, an ancient, single-arched stone bridge, much painted by local artists because of its beautiful setting. Today, Glaisdale is a tranquil village, enfolded by quiet hills. But just over a century ago these same hills were clamorous with the sounds of iron-smelting, and blast furnaces belched their smoke into the air. By the 19th century, however, the seam of ironstone that had been worked in the dale since the 13th century was exhausted.

A pleasant 3 mile walk from Glaisdale to Egton Bridge and back leads through the wooded gorge of the River Esk. Cars can be parked beneath the railway arches near Beggar's Bridge. Cross the bridge and climb the steps that lead into Arncliff Wood. On the far side of the wood the path reaches a minor road; follow the road north-east to the Horseshoe Hotel before Egton Bridge. Just north of the hotel, down a curving flight of steps, the river can be crossed by a set of stepping-stones. If the river is high, it is more sensible to go back to the road and cross by the bridge.

After crossing the river, follow the path west that leads under the railway bridge, then turn left immediately after the stables into Limber Hill Wood. A steep climb through larch trees leads to a bridleway that can be followed back to Glaisdale.

▶ *The walk can be started from either Glaisdale or Egton Bridge. Both are reached by a minor road south off the A171, 4½ miles west of Whitby, signposted Egton. For Glaisdale, turn west at Egton; for Egton Bridge, keep on southwards.*

❹ Robin Hood's Bay and Ravenscar

In the eternal battle between land and sea, the sea is winning handsomely at Robin Hood's Bay, eating away the cliffs at the rate of 5cm (2in) a year. The great bite it has already taken forms the bay itself. And the cliffs are under attack from another direction, too: streams running down from the moors are helping the work of erosion.

The bay is only 3 miles across, but the curve adds another mile. Allow two and a half hours to walk along the beach to Ravenscar, and set off only if the tide is out or on the way out.

At Ravenscar, a stepped path leads up the cliffs. Here, layers of rock are plainly revealed, with the oldest dating from the Jurassic Period, 180 million years ago. A geological fault can be clearly seen, the fracture line left by an earthquake millions of years ago, when the earth's surface sheared sideways along a line of weakness. The fault line today is marked by a valley that comes into view halfway up the cliff path, near the safety fence.

From the Raven Hall Hotel, a two-hour walk along the cliffs leads back to Robin Hood's Bay. The path passes quarries where alum was once mined. To the right of the path is a deep cleft, down which the alum was carried to be loaded on to waiting ships.

▶ *Robin Hood's Bay lies 5 miles south-east of Whitby. Take the A171 from Whitby and, after 2½ miles, take the B1447 signposted to the bay. There is a large car park at the top of the cliffs.*

NORTHERN ENGLAND

❺ Falling Foss

The Falling Foss forest trail provides an opportunity to learn about the trees and wildlife of the area on an easy-paced 3 mile walk along sun-dappled paths. Starting from the May Beck car park, cross the bridge and turn downstream, with the beck on the left. The trail is way-marked with a fox's head.

About half a mile from the start, the path skirts some ponds that were specially created to provide a habitat for frogs, toads, newts and pond plants. Take the left fork and cross the Falling Foss car park, then turn left at a marker stone, down into the woods. Turn right and follow a tumbledown wall.

The path descends to a bridge over the beck, and the soil becomes deeper and damper. This is reflected in the succession of trees – beech, oak and larch near the top; ash, elm and sycamore halfway down; hazel and rowan near the bottom. Near the bridge, ivy and honeysuckle wind their coils around the roots of bankside trees.

As the path begins to climb the other side of the valley it passes meadowsweet, giant horsetail, and lords-and-ladies which bears clusters of poisonous orange-red berries. Turn right and, shortly after crossing a small bridge, head left for Falling Foss. This is an exhilarating waterfall, where May Beck, after gurgling placidly down from Sneaton High Moor, plunges over mossy rocks into a dark, swirling pool 9m (30ft) below. Return to the path and a short climb brings you into open farmland, with views of the surrounding countryside. A quarter-mile walk leads back to the car park.

▶ *Falling Foss is 5 miles south of Whitby. From the A171 Whitby-Scarborough road turn west onto the B1416. After 1½ miles at the crossroads, turn south-east over a cattle grid onto a minor road to New May Beck Farm. May Beck car park is about ½ mile beyond the farm.*

❻ Mallyan Spout and Beck Hole

One of the loveliest parts of Esk Dale is the tributary valley of the Murk Esk, curving round from the south to join the main Esk Valley. An easy-paced three-hour walk from Goathland will take you through woodland, across fields and alongside tumbling becks with picturesque waterfalls.

There are plenty of places for parking in Goathland, an attractive, scattered village whose wide greens are kept close-cropped by sheep. The walk begins close to the grand edifice of the Mallyan Spout Hotel, at the south end of the

village. A footpath just to the east of the hotel leads north-west through larchwoods down to Murk Esk, known this high up as West Beck. Turn upstream and scramble alongside the beck for 180m (200yd) as it tumbles untidily over rocks and boulders. Suddenly, coming in from the left is Mallyan Spout – a spray of water arching over a moss-covered cliff, 20m (70ft) high. The fall can be wispy during spells of dry weather. Retrace your steps alongside the tumbling peat-brown beck, and follow its course beyond the path leading back up to Goathland. Over a stile, the path leads into fields, with a wood on the right. Turn right through a gate, then left after a second gate to reach the delightful little moorland village of Beck Hole, where stone-built cottages cling to a grassy slope.

Climb the slope to cut off a section of road, turn right along the road then right again, on the track that leads past Hill Farm. Follow the track on the right, that goes east and leads past another farm down to Thomason Foss. Here, the Eller Beck plunges over a set of cataracts. Further upstream, spanned by an iron foot-bridge, the beck has cut a straight-sided channel through its bedrock with the precision of a stonemason. Over the foot-bridge, a flight of steps leads to the footpath back to Goathland.

▶ *Goathland is 7 miles south-west of Whitby on a minor road west of the A169, signposted about 5 miles south-west of Whitby.*

❼ Wade's Causeway

One of the best-preserved examples of Roman road-building in Britain marches confidently over Wheeldale Moor. The moor is a bleak, wind-buffeted place today, as it must have been when captive British tribesmen sweated to bed the flat, heavy foundation stones into place for their Roman overseers.

The road originally stretched for 25 miles, from near the Roman fort at Derventio (modern Malton) to Lease Rigg, in the Esk Valley. All that can be seen today is a stretch about a mile long on Wheeldale Moor, and another north of the Roman camps at Cawthorne to the south. Research suggests that the road was built around AD 80 as a highway along which detachments of the Ninth Legion could march to overawe the recently subjugated Brigantes tribe.

The name Wade's Causeway arises from a local legend that the Cleveland giant, Wade, built it as a track along which his wife, Bel, could drive her cattle out to pasture.

▶ *Wade's Causeway is 5 miles south of Egton Bridge. It meets the minor road that runs south from the village up to the moor.*

8 Hole of Horcum and Blakey Topping

The Cleveland giant, Wade, was mighty in his rages, as well as in his proportions. One day, his wife, Bel, angered him so much that he scooped up a handful of earth and flung it at her. Bel ducked, and the mountain of soil sailed over her head to land a couple of miles away, where it became known as Blakey Topping. The hollow left behind was the Hole of Horcum.

That, at least, is one legend explaining the origin of this huge natural amphitheatre, just off the main road between Pickering and Whitby. The top of the Hole commands one of the finest views on the moors – south over the Vale of Pickering and west over the Hole itself, floored with green fields that look flat from above but in fact have a pronounced slope.

This spectacular bowl, curving at its southern end into a narrow valley, is the result of what geologists call spring tapping – the deepening and widening of a natural hollow by the erosive action of springs whose water cannot seep away through the underlying clay.

A short walk from the roadside car park leads to a gate and stile near the hairpin bend called Devil's Elbow. This is the start of a walk around the Hole. The wind is fierce and persistent at the edge, and the steep northern slopes have become a launching ground for hang-gliders. A track through the heather leads past the lip of the Hole and then, after about 1¼ miles, to Seavy Pond on Levisham Moor. Half a mile beyond the pond, there are Iron Age earthworks across the path and on high ground to the left.

Continue to Dundale Pond and turn left, taking the track down the valley to Levisham Beck. The rocky ravine beside the track provides shelter after the rigours of the open moor, and mossy oak trees have established themselves along its course. Turn left at the bottom of the ravine and cross Levisham Beck. Then turn left again, keeping the beck on your left and a drystone wall on the right. The path leads past woodland and a deserted farm, Low Horcum, romantic in its solitude. Follow the path north-east. Where it forks, you can either go left, up the western side of the Hole or turn right and walk along the bottom of the Hole.

Blakey Topping, an isolated conical hill about 2 miles from the Hole, is a good viewpoint reached by taking the road east from near the car park to Newgate Foot. From there, the walk is mostly on a metalled road, but cars are not allowed beyond the gate at the start. The best view is north towards the large truncated pyramid which is part of the Fylingdales Ballistic Missile Early Warning System. Follow the track that swings eastwards along the escarpment; below are the remains of a Bronze Age stone circle. Three stones remain in position, and depressions in the ground mark where other stones once stood.

▶ *The Hole of Horcum lies west of the A169 Pickering-Whitby road, about 6½ miles north-east of Pickering.*

9 Dalby Forest

More than 4,000 years ago, Bronze Age farmers began the first serious assault on the forests of north Yorkshire. They slashed and burned great stands of oak, ash and elm to make grazing runs for their flocks and herds.

Today, man is restoring the forests that he once destroyed, though for the most part with fast-growing conifers instead of the broad-leaved trees of the past. Dalby Forest, near Thornton-le-Dale, proves that just because a forest is man-made it need not lose its natural look. It is owned by the Forestry Commission.

The forest contains 10 waymarked trails varying in length from a short half-mile walk to a longer walk to The Bridestones. On any of them there is the chance of seeing roe deer, grey squirrels, rabbits and foxes, as well as crossbills, goldcrests, siskins, great spotted woodpeckers, pheasants, jays, sparrowhawks and kestrels.

The best way to get the general feel of Dalby Forest is to drive through it. A 10 mile forest drive winds through conifer-clad hills that seem more like the foothills of the Canadian Rockies than part of Yorkshire. On the way it passes a Visitor Centre, where there are displays on the history and natural history of the forest, and you can consider which of the waymarked trails best meets your taste.

Just before the forest drive ends, a sign-posted track to the west leads to the Crosscliff viewpoint, high above Crosscliff Wood. It is only a 230m (250yd) walk from the car park along a woodland path to the viewpoint. The hollows beside the path are Dargate Dykes, the remains of early Saxon or medieval earthworks. At the viewpoint there is an indicator that points out distant landmarks and types of trees. As well as features such as Blakey Topping and the blue bulk of Lockton High Moor, you will see stands of oak, beech, alder, Scots pine, Norway spruce and Sitka spruce.

▶ *Dalby Forest lies 4 miles north-east of Pickering. Turn north on to a minor road at Thornton-le-Dale on the A170 and, after 1½ miles, turn right to Low Dalby. The forest drive is a toll road.*

NORTHERN ENGLAND

MEADOWS FULL OF NODDING DAFFODILS
RIVER DOVE

10 Gillamoor and Farndale

Nothing about the gentle approach to Gillamoor from the south gives any indication of the village's treasure – its surprise view. Just past the church, the road swings north-west, and suddenly the view opens out. It is a tapestry of green farmland dotted with clumps of trees and brave little moorland roads tackling the heights of Spaunton Moor. All is held together by the winding Dove Valley, with everything arranged perfectly, like the backdrop of some gigantic open-air theatre.

The surprise view is a bonus on the way to Farndale. This secluded valley, enfolded by the mighty arms of Rudland Rigg, Blakey Ridge and Farndale Moor, puts on a remarkable display of wild daffodils in the spring. A well-marked footpath, beside the eastern bank of the meandering Dove, begins at the Low Mill car park. It leads for about 1½ miles through meadows full of nodding daffodils, past an old abandoned mill then up a short stretch of road to Church Houses. The area is a nature reserve and the daffodils are protected.

The bridge over the Dove just west of Church Houses was, according to local legend, the setting for a romantic tragedy. The beautiful daughter of a local landowner fell in love with a farmer's boy, and when her parents forbade the match the despairing girl jumped off the bridge to her death. How she managed to do more than get her feet wet in the shallow water is a matter of conjecture.

▶ *Gillamoor is 3 miles north-west of Kirkbymoorside on the A170. The Low Mill car park is 3 miles north of Gillamoor along a minor road that follows the Dove valley.*

⑪ The Bridestones

Despite their romantic name and monolithic shapes, the Bridestones have no connection with prehistoric marriage rituals. The name comes from the Norse word *brinka*, meaning hillside or edge. Weathered into fantastic shapes, these massive rocks were once thought to be Stone Age monuments or, later, to have been brought down from the moorland plateau by glaciers. It is now known that the stones were shaped by the action of wind, rain and frost.

There are two sets of Bridestones, the upper outcrop in a horseshoe shape, the lower stones in a straight line. Some are top-heavy, like gigantic mushrooms, some only half emerge from the hillside. In one, the wind has sculpted a complete tunnel. These 150-million-year-old rocks have taken on strange shapes because they are composed of alternate layers of hard and soft sandstone, which erode at different rates.

The best approach to the Bridestones is from the High Staindale car park on the Dalby Forest Drive. Cross the stile and there is a choice of paths, which join up after a mile near the stones. The path west leads fairly gently to the open moor, through woodland that is mainly oak. The path east climbs steeply, along the pretty ravine of Jonathan Gill.

From Low Bridestones the path leads to High Bridestones, dipping to cross Bridestones Griff. 'Griff' is a local word for a ravine cut by a stream, and may be Scandinavian in origin. After leaving High Bridestones the path swings south, in a steep descent down Needle Point to Dovedale Griff.

▶ *High Staindale car park is on the northern part of the Dalby Forest Drive, which is a toll road. To reach the drive, take the minor road north from Thornton-le-Dale on the A170. After about 1 mile turn east on to the road for Low Dalby and carry on for 3 miles.*

⑫ Kirk Dale

In 1821, workmen digging for road-stone in a quarry at Kirk Dale made a remarkable discovery. They broke through the mouth of a cave and found its floor littered with thousands of bones – relics of prehistory. Kirk Dale was once the home, over a period of many years, of mammoths, cave lions, cave bears, tigers, rhinoceroses, hippopotamuses, bison, Irish elks and giant oxen. The cave was probably the den of hyenas, and over an immense period of time they dragged in their victims. About 20,000 years ago, during the last Ice Age, the cave was submerged under a meltwater lake, and the cave mouth was sealed, to be discovered only in the 1820s.

It is easily reached from the road near the ford at the lower end of Kirk Dale. Take the path east of the river into the woods, just beyond the ford, and follow it as it swings right, back to the roadside quarry. The cave openings are little more than slits, through which sightseers must crawl.

Apart from the cave, there are a number of pleasant walks through Kirk Dale. One starts from the ancient church, St Gregory's Minster, where a Saxon sundial above the south door records that the church was rebuilt 'in the days of Edward the King and Tosti the Earl'. The Edward referred to was Edward the Confessor, and Tosti was the Earl of Northumberland. The footpath leads through woods on the eastern bank of the Hodge Beck.

▶ *Kirk Dale lies north of the A170 along a minor road 1½ miles west of Kirkbymoorside.*

⑬ Rye Dale, Rievaulx Abbey and Old Byland

The graceful ruins of Rievaulx Abbey stand in Rye Dale on a shelf of land overlooking a loop of the River Rye. They are overlooked in turn by elegant terraces of verdant lawns, complete with Grecian temples, laid out in 1758. Framing the terraces and the abbey is a huge sweep of wooded hillside, where noble oaks stand side by side with ash and sycamore.

This is marvellous walking country, and one of the best starting points is Old Byland, itself once the site of an abbey. A three-hour circular walk leads to Rye Dale and Rievaulx Abbey. Take the road to Cold Kirby, and after about a quarter of a mile turn off left to Grange Farm. Past the farm, turn south just before a cattle grid, along a path that is ill-defined in places. Swing east, and down through Callister Wood, then cross a wooden bridge, a stile and a plank bridge. Take the track that goes east, past three large ponds. A metalled road leads east to Ashberry Farm, and to a three-quarter mile detour across the River Rye to the abbey. A pleasant hour can be spent walking round Ashberry Hill, reached by crossing the stile at the side of Ashberry Farm.

To get back to Old Byland from the abbey, return to Ashberry Farm, turn north and follow the road for about a quarter of a mile as it starts to climb, then turn west. This track leads back to Old Byland.

▶ *Rievaulx Abbey is ½ mile west of the B1257, 2½ miles north-west of Helmsley on the A170. It can also be reached from Old Byland, 2 miles north-west of the abbey. For Old Byland, take the road to Cold Kirby from the Sutton Bank car park on the A170, 6 miles west of Helmsley. Turn left just before Cold Kirby, then right at the T-junction.*

NORTHERN ENGLAND

⑭ Kilburn White Horse and Roulston Scar

The Hambleton Hills, above the pretty village of Kilburn, have been noted for their horses since Viking days. It was the Vikings who introduced horse-racing to the area and today there are still gallops on the hills, where thoroughbreds are brought to racing condition. John Hodgson, a local schoolmaster, clearly had the long association between the hills and horses in mind when, in 1857, he decided to mark out a massive white horse on the slopes above Kilburn. He had 30 helpers for the task, and they used 6 tonnes of lime to whiten the figure. For, unlike the white horses in southern Britain, Kilburn's is not cut into chalk; it rests on a foundation of gritty limestone that has to be freshened every few years. At 96m (314ft) long and 69m (228ft) high, the horse was meant to be seen from a distance, rather than close up, and sightings have been reported from as far off as Leeds, some 30 miles away.

Steps lead to the top of the white horse from a car park at its base, about a mile north of Kilburn village. This is also the start of a pleasant 1½ mile Ampleforth Forest walk, that leads along the edge of cliffs to Roulston Scar, a creamy limestone crag with magnificent views across the chequer-board Vale of York. More than 30 miles away rise the Pennine heights. Just across the valley is cone-shaped Hood Hill, where in pre-Roman times the Druids are said to have practised human sacrifice.

The promontory on which Roulston Scar lies is defended by two prehistoric earthworks, both called the Casten Dike. The southern section is about a quarter of a mile long, while the northern section is about 23m (25yd) wide and some two-thirds of a mile long – a prodigious feat of engineering for people whose main digging tool was probably the antler pick.

The forest walk leads down into Happy Valley below the scar, where rowan trees, elderberries, hazels and hawthorns all struggle for a footing among a profusion of fallen boulders.

▶ *Kilburn is 5 miles east of Thirsk. 2 miles east from Thirsk on the A170, turn south onto a minor road towards Bagby. Turn east at Bagby and the road leads to Kilburn. The White Horse car park is signposted about a mile north of the village.*

⑮ The Hambleton Drove Road

In the middle of the 19th century, one of the busiest roads in Britain ran along the ridge of The Hambleton Hills. Columns of shaggy West Highland cattle and black Galloways stretched back for miles. Collie dogs, ears alert for their masters' whistling, threaded their way through a seeming confusion of pigs, sheep, waddling geese and clacking turkeys. Scottish drovers were taking their flocks and herds to market along the ancient drove road which crossed the Tees near Yarm and then climbed the moors, thus avoiding the tolls that were charged on the turnpike roads below.

Parts of this ancient highway are now metalled, making a scenic drive. But there is a 6 mile stretch of moorland track, beginning just above the village of Nether Silton, that is ideal for walkers. Take the road east then north from Nether Silton, signposted to Over Silton, but turn right after about 180m (200yd), along a road that climbs steeply at first. Park beyond the cattle-grid and follow the Forestry Commission track that leads to the northern flank of 399m (1,309ft) high Black Hambleton. After about an hour's steady walking, with conifers on either side, the track meets the drove road.

For those who turn right, the promise of the open road – wild, bracing and free – is abundantly fulfilled. The first section of the ancient moorland track leads over the hunched shoulder of Black Hambleton to Arden Great Moor. Once on the rim of the hills, there is a purple sea of heather to the left and glorious views of the Vale of York to the right.

You can retrace your steps at any time, or decide to carry on to complete an 8 mile circular hike. This leads past some disused quarries, to the east of the track about 1½ miles from the crest of Black Hambleton. About a mile further on is a crossroads, with a gate on the right, and a track leading west down to Kepwick. Keep west through Kepwick and follow the signs back to Nether Silton. Just beyond Nether Silton, before you reach the parking place, the landscape obligingly stretches out like a panoramic map, to show much of the route you have walked.

▶ *Nether Silton lies 6½ miles north of Thirsk. To reach it, take the signposted road east off the A19, 5½ miles north of Thirsk.*

⑯ Sutton Bank

Like a rousing overture played as the curtain rises on a grand opera, Sutton Bank gives a foretaste of all that is to come in the North York Moors – exhilarating views, prehistoric remains and abundant wildlife. There could be no finer entry point to the National Park. To the west the view stretches out across the broad Yorkshire plain to Swaledale, Wensleydale and the Pennines, with Great Whernside on the horizon more than 30 miles away. The plain is punctuated by such landmarks as Fountains Abbey, 17 miles away, and Knaresborough Castle, 19 miles to the south-west. Roulston Scar juts out assertively along the cliffs to the south, and just below sparkles Gormire Lake, an enchanting (and some say

enchanted) lake, whose waters were trapped by a landslip at the end of the last Ice Age. Ahead lies a scenic drive along the southern edge of the moors, passing wooded dales that lead to the high moorland plateau.

The A170 from Thirsk zigzags like an Alpine pass to climb Sutton Bank, and still leaves motorists with a punishing 1-in-4 gradient. Near the elbow of the zigzag, a roadside plaque marks a Bronze Age burial site, dating back to about 1400 BC. The Bronze Age people of the moors usually sited their graves where there were marvellous views; and this one looks south along the cliffs towards the bluff of Roulston Scar and the conical shape of Hood Hill.

▶ *Sutton Bank is on the A170, about 5 miles east of Thirsk. Stopping is prohibited on the road, but there is a car park at the top of the hill.*

SUTTON BANK

The Pennine Way is the jewel in the crown of long-distance footpaths. But there are many others ... by which you can come to grips with this wonderful wild countryside.

Walking wild

The long-distance footpaths of Northern England take walkers into amazing countryside no car can reach.

There are both penances and pleasures to be had when walking in the wild country of northern England. The wind blows harder, the rain falls wetter and the mist swirls thicker than down in the gentle uplands of the south – or so it usually feels. But there is a sharper pleasure, too, in measuring oneself against the harsh moorlands and rugged fells of the north. Nothing can beat the reward, after a long, hard slog to the summit, of a staggeringly beautiful, jaw-dropping view, like the great hundred-mile vistas from the tops of the Yorkshire and Lancashire moors, the fells of Cumbria and Durham, and the remote border hills of Northumberland.

The 190 mile Coast-to-Coast Walk, devised by Alfred Wainwright, from St Bees Head, in Cumbria, to Robin Hood's Bay, in Yorkshire, is the most popular long-distance walk in the UK by virtue of the terrain it covers – Lake District fells, Pennine hills and dales, North Yorkshire moors, all high, all wild and all lonely. Northern landscapes, it seems, call forth a unique response in a walker's soul.

The Pennine Way National Trail, all 270 miles of it between Edale in the Dark Peak of Derbyshire and Kirk Yetholm in the billowing Cheviot uplands of the Scottish Border, is by common consent the most challenging long-distance trek in England. There is something truly exhilarating about travelling the rainy watershed of the north, forging slowly up the backbone of Britain along the pathway of high ground between the former textile towns of Yorkshire and Lancashire, up across the open moorlands of Durham and Cumbria among the

❻ Parlick Fell

It is a tough climb to the 432m (1,417ft) summit of Parlick Fell, for the hill has convex slopes. The first part of the climb is the steepest stretch and the most slippery, since it is over shale. But the views from the top make the climb worth the effort. Parlick is among the southern Bowland fells and, jutting well out from the main mass, it commands tremendous views – over the valleys of the Loud and Ribble rivers, over the wide Lancashire plain, across Morecambe Bay towards the southern hills of the Lake District, and even, when the weather is fine, as far as the Isle of Man and the distant mountains of Snowdonia some 80 miles away.

Off the road that climbs up to Parlick from Chipping there is a rough farm track, just where the road makes a steep left bend at the foot of the fell. From the gate at the far end of the track, one path, with a gully on the right, climbs straight up the fell. A longer but easier path, to the left of the first, reaches the top of the fell in a series of zigzags.

Sheltering beneath the great rise of the fell is the village of Chipping. It lies in the valley of the River Loud, on a shelf about 50ft above the river. Everywhere the valley is lush. Cattle graze on the rich, green grass between the woods and coppices, and lines of windbreak trees punctuate the landscape. Areas of ancient forest shelter some of the finest bluebell woods in England.

In winters long ago, it is said, the wolves that lived above the village on Wolf Fell used to come down to search for food in Chipping. Standing here today, it is hard to imagine that anything has ever disturbed the peace of the place. Its name, recorded in the Domesday Book as Chippenden, derives from the old word for a market, and for centuries the village was the principal meeting-place for local farmers.

▶ *Longridge is on the B5269, which branches off the A6, 3 miles north of Preston. From Longridge signposted minor roads lead to Chipping, 5 miles to the north, and beyond it to the foot of Parlick Fell.*

❼ Beacon Fell

In the days when national victories or approaching dangers were proclaimed by lighting fires on hilltops, Beacon Fell was an important link in the chain. Its broad dome is clear of vegetation and commands far, all-round views. Indeed, a view indicator on the summit optimistically points to the Welsh mountains some 80 miles away, but the chance of actually seeing them is rare; 150cm (60in) of rain falls annually on the fell.

For all its impressive views, Beacon Fell is only 266m (873ft) high and it is easily climbed. It consists of Bowland shale capped with gritstone, and the line where the two rocks meet is the birthplace of myriad springs. One of them feeds the pond by the Fell House car park, from which a delightful walk leads around the thickly wooded hillsides. Tawny owls haunt the forest. In Bull Coppice, south-west of the summit, 1.5m (5ft) high stumps have been left during thinning operations to provide night perches for the birds.

Among the predominant spruces there are stands of sycamore, rowan, wild cherry, oak, alder and beech. The open summit is dressed with purple moor-grass – at its colourful best in July and August – and with ling, bell heather, bilberry, crowberry and mat-grass. You may even be lucky enough to see a hen harrier, one of the country's most endangered birds of prey. The Forest of Bowland is home to 80 per cent of the English breeding population of this graceful upland bird. Peregrine falcons and merlins are among the other rare birds of prey found in the area.

▶ *Beacon Fell is 9 miles north of Preston. It can be reached by minor roads leading east from Bilsborrow on the A6, 7 miles north of Preston. A one-way, clockwise ring road circles the fell.*

❽ Waddington Fell

When the guns open up at the start of the grouse-shooting season on the 'Glorious Twelfth' of August, the footpaths on the moors round Waddington Fell are closed to the public. Red grouse are practically an industry hereabouts, and even out of season their importance is apparent from the number of shooting butts scattered about the moors. But in spring and early summer it is the views, not the birds, that are the fell's main attractions.

A moorland road climbs to the summit of the fell from the village of Waddington, which lies to the south. Just after the road has surmounted the fell and dropped over the other side, it passes a spring bubbling into a stone trough on the left – Walloper Well.

Climb the hill above the well, and at once there is a lovely view of the Bowland fells across the River Hodder. Or park a little downhill from the well and take the path that runs northwards down to the hamlet of Easington. From anywhere along the path, near the plateau edge, there are fine views across the water-meadows of the Hodder to Beatrix and Burn fells, and to Dunsop Fell beyond the valley.

▶ *Waddington is 2 miles north-west of Clitheroe along the B6478. This is the road that continues over the summit of Waddington Fell.*

NORTHERN ENGLAND

❾ Pendle Hill

There is no denying its domination. Such is the bulk of Pendle Hill that it overshadows the Ribble Valley and the surrounding countryside for miles around. The hill is 7 miles long so wherever you are, the commanding presence of Pendle is with you, watching you. The summit reaches 557m (1,827ft), and is capped by a flat, east-west sloping plateau of gritstone, with patches of bare peat and angular, frost-fractured fragments of grit. There are no trees or walls, either on Pendle's plateau or on its steeply sloping sides. It is a bare hill, and when the mists swirl over it, as they often do, it is easy to imagine that something sinister lingers here – perhaps a last spell cast by the poor women, known as the witches of Pendle, who were tried for sorcery in Lancaster in 1612.

Access to the top of Pendle is easy, in the sense that there are many paths – all of them steep. Perhaps the best approaches, apart from the path that starts at Nick of Pendle, are from the villages of Barley and Downham. Both are at the 'Big End', or eastern end. The paths from Barley are shorter, those from Downham more numerous, but, since Pendle has concave slopes, all paths end with a difficult last 240m (800ft).

Nevertheless, the climb is worth while for the 270 degree prospect – the view to the south-west is blocked by the hill's own bulk – when the day is clear, with the whole Pennine range wide open to the east. For such a bare-looking hill, Pendle supports an astonishing variety of plants, including two kinds of club moss, cotton-grass and its less common relative hare's-tail cotton-grass, common butterwort, heather, several mountain grasses, and that unusual orange cousin of the raspberry, the cloudberry.
▶ *Pendle Hill lies between Clitheroe and Nelson. Downham is 3 miles north-east of Clitheroe east of the A59. From the A682 north of Nelson, minor roads lead west to Barley*

❿ Nick of Pendle

The slumbering-lion shape of Pendle Hill sprawls to the east of Pendleton village, its head pointing north-east, its rump south-west. The rise of the rump – the 'Little End' of Pendle – is grooved by a col called the Nick of Pendle. Pendleton village is stone-built, with a stream running down its street and the green fields of the Ribble Valley spreading about it. But the moment the village is left behind and the first cattle-grid crossed, the scene changes instantly to one of bleak, sweeping moorland. Clumps of rushes and sedge dot the poor, close-cropped grass, and rocks stick up through the thin soil. Ahead, the road rises up the Nick.

From the top of the pass, where the small quarries just over the crest make convenient car parks, climb the sloping slabs of rock to the west. Enormous views spread in every direction. The cotton towns lie to the south, and to the west stretch the crops on the plain of Fylde with the Irish Sea beyond. The Pennines dominate the eastern skyline, and to the north is the beautifully wooded valley of the Ribble, planted 200 years ago with more than a million oak trees. Beyond this belt of green, rise the purple crags and moors of the Forest of Bowland, filling the whole horizon.

On the east side of the Nick, a path runs away to the bulk of Pendle Hill. It climbs and climbs, and then suddenly steepens to scramble up the lion's flank. It is a rough track of gritstone fragments, and fairly hard going, but it is a wonderful, exhilarating walk all the way and well worth the effort. You will see rabbits, hares and Swaledale sheep, as well as birds such as skylarks meadow pipits and plaintive lapwings. There are no trees, only the small, erect shrubs that bear the orange-coloured fruits called cloudberries.

Pendle Hill has always been a natural barometer for local people, 'a vast black mountain which is the morning weather glass of the country people', according to the 18th-century traveller William Stukeley.

At haymaking time the people of Barley, on the eastern side, used to post a sentinel with a flag on the hill. If he saw a storm brewing in the west, he would wave the flag as a warning to the farmers, telling them to bring in the hay as quickly as possible.
▶ *Pendleton is on a minor road 2 miles south-east of Clitheroe close to the A59.*

The LAKE DISTRICT

Spectacular and inspiring scenery has been attracting tourists to the Lake District since the early 19th century and today England's largest National Park draws in more than 14 million visitors a year.

❶ The Solway Coast

The tide calls the tune in Solway Firth, the sea-gash between south-west Scotland and north-west England. As the Firth narrows, the currents become faster; and with the sudden arrival and departure of the all-engulfing tide, the inner reaches of the Solway become one of the most dramatic of British estuaries.

The landscape on both sides of the Firth is flat; only the mass of Criffel on the Scottish shore and the peaks of the Lake District relieve the endless vistas of mud-flats and marsh. The wide marshes are on the English shore – between Grune Point at the mouth of Moricambe bay and the head of the estuary, near Gretna. At low tide the sands and mud-flats are bare and silent, except for the calls of wading birds searching for food. Then suddenly the tide rushes in, drowning the tawny sand in a gleaming expanse of steel-grey water.

In this endless advance and retreat, the sea is gradually losing its hold. The surrendered territory, bound fast by advancing grasses, becomes salt-marsh; and here, where water and land meet in uneasy alliance, nature is at its most abundant. The innermost marsh, Rockcliffe, borders Gretna between the English River Eden and Scotland's

Esk. From Rockcliffe Cross a lane leads to Esk Boathouse, on the very edge of the marsh. From this desolate spot the marshes of the estuary spread to the west. On Burgh Marsh stands a slender column – man's only intrusion in the emptiness of marsh, sea and sky – a Victorian monument to Edward I, who died here of dysentery in 1307 while fighting the Scots. Burgh Marsh can be reached by car and then footpath from Burgh by Sands.

Following the coast westwards, through Drumburgh, Port Carlisle and Bowness-on-Solway, there are three other vast marshlands: Cardurnock Flatts and Newton and Skinburness Marshes on the south shore of Moricambe bay.

These Moricambe marshes are enclosed by the arm of Grune Point, a shingle spit running north-east from Skinburness village. Mixed woodland and small fields cover the peninsula and a path runs round both shores. The view from the end of the point is unforgettable; acres of sea-washed turf, the tide stealing up narrow creeks and the rippling waters making a world ruled by the ebb and flow of the tide.

▶ *The Esk Boathouse, close to Rockcliffe Cross, lies along minor roads to the west of the M6 north of Carlisle. A path from Skinburness, off the B5302, leads to Grune Point.*

A WORLD RULED BY THE EBB AND FLOW OF THE TIDE
THE SOLWAY FIRTH, LOOKING TOWARDS SCOTLAND

❷ Bowscale Tarn

The surface of Bowscale Tarn is like a black mirror reflecting the bleak, scree-laden cliffs of Tarn Crags. It seems to concentrate in one place all the loneliness of the landscapes around it. Only the croak of a raven or carrion crow, echoing off the rocks, disturbs the deep quiet.

The climb to the tarn starts low down in the valley of the River Caldew and leads up through rough moorland to the great dam of Ice Age litter which holds back the tarn's dark waters.

The path begins just beyond a row of cottages where the road turns sharply through the hamlet of Bowscale. There a gate leads on to open fellside and the path climbs steeply to the west for a few metres before levelling out.

Across the valley, the slopes of Carrock Fell sweep down in a cascade of scree. Geologically the fell is exceptionally complex, and 23 minerals have been found there including lead, arsenic, iron and tungsten which was mined until the 1980s.

The path crosses Drycombe Beck, then winds round the next bluff before climbing diagonally up the moraine dam to Bowscale Tarn. The land is littered with boulders, many of them scratched or smoothed by the glacier which deposited them at the end of the last Ice Age. Everywhere Skiddaw Slate breaks through, the rock from which the whole of this area is formed. And then, over the brow of the dam, lies the tarn – black, menacing and to all appearances devoid of life.

▶ *A minor road to Mungrisdale turns north about 6 miles north-east from Keswick along the A66. Bowscale is 1 mile further on.*

❸ Ullock Pike

The shapely summit of Ullock Pike, 680m (2,230ft) high, offers panoramic views across northern lakeland. Yet, in spite of the mountain's proximity to Keswick, it remains one of the least visited of the Skiddaw and Saddleback mountain group. The final part of the ascent is the most exciting, along the heather-clad ridge, looking steeply down over the wilderness of Southerndale to the north-east, and over the 4 mile long Bassenthwaite Lake to the west – the most northern of all the lakes and the only one to be called a lake, and not a water or mere.

There are two routes up Ullock Pike from the road, both starting from a creosoted gate and stile 27m (30yd) south of the Ravenstone Hotel. The first path climbs to the right through the Forestry Commission plantation – first larch, oak, sycamore and Scots pine, then Sitka spruce and other softwoods – to the tree-line at 180–210m (600–700ft). Then follows a steep scramble

through bracken and heather and bare outcrops of rock to the ridge about 300m (1,000ft) above. The second path meets the ridge about a mile further north, after climbing behind the hotel and following a wall north-eastwards above the tree-line, then following an old drove road.

The safest way back is to return along the ridge, for the sides are very steep and rocky. But it is possible to drop into Southerndale further down, picking up the path on the east of the valley and following it to the footbridge below the natural standing stones known as The Watches. A path leads from the gate below the footbridge to the minor road leading from Orthwaite to High Side, a hamlet about half a mile north of the Ravenstone Hotel.

▶ *Ullock Pike is 4 miles north-west of Keswick. The Ravenstone Hotel is on the A591, 4½ miles north-west of Keswick.*

❹ Holme Wood

Seen from the road along the north-eastern shore of Loweswater, across the lake's gently rippling surface, Holme Wood is a beautiful mile-long strip of mixed woodland running from the water's edge up to the 300m (900ft) contour. The blanket of trees clings close below the crags of Burnbank Fell and Carling Knott and then steals up the shelter of Holme Beck. Its reflection melts into the water. But the real beauty of the wood is in the heart of the woodland, between the conifers on the highest slopes and the delicate alders overhanging the lake. Here mature, broad-leaved trees are seen at their best, a whispering canopy of oak, ash, sycamore, mountain ash, elm, birch, large-leaved lime and the great, palmate-leaved chestnut.

The best way to savour this beauty is to walk through the woods. Go to the south-east end of the lake and walk through Watergate Farm and along the shoreline. Ford the Holme Beck and turn up along the stream. The roar of water announces Holme Force, a series of sparkling cascades tumbling among the trees. Return through the woods to the shore and look out across the water to the gentle, bracken-covered slopes of Darling Fell. Walk on to the northern end of the lake and look back at the views behind. Climb to the terrace on the 300m (900ft) contour and return round the top side of the wood. On a summer's day the scene is one of matchless tranquillity, a perfect blend of woodland, water and hills with the sun and clouds playing hide-and-seek across the sky.

▶ *The easiest approach to Holme Wood is along the A5086 south-west from Cockermouth. After 5 miles turn south-east, Loweswater is 3 miles further on.*

Basic Computer Coaching

Please fill in the details below to add your name to the waiting list

Name	
Telephone Number	
Library Card Number	
Available for 6 weeks in a row?	☐ Yes ☐ No

Have you used a computer before?	Are you familiar with the Keyboard and Mouse?	Do you have an email address?
☐ Yes ☐ No	☐ Yes ☐ No	☐ Yes ☐ No

SKIDDAW AND BASSENTHWAITE LAKE FROM CAT BELLS

⑤ Newlands Pass

Until the 18th century, no road suitable for wheeled transport led to the village of Buttermere. It was named by the Angles who came this way in the 6th century and made good butter from the cattle they pastured by the lakeside – and farming was to remain the village's chief occupation until the building of the Newlands Pass road in the 1770s.

Father Thomas West, who wrote the first guide to the Lake District, published in 1778, described the pass as 'Alpine views and pastoral scenes in a sublime style'. Even today, the narrow, steep road twisting through the fells provides its excitements, and is perhaps more 'sublime' for the passenger than the driver.

For almost 3 miles from Braithwaite, the road runs along a ledge high above the Newlands valley, with fine views to the east and south-east of wooded Swinside and cosy-looking Cat Bells – the hill where Beatrix Potter's Mrs Tiggy-Winkle lived.

Stretching flat and green below, criss-crossed by stone walls, the Newlands valley is remote and peaceful. Yet in Elizabethan times it was a busy mining centre, with copper and silver recovered from the local Goldscope Mine. The mine was worked by experts brought in from Germany by the Mines-Royal Company; the name Goldscope is said to come from the German *Gottsgabe* – 'God's gift'. During the peak years of mining in the 16th century, ore was smelted near Keswick and local woods were turned over to charcoal production to feed the furnaces.

After crossing Rigg Beck the road swings westwards from the Newlands valley along the much narrower Keskadale valley, below the steep fells of Ard Crags to the right. It is well worth parking by the hairpin bend over Ill Gill and scrambling up beside the beck for a glimpse of the Keskadale Oakwood. The 5.5ha (14 acre) oakwood is now a protected area; in company with the Birkrigg Oakwood, on the slopes of Causey Pike to the north-east, it is thought to be the last surviving remnant of the great oak forests that once covered the lakeland fells. The trees are small and wind-swept sessile oaks, recognised by their stalkless acorns.

The road climbs steeply to Newlands Hause, approaching close to the point where Moss Force cascades spectacularly over a line of crags below the sodden Buttermere Moss.

▶ *To reach Newlands Pass, leave Keswick by the A66 towards Cockermouth; 1 mile beyond Portinscale turn left along the B5292 through Braithwaite. From here follow signs to Newlands Pass and Buttermere, a drive of about 7 miles.*

6 Aira Force

The waterfall is one of the Lake District's most romantic spots – a silver stream of water tumbling some 20m (70ft) between gleaming, precipitous walls of rock. Here Aira Beck, which rises high in the wilderness of Matterdale Common, makes its last dramatic gesture before flowing into Ullswater.

Legend tells that Aira Force was once the scene of a tragic love story. Its heroine, Emma, lived in the nearby Lyulph's Tower, and loved a knight called Sir Eglamore. For some reason he left her, and in despair she took to sleep-walking beside Aira Force, the place where they had first met. One night Sir Eglamore came back and found Emma at the waterfall; but when he called her name she awoke suddenly, tripped, and fell to her death in the foaming waters. The grieving knight became a hermit, and lived out his life near the spot where she had died.

A gate from the car park at the foot of Aira Beck leads into a field, and from the right of the field a stile leads into the woods and over a foot-bridge across the beck. The path follows the beck up through the woods – a delightful mixture of oak, ash, alder, willow, beech and the occasional wych elm. Many orchids can be seen, especially early purple orchids in late spring and common spotted orchids in early summer.

Two bridges span the gorge, one above and one below Aira Force; cross the top bridge and follow the beck upstream on its right-hand side to another beautiful waterfall called High Force. The rock slabs around it seem perfectly made for sitting and contemplating for a while, as the water leaps loud and white towards its dark and silent ending in the lake.

▶ *Aira Force car park is near the shore of Ullswater, a few metres north of the A592 and A5091 junction.*

7 Moor Divock

This wide, windswept plateau off the north-east shore of Ullswater is littered with cairns, standing stones, stone circles, mounds and pits, all of them dating back some 4,000 to 3,000 years. Many of the smaller relics are almost lost in the bracken; but the larger ones, such as the Cop Stone, stand up from the Moor Divock like the last, indestructible memorials to an otherwise forgotten people. The relics suggest a purpose, but that purpose remains unknown. Why prehistoric man dug the Wofa Holes, the Pulpit Holes and the Dew-pot Holes is as much a matter of mystery as his reason for raising the Cop Stone or any other of the stones round about it.

The Romans also left their mark on the moor, but they were chiefly concerned with crossing it, not with stopping. The old Roman road called High Street ran across the moor, on its way south to the Troutbeck valley and the central lakes. To this day the huge mountain over which the road ran is still called High Street. Careful searching of the moor can still reveal traces of the old road.

This is perfect walking country, criss-crossed with green paths of springy turf. Skylarks spiral into the sky in full song and wild ponies roam the moor. Nothing expresses the spirit of the place better than the sight of a herd of these shy creatures wheeling away from one of the tiny moorland becks, and galloping into the distance.

▶ *Moor Divock can be reached by car along a minor road south-west from Helton, which is about 5 miles south of Penrith off the B5320. Alternatively, from Pooley Bridge on the B5320 at the northern end of Ullswater, a footpath runs south-east across the moor.*

8 Hallin Fell

It is not always the highest peaks that provide the finest views. Hallin Fell is not much more than 380m (1,260ft) above sea-level, and yet a superb lakeland panorama is visible from its neatly built summit cairn. The mountain is tucked into the inside of Ullswater's 'elbow', and commands views down both stretches of the lake. Across the water are the craggy splendours of Gowbarrow Park. To the north-west lies the Skiddaw massif. The great ridge of Helvellyn dominates the south-west. To the south are the beautiful valleys of Boardale, Bannerdale and Rampsgill, flat-bottomed and U-shaped in perfect lakeland style. The valley bottoms are stone-walled, carefully tended, green and lush; but beyond the walls bracken sweeps over the fell, a dark blanket broken only by the darker outlines of naked crags.

The path to the summit of Hallin Fell starts from opposite Martindale Church. It is said that the fell can be climbed comfortably from the church in bare feet, so velvety is the turf.

Hallin Fell is also a good starting point for a fine walk of about 5 miles along the lake shore, from the hamlet of Howtown, at the foot of the fell, to Patterdale; in parts it is woodland walking at its finest, through oak, beech and sycamore with the shining waters of the lake visible through the trees. The stretch of juniper scrub on Birk Fell is the most extensive in the Lakes. It is possible to return to Howtown by lake steamer.

▶ *Howtown is on the minor road running south-west along the eastern side of Ullswater from Pooley Bridge on the B5320. Martindale Church is ½ mile south-west of Howtown.*

❾ Lanty's Tarn

The tarn is tiny, tucked away and unknown to most visitors to the Lake District, and even in the height of summer it offers the determined walker a rare peace and solitude, wrapped in the deep quiet of the mountains. The 1½ mile walk across the fells leads south from the village of Glenridding, at the southern end of Ullswater. Take the road past the shops, keeping the car park on the right, and cross the stream beyond the cottages. Through the gate the path climbs very steeply upwards into typical fell countryside. Outcrops of rock stand bare and forbidding among patches of bracken; scattered trees, including oaks, ashes, birches and Scots pines, raise their branches to the sky. In early summer butterworts bloom beside thin streams trickling down towards the lake, and tormentil and sheep's sorrel add a twinkle of colour to the dark undergrowth.

The tarn, ringed with conifers, is wasp-waisted, heavily sedimented and full of fish – though most are very small. It is possible to walk on past its quiet waters, following the path through the bracken. Turn left where the path forks – the right-hand fork leads up to the heights of Striding Edge and then on to Helvellyn, a spectacular but long ascent. To the left the path drops down to Grisedale Beck and then east through the woods to the main road; turn left for Glenridding, half a mile away.

▶ *Glenridding is on the A592, at the southern end of Ullswater.*

❿ Stonethwaite Beck

Any walk around Stonethwaite is almost bound to be wet, for this was once the eastern limb of a great lake that covered the flat-lands of Borrowdale. The lake was connected by a river to Derwent Water in the north. Over thousands of years the streams rushing down from the ring of high fells around the lake swept more and more debris into it, and eventually filled it. Even today, after a spell of heavy rain, the flat-lands become a lake again and large boulders are carried there by the tumultuous, flooding becks.

On these damp uplands there is a chance of seeing the mountain ringlet during June and July. This little butterfly, with dark, velvety-brown wings, blotched with orange, is found only in lakeland and the Grampians.

Stonethwaite Beck is formed by two streams, Langstrath Beck and Greenup Gill, which meet below the fierce bluff of Eagle Crag. The crag can be reached by turning east out of Stonethwaite village, crossing the bridge, turning right and following the track through the woods. At the meeting of the two becks lies Smithymire Island, where the monks of Furness Abbey, 25 miles to the south, used to smelt iron ore. Beyond, rough, wet beck-side paths lead through wild, lonely country overhung by beetling crags.

By way of old packhorse trails, the Greenup Gill route leads eventually to Grasmere (6 miles away), and from Langstrath, a climb through Ore Gap and down Mosedale and the Duddon valley leads eventually to the distant Furness peninsula.

▶ *For Stonethwaite, take the B5289 south from Keswick, and after 7 miles, at Borrowdale, turn southeast along the minor road for ½ mile.*

⓫ Angle Tarn

Many people consider Angle Tarn the loveliest of all lakeland tarns, for it has something more than the wildness, isolation and scenic grandeur common to most tarns. Its shoreline is deeply indented, which gives it a very individual beauty, and two small islands standing far out on its trout-filled waters set off the scenery around them perfectly.

Above the tarn rise the peaks named after it – Angletarn Pikes, a summit with two separate peaks, rocky outcrops with a peat-bog in the depression between them. The views from the summit are not particularly extensive, but the surrounding countryside is glorious. This is part of the Martindale deer forest, and herds of red deer can sometimes be seen watering at the tarn. Fell ponies, almost as wild as the deer, also use the tarn as a watering-place, especially at daybreak and twilight.

There are several routes to the tarn, and one of the loveliest is from Dale Head Farm in Bannerdale. The path climbs diagonally past a stone ruin and a sheep-fold before crossing the screes between Heck Crag and Buck Crag.

Then, quite suddenly, the tarn comes into view in all its glory. Other ascents start at Patterdale and Hartsop, beginning in wooded lowlands and climbing through boulder-strewn, bracken-covered fells to the craggy heights.

From the tarn a path runs half a mile south-east to Satura Crag, from where there is a splendid view back down Bannerdale.

▶ *Patterdale is on the A592, ½ mile from the southern end of Ullswater. Bannerdale can be reached by following the minor road from Pooley Bridge (on the B5320 at the northern end of Ullswater) to Howtown. Beyond the top of the col, or 'pause', the road drops steeply to Hause Farm. From here the left turn leads down to Dale Head Farm beside Bannerdale Beck.*

NORTHERN ENGLAND

⑫ Harter Fell

The fearsome crags of Harter Fell are impressive on their own; but they become doubly impressive when seen in combination with the man-made wonders of Haweswater Reservoir and the jewel-like beauty of Small Water. Every approach to the fell, celebrates the marriage of rock and water. Climb up the Gatescarth Pass from Longsleddale, with the infant River Sprint tumbling beside the track and the enormous masses of Goat Scar and Buckbarrow Crag towering over it, and from the top of the col there is a breathtaking view over Haweswater. In a series of gigantic steps the north face of the fell plunges 550m (1,800ft) to the head of the lake. Continue north-west from the pass along the crag top, and Small Water lies like a sparkling teardrop far below.

A path drops diagonally down Small Water's corrie walls, and continues to the valley of the Small Water Beck. On its way to Haweswater, the stream tumbles down waterfalls, gurgles in deep pools and potholes, and races down long waterslides. From crevices in the rock, rowan trees grow at giddy angles, while the tremendous scatter of drumlins – hummocks of rubble left by melting Ice Age glaciers – makes the landscape wild and strange.

Another approach to Harter Fell is from Bampton by the lakeside road on the south-eastern shore of Haweswater. Once through the woods at the north-eastern end of the lake, the valley is walled in by the crags of Whelter, Bason, Lad and Laythwaite and by the great masses of Harter Fell and High Street.

Two paths lead on from the car park at the end of the road. The one to the left goes to the Gatescarth Pass, a mile away; the one straight ahead climbs some 200m (700ft) to Small Water. Beyond Small Water the path strikes up the formidable corrie slope at the western end; and the backward views from here are superb. But for many it will be enough just to sit on one of the slabs of rock which surround this lovely lake, and to gaze up at the mighty bulk of Harter Fell above it.

▶ *Longsleddale starts 4 miles north of Kendal and is reached by a minor road off the A6. Alternatively, from the south-eastern shore of Haweswater, take the minor road west from Shap on the A6 to Bampton, then turn south following signposts to Haweswater Reservoir.*

⓭ Easedale Tarn

Walled round by cliff-like mountainsides, Easedale preserves a sense of seclusion. Even on fine days the dark mountain shadows seem to fall ominously across the valley, and there is a sinister violence about the stream that rushes past the tiny green fields, aptly named Sour Milk Gill because of the curdling whiteness of its churned water. A mile further up the valley, it issues from Easedale Tarn.

The 2 mile walk to Easedale Tarn, very steep and wet in places, is dominated at first by the immense mass of Helm Crag to the north, with its fantastic rock formation known as The Lion and The Lamb. The walk starts from Easedale Road in Grasmere. Follow it across Goody Bridge then, ignoring the turn on the right, cross Easedale Beck by the next bridge. For the rest of the walk the beck remains on the right.

Large boulders litter the valley. These are the so-called sheep rocks of the Ice Ages, whose shapes, when seen from a distance, resemble those of sheep sleeping on the hillside. Glaciers smoothed the backs of the rocks, and carved out their downhill faces.

HAWESWATER AND HARTER FELL

The stony path climbs steeply upwards until, suddenly, the tarn lies ahead with Tarn Crag towering some 270m (900ft) above the water. The best time to see it is in the morning or early afternoon, when the sun is still catching its sheer, gleaming precipices.

▶ *The easiest way to Easedale Tarn is to turn west off the Keswick road as Grasmere village ends. There is a car park at the start of the walk. Grasmere is off the A591, 3 miles north-west of Ambleside.*

⓮ Burnmoor Tarn

From Eskdale Green to Boot is only a couple of miles along the flat road beside the River Esk; but a delightful 6 mile valley walk connects the two villages, climbing up Miterdale from Eskdale Green, turning round the windswept waters of Burnmoor Tarn, and dropping down again to Boot beside the Whillan Beck.

The first part of the walk north-east up Miterdale leads through Forestry Commission plantations, with many broad-leaved trees mixed in with the usual conifers, a wide variety of wayside and woodland flowers, and the River Mite always close at hand. After about a mile, at Low Place, the forest ends and a foot-bridge leads across the river. On the east side of the valley the fell is bare and stony, with some prehistoric stone circles and cairns up on Low Longrigg. There are impressive views northwards of the backs of Illgill Head and Whin Rigg, the fells which, on their north-west sides, form Wast Water's famous Screes.

The path climbs steadily north-east towards the isolated depression between Tongue Moor and Eskdale Moor, passing a lovely small amphitheatre on the right, with cliffs, waterfalls and a delightful greensward. Soon afterwards it reaches the graceful Burnmoor Tarn, where the view to the north-east is particularly impressive. The ridge ahead is Scafell and, beyond Slight Side, the southernmost summit, the well-named Crinkle Crags can be seen in the distance.

The path south-west down to Boot starts from the north-eastern corner of the tarn, where a complicated maze of tiny streams marks the point where Whillan Beck flows out of the tarn and Hardrigg Gill flows into it. The path is dry and follows the course of Whillan Beck a short distance above it on the fellside.

▶ *Eskdale Green is 4 miles north-east of Ravenglass. Follow minor roads through Santon Bridge and onto Eskdale Green from the A595, 2 miles north of Ravenglass. Alternatively, from Ambleside, leave the A593 and take the minor road over Wrynose and Hard Knott passes, both with steep gradients and sharp bends.*

NORTHERN ENGLAND

⑮ Wast Water

No other lake is so fierce and austere as Wast Water, at 79m (258ft) the deepest of the lakeland lakes. Sometimes it is as smooth as glass, sheltered by the highest mountains in England and reflecting them on its surface. At other times, when the peaks are lost in cloud and mist and wild winds squall up the valley, cold spray can be felt even high up on the slopes and waves race madly up the three dark miles of the lake's length. Above all it is the Screes cliff on the eastern shore that sets the lake apart – nearly 600m (2,000ft) of loose rock fragments spilling into the water. Under bleak, overcast skies, the Screes look black and threatening, but when the skies clear, they are full of colour.

There are many places from which to view the lake, and one of the best is from the south-west end in the area of Wasdale Hall. On the left the crags of Buckbarrow give way to the immense jumble of rocks – Long Crag – which forms the lower slopes of Middle Fell. The valley of Nether Beck slices through the heights, and beyond it are the crag-stepped ridge of Yewbarrow, the Mosedale valley and the great mass of Kirk Fell. To the north-east, at the head of the valley, stands the triumphant shape of Great Gable. On the south-east side are the twin summits of Illgill Head and Whin Rigg, the boundaries of the scree slopes.

The two ends of the lake are totally different. In the south-west, Nether Wasdale is sheltered and thickly wooded, with an abundance of flowers on the forest floor and moss and lichen everywhere. Wasdale Head in the north-east is the very core of the highest part of England, rough and wild above drystone walls that enclose the arable fields on the valley floor.

The waters of the lake are acidic and poor in nutrients. However, Wast Water is home to the Arctic char, a rare fish in Britain, found only in the deepest, coldest lakes.

▶ *From the east, Wast Water can be approached from Ambleside by the very steep Wrynose and Hard Knott passes. From the west, the way is from Ravenglass or Gosforth on the A595.*

⑯ Longsleddale

Among the most charming of the Lake District valleys, Longsleddale is lonely yet well inhabited, intensely private and yet easy to reach. The narrow road into the valley drops steeply away from the A6, winding through the trees to Garnett Bridge. As the road probes deeper into the valley, the impression grows that nothing has changed here for centuries.

The narrow valley, with its string of old stone farms and its pleasant patchwork of fields, forms a passage between the steep fells. The Cumberland poet, Norman Nicholson, said that in wet winters 'water pours down gill after gill till the dale looks like a street of terraced houses with the roof gutters all burst'. This mighty deluge of waterfalls feeds the aptly named River Sprint and enriches the fields on the narrow valley floor. The church, built in 1712, is in a lovely setting halfway along the valley, with broad-leaved woods closing in on both sides.

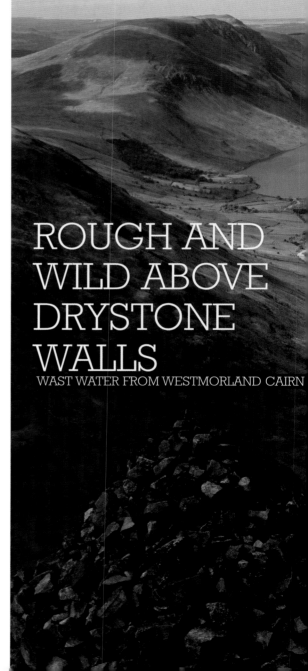

ROUGH AND WILD ABOVE DRYSTONE WALLS
WAST WATER FROM WESTMORLAND CAIRN

Beyond, the fells close in and the landscape becomes starker. In front, visible through the roadside trees, Goat Scar and Buckbarrow Crag tower over the valley head. The road ends at Sadgill, the highest farm, but on the east side of the valley a track leads on towards a distant col. This is Gatescarth Pass, between the heights of Harter Fell and Artle Crag. This path linked the valley with Mardale Green, the village drowned beneath Haweswater Reservoir.

▶ *Garnett Bridge is 4 miles north of Kendal and is reached by a minor road north-west off the A6.*

⑰ Claife Heights

Strange stories are told of Windermere, where an unbroken succession of ferrymen have plied their trade for a thousand years or more. One stormy night, many centuries ago, strange cries were heard from the Claife shore of the lake. A young ferryman set out to collect the passenger and returned, apparently alone, but struck dumb with fear; he died the very next day. According to local legend he had brought back a phantom passenger, the Crier of Claife. The ghost was eventually exorcised by a priest and put to rest in an old quarry known now as Crier of Claife Quarry.

On a fine day, such hauntings seem impossible in this lovely place, with its wooded isles reflected in calm water beneath the tree-clad heights of Claife. The gently rolling countryside of Claife, lying between Esthwaite Water and the enclosing curve of Windermere, provided an appropriate background for the stories of Beatrix Potter. Six of her books are set at Hill Top Farm at Near Sawrey (owned by the National Trust), and many others contain her exquisite miniature water-colours of the surrounding woods and fields that she loved.

One of the most interesting of the walks on Claife Heights begins just below Hill Top Farm. Take the path north from opposite the Tower Bank Arms in Near Sawrey. The surrounding countryside is typical of the southern lakes – partly woods, where roe deer roam, and partly fertile grazing land, with occasional outcrops of shale. The path climbs upwards through some very large rock outcrops and soon reaches Moss Eccles Tarn. Here ducks and the occasional diver and grebe may be seen, while coots and moorhens dodge among the reeds. A colony of black-headed gulls also breed here. Larches, copper beeches and huge rhododendrons fringe the banks of the tarn. Further on lies Wise Een Tarn, wrapped like a silver boomerang around a dark mass of conifers. Ahead there are wonderful views of the central Lake District, stretching from The Old Man of Coniston through Langdale to the shoulder of Skiddaw.

▶ *Near Sawrey is 6 miles south of Ambleside. From the A593, follow the B5286 then the B5285 through Hawkshead. Alternatively, take the A592 south from Windermere and cross the lake on the ferry.*

NORTHERN ENGLAND

⑱ Walna Scar Road

Walking across Coniston Fells by the Walna Scar Road is like travelling back through time, for this is one of the oldest roads in the Lake District. It has been walked or ridden throughout history by shepherds and weavers, pedlars and traders, wool-buyers, merchants and, of course, lovers of landscape.

But for a thousand years or more the chief traffic was provided by pack-ponies, heavily laden with copper ore from the Coniston mines. They are the oldest mines in the Lake District, dating from Roman times. The route from them crossed the Duddon at Seathwaite and led on over Birker Fell to Eskdale and then down to the Roman port of Ravenglass. In the early 19th century, when the mines were at their peak, several hundred men and boys were employed. The boys were trained to wash and sort the ore, using water diverted from mountain streams and tarns. Some of the old waterways can be found above the mine workings on the Coniston Fells. Mine entrances, often no more than about 1.5m (5ft) high and 46cm (18in) wide, can be found in the area. It is unsafe to enter them.

The road starts at the foot of Coniston Fells. It can be reached by driving at least part way up the signposted steep, rough road, just south of the centre of Coniston. Beyond the second gate there is no choice but to walk. Walna Scar Road leads straight ahead; the track to the right along Church Beck climbs to the top of Wetherlam.

The old road winds steadily upwards beneath the crags of Little Arrow Moor, passing various tiny stretches of water, including Boo Tarn. A path northwards leads to Goat's Water, in a magnificent example of an Ice Age corrie, with Dow Crag soaring 778m (2,555ft) on its western shore.

Once the col between Walna Scar and Brown Pike has been reached, the view ahead is breathtaking. Away in the far south-west is the huge bulk of Black Combe; across the foreground lies the lovely expanse of the Duddon valley. To the north-west is Harter Fell, behind which and further to the north is the mighty jumble of mountains leading to Scafell Pike, at 977m (3,206ft) the highest peak in England.

The return to Coniston can be made by walking back along the road, or by following the ridge walk north to the summit of Dow Crag, and then swinging round to the top of The Old Man of Coniston. From there the path down is steep but passable, although the area around it is riddled with old mine workings and shafts, and it is dangerous to stray from the path.

▶ *Coniston is 6 miles south-west of Ambleside, along the A593.*

⑲ Stanley Ghyll and Devoke Water

It is not its height but its spectacular setting in a narrow, thickly wooded gorge that has made Stanley Force, the waterfall in Stanley Ghyll, such an attraction. When Ice Age glaciers carved out the lakeland valleys, they cut off many river tributaries and left them hanging in the air – places today where lovely waterfalls tumble to the valley bottoms. Stanley Ghyll was created in this way when the glacier deepening the River Esk valley cut across its course.

A nature trail leads up to the falls by way of Stanley Beck, passing the old farmhouse of Dalegarth Hall, the home of the Stanleys from whom the ghyll takes its name. Oaks, sycamores, rowans and hazels borders the beck, while bilberries, wood sage and mats of white-flowered heath bedstraw grow along the banks.

Pick your way through the boulders brought down by previous floods until the path meets the beck again. Mosses and liverworts, including the light green bog moss, thrive in the damp atmosphere. Rhododendrons bloom among the rocks in June, naturalised from earlier plantings when part of the ghyll was a woodland garden.

All the way to the third wooden bridge across the beck the path remains steep and rocky, and beyond the bridge it becomes very wet and dangerous. But there is no need to go further. You are now standing at the bottom of the waterfall, with fine views from the bridge of the thin wall of water tumbling down its gorge of 400-million-year-old Eskdale granite.

High on Birker Fell above Stanley Ghyll lies the wild and lonely Devoke Water (it is pronounced 'Dev-ock'), surrounded by heather moors. Part of the Muncaster Castle estate, it is noted for its trout and its birds – red-throated and black-throated divers have been seen here in winter. The many cairns around its shores (which are boggy in places) are remains of the Bronze Age settlements of more than 3,000 years ago. The view north-eastwards as you walk back to the road is staggering – most of the major peaks, from nearby Harter Fell swinging northwards round to Great Gable, form a superb backcloth.

▶ *Stanley Ghyll and Devoke Water lie east of Ravenglass. Stanley Ghyll can be reached by the Ravenglass and Eskdale Miniature Railway to Beckfoot or Dalegarth stations. By car, follow a minor road from the A595 2 miles east of Ravenglass; cars can be parked at Dalegarth railway station. To continue to Devoke Water, take the signposted road to Ulpha, 2 miles west of Dalegarth Station. After 2 miles, park at the crossroads and follow the short track south-west to the lake.*

20 Wallowbarrow Gorge

In the last Ice Age, glaciers scoured out the deep cleft now called Wallowbarrow Gorge. Here, in its most spectacular stretch, the River Duddon flows straight through a fell instead of round it, walled in to the west by Wallowbarrow Crag and to the east by Hollin House Tongue. Both sides of the gorge are very steep – in some places vertical – and thickly wooded. When the river breaks out of the gorge it begins to meander across the wide flood plain, where it is joined by its tributary, the Tarn Beck.

Shortly before the Newfield Inn, in Seathwaite, a signpost marked 'To the Stepping Stones' points the way to the gorge, which leads through a mixed wood. If the stepping-stones become impassable, there is a single-arch bridge a little further upstream.

The path carries on through another wood to the flood plain, with the southern end of the Wallowbarrow Crags towering above. From here it is possible to walk up the gorge, although the going is rough. Another path striking off to the west of Wallowbarrow Crags leads to Grassguards Farm. Then it drops down to more stepping-stones below Fickle Crag, before climbing back south-eastwards through bracken and a scattering of oaks to the road – about three-quarters of a mile north of Seathwaite. An alternative path leads from Grassguards Farm through the woods to Birks Bridge, which lies on the same road about 2 miles north of Seathwaite.

▶ *A turning north off the A595, close to Duddon Bridge, leads through Ulpha to Seathwaite 6 miles up the valley. Parking is not easy in the village, but there is a car park at Birks Bridge.*

21 Black Combe

A soft, sweetly scented cushion of heather covers the summit of Black Combe, and on a clear summer day this is an ideal mountain for views. It stands alone in the extreme south-west of the Lake District, and so commands both land and sea. Snowdon is visible in the far south; the Isle of Man can be seen across the sea; and to the north, Scotland shimmers beyond the Solway Firth. Inland the view swings from the Forest of Bowland right round to the heights of Skiddaw in the distant north-east, with the majestic summits of Scafell Pikes in front of them. The only sound is the sighing and buffeting of the wind sweeping in from the sea. Birds are the only company – perhaps a kestrel hovering far below in the sun, red grouse starting from the heather or meadow pipits on flickering wings darting from one patch of cover to another.

This most undramatic of mountains has attracted more than its share of folklore, possibly because of the Swinside stone circle on its north-eastern flank. The Bronze Age circle is known locally as Sunken Kirk and was once believed to be a supernatural spot.

The easiest ascent of Black Combe is from the little church at Whicham, about a mile from the sea. A path between the church and the school leads to a narrow lane lined with brambles and wild roses, foxgloves and harebells. Beyond a farmhouse, a track leads over a stile and up a valley on the right. The going is always easy; and after about 2 miles of leisurely zigzagging the path arrives at the summit.

▶ *Whicham is on the A595, about 6 miles south-west of Broughton in Furness.*

239

The PEAK DISTRICT

England's first National Park, the Peak District is a land of rock and stone. Limestone forms the core of that part of the Park known as the White Peak; the Dark Peak has a heart of Millstone Grit.

❶ Bleaklow

At 633m (2,077ft), Bleaklow is very nearly the highest point in the Peak District; it is exceeded only by Kinder Scout – and that by a mere 3m (11ft). But it is a much larger area than Kinder and its dangers are the greater in consequence; therefore traverse it with even more care. Warm clothing, sound boots, and map and compass (and the knowledge to use them) are mandatory.

However, for those in whom the pioneering spirit burns less brightly, a fine impression of the place may be gathered from the Snake Road, the name given to the Peak District portion of the A57 which runs from Manchester to Sheffield. At the highest point of the road, just where it is crossed by the Pennine Way on its journey to the Scottish border, Bleaklow can be seen rising to the north. It is a high, almost featureless plateau, but at its western end is the noble gritstone edge of the Wain Stones, looming above the head of Dowstone Clough and the Yellowslacks Brook, which rises just below the crags.

Bleaklow is aptly named. Kinder Scout excepted, it is just about the toughest stretch of the Pennine Way, and offers little comfort to the traveller. Nevertheless, it has a wild, rare beauty. Mile after mile of dark peat drops slowly away eastwards from Bleaklow Head, and the only colour in all this is the green of bilberry, the purple of heather and the white feathers of cotton-grass. On bad days, even these disappear in the all-enshrouding mist, but on good ones there is the blue upturned bowl of the sky above you, and for company, a clattering red grouse or a lolloping mountain hare.

Though it may not seem so, you are not the first to pass this way or to see these things. Running off the Snake Road there is a track called Doctor's Gate; in fact, this is the old Roman road that ran from Navio fort at Brough in the Hope valley to Melandra fort at Brookfield, 2 miles north-west of Glossop. It makes a fine, firm path across the moors, as well it might; its foundations were firmly laid by the Romans nearly 2,000 years ago.

▶ *Access to Bleaklow is by the Pennine Way from north or south; from Glossop; or by Doctor's Gate, which starts ½ mile east of the summit on the A57.*

❷ Kinder Scout

The moorland plateau of Kinder Scout is, at 636m (2,088ft), the highest part of the Peak District National Park. It is flat, bleak, nearly featureless, a wasteland of peat criss-crossed by hundreds of groughs, or natural drainage channels. These can be deep, for the peat is thick, having been 8,000 years in the forming, and in winter when the groughs are filled with snow, they become traps that can be fatal to the unwary.

But if the place still attracts you, it might be better to avoid the interior of the plateau and to take instead the well-defined gritty paths that trace its periphery. You can come to the summit by many ways; from the A57, where a path about half a mile south-east of the Snake Inn crosses Woodlands Valley and climbs up Fairbrook Naze to the northern edges; or from Edale along the early stretches of the Pennine Way that begins at The Nag's Head. Both are excellent routes among a number of others equally good, but whichever way you approach Kinder, all paths seem in the end to lead to Kinder Downfall on the western edge, where, the Kinder river makes a spectacular 30m (100ft) plunge.

Kinder Scout is wild and fascinating, but treat it with respect, especially in winter. The perimeter walk is 17 miles, and most is fairly tough going, requiring proper equipment and a good level of physical fitness. If you have doubts about either, view the place instead from, say, Mam Tor; better that than find yourself tired and stranded at nightfall, miles away from shelter.

▶ *Kinder Scout can be approached from the A57; or from Hayfield, Edale and many other points. There is a National Park Visitor Centre in Edale, where details about routes and weather conditions may be obtained.*

❸ Derwent Edge

The lakes of the Peak District are highly picturesque, yet the most famous of them are not even a century old yet. They are, in fact, reservoirs serving Sheffield, Derby, Leicester and Nottingham, and were created by drowning two valleys – the Woodlands, which separates the Bleaklow massif from Kinder Scout, and the Derwent, which forms the eastern boundary of the Bleaklow moors. The interlinking system of dams and reservoirs was begun in 1912 with the building of the Howden dam, followed by the Derwent, lower down, in 1916, and finally by the great Ladybower, completed in 1943. Beneath the waters of the last reservoir there lie the remains of two villages, Derwent and Ashopton, and a 17th-century manor house, Derwent Hall.

The scars of construction in the valleys have long faded, and apart from the dams, the reservoirs now look entirely natural, making a drive along their wooded shores a delight. Even more exhilarating are the views from the paths that climb Derwent Edge, high up on the east side of the valley. From here you can see the whole 7 miles of the system, the endless conifers planted by the Forestry Commission, and the long arms of water reaching up the side valleys, glittering in the sun. And after rain there is the additional bonus of seeing great cataracts, sliding majestically over the dams.

The top of the edge is decorated with an extraordinary series of sculptures, carved out of the Millstone Grit by aeons of weathering, yet looking for all the world like some outdoor exhibition of modern statuary. Equally impressive from close to, or from far down on the western shore of the reservoir, they have even been given names according to fancied resemblances – the Wheel Stones, the Salt Cellar and the Cakes of Bread.

▶ *Derwent Edge can be reached from the northern side of the A57, to the east of the point where it crosses the Ashopton Viaduct, near the Ladybower dam.*

❹ Vale of Edale

The flat-bottomed valley, threaded by the River Noe, is best appreciated from Mam Tor or Hollins Cross, from where the full glory of the green chequerboard fields is laid out in its entirety. Down on the valley floor there are pretty hamlets and field paths to wander along, surrounded by the high ring of the hills.

The first part of the track that starts at The Old Nag's Head in Edale village – it is actually the beginning of the Pennine Way – runs through lush meadows, dotted with sycamore, oak and beech. But once across the little stream that runs out of Golden Clough, the rich pasture changes to poorer, thin grazing, and soon to vegetation so sparse as to be almost non-existent. This is wild country, where warm clothing and stout boots are essential, and if you are going as far as Edale Moor, take a map and compass too.

▶ *The Vale of Edale is best reached from the east, where a road runs up from Hope on the A6187, 4 miles west of Hathersage. Access from the west is more spectacular, since it involves taking minor roads west then north from Castleton, and climbs up to 450m (1,500ft) in the shadow of Mam Tor.*

THE SALT CELLAR

MAM TOR

⑤ Mam Tor

The name, in a mixture of Celtic and Old English, means Mother Hill; though whether it is derived from the great bosomy swell of Mam Tor itself, or from the fact that the Iron Age fortification that tops the near 520m (1,700ft) summit is the largest, and maybe the oldest, one of its kind in Derbyshire, is uncertain.

However, there is no doubt about 'Shivering Mountain', the alternative local name. A little to the east of the triangulation point at the summit, there is a tremendous cliff whose face is constantly in movement. It is made up of layers of sandstone and shale, and when water seeps through fissures in the sandstone, it lubricates the surface of the shale beneath, so dispatching great masses of rock into the valley below. From the top of the precipice you can see the evidence of hundreds of such slips which quite often take the Chapel-en-le-Frith to Castleton road with them.

The precipice is appalling, and, edged as it is with slippery, sheep-cropped grass, fairly dangerous. But the views are stupendous, and

the ridge that runs from Rushup Edge to the west, then north-east from Mam Tor to Lose Hill by way of Hollins Cross, is easily the best ridge walk in the Peak. On either side the green slopes slide down – into the lovely, U-shaped chequerboard of Edale to the north and into the wide expanse of the Hope Valley to the south. So handsome is the Hope Valley that the huge limestone quarry and cement works in its midst dents its majestic appearance scarcely at all.

The best place to begin the walk is from a point on a minor road off the A6 about 2 miles north-east of Chapel-en-le-Frith; though not signposted the beginning is fairly obvious, since it is part of an old, paved packhorse route. The track climbs up Rushup Edge, reaching the highest point, in this first section, at a Bronze Age tumulus on Lord's Seat. Whoever was buried here, with all the countryside laid before him, must have been a great lord indeed.

Now the path drops steadily down to the Edale road, which cuts through Rushup Edge via the Mam Nick Pass, before climbing once more, but not too exhaustingly, to the summit of Mam

Tor. The remainder of the high, exhilarating ridge lies before you. It is always windy up here, and skylarks sing perpetually overhead. Below, you can see the brown backs of hovering kestrels, crows flapping their weary way into the wind, and rooks, those aerial comedians, falling and tumbling about in the breeze.

The view is completely splendid. To the south is the gleaming White Peak, the limestone area of Derbyshire, while to the north is the sombre gritstone of the Dark Peak. And the ridge you are standing upon is the place where those two extraordinarily contrasting rock formations meet.

▶ *Mam Tor can be reached by the footpath which climbs up from the picnic site at the foot of the Edale road, which runs north from a minor road about 2 miles west of Castleton which is on the A6187.*

❻ Hathersage

Charlotte Brontë stayed at Hathersage vicarage, and incorporated both the house and village in *Jane Eyre*. Robin Hood was a frequent visitor, too, to judge from his well near the Fox House Inn, 3 miles along the Sheffield road; his cave, 1½ miles north-east of the village; and the 3.3m (11ft) grave in the churchyard that is said to contain the bones of Little John. Though what the outlaws were doing here on the gritstone edge of Hallam Moors, and so far from Sherwood Forest, history does not relate.

But on the moors there is solid evidence of residents that predate even Robin and his men – the mound of a Norman castle at Camp Green, the mighty and mysterious Carl Wark fort and a scattering of tumuli and stone circles. Among these are a number of natural curiosities, such as the Rocking Stone in Lawrence Field, 1½ miles south-east of Hathersage, and the Toad's Mouth rock near the bridge north-west of the Fox House Inn. With a pluck at the imagination, it really does look a bit like a toad. Close by is Longshaw Country Park, with pastures made bright with common dog violets, wood-sorrel, mosses and lesser celandine, and watered by the murmuring Burbage Brook. There is also a disused quarry, where you can see half-finished millstones abandoned a century and more ago.

From the top of Stanage Edge and the Burbage Rocks there are dramatic views of the moors and Carl Wark, while Millstone Edge, west of Toad's Mouth, has a surprise view of the valley of the Derwent lying to the north-west, and its western tributary, the Noe, which rises in Edale and joins the Peakshole Water at Hope village.

▶ *Hathersage is situated on the A6187, about 5 miles from the outskirts of Sheffield.*

❼ Carl Wark

It was long presumed that the fortifications of Carl Wark were Iron Age work, but recent investigation has suggested that it belongs to a much later period, perhaps the 6th or 7th century AD. In which case, who built it, and why?

Whoever it was had a fine eye for a defensive position. The fort is built on a kind of promontory that juts out south of Higger Tor, so that on three sides its defences are natural rock faces, supplemented by gritstone boulders. The fourth side, the neck of the promontory, is blocked by a great drystone wall, some 3m (10ft) high and 27m (30yd) long, and backed, on the fort side, by an earthen embankment.

To the north is the high outcrop of Higger Tor, whose summit is a jumble of boulders weathered into fantastic shapes. The view from here is breathtaking.

▶ *Carl Wark and Higger Tor are best approached from the footpaths leading from the minor road that runs off the A6187 at Hathersage Booths.*

❽ Miller's Dale

The valley of the River Wye has acquired many different names on its long route between Buxton and Bakewell. South of Tideswell village it is called Miller's Dale, a name derived from two mills built in the valley in the 18th century. The one at Cressbrook was owned by Sir Richard Arkwright and staffed by workhouse boys, housed in cottages near by. The other, further upstream at Litton Mill, had a reputation for the treatment of its apprentices, that rivalled that of the fictional Dotheboys Hall.

The path from Cressbrook leads through Litton Mill alongside the quiet river, a stretch that is known, quite delightfully, as Water-cum-Jolly-Dale. From Litton Mill, the path becomes a road, but it is little used and is never more than a metre or so from the Wye just after the hamlet of Miller's Dale, continues along the north bank.

From now on, the valley is called Chee Dale, and is quite magnificent. Here is Chee Tor, arguably the finest single limestone crag in the Park. The footpath follows the river round on its winding course, in one of the most delightful walks even this area has to offer, until finally it reaches the A6 near Topley Pike, about 3 miles east of Buxton. Deservedly, the dale is now a nature reserve.

▶ *The best way to Miller's Dale is by the B6049, which runs north-east from the A6 some 4 miles east of Buxton. A good place to park your car before exploring the area is at Monsal Head on the B6465.*

NORTHERN ENGLAND

243

➒ Taddington Moor

Moors are unusual hereabouts, since in Derbyshire the term is generally reserved for the dark uplands of the gritstone Peak. But Taddington Moor is a limestone ridge, whose highest point Sough ('Suff') Top reaches up to 438m (1,438ft) above the surrounding wind-combed solitudes; so perhaps 'moor' is appropriate here, too, even though it is now mainly pasture, box-patterned with the drystone walls so characteristic of Derbyshire.

The views stretch out to Kinder Scout in the north, the Sheffield moors to the east and due west to Axe Edge. Taddington Moor's best-known attribute is the highest Neolithic monument in England. It shows on the Ordnance Survey map as a 'Chambered Cairn', but local people have always known it as Five Wells. Originally, it was a huge oval barrow, some 24m (80ft) by 18m (60ft), and probably about 6m (20ft) high. When it was built, some 4,500 years ago, a great mound of earth covered its two limestone burial chambers and passages, but this has long eroded away, leaving them open to the sky and revealing the massive stone slabs of their construction. Excavations showed that at least 12 people were buried in the barrow, accompanied by pottery, flint tools and other grave goods.

▶ *Access to Five Wells is by a track near the hotel that stands on the A6 just west of the Taddington by-pass. Alternatively, there is a path across the moor from Chelmorton to Taddington which forks after a few hundred metres. The left fork leads to the tomb. Though these paths are generally open, they are not actually public rights-of-way.*

➓ Axe Edge

Two of the loveliest rivers in England, the Dove and the Manifold, are born in the moorlands just below Axe Edge, the highest point on the magnificent road between Leek and Buxton. On the way out of Leek, the road passes the superbly jagged Ramshaw Rocks, and that last breath of the Pennines, The Roaches. It also passes Flash, which at 463m (1,518ft) is said to be the highest village in England. Once, this was

the headquarters of a gang of coiners and, in some circles, 'flash' is still a name given to counterfeit money.

The views are splendid throughout the journey, but the real sense of spaciousness comes immediately below Axe Edge itself. The highest point on Edge is a chilly 551m (1,807ft) above sea-level, so providing a prospect as vast as any in Derbyshire. To the south-east, the infant Dove and Manifold begin to carve their separate valleys down to their eventual meeting place near Ashbourne, while to the west and north-west are the conical peaks of Shutlingsloe and Shining Tor. Slightly further to the north is the deep trench of the Goyt valley, and to the north-east, beyond Buxton, is the limestone section of the High Peak.

▶ *Axe Edge is west of the A53, 3 miles south-west of Buxton.*

⓫ Three Shire Heads

The triangle of high moorland between Leek and Macclesfield in the west and Buxton to the east is the birthplace of five rivers and the meeting place of three counties – Staffordshire, Derbyshire and Cheshire. The actual meeting place, called Three Shire Heads, is in the upper valley of the River Dane where the infant stream divides into two branches; the northerly one is generally taken to be the Dane's source.

The wide, rolling moorland is slashed across by tributaries of the Dane which have eroded through the sandstone and shales of the dip slope to produce attractively named edges such as Cutthorn Hill and Turn Edge; there is also a spot called the Hawk's Nest, which gives a delightful view down the Dane valley towards The Roaches, with Wolf Edge to the east.

About 2 miles north of Three Shire Heads, on the A537, is the Cat and Fiddle Inn which, at 515m (1,690ft), is one of the highest pubs in England. According to the weather, it provides either a panoramic view over Macclesfield Forest, or a shelter from the stormy blast.

▶ *The easiest access to Three Shire Heads is by the path that runs from the A54 just below Dane Bower quarries, 4 miles south-west of Buxton.*

THE APPEARANCE OF THE

⑫ The Roaches

The Pennines have kept a special triumph to mark the very end of their long march down Britain – the fantastic, battlemented ridge called The Roaches. Like nearby Ramshaw Rocks that overhang the A53, whose base is the old Roman road to Buxton, and the oddly named Hen Cloud, The Roaches are a last outcrop of the Millstone Grit from which the bones of the North Country were formed. Though they never rise to more than 520m (1,700ft), their weird, weathered shapes and their foreign appearance in the landscape make them enormously impressive.

The best side from which to tackle The Roaches is the south-west, the way the gritstone edge faces. From Upper Hulme a minor road takes you up the first part of the climb, then just past Hen Cloud there is a path on the right that slopes northwards up the escarpment. Halfway up there is surprising wooded pasture where a bed of shale, sandwiched between the gritstone, results in richer soils and easier slopes. But the final 60m (200ft) or so up to the top is something of a scramble.

The views, however, are well worth the breathlessness after the climb. Away to the north-east the land dips and rises to the heights of Axe Edge, and to the south-west, shimmering in the haze, is the eccentric shape of Tittesworth Reservoir. Almost due west is The Cloud, the hill that stands over Congleton, and beyond that the rolling Cheshire Plain.

The path along the top of The Roaches climbs steadily northwards towards the triangulation point marking the summit at 505m (1,658ft); shortly before you reach it, there is a little pool crouched behind the ramparts of the ridge. Surrounded by flat-topped boulders, it is a perfect place to take a mid-climb breather.

From the triangulation point to the north, can be seen the pyramid cone of Shutlingsloe, the rolling moorlands of Goyt's Moss, and the gritstone country that surrounds the central Peakland core of white limestone.

▶ *Access to The Roaches is by Upper Hulme village, which lies west of the A53, 3 miles north-east of Leek.*

⑬ Lathkill Dale

Charles Cotton, Izaak Walton's friend, described the waters of Lathkill Dale as 'the purest and most translucent stream that ever I saw either at home or abroad' – and as author of the fly-fishing section that was added to the fifth edition of *The Compleat Angler*, his opinion carries more weight than most. The appearance of the waters has not changed at all since he wrote of them in the 17th century, and the valley that gives them birth remains quiet and peaceful, smaller than the more famous dales, such as Dove Dale and the Manifold Valley.

The head of the dale lies a little to the east of Monyash, and the Lathkill river, after rain at least, leaps full-fledged to life from a cave about a quarter of a mile below. In dry weather, however, the cave dries up and the river is born piecemeal from a series of springs further down the valley.

The footpath hugs the north bank and runs beside the trout pools that gladdened the hearts of Cotton and Walton, and has delightful views of the woods on the opposite shore. Most of the dale is a National Nature Reserve, and, understandably, admission is restricted to the public footpaths. Jacob's ladder, one of Britain's rarest plants, is found in the valley; it is native to only a few sites, all in Northern England.

Carter's Mill, at the junction with a tiny dale coming down from Haddon Grove direction, was a corn-mill, but now all that remains are its millstones and the weir. Then, a few metres further downstream is another, much larger, pool. Once, this powered the water-wheels that drained the nearby Lathkill and Mandale lead mines, whose derelict buildings add a touch of melancholy to the beauty of the valley.

At Conksbury, the path crosses the river by a medieval bridge on the road from Bakewell, then runs downstream to Alport where the Lathkill marries with the Bradford. From here, their united waters flow on for 2 miles to lose themselves in the River Wye, a little below Haddon Hall.

▶ *Monyash is 4½ miles west of Bakewell on the B5055, which joins the A515 about 7 miles south-east of Buxton.*

NORTHERN ENGLAND

WATERS HAS NOT CHANGED

LATHKILL DALE

⑭ Stanton Moor

Just south of the point where the Derwent and Wye rivers meet there is a stretch of moorland which is never more than 323m (1,060ft) high, yet somehow gives the feeling that you have reached the top of the world.

During the Bronze Age, Stanton Moor must have had considerable religious significance, for more than 70 barrows have been identified here, many of which have been excavated; finds are now in the Sheffield Museum at Weston Park.

The barrows have been worn down by time, and the heather is deep, so they are not always easy to find. However, there is a little stone circle called the Nine Ladies, with the separate King's Stone standing near by, at the northern end of the plateau. By the path running north-eastwards towards the Nine Ladies, the remains of two mounds can be seen, and careful searching will reveal many others all over the moor, but especially in the south and east. Whether you are successful or not, the search gives added interest to a pleasant walk along sandy paths and through heather, among surroundings of great charm.

▶ *Stanton Moor can be reached from Stanton Lees, which is 3½ miles north-west of Matlock on a minor road leading from the B5057 at Darley Bridge.*

⑮ Arbor Low

This is the Stonehenge of the Peak District. Not quite so impressive, perhaps, as its Wiltshire counterpart, since all of its massive limestone slabs save one now lie flat on the ground. But stand among them, at twilight especially, and you can feel the enormous significance this place once possessed.

When Arbor Low was constructed some 4,000 years ago, the 40-odd stones, each weighing 8 tonnes and more, may have stood on end and the whole formation was surrounded by a rampart and ditch about 75m (250ft) in diameter. Considering the tools of the period – picks and shovels of stone, bone and antler – the labour involved was prodigious, and could only have been inspired by a devotion to some long-forgotten faith. Yet the site was regarded as sacred for a very long time, to judge from the numerous burial mounds in the vicinity. One of these is actually built into the bank, and there is another, Gib Hill, about 320m (350yd) to the south-west. These, like the earthwork that leads to the south entrance of Arbor Low, may have been built 1,000 years later than the stone circle.

▶ *Arbor Low is about 9 miles south-east of Buxton near a minor road leading east off the A515.*

⑯ Dove Dale

Correctly – or cartographically, anyway – Dove Dale is that wooded, limestone, highly picturesque part of the valley of the Dove that lies just to the north of Thorpe. But almost every part of the little river's course is pleasant, whatever names its banks are given. Much of it can be followed by footpath, all the way from its birthplace among the gritstone and shales of Axe Edge down to Burton, where it joins the Trent.

Perhaps as good a place as any to start is at Crowdecote, near Longnor, from which a footpath runs past Pilsbury Castle to Hartington. Incidentally, there are no riverside roads; you can drive down to the Dove, but not along it. Below Hartington, the valley is called Beresford Dale, and it was in Beresford Hall – now sadly demolished – that Izaak Walton stayed with his friend Charles Cotton. Cotton taught him fly-fishing along the Dove, and later added a section on the art to *The Compleat Angler*.

The next stretch of the river is called Wolfscote Dale after Wolfscote Hill above. Here, the stream's flow is slowed by a number of tiny weirs that create resting pools to encourage trout and grayling to linger. Downstream is Milldale and Viator Bridge, an old packhorse bridge whose narrowness was remarked upon in *The Compleat Angler* – confirmation that it is not passable by modern motor vehicles.

Below Milldale are the Dove Holes, caves carved deep into the limestone long ago before the Dove had worn its way down to its present level. Here, Dove Dale proper begins, a deep gorge heavily clad with ash and alders, out of whose dense cover limestone crags and pinnacles leap skywards. Surely in all England there can be few grander spectacles than the river at this point, guarded by Ilam Rock with its flat, grassy top on one side, and by the multiple spires of Pickering Tor on the other. Further south still is Reynard's Cave, and a natural arch formed by the collapse of part of the cave roof.

Everywhere there are pillars, spurs and outcrops of limestone – Jacob's Ladder, The Twelve Apostles, Tissington Spires, Lovers' Leap. The river makes one last great sweep round Dovedale Castle – a crag, not a fortification – and runs on to break through the southerly guardian hills of Bunster and Thorpe Cloud, leaving the limestone behind to hurry on through the shales past Ashbourne to Burton.

▶ *Longnor is on the B5053, 6 miles south of Buxton. Crowdecote is 1 mile east of Longnor on minor roads between the B5053 and A515.*

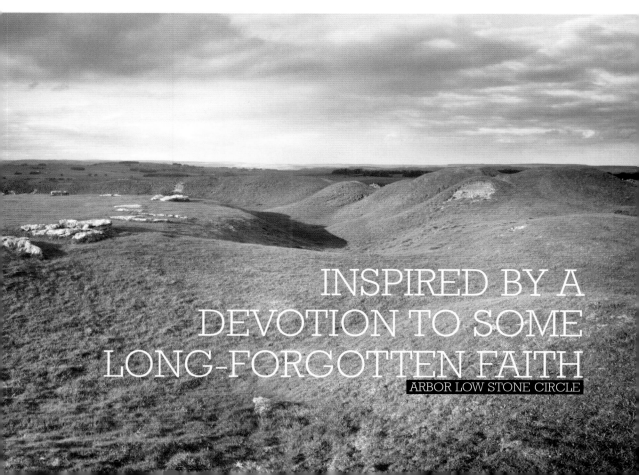

INSPIRED BY A DEVOTION TO SOME LONG-FORGOTTEN FAITH

ARBOR LOW STONE CIRCLE

NORTHUMBERLAND'S COAST and HILLS

Northumberland is border country, the place where England meets Scotland. Bounded by the North Sea to the east, that ancient frontier, Hadrian's Wall, still marches across its southern reaches.

❶ Holy Island

Across a mile-long causeway, which is impassable for about five hours during high water, lies Holy Island. Its long green spit runs into the North Sea and thrusts up dramatically at the south-eastern tip into a sharp cone round whose apex Lindisfarne Castle clings in a spiral.

The castle was built from the stones of Lindisfarne Priory, half a mile away. After the Dissolution of the Monasteries, the priory had been abandoned by the Benedictine order who built it in 1093 and lived comfortably on the island by farming. Gaunt, roofless ruins, with sandstone arches framing the sky, are all that remain of the priory. They stand in the village, where now the island's only road leads from the causeway. All exploring is on foot.

The Benedictines were not the first monks to live on Holy Island. It had been Saxon England's greatest centre of religious and intellectual life. It was chosen as a monastery by St Aidan when he came from Iona in 635 to be Bishop of Northumbria. He trained missionaries who went all over Britain, and even to the Low Countries. The sumptuously illuminated manuscript known as the *Lindisfarne Gospels* was created by the monks in the late 7th century. But in 793 the Vikings came raiding and destroyed the abbey. The monks rebuilt it, but in 875 they finally fled as the raiders plagued the area again and again. The island stood desolate until the Benedictines came.

Holy Island's historic stones are now extra adornments on its 3 sq miles of dunes, rugged cliffs, rocky beaches and, above all, teeming birdlife. The whole east-coast path is a birdwatcher's paradise, with Emmanuel Head at the island's north-east corner the best viewing point. Gannets, cormorants, Bewick's swans, greylag geese, guillemots, divers, redshanks, oystercatchers, kestrels, long and short-eared owls, varied ducks and grebes – the variety and vast numbers amaze the eye and stun the ear.
▶ *The causeway to Holy Island is reached by a signposted minor road that turns off the A1, 8 miles south-east of Berwick-upon-Tweed. A tide-table is displayed at the approach to the causeway.*

❷ Farne Islands

The sharp, fluted outlines of the Farne Islands stand in the waters off Seahouses like the broken pillars of an ancient ruin, rising vertically to 20m (70ft) in places. The 15, 20 or 26 islands – for some emerge and submerge with the tides – are scattered like stepping-stones, each with a creamy collar of foam.

The islands, owned by the National Trust, are in two groups divided by the mile-wide water of Staple Sound. Nearest to the shore, about 1½ miles out, are the inner islands with 6.5ha (16 acre) Inner Farne the largest of the group. The outer group include Staple Island, Brownsman, Longstone and the North and South Wamses. The rest of this group are mostly barren rocks which hardly qualify as islands since they are underwater most of the time. Each group has its own lighthouse – on Longstone and on Inner Farne. They are both now automatic with the last lighthouse keeper leaving Longstone in 1990.

Sea-birds breed and nest on the islands in vast numbers. Puffins come home from their fishing in hordes each evening to their nest-holes in the ground. Ranks of bronze cormorants and green shags stand with their wings outspread to dry. Chocolate-coloured guillemots are so crowded on the rock ledges that their eggs often get pushed off. Razorbills, eider ducks, rock pipits, fulmars, gulls and terns team over the rocky islands.

St Cuthbert, a prior at Lindisfarne, came to Inner Farne in 676, and stayed there in a rough shelter. A small monastic group lived on the island from 1255, and the ruins of their buildings remain. The monks sold sea-bird eggs and fish, salvaged wrecks and made a profit on their surplus barley. There are no trees on the Farnes, but the peaty soil over the hard dolerite rock bears an abundance of wild flowers as well as mosses and lichens.
▶ *Landing is allowed only on Inner Farne and Staple Island, and not even there from May 15 to July 15, when the birds are breeding. The islands are reached by boat from Seahouses, which is on the B1340, 3 miles south-east of Bamburgh.*

❸ Bamburgh

The red-sandstone castle seems to grow out of the massive rock on which it stands, towering over Bamburgh on one side and over windswept sand on the other. There has been a castle of one kind or another at Bamburgh since almost the dawn of English history. The Saxon Ida the Flamebearer became king of Bernicia, as the area was known, in 547 and founded his capital at the site. His grandson Ethelfrith became king of all Northumbria and named the capital Bebbanburh in honour of Bebba, his wife. Three times it survived Viking attacks. The Normans took it from Matilda, Countess of Northumberland, who surrendered it to William Rufus rather than have him put out the eyes of her captive husband, Robert.

It was the Normans who built the vast, square keep that still stands. Much of the present building, however, dates from 1894 when the castle was restored and modernised by Lord Armstrong. Below the castle walls, a wide stretch of sandy beach runs for 2½ miles to Seahouses. Such a magnificent beach attracts many visitors, but there is room for all and a walk along it is invigorating. Sand-dunes roll away inland to the main road that is parallel to the beach, and always in view are the rocky Farne Islands.

▶ *Bamburgh is reached from the B1341 or the B1342, which turn off the A1 midway between Alnwick and Berwick.*

❹ Budle Bay

Greylag geese use Budle Bay as a winter roosting place, and hosts of gulls and wildfowl come here all the year round to search for food among its mud-flats. The shallow estuary, almost totally enclosed by a finger of Ross Back Sands pointing across to Budle Point, fills with water only at high tide. Then the sea curls in, swift, deep and dangerous in the channel below the headland.

The whole of the bay, a mile wide and 1½ miles long, is within the Lindisfarne National Nature Reserve. The road along the southern tip makes an ideal viewpoint for bird-watchers – and a good parking spot. Only a grass verge and a fence separate the road from the bay. Another good vantage point is the high ground beyond Budle Point, just over a mile from Bamburgh along a footpath that makes its way round the edge of the golf course.

In the 13th century Budle Bay was the port of Bamburgh, and schooners and barges crossed to the creek at its southern tip to reach Waren Mill which dates from Norman times and, until recently, produced malted barley for brewing.

▶ *Budle Bay is 2½ miles east of Belford on the A1, north of the B1342 from Belford to Bamburgh.*

BAMBURGH CASTLE

❺ Kirknewton

History and beauty crowd the hills above Kirknewton, a sturdy Border village of thick-walled buildings on the northern edge of the Cheviots. Scarcely a hilltop is without its prehistoric fort or enclosure. The most extensive Iron Age camp in Northumberland sprawls over 5ha (13 acres) on top of Yeavering Bell, an aptly named dome of a hill a mile to the south-east. Inside the stone rampart are the foundations of some 130 circular or oval huts.

The hill is close to the road, and its 361m (1,182ft) summit, reached with no more than a modest walk, gives a generous reward: a magnificent view over the valleys of the Tweed and the Till in the north, the hills above Chatton to the east, and layer upon layer of hills in the west swirling round to the Cheviots in the south.

Below Yeavering Bell, Edwin, Saxon king of Northumbria, had his summer palace, Gefrin. When it was discovered and excavated in the late 1950s, timber halls and stockades came to light, and also shrines both pagan and Christian. Edwin married a Christian, Ethelberga, who brought with her Paulinus, one of the missionaries who came with Augustine from Rome in 597 to bring their religion to the English. Paulinus converted Edwin in 627. Many of the king's people followed his example. Paulinus spent 36 days at Gefrin teaching and baptising the converts. A plaque marks the site of the palace.
▶ *Kirknewton is 5 miles west of Wooler along the A697, then the B6351.*

❻ Hepburn Wood

Hepburn Wood clothes a steep escarpment of fell sandstone crags below the wild expanse of Hepburn Moor. The crags are part of a fault that curves from Kyloe in the north towards Otterburn in the south-west. The waymarked Woodland Walk, taking about an hour, follows forest roads and grassy rides between the conifer and beech plantations. Woodpeckers, redstarts and other woodland songbirds can be seen and heard. Along the way an optional steep path branches up the crag to give a magnificent view from the edge of the scarp across to the Cheviot Hills in the west.

Hepburn Crag Walk turns off the Woodland Walk. The waymarked track takes an hour longer and involves some steep, hard walking. But it rises through the plantations, crosses open moorland and the remains of a 4,000-year-old hill-fort – with Chillingham Park and a ruined 'bastle', or fortified farmhouse, below – and finally leads along the crag top to one of the finest views in Northumberland.

The viewpoint is Ross Castle, the site of a double-rampart hill-fort 3,000 years old, with some traces left of the stone-built camp. The Cheviots roll across to the west; the sea shines in the east. On a clear day the seven castles of Lindisfarne, Bamburgh, Dunstanburgh, Warkworth, Alnwick, Ford and Chillingham show up like tiny models. Here, at 315m (1,035ft), the National Trust and the Forestry Commission have built a viewing platform to reward visitors with the full panorama.

In Napoleonic times, Ross Castle was a beacon point with its fire kept ready for lighting to spread the alarm if Bonaparte and his French forces landed in England. On January 31, 1804, the men on evening watch spotted a fire away to the north and lit their beacon. It started a chain of beacons running for miles before messengers could stop them with the reassuring news that the fire in the north was only gorse alight on the Lammermuir Hills.
▶ *Hepburn Wood is 6 miles south-east of Wooler. Take the B6348, turn off at Chatton towards Chillingham, and follow the signs after Chillingham.*

❼ Craster and Dunstanburgh Castle

A tiny harbour set in a cluster of cottages is the heart of Craster, a village named after the family that owned the district even before the Norman Conquest. The Crasters enlarged the harbour in 1906, not for the fishing boats but for the barges and coasters that came to get setts and chippings of the hard whinstone cut from the family's quarries behind the village. The setts were taken to pave the streets of cities as far away as London.

The few brightly coloured cobles in the harbour are the remnant of a much larger fleet. They fish for salmon, crabs and the sweet-

A TINY HARBOUR SET

flavoured lobsters that thrive on the limestone rocks protecting the harbour. The coble, the distinctive fishing craft of the north-east coast, has a bow both deep and high to breast the rough seas, and an iron-shod flat-bottomed stern that can be hauled on to the shore for landing.

To the north of the harbour, through the village, a wicket gate marks the start of a 3 mile walk along the coastal path dominated by the spectacular ruin of Dunstanburgh Castle. To the west lie rich meadows and pasturelands; on the east the sea washes the foot of the cliff columns where many fulmars nest. The path is the only way to the 4.5ha (11 acre) site of the castle.

This great size had no practical purpose. It was determined by the natural defences of the spot. The castle stands on an outcrop of the Great Whin Sill, with the steep drop and the sea protecting it more than its long curtain walls. Only the south wall was approachable, and here it had towers built about every 27m (30yd).

After the Wars of the Roses, in the late 15th century, the castle fell into ruin. The main road to the north was developed inland, away from Dunstanburgh; the siege cannon ended its impregnability; and even its harbour silted up behind a shingle bar to form the low-lying pasture that is there now.

From the ruins there is a sweeping view stretching from Coquet Island in the south to the Farne Islands in the north. Sea-birds, and kittiwakes in particular, wheel round the cliffs where they breed. Down on the foreshore 'Dunstanburgh diamonds' – tiny quartz fragments – glint between the rocks. The path continues north beyond the castle, dipping down to the sandy beach to skirt the golf-course, and crossing Embleton Burn where stonechats nest in the hawthorn bushes. Linnets, yellowhammers and whitethroats love the gorse-covered crag. The path ends at Low Newton-by-the-Sea, beside fields where lapwings make their home.

▶ *Craster and Low Newton-by-the-Sea are 6 miles and 8 miles north-east of Alnwick on signposted minor roads leading off the B1339 and B1340 respectively.*

8 Warkworth

Here the River Coquet makes its final serpentine coil before entering the sea. Emerging from its steep, wooded valley, it winds round the little town of Warkworth in a great horseshoe, slipping past the beautiful Norman church before, overlooked by the stately remains of the castle, it passes unhurriedly beneath a fortified medieval bridge and flows to the sea at Amble.

Warkworth Castle, built early in Norman times on a fortified Saxon site, came into the hands of the Percy family – the Earls of Northumberland – in 1331. They strengthened it, gave it the magnificent cruciform keep, and added some domestic comforts. That straightforward soldier Harry Hotspur was brought up here. He helped Henry Bolingbroke to seize the crown of England from Richard II but later, his loyalty cooled by Henry's autocracy, plotted against him.

Warkworth Castle sits high on its green velvet mount, the grassy slopes running down from it to the water's edge. A path along the river leads to a 14th-century hermitage half a mile upstream; an even more pleasant approach is by boat. The cell and its tiny, vaulted chapel are cut into the sandstone cliffside. At the entrance the inscription *Fuerunt mihi lacrymae panes nocte et die* sets a sad mood – 'Tears have been my portion night and day'.

Between Warkworth and Amble, the road runs beside Warkworth Harbour. A mile off the harbour lies the flat-topped, rocky Coquet Island. Boat trips give a good view of the island, but landing is forbidden for it is a bird sanctuary and the most southerly breeding ground in eastern Britain of the eider duck.

▶ *Warkworth is on the A1068, 6 miles south-east of Alnwick.*

N A CLUSTER OF COTTAGES

9 Rothbury

The attractive 'capital' of Coquetdale is Rothbury, a large, elegant, unspoiled village. Old stone houses and wide streets climb from the sloping green, shaded by sycamore trees, up the hill on the north bank of the Coquet.

The Simonside Hills lie south of Rothbury. Their dark, rugged outlines are clad with pines, silver birches and rowans on the northern slopes and rise like steps to the highest point at Tosson Hill, 440m (1,444ft) above sea-level, and the craggy sandstone bluff of Simonside. The views from Simonside are enormous, an unhindered sweep stretching from Cumbria round to the east coast and including almost all of the Coquet from source to mouth.

From the road between Great Tosson and Lordenshaw, waymarked Forestry Commission paths lead through the forest on walks taking half an hour to two and a half hours. Paths lead to Simonside Ridge and Ravens Heugh. A short diversion on Simonside leads to Little Church Rock, a great sandstone boulder cleft from top to bottom as if by some gigantic sword. Ravens Heugh crags face west, and there is no finer place to be on a late summer afternoon when Coquetdale and the distant Cheviots are bathed in golden sunlight.

Great Tosson was the legendary home of the Duergars, elves who plagued the local folk with their tricks. It was also the scene of many Border raids, and the remains of its pele tower still rise 9m (30ft) above the farm buildings of the tiny hamlet. The stone facings near ground level have been stolen for other buildings, and the rubble masonry within is revealed. When raiders came over the border the villagers would crowd into the pele tower, first driving their cattle in on the ground floor and then retreating to the floor above up the wooden stairs. As a last resort, the stairs could be burned to prevent the raiders from reaching the villagers.

Just above Lordenshaw there is a Bronze Age camp on a spur of the hillside, at the junction of four ancient tracks. The camp is 37m (40yd) across, with the remains of the rough huts protected by a double circle of banks and ditches. The rocks around the camp bear Britain's largest collection of the strange, and unexplained, 'cup-and-ring' markings.

▶ *Rothbury is 11 miles south-west of Alnwick on the B6341. Great Tosson is 2 miles away along the marked minor road that leaves Rothbury to the south and then turns west.*

10 Holystone

An ancient holy well, an oakwood glen, an enchanted waterfall and an Iron Age hill-fort are among the delights to be discovered around the small village of Holystone. The well was a watering place for the Romans; early Christians were baptised there, so tradition claims, and this sacred association attracted Augustinian nuns to found a priory there soon after 1100. They dedicated it to St Mary the Virgin, and the well soon became known as the Lady's Well. It is still the source of fresh water for the village. A way marked half-hour walk leads to the well. It is the shortest of three Forestry Commission walks in Holystone Forest, all starting from the car park almost half a mile west of the village.

In a glade among the trees, the smooth surface of the large well, contained within its square wall, reflects the Celtic cross that was placed in the centre more than 200 years ago when the wall was repaired. At the same time, a medieval statue from Alnwick was set beside the water. The bearded, long-robed man, now half hidden by laurels, has a broken nose that gives him a curiously pugnacious look.

The longest of the walks, taking two and a half hours, follows Dove Crag Burn up to Dove Crag itself. Here the stream tumbles over a mass of rocks – a wonderful sight after a storm, but often dry in summer. There is magic in this place; local folklore tells that on summer evenings fairies, elves and goblins – perhaps the spirits of the ancient Celts – take over this spot for feasting and dancing.

The Farm Walk, which takes about an hour, leads through Campville Farm near to the two concentric earthwork ridges of an Iron Age settlement. Its earlier name was the sweeter-sounding Lanternside. Timber palisades topped the ridges 2,500 years ago, protecting the village of thatched huts.

Oakwoods are rare in Northumbria, but there is one along the Holystone Burn which used to be coppiced: the trunks were cut down to stumps from which a ring of shoots sprouted and, after several years, produced a crop of stout poles. The oak was used to make charcoal, employed as fuel for iron smelting until coke replaced it in the early 18th century. Mines also used the oak poles for pit props.

▶ *Holystone is 6 miles west of Rothbury and reached from there by the B6341, then by a minor road forking right 1 mile after Hepple.*

⑪ Coquet Head

Of all the valleys carved from the great mass of the Cheviots, Upper Coquetdale is perhaps the most exhilarating. For 12 miles or so, running west from Alwinton, a remote mountain road follows the course of the Coquet to its head, twisting and turning along the sinuous valley floor while the hills close in on either side and all signs of civilisation are left far behind. Along the way streams come to join the main artery of the Coquet, threading their way down through the moors from Shillhope Law, Barrow Law, Yearning Law, Deerbush Hill and Deel's Hill, all more than 300m (1,000ft) high. As it approaches Coquet Head the road dips to skirt around Thirl Moor, the highest of all at 558m (1,829ft).

At the head of the valley the road comes within metres of the Scottish Border at Chew Green. Here are the remains of a group of Roman marching camps which lie on Dere Street, the Roman road from York to Scotland.

The earthworks of two superimposed camps are clearly defined – one with ditches defending two enclosures and a labour camp, the other a temporary camp large enough to hold a legion of 5,300 men.

The lines of the camp show up clearly from a distance. There is a dramatic view of the layout from half a mile along Gamel's Path, up which the road swings to the south away from Chew Green. Gamel's Path was one of the meeting places for the Wardens of the Middle Marches, who vainly attempted to settle Border disputes in Tudor times. The track was also used as a smugglers' route.

Gamel's Path now leads through the vast Redesdale artillery range, which also runs all along the south side of the road from Alwinton to Chew Green. Do not stray from the road, and watch out for any signs warning of military activity in the area.

▶ *The road to Coquet Head is marked from Alwinton, which is 9 miles west of Rothbury along the B6341 and then along a signposted minor road.*

CARVED FROM THE GREAT MASS OF THE CHEVIOTS

UPPER COQUETDALE

⑫ Carter Bar

Up through Redesdale between forests and hills the A68 climbs to Scotland, slowly at first then sharply – 170m (550ft) in a mile – to reach 418m (1,371ft) and Carter Bar, the most dramatic crossing point on the Border. Behind lie the Cheviots, but spread out ahead are the green fields of the Scottish Lowlands; across them Edinburgh and the Firth of Forth, 50 miles away, are visible on a clear day. The Eildon Hills rise at Melrose, 18 miles away to the north-west.

Four miles south-east of Carter Bar the River Rede has been dammed to form Catcleugh Reservoir. Across its dam, a footpath runs for a mile beside the water then crosses the Chattlehope Burn to join a walk curving north-west through a wood to meet the reservoir again and run with it back to the road 1½ miles above the dam. The water, woods and enclosing hills make a delightful setting for the walk.

On the northern side of the valley, half a mile after the Rede re-emerges from the reservoir, a path leads from the A68 north-west through the forest to Hungry Law. The path leads on from the summit along the Border to Phillip's Cross, where a cairn stands on the old drovers' road from Scotland. Ruts worn by the cattle being driven to market still mark the ground.

▶ *Carter Bar is on the main A68, 9 miles south of Jedburgh.*

⑬ Bellingham

A small market town of less than 1,000 people, Bellingham (pronounced 'bellinjum') lies on the River North Tyne, one of Northumberland's prettiest stretches of water. Its course runs below the bare fells and across Kielder Forest Park, sometimes shaded by wooded banks and sometimes winding through lush grazing lands. Where rushing tributaries have carried stones and silt from above, large islands have formed in the river. There are delightful walks along the banks to east and west. Meadowsweet, great burnet, devil's-bit scabious, ladies' bedstraw and the melancholy thistle are among the summer's wild plants. Brown trout flicker in the glinting water, dippers bob above it, and among the trees green woodpeckers laugh and great spotted woodpeckers drum.

Three long walks into the Forest Park, all 15–20 miles, start at Bellingham and include fine views, but one of the best sights is close at hand. A footpath running north alongside the Hareshaw Burn passes the site of an old iron works, enters a wooded valley, criss-crosses the burn, and after about a mile reaches Hareshaw Linn. Here the burn slides more than 9m (30ft) down a sandstone outcrop. After heavy rain it is spectacular – but the path becomes very slippery.

▶ *Bellingham is 13 miles north-west of Hexham. Take the A6079 north from Hexham. At Low Brunton, turn on to the B6320 and follow the signposts to Bellingham.*

⑭ Kielder Water and Forest Park

This is an area of superlatives. Kielder Water is northern Europe's largest man-made lake and Kielder Forest is England's largest forest. With a 27 mile shoreline, Kielder Water shines or broods, depending on the quality of light, at the heart of the forest. The lake also provides a focus for recreational activities, especially along its southern and western shores.

Few forests have so many streams, every one providing beautiful scenery of rock and water among the trees. The Kielder Burn is a spawning ground for salmon and sea trout, and occasionally an otter shows itself. The streams are the haunt of ringed plovers, dippers, grey wagtails, goosanders, mallards and grey herons.

Even a short walk holds the promise of seeing some of the forest's shy wildlife – foxes, perhaps one of the plentiful roe deer, or possibly a red deer that has strayed over the Border from Scotland. Or maybe even a red squirrel as the forest is one of the few strongholds in England of this native British species. There are blue hares on the high, open moors, and herds of wild goats with magnificent curved horns and long coats. Farmland and moors hold kestrels, lapwings, sky larks, meadow pipits, red grouse, dunlin and golden plovers underfoot a variety of mosses, ferns and rushes thrive.

At the northern tip of Kielder Water is Kielder Castle, once a hunting lodge for the Duke of Northumberland and now a forest information centre. A number of waymarked walks and cycle trails start from here including the Duchess Trail to the Kielder Burn, and also the 12 mile Forest Drive along an unsealed forest road for which a toll is payable. This links north Tynedale with Redesdale, and crosses some of the remotest country in Northumberland as it climbs to 450m (1,500ft) at Blakehope Nick. It skirts the wild moorland of Oh Me Edge and then re-enters the forest to follow the Blakehope Burn down to the Rede just below Byrness on the A68.

▶ *Kielder Water and Forest Park lie 10 miles north-west of Bellingham, and are reached by signposted minor roads which head west from the B6320.*

⓯ Wark Forest

Wark Forest is the southern extension of Kielder Forest and lies within the Northumberland National Park. Managed by the Forestry Commission, the traditional style of planting serried rows of conifers is being broken up by stands of native broadleaves to give a more natural feel to the forest. With over 60 miles of public footpaths and 40 miles of bridleways, public access is encouraged.

The Commission has marked two delightful walking trails at Warksburn that offer a short half mile walk and a slightly longer 1½ mile stroll alongside a trickling burn, under plantations of conifers, through mixed woodland, and across meadows with views of the North Tyne Valley.

The trails start and finish near the village of Stonehaugh, which was built for the forest workers. Along much of the way the sound of water, the sweet smell of pine and the chorus of bird-song are welcome companions. Warks Burn winds through the forest, following a stone-strewn course where trout lie in the shallows.

The forest is made up mostly of Scots pine, Norway spruce and Japanese larch. Each species has its own function. Scots pine, a native of Britain, produces the timber known as red deal, while the Norway spruce is felled for Christmas trees as well as for white deal. Japanese larches, deciduous conifers, are planted along the forest roads as fire-breaks. They grow fast, and quickly suppress grasses which spread fire.

At dawn or dusk you may spot a roe deer emerging cautiously into an open glade with nose twitching and ears erect. These graceful creatures are common in this area and, although shyness keeps them largely out of sight, there is ample evidence of their presence – frayed bark on the trees where they rub the velvet from their new spring antlers, and stunted trees where they have browsed on the young shoots.

▶ *Stonehaugh is 5 miles west of Wark on the B6320, and is reached by signposted minor roads.*

⓰ Hadrian's Wall

While the Romans occupied Britain, Hadrian's Wall was their principal deterrent against invasion from the north. Across the entire width of the land, from the Tyne estuary to the Solway Firth, this impregnable barrier ran for 80 Roman miles – a little over 73 miles. It was built between AD 122 and AD 130 by order of the Emperor Hadrian after he had visited Britain and decided not to attempt to push the empire any further north.

In the absence of a natural frontier the Romans created an artificial one, running from one natural strongpoint to the next until it had spanned the country. Hadrian's Wall, stone-built in the east and turf-built in the west, became the northernmost frontier of the Roman Empire. It was manned by 5,500 cavalry and 13,000 infantry auxiliaries from all parts of the empire.

Some of the best-preserved parts of the wall run through the Northumberland National Park, between Chollerford and Gilsland. Mile after mile the grey line of stones, built to 4m (14ft) high in places, marches across the countryside with the ruins of forts, milecastles and signal turrets set along its length at regular intervals. On the northern side runs a ditch, about 8m (27ft) wide and 2.7m (9ft) deep – except where cliffs make it unnecessary. A short distance to the south lies the *vallum*, a flat-bottomed ditch about 3m (10ft) deep and 6m (20ft) wide, flanked on each side by a turf mound originally about 2m (6ft) high. The *vallum* probably served as a road, and marked the southern boundary of the military zone.

One of the best-preserved of the 17 forts is at Vercovicium, the modern Housesteads; it could garrison 1,000 infantry within its 2ha (5 acres) and was built to guard the point where the Knag Burn breaches the ridge.

At Cawfields there is a good example of a milecastle. These fortlets for about 30 men were built between the forts at every Roman mile (1,481m or 1,620yd), with two signal turrets equally spaced between them.

The Romans withdrew from the wall in AD 383, when Rome itself was under threat from invading Goths, Vandals and Huns, and troops were needed to defend the city. Eventually Rome fell, but Hadrian's Wall survived – a monument to the time when Britain was part of that great empire.

▶ *Cawfields is found on a minor road 2 miles north of Haltwhistle and just north of the B6318. Housesteads lies just off the B6318, 6 miles north-east of Haltwhistle.*

NORTHERN ENGLAND

Scotland

A land of mighty granite heights slashed through with deep, forested glens, lonely lochs and scattered remote islands, Scotland is Britain's crowning glory. The unspoilt splendour of its landscape, dotted with prehistoric sites and age-old castles, never fails to impress.

14
NORTH UIST

The SCOTTISH LOWLANDS

Stretching from the Solway Firth in the south-west, to the mouth of the Tweed and the North Sea in the north-east, the Lowlands can be found in that much-disputed territory, the Scottish Borders.

❶ The Lomond Hills

East of Loch Leven, the Lomond Hills rise above the plain of Kinross. The lie of the land here is evidence of the movement of the last Ice Age glaciers. On the side which took the brunt of the glacier's advance, the map shows the contour lines packed together. On the other side, the gradients are gentler.

The escarpment above Loch Leven, and the long hill of Benarty south of the loch, make the Lomonds, with their thermal currents and upward-sweeping winds, the finest site in Scotland for gliding. Walkers on the Lomonds should be prepared for the sudden, silent approach of a glider as it searches for height from the launching ground at Portmoak below.

Falkland and its palace, a favourite home of the Stuart kings of Scotland, lies at the foot of the northern slopes, separated from the upland moors and summits by a bank of conifer plantations. This is not the same Forest of Falkland where the Scottish kings used to hunt – that was north of the little town, on the level ground seen from East Lomond Hill, towards the course of the River Eden. The original oak forest was felled by Cromwell's troops in 1652. The year before, Charles II was the last king to stay in the palace.

The Lomond Hills are well served by footpaths. They go to both the main summits, West Lomond and East Lomond. On the rounded top of East Lomond, the view takes in not only the North Sea coast and the mountains of the Highland Line, the Moorfoots and the Lammermuirs to the south but also, on a clear day, Cairn Toul in the distant Cairngorms.

From West Lomond, all the rich farmlands around Kinross come into view. But the most spectacular sight is on the hills themselves. Almost 300m (1,000ft) lower than the summit of West Lomond is the curious Bannet Stane. Balanced on an outcrop, it seems to defy the force of gravity – a mushroom of sandstone with a slim supporting pillar. Whether caused by erosion or by some long-ago action of the glaciers is a matter of continuing debate.

▶ *The Lomond Hills lie to the south-west of Falkland, from where a minor road leads across them to Leslie. Near the summit, there is a car park, signposted Craig-mead. From it, walks lead to the East and West Lomond Hills.*

❷ Loch Leven

Many of Scotland's inland lochs have been deepened and increased in size to provide extra water supplies. But at Loch Leven, east of the old county town of Kinross in the angle between Benarty Hill and the Lomonds, exactly the opposite was done. In 1830 the River Leven, which runs from the south-east corner of the loch, was deepened and straightened, partly to regulate the essential water supplies to the paper and textile mills of towns like Leslie and Markinch. In lowering the level of the loch by 1.4m (4½ft), much of the rich alluvial soil at the edges could be drained and ploughed.

From Findatie, near the outlet from the loch, the 'new cut' of 1830 can still be seen, running dead straight from the sluices for more than 3 miles across the almost level farmlands to Auchmuirbridge, where the original course of the river takes over.

The lowering of the water level in the loch also increased the size of its six islands. On St Serf's, the biggest, is the ruined tower of a 9th-century priory. Castle Island is known for the

remains of the stronghold where Mary, Queen of Scots was imprisoned in 1567, and from which she made a daring escape in May, 1568.

The whole loch, with its 11 miles of shore, was declared a National Nature Reserve in 1964. It is one of the finest places in Scotland to see wintering ducks, geese and swans and in the summer you may even see ospreys. In the autumn, thousands of pink-footed geese gather on St Serf's and the lochside farmlands. Vane Farm, near Findatie, is an RSPB reserve, with an information centre and nature trail.

▶ *Kinross, at the western end of Loch Leven, is at the A977/A922 junction. Access to the loch shore is restricted to three places — car parks near Findatie beside the B9097 on the south side, at Burleigh Sands on the north side, and at Kirkgate Park in Kinross, from where a summertime ferry runs to Castle Island.*

❸ Cornalees

As the towns of Greenock, Port Glasgow and Gourock grew and prospered in the 19th century, they began to run short of water for their factories, mills and increasing numbers of houses. A civil engineer, Robert Thom, devised a water system based on a series of new reservoirs near Cornalees on the hilly plateau above Greenock, out of sight of the town itself.

At the heart of his scheme was the Great Reservoir. Local people from the towns called it the 'Little Caspian' but in the end it was officially named Loch Thom. Robert Thom also built the Greenock Cut, a channel that lead the water to the top of the town, and he constructed the Kelly Cut, which approached Loch Thom from the south, to bring supplies from another reservoir above Wemyss Bay. Pathways, which still survive, were built along the sides of the cuts.

In 1971 the original channels were replaced by modern tunnels. A year later, the older system was declared an ancient monument, and in 1973 a visitor centre was opened at Cornalees Bridge.

This is fresh, airy walking country, with extensive views across the Firth of Clyde to the mountains of Cowal, Ardgoil and Loch Lomond. Grey herons stalk the shallows of Loch Thom, whooper swans winter there, and buzzards and kestrels patrol the moors where red grouse live. But the real fascination is to walk alongside the cuts, now with slow-moving shallow water instead of the bustling currents of their busier days. After heavy rain, the sluice-gates are opened at Cornalees Bridge, and great foaming falls pour out into the narrow valley of the Kip Water.

A nature trail wanders deep into the heart of Shielhill Glen, where the Kip Water suddenly plunges out of the bare moorland above into a chasm of birches, ashes, oaks and rowans, one of the last remaining deciduous woodlands in this corner of the lowlands.

▶ *Cornalees is 2½ miles south of Greenock. Minor roads lead to it from Greenock, and also from the A78 at Inverkip.*

LOCH LEVEN FROM THE PAP OF GLENCOE

4 Glencorse

Sweeping south-westwards beyond the boundaries of the city of Edinburgh are the Pentland Hills. From the hamlet of Swanston, boyhood home of Robert Louis Stevenson, by the battlefield of Rullion Green and the Roman road along the eastern edge, to the hill burns and wooded reservoirs, the Pentlands are a carefully preserved natural world apart from the busy streets for which they form the skyline.

The hills are criss-crossed by walking routes, on pathways signposted for more than 120 years by the Scottish Rights of Way and Access Society. And this is genuine walking country. No public roads penetrate the lonely passes of the Maiden's Cleuch and the Cauldstane Slap, among the grassy, heathery hills with names like Allermuir, Carnethy and Caerketton.

Flotterstone, a stone inn off the Edinburgh–Biggar road, is a favourite access point to the hills. A mile from it is Glencorse Reservoir, opened in 1822 and the first one in the Pentlands to supply water to Edinburgh. But this is no tame Lowland waterway. Curving through a steep-sided valley, it is uncompromisingly Highland in aspect, an impression helped by the windswept pines along its north-eastern shore, a wooded island and the conical peak of West Kip hill above the more rounded slopes on the south-western skyline.

Where the reservoir bends, a path goes uphill across the Maiden's Cleuch, on the line of an old drovers' road, leading to Balerno village and the reservoir at Threipmuir.

▶ *Glencorse lies about 3 miles from the southernmost outskirts of Edinburgh; Flotterstone is east off the A702, 1 mile south of Easter Howgate.*

GLENCORSE RESERVOIR

❺ St Abb's Head

The highest cliffs on Scotland's eastern coast, rising to a little over 90m (300ft), are near the little fishing village of St Abb's, clustering around its harbour. North of the village, the wild coastline and the gentler landscape above the cliffs together make up the St Abb's Head National Nature Reserve, owned by the National Trust for Scotland.

St Abb's Head is the highest point of the reserve, marked by a lighthouse built in 1862. The all but inaccessible cliffs, rock stacks and inlets around it are the home, at all levels, of thousands of sea-birds. There are kittiwakes and guillemots, razorbills, fulmars and herring gulls. A few puffins breed here too. Among the sea-birds to be seen off-shore are terns, skuas and shearwaters, and gannets can often be glimpsed, cruising by on their way to and from their great nesting ground on the Bass Rock.

Perhaps the best view of the structure of this coastline is from Pettico Wick, a steep bay on the northern edge of the reserve. It marks the fault-line between the volcanic rocks of the headland and the shales and greywackes to the north.

The fault-line south-east from Pettico Wick provided a route for the melting waters of an Ice Age glacier. The narrow valley, once bog-land, was dammed in 1900 to create the Mire Loch, which now provides the reserve with a home for other than coastal birds. Grebes and moorhens nest here, and the grazing and arable lands around it attract wheatears and skylarks, stonechats and yellowhammers, and rare migrants such as wrynecks. Sheep grazing on the grasslands of the reserve keep much of the vegetation trimmed. But on the cliffs, well out of reach, there are sea campion and rose-root, vetches and lovage.

▶ *The village of St Abb's is on the B6438, 1½ miles north-east of Coldingham. Footpaths to St Abb's Head start near the church in the village.*

❻ Abbey St Bathans

Spreadeagled across the boundary of the Scottish Borders and East Lothian are the Lammermuir Hills. There is no drama in their gentle summits but they have their own almost secret and rarely visited corners.

One substantial river valley cuts through the hills, where the Whiteadder Water gathers the burns on the old Dunbar Common and then sidles down to the rich farmlands of the Merse of Berwickshire. The Whiteadder's main tributaries – the Bothwell, the Faseny, the Monynut and the Dye – provide their own lonelier valleys. Down the Faseny Water runs the course of an old 'herring road', which the people of Lauderdale followed on their way to buy winter supplies of salt herring from the fishermen of Dunbar.

Villages in this predominantly sheep-rearing landscape are few and far between. Most are on sites originally chosen to be out of sight of wandering marauders. One such village is Abbey St Bathans on the Whiteadder, downstream of the point where it is joined by the Monynut Water. A foot-bridge over the river leads up through birchwoods to an open hillside beyond. To the south-east, a fine walking route goes past Edin's Hall – the remains of an Iron Age broch. This partly reconstructed circular building, of a style more often seen in the north, has double walls, up to 5.5m (18ft) thick, that once held the rooms of a family stronghold. From the traces of earlier ditches and earthen ramparts that surround the site, this was a fortress in even more remote times than the broch-builders knew.

▶ *Abbey St Bathans is 5½ miles north of Duns. A minor road leads to the village from the B6355, which runs westwards from the A6112 at Preston.*

❼ Glentress Forest

In 1919, when the Forestry Commission came into being, one of it's first acquisitions was 405ha (1,000 acres) of land on the Haystoun estate near Peebles. This was the beginning of Glentress Forest, which today extends to more than ten times the original area on the hills around the Tweed Valley.

Glentress is made up of nearly 30 separate plantation areas. The centre of the forest is a fine sweep of hillside east of the town of Peebles, with forest walks and trails extending to a height of almost 460m (1,500ft), rising on both sides of the Glentress Burn. The higher the road or pathway, the more widely does the view open out over the rich landscape of Tweeddale.

The modern forest is made up largely of Norway and Sitka spruce, Douglas and silver firs, Scots pines, Japanese and European larch. Beech and sycamore have been planted to give variety and add to the attractions of these hillside plantations. With its variety of tree cover, Glentress attracts much wildlife. Birds range from crossbills and woodpeckers to sparrowhawks and hen harriers. In recent years, ospreys have successfully bred in the forest. There are red squirrels here, and groups of delicate roe deer can often be seen browsing in the early morning and at dusk.

▶ *The entrance to Glentress Forest is at Glentress village, off the A72, 2 miles east of Peebles.*

SCOTLAND

❽ Eildon Hills

More than 2,000 years ago, the summit of North Eildon Hill was a settlement of one of the shadowy tribes who lived in Tweeddale. Here they built a circular fort, with banks and ditches which can still be followed today. And inside that protecting circle the foundations of more than 300 stone buildings have been traced.

Then came the Romans. On the same summit they built a signal station for their great military road, now known as Dere Street, which ran from the Cheviots to the east side of the Eildons, and on to Inveresk on the Forth.

Their main fort in the Borders was on the north-east side of the hills; they called it Trimontium, after the triple peaks of the Eildon Hills. The site is marked, but nothing remains above ground. However, the village of Newstead alongside claims to be the oldest continuously inhabited settlement in Scotland.

There are footpaths to the Eildon summits, past farmlands on the lower slopes, but then more steeply over a grassy moorland with gorse, bracken and heather. The views, especially from the northern summit, are superb. Down below is the town of Melrose, with its ruined abbey where the heart of Robert Bruce is said to be buried. The Tweed winds its way by Dryburgh and St Boswells to the hazy farmlands of the Berwickshire Merse. And on the southern horizon, just as it was when Roman lookouts scanned it almost 20 centuries ago, is the line of the faraway Cheviot Hills.

▶ *The Eildon Hills rise on the southern outskirts of Melrose. The path to the summits, the Eildon Walk, starts near the old station car park on the B6359.*

❾ The Grey Mare's Tail

There are several waterfalls in south-west Scotland called the Grey Mare's Tail. By far the most impressive is the one high up in the valley of the Moffat Water, near the head of the pass which leads north-east towards St Mary's Loch and Selkirk. The summit of the pass is at the lonely house of Birkhill, once a welcome sign to drivers of horse-drawn coaches that the long haul up from Moffat was coming to an end.

Near the summit of the road the Tail Burn plunges down from Loch Skeen, far out of sight in its craggy and ice-scooped hollow to the north-west. The spurs of the eroded hillside interlock among each other, from the left bank and then from the right of the Tail Burn. A nick on the skyline marks the point where the burn begins its precipitous descent.

In the wild and lonely hill country of rough grassland, heather, bracken, rock and scree which marks the head of the Moffat Water, the Grey Mare's Tail is a suitable climax. In 1962 the fall itself, Loch Skeen and the crags which circle it passed into the possession of the National Trust for Scotland, when they bought 963ha (2,380 acres) of Birkhill Farm.

A pathway to the left of the Tail Burn leads to the foot of the waterfall. Another on the far bank rises steeply to the outflow of Loch Skeen. This is very difficult country, and great care is needed on the higher reaches because of the steep and slippery slopes.

▶ *The Grey Mare's Tail is 8 miles north-east of Moffat, on the A708.*

❿ The Lowther Hills

In the heart of the Lowther Hills stand two remote villages, Leadhills and Wanlockhead, at more than 400m (1,300ft) the highest in Scotland. The approaches to them are long and winding, climbing up from Clydesdale and Nithsdale by valleys among grassy, heathery hills managed for sheep and grouse.

In these quiet hills above the Elvan Water, the Glengonnar, the Wanlock and the Mennock, there used to be such a concentration of mineral wealth that the Lowthers were known as 'God's Treasure House in Scotland'.

Gold was once mined here but from the 18th century onwards it was lead that made the fortunes of the great Lowther landlords: Leadhills lay in the estates of the Earl of Hopetoun, and Wanlockhead on the lands of the Duke of Buccleuch. Lead-mining has finished now but at Leadhills the library founded by the miners in 1741 is still open, with extensive records and maps of the lead-mining ventures in the area from 1739 to 1854. The miners named the library after Allan Ramsay, who was born in Leadhills in 1686; he was a poet and the author of *The Gentle Shepherd*.

At Wanlockhead there is an open-air mining museum. But disregarding industrial archaeology, the Lowthers are invigorating. There are fine

WHERE THE BURN BEGINS

footpaths over the hills and through the glens, especially around the Mennock Pass. And take heart from John Taylor's memorial in the hilltop graveyard at Leadhills. After a century of working in the mines, he died at the reputed age of 137. His longevity is attributed to the fresh, clean air of the uplands.

▶ *Leadhills and Wanlockhead are 7 and 6 miles east of Sanquhar on the B797, which runs across the Lowther Hills between the A76 and the A74(M). The B7040 from Elvanfoot, which lies on the A702, also leads to Leadhills.*

⑪ Mabie Forest

South-west of Dumfries, on high ground that was once open grazing, are the conifer plantations of the Forestry Commission's Mabie Forest. On the lower slopes, around Mabie House, there were 'policy' woodlands – the Scots name for ornamental grounds.

Samples of the more exotic trees are preserved in an arboretum, including cypresses from Japan and a giant redwood from California. Around them, and away into the highest reaches of the forest, walks and trails fan out to reach a series of panoramic viewpoints.

In spring, rides among the trees are deep in bluebells. On the lower slopes there are mixed woodlands of beeches and oaks, and by the side of tumbling burns there are alders and elms. The main plantations are spruce and larch, pine and Douglas fir. They are saved from monotony by the contours of the forest, which rises in a series of hills and glens where, on gloomy days, wisps of mist trail through the trees. A water system built to drive a Victorian sawmill can still be traced. And a tiny reservoir beside one of the walks, high up on the Mabie Burn, once topped up the water tanks of Mabie House.

Five major viewpoints have been cleared along the forest trails. One is over the narrow tidal channel of the River Nith, another looks down to Mabie House, a third to the marshy coastline of the Caerlaverock Nature Reserve and a fourth south to Criffel peak. The fifth looks inland, to the long valley of Nithsdale and the northern horizon of the Lowther Hills.

▶ *Mabie Forest is 3 miles south-west of Dumfries. The road to the start of the forest walks, signposted 'Solway Forest', runs from the A710, 3 miles north of New Abbey.*

⑫ Mote of Mark

Excavations in 1913 and 1973 revealed an early settlement on Mote of Mark, a hilltop site in one of the most beautiful areas of the Solway coast, now in the care of the National Trust for Scotland. It lies between the villages of Rockcliffe and Kippford on the estuary of the Urr Water, and was probably first settled in the 5th or 6th century. There are remains of ditched fortifications here, and at one time the defences included heaped-up stones supported by timber frames. As with so many similar sites, the timber was burned, perhaps in some 7th-century attack by invading Angles, and in the intense heat the stonework vitrified.

Signs of a gateway and metal-working areas have been discovered, and excavations have brought to light examples of Celtic craftsmanship – decorated clay moulds, and bronze and iron implements. Evidence has also been found of the international trade of those early years. There were pieces of Bordeaux pottery, glass from the Rhineland, ornaments of Yorkshire jet, and iron tools forced from Lake District ore.

The splendid outlook from Mote of Mark is over a rugged coast of bays and rocky islands, plantations and natural woods, with the stately heights of Bengairn and Screel Hill across the estuary. This was once smugglers' country. In the days when French brandy, wine and lace were shipped openly to the Isle of Man, then brought by night to secret creeks and inlets on the Solway shore, White Horse Bay on the Almorness peninsula was a favourite landing place. So was Hestan Island, off the southern tip. Beyond Almorness, the view from Mote of Mark takes in the promontory of Balcary Hill, where the smugglers were so confident and so well organised that they built a mansion for their headquarters – all that remains is a ruined tower below the hill.

Between the two villages of Rockcliffe and Kippford, a maze of footpaths leads across the hillside and along the shore. On the ebb tide, you can cross the causeway known as The Rack to the bird sanctuary on Rough Island. Do not cross when tides are rising as the currents here are very fast.

▶ *Rockcliffe, the nearest village to Mote of Mark, is on a minor road which leads west from the A710, 4½ miles south of Dalbeattie.*

ITS PRECIPITOUS DESCENT

THE GREY MARE'S TAIL

A CURIOUS AND INDIVIDUAL COASTLINE
THE NATURE RESERVE AT BROW WELL

⑬ Caerlaverock

The parish of Caerlaverock is off the beaten track to the south-east of Dumfries. On the west it is bounded by the River Nith, where, near the one-time port and boat-building village of Glencaple, salmon-fishing is still carried on by haaf-netters. They wade out carrying rectangular nets on long poles, stand in line and whip the nets out of the water as salmon tumble in.

Between Glencaple and Brow Well is a curious and individual coastline – the Merse of Caerlaverock, an expanse of tidal salt-marsh. In 1957, 6 miles of it were declared a National Nature Reserve, together with some farmland and the extensive foreshore, covered and uncovered by the fast-moving, treacherous Solway tides.

A sanctuary area, administered by the Wildfowl and Wetlands Trust, it is one of the finest refuges in Britain for wintering wildfowl. All the barnacle geese which spend a brief, far-northern summer breeding on the Norwegian

Arctic island of Spitsbergen have their traditional wintering ground at Caerlaverock. Around 10,000 pink-footed geese roost on the reserve, flying inland during the day. Hundreds of greylag geese also roost here.

On the lands of Eastpark Farm, the Wildfowl Trust has erected a series of watchtowers and hides. Many of the hides are approached along roads that are bounded by high banks, so that the birds will not notice the human observers.

To the west is one of the great castles of southern Scotland. Caerlaverock Castle was built of red sandstone towards the end of the 13th century using a curious triangular ground plan. For several hundred years, its Maxwell lairds were the most powerful family in the county of Dumfries. But it was never lived in again after a siege by Covenanters in 1640.

▶ *The Caerlaverock district lies about 6 miles to the south-east of Dumfries and is reached by the B725 which skirts the east bank of the River Nith. The castle and nature reserve are south of the B725 where it turns inland.*

⑭ The Queen's Way

At the time of Queen Elizabeth II's Silver Jubilee in 1977, the Forestry Commission gave the title of the Queen's Way to the stretch of the A712 that runs through Bennan, Clatteringshaws and Kirroughtree forests.

This is far more than a landscape simply engulfed in trees. One stroll through the forest fringe beside Clatteringshaws Loch, for example, leads to the battlefield of Raploch Moss. In 1307 this was the site of one of Robert Bruce's earliest victories against the English.

The loch was created by a dam on the Black Water of Dee. The rocky course of the river below Clatteringshaws is low in water because most of the outflow is tunnelled eastwards to feed the great Kendoon hydroelectric scheme.

Among the sheltering pines by the lochside, the white house of Clatteringshaws has been turned into a visitor centre incorporating a deer museum with displays of other wildlife from the area. West of the loch, a dead-end public road heads northwards through a lonely landscape to a forest road which walkers may use to hike up through the plantations of Garraries Forest to the desolate country of the Merrick range.

Nearer at hand, off the lochside road, lower-level walking routes lead to Lillie's Loch, and along the course of the old Edinburgh–Wigtown road, used by honest travellers and smugglers alike hundreds of years ago.

A forest road which turns south off the Queen's Way is used as a public scenic drive. Called the Raiders' Road, this was a route used by the tough and troublesome cattle thieves of the 18th century – the Faas and the Marshalls. Buzzards, ravens and sparrowhawks can be seen flying overhead, while crossbills and siskins might be glimpsed among the trees.

Natural history takes over again at Brockloch Hill on the north side of the Queen's Way, where there is a red-deer range. And among the bracken and heathery crags of Craigdews Hill there is a car park on the A712 where you can get close to wild goats.

Beyond Craigdews, at Talnotry, there is a fine waterfall and the start of a network of hill and forest walks which include part of the old Edinburgh road. Relics of lead and nickel mines can be seen on the way. From the summit of Blackcraig, south by the A75, a panoramic view extends over forests and sturdy hills to Wigtown Bay and the farmlands of the Machars on the southern horizon.

▶ *The Queen's Way is part of the A712, between New Galloway and Newton Stewart. The Raiders' Road starts about 2 miles west of New Galloway.*

⑮ Glen Trool

A couple of hundred square miles of south-west Scotland make up the Galloway Forest Park. As so often in Scotland, 'park' is a very mild word for the wild and rugged landscape within its boundaries. There are mountain ranges, not simply single peaks; harsh upland lochs; and, above the tree-line, a wilderness fit only for minor expeditions, not casual strolls.

In the heart of the forest park is the almost Highland scenery of Glen Trool. Its entrance is spectacular, at the Black Linn on the Water of Minnoch. There are rapids above a bridge, and tumbling falls that foam down a winding gorge, as the Minnoch battles through plantations of larch and pine to join the Water of Trool.

Forest walks spread north and south from Glen Trool, but the public road heads eastwards up the glen until it stops high above the north shore of Loch Trool. A granite memorial, the Bruce Stone, stands on a hilltop – a magnificent viewpoint over the curving shores of the loch. Below it lie the beautifully preserved Buchan oak-woods which in past years were coppiced for commercial use. The woods are quiet now, and the only sound is of the falls of the Buchan Burn, crashing down a granite ravine among the woodlands. Opposite, forest plantations climb the steep flanks of Mulldonoch.

The Bruce Stone stands where Robert Bruce is traditionally believed to have stood one spring day in 1307, directing his men in action against the English at the Steps of Trool on the slopes of Mulldonoch on the far bank. This was at the start of his seven-year campaign to assert his position as King of Scotland, which ended with his victory over Edward II's army at Bannockburn in 1314. The Steps of Trool can still be seen today, where a burn tumbles down the steep hillside to the loch. As an English force made its way across the face of the hill, Bruce's men hurled boulders down on them, then swept down to finish the fight man to man.

North-west of the viewpoint rise the rugged crags of the Fell of Eschoncan: rock faces, scree runs and heather ledges. A footpath heads beyond it into even wilder country, towards the summit of the Merrick, at 843m (2,765ft) the highest point in the south of Scotland.

The names of the mountain features are as intriguing as the landscape: the Rig of the Jarkness, Mullwharchar, the Round Loch of the Dungeon, the Murder Hole of Loch Neldricken, Curleywee and the Range of the Awful Hand.

▶ *Glen Trool is 9 miles north of Newton Stewart. The road leading into the glen starts at Glentrool Village, on a minor road 1 mile east of the A714.*

ARGYLL and LOCH LOMOND

Where the Lowlands meet the Highlands, there lies Loch Lomond. South of its bonnie banks, the landscape is one of rolling hills and gentle pastures; to the north stand stern mountains and wild lochs.

❶ Rannoch Moor

A jigsaw of lochs, pools and meandering burns within miles and miles of soggy peat bog with hummocks of glacial debris, pine-tree roots from the original Caledonian Forest, and a surrounding ring of mountains. This is Rannoch Moor, the most famous and perhaps the wildest extent of moorland in the whole of Scotland. One of the last great Ice Age glaciers spread over Rannoch and its granite underlay, with ice flows running in all directions down the valleys and channels of pre-glacial times. The ice created the moor as it is today; the watery, jumbled wasteland draining through Loch Bà and Loch Laidon east into the River Gaur and Loch Rannoch, and eventually to the North Sea.

Roads touch only the fringes of the moor, and the railway that runs across it was built by Victorian navvies with immense difficulty, laying piles of brushwood across the bog to support the causeway. The surrounding mountains seem to emphasise the isolation. From the road between Loch Bà and Lochan na h-Achlaise, the view

westwards is to the deer-forest peaks of Clach Leathad and Stob Ghabhar, separated by one of the most striking corries in Britain, Coireach a' Ba. To the south lie the ridges of Beinn Achaladair, and to the north the bleak hills of Black Corries. And away to the east is the long vista of the heart of the moor, with the cone of Schiehallion on the horizon.

In wet and misty weather the moor is eerie, forbidding and dangerous, a misery of peat bogs and treacherous spongy ground. On a fine day, it is still a desolate, lonely place, but with a certain wild beauty. The tangled waterways are thronged with ducks, divers, dunlin, plovers, greenshank and swans, the sky rings with the singing of skylarks and the damp places twinkle with bog cotton, asphodel and tiny orchids.

▶ *The A82 between Bridge of Orchy and Glencoe crosses the western fringe of Rannoch Moor: parking near Loch Bà and picking out a short route along its southern bays is a pleasant introduction to the moor. The B846 from Tummel Bridge to Rannoch Station along the northern shore of Loch Rannoch ends on the north-eastern edge of the moor.*

❷ Inveroran

Two of the old roads over the edge of Rannoch Moor to the Black Mount converge at Inveroran, a whitewashed hotel, built about 1820. From Bridge of Orchy, on the A82, the old military route of the 1750s – now a track for walkers only – heads direct for Inveroran, over the pass of Mam Carraigh. It can also be reached by car, along a lower road by the southern shore of Loch Tulla which passes through the wood of Doire Darach, a protected remnant of the old Caledonian pine forest.

The main road to Glencoe came this way until the 1930s, when the present A82 was opened up to the east of Loch Tulla. Beyond Inveroran, a mile or so of the former road remains public, leading to the gate at Forest Lodge; beyond here stretches out the West Highland Way for walkers only, through some superb mountain scenery. The ridges and corries of the Black Mount provide a striking background to the wooded areas around Loch Tulla. It is a 9 mile hike north along the old road which eventually meets the A82, 5½ miles east of the Pass of Glencoe. There are wide-ranging views from Ba Bridge on the way – eastwards over the vast expanse of Rannoch Moor, and west to Coireach a' Bà in the heart of the Black Mount.

▶ *To reach Inveroran and Forest Lodge, turn west onto a minor road off the A82 at Bridge of Orchy.*

❸ Braes of Balquhidder

The narrow glen road beneath the soaring heights of the Braes of Balquhidder leads to some of the most striking scenery in the Central Highlands. West of Balquhidder village the road climbs high above Loch Voil, then darts down to the water's edge. Conifer plantations cover the hillsides on both banks of the loch, and there are many acres of recently planted land. But by the waterside the old natural woodland survives round little bays and curving inlets.

Separated by a narrow spit of land from Loch Voil is Loch Doine. Once the two lochs were joined together, but earth and stones washed down from the braes by the Monachyle Burn, which still forms a fine roadside waterfall, finally divided them. It is probable that at one time they were also joined to Loch Lubnaig, which lies south-east of Balquhidder village.

The public road ends before the farm of Inverlochlarig. The view ahead is magnificent, into the heart of the mountain country north of Loch Katrine and east of Loch Lomond. A lovely panorama of shapely peaks and steep-sided glens spreads out before the eye – a delight in summer, but cold and inhospitable in winter when only red deer and hardy Blackface sheep can survive.

▶ *The road to Balquhidder turns west from the A84 at Kingshouse, north of Strathyre. There is a car park and information point at Inverlochlarig.*

RANNOCH MOOR

❹ Glen Nant

In the narrow, rocky valley of the River Nant, south of Taynuilt in Argyll, two nature reserves face each other. On the east bank is a National Nature Reserve and on the other side of the river is a Forest Nature Reserve.

From 1753 to 1870 the woodlands of the forest reserve were exploited to provide charcoal for the Lorn Furnace at Bonawe, on the shore of Loch Etive. The furnace was established by a firm of ironmasters from the Furness district of Lancashire, where fuel was growing scarce. Something like 30ha (75 acres) of woodland had to be felled each year to keep it burning, but fortunately for Glen Nant the felling was carefully controlled, with woods being coppiced so that after 20 years or so there was a new crop of poles ready to be thinned once again.

Since 1870 the open oak and birch woods and mature conifer plantations of Glen Nant have been left to develop naturally, and a walk along the nature trail laid out through them shows how well they have recovered. But there are still signs of the old industry – the sites of the hearths where the charcoal was made, for instance, before being taken by packhorse to Bonawe. At Bonawe itself the furnace has been rebuilt as an industrial monument. Standing on a rise of ground between the River Nant and the River Awe, the furnace, the casting house and the storage sheds look exactly as they did in 1753. Kelly's Pier, by contrast, where pig-iron was shipped in and cast-iron out, is in ruins. And its old, unofficial importance to smugglers – excise men once snatched 34 casks of brandy hidden there – is no more than a memory.

A different industry exploits the natural resources of the district today – the hidden hydroelectric scheme buried deep in the heart of Ben Cruachan. It causes sudden fluctuations in the level of the River Awe. But herons still hunt their prey along the river mouth, and the mountain and lochside scenery is still as marvellous as it has always been, and so far remains untroubled by industry.
▶ *Glen Nant is reached by the B845, which turns south off the A85 on the east side of Taynuilt. A bridge on the west side of the B845, about 2 miles on from Taynuilt, leads to the forest trail. To reach Bonawe Furnace, follow the signposts from the crossroads in Taynuilt.*

❺ Inverliever Forest

Inverliever Forest is the oldest state-owned forest in Argyll; planting was begun by the Office of Woods in 1908, before the Forestry Commission had been established. Some 36 of its 78 sq miles are tree-covered. In the forest there are many lochans (small lochs), burns, glens, forest roads and tracks; there are Loch Avich and Loch Nant and 17 miles of the shore of Loch Awe; there is a crannog, a long-ago loch dwelling linked by a causeway to the shore; there is the River Avich, draining Loch Avich to Loch Awe and one of the shortest rivers in Scotland; and there is a ruined settlement called Newyork, a relic of the York Timber Company of London, which took over many forfeited estates after the Jacobite rising of 1715. There are also eight forest walks and cycle trails, most of them in the plantations rising high on the western hills, or down by the loch shore. In places the trees have been cleared to provide breathtaking views along the meandering course of Loch Awe.

Lurking among the shadows of the woods there are red deer and roe deer, badgers and, on rare occasions, wildcats. Buzzards, kestrels, sparrowhawks and even golden eagles circle overhead, and in the forest jays, crossbills and woodpeckers are common. Probably the strangest sight on the open moorland is the 'lek' – the spring courtship display of black grouse.
▶ *The Ford-to-Kilchrenan road along the west side of Loch Awe gives access to all the Inverliever Forest walks. The forest office is in Dalavich, 1 mile south of the junction of the Kilchrenan and Kilmelford roads.*

❻ Ardgoil

Once this mountainous triangle of land lying between Loch Long and Loch Goil was on the route used by the Earls and Dukes of Argyll, when they needed to move quickly from their stronghold at Inveraray to the Lowlands without crossing hostile clan territory. They would be ferried across Loch Fyne and then ride to Lochgoilhead. Here a half-secret track, much of which can still be traced, once lead to Mark, on the west shore of Loch Long, and a ferry across to Portincaple, in the Lowlands.

The Helensburgh to Arrochar road above Portincaple still offers one of the most striking views of this wild region; across the shimmering

LURKING AMONG THE

waters of the loch the mountains climb towards the sky, reaching as high as 761m (2,497ft) at the summit of Cnoc Coinnich – evidence that the rugged Highlands are close at hand. Many of the hillsides are forested, for the estate has belonged to the Forestry Commission for many years and is now part of the Argyll Forest Park. Some of the oldest woods stand along the shore of Loch Long, from Coilessan to Mark. There are oaks and birches, hazels and rowans, with the conifer plantations soaring above. Off the rugged shore, wild duck gather in winter, and grey herons patrol all year.

Although several of the gravelled forest tracks head southwards, there is no reasonable route round the tip of the peninsula. But the main forest track from Coilessan ends at a splendid viewpoint, backed by rock and overlooking the meeting of the two lochs. At this point, the track has already passed the bare hillside below Corran Lochan, about 260m (850ft) above the sea. Experienced hill walkers leave the path here to head north through a pass leading to the head of Loch Goil – the pass once used by the Dukes of Argyll.

▶ *Walking routes in Ardgoil start at Ardgartan on the A83; near the western end of the B828 near Lochgoilhead; at the foot of Glen Croe; and at Lochgoilhead itself.*

❼ Inversnaid

The lonely farm called Garrison of Inversnaid, which looks down on Loch Lomond, once belonged to Rob Roy; but his house there was destroyed in 1712, and the government built a garrison fort instead, to keep the MacGregors in check after the first Jacobite rising. Across a bridge beyond the church, above the ravine of the Snaid Burn, there is a splendid viewpoint looking out to the shapely peaks of the 'Arrochar Alps' – Narnain, Beinn Ime, Ben Vorlich and Ben Vane – across the narrows of Loch Lomond.

From the hilltop the road plunges towards the loch, to the Victorian hotel, the tiny harbour and the steamer pier. In Victorian times, parties of tourists used to come here in coaches-and-four, keeping the brake hard on down the steep and winding hill. Above the toy-town-like harbour, a lovely waterfall pounds over a rock step to a dark pool below. A foot-bridge across

the fall leads on to the West Highland Way to Rowardennan, seven hard but beautiful miles south beside the loch.

▶ *Inversnaid can be reached along the B829 from Aberfoyle, taking the left turn at the T-junction at the east end of Loch Arklet. Walkers can come from north or south along the West Highland Way.*

❽ Loch Katrine

The Trossachs is the name now used to describe most of the splendid landscape of mountains, lochs and forests west of Callander and north of Aberfoyle. But to Sir Walter Scott, whose poem 'The Lady of the Lake' made the district famous, it meant the tangle of hills and woodlands around the pass between Loch Achray and Loch Katrine. It was also the country of the outlaw Rob Roy, who was born at Glengyle, a farm on the far north-west corner of Loch Katrine.

The rustic Trossachs Pier is the most accessible point on the beautifully wooded lochside. This is the base for the turn-of-the-century steamer *Sir Walter Scott*, which makes summer cruises on the loch.

The road beyond Trossachs Pier, which follows the north side of the loch, is restricted to pedestrians and cyclists. Beyond Glengyle it curves round the head of the loch and turns back along the south side to Stronachlachar. Motorists can reach there by a much more roundabout route, which doubles back by Aberfoyle, Loch Ard and Loch Chon.

In spite of its remoteness, Stronachlachar is no quaint Highland clachan, but a flamboyant display of Victorian architecture set among wooded headlands, pines and rhododendrons. It was built by the Corporation of the City of Glasgow, when the loch was made the city's main reservoir. Royal Cottage, to the east of Stronachlachar, is where Queen Victoria stayed when she came to open the mighty water scheme in 1859. Ornamental milestones can still be seen along the Stronachlachar road, marking the royal route.

A fine summer excursion is to walk or cycle from Trossachs Pier along the private road by Glengyle to Stronachlachar, and then take the *Sir Walter Scott* for the return journey.

▶ *Trossachs Pier lies on the A821, 9 miles west from Callander or 4 miles north from Aberfoyle.*

SHADOWS OF THE WOODS
INVERLIEVER FOREST

SCOTLAND

❾ Achray Forest

At the village of Aberfoyle there is a sudden and dramatic change in the landscape, because this is one of the gateways to the Highlands, built exactly on the geological dividing line known as the Highland Boundary Fault. The approach from the south is through undulating farmland, but immediately behind the village rise the steep, wooded slopes of the Menteith Hills and the rugged outliers of Ben Venue. Here, in the hills, the finest viewpoints, woodlands, rivers and lochs fall within the bounds of Achray Forest, part of the Queen Elizabeth Forest Park.

Waymarked forest trails start from the David Marshall Lodge, the park information centre on a summit directly above Aberfoyle. The lodge itself is a splendid viewpoint, with an outlook extending for miles to the south, across the lower-lying Loch Ard Forest. The view also takes in the scattered plantations on the former bogland of Flanders Moss, around the winding course of the River Forth. Looking at the landscape, mostly rich, black farming country, it is hard to believe that only 200 years ago it was a vast wilderness of peat bog.

A spectacular route over the Duke's Pass, called the Duke's Road, splits Achray Forest from north to south. The original toll-road was built in 1820 by the Duke of Montrose, partly to cope with the flood of visitors attracted to the district where Sir Walter Scott's novel *Rob Roy* and his epic poem 'The Lady of the Lake' were set. The Forestry Commission bought the lands of what is now Achray Forest in 1931, and only then was the road transferred to public ownership. Now it is the twisting, swooping A821, which leads past picnic areas and forest trails.

It passes the entrance to the old Aberfoyle slate quarry, closed in 1958 and now a fascinating relic of the area's industrial past. It also leads to a forest drive, open from March to October. The drive winds for 7 miles through the plantations, to information areas, walks and viewpoints, including Larch Point, Pine Ridge, Spruce Glen and Birch Bay. Some of these are above the shore of Loch Drunkie which, before the drive was opened, was only visible to motorists as a glint of water in the heart of the forest. A nearby mansion used to have the same name as the loch, until just before Queen Victoria was due to visit it, when it was discreetly re-christened Invertrossachs House.

▶ *Aberfoyle is on the A821, off the A81 north of Glasgow. Follow the A821 through the village for the start of the Duke's Road. The David Marshall Lodge, where there is parking, is ½ mile up this road.*

❿ Loch Ard Forest

Since the 18th century, commercial woodlands have covered the lower slopes of this splendid sweep of country, from the shores of Loch Lomond to the heart of the Trossachs. The trees planted in the early days were mostly oak, ash, alder and birch. In 1928, the Forestry Commission started buying land in this area; now commercial plantations of spruce, pine and larch have largely taken the place of the older woodlands. In 1953, at the time of the Coronation, the Queen Elizabeth Forest Park was created, with Loch Ard as part of it.

There are walks and trails on forest paths and roads, and some longer routes lead westwards to Ben Lomond and Rowardennan. There are intimate corners of the forest: a footbridge makes the mighty leap from the Lowlands to the Highlands, for the burn it crosses marks the line of the Highland Boundary Fault. By the sparkling Duchray Water are the ruins of the township of Daldannet, deserted two centuries ago when the land was taken from the crofters to make way for sheep farming.

Wildlife is abundant in the forest. At Lochan Spling, near the forest's northern edge, there are goosanders, red-breasted mergansers, moorhens, coots, swans and grebes; elsewhere roe deer and red deer may be seen, as well as stoats, foxes, weasels, otters and, just possibly, a solitary hunting mountain burns, can be bitterly cold even on a summer's day. Glenmore is also the home of Britain's only herd of reindeer, introduced from Lapland in 1952, who can be seen browsing on the lichen higher up.

For hill-walkers, Glenmore is a paradise. They can follow the tracks on which old-time cattle thieves hustled their stolen herds through the Pass of Ryvoan to Nethy Bridge. Or hike to Glen Einich and its loch in a scooped-out glacial hollow. Or attempt an expedition through Lairig Ghru, a high and formidable mountain pass, often buffeted by piercing winds.

▶ *Loch Morlich, in the heart of Glenmore Forest Park, is 5 miles east of Aviemore. The road into the forest starts from the B970, 2 miles east of Aviemore.*

❼ Loch an Eilein

In the heart of Rothiemurchus, a district once completely covered by the Caledonian pine forest, lies Loch an Eilein. Although most of the ancient forest has long since been felled, natural woodland of tall Scots pines surrounds the loch, with the wall of the Cairngorm plateau soaring up beyond.

Milton Burn, which drains the loch, still has the remains of a stone dam across it. This was once used to control the level of the water as felled pine logs were floated downstream to saw-mills closer to the Spey. Many of the trees were cut down during the two World Wars, but now Scottish Natural Heritage is trying to preserve the woods round Loch an Eilein. The conifers provide food for a varied wildlife: both red squirrels and crossbills feed on the seeds.

In this natural woodland, roe deer and foxes may be glimpsed by early morning visitors. Goldcrests, the smallest of British birds, are often seen among the trees on the northern shore. Grey herons fish on the margins of the loch, standing motionless for long minutes, observing the water and their selected prey before that final downward dart. Mallards, wigeons, tufted ducks, goldeneyes, red-breasted mergansers and whooper swans are here in their season. Ospreys sometimes swoop over the loch, snatching up fish with their talons.

Until 1899 ospreys nested at Loch an Eilein, on the ruined 15th-century castle on the island which gives the loch its Gaelic name. But the nest was repeatedly plundered, and the birds were hunted out of the district. Those seen at Loch an Eilein nowadays come from nesting places elsewhere, and the ruin of the castle now provides a haunt for jackdaws.

▶ *Loch an Eilein is 2 miles south of Aviemore, and is reached by a road running south-east from the B970.*

A HIGH AND FORMIDABLE MOUNTAIN PASS
LAIRIG GHRU

WOODLAND NEAR GANNOCHY BRIDGE

❽ Creag Far-leitire

Pine and birch, heather moors and lochs, rocky crags and distant mountains are at the heart of many Highland views. But they are rarely gathered together in so small a compass as at Creag Far-leitire, which lies in the heart of Inshriach Forest.

Creag Far-leitire is a little ridge pointing north-west and south-east, against the usual run of landforms in this area. The ridge rises from woods of pine and birch, and carpets of heather. There are old Scots pine trees, well spaced out, as well as denser, younger woods. From the summit, Inshriach Forest lies spread out, and there is a long view north-east down the Spey Valley.

Just to the north is Loch Insh, marking the end of the marshy country through which the Spey meanders on its way from Kingussie to Kincraig. East and south-east the view is to the mountain wall on the far side of Glen Feshie, marking the start of the main Cairngorm range. This is fine country for walkers and climbers, with farmland on the valley floor, forests rising on either side, and deer-stalking grounds in the wild and lonely corries above.

A far different landscape from this nestles at the south-east end of the Creag Far-leitire ridge. Set among open heather moors, ringed by pines and birches, lie Uath Lochan and the three smaller Rock Wood Ponds. Crossbills, goldcrests and treecreepers nest in the deeper woodland.

The moors attract grouse, curlews, meadow pipits, whinchats, redpolls and willow warblers. The woodland edges are home to black grouse and sparrowhawks. Above the crags, golden eagles and buzzards hunt.

To complete the amazing variety of landscape, a half-hidden alleyway through the woodland leads to a hide where wigeon, teal and goldeneye can be seen on Uath Lochan, with tufted duck on the reed-beds.

▶ *Creag Far-leitire is on the B970, 5 miles east of Kingussie. A road signposted to Glen Feshie leaves the B970 southwards at Fair, and just over 1 mile along this road is the entrance to the Forestry Commission's car park for Rock Wood Ponds.*

❾ Morrone

On Upper Deeside, the woods are mostly of old Scots pine. But at Morrone, the hill rising above Braemar in the angle between the River Dee and the Clunie Water, there is one of the most fascinating birkwoods, or birchwoods, in Scotland. The trees are not the tall, upstanding birches of lower ground. Close to the upper limit of tree growth in the Highlands, they are gnarled and twisted, scattered over the hillside. Under their shelter is a carpet of juniper, which in its turn protects a great variety of tiny alpine plants.

Constant heavy grazing by deer and sheep reduced the birkwood in quality and extent and in 1978 the Nature Conservancy (now Scottish

Natural Heritage) fenced off large areas to protect them from the depredations of red and roe deer. However, there are still many tracks and pathways open. One of them winds up to a view indicator set in place by the Deeside Field Club. Although on the hill's lower slopes, it identifies the dramatic view towards the main range of the Cairngorms. Three of Britain's loftiest peaks, which reach more than 1,200m (4,000ft), are visible: Ben Macdui, Braeriach and Cairn Toul.

Morrone itself is 859m (2,819ft) high, and a stiff walk leads all the way to its summit. Clouds and mist can descend suddenly, so do not start the walk if the weather is doubtful. Avoid it also during the grouse-shooting season, from August 12 to December 10.

Eastwards from the view indicator the track passes behind one of the buildings of the farm of Tomintoul, some of whose fields at over 425m (1,400ft) are reckoned to be the highest cultivated land in Britain. On the right, a pathway marked by cairns heads uphill over grass and heather moors to the summit of Morrone and its ever-widening panorama of the Cairngorms and the Forest of Mar.

▶ *Braemar is on the A93, 15 miles west of Ballater. Morrone is to the south-west of Braemar, and the path to the summit starts from a car park in Chapel Brae.*

⑩ Glen Esk

Of all the valleys which slice into the south-eastern Grampians, the one with the grandest yet most unexpected entrance is Glen Esk. Let into a wall beside Gannochy Bridge on the road from Edzell to Fettercairn there is a wooden door. Open it, and from the neatly farmed and forested country around Edzell you are suddenly plunged into a landscape of cliffs, whirlpools, cascades and weird rock formations.

This is where the North Esk has gouged its way through the sandstone along the Highland Boundary Fault. For just over a mile a dramatic pathway above the east bank, planted with trees 200 years ago to relieve the harsh rock formations, keeps pace with the natural sculpture of the Loups of Esk and the Rocks of Solitude. Eventually, this pathway joins the public road which matches the river's windings until it ends at remote Loch Lee and the ruined 16th-century tower of Invermark.

Glen Esk was once a centre for mining but there was also another lucrative and more secret trade. In little settlements, now all but disappeared, whisky was produced in illicit stills. Glen Esk is still crossed by the route of an old whisky road, along which smugglers took the tax-free spirit to the Lowlands.

North-west of Invermark stands a monument in the shape of an imperial crown, almost 6m (20ft) high, that marks a spring where Queen Victoria paused during a pony expedition in 1861. St Andrew's Tower lies 2½ miles south-east of Tarfside on a hidden stretch of the old Glen Esk road, out of sight of the modern route. It was built in 1826 as a shelter for travellers.

▶ *Gannochy Bridge is 1 mile north of Edzell on the B966. The doorway to the riverside path is on the north side of the bridge, and just beyond it a minor road leads north-westwards and follows the river to Invermark and Loch Lee.*

⑪ Cairn o' Mount

One of the all-but-forgotten place-names of Scotland is The Mounth, denoting the great hill-mass running eastwards from the Pass of Drumochter to the plains of Strathmore. Ancient rights of way like the Fir Mounth and the Tolmounth preserve the name. But the most familiar now is the Cairnamounth, which appears on today's maps as Cairn o' Mount.

This is the only one of the old routes which has become a modern through-road, sweeping steeply up from Fettercairn to a summit at 455m (1,488ft), before continuing its hard-fought way north to Deeside. At the summit, a rocky cairn is a splendid viewpoint over two entirely different landscapes. To the north and west is the genuine Mounth, a land of empty hills and secret glens, but in other directions there is much softer country. To the north-east lie the rounded heather moors of Kerloch. Eastwards, Drumtochty Forest sweeps down to Strath Finella, and beyond spread the fields around Drumlithie and Glenbervie. South-east of the summit is the grassy ridge of Strathfinella Hill, while to the south stretches the rich arable land of the Howe of the Mearns.

Cairn o' Mount can suffer from savage weather. Snow poles along the roadside, and fences above it to catch the drifting snow, show that this is a far harder landscape than the settled farmlands in the plains below.

The Mounth hills are mainly rounded but one sturdy exception, to the north-west, is Clachnaben – literally, 'the Stone on the Mountain' – whose summit is a sudden granite tor. It can be identified by a curious notch in the ridge, as it falls away to the east. There are grouse moors at Cairn o' Mount and outside the shooting season, from August 12 to December 10, Clachnaben may be climbed from Glen Dye, the first main valley north of Cairn o' Mount.

▶ *Cairn o' Mount is 10 miles south of Banchory, and lies on the western side of the B974.*

SCOTLAND

⑫ Glen Clova

With seemingly outlandish names like Mayarand Driesh, Cairn Inks and the Shank of Drumfollow, the mountains at the head of Glen Clova lose none of their remote wildness by being clothed with man-made forest on their lower slopes. As the glen marches into the heart of the mountains, so it narrows, steepens and becomes a far different place from the lushly wooded arable country which it leaves behind on the fertile plain of Strathmore.

Beyond Clova, the village of the glen, the hillsides begin to close in. Bare rocky crags and fallen boulders loom over the road, and individual peaks dominate the skyline ahead.

At its head, the glen splits into two much narrower valleys, each of them containing an old drove road – today these tracks are open only to walkers. One road, the Tolmounth, goes north-west over the hills to Braemar; the other, Capel Mounth, heads northwards, passing through Glen Muick, to Ballater.

There are low and high-level ways to explore the head of the glen. Walks along the old drove roads give an idea of the wild hill country around, country which is not to be tackled lightly or by inexperienced walkers. Forest walks through Glen Doll are towered over by cliffs and scree-runs, as they amble through Scots pine and Japanese larch.

For botanists, the hillsides of Glen Clova and Glen Doll are most rewarding research grounds. One of the first to realise this was a Forfar gardener, George Don, the author of Herbarium Britannicum, published in 1804. For 30 years at the turn of the 18th and 19th centuries Don combed the Clova area and other Scottish mountains, recording rarity after rarity, from hawkweeds and saxifrages to tiny mountain bog sedge and russet sedge.

In 1650 the glen was the scene of the so-called 'Start' – an abortive attempt by Charles II to escape from the Presbyterians who were demanding too many concessions from him in return for their support. He arranged a rendezvous with Royalist chiefs at Glen Clova, but they failed to appear; in their stead there arrived a troop of Presbyterian horse who returned him to their headquarters at Perth.

The mountain tops above Glen Clova, despite their often spiky appearance, lead on to a high grassy tableland well out of sight of travellers in the valley below – the country of red deer, wildcat and ptarmigan.

▶ *The southern end of Glen Clova lies 7 miles north of Kirriemuir. The B955 runs on both sides of the glen, following the River South Esk, as far as Clova.*

⑬ Loch Faskally

One of Scotland's newest lochs is Loch Faskally, formed in 1950 when a dam was built across the narrow gorge of the River Tummel at Pitlochry for a hydroelectric power station. The loch winds between wooded banks, each curving section hidden from the next, with pathways for most of its length.

Faskally Woods on the eastern shore are a blaze of varied colours in autumn, and throughout the year the woodland paths are full of interest. Lime, elm, ash and sycamore, beech and gean – wild cherry – Douglas fir and Silver fir, rhododendron, pine and birch have all been preserved by the Forestry Commission; some of the specimens are more than 200 years old. In the heart of the woods lies little Loch Dunmore, its surface dappled with water-lilies. The loch was created as part of a woodland garden more than a century ago.

On the west shore, beside the road from Logierait to Foss, there are birchwoods along the winding banks. And at the northern end, where the River Garry joins the Tummel and their combined waters feed the loch, is a forest nature trail. Part of the trail crosses the Bonskeid estate, where there is a fine specimen of Douglas fir – the species introduced into Britain in 1828 by David Douglas of Perth.

Once called the Falls, this place has been known as the Linn of Tummel since construction of the hydroelectric complex. Dippers and grey wagtails can be seen, and there are roe deer and capercaillies in the higher woodlands.

Greylag geese, wigeon and goldeneye winter on the loch, and Faskally is a noted place for salmon and trout. A special fish ladder, with 34 pools, allows salmon to fight upwards to their ancient spawning grounds past the dam which closes the southern end.

▶ *Pitlochry is 24 miles north-west of Perth. The A9 bypasses the town and crosses Loch Faskally.*

⑭ Queen's View

In her travels around the Highlands, Queen Victoria stopped to admire many a splendid view. The most famous Queen's View is above Loch Tummel, on a knoll looking westwards to the cone of Schiehallion, 1,083m (3,553ft) high but not at all a mountain in the rock-climber's sense of the word. Beyond it the view stretches away to the wild lands of Rannoch.

The modern view is not the same as the one the Queen admired. She looked down on a Loch Tummel only half the size it is today. The valley was flooded in 1950 as part of a scheme to

THE VIEW STRETCHES AWAY TO THE WILD LANDS

LOCH TUMMEL FROM QUEEN'S VIEW

create hydroelectric power, and the loch extended by some 4 miles, so the little wooded islands below the viewpoint are actually the tops of former hills.

Above the Queen's View, the bare hillside was planted with trees in 1948. And that view is repeated, from higher levels, at several places on the Allean Forest walks. The walks curl upwards through plantations mainly of pine and spruce trees, but there are stands of larch, as well, brightening up the autumn forest.

One forest road cuts through a partly restored clachan, or hamlet, whose inhabitants used to eke out a bare living on this windy hillside long before the forest came. So remote and tiny was this place, with only three houses, that there is no definite record of its occupants or even of its name. It may have been Tombuie.

Whatever it was called; and whoever originally lived here, in one of the periods of occupation the thick-walled stone cottage now known simply as House I was used for carding fleeces and dyeing wool. An old corn-drying kiln alongside was converted to burn limestone for fertiliser. The clachan was probably lived in, and crops were grown in its tiny walled-off fields in the early 18th century. This miniature but self-contained and self-sufficient community has been deserted for at least 175 years. At another site beside one of the forest roads stand the ruins of a far more ancient building – a ring-fort used for defence by even more remote Highlanders 1,000 years ago.

▶ *Queen's View is on the B8019, 6 miles west of Pitlochry. The car park for the Allean Forest walks is about 1 mile further west along the B8019.*

SCOTLAND

⓳ Black Wood of Rannoch

In the Black Wood of Rannoch, 'black' means dark, for this is a pinewood rather than one of oak or birch. It is one of the original stretches of the great Caledonian Forest which once smothered most of the Highlands. It sweeps up from the south shore of Loch Rannoch, a defiant survivor of centuries of exploitation. Once it was the home of hunted outlaws and desperadoes. Then, burning, cutting and overgrazing reduced it relentlessly in size.

The wood was used by many: there were illicit whisky stills far out of reach of the Revenue men; there were charcoal burners; and splinters of Rannoch pine had a vogue as torches. Deer browsed off the young shoots, and crofters put their cattle and sheep to graze here in summer, having burned off old growth in the spring to bring on fresh green grass.

Early in the 19th century the owners sold the trees of the Black Wood to a timber company. Canals and sluices were built in the higher reaches. Stacked behind dams, logs would be released to plunge down wooden ramps, up to a mile long, into the waters of the loch. Only the financial failure of the company stopped the entire Black Wood from being felled.

In the First World War, it again narrowly escaped being obliterated. And in the Second World War, the Canadian Forestry Corps felled the central and southern parts of the wood. When bought by the Forestry Commission in 1947, the old and almost exhausted woodland harboured a miserable stock.

The square-mile heart of the original Black Wood is now a forest reserve, fenced off and being rejuvenated. To the east of it, in the modern Rannoch Forest, a series of low and high-level walks head into the hills from the rocks and falls of the Carie Burn.

There are fine views of the Black Wood and over the loch. Old stands of pine and birch mingle with more recent spruce and larch, Scots and Lodgepole pine. In the heart of the forest, treecreepers and crossbills, black grouse and owls, and bird as different in size as the tiny goldcrest and that huge grouse, the capercaillie, find their food. Jays and woodpeckers, wrens and chaffinches throng the woodland edge. Deer are not encouraged, but foxes prowl the area, red squirrels race up and down the pines, and in remote corners wildcats still have their dens.

▶ *The Black Wood of Rannoch is beside the minor road on the south side of Loch Rannoch, between Kinloch Rannoch and Bridge of Gaur. There is a Forestry Commission car park at Carie, with access to the forest, about 3½ miles west of Kinloch Rannoch.*

⓰ Glen Lyon

The longest glen in Scotland – more than 30 miles of it – is Glen Lyon. And yet from the village of Fortingall at its entrance it is invisible. Fortingall itself is a curious place. Many of its houses are thatched, to an English pattern. In the churchyard is a gnarled and twisted yew, thought to be little less than 1,500 years old and one of the oldest living trees in Britain. A persistent legend claims that Fortingall was the birthplace of Pontius Pilate, when his father was a Roman emissary to one of the Pictish kings.

West of the village, Glen Lyon sneaks into the mountains by a narrow pass, curling through what looks like an impossible gap between the bulk of the Culdares Hills and the steep slopes of Creag Mhor. At one point in the rocky ravine is MacGregor's Leap, recalling an incident in the fierce days of the 16th century when the rebellious young Gregor MacGregor, an ancestor of Rob Roy, flung himself to safety on the far bank with his pursuers' bloodhounds baying at his heels.

Stories like this, and from a much earlier time, stalk you through Glen Lyon. There are ruined castles, standing stones and weird relics of the past, with Gaelic legends spun around them. It was the heart of the land of the Picts, and later a hunting ground of the Scottish kings.

Chesthill, in the lower part of the glen looking across at a fine waterfall, was the last property on his ancestral estates occupied by Robert Campbell of Glenlyon, the feckless and drunken 17th-century laird who led his clansmen at the massacre of Glencoe.

There are memories, too, of a gentler soul – St Adamnan, who had a chapel here. In 664, so the story goes, he stopped a plague by enticing it into a stone. The stone is still to be seen, although, like so many features of Glen Lyon's shadowy past, it lies little regarded by the roadside near Camusvrachan.

▶ *Fortingall is 8 miles west of Aberfeldy. It is reached by minor roads from the A827 or the B846. A minor road to the west of Fortingall leads north then west into Glen Lyon and follows the River Lyon to Loch Lyon at the end of the glen.*

⓱ Ben Lawers

The highest mountain in Scotland south of Ben Nevis is Ben Lawers, sweeping up to 1,214m (3,984ft) on the north side of Loch Tay. Almost all the south side of the mountain, up to the summit ridge, belongs to the National Trust for Scotland. It is open to the public even during deer-stalking season, when other parts of the hill can be hazardous for thoughtless wanderers.

A visitor centre has been built beside the public road over the Pass of Lochan na Lairige, which separates Ben Lawers from the Tarmachan range to the west. The view takes in the sweep of mountain country west and south.

At Ben Lawers the hillside is grassy, in contrast to the heather-covered slopes of less-fertile hills. At one time there was a forest on the middle slopes, but burning and overgrazing through the centuries left the hillside bare. Below the Trust property, conifers have been replanted. Above them, right to the summit, grows a profusion of alpine flowers. This is a National Nature Reserve, and its catalogue of plants includes alpine lady's mantle and alpine meadow rue, yellow saxifrage and mountain male fern. At different levels and in different habitats – gorges, exposed grasslands, springs, cliffs and bogs – Ben Lawers has a bewildering mixture of plants. The National Trust for Scotland offers walks to discover the animal and plant life.

▶ *The south side of Ben Lawers is traversed by the A827, and 4 miles north-east of Killin a road leads from Edramucky to the Ben Lawers Visitor Centre.*

⓲ Birks of Aberfeldy

The depths and heights of this narrow and heavily wooded ravine are startling. There are steepish pathways on both sides of the Urlar Burn. Tackle them in the direction suggested by a nature trail laid out up the northern side of the ravine and down the other side.

The uphill path leads through beech, birch, hazel, oak and alder. On the hillside to the right you may catch a glimpse of roe deer. Red squirrels dart among the trees, which provide food and nesting sites for finches, tits, warblers and other birds.

The falls are little more than a muffled rumble until a point high up the ravine where the pathway turns to the other bank. The footbridge is directly above the upper falls; there the river pours over rock slabs, then hurtles over the dizzy drop into deep pools far below.

All the way down the other side of the ravine, the sound of crashing waters is ever present. It disguises until the last possible moment one of the surprises of the eastern wall of the Moness glen – a series of tributary burns with their own smaller falls, pouring down in lacy patterns, or over natural steps of rock, down to the hidden depths of the ravine.

Robert Burns came here in August 1787. He sat on a stone seat, still at the side of the downward path today, and afterwards composed the lilting verse of 'The Birks o' Aberfeldy'. Captious critics, perhaps misled by the varied

woodland cover here, have sometimes claimed that he made a mistake; there were no birks, or birches, at Aberfeldy. Did he mix it up with Abergeldie on Deeside? But a farmer-poet, son of the gardener on a wooded estate, would know his trees. And there are birks at Aberfeldy yet.

▶ *Aberfeldy is at the A826/A827 junction, 20 miles north of Crieff. The car park for the nature trail is by the river bridge on the A826, south of the town.*

⓳ Loch of Lowes

Between Dunkeld and Coupar Angus, there lies a string of little lochs unsuspected by casual passers-by. Even the names are unfamiliar: Butterstone and Clunie, Drumellie and Fingask. They stand mostly behind a screen of trees or just far enough away from the public roads not to be noticed.

But one of them, the Loch of Lowes, is a reserve of the Scottish Wildlife Trust. Lowes is an unobtrusive loch, for all its fascination to naturalists. Its southern shore is fringed by oak and beech, sycamore and alder, pine and birch. The reserve includes the whole of the loch, this screen of woodland, and the reed-beds in the western bay. Outside the reserve area, but just to the north-west behind more woodlands, is the Loch of Craiglush. A small canal was dug between the two lochs early last century, in a miscalculated attempt to drain the marshy land for cultivation. But there is no fall of water, and so the marshland remains.

Bought by the Scottish Wildlife Trust in 1969, Lowes provided its first surprise very soon after that when ospreys nested near the west bay. An observation hide and visitors' centre were set up there, but perhaps the greatest attraction of the reserve is its opportunity for informal viewing. Lay-bys along the public road on the southern shore lead to several splendid viewing areas by the water's edge. One especially beautiful time is on a calm morning with early mist clearing slowly from the loch.

The reed-beds are favourite nesting places for grebes, coots and dabchicks. Tufted duck, goldeneye, goosander, red-breasted merganser, wigeon, mallard, teal and great-crested grebe are there all the year round, and great flocks of greylags roost in the autumn and winter.

Among the woods, siskins and redpolls feed on the birch and alder seeds in autumn and winter. Willow warblers, spotted flycatchers, wrens and treecreepers prey on the rich insect life of the woodland fringe. Look out for otters around the loch and deer in the woods.

▶ *Loch of Lowes is 1 mile north-east of Dunkeld, and is reached by a road leading east from the A923.*

SCOTLAND

Making tracks

Scotland is alive with wildlife and animal-tracking is an ideal way to enjoy it and see more of the incredible landscape.

Duncan Macdonald kneels in the snow with his nose just above a set of paw prints. 'Otter,' he pronounces. 'Not more than a couple of hours old. See how the toes are rounded, and the back foot has come down right on top of the front foot's print? That's very characteristic of an otter.' He points to the continuous groove forming a channel between the left and right footprints. 'That's where its tail has dragged through the snow. Let's see if we can find its spraints, shall we? Black and sort of slimy, with a strong smell of new-mown hay.'

Snow has swept across the north of Scotland overnight, whitening the rounded flanks of the Monadhliath Mountains and powdering the farms and fields of the Upper Findhorn valley. This timely flurry from the heavens is as welcome as an old overdue friend. If you're going animal-tracking in these mountains, a nice soft fall of snow before setting off is exactly what you want.

Duncan Macdonald works for a company dedicated to getting its clients 'up close and personal' with the rare and elusive birds and animals of Scotland's wildest highlands. As their expert tracker, Duncan is the proper man for the job. A quietly spoken, amusing and highly knowledgeable guide, he reads the whitened mountain landscape like an open book. One scarcely dreams of seeing red squirrel, red deer, red grouse, mountain hare, pine marten and golden eagle in one day, but that is the kind of wildlife feast that Duncan can lay on, with luck and the right conditions.

Out with Duncan, you also learn all kinds of amazing facts: that pine marten droppings smell like Parma violets, for example, or that – according to Duncan's grandmother's recipe – a capercaillie, a bird with an insatiable appetite for pine needles, has to be soaked in milk for 24 hours before roasting to get rid of the taste of turpentine.

MONARCH OF THE GLEN

The River Findhorn snakes fast and black through whitened meadows in the flat floor of the valley. Beyond rise the billowy foothills of the mountains, lumpy with crags, scree and steep side clefts, all powdered over with snow. A large herd of red deer comes into sight and, on the summit, a stag with magnificent antlers is outlined against the sky, creating a real Landseer moment.

To the untuned eye these hills and glens can appear barren and empty. Life above the tree line on the bare moors and mountains of the Scottish Highlands is a harsh affair of sparse pickings and intense competition for food, sex, personal space and safety. Concealment is a way of life – and if you're so cleverly camouflaged or hidden away that the ten-mile stare of a golden eagle can't spot you, the blurry eyes of the average human don't stand much of a chance. Amateur trackers can see animals on the mountainsides easily enough when the experts are there to point them out. But relying on one's own five senses is a different matter altogether. Without the guiding finger and the murmured word of encouragement, it can look as if all the slopes and hollows of the Upper Findhorn have been swept clean of life by the harshness of winter.

Pulling up by a footbridge, Duncan spots more otter tracks along the snow-powdered river bank, and with them a mysterious set of prints that have him momentarily puzzled. 'Much smaller than the otter,' he muses, 'and with these tiny sharp clawmarks. Stoat, I wonder?' He bends even

If you're going animal-tracking in these mountains, a nice soft fall of snow before setting off is exactly what you want.

closer to the little footprints. 'Too small, really ... no, I think what we're seeing is mink. Fierce little hunters, you know, and they do very well up here.'

He crunches on up a snowy track that leads into a side glen under a great slab of mountainside. A group of four red deer stags moves slowly away across the fields, and high on the hillside a great herd of nearly a hundred deer shifts by ones and twos, receding, as the humans advance, in a carefully judged adjustment of territorial boundaries. A harsh cry comes out of the white sky, and two ravens appear, tumbling and showing off to each other.

WINTER MARKINGS

Beside the track are more tiny prints, with mink-like claw marks but very slightly larger. 'Now these are stoat,' decides Duncan, 'and look here, this is what it jumped up to have a look at.' Two neat round front paw prints lie dinted close together, with a pair of hind prints falling in line behind. 'Mountain hare – and here's where he stopped and sat down to eat heather roots.' The hind footmarks have changed to a pair of parallel grooves about 10cm (4in) long, where the hare's long leg bones folded into the snow

as he squatted. 'Pretty fresh,' murmurs Duncan. 'Should still be around, if we're lucky.' He scans the hillside with his telescope. 'Got you!' he whispers.

The mountain hare is lying in the lee of a rock, face on to us and about 200m (220yd) away. He is in full winter coat of white with a faint but definite tinge of blue. His short ears are dark grey, his thickly furred and constantly twitching nose a rich creamy colour. His shiny blackcurrant eyes stay fixed on us, but he seems remarkably relaxed. A little way to his left another hare shapes itself against the snow in the telescope lens, this one nibbling heather roots.

A flight of red grouse some forty strong goes whirring across the mountainside. 'Something spooked them, for sure,' observes Duncan, and as if he has called out a stage direction, a golden eagle comes wheeling across the ridge high above, wingtip 'fingers' spread wide, circling majestically. One lift of the shoulder and he has disappeared behind the mountain. 'Oh, marvellous! Oh, you beauty!' sighs Duncan, grinning like a man who has scooped a jackpot. He gestures round the silent white bowl of mountains. There is no need for any more words. The scene is perfect, and so is the moment.

The GREAT GLEN

Around 350 million years ago, some cataclysm tore Scotland in two and created the Great Glen. Four long lochs lie within the rift, linking sea to sea through some of the wildest landscapes in the country.

❶ Port Appin

Appin is the name generally given to the wild country that lies between Loch Creran and the meeting of lochs Leven and Linnhe. For centuries, the land was feuded over by warring clans and it is dotted with landmarks that still bring these conflicts to mind.

The little whitewashed village of Port Appin looks over to Mull, with the MacLean castle on Duart Point, and to Lismore with its ruined strongholds. A little to the north is Portnacroish, facing the startlingly picturesque Castle Stalker (correctly Stalcair, 'Hunter's Castle'). Built on an offshore isle in about 1300, it has reflected the Appin fortunes ever since. In 1450 it was James IV's hunting lodge, and 18 years later its castellan, Sir Dugald Stewart, fought a bloody battle for its possession in which Stewarts, MacLarens, MacDougalls and MacFarlanes were all involved.

Possession of the castle alternated between Stewarts and Campbells for centuries, the exchanges effected through battle, treachery, shifts in the political scene and once through a fit of drunken generosity when a Stewart swapped it with a Campbell for a rowing-boat. The Campbells held the castle for the Government in the Jacobite rising of 1745, and it did not become Stewart property again until 1908. The castle is open for pre-booked tours during certain weeks of the year.

The enmity that existed between Campbells and Stewarts escalated in the aftermath of the 1745 rising when Colin Campbell of Glenure, known as 'Red Fox', was appointed Government agent for the sequestered lands of the Jacobite Stewarts of Appin. Someone shot him from behind a tree on the road between Ballachulish and Kentallen. The name of the assassin remains a mystery to this day, but a rigged Campbell court convicted a Stewart smallholder named James of the Glens and hanged him at Ballachulish. Robert Louis Stevenson tells part of the story in *Kidnapped*, but perhaps the tale becomes more haunting if you stand on the hillock behind the old ferry stage and look across the great expanse of Loch Linnhe to the mountains. This was the last sight that James saw before they hanged him.

▶ *Port Appin is reached by turning south-west from the A828 Oban–Fort William road at Tynribbie, a hamlet in the Strath of Appin.*

❷ Ardgour

At the foot of the steep mountains on the western shore of Loch Linnhe lies Ardgour. It can be reached by ferry across the Corran Narrows, or via a long detour by road. An easy walk begins just after the old post office at the end of the village street. Near its start, the path disappears into a tunnel of rhododendrons and leads past a magnificent row of old overhanging beech trees to two well-hidden small lochs.

The wooded glades – home of deer, badgers, squirrels, wildcats and rabbits – give way to the shore of the loch and the widening view south-west towards Mull and the open sea. A walk along the shore, accompanied only by the cries of gulls and the piping call of oystercatchers, can be rewarded by the sight of seals and their pups at play in a small bay that lies just behind Sallachan Point.

The walks around the inland lochs of Ardgour can be completed within an hour. But such is the beauty of the place, they may take very much longer.

▶ *The car ferry to Ardgour is 2 miles north of Onich on the Fort William road (A82). Or park just below the Corran Inn by the landing-stage and travel across as a foot passenger.*

DARK PEAKS SEEM STILL TO BROOD
TOWARDS GLEN COE

❸ Lochan Lùnn Dà-Bhrà

This lonely little loch (whose name is pronounced 'Lundavra') lies hidden among the mountains south of Fort William. It can be reached by car along an old military road whose lack of width almost seems planned to make the traveller slow down and admire the views.

There is an ancient stillness about the loch itself, with its two small islands, scattered clumps of pine and bare green hills sloping down to the water's edge. Only in spring is the scene transformed by a profusion of wild flowers. The island off the north shore, which can be reached only by boat, has an oddly regular appearance and is strongly suspected to be a crannog, a man-made island stronghold that could have been constructed at any time between the Bronze and Middle Ages. The southern island, however, is natural and quite charming; it can be visited by way of stepping-stones from the shore.

Permission to walk round the loch may be obtained from the farmhouse, Lundavra, which also issues fly-fishing permits, should you wish to try for some of the specially stocked brown and Loch Linnhe trout.

▶ *To reach the loch, take the Lundavra road signposted Upper Auchintore at the southern end of the A82 in Fort William; keep on until the road comes to an end – a distance of about 5½ miles.*

❹ Glen Coe

The bleak and sombre wilderness of Glen Coe seems a fitting setting for the infamous massacre of 1692. The dark peaks seem still to brood upon that February night when Campbell militia, on secret government orders, slaughtered some 40 MacDonalds of Glen Coe, leaving many others to die of exposure in the frozen hills. What made the crime particularly heinous in Highland eyes was that the soldiers were guests of the MacDonalds at the time. That, and the connivance of the king, William III, who had determined to make an example of the clan for its tardiness in swearing allegiance to him.

Nothing tangible remains of that terrible night except a monument to the MacDonalds and Signal Rock, now deep in woods, from which tradition says a beacon signal was given for the slaughter to begin. This is now considered doubtful, since the essence of the deed was secrecy and, in any case, the killing began simultaneously down the length of the glen, in some places out of sight of Signal Rock. But if anywhere in Scotland is haunted, it is Glen Coe.

Today, Glen Coe offers some of the finest rock climbs in Britain, and much of it is cared for by the National Trust for Scotland. Perhaps the best view of its savage splendour, and of the wild, bare peaks such as Bidean nam Bian and The Three Sisters of Glencoe, is from the rock platform called The Study, that stands above the road in the heart of the glen.

▶ *The A82 runs the length of Glen Coe; the National Trust for Scotland visitor centre is 17 miles south of Fort William.*

❺ Glen Nevis

The glen cuts deep into the mountains along the steep western slopes of Ben Nevis, and in the variety of its scenery – a swift-flowing river, steep, tree-lined gullies and great rocky crags high above the valley – is the Highlands in microcosm. To complete the picture, the head of the glen is dominated by the graceful quartzite peaks of Sgurr a' Mhàim and Stob Bàn, both rising to more than 900m (3,000ft).

At the eastern end of the glen there is a spectacular waterslide, Allt Coire Eòghainn, a 380m (1,250ft) gully of white water running down from below the summit of Ben Nevis. Just beyond the waterslide there is a car park from which a path runs through the splendid Nevis gorge to the Steall falls. This path divides once or twice at the beginning of the walk; keep to the upper branches for the best views.

High above the gorge, the track winds through pine, birch, oak and rowan. Below, the water crashes thunderously on boulders sculpted through the ages into wild forms. Suddenly, as you continue, the scene changes to a quiet meadow, at the end of which the white, feathery plumes of the Steall falls tumble from a valley high above.

For a flavour of adventure, climb at least some way up the tracks by the waterslide. These are perfectly safe, and a recognised route for experienced walkers to climb Ben Nevis. Even a short distance above the road will give you that special feel of big mountains.

▶ *Glen Nevis is signposted from the north side of Fort William; the distance to the end of the glen is 6½ miles.*

❻ Ben Nevis

The massive bulk of Ben Nevis looms above the bustling town of Fort William. It is not a particularly handsome mountain and, as often as not, clouds obscure its 1,343m (4,406ft) summit. This, together with the absence of a crowning peak, sometimes leads to Ben Nevis being dismissed as a huge but uninteresting lump on the landscape. However, a cautious glance down the precipitous North–east Buttress, or Tower Ridge, will quickly convince any doubters that the mountain does, in fact, possess an awesome grandeur all its own.

These North Face cliffs must be left to the most experienced rock climbers, but splendid views of the towering rock faces may be had by following either the Allt a' Mhuilinn footpath from a point a couple of miles along the Inverness road opposite the grounds of Inverlochy Castle, or from the branch of the path that skirts the marshy edge of Lochan Meall an t-Suidhe. But, for most people, the way to the top is by the well-trodden tourist path.

Do not be put off by the fairly strenuous start. Higher up, the climb is easier, particularly after about 760m (2,500ft) where heather and tufted hair grass give way to rocky scree among which alpine flowers, lichens and mosses grow. Those who get to the top will find their efforts amply rewarded.

From here, among the shattered lava and the multitude of cairns commemorating various people and events, you can see the superb Aonach Eagach ridge high above Glen Coe, while further off are the distant peaks of Ben Lomond, Ben Lawers and the three peaks of the Paps of Jura, 77 miles away. To the west are Rùm, Eigg and, in the distance, 92 miles off, South Uist, as well as the Cuillins on Skye.

Below Ben Nevis, the mighty rift of the Great Glen can be seen, cutting its way through the mountains from Loch Linnhe towards Inverness. In very clear weather, it is even possible to see the Antrim mountains in Northern Ireland, more than 120 miles south.

▶ *Fort William is on the A82: the summit path runs from the bridge opposite the Glen Nevis Youth Hostel, 2 miles along a minor road signposted from the north side of Fort William. There is a car park.*

❼ Glen Roy

Most National Nature Reserves are devoted to wild plants and animals, but at Glen Roy it is the 'parallel roads' which have made this glen an area of 'exceptional geological interest'. These are the three distinct horizontal stripes that can be seen clearly contouring the higher slopes on both sides of the glen. They show up as bright green against the darker shades of heather.

They are not highways, but the tide-marks left behind by ice-blocked lakes that once filled the glen. About 10,000 years ago, the last glaciers to cover the Highlands advanced up the Great Glen, and in doing so sealed off several side glens,

BOULDERS SCULPTED THROUGH

including Glen Roy and the neighbouring glens of Gloy and Spean. With no means of drainage, the glens filled up and became huge lakes. The Glen Roy lake during its largest phase was 200m (650ft) deep and 10 miles long.

The upper 'road' marks the shoreline of the lake when it was at its deepest. As the climate changed and the ice retreated, the lake dropped to successive new levels to where fresh outlets could balance the inflow of feed waters. The middle and lower 'roads' mark these newer and reduced shorelines. The best place from which to see this phenomenon is a viewing point about 3 miles along the glen, passing the small crofting village of Bohuntinville on the way.

Geology aside, Glen Roy is also a place where you can see some fascinating wildlife, including golden eagles, swooping down from the hillsides.

▶ *Roybridge, the entrance to the glen, is roughly 3 miles to the east of Spean Bridge along the A86.*

8 Achnacarry

Lying as it does within the walled estates of Cameron of Lochiel, the tiny village of Achnacarry, between the shores of Loch Arkaig and Loch Lochy, must be one of the best-hidden places in the whole of Britain. The sign 'Private Road', however, does not deny access to the village, and visitors may pass through the open gates and along the estate road between a rich variety of magnificent old trees.

The village lies beneath a wooded rocky outcrop, and consists of a farm, a few estate cottages, a small post office, the fine building of Achnacarry House and the Clan Cameron Museum. This enchanting scene is completed by a small village green and the sight of Highland cattle grazing in the surrounding fields. Under the boughs of an oak tree an old cannon sits peacefully, and behind are the moss-covered remains of a castle destroyed by the Duke of Cumberland in 1746.

A walk from the village leads through the estate and across a bridge over the River Arkaig. Turn right and you will pass a magnificent waterfall down which tumble the waters of the Chia-aig. The road continues along the Mile Dorcha (the dark mile), a straight, tree-lined avenue alongside the moss-covered estate wall. The wooden forestry houses at Clunes mark the start of the Loch Lochy section of the walk that follows the shoreline past superb old pine trees and into Bunarkaig. Just a little further round this sheltered bay is the entrance to the Achnacarry estate. The whole circuit is probably among the best 5 miles of easy walking anywhere.

▶ *The entrance to the Achnacarry estate is from the B8005 from Gairlochy, just before Bunarkaig.*

9 Loch Arkaig

The 13 mile drive along the shores of Loch Arkaig ends among some of the wildest and most remote mountains in the Western Highlands. From the head of the loch, people wishing to get to Loch Morar or Loch Nevis have to do so on foot through the long, lonely passes of Glen Pean or Glen Dessarry. Perhaps because there is no through road, Loch Arkaig has remained one of the most beautiful stretches of water in Scotland; not only beautiful, but also huge and almost deserted.

Only the far-off hum of a small outboard engine, or the occasional sound of a car, discloses the presence of fishermen. This is water renowned for its fish – salmon, trout, pike and char. But of greater fame still is the Arkaig Treasure – gold landed here by the French in 1746 to bolster the already-defeated Jacobites. It is believed that some of the gold at least may still be buried somewhere along the lochside.

At the east end of the loch there are two small islands. One is the ancient burial-place of the Lochiels, the other was noted as having been the nesting-place of ospreys during the 19th century. Now re-established in the area, ospreys regularly patrol the loch again. At this end of the loch – and indeed for most of its length – the surrounding hillsides are covered in mixed woodland reaching down to the water's edge. Across the loch are the remains of the original pine forest destroyed by a wartime blaze. But even this sad sight of desolation does not mar the overall scene. Numerous little sheltered bays provide delightful picnic places with very little chance of being disturbed. Further down the loch the scenery changes quite dramatically to that of bleaker, bare slopes and a grassy shore where blobs of white cotton-grass dance in the lightest of mountain breezes.

▶ *Loch Arkaig can be reached by following the B8005 north out of Gairlochy.*

SCOTLAND

THE AGES INTO WILD FORMS
GLEN NEVIS

GLEN GARRY

⑩ Glen Garry

Not every visitor to the Highlands wants to climb the craggy peaks, so the well-laid-out trails in Glen Garry Forest are ideal for people who prefer a pleasant stroll to a scramble. The forest consists mainly of conifers that thrive even in the poor, peaty remnants of a soil largely destroyed by overgrazing and burning during past centuries. Specimen trees are labelled, and there is an observation point from which the conical peak of Ben Tee can be seen to the south through the trees.

If you follow the nature trails through the forest, you will encounter the great cascading falls, whose waters thunder majestically down a gorge. Well-protected viewing points allow a close look. Further along the glen, the Daingean Trail offers a chance to walk among the remains of Daingean, a village abandoned during the Highland Clearances.

▶ *Forest trails start at the Ciste Dubh car park in Glen Garry Forest, 2 miles west of Invergarry, along the A87. The Daingean Trail is reached via a forest track, off the A87, 5 miles west of Invergarry.*

⑪ Loch nan Lann

The scenery on the eastern side of Loch Ness differs considerably from the better-known views offered by the main Inverness to Fort William road along the western shore. After climbing steeply out of Fort Augustus, the old military road levels out and runs across a high plateau above the eastern side. The open heather-clad moor, from which a grouse may suddenly and noisily rise, is broken by a number of small lochans, each having its own particular charm.

One such is Loch nan Lann which lies off the beaten track at the foot of Beinn a' Bhacaidh. It can be found by following the signposted minor road to Knockie Lodge, which leaves the B862 about 6 miles north-east of Fort Augustus. Motorists should park along the edge of Loch Knockie, which appears on the right after a mile or so. The path to Loch nan Lann starts another quarter of a mile further on by the side of the old shooting lodge.

The wooded path round the lochside provides an easy and pleasant walk, with only an occasional sudden splash or movement amongst the reeds to disturb the peaceful water. More energetic walkers will enjoy crossing the stepping-stones at the end of the loch. From there the path can be followed down the deep gorge to the remote and isolated boat-house 180m (600ft) below on the shore of Loch Ness.

▶ *Take the B862 from Fort Augustus towards Whitebridge. After 6 miles, a signposted minor road turns off west to Knockie Lodge and the loch.*

⑫ Falls of Divach

A rewarding walk through delightful countryside will take you to the Falls of Divach on a tributary of the River Coiltie. Start from the small village of Lewiston – a straight row of neat and brightly painted houses that is not far from Urquhart Castle and the shore of Loch Ness. A sign to the falls, which lie south of the village, points past a farm with partly ruined, but still splendid, buildings that were once part of a great estate. The old mill, now almost hidden in trees, was actually a miniature gasworks supplying piped gas up to the now demolished hall.

The land climbs steeply to a point where fine views of Loch Ness and Urquhart Bay open out. This is splendid scenery, a perfect blend of wooded hillsides, green fields and the reflecting waters of the loch below. As the land levels out a little, the thunder of falling water can be heard. On the right-hand side of the road there is a small car park from which a path cuts through woods of birch and oak to the falls.

Less impressive than those at Foyers across the loch, the Falls of Divach are majestic enough nevertheless. The natural amphitheatre set in dark woods offers the photographer magnificent opportunities, especially from the viewing point. At the end of the lane, a lovely old house overlooks the falls. This is Divach Lodge, once owned by the actress Ellen Terry. It was here, in 1904, that J. M. Barrie sat in the garden and wrote *Peter Pan*.

▶ *Lewiston is 14 miles south-west of Inverness, on the A82, at the entrance to Glen Urquhart.*

⑬ Foyers

The Falls of Foyers, on the eastern shore of Loch Ness, are one of the most famous sights in Scotland. The enormous force of water crashing through the thickly wooded gorge is best seen in full spate after heavy rain, when the peat-stained river foams and thunders through the tortuous passages of the ravine, flinging up clouds of misty spray that sparkle among the tree-tops.

The best places to see this splendid spectacle are from the vantage points along the well-protected path through the trees. This starts opposite the shop in Upper Foyers and leads down the ravine to where the river, its energy spent, flows into the broad waters of Loch Ness. It is advisable to return by the same path, since this avoids a much longer walk along the road.

Foyers is also of special interest to geologists for its long-severed connection with Strontian, away to the south-west. Both Foyers and Strontian have an identical and isolated granite composition, proving that they were once part of the same mass. These geological clues clearly show the tremendous distance the Northern and Western Highlands have slipped along the Great Glen fault; Foyers and Strontian, for example, now lie 55 miles apart.

▶ *Foyers is on the B852, off the old military road from Fort Augustus to Inverness (B862) on the east side of Loch Ness.*

⑭ Rosemarkie

The green rolling hills of the Black Isle peninsula contrast strongly with the rugged Highland scenery a few miles inland. Here, the thick glacial deposits that came to rest on the Old Red Sandstone have produced a rich farming country that rises steeply out of the wide, clear waters of the Moray Firth.

This contrast between the wooded inland glens and the peninsula goes beyond mere scenic differences. This is an area of huge horizons, clear blue skies and one of the lowest rainfalls in the United Kingdom.

A few miles along the coast past Avoch and Fortrose is the pleasant village of Rosemarkie, where fishermen cast their drag-nets from the sandy beaches to catch the salmon. There has been a settlement here since Pictish times and a collection of carved Pictish stones, all from the village, can be seen in the local museum.

A walk along the headland, populated mainly by rabbits that bob in and out of the undergrowth, is a delight, particularly in spring when gorse flares yellow on the hills and the Nairn coast lies in blue-green serenity across the Moray Firth. A path where all this can be experienced leaves the narrow minor road along the headland about 4 miles out of Rosemarkie towards Cromarty. After skirting the side of a wood, it descends steeply through a bracken-covered hillside down to a remote fishing station on a deserted sandy, shore. Here, your only likely companions will be sea-birds.

▶ *Rosemarkie lies on the A832, between Muir of Ord and Cromarty.*

The NORTH-WEST HIGHLANDS

The Highlands sometimes seem like the ends of the earth, with the most northerly and westerly points in the British mainland – Dunnet Head and Ardnamurchan – both found north of the Great Glen.

❶ Dunnet Head

Dunnet Head is the most northerly of the great capes that so dramatically terminate the Scottish mainland. It is easier of access than Cape Wrath, but feels much more remote than Duncansby Head with its John o' Groats. Dunnet Head is reached by a road crossing a wild sweep of moor and, when you reach the lookout point by the lighthouse, you are at the most northerly tip of mainland Britain. The Pentland Firth snores 104m (340ft) below, or explodes at the foot of the cliff in bullets of spray that can easily reach your vantage place. Before you, anchored against the red-gold shoals of sunset, is the towering, sinister stack of the Old Man of Hoy backed by the humps of Orkney.

The scene changes hourly or, at times, in a matter of a few minutes. For everyone who remembers a Wagnerian storm, there are many others who recall the wide sands of Dunnet Bay, glittering under a calm sky.

▶ *Take the A836 from Thurso to John o' Groats; at Dunnet turn on to the B855 and follow the signposts to Dunnet Head.*

❷ Durness and Loch Eriboll

A week or so after the end of the holiday season, motorists on the road that runs across the tip of Scotland to the Kyle of Durness begin to wave to one another. Doubtless each is relieved to discover that he is not the sole survivor of some cataclysm that has wiped every other human from the face of the earth. The moorlands hereabouts are very wild and very lonely, so that even the crofting hamlets at Durness seem bustling by comparison.

The principal attraction here is the Smoo Cave, situated at the end of a deep cleft about 1½ miles east down the coast. Actually there are three caves, but only one of them, the largest, is accessible without potholing equipment. A river, the Allt Smoo, emerges from its mouth behind which lies a tremendous cavern of cathedral-like proportions and appearance, some 60m (200ft) deep and 36m (120ft) high. It is said that the Devil once hid in the Smoo Cave. He was cornered there by the 17th-century Lord Reay, 'The Wizard of Reay', whose shadow Old Nick had stolen in Italy. Just as the wizard was about to settle accounts, the Devil blew a great hole in the roof and made his escape. By way of confirmation, the hole remains there to this

SHIMMERING LIKE A TALL SHIP ON THE HORIZON

TOWARDS AM BUACHAILLE FROM SANDWOOD BAY

day, though some prosaic people say it was really cut by the Allt Smoo which drops through the hole in a 24m (80ft) waterfall to the cave floor. From there, it runs through the gully and out to the sea. This is an unspoiled and lovely place, calm even on a wild day, when the sea explodes in spray at the gully's entrance.

From the cave, the road runs off to Tongue, making a huge loop round Loch Eriboll, down one shore and up the other. This narrow-entranced sea loch cuts deep into the Sutherland mountains, creating a fine, easily defended anchorage, and was used as such by the Home Fleet during the Second World War. Now it is more or less deserted, a place of great sweeps of heather that swim in the heat of summer and pour mist on to the loch for most of the rest of the year. Here and there, however, and around nearby Loch Hope, tumbled traces of Pictish settlements show that the area was fairly populous in early times. Roofless crofts testify that it continued to be so for many centuries after, until the evictions of the 1800s, which in this district left thousands of people homeless.

But the present emptiness has one advantage in that the loch's solitude provides one of the very few mainland breeding grounds of the grey seal. The animals can be seen sometimes around the cliffs and caves of the south shore.

▶ *Durness and Loch Eriboll are about 40 miles north-west of Lairg and can be approached on the A838, or the A836 to Tongue and thence the A838.*

❸ Sandwood Bay

The old Gaels claimed that Tir nan Og, 'the Land of Youth' – Paradise, in other words – lay somewhere far to the west, a place of quiet waters and gentle shores. Perhaps it was Sandwood Bay they had in mind, the most north-westerly beach in mainland Britain and one of the loveliest and most remote.

It is not easy of access. It is found by way of Loch Inchard and Kinlochbervie, a bright cluster of fishing boats backed by bungalows, fish sheds, a school and a hotel, all wrapped about by promontories and islands. From there, a rough road goes on to Oldshoremore with its cemetery overhanging a bay of white-gold sand and further still to Blairmore and Sheigra, at which point the road gives up in a peat bog. From a little before Sheigra, a path leads to the bay, over 4 miles of rock, peat and water, so go well-shod.

In fine weather Sandwood Bay is indeed a paradise. An odd stillness lies upon the marram grass on the dunes and upon the freshwater loch behind. The sea is mirror-calm and far off, to the north, stands the great bulk of Cape Wrath; to the south lies the sea-stack of Am Buachaille, shimmering like a tall ship on the horizon. But a brisk wind can change the sea quickly into a wild symphony of both colour and sound. White horses gallop in over the dark green Minch, smashing and exploding into the stacks of red Torridon rock as they race up to the beach.

In fair weather or foul there is a touch of the uncanny about Sandwood Bay. It has always had the reputation of being haunted, not by anything so mundane as ghosts but by shy and mysterious creatures from the sea. One such – a mermaid – was found by a shepherd named Sandy Gunn in 1900, stranded by the tide on a ledge about a mile down the coast from the bay. She had reddish-yellow hair, green eyes, a yellowish complexion and, apart from her fishy tail, looked just like any bonnie human girl. Sandy and the mermaid stared at each other in equal amazement; then his dog let out a fearful howl and tore off up the beach. This broke the spell, and Sandy, suddenly terrifyingly aware of what he was looking at, also took to his heels.

However, it seems that the mermaid came to no harm, for she, or her descendants, have been seen many times since, in and around the bay and in Loch Inchard. Sometimes she is in full view, but more often she is a swirl of golden hair just under the surface of the waves.

▶ *Kinlochbervie is on the B801 and best approached by the A838 north-west out of Lairg, or by the A894 north from Ullapool, which joins the A838 4 miles south of the junction with the B801 at Rhiconich.*

❹ Knockan Crag

About 10 miles north of Ullapool the road is overhung by a mile-long dark cliff. This is the Knockan Crag, a geological curiosity that about 150 years ago started an entirely new way of thinking about the origins of the world's mountain chains. Generally, in any rock formation, the oldest deposits are at the bottom, compressed and altered by the weight of the younger rocks above. But at Knockan Crag in 1859, Professor Nicol, a geologist, observed that the topmost layer of Moine schists was considerably more compressed and altered in structure – and therefore probably older – than the limestone and quartzite on which it rests. This, it was deduced, was the result of a tremendous upheaval that took place in the earth's crust some 400 million years ago, thrusting up ancient rock from the depths to overlie the newer surface deposits. The discovery led to the investigation of similar phenomena elsewhere, and to a more profound understanding of the forces that shaped the great mountain ranges.

Knockan Crag is now a nature trail, marked out by Scottish Natural Heritage and involving a 1½ mile walk and a climb to 320m (1,050ft). Each viewing point on the way illustrates some different aspect of the area – its geological formation, its views, and its flora and fauna. There is even a 6,000-year-old pine root to suggest that the climate was much kinder here once, kind enough to permit the covering of the whole area by forest. This is not the case now, however, and the trail must not be taken lightly. Stout boots are essential and, if the weather is wet and windy, take advice as to how much of the trail is accessible.

The cliff looks out upon the Inverpolly Reserve, some 11,000ha (27,000 acres) of savage wilderness that provides a variety of habitats from marine islands to birchwoods, lochs and rivers, much of it is a whisky-coloured wilderness of rock, peat bog and water. No one lives here, and you feel that probably no one ever has or ever will. The surface of the land is covered by the old, leathery, unadorned hide of this planet, worn by aeons of ice and weather. It is not hostile, exactly; simply ancient and utterly indifferent.

▶ *Knockan Crag and the Inverpolly Reserve lie 10 miles north from Ullapool on the A835.*

❺ Corrieshalloch Gorge

Corrieshalloch Gorge, with the Falls of Measach that pour through its entrance in a mighty 45m (150ft) spout, is an extravaganza even by Highland standards – all the more so for being so completely unexpected. On either hand, the barren sentinel peaks of An Teallach and Beinn Dearg stand over the Ullapool road, where from a car park a steep, slippery path descends through massed birch, rowan and hazel. At its end there is a little wooden platform which overhangs a world as lush as any Victorian conservatory. Rare ferns and mosses sprout from every crevice of the sheer rock walls; above them cling goat willow, guelder rose and bird cherry, and far below the River Droma tumbles.

The gorge itself is a box canyon – that is, it is as wide at the top as it is at the bottom, 60m (200ft) below. A mile long and 30m (100ft) wide, it was carved through solid metamorphic rock by floodwaters at the end of the last Ice Age.

Apart from the platform, a good view of the falls can also be obtained from the little suspension bridge that runs above them. This was built and presented by Sir John Fowler, co-designer of the Forth Bridge, towards the end of the last century. From it you can watch ravens and other birds make incredibly tight landings on the ledges and pinnacles among which they nest.

On the road to Dundonnell and Gairloch above the gorge there is another viewpoint that provides a splendid summary of the variety and contrasts of this part of the Highlands. Opposite, steep-crowding conifers clothe the lower slopes of Meall Doire Fàid, whose purple-brown 730m (2,395ft) summit disappears into the mists above. Below, the gorge opens out into the gentle oak-dotted meadows of Strath More, threaded by the River Broom. At the river's end is Loch Broom and Ullapool, where trawlers from half Europe ride at anchor. Even the very road on which the viewpoint lies is part of the region's story; known throughout the Highlands as 'Destitution Road', it was built to give men work during the potato famine of 1851.

▶ *Corrieshalloch Gorge lies on the A835 Garve to Ullapool road, 12 miles south-east of Ullapool and ½ mile north-west of the junction with the A832.*

❻ Loch Maree

Beinn Eighe is the earliest of the National Nature Reserves, set up in 1951 chiefly to conserve the fragment of the old Caledonian forest, Coille na Glasleitire, 'the wood on the grey slopes', that runs along the southern shore of Loch Maree. It was not before time, since, as elsewhere in the Highlands, the hand of man has lain heavily on the forest this last 1,500 years and more. Vikings from Orkney built their ships of Highland timber and wantonly fired any stands about them that they did not use.

In the 14th century, Alexander Stewart, the 'Wolf of Badenoch', is said to have burned the forests as an efficient means of persuading fugitives to emerge from hiding; so, too, did his grandfather, Robert Bruce, and many Highland chieftains in neighbourly squabbles. Later on, sheep runs and lumbering both took a massive toll, but now at Beinn Eighe and in other reserves, attempts are being made to regenerate not only the Scots pine forest, but the native stands of oak and birch as well.

The mountain trail at Beinn Eighe – steep and rough in places – explores the reserve and illuminates its history. Cairns mark points of particular interest and places where ptarmigan can be seen. There are wildcats and pine martens around, but you will have to be very lucky to catch sight of any. As you climb, the glorious 12 mile vista of Loch Maree, with its raft-like islands and wild mountain scenery to the north, opens up. Dominating all is the peak of the aptly named Slioch, 'the spearhead', shadowing dark Gleann Biannasdale. Up the glen there are the remains of an ironworks that in the 17th century smelted iron from bog ore. The men who did the work were recruited from the south, and to this day part of the mouth of the glen, where it opens up on to the loch shore, is known as Cladh nan Sussanach, 'the grave of the English'.

The trails through Slattadale Forest at the western end of the loch provide an insight into modern forest management and the way it helps to preserve the wildlife of the area. One of the trails, Tollie Path, is fairly rough so make sure that you are adequately shod.

▶ *The best approach to Loch Maree is by the A896 from Lochcarron, or by the A832 from Achnasheen.*

❼ Torridon

The National Trust for Scotland proclaims Glen Torridon and the wild mountains about it to be among the most spectacular mountain scenery in Scotland. Those who are sensitive to landscape may feel that 'spectacular' is not an adequate enough term to describe Torridon, which in its old, old age is truly awesome, majestic and faintly terrible.

The phrase 'as old as the hills' takes on a new significance here, for you are looking at some of the oldest shapes on earth – the mighty ridge of Liathach, with its peaks, corries and crags, and the only slightly less impressive Beinn Alligin and Beinn Dearg. They are composed mainly of reddish Torridon sandstone, a substance laid down 750 million years ago and worn into shape by time, wind and rain. By way of underlining the time scale involved, a number of the peaks are capped with white quartzite, in which are embedded the fossils of some of the first living creatures on the planet.

The weather is by no means invariably sympathetic, and in any event the stiffer hill walks should be attempted only by experienced climbers. But the less ambitious walker can, for example, take the road from the scattering of houses that make up Torridon village, round the north shore of Upper Loch Torridon to Inveralligin. The mountains rise straight from the roadside, their gullies spilling cloud over the loch whose slaty calmness is streaked with the paler lines of currents.

From Inveralligin there runs a single-track switchback road that should satisfy the most ardent lover of mountain scenery. Justly named the Bealach na Gaoithe, 'the Pass of the Winds', it clambers around the lower slopes of Beinn Alligin, then soars and swoops to the little hamlets of Upper and Lower Diabaig, among the loneliest habitations in Britain. About halfway up the pass there is a parking place. Before and around it there is the whole glorious panorama of rock and water – Loch Shieldaig, Loch Torridon and Loch Diabaig, the mountains of Shieldaig, Applecross and Torridon. Close by there is a little red letter-box. Who, you wonder, ever posts a letter here? And who collects it?

▶ *Torridon village is on a minor road off the A896, between Lochcarron and Kinlochewe, 6 miles east of Shieldaig. Continue along the minor road, past the turning for Inveralligin and over the pass to reach Upper and Lower Diabaig.*

❽ Bealach na Bà

At the Loch Kishorn end of the Bealach na Bà – 'the Pass of the Cattle' – the roads rises to a height of 626m (2,053ft) with gradients of 1 in 5 and hairpin bends. This may sound formidable but only a few years ago some of the gradients were 1 in 4 and roadside barriers were practically non-existent.

All the same, it is still one of the highest mountain roads in Britain, and perhaps the nearest thing to an Alpine pass that we have, especially in winter when it can become choked by snow. Until the building of the easier coast road from Shieldaig a few years ago, this was a serious matter for the inhabitants of Applecross, who had no other means of access except by sea.

The dramatic part of the drive is on the Loch Kishorn side, the slope down to Applecross being fairly gentle. But before beginning the climb, it is worth walking up the lower screes of Sgurr a Chaorachain by the Russel Burn and looking back at Loch Kishorn. The road ascends high above, there is a sense of immense peace broken only by the splash of a little waterfall.

The sharpest hairpins are at the top of the pass where it runs between the peaks of Chaorachain and Meall Gorm, and it seems incredible that this was the old cattle-drovers' route to Lowland markets. Just beyond, there is a rocky plateau with a viewing base from which, on the occasional clear day, you can see the Cuillins of Skye and the Outer Isles.

▶ *The Bealach na Bà lies on a minor road west from Tornapress on the A896 between Lochcarron and Shieldaig or Loch Torridon.*

❾ Glen Affric

If all the loveliest glens in the Highlands were distilled, then their yielded essence would be something very much like Glen Affric. It would be a traditional blend rather than a straight malt: two lochs, Affric and Benevean (correctly, Beinn a' Mheadhoin), a number of 'wild hanging woods and loud-roaring floods', and, for good measure, the fugitive memory of the Young Pretender, who found refuge in these parts after Culloden, in a cave above Badger Gall on the River Affric. The mountains are regular, graceful peaks that can wear snowy mantles as early as October.

Glen Affric was part of the old road that cut through the Inverness-shire hills and ran across Scotland, and in fact there is still a fine long-distance path that goes all the way to Kintail. From the 16th to the early 20th centuries, the glen was Chisholm country, secured to some extent during the 1745 rising by a judicious hedging of bets. At Culloden, the chief of Clan Chisholm and a younger son fought for Charles, while two elder brothers faced them among the redcoat ranks opposite.

About 50 years ago, a hydroelectric dam was built across the eastern end of Loch Benevean, turning hillocks into islets crowned with pine. Those who remember the place in the days before the dam say that much of its beauty is gone for ever, in which case it must have been a paradise indeed, for there can be few more glorious valleys on the face of the planet.

The best way to see it is to take one of the Forestry Commission walks from Dog Fall – actually more of a tumbling rapid – or from the car park near the narrow spit of land that divides Benevean from Affric. The walks are from one to three hours' duration and offer splendid vistas of forest, dark lochs and rapids. Examples of almost every bird species in the Highlands nest here, and as well as red and roe deer there are foxes, badgers, and if very lucky, wildcats and pine martens. Keep off the hills in the deer-stalking season, August to October; otherwise it is a gentle, friendly place.

▶ *Glen Affric is reached by a minor road branching south-west off the A831 at Cannich, which is 23 miles west of Inverness.*

❿ Glenelg and Glen Shiel

The drive through Glen Shiel coming west from Invermoriston, with the mountains rising to 900m (3,000ft) on either hand – so close you feel you could almost touch them – must be one of the most spectacular in Britain. And if you are inspired by it, you would not be the first, for it was here that Dr Johnson, riding with the faithful Boswell to Glenelg and Skye, conceived the idea of writing his *Journey to the Western Isles*.

The route they took is the same as that followed by the modern motorist, turning west at Shiel Bridge and climbing the old military road over the helter-skelter Mam Ratagain Pass. The view has been considerably obscured since Johnson's day by dark conifers, planted by the Forestry Commission, but in its usual courteous way it has made amends with a viewing base above the tree-line. Turn round, and the sight is at once breath-catching, almost too much to take in. Below in a pale green bowl lies little Loch Shiel, the head of Loch Duich and the toy shape of Shiel Bridge. Above them all, and the glen, tower the great billowing exuberant shapes of the grassy mountains known as the Five Sisters of Kintail. Wearing green in summer, old-gold in autumn and white in winter, with an occasional cloud veil to add a little mystery, they are among the loveliest of Highland hills.

The minor road west from Shiel Bridge runs on to Glenelg village and the Sound of Sleat. The village is a cluster of cottages and fishing boats on the seaweed-draped shore south of the swift-flowing strait of Kyle Rhea. Opposite the village, on Skye, are the cottages of Kylerhea, scattered at the foot of a dark glen running between the peaks of Sgurr na Coinnich and Ben Aslak. Cattle used to be ferried from Skye here, and driven over Mam Ratagain to the Lowland markets. There is still a ferry for cars and people, but it shuts down in winter.

Inland and south from Glenelg, along a minor road into Glen Beag, there is a pair of those mysterious towers called brochs – Dun Telve and Dun Trodden – reputed to be the best-preserved of their kind on the mainland. Possibly built by Iron Age Picts as a defence against Norse sea-raiders, the outer wall of Dun Telve still rises in places to a sheer 10m (33ft) of unmortared stone, pierced only by a 1.2m (4ft) high door. Within, there is a second wall, rising up to join the outer one at the top, the lower space between them being filled with galleries and chambers. A pair of windows look down from the inner wall into a courtyard, some 10m (33ft) across, that was perhaps a corral for cattle in times of trouble. Two ledges jut from a wall; but like so much else about the place, their purpose is a mystery.

▶ *Shiel Bridge is reached by the A87 from Invergarry or from Kyle of Lochalsh. Glenelg is on a minor road 9 miles west from Shiel Bridge.*

AMONG THE LOVELIEST OF HIGHLAND HILLS
THE FIVE SISTERS OF KINTAIL

⑪ Loch Morar

Above the hilly village of Morar there is a metal cross marking the spot where the first Irish missionary to these parts, said to be St Cumin, began his conversion of the local pagans. To the west, it looks out over the famous pure white quartzite sands of the beach to Rùm and, closer still, to Eigg; both islands lift out of the sea and disappear again in minutes, according to the whim of the weather.

Eastwards across a narrow neck of land there is the full 12 mile stretch of Loch Morar. If you take the narrow road to Bracora half a mile south of Morar, you come first to a thunderous weir on the short Morar river. This is the site of some once-mighty falls, but they have been largely tamed by a hydroelectric scheme. Beyond, the road opens out on to the loch's waters which, towards the eastern end, fill the deepest abyss in Britain – 310m (1,017ft), a depth that does not occur again, even in the sea, until the edge of the Continental Shelf is reached near Rockall. It is thought that the fearsome trench was scoured by a fast-moving glacier that spread and slowed at the valley's broader western end. Certainly the loch is wider and shallower at this point.

For about 2 miles the road runs between little crofting meadows, oaks and rhododendrons, with crags above which buzzards soar and glide. However, a little beyond the scattered houses of Bracora the road comes to an end. From here on, the way along the loch is on foot.

It is a fine, stony, adventurous path, constantly twisting and turning along the shore, to offer new vistas. For company there is the odd sheep and heron, fast-falling streams on the left and the splash of loch water on the right. There might also be a glimpse of Morag, Morar's monster, though she is less publicity-conscious than her relative in Loch Ness, and is said to appear only when the death of a MacDonald of Clanranald is imminent. The mountains of North and South Morar lean over the shores of the loch and its scattering of islands, on which grow fragments of the ancient Caledonian Forest.

After about 5 miles, the track turns left to Tarbet and the roadless splendours of Loch Nevis. Backed by the mountains of Knoydart, the inner and outer lochs are grander and wilder than Morar, though they are accessible only to walkers and sailors. For those who prefer tougher hikes, there are also magnificent views of Lochs Nevis and Morar from some of the peaks east of the road to Mallaig.

▶ *Morar village lies on the A830, 30 miles north-west of Fort William and 3 miles south of Mallaig ferry harbour.*

⑫ Glen Beasdale

As Glenfinnan was the pinnacle of the Jacobite rising of 1745, so Glen Beasdale was its beginning and its end, for it was on the shores of Loch nan Uamh, the little sea loch lying at the mouth of the glen, that the Young Pretender first set foot on the Scottish mainland. And it was from there, too, that he departed, closing the final chapter of the story of the House of Stuart.

Beasdale Burn tumbles down from the mountains of South Morar in a series of waterfalls until it reaches the lower end of the glen, where it plunges deeply into woods as rich as any in southern England. Oaks descended from the ancient forest that once covered this part of the country grow here, mingled with rhododendrons, birches and larches. Mossy cushions coat the rocks, and pale green streamers of lichen hang from dead branches – all in astonishing contrast to the austere hills climbing above.

Near Arisaig House, where the trees arch over the road by the Borrodale Burn, there is a track signed 'Druimindarroch' angling down towards the shore. Take it, and abruptly the woods come to an end, opening out into the brightness of Loch nan Uamh, all lumpy green islets and isthmuses, with far to the west the bulks of Rùm and Eigg rising from the sea. There is a barn at the bottom of the track, and opposite, over a grassy beach crossable at low tide, a single wind-blown oak, beyond which lies 'Prince Charlie's Cave'. It is also possible to reach the cave by a longer track, but the beach route is

BEYOND, THERE IS NOTHING BUT SEA

RÙM, MUCK AND EIGG FROM ARDNAMURCHAN

more enjoyable. The chances are that a seal will stick his head out of the water and gaze at you, as fascinated by your presence as you are by his.

In September 1746, so tradition says, the Prince and a few companions hid in the cave for ten days, awaiting a ship to France. He had been a wanderer and a fugitive ever since the Battle of Culloden, six months earlier, and by now had grown a long red beard, was bare-footed, and was dressed in a dirty shirt, a plaid and a ragged coat. However, he seemed in the best of spirits; fortitude in the face of adversity was always one of the Stuarts' most endearing traits. Eventually Charles and a number of his followers were picked up by the French ship *L'Heureux* from a cove some 2 miles east along the road. A cairn marks the spot, close by the place where he had landed with such high hopes 14 months earlier.

▶ *Glen Beasdale runs north-east from the Sound of Arisaig towards Loch Morar. The A830 from Lochailort to Arisaig traverses part of it.*

⓭ Ardnamurchan

Like Cornwall and Caithness, Ardnamurchan has an air of separateness, often expressed by the inhabitants of all three in a note of faint surprise that anyone should ever bother to go anywhere else. All, of course, are peninsulas, Ardnamurchan being the westernmost in mainland Britain. From Point of Ardnamurchan beside the lighthouse, you can see Coll, Tiree, Rùm, Muck and Eigg, and on a clear day, far out, Barra and South Uist. Beyond, there is nothing but sea until America.

Ardnamurchan is threaded through by the B8007 which runs off the A861 at Salen, and is fairly bumpy and swooping even by Western Highland single-track standards. For a time it follows the shores of Loch Sunart, dressed at first in Forestry Commission larch and spruce, but these shortly give way to banks of azaleas, fuchsias and rhododendrons. At this point, the road switchbacks inland to skirt Ben Hiant – the Holy Mountain – an extinct volcano whose jagged ramparts are quite unlike the rounded tops of the other hills near by.

The road returns to Loch Sunart again at Kilchoan, near which is the ruined Mingary Castle, a 13th-century stronghold that at various times was besieged or sacked by Campbells, MacDonalds and even the Spanish from the galleon that now lies with its treasure in Tobermory Bay. Hereabouts, and in other parts of the peninsula too, are a number of old blackhouses, traditional stone-built houses, that are either roofless now or converted into animal pens. These are evidence of the Clearances which hit Ardnamurchan hard in the middle of the last century. One of those responsible was a tenant farmer named MacColl who lies in Kilchoan churchyard. He was cursed to eternal damnation by an old woman he had evicted, who also swore that grass would never grow on his grave; and, indeed, it does not.

▶ *Take the A830 from Fort William to Lochailort. Turn south on to the A861 and follow it to Salen – the road becomes a single track, with passing places. Then take the B8007, again a single-track road, to Glenborrodale and on into Ardnamurchan.*

SCOTLAND

The ISLANDS of SCOTLAND

Britain is crowned by hundreds of islands. Some are near – Arran is just 13 miles from the mainland; others are more remote – the Shetlands stand some 130 miles to the north of Scotland.

THE CLIFFS AT ESHA NESS

The SHETLAND ISLANDS

❶ Herma Ness

This is the ragged, northernmost tip of Britain – further north than St Petersburg or Labrador, and on the same latitude as Cape Farewell in Greenland and the Kenai Peninsula in Alaska. In the summer sky, wild aerial battles take place between the great skuas, known locally as bonxies, and the gannets which throng the rock stacks and skerries. The gannets dive for fish, while the piratical skuas harry them to steal their catch. The other sea birds which breed around the cliffs – the tens of thousands of puffins on the grassy slopes, the kittiwakes, guillemots, fulmars and shags – must protect their eggs and young from the bonxies, which sometimes also strike down adult birds in flight.

Even visitors to the Hermaness National Nature Reserve are not spared the bonxies' ferocity. It takes about an hour to walk north from The Ness through the rough moorland to the top of Hermaness Hill, and down the steep grassy slopes to the cliffs; but under attack from the bonxies, which swoop down again and again in defence of their territory, it may take considerably longer. Many comments in the visitors' book in the shelter on the hill bear witness to the fact that it has never been easy to reach the top of Britain, whether because of the bonxies, or the wind, or a sudden mist, or just the climb through the heather and among the peat hags, or bogs. But the comments also confirm that the walk is well worth the trouble – partly for a close look at the bonxies, but also for the wild cliffs, and for the view. It reaches across the tide-race to the lighthouse on Muckle Flugga, and to Out Stack beyond it – the final fragment of Britain, a tiny island of rock defiantly angled against the storming of the sea.

▶ *Herma Ness is on Unst and about 3 miles north-west of Haroldswick, along the B9086 and then along a minor road. Unst can be reached by inter-island boat and bus services from Lerwick, Mainland Shetland. Mainland Shetland can be reached by car ferry from Kirkwall and Aberdeen or by flights from Aberdeen, Edinburgh, Glasgow, Inverness and Kirkwall.*

298

shades of grey and pink, delicately streaked and patterned by the immense natural forces which first gave them form. Their power and beauty is unquestionable, like the power and beauty of the landscape which surrounds them. They are known to have been quarried locally, and to have been raised some 4,000 years ago. But who raised them, and why, remains uncertain.

The stones are aligned like a Celtic cross, north to south and east to west, around a central circle. The remains of a cairn lie inside the circle. Perhaps this was a burial place or a centre for religious worship. Was the sun the supreme deity, or the moon? Or maybe some supernatural being was worshipped here.

Another theory is that the stones were arranged as an astronomical observatory, one of whose purposes was to help maintain a calendar. The cairn at the centre may not have been a cairn at all, but the central observation point for an astronomer-priest.

One thing is certain. The landscape and weather of Lewis have changed since prehistoric times – the sea-level was lower then, the land was more fertile, there was more sunshine, and there was less rain. Trees probably grew where now there is only peat-bog. So, whoever raised the Calanais stones, and the many other stone circles found in the area, had time enough to spare from the basic struggle for survival. The stones suggest that Lewis in prehistory was a more comfortable land than it is today. In a whisper from long ago they speak of warmth and plenty.

▶ *Calanais lies about 16 miles west of Stornoway, Lewis, off the A858.*

⑫ Huisinis

For 17 miles the road to Huisinis winds westwards over North Harris from the head of West Loch Tarbert. It dips and rises and dips again, always narrow, sometimes blind, sometimes with long views ahead. The road passes a salmon leap where Lochan Beag tumbles towards the sea, and turns briefly through the grounds of Amhuinnsuidhe Castle, built in 1868. Then suddenly, after passing inland behind a cluster of coastal lochs, the road rises over the crest of a hill and Huisinis comes into sight. Below the hill, a flat bed of grassland backs a bay of silver sand, and the sombre colour of the hills gives way to brilliant green.

Huisinis is a tiny crofting settlement at the neck of Rubha Huisinis, and on its northern side it looks out across half a mile of tidal strait to the island of Scarp. A century ago more than 200 people lived here, but today it is deserted. In the 1930s it was the scene of an experiment to send post by rocket, devised by a German inventor called Gerhard Zucker. His rocket, bound for the Harris shore, exploded on impact and shredded the mail – the experiment was deemed a failure.

From the pier opposite Scarp, a beautiful walk leads north-east over the fringe of the hills to the long stretch of sand which lies beyond; by turning inland it is possible to walk over the dunes and through grassland to the lonely Loch na Cleavag. Even on a wet and windswept day, the loch is exhilarating in its wildness and isolation.

▶ *Huisinis is on Harris, about 17 miles north-west of Tarbert along the B887. Harris can be reached by car ferry from Uig (on Skye) to Tarbert.*

CALANAIS STANDING STONES

⑬ Blathaisbhal

An immense labyrinth of rock and water spreads in every direction at the foot of Blathaisbhal, a hill which rises to 109m (358ft) on the eastern side of North Uist in the Outer Hebrides. From its summit can be seen Loch Maddy, to the east, an inlet so strewn with little islands that it is estimated to have more than 70 miles of shore to every mile of its length. To the south and west the inland moor is so waterlogged that it is almost impossible to tell where one loch ends and the next begins – the lochs are every shape and size and far too numerous to count.

Blathaisbhal is the first hill on the road north from Lochmaddy. Three standing stones on the north-west slope are, according to one tradition, the gravestones of three spies who were buried alive, but according to another they are the petrified bodies of three men from Skye who deserted their wives. White tufts of bog cotton rise above the heather, and the flowers on the hill include tormentil, milkwort and lousewort. Skylarks nest on the ground, or climb singing into the sky.

Blathaisbhal is small by comparison with the distant mountains of Harris to the north, and Skye to the east. But it is a simple, unbothered place, and a perfect vantage point from which to survey the half-drowned wilderness around it.
▶ *Blathaisbhal is on North Uist, about 2 miles north-west of Lochmaddy along the A865. North Uist can be reached by car ferry from Uig (Skye) to Lochmaddy. There are also flights from Glasgow to Benbecula airport, about 20 miles south-west of Lochmaddy via the A867 and A865.*

⑭ Balranald

Behind Hogha Gearraidh cemetery, the burial place of John MacCodrum, a famous 18th-century North Uist bard, the land lies low, flat and wet – a rare example of undrained machair grassland. Looking down from the bard's grave, or south from the road to Hogha Gearraidh, it is clear that the marsh and its shallow waters, rich with aquatic vegetation, are spectacular places for bird-watching. Coots and moorhens move slowly among the many species of wildfowl, including mallards, gadwalls, tufted ducks, teal, wigeon and shovelers. Dabchicks, like dark flecks on the water, vanish suddenly from view as they dive for food. In the wet pasture there are lapwings, redshanks and other waders; and occasionally a bird of prey sweeps by, solitary and menacing, a hen-harrier perhaps, or a merlin, a short-eared owl or even a peregrine.

The delights of Balranald Nature Reserve are not confined to the birds of the marshland. The reserve also includes long stretches of beach, the rocky headland of Aird an Runair, and a large expanse of cultivated machair. In spring and autumn the beaches attract huge flocks of dunlins, ringed plovers and other migrant waders, while meadow pipits, corn buntings, curlews, golden plovers and greylag geese are among the many species which descend on the cornfields around harvest time. There are colonies of Arctic terns among the breeding species on the headland. The birds defend their territories by ferociously mobbing anyone who comes too near, so it is best to stay well away; also, predators are always waiting to snap up the eggs or young when the adults leave them to mob intruders.

Even in the still of a summer's night, birds still proclaim Balranald's charm. Sometimes from far away on the grassland, sometimes from a nearby hiding place, the rarely seen corncrake rasps out its song – a double croak that sounds like the incessant ringing of a telephone.

Balranald Nature Reserve is maintained by the Royal Society for the Protection of Birds, and is open all year. An information centre explains the importance for wildlife of traditional crofting practices.
▶ *Balranald is on North Uist, about 15 miles west of Lochmaddy via the A867 and A865. North Uist can be reached by ferry and air (see Blathaisbhal).*

⑮ Quiraing

The rocks at Quiraing are so dramatic and so spectacular in their setting on Skye that afterwards the memory of them seems like an illusion. Their names are simple, and yet they describe so much – Quiraing (the Gaelic for 'pillared stronghold'), The Needle, The Prison, The Table. It was a place which Victorian travellers never failed to visit, so well did it suit their taste for grandeur.

The easiest approach to the rocks is from the hill road between Uig and Staffin, following the footpath which starts above the steep, hairpin bend. The hillside falls away sharply below the path, and there are sweeping views to the south and east. Above the path tower dark, inland cliffs, which extended much further east before the end of the last Ice Age. Quiraing and the landscape around it are the tumbled result of landslips – the slow, downward slide of layers of volcanic rock once held stable by the ice sheet.

At the end of the path, to the right, The Prison rises steeply, a brooding, castellated crag. To the left The Needle soars 36m (120ft) into the sky, standing sentinel over the narrow gully

㉖ Glen Rosa

For travellers arriving on Arran by the ferry to Brodick, the first impression of the island is created by the soaring, conical peak of Goat Fell. The mountain towers 874m (2,866ft) above Brodick Bay, making it the highest point on the island. Just to the west of it is another of Arran's wonders, sandwiched between immense mountain walls. This is Glen Rosa, which starts from sea-level at a winding river mouth cruised by mute swans and climbs into the heart of the great, granite mountain range.

Lower Glen Rosa has cottages and farmland between the forestry plantations which sweep up its sides. Between the two main blocks of woodland on the north side, a path climbs towards the summit of Goat Fell alongside the Cnocan Burn. Higher up the glen, the landscape becomes more obviously glacial. The Glenrosa Water curls down a U-shaped valley cut through mounds of glacial moraine – the debris left behind by retreating glaciers in the last Ice Age.

Near a foot-bridge where a tributary burn tumbles down from the west side of the glen, the underlying rock structure changes. Here Glen Rosa crosses into the heart of the granite country. Even the name of the stream is a clue to this – Garbh Allt means 'the Rough Burn', a name which accurately describes the obstacle course of massive granite boulders through which the stream drops.

From here the peak of Cir Mhór dominates the northward view, rising above The Saddle – the col which links Cir Mhór with Goat Fell. To one side is the bristling A'Chir ridge; ranged along the other is a wild series of rock pinnacles and gullies. Between two of these pinnacles is one of the most famous features of Arran's mountain scenery – the Witch's Step, formed by the weathering away of a dyke of soft rock intruded into the harder granite. In fact there are so many of these intrusive rocks on the island that they are known collectively as the Arran Dyke Swarm. For years they have made Arran a geologists' paradise, and the local people are no longer surprised to find 'jolly-boys', as the geologists are sometimes called, tapping away at rocks in the most remote corners of the island.

▶ *From Brodick Pier, turn west and take the B880 Blackwaterfoot road. After 180m (200yd), a road signposted 'Cart Track Glen Rosa' leads north. The tarmac gives way to an unsurfaced road, and after the footbridge this becomes a path.*

㉗ Clauchland Hills

No view shows better the two contrasting faces of Arran than that from the Thomson Memorial Seat, the highest point of the road from Brodick to Lamlash. The memorial is named after a much-respected member of the Glasgow Arran Society. To the north lie great granite mountains, rising to more than 850m (2,800ft). A gentle panorama of rolling hills, moorland and forest spreads out to the south.

East of the road are the Clauchland Hills, with footpaths and rights of way threading through the forests. One route, which starts from near the seat, leads through dark conifers and over bracken-covered hillside to another fine viewpoint overlooking Lamlash village. Backed by sweeping forest, Lamlash and its surrounding farmlands fringe the shore of a great semicircular bay, which is separated from the open waters of the Firth of Clyde by the impressive bulk of Holy Island. This is no gentle offshore islet, but a 2 mile range of cliffs, jagged rocks and rugged moorland, rising at its summit to 314m (1,030ft) – higher than any mainland Arran hill for nearly 3 miles around.

Holy Island is named in honour of the 7th-century St Molaise, who is said to have lived to be 120. His cell is on the western shore and can still be visited. There are graffiti on the walls in runic – the old Norse alphabet – carved by Norwegian sailors who gathered in Lamlash Bay before the Battle of Largs in 1263. Their defeat ended the centuries of Norse control of the Western Isles. It was also from Lamlash Bay – from Kingscross at the southern end – that Robert Bruce set sail for the Ayrshire coast in 1307, at the start of his seven-year campaign against the English that ended with his triumph at Bannockburn.

Holy Island is a centre for spiritual retreat but also welcomes visitors. There are Eriskay ponies, Soay sheep, wild goats and more than 50 species of nesting and migrant birds.

▶ *The highest point of the A841 between Brodick and Lamlash is marked by the Thomson Memorial Seat. A ferry runs from Lamlash to Holy Island.*

SCOTLAND

Index

Acknowledgments

Front Cover Getty Images Ltd/Guy Edwardes (Marshwood Vale, Dorset) **Back Cover** Collections/Graeme Peacock (Upper Coquetdale, Northumberland)

1 www.ntpl.org.uk/©NTPL/Derek Croucher (Bluebells, Ashridge Estate) **2-3** naturepl.com/Adam Burton (Buachaille Etive Mor, Glen Coe) **6-7** naturepl.com/Pete Cairns (Ancient pine forest, Strathspey) **8-9** www.britainonview.com/Guy Edwardes (View of Dartmoor from Bowerman's Nose) **10-11** www.britainonview.com/NTPL/Derek Croucher **12** Collections/Paul Watts **15** Alamy Images/Mark Stokes **16-17** www.ntpl.org.uk/©NTPL/Steve Atkins **21** www.ntpl.org.uk/©NTPL/Steve Lewis **23** www.britainonview.com **24-25** naturepl.com/ Ross Hoddinott **26-27** Alamy Images/Adam Burton **28-29** naturepl.com/David Noton **31** Collections/John Gollop **32-33** www.ntpl.org.uk/©NTPL/David Noton **36-37** naturepl.com/Gary K. Smith **38** Alamy Images/Andy Hallam **40** Alamy Images/Peter Horree **42-43** Alamy Images/Fabienne Fossez **45** naturepl.com/John Waters **51** Alamy Images/Craig Joiner Photography **52-53** www.ntpl.org.uk/©NTPL/David Sellman **54-55** Mick Sharp and Jean Williamson **56** Alamy Images/Mark Bolton Photography **58-59** Alamy Images/David Noton **62-63** Atmosphere Picture Library/Bob Croxford **66** Alamy Images/Jinny Goodman **68-69** www.ntpl.org.uk/©NTPL/John Miller (View from Leith Hill towards the South Downs) **70-71** www.britainonview.com/ Paul Felix **73** www.britainonview.com/David Sellman **74-75** www.britainonview.com/Cotswold Picture Library **79** Collections/ John Bethell **80-81** www.ntpl.org.uk/©NTPL/Michael Caldwell **85** Kit Houghton **86** www.britainonview.com/David Hall **88-89** www.ntpl.org.uk/ ©NTPL/David Noton **90-91** www.britainonview.com **93** Collections/David Askham **97** www.lastrefuge.co.uk **99** naturepl.com/Geoff Dore **102-103** www.lastrefuge.co.uk **104-105** Collections/Simon Bache **107** www.ntpl.org.uk/©NTPL/John Miller **108-109** www.britainonview.com/David Sellman **110-111** Collections/Michael St Maur Shiel **112-113** www.ntpl.org.uk/ ©NTPL/Rod J. Edwards **116-117** Frank Lane Picture Agency/Andrew Bailey (Sunset near Flatford, Dedham Vale) **119** naturepl.com/Jose B. Ruiz **120-121** Collections/Peter Wilson **124** Frank Lane Picture Agency/Gary K Smith **126-127** www.britainonview.com/Jon Gibbs **128** www.ntpl.org.uk/©NTPL/Rod J. Edwards **130-131** naturepl.com/ Chris Gomersall **132** www.ntpl.org.uk/©NTPL/David Sellman **134-135** www.britainonview.com/Rod Edwards **136-137** CADW. Crown Copyright/(Harlech Castle, Gwynedd) **139** The Photolibrary Wales/Harry Williams **142** www.ntpl.org.uk/©NTPL/Joe Cornish **144-145** The Photolibrary Wales/Graham Morley **147** www.ntpl.org.uk/©NTPL/David Noton **150** www.britainonview.com/Joe Cornish **153** The Photolibrary Wales/David Newbould **154-155** The Photolibrary Wales/Kevin Fitzmaurice Brown **156** www.ntpl.org.uk/©NTPL/Joe Cornish **160** www.ntpl.org.uk/ ©NTPL/Martin Dohrn **163** The Photolibrary Wales/John Prior **164-165** naturepl.com/Chris O'Reilly **169** www.britainonview.com/Steve Lewis **170-171** Mick Sharp and Jean Williamson **173** www.ntpl.org.uk/©NTPL/Joe Cornish **174** www.ntpl.org.uk/©NTPL/Joe Cornish **178** naturepl.com/David Noton **181** www.britainonview.com/Steve Lewis **182-183** Mick Sharp and Jean Williamson **186-187** Collections/George Wright **188** www.ntpl.org.uk/©NTPL/David Noton **193** www.britainonview.com/Joe Cornish **196** Collections/Archie Miles **198** www.lastrefuge.co.uk **201** Collections/Robert Estall **202-203** English Heritage/Paul Marsch (Hadrian's Wall) **204** Mike Kipling Photography **206-207** www.britainonview.com/Steve Walton **210-211** Collections/Dorothy Burrows **213** www.ntpl.org.uk/©NTPL/Mark Sunderland **214** www.ntpl.org.uk/©NTPL/Joe Cornish **218** www.ntpl.org.uk/©NTPL/ Mark Sunderland **221** www.britainonview.com/Joe Cornish **222-223** Mike Kipling Photography **224-225** Charlie Hedley **226** Charlie Hedley **229** Charlie Hedley **231** www.britainonview.com/Alan Novelli **234-235** www.britainonview.com/Andy Stothert **236-237** Collections/Simon Warner **239** www.ntpl.org.uk/©NTPL/Joe Cornish **240-241** www.britainonview.com/Fran Halsall **242** www.ntpl.org.uk/©NTPL/Joe Cornish **246-247** www.britainonview.com/Fran Halsall **249** naturepl.com/David Noton **253** Collections/Graeme Peacock **256-257** Scottish Viewpoint/Fran Halsall (Loch Scavaig and the Black Cuillins) **258-259** Scottish Viewpoint/Richard Nicholls **260** Scottish Viewpoint/Darren Miller **264** Scottish Viewpoint/Allan Devlin **266-267** Scottish Viewpoint/Richard Nicholls **270-271** Scottish Viewpoint/VisitScotland **275** www.britainonview.com/Duncan Shaw **276** Scottish Viewpoint/STB **279** Scottish Viewpoint/Susan Pettigrew **282-283** Scottish Viewpoint/Peter Cairns **284-285** naturepl.com/Duncan McEwan **288** www.britainonview.com/Duncan Shaw **290-291** Scottish Viewpoint/John Pringle **295** naturepl.com/David Noton **296-297** Scottish Viewpoint/Ian Macrae Young **298** Scottish Viewpoint/Rowan Greenwood **300-301** Charles Tait **302-303** www.britainonview.com/Fran Halsall **305** Scottish Viewpoint/David Osbourne **308-309** naturepl.com/Nick Garbutt **310** Scottish Viewpoint/P. Tomkins/VisitScotland